ISBN 978-0-260-59521-8
PIBN 10693317

THE A...

PRESIDENT LINCOLN

...AL OF THE CONSPIRATORS

VID E. HEROLD
... Y SPRATT
...
... LEWIS ...

THE ASSASSINATION

OF

PRESIDENT LINCOLN

AND THE

TRIAL OF THE CONSPIRATORS

DAVID E. HEROLD,	EDWARD SPANGLER,
MARY E. SURRATT,	SAMUEL A. MUDD,
LEWIS PAYNE,	SAMUEL ARNOLD,
GEORGE A. ATZERODT,	MICHAEL O'LAUGHLIN.

Containing the Orders convening the Commission; Rules for its guidance; Pleas of the accused to the Jurisdiction of the Commission, and for Severance of Trial; Testimony in full concerning the Assassination, and attending circumstances; Flight, pursuit and capture of John Wilkes Booth; Attempted Assassination of Hon. W. H. Seward, Secretary of State. Official Documents and Testimony relating to the following plots: The Abduction of the President and Cabinet, and carrying them to Richmond; The Assassination of the President and Cabinet; The Murder of President Lincoln by presents of infected clothing; The introduction of pestilence into Northern cities by clothing infected with Yellow Fever and Small Pox; Starvation and murder of Union prisoners in Southern prisons; Attempted burning of New York and other Northern cities; Poisoning the water of the Croton Reservoir, New York; Raid on St. Albans; Contemplated raids on Buffalo, Ogdensburg, etc.; Burning of Steamboats on Western rivers, Government Warehouses, Hospitals, etc.; Complicity of Jefferson Davis, Judah P. Benjamin, Jacob Thompson, George N. Sanders, Beverley Tucker, C. C. Clay, etc.; Jacob Thompson's banking account in Canada; The mining of Libby Prison, and preparations to blow it up; The "disorganisation of the North" by a system of terrorism and infernal plots; Arguments of Counsel for the Accused; Reply of Hon. J. A. Bingham, Special Judge Advocate; Findings and Sentences of the Accused, etc.

COMPILED AND ARRANGED BY BENN PITMAN,
RECORDER TO THE COMMISSION.

PUBLISHERS:
MOORE, WILSTACH & BALDWIN,
25 WEST FOURTH STREET, CINCINNATI.
NEW YORK, 60 WALKER STREET.
1865.

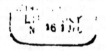

APPROVAL OF THE SECRETARY OF WAR, ETC.

MILITARY COMMISSION, PENITENTIARY, WASHINGTON, D. C., }
Tuesday, June 20, 1865. }

:RIG. GEN. JOSEPH HOLT, *Judge Advocate General:*

GENERAL—To satisfy the present public desire, and for future use and reference, it is certainly desirable that an authentic record of the trial of the assassins of the late President, as developed in the proceedings before the Military Commission, should be published: such record to include the testimony, documents introduced in evidence, discussion of points of law raised during the trial, the addresses of the counsel for the accused, the reply of the Special Judge Advocate, and the findings and sentences.

Messrs. Moore, Wilstach & Baldwin, publishers, of Cincinnati and New York, are willing to publish the proceedings in respectable book shape, and I will arrange and compile, on receiving your approval.

I respectfully refer to the printed work, "THE INDIANAPOLIS TREASON TRIALS," as an indication that my part of the work will be performed with faithfulness and care.

Very respectfully, your obedient servant,   BENN PITMAN.
Recorder to Commission.

Indorsed and approved by—

DAVID HUNTER, Maj. Gen. U. S. Vols.
AUGUST V. KAUTZ, Brev. Maj. Gen. U. S. Vols.
ALBION P. HOWE, Brig. Gen. U. S. Vols.
JAMES A. EKIN, Brev. Brig. Gen. U. S. Vols.
DAVID R. CLENDENIN, Lieut. Col. 8th Ills. Cav.
LEWIS WALLACE, Maj. Gen. U. S. Vols.
ROBERT S. FOSTER, Brev. Maj. Gen. U. S. Vols.
T. M. HARRIS, Brig. Gen. U. S. Vols.
C. H. TOMKINS, Brev. Col. U. S. Army.
JOHN A. BINGHAM, Special Judge Advocate.
H. L. BURNETT, Brev. Col. and Special Judge Advocate.

BUREAU OF MILITARY JUSTICE, *June 30, 1865.*

By authority of the Secretary of War, the publication of the work referred to in the foregoing letter, will be permitted, on the condition that it be made without cost to the Government, and that it be prepared and issued under the superintendence of Col. Burnett, who will be responsible to this Bureau for its strict accuracy.

J. HOLT, *Judge Advocate General.*

JUDGE ADVOCATE'S OFFICE, DEPARTMENT OF THE OHIO, }
CINCINNATI, *October 2, 1865.* }

In obedience to the directions of the Secretary of War, through the Judge Advocate General, I have superintended the compilation and publication, in book form, of the record of the trial of the conspirators at Washington, for the assassination of the late President, Abraham Lincoln, and the attempted assassination of the Secretary of State, Mr. Seward, other members of the Cabinet, and Lieut. Gen. Grant, and hereby certify to its faithfulness and accuracy.   H. L. BURNETT,

Judge Advocate Dept. of the Ohio, and Special Judge Advocate of the Commission.

THE entire testimony adduced at the trial of the assassins of President Lincoln is contained in the following pages. It has been arranged in narrative form, to avoid unnecessary repetitions, and to present the facts testified to by each witness in a concise and consecutive form. The phraseology is that of the witness; the only license taken with the testimony has been its arrangement in historical sequence, both as to generals and particulars.

Whenever the meaning of a witness was doubtful, or an evasive answer was given, or whenever the language of the witness admitted of a double interpretation, or of no interpretation at all, the questions of counsel, and the answers of the witness, have been retained.   B. P.

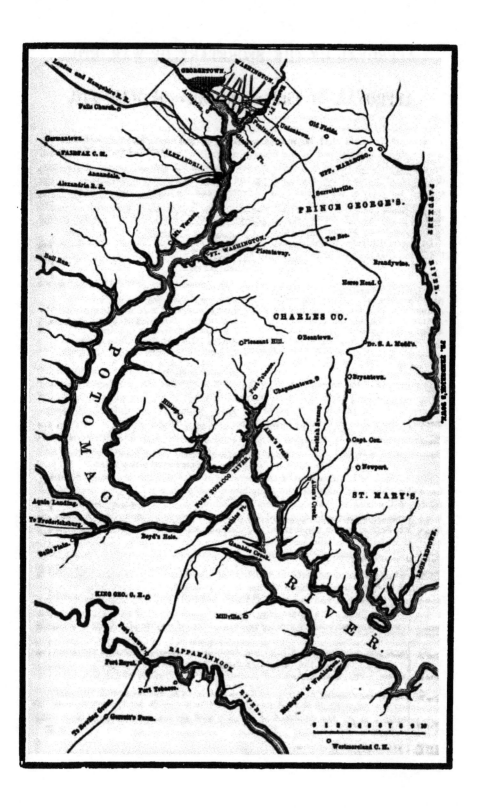

TABLE OF CONTENTS.

(7)

DEFENSE OF DR. SAMUEL A. MUDD.

DR. MUDD IN WASHINGTON DECEMBER 23, 1864.

DR. MUDD'S WHEREABOUTS FROM 1st TO 6th MARCH.

DR. MUDD IN WASHINGTON MARCH 23D.

AT GIESBORO APRIL 11th.

DR. MUDD'S ABSENCE FROM HOME.

AT BRYANTOWN APRIL 15th AND 16th.

TESTIMONY IN REBUTTAL.

MICHAEL O'LAUGHLIN.

DEFENSE OF MICHAEL O'LAUGHLIN.

SAMUEL ARNOLD.

DEFENSE OF SAMUEL ARNOLD.

APPENDIX.

ALPHABETICAL INDEX OF WITNESSES.

PROCEEDINGS

OF A

MILITARY COMMISSION,

Convened at Washington, D. C., by virtue of the following Orders:

EXECUTIVE CHAMBER,
Washington City, May 1, 1865. }

WHEREAS, the Attorney-General of the United States hath given his opinion:

That the persons implicated in the murder of the late President, Abraham Lincoln, and the attempted assassination of the Honorable William H. Seward, Secretary of State, and in an alleged conspiracy to assassinate other officers of the Federal Government at Washington City, and their aiders and abettors, are subject to the jurisdiction of, and lawfully triable before, a Military Commission;

It is *ordered:* 1st. That the Assistant Adjutant-General detail nine competent military officers to serve as a Commission for the trial of said parties, and that the Judge Advocate General proceed to prefer charges against said parties for their alleged offenses, and bring them to trial before said Military Commission; that said trial or trials be conducted by the said Judge Advocate General, and as recorder thereof, in person, aided by such Assistant and Special Judge Advocates as he may designate; and that said trials be conducted with all diligence consistent with the ends of justice: the said Commission to sit without regard to hours.

2d. That Brevet Major-General Hartranft be assigned to duty as Special Provost Marshal General, for the purpose of said trial, and attendance upon said Commission, and the execution of its mandates.

3d. That the said Commission establish such order or rules of proceeding as may avoid unnecessary delay, and conduce to the ends of public justice.

[Signed]   ANDREW JOHNSON.

WAR DEPARTMENT, ADJ'T-GENERAL'S OFFICE,
Washington, May 6, 1865. }

Special Orders, No. 211.

* * * * * * *

EXTRACT.

4. A Military Commission is hereby appointed to meet at Washington, District of Columbia, on Monday, the 8th day of May, 1865, at 9 o'clock A. M., or as soon thereafter as practicable, for the trial of David E. Herold, George A. Atzerodt, Lewis Payne, Michael O'Laughlin, Edward Spangler, Samuel Arnold, Mary E. Surratt, Samuel A. Mudd, and such other prisoners as may be brought before it, implicated in the murder of the late President, Abraham Lincoln, and the attempted assassination of the Honorable William H. Seward, Secretary of State, and in an alleged conspiracy to assassinate other officers of the Federal Government at Washington City, and their aiders and abettors.

DETAIL FOR THE COURT.

Major-General David Hunter, U. S. Volunteers.

Major-General Lewis Wallace, U. S. Volunteers.

Brevet Major-General August V. Kautz, U. S. Volunteers.

Brigadier-General Albion P. Howe, U. S. Volunteers.

Brigadier-General Robert S. Foster, U. S. Volunteers.

Brevet Brigadier-General Cyrus B. Comstock, U. S. Volunteers.

Brigadier-General T. M. Harris, U. S. Volunteers.

Brevet Colonel Horace Porter, Aid-de-Camp.

Lieutenant-Colonel David R. Clendenin, Eighth Illinois Cavalry.

Brigadier-General Joseph Holt, Judge Advocate General U. S. Army, is appointed the Judge Advocate and Recorder of the Commission, to be aided by such Assistant or Special Judge Advocates as he may designate.

The Commission will sit without regard to hours.

By order of the President of the United States.

[Signed]   W. A. NICHOLS,
Assistant Adjutant-General.

COURT-ROOM, WASHINGTON, D. C., }
May 9, 1865, 10 o'clock A. M. }

The Commission met pursuant to the foregoing Orders.

All the members present; also the Judge Advocate General.

The Hon. John A. Bingham, and Brevet Colonel H. L. Burnett, Judge Advocate, were then introduced by the Judge Advocate General as Assistant or Special Judge Advocates.

The accused, David E. Herold, George A. Atzerodt, Samuel Arnold, Lewis Payne, Michael O'Laughlin, Edward Spangler, Mary E. Surratt, and Samuel A. Mudd, were then brought into court, and being asked whether they desired to employ counsel, replied that they did.

To afford the accused opportunity to secure counsel, the Commission adjourned to meet on Wednesday, May 10, at 10 o'clock A. M.

COURT-ROOM, WASHINGTON, D. C., }
May 10, 1865, 10 o'clock A. M. }

The Commission met pursuant to adjournment.

Present, all the members named in the foregoing Order; also present the Judge Advocate General, and Assistant Judge Advocates Bingham and Burnett.

The Judge Advocate General then read the following Special Order:

WAR DEPARTMENT, ADJ'T-GENERAL'S OFFICE, }
Washington, May 9, 1865. }

Special Orders, No. 216.

EXTRACT.

* 　* 　* 　* 　* 　* 　* 　*

91. Brevet Brigadier-General Cyrus B. Comstock, U. S. Volunteers, and Brevet Colonel Horace Porter, Aid-de-Camp, are hereby relieved from duty as members of the Military Commission, appointed in Special Orders No. 211, paragraph 4, dated "War Department, Adjutant-General's Office, Washington, May 6, 1865," and Brevet Brigadier-General James A. Ekin, U. S. Volunteers, and Brevet Colonel C. H. Tomkins, U. S. Army, are detailed in their places respectively.

The Commission will be composed as follows:

Major-General David Hunter, U. S. Volunteers.

Major-General Lewis Wallace, U. S. Volunteers.

Brevet Major-General August V. Kautz, U. S. Volunteers.

Brigadier-General Albion P. Howe, U. S. Volunteers.

Brigadier-General Robert S. Foster, U. S. Volunteers.

Brevet Brigadier-General James A. Ekin, U. S. Volunteers.

Brigadier-General T. M. Harris, U. S. Volunteers.

Brevet Colonel C. H. Tomkins, U. S. Army.

Lieutenant-Colonel David R. Clendenin, Eighth Illinois Cavalry.

Brigadier-General Joseph Holt, Judge Advocate and Recorder.

By order of the President of the United States.

[Signed]　　E. D. TOWNSEND.
Assistant Adjutant-General.

All the members named in the foregoing order being present, the Commission proceeded to the trial of David E. Herold, George A. Atzerodt, Lewis Payne, Michael O'Laughlin, Edward Spangler, Samuel Arnold, Mary E. Surratt, and Samuel A. Mudd, who were brought into court, and having heard read the foregoing orders, the accused were asked if they had any objection to any member named therein, to which all severally replied they had none.

The members of the Commission were then duly sworn by the Judge Advocate General, in the presence of the accused.

The Judge Advocate General, and Assistant Judge Advocates, Hon. John A. Bingham and Brevet Colonel H. L. Burnett, were then duly sworn by the President of the Commission, in the presence of the accused.

Benn Pitman, R. Sutton, D. F. Murphy, R. R. Hitt, J. J. Murphy, and Edward V. Murphy, were duly sworn by the Judge Advocate General, in the presence of the accused, as reporters to the Commission.

The accused were then severally arraigned on the following Charge and Specification:

CHARGE AND SPECIFICATION

AGAINST

DAVID E. HEROLD, GEORGE A. ATZERODT, LEWIS PAYNE, MICHAEL O'LAUGHLIN, EDWARD SPANGLER, SAMUEL ARNOLD, MARY E. SURRATT, AND SAMUEL A. MUDD.

CHARGE.—For maliciously, unlawfully, and traitorously, and in aid of the the existing armed rebellion against the United States of America, on or before the 6th day of March, A. D. 1865, and on divers other days between that day and the 15th day of April, A. D. 1865, combining, confederating, and conspiring together with one John H. Surratt, John Wilkes Booth, Jefferson Davis, George N. Sanders, Beverly Tucker, Jacob Thompson, William C. Cleary, Clement C. Clay, George Harper, George Young, and others unknown, to kill and murder, within the Military Department of Washington, and within the fortified and intrenched lines thereof, Abraham Lincoln, late, and at the time of said combining, confederating, and conspiring, President of the United States of America, and Commander-in-Chief of the Army and Navy thereof; Andrew Johnson, now Vice-President of the United States aforesaid; William H. Seward, Secretary of State of the United States aforesaid;

and Ulysses S. Grant, Lieutenant-General of the Army of the United States aforesaid, then in command of the Armies of the United States, under the direction of the said Abraham Lincoln; and in pursuance of and in prosecuting said malicious, unlawful, and traitorous conspiracy aforesaid, and in aid of said rebellion, afterward, to-wit, on the 14th day of April, A. D. 1865, within the Military Department of Washington aforesaid, and within the fortified and intrenched lines of said Military Department, together with said John Wilkes Booth and John H. Surratt, maliciously, unlawfully, and traitorously murdering the said Abraham Lincoln, then President of the United States and Commander-in-Chief of the Army and Navy of the United States, as aforesaid; and maliciously, unlawfully, and traitorously assaulting, with intent to kill and murder, the said William H. Seward, then Secretary of State of the United States, as aforesaid; and lying in wait with intent maliciously, unlawfully, and traitorously to kill and murder the said Andrew Johnson, then being Vice-President of the United States; and the said Ulysses S. Grant, then being Lieutenant-General, and in command of the Armies of the United States, as aforesaid.

SPECIFICATION.—In this: that they, the said David E. Herold, Edward Spangler, Lewis Payne, Michael O'Laughlin, Samuel Arnold, Mary E. Surratt. George A. Atzerodt, and Samuel A. Mudd, together with the said John H. Surratt and John Wilkes Booth, incited and encouraged thereunto by Jefferson Davis, George N. Sanders, Beverly Tucker, Jacob Thompson, William C. Cleary, Clement C. Clay, George Harper, George Young, and others unknown, citizens of the United States aforesaid, and who were then engaged in armed rebellion against the United States of America, within the limits thereof, did, in aid of said armed rebellion, on or before the 6th day of March, A. D. 1865, and on divers other days and times between that day and the 15th day of April, A. D. 1865, combine, confederate, and conspire together, at Washington City, within the Military Department of Washington, and within the intrenched fortifications and military lines of the United States, there being, unlawfully, maliciously, and traitorously to kill and murder Abraham Lincoln, then President of the United States aforesaid, and Commander-in-Chief of the Army and Navy thereof; and unlawfully, maliciously, and traitorously to kill and murder Andrew Johnson, now Vice-President of the said United States, upon whom, on the death of said Abraham Lincoln, after the 4th day of March, A. D. 1865, the office of President of the said United States, and Commander-in-Chief of the Army and Navy thereof, would devolve; and to unlawfully, maliciously, and traitorously kill and murder Ulysses S. Grant, then Lieutenant-General, and, under the direction of the said Abraham Lincoln, in command of the Armies of the United States, aforesaid; and unlawfully, maliciously, and traitorously to kill and murder William H. Seward, then Secretary of State of the United States aforesaid, whose duty it was, by law, upon the death of said President and Vice-President of the United States aforesaid, to cause an election to be held for electors of President of the United States: the conspirators aforesaid designing and intending, by the killing and murder of the said Abraham Lincoln, Andrew Johnson, Ulysses S. Grant, and William H. Seward, as aforesaid, to deprive the Army and Navy of the said United States of a constitutional Commander-in-Chief; and to deprive the Armies of the United States of their lawful commander; and to prevent a lawful election of President and Vice-President of the United States aforesaid; and by the means aforesaid to aid and comfort the insurgents engaged in armed rebellion against the said United States, as aforesaid, and thereby to aid in the subversion and overthrow of the Constitution and laws of the said United States.

And being so combined, confederated, and conspiring together in the prosecution of said unlawful and traitorous conspiracy, on the night of the 14th day of April, A. D. 1865, at the hour of about 10 o'clock and 15 minutes P. M., at Ford's Theater, on Tenth Street, in the City of Washington, and within the military department and military lines aforesaid, John Wilkes Booth, one of the conspirators aforesaid, in pursuance of said unlawful and traitorous conspiracy, did, then and there, unlawfully, maliciously, and traitorously, and with intent to kill and murder the said Abraham Lincoln, discharge a pistol then held in the hands of him, the said Booth, the same being then loaded with powder and a leaden ball, against and upon the left and posterior side of the head of the said Abraham Lincoln; and did thereby, then and there, inflict upon him, the said Abraham Lincoln, then President of the said United States, and Commander-in-Chief of the Army and Navy thereof, a mortal wound, whereof, afterward, to-wit, on the 15th day of April, A. D. 1865, at Washington City aforesaid, the said Abraham Lincoln died; and thereby, then and there, and in pursuance of said conspiracy, the said defendants, and the said John Wilkes Booth and John H. Surratt, did unlawfully, traitorously, and maliciously, and with the intent to aid the rebellion, as aforesaid, kill and murder the said Abraham Lincoln, President of the United States, as aforesaid.

And in further prosecution of the unlawful and traitorous conspiracy aforesaid, and of the murderous and traitorous intent of said conspiracy, the said Edward Spangler, on said 14th day of April, A. D. 1865, at about the same hour of that day, as aforesaid, within said military department and the military lines aforesaid, did aid and assist the said John Wilkes Booth to obtain entrance to the box in said theater, in which said Abraham Lincoln was sitting at the time he was assaulted and shot, as aforesaid, by John Wilkes Booth; and also did, then and there, aid said Booth in barring and obstructing the door of the box of said theater, so as to hinder and prevent any assistance to or rescue of the said Abraham Lincoln against the murderous assault of the said John Wilkes Booth; and did aid and abet him in making his escape after the said Abraham Lincoln had been murdered in manner aforesaid.

And in further prosecution of said unlawful, murderous, and traitorous conspiracy, and in pursuance thereof, and with the intent as aforesaid, the said David E. Herold did, on the night of the 14th of April, A. D. 1865, within the military department and military lines aforesaid, aid, abet, and assist the said John Wilkes Booth in the killing and murder of the said Abraham Lincoln, and did, then and there, aid and abet and assist him, the said John Wilkes Booth, in attempting to escape through the military lines aforesaid, and did accompany and assist the said John Wilkes Booth in attempting to conceal himself and escape from justice, after killing and murdering said Abraham Lincoln as aforesaid.

And in further prosecution of said unlawful and traitorous conspiracy, and of the intent thereof, as aforesaid, the said Lewis Payne did, on the same night of the 14th day of April, A. D. 1865, about the same hour of 10 o'clock and 15 minutes P. M., at the City of Washington, and within the military department and the military lines aforesaid, unlawfully and maliciously make an assault upon the said William H. Seward, Secretary of State, as aforesaid, in the dwelling-house and bed-chamber of him, the said William H. Seward, and the said Payne did, then and there, with a large knife held in his hand, unlawfully, traitorously, and in pursuance of said conspiracy, strike, stab, cut, and attempt to kill and murder the said William H. Seward, and did thereby, then and there, and with the intent aforesaid, with said knife, inflict upon the face and throat of the said William H. Seward divers grievous wounds. And the said Lewis Payne, in further prosecution of said conspiracy, at the same time and place last aforesaid, did attempt, with the knife aforesaid, and a pistol held in his hand, to kill and murder Frederick W. Seward, Augustus H. Seward, Emrick W. Hansell, and George F. Robinson, who were then striving to protect and rescue the said William H. Seward from murder by the said Lewis Payne, and did, then and there, with said knife and pistol held in his hands, inflict upon the head of said Frederick W. Seward, and upon the persons of said Augustus H. Seward, Emrick W. Hansell, and George F. Robinson, divers grievous and dangerous wounds, with intent, then and there, to kill and murder the said Frederick W. Seward,

Augustus H. Seward, Emrick W. Hansell, and George F. Robinson.

And in further prosecution of said conspiracy and its traitorous and murderous designs, the said George A. Atzerodt did, on the night of the 14th of April, A. D. 1865, and about the same hour of the night aforesaid, within the military department and the military lines aforesaid, lie in wait for Andrew Johnson, then Vice-President of the United States aforesaid, with the intent unlawfully and maliciously to kill and murder him, the said Andrew Johnson.

And in the further prosecution of the conspiracy aforesaid, and of its murderous and treasonable purposes aforesaid, on the nights of the 13th and 14th of April, A. D. 1865, at Washington City, and within the military department and the military lines aforesaid, the said Michael O'Laughlin did, then and there, lie in wait for Ulysses S. Grant, then Lieutenant-General and Commander of the Armies of the United States, as aforesaid, with intent, then and there, to kill and murder the said Ulysses S. Grant.

And in further prosecution of said conspiracy, the said Samuel Arnold did, within the military department and the military lines aforesaid, on or before the 6th day of March, A. D. 1865, and on divers other days and times between that day and the 15th day of April, A. D. 1865, combine, conspire with, and aid, counsel, abet, comfort, and support, the said John Wilkes Booth, Lewis Payne, George A. Atzerodt, Michael O'Laughlin, and their confederates in said unlawful, murderous, and traitorous conspiracy, and in the execution thereof, as aforesaid.

And in further prosecution of said conspiracy, Mary E. Surratt did, at Washington City, and within the military department and military lines aforesaid, on or before the 6th day of March, A. D. 1865, and on divers other days and times between that day and the 20th day of April, A. D. 1865, receive, entertain, harbor, and conceal, aid and assist the said John Wilkes Booth, David E. Herold, Lewis Payne, John H. Surratt, Michael O'Laughlin, George A. Atzerodt, Samuel Arnold, and their confederates, with the knowledge of the murderous and traitorous conspiracy aforesaid, and with intent to aid, abet, and assist them in the execution thereof, and in escaping from justice after the murder of the said Abraham Lincoln, as aforesaid.

And in further prosecution of said conspiracy, the said Samuel A. Mudd did, at Washington City, and within the military department and military lines aforesaid, on or before the 6th day of March, A. D. 1865, and on divers other days and times between that day and the 20th day of April, A. D. 1865, advise, encourage, receive, entertain, harbor, and conceal, aid and assist the said John Wilkes Booth, David E. Herold, Lewis Payne, John H. Surratt, Michael O'Laughlin, George A. Atzerodt, Mary E. Surratt, and Samuel

Arnold, and their confederates, with knowledge of the murderous and traitorous conspiracy aforesaid, and with the intent to aid, abet, and assist them in the execution thereof, and in escaping from justice after the murder of the said Abraham Lincoln, in pursuance of said conspiracy in manner aforesaid.

By order of the President of the United States.   J. HOLT,
Judge Advocate General.

Charge and Specification indorsed:
"Copy of the within Charge and Specification delivered to David E. Herold, George A. Atzerodt, Lewis Payne, Michael O'Laughlin, Samuel Arnold, Mary E. Surratt, and Samuel A. Mudd, on the 8th day of May, 1865.
[Signed]   "J. F. HARTRANFT,
Brev. Maj.-Gen. and Spec. Prov. Mar. Gen."

To the Specification, all the accused severally pleaded.....................*"Not Guilty."*
To the Charge.....................*"Not Guilty."*

The Commission then considered the rules and regulations by which its proceedings should be conducted, and after discussion adopted the following:

RULES OF PROCEEDING

ADOPTED BY THE MILITARY COMMISSION CONVENED PURSUANT TO SPECIAL ORDERS Nos. 211 AND 216.

1. The Commission will hold its sessions in the following hours: Convene at 10 A. M., and sit until 1 P. M., and then take a recess of one hour. Resume business at 2 P. M.

2. The prisoners will be allowed counsel, who shall file evidence of having taken the oath prescribed by act of Congress, or shall take said oath before being permitted to appear in the case.

3. The examination of witnesses shall be conducted on the part of the Government by one Judge Advocate, and by counsel on the part of the prisoners.

4. The testimony shall be taken in shorthand by reporters, who shall first take an oath to record the evidence faithfully and truly, and not to communicate the same, or any part thereof, or any proceedings on the trial, except by authority of the presiding officer.

5. A copy of the evidence taken each day shall be furnished the Judge Advocate General, and one copy to the counsel of the prisoners.

6. No reporters but the official reporters shall be admitted to the court-room. But the Judge Advocate General will furnish daily, in his discretion, to the agent of the Associated Press, a copy of such testimony and proceedings as may be published, pending the trial, without injury to the public and the ends of justice. All other publication of the evidence and proceedings is forbidden, and will be dealt with as contempt of Court, on the part of all persons or parties concerned in making or procuring such publication.*

7. For the security of the prisoners and witnesses, and to preserve order and decorum in the trial and proceedings, the presiding officer will furnish a pass to counsel, witnesses, officers, and such persons as may be allowed to pass the guard, and be present at the trial. No person will be allowed to pass the guard without such pass, which, for greater precaution, will be countersigned by the Special Provost Marshal in attendance upon the Court.

8. The argument of any motion will, unless otherwise ordered by the Court, be limited to five minutes by one Judge Advocate, and counsel on behalf of the prisoners. Objections to testimony will be noted on the record, and decided upon argument, limited as above, on motions. When the testimony is closed, the case will be immediately summed up by one Judge Advocate, at the discretion of the Judge Advocate General, and be followed or opened, if the Judge Advocate General elects, by counsel for the prisoners, and the argument shall be closed by one Judge Advocate.

9. The argument being closed, the Court will immediately proceed duly to deliberate and make its determination.

10. The Provost Marshal will have the prisoners in attendance during the trial, and be responsible for their security. Counsel may have access to them in the presence, but not in hearing, of a guard.

11. The counsel for the prisoners will immediately furnish the Judge Advocate General with a list of the witnesses required for defense, whose attendance will be procured in the usual manner.

To allow further time for the accused to secure and communicate with counsel, the Commission adjourned to meet on Thursday, May 11th, at 10 o'clock A. M.

COURT-ROOM, WASHINGTON, D. C., }
May 11, 1865, 10 o'clock A. M. }

The Commission met pursuant to adjournment.

All the members present; also the Judge Advocate, the Assistant Judge Advocates, and all the accused.

The record of preceding session was read and approved.

The accused, SAMUEL A. MUDD, applied for permission to introduce Frederick Stone, Esq., and Thomas Ewing, jr., Esq., as his counsel.

The accused, MARY E. SURRATT, applied for permission to introduce Frederick Aiken, Esq., and John W. Clampitt, Esq., as her

*The testimony of Richard Montgomery, Sanford Conover, and James B. Merritt was, for prudential reasons, taken in secret session. At the opening of the session, on May 13th, the Judge Advocate announced that the testimony hereafter to be introduced might be given to the public without impropriety or embarrassment to the Government, and that the President of the Commission would grant permits for admission to reporters and others to an extent not to interfere with the proceedings of the Commission.

counsel, which applications were granted; and the aforesaid counsel, having first taken, in open Court, the oath prescribed by act of Congress, approved July 2, 1862, accordingly appeared.

To allow further time for the accused to secure the attendance of counsel, the Commission adjourned, to meet on Friday, May 12th, at 10 o'clock A. M.

The Commission met pursuant to adjournment.

All the members present; also the Judge Advocate, the Assistant Judge Advocates, the accused, and Messrs. Ewing, Stone, Aiken, and Clampitt, counsel for the accused.

The proceedings were read and approved.

The accused, DAVID E. HEROLD, applied for permission to introduce Frederick Stone, Esq., as his counsel.

The accused, SAMUEL ARNOLD, applied for permission to introduce Thomas Ewing, jr., Esq., as his counsel; which applications were granted, and the aforesaid counsel accordingly appeared.

The accused, GEORGE A. ATZERODT, applied for permission to introduce William E. Doster, Esq., as his counsel.

The accused, MICHAEL O'LAUGHLIN, applied for permission to introduce Walter S. Cox, Esq., as his counsel.

The accused, LEWIS PAYNE, applied for permission to introduce William E. Doster, Esq., as his counsel.

The accused, EDWARD SPANGLER, applied for permission to introduce Thomas Ewing, jr., Esq., as his counsel; which applications were granted, and Messrs. Doster, and Cox, having first taken, in open Court, the oath prescribed by act of Congress, approved July 2, 1862, accordingly appeared.

The accused, MARY E. SURRATT, applied for permission to introduce the Hon. Reverdy Johnson as additional counsel for her,

A member of the Commission (General T. M. Harris) objected to the admission of Mr. Johnson as counsel before the Commission, on the ground that he did not recognize the moral obligation of an oath designed as a test of loyalty, or to enforce the obligation of loyalty to the Government of the United States, referring to a printed letter, dated Baltimore, October 7, 1864, upon " the constitutionality, legal and binding effect and bearing of the oath prescribed by the late Convention of our State, to be taken by the voters of the State as the condition and qualification of the right to vote upon the New Constitution."

The letter, published over the signature of the Hon. Reverdy Johnson, pending the adoption of the New Constitution of Maryland, contained the following passage:

"Because the Convention transcended its power, as I am satisfied it has, that is no reason why the people should submit. On the contrary, it should lead them to adopt the only course left to redress the wrong. The taking of the oath under such circumstances, argues no unwillingness to surrender their rights. It is indeed the only way in which they can protect them, and no moral injunction will be violated by such a course, because the exaction of the oath was beyond the authority of the Convention, and, as a law, is therefore void."

MR. JOHNSON. The Convention called to frame a new Constitution for the State was called under the authority of an act of the Legislature of Maryland, and under that alone. By that legislation, their proceedings were to be submitted to the then legal voters of the State. The Convention thought that they were themselves authorized not only to impose as an authority to vote what was not imposed by the then existing Constitution and laws, but to admit to vote those who were prohibited from voting by such Constitution and laws; and I said, in common with the whole bar of the State, (and with what the bar throughout the Union would have said if they had been consulted,) that to that extent they had usurped the authority under which alone they were authorized to meet, and that, so far, the proceeding was a nullity. They had prescribed this oath; and all that the opinion said, or was intended to say, was that to take the oath voluntarily was not a craven submission to usurped authority, but was necessary in order to enable the citizen to protect his rights under the then Constitution, and that there was no moral harm in taking an oath which the Convention had no authority to impose.

The objection being then withdrawn, Mr. Johnson accordingly appeared as counsel for Mrs. Mary E. Surratt.

The accused, David E. Herold, George A. Atzerodt, Lewis Payne, Michael O'Laughlin, Edward Spangler, Samuel Arnold, Mary E. Surratt, and Samuel A. Mudd, severally, through their counsel, asked leave to withdraw for the time their plea of " Not Guilty," heretofore filed, so that they may plead to the jurisdiction of the Commission.

The applications were granted.

The accused then severally offered a plea to the jurisdiction of the Commission as follows:

—— ——, one of the accused, for plea, says that this court has no jurisdiction in the proceeding against him, because he says he is not, and has not been, in the military service of the United States.

And, for further plea, the said —— —— says that loyal civil courts, in which all the offenses charged are triable, exist, and are in full and free operation in all the places where the several offenses charged are alleged to have been committed.

And, for further plea, the said —— —— says that the court has no jurisdiction in the matter of the alleged conspiracy, so far as it is charged to have been a conspiracy to murder Abraham Lincoln, late President of the United States, and William H. Seward, Secretary of State, because he says said alleged conspiracy, and all acts alleged to have been done in the formation and in the execution thereof, are in the charges and specifications alleged to have been committed in the City of Washington, in which city are loyal civil courts, in full operation, in which all said offenses charged are triable.

And the said ——— ———, for further plea, says this Court has no jurisdiction in the matter of the crime of murdering Abraham Lincoln, late President of the United States, and William H. Seward, Secretary of State, because he says said crimes and acts done in execution thereof are in the charges and specifications alleged to have been committed in the City of Washington, in which city are loyal civil courts, in full operation, in which said crimes are triable.

Signed on behalf of the accused by counsel.

The Judge Advocate then presented the following replication:

Now come the United States, and for an-swer to the special p ea by one of the defendants, ——— ———, pleaded to the jurisdiction of the Commission in this case, say that this Commission has jurisdiction in the premises to try and determine the matters in the Charge and Specification alleged and set forth against the said defendant, ——— ———.

J. HOLT,
Judge Advocate General.

The Court was then cleared for deliberation, and on being re-opened, the Judge Advocate announced that the pleas of the accused had been overruled by the Commission.

The accused then severally made application for severance as follows:

——— ———, one of the accused, asks that he be tried separate from those who are charged jointly with him, for the reason that he believes his defense will be greatly prejudiced by a joint trial.

Signed by counsel on behalf of accused.

The Commission overruled the application for a severance.

The accused then severally pleaded:

To the Specification............" *Not Guilty.*"
To the Charge................." *Not Guilty.*"

TESTIMONY

RELATING TO THE GENERAL CONSPIRACY.

RICHARD MONTGOMERY.

Witness for the Prosecution.—May 12, 1865.

I visited Canada in the summer of 1864, and, excepting the time I have been going backward and forward, have remained there until about two weeks ago. I know George N. Sanders, Jacob Thompson, Clement C. Clay, Professor Holcomb, Beverly Tucker, W. C. Cleary, and. Harrington. I have frequently met these persons, since the summer of 1864, at Niagara Falls, at Toronto, St. Catherines, and at Montreal. Thompson passed by several other names, one of which was Carson. Clay passed by the name of Hope, also Tracy, and another was T. E. Lacy.

In a conversation I had with Jacob Thompson, in the summer of 1864, he said he had his friends (Confederates) all over the Northern States, who were ready and willing to go any lengths to serve the cause of the South; and he added that he could at any time have the tyrant Lincoln, and any other of his advisers that he chose, put out of his way; he would have but to point out the man that he considered in his way, and his friends, as he termed them, would put him out of it, and not let him know any thing about it if necessary; and that they would not consider it a crime when done for the cause of the Confederacy.

Shortly after Mr. Thompson told me what he was able to do, I repeated the conversation to Mr. Clay, who said, "That is so; we are all devoted to our cause, and ready to go any lengths—to do any thing under the sun to serve our cause."

In January of this year, I saw Jacob Thompson in Montreal several times, in one of these conversations he said a proposition had been made to him to rid the world of the tyrant Lincoln, Stanton, Grant, and some others. The men who had made the proposition, he said, he knew were bold, daring men, and able to execute any thing they would undertake, without regard to the cost.

(24)

He said he was in favor of the proposition, but had determined to defer his answer until he had consulted with his Government at Richmond, and he was then only waiting their approval. He added that he thought it would be a blessing to the people, both North and South, to have these men killed.

I have seen Lewis Payne, the prisoner at the bar, in Canada. I saw him at the Falls in the summer of 1864. I saw him again, and had some words with him, at the Queen's Hotel in Toronto. I had had an interview with Mr. Thompson, and on leaving the room I met this man Payne in the passage way, talking with Mr. Clement C. Clay. Mr. Clay stopped me, and held my hand, finishing his conversation with Payne in an undertone, and when he left me for a moment he said, "Wait for me; I will return." He then went and spoke to some other gentleman who was entering Mr. Thompson's door, and then came back and bade me good-by, asking where he could see me in half an hour. I told him, and made an appintment to meet him. While Mr. Clay was away, I spoke to this man Payne, and asked him who he was. I commenced talking about some of the topics usually spoken of in conversation among these men. He rather hesitated about telling me who he was. He said, "O, I am a Canadian;" by which I understood that I was not to question him further. In about half an hour afterward I asked Mr. Clay who this man Payne was, and he said, "What did he say?" I told him that he said he was a Canadian. Mr. Clay laughed and said, "That is so; he is a Canadian; and," he added, "we trust him."

The term "Canadian" was a common expression among the Confederates there, and was applied to those who were in the habit of visiting the States; and I understood from Mr. Clay's laugh that their intercourse was of a confidential nature.

I have been in Canada since the assassination. A few days after, I met Beverly Tucker at Montreal. He said a great deal about the wrongs that the South had received at the hands of Mr. Lincoln, and that he deserved his death, and it was a pity he did not meet with it long ago. He said it was too bad that the boys had not been allowed to act when they wanted to. "The Boys" was an expression applied to the Confederate soldiers and others in their employ, who engaged in raids, and who were to assassinate the President.

I related a portion of the conversation I had had with Mr. Thompson to Mr. W. C. Cleary, who is a sort of confidential secretary to Mr. Thompson, and he told me that Booth was one of the parties to whom Thompson had reference; and he said, in regard to the assassination, that it was too bad that the whole work had not been done; by which I understood him to mean that they intended to assassinate a greater number than they succeeded in killing. Cleary remarked, when speaking of his regret that the whole work had not been done, "They had better look out; we have not done yet." And he added that they would never be conquered—would never give up.

Cleary said that Booth had been there, visiting Thompson, twice in the winter; he thought the last time was in December. He had also been there in the summer.

Thompson told me that Cleary was posted upon all his affairs, and that if I sought him (Thompson) at any time, and he was away, I might state my business to Mr. Cleary, and it would be all the same; that I could have perfect confidence in him, and that he was a very close-mouthed man.

On my return to Canada, a few days after the assassination, I found that those parties supposed that they were suspected of the assassination. They expected to be indicted in Canada, for a violation of the neutrality law, a number of days before they were indicted, and they told me they were destroying a great many of their papers. Tucker and Cleary both told me they were destroying their papers. Tucker said, in an interview I had with him after my return, that it was too bad they had not been allowed to act when they wanted to.

[A paper containing a secret cipher, found among J. Wilkes Booth's effects, introduced in evidence, was here handed to the witness.]

I am familiar with two of the secret ciphers used by the Confederates; this is one of them. I saw this cipher in 1864, in Mr. Clay's house—the private house in which I was stopping at St. Catherines.

During my stay in Canada I was in the service of the United States Government, seeking to acquire information in regard to the plans and purposes of the rebels who were assembled there. To do this most effectually, I adopted the name of James Thompson; and leading them to suppose this was my correct name, I adopted some other name at any hotel at which I might be stopping. I was intrusted with dispatches from these Confederates to take to Richmond. I carried some to Gordonsville, with instructions to send them from there. I received a reply to these dispatches, which I carried back to Canada, bringing them through Washington, and making them known to the United States Government. I took no dispatches from the rebel Government to their agents in Canada without first delivering them to the authorities at Washington.

I received a dispatch at Gordonsville from a gentleman who represented himself as being in the rebel State Department, and sent by their Secretary of State. This dispatch I delivered to Mr. Thompson in October. Thompson, Clay, Cleary, and others represented themselves as being in the service of the Confederate Government.

I frequently heard the subject of raids upon our frontier, and the burning of cities, spoken of by Thompson, Clay, Cleary, Tucker, and Sanders. Mr. Clement C. Clay was one of the prime movers in the matter before the raids were started. They received his direct indorsement. He represented himself to me as being a sort of representative of their War Department at Richmond. The men I have reference to, more especially Mr. Clay and Mr. Thompson, represented that they were acting under the sanction of their Government, and as having full power to act with reference to that; that they had full power to do any thing that they deemed expedient and for the benefit of their cause.

I was in Canada when arrangements were made to fire the City of New York. I left Canada to bring the news to Washington, two days before the attempt was made. It originated in Canada, and had the full sanction of these men.

Before the St. Albans' raid I knew of it; I was not, however, aware of the precise point aimed at, but I informed the Government at Washington that these men were about setting out on a raid of that kind. I also informed the Government of the intended raids upon Buffalo and Rochester, and by that means prevented them. I heard Mr. Clay say, in speaking about the funds for paying these raids, that he always had plenty of money to pay for any thing that was worth paying for. I know that they had funds deposited in several different banks. They transacted considerable business with one which is, I think, called the Niagara District Bank; it was almost opposite to Mr. Clay's residence in St. Catherines.

With respect to George N. Sander's position, Mr. Clay told me I had better not tell him all the things I was bent upon, nor all the things they intrusted to me; that he was a very good man to do their dirty work. Those were Mr. Clay's words. He said Sanders was associated with men that they could not associate with; but that he was very useful in that way—a very useful man indeed.

When Mr. Jacob Thompson spoke to me of the assassination, in January of this year, he said he was in favor of the proposition that had been made to him to put the President, Mr. Stanton, General Grant, and others out of the way; but had deferred giving his answer until he had consulted his Government at Richmond, and that he was only waiting their approval. I do not know, of my own knowledge, that he received an answer; my impression, from what Beverly Tucker said, was that he had received their answer and their approval, and that they had been detained waiting for that.

Cross-examined by MR. AIKEN.

I am originally from New York City. I received from the Confederate Government, for going to Gordonsville with those dispatches, equivalent to $150, in greenbacks. I reported that fact to the War Department at Washington, and applied it on my expense account as having been received from the United States Government. On my return from Gordonsville, I handed the original dispatches over to the authorities here. All those they selected to go ahead I carried on; all those they did not, they retained.

Recalled for the Prosecution.—June 12.

[A paper was here handed to the witness by the Judge Advocate.]

That paper I received from Clement C. Clay, jr., on the evening of the 1st or 2d of November, 1864. I saw Mr. Clay write a very considerable portion of it myself, and a part of the letter was written with my own pen. It was written in his house, in St. Catherines, Canada West, which, I believe, is on Park Street. I delivered a copy of that letter to the Hon. C. A. Dana, Secretary of War, here in Washington. I was instructed to deliver the original to Mr. Benjamin, Secretary of State of the Confederate States, if I could get to Richmond, and to tell him that I was informed of the names that were to be inserted in the blanks in the original letter. There are two or three such blanks left for names. There was no signature to the letter, which was omitted principally for my safety, and also that, in the event of its being seized, it could not be used as evidence against Mr. Clay. Both of these reasons were given to me by Mr. Clay. Mr. Clay left Canada about the 1st of January.

[The original of the following letter was then read and put in evidence:]

ST. CATHERINES, C. W., November 1, 1864.

Hon. J. P. Benjamin, Secretary of State, Richmond, Virginia:

SIR: You have doubtless learned, through the press of the United States, of the raid on St. Albans, Vermont, by about twenty-five Confederate soldiers—nearly all of them es-caped prisoners—led by Lieutenant Bennett H. Young; of their attempts and failure to burn the town; and of their robbery of three banks there of the aggregate amount of about $200,000; of their arrest in Canada by United States forces, their commitment, and the pending preliminary trial. There are twelve or fourteen of the twenty-five who have been arrested, and are now in prison at Montreal, where the trial for commitment for extradition is now progressing. A letter from Hon. J. J. N. Abbott, the leading counsel for the prisoners, dated Montreal, 28th October, says to me: "We (prisoners' counsel) all think it quite clear that the facts will not justify a commitment for extradition under the law as it stands, and we conceive the strength of our position to consist in the documents we hold, establishing the authority of the raiders from the Confederate States Government. But there is no doubt that this authority might be made more explicit than it is, in so far as regards the particular acts complained of, and I presume the Confederate Government will consider it to be their duty to recognize officially the acts of Lieutenant Young and his party, and will find means to convey such recognition to the prisoners here, in such a form as can be proven before our courts. If this were accompanied or followed by a demand upon our Government that the prisoners be set at liberty, I think a good effect would be produced, although probably the application would not be received by the authorities. There will be at least a fortnight's time, and probably more, expended in the examination of witnesses; so that there will be plenty of time for any thing that may be thought advisable to be done in behalf of the prisoners."

I met Mr. Young at Halifax, on my way here, in May last. He showed me letters from men whom I know, by reputation, to be true friends of States' rights, and therefore of Southern independence, vouching for his integrity as a man, his piety as a Christian, and his loyalty as a soldier of the South. After satisfying me that his heart was with us in our struggle, and that he had suffered imprisonment for many months as a soldier of the Confederate States army, from which he had escaped, he developed his plans for retaliating on the enemy some of the injuries and outrages inflicted upon the South. I thought them feasible and fully warranted by the law of nations, and therefore recommended him and his plans to the Secretary of War. He was sent back by the Secretary of War, with a commission as Second Lieutenant, to execute his plans and purposes, but to report to Hon. —— and myself. We prevented his achieving or attempting what I am sure he could have done, for reasons which may be fully explained hereafter. Finally, disappointed in his original purpose and in all the subsequent enterprises projected, he proposed to return to the Confederate States, via Halifax, but passing through the New England States, and burning some towns, and robbing them of whatever he could convert *to the use of the Confederate Government.* This I approved as justifiable retaliation. He attempted to burn the town of St. Albans, Vermont, and would have succeeded but for the failure of the chemical preparations with which he was armed. Believing the town was already fired in several places, and must be destroyed, he then robbed the banks of all the funds he could find—amounting to more than $200,000. That *he* was not prompted by selfish or mercenary motives, and that he did not intend to convert the funds taken to his own use, but to that of the Confederate States, I am as well satisfied as I am that he is an honest man, a true soldier, and patriot; and no one who knows him well will question his title to this character. He assured me, before going on the raid, that his efforts would be to destroy towns and farm houses, not to plunder or rob; but he said if, after firing a town, he saw he could take funds from a bank, or any house, which might inflict injury on the enemy and benefit his own Government, he would do so. He added, most emphatically, that whatever he took should be turned over to the government or its representatives in foreign lands. My instructions to him, oft repeated, were "to destroy whatever was valuable; not to stop to rob; but if, after firing a town, he could seize and carry off money, or treasury or bank notes, he might do so, upon condition that they were delivered to the proper authorities of the Confederate States." That they were not delivered according to his promise and undertaking was owing, I am sure, to the failure of his chemical compound to fire the town, and to the capture of himself and men on Canadian soil, where they were surprised and overpowered by superior numbers from the United States. On showing me his commission and his instructions from Mr. Seddon—which were, of course, vague and indefinite—he said he was authorized to do all the damage he could to the enemy in the *way of retaliation.* If this be true, it seems to me the Confederate States Government should not hesitate to avow his act was fully authorized as warrantable retaliation. If the Government do not assume the responsibility of this raid, I think Lieutenant Y. and his men will be given up to the United States authorities. If so, I fear the exasperated and alarmed people of Vermont will exert cruel and summary vengeance upon them before they reach the prison at St. Albans.

The sympathies of nine-tenths of the Canadians are with Young and his men; a majority of all the newspapers justify or excuse his act as merely retaliatory, and they desire only the authority of the Confederate States Government for it to refuse their extradition. The refusal of extradition is fully warranted by the like course of the United States in many cases, cited lately in the Canadian papers, which I can not now repeat, but which you can readily find. The refusal of extradition would have a salutary political influence, it is thought, both in the British Provinces and in England. I can not now explain why. I trust, therefore, for the sake not only of the brave soldiers who attempted this daring exploit, (which has caused a panic throughout the United States bordering on Canada, and the organization of forces to resist, as well as the arbitrary and tyrannous order of General Dix touching the coming Presidential election,) but, for the sake of our cause and country, that the President will assume the responsibility of the act of Lieutenant Bennett H. Young, and that you will signify it in such form as will entitle it to admission as evidence in the pending trial.

I send the special messenger who brings this, that your answer may be brought back by him within ten days or by 11th instant. The final judgment can and will be postponed for the action of the Confederate States Government as long as possible—certainly for ten days.

I avail myself of this opportunity to bring to your notice the case of Captain Charles H. Cole, another escaped prisoner of General Forrest's command, who was taken about six weeks since in the Michigan, (the Federal war steamer on Lake Erie,) and is charged with an attempt at piracy, (for attempting to capture the vessel,) with being a spy, etc. The truth is, that he projected and came very near executing a plan for the capture of that vessel and the rescue of the prisoners on Johnson's Island. He failed only because of the return of the Captain (Carter) of the Michigan a day sooner than expected, and the betrayal (in consequence of C.'s return) of the entire plot. The only plausible ground for charging him with being a spy is that he was in Sandusky, on Johnson's Island, and in the Michigan frequently, without having on his person the Confederate uniform, but wearing the dress of a private citizen. Mr. ——— and I have addressed a letter to the commandant at Johnson's Island, protesting against his being treated as a spy for the following reasons: "That he was in the territory of the United States as a prisoner against his consent; that he escaped by changing his garb; that he had no Confederate uniform when he visited Sandusky, Johnson's Island, and the Michigan; that he did not visit them as an *emissary from the Confederate States;* that whatever he conceived, he had not executed any thing; that he had conveyed no information to his Government, and did not contemplate conveying any information to the Government." His trial has been postponed. I know not why, or to what time. His exchange should be proposed, and notice given that any punishment inflicted on him will be retaliated upon, as officer of equal rank. He is a very brave and daring soldier and patriot, and deserves the protection of his Government.

L wrote to you on the 14th of June; to the President, 25th July; and to you again on the 11th August and 12th September last. I trust you received those letters. Mr. H. (who, I see, has gotten into the Confederate States) has doubtless explained things here. I have never received a line from you or any person, except my brother, at Richmond.

I have not changed the views expressed in my former communications. All that a large portion of the Northern people—especially in the North-west—want to resist the oppressions of the despotism at Washington, is a *leader*. They are ripe for resistance, and *it may come soon after the Presidential election*. At all events, it must come, if our armies are not overcome and destroyed or dispersed. No people of the Anglo-Saxon blood can long endure the usurpations and tyrannies of Lincoln. Democrats are more hated by Northern Republicans than Southern rebels, and will be as much outraged and persecuted if Lincoln is re-elected. They must yield to a cruel and disgraceful despotism or fight. They feel it and know it.

I do not see that I can achieve any thing by remaining longer in this Province, and, unless instructed to stay, shall leave here by 20th instant for Halifax, and take my chances for running the blockade. If I am to stay till spring, I wish my wife to join me under flag of truce, if possible. I am afraid to risk a winter's residence in this latitude and climate.

I need not sign this. The bearer and the person to whom it is addressed can identify me.

But I see no reasons why your response should not be signed and sealed, so as to make it evidence, as suggested, in respect to the St. Albans' raid. A statement of prisoners' counsel has been sent by way of Halifax and Wilmington, but it may never reach you, or not in time for the deliverance of the prisoners. This is my chief reason for sending this by one I can trust. Please reply promptly, and start the messenger back as soon as possible. He will explain the character of his mission. Send under a seal that can not be broken without being discovered.

I am respectfully, your most obedient servant.

N. B. See the Secretary of War (Mr. Seddon) touching Young's case.

Recalled for the Prosecution.—June 13.

The time occupied to go by rail from Montreal to Washington City, is between thirty-six and thirty-eight hours. The train which leaves Montreal at 3 o'clock in the afternoon connects with trains for Washington, so that a person leaving at 3 o'clock on the afternoon of the 12th, would certainly reach Washington before daylight on the morning of the 14th.

WILLIAM H. ROHRER.
For the Prosecution.—June 13.

I am acquainted with Clement C. Clay, jr., formerly of the United States Senate. I have had opportunities for becoming well acquainted with his handwriting. I have examined the paper that has been testified to by Richard Montgomery, and from memory and comparison, I have no hesitation in pronouncing it the writing of Clement C. Clay.

SANFORD CONOVER.
For the Prosecution.—May 20.

I was born in New York, and educated there. Since October last, I have resided in Montreal, Canada. Previous to that, I resided a short time in Baltimore. Before that, I was conscripted, from near Columbia, S. C., into the rebel service, but was detailed as a clerk, and served as such in the rebel War Department at Richmond, for upward of six months. Mr. James A. Seddon was at that time the rebel Secretary of War. I "ran the blockade" from Richmond, by walking most of the way. I rode on the cars to Hanover Junction, and from there walked up through Snickersville to Charlestown, Va., and from there to Harper's Ferry, and so on.

While in Canada, I was intimately acquainted with George N. Sanders, Jacob Thompson, Clement C. Clay, Dr. Blackburn, Beverly Tucker, William C. Cleary, Lewis Castleman, Rev. M. Cameron, Mr. Porterfield, Captain Magruder, General Frost of Missouri, General Carroll of Tennessee, and a number of others of less note. Of the accused who visited these persons, I knew John Wilkes Booth and John H. Surratt. Booth I saw but once. That was in the latter part of October last. I think I saw him with Sanders, and also at Mr. Thompson's. I saw him principally about the St. Lawrence Hall. He was strutting about there, dissipating, playing billiards, etc.

Surratt I saw in Montreal somewhere about the 6th or 7th of April last, on several successive days. Surratt is a man of about five feet, nine, ten, or eleven inches; a spare man, light complexioned, and light hair. I saw him in Mr. Thompson's room; and, from the conversation, Surratt had just brought dispatches from Richmond to Mr. Thompson, to which their conversation referred. One dispatch was from Mr. Benjamin, the rebel Secretary of State, and there was also a letter, I think in cipher, from Mr. Davis. I had previously had some conversation with Mr. Thompson on the subject of the plot to assassinate Mr. Lincoln and his Cabinet, and I had been invited by Mr. Thompson to participate in the enterprise.

On the occasion when Surratt brought the dispatches, Thompson laid his hand on them and said, "This makes the thing all right," referring to the assent of the rebel authorities. Mr. Lincoln, Mr. Johnson, the Secretary of War, the Secretary of State, Judge Chase, and General Grant were to be victims of this plot.

Mr. Thompson said, on one of these occasions, that it would leave the Government entirely without a head. That there was no provision in the Constitution of the United States by which, if these men were removed, they could elect another President. Mr. Welles (Secretary of the Navy) was also named; but Mr. Thompson said it was not worth while to kill him.

My first interview with Mr. Thompson was at his room, in the St. Lawrence Hall Hotel, Montreal, in the early part of February last. I had called on him to make some inquiry about the intended raid on Ogdensburg, N. Y., which had failed because the United States Government had received intimation of the intentions of the rebels, and were prepared for it. Mr. Thompson said, "We will have to drop it for a time, but we will catch them asleep yet." And he added, "There is a better opportunity, a better chance to immortalize yourself and save your country." I told him I was ready to do any thing to save the country, and asked what was to be done. He said, "Some of our boys are going to play a grand joke on Abe and Andy." This led to explanations, when he informed me it was to kill them, or rather "to remove them from office." He said it was only removing them from office; that the killing of a tyrant was no murder. Thompson had blank commissions, and he told me then, or subsequently, that he had conferred one on Booth; that he had been commissioned, and that everybody that engaged in the enterprise would be commissioned; so that, if it succeeded or failed, if they escaped to Canada, they could not be successfully claimed under the Extradition Treaty.

I know, of my own personal knowledge, that the commission conferred on Bennett H. Young, the St. Albans' raider, was a blank commission, filled up and conferred by Mr. Clay. The name attached to it, when it came into the hands of these men from Richmond, was that of James A. Seddon, Secretary of War. I saw this commission, and I was asked by Mr. Thompson as to the genuineness of Seddon's signature, having been a clerk in his department. I testified before Judge Smith, in the presence of Mr. Thompson, Sanders, Young, and Mr. Abbot, the counsel in the case, that the signature of Seddon was genuine. I am well acquainted with the handwriting of James A. Seddon, and know that the blank commission was in his handwriting.

These commissions were left blank, except the signature of Seddon, the rebel Secretary of War; the names were filled up in Canada. These commissions were conferred at pleasure upon those who engaged in any enterprise, and it was understood to be a cover, so that in case they were detected they could claim

that they were rebel soldiers, and to be protected and treated as prisoners of war. Booth, I believe, was specially commissioned for the assassination project. The commission of Bennett H. Young was of this sort, and was filled up and conferred by Mr. Clay.

On the day before, or the very day of the assassination, I had a conversation with Mr. Wm. C. Cleary, at the St. Lawrence Hotel, in Montreal. We were speaking of the rejoicings in the States over the surrender of Lee and the capture of Richmond, etc, and Cleary remarked that they would put the laugh on the other side of their mouth in a day or two. The conspiracy was talked of at that time about as commonly as one would speak of the weather.

Before this I had a conversation with George N. Sanders, who asked me if I knew Booth very well. He expressed some apprehension that Booth would make a fizzle of it; that he was dissipated and reckless, and he was afraid the whole thing would prove a failure.

While in Canada I was a correspondent of the New York Tribune. I communicated to the New York Tribune the contemplated assassination of the President and the intended raid on Ogdensburg. The assassination plot they declined to publish, because they had been accused of publishing sensation stories. The plot of the assassination I communicated in March last, and also in February, I think; certainly before the 4th of March.

I saw John H. Surratt in Montreal, about the 7th to the 9th of April, within four or five days of the assassination of the President. From the whole of his conversation I inferred that he was to take his part in the conspiracy on the President and his Cabinet, whatever that conspiracy might be. I do not remember that I heard any thing said about money or compensation, but it was always well understood that there was plenty of money where there was any thing to be done. At the time of this conversation I understood that John H. Surratt was just from Richmond.

In the conversation I had with Mr. Thompson in February, he said that killing a tyrant in such a case was no murder. He asked me if I had ever read the work entitled "Killing, no Murder," a letter addressed by Col. Titus to Oliver Cromwell. Mr. Hamlin was also to have been included had the scheme been carried out before the 4th of March. In the conversation in April, Mr. Hamlin was omitted, and Vice-President Johnson put in his place.

There was a proposition before these parties to destroy the Croton Dam, by which the City of New York is supplied with water. It was supposed it would not only damage the manufactories, but distress the people generally very much. Mr. Thompson remarked that they would have plenty of fires, and the whole city would soon be destroyed by a general conflagration, without sending any Kennedy or anybody else there; and, he added, if they had thought of this scheme before, they might have saved some necks. That was said a few weeks ago, when Mr. Thompson, Sanders, Castleman, Gen. Carroll, and myself were present.

I heard a great deal of talk about the attempted descent upon Chicago last year; that they had some eight hundred men concealed there; their object, as stated by Thompson and others, was the release of the rebel prisoners at Camp Douglas.

Cross-examined by MR. DOSTER.

I do not think I ever saw either of the prisoners, Atzerodt or Payne, in Canada.

Cross-examined by Mr. AIKEN.

I left Richmond to go North in December, 1863. I afterward, while in Washington, became a correspondent of the New York Tribune, and in October of last year I went to Canada in that capacity. I received compensation for my services as correspondent to the Tribune, but have never received any pay from the Government, nor the promise of any, nor have I ever received any pay from the Confederate Government. The parties in Canada did not know that I corresponded with the Tribune. I was freely admitted to their meetings and enjoyed their confidence. My reason for communicating the intended assassination to the Tribune, and not directly to the Government, was that I supposed that the relations between the editor and proprietor of the Tribune and the Government were such, that they would lose no time in giving them information on the subject. In regard to the conspiracy, as well as to some other secrets of the rebels in Canada, I requested Mr. Gay of the Tribune to give information to the Government, and I believe he has formerly done so.

I met John H. Surratt in Mr. Thompson's room, and once in Mr. Sander's room. I spoke to Surratt, asking him what changes there were in Richmond, and how the place looked. While in Canada I went by the name of James Watson Wallace.

I heard the burning of the City of New York discussed by these parties, but I knew no particulars until after the attempt had been made. I never heard the name of Mary E. Surratt mentioned in any one of these conferences.

Cross-examined by MR. COX.

In February, I think it was, I heard the project of capturing the President and carrying him off to Richmond talked of. When Mr. Thompson first suggested that I should participate in the attempted assassination, I asked if it would meet with the approbation of the Government at Richmond; he said he thought it would, but he would know in a few days. That was early in February. It was in April, in Surratt's presence, that he referred to the dispatches that had been received from Richmond, part of which were in cipher, as having furnished the assent.

Recalled for the Prosecution.—May 22.

The Dr. Blackburn to whom I referred in my previous testimony, is the same that packed a number of trunks with infected clothing, for the purpose of introducing pestilence into the States. I have seen him associating with Jacob Thompson, George N. Sanders, his son, Lewis Sanders, Ex-Gov. Westcott of Florida, Lewis Castleman, William C. Cleary, Mr. Porterfield, Capt. Magruder, and a number of rebels of less note. Dr. Blackburn was there known and represented himself as an agent of the so-called Confederate Government, just as Jacob Thompson was an agent. In June last, I knew of Dr. Blackburn's trying to employ Mr. John Cameron, who lived in Montreal, to accompany him to Bermuda, for the purpose of taking charge of goods infected with yellow fever to bring to the cities of New York, Philadelphia, and, I understood, Washington. Cameron declined to go, being fearful of taking the yellow fever and dying himself. Compensation to the amount of several thousand dollars, he told me, had been offered him, which I understood was to be paid by Dr. Blackburn, or by other rebel agents. Mr. Jacob Thompson, I understood, was the moneyed agent; the others drew on him for what money they required. There were other parties in Montreal that Dr. Blackburn employed, or endeavored to employ, whom I knew by sight, but do not remember their names. There were two medical students. I heard Blackburn say that he went from Montreal to Bermuda, or some of the West India Islands, about a year ago last June, for the express purpose of attending cases of yellow fever, and collecting infected clothing, and forwarding it to New York, but for some reason the scheme failed. On one occasion, I remember, Jacob Thompson, Mr. Cleary, and, I think, Lewis Sanders, were present when Dr. Blackburn spoke of his enterprise. They all favored it, and were all very much interested in it.

It was proposed to destroy the Croton Dam at New York. Dr. Blackburn proposed to poison the reservoirs, and made a calculation of the amount of poisonous matter it would require to impregnate the water so far as to render an ordinary draught poisonous and deadly. He had taken the capacity of the reservoirs, and the amount of water that was generally kept in them. Strychnine, arsenic, prussic acid, and a number of others were spoken of as the poisons which he proposed to use. Blackburn regarded the scheme as feasible; Mr. Thompson, however, feared it would be impossible to collect so large a quantity of poisonous matter without exciting suspicion, and leading to the detection of the parties. Whether the scheme has been entirely abandoned or not, I do not know; but so far as the blowing up of the dam is concerned it has not been. Jacob Thompson fully approbated the enterprise, and discussed it freely, together with Mr. Lewis Sanders, Mr. Cleary, and Mr. M. A. Pallen of Mississippi, who had been a surgeon in the rebel army. The matter was discussed in June last, and I have heard it spoken of since. When Mr. Thompson made the suggestion that the collection of so large an amount of poison might attract attention to the operation, Mr. Pallen and others thought it could be managed in Europe. Pallen is a physician.

Among others that I knew in Toronto was Dr. Stuart Robinson, a Doctor of Divinity, a refugee from Kentucky, where he had been editor of a journal, called the True Presbyterian. He was present when some of these schemes were being discussed. I remember he approved of the poisoning of the Croton water. He said any thing under heaven, that could be done would be justifiable under the circumstances. He is regarded as one of the most intense of all the traitors who have taken refuge in Canada; he is, I believe, related to the Breckinridges of Kentucky. Dr. Robinson appeared to be on intimate terms with Jacob Thompson and Dr. Blackburn.

I saw John H. Surratt in Canada three or four days after the assassination of the President. I saw him in the street with a Mr. Porterfield. I learned immediately after that Surratt was suspected; that officers were on his track; and that he had decamped. Mr. Porterfield is a Southern gentleman, now a British subject, having been made so, I believe, by a special act of the Canadian Parliament. He has been for some time a broker or banker there. He is the agent who took charge of the St. Albans plunder for the Ontario bank, when prematurely given up by Judge Coursol. Porterfield is on very intimate terms with Thompson and Sanders.

When Mr. Thompson received the dispatches from Richmond in April assenting to the assassination, there were present Mr. Surratt, General Carroll of Tennessee, I think Mr. Castleman, and I believe there were one or two others in the room, sitting farther back. General Carroll participated in the conversation, and expressed himself as more anxious that Mr. Johnson should be killed than anybody else. He said that if the damned prick-louse were not killed by somebody, he would kill him himself. His expression was a word of contempt for a tailor, so I have always understood. At this interview it was distinctly said that the enterprise of assassinating the President was fully confirmed by the rebel authorities at Richmond.

Booth, whom I saw on one occasion in conversation with Sanders and Thompson, went by the nick-name of "Pet." I so heard him called by Mr. Thompson, I think; by Cleary, I am sure, and by others.

The firing of New York City was recognized among these parties as having been performed by the authority of the rebel Government, and was by the direction of Mr. Thompson. I so learned from Mr. Thompson, or at least from conversation in his presence. Thompson said Kennedy deserved to be hanged, and he was devilish glad he had been, because he was a stupid fellow, and a bungler, and had managed things badly.

I have always, in my convictions and feelings, been loyal to the Government of the United States, and escaped from the rebel service the first moment I had opportunity. I know, of my own personal knowledge, that Jefferson Davis was the head of the so-called Confederate States, and was called its President, and acted as such, controlling its armies and civil administration.

Recalled for the Prosecution.—June 27.

[The following was read by the Judge Advocate from a volume published in Montreal, by John Lovell, St. Nicholas Street, 1865, entitled "The St. Albans Raid; or, Investigation into the Charges against Lieutenant Bennett H. Young and Command for their Acts at St. Albans, Vt., on the 19th of October, 1864," at page 212:]

James Watson Wallace, of Virginia, on his oath, saith: I am a native of Virginia, one of the Confederate States. I resided in Jefferson, in the said State. I left that State in October. I know James A. Seddon was Secretary of War last year. Being shown and having examined the papers M, N, and O, I say that, from my knowledge of his handwriting, the signatures to said papers are the genuine signatures of the said James A. Seddon. I have seen him upon several occasions write and sign his name. He has signed documents, and afterward handed them to me, in my presence. I never was in the Confederate army. I was commissioned as Major to raise a battalion. I have seen a number of the commissions issued by the Confederate Government, and the commission of Lieutenant Young, marked "M," is in the usual form of all commissions issued in the army, which are always signed by the Secretary of War. I never served; I was incapacitated by an accident, and being then kidnapped by the Northerners.

I was in Richmond in September last. I then visited the War Department. It was then notorious that the war was to be carried into New England in the same way that the Northerners had done in Virginia. When I was in Virginia, I lived in my own house until I was burned out, and my family were turned out by the Northern soldiers.

The counsel for the United States object to the whole of this evidence as illegal, irrelevant, and foreign to the issue, and consequently decline to cross-examine.

[Signed]   J. WATSON WALLACE.

[The witness proceeded :]

That contains my testimony in that case, and a great deal more that I did not give. It is compounded of the testimony of myself and of a James Wallace, who also was examined in that case. There was also a William Pope Wallace, who gave testimony in that case, and I do not know but a fourth Wallace. The testimony of James Wallace is included in that of James Watson Wallace, the name under which I was there known. The testimony I gave on that occasion was correctly reported in the Witness; I think also in the Montreal Transcript. In the Gazette, and I think in the Telegraph, the report was the same as appears in that book, which was, I believe, printed from type set up in the Telegraph office.

[The following, cut from a newspaper, was then read by the Judge Advocate, and afterward offered in evidence :]

James Watson Wallace, sworn: I reside at present in this city; have been here since last October; formerly resided in the Confederate States. I know James A. Seddon; he occupied the position of Secretary of War. I should say the signatures to the papers M, N, O, are those of the said Seddon. I have on several occasions seen the signature of James A. Seddon, and have seen him on several occasions sign his name; he has signed documents in my presence, and handed them to me after signing. I never belonged to the Confederate army, but have seen many commissions issued by the Confederate Government. The commission of Lieutenant Young, marked M, is in the usual form. The army commissions are always signed by the Secretary of War. I have never seen a commission with the signature of the President or with the seal of the Government. The Confederate States, at the time I left the country, had no seal; one had been devised, but had not been prepared.

[The witness continued :]

That paragraph appeared in either the Witness or the Transcript, from one of which papers it is cut, and was published immediately after the trial, and correctly reports the testimony I gave on that occasion.

After giving my testimony here on the 20th and 22d of May, I left this city and returned to Canada, under instructions from Judge Holt to procure a certified copy of the evidence before the Court in the St. Albans case. I met Beverly Tucker, G. N. Sanders, his son, Lewis Sanders, General Carroll of Tennessee, M. A. Pallen of Mississippi, Ex-Governor Westcott of Florida, and a number of others. I had conversations with them, especially with Beverly Tucker and G. N. Sanders, in reference to events here in Washington, connected with the assassination, and the trial of the assassins. At that time they had not the slightest suspicion that I had been a witness before this Commission. They therefore received me with great cordiality, and the subject of the trial was very freely discussed.

Beverly Tucker made the remark, after dinner—I dined with them—that that scoundrel Stanton, and that blood-thirsty villain Holt, might protect themselves as long as they remained in office, and could protect themselves by a guard, but that would not always be the case, and, by the Eternal, he had a large account to settle with them. Sanders never made such vehement threats as I have heard Tucker and others make. Cleary threatened the officers of the Government for the execution of Beall. He said that Beall would have been pardoned if it had not been for Judge Holt; but, he said, "blood shall follow blood;" and added, "We have not done with them yet." He boasted of it, and reminded me, just after the killing of President Lincoln, of what he had said on a former occasion; namely, that retributive justice would come. He considered the killing of the President as an act of retributive justice.

I had been in Canada at my last visit but a short time when the parties of whom I have testified knew of my presence. I was not then aware that my testimony had been published, or I should not have gone there. While sitting in a saloon, one of the Canadian rebels came in, and, discovering my presence, immediately reported it to the rest; then there came in more than a dozen—Sanders, Tucker, Carroll, and O'Donnel, the man who boasted of setting fire to houses in New York, and others. They at once accused me of betraying their secrets in becoming a witness before this Commission. Not knowing at the time that my testimony had been published, I denied having testified. They insisted that it was so, and that they would not be satisfied unless I would give them a letter stating that I had not testified. I knew that it was only by doing something of that kind that I could get away from them. It was then arranged that I should go down to my hotel, and it was my intention, if I got out of their hands, to leave the place at once. When we got opposite the St. Lawrence Hall they said, "We will go up here." O'Donnel had a room at the St. Lawrence Hall. Just as I had entered his room, Beverly Tucker came in and said that a mere letter would not be sufficient; that, having testified before the Commission under oath, I must make an affidavit under oath, to make my denial equally strong. This, at first, I declined to do, when a dozen of them assailed me in the most furious manner, and O'Donnel, drawing from his pocket a pistol, said if I would not consent, I could not leave that room alive. I still declined for a time, when Sanders said to me, "Wallace, you see what kind of hands you are in; I hope you will not be foolish enough to refuse." It was under these circumstances that I consented.

Mr. Kerr, who defended the St. Albans raiders, was sent for to prepare the statement, when we adjourned to the room of Ex-Governor

Westcott. I then again declined giving my oath to any statement, and again pistols were held to my head by one of Morgan's guerrillas. I do not know his name, but I know him well as a rebel soldier. O'Donnel also presented his pistol at me, and assured me I must take the consequences if I would not do as they desired me. The affidavit was read to me in Westcott's room; I, however, paid little or no attention to it, and I there signed it, and went through the ceremony of taking an oath. They also brought some other man in, accompanying Mr. Kerr. Kerr had no knowledge of the menaces under which I signed the paper. Beverly Tucker said, before Kerr came, that in order to make my deposition of any value, it must seem that I did it willingly, and that I must not manifest any unwillingness to sign it before Kerr; if I did, they said they would follow me to hell.

When Kerr brought the paper for me to sign, I did so without any remark; although the statements in the body of the paper are absolutely false. The following, which appeared in the Montreal Telegraph, and afterward in the New York World, is a copy of the paper I signed.

[The paper was put in evidence.]

THE SUPPRESSED TESTIMONY.

Sanford Conover v. *James W. Wallace—Affidavits of the real Wallace—Five Hundred Dollars Reward offered for the Arrest of Conover—What Thompson said about a Proposition to Destroy Waterworks in Northern Cities—Interesting Depositions.*

[From the Montreal Evening Telegraph, June 10.]

To the Editor of the Evening Telegraph:

SIR: Please publish my affidavit now handed you, and the advertisement subjoined. I will obtain and furnish others for publication hereafter. I will add that if President Johnson will send me a safe conduct to go to Washington and return here, I will proceed thither and go before the Military Court and make *profert* of myself, in order that they may see whether or not I am the Sanford Conover who swore as stated.

JAMES W. WALLACE.

MONTREAL, *June* 8, 1865.

PROVINCE OF CANADA, DISTRICT OF MONTREAL.

James Watson Wallace, of the city and district of Montreal, counselor at law, being duly sworn upon the Holy Evangelists, doth depose and say: I am the same James Watson Wallace who gave evidence on the subject of the St. Albans raid, which evidence appears on page 212 of the printed report of the said case. I am a native of the county of Loudon, in the Commonwealth of Virginia. I arrived in Montreal in the month of October last past. I resided during a portion of last winter and spring in houses in Craig Street and Monique Street, in the city

of Montreal. I have seen and examined the report of what is called the suppressed evidence before the Court-martial now being holden at Washington City on Mistress Surratt, Payne, and others; and I have looked carefully through the report of the evidence in the New York papers of a person calling himself Sanford Conover, who deposed to the facts that while in Montreal he went by the name of James Watson Wallace, and gave evidence in the St. Albans raid investigation; that the said Sanford Conover evidently personated me before the said Court-martial; that I never gave any testimony whatsoever before the said Court-martial at Washington City; that I never had knowledge of John Wilkes Booth, except seeing him upon the stage, and did not know he was in Montreal until I saw it published, after the murder of President Lincoln; that I never was a correspondent of the New York Tribune; that I never went under the name of Sanford Conover; that I never had any confidential communication with George N. Sanders, Beverly Tucker, Hon. Jacob Thompson, General Carroll of Tennessee, Dr. M. A. Pallen, or any of the others therein mentioned; that my acquaintance with every one of these gentleman was slight; and, in fine, I have no hesitation in stating that the evidence of the said Sanford Conover personating me is false, untrue, and unfounded in fact, and is from beginning to end a tissue of falsehoods.

I have made this deposition voluntarily and in justice to my own character and name.

[Signed] J. WATSON WALLACE.

Sworn to before me, at Montreal, this eighth day of June, 1865.

G. SMITH, J. P.

I, Alfred Perry, of Montreal, do hereby certify that I was present when the said James Watson Wallace gave the above deposition, and that he gave it of his own free will; and I further declare he is the same individual who gave evidence before the Honorable Justice Smith in the case of the St. Albans raiders. ALFRED PERRY

MONTREAL, *June* 9.

Extract from suppressed testimony given at Washington before the Military Commission by Sanford Conover, *alias* J. Watson Wallace, on the first two days of the proceedings, as published in the New York papers:

Q. State whether you did testify on the question of the genuineness of that signature of Seddon?

A. I did.

Q. In what court?

A. I testified before Judge——that the signature was genuine.

Q. State to the Court whether you are acquainted and familiar with the handwriting of James A. Seddon, the rebel Secretary of War?

A. Yes, sir.

Q. State to the Court, upon your oath here, whether the signature to the blank commission you saw was his genuine signature or not?

A. It was his genuine signature.

Q. Did you go to Canada by the name of Samuel Conover?

A. No, sir.

Q. What name did you go there by?

A. James Watson Wallace.

[The witness continued:]

Of Alfred Perry, the person named in the paper, I know nothing. I never heard of such a person.

[The Judge Advocate here read the following, which was put in evidence:]

PROVINCE OF CANADA, DISTRICT OF MONTREAL.

William Hastings Kerr, of the city and district of Montreal, esquire, advocate, being duly sworn, doth depose and swear that he knows James Watson Wallace, late of Virginia, but now and for the last seven months resident in the city of Montreal, counselor at law; that he, this deponent, was one of the counsel engaged for the defense in the affair of the investigation before the Hon. Judge Smith into the St. Albans raid; that he was present in Court, and examined the said James Watson Wallace while the said investigation was going on, a report of whose testimony appears at page 12 of the printed case, published by John Lovell, of the said city of Montreal; that this deponent has frequently seen the said James Watson Wallace on private business, and has acted as the said James Watson Wallace's professional adviser in Montreal; that this deponent yesterday saw the said James Watson Wallace in the said city of Montreal; that he was present while the said James Watson Wallace denied that he, the said James Watson Wallace, was the person who, under the name of Sanford Conover, gave, before the Military Commission or Court-martial now and for some time past assembled in Washington, evidence which has since been published as the suppressed evidence in the New York papers—he, the said James Watson Wallace, then and there declaring that some person had personated him, the same James Watson Wallace, and had given testimony which, from beginning to end, was a tissue of falsehoods; that this deponent was present while the statements and denials of the said James Watson Wallace were reduced to writing in his presence, and signed by the said James Watson Wallace, and sworn to by him before G. Smith, Esq., one of her Majesty's justices of the peace; that the said James Watson Wallace then and there declared that he made the said affidavit voluntarily, and in order to clear himself from any suspicion of being the Sanford Conover in question. And this deponent saith that no force or violence was used toward the said James Watson Wallace, nor were any menaces or threats made use of toward him by any one, but he seemed to be anxious to make the said affidavit, and to use all means in his power to discover the person who had so personated him, the said James Watson Wallace, before the Military Commission; and further this deponent saith not, and hath signed.   WILLIAM H. KERR.

Sworn before me at Montreal, this ninth day of June, eighteen hundred and sixty-five.
JAS. SMITH, J. S. C.

Five hundred dollars reward will be given for the arrest, so that I can bring to punishment, in Canada, the infamous and perjured scoundrel who recently personated me under the name of Sanford Conover, and deposed to a tissue of falsehoods before the Military Commission at Washington.
JAMES W. WALLACE.

[The witness continued:]

That paper and its preparation is part of the action referred to, and was prepared under the threat to which I have testified. I can not say positively that those parties attempted to detain me in Canada; I only know that I was rescued by the United States Government, through the interposition of Major-General Dix.

NATHAN AUSER.

For the Prosecution.—June 27.

I reside in New York, and am acquainted with Sanford Conover, who has just testified: I have known him eight or ten years; his character for integrity and usefulness is good, as far as I know. I recently accompanied him to Montreal, in Canada, and was present at an interview which he had with Beverly Tucker, George N. Sanders, and that clique of rebel conspirators. After we went into O'Donnel's room, at Montreal, Mr. Cameron gave each of us a paper containing the evidence Mr. Conover gave here in Washington before the Commission, when he denied it. They told him he must sign a written paper to that effect, and if he did not, he would not leave the room alive. O'Donnel said that he would shoot him like a dog if he did not. Mr. Conover was first going to his hotel to write the paper; at first they agreed to this, but when they got as far as St. Lawrence Hall, they made up their minds they would not let him do this himself, and when they went up stairs, at the St. Lawrence Hall, they would not allow me to go up. There were, I think, twelve or fifteen of the conspirators together; among them, Sanders, Tucker, O'Donnel, Gen. Carroll, Pallen, and Cameron. They all accompanied him for the purpose of preventing his escape, and obliging him to do what they required.

JAMES B. MERRITT.

For the Prosecution.—May 13.

I was born in Canada, while my parents were on a visit there from their home, Oneida county, New York. I am a physician, and have resided for about a year in Canada; part of the time at Windsor, and part at North Dumfries, Waterloo county.

In October or November last, I met at Toronto, George Young, formerly of Morgan's command; a man named Ford, also from Kentucky; and another named Graves, from Louisville. Young asked me if I had seen Colonel Steele before leaving Windsor. Steele was a rebel, and I understood had been in the rebel service. He asked me if Colonel Steele had said any thing to me in relation to the Presidential election. I told him he had not; he then said, "We have something on the *tapis* of much more importance than any raids we have made or can make." He said it was determined that Old Abe should never be inaugurated; that, I believe, was his expression. They had plenty of friends in Washington, he said; and, speaking of Mr. Lincoln, he called him a "damned old tyrant." I was afterward introduced to George N. Sanders by Colonel Steele. I asked Steele what was going to be done, or how he liked the prospects of the Presidential election, and he replied, "The damned old tyrant never will serve another term if he is elected." Mr. Sanders then said he (Lincoln) "would keep himself mighty close, if he did serve another term."

About the middle of February, a meeting of rebels was held in Montreal, to which I was invited by Captain Scott. I should think there were ten or fifteen persons present; among them were Sanders, Colonel Steele, Captain Scott, George Young, Byron Hill, Caldwell, Ford, Kirk, Benedict, and myself. At that meeting a letter was read by Sanders, which he said he had received from "the President of our Confederacy," meaning Jefferson Davis, the substance of which was that if the people in Canada and the Southerners in the States were willing to submit to be governed by such a tyrant as Lincoln, he did not wish to recognize them as friends or associates; and he expressed his approbation of whatever measures they might take to accomplish this object. The letter was read openly in the meeting by Sanders, after which it was handed to those present, and read by them, one after another. Colonel Steele, Young, and Hill, and I think Captain Scott, read it. I did not hear any objection raised.

At that meeting Sanders named a number of persons who were ready and willing, as he said, to engage in the undertaking to remove the President, Vice-President, the Cabinet, and some of the leading Generals; and that there was any amount of money to accomplish the purpose, meaning the assassination. Booth's name was mentioned, as also were the names of George Harper, Charles Caldwell, one Randall, and Harrison, by which name Surratt was known, and whom I saw in Toronto. Another person, I think, spoken of by Sanders, was one they called "Plug Tobacco," or Port Tobacco. I think I saw the prisoner, D. E. Herold, in Canada. Sanders said that Booth was heart and soul in this project of assassination, and felt as much as any person could feel, for the reason that he was a cousin to Beall that was hung in New York. He said that if they could dispose of Mr. Lincoln, it would be an easy matter to dispose of Mr. Johnson; he was such a drunken sot, it would be an easy matter to dispose of him in some of his drunken revelries. When Sanders read the letter, he also spoke of Mr. Seward. I inferred that it was partially the language of the letter. It was, I think, that if the President, Vice-President, and Cabinet, or Mr. Seward could be disposed of, it would be satisfying the people of the North; that they (the Southerners) had friends in the North, and that peace could be obtained on better terms than could be otherwise obtained; that they (the rebels) had endeavored to bring about the war between the United States and England, and that Mr. Seward, through his energy and sagacity, had thwarted all their efforts. This was suggested as one of the reasons for removing him.

On the evening of Wednesday, the 5th of April last, I was in Toronto, and when on my way to the theater, I met Harper and Ford. They asked me to go with them and spend the evening; I declined, as I was going to the theater. The next morning I was around by the Queen's Hotel, where I saw Harper, Caldwell, Randall, Charles Holt, and a man called "Texas." Harper said they were going to the States, and were going to kick up the damnedest row that had ever been heard of. An hour or two afterward I met Harper, and he said if I did not hear of the death of Old Abe, and of the Vice-President, and of General Dix, in less than ten days, I might put him down as a damned fool. This was the 6th of April.

Booth, I think, was mentioned as being in Washington. They said they had plenty of friends in Washington, and that there were some fifteen or twenty going there. On Saturday, the 8th of April, I was at Galt, five miles from which place Harper's mother lives, and I ascertained there that Harper and Caldwell had stopped there and had started for the States.

When I found that they had left for Washington, probably for the purpose of assassinating the President, I went to Squire Davidson, a justice of the peace, to give information and have them stopped. He said that the thing was too ridiculously or supremely absurd to take any notice of; it would only appear foolish to give such information and cause arrests to be made on such grounds; it was so inconsistent that no person would believe it, and he declined to issue any process.

I was in Galt again on Friday after the assassination, and I found from Mr. Ford that Harper had been home on the day before, and had started to go back to the States again.

Some time last fall, one Colonel Ashly, a rebel sympathizer, and a broker at Windsor, handed me a letter which he had received from Jacob Thompson, asking him for funds to enable rebels to pay their expenses in going to the States to make raids, as I understood; and, referring to the letter, he asked me to contribute.

In February last I had a conversation with Mr. Clement C. Clay in Toronto. I spoke to him about the letter from Mr. Jefferson Davis that Sanders had exhibited in Montreal; he seemed to understand the nature and character of the letter perfectly. I asked him what he thought about it. He said he thought the end would justify the means; that was his expression.

Surratt was once pointed out to me, in February, in Toronto; he was pointed out to me by Scott, I think, while he and Ford and myself were standing on the sidewalk.

I saw Booth in Canada two or three times; I sat at the table with him once at the St. Lawrence; Sanders, Scott, and Steele were at the same table. Sanders conversed with Booth, and we all drank wine at Mr. Sanders's expense. I have seen Booth a good many times on the stage, and know him very well by sight.

[The witness, being here shown a photograph, identified it as that of J. Wilkes Booth.]

I received a letter from General James B. Fry, the Provost Marshal General, stating that he had received a letter written by Squire Davidson, giving information of my visit to him for the purpose of having Harper and Caldwell arrested.

[The following letter was then read, and put in evidence:]

WAR DEPARTMENT,
PROVOST MARSHAL GENERAL'S BUREAU,
Washington, D. C., April 20, 1865. }

Dr. J. B. Merritt, Ayr, Canada West:

SIR: I have been informed that you possess information connected with a plot to assassinate the President of the United States and other prominent men of this Government. The bearer has been sent to present this letter to you, and to accompany you to this city, if you will come. The Secretary of War authorizes me to pledge you protection and security, and to pay all expenses connected with your journey both ways, and in addition to promise a suitable reward if reliable and useful information is furnished. Independent of these considerations, it is hoped that the cause of humanity and justice will induce you to act promptly in divulging any thing you may know connected with the recent

tragedy in this city, or with any other plots yet in preparation. The bearer is directed to pay all expenses connected with your trip.

I am, very respectfully,
Your obedient servant,
JAMES B. FRY,
Provost Marshal General.

Cross-examined by MR. STONE.

The man called Harrison I saw in Canada two or three times; I saw him once in a saloon, about the 15th or 20th of February; he was pointed out to me by Mr. Brown, I think, and I noticed him more particularly on account of his name having been mentioned, in connection with others, at the meeting in Montreal.

Cross-examined by MR. AIKEN.

I was on confidential terms with the rebels in Canada because I represented myself as a good Southerner. The letter from Jefferson Davis, which was read by Mr. Sanders, was read to the meeting some time in February, and on the 10th of April I went to see the justice of the peace; he refused to accede to my request. I then called upon the Judge of the Court of Assizes; made my statement to him, and he said I should have to go to the grand jury. I first communicated this information to the Government, I think, two weeks ago to-day, since the assassination of the President, though I understood the Government was in possession of the information before I communicated it direct.

I saw Surratt in Toronto about the 20th of last February; he was pointed out to me on the street, and passed down by me. Ford, who was with me, and who was present at the meeting held in Montreal, said, "Doctor, that is Surratt." He is a man five feet, six, seven, or eight inches, slim, and wore a dark moustache, and was dressed in ordinary clothes, like any gentleman would be, I think of a dark color. I am not positive that it was Surratt, because I do not know the man.

I knew of the project to burn the City of New York. I heard it talked of in Windsor, and communicated the information to Colonel Hill, of Detroit, before the attempt was made. It was communicated to me by Robert Drake, and a man named Smith, both formerly of Morgan's command. They both had been to Chicago to attend the Presidential Convention there. They told me, after their return, that they went there for the purpose of releasing the rebel prisoners at Camp Douglas.

I continued my intimacy with these rebel sympathizers for the purpose of giving information, when I should find it of importance. Nine-tenths of the people in Canada are rank rebel sympathizers, and my practice was mostly among Southerners. I have never received a dollar from the Government for furnishing any information from Canada, nor have I ever received any thing from the rebels for services rendered them. I have proof in my pocket from the Provost Marshal at Detroit, that I furnished valuable information without any remuneration.

Recalled for the Prosecution.—June 27.

On Friday, the 2d of June, I was in Montreal. At the St. Lawrence Hall I saw General Carroll. I introduced myself to him as Dr. Merrill of Memphis. There was a large family of Merrills residing there, who were physicians. He expressed considerable gratification at seeing me, and he introduced me to Governor Westcott, and we conversed in reference to this trial. These men were not aware that I had testified before this Commission. My testimony was not published there until Tuesday, the 6th of June. Mr. Beverly Tucker said, in that conversation, that they had friends in Court, and were perfectly posted as to every thing that was going on at this trial. Tucker said they had burned all the papers they had received from Richmond, for fear some Yankee would break into their room and steal them, and use them against them in this trial. In that interview, I should state that Governor Westcott expressed no disloyal sentiments, and took no part in the conversation.

GEORGE B. HUTCHINSON.

For the Prosecution.—June 23.

I am a native of England, and was an enlisted man in the service of the United States, from the 12th of June, 1861, to the 12th of November, 1862. I have resided in Canada for the last seven months. I have seen Clement C. Clay, Beverly Tucker, George N. Sanders, and others of that class several times. I last saw Clement C. Clay at the Queen's Hotel, Toronto, about the 12th or 13th of February.

On the 2d of June, and on the morning of the 3d, I saw Dr. Merritt in conversation with Beverly Tucker, at the St. Lawrence Hall in Montreal. I heard Beverly Tucker say, in reply to a remark of Dr. Merritt, that he had burned all the letters, for fear some Yankee son of a bitch might steal them out of his room, and use them in testimony against him. They were at the time speaking about this trial, and the charges against them. They were talking to Dr. Merritt as to one to whom they gave their confidence.

LIEUTENANT-GENERAL U. S. GRANT.

For the Prosecution.—May 12.

Since the 4th of March, 1864, I have been in the command of the armies of the United States. I met Jacob Thompson, formerly Secretary of the Interior under President Buchanan's administration, when the army was lying opposite Vicksburg, at what is called Milliken's Bend and Young's Point. A little boat was discovered coming up near

the opposite shore, apparently surreptitiously, and trying to avoid detection. A little tug was sent out from the navy to pick it up. When they got to it, they found a little white flag sticking out of the stern of the row-boat, and Jacob Thompson in it. They brought him to Admiral Porter's flag-ship, and I was sent for to meet him. I do not recollect the ostensible business he had. There seemed to be nothing at all important in the visit, but he pretended to be under a flag of truce, and he had therefore to be allowed to go back again. That was in January or February of '63; and it was the first flag of truce we had through. He professed to be in the military service of the rebels, and said that he had been offered a commission—any thing that he wanted; but, knowing that he was not a military man, he preferred having something more like a civil appointment, and he had therefore taken the place of Inspector-General, with the rank of Lieutenant-Colonel, in the rebel service.

The military department of Washington embraces all the defenses of the city on both sides of the river.

[The commission of Lieutenant-General Grant, dated March 4, 1864, accompanied by General Orders No. 98, was here offered in evidence.]

Cross-examination by Mr. AIKEN.

All the civil courts of the city are in operation. I am not prepared to say exactly to what point the Department of Washington extends; any troops that belong to the command of Major General Augur, who commands the Department of Washington, sent out to any point, would necessarily remain under his command. Martial law, I believe, extends to all the territory south of the railroad that runs across from Annapolis, running south to the Potomac and Chesapeake.

I understand that martial law extends south of Annapolis, although I have never seen the order.

SAMUEL P. JONES.

For the Prosecution.—May 12.

I resided in Richmond during a part of the war. I have often heard the officers and men of the Confederate army conversing respecting the assassination of President Lincoln. I have heard it discussed by rebel officers as they were sitting around their tents. They said they would like to see him brought there, dead or alive, and they thought it could be done. I heard a citizen make the remark that he would give from his private purse ten thousand dollars, in addition to the Confederate amount offered, to have the President of the United States assassinated, and brought to Richmond, dead or alive. I have, besides that, heard sums offered to be paid, with the Confederate sum, for any person or persons to go north and assassinate the President. I judge, from what I heard, that there was an amount offered by the Government in their trashy paper, to assassinate any officials of the United States Government that were hindering their cause.

HENRY VON STEINACKER.

For the Prosecution.—May 12.

I was in the Confederate service as an engineer officer in the Topographical Department, with the pay of an engineer, and was on the staff of General Edward Johnson. Altogether I was in the service nearly three years. In the summer of '63, being at Swift Run Gap, near Harrisonburg, I was overtaken by three citizens, and rode with them some eighteen or twenty hours. The name of one was Booth and another Shepherd.

[A photograph of John Wilkes Booth being shown to the witness, he identified a resemblance between it and the person referred to. The photograph was offered in evidence.]

I was asked by Booth, and also by the others, what I thought of the probable success of the Confederacy. I told them, after such a chase as we had just had from Gettysburg, I thought it looked very gloomy. Booth replied, "That is nonsense. If we only act our part, the Confederacy will gain its independence. Old Abe Lincoln must go up the spout, and the Confederacy will gain its independence any how." By this expression I understood he meant the President must be killed. He said that as soon as the Confederacy was nearly giving out, or as soon as they were nearly whipped, that this would be their final resource to gain their independence. The other two engaged in the conversation, and assented to Booth's sentiments.

They being splendidly mounted, and my horse being nearly broken down, they left me the next day. Three or four days afterward, when I came to the camp of the Second Virginia Regiment, I found there three citizens, and was formally introduced by Captain Randolph to Booth and Stevens. That evening there was a secret meeting of the officers, and the three citizens were also present. I was afterward informed of the purpose of the meeting by Lieutenant Cockrell of the Second Virginia Regiment, who was present. It was to send certain officers on "detached service" to Canada and the "borders" to release rebel prisoners, to lay Northern cities in ashes, and finally to get possession of the members of the Cabinet and kill the President. This "detached service" was a nickname in the Confederate army for this sort of warfare. I have heard these things spoken of, perhaps, a thousand times before I was informed it was the purpose discussed at this meeting, but I always considered it common braggadocio. I have freely heard it spoken of in the streets of Richmond among those connected with the rebel Government. Cockrell belonged, I believe, to the Second Virginia Regiment, and to the same company to which Captain Beall belonged, who was executed at Governor's Island. Cockrell told me that Beall was on "detached service," and that we would hear of him.

I have heard mention made of the existence of secret orders for certain purposes to assist the Confederacy. One I frequently heard of was called a Golden Circle, and several times I heard the name of the "Sons of Liberty."

[No cross-examination.]

HOSEA B. CARTER.

For the Prosecution.—May 29.

I reside in New Hampshire. I was at the St. Lawrence Hall, Montreal, Canada, from the 9th or 10th of September till the 1st of February last. I met George N. Sanders, Clement C. Clay, Beverly Tucker, Dr. Blackburn, Dr. Pallen, J. Wilkes Booth, General Carroll from Memphis, an old gentleman from Florida that wore a *cue*—I think his name was Westcott—a Dr. Wood, a gentleman named Clark, and many others whose names I do not now recollect. I do not remember that I saw Jacob Thompson there. I saw him at Niagara Falls on the 17th of June. Some twenty or thirty Southerners boarded at the St. Lawrence Hall, and usually associated together, and very little with other people who came there, either English or American.

I frequently observed George N. Sanders in intimate association with Booth, and others of that class, in Montreal. I used to see a man named Payne nearly every morning. I think they called him John. He was one of the Payne brothers, two of whom were arrested for the St. Albans raid; but Lewis Payne, the accused, I do not think I have seen before.

Dr. Blackburn came to the St. Lawrence Hall when the Donegana Hotel closed, which was about the 20th of October last. He seemed to associate on terms of intimacy with all those I have named, but Booth. Whether he came there before Booth I can not say. Blackburn was one of that *clique* of men who were known there as Confederates.

Cross-examined by MR. DOSTER.

I heard that the Paynes to whom I have referred originally came from Kentucky, and that they had been in the counterfeiting business. I think I have seen Cleary in Canada in company with John Payne. I have seen them in company with Sanders and Tucker and Blackburn every day.

JOHN DEVENY.

For the Prosecution.—May 12.

I have resided in Washington, off and on, for a year or two. I was formerly a Lieutenant in company "E," Fourth Maryland Regiment. I was before that employed in Adams's Express company. In July of 1863, I was in Montreal, and left there the 3d or 4th of

February of this year. I was well acquainted with John Wilkes Booth. The first time I saw him in Canada he was standing in the St. Lawrence Hotel, Montreal, talking with George N. Sanders. I believe that was in the month of October. They were talking confidentially, and drinking together. I saw them go into Dowley's and have a drink together. I also saw in Canada, at the same time, Jacob Thompson of Mississippi, who was Secretary of the Interior under the administration of President Buchanan. I also saw Mr. Clement C. Clay of Alabama, formerly United States Senator, Mr. Beverly Tucker, and several others who were pointed out to me; but I was not personally acquainted with those gentlemen. I spoke to Booth, and asked him if he was going to play there, knowing that he was an actor. He said he was not. I then said, "What are you going to do?" He said, "I just came here on a pleasure trip." The other Southerners, whose names I have mentioned, I have seen talking with Sanders, but I can not say positively that I saw them talking with Booth.

The next time I saw Booth was on the steps of the Kirkwood House, in this city, on the night of the 14th of April, between 5 and 6 o'clock. He was going into the hotel as I was standing talking to a young man named Callan. As Booth passed into the hotel, he turned round and spoke to me, and I asked him when he came from Canada. He said he had been back here for some time, and was going to stay here for some time, and would see me again. I asked, "Are you going to play here again?" He replied, "No, I am not going to play again; I am in the oil business." I laughed at his reply, it being a common joke to talk about the oil business. A few minutes afterward I saw him come down the street on horseback, riding a bay horse. I noticed particularly what kind of a looking rig he had on the horse, though I know not what made me do it. The next I saw of him was when he jumped out of the box of the theater, and fell on one hand and one knee, when I recognized him. He fell with his face toward the audience. I said, "He is John Wilkes Booth, and he has shot the President." I made that remark right there. That is the last I ever saw of him, when he was running across the stage. I heard the words "*Sic semper tyrannus*" shouted in the President's box before I saw the man. He had a knife in his hand as he went across the stage. If he made any remark as he went across the stage I did not notice it. The excitement was very great at the time.

WILLIAM E. WHEELER.

For the Prosecution.—May 12.

I reside in Chickopee, Massachusetts. I was at Montreal, Canada, in October or November last, when I saw John Wilkes Booth, who was standing in front of the St. Lawrence

Hall, Montreal. I spoke to Mr. Booth, and asked him if he was going to open the theater there. He said he was not. He left me, and entered into conversation with a person who was pointed out to me as George N. Sanders.

[No cross-examination.]

HENRY FINEGAS.

For the Prosecution.—May 26.

I reside in Boston, Mass., and have been in the United States service since the rebellion as a commissioned officer. In the month of February last I was in Montreal, Canada, and remained there eleven days. While there I knew well, by sight, George N. Sanders, William C. Cleary, and other men of that circle, but did not make their acquaintance personally. On one occasion I heard a conversation between George N. Sanders and Wm. C. Cleary; it took place at the St. Lawrence Hall on the 14th or 15th of February. I was sitting in a chair, and Sanders and Cleary walked in from the door; they stopped about ten feet from me, and I heard Cleary say, "I suppose they are getting ready for the inauguration of Lincoln next month." Sanders said, "Yes; if the boys only have luck, Lincoln won't trouble them much longer." Cleary asked, "Is every thing well?" Sanders replied, "O, yes; Booth is bossing the job."

Cross-examined by MR. AIKEN.

The conversation took place about 5 o'clock in the evening. Sanders and Cleary were standing close together, conversing in rather a low tone of voice, I thought. I never was introduced to Sanders or Cleary, but have been introduced to men who claimed to be escaped prisoners from camps in the North. I knew Sanders and Cleary by sight well; I saw them testify in court in the St. Albans raid case. Cleary is a middle-sized man, sandy complexion, sandy hair; carries his neck a little on one side, and has reddish whiskers. Sanders is a short-sized, low, thickset man, with grayish curly hair, a grayish moustache, and very burly form.

I left Montreal on the 17th of February. I first communicated this information to the Government a few days ago, but spoke of it to two or three parties some time ago. I did not consider it of any importance at the time, but looked upon it as a piece of braggadocio.

MRS. MARY HUDSPETH.

For the Prosecution.—May 12.

In November last, after the Presidential election, and on the day General Butler left New York, as I was riding on the Third Avenue cars, in New York City, I overheard the conversation of two men. They were talking most earnestly. One of them said he would leave for Washington the day after to-morrow. The other was going to Newburg, or Newbern, that night. One of the two was a young man with false whiskers. This I observed when a jolt of the car pushed his hat forward and at the same time pushed his whiskers, by which I observed that the front face was darker than it was under the whiskers. Judging by his conversation, he was a young man of education. The other, whose name was Johnson, was not. I noticed that the hand of the younger man was very beautiful, and showed that he had led a life of ease, not of labor. They exchanged letters while in the car. When the one who had the false whiskers put back the letters in his pocket, I saw a pistol in his belt. I overheard the younger say that he would leave for Washington the day after to-morrow; the other was very angry because it had not fallen on him to go to Washington. Both left the cars before I did. After they had left, my daughter, who was with me, picked up a letter which was lying on the floor of the car, immediately under where they sat, and gave it to me; and I, thinking it was mine, as I had letters of my own to post at the Nassau Street Post-office, took it without noticing that it was not one of my own. When I got to the broker's, where I was going with some gold, I noticed an envelope with two letters in it.

[Exhibiting an envelope with two letters.]

These are the letters, and both were contained in one envelope. After I examined the letters and found their character, I took them first to General Scott, who asked me to read them to him. He said he thought they were of great importance, and asked me to take them to General Dix. I did so.

[The following letters were then read to the Commission, and offered in evidence:]

DEAR LOUIS: The time has at last come that we have all so wished for, and upon you every thing depends. As it was decided before you left, we were to cast lots. Accordingly we did so, and you are to be the Charlotte Corday of the nineteenth century. When you remember the fearful, solemn vow that was taken by us, you will feel there is no drawback—*Abe* must *die*, and *now*. You can choose your weapons. The cup, the *knife*, the *bullet*. The cup failed us once, and might again. Johnson, who will give *this*, has been like an enraged demon since the meeting, because it has not fallen upon him to rid the world of the monster. He says the blood of his gray-haired father and his noble brother call upon him for revenge, and revenge he will have; if he can not wreak it upon the fountain-head, he will upon some of the blood-thirsty Generals. Butler would suit him. As our plans were all concocted and well arranged, we separated, and as I am writing—on my way to Detroit—I will only say that all rests upon you. You know where to find your friends. Your disguises are so perfect and complete, that without one

knew *your face*, no police telegraphic dispatch would catch you. The English gentleman, *Harcourt*, must not act hastily. Remember he has ten days. Strike for your home, strike for your country; bide your time, but strike sure. Get introduced, congratulate him, listen to his stories—not many more will the brute tell to earthly friends. Do any thing but fail, and meet us at the appointed place within the fortnight. Inclose this note, together with one of poor Leenea. I will give the reason for this when we meet. Return by Johnson. I wish I could go to you, but duty calls me to the *West;* you will probably hear from me in Washington. Sanders is doing us no good in Canada.

Believe me, your brother in love,

CHARLES SELBY.

ST. LOUIS, October 21, 1864.

DEAREST HUSBAND: Why do you not come home? You left me for ten days only, and you now have been from home more than two weeks. In that long time, only sent me one short note—a few cold words—and a check for money, which I did not require. What has come over you? Have you forgotten your wife and child? Baby calls for papa until my heart aches. *We are so lonely* without you. I have written to you again and again, and, as a last resource, yesterday wrote to Charlie, begging him to see you and tell you to come home. I am so ill, not able to leave my room; if I was, I would go to you wherever you were, if in *this world*. Mamma says I must not write any more, as I am too weak. Louis, darling, do not stay away any longer from your heart-broken wife.

LEENEA.

HON. CHARLES A. DANA.

For the Prosecution.—June 9.

The letters found and testified to by Mrs. Hudspeth, came to me by mail at the War Department, inclosed in one from General Dix. The letter from General Dix bears date November 17th, and I received it, I suppose, the next day. On receiving the letters I took them to the President, Mr. Lincoln, who looked at them, but I do not think he made any special remark; he seemed to attach very little importance to them. Two or three days after the assassination of the President, I was sent by the Secretary of War to find them. I went over to the White House and searched in the President's private desk, where I found them. I kept them for some time, and afterward delivered them to Judge Bingham. The President received a great many communications of a similar nature, but he seems to have attached more importance to these than any others, because I found them among his papers in an envelope marked, in his own handwriting, "Assassination." The two letters just put in evidence, are those that were inclosed in the letter from General Dix; and the letter from General Dix is in his own handwriting, with which I am familiar.

[The following letter from General Dix was then read and put in evidence:]

HEAD-QUARTERS, DEPARTMENT OF THE EAST, }
New York City, 17th November, 1864. }

C. A. DANA, Esq.—*My Dear Sir*: The inclosed was picked up in a Third Avenue railroad car. I should have thought the whole thing got up for the Sunday Mercury, but for the genuine letter from St. Louis in a female hand. The Charles Selby is obviously a manufacture. The party who dropped the letter was heard to say he would start for Washington Friday night. He is of medium size; has black hair and whiskers, but the latter are believed to be a disguise. He had disappeared before the letter was picked up and examined.

Yours truly,   JOHN A. DIX.

Cross-examined by MR. AIKEN.

The authorities of the War Department are in the habit of receiving a great many foolish letters from anonymous correspondents and others; some of a threatening character, and others making extraordinary propositions.

MAJOR T. T. ECKERT.

For the Prosecution.—June 13.

An order was sent forward to General Butler at New York for his troops to leave on the 11th of November. General Butler made application for leave to remain until the next Monday; the Secretary of War replied to the application, "You have permission to remain until Monday, the 14th of November."

IDENTIFICATION OF KEY TO SECRET CIPHER.

LIEUTENANT WILLIAM H. TERRY.

For the Prosecution.—May 18.

I am attached to the Provost Marshal's Office in this city. On the night of the assassination, Mr. Eaton placed in my hands certain papers which he had taken from the trunk of J. Wilkes Booth, at the National Hotel.

[A paper containing a secret cipher was handed to the witness.]

This is one of the papers I received from Mr. Eaton; it was in that envelope, on which Colonel Taylor marked the word "Important," and signed his initials to it.

WILLIAM EATON.

For the Prosecution.—May 18.

On the night of the 14th of April, after the assassination, I went, under authority of the War Department, to the National Hotel, to take charge of Booth's trunk and its con-

tents. I took all the papers to the Provost Marshal's Office, and placed them in the hands of Lieutenant Terry.

COLONEL JOSEPH H. TAYLOR.

For the Prosecution.—May 19.

I am on duty at the Head-Quarters of the Department of Washington.

[A paper containing a secret cipher was handed to the witness.]

I received this paper, on the night of the 14th of April last, from Lieutenant Terry, an officer on duty in the Provost Marshal's Office, who had been sent by me to examine Booth's trunk, where it was found among Booth's papers.

HON. C. A. DANA.

For the Prosecution.—May 20.

I am Assistant Secretary of War. I was in Richmond, Va., on Wednesday, the 5th of April—Richmond being evacuated on the 3d. On the 6th of April I went into the office of Mr. Benjamin, the rebel Secretary of State. On the shelf, among Mr. Benjamin's books and other things, I found this secret cipher key.

[The secret cipher key is a model consisting of a cylinder six inches in length, and two and one-half in diameter, fixed in a frame, the cylinder having the printed key pasted over it. By shifting the pointers fixed over the cylinder on the upper portion of the frame, according to a certain arrangement previously agreed upon, the cipher letter or dispatch can readily be deciphered. The model was put in evidence.]

I saw it was a key to the official rebel cipher, and as we had a good many of them to decipher at different times at the War Department, it seemed to me of interest, and I therefore brought it away. Mr. Benjamin's offices consist of a series of rooms in succession. His own office was the inmost of all; the next room, where his library was, and which seemed to have been occupied by his most confidential clerk or assistant, was the one in which I found several interesting documents, and this cipher model among them. I sent it to Major Eckert at the War Department, who has charge of the ciphers there.

MAJOR T. T. ECKERT.

For the Prosecution.—May 20.

[A secret cipher, found among the effects of J. Wilkes Booth, already in evidence, was here handed to the witness; also the secret cipher model just testified to.]

I have examined the secret cipher found in Booth's trunk, and the other cipher just testified to by the Assistant Secretary of War, and find they are the same.

Cipher dispatches from the rebel authorities have from time to time fallen into my hands, and as I am somewhat familiar with them, they have been referred to me for examination. Some of the dispatches referred to me were worked on the same plan.

[The witness here produced cipher dispatches bearing date October 13th and 19th.]

These dispatches which I hold in my hand are copies and translations of certain cipher dispatches which came from Canada; they passed through the War Department in this city, where copies were taken of them, and the originals forwarded to Richmond. These dispatches are written in the cipher to which this model and the paper found in Booth's trunk furnish the key.

[The dispatches were then read as follows, and put in evidence:]

OCTOBER 13, 1864.

We again urge the immense necessity of our gaining immediate advantages. Strain every nerve for victory. We now look upon the re-election of Lincoln in November as almost certain, and we need to whip his hirelings to prevent it. Besides, with ·Lincoln re-elected and his armies victorious, we need not hope even for recognition, much less the help mentioned in our last. Holcombe will explain this. Those figures of the Yankee armies are correct to a unit. Our friend shall be immediately set to work as you direct.

OCTOBER 19, 1864.

Your letter of the 13th instant is at hand. There is yet time enough to colonize many voters before November. A blow will shortly be stricken here. It is not quite time. General Longstreet is to attack Sheridan without delay, and then move North, as far as practicable, toward unprotected points.

This will be made instead of movement before mentioned.

He will endeavor to assist the Republicans in collecting their ballots. Be watchful, and assist him.

CIPHER LETTER.

CHARLES DUELL.

For the Prosecution.—June 5.

I reside in Washington. I was recently engaged in business, driving piles at Morehead City, N. C. While there, I found a letter floating in the water; it was in cipher. My attention was first called to it by Mr. Ferguson, who was working there. The envelope was addressed "John W. Wise." I made inquiries relative to the person to whom it was addressed, but I could hear of no one of that name in North Carolina.

[The translation of the letter was here read, and the original put in evidence.]

WASHINGTON, April the 15, '65.

DEAR JOHN: I am happy to inform you that Pet has done his work well. He is safe, and Old Abe is in hell. Now, sir, all eyes are on you. You must bring Sherman—Grant is in the hands of Old Gray ere this. Red Shoes showed lack of nerve in Seward's case, but fell back in good order.

Johnson must come. Old Crook has him in charge.

Mind well that brother's oath, and you will have no difficulty; all will be safe, and enjoy the fruit of our labors.

We had a large meeting last night. All were bent in carrying out the programme to the letter. The rails are laid for safe exit. Old ——, always behind, lost the pop at City Point.

Now, I say again, the lives of our brave officers, and the life of the South depend upon the carrying this programme into effect. No. Two will give you this. It's ordered no more letters shall be sent by mail. When you write, sign no real name, and send by some of our friends who are coming home. We want you to write us how the news was received there. We receive great encouragement from all quarters. I hope there will be no getting weak in the knees. I was in Baltimore yesterday. Pet had not got there yet. Your folks are well, and have heard from you. Don't lose your nerve.

C. B.   No. FIVE.

The letter just read, is, I believe, a correct translation of the cipher.

Cross-examined by MR. AIKEN.

In making the translation I had the assistance of a gentleman in North Carolina, who told me he had seen the cipher before. We first supposed, by its beginning with a W, that it was dated at Wilmington. The first evening we tried it with Wilmington, but we could not make out any thing. The next evening we tried the word "Washington," and "April," and made an alphabet, and stuck figures and characters under the letters of the alphabet, and proceeding in that way we at length worked it out.

JAMES FERGUSON.

For the Prosecution.—June 5.

I have recently been at Morehead City, N. C., where I have been working under Mr. Duell. While there, I discovered a letter floating in the water when we were at work, and called his attention to it. The letter which has been read is the same as was picked up; and I identify the envelope as the same. We found it either on the 1st or 2d of May last.

THE "LON" LETTER.

CHARLES DAWSON.

For the Prosecution.—June 2.

I am a clerk at the National Hotel in this city. In looking among the initials for a letter for a gentleman whose name begins with B, I found a letter addressed "J. W. B."

The initials struck me as being rather peculiar, and I took the letter unopened to Judge Advocate Bingham, about the 24th of May.

[The letter was read as follows, and it and the envelope were put in as evidence:]

ENVELOPE.

[P. O. stamp.]
Cumberland,
May 8.

J. W. B.,
National Hotel,
Washington,
D. C.

SOUTH BRANCH BRIDGE, April 6, 1865.

FRIEND WILKES: I received yours of March 12th, and reply as soon as practicable. I saw French, Brady, and others about the *oil* speculation. The subscription to the *stock* amounts to $8,000, and I add $1,000 myself, which is about all I can stand. Now, when you *sink* your well go DEEP enough; don't fail, every thing depends on you and your *helpers*. If you can't get through on your *trip*, after you *strike ile*, strike through Thornton Gap, and cross by Capon, Romney's, and down the Branch, and I can keep you safe from all hardships for a year. I am clear of all surveillance, now that infernal Purdy is beat. I hired that girl to charge him with an outrage, and reported him to old Kelly, which sent him in the *shade*, but he suspects to (too) damn much now. Had he better be *silenced for good?* I send this up by Tom, and if he don't get drunk you will get it the 9th; at all events, it can't be understood if lost. I can't half write. I have been drunk for two days. Don't write so much highfalutin next time. No more; only Jake will be at Green's with the funds. Burn this.

Truly, yours, LON.
Sue Guthrie sends much love.

The only guest at the National Hotel that I knew of to whom the initials J. W. B. belonged was John Wilkes Booth. Any letters addressed to Mr. Booth in full would be put into his box, as he had a room at the house. These being mere initials, the letter was put in with sundry letters for those who had no room in the house.

ROBERT PURDY.

For the Prosecution.—June 16.

I reside in Marshall County, West Virginia, near the Ohio River. I have been in the service of the United States since the 11th of December, 1861. Since the 23d of August last, I have belonged to a scouting company.

The letter signed "Lon" I never saw until it was published in the public papers. I have no knowledge whatever by whom it was written. I have heard of French, who is referred to in the letter, but I do not know of any one named Brady living on South Branch.

There is a man in that region of country named Lon; his full name is Leonidas McAleer, but he generally goes by the name of Lon. I have seen his handwriting. He showed me some notes that he said he had been black-mailed about. The writing of the letter resembles his. I am the Purdy referred to in the letter.

I captured a rebel spy a few miles from Lon's house. I understood he was to meet Lon McAleer that day to carry information there. I flanked the field and captured him, in company with two men named Darnduff, and a very reliable colored scout belonging to General Kelly. Lon McAleer had been playing both sides, loyal and disloyal; but as he had been lately bragging of his Unionism, I thought he would be glad to learn that the great rebel spy had been captured, so I rode down to him and told him. He cursed me for capturing the man, and said I should have taken his money and let him go. He said, when he went out and saw a small squad of rebels who could do no great damage to the railroad, he did not report it; but when he saw a force that could operate against Cumberland and New Creek, he always reported it. A day or two after that, I overtook a girl near his house. I halted her and searched her, and found her carrying letters. This was in the winter, in January, I think. A charge, such as that alluded to in the letter was made against me, but it was entirely false, and I afterward went to McAleer to get the thing settled. McAleer had a white servant named Tom, a deaf man, who afterward married this girl. I have heard he drinks.

I do not know any person of the name of Green in that neighborhood; but there are Greens some seventy or eight miles off, and there may be other families of that name that I do not know of.

The route through Thornton Gap, crossing by Capon, Romney's, and down the Branch, is an obscure route, of which I never knew till lately. It passes right through by Green's house at Thornton Gap. Green's reputation is that of a very disloyal man.

I do not know the Sue Guthrie mentioned, but I have ascertained that she is a lady who lived with Mr. French. I once wrote a letter to French, warning him that some deserters from our army were going to commit robbery at his house. It was then that McAleer told me that French was his father-in-law.

Cross-examined by MR. AIKEN.

I am acting for the Government as detective and scout. I have been charged with writing that letter myself. I was at South Branch Bridge in January last. South Branch empties into the Potomac River, and is from twenty-one to twenty-three miles from Cumberland. There is a railroad through South Branch to Cumberland. People at South Branch Bridge are not in the habit of taking their letters to Cumberland to mail. They generally take them to Green Spring Run, about one and three-fourths miles above.

PLOT TO CAPTURE.

SAMUEL KNAPP CHESTER.

For the Prosecution.—May 12.

I am by profession an actor, and have known J. Wilkes Booth a great many years. For six or seven years I have known him intimately. In the early part of November last I met him in New York, and asked him why he was not acting. He told me that he did not intend to act in this portion of the country again; that he had taken his wardrobe to Canada, and intended to run the blockade. I saw him again on the 24th or 25th of November, about the time we were to play "*Julius Cæsar*" in New York, which we did play on the 25th. I asked him where his wardrobe was; he said it was still in Canada, in charge of a friend. I think he named Martin in Montreal.

He told me he had a big speculation on hand, and asked me to go in with him. I met him on Broadway as he was talking with some friends. They were joking with him about his oil speculations. After he left them, he told me he had a better speculation than that on hand, and one they wouldn't laugh at. Some time after that I met him again, and he asked me how I would like to go in with him. I told him I was without means, and therefore could not. He said that didn't matter; that he always liked me, and would furnish the means. He then returned to Washington, from which place I received several letters from him. He told me he was speculating in farms in lower Maryland and Virginia; still telling me that he was sure to coin money, and that I must go in with him.

About the latter part of December, or early in January, he came to New York, and called on me at my house, No. 45 Grove Street. He asked me to take a walk with him which I did. We went into a saloon known as the "House of Lords," on Houston Street, and remained there perhaps an hour, eating and drinking. We afterward went to another saloon under the Revere House, after which we started up Broadway. He had often mentioned his speculation, but would never mention what it was. If I would ask him, he would say he would tell me by-and-by. When we came to the corner of Bleecker Street, I turned and bade him good night. He asked me to walk further with him, and we walked up Fourth Street, because he said Fourth Street was not so full of people as Broadway, and he wanted to tell me about that speculation. When we got into the unfrequented portion of the street, he stopped and told me that he was in a large conspiracy to capture the heads of the Government, including the President, and to take them to Richmond. I asked him if that was the speculation that he wished me to go into. He said it was. I told him I could not do it;

that it was an impossibility; and asked him to think of my family. He said he had two or three thousand dollars that he could leave them. He urged the matter, and talked with me, I suppose, half an hour; but I still refused to give my assent. Then he said to me, "You will at least not betray me;" and added, "You dare not." He said he could implicate me in the affair any how. The party he said were sworn together, and if I attempted to betray them, I would be hunted down through life. He urged me further, saying I had better go in. I told him "No," and bade him good night, and went home.

He told me that the affair was to take place at Ford's Theater in Washington, and the part he wished me to play, in carrying out this conspiracy, was to open the back door of the theater at a signal. He urged that the part I would have to play would be a very easy affair, and that it was sure to succeed, but needed some one connected or acquainted with the theater. He said every thing was in readiness, and that there were parties on the other side ready to co-operate with them. By these parties I understood him to mean the rebel authorities and others opposed to our Government. He said there were from fifty to one hundred persons engaged in the conspiracy.

He wrote to me again from Washington about this speculation; I think it must have been in January. I did not keep my letters. Every Sunday I devoted to answering my correspondence and destroying my letters. In January I got a letter from him, saying I must come. This was the letter in which he told me his plan was sure to succeed. I wrote back, saying that it was impossible, and I would not come. Then by return mail, I think, I got another letter, with fifty dollars inclosed, saying, I must come, and must be there by Saturday night. I did not go, nor have I been out of New York since last summer. The next time he came to New York, which I think was in February, he called on me again, and asked me to take a walk with him, and I did so. He then told me that he had been trying to get another party, one John Matthews, to join him, and when he told Matthews what he wanted, the man was very much frightened, and would not join him; and he said he would not have cared if he had sacrificed him. I told him I did not think it was right to speak in that manner. He said no; but Matthews was a coward, and was not fit to live. He then urged me again to join, and told me I must do so. He said there was plenty of money in the affair; and that, if I joined, I never would want for money again as long as I lived. He said the President and some of the heads of the Government came to the theater very frequently during Mr. Forrest's engagements. I desired him not to again mention the affair to me, but to think of my poor family. He said he would ruin me in the professios if I did not go. I told him I could not help that, and begged him not to mention the affair to me.

When he found I would not go, he said he honored my mother and respected my wife, and he was sorry he had mentioned this affair to me; but told me to make my mind easy, and he would trouble me no more. I then returned him the money he had sent me. He told me he would not allow me to do so, but that he was so very short of funds, and that either he or some other party must go to Richmond to obtain means to carry out their designs.

On Friday, one week previous to the assassination, I saw him again in New York. We were in the "House of Lords," sitting at a table. We had not been there long before he exclaimed, striking the table, "What an excellent chance I had to kill the President, if I had wished, on inauguration day!" He said he was as near the President on that day as he was to me.

Cross-examination by MR. EWING.

Booth spoke of the plot to capture the President, not to assassinate him, and to take him to Richmond. By the expression "other side," I understood him to mean across the lines—across the Potomac.

Booth did not say any thing as to the means he had provided or proposed to provide for conducting the President after he should be seized. On one occasion he told me that he was selling off his horses; that was after he had told me he had given up this project of the capture. It was, I think, in February that he said he had abandoned the idea of capturing the President and the heads of the Government. The affair, he said, had fallen through, owing to some parties backing out. It was on Friday, the 7th of April, one week previous to the assassination, that he said what an excellent chance he had had for killing the President.

BOOTH'S OIL SPECULATIONS.

JOSEPH H. SIMONDS.

For the Prosecution.—May 13.

I was acquainted with J. Wilkes Booth in his lifetime, and was his business agent, particularly in the oil region. I did some little business for him in the City of Boston, but it was very little, and was entirely closed up before I left there.

Mr. Booth's interest in the oil speculations was as follows: He owned a third undivided interest in a lease of three and a half acres on the Alleghany River, near Franklin. The land interest cost $4,000. He paid $2,000—that being one-half of it. He also purchased, for $1,000, an interest in an association there owning an undivided thirtieth of a contract.

That is all that he ever absolutely purchased. There was money spent for expenses on this lease, previous to his purchase of the land interest. He never realized a dollar from any interest possessed in the oil region. His speculations were a total loss.

The first interest he acquired in any way was in December, 1863, or January, 1864. I accompanied him to the oil regions in June, 1864, for the purpose of taking charge of his business there. The whole amount invested by him in this Alleghany River property, in every way, was about $5,000, and the other investment was about $1,000, making $6,000 in all.

His business was entirely closed out there on the 27th of September, 1864.

One of the conveyances was made to his brother, Junius Brutus Booth, which was without compensation; but a consideration was mentioned in the deed. The other transfer was to me, and it was done in consideration of my services, for which I never received any other pay. There was not a dollar paid to J. Wilkes Booth at all for these conveyances, and he paid all the expenses on the transfer and the conveyances.

JACOB THOMPSON'S BANK ACCOUNT.

ROBERT ANSON CAMPBELL.

For the Prosecution.—May 20.

I reside in Montreal, Canada, and am first teller of the Ontario Bank, of that city.

I know Mr. Jacob Thompson very well. His account with the Ontario Bank I hold in my hand. It commenced May 30, 1864, and closed April 11, 1865. Prior to May 30th, he left with us sterling exchange, drawn on the rebel agents in Liverpool, for collection. The first advice we had was May 30th, when there was placed to his credit £2,061 17s. 1½d., and £20,618 11s. 4d., amounting to $109,965.63. The aggregate amount of the credits is $649,873.28, and there is a balance still left to his credit of $1,766.23; all the rest has been drawn out. Since about the first of March he has drawn out $300,000, in sterling exchange and deposit receipts. On the 6th of April last there is a deposit receipt for $180,000. The banks in Canada give deposit receipts, which are paid when presented, upon fifteen days' notice. On the 8th of April he drew a bill of £446 12s. 1d., and on the same day £4,000 sterling. On the 24th of March he drew $100,000 in exchange; at another time $19,000. This sterling exchange was drawn to his credit, and also the deposit receipt.

Mr. Jacob Thompson has left Montreal since the 14th of April last. I heard him say that he was going away. He used to come to the bank two or three times a week, and the last time he was in he gave a check to the hotel-keeper, which I cashed, and he then left the hotel. His friends stated to me that he was going to Halifax, overland. Navigation was not open then, and I was told that he was going overland to Halifax, and thence to Europe. I thought it strange at the time that he was going overland, when by waiting two weeks longer he could have taken the steamer; and it was talked of in the bank among the clerks.

The account was opened with Jacob Thompson individually; the newspaper report was that he was financial agent of the Confederate States. We only knew that he brought Southern sterling exchange bills, drawn on Southern agents in the old country, and brought them to our bank for collection. How they came to him we did not know. He was not, as far as I know, engaged in any business in Canada requiring these large sums of money. He had other large money transactions in Canada. I knew of one transaction of $50,000, that came through the Niagara District Bank, at St. Catherines; a check drawn to the order of Mr. Clement C. Clay, and deposited by him in that bank; they sent it to us, August 16, 1864, to put it to their credit.

Thompson has several times bought from us United States notes, or greenbacks. On August 25th he bought $15,000 in greenbacks, and on July 14th, $19,125. This was the amount he paid in gold, and at that time the exchange was about 55. I could not say what the amount of greenbacks was, but that is what he paid for it in gold. On March 14th, last, he bought $1,000 worth of greenbacks at 44¾, for which he paid $552.20 in gold. On the 20th of March he bought £6,500 sterling at 9¼. He also bought drafts on New York in several instances.

J. Wilkes Booth, the actor, had a small account at our bank. I had one or two transactions with him, but do not remember more at present. He may have been in the bank a dozen times; and I distinctly remember seeing him once. He has still left to his credit $455, arising from a deposit made by him, consisting of $200 in $20 Montreal bills, and Davis's check on Merchants' Bank of $255. Davis is a broker, who kept his office opposite the St. Lawrence Hall, and is, I think, from either Richmond or Baltimore. When Booth came into the bank for this exchange, he bought a bill of exchange for £61 and some odd shillings, remarking, "I am going to run the blockade, and in case I should be captured, can my capturers make use of the exchange?" I told him they could not unless he indorsed the bill, which was made payable to his order. He then said he would take $300, and pulled out that amount, I think, in American gold. I figured up what $300 would come to at the rate of exchange—I think it was 9¼—and gave him a bill of exchange for £61 and some odd shillings.

Those are the Ontario Bank bills of exchange that were sold to Booth, bearing date October 27, 1864.

BOOTH AT THE NATIONAL HOTEL.

G. W. BUNKER.

For the Prosecution.—May 12.

I am a clerk at the National Hotel in this city. John Wilkes Booth has been in the habit of stopping at that hotel when he came to the city. From the register, which I have examined, I find that Booth was not at the National Hotel during the month of October, 1864. He arrived in the evening of November 9th, and occupied room "20;" left on an early train on the morning of the 11th; returned November 14th, in the early part of the evening, and left on the 16th. His next arrival was December 12th; left December 17th by the morning train; he arrived again December 22d; left on the 24th; arrived December 31; left January 10th; arrived again January 12th; left on the 28th; arrived again February 22d; occupied room "231," in company with John T. H. Wentworth and John McCullough. Booth left February 28th in 8:15 A. M. train, closing his account to date, inclusive. His name does not appear on the register, but another room is assigned to him, and his second account commences March 1st, without any entry on the register of that date. On the 2d, 3d, and 4th he is called at 8 o'clock A. M.; 21st of March, pays $50 on account, and left that day on 7:30 P. M. train; arrived again March 25th—room "231;" took tea, and left April 1st on an afternoon train; arrived April 8th, room "228," and remained there until the assassination of the President.

[The attention of the witness was directed to the prisoners at the bar.]

The only one of the accused I know is the one with the black whiskers and imperial, [pointing to the accused, Michael O'Laughlin.] I do not know his name, but know him by sight. He frequently called on Booth at the hotel. I do not think I saw him the last few days of Booth's stay there.

[A certified memorandum of the above dates, copied from the register of the National Hotel, was here offered in evidence.]

JEFF. DAVIS AND THE ASSASSINATION.

LEWIS F. BATES.

For the Prosecution.—May 30.

I reside in Charlotte, N. C., where I have resided a little over four years. I am Superintendent of the Southern Express Company for the State of North Carolina. I am a native of Massachusetts. On the 19th of

April, Jefferson Davis stopped at my house in Charlotte, when he made an address to the people from the steps of my house. While speaking, a telegram from John C. Breckinridge was handed him.

[The following telegram was here read to the Commission:]

GREENSBORO, April 19, 1865.

His Excellency President Davis:

President Lincoln was assassinated in the theater in Washington on the night of the 11th instant. Seward's house was entered on the same night, and he was repeatedly stabbed, and is probably mortally wounded.

JOHN C. BRECKINRIDGE.

In concluding his speech, Jefferson Davis read that dispatch aloud, and made this remark, "If it were to be done, it were better it were well done." I am quite sure these are the words he used.

A day or two afterward, Jefferson Davis and John C. Breckinridge were present at my house, when the assassination of the President was the subject of conversation. In speaking of it, John C. Breckinridge remarked to Davis, that he regretted it very much; that it was very unfortunate for the people of the South at that time. Davis replied, "Well, General, I don't know, if it were to be done at all, it were better that it were well done; and if the same had been done to Andy Johnson, the beast, and to Secretary Stanton, the job would then be complete." No remark was made at all as to the criminality of the act, and from the expression used by John C. Breckinridge, I drew the conclusion that he simply regarded it as unfortunate for the people of the South at that time.

J. C. COURTNEY.

For the Prosecution.—May 30.

I reside in Charlotte, N. C., and am engaged in the telegraphing business, in connection with the Southern Express Company.

The telegram to which Mr. Bates has just testified is a true copy of the message that was transmitted to Jefferson Davis on the 19th of April last, and signed John C. Breckinridge. I was standing by the operator when the message was received. Jefferson Davis received the message at Mr. Bates's house in Charlotte, to which place he had come from Greensburg or Concord, where he had stopped the night before.

JAMES E. RUSSELL.

For the Prosecution.—June 9.

I reside in Springfield, Mass. I have known Lewis F. Bates for about twenty-five years. For the last five years I have not known any thing of his whereabouts, until I learned from him that he had been living in Charlotte, N. C. He was in business as baggage-master on the Western Railroad, Massa-

chusetts, while I was conductor, and I never heard any thing against his reputation for truth.

WILLIAM L. CRANE.

For the Prosecution.—June 9.

I am the agent of Adams's Express Company in New York Eastern Division. I have known Lewis F. Bates since 1848, and have never heard any thing against his reputation as a man of truth and integrity.

DANIEL H. WILCOX.

For the Prosecution.—June 9.

I left the South a year ago last April. I have known Mr. L. F. Bates for two or three years quite intimately; he occupied a position of great trust and responsibility, and is a man of truth and integrity. He bore the best reputation possible. His character is without reproach, as far as I know.

JULES SOULE.

For the Prosecution.—June 9.

I reside in the city of New York at present; for the past few years I have lived in Columbia, S. C. I knew Mr. L. F. Bates; he bore the reputation of a truthful and reliable man, in every respect, to the best of my knowledge. We have been intimately connected in business for the last three or four years. The position he occupied was one of high responsibility and trust.

MAJOR T. T. ECKERT.

For the Prosecution.—June 9.

Mr. L. F. Bates was brought here by the order of the Secretary of War.

PLOT TO DESTOY STEAMERS, GUN-BOATS, ETC.

REV. W. H. RYDER.

For the Prosecution.—May 18.

I reside in Chicago. On the 9th of April I left that city for Richmond, Va.; arrived there the 14th, and remained there until the 21st of that month. While there I visited the State Capitol, and found the archives of the so-called Confederate States scattered about the floor; and, in common with others, took as many of these as I chose. I collected quite a number of papers in different rooms and from among the rubbish. There were one or two persons with me, and, as we handled the papers, any thing that seemed important or interesting we put into our pockets. Among the papers so found was this letter.

[The following letter was then read and offered in evidence:]

RICHMOND, February 11, 1865.

His Excellency Jefferson Davis, Pres't C. S. A.

SIR: When Senator Johnson of Missouri and myself waited on you a few days since, in relation to the prospect of annoying and harassing the enemy by means of burning their shipping, towns, etc., there were several remarks made by you upon the subject that I was not fully prepared to answer, but which, upon subsequent conference with parties proposing the enterprise, I find can not apply as objections to the scheme.

1. The combustible material consists of several preparations and not one alone, and can be used without exposing the party using them to the least danger of detection whatever. The preparations are not in the hands of McDaniel, but are in the hands of Professor McCullough, and are known but to him and one other party, as I understand.

2. There is no necessity for sending persons in the military service into the enemy's country; but the work may be done by agents, and, in most cases, by persons ignorant of the facts, and therefore innocent agents.

I have seen enough of the effects that can be produced to satisfy me, that, in most cases, without any danger to the parties engaged, and in others but very slight, we can—1. Burn every vessel that leaves a foreign port for the United States. 2. We can burn every transport that leaves the harbor of New York or other Northern port, with supplies for the armies of the enemy in the South. 3. Burn every transport and gunboat on the Mississippi River, as well as devastate the country of the enemy, and fill his people with terror and consternation. I am not alone of this opinion, but many other gentlemen are as fully and thoroughly impressed with the conviction as I am. I believe we have the means at our command, if promptly appropriated and energetically applied, to demoralize the Northern people in a very short time. For the purpose of satisfying your mind upon the subject, I respectfully, but earnestly, request that you will have an interview with General Harris, formerly a member of Congress from Missouri, who, I think, is able, from conclusive proofs, to convince you that what I have suggested is perfectly feasible and practicable.

The deep interest I feel for the success of our cause in this struggle, and the conviction of the importance of availing ourselves of every element of defense, must be my excuse for writing you, and requesting you to invite General Harris to see you. If you should see proper to do so, please signify the time when it will be convenient for you to see him.

I am, respectfully, your obedient servant,

W. S. OLDHAM.

INDORSEMENT.

Hon. W. S. Oldham. Richmond, February 12, 1865. In relation to plans and means for burning the enemy's shipping, towns, etc. Preparations are in the hands of Professor McCullough, and are known to only one other party. Asks the President to have an interview with General Harris, formerly a member of Congress from Missouri, on the subject.

SECOND INDORSEMENT.

Secretary of State, at his convenience, please see General Harris, and learn what plan he has for overcoming the difficulty heretofore experienced. J. D.

20 Feb'y, '65·

Rec'd Feb'y 17, 1865.

JOHN POTTS.

For the Prosecution.—May 18.

I am chief clerk in the War Department, which position I have filled for upward of twenty years. While Jefferson Davis was Secretary of War, I had abundant opportunities of becoming acquainted with his handwriting, and became perfectly familiar with it. In my belief, the indorsement on that letter just read is in his handwriting.

NATHAN RICE.

For the Prosecution.—May 18.

I was requisition clerk eight years ago, when Jefferson Davis was Secretary of War, and every day he had to sign the requisitions that came to me. The indorsement on the letter signed W. S. Oldham, I should think, was in the handwriting of Jefferson Davis. I had ample opportunities of becoming acquainted with his handwriting, seeing from ten to twenty-five signatures of his every day, and sometimes they were signed in my presence.

JOSHUA T. OWEN.

For the Prosecution.—May 18.

I have known Professor McCullough, I suppose, for twenty years; he was Professor of Chemistry at Princeton College. At Jefferson College, Pennsylvania, where I graduated about 1839 or 1840, he was Professor of Mathematics, and if my recollection serves me, he was Assayer at the Mint, Philadelphia. He has, I believe, been at Richmond during the rebellion, in the service of the Confederates. He had attained some distinction as a chemist, perhaps more in that than in anything else.

GENERAL ALEXANDER J. HAMILTON.

For the Prosecution.—May 20.

I am a citizen of the State of Texas, and was formerly a member of Congress from that state. I am perfectly familiar with the handwriting of Williamson S. Oldham. The letter which has just been introduced in evidence, signed W. S. Oldham, is in his handwriting. At the time of writing this letter, he was a member of the Senate of the so-called Confederate States. I so conclude, because I was present, in 1861, when he was elected for six years, by the rebel Legislature of Texas, to a seat in the Senate of the rebel Government, and since then I have seen reports of many speeches of his, and resolutions and bills introduced by him into the rebel Senate.

DESTRUCTION OF STEAMBOATS, Etc.

EDWARD FRAZIER.

For the Prosecution.—June 8.

I am a steamboat man, and have been making St. Louis my home for the last nine or ten years. During 1864 I knew of the operations of Tucker, Minor Majors, Thomas L. Clark, and Colonel Barrett of Missouri, for burning boats carrying Government freight, transports, and other vessels on the Mississippi, Ohio, and other rivers. These men were in the service of the Confederate Government. I knew of the following steamboats having been been burned by the operations of these parties: the Imperial, Hiawatha, the Robert Campbell, the Louisville, the Daniel G. Taylor, and others, besides some in New Orleans that I do not know the name of. The Imperial was one of the largest and finest transports on the western waters. In the case of the burning of the Robert Campbell, which was destroyed in the stream, when under way, at Milliken's Bend, twenty-five miles above Vicksburg, there was a considerable loss of life. The agent who destroyed this boat was on board. These boats were all owned by private individuals.

The operations of these men were to include Government hospitals, store-houses, and every thing appertaining to the army. A United States hospital at Louisville was burned in June or July of 1864. I do not know who burned it, but a man named Dillingham claimed compensation for it.

I was in Richmond from the 20th or 25th or 26th of August last, when I had an interview with the rebel Secretary of War, the Secretary of State, and Mr. Jefferson Davis. Thomas L. Clark, Dillingham, and myself called there in connection with the boat burning, and put in claims to Mr. James A. Seddon, the rebel Secretary of War. Mr. Clark introduced me to Mr. Seddon. He told me that he had thrown up that business; that it was now in the hands of Mr. Benjamin. We went to him, and Mr. Benjamin looked at the papers we brought him, and asked me if I knew any thing about them. I told him that I did, and that I believed they were all right. He asked me if I was from St. Louis; I told him I was. He then asked Mr. Clark if he knew me to be all right, and he said I had been represented to him by Mr. Majors

as being all right. Mr. Benjamin told us all three to call next day. We did so, when he said he had shown those papers to Jefferson Davis, and he (Benjamin) wanted to know if we would not take $30,000 and sign receipts in full. We told him we would not. Mr Benjamin then said that if Dillingham was to claim this in Louisville, he wanted a statement of it. We went back to the hotel, and I wrote the statement myself. It read that Mr. Dillingham had been hired by General Polk, and that he had been sent to Louisville expressly to do that work—namely, burn the hospital. It was then talekd over, with Mr. Benjamin, and we made a settlement with him for $50,000; $35,000 down in gold, and $15,000 on deposit, to be paid in four months, provided the claims proved correct. The money was paid by a draft on Columbia for $34,800 in gold, and $200 in gold we got in Richmond. We received the gold on the draft at Columbia.

While at Richmond Mr. Benjamin told me that Mr. Davis wanted to see me. I went in with Benjamin to see Mr. Davis, and we sat and talked. The conversation first was about what was called the Long Bridge, between Nashville and Chattanooga. Mr. Davis wanted to know what I thought about destroying it. He said they had been thinking about it, and of sending some one to have it done. I told him I knew of the bridge, though I did not, for I had never been there; but I did not know what to think about destroying it. He said I had better study it over. Finally, I told him I thought it could be done. Mr. Benjamin, I believe it was, who first remarked that he would give $400,000 if that bridge was destroyed, and asked me if I would take charge of it. I told him I would not, unless the passes were taken away from those men that were now down there; and Mr. Davis said it should be done. The conversation then turned on the burning of the steamboats. I told Mr. Davis that I did not think it was any use burning steamboats, and he said no, he was going to have that stopped. The next day I saw an order in the paper taking away passes issued on or before the 23d of August. These passes were permits to do this kind of work.

I asked Mr. Davis if it would make any difference where the work of destroying bridges was done. He said it did not; it might be done in Illinois, or any place; that we might destroy railroad bridges, commissary and quarter-master stores—any thing appertaining to the army, but as near Sherman's base as possible; that Sherman was the man who was doing more harm than any body else at that time.

I presume Mr. Davis knew that the pay I received was for the work I had done; he knew I had received money there.

The papers we presented were statements written out by Mr. Clark, of the services rendered and the amount claimed.

4

Mr. Davis seemed fully aware of what we had done, and he did not condemn it. Mr. Majors and Barrett belonged to an organization known as the O. A. K., or Order of American Knights.

Q. Will you state, if you think proper to do so, whether you are also a member of that order? You are not bound to state it, if the answer will criminate you in any way.

[The witness declined to answer.]

I understood that Colonel Barrett held the position of Adjutant-General of this organization, of the Sons of Liberty, for the State of Illinois. I do not know that Majors and Barrett were in Chicago in July last, but Mr. Majors left St. Louis, either in June or July, to go to Canada, and I presume went there by way of Chicago.

THE CITY POINT EXPLOSION.

BRIG.-GEN. E. D. TOWNSEND, U. S. A.

For the Prosecution.—June 12.

I was well acquainted with G. J. Rains, who resigned as Lieutenant-Colonel of the Fifth Regiment of United States Infantry in 1861. He has, I understand, since then been Brigadier-General in the rebel service. I am acquainted with his handwriting, and, to the best of my knowledge and belief, the signature to the indorsement now shown to me is in his handwriting.

[The following letter, with the indorsement, was then read and put in evidence:]

RICHMOND, December 16, 1864.

Capt. Z. McDaniel, Com'ding Torpedo Co.:

CAPTAIN: I have the honor to report that, in obedience to your order, and with the means and equipment furnished me by you, I left this city 26th July last, for the line of the James River, to operate with the "Hozological Torpedo" against the enemy's vessels navigating that river. I had with me Mr. R. K. Dillard, who was well acquainted with the localities, and whose services I engaged for the expedition. On arriving in Isle of Wight County on the 2d of August, we learned of immense supplies of stores being landed at City Point; and, for the purpose, by stratagem, of introducing our machine upon the vessels there discharging stores, started for that point. We reached there before daybreak, on the 9th of August last, with a small amount of provisions, having traveled mostly by night, and crawled upon our knees to pass the east picket line. Requesting my companion to remain behind about half a mile, I approached cautiously the wharf, with my machine and powder covered by a small box. Finding the Captain had come ashore from a barge then at the wharf, I seized the occasion to hurry forward with my box. Being halted by one of the wharf sentinels, I succeeded in passing him by representing that the Captain had ordered me to convey the box on board.

Hailing a man from the barge, I put the machine in motion, and gave it in his charge. He carried it aboard. The magazine contained about twelve pounds of powder. Rejoining my companion, we retired to a safe distance to witness the effect of our effort. In about an hour the explosion occurred. Its effect was communicated to another barge beyond the one operated upon, and also to a large wharf building containining their stores, (enemy's,) which was totally destroyed. The scene was terrific, and the effect deafened my companion to an extent from which he has not recovered. My own person was severely shocked, but I am thankful to Providence that we have both escaped without lasting injury. We obtained and refer you to the inclosed slips from the enemy's newspapers, which afford their testimony of the terrible effects of this blow. The enemy estimate the loss of life at fifty-eight killed and one hundred and twenty-six wounded, but we have reason to believe it greatly exceeded that.

The pecuniary damage we heard estimated at four millions of dollars; but of course we can give you no account of the extent of it exactly. I may be permitted, Captain, here to remark that, in the enemy's statement, a party of ladies, it seems, were killed by this explosion. It is saddening to me to realize the fact that the terrible effects of war induce such consequences; but when I remember the ordeal to which our own women have been submitted, and the barbarities of the enemy's crusade against us and them, my feelings are relieved by the reflection that while this catastrophe was not *intended* by us, it amounts only, in the providence of God, to just retaliation.

This being accomplished, we returned to the objects of our original expedition. We learned that a vessel (the Jane Duffield) was in Warwick River, and, with the assistance of Acting-Master W. H. Hinds, of the Confederate States navy, joined a volunteer party to capture her. She was boarded on the 17th September last, and taken without resistance. We did not destroy her, because of the effect it might have had on the neighboring citizens and our own further operations. At the instance of the Captain she was bonded, he offering as a hostage, in the nature of security to the bond, one of his crew, who is now held as a prisoner of war on this condition in this city.

In the meanwhile we operated on the James, as the weather and moon co-operated, but without other success than the fear with which the enemy advanced, and the consequent retarding of his movements on the river. We neared success on several occasions. Finding our plan of operations discovered by the enemy, and our persons made known and pursued by troops landed from their boats at Smithfield, we deemed it best to suspend operations in that quarter and return to report to you, officially, our labors. Your orders were to remain in the enemy's lines as long as we could do so; but I trust this conduct will meet your approval. The material unused has been safely concealed. I have thus, Captain, presented you in detail the operations conducted under your orders and the auspices of your company, and await further orders.

Very respectfully, your obedient servant,

JOHN MAXWELL.

INDORSEMENTS.

December 17, 1864.

Report of J. Maxwell, of Captain Z. McDaniel's Company, Secret Service, of his operations on James River.

Respectfully forwarded to Brigadier-General Rains.
Z. McDANIEL,
Captain Company A, Secret Service.

FOR. BU., RICHMOND, VA.
December 17, 1864.

For Hon. Secretary of War:

Present.

Respectfully forwarded, with remark that John Maxwell and R. K. Dillard were sent by Captain McDaniel into the enemy's lines by my authority, for some such purpose, and the supposition was strong, as soon as the tremendous explosion occurred at City Point, on the 9th August last, that it was done through their agency, but, of course, no report could be made until the parties returned, which they did on Wednesday last, and gave an account of their proceedings.

This succinct narrative is but an epitome of their operations, which necessarily implies secrecy, for the advantage of this kind of service, as well as their own preservation.

John Maxwell is a bold operator and well calculated for such exploits, and also his co-adjutor, R. K. Dillard.

G. J. RAINS,
Brigadier General, Sup't.

MILLION DOLLARS FOR ASSASSINATION.

JOHN CANTLIN.

For the Prosecution.—June 27.

I reside at Selma, Alabama, and am a printer. I was foreman of the Selma Dispatch in December last.

[The following advertisement, purporting to have been clipped from the Selma Dispatch, was then read by the Judge Advocate, and offered in evidence:]

"ONE MILLION DOLLARS WANTED TO HAVE PEACE BY THE 1ST OF MARCH.—If the citizens of the Southern Confederacy will furnish me with the cash, or good securities for the sum of one million dollars, I will cause the lives of Abraham Lincoln, Wm. H. Seward, and Andrew Johnson to be taken by the 1st of March next. This will give us peace, and satisfy the world that cruel tyrants can not live in a 'land of liberty.' If this is not accomplished, nothing will be claimed beyond

the sum of fifty thousand dollars in advance, which is supposed to be necessary to reach and slaughter the three villains.

"I will give, myself, one thousand dollars toward this patriotic purpose. Every one wishing to contribute will address Box X, Cahawba, Alabama.

"*December 1, 1864.*"

That advertisement was published in the Selma Dispatch, and, as far as I remember, at the date named. It was inserted four or five times; the manuscript passed through my hands, and was in the handwriting of Mr. G. W. Gayle, of Cahawba, Ala. His signature was on the manuscript, to indicate that he was the author, and was responsible for it. I am familiar with his handwriting.

The Selma Dispatch had a circulation of about eight hundred copies, and exchanged with most, if not all, the Richmond papers.

Mr. Gayle is a lawyer of considerable reputation, and is distinguished, even in Alabama, for his extreme views on the subject of slavery and the rebellion, and as an ardent supporter of the Confederacy.

W. D. GRAVES.

For the Prosecution.—June 27.

I reside in Selma, Alabama, and am a printer. I was engaged in the office of the Selma Dispatch in December last, and remember seeing an advertisement published in that paper, signed "X," bearing date December 1st, 1864, headed, "One Million of Dollars Wanted, to have Peace by the First of March." I saw the manuscript from which the advertisement just testified to was set up. It was in the handwriting of Colonel G. W. Gayle; I am well acquainted with it, having seen it frequently in articles we had published before.

PROPOSALS TO RID THE COUNTRY "OF SOME OF HER DEADLIEST ENEMIES."

COLONEL R. B. TREAT

For the Prosecution.—May 22.

I am Chief Commissary of the Army of the Ohio, and have recently been on duty in the State of North Carolina. The army with which I have been connected captured a variety of boxes said to contain archives of the so-called Confederate States. They were delivered up by General Joseph A. Johnston, at Charlotte, N. C.

A letter was sent to General Schofield at Raleigh from General Johnston at Charlotte, stating that he had in his possession there the records and archives of the Confederacy, which he was ready to deliver on General Schofield's sending an officer to receive them. The day following, an officer on the

General's staff was sent to Charlotte, who received them and brought them to Raleigh. From that point I brought them here, and delivered them at the War Department to Major Eckert, Acting Assistant Secretary of War.

MAJOR T. T. ECKERT.

For the Prosecution.—May 22.

Yesterday morning I received at the War Department certain boxes from Colonel Treat, purporting to contain the archives or records of the War Department of the so-called Confederate States. Some of these boxes, by my direction, have been opened by Mr. Frederick H. Hall, and their contents have undergone an examination by him.

FREDERICK H. HALL.

For the Prosecution.—May 22.

I have opened certain of the boxes delivered to Major Eckert, containing the archives of the so-called Confederate States. From the box marked "Adjutant and Inspector-General's Office; Letters received July to December, 1864," I took this letter.

[The following letter was then read and offered in evidence:]

MONTGOMERY, WHITE SULPHUR SPRINGS, VA.
To his Excellency the President of the Confederate States of America:

DEAR SIR: I have been thinking some time that I would make this communication to you, but have been deterred from doing so on account of ill health. I now offer you my services, and if you will favor me in my designs, I will proceed, as soon as my health will permit, to rid my country of some of her deadliest enemies, by striking at the very heart's blood of those who seek to enchain her in slavery. I consider nothing dishonorable having such a tendency. All I ask of you is to favor me by granting me the necessary papers, etc., to travel on while within the jurisdiction of the Confederate Government. I am perfectly familiar with the North, and feel confident that I can execute any thing I undertake. I am just returned now from within their lines. I am a lieutenant in General Duke's command, and I was on the raid last June in Kentucky under General John H. Morgan. I and all of my command, excepting about three or four, and two commissioned officers, were taken prisoners; but finding a good opportunity, while being taken to prison, I made my escape from them. Dressing myself in the garb of a citizen, I attempted to pass out through the mountain; but finding that impossible, narrowly escaping two or three times from being retaken, I shaped my course north and went through to the Canadas, from whence, by the assistance of Colonel J. P. Holcombe, I succeeded in making my way around and through the blockade; but

having taken the yellow fever, etc., at Bermuda, I have been rendered unilt for service since my arrival.

I was reared up in the State of Alabama, and educated at its university. Both the Secretary of War and his assistant, Judge Campbell, are personally acquainted with my father, William J. Alston, of the Fifth Congressional District of Alabama, having served in the time of the old Congress, in the years 1849–50–51.

If I do any thing for you, I shall expect your full confidence in return. If you do this, I can render you and my country very important service. Let me hear from you soon. I am anxious to be doing something, and having no command at present, all, or nearly all, being in garrison, I desire that you favor me in this a short time. I would like to have a personal interview with you, in order to perfect the arrangements before starting.

I am, very respectfully,
Your obedient servant,
LIEUT. W. ALSTON.

INDORSEMENTS.

A, 1,390. Lieutenant W. Alston, Montgomery, Sulphur Springs, Va. [No date.] Is lieutenant in General Duke's command. Accompanied raid into Kentucky and was captured, but escaped into Canada, from whence he found his way back. Been in bad health. Now offers his services to rid the country of some of its deadliest enemies. Asks for papers to permit him to travel within the jurisdiction of this Government. Would like to have an interview and explain.

Respectfully referred, by direction of the President, to the Honorable Secretary of War.
BURTON W. HARRISON,
Private Secretary.

Received November 29, 1864.
Recorded book A. A. G. O., December 15, 1864.
A. G. for attention.
By order. J. A. CAMPBELL, A. S. W.

LEWIS W. CHAMBERLAYNE.

For the Prosecution.—May 26.

I reside at Richmond, Virginia, and have been on duty as a clerk in the War Department of the Confederate States. While so acting, I became acquainted with the handwriting of John A. Campbell, rebel Assistant Secretary of War, and late Judge of the Supreme Court of the United States; also, with that of Burton W. Harrison, the Private Secretary of Jefferson Davis. I have examined the letter of Lieutenant W. Alston, and the indorsements thereon, and the indorsement, "Respectfully referred, by direction of the President, to the Honorable Secretary of War," is, to the best of my knowledge and belief, in the handwriting of Burton W Harrison, who was recognized in the War

Office at Richmond as the private secretary of Jefferson Davis.

The other indorsement,

"A. G. for attention.

"By order.

[Signed] "J. A. CAMPBELL, A. S. W." is in the handwriting of Judge Campbell.

COMMISSIONS FOR RAIDERS.

GEORGE F. EDMUNDS.

For the Prosecution.—May 27.

I reside at Burlington, Vt., and am counselor at law. At the recent trial of the St. Albans raiders that took place in Canada, I appeared as counsel in behalf of the Government of the United States.

In the performance of my duty there, I became acquainted with Jacob Thompson, William C. Cleary, Clement C. Clay, George N. Sanders, and others of that *clique.* They assumed to be officers of the Confederate Government in defending these raiders. I have no personal knowledge of their real authority, but they were notoriously understood there to be the representatives of the rebel cause. Mr. Cleary was examined as a witness on the part of the defendants; he represented that the persons engaged in this raid were acting under the authority of the Confederate Government. All those who testified stood upon that defense.

The volume entitled "The St. Albans Raiders, or Investigation into the Charges against Lieutenant Bennett H. Young, and Command for their acts at St. Albans, Vt., on the 19th of October, 1864, compiled by L. N. Benjamin, B. C. L., printed at Montreal by John Lovell," contains, on page 216, a copy of a paper marked R, the original of which was given in evidence at the trial, on the part of the defendant, Mr. Young, and others. I examined the original very critically, and I am able to swear that this is substantially a copy, and I have no doubt it is a literal one.

[The following was then read and put in evidence:]

PAPER R.

CONFEDERATE STATES OF AMERICA, WAR DEPARTMENT, Richmond, Va., June 16, 1864.

To Lieutenant Bennett H. Young:

LIEUTENANT: You have been appointed temporarily first lieutenant in the provisional army for special service.

You will proceed, without delay, to the British Provinces, where you will report to Messrs. Thompson and Clay for instructions.

You will, under their direction, collect together such Confederate soldiers who have escaped from the enemy, not exceeding twenty in number, as you may deem suitable for the purpose, and will execute such enterprises as may be intrusted to you. You will take care to commit no violation of the local law, and

to obey implicitly their instructions. You and your men will receive from these gentlemen transportation, and the customary rations and clothing, or the commutation therefor.

JAMES A. SEDDON, VA., June 16. *Secretary of War.*

Bennett H. Young, who was on trial, produced that document as his authority for the acts he did at St. Albans.

HENRY G. EDSON.

For the Prosecution.—June 10.

I reside at St. Albans, Vt., and am an attorney and counselor at law. I was in Canada during the judicial investigations in connection with the St. Albans raid, acting as counsel in behalf of the bank and the United States. I saw there George N. Sanders, Jacob Thompson, Clement C. Clay, and others of that circle of rebels.

I heard a conversation between George N. Sanders and other parties at St. John's, in regard to movements in the States contemplated by the rebel authorities. I made a memorandum in my diary of this conversation at the time.

In speaking of the so-called St. Albans raid, George N. Sanders said he was ignorant of it before it occurred, but was satisfied with it. He said that it was not the last that would occur; but it would be followed up by the depleting of many other banks, and the burning of many other towns on the frontier, and that many Yankee sons of —— (using a course, vulgar expression) would be killed. He said that they had their plans perfectly organized, and men ready to sack and burn Buffalo, Detroit, New York, and other places, and had deferred them for a time, but would soon see the plans wholly executed; and any preparation that could be made by the Government to prevent them would not, though it might defer them for a time. He made other statements in connection with the case; that he had hired a house in St. John's, which he intended to furnish himself, to accommodate his friends and attorneys; that he had employed twenty or thirty counsel in Canada.

Sanders claimed to be acting as an agent of the so-called Confederate Government. He said that he had retained the counsel who had acted in the case, and that Mr. Clement C. Clay, from the Clifton House, was also to aid.

PLOT TO BURN NEW YORK CITY.

COLONEL MARTIN BURKE.

For the Prosecution.—May 29.

I knew Robert C. Kennedy, who was hanged in New York in March last. I had charge of him and had him hung. I hold in my hand a confession made by him in my presence, a day or so before his execution.

[The following was then read and put in evidence:]

CONFESSION OF ROBERT C. KENNEDY.

After my escape from Johnson's Island, I went to Canada, where I met a number of Confederates. They asked me if I was willing to go on an expedition. I replied, "Yes, if it is in the service of my country." They said, "It is all right," but gave no intimation of its nature, nor did I ask for any. I was then sent to New York, where I staid some time. There were eight men in our party, of whom two fled to Canada. After we had been in New York three weeks, we were told that the object of the expedition was to retaliate on the North for the atrocities in the Shenandoah Valley. It was designed to set fire to the city on the night of the Presidential election; but the phosphorus was not ready, and it was put off until the 25th of November. I was stopping at the Belmont House, but moved into Prince Street. I set fire to four places—in Barnum's Museum, Lovejoy's Hotel, Tammany Hotel, and the New England House. The others only started fires in the house where each was lodging, and then ran off. Had they all done as I did, we would have had thirty-two fires, and played a huge joke on the fire department. I know that I am to be hung for setting fire to Barnum's Museum, but that was only a joke. I had no idea of doing it. I had been drinking, and went in there with a friend, and, just to scare the people, I emptied a bottle of phosphorus on the floor. We knew it would n't set fire to the wood, for we had tried it before, and at one time concluded to give the whole thing up.

There was no fiendishness about it. After setting fire to my four places, I walked the streets all night, and went to the Exchange Hotel early in the morning. We all met there that morning and the next night. My friend and I had rooms there, but we sat in the office nearly all the time, reading the papers, while we were watched by the detectives, of whom the hotel was full. I expected to die then, and if I had, it would have been all right; but now it seems rather hard. I escaped to Canada, and was glad enough when I crossed the bridge in safety.

I desired, however, to return to my command, and started with my friend for the Confederacy, via Detroit. Just before entering the city, he received an intimation that the detectives were on the lookout for us, and, giving me a signal, he jumped from the cars. I did n't notice the signal, but kept on, and was arrested in the depot.

I wish to say that killing women and children was the last thing thought of. We wanted to let the people of the North understand that there were two sides to this war, and that they can't be rolling in wealth and comfort, while we at the South are bearing all the hardships and privations.

In retaliation for Sheridan's atrocities in the Shenandoah Valley, we desired to destroy property, not the lives of women and children, although that would, of course, have followed in its train.

Done in the presence of
LIEUT-COL. MARTIN BURKE,
And J. HOWARD, JR.
March 24, 10:30 P. M.

INTRODUCTION OF PESTILENCE.

GODFREY JOSEPH HYAMS.

For the Prosecution.—May 29.

I am a native of London, England, but have lived South nine or ten years. During the past year, I have resided in Toronto, Canada. About the middle of December, 1863, I made the acquaintance of Dr. Blackburn; I was introduced to him by the Rev. Stewart Robinson, at the Queen's Hotel, in Toronto. I knew him by sight previously, but before that had had no conversation with him. I knew that he was a Confederate, and was working for the rebellion. Dr. Blackburn was then about to take South some men who had escaped from the Federal service, and I asked to go with him.

He asked me if I wanted to go South and serve the Confederacy. I said I went. He then told me to come up stairs; he wanted to speak to me. He took me up stairs to a private room, and pledged his word, as a Freemason, and offered his hand in friendship, that he would never deceive me; he said he wanted to confide to me an expedition. I told him I would not care if I did. He said I would make an independent fortune by it, at least $100,000, and get more honor and glory to my name than General Lee, and be of more assistance to the Confederate Government, than if I was to take one hundred thousand soldiers to reinforce General Lee. I pledged my word that I would go, if I could do any good. He then told me he wanted me to take a certain quantity of clothing, consisting of shirts, coats, and underclothing into the States, and dispose of them by auction. I was to take them to Washington City, to Norfolk, and as far South as I could possibly go, where the Federal Government held possession and had the most troops, and to sell them on a hot day or of a night; that it did not matter what money I got for the clothes; I had just to dispose of them in the best market, where there were most troops, and where they would be most effective, and then come away.

He told me I should have $100,000 for my services; $60,000 of it directly after I returned to Toronto; but he said that would not be a circumstance to what I should get. He said I might make ten times $100,000.

I was to stay in Toronto, and go on with my legitimate business, until I heard from him. He told me to keep quiet, and if I moved anywhere, I was to inform Dr. Stuart Robinson where I went to, and he would telegraph for me, or write to me through him. Some time in the month of May, 1864, I went to my work, and worked on until the 8th day of June, 1864; it was on a Saturday night; I had been out to take a pair of boots home to a customer of mine; and when I returned home, my wife had a letter for me from Dr. Blackburn, which Dr. Stuart Robinson had left in passing there. I read the letter, and went out to see Dr. Robinson. I asked him what I was to do about it; he said he did not know any thing at all about it; that he did not want to furnish any means to commit an overt act against the United States Government. He advised me to borrow from Mr. Preston, who keeps a tobacco manufactory in Toronto, enough money to take me to Montreal, which I did. I went down to Montreal, and there got money from Mr. Slaughter, according to the directions contained in the letter. The letter instructed me to proceed from Montreal to Halifax to meet Dr. Blackburn; it was dated "Havana, May 10, 1864." I went to Halifax, to a gentleman by the name of Alexander H. Keith, jr., and remained under his care until Dr. Blackburn arrived in the steamer Alphia, on the 12th of July, 1864. When Dr. Blackburn arrived, he sent to the Farmer's Hotel, where I was staying, for me. I went to see him, and he told me that the goods were on board the steamer Alphia, and that the second officer on the steamer would go with me and get the goods off, as they had been smuggled in from Bermuda. Mr. Hill, the second officer, told me to get an express wagon and take it down to Cunard's steamboat wharf; I did so, and there got eight trunks and a valise. I was directed to take them to my hotel, and put them in a private room. I put them in Mr. Doran's private sitting-room.

I then went around to Dr. Blackburn and told him I had got the goods off the steamer. He told me that the five trunks tied up with ropes were the ones for me to take, and asked me if I would take the valise into the States, and send it by express, with an accompanying letter, as a donation to President Lincoln. I objected to taking it, and refused to do it. I then took three of the trunks and the valise around to his hotel. He was then staying at the Halifax Hotel. The trunks had Spanish marks upon them, and he told me to scrape them off; and that Mr. Hill would go with me the next morning, and make arrangements with some captain of a vessel to take them. There were two vessels there running to Boston, and I was to make an arrangement with either of them

to smuggle the trunks into Boston. The next morning I went down with Mr. Hill to the vessels.

Mr. Hill had a private conversation with Captain McGregor, the captain of the first vessel to whom we applied, and he refused to take the goods. We then went to see Captain John O'Brien of the bark Halifax. Hill told him that I had some presents in my trunks, consisting of silks, satin dresses, etc., that I wanted to take to my friends. The Captain and Mr. Hill had a private conversation, and when the Captain came out, he consented to take them. I was to give him a twenty-dollar gold piece for smuggling them in. I put them on board the vessel that day, and he stowed them away. The vessel laid five days at Boston before he could get a chance to get them off, but he finally succeeded in getting them off, and expressed them to Philadelphia, where I received them, and brought them to Baltimore. I then took out the goods, which were very much rumpled, smoothed them out, and arranged them, bought some new trunks, and repacked them, and brought them to this city.

Dr. Blackburn, by way of caution, asked me before leaving if I had had the yellow fever; and on my saying "No," he said, "You must have a preventive against catching it. You must get some camphor and chew it, and get some strong cigars, the strongest you can get, and be sure to keep gloves on when handling the things." He gave me some cigars that he said he had brought from Havana, which he said were strong enough for any thing.

When I arrived in this city, I turned over five of the trunks to Messrs. W. L. Wall & Co., commission merchants in this city, and four to a man by the name of Myers from Boston, a sutler in Sigel's or Weitzel's division. He said he had some goods which he was going to take to Newbern, North Carolina, and I told him that I had a lot of goods that I wanted to sell, and to make the best market I could for them, I would turn them over to him on commission. I also told him I would shortly have more, and mentioned that I had disposed of some to Wall & Co., of this city. Dr. Blackburn told me, when I was making arrangements, that I should let the parties to whom I disposed my goods know that I would have a big lot to sell, as it was in contemplation to get together about a million dollars' worth of goods and dispose of them in this way.

Dr. Blackburn stated that his object in having these goods disposed of in different cities, was to destroy the armies or anybody that they came in contact with. All these goods, he told me, had been carefully infected in Bermuda with yellow fever, small-pox, and other contagious diseases. The goods in the valise, which were intended for President Lincoln I understood him to say, had been infected both with yellow fever and small-pox. This valise I declined taking charge of, and turned it over to him at the Halifax Hotel, and I afterward heard that it had been sent to the President.

On the five trunks that I turned over to W. L. Wall & Co., I got an advance of $100. Among these five trunks there was one that was always spoken of by Blackburn to me as " Big No. 2," which he said I must be sure to have sold in Washington.

On disposing of the trunks, I immediately left Washington, and went straight through until I got to Hamilton, Canada. In the waiting-room there I met Mr. Holcombe and Mr. Clement C. Clay. They both rose, shook hands with me, and congratulated me upon my safe return, and upon my making a for-tune. They told me I should be a gentleman for the future, instead of a working-man and a mechanic. They seemed perfectly to under-stand the business in which I had been engaged. Mr. Holcombe told me that Dr. Blackburn was at the Donegana Hotel in Montreal, and that I had better telegraph to him, stating that I had returned.

As Dr. Blackburn had requested me to telegraph to him, as soon as I got into Canada, I did so; and the next night, be-tween 11 and 12 o'clock, Dr. Blackburn came up and knocked at the door of my house. I was in bed at the time. I looked out of the window and saw Dr. Blackburn there. Said he, " Come down, Hyams, and open the door; you're like all damned rascals who have been doing something wrong—you're afraid the devil is after you." He was in company with Bennett H. Young. I came down and let him in. He asked me how I had disposed of the goods, and I told him. " Well," said he, " that is all right, as long as big No. 2 went into Washington; it will kill them at sixty yards' distance." I then told the Doctor that every thing had gone wrong at my home in my absence; that I needed some funds; that my family needed money. He said he would go to Colonel Jacob Thompson and make arrangements for me to draw upon him for any amount of money I required. He then said that the British authorities had solicited his services in attending to the yellow fever that was then raging in Bermuda; that he was going on there; and that as soon as he came back he would see me. I went up to Jacob Thompson the next morning, and told him what Dr. Blackburn had said. He said, " Yes; Dr. Blackburn had been there, and had made arrangements for me to draw $100 whenever it was shown that I had made disposition of the goods according to his direction." I told him I needed money; that I had been so long away from home that every thing I had was gone, and I wanted money to pay my rent, etc. He said, " I will give you $50 now, but it is against Dr. Blackburn's request; when you show me that you have sold the goods, I will give you the balance." He asked me to give him a receipt, which I did: " Received of Jacob Thompson the sum of $50, on account of Dr. Blackburn." That was about the 11th or 12th of August last. The next day I wrote to Messrs. Wall & Co., of Washington, desiring them to send me an account of the sales, and the balance due me. When I received their answer, I took it up to show to Colonel Thompson. He then said he was perfectly satisfied I had done my part, and gave me a check for $50 on the Ontario Bank. I gave him a receipt: "Received from Jacob Thompson $100, in full, on account of Dr. Luke P. Blackburn."

I told Jacob Thompson of the large sum which Dr. Blackburn had promised me for my services, and that he and Mr. Holcombe had both told me that the Confederate Gov-ernment had appropriated $200,000 for the purpose of carrying it out; but he would not pay me any thing more.

When Dr. Blackburn returned from Ber-muda, I wrote to him at Montreal, and told him I wanted some money, and that he ought to send me some; but he made no reply to my letter. I was then sent down to Mon-treal with a commission for Bennett H. Young, to be used in his defense in the St. Albans raid case. I there met Dr. Black-burn. He said I had written some hard let-ters to him, abusing him, and that he had no money to give me. He then got into his car-riage at the door, and rode off to some races, I think, and never gave me any more satisfac-tion. As I wanted money before leaving for the States, I went to the Clifton House, Niagara. Dr. Blackburn told me he had no money with him then, but that he would go to Mr. Holcombe and get some, as he had Confed-erate funds with him. Blackburn said that when I returned he would get the money for the expedition, from either Holcombe or Thompson, it did not matter which. From this, and from Holcombe and Clay both shaking hands with me, and congratulating me at Hamilton upon my safe return, I thought, of course, they knew all about it.

I do not know that Dr. Stuart Robinson knew of the business in which I was engaged, but he took good care of me while I was at Toronto, in the fall, and until Dr. Blackburn wrote for me in the spring; and when he gave me Dr. Blackburn's letter, he told me to borrow the money from Mr. Preston to take me to Montreal, as he said he did not want to commit an overt act against the United States Government him-self. Mr. Preston lent me $10 to go to Montreal. On arriving at that place, accord-ing to the directions in Dr. Blackburn's letter, I went to Mr. Slaughter to get the means to take me to Halifax. Mr. Slaughter was short of funds, and had only $25 that he could give me. He said that I had better go to Mr. Holcombe, who was staying at the Donegana Hotel, and he would give me the balance. I went to the hotel and sent up my name. Mr. Holcombe had heard of my name, and he sent for me to come up. I told him that I wanted some money to take me to Halifax; he asked me how much I wanted; I told him as much as would make up $40; he said, "You had better take $50;" but as I did not want that much, I only took enough to make up $40. When I came to Washington to dispose of the goods, which was on the 5th of August, 1864, I put up at the National Hotel; registered my name as J. W. Harris, under which name I did business with Wall & Co.

W. L. WALL.

For the Prosecution.—May 29.

I am an auction and commission merchant in this city. In August last, while I was out of town, a person named Harris called at my store, and told my book-keeper that he had some shirts that he wanted to sell at auction, and asked him if he would sell them the next morning. The clerk told him he would. Harris then asked for an advance of $100. The money was given him, and the shirts were sold the next morning.

A. BRENNER.

For the Prosecution.—May 29.

During last summer I was a clerk in the service of Mr. Wall, of this city. In the month of August a man named J. W. Harris came to the store late one evening. I supposed him to be a sutler returning home. He said he had some twelve dozen shirts and some coats, which he asked me to sell. I advanced him $100 on them, and sold them the next morning. They were packed in five trunks.

On the 1st of September he wrote from Toronto, for an account of sales and the balance of the money, as follows:

Messrs. Wall & Co., Auction and Commission Merchants:

GENTLEMEN: On Friday, the 5th of August, last month, I left in your care five trunks, containing one hundred and fifty fancy woolen shirts and twenty-five coats, to be sold at auction on the next morning, and business calling me to Toronto, I have not been able to go to the States since. I beg most respectfully that you will send me an account of sales, and a check on New York for the proceeds. I have written before, but I have received no answer. I shall come over in October, about the 10th, with some five or six thousand pairs of boots and shoes.

Yours most respectfully,
J. W. HARRIS,
Care of Post-office Box No. 126, Toronto, C. W.

I sent him the following account of the sales, and the balance of the money:

The shirts I bought were tossed into the trunks promiscuously, and I supposed the packing had been done in a hurry. When I first opened the trunks I was in doubt about the money I had advanced being a safe investment, but a close inspection of the clothing showed it to be new, and that it had not been worn.

STARVATION OF UNION PRISONERS.

SALOME MARSH.

For the Prosecution.—May 25.

I entered the United States service in 1861 as Lieutenant of the Fifth Maryland Volunteer Infantry, and served until the 31st of August, 1864. At the time I quit the service I held the rank of Lieutenant-Colonel.

While Major, I was a prisoner of war, confined at Libby Prison, from the 15th of June, 1863, to the 21st of March, 1864.

I was captured near Winchester, on the Martinsburg road, on the 15th of June. I was then in General Milroy's command, and at the time of my capture I was in command of my regiment. I was captured by General Ewell's corps, of the rebel army. I was taken to Winchester, and, on account of ill health, was kept there two weeks in hospital. I was somewhat sick at the time of my capture, from excessive duty, exposure, etc. At the expiration of two weeks my health somewhat improved. I was then compelled to march to Staunton in a feeble condition; and on the road was treated very kindly by the officer in charge of the squad. I arrived in Libby Prison, and was incarcerated there. The rations we received there when I first arrived were small, but such as they gave us at first were tolerably fair. There was about one loaf of bread allowed to two men—half a loaf per man—and, I judge, about four ounces of meat, and about three spoonfuls of rice. That constituted the ration that we received at first. After I had been there about four months, the meat was stopped, and we only received it occasionally. Then they took the bread from us, and gave us instead what they called corn-bread, but it was of a very coarse character. I have known the officers there to be without meat for two or three weeks at a time, and receive nothing but the miserable corn-bread that they gave us. Occasionally they would distribute some few potatoes, but of the very worst character, rotten, etc., such as the men could hardly eat. This continued for some time. The officers held a meeting there in regard to the treatment we were receiving, and a letter was sent to General Ould, the rebel Commissioner of Exchange, signed by Colonel Streight, I think, who was chairman of the meeting at the time, complaining of our treatment, and asking that we should receive better treatment. General Ould sent a written reply, stating that our treatment was good enough, better than their prisoners were receiving in our prisons, at Fort Delaware and other places.

When I had been there some five months, I was taken sick with the dropsy, for the want of proper nourishment, proper diet, etc., and was quite ill, and was sent to the hospital. I remained there some few weeks. During my stay in the hospital I saw some enlisted men brought in from Belle Isle. The condition of these men was horrible in the extreme. I am satisfied from their appearance that they were in a starving condition. Out of a squad of forty that were brought in, at least from eight to twelve died the first night they were brought there. I asked the Assistant Surgeon in charge of the officers' department of the hospital—I forget his name; he was very kind to us, though, and very much of a gentleman—what was the matter with these men. He stated that their condition was owing to the want of proper treatment; that they did not receive the nourishment that they ought to have for such men. I suppose I had been in that hospital about two weeks when two of the officers made their escape. Major Turner, the keeper of Libby Prison—who was a very passionate man, and very insulting to the officers, always insulting in his remarks whenever he had occasion to speak to any of them, and very ungentlemanly—took it into his head to remove us from that place, and take us back to Libby Prison. He had a room washed out for us in Libby, and, removed us to that room while it was in a wet condition, although some of the officers who were in the hospital were in a dying state. We were placed in that wet room and compelled to remain there twenty-four hours, without cot, bed, or any thing else to lie upon, and without a morsel to eat, as a punishment, because those two men had escaped. The treatment generally to prisoners was of a very harsh character.

Colonel Powell spoke to Turner in regard to the treatment he had inflicted upon those men. Colonel Powell said he thought it was wrong to punish a parcel of sick and dying men for the sa e o two who had attempted to escape. His reply was, as near, as I can recollect, "It is too damned good for you."*

The only opportunity I had of knowing the treatment enlisted men received, was from

seeing those men that were brought to the hospital while I was there. They were in an emaciated condition, and their whole appearance indicated that they were suffering for want of food, and were in a state of starvation. I noticed that, though in a tottering and feeble condition, they were eager to obtain something to eat, and would grasp at any thing that was offered them in the shape of victuals; and I am satisfied that the prisoners brought to the hospital died simply of neglect, and the want of proper food—of starvation.

The only reason that I could hear from the rebel authorities for their treatment of Union prisoners, was that it was a matter of retaliation; they said that their prisoners were treated in a worse manner than we were.

As to the quantity of food given us, a man might possibly live on what they gave us at first, although it was not near what we would call a full ration. Subsequently, the quantity given could not possibly support life for any length of time. The corn-bread which they gave us was corn-meal and bran; it was very coarse, baked in a rough condition, and very often we had to live on that and water alone for days at a time.

FREDERICK MEMMERT.
For the Prosecution.—May 25.

I have held the rank of Captain in the United States service for two years and ten months. On the 15th of June, 1863, I was taken prisoner, and was exchanged on the 1st of May, 1864. I was confined in the Libby Prison, and the treatment we received there was simply awful.

When we went there first, we had half a loaf of wheat-bread, between three and four ounces of meat, and about two tablespoonfuls of rice. That was continued for about

---

* In contrast with the above, and to show how Confederate prisoners were treated in "Northern" prisons, we give the following extract from a letter received by us during the progress of this trial:

"BALTIMORE, June 21, 1865.

* * * "When South Carolina took the fatal step of secession, I was lecturing in the University of Virginia, having an engagement which would have paid me $600 for two weeks more work. I cast in my lot with the Southern Confederacy, and with that was wrecked on the 'Lee' shore.

"I was taken prisoner on the 26th of January, 1864, and held as a prisoner of war until the 5th of June, 1865, when I was released, and took the oath of allegiance to the United States. Fourteen months of my imprisonment were spent as superintendent of a prisoners' school at Point Lookout. This school had a library of 3,000 volumes, mostly school books. There were 1,200 pupils and 50 teachers. We taught many poor fellows to read and write who had never understood such mysteries before.

"But we did not confine ourselves to the lower branches. We taught all the English branches, Latin, Greek, French, German, and mathematics through trigonometry.

"I was appointed agent for the distribution of supplies furnished by the C. S. for the prisoners at Point Lookout, and as such distributed over $200,000 worth of goods. Afterward I was promoted to the high position of 'Mayor of the City of Canvas,' and was charged with the duty of maintaining law and order among my 22,000 comrades. Thus I have passed sixteen long months a prisoner"

STARVATION OF UNION PRISONERS.

four months; after that the treatment was very bad. We had a meeting, at which Colonel Streight presided, and of which Colonel Irvine, who was afterward our Assistant Exchange Commissioner, was Secretary. We sent a communication to Judge Ould, which he sent to the rebel Secretary of War, Seddon. We received for answer that they could do nothing for us; that it was good enough for Yankees; that their prisoners were treated just as badly as we were; and that they could not help us in any way. We then sent another communication, asking them to give us our money, (which they had taken away from us when we came to the Libby,) that we might have something to buy food with, but they would not do that. I had my money hid under my shoulder-straps, and kept it there; but the others had given theirs up, and it was never returned.

We often had no meat for twenty days. After I had been there four months, they stopped the meat for five or six days, and gave us bread and water, a little beans and rice. At this time we got half a loaf of corn-bread, or about ten ounces, I guess. When I left Libby, we had had nothing but corn-bread and water for twenty days. The prisoners were very much reduced and emaciated by this treatment, and a great many of them had the scurvy.

The bearing of the keepers of the prison was rough and insulting, and they abused us in every way they could. I went to the hospital two or three times when our Lieutenant-Colonel died, and the prisoners who were brought in looked awful; I can not find any word to describe how they looked. Their condition was the result of starvation.

After the battle of Chickamauga, and the wounded prisoners from the West were brought in, I saw some fifteen or sixteen amputated cases placed on a cart, and a rope tied around them, so that they could not fall off; and they were carried in that way from the depot to the hospital, although right opposite Libby, not more than one thousand yards off, I guess, there were twenty or twenty-five ambulances not in use.

At the time I left Libby, I had the scurvy so badly that I could hardly walk, and I have been sick pretty much ever since; and, though I have now recovered, I still feel it, and have not the strength I used to have.

When Turner, the keeper of the prison, came up, which was very seldom, we spoke to him about ameliorating the condition of the prisoners. We also spoke to a committee from their Senate that was appointed to go through the Libby and examine our condition; they reported favorably, although we showed them the bread we got, and told them we received no meat, and little of any thing else.

I went to Turner once and told him I wanted to get some medicine; that I was getting worse, and could hardly walk; and that the doctor would not give me any. Turner said he had not got any. His words were, "You can not have any; it do n't make any difference to me. What the hell have I to do with it?" When I told him that I had nothing to eat, and no money to buy any thing, he said, "That's good enough for Yankees."

We once remonstrated with Dick Turner, who was an inspector there, and told him that we did not get any thing to eat, and how things were. He said, "That's good enough for you. Our prisoners are just as badly treated by your fellows as you are here, and you have no business to come down here. I wish to kill you off. If I had the command, I would hang every God damned one of you."

BENJAMIN SWEERER.
For the Prosecution.—May 25.

I am Color-sergeant of the Ninth Maryland Regiment. I was captured on the 18th of October, 1863, and was held prisoner at Belle Island for over five months, and seven days at Scott's Building. There were about thirteen thousand prisoners, about half of whom were provided with shelter; the rest were just on the naked sands of the island. I lay there two months without ever putting my head under shelter, although it was in the winter time. The treatment of the prisoners was brutal, and we had not half enough to live on. There were twenty-five pounds of meat, the biggest part of which was bone, served out for a hundred men, and corn-bread with the husks ground up in it. Not having fuel enough to warm us, and not provisions enough to live on, I saw the men freezing to death on the island. I saw them starving to death; and, after they were dead, I saw them lying, for eight or nine days, outside of the intrenchments, where we were kept, and the hogs eating them. We were refused permission to bury them. I asked myself, as a favor, to be allowed to bury our prisoners, and was refused permission. I spoke to Lieutenant Bossieux, who had charge of the island, about the treatment of our men; and he told me he had nothing to do with it; that it was in accordance with the orders he had received from Major Turner, the keeper of the rebel prison. The deaths of the prisoners were caused mostly by starvation. I helped to carry out from ten to fifteen and twenty a day.

A great many of the prisoners, to my knowledge, volunteered to work at shoe-making and building a furnace on the island, in order to support themselves.

When I came home I weighed one hundred and twenty-three pounds; my ordinary weight in health is one hundred and seventy or one hundred and eighty. I do not think I could have lasted a month longer there; I was pretty nearly gone when I left.

WILLIAM BALL.

For the Prosecution.—May 25.

I enlisted in the service of the United States in April, 1862, and was captured by the enemy on the 7th of May, 1864. I was a prisoner of war at Andersonville, Georgia, eleven months and twenty-three days. At the time I was there, there were about thirty-two thousand prisoners. The treatment of the prisoners was poor indeed; they were turned into a swamp, with no shelter whatever, and were stripped of all their clothing, blankets, hats, caps, shoes, money, and whatever they had. Where we were confined there was no shelter and no trees, although there were plenty of pine woods about there. The encampment was nothing but an open swamp, with a hill on each side.

Every morning, about nine or ten o'clock, they would bring a wagon on the ground, with corn-meal and some bacon. Of the corn-meal, which was ground up, cobs and all, and was full of stones and one thing and another, they gave each man half a pint, and two ounces of bacon, which was all alive, rancid, and rotten, and a half spoonful of salt. This was to last us twenty-four hours. Once in a while we would get hold of a good piece of bacon, but that was not often. The provisions served out to us were of such a character that no man would eat them unless he was in a starving condition; and from the amount and character of the food served out, it would not be possible to sustain human life for any length of time.

The effect of this treatment upon the health of the prisoners was very bad; it killed them off rapidly. The deaths averaged from sixty to a hundred a day; and one day one hundred and thirty-three died. These deaths were caused principally by starvation. There was some remonstrance addressed to the rebel authorities by the prisoners in regard to their treatment; but they said they did the best they could for them, and they did not care a damn whether the Yankees died or not.

I remember Howell Cobb visiting Andersonville some time in February. He is the man who was formerly the Secretary of the Treasury. He made some very bitter remarks, in a speech to the rebels, in reference to our prisoners. As to our treatment, he said that was the best that could be done for us; but if the authorities liked to do better they probably could, but they did not seem to care much about it. I remember he made some reference in his speech to a plan on hand to burn and plunder Northern cities.

The heat in the open sun was very intense, and the water was very poor indeed. You could get water by digging down half a foot. There was a place a little way above into which they threw all the dirt and garbage that came from Andersonville, and the water we were obliged to drink ran through all this filth. Whether this was designed or not, I do not know, but they did not seem to care. A committee from the prisoners was sent to Captain Wirz, who was in command of the interior of the prison, in respect to this, and he said he did not care a damn whether the water ran through the garbage or not, or whether we got any or none.

When we first went there, there were on an average as many as six or eight of the prisoners shot every day. If a man would stick his nose half a foot over the line, he would be shot. It was said the rebel soldiers were rewarded with thirty days' furlough for shooting a Yankee; and I never heard of their wantonness in shooting our soldiers being rebuked by the rebel authorities.

The treatment of the prisoners in the hospital was very poor. All they would give them was pitch-pine pills; pitch-pine pills for diarrhea, and pitch-pine pills for the scurvy, the head-ache, or anything else. These pills were made out of the pitch that runs out of the trees there, and a little vinegar. They got no medicine. Medicines, it was said, were sent there by the Confederate Government, but they were sold by the doctor in charge for greenbacks.

The money that was taken from the prisoners was never returned to them—not a cent of it. When I was captured, they took my shoes off, and I walked bare-foot on the pike from near Waterford to Gordonsville, and then they took my money and clothes. I had nothing but a pair of drawers and shirt for nine months in Andersonville. I lay there for this whole nine months in the open field without a bit of shelter; and there were thousands in the same fix. The men would die there in the morning, and by night nobody could go within fifty feet of them. They had to be put into the wagons with long wooden pitch-forks, when they were carried off and put into the trenches.

Colonel Gibbs was in command of the post, and Captain Wirz was in command of the interior of the prison. Clothing that was sent to Andersonville by our Government, consisting of blankets, pants, socks, and other things, Wirz took himself, and put into his own house, and sold.

Up to March 24th, when I left Andersonville, 16,725 of the prisoners had died; that was the number I took from the books myself, and there were at that time about 1,500 not able to be moved. It was the rations they got that brought on their sickness, and when they got sick they could not eat the stuff served out, and, of course, they starved. As to medical treatment, there was nothing at all of any benefit.

CHARLES SWEENEY.

For the Prosecution.—May 26.

My present home is in the State of New York. I was a private in the United States service, and was captured by the rebels twice.

The first time I was taken prisoner, I was confined two months and ten days at Libby; the second time I was a prisoner fifteen months, of which I spent two months in Belle Isle hospital, near Richmond; about six months at Andersonville, in Georgia; and the rest of the time at Savannah.

At Belle Isle I had less than half a pound of bread a day, and once in a while got a little rice soup. For about six weeks I do not believe I had a piece of meat as big as my two fingers. When I went to the hospital, the bread was a little better, but there was very little meat. They pretty nearly starved me. For about four or five months after I got to Andersonville they gave me a pretty good ration of the kind it was. I had all I wanted to eat of corn-meal, but the bacon was pretty strong. After August they began to cut down our ration, and our allowance was very short.

Old Captain Wirz told the guard that they must shoot every Yankee caught with his hand or his head over the dead-line; and that for every man shot the guard would get a furlough of thirty days; so they used to kill our men as though they were brutes.

I had a brother at Andersonville, who was very sick and dying. For about eight days, to my knowledge, he had nothing to eat. He could not eat their corn-meal, and what they gave him, for it was not fit for a dog to eat. I had a little money that I used to gather about the camp, and I bought a few biscuits for him, but I could not get enough to feed him on long, and he lay in his tent and starved. I went to the doctor and told him my brother was dying, and asked him to see him; but he said, "No, I can not do it." Before he died, my brother said, "Keep good courage; stick to your Government; never take an oath to *that* Government." I told him I would, and I have done it.

I made my escape; but after I got over the stockade, they caught me, took me back, and gagged me for six hours. It was very cold, and when I got up I could hardly walk, and I was sick in the hospital; but in the month of June I was able to be up, and I thought I would try again to make my escape and get to Stoneman, who was making a raid, I heard. I got out of the hospital, and traveled that night in the swamps and mud, clear up to my neck, and made four miles. The pickets, however, caught me, and took me back to Captain Winder. He told them to put me in the stockade, with a ball and chain; and at Wirz's head-quarters I was put in the stockade all day in the hot sun, with my arms stretched out. The sun affected me so much that the next day I was sick, and for six days I could neither eat nor drink any thing. It is God only who has let me live this long.

General Cobb came there on the 4th day of March. He preached up to the guard the way the war was going on. The guards around there were only old men and boys that never knew any thing. He said to them, "You see this big graveyard; all those in the stockade will be in the graveyard before long." He expected we were all going to be starved to death, if we were held long enough. He said they would all perish before they would come back to the Union again. He also said they would hang Old Abe if they caught him, as he supposed Old Abe would hang him if he caught him.

JAMES YOUNG.

For the Prosecution.—May 26.

I was a prisoner of war nine months and two days. I was confined in Andersonville, Ga., and Charleston and Florence, S. C. At Andersonville the greater portion of the rations were cooked, but in a very inferior way—corn-bread and mush, boiled rice and boiled bacon. The ration of bread for the day was about four inches long, three wide, and two thick; with that we got about two or three ounces of boiled pork. The effect of this stinted diet upon the health of the men was very injurious; they were wasting and dying all the time. The number of deaths for August, I understood, was three thousand and forty-four. We were exposed to the sun, without any shelter, though there was woodland all around us. The stockade, where we were was chopped out of it but we were all exposed. The heat during the day was extreme, but the nights were cool.

The water was very poor; it was infected by the garbage and filth through which it ran.

At Florence I heard some hard threats made against the "Yanks," as they called us. Our cavalry were raiding, destroying their country, they said, and they would starve us, they said, in retaliation. We received worse treatment at Florence than at Andersonville, and got less rations. The amount of food was not sufficient to sustain life for any long period of time. Men that were destitute of any little means of their own, or had no watches or trinkets that they could sell, kept running down till they died. I had some money, and I bought some extra provisions, and kept my health tolerably good.

At Charleston I was imprisoned about three weeks. We were treated very well there, with the exception of the shooting of our men inside the inclosure by the guards; that occurred often, and seemed to be encouraged by the officers. I never knew of a man being rebuked or punished for such shooting. At Andersonville the general report in camp was that the rebel authorities offered their men a thirty days' furlough for every "Yank" they would shoot inside of the stockade.

LIEUTENANT J. L. RIPPLE.

For the Prosecution.—June 10.

I entered the United States service, in the Thirty-Ninth Illinois, as a private, on the 28th of October, 1861. I was a prisoner of war for six months at Andersonville, Ga. The character of the food furnished to the prisoners was poor, and the quantity very small. We got only half a pint of corn-meal daily, and from two to four ounces of meat. The result was the prisoners died in large numbers, occasioned, without doubt, in many cases, by starvation and the horrible treatment they received.

I heard rebel officers approve of the kind of treatment we received; they said it was good enough for us. I remember Captain Wirz saying, on the 1st of July, "It is good enough for you; I wish you 'd all die." The location of the camp at Andersonville, and the arrangements to which the prisoners were subjected, seemed to show that the Confederate authorities intended the infliction of all possible suffering, short of putting the men to death. At Millen it was somewhat better.

A pack of blood-hounds was kept at Andersonville, and I heard some of the men who went after them say that some of the prisoners who had escaped were pursued and torn by the blood-hounds.

While at Andersonville I knew Quartermaster Hume. I heard him say, previous to the election, that if Mr. Lincoln were re-elected, he would not live to be inaugurated. He said that a party North would attend to him, and to Mr. Seward also. I also heard a lieutenant, who was in charge of the guard, say something to the same effect.

MINING OF LIBBY PRISON.

LIEUTENANT REUBEN BARTLEY.

For the Prosecution.—May 22.

I have been in the United States service since 1862, and since August the 3d have been in the signal corps. I was confined in Libby Prison from the 3d of March to the 16th of July, 1864, and at other prisons until the 10th of December, 1864.

On being taken to Libby, we were informed, when taken into the hall, that the place had been mined. The next morning we were taken into a dungeon in the cellar part of the building. In going to the door of the dungeon, we had to go round a place where there was fresh dirt in the center of the cellar. The guard would allow no person to pass over it or near it. On inquiring why, we were told that that was the place where the torpedo had been placed. It remained there while we were in the dungeon, and for some time after we were taken up stairs.

I learned also from the officers who accompanied and had charge of us that the torpedo was buried there. It was always spoken of as *the* torpedo. The place that had been dug out was about six feet in diameter. The ground was a little raised, as if the dirt had been dug out and put back again. It was directly under the center of the prison. Rebel officers and others told us that the prison had been mined on account of Colonel Dahlgren's raid, and that if we succeeded in getting into the city, they would blow up the prisoners rather than liberate them.

ERASTUS W. ROSS.

For the Prosecution.—May 25.

I was in the service of the rebel Government; I was conscripted and detailed as a clerk at the Libby Prison, and never served in the army.

In March, 1864, General Kilpatrick was making a raid in the direction of Richmond. About that time the prison was mined. I saw the place where I was told the powder was buried under the building; it was in the middle of the building. The powder was put there secretly in the night; I never saw it; but I saw the fuse; it was kept in the office safe. I was away at my uncle's the night the powder was placed there, and was told of it the next morning by one of the colored men at the prison. There were two sentinels near the place to prevent any person's approaching it. The excavation made was about the size of a barrel-head, and the earth was thrown up loosely over it. Major Turner, the commandant of the prison, had charge of the fuse. He told me that the powder was there, and that the fuse was to set it off; that it was put there for the security of the prisoners, and if the army got in, it was to be set off for the purpose of blowing up the prison and the prisoners.

The powder was secretly taken out in May, and the whole building was then shut up. The prisoners had all been sent to Macon, Georgia.

I suppose the powder was placed there by the authority of General Winder, or the Secretary of War. Major Turner said he was acting under the authority of the rebel War Department, though I never saw any written orders about it.

JOHN LATOUCHE.

For the Prosecution.—May 25.

I was First Lieutenant in Company B, Twenty-fifth Virginia Battalion, C. S. A. I was detailed to post duty in Richmond, to regulate the details of the guards of the military prisons there, and in March, 1864, I was on duty at Libby Prison. Major Turner, the keeper of the prison, told me he was going to see General Winder about the guard. On his return he told me that General Winder himself had been to see the Secretary of War, and that they were going to put powder under the prison. In the evening of the same day, the powder was brought. There were two kegs, of about twenty-five pounds each, and a box which contained, I suppose, about as much as the two kegs. A hole was dug in the center of the middle basement, and the powder was put down there. The box, when put in, just came level with the ground, and the place was covered over with gravel. I did not see any fuse to it then. I placed a sentry over this powder, so that no accident might occur; and the next day Major Turner, who had charge of the fuse, showed it to us in his office; he showed it to everybody there. It was a long fuse, made of gutta-percha; such a one as I had never seen before.

In May, I think it was, Major Turner went South, and all the prisoners were sent out of the Libby building proper to the South; and General Winder sent a note down to the office, with directions to take up the powder as privately or as secretly as possible; I forget the exact word. The note was delivered into my hands for the inspector of the prison, to whom I either gave or sent it. I afterward heard Major Turner say that, in the event of the raiders coming into Richmond, he would have blown up the place. I understood him to say that those were his orders.

THE BEN. WOOD DRAFT.

DANIEL S. EASTWOOD.

For the Prosecution.—June 16.

I am assistant manager of the Montreal branch of the Ontario Bank, Canada. I was officially acquainted with Jacob Thompson, formerly of Mississippi, who has for some time been sojourning in Canada, and have knowledge of his account with our bank, a copy of which was presented to this Commission by Mr. Campbell, our assistant teller.

The moneys to Mr. Thompson's credit accrued from the negotiation of bills of exchange, drawn by the Secretary of the Treasury of the so-called Confederate States, on Frazier, Trenholm & Co., of Liverpool. They were understood to be the financial agents of the Confederate States at Liverpool, and the face of the bills, I believe, bore that inscription. Among the dispositions made from that fund, by Jacob Thompson, was $25,000, paid in accordance with the following requisition:

$329.   MONTREAL, Aug. 10th, 1864.
Wanted from the Ontario Bank, 3 days sight,
On N. York,
Favor Benjamin Wood, Esq..
           $25,000
For ——— current funds.
           10,000
Deliv. 60 p. c.   A. M.
Ex. 15,000.

[The requisition, having been read, was put in evidence.]

The "$10,000" underneath the $25,000, is the purchase money in gold of $25,000 worth of United States funds.

At Mr. Thompson's request, the name of Benjamin Wood was erased, (the pen just being struck through it,) and my name, as an officer of the bank, written immediately beneath it, that the draft might be negotiable without putting any other name to it.

I have in my hand, it having been obtained from the cashier of the City Bank in New York, the original draft for the $25,000, for which that requisition was made by Mr. Thompson, in the name of Benjamin Wood. It reads:

$25,000.   THE ONTARIO BANK.   No. 4,329.

MONTREAL, 10TH AUGUST, 1864.
At three days' sight, please pay to the order of D. S. Eastwood, in current funds, twenty-five thousand dollars, value received, and charge the same to account of this branch.

U. S. INTER. REV.   To the Cashier,   H.Y. STARNS,
   2 cts.   City Bank,   Manager
BANK CHECK.   New York.

INDORSED:
Pay to the Hon. Benj. Wood, Esq.,
   or Order.
         D. S. EASTWOOD,
         B. WOOD.

[The draft, having been read, was put in evidence.]

I found this draft in the hands of the payee of the City Bank, in New York, and I understand from the cashier it has been paid.

Mr. Thompson was frequently in the habit of drawing moneys in the name of an officer of the bank, so as to conceal the person for whom it was really intended. A good deal of Thompson's exchange was drawn in that way, so that there is no indication, except from the bank or the locality on which the bill was drawn, to show where use was to be made of the funds. Large amounts were drawn for, at his instance, on the banks of New York, but we were not acquainted with the use they were put to.

The Benjamin Wood, to whom the draft was made payable, is, I believe, the member of Congress, and the owner of the New York News.

[Jacob Thompson's bank account, already in evidence, was handed to the witness.]

This is a copy of Jacob Thompson's banking account with us, as testified to by Robert Anson Campbell. I see in the account, entries of funds that were used for the purpose of exchange on New York and also on London. The item, $180,000, on the 6th of April, 1865, was issued in deposit receipts, which may be used anywhere.

John Wilkes Booth purchased a bill of exchange at our bank, about the beginning of October, and made a deposit at the same time, which remains undrawn to this day. I do not know of his having been in our bank but once. John H. Surratt's name I never heard mentioned.

Cross-examined by MR. AIKEN.

I do not remember any drafts cashed at our bank in favor of James Watson Wallace, Richard Montgomery, or James B. Merritt. I have no recollection of the names.

GEORGE WILKES.

For the Prosecution.—June 16.

I am acquainted with Benjamin Wood of New York, and am familiar with his handwriting.

[The $25,000 draft was here handed to the witness.]

The signature at the back of that bill of exchange I should take to be his. At the date of this bill Benjamin Wood was a member of Congress of the United States. He was editor and proprietor of the New York News; so he told me himself. The paper,

I have heard, has been recently managed by John Mitchell, late editor or assistant editor of the Richmond Examiner and the Richmond Enquirer.

ABRAM D. RUSSEL.

For the Prosecution.—June 16.

I am City Judge for the City of New York, judge of the highest criminal court in the State. I am acquainted with Benjamin Wood of the City of New York, and also with his handwriting.

[The bill of exchange was here handed to the witness.]

The indorsement on this bill of exchange is in the handwriting of Benjamin Wood. I have no doubt it is his. He was at that time member of Congress of the United States and editor and proprietor of the New York News.

DEFENSE.

TESTIMONY TO IMPEACH H. VON STEINACKER, MAY 30.

[EDWARD JOHNSON was called as a witness for the defense on the part of Mary E. Surratt. On appearing on the stand, General HOWE said:]

Mr. President: It is well known to me, and to very many of the officers of the army, that Edward Johnson, the person who is now introduced as a witness, was educated at the National Military Academy at the Government expense, and that, since that time, for years he held a commission in the army of the United States. It is well known in the army that it is a condition precedent to receiving a commission, that the officer shall take the oath of allegiance and fidelity to the Government. In 1861 it became my duty as an officer to fire upon a rebel party, of which this man was a member, and that party fired upon, struck down, and killed loyal men that were in the service of the Government. Since that time, it is notorious to all the officers of the army that the man who is introduced here as a witness, has openly borne arms against the United States, except when he has been a prisoner in the hands of the Government. He is brought here now as a witness to testify before this Commission, and he comes with his hands red with the blood of his loyal countrymen, shed by him or by his assistance, in violation of his solemn oath as a man, and his faith as an officer. I submit to this Commission that he stands in the eye of the law as an incompetent witness, because he is notoriously infamous. To offer as a

witness a man of this character, who has openly violated the obligation of his oath, and his faith as an officer, and to administer the oath to him and present his testimony, is but an insult to the Commission, and an outrage upon the administration of justice. I move, therefore, that this man, Edward Johnson, be ejected from the Court as an incompetent witness on account of his notorious infamy, on the grounds I have stated.

General EKIN. I rise, sir, to second the motion, and I am glad the question is now presented to the Commission. I regard the gentleman clearly incompetent as a witness. That one who has been educated, nourished, and protected by the Government, and, in direct violation of his oath, has taken up arms against the Government, should present himself as a witness before this Commission, I regard as the hight of impertinence, and I trust, therefore, that the motion will be adopted without a moment's hesitation.

Mr. AIKEN. I was not aware that the fact of a person's having borne arms against the United States disqualified him from becoming a witness in a court of justice; and, therefore, it can not be charged upon me, that I designed any insult to the Commission in introducing General Johnson as a witness here. It will be recollected that Mr. Jett, who has also borne arms against the Government, was introduced here as an important witness by the prosecution; and he, according to his own statement, had never taken the oath of allegiance, and his testimony, at that time, was not ojected to.

General KAUTZ. This is not a volunteer witness, is he?

Mr. AIKEN. No, sir.

The JUDGE ADVOCATE. If it please the Court, the rule of law on this point is, that before a witness can be renderd so infamous as to become absolutely incompetent to testify, he must have been convicted by a judicial proceeding, and the record of his conviction must be presented as a basis of his rejection. All evidences of his guilt that fall short of that conviction affect only his credibility. This Court can discredit him just as far as they please upon that ground; but I do not think the rule of law, as now understood, would authorize the Court to declare him an incompetent witness, and incapable of testifying, however unworthy of credit he may be.

General WALLACE. For the sake of the character of this investigation, for the sake of public justice—not for the sake of the person introduced as a witness, but for the persons who are at the bar on trial—I ask the General who makes the motion to withdraw it.

General HOWE. On the statement of the Judge Advocate General, that this witness is technically and legally a competent witness, I withdraw the objection.

Examined by MR. AIKEN.

[The witness, being duly sworn by the Judge Advocate, testified as follows:]

I am, at present, a United States prisoner of war, confined at Fort Warren, Boston Harbor. I was captured at Nashville about the 15th of December last. Since February, 1863, I have been a Major-General in the Confederate States army.

I am acquainted with the man who went by the name of Henry Von Steinacker. He was a private on engineer duty; but was not an officer either of the engineers, the staff, or of the line. He belonged to the Second Virginia Infantry, of the Stonewall Brigade, which was one of the brigades of my division. In the month of May, 1863, a man accosted me in Richmond, on the Capitol Square, by my rank and name, and with the rank I had borne in the United States army, as Major Johnson; he told me he had served under me as a private, and applied to me for a position in the engineer corps. He told me that he was a Prussian by birth, and an engineer by education. It was not in my power to give him a position, and he left me that evening. He afterward made a second application to me for a position. I was then ordered off to my division at Fredericksburg, and in about a week after my arrival there this man appeared in my camp again, and made application for a position in the engineer corps, or on my staff. I told him I could not give him a position

in either; but if he would enlist himself as a private, and if he was what he represented himself, an engineer and draftsman, I would put him on duty, as a private, under an engineer officer of my staff. Under these conditions he enlisted. I attached him to headquarters, and assigned him to special duty under an engineer officer, Captain Oscar Hendricks, with whom he acted as draftsman and assistant from that time until he left.

Q. Was he the subject of a court-martial at any time in your camp; and, if so, for what?

Judge Advocate BINGHAM. I object to the question. The record of such a court-martial would be the only competent evidence of conviction, and if the record were here, it would not impart any verity. I do not think there were any courts in Virginia in those days that could legally try a dog.

Mr. AIKEN. Under the circumstances, parol testimony of the fact is the best that can be offered, and therefore I presume it will not be seriously objected to.

[The Commission sustained the objection.]

Soon after the battle of Gettysburg, our encampment was near Orange Court-House, Orange County, Virginia. I know nothing of, and never heard of, any secret meeting of the officers of the Stonewall Brigade, at the camp of the Second Virginia Regiment. I never knew of any plans discussed for the assassination of the President of the United States, and I never heard his assassination alluded to by any officer of my division as an object to be desired; nor did I ever hear, while in the South, of a secret association called the Knights of the Golden Circle, or Sons of Liberty, nor have I ever known of any one belonging to them, or reputed to belong to them.

I never saw John Wilkes Booth, and never heard of him till after the assassination of the President.

I do not know that H. Von Steinacker was a member of General Blenker's staff, though he told me he was; but he also told me that he was a deserter from the United States service, or that he attempted to desert and had been apprehended.

Cross-examined by ASSISTANT JUDGE ADVOCATE BINGHAM.

I graduated at West Point Military Academy in 1838, and was in the United States service till the breaking out of the rebellion. My rank at that time was that of Captain and Brevet Major of the Sixth Infantry, United States army. I tendered my resignation in May, I think, and received notice of its acceptance in June, 1861. I then went to my home in Virginia, and in a few weeks I entered the Confederate States service, in which I have since remained.

OSCAR HEINRICHS.

For the accused, Mary E. Surratt.—May 30.

Examined by MR. AIKEN.

I served as engineer officer on the staff of General Edward Johnson, and on the staff of other general officers of the Confederate States army.

I am acquainted with Henry Von Steinacker; he was detailed to me as draftsman shortly after General Johnson took command of my division, and I employed him as such. He had neither the rank nor the pay of an engineer officer.

I am not acquainted with J. Wilkes Booth, the actor. I never saw a person calling himself by that name in our camp; nor did any secret meeting of officers ever, to my knowledge, take place in that camp, where plans for the assassination of President Lincoln were discussed.

H. K. DOUGLAS.

For the accused, Mary E. Surratt.—May 30.

Examined by MR. AIKEN.

I have held several commissions in the Confederate States service; my last was that of Major and Assistant Adjutant-General. During the last campaign I served on the staff of six general officers—Generals Edward Johnson, Early, Gordon, Pegram, Walker, and Ramsey.

I know a man named Von Steinacker; he was in the Second Virginia Infantry, the Stonewall Brigade. At the battle of Gettysburg I was wounded and taken prisoner, and remained prisoner for nine months. I did not see Steinacker in camp after I returned to duty, but I got a letter from him.

I do not know of any secret meeting being held in our camp for the discussion of plans for the assassination of the President of the United States.

I wish to say of the officers of that brigade, that their integrity as men, and their gallantry as soldiers, would forbid them from being implicated in any such plot as the assassination of Mr. Lincoln; and in their behalf I desire to say, that I do not believe they knew any thing about it, or in the least degree sympathized with so unrighteous an act.

Steinacker acknowledged to me, on several occasions, that he was a deserter from the Northern army. I have never heard of the existence of any secret treasonable societies, organized for the assassination of the President of the United States. I never was a member of the Knights of the Golden Circle or Sons of Liberty, nor do I know of any of the General's staff being connected with that organization. I never heard it declared in Richmond that President Lincoln ought to be assassinated.

MR. EWING. I move that the cipher letter introduced in evidence, June 5th, and its translation, be rejected as testimony, and that it be so entered upon the record. My reason is a twofold one. In the first place, I really believe the letter to be fictitious, and to bear upon its face the evidence that it is so. In the second place, it is testimony that is wholly inadmissible under the plainest rules of evidence. It is not signed; the handwriting was not proved; it was in cipher; it was not shown at all that it was traced to anybody proved or charged to be connected with this conspiracy, or that it was in the possession of anybody shown or charged to be connected with this conspiracy. The rule in regard to declarations in cases of conspiracy is, that they may be admitted when they are declarations of one of the conspirators. This is not shown to be the declaration of one of the conspirators; and when the declarations are those of a conspirator, they must accompany some act of the conspiracy,. being not merely a declaration of what had been done, or was going to be done, but some declaration connected with an act done in furtherance of the common design. The rule is very succinctly stated in Benét on Military Law and Courts-Martial, page 289:

"In like manner, consultations in furtherance of a conspiracy are receivable in evidence, as also letters, or drafts of answers to letters, and other papers found in the possession of co-conspirators, and which the jury may not unreasonably conclude were written in prosecution of a common purpose, to which the prisoner was a party. For the same reason, declarations or writings explanatory of the nature of a common object, in which the prisoner is engaged, together with others, are receivable in evidence, provided they accompany acts done in the prosecution of such an object, arising naturally out of these acts, and not being in the nature of a subsequent statement or confession of them. But where words or writings are not acts in themselves, nor part of the *res gestæ*, but a mere relation or narrative of some part of the transaction, or as to the share which other persons have had in the execution of a common design, the evidence is not within the principle above mentioned; it altogether depends on the credit of the narrator, who is not before the court, and therefore it can not be received."

In this case, it is a declaration not only of some person who is not shown to be connected with the conspiracy, but it is a declaration of some person whose existence nobody knows any thing of—a nameless man. The letter is as completely unconnected with the subject of investigation as the loosest newspaper paragraph that could be picked up anywhere.

Assistant Judge Advocate BINGHAM. If the Court please, there is a great deal in what the gentleman says that exactly states the law of conspiracy; but there is one thing I beg him to notice, that while that limitation which he has named obtains in regard to third persons, there are two principles of the law touching conspiracy which are just about as old as the crime itself, and as old as the common law, which itself is the growth of centuries— namely, that every declaration made, whether it is in the formation of a conspiracy, in the prosecution of a conspiracy, before it is shown to have been organized, or after it is shown to be completed, is always evidence against the party himself.

There is an allegation in the charge and specification that this conspiracy was entered into with the parties named, and with others unknown, which is also a mode of proceeding known to the administration of justice wherever the common law obtains. There is a rule in connection with this that can not be challenged, and that is that the declarations of parties who are neither indicted nor on trial, are admissible in the trial of those who are indicted and upon trial touching the conspiracy. In the first place, you find it proved, beyond any question of doubt, that Booth, during the month of October, 1864, was in Canada, plotting this assassination with the declared agents of this revolt. You find that about the 14th of November, 1864, after he had so plotted this assassination with those who had weighed him out the price of blood, he is on his way to Washington City for the purpose of hiring his assistants; he is in the City of New York; he is in conversation with one of his co-conspirators, and, in my judgment, with one of them who is now within the hearing of my voice.

In that conversation they disclosed the fact that they are conspirators, as detailed by the witness who was present, Mrs. Hudspeth. Upon one of them the lot has fallen to go to Washington, to carry out the conspiracy, to hire the assassins—to go to Washington to strike the murderous blow in aid of this rebellion; and what of the other? The other has been ordered, according to the testimony, to go to Newbern, North Carolina—Newbern, which became the doomed city afterward among these conspirators for the importation of pestilence. After the introduction of proof of this sort against these unknown conspirators, who are numbered by fifties and hundreds, as Booth himself testified when he was trying to hire with his money a man who could not be hired to do murder, Mr. Chester—after such facts as these are proved, in the very vicinity of Newbern this infernal thing is found floating as a waif on the waters, bearing witness against these villains. Although you can not prove the writer of it, I say it is admissible in evidence. It is alleged that there are conspirators here unknown. There are facts here to prove that one of them was to go to Newbern. The letter is found in the vicinity of Newbern, in North Carolina, at the dock in Morehead City. The foundation has been laid for the introduction of it.

Allow me to say one other word in this connection. There are, I know, some rules of law that draw very harshly on conspirators that are engaged in crime. It may seem very hard that a man is to be affected in the remotest degree by a letter written by another who is not upon his trial, or a letter that has never been delivered, which could only speak from the time of its delivery; and yet the gentleman knows very well that upon principle it has been settled that a letter written and never delivered is admissible upon the trial of conspirators.

Mr. EWING. Written by a co-conspirator.

Assistant Judge Advocate BINGHAM. Of course. But the fact that it was written by a co-conspirator is patent on its face, and gathered from the other facts in proof in the case. The point about it is that he is an unknown conspirator. Suppose it had been found in possession of Booth, addressed to him through the post-office, instead of being sent by hand, as the cipher letter shows they must do, because the detectives are on their track; suppose it had been found in the possession of Booth, will any man say that it would not be admissible in evidence against him and everybody else who conspired with him in this infernal plot? What difference does it make that it had not reached him, or the other hired assassin, that was on the track of Sherman, to creep into his tent and murder him, as they crept into the tent of the Commander-in-chief of your army and murdered him. I say it is evidence.

Mr. COX. If the Court will allow me, I desire to submit a word in support of the motion made by General Ewing. When it was announced that a cipher letter was about to be offered in evidence, the counsel for the defense took it for granted that it belonged to that general class of evidence relating to the machinations of the rebel agents in Canada, which had been generally admitted here without objection. The counsel for the defense have had no objection to the exposure of those machinations; their only concern has been to show that their clients were not involved in them. The whole of the evidence of this description of a secret character heretofore has been evidence relating to the contrivances and machinations of the rebel agents in Canada, either on their own responsibility, or in connection with the authorities in Richmond. Therefore, no objection was made to the introduction of that evidence; nor was it perceived, until the letter was read before the Court, that it purported to come from somebody in immediate connection with the act of assassination itself. Therefore the counsel were taken by surprise, and allowed the letter to be read to the Court without objection, without even inspecting it, as they had a right to do, if they desired to submit objections to its introduction as evidence.

The rule stated by the learned Judge Advocate is undoubtedly true, in general, that the declarations of conspirators are admissible in evidence against their co-conspirators; but that is subject to this limitation, that the conspiracy must first be established between the author of the declaration, whether oral or written, and the party accused. That conspiracy being first proved by evidence *aliunde*, by other proof than the declaration itself, then the declaration may be offered in evidence to show the scope and design of the conspiracy; and if it had been established that this letter emanated from somebody between whom and any one of the accused the conspiracy had been established, unquestionably it would have been evidence against the accused, supposing it to be made in the prosecution of the conspiracy. But there has not been a particle of proof produced to the Court showing that the letter did emanate either from Booth, or any one of his associates. The logic of my learned friend on the other side seems to be this: It is sufficiently established, at least by *prima facie* evidence before the Court, that Booth was engaged in a conspiracy with some unknown persons; this letter comes from an unknown person; *ergo*, it is a letter from somebody connected with Booth in this conspiracy.

Assistant Judge Advocate BINGHAM. Not all the logic.

Mr. Cox. But, as far as it goes, it seems to be the logic of the other side. He says the charge is that these accused were engaged in a conspiracy with somebody unknown; this letter comes from somebody unknown; therefore it is admissible in evidence. That is about the substance of it. I submit to the Court that this is chop-logic. The rule of law is that the author of a declaration must first be shown, and when a letter is produced here, and read in evidence, it must be first shown whose the handwriting is; that it is really the production of somebody whose declarations, oral or written, are evidence against the accused; and until that is proved the letter is clearly inadmissible.

If the Court will look at the face of the letter, although that is a matter for argument, in case it is fairly before the Court as evidence, I think the Court will perceive that it does bear on its very face the marks of fabrication. The letter is picked out of the water at Morehead City, no more blurred, I think, than any paper on this table. It looks as if it had been written and dropped in the water immediately before it was found, for the very purpose of being picked up by the Government agents, to be used as evidence. It declares that, "Pet" (who, I suppose, is intended to mean Booth) "has done his work well." "We had a large meeting last night" (the Friday night when these conspirators were flying from the city for their lives.) "I was in Baltimore yesterday." That was Friday. "Pet had not got there." Of course he had not got there when

the work of conspiracy was to be done that very night, Friday; yet this letter assumes that he had done the work before, and was to get there "yesterday," Friday, in Baltimore. Every thing about it is suspicious. That, however, is a matter of argument to the Court, as a question of evidence, when it is before the Court as evidence. In support of the motion of my learned friend, I submit that the letter was read and admitted in evidence by surprise; it is not legitimate evidence, and therefore should be so entered upon the record.

Assistant Judge Advocate BINGHAM. I have only to say that the motion of the learned counsel will come more fitly when he makes his final argument. It is competent for him to say then to the Court, "You are not entitled to consider this evidence;" but I object to commencing the argument of the case in the middle of the trial, and asking the Court to decide a part of the case at one time, and another part of it at another. That is a new system of practice.

In regard to the remarks of my learned friend who has just spoken, his tongue certainly tripped, and he forgot himself, when he said that, in cases of conspiracy, written evidence could not be admitted without proving the handwriting. I asked him, and challenged him, to produce a single authority that showed any such limitation, where a paper was found relating to the conspiracy, no matter who wrote it. Will the gentleman say here that because we did not prove who wrote the cipher that was found in Booth's possession, which accords exactly with the cipher found in Davis's or Benjamin's possession at Richmond, it is not evidence? It is no matter who wrote it; he had it, and let him account for his possession of it, and let him account for the uses he was making of it. This letter was found on the premises under the control and occupied by the enemy, who were engaged in this conspiracy. The gentleman said that "Pet" is referred to in the letter. He is, and it is proved that "Pet" is the name by which Booth was known among his co-conspirators in Canada; it is so proved by Conover. How would Conover know any thing about the contents of this letter? Who has proved that he was in North Carolina at the time of the flight?

The letter is dated Washington, April 15th, which is the day after the murder, and the day of the death of the President of the United States. It does not follow, by any means, that it was written in Washington; but that is what is on its face. Now, let us see whether there is any thing of this supposed contradiction on the face of it.

"I am happy to inform you that Pet has done his work well. He is safe, and Old Abe is in hell."

Is there any contradiction here in dates, or time, or fact? Did not Abraham Lincoln die on the morning of the 15th of April, and is not that in proof? The conclusions of this miserable monster, of course, are not statements of facts; but, monster as he is, he knows enough to state the fact, which he does state, that "Pet has done his work well," after their method of well-doing, and that his victim, Abraham Lincoln, is dead. That is the fact that he states; there is no contradiction there. "Now, sir, all eyes are on you." Who? "You." "You must bring Sherman. Grant is in the hands of Old Gray ere this." Who in America knew that, except a man in this conspiracy, on the 15th of April?

Mr. Cox. We do not know that it was written on that day.

Assistant Judge Advocate BINGHAM. We are taking things as we find them. "Red Shoes showed lack of nerve in Seward's case, but fell back in good order." Who knew in what sort of order he fell back, except a co-conspirator? We know who Red Shoes was. He did fall back.

Mr. Cox. When was the letter found?

Assistant Judge Advocate BINGHAM. On the second day of May.

Mr. Cox. Three weeks after.

Assistant Judge Advocate BINGHAM. Yes; but the gentleman assumes in his criticism that it bears date the day it purports to have been written. "Johnson must come. Old Crook has him in charge." Who knew on the 15th of April who had him in charge? "Mind well that brother's oath." Who knew then about the oath? It is all abundantly proved here, however. "And you will have no difficulty. All will be safe, and enjoy the fruit of our labors." That is, the price. "We had a large meeting last night. All were bent on carrying out the programme to the letter." The gentleman says there is a contradiction. Wherefore? "The rails are laid for safe exit. Old ——, always behind—missed the pop at City Point. I say again, the lives of our brave officers, and the life of the South, depend on carrying this programme into effect." Which was the original design. "Number 2 will give you this. When you write sign no real name. I was in Baltimore yesterday. Pet had not got there yet." The gentleman says there is a contradiction. Wherefore? Was not "yesterday" until midnight at least of the 14th of April? "I was in Baltimore yesterday." Assuming that he was in Washington on the 15th, he was in Baltimore the day before the day of the murder. "Pet had not got there yet." Where? At midnight yesterday, under cover of the same darkness which he sought when he inflicted the mortal wound upon Abraham Lincoln. If he had got the benefit of the trains, everybody knew he would have been there "yesterday." Where is the contradiction?

I submit to the Court that this is no time to decide the effect of this letter upon the case or upon the Court.

Mr. Cox. The argument of the learned counsel for the Government is, that the handwriting of a letter need not be proved when it is found in the custody of parties implicated in the conspiracy. That I may admit, but that assumes the whole question. The letter was not found in the custody of any person. It was found floating upon the water, and *non constat* that the letter may not have been written the very day when it was found, and a few minutes before it was found; and written by somebody who had possessed himself of sufficient knowledge of the facts charged against the conspirators to enable him to fabricate a letter specious on its face, and appearing to have some bearing on the conspiracy itself.

Assistant Judge Advocate BINGHAM. Pardon me for saying to the gentleman, that while his statement is correctly made as regards what I said, I did also say, in that connection, that we must lay a foundation, and show that it had been in the custody of one of the conspirators. I think we have done it by showing that "Pet" was the name of one of the party; by showing that the object of the conspiracy, as narrated in the letter, was the object agreed upon; by showing that that was not a matter of notoriety, nor a matter known to anybody except the conspirators themselves on the day of its date; and by showing that all the evidence in this case, so far as this letter can be understood to-day, corroborates the fact which I assert, that the writer of the letter, on the 15th day of April, was a party to this conspiracy—a fact clearly enough shown, I think, to hang him if he were found with that paper in his pocket, though no man knew his name, and no man ever testified about the writer, unless he could explain how he came by it.

The Commission overruled the motion of Mr. Ewing.

TESTIMONY

RELATING TO JOHN WILKES BOOTH, AND CIRCUMSTANCES ATTENDING THE ASSASSINATION.

ROBERT R. JONES.

For the Prosecution.—May 13.

I am a clerk at the Kirkwood House in this city. The leaf exhibited to the Commission is from the register of the Kirkwood House. It contains the name of G. A. Atzerodt, Charles County.

[The leaf from the hotel register was offered in evidence.]

It appears from the register that Atzerodt took room No. 126 on the morning of the 14th of April last, I think before 8 o'clock in the morning. I was not present when his name was registered, and did not see him until between 12 and 1 in the day. I recognize Atzerodt among the accused. That is the man, I think.

[The witness here pointed to the accused, G. A. Atzerodt.]

I went to the room occupied by Atzerodt after it had been opened by Mr. Lee, on the night of the 15th of April, and I saw all the articles that were found there. I can not identify the knife, though it was similar to the one just shown me. It was between the sheet and the mattress. The bed had not been occupied on the night of the 14th, nor had the chambermaid been able to get into the room the next day. A young man spoke to Atzerodt when I saw him standing at the office counter. I do not know his name. Atzerodt before that asked me if any one had inquired for him within a short time. From the book it appears that Atzerodt paid one day in advance. I had never seen him in the hotel before.

During that day I gave a card of J. Wilkes Booth to Colonel Browning, Mr. Johnson's secretary. It was put in his box. I am not positive that I received it from J. Wilkes Booth, although I may have done so.

Cross-examination by MR. DOSTER.

I do not think I could identify the particular pistol found in Atzerodt's room. It

(70)

was quite a large one, such as cavalry officers wear, and was loaded and capped.

WILLIAM A. BROWNING.

For the Prosecution.—May 16.

I am the private secretary of President Johnson. Between 4 and 5 o'clock in the afternoon of the 14th of April last, I left the Vice-President's room in the Capitol, and went to the Kirkwood House, where we both boarded. On going to the office of the hotel, as was my custom, I noticed a card in my box, which was adjoining that of Mr. Johnson's, and Mr. Jones, the clerk, handed it to me. It was a very common mistake in the office to put cards intended for me into the Vice-President's box, and his would find their way into mine; the boxes being together.

[A card was here handed to the witness.]

I recognize this as the card found in my box. The following is written upon it in pencil:

Don't wish to disturb you; are you at home?   J. WILKES BOOTH.

[The card was offered in evidence.]

I had known J. Wilkes Booth when he was playing in Nashville, Tenn.; I met him there several times; that was the only acquaintance I had with him.

When the card was handed to me, I remarked to the clerk, "It is from Booth; is he playing here?" I thought perhaps he might have called upon me, having known me; but when his name was connected with the assassination, I looked upon it differently.

Cross-examined by MR. DOSTER.

The Vice-President was, I believe, at the Capitol the greater part of the forenoon of that day. He was at dinner at the Kirkwood at 5 o'clock, and I do not think he was out afterward. He was in his room for the balance of the evening. I was there, I think, up to 6 or 7 o'clock, when I left, and did not return until about 11 or 12 o'clock, after the assassination.

CHARLES DAWSON.

For the Prosecution.—May 26.

I am acquainted with the handwriting of J. Wilkes Booth, and the signature on the card shown to me is undoubtedly that of John Wilkes Booth.

THOMAS L. GARDINER.

For the Prosecution.—May 26.

I saw at the Government stables in this city, Seventeenth and I Streets, a dark-bay one-eyed horse on the 8th of this month. It is the same horse that was sold some time in the latter part of November, by my uncle, George Gardiner, to a man named Booth. Booth came to my uncle's with Dr. Samuel A. Mudd, and Booth selected this one out of three horses my uncle had for sale. In accordance with this request, I delivered it to him the next morning at Bryantown. Booth and Dr. Mudd came on horseback, and after the purchase they left together. Booth made the agreement, and Dr. Mudd took no part or interest in the purchase that I saw.

Cross-examined by MR. STONE.

My uncle's house is but a short distance from Dr. Mudd's, not over a quarter of a mile. Booth said he wanted a horse to run in a light buggy to travel over the lower counties of Maryland, that he might look at the lands, as he desired to buy some. My uncle told him he had but one horse that he could recommend as a buggy-horse, and that he could not spare, as he wanted it for his own use. He then offered to sell him a young mare, but Booth said a mare would not suit him. My uncle then said that he had an old saddle-horse that he would sell him if it would suit him. Booth examined the horse, and said he thought it would suit, as he only wanted it for one year. He bought the horse, and paid for him.

I think I have heard of Booth being in the neighborhood of Bryantown some time before that, but I never heard of his being at Dr. Mudd's house.. Our farms were adjoining, and I very often saw Dr. Mudd; sometimes two or three times a week.

BROOKE STABLER.

For the Prosecution.—May 15.

I am manager at Howard's livery stable, on G Street. I was acquainted with J. Wilkes Booth, John H. Surratt, and George A. Atzerodt. They were frequently at the stable together; they almost always came

together, and were sometimes there three or four times a day. Mr. Surratt kept two horses at the stable, and Atzerodt rode out occasionally with Surratt.

I have in my hand a note from Mr. Surratt, which reads:

Mr. Howard will please let the bearer, Mr. Atzerodt, have my horse whenever he wishes to ride, also my leggings and gloves, and oblige, Yours, etc.,
[Signed] J. H. SURRATT.
Feb. 22, 1865.

This note was sent to the stable by Mrs. Surratt, and I put it on file. Atzerodt several times rode horses from that order. It was afterward rescinded.

In the early part of April, Atzerodt told me that John H. Surratt had been to Richmond, and that in coming back he got into difficulty; that the detectives were after him; but he thought he would soon be relieved from the difficulty.

On the 31st of March, Atzerodt took away from the stable a horse blind of one eye, a fine racking horse, and another smaller bay horse, under an order from John H. Surratt. Surratt claimed the horses, but Booth paid for their keep. Atzerodt afterward brought these horses back to the stable to sell them to Mr. Howard, but failing to sell them, he took them away. The horse now at the Government stable, corner Seventeenth and I Streets, is the same one-eyed bay horse that Atzerodt took away on the 31st of March, and brought back for sale some days afterward.

WILLIAM E. CLEAVER.

For the Prosecution.—May 22.

I keep a livery stable on Sixth Street, in this city. In January last, J. Wilkes Booth kept a one-eyed bay horse at my stable, part of the time, for about a month. On the 30th of January he sold the horse to the prisoner, Samuel Arnold, so Booth told me, and Arnold paid me eight dollars for the eight days that the horse remained there after the sale.

John H. Surratt used to hire horses from me in January last, to go down into the country to parties. He was generally with Mr. Booth, but after three or four visits down the country, Booth left word that Mr. Surratt was to have his horse any time he came for it.

I have seen Atzerodt at our stable once; he was there with horses for sale. I have seen the one-eyed horse now at the Government stables on Seventeenth and I Streets, and it is the same that Arnold bought of Booth.

Cross-examined by MR. EWING.

I have only seen Arnold twice; on the 8th of February when he paid me, and once since.

JAMES W. PUMPHRY.

For the Prosecution.—May 15.

I reside in Washington City, and keep a livery stable. I was acquainted with J. Wilkes Booth. He came to my stable about 12 o'clock of the 14th of April last, and engaged a saddle-horse, which he said he wanted about 4 or half-past 4 that day. He had been in the habit of riding a sorrel horse, and he came to get it, but that horse was engaged, and he had in its place a small bay mare, about fourteen or fourteen and a half hands high. She was a bay, with black legs, black mane and tail, and a white star in the forehead. I think the off front foot had white spots. I have never seen the mare since. He asked me to give him a tie-rein to hitch the horse. I told him not to hitch her, as she was in the habit of breaking the bridle. He told me he wanted to tie her while he stopped at a restaurant and got a drink. I said, "Get a boy at the restaurant to hold her." He replied that he could not get a boy. "O," said I, "you can find plenty of bootblacks about the streets to hold your horse." He then said, "I am going to Grover's Theater to write a letter; there is no necessity of tying her there, for there is a stable in the back part of the alley; I will put her there." He then asked where was the best place to take a ride to; I told him, "You have been some time around here, and you ought to know." He asked, "How is Crystal Spring?" "A very good place," I said, "but it is rather early for it." "Well," said he, "I will go there after I get through writing a letter at Grover's Theater." He then rode off, and I have never seen Booth since.

About six weeks before the assassination, Booth called at my stable, in company with John H. Surratt. He said he wanted a good saddle-horse. I said, "Before you get him you will have to give me a reference; you are a stranger to me." He replied, "If you do n't know me you have heard of me; I am John Wilkes Booth." Mr. Surratt spoke up and said, "This is John Wilkes Booth, Mr. Pumphry; he and I are going to take a ride, and I will see that you are paid for the horse." I let him have the horse, and I was paid.

Cross-examined by MR. AIKEN.

Mr. Surratt never came to my place with Booth after the first time. I do not know any of the prisoners at the bar.

PETER TALTAVUL.

For the Prosecution.—May 15.

I was acquainted with John Wilkes Booth. I kept the restaurant adjoining Ford's Theater, on the lower side. Booth came into my restaurant on the evening of the 14th of April, I judge a little after 10 o'clock, walked up to the bar, and called for some whisky, which I gave him; he then called for some water, which I also gave him; he placed the money on the counter and went out. I saw him go out of the bar alone, as near as I can judge, from eight to ten minutes before I heard the cry that the President was assassinated.

I am acquainted with the prisoner, Herold; have known him since he was a boy. I saw him on the night of the murder, or the night previous to that; he came into my place and asked me if Mr. Booth had been there that afternoon. I told him I had not been there myself in the afternoon, when he asked, "Was he not here this evening?" I said, "No, sir;" and he went out.

Cross-examined by MR. STONE.

I can not positively swear as to whether that was Thursday or Friday evening. I think Herold came alone to the bar. I did not see anybody come in there with him. As near as I can recollect, the time was between 6 and 7 o'clock.

SERGEANT JOSEPH M. DYE.

For the Prosecution.—May 15.

On the evening of the 14th of April last, I was sitting in front of Ford's Theater, about half-past 9 o'clock. I observed several persons, whose appearance excited my suspicion, conferring together upon the pavement. The first who appeared was an elegantly-dressed gentleman, who came out of the passage, and commenced conversing with a ruffianly-looking fellow; then another appeared, and the three conversed together. It was then drawing near the second act. The one that appeared to be the leader, the well-dressed one, said, "I think he will come out now," referring to the President, I supposed. The President's carriage was standing in front of the theater. One of the three had been standing out, looking at the carriage, on the curbstone, while I was sitting there, and then went back. They watched awhile, and the rush came down; many gentlemen came out and went in and had a drink in the saloon below. After the people went up, the best-dressed gentleman stepped into the saloon himself; remained there long enough to get a drink, and came out in a style as if he was becoming intoxicated. He stepped up and whispered to this ruffian, (that is, the miserablest-looking one of the three), and went into the passage that leads to the stage from the street. Then the smallest one stepped up, looked at the clock in the vestibule, called the time, just as the best-dressed gentleman appeared again. Then he started up the street, remained there awhile, and came down again, and called the time again. I then began to think there was something going on, and looked toward this man as he called the time. Presently he went up again, and then came down and called the time louder. I think it was ten minutes after 10 that he called out the last time. He was announcing the time to the other two, and then started on a fast walk up the street, and the best dressed one went inside the theater.

I was invited by Sergeant Cooper to have some oysters; and we had barely time to get seated in the saloon and order the oysters, when a man came rushing in and said the President was shot.

[A photograph of J. Wilkes Booth was handed to the witness.]

That was the well-dressed man; but his moustache was heavier and his hair longer than in the photograph, but these are his features exactly.

The ruffianly man I saw was a stout man, with a rough face, and had a bloated appearance; his dress had been worn a considerable time. The prisoner, Edward Spangler, has the appearance of the rough-looking man, except that he had a moustache.

The one that called the time was a very neat gentleman, well dressed, and he had a moustache. I do not see him among the prisoners. He was better dressed than any I see here. He had on one of the fashionable hats they wear here in Washington, with round top and stiff brim. He was not a very large man, about five feet, six inches high; his coat was a kind of drab color, and his hat was black.

Cross-examined by Mr. Ewing.

During the half hour or more that I sat in the front of the theater, the man in slouched clothes was there; he stood on the pavement at the end of the passage. His moustache was black, and he had on a slouched hat, one that had been worn some time. I did not pay particular attention so as to observe the color of his dress. Booth entered the theater the last time at the front door; he whispered to the man, and left him, and went into the theater by the front door. I did not see the man in the slouched dress change his position, because I was observing Booth. The other man went up the street on a fast walk. I suppose it was about fifteen minutes after Booth entered the theater, that we heard the news of the assassination, while we were in the saloon.

JOHN E. BUCKINGHAM.

For the Prosecution.—May 15.

I am night door-keeper at Ford's Theater. In the daytime I am employed at the Washington Navy Yard.

I know John Wilkes Booth by sight. About 10 o'clock on the evening of the 14th he came to the theater, walked in and went out again, and returned in about two or three minutes. He came to me and asked

what time it was. I told him to step into the lobby and he could see. He stepped out and walked in again, entering by the door that leads to the parquette and dress-circle; came out again, and then went up the stairway to the dress-circle. The last I saw of him was when he alighted on the stage from the box, and ran across the stage with a knife in his hand. He was uttering some sentence, but I could not understand it, being so far from him.

Cross-examined by Mr. Ewing.

I know the accused, Edward Spangler. I am perfectly satisfied that he was not in front of the theater during the play on the night of the 14th of April; had he come out, I must have seen him. I have never known Spangler wear a moustache.

JOHN F. SLEICHMANN.

For the Prosecution.—May 15.

I am assistant property man at Ford's Theater, and have to set the furniture, etc., on the stage. I was at the theater on the night of the assassination of the President. About 9 o'clock that night I saw John Wilkes Booth. He came up on a horse, and entered by the little back door to the theater. Ned Spangler was standing by one of the wings, and Booth said to him, "Ned, you 'll help me all you can, won't you?" and Ned said, "O yes." Those were the first words that I heard.

I just got a glimpse of Booth after the President was shot, as I was going out at the the first entrance on the right-hand side near the prompter's place. I saw Booth on the afternoon of the 14th, between 4 and 5 o'clock, in the restaurant next door. I went in to look for James Maddox, and I saw Booth, Ned Spangler, Jim Maddox, "Peanuts," and a young gentleman by the name of John Mouldey, I think, drinking there.

Cross-examined by Mr. Ewing.

Booth spoke to Spangler right by the back-door. I saw his horse through the open door, but as it was dark I could not see if any one was holding it.

I was on the stage that night, except when I had to go down to the apothecary's store to get a few articles to use in the piece, and when I went into the restaurant next door. Spangler's business on the stage is shoving the scenes. I went to the front of the theater by the side entrance, on the left-hand side. When I was in front, I noticed the President's carriage there, but did not see Spangler; had he been there, I guess I should have seen him. I have never seen Spangler wear a moustache. I was in front of the theater two or three times, but was on the stage during the third act. I think it was ten or fifteen minutes before the close of the second act that I was in the restaurant next door.

About ten minutes, I suppose, after the

assassination, Spangler was standing on the stage by one of the wings, with a white handkerchief in his hand. He was very pale, and was wiping his eyes. I do not know whether he was crying or not.

Booth was very familiar with the actors and employees of the theater, and was backward and forward in the theater frequently. He had access to the theater at all times, and came behind the scenes, and in the green-room, and anywhere about the theater, just as though he was in the employment of Mr. Ford.

When Booth spoke to Spangler, they were about eight feet from me, but Booth and Spangler were not more than two or three feet apart. After Booth had spoken, he went behind the scenes. I do not know whether Booth saw me, but he could have seen me from where he was standing; no one else was by at the time that I noticed. Spangler is, I think, a drinking man; whether he was in liquor that night I do not know.

JOSEPH BURROUGHS, *alias* "PEANUTS."

For the Prosecution.—May 16.

I carry bills for Ford's Theater during the daytime, and stand at the stage-door at night. I knew John Wilkes Booth, and used to attend to his horse, and see that it was fed and cleaned. His stable was immediately back of the theater. On the afternoon of the 14th of April, he brought his horse to the stable, between 5 and 6 o'clock. He hallooed out for Spangler; when he came, Booth asked him for a halter. He had none, and sent Jake up stairs after one. Jim Maddox was down there too. Between 9 and 10 o'clock that night, I heard Deboney calling to Ned that Booth wanted him out in the alley. I did not see Booth come up the alley on his horse, but I saw the horse at the door when Spangler called me out there to hold it. When Spangler told me to hold the horse, I said I could not; I had to go in to attend to my door. He told me to hold it, and if there was any thing wrong to lay the blame on him; so I held the horse. I held him as I was sitting over against the house there, on a carpenter's bench.

I heard the report of the pistol. I was still out by the bench, had not got off when Booth came out. He told me to give him his horse. He struck me with the butt of a knife, and knocked me down. He did this as he was mounting his horse, with one foot in the stirrup; he also kicked me, and rode off immediately.

I was in the President's box that afternoon when Harry Ford was putting the flags around it. Harry Ford told me to go up with Spangler and take out the partition of the box; that the President and General Grant were coming there. While Spangler was at work removing it he said, "Damn the President and General Grant." I said to him, "What are you damning the man for—a man

that has never done any harm to you?" He said he ought to be cursed when he got so many men killed.

I only saw one horse in the stable when I was there between 5 and 6 o'clock, and I was not there afterward. There was another horse there some days before. Booth brought a horse and buggy there; it was a little horse; I do not remember the color. The fellow that brought the horse there lived at the Navy Yard. I think he used to go with Booth very often. I do not see him among the prisoners.

[Probably Herold, though the witness failed to recognize him among the prisoners and the guards.]

I saw Booth as he came out of the small door. I did not see anybody else. I did not see Spangler come in or go out while I was sitting at the door.

Cross-examined by MR. EWING.

It was about six or eight minutes after Deboney called Spangler that Spangler called me. I was sitting at the first entrance on the left, attending to the stage-door. I was there to keep strangers out, and prevent those coming in who did not belong there.

When I was not there, Spangler used to hitch up Booth's horse, and hold him or feed him. Between 5 and 6 that evening, Spangler wanted to take the saddle off Booth's horse, but Booth would not let him; then he wanted to take the bridle off, but Booth would not agree to it; so Spangler just put a halter round the horse's neck, but he took the saddle off afterward.

I was out in front of the theater that night while the curtain was down; I go out between every act. When the curtain is up, I go inside. I did not see Booth in front of the theater that night, nor Spangler. I never saw Spangler wear a moustache.

Booth was about the theater a great deal; he sometimes entered on Tenth Street, and sometimes from the back. The stable where Booth kept his horses is about two hundred yards from the back entrance to the theater. When I went to hold the horse for Booth that night, I think they were playing the first scene of the third act.

Spangler always worked on the left-hand side of the stage; that is the side the President's box was on, and it was on that side I attended the door. When I was away, Spangler used to attend the door for me; that was the door that went into the alley from Tenth Street. A man by the name of Simmons worked with Spangler on that side of the stage, and on the other side, Skeggy, Jake, and another man worked. While the play was going on, these men were always about there. It was their business to shove the scenes on. They usually staid on their own side of the stage, but when a scene stood the whole of the act, they might go round on the other side; sometimes they would go out, but not very often.

Recalled for the Prosecution.—May 22.

The stable in the rear of the theater was fitted up for Booth in January, by Spangler and a man by the name of George. It was raised up a little higher for the buggy, and two stalls put in it. Booth occupied that stable until the assassination. First he had a saddle-horse, which he sold; then he got a horse and buggy. The buggy he sold on Wednesday before the assassination. Ned Spangler, the prisoner, sold it for him.

Cross-examined by Mr. EWING.

I do not know to whom Spangler sold it. Booth and Gifford told Spangler on the Monday, to take it to the bazar on Maryland Avenue; but he could not get what he wanted for it there, and sold it afterward to a man that kept a livery stable.

MARY ANN TURNER (colored.)

For the Prosecution.—May 16.

I reside in the rear of Ford's Theater; my front-door fronts to the back of the theater. I knew John Wilkes Booth when I saw him. I saw him on the afternoon of the 14th, standing in the back-door of Ford's Theater, with a lady by his side. Between 7 and 8 o'clock that night, he brought a horse up to the back door of the theater, and, opening it, called "Ned" three times.

Ned came to him, and I heard him say, in a low voice, "Tell Maddox to come here." When Maddox came, Booth said something in a very low voice to him, and I saw Maddox reach out his hand and take the horse. Where Ned went I can not tell. Booth then went into the theater. After the assassination, I heard the horse going very rapidly out of the alley. I ran immediately to my door and opened it, but he was gone. The crowd then came out, and this man, Ned, came out of the theater.

[The witness here identified the accused, Edward Spangler.]

When I saw him, I said, "Mr. Ned, you know that man Booth called you." Said he, "I know nothing about it."

MARY JANE ANDERSON (colored.)

For the Prosecution.—May 16.

I live right back of Ford's Theater, adjoining Mrs. Turner's house. I knew John Wilkes Booth by sight. I saw him on the morning of the 14th of April down by the stable, and again between 2 and 3 o'clock in the afternoon, standing in the theater back-door, in the alley, talking to a lady. I stood in my gate and looked right wishful at him. He and this lady were pointing up and down the alley, as if they were talking about it. They stood there a considerable time, and then Booth went into the theater.

After I had gone up stairs that night, a carriage drove up, and after that I heard a horse step down the alley. I looked out of the window, and it seemed as if the gentleman was leading the horse down the alley. He did not go further than the end of it, and in a few minutes he came back up to the theater door, holding his horse by the bridle. He pushed the door open, and said something in a low voice, and then in a loud voice he called "Ned" four times. There was a colored man up at the window, who said, "Mr. Ned, Mr. Booth wants you." This is the way I came to know it was Mr. Booth, for it was dark and I could not see his face. When Ned came, Mr. Booth said, in a low voice, "Tell Maddox to come here."

Then Ned went back and Maddox came out, and they said something to each other. Maddox then took off the horse from before my door, round to where the work bench was, that stood at the right side of the house. They both then went into the theater. The horse stood out there a considerable time, and kept up a great stamping. After awhile, the person who held the horse kept walking backward and forward; I suppose the horse was there an hour and a half altogether. Then I saw Booth come out of the door with something in his hand, glittering. He came out of the theater so quick that it seemed as if he but touched the horse, and it was gone like a flash of lightning. I thought to myself that the horse must surely have run off with the gentleman. Presently there was a rush out of the door, and I heard the people saying, "Which way did he go?" I asked a gentleman what was the matter, and he said the President was shot. I asked who shot him. Said he, "The man who went out on the horse."

I went up to the theater door, and saw Mr. Spangler. When he came out, I said to him, "Mr. Spangler, that gentleman called you." Said he, "No, he didn't." Said I, "Yes, he did." He said, "No, he didn't call me." He denied it, and I kept on saying so.

Cross-examined by Mr. EWING.

When Mr. Maddox took the horse round out of my sight, I could not see who held him. He came back after a little while, and went into the theater again. Mr. Spangler came out when Booth called him, and told him to tell Maddox to come out, but I am not certain that Spangler came out again.

JAMES L. MADDOX.

For the Prosecution.—May 22.

I was employed at Ford's Theater as property man. In December last, I rented from Mrs. Davis, for John Wilkes Booth, the stable where he kept his horse up to the time of the murder of President Lincoln. Mr. Booth gave me the rent money monthly, and I paid it to Mrs. Davis.

I saw Harry Ford decorating the Presi-

dent's box on the afternoon of the 14th of
April, but do not remember seeing any one
else in the box. I was in there but once.

I saw Joe Simms, the colored man, coming
from Mr. Ford's room, through the alley
way, carrying on his head the rocking-chair
that the President was to use in the evening.
I had not seen that chair in the box this
season; the last time I saw it before that
afternoon was in the winter of 1863, when
it was used by the President on his first visit
to the theater.

Cross-examined by MR. EWING.

My duties require me to be on the stage
while the performance is going on, unless, as
sometimes happened, there is nothing at all
to do, when I go out. My business is to see
that the furniture is put on the stage aright,
and to get the actors any side properties that
may be required for use in the play.
The passage way by which Booth escaped
is usually clear. Only when we are playing
a heavy piece, and when in a hurry, do we
run things in there. The "American Cousin,"
which was performed on that night, is not a
heavy piece, and the passage would therefore
be clear of obstruction.

Spangler's position on the stage was on
the left-hand side, facing the audience, and
the same side that the President's box was
on. I saw Spangler during nearly every
scene. If he had not been at his place, I
should certainly have missed him. If he
had missed running off a single scene, I
should have known it. Sometimes a scene
lasts twenty minutes, but in the third act
of the "American Cousin" there are seven
scenes, the way Miss Keene plays it, and had
Spangler been absent five minutes after the
first scene of this act we should have noticed
it. In the second act, I guess, he has a half
hour, and in the first scene of the third act
he has twenty-five minutes, and after this the
scenes are pretty quick.

I was at the front of the theater during the
second act, but did not see Spangler there.
I have never seen Spangler wear a moustache
during the two years that I have known him.

I was in the first entrance to the stage, the
side the President's box is on, at the moment
of the assassination. Three or four minutes
before that, while the second scene of the
third act was on, I crossed the stage with the
will, and saw Spangler in his place. After
the pistol was fired, I caught a glimpse of
Booth, when he was about two feet off the
stage. I ran on the stage and heard a call
for water; I ran and brought a pitcher full,
and gave it to one of the officers. I did not
see Spangler after that, that I remember,
until the next morning. I may have seen
him, but not to notice him.

I heard about 12 o'clock that the President was coming to the theater that night; I
was told so by Mr. Harry Ford. I heard a
young man, one of the officers connected with

the President's house, say that night that he
had come down that morning and engaged
the box for the President.

JAMES P. FERGUSON.
For the Prosecution.—May 15.

I keep a restaurant, adjoining Ford's
Theater, on the upper side. I saw J. Wilkes
Booth, on the afternoon of the 14th, between
2 and 4 o'clock, standing by the side of
his horse—a small bay mare; Mr. Maddox
was standing by him talking. Booth remarked, "See what a nice horse I have got;
now watch, he can run just like a cat;" and,
striking his spurs into his horse, he went off
down the street.

About 1 o'clock Mr. Harry Ford came
into my place and said, "Your favorite, General Grant, is to be at the theater to-night,
and if you want to see him you had better go
and get a seat." I went and secured a seat
directly opposite the President's box, in the
front dress-circle. I saw the President and
his family when they came in, accompanied
by Miss Harris and Major Rathbone.

Somewhere near 10 o'clock, during the second scene of the third act of "Our American
Cousin," I saw Booth pass along near the
President's box, and then stop and lean
against the wall. After standing there a
moment, I saw him step down one step, put
his hands on the door and his knee against
it, and push the door open—the first door
that goes into the box. I saw no more of
him until he made a rush for the front of the
box and jumped over. He put his left hand
on the railing, and with his right he seemed
to strike back with a knife. I could see the
knife gleam, and the next moment he was
over the box. As he went over, his hand
was raised, the handle of the knife up, the
blade down. The President sat in the left-
hand corner of the box, with Mrs. Lincoln
at his right. Miss Harris was in the right-
hand corner, Major Rathbone sitting back at
her left, almost in the corner of the box. At
the moment the President was shot, he was
leaning his hand on the railing, looking down
at a person in the orchestra; holding the flag
that decorated the box aside to look between
it and the post, I saw the flash of the pistol
right back in the box. As the person jumped
over and lit on the stage, I saw it was Booth.
As he struck the stage, he rose and exclaimed,
"Sic semper tyrannus!" and ran directly across
the stage to the opposite door, where the actors
come in.

I heard some one halloo out of the box,
"Revenge for the South!" I do not know
that it was Booth, though I suppose it must
have been; it was just as he was jumping
over the railing. His spur caught in the blue
part of the flag that was stretched around the
box, and, as he went over, it tore a piece of
the flag, which was dragged half way across
the stage on the spur of his right heel.

Just as Booth went over the box, I saw the President raise his head, and then it hung back. I saw Mrs. Lincoln catch his arm, and I was then satisfied that the President was hurt. By that time Booth was across the stage. A young man named Harry Hawk was the only actor on the stage at the time.

I left the theater as quickly as I could, and went to the police station on D Street, to give notice to the Superintendent of Police, Mr. Webb. I then ran up D Street to the house of Mr. Peterson, where the President was taken. Colonel Wells was standing on the steps, and I told him that I had seen it all, and I knew the man who jumped out of the box.

Next morning I saw Mr. Gifford, who said, "You made a hell of a statement about what you saw last night; how could you see the flash of the pistol when the ball was shot through the door?" On Sunday morning Miss Harris, accompanied by her father, Judge Olin, and Judge Carter, came down to the theater, and I went in with them. We got a candle and examined the hole in the door of the box through which Mr. Gifford said the ball had been shot. It looked to me as if it had been bored by a gimlet, and then rimed round the edge with a knife. In several places it was scratched down, as if the knife had slipped. After this examination, I was satisfied that the pistol had been fired in the box.

Mr. Gifford is the chief carpenter of the theater, and I understood had full charge of it. I recollect when Richmond was surrendered I said to him, "Have you not got any flags in the theater?" He replied, "Yes, I have; I guess there is a flag about." I said, "Why do you not run it out on the roof?" He answered, "There's a rope, is n't that enough?" I said, "You are a hell of a man, you ought to be in the Old Capitol." He did n't like me any how.

Cross-examined by MR. EWING.

We looked for the bar that had been used to fasten the box-door, but could not find it. I know Mr. Spangler very well. I never saw him wear a moustache, that I recollect.

JAMES J. GIFFORD.

For the Prosecution.—May 19.

I was the builder of Ford's Theater, and am stage-carpenter there. I noticed Mr. Harry Clay Ford in the President's box, on the 14th of April last, putting flags out; I think I saw Mr. Raybold with him. When I was in the box on Saturday, the 15th, I saw the large rocking-chair. I do not know whether or not it has been previously used this season, but I saw it there last season. It was part of a set of furniture—two sofas and two high-backed chairs—one with rockers and one with castors. I have sometimes seen the one with castors in the box this season, but not the rocking-chair. The last time I saw the chair before it was placed in the President's box was in Mr. Ford's room, adjoining the theater.

On Monday morning, after the assassination, I was trying to find out how the door of the President's box had been fastened, when I first saw the mortise in the wall. The Secretary of War came down to the theater to examine the box, and he told me to bring a stick and fit it in the door. I found that a stick about three feet six inches long, if pressed against it, would prevent the door from being opened on the outside, but if the door was shaken, the stick would fall. The mortise in the plastering looked as though it had been recently made, and had the appearance of having been made with a knife. Had a chisel or hammer been used, it would have made a sound, but with a knife it could have been done quietly. It might have required some ten or fifteen minutes to make it. I had not been in the box, I think, for a week. Had the marks been there then, I think I should have observed it, as I am particular in looking around to see the place is clean. It was the duty of Mr. Rayboltd, the upholsterer, to decorate the box; but he had a stiff neck, and got Mr. Clay Ford to do it for him, so he told me afterward.

At the moment of the assassination I was in front of the theater; twenty minutes before, I was behind the scenes where I saw Spangler; he was then waiting for his business to change the scene.

Cross-examined by MR. EWING.

The passage on each side of the entrances is always kept free. The entrances are always more or less filled with tables, chairs, etc. The passage way through which Booth passed to the outer door is about two feet eight inches to three feet wide; some places a little wider, some a little narrower; but it is never obstructed, except by people when they have a large company on the stage; never by chairs, tables, etc. It is necessary to keep this passage way clear to allow the actors and actresses to pass readily from the green-room and dressing-rooms to the stage. I was on the stage until the curtain went up at each act, and saw Spangler there each time. The last time I saw him was about half-past 9 o'clock.

I was in front of the theater a part of the time between the second and third acts. I did not see Spangler in front of the theater at all; I do not think he could have been there without my knowing it, because the scenes would have gone wrong had he left the stage for any length of time. I never knew Spangler to wear a moustache.

In the play of the "American Cousin" there are, I believe, some five or six scenes in each act, and Spangler's presence on the stage would have been indispensable to the performance. Ritterspaugh was on duty with Spangler on his side of the stage that night.

I know nothing more of Booth's connection with Spangler than that it was friendly. Everybody about the house, actors and all, were friendly with Booth; he had such a winning way that he made every person like him. He was a good-natured, jovial kind of man, and the people about the house, as far as I know, all liked him. He had access to the theater by all the entrances, just as the employees of the theater had. Spangler appeared to be a sort of drudge for Booth, doing such things as hitching up his horse, etc.

CAPTAIN THEODORE McGOWAN.
For the Prosecution.—May 15.

I was present at Ford's Theater on the night of the assassination. I was sitting in the aisle leading by the wall toward the door of the President's box, when a man came and disturbed me in my seat, causing me to push my chair forward to permit him to pass; he stopped about three feet from where I was sitting, and leisurely took a survey of the house. I looked at him because he happened to be in my line of sight. He took a small pack of visiting-cards from his pocket, selecting one and replacing the others, stood a second, perhaps, with it in his hand, and then showed it to the President's messenger, who was sitting just below him. Whether the messenger took the card into the box, or, after looking at it, allowed him to go in, I do not know; but, in a moment or two more, I saw him go through the door of the lobby leading to the box, and close the door.

After I heard the pistol fired, I saw the body of a man descend from the front of the box toward the stage. He was hid from my sight for a moment by the heads of those who sat in the front row of the dress-circle, but in another moment he reappeared, strode across the stage toward the entrance on the other side, and, as he passed, I saw the gleaming blade of a dagger in his right hand. He disappeared behind the scenes in a moment, and I saw him no more.

I know J. Wilkes Booth, but, not seeing the face of the assassin fully, I did not at the time recognize him as Booth.

MAJOR HENRY R. RATHBONE.
For the Prosecution.—May 15.

On the evening of the 14th of April last, at about twenty minutes past 8 o'clock, I, in company with Miss Harris, left my residence at the corner of Fifteenth and H Streets, and joined the President and Mrs. Lincoln, and went with them, in their carriage, to Ford's Theater, on Tenth Street. On reaching the theater, when the presence of the President became known, the actors stopped playing, the band struck up "Hail to the Chief," and the audience rose and received him with vocif-

erous cheering. The party proceeded along in the rear of the dress-circle and entered the box that had been set apart for their reception. On entering the box, there was a large arm-chair that was placed nearest the audience, farthest from the stage, which the President took and occupied during the whole of the evening, with one exception, when he got up to put on his coat, and returned and sat down again. When the second scene of the third act was being performed, and while I was intently observing the proceedings upon the stage, with my back toward the door, I heard the discharge of a pistol behind me, and, looking round, saw through the smoke a man between the door and the President. The distance from the door to where the President sat was about four feet. At the same time I heard the man shout some word, which I thought was "Freedom!" I instantly sprang toward him and seized him. He wrested himself from my grasp, and made a violent thrust at my breast with a large knife. I parried the blow by striking it up, and received a wound several inches deep in my left arm, between the elbow and the shoulder. The orifice of the wound was about an inch and a half in length, and extended upward toward the shoulder several inches. The man rushed to the front of the box, and I endeavored to seize him again, but only caught his clothes as he was leaping over the railing of the box. The clothes, as I believe, were torn in the attempt to hold him. As he went over upon the stage, I cried out, "Stop that man." I then turned to the President; his position was not changed; his head was slightly bent forward, and his eyes were closed. I saw that he was unconscious, and, supposing him mortally wounded, rushed to the door for the purpose of calling medical aid.

On reaching the outer door of the passage way, I found it barred by a heavy piece of plank, one end of which was secured in the wall, and the other resting against the door. It had been so securely fastened that it required considerable force to remove it. This wedge or bar was about four feet from the floor. Persons upon the outside were beating against the door for the purpose of entering. I removed the bar, and the door was opened. Several persons, who represented themselves as surgeons, were allowed to enter. I saw there Colonel Crawford, and requested him to prevent other persons from entering the box.

I then returned to the box, and found the surgeons examining the President's person. They had not yet discovered the wound. As soon as it was discovered, it was determined to remove him from the theater. He was carried out, and I then proceeded to assist Mrs. Lincoln, who was intensely excited, to leave the theater. On reaching the head of the stairs, I requested Major Potter to aid me in assisting Mrs. Lincoln across the street to the house where the President was being conveyed. The wound which I had received had been bleeding very profusely, and on reaching the house, feeling very faint from the loss of blood, I seated myself in the hall, and soon after fainted away, and was laid upon the floor. Upon the return of consciousness I was taken to my residence.

In a review of the transactions, it is my confident belief that the time which elapsed between the discharge of the pistol and the time when the assassin leaped from the box did not exceed thirty seconds. Neither Mrs. Lincoln nor Miss Harris had left their seats.

[A bowie-knife, with a heavy seven-inch blade, was exhibited to the witness, stains of blood being still upon the blade.]

This knife might have made a wound similar to the one I received. The assassin held the blade in a horizontal position, I think, and the nature of the wound would indicate it; it came down with a sweeping blow from above.

[The knife was offered in evidence.]

WILLIAM WITHERS, JR.

For the Prosecution.—May 15.

I am the leader of the orchestra at Ford's Theater. I had some business on the stage with our stage-manager on the night of the 14th, in regard to a national song that I had composed, and I went to see what costume they were going to sing it in. After talking with the manager, I was returning to the orchestra, when I heard the report of a pistol. I stood with astonishment, thinking why they should fire off a pistol in "Our American Cousin." As I turned round I heard some confusion, and saw a man running toward me with his head down. I did not know what was the matter, and stood completely paralyzed. As he ran, I could not get out of his way, so he hit me on the leg, and turned me round, and made two cuts at me, one in the neck and one on the side, and knocked me from the third entrance down to the second. The scene saved me. As I turned, I got a side view of him, and I saw it was John Wilkes Booth. He then made a rush for the back door, and out he went. I returned to the stage and heard that the President was killed, and I saw him in the box apparently dead.

Where I stood on the stage was not more than a yard from the door. He made one plunge at the door, which I believe was shut, and instantly he was out. The door opens inward on the stage, but whether he opened it, or whether it was opened for him, I do not know. I noticed that there was nothing to obstruct his passage out, and this seemed strange to me, for it was unusual.

Cross-examined by MR. EWING.

On that night the passage seemed to be clear of every thing. I do not think it

wanted many minutes until the scene changed, and it was a time in the scene when the stage and passage way would have been somewhat obstructed by some of the scene-shifters, and the actors in waiting for the next scene, which requires their presence. I never remember seeing Spangler wear a moustache.

JOSEPH B. STEWART.

For the Prosecution.—May 20.

I was at Ford's Theater on the night of the assassination of the President. I was sitting in the front seat of the orchestra, on the right-hand side. The sharp report of a pistol at about half-past 10—evidently a charged pistol—startled me. I heard an exclamation, and simultaneously a man leaped from the President's box, lighting on the stage. He came down with his back slightly toward the audience, but rising and turning, his face came in full view. At the same instant I jumped on the stage, and the man disappeared at the left-hand stage entrance. I ran across the stage as quickly as possible, following the direction he took, calling out, "Stop that man!" three times. When about twenty or twenty-five feet from the door through which the man ran, the door slammed to and closed. Coming up to the door, I touched it first on the side where it did not open; after which I caught hold at the proper place, opened the door, and passed out. The last time that I exclaimed "Stop that man," some one said, "He is getting on a horse at the door;" and almost as soon as the words reached my ears I heard the tramping of a horse. On opening the door, after the temporary balk, I perceived a man mounting a horse. The moon was just beginning to rise, and I could see any thing elevated better than near the ground. The horse was moving with a quick, agitated motion—as a horse will do when prematurely spurred in mounting—with the reins drawn a little to one side, and for a moment I noticed the horse describe a kind of circle from the right to the left. I ran in the direction where the horse was heading, and when within eight or ten feet from the head of the horse, and almost up within reach of the left flank, the rider brought him round somewhat in a circle from the left to the right, crossing over, the horse's feet rattling violently on what seemed to be rocks. I crossed in the same direction, aiming at the rein, and was now on the right flank of the horse. He was rather gaining on me then, though not yet in a forward movement. I could have reached his flank with my hand when, perhaps, two-thirds of the way over the alley. Again he backed to the right side of the alley, brought the horse forward and spurred him; at the same instant he crouched forward, down over the pummel of the saddle. The horse then went forward, and soon swept rapidly to the left, up toward F Street. I still ran after the horse: some forty or fifty yards, and commanded the person to stop. All this occupied only the space of a few seconds.

After passing the stage, I saw several persons in the passage way, ladies and gentlemen, one or two men, perhaps five persons.

Near the door on my right hand, I saw a person standing, who seemed to be in the act of turning, and who did not seem to be moving about like the others. Every one else that I saw but this person, seemed intensely excited, literally bewildered; they were all in a terrible commotion and moving about, except this man. As I approached the door, and only about fifteen feet from it, this person was facing the door; but, as I got nearer, he partially turned round, moving to the left, so that I had a view of him as he was turning from the door and toward me.

[The witness was directed to look at the prisoners, to see if he recognized among them the person he saw standing at the door.]

That man [pointing to Edward Spangler] looks more like the person I saw near the door than anybody else I see here. He recalls the impression of the man's visage as I passed him. When the assassin alighted on the stage, I believed I knew who it was that had committed the deed; that it was J. Wilkes Booth, and I so informed Richards, Superintendent of the Police, that night. I knew Booth by sight very well, and when I was running after him, I had no doubt in my mind that it was Booth, and should have been surprised to find that it was anybody else. I felt a good deal vexed at his getting away, and had no doubt when I started across the stage that I could catch him. From the time I heard the door slam until I saw the man mounting his horse, was not over the time I could make two steps.

I am satisfied that the person I saw inside the door was in a position and had an opportunity, if he had been disposed to do so, to have interrupted the exit of Booth, and from his manner, he was cool enough to have done so. This man was nearest of all to the door, and could have opened and gone out before I did, as it would have been but a step to the right and a reach to open it.

Cross-examined by MR. EWING.

The man I have spoken of stood about three feet from the door out of which Booth passed; I noticed him just after the door slammed. From the position in which he stood, he might have slammed it without my noticing it. The lock of the door, as I approached it, was on the right-hand side, the hinges to the left. If the door had been open and I had not been stopped, I could have got the range of the horse outside.

As I passed out of the door, a person, a small person, passed behind me, directly under my right elbow, [the witness was a tall man,] and as I approached the horse at the nearest point, some one ran rapidly out of the alley. The one who passed me is not so tall as Spangler by, perhaps, four or five inches.

I did not notice that the person whom I now suppose to be Spangler wore whiskers or a moustache; my impression is that he was slightly bearded. It was his visage, the side face, that struck me. I do not undertake to swear positively that the prisoner, Edward Spangler, is the person I saw near that door; but I do say that there is no one among these prisoners, who calls that man to my mind, except the one who, I am told, is Mr. Spangler; but I am decided in my opinion, that Spangler resembles the person I saw there.

As I got to the door, Booth was just completing his balance in the saddle. I think, from his position and the motion of the horse, that the moment he got one foot in the stirrup he spurred the horse, and, having the rein drawn more on one side than the other, lost control of him for the moment, so far as making him take a straight forward movement; he was circling round, moving with a quick sort of motion, apparently making more exertion than headway, but still going pretty fast.

Hearing the report of a loaded pistol, and seeing the man jump from the President's box with a dagger in his hand. my impression was that the person had assassinated, or attempted to assassinate, the President, and every effort I made after I started to get upon the stage was under this conviction; so much so that I stated to the people in the tenement houses in the rear, before I returned to the theater, that the person who went off on that horse had shot the President.

JOE SIMMS (colored.)

For the Prosecution.—*May* 15.

I have worked at Ford's Theater for the past two years. On the day of the President's assassination, during the performance, while I was up on the flies to wind up the curtain, I heard the fire of a pistol, and looking down I saw Booth jump out of a private box down on to the stage, with a bowie-knife in his hand, and then making his escape across the stage. Between 5 and 6 o'clock that day, I was in front of the theater, when I saw Booth go into the restaurant by the side of the theater. Spangler was sitting out in front, and Booth invited him to take a drink. I did not hear a word spoken between them. Booth and Spangler were very intimate. I have often seen them together, and drinking together.

Cross-examined by MR. EWING.

Spangler had charge of Booth's horses. There was a young man hired by Booth, but I suppose Mr. Booth thought he might not do right by his horses, so he got Spangler to see to their being fed and watered.

Spangler's place on the stage is at the back part of the stage, next to the back-door leading out to the side alley. The President's box is on the left-hand side as you look toward the audience. My position is on the flies on the opposite side of the President's box, and Mr. Spangler's place was on the opposite side below, the side the President's box is on. I saw him in the first act. I do not remember seeing him in the second, but I was not looking for him. When I saw Mr. Spangler, he had his hat on. I never saw him wear a moustache. Mr. Spangler was on the stage attending to his business as usual that night. He was obliged to be there. From my position on the flies I could see him very well.

Recalled for the Prosecution.—May 18.

On the afternoon of the day of the assassination, I saw Mr. Harry Ford and another gentleman fixing up the box. Mr. Ford told me to go to his bed-room and get a rocking-chair, and bring it down and put it in the President's box. I did so. The chair had not been there before this season. It was a chair with a high back to it and cushioned. Mr. Spangler was at the theater during the afternoon. He worked there altogether, the same as I did.

Cross-examined by MR. EWING.

I did not notice Mr. Spangler there in the afternoon, but his business was to be there. It was about 3 o'clock in the afternoon when Mr. Harry Ford and, I think, Mr. Buckingham were in the private box. I did not see Spangler in the President's box in the afternoon, nor did I see him when I came away from the private box.

JOHN MILES (colored.)

For the Prosecution.—May 15.

I work at Ford's Theater. I was there on the day of the assassination of the President. About 3 o'clock in the afternoon Booth put his horse in the stable, and Ned Spangler and Jim Maddox were with him. The stable is not more than five yards from the theater. Between 9 and 10 o'clock that night, J. Wilkes Booth brought a horse from the stable, and, coming to the back door of the theater, called "Ned Spangler" three times. When Booth first called Spangler, some person told him that Booth called him, and he ran across the stage to him. I saw nothing more of Spangler or Booth until I heard the pistol go off. In a minute or two I heard the sound of a horse's feet going out of the alley. Before this I saw a boy holding the horse in the alley, perhaps for fifteen minutes. That was after Booth had called Spangler.

Cross-examined by MR. EWING.

When Booth called Spangler I was up on the flies, about three and a half stories from

the stage. It was, I think, in the third act; and from the time Booth brought his horse there until the President was shot was, I think, about three-quarters of an hour. I I was at the window pretty nearly all the time. From the time Booth brought the horse until he went away, and from the time I looked out of the window, John Peanuts was lying on the bench holding the horse; I did not see any one else holding it.

John Peanuts attended to Mr. Booth's horses. I have seen Spangler hold Booth's horses or hitch them up, but I never saw him put any gearing on them. Spangler's place on the stage was on the same side as the President's box, and he was there when Booth called him. There was another man working with Spangler to help him shove the scenes.

After the President was shot, I came down the stairs, and I saw Spangler out there at the door Booth went out of. There were, I think, two or three other or more men out there, some of whom were strangers. When I came down, I went toward the door, and Spangler came out, and I asked him who it was that held the horse, and he said, "Hush! do n't say any thing about it;" and I did n't say any more, though I knew who it was, because I saw the boy holding the horse. Spangler, I suppose, when he said this, was about a yard and a half from the door, outside the door. Spangler appeared to be excited; every person appeared to be very much excited. By the time I got down stairs, the door through which Booth had passed was open. I never saw Spangler wear a moustache.

DR. ROBERT KING STONE.

For the Prosecution—May 16.

I am a practicing physician in this city, and was the family physician of the late President of the United States.

I was sent for by Mrs. Lincoln immediately after the assassination. I arrived in a very few moments, and found that the President had been removed from the theater to the house of a gentleman living directly opposite; and had been carried into the back room of the residence, and was there placed upon a bed. I found a number of gentlemen, citizens, around him, and, among others, two assistant surgeons of the army, who had brought him over from the theater, and had attended to him. They immediately gave the case over to my care, knowing my relations to the family. I proceeded to examine the President, and found that he had received a gun-shot wound in the back part of the left side of his head, into which I carried my finger. I at once informed those around that the case was a hopeless one; that the President would die; that there was no positive limit to the duration of his life; that his vital tenacity was very strong, and he would resist as long as any man could; but that death certainly would soon close the scene. I remained with him, doing whatever was in my power, assisted by my friends; but, of course, nothing could be done, and he died from the wound the next morning at about half-past 7 o'clock. It was about a quarter past 10 that I reached him.

The next day, previous to the process of embalmment, an examination was made in the presence of Surgeon-General Barnes, Dr. Curtis, and Dr. Woodward, of the army. We traced the wound through the brain, and the ball was found in the anterior part of the same side of the brain, the left side; it was a large ball, resembling those which are shot from the pistol known as the Derringer; an unusually large ball—that is, larger than those used in the ordinary pocket revolvers. It was a leaden hand-made ball, and was flattened somewhat in its passage through the skull, and a portion had been cut off in going through the bone. I marked the ball "A. L.," the initials of the late President, and in the presence of the Secretary of War, in his office, inclosed it in an envelope, sealed it with my private seal, and indorsed it with my name. The Secretary inclosed it in another envelope, which he indorsed in like manner, and sealed with his private seal. It was left in his custody, and he ordered it to be placed among the archives of his department.

[An official envelope, sealed with the official seal of the Secretary of War, was here opened by the Judge Advocate in the presence of the witness, from which was taken a Derringer pistol and an envelope containing a leaden ball in two pieces.]

This is the ball which I extracted from the head of the President; I recognize it from the mark which I put upon it with my pen-knife, as well as from the shape of the ball. This smaller piece is the fragment which was cut off in its passage through the skull. The ball was flattened, as I have before described.

[The ball was then offered in evidence.]

WILLIAM T. KENT.

For the Prosecution.—May 16.

About three minutes after the President was shot, I went into his box; there were two other persons there and a surgeon, who asked me for a knife to cut open the President's clothes. On leaving the theater I missed my night-key, and thinking I had dropped it in pulling out my knife, I hurried back, and on searching round the floor of the box, I knocked my foot against a pistol, which I picked up, and, holding it up, I cried out, "I have found the pistol." I gave it up to Mr. Gobright, the agent of the Associated Press. The next morning I went round to the police station and identified it there.

[A Derringer pistol, about six inches in length, was handed to the witness.]

This is the pistol I picked up in the President's box on the night of the 14th of April.

[The pistol was offered in evidence.]

ISAAC JACQUETTE.

For the Prosecution.—May 18.

I was present at Ford's Theater on the night of the assassination. Soon after the President was carried out, I went to the box with several others.

[A wooden bar, about two inches square and three feet long, was handed to the witness.]

This wooden bar was lying on the floor inside of the first door going into the box. I picked it up and took it home with me. There was an officer stopping at my boarding-house, and he wanted a piece of it, which I sawed off for him, but he concluded afterward not to take it. It is nearly covered with spots of blood which were fresh at the time when I found it.

[The bar was offered in evidence.]

JUDGE A. B. OLIN.

For the Prosecution.—May 18.

On Sunday, the 16th of April, accompanied by Miss Harris, I visited Ford's Theater, and made an examination of the President's box, doors, locks, etc. My attention was called to the incision into the wall that was prepared to receive the brace that fitted into the corner of the panel of the outer door; the brace was not there. The door opens into the passage leading to the box at an angle with the wall, and a brace, fitted against the wall to the corner of the door, fastens the door very securely. I discovered that, and looked for the remains of the plastering that had been cut from the wall to make this incision. That, so far as I could observe, had been carefully removed from the carpet, where it must have fallen, as it was cut by some sharp instrument.

The indentation upon the panel of the door where the brace might have been fixed from against the wall, was quite perceptible, and the brace was so fixed that it would be very difficult to remove it from the outside. I think it could not have been done without breaking the door down. The more pressure that was made upon it from the outside, or the dress-circle, the firmer it would have been held in its place.

It had been said that the pistol was discharged through the panel of the door. As the passage way is somewhat dark, I procured a light and examined very carefully the hole through the door. I discovered at once that that was made by some small instrument in the first place, and was, as I supposed, cut out then by a sharp instrument like a penknife; and, by placing the light near the door, I thought I saw marks of a sharp cutting knife used to clean out the hole. I examined to see if I could discover the chips that must have been made by boring and cutting this small hole, but they had been removed. It was a freshly-cut hole, the wood apparently being as fresh as it would have been the instant it was cut.

I then discovered that the clasp which fastens the bolt of the outer door had been loosened. The upper screw holding the clasp had been loosened in such a way that when the door was locked I could push it open with my forefinger.

I then placed the chair in which the President sat in the position, as nearly as Miss Harris could recollect, it had occupied on the night of the assassination. Seating myself in it, and closing the door, it was found that my head—about midway from the base to the crown—would be in the range of the eye of a person looking through the hole in the door. It was a large high-backed arm-chair, with satin cushions, not a rocking-chair, I think.

DAVID C. REED.

For the Prosecution.—May 15.

On the 14th of April, about 2 o'clock, as I was standing just below the National Theater, I saw John H. Surratt, and we bowed to each other as he passed. I am quite positive that it was John H. Surratt. He was dressed in a country-cloth suit of drab, very fine in its texture and appearance, and very genteelly got up. I took particular notice of his clothing, for it was my business to make clothes. He had a little, round-crowned drab hat. He was on foot, but I particularly noticed he wore a pair of new, brass-plated spurs, with very large rowels.

I have known John H. Surratt a great while. I knew him when quite a boy, at his father's house, and have seen him out gunning. He had grown pretty much out of my recollection; still I knew him, though I had no intimacy with him.

Cross-examined by Mr. AIKEN.

I last saw John H. Surratt before the 14th of April, I think, in October. In appearance, John H. Surratt is light complexioned, with rather singular colored hair; it is not red, it is not white, it is a kind of sandy. It was cut rounded, so as to lay low on his collar, and a little heavy. I did not notice whether he wore a moustache or a goatee, for I was more interested in his clothing.

I never saw him in that dress before. In hight, I suppose he is about five feet, ten inches; he is not a stout man, but rather delicate. I do not suppose he would weigh over one hundred and forty pounds, judging from his build. In walking, he stoops a little. He was on the same side of the avenue that I was, and passed within three feet of me. I am as certain that it was Surratt as that I stand here.

JOHN F. COYLE.

For the Prosecution.—May 17.

I am connected with the National Intelligencer. I knew J. Wilkes Booth in his lifetime, though not intimately.

The statement that Booth, on the night before the assassination, wrote an article in which he set forth the reasons for his crime, and left it with one of the editors of the National Intelligencer, is not correct. No such paper was ever received, to my knowledge.
See testimony of C. D. Hess, page 99.

PURSUIT AND CAPTURE OF BOOTH AND HEROLD.

JOHN FLETCHER.

For the Prosecution.—May 17.

David E. Herold came to our stable, in company with the prisoner, Atzerodt, about a quarter to 1 o'clock, on the 14th of April, and engaged a horse, which he told me to keep for him, and he would call for it at 4 o'clock. At a quarter past 4 he came and asked me how much I would charge him for the hire of the horse. I told him five dollars. He wanted it for four. I told him he could not have it for that. He knew the horse, and inquired for that particular one. I went down to the stable with him, and told him to take a mare that was in the stable; but he would not have her. I then told him I would give him the other horse. He then wanted to see the saddles and bridles. I showed him a saddle, and he said it was too small. Then I showed him another. That suited him very well, only that it had not the kind of stirrups he wanted. The stirrups were covered with leather, and he wanted a pair of English steel stirrups. He then wanted to see the bridles. I took him into the office and showed him the bridles, and he picked out a double-reined bridle. Before he mounted the horse he asked me how late he could stay out with him. I told him he could stay out no later than 8 o'clock, or 9, at furthest. After that hour I became very uneasy about the horse, and wanted to see about it before I closed up the stable; and that is how I got to see Atzerodt and Herold.

At about 10 o'clock, having a suspicion that Herold was going to take the horse away, I went across E Street, and up Fourteenth Street, till I came upon Pennsylvania Avenue, close to Willard's, where I saw Herold riding the roan horse. He seemed as if he was coming down from the Treasury upon the Avenue. He was passing Fourteenth Street; the horse was pulling to get to the stable, for he was a horse very well acquainted with the stable. I suppose Herold knew me by the light of the lamp, for he turned the horse around, and I hallooed to him, "You get off that horse now; you have had it long enough;" but he put spurs to it, and went, as fast as the horse could go, up Fourteenth Street, making no reply to me. He was a very fast horse, and all the time used as a lady's saddle-horse; any one could ride him, he was so gentle and nice; his pace was a single foot rack. He would trot if you would let the bridle go slack. He was a light roan horse, black tail, legs, and mane, and close on fifteen hands high. I kept sight of him until he turned to the east of F Street. That was about twenty-five minutes past 10.

I then returned to the stable for a saddle and bridle and horse myself, and went along the avenue until I came to Thirteenth Street; went up Thirteenth Street to E; along E until I came to Ninth, and turned down Ninth Street to Pennsylvania Avenue again. I went along the avenue to the south side of the Capitol. I there met a gentleman, and asked him if he had passed any one riding on horseback. He said yes, and that they were riding very fast. I followed on until I got to the Navy Yard bridge, where the guard halted me, and called for the sergeant of the guard. He came out, and I asked him if a roan horse had crossed that bridge, giving him a description of the horse, saddle, and bridle, and the man that was riding. He said, "Yes, he has gone across the bridge." "Did he stay long here?" I asked. He replied, "He said that he was waiting for an acquaintance of his that was coming on; but he did not wait, and another man came riding a bay horse or a bay mare, right after him." "Did he tell you his name?" "Yes, he said his name was Smith." I asked if I could cross the bridge after them. He said, "Yes, you can cross, but you can not return." I said, "If that is so, I will not go." So I turned around and came back to the city again. When I came to Third Street, I looked at my watch, and it wanted ten minutes to 12. I rode pretty fast going down to the Navy Yard, but I rode slowly coming back. I went along E Street until I got to Fourteenth Street, and inquired of the foreman at Murphy's stable, by the name of Dorsey, whether this roan horse had been put up there. He said, "No; but," said he, "you had better keep in, for President Lincoln is shot and Secretary Seward is almost dead." I then returned to the stable, put up the horse, came outside of the office window, and sat down there; it was half-past 1 o'clock.

Cross-examined by MR. STONE.

When I caught sight of Herold on the horse, near Willard's, the horse seemed somewhat tired, and as if he wanted to go to the stable, and appeared as if he had been ridden a right smart distance. He was then going an easy kind of pace. I am quite satisfied that it was Herold I saw on my horse.

I became acquainted with Herold by his calling at our stable, about the 5th or 6th of April, inquiring for the man Atzerodt, but he did not inquire for him by name; he wanted to know if the man that kept the horse in the side stable had been there that day. He came to our stable every day, from about the 5th or 6th of April until the 12th, inquiring for Atzerodt, and I saw him ride with him. One day Atzerodt went out riding, and sent the horse back by Herold, and the next day Atzerodt asked, "How did he bring the horse back?" and if he rode him fast.

SERGEANT SILAS T. COBB.

For the Prosecution.—May 16.

On the night of the 14th of April, I was on duty at the Navy Yard bridge. At about half-past 10 or 11 o'clock, a man approached rapidly on horseback. The sentry challenged him, and I advanced to see if he was a proper person to pass.

I asked him, "Who are you, sir?" He said, "My name is Booth." I asked him where he was from. He made answer, "From the city." "Where are you going?" I said; and he replied, "I am going home." I asked him where his home was. He said it was in Charles. I understood by that that he meant Charles County. I asked him what town. He said he did not live in any town. I said, "You must live in some town." Said he, "I live close to Beantown; but do not live in the town." I asked him why he was out so late; if he did not know the rule that persons were not allowed to pass after 9 o'clock. He said it was new to him; that he had had somewhere to go in the city, and it was a dark night, and he thought he would have the moon to ride home by. The moon rose that night about that time. I thought he was a proper person to pass, and I passed him.

[A photograph of J. Wilkes Booth was shown the witness.]

That is the man that passed first. He rode a small-sized horse, rather an under-sized horse, I should think, a very bright bay, with a shining skin, and it looked as though he had just had a short burst—a short push—and seemed restive and uneasy, much more so than the rider. In all, I had some three or four minutes' conversation with him before I allowed him to pass.

In perhaps five or seven, or, at the outside, ten minutes, another person came along. He did not seem to be riding so rapidly as the first, or his horse did not show signs of it as much as the first. I asked who he was, and he said that his name was Smith, and that he was going home; that he lived at the White Plains. I asked him how it was that he was out so late. He made use of a rather indelicate expression, and said that he had been in bad company. I brought him up before the guard-house door, so that the light shone full in his face and on his horse.

[The accused, David E. Herold, was directed to stand up for identification.]

He is very near the size of the second horseman; but, I should think, taller, although I can not be sure, as he was on horseback. He had a lighter complexion than this man. After his explanation, I allowed him to pass. He rode a medium-sized, roan horse. I should think the horse was going at a heavy racking pace, or something like that. The horse did not move like a trotting horse. He carried his head down.

Afterward, a third horseman rode up, and made inquiry after a roan horse; after a man passing on a roan horse. He made no inquiry about the other horseman who had passed first. He did not seem to have any business on the other side of the bridge that I considered of sufficient importance to pass him, and so I turned him back.

I do not think the moon was up at that time, but rose after the horsemen had gone forward.

POLK GARDINER.

For the Prosecution.—May 16.

On the night of the 14th of April last, I was on the Bryantown road, coming to Washington, and about 11 o'clock, when on Good Hope Hill, I met two horsemen, one about half a mile behind the other, and both riding very fast. The first, who was on a dark horse, I think a bay, asked me if a horseman had passed ahead; he then asked me the road to Marlboro, and if it did not turn to the right. I told him no; to keep the straight road.

As the second horseman rode up, a lot of teamsters were passing at the time, and I heard him ask them whether a horseman had passed ahead; I do not know whether he asked them or me; I did not answer. He rode a roan horse, a light horse, a roan or an iron-gray.

Cross-examined by MR. COX.

I met the first horseman two miles and a half or three miles from the city, half-way up the hill. It was not over five or ten minutes before the second horseman came along. Both of them were riding very fast. I got off the hill entirely before I met the second man.

JOHN M. LLOYD.

For the Prosecution.—May 13.

I reside at Mrs. Surratt's tavern, Surrattsville, and am engaged in hotel-keeping and farming. Some five or six weeks before the assassination of the President, John H. Surratt, David E. Herold, and G. A. Atzerodt came to my house. Atzerodt and Surratt drove up to my house in the morning first, and went toward T. B., a post-office about five miles below there. They had not been gone more than half an hour, when they returned with Herold. All three, when they came into the bar-room, drank, I think. John Surratt then called me into the front parlor, and on the sofa were two carbines, with ammunition; also a rope from sixteen to twenty feet in length, and a monkey-wrench. Surratt asked me to take care of these things, and to conceal the carbines. I told him there was no place to conceal them, and I did not wish to keep such things. He then took me into a room I had never been in, immediately above the store-room, in the back part of the building. He showed me where I could put them underneath the joists of the second floor of the main building. I put them in there according to his directions.

I stated to Colonel Wells that Surratt put them there, but I carried the arms up and put them in there myself. There was also one cartridge-box of ammunition. Surratt said he just wanted these articles to stay for a few days, and he would call for them. On the Tuesday before the assassination of the President, I was coming to Washington, and I met Mrs. Surratt, on the road, at Uniontown. When she first broached the subject to me about the articles at my place, I did not know what she had reference to. Then she came out plainer, and asked me about the "shooting-irons." I had myself forgotten about their being there. I told her they were hid away far back, and that I was afraid the house might be searched. She told me to get them out ready; that they would be wanted soon. I do not recollect distinctly the first question she put to me. Her language was indistinct, as if she wanted to draw my attention to something, so that no one else would understand. Finally she came out bolder with it, and said they would be wanted soon. I told her that I had an idea of having them buried; that I was very uneasy about having them there.

On the 14th of April I went to Marlboro to attend a trial there; and in the evening, when I got home, which I should judge was about 5 o'clock, I found Mrs. Surratt there. She met me out by the wood-pile as I drove in with some fish and oysters in my buggy. She told me to have those shooting-irons ready that night, there would be some parties who would call for them. She gave me something wrapped in a piece of paper, which I took up stairs, and found to be a field-glass. She told me to get two bottles of whisky ready, and that these things were to be called for that night.

Just about midnight on Friday, Herold came into the house and said, "Lloyd, for God's sake, make haste and get those things." I did not make any reply, but went straight and got the carbines, supposing they were the parties Mrs. Surratt had referred to, though she didn't mention any names. From the way he spoke he must have been apprised that I already knew what I was to give him. Mrs. Surratt told me to give the carbines, whisky, and field-glass. I did not give them the rope and monkey-wrench. Booth didn't come in. I did not know him; he was a stranger to me. He remained on his horse. Herold came into the house and got a bottle of whisky, and took it out to him, and he drank while sitting on his horse. Herold, I think, drank some out of the glass before he went out.

I do not think they remained over five minutes. They only took one of the carbines. Booth said he could not take his, because his leg was broken.

Just as they were about leaving, the man who was with Herold said, "I will tell you some news, if you want to hear it," or something to that effect. I said, "I am not particular; use your own pleasure about telling it." "Well," said he, "I am pretty certain that we have assassinated the President and Secretary Seward." I think that was his language, as well as I can recollect. Whether Herold was present at the time he said that, or whether he was across the street, I am not positive; I was much excited and unnerved at the time.

The moon was shining when the men came. The man whose leg was broken was on a light-colored horse; I supposed it to be a gray horse, in the moonlight. It was a large horse, I suppose some sixteen hands high; the other, ridden by Herold, was a bay, and not so large.

Between 8 and 9 o'clock the next morning the news was received of the assassination of the President, and I think the name of Booth was spoken of as the assassin.

I have heard Atzerodt called by the nickname of "Port Tobacco." I used to call him "Miserable," and then I called him, for a long time, "Stranger." I do not think I had been acquainted with him over two months before the assassination.

[Two carbines, Spencer rifles, were exhibited to the witness.]

The carbines were brought in covers. The cover that is on this one looks like the cover in which it was brought to me. I took the cover off one, and the peculiar kind of breech attracted my attention, never having seen one like it before. They look like the carbines that were brought to my place.

I rented Mrs. Surratt's house at Surrattsville, about the first of December last, and Mrs. Surratt frequently came there after that. When I met Mrs. Surratt on the Tuesday preceding the assassination, I was coming to Washington, and she was going to my place, I supposed. I stopped, and so did she. I then got out and went to her buggy. It had been raining, and was very muddy. I do not know that the word "carbine" was mentioned. She spoke about those shooting-irons. It was a very quick and hasty conversation. I am confident that she named the shooting-irons on both occasions; not so positive about the first as I am about the last; I know she did on the last occasion. On the Friday I do not think Mrs. Surratt was there over ten minutes.

When I first drove up to the wood-yard, Mrs. Surratt came out to where I was. The first thing she said to me was, "Talk about the devil, and his imps will appear," or something to that effect. I said, "I was not aware that I was a devil before." "Well," said she, "Mr. Lloyd, I want you to have those shooting-irons ready; there will be parties here to-night who will call for them." At the same time she gave me something wrapped up in a newspaper, which I did not undo until I got up stairs.

The conversation I had with Mrs. Surrat about the shooting-irons was while I was carrying the fish and oysters into the house. Mrs. Surratt then requested me to fix her buggy for her. The front spring bolts were broken; the spring had become detached from the axle. I tied them with some cord; that was the only fixing I could give them. Mrs. Offutt, my sister-in-law, was, I believe, in the yard; but whether she heard the conversation or not, I do not know.

The first information that I gave of this occurrence was to Lieutenant Lovett and Captain Cottingham, some time about the middle of the week; but I did not detail all the circumstances. I told these officers that it was through the Surratts that I had got myself into the difficulty. If they had never brought me on the scene, I never would have got myself into difficulty, or words to that effect; and I gave full information of the particulars to Colonel Wells, on the Saturday week following.

When Booth and Herold left my house, they took the road toward T. B. Herold came up toward the stable between me and the other man, who was on the light-colored horse, and they rode off at a pretty rapid gait. When Herold brought back the bottle from which Booth had drank the whisky, he remarked to me, "I owe you a couple of dollars;" and said he, "Here." With that he offered me a note, which next morning I found to be one dollar, which just about paid for the bottle of liquor they had just pretty nearly drank.

I think I told Mrs. Offutt, after Mrs. Surratt went away, that it was a field-glass she had brought. She did not tell me that Mrs. Surratt gave her a package.

By Mr. Doster.

I did not know his name to be Atzerodt until, I suppose, two or three weeks at the farthest.

By Mr. Stone.

Booth did not take a carbine with him. I only brought one carbine down; Booth said he could not carry his; I had the carbine then in my bed-chamber. It was no great while after Mrs. Surratt left, when, according to her orders, I got them from the store-room and carried them to my bed-room to have them ready. I brought the carbine and gave it to Herold before they said they had killed the President; they never told me that until they were about riding off. I was right smart in liquor that afternoon, and after night I got more so. I went to bed between 8 and 9 o'clock, and slept very soundly until 12 o'clock. I woke up just as the clock struck 12. A good many soldiers came there on Saturday, and on Sunday night others came and searched the place. When they asked if I had seen two men pass that way in the morning, I told them I had not. That is the only thing I blame myself about. If I had given the information they asked of me, I should have been perfectly easy regarding it. This is the only thing I am sorry I did not do.

Recalled for the Prosecution.—May 15.

Cross-examined by Mr. Aiken.

When the party brought the carbines to my house, Mr. Surratt assisted me in carrying them up stairs, together with the cartridge-boxes, and they were immediately concealed between the joists and ceiling of an unfinished room, where they remained until that Friday when Mrs. Surratt gave me information that they would be wanted that night. I then took them out, according to her direction, and put them in my bed-room, so as to have them convenient for any parties that might call that night. I was out by the wood-pile when Mrs. Surratt handed the package to me. I prepared two bottles of whisky, according to her directions.

Lieutenant Alexander Lovett.

For the Prosecution.—May 16.

On the day after the assassination of the President, I went with others in pursuit of the murderers. We went by way of Surrattsville to the house of Dr. Samuel A. Mudd, which is about thirty miles from Washington, and about one-quarter of a mile or so off the road that runs from Bryantown, arriving there

on Tuesday, the 18th of April. Dr. Mudd, whom I recognize among the accused, did not at first seem inclined to give us any satisfaction; afterward he went on to state that on Saturday morning, at daybreak, two strangers had come to his place; one of them rapped at the door, the other remained on his horse. Mudd went down and opened the door, and with the aid of the young man who had knocked at the door helped the other, who had his leg broken, off his horse, took him into his house and set his leg.

On asking him who the man with the broken leg was, he said he did not know; he was a stranger to him. The other, he said, was a young man, about seventeen or eighteen years of age. Mudd said that one of them called for a razor, which he furnished, together with soap and water, and the wounded man shaved off his moustache. One of our men remarked that this was suspicious, and Dr. Mudd said it did look suspicious. I asked him if he had any other beard. He said, "Yes, he had a long pair of whiskers." He said the men remained there but for a short time, and I understood him that they left in the course of the morning. He said that the wounded man went off on crutches that he (Mudd) had had made for him. He said the other led the horse of the injured man, and he (Mudd) showed them the way across the swamp. He told me that he had heard, at church, on Sunday morning, that the President had been assassinated, but did not mention by whom. We were at his house probably an hour, and to the last he represented that those men were entire strangers to him.

It was generally understood at this time that Booth was the man who assassinated the President; even the darkeys knew it; and I was told by them that Booth had been there, and that he had his leg broken.

On Friday, the 21st of April, I went to Dr. Mudd's again, for the purpose of arresting him. When he found we were going to search the house, he said something to his wife, and she went up stairs and brought down a boot. Mudd said he had cut it off the man's leg, in order to set the leg. I turned down the top of the boot, and saw the name "J. Wilkes" written in it.

I called Mudd's attention to it, and he said he had not taken notice of it before. Some of the men said the name of Booth was scratched out, but I said that the name of Booth had never been written.

[A long riding boot, for the left foot, slit up in front for about eight inches, was exhibited to the witness.]

That is the boot.

[The boot was offered in evidence.]

At the second interview, he still insisted that the men were strangers to him. I made the remark to him that his wife said she had seen the whiskers detached from his face, and I suppose he was satisfied then, for he subsequently said it was Booth. After we left his house, one of the men showed him Booth's photograph, and Mudd remarked that it did not look like Booth, except a little across the eyes. Shortly after that, he said he had an introduction to Booth in November or December last, at church, from a man named Johnson or Thompson. On being questioned, he said he had been along with Booth in the country, looking up some land, and was with him when he bought a horse of Esquire Gardiner, last fall.

Although I was in citizen's clothes at the time, and addressed no threats to him, Dr. Mudd appeared to be much frightened and anxious. When asked what arms the men had, Dr. Mudd stated that the injured man had a pair of revolvers, but he said nothing about the other having a carbine, or either of them having a knife; his manner was very reserved and evasive.

Cross-examined by MR. EWING.

At the time that Dr. Mudd was describing to me the "two strangers" that had been to his house, I did not tell him of my tracking Booth from Washington; I did not mention Booth's name at all; it was not my business to tell him whom I was after.

On my second visit, Dr. Mudd was out, and his wife sent after him; I walked down and met him. I was accompanied by special officers Simon Gavacan, Joshua Lloyd, and William Williams. After we entered the house, I demanded the razor that the man had used. It was not until after we had been in the house some minutes, and one of the men said we should have to search the house, that Dr. Mudd told us the boot had been found, and his wife brought it to us.

I asked him if that might not be a false whisker; he said he did not know. I asked this because Mrs. Mudd had said that the whisker became detached when he got to the foot of the stairs. The Doctor never told me that he had Booth up stairs; he told me he was on the sofa or lounge.

Mudd stated, at our first interview, that the men remained but a short time; afterward his wife told me that they had staid till about 3 or 4 o'clock, on Saturday afternoon. I asked Mudd if the men had much money about them. He said they had considerable greenbacks; and, in this connection, although I did not ask him if he had been paid for setting the man's leg, he said it was customary to make a charge to strangers in such a case. When Dr. Mudd said he had shown the men the way across the swamps, I understood him to refer to the swamps a thousand yards in the rear of his own house. He told us that the men went to the Rev. Dr. Wilmer's, or inquired for Parson Wilmer's; that he took them to the swamps; that they were on their way to Allen's Fresh; but I paid no attention to this at the time, as I considered it was a blind to throw us off our track. We, however, afterward searched

Mr. Wilmer's, a thing I did not like to do, as I knew the man by reputation, and was satisfied it was unnecessary. We tracked the men as far as we could. We went into the swamp and scoured it all over; I went through it half a dozen times; it was not a very nice job though. I first heard from Lieutenant Dana that two men had been at Mudd's house. I afterward heard from Dr. George Mudd that a party of two had been at Dr. Samuel Mudd's.

Cross-examined by MR. STONE.

When we first went to Dr. Samuel Mudd's house, we were accompanied by Dr. George Mudd, whom we had taken from Bryantown along with us. Our first conversation was with the Doctor's wife. When we asked Dr. Mudd whether two strangers had been there, he seemed very much excited, and got as pale as a sheet of paper, and blue about the lips, like a man that was frightened at something he had done. Dr. George Mudd was present when I asked if two strangers had been there. He had spoken to Dr. Samuel Mudd previous to that. He admitted that two strangers had been there, and gave a description of them.

In my first interview with Mudd on the Tuesday, I did not mention the name of Booth at all; and it was not till I had arrested him, when on horseback, that he told me he was introduced to Booth last fall, by a man named Johnson or Thompson.

LIEUTENANT DAVID D. DANA.

For the Prosecution.—May 20.

On Saturday, the day after the assassination of the President, I sent a guard of four men ahead of me to Bryantown, and they arrived about half an hour before me. I arrived there about 1 o'clock. I communicated the intelligence of the assassination, and the name of the assassin, to the citizens; it spread through the village in a quarter of an hour. Some of the citizens asked me if I knew for a certainty it was J. Wilkes Booth, and I told them yes, as near as a person could know any thing.

WILLIAM WILLIAMS.

For the Prosecution.—May 17.

On Monday, the 17th of April, in company with some cavalry, I proceeded to Surrattsville. On the next day, Tuesday, I arrived at Dr. Mudd's. He was not at home, and his wife sent for him. I asked if any strangers had been that way, and he said there had not. Some of the officers then talked with him. I think he stated that he first heard of the assassination of the President at church, on the Sunday morning. He seemed to be uneasy, and unwilling to give us any information without being asked directly.

On Friday, the 21st, we went there again for the purpose of arresting Dr. Mudd. He was not at home, but his wife sent for him. I asked him concerning the two men who had been at his house, one of them having a broken leg. He then said that they had been there. I asked him if those men were not Booth and Herold. He said they were not. He said he knew Booth, having been introduced to him last fall by a man by the name of Thompson, I believe.

After we had arrested him, and were on our way to Bryantown, I showed him Booth's picture, and asked him if that looked like the man who had his leg broken. After looking at the picture a little while, he said it did not; he did not remember the features; after awhile, however, he said it looked something like Booth across the eyes.

At our second visit to Dr. Mudd's house, I informed Mrs. Mudd that we had to search the house. She then said—

Mr. EWING. You need not state what Mrs. Mudd said.

The JUDGE ADVOCATE. Any thing that was said in Dr. Mudd's presence is admissible.

The witness continued. This was said, I believe, in Dr. Mudd's presence. She said that the man with the broken leg had left his boot in the bed. She then went and brought the boot down. It was a long riding-boot, with "J. Wilkes" and the maker's name, "Broadway, N. Y.," written inside. The boot was cut some ten inches from the instep.

Dr. Mudd said that the men had arrived before daybreak, and that they went away on foot between 3 and 4 o'clock on the afternoon of Saturday. He had set the man's leg, and had had crutches made for him by one of his men.

Cross-examined by MR. STONE.

Lieutenant Lovett was present at this conversation. I believe it was on Friday that Dr. Mudd said that the first knowledge he had of the assassination was received at church on the Sunday before. I asked him the question on Friday, if "two strangers" had been there. He said that there had been. Two men had come there at daybreak; one, a smooth-faced young man, apparently seventeen or eighteen years of age, and that he had set the leg of one of them. They had come to his door and knocked, and he had looked out of the window up stairs, and asked them who they were. I believe he said their reply was that they were friends, and wanted to come in. Dr. Mudd then came down stairs, and, with the assistance of the young man, got the wounded man off his horse into the parlor, and examined his leg on the sofa. The wounded man had a moustache, he said, and pretty long chin-whiskers. I asked him if he thought the whiskers were natural. He said he could not tell. The injured man

had a shawl round his shoulders. Dr. Mudd said that on leaving they asked him the road to Parson Wilmer's, and that he had shown them the way down to the swamp. I did not pay much attention to their going to Parson Wilmer's at first, because I thought it was to throw us off the track; but we followed the road as far as we could, after which we divided ourselves, and went all through the different swamp roads. The road is not much frequented. We found horses' tracks, but not such as satisfied me that they were the tracks of these men, and we heard nothing of them on the road. We got to the Rev. Mr. Wilmer's, I think, on the Wednesday evening. We were acting under the orders of Major O'Beirne, and Lieutenant Lovett had charge of our squad.

SIMON GAVACAN.

For the Prosecution.—May 17.

I was at Dr. Mudd's house on the forenoon of Tuesday, the 18th of April, in pursuit of the murderers of the President. We inquired if two men passed there on the Saturday morning after the assassination, and Dr. Mudd said no. Then we inquired more particularly if two men had been there, one having his leg fractured. He said yes. In answer to our questions, he told us that they had come about 4, or half-past 4, on Saturday morning, and rapped at his door; that he was a little alarmed at the noise, but came down and let them in; that he and the other person assisted the man with the broken leg into the house, and that he attended to the fractured leg as well as he could, though he had not much facilities for doing so. I believe he said the wounded person staid on the sofa for awhile, and after that was taken up stairs, and remained there until between 3 and 5 o'clock in the afternoon of Saturday. He said that he went out with the other man to find a buggy to take away the wounded man, but could not get one. I understood him to say that on leaving his house they first inquired the road to Allen's Fresh, and also to the Rev. Dr. Wilmer's, and that he took them part of the way to show them the road. He told us he did not know the persons at all.

On Friday, the 21st, we went to Dr. Mudd's again, for the purpose of arresting him and searching his house. He was not in, but his wife sent for him. When he came, we told him that we would have to search his house. His wife then went up stairs and brought down a boot and a razor. Inside the leg of the boot we found the words, "J. Wilkes." We asked him if he thought that was Booth, and he said he thought not. He said the man had whiskers on, but that he thought he shaved off his moustache up stairs. When we inquired of him if he knew Booth, he said that he was introduced to him last fall by a man named Thompson, but he thought the man who had been there was not Booth.

Cross-examined by MR. EWING.

Our conversation with Dr. Mudd lasted probably an hour. He was asked questions by all of us. Lieutenant Lovett was there all the time. When Mrs. Mudd brought down the boot and razor, we thought we had satisfactory evidence that Booth and Herold had been there, and did not search the house further. I believe there was a photograph of Booth shown to Dr. Mudd on Tuesday, and he said he did not recognize it, but said there was something about the forehead or the eyes that resembled one of the parties.

JOSHUA LLOYD.

For the Prosecution.—May 16.

I was engaged with others in the pursuit of the murderers of the President in the direction of Surrattsville. We got to Dr. Mudd's on Tuesday, the 18th. I asked him if he had not heard of the President being assassinated; he said yes. I then asked him if he had seen any of the parties—Booth, Herold, or Surratt; he said he had never seen them.

On Friday, the 21st, at the second interview, he said two men came there about 4 o'clock on the Saturday morning, and remained there until about 4 in the afternoon. They came on horseback; one of them had a broken leg, and when they left his house one was riding and the other walking, leading his horse.

As we were sitting in the parlor, Mrs. Mudd seemed very much worried, so did the Doctor, and he seemed to be very much excited. At this interview Lieutenant Lovett and Mr. Williams did most of the talking; I was not well. Dr. Mudd said that he had been in company with Booth; that he had been introduced to him by a man named Thompson, I think he said, at church. He offered no explanation of his previous denial. When the men left, he said they went up the hill toward Parson Wilmer's, and I think he said he showed them the road. I understood him to say that the man's leg was broken by the fall of the horse.

Cross-examined by MR. STONE.

It was late on Tuesday evening when we were there. Each time that we went to his house Dr. Mudd was out, but not far away, for he was not long in returning with the messenger sent for him. At the first interview, I asked if any strangers had passed that way, and then if Booth and Herold had passed; I described them to him, and the horses they rode, and he denied either that any strangers or Booth and Herold had passed. The interview only lasted a few minutes.

Booth's portrait was shown to Dr. Mudd. He told us that Booth had been down there last fall, when he was introduced to him by Mr. Thompson. I think he said Booth was there to buy some property.

Before he came to the house, Mrs. Mudd brought us the boot, and when the Doctor saw that we had the boot, he admitted that Booth had been there. Dr. Mudd then brought the razor down himself, and gave it to Lieutenant Lovett.

WILLIE S. JETT.

For the Prosecution.—May 17.

I was formerly a member of the Ninth Virginia Cavalry. More recently, I was stationed in Caroline County, Virginia, as commissary agent of the Confederate States Government. I was on my way from Fauquier County (where I had been with Mosby's command) to Caroline County, Virginia, in company with Lieutenant Ruggles and a young man named Bainbridge. At Port Conway, on the Rappahannock, I saw a wagon down on the wharf, at the ferry, on the Monday week after the assassination of President Lincoln. A young man got out of it, came toward us, and asked us what command we belonged to. We were all dressed in Confederate uniform. Lieutenant Ruggles said, "We belong to Mosby's command." He then said, "If I am not inquisitive, can I ask where you are going?" I spoke, then, and replied, "That's a secret, where we are going." After this we went back on the wharf, and a man with crutches got out of the wagon. One of us asked him what command he belonged to, and he replied, "To A. P. Hill's corps." Herold told us their name was Boyd; that his brother was wounded below Petersburg, and asked if we would take him out of the lines. We did not tell him where we were going. Herold asked us to go and take a drink, but we declined. We then rode up to the house there, and having tied our horses, we all sat down. After we had talked a very short time, Herold touched me on the shoulder and said he wanted to speak to me; he carried me down to the wharf, and said, "I suppose you are raising a command to go South?" and added that he would like to go along with us. At length I said, "I can not go with any man that I do n't know any thing about." He seemed very much agitated, and then remarked, "We are the assassinators of the President." I was so much confounded that I did not make any reply then that I remember. Lieutenant Ruggles was very near, watering his horse; I called to him, and he came there, and either Herold or myself remarked to Lieutenant Ruggles that they were the assassinators of the President. Booth then came up, and Herold introduced himself to us, and then introduced Booth. Herold passed himself off to us first as Boyd, and said he wanted to pass under that name. He afterward told us their true names were Herold and Booth, but they kept the name of Boyd. Booth, I remember, had on his hand "J. W. B." We went back then to the house, and sat down there some time on the steps. Then we went across the river. Booth rode Ruggles's horse. Herold was walking. When we got on the other side of the river, before they got out of the boat, I got on my horse and rode up to Port Royal, went into a house, and saw a lady. I asked her if she could take in a wounded Confederate soldier, just as he represented himself to me, for two or three days. She at first consented; then afterward she said she could not. I walked across the street to Mr. Catlitt's, but he was not at home. We then went on up to Mr. Garrett's, and there we left Booth. Herold and all of us went on up the road, then, to within a few miles of Bowling Green. Bainbridge and Herold went to Mrs. Clark's, and Ruggles and myself to Bowling Green. The next day Herold came to Bowling Green, spent the day, had dinner, and left in the evening, and that was the last I saw of him, except the night that they were caught, when I went down there; I saw him the next morning in the custody of the officers. I recognize the prisoner Herold as the man that I saw with Booth.

Cross-examined by MR. STONE.

Herold said he wanted us to help in getting Booth further South, but we had no facilities; and he seemed a good deal disappointed after we made known our real object, that we were going on a visit. Booth was not present when Herold told me they were the assassinators of the President; when he came up, he said he would not have told, that he did not intend telling. Herold did not appear very self-possessed; his voice trembled very much, and he was a good deal agitated. His language was, "We are the assassinators of the President;" and then, pointing back to where Booth was standing, he said, "Yonder is J. Wilkes Booth, the man who killed the President," or he may have said "Lincoln." I have never taken the oath of allegiance, but am perfectly willing to take it.

EVERTON J. CONGER.

For the Prosecution.—May 17.

I assisted in the pursuit of the murderers of the President.

JUDGE ADVOCATE. Will you please take up the narrative of the pursuit at the point where you met with Willie Jett, and state what occurred until the pursuit closed.

WITNESS. On the night of the capture, I found Jett in bed in a hotel in Bowling Green. I told him to get up; that I wanted him. He put on his pants, and came out to me in the front part of the room. I said, "Where are the two men who came with you across the river?" He came up to me and said, "Can I see you alone?" I replied, "Yes, sir, you can." Lieutenant Baker and Lieutenant Doherty were with me. I asked them to go out of the room. After they were gone, he reached out his hand to me and said, "I know who you want, and I will tell you where they can be found." Said I, "That's what I want to know." He said, "They are on the road to Port Royal, about three miles this side of that." "At whose house are they?" I asked. "Mr. Garrett's," he replied; "I will go there with you and show you where they are now, and you can get them." I said, "Have you a horse?" "Yes, sir." "Get it, and get ready to go." I said to him, "You say they are on the road to Port Royal?" "Yes, sir." I said to him, "I have just come from there." He stopped a moment, and seemed to be considerably embarrassed. Said he, "I thought you came from Richmond. If you have come that way, you have come past them. I can not tell you whether they are there now or not." I said it did not make any difference; we would go back and see. He dressed; had his horse saddled; we gathered the party around the house together, and went back to Mr. Garrett's house. Just before we got to the house, Jett, riding with me, said, "We are very near now to where we go through; let us stop here and look around." He and I rode on together. I rode forward to find the gate that went through to the house, and sent Lieutenant Baker to open another. I went back for the cavalry, and we rode rapidly up to the house and barn, and stationed the men around the house and quarters.

I went to the house and found Lieutenant Baker at the door, telling somebody to strike a light and come out. I think the door was open when I got there. The first individual we saw was an old man, whose name was said to be Garrett. I said to him, "Where are the two men who stopped here at your house?" "They have gone." "Gone where?" "Gone to the woods." "Well, sir, whereabouts in the woods have they gone?" He then commenced to tell me that they came there without his consent; that he did not want them to stay. I said to him, "I do not want any long story out of you; I just want to know where these men have gone." He commenced over again to tell me, and I turned to the door and said to one of the men, "Bring in a lariat rope here, and I will put that man up to the top of one of those locust trees." He did not seem inclined to tell. One of his sons then came in and said, "Do n't hurt the old man; he is scared; I will tell you where the men are you want to find." Said I, "That is what I want to know; where are they?" He said, "In the barn."

We then left the house immediately and went to the barn, and stationed the remaining part of the men. As soon as I got there, I heard somebody walking around inside on the hay. By that time another Garrett had come from somewhere; and Lieutenant Baker said to one of them, "You must go in the barn and get the arms from those men." I think he made some objection to it; I do not know certainly. Baker said, "They know you, and you can go in." Baker said to the men inside, "We are going to send this man, on whose premises you are, in to get your arms, and you must come out and deliver yourselves up." I do not think there was any thing more said. Garrett went in, and he came out very soon and said, "This man says 'Damn you, you have betrayed me,' and threatened to shoot me." I said to him, "How do you know he was going to shoot you?" Said he, "He reached down to the hay behind him to get his revolver, and I came out." I then directed Lieutenant Baker to tell them that if they would come out and deliver themselves up, very well; if not, in five minutes we would set the barn on fire. Booth replied: "Who are you; what do you want; whom do you want?" Lieutenant Baker said, "We want you, and we know who you are; give up your arms and come out." I say Booth; for I presumed it was he. He replied, "Let us have a little time to consider it." Lieutenant Baker said, "Very well;" and some ten or fifteen minutes probably intervened between that time and any thing further being said. He asked again, "Who are you, and what do you want?" I said to Lieutenant Baker, "Do not by any remark made to him allow him to know who we are; you need not tell him who we are. If he thinks we are rebels, or thinks we are his friends, we will take advantage of it; we will not lie to him about it, but we need not answer any questions that have any reference to that subject, but simply insist on his coming out, if he will." The reply was made to him, "It don't make any difference who we are; we know who you are, and we want you; we want to take you prisoners." Said he, "This is a hard case; it may be I am to be taken by my friends." Some time in the conversation he said, "Captain, I know you to be a brave man, and I believe you to be honorable; I am a cripple. I have got but one leg; if you will withdraw your men in 'line' one hundred yards from the door, I will come out and fight you." Lieutenant Baker replied that he did not come there to fight; we simply came there to make him a prisoner; we did not want any fight with him. Once more after this he said, "If you'll take your men fifty yards from the door, I'll come out and fight you; give me a chance for my life." The same reply was made to him. His answer to that was, in a singular theatrical voice, "Well, my brave boys, prepare a stretcher for me."

Some time passed before any further conversation was held with him. In the mean time I requested one of the Garretts to pile some brush up against the corner of the barn—pine boughs. He put some up there, and after

awhile came to me and said, "This man inside says that if I put any more brush in there he will put a ball through me." "Very well," said I, "you need not go there again." After awhile Booth said, "There's a man in here wants to come out." Lieutenant Baker said "Very well; let him hand his arms out, and come out." Some considerable talk passed in the barn; some of it was heard, some not. One of the expressions made use of by Booth to Herold, who was in the barn, was, "You damned coward, will you leave me now? Go, go; I would not have you stay with me." Some conversation ensued between them, which I supposed had reference to the bringing out of the arms, which was one of the conditions on which Herold was to come out. It was not heard; we could simply hear them talking. He came to the door and said, "Let me out." Lieutenant Baker said to him, "Hand out your arms." The reply was, "I have none." He said, "You carried a carbine, and you must hand it out." Booth replied, "The arms are mine, and I have got them." Lieutenant Baker said, "This man carried a carbine, and he must hand it out." Booth said, "Upon the word and honor of a gentleman, he has no arms; the arms are mine, and I have got them." I stood by the side of the Lieutenant and said to him, "Never mind the arms; if we can get one of the men out, let us do it, and wait no longer." The door was opened, he stuck out his hands; Lieutenant Baker took hold of him, brought him out, and passed him to the rear. I went around to the corner of the barn, pulled some hay out, twisted up a little of it, about six inches long, set fire to it, and stuck it back through on top of the hay. It was loose, broken-up hay, that had been trodden upon the barn-floor. It was very light, and blazed very rapidly—lit right up at once.

I put my eye up to the crack next to the one the fire was put through, and looked in, and I heard something drop on the floor, which I supposed to be Booth's crutch. He turned around toward me. When I first got a glimpse of him, he stood with his back partly to me, turning toward the front door. He came back within five feet of the corner of the barn. The only thing I noticed he had in his hands when he came was a carbine. He came back, and looked along the cracks, one after another, rapidly. He could not see any thing. He looked at the fire, and from the expression of his face, I am satisfied he looked to see if he could put it out, and was satisfied that he could not do it; it was burning so much. He dropped his arm, relaxed his muscles, turned around, and started for the door at the front of the barn. I ran around to the other side, and when about half round I heard the report of a pistol. I went right to the door, and went into the barn and found Lieutenant Baker looking at Booth, holding him, or raising him up, I do not know which. I said to him, "He shot himself." Said he, "No, he did not, either." Said I, "Whereabouts is he shot—in the head or neck?" I raised him then, and looked on the right side of the neck, and saw a place where the blood was running out. I said, "Yes, sir; he shot himself." Lieutenant Baker replied very earnestly that he did not. I then said, "Let us carry him out of here; this wil! soon be burning." We took him up and carried him out on the grass, underneath the locust-trees, a little way from the door. I went back into the barn immediately to see if the fire could be put down, and tried somewhat myself to put it out, but I could not; it was burning so fast, and there was no water and nothing to help with. I then went back. Before this, I supposed him to be dead. He had all the appearance of a dead man; but when I got back to him, his eyes and mouth were moving. I called immediately for some water, and put it on his face, and he somewhat revived, and attempted to speak. I put my ear down close to his mouth, and he made several efforts to speak, and finally I understood him to say, "Tell mother I die for my country." I said to him, "Is that what you say?" repeating it to him. He said, "Yes." They carried him from there to the porch of Mr. Garrett's house, and laid him on an old straw bed, or tick, or something. By that time he revived considerably; he could then talk in a whisper, so as to be intelligibly understood; he could not speak above a whisper. He wanted water; we gave it to him. He wanted to be turned on his face. I said to him, "You can not lie on your face;" and he wanted to be turned on his side; we turned him upon his side three times, I think, but he could not lie with any comfort, and wanted to be turned immediately back. He asked me to put my hand on his throat and press down, which I did, and he said, "Harder." I pressed down as hard as I thought necessary, and he made very strong exertions to cough, but was unable to do so—no muscular exertion could he make. I supposed he thought something was in his throat, and I said to him, "Open your mouth and put out your tongue, and I will see if it bleeds." Which he did. I said to him, "There is no blood in your throat; it has not gone through any part of it there." He repeated two or three times, "Kill me, kill me." The reply was made to him, "We do n't want to kill you; we want you to get well." I then took what things were in his pockets, and tied them up in a piece of paper. He was not then quite dead. He would—once, perhaps, in five minutes—gasp; his heart would almost die out, and then it would commence again, and by a few rapid beats would make a slight motion. I left the body and the prisoner Herold in charge of Lieutenant Baker. I told him to wait an hour if Booth was not dead; if he recovered, to wait there and send over to Belle Plain for a surgeon

from one of the gun-ships; and, if he died in the space of an hour, to get the best conveyance he could, and bring him on.

I staid there some ten minutes after that was said, when the doctor there said he was dead

[A knife, pair of pistols, belt, holster, file, pocket compass, spur, pipe, carbine, cartridges, and bills of exchange were shown to the witness.]

That is the knife, belt, and holster taken from Booth; the pistols I did not examine with any care, but they looked like these. That is the pocket compass, with the candle grease on it, just as we found it; the spur I turned over to Mr. Stanton, and I judge this to be the one taken from Booth. That is the carbine we took; it is a Spencer rifle, and has a mark on the breech by which I know it. Both the pistols and carbine were loaded. I unloaded the carbine myself in Mr. Secretary Stanton's office, and these are the cartridges that I took out; there was one in the barrel, and the chamber was full. These are the bills of exchange; I put my initials on them.

[All these articles were put in evidence; also the bill of exchange in triplicate. The first of the set was read as follows:]

No. 1492.
[Stamp.]

THE ONTARIO BANK,
Montreal Branch.
EXCHANGE FOR £61 12s. 10d.

Montreal, 27 Oct'r, 1864

Sixty days after sight of this first of exchange, (second and third of the same tenor and date unpaid,) pay to the order of J. Wilkes Booth sixty-one pounds twelve shillings and ten pence sterling. Value received, and charge to acc't of this office.
To Messrs. Glynn Mills & Co., London.
[Signed] H. STANUS, MANAGER.

The farm of Mr. Garrett, in whose barn Booth was captured and killed, is in Caroline County, Va., about three miles from Port Royal, on the road to Bowling Green.

I had seen John Wilkes Booth in Washington, and recognized the man who was killed as the same. I had before remarked his resemblance to his brother, Edwin Booth, whom I had often seen play.

I recognize among the accused, the man Herold, whom we took prisoner on that occasion, in the barn. We found on Herold a small piece of a school map of Virginia, embracing the region known as the Northern Neck, where they were captured.

Cross-examined by MR. STONE.

We found no arms on Herold. He had some conversation with Booth while in the barn, in which Booth called him a coward; and when the question of delivering up the arms was raised, Booth said that the arms were all his. When Booth said, "There is a man in here who wants to get out," I think he added, "who had nothing to do with it."

I think we got to Garrett's barn about 2 o'clock in the morning, and it was about fifteen minutes past 3 that Booth was shot and carried out on the grass.

SERG'T BOSTON CORBETT.

For the Prosecution.—May 17.

THE JUDGE ADVOCATE. Conger has just detailed to the Commission the circumstances connected with the pursuit, capture and killing of Booth, in which, I believe, you were engaged. I will ask you to state what part you took in the capture and killing of Booth, taking up the narrative at the point when you arrived at the house.

Sergeant BOSTON CORBETT. When we rode up to the house, my commanding officer, Lieutenant Doherty, told me that Booth was in that house, saying, "I want you to deploy the men right and left around the house, and see that no one escapes." Which was done. After making inquiries at the house, it was found that Booth was in the barn. A guard was then left upon the house, and the main portion of the men thrown around the barn, closely investing it, with orders to allow no one to escape. We had been previously cautioned to see that our arms were in readiness for use. After being ordered to surrender, and told that the barn would be fired in five minutes if he did not do so, Booth made many replies. He wanted to know who we took him for; he said that his leg was broken; and what did we want with him; and he was told that it made no difference. His name was not mentioned in the whole affair. They were told that they must surrender as prisoners. Booth wanted to know where we would take them, if they would give themselves up as prisoners. He received no satisfaction, but was told that he must surrender unconditionally, or else the barn would be fired. The parley lasted much longer than the time first set; probably a full half hour; but he positively declared that he would not surrender. At one time he made the remark, "Well, my brave boys, you can prepare a stretcher for me;" and at another time, "Well, Captain, make quick work of it; shoot me through the heart," or words to that effect; and thereby I knew that he was perfectly desperate, and did not expect that he would surrender. After awhile we heard the whispering of another person—although Booth had previously declared that there was no one there but himself—who proved to be the prisoner Herold. Although we could not distinguish the words, Herold seemed to be trying to persuade Booth to surrender. After awhile, he sang out, "Certainly," seeming to disdain to do so himself. Said he, "Cap, there is a man in here who wants to surrender mighty bad." Then I suppose words followed inside that we could not here. Herold, perhaps, thought he had better stand by him, or something to that effect. Then Booth said, "O, go out and save yourse f, my boy, if you can;" and then he said, "I declare before my Maker that this man here is innocent of any crime whatever," seeming willing to take all the blame on himself and trying to clear Herold.

He was told to hand out his arms. Herold declared that he had no arms, and Booth declared that the arms all belonged to him, and that the other man was unarmed. He was finally taken out without his arms.

Immediately after Herold was taken out, the detective, Mr. Conger, came round to the side of the barn where I was, and passing me, set fire to the hay through one of the cracks of the boards a little to my right. I had previously said to Mr. Conger, though, and also to my commanding officer, that the position in which I stood left me in front of a large crack — you might put your hand through it—and I knew that Booth could distinguish me and others through these cracks in the barn, and could pick us off if he chose to do so. In fact, he made a re mark to that effect at one time. Said he, "Cap, I could have picked off three or four of your men already if I wished to do so. Draw your men off fifty yards, and I will come out," or such words. He used such language many times. When the fire was lit, which was almost immediately after, Herold was taken out of the barn. As the flame rose, he was seen. We could then distinguish him about the middle of the barn, turning toward the fire, either to put the fire out or else to shoot the one who started it; I did not know which; but he was then coming toward me, as it were, a little to my right—a full front breast view. I could have shot him then much easier than when I afterward did, but as long as he was there, making no demonstration to hurt any one, I did not shoot him, but kept my eye on him steadily.

Finding the fire gaining upon him, he turned to the other side of the barn, and got toward where the door was, and as he got there I saw him make a movement toward the door. I supposed he was going to fight his way out. One of the men, who was watching him, told me that he aimed the carbine at me. He was taking aim with the carbine, but at whom I could not say. My mind was upon him attentively to see that he did no harm, and when I became impressed that it was time I shot him, I took steady aim on my arm, and shot him through a large crack in the barn. When he was brought out I found that the wound was made in the neck, a little back of the ear, and came out a little higher up on the other side of the head. He lived, I should think, until about 7 o'clock that morning; perhaps two or three hours after he was shot. I did not myself hear him speak a word after he was shot, except a cry or shout as he fell. Others, who were near him and watching him constantly, said that he did utter the words which were published.

I recognize the prisoner Herold among the accused as the man we took out of the barn. I had never seen Booth before, but from a remark made by my commanding officer, while on the boat going down to Belle Plain, that

Booth's leg was broken, I felt sure it was Booth that I fired at; for when the men in the barn were summoned to surrender, the reply of the one who spoke was that his leg was broken, and that he was alone. I knew also, from his desperate language, that he would not be taken alive, and such remarks, that it was Booth, for I believe no other man would act in such a way.

Cross-examined by MR. STONE.

From the conversation in the barn, I judge that Herold was at first anxious to surrender, and upon Booth's refusing to do so, I rather thought he desired to stay with him; but I can not say whether it was before or after that that Booth declared before his Maker that the man with him was innocent of any crime whatever.

I wish to state here, as improper motives have been imputed to me for the act I did, that I twice offered to my commanding officer, Lieutenant Doherty, and once to Mr. Conger, to go into the barn and take the man, saying that I was not afraid to go in and take him; it was less dangerous to go in and fight him than to stand before a crack exposed to his fire, where I could not see him, although he could see me; but I was not sent in. Immediately when the fire was lit, our positions were reversed; I could see him, but he could not see me. It was not through fear at all that I shot him, but because it was my impression that it was time the man was shot; for I thought he would do harm to our men in trying to fight his way through that den, if I did not

CAPT. EDWARD DOHERTY.

For the Prosecution.—May 22.

I had command of the detachment of the Sixteenth New York Cavalry that captured Booth and Herold.

JUDGE ADVOCATE. The circumstances of the capture having been fully detailed by other witnesses, I will ask you to state the part you took, if any, in the capture of the prisoner Herold, and all he said on that occasion.

WITNESS. There had been considerable conversation with reference to the arms that Booth and Herold had inside of Garrett's barn. We requested Booth and Herold to come out of the barn. Booth at first denied that there was anybody there but himself, but finally he said, "Captain, there is a man here who wishes to surrender awful bad." Mr. Baker, one of the detectives who was there, said, "Let him hand out his arms." I stood by the door and said, "Hand out your arms and you can come out." Herold replied, "I have no arms." Mr. Baker said, "We know exactly what you have got." I said, "We had better let him out." Mr. Baker said, "No, wait until Mr. Conger comes here." I said, "No; open that door," directing a man to open the door; "I will take that man out

myself." The door was opened, and I directed Herold to put out his hands; I took hold of his wrists and pulled him out of the barn. I then put my revolver under my arm and ran my hands down him to see if he had any arms, and he had none. I then said to him. "Have you got any weapons at all about you?" He said, "Nothing at all but this," pulling out of his pocket a piece of a map of Virginia. Just at this time the shot was fired and the door thrown open, and I dragged Herold into the barn with me. Booth had fallen on his back. The soldiers and two detectives who were there went into the barn and carried out Booth. I took charge of Herold; and when I got him outside he said, "Let me go away; let me go around here; I will not leave; I will not go away." Said I, "No, sir." Said he to me, "Who is that that has been shot in there in the barn?" "Why," said I, "you know well who it is." Said he, "No, I do not; he told me his name was Boyd." Said I, "It is Booth, and you know it." Said he, "No, I did not know it; I did not know that it was Booth."

I then took him and tied him by the hands to a tree opposite, about two yards from where Booth's body was carried, on the verandah of the house, and kept him there until we were ready to return. Booth in the mean time died, and I sewed him up in a blanket. Previous to this I had sent some cavalry for the doctor; and we got a negro who lives about a mile from there, with a wagon, and put the body on board the wagon, and started for Belle Plain.

Herold told me afterward that he met this man by accident about seven miles from Washington, between 11 and 12 o'clock on the night of the murder. He said that after they met they went to Mathias Point, and crossed the Potomac there. He did not mention the houses at which they stopped. Dr. Stewart's house was mentioned by some one as a place at which they had stopped, but whether it was by Herold or not I do not remember.

Cross-examined by MR. STONE.

Booth said, while in the barn, that he was the only guilty man, and that this man Herold was innocent, or words to that effect. Herold made no resistance after he was captured.

SURGEON-GENERAL J. K. BARNES.

For the Prosecution.—May 20.

I examined the body of J. Wilkes Booth after his death, when he was brought to this city. He had a scar upon the large muscle of the left side of his neck, three inches below the ear, occasioned by an operation performed by Dr. May of this city for the removal of a tumor some months previous to Booth's death. It looked like the scar of a burn instead of an incision, which Dr. May explained by the fact that the wound was torn open on the stage when nearly well.

DEFENSE OF DAVID E. HEROLD.

CAPTAIN ELI D. EDMONDS, U. S. N.—*May 27*.

By MR. STONE.

I know David E. Herold, one of the prisoners; I saw him at his home in Washington on the 20th and 21st of February. I am positive in my recollection of it.

FRANCIS S. WALSH.—*May 30*.

I reside in Washington, on Eighth Street, east. I have known the prisoner, David E. Herold, since he was a boy; have known him intimately since October, 1863. I am a druggist, and employed Herold as a clerk eleven months. During this time, he lived in my house, and I knew of nothing objectionable in his character. He was light and trifling in a great many things, more like a boy than a man, but I never saw any thing to find fault with in his moral character. He was temperate in his habits, and regular in his hours. He was easily persuaded and led, more than is usually the case with young men of his age; I considered him boyish in every respect. I should suppose him to be about twenty-two years of age.

JAMES NOKES.—*May 30*.

By MR. STONE.

I have lived in Washington since 1827; reside in that part called the Navy Yard. I have known the prisoner, Herold, from his birth—about twenty-three years, I believe. With his family I have been intimate for eighteen or nineteen years; there are seven children living, I believe, and he is the only boy. I have always looked upon him as a light and trifling boy; that very little reliability was to be placed in him; and I consider him more easily influenced by those around him than the generality of young men of his age. I have never heard him enter into any argument on any subject in the world, like other young men; all his conversation was light and trifling.

WILLIAM H. KEILOTZ.—*May 30*.

By MR. STONE.

I have lived next door to Mr. Herold for thirteen years, and know the prisoner, David

E. Herold, well. During last February, I was home, my wife being sick, and I saw the prisoner a good deal then; I may have seen him every day, except, perhaps, four or five. I consider his character very boyish. I see him often with boys; he is very fond of their company, and never associates with men. He is fond of sport, gunning, dogs, etc.

EMMA HEROLD.—*May 30*.

By MR. STONE.

I am sister of David E. Herold. I know that my brother was home on the 15th of February last; I remember it from my having sent him a valentine, which he received on the 15th; and my sisters talked with him about it. I also knew that he was at home on the 19th of February; it was the Sunday after Valentine's day. I remember taking a pitcher of water up stairs, and my brother met me in the passage and wanted it; but I would not give it to him; he then tried to take it from me, and we both got wet from the water being spilled. He was also at home between those days.

MRS. MARY JENKINS.—*May 30*.

By MR. STONE.

I know the prisoner, David E. Herold. He was at my house on the 18th of February last, and received my rent. I have his receipt of that date to show it.

MRS. ELIZABETH POTTS.—*May 30*.

By MR. STONE.

I know the accused, David E. Herold. I can not say whether he was in Washington on the 20th of last February, but I know he was there on the 19th, for he came to my house for his money. As I was not prepared, I told him I would send it to him the next day, which I did, and I have his receipt for the money, dated the 20th.

DR. CHARLES W. DAVIS.—*May 31*.

By MR. STONE.

I reside in Washington City, near the Navy Yard. I was formerly in the Quartermaster's Department on General Wool's staff. I have known the prisoner, Herold, from early boyhood, having lived a great part of the time next door. At present I live four or five squares off, but I see him frequently. I do not know that I can describe his character in better terms than to say that he is a boy; he is trifling, and always has been. There is very little of the man about him. From what I know of him, I should say he is very easily persuaded and led; I should think that nature had not endowed him with as much intellect as the generality of people possess. I should think his age is about twenty-two or twenty-three, but I consider him far more of a boy than a man.

Dr. Samuel A. H. McKim.—May 31.

By Mr. Stone.

I reside in Washington City, the eastern part. I am acquainted with the prisoner, Herold; can scarcely say when I did not know him; I have known him very well for the last six years. I consider him a very light, trivial, unreliable boy; so much so that I would never let him put up a prescription of mine if I could prevent it, feeling confident he would tamper with it if he thought he could play a joke on anybody. In mind, I consider him about eleven years of age.

TESTIMONY CONCERNING EDWARD SPANGLER.

Jacob Ritterspaugh.
For the Prosecution.—May 19.

I know the prisoner, Edward Spangler. He boarded where I did, at Mrs. Scott's, on the corner of Seventh and G Streets. He had no room in the house; he took his meals there, and slept at the theater. He used to keep his valise at the house, and when the detectives came and asked if Spangler had any thing there, I gave it to them. He had no clothes there, nothing but that valise; I do not know what it contained. I am commonly called Jake about the theater.

Recalled for the Prosecution.—May 30.

I was a carpenter in Ford's Theater down to the 14th of April last, and was there on that night when the President was shot. He occupied the upper box on the left-hand side of the stage, the right as you come in from the front. My business was to shift wings on the stage and pull them off, and fetch things out of the cellar when needed.

I was standing on the stage behind the scenes on the night of the 14th, when some one called out that the President was shot, and directly I saw a man that had no hat on running toward the back door.

He had a knife in his hand, and I ran to stop him, and ran through the last entrance, and as I came up to him he tore the door open. I made for him, and he struck at me with the knife, and I jumped back then. He then ran out and slammed the door shut. I then went to get the door open quick, and I thought it was a kind of fast; I could not get it open. In a moment afterward I opened the door, and the man had just got on his horse and was running down the alley; and then I came in. I came back on the stage where I had left Edward Spangler, and he hit me on the face with the back of his hand, and he said, "Do n't say which way he went." I asked him what he meant by slapping me in the mouth, and he said, "For God's sake, shut up;" and that was the last he said.

The man of whom I speak is Edward Spangler, the prisoner at the bar. I did not see any one else go out before the man with the knife. A tall, stout man went out after me.

Cross-examined by Mr. Ewing.

When I heard the pistol fired I was standing in the center of the stage, listening to the play, and Spangler was at the same place, just about ready to shove off the scenes; I stood nearest the door. I am certain we both stood there when the pistol was fired. I did not at first know what had happened. Some one called out "Stop that man;" and then I heard some one say that the President was shot, and not till then did I know what had occurred. When I came back, Spangler was at the same place where I had left him. There was a crowd in there by that time, both actors and strangers. When Spangler slapped me there were some of the actors near who had taken part in the play; one they called Jenny—I do not know what part she took—was standing perhaps three or four feet from me; I do not know whether she heard what he said; he did not say it so very loud. He spoke in his usual tone, but he looked as if he was scared, and a kind of crying. I heard the people halloo, "Burn the theater!" "Hang him and shoot him!" I did not, that I know of, tell a number of persons what Spangler said when he slapped me. I did not tell either of the Messrs. Ford; I told it to nobody but Gifford, the boss. At Carroll Prison, the same week that I was released, I told him that Spangler said I should not

7

say which way the man went. I told a detective that Spangler hit me in the mouth
with his open hand. I do not know his name;
he was one of Colonel Baker's men; had black
whiskers and moustache, and weighed about
one hundred and forty pounds, I should think.
He came up to the house where I board in
the afternoon of the day on which I was released, and I told him then. I have no recollection of telling any one else, though I might
have said something at the table, and the rest
might have heard.

I saw Booth open the back door of the
theater and shut it, but I did not know who
he was then; I did not see his face right. I
was the first person that got to the door after
he left; I opened the door, but did not shut
it. The big man that ran out after me might
have been five or six yards from me when I
heard him, or it might have been somebody
else, call out, "Which way?" I cried out,
"This way," and then ran out, leaving the
door open. By that time the man had got
on his horse and gone off down the alley. I
saw the big man outside, and have not seen
him since. I did not take particular notice
of him; but he was a tolerably tall man. It
might have been two or three minutes after I
went out till I came back to where Spangler
was standing, and found him kind of scared,
and as if he had been crying. I did not say
any thing to him before he said that to me.
It was Spangler's place, with another man, to
shove the scenes on; he was where he ought to
be to do the work he had to do. I did not
hear any one call Booth's name. It was not
till the people were all out, and I came outside, that I heard some say it was Booth, and
some say it was not. Spangler and I boarded
together; we went home to supper together,
on the evening of the assassination, at 6
o'clock, and returned at 7.

WILLIAM EATON.

Recalled for the Prosecution.—May 19.

I arrested the prisoner, Edward Spangler,
in a house on the South-east corner, I think,
of Seventh and H; I believe it was his board-

ing-house. It was the next week after the
assassination. I did not search him; my
orders were to arrest him.

CHARLES H. ROSCH.

For the Prosecution.—May 19.

After the arrest of the prisoner, Edward
Spangler, I went, in company with two of
the Provost Marshal's detectives, to the
house on the north-east corner of Seventh
and H Streets, where he took his meals.
When we inquired for his trunk, we were
told that he kept it at the theater; but the
man at the house handed us a carpet-bag,
in which we found a piece of rope measur-
ing eighty-one feet, out of which the twist
was very carefully taken. The bag was
locked, but we found a key that unlocked it.
It contained nothing but the rope, some
blank paper, and a dirty shirt-collar. I was
not present when Spangler was arrested. I
went to his house between 9 and 10 o'clock
on the night of Monday, April 17.

Cross-examined by MR. EWING.

It was a man called Jake, apparently a
German, that told me it was Spangler's bag,
and that it was all he had at the house. He
said he worked at the theater with Spangler.
There were two other persons there, board-
ers I presume. We got the rope from a
bed-room on the second floor that faced
toward the south; the bag was right near
where Jake had his trunk. I am satisfied
that the coil of rope I see here now is the
same that I took from Spangler's carpet-bag.

See testimony of

DEFENSE OF EDWARD SPANGLER.

C. D. HESS.

For the Defense.—May 31.

By MR. EWING.

I am manager of Grover's Theater, and I have been in the habit of seeing John Wilkes Booth very frequently. On the day before the assassination he came into the office during the afternoon, interrupting me and the prompter of the theater in reading a manuscript. He seated himself in a chair, and entered into a conversation on the general illumination of the city that night. He asked me if I intended to illuminate. I said yes, I should, to a certain extent; but that the next night would be my great night of the illumination, that being the celebration of the fall of Sumter. He then asked, "Do you intend to" or "Are you going to invite the President?" My reply, I think, was, "Yes; that reminds me I must send that invitation." I had it in my mind for several days to invite the Presidential party that night, the 14th. I sent my invitation to Mrs. Lincoln. My notes were usually addressed to her, as the best means of accomplishing the object.

Booth's manner, and his entering in the way he did, struck me as rather peculiar. He must have observed that we were busy, and it was not usual for him to come into the office and take a seat, unless he was invited. He did upon this occasion, and made such a point of it that we were both considerably surprised. He pushed the matter so far that I got up and put the manuscript away, and entered into conversation with him.

It is customary in theaters to keep the passage-way between the scenes and the green-room and the dressing-rooms clear, but much depends upon the space there is for storing scenes and furniture.

[The counsel was eliciting from the witness the position of the box usually occupied by the President on visiting Grover's Theater, and the nature of the leap that an assassin would have to make in endeavoring to escape from the box, when objection was made to the testimony as irrelevant.]

MR. EWING. I wish merely to show that, from the construction of Ford's Theater, it would be easier for the assassin to effect his escape from Ford's Theater than it would be from Grover's. The purpose is plainly to show that Ford's Theater was selected by Booth, and why Ford's Theater is spoken of by him as the one where he intended to capture or assassinate the President, and to relieve the employees of Ford's Theater, Mr. Spangler among them, from the imputation which naturally arises from Booth's selecting that theater as the one in which to commit the crime.

The Commission sustained the objection.

H. CLAY FORD.

For the Defense.—May 31.

By MR. EWING.

On the 14th of April last I was treasurer of Ford's Theater. I returned to the theater from my breakfast about half-past 11 o'clock that day, when my brother, James R. Ford, told me that the President had engaged a box for that night. John Wilkes Booth was at the theater about half an hour afterward. I do not know that the fact of the President's going to the theater that night was communicated to Booth, but I think it is very likely he found it out while there. I saw him going down the street while I was standing in the door of the theater; as he came up he commenced talking to the parties standing around. Mr. Raybold then went into the theater and brought him out a letter that was there for him. He sat down on the steps and commenced reading it. This was about 12 o'clock. He staid there perhaps half an hour. I went into the office, and when I came out again he was gone.

I told Mr. Raybold about fixing up and decorating the box for the President that night, but he had the neuralgia in his face, and I fixed up the box in his place. I found two flags in the box already there, which I got Mr. Raybold to help me put up. Another flag I got from the Treasury Department. It was the Treasury regimental flag. I put this blue regimental flag in the center, and the two American flags above. There was nothing unusual in the decorations of the box, except the picture of Washington placed on the pillar in the middle of the box. This had never been used before. We usually used small flags to decorate the box; but as General Grant was expected to come with the President, we borrowed this flag from the Treasury regiment to decorate with.

The furniture placed in the box consisted of one chair brought from the stage and a sofa, a few chairs out of the reception-room, and a rocking-chair, which belonged to the same set, I had brought from my bed-room. This chair had been in the reception-room, but the ushers sitting in it had greased it with their hair, and I had it removed to my room, it being a very nice chair. The only reason for putting that chair in the box was that it belonged to the set, and I sent for it to make the box as neat as possible

I received no suggestions from any one as to the decoration of the box, excepting from Mr. Raybold and the gentleman who brought the flag from the Treasury Department.

All that Spangler had to do with the box was to take the partition out. There are two boxes divided by a partition, which, when the President attended the theater, was always removed to make the box into one. Spangler and the other carpenter, Jake, removed it. The President had been to the theater, I suppose, about six times during the winter and spring; three or four times during Mr. Forrest's engagements, and twice during Mr. Clark's engagement. These are the only times I remember.

I did not direct Spangler with respect to the removal of the partition; I believe Mr. Raybold sent for him. While we were in the box Spangler was working on the stage; I think he had a pair of flats down on the stage, fixing them in some way. I called for a hammer and nails; he threw up two or three nails, and handed me the hammer up from the stage.

Spangler, of course, knew that the President was coming to the theater that evening, as he assisted in taking out the partition.

In decorating the box I used my penknife to cut the strings to tie up the flags, and left it there in the box.

Three or four times during the season Booth had engaged box No. 7, that is part of the President's box, being the one nearest the audience. He engaged no other box.

During the play that evening, the "American Cousin," I was in the ticket-office of the theater. I may have been out on the pavement in front two or three times, but I do not remember. I did not see Spangler there. I never saw Spangler wear a moustache.

Cross-examined by ASSISTANT JUDGE ADVOCATE BINGHAM.

None of the other boxes were occupied on the night of the President's assassination, and I do not remember any box being taken on that night. I certainly did not know that the boxes were applied for, for that evening, and that the applicants were refused and told that the boxes were already taken. The applicants did not apply to me. Booth did not apply to me, or to any one, for those boxes, to my knowledge, nor did any one else for him. There were four of us in the office who sold tickets. There were not, to my knowledge, any applications for any box except the President's. There may have been applications without my knowledge.

I know nothing of the mortise in the wall behind the door of the President's box. I heard of it afterward, but have never seen it, nor did I see the bar said to have been used to fasten the door, nor did I see the hole bored through the first door of the President's box, though I have since heard there was one. I have not been in the box since.

The screws of the keepers of the lock to the President's box, I understand, were burst some time ago. They were not, to 'my knowledge, drawn that day, and left so that the lock would not hold the door on its being slightly pressed. It was not done in my presence, and if it was done at all, it was without my knowledge.

I do not remember any conversation with Mr. Ferguson before the day of the assassination about decorating the theater in celebration of some victory.

By MR. AIKEN.

The letter that Booth received on the day of the assassination, and read on the steps of the theater, was a long letter, of either four or eight pages of letter-paper—whether one or two sheets I do not know, but it was all covered with writing. He sat on the steps while reading his letter, every now and then looking up and laughing. It was while Booth was there that I suppose he learned of the President's visit to the theater that evening. There were several around Booth, talking to him. Mr. Gifford was there; Mr. Evans, an actor, and Mr. Grillet, I remember, were there at the time.

The President's visit to the theater that evening could not have been known until 12 o'clock, unless it was made known by some one from the Executive Mansion. It was published in the Evening Star, but not in the morning papers.

I am not acquainted with John H. Surratt. [Photograph of John H. Surratt exhibited to the witness.]

I never saw that person that I know of.

By MR. EWING.

I have never, to my knowledge, seen the prisoner, Herold.

The mortise in the passage-way was not noticed by me; the passage was dark, and when the door was thrown back against the wall, as it was that day, I should not be likely to notice it had it been there at that time. Had the small hole been bored in the door, or had the screws been loosened, it is not likely I should have noticed them.

By the COURT.

I might have stated in the saloon on Tenth Street that the President was to be at the theater that evening, and also that General Grant was to be there.

JAMES R. FORD.

For the Defense.—May 30.

By MR. EWING.

At the time of the assassination, I was business manager of Ford's Theater. I was first apprised of the President's intended visit to the theater on Friday morning, at half-past 10 o'clock. A young man, a messenger from the White House, came and engaged the box. The President had been previously invited to the theater that night, and I had no knowledge of his intention to visit the theater until the reception of that message. I saw John Wilkes Booth about half-past 12, two hours after I received this information. I saw him as I was coming from the Treasury Building, on the corner of Tenth and E Streets. I was going up E Street, toward Eleventh Street; he was coming from the direction of the theater.

Q. State whether, upon any occasion, you have had any conversation with Booth as to the purchase of lands, and, if so, where?

Assistant Judge Advocate BINGHAM. I object to the question.

Mr. EWING. Testimony has already been admitted on that point.

Assistant Judge Advocate BINGHAM. I know, but it is unimportant as to this man; there is no question about this man in the case.

Mr. EWING. It is very important as to one of the prisoners.

Assistant Judge Advocate BINGHAM. This witness can not be evidence for any human being on that subject, no matter what Booth said to him about it. I object to it on the ground that it is entirely incompetent, and has nothing in the world to do with the case. If this witness had been involved in it, I admit it might be asked, with a view to exculpate him from any censure before the public.

Mr. EWING. The Court will recollect that in Mr. Weichman's testimony there was evidence introduced by the prosecution of an alleged interview between Dr. Mudd and Booth at the National Hotel, in the middle of January, which was introduced as a circumstance showing his connection with the conspiracy, which Booth is supposed to have then had on foot. The accused, Dr. Mudd, is represented to have stated that the conversation related to the purchase of his lands in Maryland. I wish to show by this witness that Booth spoke to him frequently, through the course of the winter, of his speculations, of his former speculations in oil lands, which are shown to have been actual speculations of the year before, and of his contemplating the investment of money in cheap lands in Lower Maryland. The effect of the testimony is to show that the statement, which has been introduced against the accused, Dr. Mudd, if it was made, was a *bona fide* statement, and related to an actual pending offer, or talk about the sale of his farm to Booth.

Assistant Judge Advocate BINGHAM. The only way, if the Court please, in which they can do any thing in regard to this matter of the declaration of Mudd, if it was made, (and, if it was not made, of course it does not concern anybody,) is simply to show by legitimate evidence that there was such a negotiation going on between himself and Booth. The point I make is, that it is not legitimate

evidence, or any evidence at all, to introduce a conversation between Booth and this witness at another time and place. It is no evidence at all, it is not colorable evidence, and the Court have nothing in the world to do with it. It would be impossible to ask the witness any questions that would be more irrelevant or incompetent than the question that is now asked him.

Mr. EWING. I will state to the Court further that it has already received testimony, as explanatory of the presence of Booth in Charles County, of his avowed object in going there—testimony to which the Judge Advocate made no objection, and which he must have then regarded as relevant. This testimony is clearly to that point of explanation of Booth's visit in Lower Maryland, as well as an explanation of the alleged conversation with Mudd in January.

Assistant Judge Advocate BINGHAM. The difference is this: the defense attempted to prove negotiations in Charles County, and we thought we would not object to that; but this is another thing altogether. It is an attempt to prove a talk, irrespective of time or place, or any thing else.

The Commission sustained the objection.

By Mr. EWING.

Q. Do you know any thing of the visit made by Booth into Charles County last fall?

A. He told me ——

Assistant Judge Advocate BINGHAM objected to the witness giving the declarations of Booth.

The WITNESS. I have never known Booth to go there.

Q. Have you ever heard Booth say what the purpose of any visit which he may have made last fall to Charles County was?

Assistant Judge Advocate BINGHAM renewed his objection.

The Commission sustained the objection.

By Mr. AIKEN.

The notice in the Evening Star that announced the President's intended visit to the theater, also said that General Grant would be there.

By Assistant Judge Advocate BURNETT

I wrote the notice for the Star in the ticket-office of the theater about half-past 11 or 12 o'clock, and sent it to the office immediately; I at the same time carried one myself to the National Republican. The notice appeared in the Star about 2 o'clock. Before writing the notice I asked Mr. Phillips, an actor in our establishment, who was on the stage, to do it; he said he would after he had finished writing the regular advertisements. I also spoke to my younger brother about the propriety of writing it. I had not seen Booth previous to writing the notice, nor do I remember speaking to any one else about it.

By MR. AIKEN.

I had sent the notice to the Star office before seeing Booth.

[Exhibiting the photograph of John H. Surratt.]

I do not know Surratt. I never remember seeing him.

John McCullough, the actor, left this city the fourth week in January. He returned with Mr. Forrest at his last engagement. I do not know exactly when, but about the 1st of April.

JOHN T. FORD.

For the Defense.—May 31.

I reside in Baltimore, and am proprietor of Ford's Theater in the city of Washington. The prisoner, Edward Spangler, has been in my employ three or four years at intervals, and over two years continuously.

Spangler was employed as a stage hand, frequently misrepresented as the stage-carpenter of the theater. He was a laborer to assist in shoving the scenery in its place, as the necessity of the play required. These were his duties at night, and during the day to assist in doing the rough carpenter work incidental to plays to be produced.

Q. State whether or not his duties were such as to require his presence upon the stage during the whole of a play.

A. Strictly so; his absence for a moment might imperil the success of a play, and cause dissatisfaction to the audience. It is very important to the effect of a play that the scenery should be well attended to in all its changes; and he is absolutely important there every moment from the time the curtain rises until it falls. There are intervals, it is true, but he can not judge how long or how brief a scene may be.

On Friday, the day of the assassination, I was in Richmond. Hearing of the partial destruction of that city by fire, I went there, anxious to ascertain the condition of an uncle, a very aged man, and my mother-in-law. I did not hear of the assassination until Sunday night, and then I heard that Edwin Booth was charged with it. On Monday morning I started for Washington by the 6 o'clock boat. While on the boat I saw the Richmond Whig, which confirmed the report I had heard of the assassination on Sunday night.

During the performance of the "American Cousin," Spangler's presence on the stage would be necessary. The first scene of the third act is quick, only of a few moments' duration. The second scene is rather a long one, longer perhaps than any other scene in that act, probably eight, ten, or twelve minutes long. Spangler's presence would be necessary unless positively informed of the duration of the scene.

The second act depends very much upon the action and the spirit of the actors engaged in it. Sometimes it is much more rapid than at others. In the second act I hardly think there is an interval of more than five or eight minutes between the times that Spangler would have to move the scenes. His constant presence upon the stage would be absolutely necessary if he attended to his duties.

In the intervals between the scenes, he should be preparing for the next change, to be ready at his scene, and to remain on the side where the stage-carpenter had assigned him his post of duty; besides, emergencies often arise during an act that require extra services of a stage hand.

J. B. Wright was the stage-manager, James J. Gifford the stage-carpenter. The stage-manager directs, the stage-carpenter executes the work belonging to the entire stage. The duty of keeping the passage-way clear and in a proper condition belongs to Gifford's subordinates, the stage hands who were on the side where this passage is. It is the duty of each and every one to keep the passage-way clear, and is as indispensable as keeping the front door clear. The action of the play might be ruined by any obstruction or hinderance there.

My positive orders are to keep it always clear and in the best order. It is the passage-way used by all the parties coming from the dressing-rooms. Where a play was performed like the "American Cousin," the ladies were in full dress, and it was absolutely necessary that there should be no obstruction there, in order that the play should be properly performed. Coming from the dressing-rooms and the green-room of the theater, every one had to use that passage. The other side of the stage was not used more than a third as much, probably. Most of the entrances by the actors and actresses are made on the prompt side; but many are essential to be made on the O. P. side. By entrances to the stage, I mean to the presence of the audience. The stage-manager was a very exacting man in all those details, and I have always found the passage clear, unless there was some spectacular play, in which he required the whole spread of the stage. Then at times it would be partly incumbered, but not enough so to prevent the people going around the stage, or going to the cellar-way and underneath, and passing to the other side by way of the cellar.

The "American Cousin" was a very plain play; no obstruction whatever could be excused on account of that play; it was all what we call flats, except one scene. The flats are the large scenes that cross the stage.

The prompt side, the side on which the prompter is located, is the position of the stage-carpenter, and opposite to where Spangler worked, which is on the O. P. side, opposite the prompter's place. Keeping the passage-way clear would not be a duty of Spangler's, unless he was specially charged with it.

Spangler, I know, considered Baltimore his home. He buried his wife there about a year ago, or less, while in my employ. He usually spent his summer months there, during the vacation of the theater, chiefly in crab-fishing. I have understood he was a great crab-fisher; we used to plague him about it.

[Exhibiting a coil of rope found at Spangler's boarding-house, in his carpet-bag.]

That rope might be used as a crab-line, though it is rather short for that purpose. Professional crab-fishers use much longer ropes than this, four hundred or five hundred feet long, though I have seen ropes as short as this, which I understand is eighty feet, used by amateurs in that sport. The rope is supported by a buoy, and to it are attached smaller ropes or lines.

Spangler seemed to have a great admiration for J. Wilkes Booth; I have noticed that in my business on the stage with the stage-manager.

Booth was a peculiarly fascinating man, and controlled the lower class of people, such as Spangler belonged to, more, I suppose, than ordinary men would. Spangler was not in the employ of Booth, that I know, and only since the assassination have I heard that he was in the habit of waiting upon him. I have never known Spangler to wear a moustache.

I have known John Wilkes Booth since his childhood, and intimately for six or seven years.

Q. State whether you have ever heard Booth speak of Samuel K. Chester, and, if so, in what connection and where.

Assistant Judge Advocate BINGHAM. I object to any proof about what he said in regard to Chester.

Q. [By Mr. EWING.] State whether or not Booth ever applied to you to employ Chester, who has been a witness for the prosecution, in your theater.

Assistant Judge Advocate BINGHAM. That I object to. It is certainly not competent to introduce declarations of Booth made to anybody in the absence of a witness that may be called, relative to a transaction of his, to affect him in any way at all. I object to it as wholly incompetent.

Mr. EWING. It is not to attack Chester, may it please the Court, that I make this inquiry, but rather to corroborate him; to show that Booth, while manipulating Chester to induce him to go into a conspiracy for the capture of the President, was actually at the same time endeavoring to induce Mr. Ford to employ Chester, in order that he might get him here to the theater and use him as an instrument; and it goes to affect the case of several prisoners at the bar—the

case of the prisoner, Arnold, who in his confession, as orally detailed here, stated that the plan was to capture the President, and Chester corroborates that; and also to assist the case of the prisoner, Spangler, by showing that Booth was not able to get, or did not get, in the theater any instruments to assist him in the purpose, and was endeavoring to get them brought there—men that he had previously manipulated. I think it is legitimate.

Assistant Judge Advocate BINGHAM. Nothing can be clearer, if the Court please, than that it is utterly incompetent. It is not a simple question of relevancy here; it is absolute incompetency. A party who conspires to do a crime may approach the most upright man in the world with whom he has been, before the criminality was known to the world, on terms of intimacy, and whose position in the world, was such that he might be on terms of intimacy with reputable gentlemen. It is the misfortune of a man that is approached in that way; it is not his crime, and it is not colorably his crime either. It does not follow now, because Booth chose to approach this man Chester, that Booth is therefore armed with the power, living or dead, to come into a court of justice and prove on his own motion, or on the motion of anybody else, what he may have said touching that man to third persons. The law is too jealous of the reputation and character of men to permit any such proceedings as that.

The Commission sustained the objection.

Q. Do you think that the leap from the President's box upon the stage would be at all a difficult one for Booth?

A. I should not think so; I have seen him make a similar leap without any hesitation, and I am aware that he usually introduced such a leap into the play of "Macbeth."

Q. Do you think, then, from your knowledge of the physical powers of Booth, that that leap was one that he would not need to rehearse?

A. I should not think a rehearsal of it was needed. He was a very bold, fearless man; he always had the reputation of being of that character. He excelled in all manly sports. We never rehearse leaps in the theater, even when they are necessary to the action of the play; they may be gone over the first time a play is performed, but it is not usual. Booth had a reputation for being a great gymnast. He introduced, in some Shaksperian plays, some of the most extraordinary and outrageous leaps—at least they were deemed so by the critics, and were condemned by the press at the time.

I saw him on one occasion make one of these extraordinary leaps, and the Baltimore Sun condemned it in an editorial the next day—styling him "the gymnastic actor." It was in the play of "Macbeth," the en-

trance to the witch scene; he jumped from
a high rock down on the stage, as high or
perhaps higher than the box; I think nearly
as high as from the top of the scene; and he
made the leap with apparent ease.

Booth was in the habit of frequenting
Ford's Theater at Washington. I seldom
visited the theater but what I found him
about or near it, during the day, while I was
there. I usually came down to the theater
three days a week, devoting the other three
to my business in Baltimore, and being there
between the hours of 10 and 3. I would
nearly always meet Booth there when he
was in the city. He had his letters directed
to the theater, and that was the cause of
his frequent visits there, as I thought then.
The last time I saw Booth was some two or
three weeks before the assassination.

The last appearance of John McCullough
at my theater in Washington was on the 18th
of March, the night, I believe, when the
"Apostate" was played. Mr. McCullough
always appears with Mr. Forrest, and he has
since appeared in New York.

Cross-examined by ASSISTANT JUDGE ADVOCATE
BINGHAM.

I can not state positively that the private
boxes are locked when not in actual use;
that is our custom in Baltimore. Mr. Gifford, who had control of the whole theater,
is the responsible party whom I should
blame for any thing wrong about the boxes.
We keep the boxes locked, and the keys in
the box-office; here, I understand, the custom
is for the ushers to keep the keys. James
O'Brien was the usher of the dress-circle,
and James R. Ford and Henry Clay Ford
were the parties authorized to sell tickets for
those boxes that day.

Q. Do you know as a fact that none of
the boxes were occupied that night, except
that occupied by the President?

A. I have only heard so.

Q. Is the play of the "American Cousin"
a popular one? Does it attract considerable
audiences?

A. It was, when originally produced, an
exceedingly attractive play; of late years it
has not been a strong card, but a fair at-
traction.

Q. Is it not a very unusual thing, when
such plays are produced, for your private
boxes to be entirely empty?

A. Washington is a very good place for
selling boxes usually. They are generally in
demand, and nearly always two or three
boxes are sold.

Q. Can you recall any occasion on which
a play, so popular and attractive as that was,
presented when none of your private boxes,
save the one occupied by the President, was
used?

A. I remember occasions when we sold
no boxes at all, and had quite a full house—
a good audience; but those occasions were

rare. My reason for constructing so many
boxes to this theater was, that usually private boxes were in demand in Washington—
more so than in almost any other city. It
is not a favorable place to see a performance,
but it is a fashionable place here to which
to take company.

Recalled for the Defense.—June 9.

By MR. EWING.

I have known Edward Spangler for nearly
four years. He has been in my employ most
of that time. He was always regarded as a
very good-natured, kind, willing man. His
only fault was in occasionally drinking more
liquor than he should have done, not so as
to make him vicious, but more to unfit him
to work. Since he has been in my employ
I never knew him to be in but one quarrel,
and that was through drink. He was always
willing to do any thing, and was a very good,
efficient drudge. He was considered a very
harmless man by the company around the
theater, and was often the subject of sport
and fun. I do not think he was intrusted
with the confidence of others to any extent.
He had not many associates. He had no
self-respect, and was a man that rarely slept
in a bed; he usually slept in the theater.
I never knew any thing of his political sentiments in this city; never heard from him an
expression of partisan or political feeling.
In Baltimore he was known to be a member
of the American Order.

By MR. CLAMPITT.

I never met J. Z. Jenkins except in Carroll
Prison.

JOSEPH S. SESSFORD.

For the Defense.—June 3.

I was seller of tickets at Ford's Theater.
My business commenced about half-past 6 in
the evening.

None of the private boxes, except that
occupied by the party of the President, were
applied for on the evening of the assassination, nor had any been sold during the day
that I know of.

WILLIAM WITHERS, JR.

Recalled for the Defense.—May 31.

By MR. EWING.

The door leading into the alley from the
passage was shut when Booth rushed out.
After he made the spring from the box, and
ran across the stage, he made a cut at me,
and knocked me down to the first entrance;
then I got a side view of him. The door was
shut, but it opened very easily; I saw that
distinctly. He made a plunge right at the
knob of the door, and out he went, and pulled
the door after him. He swung it as he went
out. I did not see Booth during the day.

HENRY M. JAMES.

For the Defense.—May 31.

By MR. EWING.

I was at Ford's Theater on the night of the assassination. When the shot was fired, I was standing ready to draw off the flat, and Mr. Spangler was standing right opposite to me on the stage, on the same side as the President's box, about ten feet from me. From his position he could not see the box, nor the side of the stage on which Booth jumped. I had frequently during the play seen Spangler at his post. I saw no one with him. The passage-way was clear at the time; it was our business to keep it clear; it was more Spangler's business than mine.

I saw Spangler when the President entered the theater. When the people applauded on the President's entry, he applauded with them, with both hands and feet. He clapped his hands and stamped his feet, and seemed as pleased as anybody to see the President come in.

I did not see Jacob Ritterspaugh near Spangler that evening. He might have been there behind the scenes, but I did not see him. I can not say how long I staid in my position after the shot was fired; it might have been a minute. I did not see Spangler at all after that happened.

By ASSISTANT JUDGE ADVOCATE BINGHAM.

Jacob Ritterspaugh was employed there, and it was his business to be there behind the scenes, though I did not see him.

J. L. DEBONAY.

For the Defense.—May 31.

By MR. EWING.

I was playing what is called "responsible utility" at Ford's Theater at the time of the assassination. On the evening of the assassination, Booth came up to the alley door and said to me, "Tell Spangler to come to the door and hold my horse." I did not see his horse. I went over to where Mr. Spangler was, on the left-hand side, at his post, and said, "Mr. Booth wants you to hold his horse." He then went to the door and went outside, and was there about a minute, when Mr. Booth came in. Booth asked me if he could get across the stage. I told him no, the dairy scene was on, and he would have to go under the stage and come up on the other side. About the time that he got upon the other side, Spangler called to me, "Tell Peanut John to come here and hold this horse; I have not time. Mr. Gifford is out in the front of the theater, and all the responsibility of the scene lies upon me." I went on the other side and called John, and John went there and held the horse, when Spangler came in and returned to his post.

I saw Spangler three or four times that evening on the stage in his proper position. I saw him about two minutes before the shot was fired. He was on the same side I was on—the same side as the President's box. About five minutes after the shot was fired I again saw Spangler standing on the stage, with a crowd of people who had collected there.

I saw Booth when he made his exit. I was standing in the first entrance on the left-hand side. When he came to the center of the stage, I saw that he had a long knife in his hand. It seemed to me to be a double-edged knife, and looked like a new one. He paused about a second, I should think, and then went off at the first entrance to the right-hand side. I think he had time to get out of the back door before any person was on the stage. It was, perhaps, two or three seconds after he made his exit before I saw any person on the stage in pursuit. The first person I noticed was a tall, stout gentleman, with gray clothes on, I think, and I believe a moustache. Booth did not seem to run very fast across the stage; he seemed to be stooping a little when he ran off. The distance he ran would be about thirty-five or forty feet; but he was off the stage two or three seconds before this gentleman was on, and of the two, I think Booth was running the fastest.

By MR. AIKEN.

I was at the theater at 12 o'clock that day. I did not see Booth there.

Recalled for the Prosecution.—June 13.

When the shot was fired on the night of the assassination, I was standing on the left-hand side of the first entrance, the side the President's box was on. About a minute and a half or two minutes after Mr. Stewart left the stage, or about time to allow of his getting to the back door, I saw Spangler above the scene back to give the whole stage to the people who came on. I do not know who assisted him. Spangler then came to the front of the stage with the rest of the people. There was then a cry for water. I started to the green-room, and he came the same way. About a half dozen of us went to get some water to carry it to the private box.

When Booth wanted Spangler to hold his horse, and I went over to tell him, Spangler and Sleichman were standing close to each other on the opposite side of the stage, the side of the President's box. Spangler then left; I saw him go out to Booth, and in about a minute or a minute and a half Booth came in.

I heard no conversation between Spangler and Booth. Booth met Spangler at the door, and was standing at the door on the outside; the door was about half open when Spangler went out. If any person had followed Spangler I should have seen him. I was half-way between the back door and the green-room,

about eighteen or twenty feet distant, I suppose. Booth, when he came in, went under
the stage to the opposite side, and went out
of the side door; I went under the stage and
crossed with him. I did not see him speak
to any one. I was in front of the theater
about five minutes before the assassination;
I did'not see Spangler there.

I have known Spangler for about six
months. I have never seen him wear a moustache. He is a man that has been a little
dissipated a considerable portion of his time—
fond of spreeing round. He is free in conversation, especially when in liquor.

Cross-examined by the JUDGE ADVOCATE.

When Booth passed under the stage, he
went through the little side passage, level with
the lower floor of the theater, that leads out
into Tenth Street; that side passage also
leads up to Mr. Ford's room. I went out
through that passage to the front of the
theater, and returned by the same way, and
had taken my place on the stage when the
pistol was fired. I was not doing any thing,
but was leaning up against the corner of the
scene at the time. We were waiting for the
curtain to drop. Mr. Harry Hawk was on
the stage at the moment, playing in a scene.

By MR. EWING.

I played in the piece, taking the part of
John Wigger, the gardener.

WILLIAM R. SMITH.
For the Defense.—June 2.
By MR. EWING.

I am Superintendent of the Botanical Garden, Washington. I was in Ford's Theater
at the time of the assassination. I saw J.
Wilkes Booth pass off the stage, and Mr.
Stewart get on it. Mr. Stewart was among
the first to get on; but my impression is that
Booth was off the stage before Mr. Stewart
got on it. I did not notice him after he got
on the stage.

J. P. FERGUSON.
Recalled for the Defense.—May 31.

I saw the gentleman who first got upon the
stage after Booth got off. He was a large
man, dressed in light clothes, with a moustache. This gentleman was the first that got
upon the stage, and I suppose it was probably
two or three minutes—about that long—after
Booth went off the stage that this man went
out of the entrance. I saw no one else run
out of the entrance except Hawk, the young
man who was on the stage at the time Booth
jumped from the box. If any one had run
out of the entrance following Booth, I should
probably have seen him, because I thought
it was very singular that those who were near
the stage did not try to get on it.

Cross-examined by ASSISTANT JUDGE ADVOCATE BINGHAM.

I sat in the dress-circle on the north side,
the same side as the entrance through which
Booth passed. From the place where I sat I
could not distinctly see the mouth of the
entrance.

JAMES LAMB.
For the Defense.—June 2.
By MR. EWING.

For over a year I have been employed at
Ford's Theater as artist and scene-painter.

[The rope found in Spangler's bag exhibited to the witness.]

I have seen ropes like this at the theater.
There are probably forty or fifty of such ropes
in use there. They are called border-ropes,
and are about seventy or eighty feet in length,
used for suspending the borders that hang
across the stage. The borders are long strips
of canvas, painted to represent some exteriors,
others interiors, and as they are required to
be changed for the scene that is on, they are
raised or lowered by means of such ropes as
these. This rope has the appearance of
having been chafed; a new rope would be a
little stiffer in its texture than this. I should
say this is a new rope, but has been in use,
though I can not detect any thing that would
lead me to say it has been in use as a border-
rope; if it had been, there would have been
a knot fastening at the end, or have the appearance of having been tied.

Cross-examined by ASSISTANT JUDGE ADVOCATE BINGHAM.

I think it is a rope very similar to the
ones used at the theater, but I should be very
sorry to swear that it was one of them. I
should say the material was manilla.

I know John Wilkes Booth by sight. I
never spoke a word to him in my life. I did
not hear him say any thing in March or
April last about the President. I never was
in his company.

By MR. EWING.

From an examination of the rope, I have
no reason to believe that it was not used as
a border-rope. I was in the theater the
whole of Saturday, the day after the President was assassinated, from 10 o'clock until
the military guard took possession, and I saw
Spangler there several times during the day.

By ASSISTANT JUDGE ADVOCATE BINGHAM.

I saw him on the stage. Maddox, Jake,
Mr. Gifford, and Mr. Wright, the stage-manager, were in and out occasionally. Carland
was also there with Spangler, Maddox, and
myself, in the forenoon, loitering and walking about, sometimes sitting down; there
was no companionship particularly. I have
not seen Spangler since until this morning.

JACOB RITTERSPAUGH.

Recalled for the Defense.—June 2.

By MR. EWING.

When I was in the theater with Mr. Lamb, the next day after the assassination, I told him about Spangler slapping me and saying, "Shut up; do n't say which way he went;" and on the night of the assassination, when Carland came up to Mr. Gifford's room, he woke me up and asked where Ned was. I told him I did not know, and then I told him that Ned had slapped me in the mouth, and said, "Don't say which way he went."

As I was on the stage with Spangler on the day of the assassination, we saw a man in the dress-circle smoking a cigar. I asked Spangler who it was, but he did not know; and I said we ought to tell him to go out; but Spangler said he had no charge on that side of the theater, and had no right to do so. I took no more notice of him, and went to my work again. After awhile I saw him sitting in the lower private box, on the right-hand side of the stage. He was looking at us. I told Ned, and he spoke to him, and then the man went out. That was about 6 o'clock on the evening of the day on which the President was assassinated. That was about 6 o'clock in the evening.

Cross-examined by ASSISTANT JUDGE ADVOCATE BINGHAM.

I never saw the man before. He wore a moustache. I saw him first in the dress-circle, then in the lower private box on the right-hand side of the stage, the left-hand when you come in from the front of the theater.

JAMES LAMB.

Recalled for the Defense.—June 2.

I saw Ritterspaugh on the stage on Saturday, the day following the President's assassination. Ritterspaugh was grumbling, and saying that it was well for Ned that he had n't something in his hand at the time. I asked him why. He replied, "He struck me last night a very hard blow, and he said at the same time, 'Shut up; you know nothing about it.'" This was said in connection with Ritterspaugh having said it was Booth that ran across the stage. Ritterspaugh said he called out, "I know him; I know who it was; it was Booth," or something of that kind, and then Ned struck him and said "Hush up; be quiet. What do you know about it?" That was while Mr. Booth, or whoever it was, was leaving the stage. It was when he was making his escape that this man Jake said he was rushing up and made this exclamation, "That was Booth; I know him; I know him; I will swear that was Booth;" when Ned turned round and struck him in the face with his hand. Ritterspaugh said, "It is well for him I had not something in my hand to return the blow." Then he represented Spangler as saying, when he slapped him, "Hush up; hush up; you know nothing about it. What do you know about it? Keep quiet;" hushing him up.

Ritterspaugh did not say to me that when Spangler hit him on the face he said, "Do n't say which way he went." I am certain Ritterspaugh did not say that to me, or words to that effect.

Cross-examined by ASSISTANT JUDGE ADVOCATE BINGHAM.

Q. Can you tell just exactly the words he did say, that you have sworn to already?
A. Yes, sir.
Q. State them.
A. "Shut up; what do you know about it? Hold your tongue."
Q. That is what Jake said?
A. That is what Spangler said to Jake.
Q. Are you now reporting what Jake said, or reporting what Spangler said?
A. I am reporting what Spangler said and what Jake said.
Q. We are not asking you for what Spangler said; we are asking you what Jake said. State, if you please, what Jake said on that occasion, and exactly what you have sworn he said, and all he said.
A. I will, as near as I can recollect. As he told me, he said, "I followed out the party, was close at his heels, or near to him, and I said that is Booth. I know him; I know him;" or words to that effect, as near as can be.
Q. Jake said he followed out the party, close to his heels?
A. Near to him.
Q. And that he knew who that was?
A. He did not say that he followed the party.
Q. I am asking you what he said. Did you not swear just now that he said he followed the party close to his heels?
A. He was near to him.
Q. Did you or did you not swear that he said he followed the party close to his heels?
A. You know whether I swore it or not.
Q. I ask you whether you did swear to it or not?
A. I say he did.
Q. Very well, then, stick to it. Then Jake said he followed the party close to his heels?
A. Yes, sir.
Q. And he knew who he was?
A. Yes, sir.
Q. What more did Jake say? Did he say he came back after following him close to his heels?
A. No; he received a blow from Spangler, and that shut him up.
Q. Do you swear now that Spangler followed the man close to his heels?

A. No, sir.

Q. Then how did they fix it?

A. Spangler was standing in the way.

Q. While Jake was following the man close to his heels?

A. No, not at all.

Q. How was that?

A. Spangler, I suppose—

Q. You need not state what you suppose. State what Jake said. That is the only question before the Court.

A. That is what I have stated.

LOUIS J. CARLAND.

For the Defense.—June 12.

By MR. EWING.

I am acquainted with Jacob Ritterspaugh. On the night of the assassination I went to Mr. Gifford's room, and Ritterspaugh was there asleep. I woke him up, and asked him where Spangler was. He seemed frightened, and thought I was Mr. Booth.

I asked him where Mr. Spangler was. He told me he did not know where he was now; the last he had seen of Mr. Spangler was when he was standing behind the scenes, and that he did not know where he had gone; that when the man was running past he had said that was Mr. Booth, and Spangler had slapped him in the mouth and said to him, "You do n't know who it is; it may be Mr. Booth, or it may be somebody else."

He did not say then that Spangler slapped him on the face with the back of his hand and said, "Do n't say which way he went," nor any thing to that effect.

I did not see Spangler until the next day; then I saw him in the theater, on the stage. When he went up stairs to bed on the Saturday night after the assassination, he said there was some talk that the people were going to burn the theater, and as he slept very heavily, he was afraid to sleep up there; so I took him into my room, and he was there all night. He was put under arrest that night in my room. At half-past 9 o'clock on Sunday morning the guard came and relieved him, and when I was discharged we both went into the street. I went to church, and in the afternoon saw Spangler again in the street near the theater. We walked round together that afternoon, and in the evening went down to Mr. Bennett's, and to Mr. Gurley's on C street. Some one came there and told him he was going to be arrested, and I advised him at once to go and see the detectives, and not have them come after him when he was asleep and take him out of his bed. I went to Mr. Barry, one of the detectives, and asked him if there was any such report at the police head-quarters, and he said no. I know that Spangler had very little money those two days, for he wanted to see Mr. Gifford to get some.

Booth frequented the theater very famil-

iarly before the assassination. He was there a great deal, and was very intimate with all the employees, and called them by name. He was a gentleman who would soon get acquainted, and get familiar with people on a very short acquaintance.

[Exhibiting to witness the rope found in Spangler's bag.]

We use just such ropes as that in the theater to pull up the borders and scenes, and for bringing up lumber to the top dressing-rooms, because the stairs are too narrow. About two weeks before the assassination, we used such a rope as that to haul up some shelving for my wardrobe, through the window, to the fourth story; Spangler and Ritterspaugh brought it up. I do not know that the rope we used was an extra one; there were a great many ropes around the theater. I am not qualified to judge about how much the rope has been used; this one does not look like an entirely new rope; it is not such as I would buy for a new one; it looks as if it had been exposed out of doors, or in the rain.

Cross-examined by ASSISTANT JUDGE ADVOCATE BINGHAM.

Spangler used to sleep in the theater before the assassination, and he slept there on that night, but not in the room he usually slept in. On that night he slept in the carpenter's shop attached to the theater. I do not know where he slept on Sunday night.

It was about 12 o'clock on Friday night when I woke Ritterspaugh up; there was no one with me, but a policeman stood in the passage-way. Mr. Gifford's bed is in the manager's office, on the first floor of the green-room; that is where I found Ritterspaugh. He was frightened when I woke him up, and thought it was Booth. He did not say any thing to me about Booth drawing a knife on him. When I asked, "Where is Ned?" he said he did not know where he was; that he supposed he was up. I made no reply, and he went on and said that when Booth ran out through the passage-way, while he and Ned were standing behind the scenes, he made the remark, "That is Mr. Booth," and Ned slepped him in the mouth and said, "You do n't know whether it is Mr. Booth, or who it is." That is all that I remember he said.

I never told it to any one but Mr. William Withers, jr. I dined with him on the Sunday after the assassination, and told him then.

By MR. EWING.

The carpenter-shop is attached to the theater just the same as my wardrobe is. It is not in the theater building, but it is included in the theater. You do not have to go into the street to get to it. You leave the theater, and there is a passage-way to go up, the same as we have to go to the green-room and the dressing-rooms.

Ritterspaugh had fully waked up when he

told me that; he stood up and recognized me. He knew who it was before he began to speak.

The theater was guarded on Sunday night, but any of the employees who slept there could get in. Mr. Spangler had a pass from the captain or officer of the guard to go in and out when he liked, and on Saturday I had a pass for that purpose.

JAMES J. GIFFORD.

Recalled for the Defense.—May 30.

By MR. EWING.

On Monday evening of the week previous to the assassination, I heard Booth tell Spangler to take his horse and buggy down to Tattersall's, the horse-market, and sell it. I presume Spangler sold it. He brought the man up with him, and asked me to count the money and give him a receipt. I took the money and handed it over to Booth.

Q. State whether or not, since the assassination, and previous to his release from Carroll Prison, Ritterspaugh told you at the prison that the prisoner, Edward Spangler, directly after the assassination of the President in the theater, hit him in the face with the back of his hand and said, "Don't say which way he went."

A. To the best of my knowledge, I never heard him say so. He asked me if he could amend the statement that he had made. He said he had not told all he knew, and he asked me if he could amend it. I told him certainly, but he ought to be particular and state the truth of what he knew. That is all the conversation we ever had regarding it. He told me he had made a misstatement, and had not told all he knew. He did not say what he had omitted; if he had, I should surely have remembered it, for I have had nothing but this case to think about since I have been in the Old Capitol Prison.

If any thing was wrong about the locks on the private boxes at the theater, it was the duty of the usher to inform me, and for me to have them repaired. No repairing was done to any door leading to the President's box since August or September of last year.

I have frequently heard of Spangler going crab-fishing, but I never saw him. He has told me of going down to the Neck on the Saturday night, and staying till Monday morning; and I have heard others say that they had gone crabbing with him.

[Exhibiting to the witness the rope found in Spangler's bag.]

They use a line of that sort, with small lines tied to it, about three feet apart, and pieces of meat attached as bait. The line is trailed along, and as the crabs seize the bait they are dragged along and taken. I have seen ropes similar to this used, and sometimes a little longer. As there is but little strain upon the rope, it is not particular about the size.

By MR. AIKEN.

I saw J. Wilkes Booth, about half-past 11 or 12 o'clock on the 14th, pass the stage entrance and go to the front door. He bowed to me, but we had no conversation.

Cross-examined by ASSISTANT JUDGE ADVOCATE BINGHAM.

It is fully three weeks ago that Ritterspaugh said he was scared, and that he could not tell what he was doing; but I do not remember his precise words. He seemed to be troubled about it, and asked me if he could not make a correct statement, and I told him certainly he could.

THOMAS J. RAYBOLD.

For the Defense.—June 2.

By MR. EWING.

I have been engaged at Ford's Theater since the first Monday of December a year ago. I was employed to take charge of the house; to see to the purchasing of every thing required in the house, and if any repairs were needed, they were done through my order. In the absence of the Messrs. Ford, I was in the box-office and sold the tickets.

I know of the lock on the door of box 8, the President's box, as it is called, being burst open during Mrs. Bowers's engagement in March. On the 7th of March Mr. Merrick, of the National Hotel, asked me, while at dinner, to reserve some seats in the orchestra for some company, which I did. It is customary, after the first act is over, for reserved seats, which have not been occupied, to be taken by any person wanting seats. Mr. Merrick did not come by the end of the first act, and the seats were occupied. Shortly afterward word was sent to me in the front office, saying that Mr. Merrick and his friends were there, and inquiring for the seats. I took them up stairs to a private box, No. 6, but it was locked, and I could not get in; I went then to boxes 7 and 8, generally termed the President's box, and they were also locked. I could not find the keys, and I supposed the usher had them; but he had left the theater, as he frequently does, when the first act is over; so I put my shoulder against the door of No. 8, the box nearest the stage, to force it open, but it did not give way to that, and I stood from it with my back and put my foot against it close to the lock, and with two or three kicks it came open. There is another lock in the house to which I did the same thing when I could not find the key. When the President came to the theater, boxes 7 and 8 were thrown into one by the removal of the partition between them. The door to No. 8—the one I burst open—was the one always used, and was the door used on the night of the assassination. The other door could not be used.

I do not know whether the lock was ever repaired after I burst it open. It was my place to report it to Mr. Gifford and have it repaired, but I never thought of it from that time. I frequently entered the box afterward, and always passed in without a key. I never said a word to Mr. Gifford about repairing the lock, and never thought even of examining it to see what condition it was in. The locks were only used to keep persons out when the boxes were not engaged. I have frequently had to order persons out when the boxes were left open.

About two weeks prior to the 14th of April, J. Wilkes Booth engaged a private box, No. 4, at Ford's Theater, and in the afternoon he came again to the office and asked for an exchange of the box, and I believe it was made to box 7. I can not be positive whether it was box 7 or 8, that he occupied that night, but I think it was 7. It is the door leading into box 7 that has the hole bored in it.

To the best of my knowledge, there were no tickets sold up to the time of the opening of the theater on the night of the assassination; I can not say positively, for I had been sick with neuralgia for several days, and was not in the office the whole of the day. I was there in the morning, between 10 and 11, when the messenger obtained tickets for the President, and again in the afternoon, but do not know of any applications, and if there had been, I should have seen when I counted the house at night, which I did on the night of the assassination, at 10 o'clock, as usual.

I saw Booth on the morning of the 14th at the office; I do not know whether before or after the box was engaged for the President. I know he got a letter from the office that morning. Booth's letters were directed to Mr. Ford's box at the post-office, and he generally came every morning for them. Mr. Ford would get the letters as he came from breakfast in the morning, and bring them to the office, when the letters that belonged to the stage would be sent there, and those belonging to Booth would be called for by him.

The rocking-chair was placed in the position it occupied in the President's box simply because, in any other position, the rockers would have been in the way. When the partition was taken down, it left a triangular corner, and the rockers went into that corner at the left of the balustrade of the box; they were there out of the way. That was the only reason why I put it there. I had it so placed on two occasions before; last winter a year ago, when Mr. Hackett was playing, when the President was there. The sofa and other parts of the furniture had been used this last season, but up to that night the chair had not.

[Exhibiting to the witness the coil of rope found in Spangler's carpet-bag.]

I can not swear that this rope has been used at the theater, but we used such ropes as this at the time of the Treasury Guard's ball, from the lobby to the wings, to hang the colors of different nations on. It is like the kind of rope we use in the flies for drawing up the different borders that go across from one wing to the other. From its appearance, I judge this rope has been used. It would be lighter in color if it had not been.

Cross-examined by ASSISTANT JUDGE ADVOCATE BINGHAM.

Any rope that was used about the theater, I should judge, ought to stay there; I do not think its proper place would be in a carpet-sack half a mile off. We use a great many such ropes; and sometimes, when they are taken down, they lie upon the scene-loft until we need them again.

The outer door, or door of the passage to the President's box, never had a lock on; I do not think it has even a latch on. I do not know whether the force I employed against the door burst the lock or the keeper off; I supposed at the time that it started the keeper. The fastening on the door is of pine I believe; I do not know whether it was split or not; I did not examine it. I did not touch box 7.

The last time I was in the President's box was on the morning after the assassination; I went in with some gentlemen to look at the hole in the door. I did not see the mortise in the wall, nor any piece of wood to fasten the door with, nor did I see the mortise the previous afternoon. I was there but for about five minutes, while the flags were being put up. The chair was in the box when I went in to help put up the flags; it was placed behind the door of box No. 7, with the rockers in the corner toward the audience. I did not see him in the box, but my opinion is that the way the chair was placed, the audience was rather behind the President as he sat in the chair.

I can not say the precise day on which Booth occupied box No. 7. Mr. Ford was the one who sold him the box and exchanged it. There were ladies and men with Booth, I think.

By MR. EWING

I can not state whether it was after Booth played *Pescara* that he occupied that box. To the best of my recollection, it was about two weeks before the assassination; it might have been more. He had the box on two occasions. Once when he engaged it, he did not use it; he told me that the ladies at the National Hotel had disappointed him.

I do not know any thing at all as to whether Spangler got that rope from the theater rightfully or not.

Recalled for the Defense.—June 2.

By Mr. Ewing.

Since I was upon the stand, I have visited Ford's Theater, and examined the keepers of the locks of boxes Nos. 7 and 8. The lock of box 8 is in the condition that I stated this morning. It has been forced, and the wood has been split by forcing the lock. The screw in the keeper is tight, and the keeper has been forced aside. The lock on the door of box 7 has been forced, which I was not aware of until I saw it just now. You can take the upper screw out with your finger, and push it in and out; you can put your thumb against it, and put it in to the full extent of the screw. I can not say as to its having been done with an instrument. It must have been done by force; I know that No. 8 was done by force applied to the outside of the door; the other has a similar appearance.

Cross-examined by Assistant Judge Advocate Bingham.

The wood in box 7 is not split a particle. The reason why I think force has been used with that lock is, that if the screw was drawn by a screw-driver, when it went back again it would have to be put back by the driver, but when force has been used, it would make the hole larger, and you could put the screw in and out just as you can the screw in the door of box 7.

By Mr. Aiken.

I do not know John H. Surratt. I do not know any of the prisoners except Spangler. He is the only one I ever saw with the exception of one, [Herold,] whom I knew when he was quite a boy.

Henry E. Merrick.

For the Defense.—June 2.

By Mr. Ewing.

I am a clerk at the National Hotel, Washington. On the evening of the 7th of March, in company with my wife, Mr. Marcus P. Norton of Troy, N. Y., Miss Engels, and Mrs. Bunker, I went to Ford's Theater. Mr. Raybold took us to a private box. We passed down the dress-circle on the right-hand side, and entered the first box; there was a partition up at the time between the two boxes. Mr. Raybold went to the office for the key, but could not find it. He then placed his shoulder, I think, against the door and burst it open. The keeper was burst off I think; at least the screw that held the upper part of the keeper came out, and it whirled around, and hung by the lower screw.

Our books show that John McCullough, the actor, left the National Hotel on the 26th of March; since then I have not seen him.

I have never known him to stop at any other hotel than the National.

Cross-examined by Assistant Judge Advocate Bingham.

Mr. McCullough may have called on some friend in the house, and I not see him. I have not seen him since the 26th of March.

It was the very first box that we went into on visiting the theater on the 7th of March; the partition was between the box we occupied and the one to our right, further on toward the stage. The box nearest the stage we did not enter at all. It was the very first box we came to that we entered, and it was the door of this box that was burst open. The upper screw came out entirely, and the keeper swung round on the lower screw, and left the lock without any fastening at all.

James O'Brien.

For the Defense.—June 3.

I have been employed as clerk in the Quarter-master General's office. I also had an engagement at night as usher at Ford's Theater.

Some time before the assassination I noticed that the keeper of box 8 had been wrenched off. I was absent one evening, at home sick, and when I came next I found that the keeper was broken off; but, as the door shut pretty tight, I never thought of speaking about it. You might lock the door, but if you were to shove it, it would come open.

The keeper on box No. 7 appeared to be all right; I always locked that box. The door of No. 8 was used when the Presidential party occupied the box; when the party occupying the Presidential box entered, the door was always left open. The door of the passage leading to the two boxes had no lock on it, or fastening of any kind.

Joseph T. K. Plant.

For the Defense.—June 2.

By Mr. Ewing.

My occupation at present is that of a dealer in furniture; ever since I was fourteen years old I have been, more or less, engaged in cabinet work. I have visited Ford's Theater to-day, and have examined the keepers on boxes No. 7 and No. 8. To all appearances they have both been forced. The wood-work in box 8 is shivered and splintered by the screws. In box 7, I could pull the screw with my thumb and finger; the tap was gone clear to the point. I could force it back with my thumb. In box 4, which is directly under box 8, the keeper is gone entirely.

I should judge that the keepers in boxes 7 and 8 were made loose by force; I could not see any evidence of an instrument having been used to draw the screws in either of them.

I noticed a hole in the wall of the passage behind the boxes; it had the appearance of having been covered with something; I could not see what, as no remnant of it was left, in size about five by seven and a half or eight inches. I noticed also a hole, a little more than one-fourth of an inch in diameter, in the door of box 7. It is larger on the outside than it is on the inside. The left side of the hole feels rough, as if cut by a gimlet, while the lower part on the right-hand side appears to have been trimmed with a penknife or some sharp instrument. The hole might, I think, have been made by a penknife, and the roughness might have been caused by the back of the knife.

G. W. BUNKER.
For the Defense.—June 2.

I am clerk at the National Hotel. The day after the assassination I packed Booth's effects at the National, and had his trunk removed into our baggage-room. In his trunk I found a gimlet with an iron handle.* I carried it to my room, and afterward gave it to Mr. Hall, who was attending to Mr. Ford's business.

John McCullough, who always made his home at the National, I find registered his name the last time on March 11; he left on the 26th of March.

---

* The gimlet would bore a hole three-sixteenths of an inch in diameter.

CHARLES A. BOIGI.
For the Defense.—June 2.
By MR. EWING.

I know the accused, Edward Spangler; he boarded at the house where I boarded. He boarded there five or six months, I presume, before the assassination, and I saw him at and about the house as usual for several days afterward. They had him once or twice in the station-house, I believe, before he was finally arrested; I do not recollect the date of his final arrest.

JOHN GOENTHER.
For the Defense.—June 2.
By MR. EWING.

I boarded in the same house with the accused, Edward Spangler, previous to his arrest. He boarded there on and off for six or seven months, perhaps longer. I have lived there off and on for the last three years. To my certain knowledge, I saw Spangler about the house for two or three days before the assassination; I never saw him wear a moustache.

Cross-examined by ASSISTANT JUDGE ADVOCATE BINGHAM.

I am not certain what days it was that I saw Spangler at the house. He did not sleep there. I used to see him in the morning, and of evenings when I came from work. I work in the arsenal, and generally take my dinner with me.

TESTIMONY

MRS. MARY E. SURRATT.

[See testimony of John M. Lloyd, page 85.]

LOUIS J. WEICHMANN

For the Prosecution.—May 13.

I have been clerk in the office of General Hoffman, Commissary-General of prisoners, since January 9, 1864.

My acquaintance with John H. Surratt commenced in the fall of 1859, at St. Charles College, Maryland. We left college together in the summer of 1862, and I renewed my acquaintance with him in January, 1863, in this city. On the 1st of November, 1864, I went to board at the house of his mother, Mrs. Surratt, the prisoner, No. 541 H Street, between Sixth and Seventh, and boarded there up to the time of the assassination.

On the 2d of April, Mrs. Surratt asked me to see J. Wilkes Booth, and say that she wished to see him on "private business." I conveyed the message, and Booth said he would come to the house in the evening, as soon as he could; and he came.

On the Tuesday previous to the Friday of the assassination, I was sent by Mrs. Surratt to the National Hotel to see Booth, for the purpose of getting his buggy. She wished me to drive her into the country on that day. Booth said that he had sold his buggy, but that he would give me $10 instead, that I might hire one. He gave me the $10, and I drove Mrs. Surratt to Surrattsville on that day, leaving this city about 9 and reaching Surrattsville about half-past 12 o'clock. We remained at Surrattsville half an hour, or probably not so long. Mrs. Surratt stated that she went there for the purpose of seeing Mr. Nothe, who owed her some money.

On Friday, the day of the assassination, I went to Howard's stable, about half-past 2 o'clock, having been sent there by Mrs. Surratt for the purpose of hiring a buggy. She herself gave me the money on that occasion, a ten-dollar note, and I paid $6 for the buggy. I drove her to Surrattsville the same day, arriving there about half-past 4. We

8

stopped at the house of Mr. Lloyd, who keeps a tavern there. Mrs. Surratt went into the parlor. I remained outside a portion of the time, and went into the bar-room a part of the time, until Mrs. Surratt sent for me. We left about half-past 6. Surrattsville is about a two-hours' drive to the city, and is about ten miles from the Navy Yard bridge.

Just before leaving the city, as I was going to the door, I saw Mr. Booth in the parlor, and Mrs. Surratt was speaking with him. They were alone. He did not remain in the parlor more than three or four minutes; and immediately after he left, Mrs. Surratt and I started.

I saw the prisoner, Atzerodt, at Howard's stable, when I went to hire the buggy that afternoon. I asked him what he wanted, and he said he was going to hire a horse, but Brook Stabler told him he could not have one.

I remember going with John H. Surratt to the Herndon House, about the 19th of March, for the purpose of renting a room. He inquired for Mrs. Mary Murray, who kept the house; and when she came, Surratt said that he wished to have a private interview with her. She did not seem to comprehend; when he said, "Perhaps Miss Anna Ward has spoken to you about this room. Did she not speak to you about engaging a room for a delicate gentleman, who was to have his meals sent up to his room?" Then Mrs. Murray recollected, and Mr. Surratt said he would like to have the room the following Monday, I think, the 27th of March, when the gentleman would take possession of it. No name was mentioned. I afterward heard that the prisoner, Payne, was at the Herndon House. One day I met Atzerodt on the street, and asked him where he was going. He said he was going to see Payne. I then asked, "Is it Payne who is at the Herndon House?" He said, "Yes." That was after the visit John H. Surratt had made to engage the room.

About the 17th of March last, a Mrs.

Slater came to Mrs. Surratt's house, and stopped there one night. This lady went to Canada and Richmond. On Saturday, the 23d of March, John Surratt drove her and Mrs. Surratt into the country in a buggy, leaving about 8 o'clock in the morning. He hired a two-horse team, white horses, from Howard's. Mrs. Surratt told me on her return that John had gone to Richmond with Mrs. Slater. Mrs. Slater, I understood, was to have met a man by the name of Howell, a blockade-runner; but he was captured on the 24th of March, so Surratt took her back to Richmond. Mrs. Slater, as I learned from Mrs. Surratt, was either a blockade-runner or a bearer of dispatches.

Surratt returned from Richmond on the 3d of April, the day the news of the fall of Richmond was received. I had some conversation with him about the fall of Richmond, and he seemed incredulous. He told me he did not believe it; that he had seen Benjamin and Davis in Richmond, and they had told him that Richmond would not be evacuated.

Surratt only remained in the house about an hour, when he told me he was going to Montreal, and asked me to walk down the street with him and take some oysters. He left that evening, saying he was going to Montreal, and I have not seen him since.

I saw about nine or eleven $20 gold pieces in his possession, and $50 in greenbacks, when he came back from Richmond; and just before leaving for Canada, he exchanged $40 of gold for $60 in greenbacks, with Mr. Holahan.

I afterward learned in Montreal that Surratt arrived there on the 6th of April, and left on the 12th for the States; returned on the 18th, and engaged rooms at the St. Lawrence Hall, and left again that night, and was seen to leave the house of a Mr. Porterfield, in company with three others, in a wagon. I arrived at Montreal on the 19th, and my knowledge was derived from the register of St. Lawrence Hall.

I saw a letter from John Surratt to his mother, dated St. Lawrence Hall, Montreal, April 12th, which was received here on the 14th; I also saw another letter from him in Canada to Miss Ward, but that was prior to the letter to his mother.

About the 15th of January last I was passing down Seventh Street, in company with John H. Surratt, and when opposite Odd Fellows' Hall, some one called "Surratt, Surratt;" and turning round, he recognized an old acquaintance of his, Dr. Samuel A. Mudd, of Charles County, Md.; the gentleman there [pointing to the accused, Samuel A. Mudd.] He and John Wilkes Booth were walking together. Surratt introduced Dr. Mudd to me, and Dr. Mudd introduced Booth to both of us. They were coming down Seventh Street, and we were going up. Booth invited us to his room at the Na-

tional Hotel. When we arrived there, he told us to be seated, and ordered cigars and wines for four. Dr. Mudd then went out into a passage and called Booth out, and had a private conversation with him. When they returned, Booth called Surratt, and all three went out together and had a private conversation, leaving me alone. I did not hear the conversation; I was seated on a lounge near the window. On returning to the room the last time Dr. Mudd apologized to me for his private conversation, and stated that Booth and he had some private business; that Booth wished to purchase his farm, but that he did not care about selling it, as Booth was not willing to give him enough. Booth also apologized, and stated to me that he wished to purchase Dr. Mudd's farm. Afterward they were seated round the center-table, when Booth took out an envelope, and on the back of it made marks with a pencil. I should not consider it writing, but from the motion of the pencil it was more like roads or lines.

After this interview at the National Hotel Booth called at Mrs. Surratt's frequently, generally asking for Mr. John H. Surratt, and in his absence for Mrs. Surratt. Their interviews were always apart from other persons. I have been in the parlor in company with Booth, when Booth has taken Surratt up stairs to engage in private conversation. Sometimes, when engaged in general conversation, Booth would say, "John, can you go up stairs and spare me a word?" They would then go up stairs and engage in private conversation, which would sometimes last two or three hours. The same thing would sometimes occur with Mrs. Surratt.

When I saw Booth at the National Hotel on the Tuesday previous to the assassination, to obtain his buggy for Mrs. Surratt, he spoke about the horses that he kept at Howard's stable, and I remarked, "Why, I thought they were Surratt's horses." He said, "No, they are mine."

John H. Surratt had stated to me that he had two horses, which he kept at Howard's stable, on G Street.

Some time in March last, I think, a man calling himself Wood came to Mrs. Surratt's and inquired for John H. Surratt. I went to the door and told him Mr. Surratt was not at home; he thereupon expressed a desire to see Mrs. Surratt, and I introduced him, having first asked his name. That is the man [pointing to Lewis Payne, one of the accused.] He stopped at the house all night. He had supper served up to him in my room; I took it to him from the kitchen. He brought no baggage; he had a black overcoat on, a black dress-coat, and gray pants. He remained till the next morning, leaving by the earliest train for Baltimore. About three weeks afterward he called again, and I again went to the door. I had forgotten his name, and, asking him, he gave the name of Payne.

I ushered him into the parlor, where were Mrs. Surratt, Miss Surratt, and Miss Honora Fitzpatrick. He remained three days that time. He represented himself as a Baptist preacher; and said that he had been in prison in Baltimore for about a week; that he had taken the oath of allegiance, and was now going to become a good and loyal citizen.

Mrs. Surratt and her family are Catholics. John H. Surratt is a Catholic, and was a student of divinity at the same college as myself. I heard no explanation given why a Baptist preacher should seek hospitality at Mrs. Surratt's; they only looked upon it as odd, and laughed at it. Mrs. Surratt herself remarked that he was a great looking Baptist preacher. In the course of conversation one of the young ladies called him "Wood." I then recollected that on his first visit he had given the name of Wood. On the last occasion he was dressed in a complete suit of gray; his baggage consisted of a linen coat and two linen shirts.

The only evidence of disguise or preparation for it, that I know of, was a false moustache, which I found on the table in my room one day. I put the moustache into a little toilet-box that was on my table. Payne afterward searched round the table and inquired for his moustache. I was sitting on a chair and did not say any thing. I retained the moustache, and it was found in my baggage that was seized.

On returning from my office one day, while Payne was there, I went up stairs to the third story and found Surratt and Payne seated on a bed, playing with bowie-knives. There were also two revolvers and four sets of new spurs.

[A spur, a large bowie-knife, and a revolver, found in Atzerodt's room at the Kirkwood House, were exhibited to the witness.]

That is one of the spurs. There were three spurs similar to that in a closet in my room when I was last there, and those three belonged to the eight that had been purchased by Surratt. The knives they were playing with were smaller than that knife. The revolvers they had were long navy revolvers, with octangular barrels; that has a round barrel.

I met the prisoner, David E. Herold, at Mrs. Surratt's, on one occasion; I also met him when we visited the theater when Booth played *Pescara;* and I met him at Mrs. Surratt's, in the country, in the spring of 1863, when I first made Mrs. Surratt's acquaintance. I met him again in the summer of 1864, at Piscataway Church. These are the only times, to my recollection, I ever met him. I do not know either of the prisoners, Arnold or O'Laughlin. I recognize the prisoner Atzerodt. He first came to Mrs. Surratt's house, as near as I can remember, about three weeks after I formed the acquaintance of Booth, and inquired for John H.

Surratt, or Mrs. Surratt, as he said. Since then he must have been at the house ten or fifteen times. The young ladies of the house, not comprehending the name that he gave, and understanding that he came from Port Tobacco, in the lower portion of Maryland, gave him the nickname of "Port Tobacco." I never saw him in the house with Booth.

At the time Booth played the part of *Pescara,* in the "Apostate," he gave Surratt two complimentary tickets, and as Surratt and I were going to the theater, we met Atzerodt at the corner of Seventh Street and Pennsylvania Avenue, and told him where we were going. He said he was going there too; and at the theater we met David E. Herold [pointing to the accused, David E. Herold, who smiled and nodded in recognition.] We also met Mr. Holahan, who boarded at Mrs. Surratt's.

After the play was over, all five of us left the theater together—Mr. Surratt, Holahan, and myself, in company. We went as far as the corner of Tenth and E Streets, when Surratt, turning round, noticed that Atzerodt and Herold were not following; and desired me to go back after them. When I went back, I found Atzerodt and Herold in the restaurant adjoining the theater, talking very confidentially with Booth. On my approach they separated, and Booth said, "Mr. Weichmann, will you not come and take a drink?" which I did. We then left the restaurant, and joined the other two gentlemen on E Street; went to Kloman's and had some oysters; after that we separated—Surratt, Holahan, and myself going home, and the others going down Seventh Street.

Cross-examined by HON. REVERDY JOHNSON.

When I went to board with Mrs. Surratt, in November, 1864, she rented her farm at Surrattsville to Mr. Lloyd, and removed to this city. Her house is on H Street, and contains eight rooms—six large and two small. Mrs. Surratt rented her rooms and furnished board. Persons were in the habit of coming from the country and stopping at her house. Mrs. Surratt was always very hospitable, and had a great many acquaintances, and they could remain as long as they chose. During the whole time I have known her, her character, as far as I could judge, was exemplary and lady-like in every particular; and her conduct, in a religious and moral sense, altogether exemplary. She was a member of the Catholic Church, and a regular attendant on its services. I generally accompanied her to church on Sunday. She went to her religious duties at least every two weeks, sometimes early in the morning and sometimes at late mass, and was apparently doing all her duties to God and man up to the time of the assassination. I visited Mrs. Surratt several times during '63 and '64, while she lived in the country. I made her acquaintance through her son, who had been a college-mate of mine for three years.

During the winter of 1864, John Surratt was frequently from home; in the month of November, especially, he was down in the country almost all the time. His stay at home was not at all permanent; sometimes he would be at home for half a week, and away the other half; sometimes he would be three or four weeks at a time in the country. I do not know of his being in Canada in the winter of '64–5, although he could have gone without my knowledge. I was upon very intimate terms with him, seeing him almost every day when he was at home; we sat at the same table, roomed together, and shared the same bed.

He never intimated to me, nor to any one else to my knowledge, that there was a purpose to assassinate the President. He stated to me, in the presence of his sister, shortly after he made the acquaintance of Booth, that he was going to Europe on a cotton speculation; that $3,000 had been advanced to him by an elderly gentleman, whose name he did not mention, residing somewhere in the neighborhood; that he would go to Liverpool, and remain there probably only two weeks to transact his business; then he would go to Nassau; from Nassau to Matamoras, Mexico, and find his brother Isaac, who had been in Magruder's army in Texas since 1861.

At another time he mentioned to me that he was going on the stage with Booth; that he was going to be an actor, and they were going to play in Richmond.

His character at St. Charles College, (Catholic,) Maryland, was excellent. On leaving college he shed tears; and the president, approaching him, told him not to weep; that his conduct had been so excellent during the three years he had been there, that he would always be remembered by those who had charge of the institution.

On the occasion of Mrs. Surratt's visit to Surrattsville, on the 11th of April, she told me she had business with Mr. Nothe; that he owed her a sum of money, $479, and the interest on it, for thirteen years. On arriving there, about half-past 12, she told Mr. Nott, the bar-keeper, to send a messenger immediately to Mr. Nothe. In the mean time, Mrs. Surratt and myself went to Captain Gwynn's place, three miles lower down, took dinner there, and remained about two hours. At Mrs. Surratt's desire, Captain Gwynn returned with us to Lloyd's. When we arrived there, Mr. Nott said that Mr. Nothe was in the parlor. They went in and transacted their business; but I did not go in, and did not see Mr. Nothe.

Mrs. Surratt's second visit to Surrattsville was on the afternoon of the 14th of April. She rapped at my room-door on that afternoon, and told me she had received a letter from Mr. Charles Calvert in regard to that

money that Mr. Nothe owed her, and that she was again compelled to go to Surrattsville, and asked me to take her down. Of course I consented. I did not see the letter. We took with us only two packages; one was a package of papers about her property at Surrattsville; and another package, done up in paper, about six inches, I should think, in diameter. It looked to me like perhaps two or three saucers wrapped up. This package was deposited in the bottom of the buggy, and taken out by Mrs. Surratt when we arrived at Surrattsville. We returned to Washington about half-past 8 or 9. About ten minutes after we got back, some one rang the front-door bell. It was answered by Mrs. Surratt, and I heard footsteps go into the parlor, immediately go out again, and down the steps. I was taking supper at the time.

I first heard of the assault on President Lincoln and the attack on Secretary Seward at 3 o'clock on Saturday morning, when the detectives came to the house and informed us of it.

The first time that Payne came to Mrs. Surratt's, when he gave the name of Wood, he had on a black coat; and when he went into the parlor he acted very politely. He asked Miss Surratt to play on the piano, and he raised the piano-cover, and did every thing which indicated a person of breeding. The moustache that I found upon my table was black, and of medium size; it was sufficiently large to entirely change the appearance of the wearer. When I found it I thought it rather queer that a Baptist preacher should use a moustache; I thought no honest person had any reason to wear one. I took it and locked it up, because I did not care to have a false moustache lying round on my table. I remember exhibiting it to some of the clerks in our office, and fooling with it the day afterward; I put on a pair of spectacles and the moustache, and was making fun of it.

Atzerodt, to my knowledge, stopped in the house only one night; he slept alone in the back room in the third story. John Surratt was out in the country; he returned that evening; and Atzerodt, who had, I understood, been waiting to see John, left the next day. I afterward heard Miss Anna and Mrs. Surratt say that they did not care about having him brought to the house. Miss Anna Surratt's expression was, she did n't care about having such sticks brought to the house; that they were not company for her.

John Surratt is about six feet high, with very prominent forehead, a very large nose, and sunken eyes; he has a goatee, and very long hair of a light color. The day he left for Montreal he wore cream-colored pants, gray frock-coat, gray vest, and a plaid shawl thrown over him.

When he returned from Richmond, he

had nine or eleven $20 gold pieces; he did not tell me from whom he got them, nor did I make any inquiries. I know he had no gold about him when he left for Richmond.

On the evening of the 14th, Mrs. Surratt showed me the letter she had received that day from John. It was a letter on general subjects. He said he was much pleased with the city of Montreal, and with the French cathedral there; that he had bought a French pea-jacket, for which he had paid $10 in silver; that board was too high at St. Lawrence Hall, $2.50 a day in gold, and that he would probably go to some private boarding-house, or that he would soon go to Toronto. The letter was signed "John Harrison," not his full name; his name is John Harrison Surratt.

By MR. EWING.

Dr. Mudd introduced Booth to John H. Surratt and myself about the 15th of January. I could fix the exact date, if reference could be had to the register of the Pennsylvania House, where Dr. Mudd had a room at the time. I am sure it was after the 1st of January, and before the 1st of February. It was immediately after the recess of Congress. The room that was occupied by Booth at the National Hotel had been previously occupied, so Booth said, by a member of Congress. Booth, I remember, walked round the room, put his hand on the shelf, and took down some Congressional documents, and remarked, "What a good read I shall have when I am left to myself." It was the first day of Booth's arrival in the city, and of his taking possession of the room, I understood. Most of the Congressmen had returned; Congress was in session at the time. When Booth and Dr. Mudd met Surratt and myself, on Seventh Street, Surratt first introduced Dr. Mudd to me, and then Dr. Mudd introduced Booth to both of us. Booth then invited us down to his room at the National Hotel. As we walked down Seventh Street, Mr. Surratt took Dr. Mudd's arm, and I walked with Booth. The conversation at the National lasted, I suppose, three-quarters of an hour. When Booth took the envelope out of his pocket, and with a pencil drew lines, as it were, on the back of this envelope, Mr. Surratt and Dr. Mudd were looking on. All the while he was doing it they were engaged in deep private conversation, which was scarcely audible. I was sitting about eight feet from them and could hear nothing of it. When Booth went out of the room with Dr. Mudd, they remained not more than five or eight minutes. They went into a dark passage, and I judge they remained there, as I heard no retreating footsteps, and they did not take their hats. Almost immediately after their return Surratt went out, and all three staid out about the same length of time as at the first interview.

After their return to the room, we remained probably twenty minutes; then left the National Hotel and went to the Pennsylvania House, where Dr. Mudd had rooms. We all went into the sitting-room, and Dr. Mudd came and sat down by me; and we talked about the war. He expressed the opinion that the war would soon come to an end, and spoke like a Union man. Booth was speaking to Surratt. At about half-past 10, Booth bade us good night, and went out: Surratt and I then bade Dr. Mudd good night. He said he was going to leave next morning. I had never seen Dr. Mudd before that day. I had heard the name of Mudd mentioned in Mrs. Surratt's house, but whether it was this Dr. Samuel Mudd I can not say. I have heard of Dr. George Mudd and Dr. Samuel Mudd.

By MR. STONE.

I first saw Herold in the summer of 1863, at Surrattsville, at a serenade there. A band had gone down from the city to serenade the officers who had been elected, and the band stopped at Mrs. Surratt's, on the way down, and serenaded us; on returning in the morning, they stopped and serenaded us again. Herold was with this party, and it was on this occasion that John Surratt introduced him to me.

By MR. CLAMPITT.

There was nothing in the conversation between Dr. Mudd, Booth, and Surratt, at the National Hotel, that led me to believe there was any thing like a conspiracy going on between them.

When Mrs. Surratt sent me to Booth, and he offered me the ten dollars, I thought at the time that it was nothing more than an act of friendship. I said to Booth, "I am come with an order for that buggy that Mrs. Surratt asked you for last evening." He said, "I have sold my buggy, but here are ten dollars, and you go and hire one." I never told Mrs. Surratt that.

Mrs. Surratt would sometimes leave the parlor on being asked by Booth to spare him a word. She would then go into the passage and talk with him. These conversations would not, generally, occupy more than five or eight minutes.

By MR. AIKEN.

On the 14th of April, when I drove Mrs. Surratt to Surrattsville, I wrote a letter for her to this man Nothe; it was, I remember, "Mr. Nothe: Sir—Unless you come forward and pay that bill at once, I will bring suit against you immediately." I also remember summing up the interest for her on the sum of $479 for thirteen years.

By MR. DOSTER.

Atzerodt has been frequently to Mrs. Surratt's house, and had interviews with John

H. Surratt in the parlor. I knew nothing of what took place between them. On the occasion of Payne's last visit to the house, Atzerodt came to see Surratt, and I saw Payne and Atzerodt together, talking in my room. I do not know of any conversation that passed between Atzerodt and Booth, or Atzerodt and Payne, having reference to a conspiracy.

Surratt was continually speaking about cotton speculations, and of going to Europe, and I heard Atzerodt once remark that he also was going to Europe, but he was going on horseback; from that remark I concluded he was going South.

At half-past 2 o'clock, on the afternoon of the 14th, I saw Atzerodt at the livery-stable, trying to get a horse. The stable-keeper, in my presence, refused to let him have one. I asked Atzerodt where he was going, and he said he was going to ride in the country, and he said he was going to get a horse and send for Payne. I met Atzerodt one day on Seventh Street, and asked him where he was going. He said he was going to see Payne. I asked him if it was Payne who was at the Herndon House. He said, "Yes." When Payne visited the Surratts, his business appeared to be with Mr. Surratt. On the occasion of his first visit, I was in the parlor during the whole time. I did not notice any other disguise than the false moustache spoken of, nor any thing else to show that Payne wanted to disguise himself. He appeared to be kindly treated by Mr. Surratt, as if he was an old acquaintance.

I do not know whether the Surratt family regarded him as a man in disguise or as a Baptist minister. One of the young ladies looked at him, and remarked that he was a queer-looking Baptist preacher, and that he would not convert many souls.

Recalled for the Prosecution.—May 18.

[A telegraphic dispatch was handed to the witness.]

I received this dispatch and delivered it to John H. Surratt on the same day. I can not say that I received it on the 23d of March, but it was after the 17th of March.

NEW YORK, March 23, 1865.

To Weichmann, Esq., 541 H *Street:*
Tell John to telegraph number and street at once. [Signed] J. BOOTH.

[The original of the above dispatch was offered in evidence:]

This is in Booth's handwriting. I have seen Booth's handwriting, and recognize his autograph. When I delivered the message to John Surratt, I asked him what particular number and street was meant, and he said, "Do n't be so damned inquisitive."

During Payne's second visit to Mrs. Surratt's house, some time after the 4th of March, I returned from my office one day at half-past 4 o'clock. I went to my room, and ringing the bell for Dan, the negro servant, told him

to bring me some water, and inquired at the same time where John had gone. He told me Massa John had left the front of the house, with six others, on horseback, about half-past 2 o'clock. On going down to dinner, I found Mrs. Surratt in the passage. She was weeping bitterly, and I endeavored to console her. She said, "John is gone away; go down to dinner, and make the best of your dinner you can." After dinner, I went to my room, sat down, commenced reading, and about half-past 6 o'clock Surratt came in very much excited—in fact, rushed into the room. He had a revolver in his hand—one of Sharpe's revolvers, a four-barrelled revolver, a small one, you could carry it in your vest-pocket. He appeared to be very much excited. I said, "John, what is the matter; why are you so much excited?" He replied, "I will shoot any one that comes into this room; my prospect is gone, my hopes are blighted; I want something to do; can you get me a clerkship?" In about ten minutes after, the prisoner, Payne, came into the room. He was also very much excited, and I noticed he had a pistol. About fifteen minutes afterward, Booth came into the room, and Booth was so excited that he walked around the room three or four times very frantically, and did not notice me. He had a whip in his hand. I spoke to him, and, recognizing me, he said, "I did not see you." The three then went up stairs into the back room, in the third story, and must have remained there about thirty minutes, when they left the house together. On Surratt's returning home, I asked him where he had left his friend Payne. He said, "Payne had gone to Baltimore." I asked him where Booth had gone; he said Booth had gone to New York. Some two weeks after, Surratt, when passing the post-office, inquired for a letter that was sent to him under the name of James Sturdey. I asked him why a letter was sent to him under a false name; he said he had particular reasons for it.

The letter was signed "Wood," and the substance of it was, that the writer was at the Revere House in New York, and was looking for something to do; that he would probably go to some boarding-house on West Grand Street, I think. This must have been before the 20th of March.

When I asked the negro servant to tell me who the seven men were that had gone out riding that afternoon, he said one was Massa John, and Booth, and Port Tobacco, and that man who was stopping at the house, whom I recognized as Payne. Though they were very much excited when they came into the room, they were very guarded indeed. Payne made no remark at all. Those excited remarks by Surratt were the only ones made.

Cross-examined by MR. AIKEN.

I did not hear the conversation that took place between Mrs. Surratt and Mr. Lloyd at Uniontown. Mrs. Surratt leaned sideways in the buggy, and whispered, as it were, in Mr. Lloyd's ear.

I have seen Mrs. Slater at Mrs. Surratt's house only once, though I understand she has been there twice. Mrs. Surratt told me that she came to the house with Mr. Howell; that she was a North Carolinian; I believe that she spoke French, and that she was a blockade-runner or bearer of dispatches. Mrs. Surratt said if she got into trouble there was no danger, because she could immediately apply to the French Consul, speaking French as she did. At the time I saw her, she drove up to the door in a buggy; there was a young man with her. Mrs. Surratt told me to go out and take her trunk. She wore a crape mask vail. That was some time in the month of February. When Howell was at Mrs. Surratt's, he gave the name of Spencer. They refused to tell me his right name, but I afterward learned from John Surratt that his name was Augustus Howell. His nickname in the house was Spencer. He was well acquainted with Mrs. Surratt. I was introduced to him, and had some conversation with him. I told him I would like to be South. I had been a student of divinity, and I was studying for the diocese of Richmond. I told him that I would like to be in Richmond for the purpose of continuing my theological studies.

By Mr. CLAMPITT.

Q. Why had you a greater desire to continue your studies in Richmond than the North?

Assistant Judge Advocate BINGHAM. I object to that question. It is wholly immaterial what reason he had.

Mr. CLAMPITT. It is important, and concerns the *res gestæ* of the case.

Assistant Judge Advocate BINGHAM. Supposing he should give an answer, how would you dispose of it?

Mr. CLAMPITT. By further testimony that we may adduce hereafter. It may be a connecting link.

Assistant Judge Advocate BINGHAM. You can not do it in that way. If you had asked him for his declarations, I could understand it; but this is an attempt to get at the interior motive of the witness, which you can not do, unless you can obtain the power of omnipotence.

The question was waived.

WITNESS. I spoke about Mr. Howell to Captain Gleason, a clerk in our office, and said to him, "There is a blockade-runner at Mrs. Surratt's; shall I have him delivered up?" I agitated the question with myself for three days, and decided in favor of Surratt; I thought it would be perhaps the only time the man would be there, and that I would let him go, in God's name.

By Mr. AIKEN.

While I was a clerk in the War Department, this man Howell taught me a cipher alphabet, and how to use it. He said nothing about its being a cipher used at Richmond, nor did he give it to me with any idea of corresponding in it; and the only use I ever made of it was to write out a poem of Longfellow's in it, which I showed to Mr. Cruikshank, a clerk in the War Department. He was in the habit of making puns and enigmas himself; and I told him I would give him an enigma which he could not make out. The cipher alphabet was in my box, and no doubt was found among my things when they were seized.

I read in the paper, the morning after the assassination, the description of the assassin of Secretary Seward; he was described as a man who wore a long gray coat, and I went to the stable on G Street and told Brook Stabler that I thought it was Atzerodt. I afterward met Mr. Holahan, and he also communicated similar suspicions to me, and after breakfast we gave ourselves up to Superintendent Richards, of the Metropolitan Police force. I told Officer McDevitt about Payne, and where he was stopping, and what I knew of Surratt, Atzerodt, and Herold. No threats were made in case I did not divulge what I knew, and no offers or inducements if I did. My only object was to assist the Government. I surrendered myself because I thought it was my duty. It was hard for me to do so, situated as I was with Mrs. Surratt and her family, but it was my duty, and so I have always regarded it since.

I can not say that any objection was ever made by any of the prisoners at the bar to my being present at any of their conversations, but they would withdraw themselves. When Booth would call, he would converse perhaps five or ten minutes, and then I noticed that John would tap or nudge Booth, or Booth would nudge Surratt; then they would go out of the parlor and stay up stairs for two or three hours. I never had a word of private conversation with them which I would not be willing to let the world hear. Their conversations, in my presence, were on general topics. I never learned any thing from the conversations of any of the prisoners at the bar of any intended treason or conspiracy. I would have been the last man in the world to suspect John Surratt, my school-mate, of the murder of the President of the United States. My suspicions were aroused by Payne and Booth coming to the house, and their frequent private conversations with John Surratt, and by seeing Payne and Surratt playing on the bed with bowie-knives, and again by finding a false moustache in my room; but my suspicions were not of a fixed or definite character. I did not know what they intended to do. I made a confidant of Captain Gleason in the War Department. I told him that Booth was a secesh sympathizer, and mentioned snatches of conversation I had heard from these parties; and I asked him, "Captain, what do you think of all this?" We even talked over several things which they could do. I asked him whether they could be bearers of dispatches or blockade-runners. I remember seeing in the New York Tribune, of March 19th, the capture of President Lincoln fully discussed, and I remarked to Captain Gleason, "Captain, do you think any party could attempt the capture of President Lincoln?" He laughed and hooted at the idea. This happened before the horseback ride of Surratt and the six others. I remarked to the Captain, the morning after they rode, that Surratt had come back, and I mentioned to Gleason the very expressions Surratt had used, and told him that, to all appearances, what they had been after had been a failure; and that I was glad, as I thought Surratt would be brought to a sense of his duty.

Q. How came you to connect the discussion which you read in the papers with any of these parties, and have your suspicions aroused against them?

Assistant Judge Advocate BINGHAM. I object to the question. It is no matter how the man's mental processes worked. We can not inquire into that.

Mr. AIKEN. It will be recollected that yesterday a witness was asked what his impressions were, and it was not objected to.

Assistant Judge Advocate BINGHAM. The question is now, how he came to form certain conclusions. We can not try a question of that sort. No court on earth could do it. It is a thing we can not understand, nor anybody else; and perhaps the witness himself would not now be able to state what controlled his mental operations at that time.

Mr. AIKEN. I insist on my question.

Assistant Judge Advocate BINGHAM. The witness has already gone on and told all he can tell, and given declarations; and now he is asked to state how he came to connect them with the newspaper article. Of what use is that to anybody? I object to it as a wholly immaterial and irrelevant question. No matter how the witness answers, it can throw no light on the subject, in favor of or against the prisoners.

Mr. AIKEN. But the Judge Advocate is aware that the witness did not tell all he wished to know in the examination in chief, and in his re-examination went into matter not brought out in the examination in chief, or in the cross-examination, which also was not objected to by us.

The Court sustained the objection.

WITNESS. I had been a companion of John H. Surratt's for seven years. I did not consider that I forfeited my friendship to him in mentioning my suspicions to Mr. Gleason; he forfeited his friendship to me by placing me in the position in which I now stand, testifying against him. I think I was more of a friend to him than he was to me. He knew that I permitted a blockade-runner at the house, without informing upon him, because I was his friend. But I hesitated about it for three days; still, when my suspicions of danger to the Government were aroused, I preferred the Government to John Surratt.

By MR. EWING.

The ride of the parties spoken of, I think, took place after my reading the article in the Tribune of March 19th. I also saw in the Republican, some time in February, that the assassination of President Lincoln was contemplated, and Surratt once made the remark to me that if he succeeded in his cotton speculation, his country would love him forever, and that his name would go down green to posterity.

I do not know what were his intentions, but he said he was going to engage in cotton speculations; he was going to engage in oil.

My remark to Captain Gleason about the possibility of the capture of the President was merely a casual remark. He laughed at the idea of such a thing in a city guarded as Washington was. It was the morning after the ride that I stated to Captain Gleason that Surratt's mysterious and incomprehensible business had failed; and I said, "Captain, let us think it over, and let us think of something that it could have been." I mentioned a variety of things—blockade-running, bearing dispatches; and we then thought of breaking open the Old Capitol Prison; but all those ideas vanished; we hit upon nothing. I will state that since that ride my suspicions were not so much aroused as before, because Payne has not been to the house since; and Atzerodt, to my knowledge, had not been to the house since the 2d of April. The only one that visited the house during that time was this man Booth.

Recalled for the Prosecution.—May 19.

[The accused, Lewis Payne, was here attired in the coat and vest in which he was arrested at the house of Mrs. Surratt.]

Payne wore that coat and vest the last time he came to Mrs. Surratt's, when he staid three days, on the 14th, 15th and 16th of March, and it was on the 16th that the party took that horseback ride. The next day after that I mentioned my suspicions to Captain Gleason. I had spoken to him previously, on various occasions, about this blockade-runner, and about Mrs. Slater, but I can not fix the precise date. I am enabled to fix the date of Payne's last visit to the house, from the fact that he went with John Surratt, Miss Fitzpatrick, and Miss Dean to see "Jane Shore" played at the theater. Forrest was playing there at that time, and Surratt had got a ten-dollar ticket. It was the next day that this horseback ride occurred.

A. R. REEVES.

For the Prosecution.—May 18.

I reside in Brooklyn, N. Y. I am a telegraphic operator.

[A telegraphic dispatch was handed to the witness.]

This is the original dispatch that was handed to me by John Wilkes Booth, at the St. Nicholas Hotel, New York, to be sent to Washington. It reads:

NEW YORK, March 23, 1865.

To Weichmann, Esq., 541 H Street:

Tell John to telegraph number and street at once. [Signed] J. BOOTH.

It was sent on the 23d. I remember Booth's signing "J. Booth," instead of John Wilkes Booth, knowing that to be his name; I noticed at the time that Wilkes was left out.

[A photograph of Booth was exhibited to the witness.]

This is the gentleman who handed the dispatch to me.

MISS HONORA FITZPATRICK.

For the Prosecution.—May 22.

I resided at the house of Mrs. Mary E. Surratt, the prisoner at the bar, last winter. During the month of March last, I saw John Wilkes Booth and John H. Surratt there, and of the prisoners, Mr. Wood, [pointing to the prisoner, Lewis Payne,] I do not know him by any other name, and Mr. Atzerodt [pointing to the accused, George A. Atzerodt.] I never saw David E. Herold there. I only saw Mr. Wood at Mrs. Surratt's twice; once was in March. Atzerodt was there but a short time; he staid over night once.

Some time in March, in company with Mr. Surratt, Wood, [Payne,] and Miss Dean, I went to Ford's Theater. I do not know what box we occupied, but think it was an upper box. John Wilkes Booth came into the box while we were there. The day after this visit to the theater I went to Baltimore, and was absent for about a week.

MRS. EMMA OFFUTT.

For the Prosecution.—May 17.

On Tuesday, the 11th of April, I was in the carriage with Mr. Lloyd, my brother-in-law. When somewhere about Uniontown we met Mrs. Surratt. Our carriage passed before we recognized that it was her, when Mr. Lloyd got out. Whether Mrs. Surratt called him I do not know. I did not hear their conversation, for I was some distance off.

On Friday, the 14th, I saw Mrs. Surratt at Mr. Lloyd's house. She came into the parlor. Mr. Lloyd had been to Marlboro that day, attending court; he had just returned, and had brought some oysters and fresh fish with him, and had driven round to the back part of the yard. Having occasion to go through to the back part of the house, she came with me, and I saw her and Mr. Lloyd conversing together in the back yard. I paid no attention at all to them, and could not tell a word that passed between them.

Cross-examined by MR. AIKEN.

When the two carriages passed at Uniontown, and Lloyd got out, it was misty and raining a little. The carriages were two or three yards apart, I suppose. I never looked out of the carriage at all after Mr. Lloyd left it, and Lloyd said nothing to me about his conversation with Mrs. Surratt.

Mrs. Surratt arrived at Mr. Lloyd's about 4 o'clock on the afternoon of the 14th. I had a conversation with her before Mr. Lloyd came in.

Q. Did you learn any thing of her business there that day?

Assistant Judge Advocate BINGHAM objected to the question. Statements of Mrs. Surratt, in the absence of Mr. Lloyd, were not admissible.

WITNESS. Mrs. Surratt gave me no charge in reference to her business, only concerning her farm, and she gave me no packages.

Q. During your visit to Mr. Lloyd's, did you ever hear any conversation there with reference to "shooting-irons?"

Assistant Judge Advocate BINGHAM objected to the question. The witness had already stated that she did not hear the conversation between Mr. Lloyd and Mrs. Surratt.

Mr. Aiken claimed the right to ask the question, in order to impeach the credibility of the previous witness, Lloyd.

The Commission sustained the objection.

MAJOR H. W. SMITH.

For the Prosecution.—May 19.

I was in charge of the party that took possession of Mrs. Surratt's house, 541 H Street, on the night of the 17th of April, and arrested Mrs. Surratt, Miss Surratt, Miss Fitzpatrick, and Miss Jenkins. When I went up the steps, and rang the bell of the house, Mrs. Surratt came to the window, and said, "Is that you, Mr. Kirby?" The reply was that it was not Mr. Kirby, and to open the door. She opened the door, and I asked, "Are you Mrs. Surratt?" She said, "I am the widow of John H. Surratt." And I added, "The mother of John H. Surratt, jr.?" She replied, "I am." I then said, "I come to arrest you and all in your house, and take you for examination to General Augur's head-quarters." No inquiry whatever was made as to the cause of the arrest. While we were there, Payne came to the house. I questioned him in regard to his occupation, and what business he had at the house that time of night. He stated that he was a laborer, and had come there to dig a gutter at the request of Mrs. Surratt. I went to the parlor door, and said, "Mrs. Surratt, will you step here a minute?" She came out, and I asked her, "Do you know this man, and did you hire him to come and dig a gutter for you?" She answered, raising her right hand, "Before God, sir, I do not know this man, and have never seen him, and I did not hire him to dig a gutter for me." Payne said nothing. I then placed him under arrest, and told him he was so suspicious a character that I should send him to Colonel Wells, at General Augur's headquarters, for further examination. Payne was standing in full view of Mrs. Surratt, and within three paces of her, when she denied knowing him.

Cross-examined by MR. AIKEN.

A variety of photographs were found in a photograph-album and in various parts of Mrs. Surratt's house.

Payne was dressed that night in a gray coat, black pantaloons, and rather a fine pair of boots. He had on his head a gray shirt-sleeve, hanging over at the side. His pantaloons were rolled up over the tops of his boots; on one leg only, I believe.

I have known some loyal people who have had in their possession photographs of the leaders of the rebellion. I can not say that I have seen on exhibition at bookstores, or advertised by newspaper dealers and keepers of photographs, cartes-de-visite of the leaders of the rebellion. I have seen photographs of Booth, but only since this trial.

Re-examined by the JUDGE ADVOCATE.

Payne was dressed at the time in a gray coat and black pantaloons.

[Exhibiting to the witness a brown and white mixed coat.]

That is the coat Payne wore, to the best of my belief.

By MR. DOSTER.

I am certain that this is the coat; I remember it by its color and general look. As near as I could judge by the light that was in the hall at the time, that was the coat.

[Submitting to the witness a dark-gray coat.]

The coat now shown me is the one worn by Payne on the night of his arrest. I recognize it by the buttons. All that was wanting in the other coat was the buttons, but it was difficult in the light in which I was standing to tell. The coat just shown me is the one.

[The gray coat was offered in evidence.]

By MR. AIKEN.

I think, if I saw a gentleman dressed in black, with a white neck-cloth, representing himself as a Baptist preacher, and two months afterward I met the same person, with a shirt-sleeve on his head, an old gray coat, his pantaloons stuffed into his boots, with a pickaxe on his shoulder, presenting himself as a laborer, and in the night-time, I think that, were I very familiar with his countenance, I should recognize him as the same person.

R. C. MORGAN.

For the Prosecution.—May 19.

On the night of the 17th of April, I was in the service of the War Department, acting under the orders of Colonel Olcott, special commissioner of that department. About twenty minutes past 11 o'clock, on the evening of the 17th of April, Colonel Olcott gave me instructions to go to the house of Mrs. Surratt, 541 H Street, and superintend the seizing of papers, and the arrest of the inmates of the house. I arrived there about half-past 11 o'clock, and found Major Smith, Captain Wermerskirch, and some other officers, who had been there about ten minutes. The inmates were in the parlor, about ready to leave.

I had sent out for a carriage to take the women arrested in the house to head-quarters, when I heard a knock and a ring at the door. At the same time Captain Wermerskirch and myself stepped forward and opened the door, when the prisoner, Payne, [pointing to Lewis Payne,] came in with a pickaxe over his shoulder, dressed in a gray coat, gray vest, black pants, and a hat made out of, I should judge, the sleeve of a shirt or the leg of a drawer. As soon as he came in, I immediately shut the door. Said he, "I guess I am mistaken." Said I, "Whom do you want to see?" "Mrs. Surratt," said he. "You are right; walk in." He took a seat, and I asked him what he came there at this time of night for. He said he came to dig a gutter; Mrs. Surratt had sent for him. I asked him when. He said, "In the morning." I asked him where he last worked. He said, "Sometimes on I Street." I asked him where he boarded. He said he had no boarding-house; he was a poor man, who got his living with the pick. I put my hand on the pick-axe while talking to him. Said I, "How much do you make a day?" "Sometimes nothing at all; sometimes a dollar; sometimes a dollar and a half." Said I, "Have you any money?" "Not a cent," he replied. I asked him why he came at this time of night to go to work. He said he simply called to find out what time he should go to work in the morning. I asked him if he had any previous acquaintance with Mrs. Surratt. He said, "No." Then I asked him why she selected him. He said she knew he was working around the neighborhood, and was a poor man, and came to him. I asked him how old he was. He said, "About twenty." I asked him where he was from. He said he was from Fauquier County, Virginia. Previous to this he pulled out an oath of allegiance, and on the oath of allegiance was, "Lewis Payne, Fauquier County, Virginia." I asked him if he was from the South. He said he was. I asked him when he left there. "Some time ago; in the month of February," I think he said. I asked him what he left for. He said he would have to go in the army, and he preferred earning his iving by the pickaxe. I asked him if he could read. He said, "No." I asked him if he could write. He said he could manage to write his name.

I then told him he would have to go up to the Provost Marshal's office and explain. He moved at that, but did not answer. The carriage had returned then that had taken off the women, and I ordered Thomas Samson and Mr. Rosch to take him up to the Provost Marshal's office. He was then taken up and searched. I then proceeded, with Major Smith and Captain Wermerskirch, to search through the house for papers, and remained there until 3 o'clock in the morning.

[A pickaxe was here exhibited to the witness.]

That is the pickaxe he had on his shoulder.

[It was then offered in evidence.]

When Payne knocked at the door, Mrs. Surratt and the inmates of the house were all in the parlor, prepared to leave. Mrs. Surratt had been directed to get the bonnets and shawls of the rest of the persons in the house, so that they could not communicate with each other

The next morning I went down to the house and found cartes-de-visite of Jefferson Davis, Beauregard, and Alexander H. Stephens; and Lieutenant Dempsey, the officer in charge, showed me a photograph of J. Wilkes Booth, that he had found behind a picture, which he turned over to the Provost Marshal.

[An envelope containing two photographs of General Beauregard, one of Jefferson Davis, one of Alexander H. Stephens, and a card with the arms of the State of Virginia and two Confederate flags emblazoned thereon, with the inscription

"Thus will it ever be with tyrants,
Virginia the Mighty,
Sic Semper Tyrannis."]

I found all these at the house of Mrs. Surratt.

Cross-examined by Mr. AIKEN.

I do not recollect having seen photographs of J. Wilkes Booth at book-stores before the assassination of the President; and I never had photographs of Jefferson Davis and other prominent leaders of the rebellion in my hand, until I had these, found at Mrs. Surratt's. I have not seen people with photographs of these men since the rebellion, though they might have had them before.

CAPTAIN W. M. WERMERSKIRCH.

For the Prosecution.—May 19.

On the night of the 17th of April I was at the house of Mrs. Surratt, in this city, and was present when the prisoner, Payne, came in, about midnight. Major Smith asked Mrs. Surratt whether she knew him, and Mrs. Surratt, in the presence of Payne, held up one or both her hands, and said, "Before God, I have never seen that man before. I have not hired him; I do not know any thing about him;" or words to that effect. The prisoner at the bar [pointing to Lewis Payne] is the man of whom I speak, and Mrs. Surratt [pointing to the prisoner, Mary E. Surratt] is the woman of whom I speak.

Cross-examined by Mr. AIKEN.

I made a search of Mrs. Surratt's house, and found a number of photographs, papers, a bullet-mold, and some percussion-caps. The bullet-mold and percussion-caps were found in the back room of the lower floor, which, I believe, was Mrs. Surratt's room.

I found cartes-de-visite, lithographic ones I think, but got up in the same shape as photographic cartes-de-visite, of Jefferson Davis, Alexander H. Stephens and Beauregard. I also saw a photograph of General McClellan there.

When Mrs. Surratt made the asseveration with regard to Payne, I was standing in the hall, very near the front parlor; she was in the parlor very near the hall-door, or standing in the door-way.

When Major Smith informed Mrs. Surratt that the carriage was ready to take her to the Provost Marshal's office, she requested a minute or so to kneel down and pray. She knelt down; whether she prayed or not I can not tell. Payne was dressed in a dark coat; pants that seemed to be black, and seemingly a shirt-sleeve, or the lower part of a pair of drawers, on his head, that made a very closely-fitting head-dress, hanging down about six or seven inches.

[The prisoner, Lewis Payne, by direction of the Judge Advocate, was then dressed in a dark-gray coat, and a shirt-sleeve for a head-dress.]

That is the coat he wore, and that is the way he had the head-dress on. I would not positively swear to the coat, but it is as near the color and shape of that coat as can be.

[The coat and shirt-sleeve were put in evidence.]

He was full of mud, up to his knees, nearly.

I have seen, in Baltimore, in booksellers, stores, pictures of Jefferson Davis, Alexander H. Stephens, etc., exhibited for sale; and I have seen photographs of Booth in the hands of persons, but only in the hands of those who took an interest in having him arrested. I do not remember seeing a photograph of him before the assassination.

If I had seen a person dressed genteelly in black clothes, with a white neckerchief, representing himself as a Baptist minister, I think I would recognise him in the garb Payne wore, for he had taken no particular pains to disguise himself; his face looked just the same as it does now, and the only difference was in the clothes.

By Mr. CLAMPITT.

The photographs were found all over the house—in the front parlor, in the back parlor, and in the two rooms up stairs. There were three albums containing photographs, besides loose pictures.

[A small framed colored lithograph, representing Morning, Noon, and Night, was exhibited to the witness.]

I saw this picture in Mrs. Surratt's house, in the back room of the lower floor, standing on the mantel-piece, I believe. I left it there, because I did not think any thing of it. This picture was all that was visible.

LIEUTENANT JOHN W. DEMPSEY.

For the Prosecution.—May 19.

[Exhibiting to the witness the picture Morn, Noon, and Night.]

I found this in the back room of the first floor of Mrs. Surratt's house. The back part was all sealed, and my curiosity was excited by noticing a piece torn off the back. I opened the back and found the likeness of J. Wilkes Booth, with the word "Booth" written in pencil on the back of it.

Cross-examined by MR. AIKEN.

I may have seen photographs of Davis, Lee, and other leaders of the rebellion in newspapers—the Sunday newspapers partic-ularly; and I have seen some of eminent actors—Forrest, Macready, and others—ex-posed for sale at different places. I was a prisoner for thirteen months, and during that time I saw a good many of the leaders of the rebellion, both personally and in pictures, but I have not seen them in the loyal states, except as I have mentioned.

Recalled for the Prosecution.—June 3.

[A photograph of J. Wilkes Booth, side view, was ex-hibited to the witness.]

This is the photograph I found at the back of the picture "Morn, Noon, and Night," which was found on the mantel-piece in the back room of the first floor, known, I believe, as Mrs. Surratt's room. It was marked, in pencil, "Booth." The pencil words, "J. Wilkes Booth," I wrote when I found it. I showed the photograph to an officer in the house, and then turned it over to Colonel Ingraham.

[The picture and photograph were put in evidence.]

DEFENSE OF MRS. MARY E. SURRATT.

GEORGE COTTINGHAM.

For the Defense.—May 25.

By MR. AIKEN.

I am special officer on Major O'Beirne's force, and was engaged in making arrests after the assassination. After the arrest of John M. Lloyd by my partner, Joshua A. Lloyd, he was placed in my charge at Roby's Post-office, Surrattsville. For two days after his arrest Mr. Lloyd denied knowing any thing about the assassination. I told him that I was perfectly satisfied he knew about it, and had a heavy load on his mind, and that the sooner he got rid of it the better. He then said to me, "O, my God, if I was to make a confession, they would murder me!" I asked, "Who would murder you?" He re-plied, "These parties that are in this con-spiracy." "Well," said I, "if you are afraid of being murdered, and let these fellows get out of it, that is your business, not mine." He seemed to be very much excited.

Lloyd stated to me that Mrs. Surratt had come down to his place on Friday between 4 and 5 o'clock; that she told him to have the fire-arms ready; that two men would call for them at 12 o'clock, and that two men did call; that Herold dismounted from his horse, went into Lloyd's tavern, and told him to go up and get those fire-arms. The fire-arms, he stated, were brought down; Herold took one, and Booth's carbine was carried out to him; but Booth said he could not carry his, it was as much as he could do to carry him-self, as his leg was broken. Then Booth told Lloyd, "I have murdered the President;" and Herold said, "I have fixed off Seward." He told me this when he came from Bryantown, on his way to Washington, with a squad of cavalry; I was in the house when he came in. He commenced crying and hallooing out, "O, Mrs. Surratt, that vile woman, she has ruined me! I am to be shot! I am to be shot!"

I asked Lloyd where Booth's carbine was; he told me it was up stairs in a little room, where Mrs. Surratt kept some bags. I went up into the room and hunted about, but could not find it. It was at last found behind the plastering of the wall. The carbine was in a bag, and had been suspended by a string tied round the muzzle of the carbine; the string had broken, and the carbine had fallen down. We did not find it where Lloyd told me it was. When Lloyd made these statements to me no one was present but Mr. Jenkins, a brother of Mrs. Surratt's. Lloyd said that Mrs. Surratt spoke about the fire-arms be-tween 4 and 5 o'clock on the day of the assassination.

At the last interview I had with him, when he came to the house to go to Washing-ton, he cried bitterly, and threw his hands over his wife's neck, and hallooed for his prayer-book. Lloyd's wife and Mrs. Offutt were in the room, and heard all the conver-sation.

Recalled for the Defense.—May 25.

By MR. AIKEN.

Q. Will you state the precise language that Lloyd used with reference to Mrs. Surratt in his confession to you?

The Judge Advocate objected to the repetition of the question. Mr. Aiken stated that he proposed to follow it up by asking the witness if he had not made a different statement to him (Mr. Aiken) in reference to what Lloyd had said. "I ask the witness now what I stated to him."

WITNESS. I met Mr. Aiken at the Metropolitan Hotel on Saturday evening last, I think. He asked me to take a drink. I went up and drank with him. He then said, "I am going to have you as a witness in this case." He asked me to sit down on a sofa and have some conversation. I said no; it would not look well for me to be sitting there, but I would go outside and take a walk. When we went outside, the first question Mr. Aiken put to me was, whether I was a Catholic. I said I was not. We walked along, and he said, "Lloyd has made a confession to you." Said I, "Yes." He then said, "Will you not state that confession to me?" I declined to do it, but told him he might ask any questions, and I would answer them. He put the question to me, if Lloyd had stated that Mrs. Surratt had come down there and told him to have the fire-arms ready. I said not. I had an object in that answer. I am now on my oath, and when on my oath I speak the truth, and I can have witnesses to prove what I say— six cavalrymen, Mr. Lloyd's wife, and Mrs. Offutt. He wanted to pick facts out of me in the case, but that is not my business; I am an officer, and I did not want to let him know any thing either way; I wanted to come here to the Court and state every thing that I knew. I told him distinctly that I would not give him that confession; that I had no right to do so.

Q. Did I ask you if Mr. Lloyd, in his confession, said any thing at all in reference to Mrs. Surratt?

A. You asked me first whether Lloyd had made a confession to me, and I said, "Yes." Said you, "What is that confession? I should like to know it." My answer to you was, "I decline giving you that confession; but if you will ask a question, I will answer you." That question you put to me, and I answered; I said "No."

Q. That Mr. Lloyd did not say so?

A. I did say so. I do not deny that.

Q. Then what did you tell me this afternoon with reference to it?

A. I told you the same thing over again in the witness-room, when you asked me, before I came up on the stand. It is a part of my business (I am a detective officer) to gain my object. I obtained the confession from Lloyd through strategy.

Q. Then you gave me to understand, and you are ready now to swear to it, that you told me a lie?

A. Undoubtedly I told you a lie there; for I thought you had no business to ask me.

Q. No business! As my witness, had I not a right to have the truth from you?

A. I told you you might call me into court; and I state here that I did lie to you; but when put on my oath I will tell the truth.

MRS. EMMA OFFUTT.

Recalled for the Defense.—June 13.

By MR. AIKEN.

On the evening of the 14th of April, Mr. Lloyd was very much in liquor, more so than I have ever seen him in my life. I insisted on his lying down, and I had to help him take off his coat. In a few minutes he got up and said he was too sick, and would go into the dining-room; but he went into the bar-room after that. For the last four or five months I have noticed his drinking free y.

I did not hear his full confession to Captain Cottingham; but I heard some remarks he made on the Sunday night when he was brought up from Bryantown, on his way to Washington. I was there all the time, and I did not hear him say, referring to Mrs. Surratt, "That vile woman, she has ruined me."

Mr. AIKEN. I wish to state to the Court that at the time Mrs. Offutt gave her testimony before, she came here very unwell. If I have been correctly informed, she had been suffering severely from sickness, and had taken considerable laudanum. Her mind was considerably confused at the time, and she now wishes to correct her testimony in an important particular.

WITNESS. After I left here the other day, I thought of my reply to a question that was asked me, and it has been on my mind ever since, and I requested Mr. Aiken to mention it to the Court.

I was asked by the Judge Advocate if Mrs. Surratt handed me a package, and I said "No;" but she did hand me a package, and said she was requested to leave it there. That was about half-past 5 o'clock, and before Mr. Lloyd came in. After that I saw the package lying on the sofa in the parlor. Shortly afterward Mr. Lloyd came in. When I saw Mrs. Surratt and Mr. Lloyd talking together at the buggy in the yard, I was in and out all the time. I did not see Mr. Lloyd go into the parlor, but I saw him on the piazza, and I think from that that he must have gone into the parlor. He had a package in his hand, but I did not see Mrs. Surratt give it to him. After the package was handed to me, it might have been taken by Mrs. Surratt and handed to Lloyd, but I did not see her give it to him.

I learned from Mrs. Surratt that she would

not have come down to Surrattsville that day, had it not been for the letter she received; and I saw business transacted while she was there.

Since January last I have met Mrs. Surratt several times. I never heard from her a word concerning any plot or conspiracy, and never heard any disloyal expressions from her.

I know that Mrs. Surratt's sight is defective. On one occasion, last December, she came down to see her mother, who was lying very sick. On being told by a servant that Mrs. Surratt was coming toward the door, I went there to her, and said, "Why, Mrs. Surratt!" When she said, "O, Mrs. Offutt, is that you?" and then she added, "I can scarcely see." I led her into the parlor, and she told me that her eyes were failing very fast.

GEORGE H. CALVERT.

For the Defense.—May 25.

By MR. AIKEN.

I reside in Bladensburg, and am acquainted with the prisoner, Mrs. Mary E. Surratt. On the 12th of April last I addressed a business letter to her. I addressed more than one to her, but the last was on the 12th of April.

[Mr. AIKEN called upon the Government to produce the letter, stating that he would suspend further examination of the witness till it could be produced.]

Recalled for the Defense.—May 26.

By MR. AIKEN.

[A letter was handed to the witness.

RIVERSDALE, April 12, 1865.
Mrs. M. E. Surratt:
DEAR MADAM—During a late visit to the lower portion of the county, I ascertained of the willingness of Mr. Nothey to settle with you, and desire to call your attention to the fact, in urging the settlement of the claim of my late father's estate. However unpleasant, I must insist upon closing up this matter, as it is imperative, in an early settlement of the estate, which is necessary.

You will, therefore, please inform me, at your earliest convenience, as to how and when you will be able to pay the balance remaining due on the land purchased by your late husband.

I am, dear madam, yours respectfully,
GEO. H. CALVERT, JR.

That is the letter I addressed to Mrs. Surratt on the 12th of April.

[The letter was read and offered in evidence.]

B. F. GWYNN.

For the Defense.—May 25.

By MR. AIKEN.

I reside in Prince George's County, near Surrattsville. I have been acquainted with Mrs. Surratt seven or eight years.

On Friday, the day of the murder of the President, as I was passing in my buggy, some one hailed me, and said Mrs. Surratt wanted to see me in the tavern. She gave me a letter for Mr. Nothey, and asked me to read it to him, which I did. I have transacted some business for her relative to the sale of lands her husband had sold to Mr. Nothey; and I have personal knowledge of Mr. Nothey buying land from Mrs. Surratt's late husband; I was privy to the transaction.

About half-past 4 on that day, the 14th, I parted with Mr. Lloyd on the road from Marlboro, about five miles from Surrattsville, and did not see him afterward. He had been drinking right smartly.

Recalled for the Defense.—May 26.

By MR. AIKEN.

[A letter was handed to the witness.]

This is the letter I carried to Mr. Nothey from Mrs. Surratt, and which I read to him on the 14th of April:

SURRATTSVILLE, MD., April 14, 1865.
Mr. John Nothey:
SIR—I have this day received a letter from Mr. Calvert, intimating that either you or your friend have represented to him that I am not willing to settle with you for the land.

You know that I am ready, and have been waiting for the last two years; and now, if you do not come within the next ten days, I will settle with Mr. Calvert, and bring suit against you immediately.

Mr. Calvert will give you a deed, on receiving payment.
M. E. SURRATT,
Administratrix of J. H. Surratt.

JOHN NOTHEY.

For the Defense.—May 26.

By MR. AIKEN.

I reside about fifteen miles from Washington, in Prince George's County. Some years ago I purchased seventy-five acres of land from Mr. John Surratt, sen. Mrs. Surratt sent me word that she wanted me to come to Surrattsville to settle for this piece of land. I owed her a part of the money on it. I met her there on Tuesday in regard to it. On Friday, the 14th of April, Mr. Gwynn brought me a letter from Mrs. Surratt, but I did not see her that day.

JOSEPH T. NOTT.

For the Defense.—May 30.

By Mr. AIKEN.

For the past two or three months I have been tending bar at Mr. Lloyd's tavern at Surrattsville.

On the 14th of April I saw Mr. Lloyd in the morning, and again at sundown. He had been to Marlboro on that day; and when he returned, he brought some fish and oysters, which he carried round to the kitchen in the back yard. For some weeks past Mr. Lloyd had been drinking a good deal; nearly every day, and night, too, he was pretty tight. At times he had the appearance of an insane man from drink. I saw him at the buggy in which Mrs. Surratt was, assisting in fixing it. He was pretty tight that evening.

By MR. CLAMPITT.

I first saw Mr. Lloyd that evening after his return from Marlboro, driving round to the kitchen. I was at the stable, and coming out I saw him going round there. Mr. Weichmann was there, and Captain Bennett F. Gwynn drove up in front of the bar-room.

Recalled for cross-examination.—June 2.

By ASSISTANT JUDGE ADVOCATE BURNETT.

I have never, to my knowledge, done or said any thing against the Government, or the Union party in Maryland, during this struggle. I have never taken sides with the secession element there, nor said any thing against the officers of the Government or the Executive.

I know Mr. Edward Smoot. I do not remember saying to him, after the murder of the President, on his stating that John H. Surratt was one of the murderers, that he was undoubtedly in New York by that time; I may or may not have said so; and I might have said, "John knows all about this matter;" but I do not recollect it; and I have no recollection whatever of saying that six months ago I could have told all about this matter; nor do I remember telling him not to mention any thing about the conversation I had had with him. I think if I had said so to Mr. Smoot, I should remember it, but I do not. Indeed, I do not recollect seeing Mr. Smoot.

By MR. AIKEN.

I may have seen Mr. Smoot on Saturday, the 15th of April last, but I have no recollection of it; nor of any such conversation with him.

By the COURT.

I do not think I rejoiced at the success of the rebels at the first battle of Bull Run. I belong to the Catholic Church when I belong to any Church at all. I have not belonged to any Church for seven years.

ANDREW KALLENBACH.
For the Defense.—June 13.

By MR. AIKEN.

I was present in the back room of Mr. Lloyd's house when he came from Bryantown, at the time of his arrest. I did not hear Lloyd say to Captain Cottingham, "Mrs. Surratt, that vile woman, she has ruined me."

Cross-examined by ASSISTANT JUDGE ADVOCATE BINGHAM.

The conversation began directly Mr. Lloyd came into the house, and lasted about five minutes. Mr. Lloyd, Mrs. Lloyd, and Mrs. Offutt were there. Lloyd told Cottingham that he was innocently persuaded into this matter by Mrs. Surratt, or Mrs. Surratt's family, I believe he said, but I will not say positively that he said by whom, or that Mrs. Surratt's name was mentioned in the conversation. Lloyd told Cottingham that the carbine was hid up stairs, and after Lloyd was gone Mr. Cottingham went up for it.

J. Z. JENKINS.
For the Defense.—May 30.

By MR. AIKEN.

I reside in Prince George's County, Maryland. I was at Mr. Lloyd's on the 14th, when Louis J. Weichman and Mrs. Surratt drove up to the house. Mrs. Surratt showed me a letter from George Calvert, also two judgments that Mr. Calvert obtained in the Circuit Court of our county against Mr. Surratt, sen. She said this letter brought her there, and I made out the interest on those judgments for her. She expressed no wish to see John M. Lloyd, and she was ready to start some time before he came, and was on the point of going when Lloyd drove up. Her business was with Captain Gwynn, and when he came in sight she went back and staid. Lloyd was very much intoxicated at the time.

My intercourse with Mrs. Surratt has been of an intimate character. She has never, to my knowledge, breathed a word that was disloyal toward the Government; nor have I ever heard her make any remark showing her to have knowledge of any plan or conspiracy to capture or assassinate the President or any member of the Government. I have known her frequently to give milk, tea, and such refreshments as she had in her house, to Union troops when they were passing. Sometimes she received pay for it; at other times she did not. I recollect when a large number of horses escaped from Giesboro, many of them were taken up and put on her premises. These horses were carefully kept and fed by her, and afterward all were given up. She received a receipt for giving them up, but never got any pay, to my knowledge.

I know that Mrs. Surratt's eyesight is defective. I have seen a man by the name of A. S. Howell stopping, I believe twice, at Mrs. Surratt's hotel. He was stopping there as other travelers do.

By MR. CLAMPITT.

I saw Mrs. Surratt, at Surrattsville, a few days before the assassination of the President.

Q. At that meeting did she not state to

you, when you asked for the news, that our army had captured General Lee's army and taken Richmond?

Assistant Judge Advocate BURNETT objected to the question as incompetent and irrelevant.

Mr. CLAMPITT stated that the object of the question was to show that the accused, Mary E. Surratt, had, a few days before the assassination, exhibited in her expressions a loyal feeling.

Assistant Judge Advocate BURNETT stated that the way to prove her character for loyalty was by bringing witnesses who knew her reputation in that respect, and not by bringing in her own declarations.

Mr. CLAMPITT waived the question.

Mrs. Surratt's reputation for loyalty was very good. I never heard it questioned, and I never heard her express any disloyal sentiments.

Cross-examined by ASSISTANT JUDGE ADVOCATE BINGHAM.

Mrs. Surratt is my sister. I live about a mile and a half this side of her place. I was arrested by the Government about ten days ago. About 10 or 11 o'clock the night before, I met a man by the name of Kallenbach, and another by the name of Cottingham. All that I said on that occasion, that I remember, was that my sister had fed his family (Kallenbach's); but I did not say that if Kallenbach or any one else testified against my sister, that I would send him to hell, or see that they were put out of the way, nor did I use any threats against him in case he appeared as a witness against Mrs. Surratt. What I did say was, that I understood he was a strong witness against my sister, which he ought to be, seeing that she had raised his family of children. I disremember calling him a liar during the conversation, and if there was any angry or excited conversation, I did not mean it any how. He said nothing to me about John H. Surratt going to Richmond with the full knowledge and consent of his mother. Mrs. Lloyd was there and heard our conversation, and so also was Mr. Cottingham.

On the 14th of April, when Mrs. Surratt was at Lloyd's, I saw Mr. Gwynn there, and perhaps from ten to fifteen others, during that time; among them, Kallenbach and Walter Edelin. I was there from between 2 and 3 o'clock until a little after sundown. I saw Mr. Surratt speaking to Mr. Gwynn in the parlor; Weichmann also was in the parlor, I think. Gwynn left the house before Mrs. Surratt.

I think that during the war my attitude toward the Government has been perfectly loyal. During the revolution, I have spent $3,000 in my district to hold it in the Union, and during the struggle I have taken no part

against the Government. I have been entirely on the side of the Government during the whole war, and never, by act or word, have I aided or abetted the rebellion, and never has the scrawl of a pen gone from me across to them, nor from them to me. I have never fed any of their soldiers, nor induced any soldiers to go into their army, nor aided and assisted them in any way.

Re-examined by MR. AIKEN.

I am under arrest, but I do not know what for. The commissioners of our county offered $2,000 for any information that could be given, leading to the arrest of any party connected with the assassination, which Mr. Cottingham claimed on account of having arrested John M. Lloyd, and he asked me if I would not see the State's Attorney and see whether he could get it or not.

When I said that Mr. Kallenbach ought to be a strong witness against my sister, on account of her bringing his children up, I spoke ironically.

J. Z. JENKINS.

Recalled for the Defense.—June 7.

By MR. AIKEN.

In 1861, about the time of the first Bull Run fight, I got a United States flag from Washington, which I and several of our Union neighbors raised. There came a report shortly after that it was going to be taken down by the secesh sympathizers. I went round the neighborhood and collected some twenty or thirty men with muskets, double-barreled guns, or whatever they had, and we lay all night round the flag to keep it up. I was there one night and a day, I think. At the time of the election, when they were all Democrats round there except myself, I used money, when I had n't it to spare and my family needed it, to get Union voters into Maryland. I remember bringing Richard Warner from the Navy Yard, Washington, to the polls. He had not been away long enough to lose his vote. I have never had any intercourse, one way or another, with the enemies of my country. At the election for Congress, in 1862, I was not allowed to vote; I was arrested on the morning of the election. I took the oath of allegiance at the time they were voting on the adoption of the new constitution, and voted that day. The last time I voted for member of Congress was for Harris; then, for the first time in my life, I voted the Democratic ticket. I have been an old-line Whig. I have suffered from the war in the loss of my negroes; but I never, to my recollection, made any complaint about that. When the State declared her new constitution, I was willing for them to go.

RICHARD SWEENEY.

For the Defense.—June 12.

By MR. AIKEN.

I met John M. Lloyd at Marlboro on the 14th of April last, and rode back with him part of the way toward his home. He was considerably under the influence of liquor, and he drank on the road.

By MR. CLAMPITT.

I am acquainted with J. Z. Jenkins, the brother of Mrs. Surratt. I have known him for ten years, and can speak confidently of his reputation as a loyal man. At the outset of those difficulties he was a zealous Union man. A Union flag was erected within one hundred yards of where I boarded, and there was a rumor that it was to be cut down, and Jenkins was one of the men who took a gun and remained there all night for the purpose of guarding the flag.

Cross-examined by the JUDGE ADVOCATE.

Lloyd returned from Marlboro to Surrattsville in his buggy; I was on horseback. We both drank; I do not know which drank the most; we drank from the same bottle. Lloyd was excited in his conversation and deportment generally; but he kept the road straight, and I did not see him deviate from it. It was six miles to Surrattsville from where we parted. I thought he could take care of himself.

Q. Have you been entirely loyal yourself during the rebellion?

A. I suppose so, and think so. I have never done any thing inimical to the interests of the Government, that I know of.

Q. Have you never desired the success of the rebellion?

A. No, sir; I never expressed any desire for its success.

Q. Have you always desired that the Government should succeed in putting down the rebellion?

A. I can not say but what my feelings were neutral in the matter.

Q. Are you quite sure they were neutral? It is very difficult to be neutral in such a war as this has been.

A. I think I was about as strictly neutral as anybody else.

Q. When you examine your feelings closely, if you can recall them, have you not an impression that at some time or other you preferred that the rebellion should succeed?

A. I may possibly have done so. I think I exercised a neutral feeling very nearly.

Q. You were neutral in your conduct?

A. And in my feelings—as strictly neutral, I think, as anybody else.

Q. You think you were perfectly indifferent whether the Government succeeded or failed.

A. I was.

9

JAMES LUSBY.

For the Defense.—June 2.

By MR. AIKEN.

I reside in Prince George's County, Md. I was at Marlboro on Good-Friday, the day that Mr. Lincoln was killed. Mr. Lloyd and I returned from Marlboro to Surrattsville together. He was very drunk on that occasion; I got there about a minute and a half, perhaps, before he did. I drove to the bar-room door, and he went round to the front door. I saw Mrs. Surratt just as she was about to start to go home. Her buggy was standing there at the gate, when we drove up, and she left in fifteen or twenty minutes after that.

Cross-examined by ASSISTANT JUDGE ADVOCATE BINGHAM.

When I got out of my wagon, I went into the bar-room to get a drink; and I do not know what took place in the mean time, when Lloyd went round the house. I am quite sure Lloyd was drunk. I had been quite smart in liquor in the course of the day before I met Lloyd, and then took drinks with Lloyd; but I do not think I was as tight as he; nor do I think I am altogether mistaken as to who was drunk that day. I did not see him take the fish out of his buggy. He did not drive into the yard; he drove to the front gate, I know; I did not see him go out. It is twelve miles from Marlboro to Surrattsville—about two and a half hours' drive. We drove along pretty brisk.

J. V. PILES.

For the Defense.—June 13.

By MR. AIKEN.

I live about ten miles from Washington, in Prince George's County, Md. I am personally acquainted with J. Z. Jenkins, and have known him ever since I was a little boy. I regarded him, formerly, as one of the most loyal men in that part of the country. I thought that he and I were two of the most loyal men there, at the beginning of the rebellion. A flag was raised, sent down, as I understood, by Mr. John Murphy, the butcher, who lived at the Navy Yard, Washington, about a month before the riots in Baltimore. A little while after, the news was spread, that a party from the Southern States, or from the lower counties of Maryland, were coming to cut it down. About twenty men were raised in our neighborhood, who armed themselves to protect the flag, and Mr. Jenkins, I believe, was among the number who staid with us that night. I have never heard a disloyal sentiment from Mr. Jenkins, nor do I know of any overt act on his part that might be construed into disloyalty; but I have not been in his company of late. About six months ago I hud some conversation with him, when he said he was as good a loyal man as I was. Whether he regarded me disloyal, and himself too, or whether he regarded us both loyal, I can not say.

Cross-examined by ASSISTANT JUDGE ADVOCATE BURNETT.

Since 1862 I have not heard any direct expression of opinion from him; but since his negroes have been taken from him, rumor says he is not quite so good a Union man as he was in the beginning. That is the general rumor.

J. C. THOMPSON.

For the Defense.—June 7.

By MR. AIKEN.

I live at Tee Bee, Prince George's County, Maryland. I have known J. Z. Jenkins since 1861, and have always considered him a loyal man.

Cross-examined by ASSISTANT JUDGE ADVOCATE BURNETT.

I do not know that I am a competent judge of loyalty; I have always considered myself loyal, and I think that such has been my reputation. I have never desired the success of the Southern rebellion, and have been all the time on the side of the Government.

DR. J. H. BLANDFORD.

For the Defense.—June 7.

By MR. AIKEN.

I am acquainted with J. Z. Jenkins, and have regarded him as loyal to the Government of the United States. I never heard him express any disloyal sentiments; and at the beginning of the war, he was generally avoided by those who were not thoroughly in favor of the administration. Mr. Jenkins, I know, supported the opposition candidates to the Democracy.

I know Andrew Kallenbach; he is a Democrat, and has always acted with the Democratic party.

WM. P. WOOD.

For the Defense.—June 5.

By MR. CLAMPITT

I am at present Superintendent of the Old Capitol Prison. I know J. Z. Jenkins, and have been intimately acquainted with him for five years. In 1860 and 1861, Mr. Jenkins was counted as one of the most reliable Union men in that district, and I know that up to 1862 he labored himself, and urged his friends to labor, and spent his means freely, to keep the State of Maryland in the Union. In 1862 and 1863, I understood that he came to this city to obtain voters who

had left the State of Maryland, but who had not lost their residence, to return to Maryland to vote the Union ticket.

I do not know of my own knowledge, but it was generally understood by those acting with the administration, that after the first battle of Bull Run, Mr. Jenkins procured a United States flag and hoisted it in his county, and that, when certain rebel sympathizers threatened to haul it down, he gathered a band of from twenty to fifty Union men, and stood by it all night to protect it. I believe Mr. Jenkins to be a loyal man. I never heard him utter any sentiments against the Government of the United States, but he is very bitter on the administration on account of the negroes. Outside of this, I believe him to be a truly loyal man. The people down there, who, in the early part of the war, acted with the administration, are now dissatisfied with it on account of its action on the subject of slavery, and there is scarcely a single friend of the administration in that county now.

I never heard him express any desire for the success of the South; but I have heard him express himself very positively the other way. Mr. Jenkins is now under arrest at the Old Capitol Prison, but I do not know what for.

Cross-examined by the JUDGE ADVOCATE.

Q. Do you not regard such bitter hostility to the Government, in a civil war like this, as in the interest of the public enemy, and therefore disloyal?

A. Lately I have not considered him sound on the subject, and have had very little to do with him, except on account of former friendship in past times. I thought then he was as loyal as any man in the county, and regarded him as such, and treated him as a friend; but at the last election he voted for Harris, and was in with these other parties, and I did not like that state of affairs, and hence had not that political confidence in him that I had previously.

MISS ANNA E. SURRATT.

For the Defense.—May 30.

By MR. AIKEN.

I was arrested on the 17th of April, and have since been confined at Carroll Prison.

I have met Atzerodt, the prisoner at the bar, at our house in Washington City. I do not think he remained over night but once. He called very often, and asked for that man Weichman. He was given to understand that he was not wanted at the house; ma said she did not care about having strangers there. The last time Atzerodt was there, Weichman engaged the room for him, and asked ma to allow him to stay there all night. They were sitting in the parlor, and made several signs over to each other. Weichman and he then left the room, and presently

Weichman came back and asked ma if she would have any objections to Atzerodt remaining there that night; that he did not feel at home at an hotel. After thinking for some time, ma said, "Well, Mr. Weichman, I have no objections." Mr. Weichman was a boarder at my mother's house, and was but too kindly treated there. It was my mother's habit to sit up for him at night, when he was out of the house; she would sit up and wait for him the same as for my brother.

Payne first came to our house one night after dark, and left very early the next morning. That was not long after Christmas. Some weeks afterward, he came one night when we were all in the parlor. Weichman went to the door and brought the gentleman in, and I recognized him as the one who had been there before under the name of Wood. I did not know him by the name of Payne at all. I went down stairs to tell ma that he was there. She was in the dining-room. She said she did not understand why strange persons should call there, but she supposed their object was to see my brother, and she would treat them politely, as she was always in the habit of treating every one. He called two or three times after that—perhaps the same week, or two weeks after—I can not say exactly. On this visit, as we were sitting in the parlor, he said, "Mrs. Surratt, if you have no objection, I will stay here to-night; I intend to leave in the morning." And I believe he did leave the next morning.

I have met John Wilkes Booth at our house. The last time he was there was on Friday, the 14th, I think; I did not see him; I heard he had been there.

My mother went to Surrattsville on the Friday of the assassination, and I think her carriage was at the door at the time Mr. Booth called. I heard some one come up the steps as the buggy was at the door, and ma was ready to start. Ma had been talking about going during the day, before Booth came, and perhaps the day before; she said she was obliged to go on some business in regard to some land. Mr. Booth only staid a very few minutes. He never staid long when he came.

[A picture, called "Morning, Noon, and Night," was exhibited to the witness.]

That picture belonged to me; it was given to me by that man Weichman, and I put a photograph of John Wilkes Booth behind it. I went with Miss Honora Fitzpatrick to a daguerrean gallery one day to get her picture; we saw some photographs of Mr. Booth there, and, being acquainted with him, we bought two and took them home. When my brother saw them, he told me to tear them up and throw them in the fire, and that, if I did not, he would take them from me. So I hid them. I owned photographs of Davis, Stephens, Beauregard, Stonewall Jackson, and perhaps a few other leaders of the rebel-

lion. My father gave them to me before his death, and I prize them on his account, if on nobody else's. I also had in the house photographs of Union Generals—of General McClellan, General Grant, and General Joe Hooker.

The last time I saw my brother was on Monday, the 3d of April; I have never seen him since. He may have been on friendly terms with J. Wilkes Booth. Mr. Booth called to see him sometimes. I never asked him what his friendship was to Booth. One day, when we were sitting in the parlor, Booth came up the steps, and my brother said he believed that man was crazy, and he wished he would attend to his own business and let him stay at home. He told me not to leave the parlor, but I did.

Assistant Judge Advocate BURNETT. Miss Surratt, you ought to be cautioned here, that the statements or conversations of Mr. Surratt, or Mr. Booth, or your mother, are not competent testimony. You should state simply what was done, and not give the statements of the parties; and the counsel ought not to ask for such statements.

Mr. AIKEN. [To witness.] In giving your evidence you will avoid giving statements that you heard your brother make, and the language he used. State only what you know, as far as your knowledge goes.

My brother was at St. Charles's College, near Ellicott Mills, Maryland, in 1861; but he was not a student of divinity. He was there, I think, three scholastic years, and spent his vacations, in August, at home. During the time he was not at home for vacation he was at college.

I never, on any occasion, heard a word breathed at my mother's house of any plot or conspiracy to assassinate the President of the United States; nor have I ever heard any remarks in reference to the assassination of any member of the Government; nor did I ever hear discussed, by any member of the family, at any time or place, any plan or conspiracy to capture the President of the United States.

My mother's eyesight is very bad, and she has often failed to recognize her friends. She has not been able to read or sew by gaslight for some time past. I have often plagued her about getting spectacles, and told her she was too young-looking to wear spectacles just yet; and she has replied that she could not read or see without them.

By MR. EWING.

My brother left college in 1861 or 1862, the year my father died. I was at school at Bryantown from 1854 until 1861; I left on the 16th of July. Surrattsville, where we formerly resided, is on the road between Washington and Bryantown.

I never saw Dr. Samuel Mudd in my mother's house in Washington.

Recalled for the Defense.—June 7.

By Mr. Aiken.

[Submitting to the witness the card containing the arms of the State of Virginia, with the motto "*Sic semper tyrannis.*"]

I recognize that card; it belongs to me, and was given me by a lady about two and a half years ago.

By Mr. Ewing.

We commenced moving from Surrattsville to the house on H Street about the 1st of October last; I went there myself about the first week in November. We have occupied no other house in Washington.

I have never seen Judson Jarboe at our house; he never visited the house at all. I have seen him pass in his buggy in the country, but I have never seen him to speak to him. I never saw Dr. Samuel Mudd at my mother's house in the city, nor heard of his being there.

Miss Honora Fitzpatrick,
For the Defense.—May 25.

By Mr. Aiken.

I boarded at the house of Mrs. Surratt, on H Street, from the 6th of October last till I was arrested. I met the prisoner Payne at breakfast one morning, I think in March or April last. I have seen him there twice; the last time was in March.

I know the prisoner, Atzerodt. I have seen him at Mrs. Surratt's, but I do not know in what month. He only stayed there a short time; I think Mrs. Surratt sent him away. I occupied the same room as Mrs. Surratt, and Miss Surratt slept in the same room for a time.

[The picture, "Morning, Noon, and Night," was exhibited to the witness.]

I know this picture; it belonged to Miss Surratt, and was kept on the mantle-piece, but I do not know of any photograph placed behind it. I bought a photograph of J. Wilkes Booth, and took it to Mrs. Surratt's house; Miss Anna Surratt also bought one. The last time I saw Mr. Booth at Mrs. Surratt's was on the Monday before the assassination. John Surratt had left a fortnight before, and I never saw him after.

I am acquainted with Louis J. Weichman; he was treated in Mrs. Surratt's house more like a son than a friend.

Mrs. Surratt has complained that she could not read or sew at night on account of her sight. I have known of her passing her friend, Mrs. Kirby, on the same side of the street, and not see her at all.

Cross-examined by the Judge Advocate.

The photographs of Stephens, Beauregard, and Davis did not belong to me.

Recalled for the Defense.—June 9.

By Mr. Aiken.

I was at communion with Mrs. Surratt on Thursday morning, the 13th of April. I was present at the time of Payne's arrest at Mrs. Surratt's house. I did not recognize him at the house, but I did at General Augur's office, when the skull-cap was taken off his head.

I know Mrs. Surratt's eyesight is defective; I have often threaded a needle for her when she has been sewing during the day, because she could not see to do it herself, and I have never known her to sew or read by gaslight. I never saw Judson Jarboe until I got acquainted with him at Carroll Prison. I never saw Dr. Samuel Mudd at Mrs. Surratt's house, and never heard his name mentioned there.

Cross-examined by Assistant Judge Advocate Burnett.

When we were at General Augur's headquarters, Mrs. Surratt was taken in another room. Payne was down behind the railing, in the room in which Miss Surratt, Miss Jenkins, and myself were. The only time that Mrs. Surratt was in the room with us was when Miss Surratt gave way to her feelings, because some one suggested that this man Payne was her brother, John H. Surratt. I do not remember that Mrs. or Miss Surratt said there that they had never seen that man before. Miss Surratt remarked that that ugly man was not her brother, and she thought whoever called him so was no gentleman. He had his cap off at that time. I did not hear her deny that she had ever seen him.

I do not remember whether the officers called Mrs. Surratt out to see Payne at the time of his arrest at the house; I remained in the parlor all the time.

Mrs. Eliza Holahan
For the Defense.—May 25.

By Mr. Aiken.

I boarded with Mrs. Surratt from the 7th of February until two days after the assassination. I know the prisoner at the bar who called himself "Wood," [Payne;] I saw him at Mrs. Surratt's in February, and the second time, I think, about the middle of March. He was introduced to me as Mr. Wood, but I never exchanged a word with him on either visit. I asked Miss Anna Surratt who he was, and she said he was a Mr. Wood, a Baptist minister. I said I did not think he would convert many souls; he did not look as if he would. He was there but one night on his first visit, and on the second, two or three days, I think; it was after the inauguration. I have seen the prisoner Atzerodt at Mrs. Surratt's, though I never heard of him by that name; he called himself, and the young ladies called him, " Port Tobacco." I saw him come in at times, and he dined there once or twice. I heard Mrs. Surratt say she objected to Mr. Atzerodt; she did not like him, and that she would rather he did not come there to board. I can not say that I was intimate with Mrs. Surratt; I liked her very much; she was a very kind lady to board with; but I was more intimate with her daughter than I was with her.

Q. In all the time you boarded in her house did you ever hear Mrs. Surratt say any thing with reference to the existence of a conspiracy to assassinate the President?

Assistant Judge Advocate BINGHAM objected to the question. The law so hedges about this matter of crime that those who are charged with it are never permitted to prove their own declarations in their own favor, because, if it were so, the greatest criminal that ever cursed the earth and disgraced our common humanity could make an abundant amount of testimony out of the mouth of the most truthful people living.

Mr. AIKEN replied, that if the witness had heard Mrs. Surratt make any remarks with reference to a conspiracy, and disclosed to her any knowledge of that fact, it would be valuable evidence on the part of the Government, and it would be just as valuable to the defense if she did not.

The question was waived.

I have seen John Wilkes Booth at Mrs. Surratt's three or four times. When he called, he spent most of his time in company with Mrs. Surratt, I believe; he would ask for Mr. John Surratt, as I understood; if he was not there, for Mrs. Surratt.

Mrs. Surratt's eyesight was defective. I never saw her read or sew after candlelight. I went to Church with Mrs. Surratt during Lent very often; she was very constant in her religious duties.

I have not seen John Surratt since early in March, when he was last at home.

GEORGE B. WOODS.

For the Defense.—May 25.

I reside in Boston. I have been in the habit of seeing, in Boston, photographs of the leaders of the rebellion exposed for sale, the same as Union celebrities.

Q. Have you not seen them in the possession of persons supposed to be loyal?

Assistant Judge Advocate BINGHAM objected to the question as immaterial.

Mr. AIKEN waived the question.

AUGUSTUS S. HOWELL.

For the Defense.—May 27.

My name is Augustus Howell. I first became acquainted with Mrs. Surratt and John H. Surratt about a year and a half ago, at Sur-

rattsville. I was present one evening, when she handed me a newspaper to read for her; and I called one evening at her house, about the 20th of February, and, although the gas was lit in the hall, she failed at first to recognize me

I met Louis J. Weichman once at Mrs Surratt's; I remained there two days or more. I had no particular business, and I went to Mrs. Surratt's because I knew them, and because it was cheaper than at a hotel.

When I saw Mr. Weichman I showed him a cipher, and how to use it. Weichman then made one himself.

[The cipher found among Booth's effects was exhibited to the witness.]

The cipher I showed to Mr. Weichman was the same as this.

Q. Did Mr. Weichman at that time give you any information in regard to the number of prisoners that we had on hand?

Assistant Judge Advocate BINGHAM objected to the question, inasmuch as Mr. Weichman was never asked any question in relation to that matter in his cross-examination.

The question was waived.

I had some conversation with Mr. Weichman with respect to his going South; he said he would like to go South, or intended to go South.

Q. Did he say any thing, in connection with his wishes to go South, of his sympathies?

Assistant Judge Advocate BINGHAM objected to the question, inasmuch as Mr. Weichman had not been asked, on his cross-examination, whether he had stated any thing to Mr. Howell about his sympathies at that time and place.

The question was waived.

Mr. Weichman said he would like to go South with me, but he was not ready, he said, to go at that time; but as soon as he got his business arranged he was going. He asked me if I thought he could get a position in Richmond; I told him I did not know whether he could or not, as the wounded and invalid soldiers generally had the preference in the offices there by an order of the War Department. He told me that his sympathies were with the South, and that he thought it would ultimately succeed. I believe he said he had done all he could for that Government—referring to the South. We had some conversation in regard to the number of prisoners on hand, and he stated to me the number of Confederate prisoners the United States Government had on hand, and the number they had over that of the Confederate Government. I doubted it at the time, but he said it could not admit of doubt; that he had the books in his own office to look at.

In that conversation, I think, Mr. Weichman said he had done all he could for the South; he expressed himself as a friend of the South, as a Southern man or a secesh sympathizer would.

Cross-examined by ASSISTANT JUDGE ADVOCATE
BURNETT.

Before the war, I resided principally in
Prince George's County, Md.; for about two
years, off and on, I have lived in King
George County, Va.

Q What has been your business for the
last year and a half?

Mr. AIKEN. I object to the question. In
the examination in chief, the witness was
asked nothing at, all with reference to his
business, one way or the other. I do not
object to his stating it, if he wishes to do so,
but I do not think it is relevant.

Assistant Judge Advocate BURNETT. The
Court has the right to know the status of the
witness. We have a right to know whether
his employment was loyal or disloyal, and
whether that fact was known to the family
of Surratts. It is always competent to give
to the Court the full status of the witness
during the time about which he testifies. It
is but the ordinary course of cross-examination.

General WALLACE. I should like to hear
the reason of the objection.

Mr. AIKEN. It is objected to, first, because
no question was asked the witness in the examination in chief, in reference to what his
business has been; and, secondly, because it
is entirely irrelevant to the issue now before
us, in every way and shape.

The Commission overruled the objection.

Mr. AIKEN. I now object to the witness
answering the question. He is not obliged
to do so, if his answer will tend in any way to
criminate himself as to any thing in which
he has been engaged; and if he does not
wish to answer the question, he has the privilege not to do it.

Assistant Judge Advocate BURNETT. If it
is placed on the ground of personal security,
if the witness claims that privilege at the
hands of the Court, he can make that claim,
and I will not press that portion of the question. [To the witness.] It is your right, and
I apprise you of it now, to claim protection at
the hands of the Court against any matter
that will criminate yourself.

WITNESS. I have had no particular occupation since I came out of the Confederate
army. I was in the First Maryland Artillery
of the Confederate service, during the first
year of the war, up to July, 1862, I believe.
Since then I have not been employed in any
particular business. I have been to Richmond occasionally. Sometimes I went once
a month, sometimes once in two or three
months. I do not think I have been but
twice the last year. I was there in December, and again in February, I think. Some
one might have gone with me in December,
but I do not remember who it was. In February, some half dozen accompanied me, but
they were principally from the neighborhood
in the county. I had no particular business

in Richmond but to see some friends, and to
get some drafts. Our Maryland boys generally sold drafts, and I used to go down
to Richmond occasionally to buy drafts for
them.

Q On whom did you buy drafts?

A. That would be implicating others, and
I do not wish to answer that question.
Any thing relative to myself I will answer
willingly.

Assistant Judge Advocate BURNETT. Protection on the stand only applies to yourself,
not to others.

WITNESS. They were upon some of my
friends in Maryland. They were not upon
any of the accused, or any person in Washington. I never carried any dispatches in
my life.

I have been at Richmond about half a
dozen times since I have known the Surratts.
I can not say that I was known to my
friends as a blockade-runner.

My name is Augustus Howell; that is my
correct name. I generally write my name
A. S. Howell. "S" stands for Spencer. My
friends call me Spencer, but I seldom use
the "S" in my name.

The cipher I showed to Weichmann I
learned out of a magician's book. I have
been acquainted with it for six or seven
years.

I never met a person by the name of Mrs.
Slater at Mrs. Surratt's house. I met a lady
by that name in Washington, about the 20th
or 22d of February, and had some convar-
sation with her in front of Mrs. Surratt's house.
We went to Virginia together. John H. Surratt was with her in the buggy. I met Mrs.
Slater in Richmond about the last of February. It was soon after I saw her in front
of Mrs. Surratt's house, that I met her in
Richmond.

I staid about two days and a half at Mrs.
Surratt's in February. I told them that I
had been to Richmond. I do not know that
they knew my business. I had some conversation with Mrs. Surratt, and judged she
knew I was from Richmond. I think Atzerodt was at Mrs. Surratt's house during the
time I was there, but I never saw Payne.

I used to meet Dr. Mudd occasionally,
when I was at Bryantown. He never sent
messages by me to Richmond, nor did I
bring any back to him. I was at his house
about a year ago, but never made it a stop-
ping-place. I had lost a pistol which I left
at a house in Bryantown, and I asked him
to go there and get it for me, but he did not.
I was going up into the country, and did not
miss the pistol until I was passing Dr. Mudd's
place. It was because his house was the
nearest that I went in and asked him to get
it for me.

I brought one draft from Richmond, from
young Marriott, in Prince George's County,
Maryland, for his sister, of $200, and for which
I paid at the rate of $300 of Confederate for

$100 of United States money. Another from young Tolson, which I have not yet collected, and another from a young man by the name of Chew, on his brother in Anne Arundel County.

I do not know any thing of Weichman's having quarreled with the Surratt family, because he was loyal and they were disloyal, nor did I know that it was his intention to glean from me all I knew for the purpose of turning me over to the military authorities; if so, he did not succeed. I never took the oath of allegiance to the United States.

By Mr. Ewing.

I frequently saw Dr. Mudd at Bryantown before the war. I have never had any communication with him, except in regard to that pistol.*

Miss Anna Ward.

For the Defense.—June 3.

By Mr. Aiken.

I reside at the Female [Catholic] School, on Tenth Street, Washington. I have been acquainted with Mrs. Surratt between six and eight years. I know Mrs. Surratt's eyesight to be defective; she has failed to recognize me on the street. On one occasion, at her house, I gave her a letter to read, and she handed it back, saying she could not see to read by gaslight. I am near-sighted myself. On one occasion something was pointed out to me, and I was laughed at for not seeing it, as it was pretty close by, and Mrs. Surratt remarked that she supposed I was something like herself; I could not see; and that she labored under the same difficulty.

I have not been very intimate with Mrs. Surratt. She always bore the character of a perfect lady and a Christian, as far as my acquaintance with her extended.

Cross-examined by Assistant Judge Advocate Bingham.

My last visit to Mrs. Surratt's house was on the day of the assassination. Some time in February or March, perhaps, I went to the Herndon House to ask if there was a vacant room. I did not engage a room; I simply went there to ask if there was a vacant room. I said nothing about its being for a delicate gentleman, for I did not known for whom it was intended. I have met Mr. Weichman, Mr. Holahan, and Mr. Booth at Mrs. Surratt's, but do not know that I ever met any of the prisoners at the bar there. I can not see them well enough to know them, but do not think I have.

I received two letters from John H. Surratt, post-marked Montreal, C. E., for his mother. I do not recollect the date of the first I received; it was probably one or two days before the second, and that I received on the day of the assassination; it was that which took me to Mrs. Surratt's on that day. He inclosed them in letters to me. I answered his letters to me, and left them with his mother, as I supposed she would be glad to hear from him. I have not seen them since.

Rev. B. F. Wiget.

For the Defense.—May 25.

By Mr. Aiken.

I am President of the Gonzaga College, F Street, between Ninth and Tenth. It is about ten or eleven years since I became acquainted with Mrs. Mary E. Surratt. I knew her well, and I have always heard every one speak very highly of her character as a lady and as a Christian. During all this acquaintance, nothing has ever come to my knowledge respecting her character that could be called unchristian.

Q. Is there an institution in the city of Richmond for theological studies?

Assistant Judge Advocate Bingham. I object to that question as wholly immaterial. What is the necessity of inquiring into that? You might as well ask whether it was an octagon or not; whether it was two stories or forty stories high. If immaterial questions were allowed to be asked and answers obtained, and the witnesses contradicted, the case would never end, if the Court lived to be as old as Methusalah, provided a succession of counsel could be obtained to keep up the fire. Wharton's American Criminal Law, p. 434, section 817, says: "The credit of a witness may be impeached by proof that he has made statements out of court contrary to what he has testified at the trial. But it is only in such matters as are relevant to the issue that the witness can be contradicted. Therefore, a witness can not be examined as to any distinct collateral fact irrelevant to the issue for the purpose of impeaching his testimony afterward by contradicting his statements."

Mr. Aiken said he would recall the recollection of the learned Assistant Judge Advocate to the fact that the answer of Mr. Weichman was on the record that he was a student of divinity, and that he desired to go to Richmond to continue his studies there. Mr. Weichman was interrogated as to these points, and the foundation was thus laid for impeaching his credibility as a witness. These questions to the witness now on the stand (which I have a right to put) are for that very purpose.

General Wallace. The witness Weichman did not state that there was a theological academy, or any thing of that kind, in Richmond.

Mr. Aiken. He said that he belonged to that diocese, and wanted to go to that diocese to finish his studies.

The Judge Advocate. He said nothing about a theological school there. He said he

---

* We can not present the contradictions and prevarications of this witness without occupying many pages. In each case we give his last statements, many of them flatly contradicting those made a few moments before.

wished to go there for the purpose of continuing his theological studies.

Mr. AIKEN. The inference was, if he was going to complete his theological studies, that there was a school there.

Assistant Judge Advocate BINGHAM. You do not propose to contradict inferences I suppose?

The Commission sustained the objection.

Cross-examined by the JUDGE ADVOCATE.

I have a personal knowledge of her general character as a Christian, but not of her character for loyalty. My visits were all short, and political affairs were never discussed; I was not her pastor. I first became acquainted with Mrs. Surratt from having had two of her sons with me. I have seen her perhaps once in six weeks. I can not say I remember hearing her utter a loyal sentiment since the beginning of the rebellion; nor do I remember hearing any one talk about her as being notoriously disloyal before her arrest.

REV. FRANCIS E. BOYLE.
For the Defense.—May 25.
By MR. AIKEN.

I am a Catholic priest. My residence is at St. Peter's Church. I made the acquaintance of Mrs. Mary E. Surratt eight or nine years ago, and have met her perhaps three or four times since. I have heard her always well spoken of as an estimable lady, and never heard any thing to her disadvantage. I have never heard her utter any disloyal sentiments.

Cross-examined by the JUDGE ADVOCATE.

I have never heard much of her sentiments, and do not undertake to say what her reputation for loyalty is.

REV. CHARLES H. STONESTREET.
For the Defense.—May 25.
By MR. AIKEN.

I am the pastor of St. Aloysius Church in this city. I first became acquainted with Mrs. Mary E. Surratt twenty years ago. I have only occasionally seen her since. During the last year or two, I have scarcely seen her. I have always looked upon her as a proper Christian matron. At the time of my acquaintance with her, there was no question of her loyalty.

Cross-examined by the JUDGE ADVOCATE.

I do not remember having seen Mrs. Surratt, though I may have done so transiently, since the commencement of the rebellion; and of her character for loyalty since then I know nothing but what I have read in the papers.

REV. PETER LANIHAN.
For the Defense.—May 25.
By MR. AIKEN.

I am a Catholic priest, and reside near Beantown, St. Charles County, Maryland. I have been acquainted with Mrs. Mary E. Surratt, the prisoner at the bar, for about thirteen years; intimately so for about nine years. In my estimation, she is a good Christian woman, and highly honorable. I never heard her on any occasion express disloyal sentiments.

Cross-examined by ASSISTANT JUDGE ADVOCATE BINGHAM.

Mrs. Surratt's character in her neighborhood is that of a good Christian woman. I have conversed with her since the rebellion in regard to current events and public affairs, and do not remember having heard any expression of disloyal sentiments, and I have been very familiar with her, staying at her house. I do not remember having heard her reputation for loyalty spoken of.

REV. N. D. YOUNG.
For the Defense.—May 26.
By MR. AIKEN.

I am a Catholic priest; I reside at the pastoral house of St. Dominick's Church, on the Island, on Sixth Street, in Washington City. I became acquainted with Mrs. Mary E. Surratt about eight or ten years ago. My acquaintance has not been intimate. I have occasionally seen her and visited her. I had to pass her house about once a month, and generally called there—sometimes staid an hour. Her reputation, as far as I have heard, is that of a Christian lady, in every sense of the word. I have heard her spoken of with the greatest praise, and never heard any thing of her but what was highly favorable to her character. She never expressed any disloyal sentiments to me.

Cross-examined by the JUDGE ADVOCATE.

I never heard her speak upon current events in any manner, loyal or disloyal.

WILLIAM L. HOYLE.
For the Defense.—May 26.
By MR. AIKEN.

I reside on Missouri Avenue, Washington. I am not particularly acquainted with Mrs. Surratt. I have a store acquaintance only; I know nothing of her, and have heard nothing against her. I never heard her express any disloyal sentiments; I never had any political conversation with her.

I know John H. Surratt by sight. I last saw him in this city about the end of February or the beginning of March. Just prior to the draft I saw him in the store. In appearance he is rather delicate looking; tall, about six feet in hight, of light complexion, and about twenty-two or twenty-three years of age. I think he had neither goatee nor moustache when I saw him, though I will not be positive.

Cross-examined by ASSISTANT JUDGE ADVOCATE BINGHAM.

I never heard Mrs. Surratt utter any political sentiment, loyal or disloyal; it was only as a customer that I knew her.

JOHN T. HOXTON.
For the Defense.—June 13.
By MR. AIKEN.

I have resided in Prince George's County, Maryland, about a mile from Surrattsville, for the last forty-five or fifty years. I have known Mrs. Mary E. Surratt for a number of years, but mostly since she came to reside in our neighborhood, about ten or twelve years ago. Since the rebellion I have not met her very frequently. Of late years I have gone from home but little; I have not visited her house often, and when there I have staid but a short time. I never had any conversation with her on political subjects. Her reputation in the neighborhood, as a truthful, Christian, kind lady, is very good, I believe. I never heard any thing to the contrary.

I am very well acquainted with J. Z. Jenkins. He was a good Union man up to 1862, I think. At the election of that year he was arrested, and since then I have understood that he had secession proclivities. I believe that he once assisted in defending the Union flag with arms in his hands. Mr. Jenkins was a good Union man two years ago, but I have known very little of him since that time. The report in the neighborhood is, that he is not at this time a very loyal man. I have never known of Mr. Jenkins committing a disloyal act, nor have I heard from him an expression unfriendly to the Government, during the past two years.

I know the Rev. W. A. Evans. There is so Presbyterian Church in Prince George's County that I know of. I can not exactly say what is the reputation of Mr. Evans in that neighborhood for veracity. Mr. Evans was impeached some years ago.

Assistant Judge Advocate BINGHAM. You need not state that.

Q. From your knowledge of his character and his reputation, would you believe him on oath where any of his interests were involved?

Assistant Judge Advocate BINGHAM objected to the question. The witness should first state whether he knew the general reputation of Mr. Evans for truth among his neighbors.

Q. Are you acquainted with the reputation

of the Rev. Mr. Evans in your community—in your neighborhood?

A. No, except by rumor.

By ASSISTANT JUDGE ADVOCATE BINGHAM.

Q. In Evans's neighborhood?

A. Evans kept school in the neighborhood where I live, some ten or twelve years ago.

Q. The question is as to his reputation now.

A. I know nothing of his reputation now.

By MR. AIKEN.

Q. Has his reputation in his neighborhood, and where he has taught school, been notoriously bad?

Assistant Judge Advocate BINGHAM. I object to any such question. The witness has disclosed the fact that he does not know what the present reputation of Mr. Evans among his own neighbors for truth and veracity is. The law, in its humanity and in its justice, has said that no man called into a court as a witness shall be put upon trial for every act of his life; the question is as to his general reputation at the time he appears as a witness. Now it is proposed to go back ten years. It is supposed in law that in ten years a man can live down a slander.

The question was waived.

[See testimony of Rev. W. A. Evans, page 174.]

WILLIAM W. HOXTON.
For the Defense.—June 13.
By MR. AIKEN.

I reside about a mile from Surrattsville, in Prince George's County, Md. I have known Mrs. Surratt, the prisoner at the bar, for about twelve years. She has always been looked upon as a very kind lady—to the sick especially—and a church-going woman. I have seen her very often during the last four or five years, and never heard her utter a disloyal word.

I am acquainted with J. Z. Jenkins; he lives about a mile and a half from me. He was the strongest Union man I ever saw when the war broke out; but I have heard that he changed when he lost his negroes, though I never heard him say any thing disloyal when he lost them, and I have never heard of any disloyal or overt act of his against the Government.

RACHEL SEMUS (colored.)
For the Defense.—June 13.
By MR. AIKEN.

I have lived at Mrs. Surratt's house for six years; was hired to her by Mr. Wildman. She treated her servants very well all the time I was with her; I never had reason to complain. I remember Mrs. Surratt has fed Union soldiers at her house, sometimes a good many of them; and I know that she always tried to do the best for them that she could, because I always cooked for them

She always gave them the best she had, and very often she would give them all she had in the house, because so many of them came. I recollect her cutting up the last ham she had in the house, and she had not any more until she sent to the city. I never knew of her taking any pay for it. I never heard her express herself in favor of the South; if she used such expressions, I did not hear them. Her eyesight has been failing for a long time; very often I have had to go up stairs and thread her needle for her because she could not see to do it; I have had to stop washing to go up and thread it for her in the day-time. I remember one day telling her that Father Lanihan was at the front gate, coming to the house, and she said, "No, it was not him, it was little Johnny"—meaning her son.

DAVID C. REED.

Recalled for the Defense.—June 3.

By Mr. AIKEN.

The last time I saw John H. Surratt was about half-past 2 o'clock on the day of the assassination, the 14th of April last. I was standing on the stoop of Hunt & Goodwin's military store, and Mr. Surratt was going past the National Hotel. I noticed his hair was cut very singularly, rounding away down on his coat-collar. I did not notice whether he had whiskers or moustache, as I was more attracted by the clothing he had on. His appearance was very genteel, remarkably so. He did not look like a person just from a long journey; his clothing was clean, and remarkably nice and genteel. I can not say that I have had any connection with Mr. Surratt since he was quite a child; I knew him by sight, and we had just a bowing or speaking acquaintance as we passed each other.

Cross-examined by ASSISTANT JUDGE ADVOCATE BINGHAM.

[A recent and large-sized photograph of John H. Surratt was handed to the witness.]

This is a fair picture of John H. Surratt; the only thing I notice is that his hair is not cut as I noticed his on the 14th of April, but the shape of the coat, the style in which it is cut, is precisely the same.

By Mr. AIKEN

If that picture had been shown to me without being told it was the picture of Mr. Surratt, I do not know that I should recognize it, if I saw it hanging in a window; but if I looked at it and examined it, I should recognize it as John H. Surratt. It is a remarkable face.

TESTIMONY IN REBUTTAL.

JOHN RYAN.

For the Prosecution.—June 7.

I have known Louis J. Weichman about a year, not perhaps intimately, but he has been quite friendly and communicative in his conversation with me. As far as my knowledge goes, he has always borne a good character as a moral young man, and I know nothing against his character for truth. I do not believe he would tell a falsehood, and I would believe him whether under oath or not. As regards his loyalty, I only remember one conversation that distinctly bore on that question, and from that conversation my impression was that he rejoiced at the restoration of the Union. I have no recollection of his ever expressing sentiments that left a contrary impression on my mind.

Cross-examined by Mr. AIKEN.

I was not a visiting friend of Mr. Weichman; our meetings were casual. I am a clerk in the War Department, but in a different department to Mr. Weichman's. He never represented himself to me as being in confidential relations to that department as

a detective. I have never heard any thing said against his character relative to money matters, veracity, or any thing of that kind

FRANK STITH.

For the Prosecution.—June 7.

I have known Louis J. Weichman intimately for about sixteen months. His reputation as an honest, truthful man is very good indeed, as far as I have heard. I have never heard it questioned. We were both in the public service, in the same office. His reputation for loyalty was excellent, and he was open and outspoken in his friendship for the Government. He was a member of the volunteer military organization formed for the defense of this city.

Cross-examined by Mr. AIKEN.

My relations to Mr. Weichman, outside of the office, were not very intimate. I never heard of his being a detective in the department. It might have been considered that a refusal to join that military organization would be equivalent to a dismissal from the office. Mr. Weichman did not always wear blue pantaloons about the office. I can not say that he only wore his blue pantaloons on drill and rainy days, or that he made use of hateful expressions on putting them on, and immediately retired to change them for his citizen's dress when drill was over.

JAMES P. YOUNG.

For the Prosecution.—June 7.

I am in General Meig's office in the War Department. I am intimately acquainted with Louis J. Weichman; have known him since 1856. I was a college class-mate of his at the Philadelphia High School; we both entered it in 1856. He remained at that college for two or three years, then left and went to Maryland to another college. I frequently heard from him, and about eighteen months ago I met him in this city, and have been very intimate with him since. His reputation as an honest and truthful man is excellent, and his character without any reproach whatever. I have had many conversations with him on political matters, and he was always most free and unequivocal in his expressions of loyalty to the Government. I regard him as a very radical, loyal man. Both he and I are members of the Union League.

Cross-examined by MR. AIKEN.

I have never known him as a detective in the employ of the Government.

P. T. RANSFORD.

For the Prosecution.—June 7.

I have known Louis J. Weichman since last September. I am a clerk in the War Department, and he was a clerk in another branch of the War Department; he has visited me at my own rooms. His reputation for integrity and truth I have always regarded as being very good indeed. I have had very little conversation with him about political matters, and am not competent to give an opinion as to his loyalty.

Cross-examined by MR. AIKEN.

Mr. Weichman and myself belonged to the same military organization, called the War Department Rifles. A refusal to become a member of that organization I understood to be equivalent to a dismissal from office. I have simply met Mr. Weichman as a friend.

JOHN T. HOLAHAN.

For the Prosecution.—June 7.

During the winter and spring, and up to the night of the assassination, I boarded with Mrs. Surratt. While there, I saw Atzerodt several times, though I did not know him by that name; he seemed to be with John Surratt most of the time. I also saw Payne there once at breakfast. The name by which I knew him was Wood. John Wilkes Booth, I have seen there frequently. I have seen him in the parlor with Mrs. Surratt and the young ladies. I never knew the prisoner, David E. Herold, to call there. I remember, about two weeks before the assassination, seeing a carriage at Mrs. Surratt's door, and a person, whom I afterward learned to be Mrs. Slater, got into it one morning as I was dressing. Mrs. Surratt was on the pavement talking to this person as she was getting into the carriage. John Surratt was with this Mrs. Slater. This was the last time I saw John Surratt previous to the 3d of April. The last time I saw him was on the night of the 3d of April, the day on which the news of the fall of Richmond was received. He knocked at the door of my room at about 10 o'clock, after I was in bed, and wished me to exchange some gold for greenbacks; and I gave him $60 in paper for $40 in gold. He said he wanted to go to New York, and that he could not get it exchanged in time to leave by the early train in the morning.

I never knew any thing of Mrs. Surratt's defective eyesight while I lived with her; I do not remember its being alluded to by any member of the household.

Cross-examined by MR. AIKEN.

Atzerodt passed by a nickname when he was at Mrs. Surratt's. I was usually from home in the evening, and therefore can not say whether Mrs. Surratt could read or sew by gaslight. I never heard any political conversation at Mrs. Surratt's, and never heard of any plot to capture the President, or of any plot or conspiracy to assassinate the President, or any members of his cabinet; if I had, I should have endeavored to prevent it.

By MR. EWING.

MR. EWING. I have two or three questions to ask the witness. It is not properly a cross-examination; but I propose to treat him as my witness, if there is no objection.

Assistant Judge Advocate BURNETT. The gentleman announces that he desires to ask some questions, making the witness his own; as we shall be entitled to rebut, there is no objection.

I never saw or knew of Mr. Judson Jarboe, or of any person by the name of Jarboe coming to Mrs. Surratt's, nor have I ever known of Dr. Mudd coming there; I never heard his name mentioned.

Mrs. Surratt's house is on the south side of H Street, about forty-five feet from Sixth Street. It is the first house from the corner of Sixth Street; a brick house, painted drab or lead color, with a basement and a flight of eight or ten steps up to the front door.

Q. Will you state whether Mr. Weichman gave himself up after the assassination of the President?

Assistant Judge Advocate BURNETT. You need not state that.

MR. EWING. My inquiry in regard to Mr. Weichman is for the purpose of proving acts in regard to him in association with Booth and other men connected with the conspiracy. I want to show by his acts at that time that he was really a guilty party in the plot to kill the President. If I show that he was, and that instead of being indicted he appears here turning State's evidence, it will tend very much, I think, to impair the value of his testimony. It is not the ordinary form of impeachment of a witness by laying the foundation in his examination for contradicting his statements upon the stand. That is not the purpose, but it is to show that he occupied the position of a co-conspirator, and that he comes here clearing himself by being a swift witness against others.

Assistant Judge Advocate BINGHAM. What the gentleman calls the act of Weichman never can be proved by any human being but by Weichman himself. He has testified that he was taken into custody. Nobody doubts it. He has testified that he was in custody when he was brought on the stand. Nobody questions it. It is utterly incompetent for the gentleman to prove any thing he said about that matter, until he has first laid the foundation by a cross-examination of Weichman, and then it is never competent, except by way of contradiction. There is no such foundation laid, and it is therefore incompetent and illegal at any stage of the case, either now or any other day.

The Commission sustained the objection.

I saw Mr. Weichman the morning after the murder; he was a good deal excited. About 2 o'clock on that morning, Mr. McDevitt and Mr. Clarvoe, detectives of the Metropolitan Police, entered Mrs. Surratt's house. Mr. Weichman opened the door for them. These officers were in the passage when my wife woke me up. Whether Mr. Weichman was in bed or dressed when the officers called, I do not know. I slept in the front room, and he in the back room on the same floor.

Q. Was Weichman then arrested?
A. I took Weichman down myself to Superintendent Richards.

Q. When?
A. In the morning, after breakfast.

Q. When you took him down, did you know he was to be arrested?

Assistant Judge Advocate BINGHAM objected to the question, and it was waived.

Q. How did you come to take him down?
A. From an expression he made to me.

Assistant Judge Advocate BINGHAM. You need not state any thing he said.

Q. Was that expression the expression of a wish to be delivered up?
A. No, sir.

Assistant Judge Advocate BINGHAM. You need not state any thing about his expressions.

By Assistant Judge Advocate BURNETT.

The excitement on account of the assassination was very general throughout the city. It was some weeks after Mrs. Slater had been there that Mrs. Surratt told me the team in which John Surratt and Mrs. Slater went away was a hired one, and that John was then down in the country. When Mr. Howell was at Mrs. Surratt's, it might have been about the 1st of March; he remained, I think, three or four days.

JAMES McDEVITT.

For the Prosecution.—June 7.

On the night of the assassination, I went to Mrs. Surratt's house with Mr. Clarvoe, and several other officers of the department. We rang the bell, when a lady put her head out of the window and asked who was there. We said we wished to enter the house. As she retired, Mr. Weichman opened the door; he was in his shirt, which was all open in front; he had his pants on, and was, I think, in his stocking feet. He appeared as if he had just got out of bed. He had time from the moment we rang to dress himself to that extent. We did not arrest Mr. Weichman then, but we did subsequently when he came to our office. Mr. Weichman accompanied me to Canada; I took him to identify John H. Surratt. He went with me willingly in pursuit of the assassins, and was zealous and earnest in performing the part allotted him in the pursuit; and though he had every opportunity to escape, he did not. I left him in Canada when I returned to New York. I could not state, from my own knowledge of John Surratt's writing, that the entry on the register of the St. Lawrence Hall is his.

Cross-examined by MR. AIKEN.

Mr. Weichman came to our office the morning after the assassination, with Mr. Holahan. Weichman made no confession in regard to himself. We did not find John H. Surratt in Canada. I saw that he was registered on the books of the St. Lawrence Hall as "John Harrison, Washington, D. C.," on the 6th of April, and again by the same name on the 18th of April, but without any city or State address. I received the first intimation that John H. Surratt would be likely to be found in Canada from Mr. Weichman. Mrs. Surratt also told me, on the morning after the assassination, that she had received a letter from him on the 14th, dated in Canada. We were inquiring for her son, when she said she had not seen him for two weeks, and that there was a letter somewhere in the house, which she had received from him that day. I asked her for the letter, but it could not be found.

ANDREW KALLENBACH.

For the Prosecution.—June 7.

I reside near Surrattsville, Prince George's County, Maryland. On the evening of the 17th of April last, I had a conversation with Mr. J. Z. Jenkins, at Mr. Lloyd's house at Surrattsville. He said that I was a liar; that he understood I had been telling some lies on him, and if he found it to be true, he would give me the damnedest whipping I ever had. He further said that if I testified against him, or any one connected with him, he would give me a damned whipping. This was said in the presence of Mr. Cottingham and Mr. Joshua Lloyd. Jenkins had been drinking, but I can not say that he was drunk on the occasion. I have known Mr. Jenkins about ten years, I think. He has always said in my presence that he was a Union man; and I have never heard him express any disloyal sentiments. I can not say what his reputation for loyalty is in the neighborhood.

Cross-examined by MR. AIKEN.

Nothing had been said by me that night to induce Jenkins to call me a liar. I have a son in the rebel army; he went there of his own choice, and without my consent. He returned about three weeks ago. I judge he has been in the rebel army during the war. I did not place any restrictions in the way of his going.

I have lived as a neighbor of Mrs. Surratt's for many years. She had never been more than neighborly with me and my family, nor has she given things to my family more than any neighbor will do for another. In politics I have been a Democrat all my life. I have never expressed any disloyal sentiments, and have never said that I wished the South would succeed.

E. L. SMOOT.

For the Prosecution.—June 2.

I live in Prince George's County, Maryland, about a mile from Surrattsville. I am acquainted with J. Z. Jenkins of Surrattsville, Mrs. Surratt's brother. He was represented as a Union man during the first year of the war, but after that, by most persons, he was looked upon as a Southern sympathizer; I know of no exception to this among the Union men. I never heard his reputation for loyalty talked of much, but I have heard him say, I think, he was a friend to the South, and an enemy to the Government during the struggle.

I know Joseph T. Nott, of Surrattsville. On the day after the President's murder, I met two young men connected with General Augur's head-quarters, one of whom told me that John H. Surratt was supposed to be the man who attempted to kill Mr. Seward. I asked Mr. Nott if he could tell me where John Surratt was; he smiled and told me

he reckoned John was in New York by that time. I asked him why he thought so, and he said, "My God! John knows all about the murder; do you suppose he is going to stay in Washington and let them catch him?" I pretended to be very much surprised and said, "Is that so?" He replied, "It is so, by God! I could have told you that this thing was coming to pass six months ago." Then he put his hand on my shoulder and said, "Keep that in your own skin, my boy. Don't mention that; if you do, it will ruin me forever." The Mr. Nott who said this is the Joseph T. Nott who testified here to-day. I have heard him speak against the Government frequently, and denounce the administration in every manner and form; I heard him say that, if the South did not succeed, he did not want to live another day.

Cross-examined by MR. AIKEN.

I have a brother-in-law named William Ward, who was in the Southern army; he was brought home under a guard of soldiers. I did not, on the occasion of his return, tell him that he had done just right, and that I wished I had been there to help him. I did not express opposition to his coming back in any way, nor did I express sentiments against the Government and friendly to the South. I begged my brother-in-law to take the oath and remain at home.

At the breaking out of the rebellion, I resided in Charles County, and was a member of Captain Cox's military company, which was organized before the war. It disbanded in the spring of 1861. I withdrew from it as soon as a rebel flag was brought and presented to it.

I have known Mr. Jenkins for about five years, I think. I do not exactly recollect when I had any political conversation with him. The last time I talked with him was about the 1st of April last, at Upper Marlboro. He came to me and told me that Roby was applying for the position of constable in the county, and asked me why I did not apply for it. I told him I did not wish it. He said, "You ought to take it to keep Roby from getting it;" and he added that he had told the County Commissioners that if they appointed Mr. Roby, or any other man of his party, he would spend every dollar he had to defeat them, if they became candidates for any other office.

I did not vote at the last Congressional election; I did not know any thing about either of the candidates. I have not been an active Union man. I have not meddled either way. The conversation with Mr. Nott occurred in the bar-room at Surrattsville, on the 15th of April. It was all the conversation we had at that time. He did not state what time he last saw John Surratt, nor what reason he had to believe him to be connected with the affair. Some gentlemen came in while he was talking with me, and he had to wait on the bar. On the next day, Sunday, I communicated this remark verbally to General Augur, Colonel Baker, and Colonel Wells. Mr. Nott did not inform me how he knew John Surratt was connected with it, and I did not ask him. He only said he could have told me six months ago that this thing was going to happen. I never knew Mr. Jenkins to do any thing disloyal, but he has denounced the administration frequently when talking with me. I do not recollect particularly to what he referred. I have heard many do the same so frequently, that I do not recollect what Mr. Jenkins said on any particular occasion. I never heard any man whom I regarded as a loyal man denounce the administration.

A. V. ROBY.

For the Prosecution.—June 2.

I reside close to Surrattsville, Prince George's County, Maryland. Since June 12, 1863, I have been enrolling officer. I have known J. Z. Jenkins since 1861, but not very intimately till 1863. Mr. Jenkins's reputation in that neighborhood, during the year 1861, was that of a Union man; but since that time he has been looked upon as a sympathizer with the South. Since 1862 he has been in the attitude of an enemy to the Government, and has opposed all its measures. Mr. Jenkins took the oath prescribed by the Legislature of Maryland, and then voted.

Cross-examined by MR. AIKEN.

The first time I saw Mr. Jenkins was when he came to the armory of Captain Mark's company, in Washington, of which I was a member. Some time between April and July of 1861 he came there begging for money for some Union man who had been killed. The next time I saw him was at my house, when he was opposing the nominees of the Union party. Dr. Bayne was a candidate for Senator; Mr. Sasser was candidate for Clerk of the County, and Mr. Grimes for Sheriff. I think Mr. John M. Brook was the disunion candidate for Senator; I do not know that Mr. Brook has been in the rebel army; I know that he was South, and staid until he came home under the President's Amnesty Proclamation.

I have been living near Surrattsville since September, 1863. I have seen Mr. Jenkins nearly every day. All this time Mr. Jenkins has been talking against the Government. At the April election, in 1864, when we voted for a convention to make a new constitution, he said he had been offered office under the damned Government, but he would not hold office under any such damned Government. He said this before a great crowd at the polls. I had just objected to his vote. I asked Mr. Jenkins if he would vote for such a man as Harris; he said he wanted the South to succeed, and he said he would vote for Harris against anybody. I consider a man disloyal

who opposes the acts of the administration. I never knew of any act of disloyalty on the part of Mr. Jenkins, except his abuse of the Government.

With respect to Mr. Jenkins spending $3,000 to sustain the Union and the Government, I do not think he ever had it to spend. I have never heard of his spending any thing, except from his own lips.

DORLEY B. ROBY.

For the Prosecution.—June 5.

I have known Mr. J. Z. Jenkins for several years. For the last three years he has been one of the most disloyal men in the county. It is from personal knowledge of his conduct and observations that I pronounce him disloyal. He got so outrageous that I had to apply to General Wallace, at Baltimore, to have him arrested. Since that time he has behaved himself a little better. He is known and recognized in that neighborhood as an open and outspoken enemy of the Government. I have heard him curse the President, and damn him to all intents and purposes. He said old Lincoln, the damned old son of a bitch, had offered him an office, but that he would not hold office under any such damned creature, or any such damned Government.

Cross-examined by MR. CLAMPITT.

I have known Mr. Jenkins for four or five years. I was not a resident of the county in 1861 and 1862; I was in 1863. I was born in Charles County, and raised in Prince George's; and I have been backward and forward through there all the time. In 1862 I knew Mr. Jenkins very well. I knew him to be a Union man till about three years ago. He was a very strong Know-Nothing, and I was a Know-Nothing too. Jenkins abandoned the Union party about three years ago this fall. He lost a negro man; and it seemed that his loyalty to his Government only lasted as long as his negro was protected. As soon as he lost the negro, he abandoned his Union principles.

The flag that was raised, and which Mr. Jenkins is said to have protected, was understood to be a Know-Nothing flag; a Union flag raised by the Know-Nothing party. The Know-Nothings were generally considered Union men, but there were a good many who, like Mr. Jenkins, went over to the rebels as soon as there was a division of parties.

There is no suit pending between me and any citizen of Maryland; there is a suit pending against my son, Andrew V. Roby. He was appointed Deputy Provost Marshal for the purpose of carrying out General Schenck's order at the election. He was ordered to have every man arrested who interfered with the election. This man Jenkins behaved very badly at the election. Colonel Baker had a company of men there, and my son suggested to the Captain that Jenkins should be arrested. He was arrested, placed on a chair, and a bottle of whisky taken from his pocket. At night I thought the poor fellow had got sober; he looked very penitent, and I suggested to the Captain that it was not worth while to take him up to Colonel Baker's, that he should allow him to go; and he acted on my suggestion. The suit pending between my son and Mr. Jenkins is for false imprisonment.

By ASSISTANT JUDGE ADVOCATE BINGHAM.

The prosecution against my son is for attempting to execute the Federal authority. The authorities, who have the management of the case, have taken steps to have it removed to the United States Court.

WILLIAM A. EVANS.

For the Prosecution.—June 5.

I reside in Prince George's County, Md., and am a Presbyterian minister. I was compelled to leave my Church in 1861 because of my loyalty and devotion to the Union. Prince George's County is a very disloyal neighborhood.

I know J. Z. Jenkins very well. He pretended to be a loyal man in 1861, as a great many in Prince George's, St. Mary's, and those lower counties did, but I never considered him a loyal man, because, if he had been, he would have co-operated with me and several others, who were endeavoring to discharge our duty to our country. His reputation and conduct since 1861, has been disloyal. I call him a rebel. His sympathy with the rebels has been open and outspoken.

Cross-examined by MR. CLAMPITT.

I have known Mr. Jenkins about fifteen years. I lived in the same county as he did in 1861, but because of my abolition proclivities, I was not, at times, permitted to remain in the county or the State. There was a writ out for me in 1861, and I was only permitted to visit my house in secrecy. Everybody that knows Mr. Jenkins knows that he is a rebel. In 1861, he pretended to be a Union man; but I knew him to be a hypocrite. I judged him to be a rebel by his conduct; saying that the country would go to ruin, and that the South would be successful. He said this to other gentlemen, and they repeated it to me. I held a secret commission under the Government. I know nothing of his labors to obtain Union votes in the State of Mary-

land, and if he has done any thing to protect the Union flag when it was threatened to be torn down by secession sympathizers, I have known nothing of it. I have known him to call at the different polls on election times, and endeavor to dissuade men from voting for the Union cause. Even at the last election, in 1864, he said he would not vote for the damned abolition Government to save anybody's life.

By the JUDGE ADVOCATE.

I do not know a loyal man in that neighborhood except Mr. Roby, his son, and a few others. We were in danger all the time, so much so that I had to call upon General Augur for a guard.

I belong to the New School Presbyterian Church, and I am a member of the Presbytery of the District of Columbia.

JOHN L. THOMPSON.

For the Prosecution.—June 5.

I have known J. Z. Jenkins ever since I can remember. For the last two years and six months he has not been a loyal man; for the four years preceding that he was. He is regarded as a disloyal man in that community; his disloyalty is open and outspoken.

I have had a difficulty with Mr. Jenkins, which grew out of my being drafted, and going to Mr. Roby's son to aid me, Jenkins said he would cut my throat in consequence of it, and drew his knife. a small pen-knife, against me. The only reason that I know for his conduct was, that he hated the Government. Jenkins said that, in case he was forced to fight, he would go with the South.

I lived in Mrs. Surratt's family for two years. I do not think she was a loyal woman. I judge so by her conversation, which was against the Government.

Cross-examined by MR. CLAMPITT.

I have known Mr. Jenkins ever since he was a child. He was considered a loyal man in 1861, but not in 1863. I know nothing of Mr. Jenkins coming to Washington to obtain votes for the Union Government. I know of his assisting to raise the Union flag, and with a band of men assisting in protecting it; but that was in 1861. I have heard him make disloyal remarks many a time. He said that he hated the Government the worst on earth, and he said that emancipation was all wrong.

TESTIMONY CONCERNING GEORGE A. ATZERODT

ROBERT R. JONES.

For the Prosecution.—May 13.

I am a clerk at the Kirkwood House in this city. The leaf exhibited to the Commission is from the register of the Kirkwood House. It contains the name of G. A. Atzerodt, Charles County. It appears from the register that Atzerodt took room No. 126 on the morning of the 14th of April last, I think before 8 o'clock in the morning. I was not present when his name was registered, and did not see him until between 12 and 1 in the day. I recognize Atzerodt among the accused. That is the man, I think.

[The witness here pointed to the accused, G. A. Atzerodt.]

I went to the room occupied by Atzerodt after it had been opened by Mr. Lee, on the night of the 15th of April, and I saw all the articles that were found there. I can not identify the knife, though it was similar to the one just shown me. It was between the sheet and the mattress. The bed had not been occupied on the night of the 14th, nor had the chambermaid been able to get into the room the next day. A young man spoke to Atzerodt when I saw him standing at the office counter. I do not know his name. Atzerodt, before that, asked me if any one had inquired for him within a short time. From the book it appears that Atzerodt paid one day in advance. I had never seen him in the hotel before.

JOHN LEE.

For the Prosecution.—May 13.

I belong to the military police force of this city. On the night of the 15th of April I went, by order of Major O'Beirne, to the Kirkwood House. When I got there a person employed in the house, whom I knew, told me there had been a rather suspicious-looking man there, who had taken a room the day previous. On the hotel register I found a name written very badly—G. A. Atzerodt. I went to the room occupied by this man; the door was locked, and the key could not be found. With permission of one of the proprietors I burst open the door. I found in the room a black coat hanging on the wall; underneath the pillow, or bolster, I found a revolver, loaded and capped. In the pocket of the coat I found a bank-book of J. Wilkes Booth, showing a credit of $455, with the Ontario Bank, Montreal, and also a map of Virginia; a handkerchief marked "Mary R. Booth;" another marked "F. M." or "F. A. Nelson;" another handkerchief with the letter "H" in the corner. In the

bank-book was an envelope with the frank of the Hon. John Conners. There was also a pair of new gauntlets, a colored handkerchief, three boxes of cartridges, a piece of liquorice, and a tooth-brush. On the corner of the bank-book was "J. W. Booth, 53." On the inside of the book was "Mr. J. Wilkes Booth in account with the Ontario Bank, Canada. 1864: October 27; by deposit, cr. $455."

There was also a brass spur, a pair of socks, and two collars. Between the sheets and mattresses I found this large bowie-knife.

[These articles were all offered in evidence.]

The room in which these things were found was No. 126, and is on the floor above the room then occupied by Vice-President Johnson.

Cross-examined by MR. DOSTER.

The person I met at the Kirkwood House, who spoke of the suspicious-looking man being there, said, "I believe that he had a gray coat on." I did not find the signature of Atzerodt, or any thing in the room; I only know it was his room because it said so on the register.

By the JUDGE ADVOCATE.

In coming down from room 126, to reach the office of the hotel, a person would pass the door of the room occupied by Vice-President Johnson. When I came down, there was a soldier at the door. A man of any courage, coming down the stairs, could easily throw a handful of snuff in the soldier's eyes and go right into Mr. Johnson's room.

LYMAN S. SPRAGUE.

For the Prosecution.—May 15.

I am clerk at the Kirkwood House in this city. I went up to the room of the prisoner, Atzerodt, with Mr. Lee, and was present when it was broken open. All I saw found, as I went in, was the revolver under the pillow. No one inquired for Atzerodt on the 14th while I was in the office.

Cross-examined by MR. DOSTER.

I was at the desk of the Kirkwood House that day from 8 in the morning till 12 at noon; no one called for Atzerodt during that time.

COLONEL W. R. NEVINS.

For the Prosecution—May 27.

I was in this city on the 12th of April, and stopped at the Kirkwood House. While there, I saw that man [pointing to the accused, George A. Atzerodt] in the passage that leads to the dining-room, when he asked me if I knew where President Johnson was. I believe that was his first question. I showed him where Mr. Johnson's room was, on the left-hand side of the passage; "However," said I, "the Vice-President is now eating his dinner." I thought he was a stranger, and referred him to the Vice-President's servant, a colored man, who was standing behind him. He looked into the dining-room; whether he went in or not I do not know.

Cross-examined by MR. DOSTER.

This was between 4 and 5 o'clock. There was no other person at dinner at the time but the Vice-President and myself. This man met me near the two or three steps that come down into the dining-room. I showed him where the Vice-President was sitting at the further end of the room, with his yellow man behind him. Atzerodt had on dark clothes at the time, and, I believe, a low-crowned llack felt hat. I noticed his countenance more than his clothes, but I could tell him among fifty thousand. I am now sixty-five years of age.

By JUDGE ADVOCATE BURNETT.

When I first came into Court this morning, I was asked to point out, among the prisoners, the man I had seen at the Kirkwood House, and I designated the prisoner, Atzerodt, before his name was mentioned to me.

JOHN FLETCHER.

For the Prosecution.—May 17.

I am foreman at J. Naylor's livery-stable, in this city. On the 3d of April, Atzerodt and another gentleman came to the stable with two horses, and inquired for Mr. Naylor. Atzerodt said they wanted to put up the horses at the stable, and I ordered them to be put up. The other gentleman said he was going to Philadelphia, and that he would leave the sale of his horse to Atzerodt; he left, and I have not seen him since. Atzerodt kept the horses at the stable until the 12th of April, when he sold one of them to Thompson, the stage contractor, and took the other, a brown horse, away. This was a very heavy, common work horse, blind of one eye; it was a dark-brown, with a heavy tail, and heavy fetlocks down to the feet.

I saw Atzerodt no more till 1 o'clock, on the 14th of April, when he and Herold came to the stable with a dark-bay mare. He said he had sold the brown horse and saddle and bridle in Montgomery County, and had bought this mare, with saddle and bridle. He then told me to put up the mare in the stable. I went to my supper at half-past 6, and when I came back the colored boy had the mare at the door, with saddle and bridle on her. Atzerodt paid the boy fifty cents for her keep, and asked me if that was right; I said, "Yes." "If I stay until morning," he asked, "how much more are you going to charge me?" "Only fifty cents," I said. He then went out and staid about three-quarters of an hour, when he returned. He told me not to take the bridle or saddle off the mare until 10 o'clock, and to keep the stable open for him. I said I would do so, and that I would be there myself at that time. At 10 o'clock he came after the mare. He asked me to take a drink with him, and I did, at the Union Hotel, corner of Thirteen-and-a-half and E Streets. I had a glass of beer and he drank some whisky. Returning to the stable he said, "If this thing happens to-night, you will hear of a present," or "Get a present." He seemed to me about half-tight, and was very excited-looking. I did not pay much attention to him. As he mounted the mare I said, "I would not like to ride that mare through the city in the night, for she looks so skittish."

"Well," said he, "She's good upon a retreat." I then said to him, "Your acquaintance is staying out very late with our horse;" that was Herold. "Oh," said he, "He'll be back after awhile." Atzerodt then left, and I followed him until he went down E Street and passed Thirteen-and-a-half Street, and saw him go into the Kirkwood House. I watched until he came out and mounted the mare again. He went along D Street and turned to Tenth Street, to the left of D and Tenth Streets. I then returned to the stable.

WASHINGTON BRISCOE.

For the Prosecution.—May 18.

I have known the prisoner, George Atzerodt, for seven or eight years. On the night of the 14th of April, between half-past 11 and 12, he got on a Navy-Yard car at Sixth Street. I was in the car, but he did not recognize me till I spoke to him. I asked him if he had heard the news, and he said he had. Then he asked me to let him sleep in the store, down at the Navy Yard, with me. I told him he could not. His manner was excited, and he was very anxious to sleep there; he urged me to let him. I told him again he could not; that the gentleman I was with was there, and I had no right to ask him. He rode down as far as I did, then got out and asked me again. When he left me, he said he would go back to the Pennsylvania House, on C Street, where he was stopping.

Cross-examined by MR. DOSTER.

I did not notice the precise time when I met Atzerodt, but I think it was between half-past 11 and 12. I was going to the Navy Yard, my home, and he rode down in the car with me to I Street, near my store, and got out where I did. I waited with him on the corner of I and Garrison Streets, till

10

the car came back. I think it was near 12 when he got into the car again and left me. I hardly know whether he had been drinking; but, judging from his manner, he was a little excited.

JOHN GREENAWALT.
For the Prosecution.—May 17.

I keep the Pennsylvania House, on C Street, between Four-and-a-half and Sixth Streets. I know the prisoner, Atzerodt. A person frequently called on Atzerodt, who, I have since found, was J. Wilkes Booth.

[A photograph of J. Wilkes Booth was exhibited to the witness.]

That is the person. Sometimes Booth would come through the hall where Atzerodt would be sitting; at other times Booth would walk in and walk back, when Atzerodt would get up and follow him. They have had frequent interviews in front of my house; and several times, as I walked on the steps, they would leave and walk toward the National Hotel, where they stood and had their interview.

On one occasion several young men from Port Tobacco met Atzerodt at the Pennsylvania House. They had been drinking, and Atzerodt asked me to take a drink, which I did, when he said, "Greenawalt, I am pretty nearly broke, but I have always got friends enough who will give me as much money as will see me through." He added, "I am going away some of these days, and I will return with as much gold as will keep me all my lifetime." This was said about the 1st of April, nine or ten days after he first came to my house, which was on the 18th of March last. Atzerodt was in the habit of stopping at my house. He never stopped any length of time. He left my house on the Wednesday before the assassination. He had no baggage with him. I saw him next on the Saturday morning after the assassination, between 2 and 3 o'clock.

I had just come in the house myself, and had gone to my room. About five minutes afterward came up with a five-dollar bill and said, "There is a man come in with Atzerodt who wants lodging, and wants to pay for it." So I went down and gave the man his change. I had an uneasiness about the thing myself; thought there was something wrong.

Atzerodt asked for his old room, and I told him it was occupied. I told him he would have to go with this gentleman. So I gave this man Thomas his change, and told the servant to show him to his room, and Atzerodt was going to follow him, when I said, "Atzerodt, you have not registered." Said he, "Do you want my name?" I replied, "Certainly." He hesitated some, but stepped back and registered, and went to his room. He had never before hesitated to register his name. The man who was with Atzerodt was about five feet seven or eight

inches high, and his weight was about one hundred and forty pounds, I should judge. He was poorly dressed, in dark clothes. His pants were worn through at the back near the heels. I took notice of that as he walked out of the door to go to his room. He was quite dark-complexioned and very much weather-beaten. He had dark hair.

Neither of the men seemed excited. This man Thomas, I noticed, kept a close eye on me as I came in. It was Thomas who asked for the room. Atzerodt was lying on the settee in the corner of the room when I came in. Atzerodt asked for his old room; I told him it was occupied, and that he would have to go with this man. It was a large room, with six beds in it. There were other persons in the room before Thomas and Atzerodt went there.

Thomas had the appearance of a laboring man. I think he wore a broadcloth coat, though it was very much worn, but I judged that his clothes were worn as a disguise. His hair, moustache, and whiskers were black. The name he gave was Samuel Thomas. He got up about 5 o'clock and left the house, so the servant told me. A lady who was stopping at the house had given orders for a carriage to take her to the 6:15 train. She left before I got up, and as the servant was going out of the door, this man Thomas went out and asked the way to the railway depot. He had no baggage.

Atzerodt left shortly afterward, and walked toward Sixth Street. As the servant came back from getting the carriage, he met Atzerodt, and said to him, "What brings you out so early this morning?" "Well," said he, "I have got business." He left without paying his bill, and I have never seen him since until now. There he sits, [pointing to the accused, George A. Atzerodt.]

In March, Atzerodt showed me a revolver he had just bought. I told him I wished I had known he wanted one, for I had a new one for which I had no use.

[The revolver found by John Lee, at the Kirkwood House, was here exhibited to the witness.]

The revolver Atzerodt had was similar to that, but I do not think that is the same.

Cross-examined by MR. DOSTER.

Atzerodt left my house on the 12th of April. He had been there from the 18th of March. On the 27th of March he left and staid away over night, and returned with a man named Bailey.

Atzerodt once handed a large revolver into the office for me to keep for him. I saw no other arms. He may have had others; in the office he said he had a knife.

When Mr. Bailey left my house, he wanted to pay his stage fare, and I bought of him some eight or nine $2.50 gold-pieces, and, I think, about seven dollars' worth of silver. I can not say that Thomas and Atzerodt were acquainted previously to their calling at my house on the night of the 14th. Atzerodt did not seem sleepy, and he was not in liquor. I did not see them come in; the servant told me they came in together; but that is the only reason I had for thinking they came together. I told Atzerodt that he would have to room with that man, and he had no objection. I do not recognize the man Thomas among the prisoners.

That man [pointing to the accused, Edward Spangler] resembles him somewhat, but is not so dark, and he has not got the beard on that Thomas had then. I could not be positive it is the same man.

[The coat found by John Lee at the Kirkwood House was handed to the witness.]

I never saw Atzerodt wear that coat.

Cross-examined by Mr. Ewing.

The man Thomas had black hair and a heavy black moustache, and he had whiskers and beard in front. ●

By the Court.

I do not know why Atzerodt and the man Thomas got up at the same time in the morning. They did not occupy the same bed. On the Wednesday before the assassination, when Atzerodt left, he told me he was going away, and he said, "Greenawalt, I owe you a couple of days' board; will it make any difference to you whether I pay for it now or when I come back?" He said he was going to Montgomery County.

I never saw the prisoner, O'Laughlin, at my house.

JAMES WALKER (colored).

For the Prosecution.—May 18.

My business at the Pennsylvania House, in this city, is to make fires, carry water, and to wait on gentlemen that come in late and early. I have seen the prisoner, Atzerodt, [pointing to the accused, George A. Atzerodt,] at the house. He came there between 12 and 1 o'clock, I think, on Friday night, the 14th of April; I held his horse while he went into the bar. When he came out, he asked me to give him a stick or a switch, as the horse was shy of the light; I gave him a piece of a hoop, and he went off. I do not know whether he had any arms; I did not see any. About 2 o'clock in the morning he came back again, on foot this time. I had to get up to let him in. He wanted to go to room 51, which he had commonly occupied; but that was taken up, and he went to 53. He left between 5 and 6 in the morning. As I was going out for a hack to take a lady to the 6:15 train, I overtook him about thirty steps from the door; he was walking along slowly. Another man came to the house about the same time that night, and occupied the same room. He went away a little earlier, to take the 6:15 train; I opened the door and let him out. He had no baggage that I saw. The gas was down pretty low

when they came in; but the man seemed to have on dark clothes and a slouch hat. He paid in advance, and went straight to the room. I do not know that I would know him. I can not say that any of the prisoners resemble him. I was not so well acquainted with him as with Mr. Atzerodt, who had been stopping there a couple of weeks.

Cross-examined by Mr. Doster.

[A coat found at the Kirkwood House by John Lee was exhibited to the witness.]

I do not recollect seeing that coat before. I have cleaned Mr. Atzerodt's clothes and boots, but I never saw that coat. We generally close the house at half-past 12 or 1 o'clock, and we had not closed on the Friday night when Mr. Atzerodt came first; we closed soon afterward. The horse that I held for him then was a light-bay horse, small; it seemed to be young, and had plenty of spirit. I opened the door for Mr. Atzerodt on the second visit, and took him and the other man to their room. They had no conversation in my presence.

I have seen Mr. Atzerodt have a belt, with a pistol and a knife, but I never saw the knife out of the sheath. That was probably four or five days before that Friday.

By the Judge Advocate.

[Exhibiting to the witness the knife found by John Lee at the Kirkwood House.]

I can not tell whether that was the knife. It was in the sheath, fastened to the belt.

[Exhibiting a bowie-knife found on Atzerodt.]

It was something more like that.

[The knife was offered in evidence.]

LIEUTENANT W. R. KEIM.

For the Prosecution.—May 18.

I was at the Pennsylvania House, in this city, on the night of the 14th of April last. I went to the hotel about 4 o'clock on the Saturday morning, and Atzerodt was in bed when I went into the room. His bed was opposite mine. I asked him if he had heard of the assassination of the President, and he said he had; that it was an awful affair. When I awoke in the morning, he was gone. I did not see any arms with him. About a week or ten days before the assassination I occupied room 51 with Atzerodt.

[The large bowie-knife found at the Kirkwood House was exhibited to the witness.]

I would not swear that is the knife I have seen in Atzerodt's possession, but it was one about that size. Atzerodt went out of the room one morning and left the knife in his bed. I got up and took it, and put it under my pillow. In a few minutes he returned, went to his bed and looked about, and then said, "Have you seen my knife?" I replied, "Yes; here it is." Then he said, "I want that; if one fails, I want the other;" and I gave it to him. His pistol, a revolver, he always carried round his waist.

Cross-examined by MR. DOSTER.

I did not know the prisoner, Atzerodt, before meeting him at the Pennsylvania House. On the Saturday morning after the assassination, when I went into the room where he was, I did not speak to him immediately; it was perhaps five or ten minutes before I spoke. He was in bed, but whether undressed or not I can not say. When I spoke to him about the assassination, he said it was an awful thing, and that was about all he said. I did not see him after that. He always addressed me as " Lieutenant." It was about a week or ten days before the assassination that I took the knife from his bed. We had been drinking together, as we lay in bed; had had, perhaps, two or three whisky-cocktails apiece. His words, as near as I remember, when I gave him back the knife, were, " If this fails, the other will not."

JOHN CALDWELL.

For the Prosecution.—May 25.

I reside in Georgetown. On the morning after the assassination, at about 8 o'clock, I was at Matthews & Co.'s store, 49 High Street, Georgetown, when that man, [pointing to the accused, George A. Atzerodt,] whom I knew, came in; and, after my asking him how he was, and so on, said he was going into the country, and asked me if I did not want to buy his watch. I told him I had a watch of my own, and did not want another. He then asked me to lend him $10. I told him I had not the money to spare. He then took his revolver off, and said, " Lend me $10, and take this as security, and I will bring the money or send it to you next week. I thought the revolver was good security for the money, and I let him have the money, expecting him to pay it back.

[A new revolver, loaded and capped, was handed to the witness.]

This is the revolver. It was loaded and capped as it is now. I did not inquire of him why it was loaded and capped.

[The revolver was offered in evidence.]

Cross-examined by MR. DOSTER.

I have known Atzerodt for three or four years. We were not on very intimate terms; we were always civil to each other when we met. I had never loaned Atzerodt any money before.

WILLIAM CLENDENIN.

For the Prosecution.—May 18.

[A bowie-knife was shown to the witness.]

I have had that knife in my hands before. I saw a colored woman pick up something out of a gutter, on F Street, as I was passing down on the morning after the assassination. She was about ten feet from me, and I went to her and asked what it was, and she gave me this knife in a sheath. A lady in the third story window of the house next to Creaser's

shoe-store, told me she saw it in the gutter, and sent the colored woman down to get it, but that she did not want it to come into the house. I told her that I would take it to the Chief of Police, which I did.

Cross-examined by MR. DOSTER.

It was about 6 o'clock in the morning when I saw the woman pick it up. It lay in the gutter on F Street, in front of Creaser's house, under the carriage step, as if the intention were to throw it there. Creaser's is on F Street, between Eighth and Ninth, opposite the Patent Office.

MARSHAL JAMES L. McPHAIL.

For the Prosecution.—May 18

I am Provost Marshal of the State of Maryland. I received an intimation from the prisoner, Atzerodt, that he desired to see me. I went to him, and he stated to me that, on the night of the assassination of the President, he had thrown his knife away in the streets of Washington. I made no promise or threat to him, in any way, in connection with the confession.

By MR. DOSTER.

Q. Was he not in irons at the time?

A. Yes, sir; he was in a cell in the prison, and in irons.

MR. DOSTER. I respectfully submit that a confession made under such circumstances is not admissible, because it was made under duress, which put the mind of the prisoner in a state of fear.

The JUDGE ADVOCATE. There was neither threat nor promise, and the fact that the man was in prison, or even in irons, does not affect the question of his mental liberty. A man's limbs may be chained, and his mind be perfectly free to speak the truth, or to conceal it, if he chooses.

MR. DOSTER, in support of his objection, quoted from the case of Commonwealth *v.* Mosler, 4 Barr's Reports, 265, to the effect that a confession to an officer, as well as to a private person, must be unattended with any inducement of hope or fear, and must be founded on no question calculated to entrap the prisoner; and referred also to 1 Leech, 263; 2 East's Pleas of the Crown; 2 Russell on Crimes, 644; 1 Washington's Circuit Court Reports, 625; 1 Chitty's Criminal Law, 85; 1 Greenleaf on Evidence, 214; 2 Starkie, 36.

I claim that the prisoner was under the influence of fear when he made that confession, and without that influence would not have made it.

The JUDGE ADVOCATE. I think it is due to the witness that he should be allowed to state precisely under what circumstances this confession was made, and if there is a trace of fear, or hope, or incitement of that kind, I shall not insist for a moment on the answer being heard.

WITNESS. I should state that a brother-in-law of Atzerodt is on my force, and for a time a brother of the prisoner was on it, and they repeatedly told me that Atzerodt desired to see me. After consulting with the Secretary of War, a pass was given me, and I saw the prisoner. I saw him first on the gun-boat, and afterward in his cell. There was no threat, or promise, or inducement of any kind made. On the contrary, I told him that I could make no promises to him; if he had any thing to say to me, he might say it, but I had nothing to say to him. I did not ask him a single question to induce him to make a confession.

[The Commission overruled the objection.]

Atzerodt said he had thrown his knife away, just above the Herndon House, which, I think, is on the corner of Ninth and F Streets.

Cross-examined by Mr. Doster.

Atzerodt stated that his pistol was in the possession of a young man by the name of Caldwell, at Matthews & Co.'s store, Georgetown. He had gone to Caldwell, and borrowed $10 on it, on the morning of the 15th of April. He also spoke of a certain coat hanging in the room at the Kirkwood House, and of a pistol, bowie-knife, and other articles there, all of which he stated belonged to the accused, David E. Herold.

Mr. STONE. I must object to that.

Mr. DOSTER. The answer has been obtained. I do not wish to press it further.

HEZEKIAH METZ.

For the Prosecution.—May 17.

I reside in Montgomery County, Md., about twenty-two miles from Washington City. On the Sunday following the death of Mr. Lincoln, the prisoner, George A. Atzerodt, was at my house, and eat his dinner there. That is the man, [pointing to the accused, George A. Atzerodt.] He was just from Washington. We were inquiring about the news, and a conversation came up about General Grant's being shot—for we had understood that he had been shot on the cars—when Atzerodt said, as I understood, "If the man that was to follow him had followed him, it was likely to be so."

Atzerodt passed in the neighborhood by the name of Andrew Attwood; that was the name by which I knew him. When I saw him, he represented himself as coming from Washington, and was traveling in the direction of Barnsville.

Cross-examined by Mr. Doster.

It is two or three years since I first became acquainted with Atzerodt. I had but a slight acquaintance with him; I knew him when I saw him. He went by the name of Andrew Attwood around our neighborhood, and he has gone by that name ever since I have known him. My house is about a mile from the road that leads to Barnsville. It was between 10 and 11 o'clock on Sunday that Atzerodt came there; he remained some two or three hours. Two young men named Leaman were in the room when Atzerodt made the remark about somebody following General Grant. I do not remember that Atzerodt said any thing about the assassination; they might have been talking about it before I came into the room. The conversation about General Grant occurred after I got into the room.

SERGEANT L. W. GEMMILL.

For the Prosecution.—May 17.

I arrested the prisoner, George A. Atzerodt, [pointing to the accused,] on the 20th of April, about 4 o'clock in the morning, at the house of a man named Richter, near a place called Germantown. I was sent there for the purpose by Captain Townsend, with a detail of six men. I first went to Mr. Purdon's house to get him as guide to Mr. Richter's. When I knocked at the door, Richter asked me twice who it was before he would let me in. I told him to come and see. When he came to the door, I asked him if there was a man named Attwood there; he said no, there was no one there; that he had been there, but had gone to Frederick, or to that neighborhood. I then told him that I was going to search the house, when he said that his cousin was up stairs in bed. His wife then spoke up, and said that as for that there were three men there. He got a light, and taking two men with me, went up stairs, where I found Atzerodt lying on the front of the bed. I asked him his name, and he gave me a name that I did not understand, and which I thought was a fictitious one. I told him to get up and dress himself; and I took him to Mr. Leaman, a loyal man, who knew him. Mr. Leaman told me it was the man. Atzerodt made no inquiry as to why he was arrested; but denied having given me a fictitious name. I asked him if he had left Washington lately, and he said no. I then asked him if he had not something to do with the assassination, and he told me that he had not.

Cross-examined by Mr. Doster.

My orders from Captain Townsend were to arrest a man by the name of Attwood; and I was ordered to go to Mr. Purdon and get a description of him, and to press him as a guide to the house of Richter. I do not remember the name Atzerodt gave me, and would not swear that it was not "Atzerodt;" he afterward insisted that that was the name he gave me. He spoke in German, and that is the reason why I did not understand the name.

MARCUS P. NORTON.

Recalled for the Prosecution.—June 3.

Assistant Judge Advocate BURNETT stated to the Commission that since the case was closed on the part of the prosecution, testimony of importance had been discovered, tending to implicate George A. Atzerodt, Michael O'Laughlin, and Samuel A. Mudd, in connection with J. Wilkes Booth.

Mr. Cox objected to the introduction of any evidence that would affect the prisoners individually, the understanding being that the prosecution was closed, except as to evidence reflecting light on the general conspiracy. It was contrary to the practice of civil courts to allow the introduction of testimony after the prosecution had been closed, except what was strictly in rebuttal.

Assistant Judge Advocate BURNETT stated that in military courts, even after the case had been closed on both sides, it was allowable to call new witnesses at the discretion of the Court.

The Commission decided to admit the testimony.

I reside in the city of Troy, New York. From about the 10th of January until about the 10th of March, I was stopping at the National Hotel in this city. I knew J. Wilkes Booth, having seen him several times at the theater. I saw the prisoners, George A. Atzerodt and Michael O'Laughlin, prior to the inauguration of President Lincoln. I saw Atzerodt twice, and O'Laughlin three or four times, in conversation with Booth. On one occasion I accidentally heard some conversation between Atzerodt and Booth, as I sat on the same seat with them; it was on the evening of either the 2d or 3d of March last; I think the 3d. I can not give the precise language used in the conversation, but the substance of it was, that if the matter succeeded as well with Mr. Johnson as it did with old Buchanan, their party would get terribly sold.

Cross-examined by MR. DOSTER.

The conversation between Atzerodt and Booth took place in the rotunda office of the National Hotel, early in the evening, as I was sitting, perhaps, within two or three feet of them. I remember the prisoner, Atzerodt, by his countenance and general features, though I do not think he had as much of a scowl on his face as he has now.

Recalled for the Prosecution.—June 8.

Cross-examined by MR. DOSTER.

I have seen Booth play in Washington, in New York, and once, I think, in Boston, but I can not recall how many times, nor the pieces in which I saw him. At the time of hearing the conversation between Booth and Atzerodt at the National Hotel, I did not consider it as having reference to an attempt to poison Mr. Johnson; but the assassination of the President, and Booth being coupled with it, is what has turned my attention to the conversation.

DEFENSE OF GEORGE A. ATZERODT.

CAPTAIN FRANK MONROE, U. S. N.
For the Defense.—May 30.

By MR. DOSTER.

I had the custody of the prisoner at the bar on board the monitors Saugus and Montauk.

MR. DOSTER. Before going further with the examination of the witness, I wish to submit an application of the prisoner in writing.

[The paper was handed to the Judge Advocate, who, having read it, said:]

This is a proposal on the part of the prisoner, Atzerodt, that his confessions made to the witness shall be heard by this Court as testimony in his favor—confessions in regard to which no evidence whatever has been introduced by the Government. I can not understand on what grounds such an application can be urged.

MR. DOSTER. The prisoner desires to make a full statement of his guilt in this transaction, if there is any guilt, and of his innocence, if there is any evidence of it. He asks his statement to be placed on record, because he has been debarred from calling any other prisoners who might be his witnesses, for the reason that they are co-defendants. He therefore asks that he may be allowed to speak through Captain Monroe, as he would otherwise speak through one of his co-defendants. I ask this as a matter of fairness and liberality at the hands of the Commission.

The JUDGE ADVOCATE. It is greatly to be deplored that the counsel for the accused will urge upon the Court proposals which they know to be contrary to law.

MR. DOSTER. I have no more to ask the witness then.

MATTHEW J. POPE.

For the Defense.—June 2.

By MR. DOSTER.

I live at the Navy Yard, and keep a livery-stable; until recently I kept a restaurant. A few days before the assassination of the President, perhaps about the 12th of April—I do not know the exact day—a gentleman called at my stable to sell a bay horse; it was a large bay horse, and blind of one eye.

[The prisoner, George A. Atzerodt, was desired to stand up for identification.]

That man has something of the same features; he was very much such a looking man; but if it is the same, he is not near so stout as when he brought the horse to my stable. I can not say positively that it is the same. There are many applications at my stable to buy and sell horses, that I did not take much notice of him. I told him I did not want to buy the horse; that I had more horses than I had use for. It was some time after 12 or 1 o'clock at noon that he came. The horse was put into my stable, and the gentleman went over to my restaurant and took a drink. He left there with a man named Barr, a wheelwright in the Navy Yard. They came back together, and the gentleman took his horse out and rode him away. The horse was in the stable, I think, some two or three hours. Barr was not sober at the time; he had been drinking a little.

JOHN H. BARR.

For the Defense.—June 5.

By MR. DOSTER.

I have seen Atzerodt, the prisoner at the bar, once before. I was coming from my work at the Navy Yard one evening, and stopped at Mr. Pope's restaurant, and there met this gentleman. I did not know him at the time, but we had several drinks together. I proposed to him to go home and take supper with me, and he did so. After supper, we went back to Mr. Pope's restaurant, and had, I think, a couple of drinks. We then went out, returned to the restaurant again, and took two more glasses, and from there went to Mr. Pope's stable. The gentleman took his horse out, and I saw him get on and ride off. That is the last I saw of him. By referring to my book, I can tell the exact day on which this occurred, because I know the work that I did that day; I made two spring blocks for Sanderson & Miller. I find it was the 12th of April.

JAMES KELLEHER.

For the Defense.—May 30.

By MR. DOSTER.

I am one of the proprietors of the livery-stable on Eighth and E Streets. On the 14th of April last, about half-past 2 in the day, I let the prisoner, Atzerodt, [pointing to the accused, George A. Atzerodt,] have out of my stable a small bay mare, sixteen and a half hands high. He paid me five dollars for the hire. The horse was returned, to the best of my knowledge, between 9 and half-past 9 that night.

Q. When Atzerodt engaged the horse, did you have a conversation with him?

A. Yes, sir.

Q. State what that conversation was.

Assistant Judge Advocate BURNETT objected to the question as incompetent.

The question was waived.

Atzerodt wrote his name on the slate in a tolerably good hand; and he gave me several references willingly. He first gave a number of persons in Maryland. He said he knew a good many persons there, and that he was a coach-maker by trade. Stanley Higgins was one to whom he referred; I can not recall any other. He also gave me the name of John Cook in Washington as a reference, and several other names in Washington, but I do not remember them.

Cross-examined by ASSISTANT JUDGE ADVOCATE BURNETT.

I was not there when the horse was returned. When I went to the stable next morning, the horse was there.

SAMUEL SMITH.

For the Defense.—May 30.

By MR. DOSTER.

I am a stable-boy at Mr. Kelleher's stable. I was at the stable on the night of the 14th of April last. The bay mare that was let out about 2 o'clock in the afternoon was returned in the course of the evening; to the best of my knowledge, it was about 11 o'clock. She was about in the same condition as when she was taken out.

Cross-examined by ASSISTANT JUDGE ADVOCATE BURNETT.

I did not notice the person who brought back the mare; there was a little light in the stable, but it was very dim; and there was no light on the sidewalk. The man stopped outside the door, and I went out there and brought the mare in. It was by feeling her that I could tell she had not been ridden hard.

LEONARD J. FARWELL.

For the Defense.—June 3.

By MR. DOSTER.

On the evening of the 14th of April last, on leaving Ford's Theater, I went immediately to the Kirkwood House, to the room of Vice-President Johnson. I should think it was between 10 and half-past 10 o'clock. I found the room door locked. I rapped, but receiving no answer, I rapped again, and said, in a loud voice, "Governor Johnson, if you are in the room, I must see you." I believe the door was locked, but am not certain. I can not say whether I took hold of the handle or not. I did not see any one apparently lying in wait near Mr. Johnson's door.

I remained in Mr. Johnson's room about half an hour. I took charge of the door, and locked and bolted it on the inside. A number of persons came to the door, but I did not allow any of them to come in, unless he was some gentleman personally known to the Vice-President. I also rang the bell and had a guard placed at the door.

[The witness was here requested to look at the prisoner, George A. Atzerodt.]

I do not know that I have seen the prisoner before.

MISS JANE HEROLD.

For the Defense.—May 30.

By MR. DOSTER.

I am the sister of David E. Herold, the prisoner at the bar.

[Exhibiting to the witness the black coat found at the Kirkwood House, also the handkerchief marked "H."]

I think I never saw that coat in the possession of my brother. The handkerchief does not belong to him.

F. H. DOOLEY.

For the Defense.—May 31.

By MR. DOSTER.

I am an apothecary, on the corner of Seventh Street and Louisiana Avenue. The tooth-brush and liquorice found at the Kirkwood House have trade-marks on them that I am positive do not belong to my establishment.

SOMERSET LEAMAN.

For the Defense.—May 30.

By MR. DOSTER.

I have known the prisoner, George A. Atzerodt, ever since he was a boy. I was at the house of Hezekiah Metz on the Sunday morning following the assassination of the President, and met Atzerodt there. As I approached him, I said, in the way of a joke, "Are you the man that killed Abe Lincoln?" "Yes," said he, and laughed. I said, "Well, Andrew"—he went by the name of Andrew there — "I want to know the truth of it; is it so?" I asked him if the President was assassinated, and he said, "Yes, it is so; and he died yesterday evening about 3 o'clock." I then asked him if it was true that Mr. Seward's throat was cut, and two of his sons stabbed, and he replied, "Yes, Mr. Seward was stabbed, or rather cut at the throat, but not killed, and two of his sons were stabbed." I then asked him if what we heard about General Grant was correct, that he was assassinated on the same night. He answered, "No, I don't know whether that is so or not; I do n't suppose it is so; if it had been, I should have heard it."

While we were at the dinner-table, my brother asked him the question again, whether General Grant was killed or not, and he said, "No, I do n't suppose he was; if he was killed, he would have been killed probably by a man that got on the same car"—or the same train, I do not remember which—"that Grant got on."

I was not in Atzerodt's company more than half an hour, and that was about all that passed in reference to this in my presence.

I thought Atzerodt seemed somewhat confused at the dinner-table. He had been paying his addresses to the daughter of Mr. Metz, and it appeared that she had been showing him the cold shoulder that day, and he was down in the mouth in consequence. There was no remark made at the dinner-table that I did not hear.

Atzerodt's father had settled in our neighborhood, but moved away when Atzerodt was quite a boy, and I had seen but little of him until the last year or two. He visited among the neighbors there, many of whom were respectable people.

JAMES E. LEAMAN.

For the Defense.—May 30.

By MR. DOSTER.

I have known the prisoner, George A. Atzerodt, for about two years. I was at the house of Mr. Metz on the Sunday morning following the assassination. I broached the subject of General Grant being assassinated, and asked him whether it was so or not. He said he did not suppose it was; and he added, "If it is so, some one must have got on the same cars that he did." That was all the conversation that I had with him, with the exception that when he and I were out in the yard he said—

Mr. DOSTER. That is unnecessary; you need not state what he said in the yard.

By ASSISTANT JUDGE ADVOCATE BURNETT.

Q. Go on and state what he said to you in the yard.

A. He said, "O, my! what a trouble I see." I said to him, "Why, what have you to trouble you?" Said he, "More than I will ever get shut of."

By MR. DOSTER.

Q. That was immediately after you had been speaking of the assassination, was it?

A. No, sir; some time afterward. I took it for granted—

Assistant Judge Advocate BURNETT. You need not state what you took for granted. Give the words, and nothing else.

A. That was about all he said at that time. Atzerodt had been paying his addresses to Mr. Metz's daughter, and she had slighted him some time before he went out into the yard.

HARTMAN RICHTER.
For the Defense.—May 31.
By MR. DOSTER.

I live in Montgomery County, Maryland, and am a cousin of the prisoner, George A. Atzerodt. He came to my house about 2 or 3 o'clock on Sunday afternoon. I met him in the morning, on my road to church. I did not have much conversation with him, and I noticed nothing peculiar about him. He remained at my house from Sunday till Thursday morning, and occupied himself with walking about, working in the garden a little, and going among the neighbors. He did not attempt to get away, or to hide himself. When he was arrested he seemed very willing to go along. He had on a kind of gray overcoat when he came to my house.

SAMUEL McALLISTER.
For the Defense.—May 30.
By MR. DOSTER.

During the month of April I saw a pistol and a dirk in Atzerodt's possession. He gave them to me to keep for him.

[The knife and pistol found at the Kirkwood House were exhibited to the witness.]

Those are not the knife and pistol.

[The knife found near F and Ninth Streets on the morning of the 15th of April was exhibited.]

That looks very much like the knife; it was a knife of that description.

[Exhibiting to the witness the pistol identified by John Caldwell, on which he loaned $10.]

That looks very much like it.

On the evening of the 14th of April, at about 10 o'clock, he rode up to the door [Pennsylvania House] and called the black boy out to hold his horse. I did not take particular notice of him, or notice whether he was excited or not.

Q. Do you know any thing about his reputation for courage?

Assistant Judge Advocate BINGHAM. I object to that; I do not think we are going to try his character for courage.

Mr. DOSTER. May it please the Court, I intend to show that this man is a constitutional coward; that if he had been assigned the duty of assassinating the Vice-President, he never could have done it; and that, from his known cowardice, Booth probably did not assign him to any such duty. Certainly it is just as relevant as any thing can be.

Assistant Judge Advocate BINGHAM. If the counsel wishes to prove that the prisoner, Atzerodt, is a coward, I will withdraw my objection.

WITNESS. I know nothing of his reputation for cowardice, save what I have heard from others. I have heard men say that he would not resent an insult.

ALEXANDER BRAWNER.
For the Defense.—June 8.
By MR. DOSTER.

I live in Port Tobacco, Md. I have known the prisoner, Atzerodt, six or eight years. He was at Port Tobacco about the last of February or the beginning of March. I think he came from Bryantown; he rode a sorrel horse. I had some business in the country, and he went along with me.

I never considered Atzerodt a courageous man, by a long streak. I have seen him in scrapes, and I have seen him get out of them very fast. I have seen him in bar-room scrapes, little scrapes, and where pistols were drawn, and he generally got out of the way, and made pretty fast time. His reputation is that of a notorious coward.

LOUIS B. HARKINS.
For the Defense.—June 8.
By MR. DOSTER.

I have known Atzerodt for probably ten years. He was down at Port Tobacco about the latter part of February or the beginning of March. I think I saw him for a day or two. He is looked upon down there, by folks that know him, as a good-natured kind of a fellow. We never gave him credit down our way for much courage. I call to mind two difficulties in which I saw him—one happened in my shop, and the other in an oyster saloon—in both of which I thought he lacked courage.

WASHINGTON BRISCOE.
For the Defense.—May 30.
By MR. DOSTER.

I have known the prisoner, Atzerodt, six or seven years at Port Tobacco. He has always been considered a man of little courage, and remarkable for his cowardice.

TESTIMONY CONCERNING LEWIS PAYNE.

MRS. MARTHA MURRAY.

For the Prosecution.—May 19.

My husband keeps the Herndon House, corner of Ninth and F Streets, opposite the Patent Office, cat-a-cornered. The only one of the prisoners I recognize as having seen before is that man, [pointing to the accused, Lewis Payne.] I think I have seen him; his features are familiar to me, but I would not say for certain. He was two weeks in our house, and he left on the Friday, the day of the assassination. He left on the 14th day, about 4 o'clock. We have dinner at half-past 4, and this gentleman came into the sitting-room and said he was going away, and wanted to settle his bill; and he wished to have dinner before the regular dinner; so I gave orders for the dinner to be cut off and sent up to him. He went into the dining-room to eat his dinner, and I have not seen him since.

I do not recognise either of the prisoners as having visited this man. I remember that he once came in with two gentlemen to supper. I do not remember that any one spoke to me about engaging a room for this man. I am spoken to by so many that I could not remember any particular circumstance of that kind.

WM. H. BELL (colored.)

For the Prosecution.—May 19.

I live at the house of Mr. Seward, Secretary of State, and attend to the door. That man [pointing to the accused, Lewis Payne] came to the house of Mr. Seward on the night of the 14th of April. The bell rang and I went to the door, and that man came in. He had a little package in his hand; he said it was medicine for Mr. Seward from Dr. Verdi, and that he was sent by Dr. Verdi to direct Mr. Seward how to take it. He said he must go up. I told him that he could not go up; then he repeated the words over, and was a good while talking with me in the hall. He said he must go up; he must see him. He talked very rough to me in the first place. I told him he could not see Mr. Seward; that it was against my orders to let any one go up, and if he would give me the medicine and tell me the directions, I would take it up, and tell Mr. Seward how to take it. He was walking slowly all the time, listening to what I had to say. He had his right hand in his coat-pocket, and the medicine in his left. He then walked up the hall toward the steps. I had spoken pretty rough to him, and when I found out that he would go up, I asked him to excuse me. He said, "O! I know; that's all right." I thought he might, perhaps, be sent by Dr. Verdi, and he might go up and tell Mr. Seward that I would not let him go up, or something of that kind. I got on the steps and went up in front of him. As he went up I asked him not to walk so heavy. He met Mr. Frederick Seward on the steps this side of his father's room. He told Mr. Frederick that he wanted to see Mr. Seward. Mr. Frederick went into the room and came out, and told him that he could not see him; that his father was asleep, and to give him the medicine, and he would take it to him. That would not do; he must see Mr. Seward. He must see him; he said it in just that way. Mr. Frederick said, "You can not see him." He kept on talking to Mr. Frederick, saying, that he must see him, and then Mr. Frederick said, "I am the proprietor here, and his son; if you can not leave your message with me, you can not leave it at all." Then he had a little more talk there for a while, and stood there with the little package in his hand. Mr. Frederick would not let him see Mr. Seward no way at all, and then he started toward the step and said, "Well, if I can not see him—" and then he mumbled some words that I did not understand, and started to come down. I started in front of him. I got down about three steps, I guess, when I turned around to him and said, "Don't walk so heavy." Then by the time I turned around to make another step, he had jumped back and struck Mr. Frederick. By the time I could look back, Mr. Frederick was falling; he threw up his hands and fell back in his sister's room; that is two doors this side of Mr. Seward's room. Then I ran down stairs and out to the front door, hallooing "murder," and then ran down to General Augur's head-quarters. I did not see the guard, and ran back again. By that time there were three soldiers who had run out of the building and were following me. When I got way back to the house, turning the corner there, I saw this man run out and get on his horse. He had on a light overcoat, but he had no hat on when he came out and got on his horse. I did not see his horse when he came to the house, and did not know he had a horse until I saw him get on it. I hallooed to the soldiers, "There he is, going on a horse!" They slacked their running, and ran out into the street, and did not run any more until he got on his horse and started off. I followed him up as far as

I Street and Fifteen-and-a-half Street, and he turned right out into Vermont avenue, where I lost sight of him. He rode a bay mare; it was a very stout animal, and did not appear to be a very high horse. He did not go very fast until he got to I Street. I must have been within twenty feet of him, but at I Street he got away from me altogether.

I do not know what he struck Mr. Frederick Seward with. It appeared to be round, and to be mounted all over with silver, and was about ten inches long. I had taken it for a knife, but they all said afterward it was a pistol. I saw him raise his hand twice to strike Mr. Frederick, who then fell. I did not wait any longer, but turned round and went down stairs. When he jumped round, he just said, "You," and commenced hitting him on the head; but I had hardly missed him from behind me until I heard him say that word.

I never saw this man about the door that I know of, nor did I see any person on the pavement when I came out.

Cross-examined by MR. DOSTER.

I do not know how old I am; I guess I am between nineteen and twenty. I was at school four or five years. I have been at Mr. Seward's nine months, and am second waiter. The talk with the man was inside; he came in and I closed the door. He had a very fine voice.

I noticed his hair and his pantaloons, and I noticed his boots that night. He talked to Mr. Frederick at least five minutes while up there near his father's door, in the third story. He had on very heavy boots at the time, black pants, light overcoat, and a brown hat. His face was very red at the time he came in; and he had very black, coarse hair.

I saw the same boots on him the night they captured him, and the same black pants.

The first time I saw the prisoner after that night was on the 17th of April. They sent for me about 3 o'clock in the morning to go down to General Augur's head-quarters. A Colonel there, with large whiskers and moustache, [Colonel H. H. Wells,] asked me to describe this man. I told him he had black hair, a thin lip, very fine voice, very tall, and broad across the shoulders, so I took him to be. There were twenty or thirty gentlemen in the room at the time, and he asked me if any gentleman there had hair like him, and I told him there was not. He then said, "I will bring a man in here and show him to you." I was leaning down behind the desk so that I could not be seen. The light was then put up, and a good many men walked into the room together. I walked right up to this man, and put my finger right here, [on the lip,] and told him I knew him; that he was the man. Nobody had offered me any money for giving the information, and no threats had been made to me.

When he struck Mr. Frederick Seward,

and I ran out, I did not observe any horse; but when I saw him run out of the house, I followed him to I Street; it seems to me he went very slow, because I kept up with him till he got to I Street.

WILLIAM H. BELL.

Recalled for the Prosecution.—May 19.

[By direction of the Judge Advocate the handcuffs were removed from the prisoner Payne, who put on the dark-gray coat, and over it the white and brown mixed coat, and the hat identified by Colonel Wells.]

When he came to Mr. Seward's he had on that coat, and that is the very same hat he had on; one corner of it was bent down over his eye. He had on a white collar, and looked quite nice to what he looks now. He had the same look as he has now, but he looked pretty fiery out of his eyes at me, the same way he looks now.

SERGEANT GEORGE F. ROBINSON.

For the Prosecution.—May 19.

On the 14th of April last I was at the residence of Mr. Seward, Secretary of State, acting as attendant nurse to Mr. Seward, who was confined to his bed by injuries received from having been thrown from his carriage. One of his arms was broken and his jaw fractured.

That man [pointing to the accused, Lewis Payne] looks like the man that came to Mr. Seward's house on that Friday night. I heard a disturbance in the hall, and opened the door to see what the trouble was; and as I opened the door this man stood close up to it. As soon as it was opened, he struck me with a knife in the forehead, knocked me partially down, and pressed by me to the bed of Mr. Seward, and struck him, wounding him. As soon as I could get on my feet, I endeavored to haul him off the bed, and then he turned upon me. In the scuffle, some one [Major Seward] came into the room and clinched him. Between the two of us we got him to the door, or by the door, and he, unclinching his hands from around my neck, struck me again, this time with his fist, knocking me down, and then broke away from Major Seward and ran down stairs.

I saw him strike Mr. Seward with the same knife with which he cut my forehead. It was a large knife, and he held it with the blade down below his hand. I saw him cut Mr. Seward twice that I am sure of; the first time he struck him on the right cheek, and then he seemed to be cutting around his neck. I did not hear the man say any thing during this time.

I afterward examined the wounds, and found one cutting his face from the right cheek down to the neck, and a cut on the neck, which might have been made by the same blow, as Mr. Seward was partially sitting in bed at the time; and another on the left side of the neck. Those were all I noticed, but there may have been more, as it was all bloody when I saw it. Mr. Seward received all his stabs in bed; but after the man was gone, and I went back to the bed, I found that he had rolled out, and was lying on the floor.

I did not see Mr. Frederick Seward down on the floor; the first I saw of him was after the man was gone; when I came back into the room he was inside the door, standing up. The man went down stairs immediately after he unwound his arm from round my neck, and struck me with his fist. I did not see him encounter Major Seward.

After he was gone we picked up a revolver, or parts of one, and his hat.

[A slouch felt hat was exhibited to the witness.]

I should judge that to be the hat; it looks like the one found there.

[A revolver was exhibited to the witness.]

That is the revolver picked up; I did not see this part, [the ramrod, which was disconnected.]

[The hat and revolver were both offered in evidence.]

[At the request of the Court, the guard was directed to place the hat on the head of the prisoner, Payne, to see if it fitted him or not, which was done, Payne smiling pleasantly. It was found to fit him.]

Recalled for the Prosecution.—May 19.

[The accused, Lewis Payne, clad in the coat and vest in which he was arrested, and the hat found at Mr. Seward's, was directed to stand up for recognition.]

He looks more natural now than he did before. I am not sure about it, but I think that is the man that came to Secretary Seward's house on the night of the 14th of April, a little after 10 o'clock. The pistol that was picked up in the room after he left was loaded. I examined it.

MAJOR AUGUSTUS H. SEWARD.

For the Prosecution.—May 26.

I am the son of the Hon. William H. Seward, Secretary of State, and was at his home in this city on the night of the 14th of April last. I saw that large man, with no coat on, [pointing to the accused, Lewis Payne,] at my father's house that night.

I retired to bed at half-past 7 on the night of the 14th, with the understanding that I was to be called about 11 o'clock to sit up with my father. I very shortly fell asleep, and so remained until awakened by the screams of my sister, when I jumped out of bed and ran into my father's room in my shirt and drawers. The gas in the room was turned down rather low, and I saw what appeared to me to be two men, one trying to hold the other at the foot of my father's bed. I seized by the clothes on his breast the person who was held, supposing it was my father, delirious; but, immediately on taking hold of him, I knew from his size and strength it was not my father. The thought then struck me that the nurse had become delirious sitting up there, and was striking about the room at random. Knowing the delicate state of my father, I shoved the person of whom I had hold to the door, with the intention of getting him out of the room. While I was pushing him, he struck me five, or six times on the forehead and top of the head, and once on the left hand, with what I supposed to be a bottle or decanter that he had seized from the table. During this time he repeated, in an intense but not strong voice, the words, "I'm mad! I'm mad!" On reaching the hall he gave a sudden turn, and sprang away from me, and disappeared down stairs. When near the door of my father's room, as I was pushing him out, and he came opposite where the light of the hall shone on him, I saw that he was a very large man, dark, straight hair, smooth face, no beard, and I had a view of the expression of his countenance. I then went into my room and got my pistol. It may possibly have taken me a minute, as it was in the bottom of my carpet-bag, to find it. I then ran down to the front door, intending to shoot the person, if he attempted to return. While standing at the door, the servant boy came back and said the man had ridden off on a horse, and that he had attacked the persons in the house with a knife. I then realized for the first time that the man was an assassin, who had entered the house for the purpose of murdering my father.

I suppose it was five minutes before I went back to my father's room. Quite a large crowd came around the door; I sent for the doctors, and got somebody to keep the crowd off before I went up to his room. It might not have been five minutes, but certainly three, before I got back; I think nearer five.

I was injured pretty badly myself, I found, when I got up stairs again. After my father's wounds were dressed, I suppose about an hour, and after my own head had been bandaged, I went in and saw my father, and found that he had one very large gash on his right cheek, near the neck, besides a cut on his throat on the right-hand side, and one under the left ear. I did not examine my brother's wounds; in fact, I went into his room but for a short time that night. I did not know how badly hurt he was. The next day he was insensible, and so remained; and it was four or five days before I saw what his wounds were. I found then that he had two wounds, one on the scalp, that was open to the brain, and another one over the ear. After the pieces of fractured skull were taken out, it left the covering of the brain open. It was such a wound that I should have supposed could have been made with a knife, but the surgeons seemed to think it was made by the hammer of a pistol. I heard that a pistol was picked up in the house, but I did not see it. I saw the hat that was found, and think I should recognize it.

[A slouch felt hat was exhibited to the witness.]

I am quite certain that is the hat. I did not see it the night it was picked up, but the next day it was taken out of the bureau-drawer, where it had been put the night before, and shown to me.

The surgeons think it was a knife with which I was struck, and after the servant boy told me what the man had been doing, I supposed so myself, though at the time I thought I was being struck with a bottle or a decanter. Not having any idea that it was a man with a knife, I did not think any thing about it.

I feel entirely satisfied that the prisoner at the bar, Payne, is the same man that made the attack on that night.

Cross-examined by Mr. Doster.

This is not the first time I have seen the prisoner since the attack; I saw him on board the monitor the day after he was taken. He was brought up on deck of the monitor, and I took hold of him the same way I had hold of him when I shoved him out of the room, and I looked at his face, and he had the same appearance, in every way, that he had the few moments that I saw him by the light in the hall; his size, his proportions, smooth face, no beard, and when he was made to repeat the words, "I'm mad! I'm mad!" I recognized the same voice, varying only in the intensity.

Surgeon-General Joseph K. Barnes.

For the Prosecution.—May 19.

I was called on the night of the 14th of April, a few minutes before 11 o'clock, to go to Mr. Seward, the Secretary of State. On arriving at his house, I found the Secretary wounded in three places; Mr. Frederick W. Seward insensible and very badly wounded in the head; the rest of the family I did not see, as I was occupied with them. The Secretary was wounded by a gash in the right cheek, passing around to the angle of the jaw; by a stab in the right neck, and by a stab in the left side of the neck.

Mr. Frederick Seward was suffering from a fracture of the cranium in two places; he was bleeding very profusely, exceedingly faint, almost pulseless, and unable to articulate. The wounds seem to have been inflicted by some blunt instrument—the butt of a pistol, a loaded bludgeon, or something of that kind.

Mr. Seward, the Secretary of State, had been progressing very favorably. He had recovered from the shock of the accident of ten days previously, and was getting along very well. His right arm was broken close to the shoulder-joint, and his jaw was broken in two places; but the serious injury of the first accident was the concussion.

The wounds of Mr. Seward were of a very dangerous character, and he is still suffering from them.

I saw Major Seward in the room; but I did not treat any of the wounded persons professionally, except Mr. Seward.

Doctor T. S. Verdi.

For the Prosecution—May 22.

I am a physician. On Friday night, the 14th of April, about half-past 10 o'clock, perhaps a little sooner, I was summoned to the house of Mr. Seward, the Secretary of State. I saw the Hon. William H. Seward, Mr. Frederick Seward, Major Augustus H. Seward, Mr. Robinson, and Mr. Hansell, all wounded, and their wounds bleeding. I had left Mr. Seward about 9 o'clock that evening, very comfortable, in his room, and when I saw him next he was in his bed, covered with blood, with blood all around him, blood under the bed, and blood on the handles of the doors.

I found Mr. Emrick W. Hansell on the same floor with Mr. Seward, lying on a bed. He said he was wounded. I undressed him, and found a stab over the sixth rib, from the spine obliquely toward the right side. I put my fingers into the wound to see whether it had penetrated the lungs. I found that it had not, but I could put my fingers probably two and a half inches or three inches deep. Apparently there was no internal bleeding. The wound seemed to be an inch wide, so that the finger could be put in very easily and moved all around. It was bleeding then, very fresh to all appearances; probably it was not fifteen or twenty minutes since the stab had occurred.

Cross-examined by Mr. Doster.

Mr. Frederick Seward was conscious, but had great difficulty in articulating. He wanted to say something, but he could not express himself. He knew me perfectly well. He had a smile of recognition on his lips, and as I looked upon his wound on the forehead, he was evidently impressed with the idea that the severest wound was in the back of the head, and he commenced saying, "It is, it is," and would put his finger to the back of his head. I examined the wound, and found that his skull was broken, and I said to him, "You want to know whether your skull is broken or not?" and he said, "Yes." He was sensible for some time; but probably in half an hour he went into a sleep, from which he woke in about fifteen or twenty minutes, and we attempted to put him to bed. Then he helped himself considerably. We put him to bed, and he went to sleep, in which he remained for sixty hours; he then improved in appearance, and gradually became more sensible.

I saw terror in the expression of all Mr. Secretary Seward's family, evidently expecting that his wounds were mortal. I examined the wounds, and immediately turned round to the family and said, "I congratulate you all that the wounds are not mortal;" upon which Mr. Seward stretched out his hands and received his family, and there was a mutual congratulation. This was probably twenty minutes before Doctor Barnes arrived.

Mr. Seward had improved very much from his accident, and was not in a critical condition when this attack was made. The effect of the wounds he received on the night of the 14th was principally from loss of blood, which weakened him very much, and made his condition still more delicate and difficult to rally from the shock. The wound itself created more inflammation in the cheek that had been swollen by the injury received before, and rendered the union of the bones more difficult. It is not my opinion that the wounds received by Mr. Seward tended to aid his recovery from his former accident; that idea got afloat from the fact that the cheek was very much inflated and swollen, and that by cutting into it, it would probably recover faster; but I never entertained and never expressed such an opinion.

ROBERT NELSON (colored.)

For the Prosecution.—May 20.

I live in Washington; I used to live in Virginia.

[A knife shown to the witness.]

That looks like the knife I found opposite Secretary Seward's house, on the Saturday morning after he was stabbed. I gave it to an officer at the door first, and afterward to that gentleman, [pointing to Surgeon John Wilson, U. S. A.]

Cross-examined by MR. DOSTER.

I do not say that it is the same knife, but it looks like the one I found in the middle of the street, right in front of Secretary Seward's house, between 5 and 6 o'clock in the morning.

DR. JOHN WILSON.

For the Prosecution.—May 20.

[The knife shown to Robert Nelson was exhibited to the witness.]

This is the knife I received from the colored boy who has just left the stand. He gave it to me in the library of Mr. Seward's house, about 10 o'clock on Saturday morning, the 15th of April.

THOMAS PRICE.

For the Prosecution.—May 19.

On Sunday afternoon, the 16th of April, I picked up a coat in a piece of woods that lies between Fort Bunker Hill and Fort Saratoga.

[Two coats were here submitted to the witness.]

This is the coat. It is a white and brown mixed cloth. I discovered traces of blood on the sleeve; that is how I recognize it. I found it about three miles from the city, in the direction of the Eastern Branch.

There is a road from one fort to another, and the coat was found in the piece of woods on the eastern side of the road.

COLONEL H. H. WELLS.

For the Prosecution.—May 19.

I had the prisoner, Payne, in my custody on the 17th of April, the night of his arrest. He had on a dark-gray coat, a pair of black pants, and something that looked like a skull-cap.

I took off his coat, shirt, pants, vest, and all his clothing the next day on board the monitor. He had on a white linen shirt and a woolen under-shirt, minus one sleeve; a pair of boots with a broad ink-stain on them on the inside.

[A box containing various articles of clothing was exhibited to the witness.]

These are the articles. There is a distinct mark on them by which I recognize them. I described to the prisoner at the time what I supposed was his position when he committed the assault, and told him I should find blood on the coat-sleeve in the inside. Spots of blood were found in the position I described.

[The witness exhibited the spots referred to.]

I found spots, also, on the white shirt-sleeve. I called Payne's attention to this at the time, and said, "What do you think now?" He leaned back against the side of the boat and said nothing.

[The articles were offered in evidence.]

I asked him where he had got his boots. He said he had bought them in Baltimore, and had worn them three months. I called his attention to this falsehood, as it was apparent the boots had only been slightly worn. He made no reply to that.

I took the boots away with me, and sent one of them to the Treasury Department, to ascertain, if possible, what the name was.

Cross-examined by MR. DOSTER.

I did not threaten the prisoner at any time. I think it is very possible I called him a liar. I saw stains of blood on the coat that was brought to me from Fort Bunker Hill; I called the prisoner's attention to the fact, and said, "How did that blood come there?" He replied, "It is not blood." I said, "Look and see, and say, if you can, that it is not blood." He looked at it and said, "I do not know how it came there."

CHARLES H. ROSCH.

For the Prosecution.—May 19.

I was present when the prisoner, Payne, was searched.

[A bundle of articles, including a pair of boots and a pocket-compass, was handed to the witness.]

All these articles were taken from the person of that big man there, [pointing to the accused, Lewis Payne.]

The pocket-compass he himself handed to Mr. Samson, and Mr. Samson handed it to me. I recognize the boots; they were pulled off in my presence.

SPENCER M. CLARK.

For the Prosecution.—May 19.

[Submitting to the witness a pair of boots.]

I had one of these boots yesterday for examination. I then discovered the name, which has now mostly disappeared under the effect of the acid I put upon it.

When I received the boot, it had on the inside a black mark, made apparently to cover writing. I examined it with a microscope, and found that it was one coat of ink overlaid on another. I then attempted to take off the outer coat to see what was below, and partially succeeded. The name appeared to me to be J. W. Booth. The J and W were distinct; the rest of the writing was obscure. I can not speak positively of a thing that is in itself obscure, but it left very little doubt upon my mind that the name was Booth.

Cross-examined by MR. DOSTER.

I have charge of the engraving and printing in the Treasury Department. I took off the outer coat of ink by the use of oxalic acid. Where the lower coat of ink has remained exposed to the air longer than the upper coat, it is possible to take off the upper and leave the lower or inner coat undisturbed. The reason the latter part of the name in this case was more obscure than the first, is because I left the acid too long on the outer coat, and it attacked the lower one. The upper coat is separated from the lower by washing with water as fast as it is dissolved. The acid is put on under a magnifier, and the moment the outer coat disappears, and the under one begins to show, I destroy the acid. An examination at the moment the outer coat dissolves and is washed away, shows the lower coat of writing. I supposed the lower coat had been exposed to the air longer than the outer, and made an effort to test it, which proved that it was so.

The boot was given me by Mr. Field, Second Assistant Secretary of the Treasury, who told me it had belonged to Payne. I expected to find the name of Payne, but I thought I plainly discovered the "th" at the end, when the name *Booth* came to my mind. That was before I had clearly determined upon the B. I should hesitate to swear positively to any thing so obscure as an obliterated signature, but I entertain very little doubt that the name is J. W. Booth. There is no process, that I am aware of, to restore the writing. The writing can not be said to be erased; it has been acted upon by the acid which destroys the color of the ink.

EDWARD JORDAN.

For the Prosecution.—May 19.

I am a solicitor of the Treasury. I was requested to look at the ink-marks on that

boot after it had been subjected to chemical preparations by Mr. Clark. By examining the writing through a glass, I came to the conclusion that the name written there was "J. W. Booth."

Cross-examined by MR. DOSTER.

I did not know to whom the boot belonged, or where it came from; and I had no suspicion why it was in Mr. Clark's possession. I was accidentally passing the room of the Assistant Secretary of the Treasury, when Mr. Clark said, "I have something curious to show you, I wish you would look at it," or words to that effect. The first letter, "J," was very distinct; the W and B were less so. I thought the outline of the writing was quite visible and determinable, but to say that it was distinct would not be true. I was asked what I thought the name was. My reply was, I thought it was the name of a very distinguished individual.

By the JUDGE ADVOCATE.

I arrived at the conclusion that it was the name of J. W. Booth before I had received any intimation as to what it was supposed to be.

STEPHEN MARSH.

For the Prosecution.—May 19.

That boot was shown to me by Mr. Field, Assistant Secretary of the Treasury, yesterday. On examining it, I thought I could make out certain letters on it. At first I could make out "J. W. B——h," then I thought I could trace a *t* next to the h; thus: J. W. B——th. I could not be positive as to the intervening letters; I examined them only with the naked eye, but in regard to the letters I have mentioned, I have no doubt at all. In the intervening space, between the B and th, there was room for two or three letters.

Cross-examined by MR. DOSTER.

The boot was handed to me by Mr. Field in his room. I was told to examine it, and see if I could make out what name appeared to be written there. I did so, and the result I have stated.

LIEUTENANT JOHN F. TOFFEY.

For the Prosecution.—May 17.

On the night of the 14th or the morning of the 15th of April last, it might have been a little after 1, as I was going to the Lincoln Hospital, where I am on duty, I saw a dark-bay horse, with saddle and bridle on, standing at Lincoln Branch Barracks, about three-quarters of a mile east of the Capitol. The sweat was pouring off him, and had made a regular puddle on the ground. A sentinel at the hospital had stopped the horse. I put a guard round it and kept it there until the cavalry picket was thrown out, when I reported the fact at the office of the picket, and was requested to take the horse down to the head-quarters of the picket, at the Old Capitol Prison. I there reported having the horse to Captain Lord, and he requested me to take it to General Augur's head-quarters. Captain Lansing of the Thirteenth New York Cavalry and myself took it there, where the saddle was taken off, and the horse taken charge of.

[A saddle was here shown to the witness.]

I should think that was the saddle; I know the stirrups. When I got to General Augur's head-quarters, I found that the horse was blind of one eye. Whether he had fallen or not I do not know, but as I rode him down I noticed that he was a little lame.

From the Lincoln Hospital to the Navy Yard Bridge is fully a mile.

[The saddle was put in evidence.]

Cross-examined by Mr. Doster.

The horse was on a sort of by-road that leads to Camp Barry; it turns north from the Branch Barracks toward Camp Barry to the Bladensburg road. I found him by the dispensary of the hospital. He had come running there, but from what direction I do not know.

Recalled.—May 18

I have been to General Augur's stables on Seventeenth and I Streets, and there recognized the horse I found.

See also testimony of
Louis J. Weichmann......... pages 113, 118
Miss Anna E. Surratt............... page 130
Miss Honora Fitzpatrick.......... " 132
John T. Holahan...................... " 139
Mrs. Eliza Holahan.......... .... " 132
Major H. W. Smith.................. " 121
Capt. W. M. Wermerskirch....... " 123
R. C. Morgan.......................... " 123

DEFENSE OF LEWIS PAYNE.

MISS MARGARET BRANSON.

For the Defense.—June 2.

By MR. DOSTER.

I live at No. 16 North Eutaw Street, Baltimore. I first met the prisoner, Payne, at Gettysburg, immediately after the battle there. I was a volunteer nurse, and he was in my ward. He was very kind to the sick and wounded. I do not know that he was a nurse, nor do I know that he was a soldier. As nearly as I remember, he wore blue pants, no coat, and a dark slouch hat. He went there by the name of Powell, and by the name of Doctor. The hospital contained both Confederate and Union soldiers. I was there about six weeks, and left the first week in September. I do not remember whether Powell was there the whole of that time.

I saw him again some time that fall or winter, at my mother's house. He was there but a very short time; only a few hours, and I had very little conversation with him.

Q. Did he say to you where he was going?

Assistant Judge Advocate BINGHAM. The witness need not state; what he said to her is altogether incompetent evidence.

Mr. DOSTER. May it please the Court, I intend to set up the plea of insanity, as I have already stated, in the case of the prisoner, Payne. It is very true that, under all other pleas, declarations of this kind are not considered competent evidence for the defense,

but the declaration of a person suspected of insanity is an act, and therefore admissible.

Assistant Judge Advocate BINGHAM. That is all very true; but the proper way to get at it is to lay some foundation for introducing the declarations in support of the allegation that the party was insane. In this case no foundation has been laid.

Mr. DOSTER. I claim that the whole conduct of the alleged murderer, from beginning to end, is the work of an insane man, and that any further declarations I may prove, are merely in support of that theory and of that foundation as laid by the prosecution.

Assistant Judge Advocate BINGHAM. According to that, the more atrocious a man's conduct is, the more he is to be permitted to make a case for himself by all his wild declarations, of every sort and to everybody, at every time and at every place. If he only manages to get a knife large enough to sever the head of an ox as well as the head of a man, rushes past all the friends of a sick man into his chamber, stabs him first on one side of the throat and then on the other, and slashes him across the face, breaks the skull of his son, who tries to rescue him, yelps, "I am mad! I am mad!" and rushes to the door and mounts a horse which he was careful to have tied there, he may thereupon prove all his declarations in his own defense, to show that he was not there at all.

Mr. DOSTER. It is claimed here that there is no foundation laid for the plea of insanity. In the first place, all the circumstances connected with the assassination show the work of insane men. The entrance into the house of Mr. Seward was by a stratagem which is peculiarly indicative of insane men. Then the conduct of Payne, after he entered the house, without the slightest particle of disguise, speaking to the negro for five minutes —a person that he must know would be able to recognize him again therafter; the ferocity of the crime, which is not indicative of human nature in its sane state; his leaving all the traces which men usually close up behind him. Instead of taking away his pistol and his knife and his hat, he walks leisurely out of the room, having plenty of time to take these away, and abandons them; he takes his knife and deliberately throws it down in front of Mr. Seward's door, as though anxious to be detected; and then, instead of riding off quickly, as a sane man would under the circumstances, he moves off so slowly that the negro tells you he followed him for a whole square on a walk; and afterward, instead of escaping either to the north, on the side where there were no pickets at the time, (for it was shown he had a sound horse,) or instead of escaping over the river, as he had ample opportunity of doing—because if he could not get across the Anacosta Bridge, he might have swam the river at any point—he wanders off into the woods, rides around like a maniac, abandons his horse, takes to the woods, and finally comes back to the very house which, if he had any sense, he knew must be exactly the house where he would be arrested—where there were guards at the time, and where he must have known, if he had been sane, that he would immediately walk into the arms of the military authorities. He goes to this house in a crazy disguise; because who in the world ever heard of a man disguising himself by using a piece of his drawers as a hat, supposing that a sane man would not discover the disguise. Finally, there is the conduct of this person since he has been here on trial—the extraordinary stolidity of this man, as opposed to the rest of the prisoners; instead of showing the slightest feeling, he has displayed an indifference throughout this trial. You yourselves noticed that at the time of that solemn scene, when the negro identified him he stood here and laughed at the moment when his life was trembling in the balance. I ask you, is that the conduct of a sane man? There are, besides, some physical reasons which go hand in hand with insanity, and corroborate it, of a character more delicate, and which I can not mention now, but which I am prepared to prove before the Court at any time. I say that the most probable case of insanity that can be made out has been made out by the prosecution, in the conduct of this prisoner before the assassination, during the assassination, at the time of his arrest, and during the trial.

Mr. CLAMPITT. May it please the Court, I do not rise for the purpose of denying to the counsel for the accused, Payne, the right to set up the plea of insanity, or any other plea that he thinks proper; but I do rise for the purpose of indignantly proclaiming that he has no right to endeavor to bring before this Court the house of Mrs. Surratt as a rendezvous to which Payne would naturally resort. There is no evidence which has shown that he would naturally go to her house for the purpose of hiding or for the purpose of screening himself from justice.

The Commission sustained the objection of the Judge Advocate.

WITNESS. I do not know where he went to from my mother's. In January of this year, he came again to our house. He was dressed then in citizen's dress of black, and represented himself to be a refugee from Farquier County, Va., and gave his name as Payne. He took a room at my mother's house, staid there six weeks and a few days, and left in the beginning of March. He never, to my knowledge, saw any company while there. I never saw J. Wilkes Booth, and do not know that he ever called upon Payne.

MARGARET KAIGHN.
For the Defense.—June 2.
By MR. DOSTER.

I am servant at Mrs. Branson's. I have seen the prisoner, Payne, at Mrs. Branson's boarding-house; he came there last January or February, and remained till the middle of March. I remember he asked a negro servant to clean up his room, and she gave him some impudence, and said she would not do it. She called him some names, and then he struck her; he threw her on the ground and stamped on her body, struck her on the forehead, and said he would kill her; and the girl afterward went to have him arrested.

DR. CHARLES H. NICHOLS.
For the Defense.—June 2.
By MR. DOSTER.

Q. Have I at any time given you any indication of the answers I expected you to give before this Court?
A. You have not.
Q. State what your official position is, and your profession.
A. I am a doctor of medicine, and superintendent of the Government Hospital for the Insane, which position I have occupied for thirteen years.
Q. What class of persons do you treat in your hospital?
A. Insane persons exclusively. The bulk of the patients I treat are composed of sailors and soldiers.
Q. Please define moral insanity.
A. When the moral or affective faculties

seem to be exclusively affected by disease of the brain, I call that a case of moral insanity.

Q. What are some of the principal leading causes that produce moral insanity?

A. My impression is that insanity is oftener caused by physical disease than moral causes, and that the fact that insanity takes the form of moral insanity is apt to depend on the character of the individual before he becomes deranged.

Q. Is active service in the field, among soldiers, at any time, a cause of moral insanity?

A. It is; but not a frequent cause. I have known cases of moral insanity occur among soldiers.

Q. Has or has not insanity increased very much in the country, and in your hospital, during the present war?

A. It has.

Q. Has it not increased much more, proportionately, than the increase in the army?

A. It has.

Q. How is the increase accounted for?

A. By the diseases, hardships, and fatigues of a soldier's life, I think, to which the men were not accustomed until they entered the service.

Q. Are young men who enlist more exposed to insanity than men who enlist in middle life?

A. I am not sure that they are. My impression is, that young men accommodate themselves to a change in their manner of life rather more readily than men of middle age.

Q. What are some of the leading symptoms of moral insanity?

A. The cases are as diverse as the individuals affected. If a man, for example, believes an act to be right which he did not believe to be right when in health, and which people generally do not believe to be right, I regard that as a symptom of moral insanity.

Q. Is depression of spirits at any time considered a symptom of insanity?

A. It is.

Q. Is great taciturnity considered a symptom?

A. It is a frequent symptom of insanity, but I can conceive that great taciturnity might exist without insanity.

Q. Is a disposition to commit suicide and an indifference to life considered a symptom?

A. It is.

Q. Is great cunning and subtlety in making plans concomitant of insanity?

A. The insane frequently exhibit extraordinary cunning in their plans to effect an object.

Q. Is it or is it not possible for a madman to confederate with other madmen or sane men in plans?

A. I would say that it is not impossible, but it is infrequent for madmen to confederate in effecting their plans.

Q. Do madmen never confederate in plans?

A. Very seldom.

Q. Is or is not a morbid propensity to destroy, proof of insanity?

A. Not a proof, but it is a very common attendant upon insanity.

Q. Is it not a symptom of insanity if one, apparently sane, and without provocation or cause, commits a crime?

A. I should regard it as giving rise to a suspicion of insanity, but not of itself a proof of it.

Q. Is not all conduct that differs from the usual modes of the world proof of insanity?

A. I will answer that by saying that no single condition is a proof of insanity in every instance, but that an entire departure from the usual conduct of man would be considered as affording strong ground to suspect the existence of insanity.

Q. Are madmen not remarkable for great cruelty?

A. My impression is that madmen exhibit about the same disposition in that respect that men generally do.

Q. Do or do not madmen, in committing crimes, seem to act without pity?

A. Those who commit criminal acts frequently do.

Q. If one should try to murder a sick man in his bed, without ever having seen him before, would it not be presumptive proof of insanity?

A. It would give rise, in my mind, to the suspicion that a man was insane. I should not regard it as proof.

Q. If the same person should besides try to murder four other persons in the house without having seen them before, would it not strengthen that suspicion of insanity?

A. I think it would.

Q. If the same person should make no attempt to disguise himself, but should converse for five minutes with a negro servant, walk away leisurely, leave his hat and pistol behind, throw away his knife before the door, and ride away so slowly that he could be followed for a square by a man on foot, would not such conduct further corroborate the suspicion of insanity?

A. I think it would. It is a peculiarity of the insane, when they commit criminal acts, that they make little or no attempt to conceal them; but that is not always the case.

Q. If the same person should cry out, while stabbing one of the attendants, "I am mad, I am mad," would it not be further ground for suspicion that he was insane?

A. Such an exclamation would give rise, in my mind, to an impression that the man was feigning insanity. Insane men rarely make such an exclamation, or a similar one, and they rarely excuse themselves for a criminal act on the ground that they are insane.

Q. Do not madmen sometimes unconsciously state that they are mad?

A. They do sometimes. but it is not frequent that they do.

Q. Do you not remember cases in your experience where madmen have told you they were mad?

A. They frequently do it in this way: An individual knows that he is regarded as insane, and if taken to task for any improper act, a shrewd man will excuse himself on the ground that he is an insane man, and therefore not responsible.

Q. If the same person that I have mentioned should, although in the possession of a sound horse, make no effort to escape, but should abandon his horse, wander off into the woods, and come back to a house surrounded with soldiers, and where he might expect to be arrested, would that not be additional ground for the suspicion that he was insane?

A. I should regard every act of a man who had committed a crime, indicating that he was indifferent to the consequences, as a ground for suspecting that he was insane.

Q. If the same person should return to this house I have spoken of, with a piece of his drawers for his hat, at a time when he saw the soldiers in its possession, would not that be additional proof of insanity?

A. I can hardly see what bearing that would have upon the question of insanity.

Q. I understood you to say before that madmen seldom disguise themselves. The disguise in question consisted of a piece of drawers being used for a hat. I ask whether that disguise may properly be presumed to be the disguise of a sane man or an insane man?

A. It would depend upon circumstances. It is a common peculiarity of insane men, that they dress themselves in a fantastic manner; for example, make head-dresses out of pieces of old garments. They do it, however, apparently from a childish fancy for something that is fantastic and attracts attention; and I do not recollect a case of an insane person dressing himself in a garment or garments of that kind for the sake of disguising himself.

Q. If this same person, after his arrest, should express a strong desire to be hanged, and express great indifference of life, would that be additional ground for suspicion of insanity?

A. I think it would.

Q. Would it be further ground for suspicion if he seemed totally indifferent to the conduct of his trial, laughed when he was identified, and betrayed a stolidity of manner different from his associates?

A. I think it would.

Q. Please state to the Court what physical sickness generally accompanies insanity, if any there is.

A. I believe that disease, either functional or organic, of the brain always accompanies insanity. No other physical disease necessarily, or perhaps usually, accompanies it.

Q. Is long-continued constipation one of the physical conditions that accompany insanity?

A. Long-continued constipation frequently precedes insanity. Constipation is not very frequent among the actual insane.

Q. If this same person that I have described to you, had been suffering from constipation for four weeks, would that be considered additional ground for believing in his insanity?

A. I think it would. I think some weight might be given to that circumstance.

Q. If the same person, during his trial and during his confinement, never spoke until spoken to, at a time when all his companions were peevish and clamorous; if he never expressed a want when all the rest expressed many; remained in the same spirits when the rest were depressed; retained the same expression of indifference when the rest were nervous and anxious, and continued immovable, except a certain wildness in his eyes, would it not be considered additional ground for believing in his insanity?

A. I think it would.

Q. If this same person, after committing the crime, should, on being questioned as to the cause, say he remembered nothing distinctly, but only a struggle with persons whom he had no desire whatever to kill, would not that be additional ground for suspicion of insanity?

A. I think it would.

Q. What are the qualities of mind and person needed by a keeper to secure control over a madman?

A. Self-control.

Q. Are not madmen easily managed by persons of strong will and resolute character?

A. Yes, sir; they are.

Q. Are there not instances on record of madmen who toward others were wild, while toward their keepers, or certain persons whom they held to be superiors, they were docile and obedient, in the manner of dogs toward their masters?

A. I think the servile obedience which a dog exhibits to his master is rarely exhibited by the insane. It is true, that the insane are comparatively mild and obedient to certain persons, when they are more or less turbulent and violent toward other persons.

Q. Would it not be possible for such a keeper, exercising supreme control over a madman, to direct him to the commission of a crime, and secure that commission?

A. I should say that would be very difficult, unless it was done in the course of a few minutes after the plan was laid and the direction given. I should say, generally, it would be very difficult.

Q. Is not the influence of some persons over madmen so great that their will seems to take the place of the will of the madman?

A. There is a great difference in the control that different individuals have over insane persons, but I think it an error that that control reaches the extent you have described, or the extent, I may add, that is popularly supposed.

Q. Do you or not recognize a distinction between mania and delusion?

A. A certain distinction, inasmuch as delusion may accompany any form and every form of insanity, and mania is the name given to a particular form, which may or may not be accompanied by delusion.

Q. Are not instances of insane delusion more frequent during civil war than any other kind of insanity?

A. My impression is, that cases in which delusions are entertained are not as frequent. Insanity is of a more general character—so far as my experience goes, has been during the war, among soldiers—than it usually is.

Q. Does or does not constant dwelling on the same subject lead to an insane delusion?

A. It frequently does, I think.

Q. If a body of men, for instance, who owned slaves, were constantly hearing speeches and sermons vindicating the divine right of slavery, burned men at the stake for attempting to abolish slavery, and finally took up arms to defend slavery, when no man was really attacking it, would not that be evidence that some of these men were actually deluded?

A. I think it would; but it does not follow that the delusion is what I technically denominate an insane delusion, arising from disease of the brain, and for which a man is not responsible.

Q. If one of those same men who owned slaves, and believed in the divine origin of slavery, and had fought in its defense, and believed that he had also fought in defense of his home and friends, should attempt, on his own motion, to kill the leaders of the people, who he believed were killing his friends, would not that conduct be esteemed a fanatical delusion?

Assistant Judge Advocate BURNETT. Unless Mr. Doster can give us some idea when this species of examination will be brought to a close, we must here interpose objection. It certainly has nothing whatever to do with the case. He is imagining facts that do not exist, and he is examining upon a basis that he has not laid, and it is certainly irrelevant and foreign to the issue. Will Mr. Doster state if he is nearly through with his examination?

Mr. DOSTER. The course of examination that I propose is not a great deal longer. I mentioned the other day that it was impossible for me to secure the attendance of witnesses from Florida. Regularly, I ought not to have called Dr. Nichols before these witnesses had been here and had been examined. I have been unwilling to detain Dr. Nichols here, and have endeavored to go over the whole ground with him, so that I need not call him twice, as I would have to do if I were to call these witnesses from Florida first.

WITNESS. If I may be allowed, I would like to give an explanatory answer. I have

given just a categorical one to all the questions that have been asked me, I believe; I am, personally, and as an expert, very much opposed to giving an opinion in respect to hypothetical cases, for the simple and best of reasons, as I conceive that I have none, and I could give no definite opinion upon the facts implied in the questions submitted to me. Every case of insanity is a case of itself, and has to be studied with all the light that can be thrown upon it, and it is impossible for me to give an opinion upon a hypothetical case.

DR. JAMES C. HALL.
For the Defense.—June 13.

This morning I spent three-quarters of an hour in an examination of the prisoner, Lewis Payne. I first examined him with regard to his physical condition. His eye appeared to be perfectly natural, except that it appeared to have very little intellectual expression; but it was capable of showing a great deal of passion and feeling. I discovered a remarkable want of symmetry in the two sides of his head. The left side is much more developed than the right. His pulse I counted twice carefully; I found it to be a hundred and eight, which is about thirty strokes above a natural healthy pulse. In other respects his health seemed to be good, with the exception of another habit, which, I believe, the Court is informed of—namely, constipation. His general muscular development is perfectly healthy.

I questioned him first to test his memory. I found that it acted very slowly. He appeared to answer my questions willingly, but his mind appeared to be very inert, and it took some time before he would give me an answer to a very simple question, though he did not seem to be at all reluctant in giving me the information I was seeking for. His intellect appears to be of a very low order; and yet I could not discover that there was any sign of insanity. His mind is naturally dull and feeble, and, I presume, has not been cultivated by education.

I asked him certain questions which I thought would draw out his moral nature and feelings, and the conclusion to which I came was, that he would perform acts, and think himself justified in so doing, which a man of better moral nature and of a better mind would condemn.

Q. Did you or not state the case to him of a person committing the crime with which he is charged, and ask his opinion in reference to the moral right to commit it?

A. I did. I mentioned it as a supposed case, and he said he thought a person in performing such an act as I described would be justified. "I wish you would give me some reason," I said, "why you think he would be justified; why you think an act which I think wrong, and which everybody else thinks wrong, could be justified." His answer amounted to this, that he thought in war a person was entitled to take life. That was the reason he assigned why he thought such an act could be justified.

I should say that, from the whole examination, there was reasonable ground for suspicion of insanity. It seems to me that no man could, if he were perfectly sane, exhibit the utter insensibility that he does and did in my presence. I do not think there was any attempt at deception. He answered the questions, so far as his mind would permit him, plainly and clearly, without any attempt at deceiving me or misleading me. I can not give a positive opinion that he is laboring under either moral or mental insanity. To decide on a case of this kind, one ought to see the person at various times and under various circumstances. I never saw this man before.

Cross-examined by the JUDGE ADVOCATE.

I can not discover any positive signs of mental insanity, but of a very feeble, inert mind; a deficiency of mind rather than a derangement of it; a very low order of intellect. His memory appears to be very slow in acting.

Q. Did he or not seem to have a distinct recollection of his crime, and also of the motives and course of reasoning—

Mr. DOSTER. I object to that question.

WITNESS. I did not refer to it as the crime committed by himself. I asked him what he would think of a man who had committed a crime such as he was charged with, and he said he thought he would be right in doing it. I carefully avoided applying the act or crime to himself, personally; I merely spoke of it as a supposititious case. I did not think it would be right for me to receive any confession from him, and I rather avoided extorting it. I by no means regard atrocious crime as *per se* evidence of insanity.

Q. Do you regard insensibility under crime or indifference to the results of crime as indicating insanity?

A. Where a man commits crime habitually and without any adequate motive or provocation, I should be disposed then to suspect insanity. If there is an absence of motive and an absence of provocation, and if it is done habitually, these are the conditions. A single act I should be very reluctant to form an opinion upon.

Q. If a man, engaged in arms as a rebel against the Government of his country, is found assassinating its Chief Magistrate and the members of its Cabinet, would you or not regard these circumstances as indicating sufficiently the presence of motive to save him from the imputation of insanity?

A. Yes, he might have a motive. I can readily conceive that a man might think he had a sufficient motive and a sufficient justification for it.

Q. Do I or not understand you to say, Doctor, that, from the whole examination you have made, you regard the prisoner, Payne, as sufficiently sane to be a responsible being for his acts?

A. I have not altogether made up my mind on that. I do not think that the single examination which I have made would suffice to decide the question. I think there is enough to allow us a suspicion that he may not be a perfectly sane and responsible man. I can give no positive opinion on that point. His intellect is very feeble and inert.

Q. The extent, then, to which you go, is that there is ground for suspicions? You do not express any such opinion?

A. I do not express a positive opinion that he is either morally or mentally insane, but that there is sufficient ground, both from his physical condition and his mental development, for a suspicion of insanity.

Q. Do you rest that suspicion largely on his course of reasoning, and the conclusion he drew from the case which you supposed?

A. Yes, sir; I should think that was the result either of insanity or very badly cultivated mind, and very bad morals.

Q. Might it not be wholly the result of very bad morals?

A. It might entirely. I attach some importance to his physical condition. It is generally known that persons who are insane, habitually, with few exceptions, have an unusual frequency of pulse. His pulse is thirty odd strokes above the normal standard.

Q. He was aware of the purpose for which you had your interview with him, was he not?

A. I introduced myself by telling him that I was a physician, and that the Court had directed me to examine into his condition, and I referred to some matters connected with his health.

Q. Did he seem to be under any excitement?

A. Not the least. He was perfectly calm, and at times smiled. He did not seem to be playing a part at all. He appeared to answer the questions honestly and truthfully, so far as I could judge; but his memory is very slow, and it is very difficult to get from him an answer to a very simple question. I asked him in regard to his birth and his residence. He could not remember the maiden name of his mother. He said her first name was Caroline, but he could not remember her maiden name.

But I have known sane persons who forgot their own names. The celebrated John Law, of this city, would go to the post-office and be unable to call for a letter in his own name.

JOHN B. HUBBARD.

For the Defense.—June 3.

By MR. DOSTER.

I am at times in charge of the prisoner, Lewis Payne, and have at times had conversation with him.

Q. Please state the substance of that conversation.

Assistant Judge Advocate BINGHAM. That I object to.

The JUDGE ADVOCATE. Is this conversation offered as a confession, or as evidence of insanity?

Mr. DOSTER. As evidence of insanity. I believe it is a settled principle of law that all declarations are admissible under the plea of insanity.

Assistant Judge Advocate BINGHAM. There is no such principle of the law, that all declarations are admissible on the part of the accused for any purpose. I object to the introduction of the declarations of the prisoner, made on his own motion.

The JUDGE ADVOCATE. If the Court please, as a confession, of course, this declaration is not at all competent, but if it is relied upon as indicating an insane condition of mind, I think it would be better for the Court to consider it. We shall be careful, however, to exclude from its consideration these statements so far as the question of the guilt or innocence of the particular crime is concerned, and to admit them only so far as they may aid in solving the question of insanity raised by the counsel.

WITNESS. I was taking him out of the court-room, about the third or fourth day of the trial, and he said he wished they would make haste and hang him; that he was tired of life, and would rather be hung than come back here in the court-room. And about a week ago he spoke to me about his constipation; he said he had been constipated ever since he had been here. I have no personal knowledge of the truth of this.

Cross-examined by the JUDGE ADVOCATE.

I communicated this statement to Colonel Dodd or Colonel McCall, and I believe to General Hartranft, and to no one else.

JOHN E. ROBERTS.
For the Defense.—June 3.
By MR. DOSTER.

I am on duty around the prison, but have no special charge of the prisoner, Lewis Payne, more than the others. I have had a little conversation with him. After the coat and hat were taken off him, on the day that Major Seward was examined, I had to put his irons back on him, and he told me then that they were tracking him pretty close, and that he wanted to die.

COLONEL W. H. H. McCALL.
For the Defense.—June 3.
By MR. DOSTER.

I have charge of the prisoner, Payne, in connection with Colonel Frederick and Colonel Dodd; we each have eight hours' duty out of the twenty-four. My duty makes me cognizant of the conduct of the prisoner in his cell, and to the best of my knowledge he has been constipated from the 29th of April until last evening; that was his first passage. I never had any conversation with him on the subject of his death.

MRS. LUCY ANN GRANT.
For the Defense.—June 12.
By MR. DOSTER.

Mr. DOSTER. I am about to call two witnesses, and to prevent any objections being made, I will state that the reason for calling them is to show that the prisoner, Payne, three months before the alleged attempted assassination of Mr. Seward, saved the lives of two Union soldiers. It is the very essence of insanity that one violates the "even tenor" of his previous life; and, therefore, if I can show that three months before the alleged attempted assassination this person exercised a degree of honor and benevolence, which he afterward violated and turned into ferocity and malignity, it will give a high degree of probability to the plea, and his subsequent conduct can only be explained by his being under the control of fury and madness.

WITNESS. I live on the Waterloo Pike, Warrenton, Virginia. I recollect having seen one of the prisoners before; that one with the gray shirt, [pointing to the accused, Lewis Payne.] I saw him some time about Christmas in the road in front of our house; he was in charge of three Union prisoners. It was at the time of General Torbett's raid; after he had passed through Warrenton, on his return to Washington. Some men—rebel soldiers, I suppose, from their uniform—were going to kill these prisoners, and I remember seeing this man try to prevent it. He told them that he could not defend all, but if they killed or captured the one he had in charge, they would do it at the peril of their lives. They left the road then, and I do not know what became of them afterward, but I know one of the prisoners was killed, for a Confederate soldier wanted to bring him into my house, and I was scared nearly to death.

Cross-examined by the JUDGE ADVOCATE.

I never saw the man before or since; but he is the same man, I am certain. I should know him anywhere. He was dressed in a dark gray uniform, and some of the men called him "Lieutenant." I understood from a citizen to whom I was speaking about his trying to save those Union prisoners that his name was Powell.

JOHN GRANT.
For the Defense.—June 12.
By MR. DOSTER.

I am the husband of Mrs. Grant, who has just left the stand. I was about three hundred yards from my home, when the affray began in front of my house, on the first of last January. I rushed home as quickly as I could, when the pistol firing commenced; and I saw that that man, [Payne,] whose name I understood was Powell, saved the lives of two Union soldiers.

TESTIMONY IN REBUTTAL.

SURGEON-GENERAL J. K. BARNES.

For the Prosecution.—June 14.

In association with Dr. Hall and Surgeon Norris, I have made an examination this morning of the prisoner, Payne, and find no evidence of insanity—none whatever.

The evidences of sanity which struck me as present in his case are his narrative of himself, of the places he has been at, of his occupation, the coherence of his story, and, the most important evidence, his reiteration of his statements of yesterday and of his first examination this morning. That is considered a very severe test. It is called the Shakspearian test, and is one of the severest.

Cross-examined by MR. DOSTER.

I should consider the Shakspearian test a test for both moral and mental sanity.

I have not of late years had a large experience in cases of insanity; but some years ago I was in charge of the insane wards of a large hospital.

I was present when the prisoner answered Dr. Hall's question as to his moral responsibility for this crime, and heard him say that, under certain circumstances, he considered such a crime justifiable.

DR. JAMES C. HALL.

Recalled for the Prosecution.—June 14.

This morning, in connection with Dr. Norris and Dr. Porter, we had an examination of the prisoner, Lewis Payne, and since the recess of the Commission, Dr. Barnes, the Surgeon-General, joined us, and we examined him again.

I asked him very nearly the same questions I proposed to him yesterday, for the purpose of seeing whether he would give me answers consistent with those which I then received, and I found that they were very accurately the same, and he answered to-day with rather more promptness than yesterday.

I think I am now prepared to say that there is no evidence of mental insanity. Payne's mind is weak and uncultivated, but I can not discover any sufficient evidence of mental insanity.

Cross-examined by MR. DOSTER.

Q. What are you prepared to state as to his moral insanity?

A. We asked him the question to-day whether he believed in a God. He said he did, and that he believed he was a just God. He also acknowledged to me that at one time he had been a member of the Baptist Church. I asked him the question, which I believe I repeated to the Court yesterday, whether he thought that private assassination, practiced upon an enemy in public war, was justifiable. After some little hesitation, he said that he believed it was.

Q. Is it or not esteemed an evidence of a fanatical delusion that a person believes to be right what everybody else believes to be wrong?

A. In some instances it would; but I can readily conceive that there are persons whose minds and morals are such that they would believe a crime similar to that which he has committed to be justifiable and proper, even a duty.

DR. BASIL NORRIS.

For the Prosecution.—June 14.

I am a surgeon in the regular army. This morning, in association with the Surgeon-General of the army and Dr. Hall, I made an examination of the prisoner, Payne, and I arrived at the conclusion that he is not insane.

His look is natural, and his speech perfectly natural, and his manner natural; that of a man sane. There is nothing in his appearance, or speech, or manner that indicates to me that he is a man of unsound mind. In my opinion, there is nothing to indicate the presence either of moral or what may be called mental insanity. We asked him a number of questions. His reasoning faculties appeared to be good, and his judgment good, to which I attach great importance.

We could not learn of any thing in his past life, so far as we have been able to gather his history, that would indicate insanity. We learned but very little of his past history; but so far as his life has been disclosed since he has been here, his conduct and conversations, nothing that he has done, has indicated to me that he was an insane man.

Cross-examined by MR. DOSTER.

I am not familiar with cases of insanity, but I have seen some cases, and have visited institutions for the insane. I would form my opinion of a man very much as any other person.

It is not usual for madness to escape the scrutiny of physicians on a single interview, or on two interviews. I think there is something always in the appearance of a man, in his manner or in his speech, that would arouse a suspicion of a physician, or indeed of any intelligent person, even on one interview.

I have heard of cases of men who have been examined for months at a time before their madness was discovered, but none have come to my knowledge.

I do not think the conduct of the prisoner in my presence was the conduct of a madman during a lucid interval. It will be found upon scrutiny that the conduct of a madman in a lucid interval differs from the ordinary conduct of men. Upon careful examination, there will be some indication always, in my opinion, that to several medical men, or several intelligent men, will be observable. I would regard it as a very exceptional case if this man should be insane. I believe it is possible that this man might be a monomaniac on a subject not broached to him this morning; but yet a monomaniac will almost invariably—I believe myself he would invariably—in a conversation with strange persons, strike upon that subject that he had the delusion on—that subject upon which he was insane. It is my opinion that a monomaniac, in an examination of half an hour even, by strange persons especially, would strike upon the subject on which he was deluded; that he would speak upon the subject on which he was a monomaniac. I

believe there are cases on record of monomaniacs who have gone whole weeks without referring to the subject on which they were insane; but I have never seen such cases.

ASSISTANT SURGEON GEORGE L. PORTER.

For the Prosecution.—June 14.

I was associated with Surgeon-General Barnes and other medical gentlemen in an examination of the prisoner, Lewis Payne, and our conclusion was that he was a sane man, and responsible for his actions.

He has been under my eye ever since he has been confined here. I have made inspections twice each day since the 30th of April; and his conduct and conversation during that period have been such as to impress me that he is a sane and responsible man. I have not observed any indication of insanity.

Cross-examined by MR. DOSTER.

I believe that the law does not recognize moral as distinct from mental insanity. Moral insanity is where the mind of a person is perverted on moral subjects; mental insanity has regard to the intellectual more than the moral faculties. The symptoms of moral insanity are common to all cases of insanity.

Insane persons have generally some physical symptoms which I find wanting in this case. I have examined this man twice each day, and I found that his pulse, as a general rule, was lower than the pulse of the others. Recently, I have examined by the watch, and find that his has not been so frequent as that of the other prisoners. Last night it was eighty; this morning it was eighty-three or eighty-four. Another symptom of insanity is want of sleep, restlessness. In this case it has been particularly noticeable that while the other prisoners were awake when I made my inspections in the evening, I almost always found this man asleep.

TESTIMONY CONCERNING SAMUEL A. MUDD.

COLONEL H. H. WELLS.

For the Prosecution.—May 16.

During the week subsequent to the assassination, I had three interviews with Dr. Samuel A. Mudd, in each of which he made statements to me; the first and third verbal, the second in writing. He said that, about 4 o'clock on Saturday morning, the 15th of April, he was aroused by a loud knock at his door. Going to the window, he saw in

his front yard a person holding two horses, on one of which a second person was sitting. The one who held the horses he described as a young man, very talkative and fluent of speech. The person on horseback had broken his leg, and desired medical attendance. He (Mudd) assisted in bringing the person on horseback into his house, and laying him upon the sofa in the parlor. After he had lain on the sofa for some time, he was carried up stairs, and put on a bed in the front room. He then examined his leg, and found that the front bone was broken, nearly at right angles, about two inches above the instep. It seemed, in his judgment, as slight a breaking as it could possibly be. The patient complained also of a pain in his back. He examined and found no apparent cause for the pain, unless it might have been in consequence of his falling from his horse, as he said he had done. Dr. Mudd stated that he dressed the limb as well as he was able to do it with the limited facilities he had, and called a young man, a white servant, I think, to make a crutch for him. At breakfast, the younger of the two persons partoo with them. After breakfast, Dr. Mudd observed the condition of his patient. He seemed much debilitated, and pale to such an extent that he was unable to tell what his complexion might have been, light or dark. After breakfast the young man made some remark about procuring a conveyance to take his friend away. In the mean time he (Mudd) had been about, giving directions to his farm servants. I think he said the two persons remained until some time after dinner. He started out with the young man to see if a carriage could be procured at his father's, but meeting his younger brother, he ascertained from him that the carriage could not be procured, and then rode on to join the young man who had gone ahead, and together they rode into the pines a mile and a half beyond the elder Mudd's house. The young man remarked that he would not go further to get a carriage, but would go back to the house and see if he could get his friend off in some way or other. Dr. Mudd then went, as he said, to the town, or near the town, to see some friends or patients, and then returned to his house. As he came back to his house, he saw the younger man of the two pass to the left of the house toward the barn.

He said he did not recognize the wounded man. I exhibited to him a photograph of Booth, but he said he could not recognize him from that photograph.

He said he had been introduced to Booth at Church, some time in November last, as wanting to buy farming lands, and that they had some little conversation on the subject of lands. In this conversation Booth asked if there were any desirable horses that could be bought in the neighborhood cheaply; and Mudd mentioned a neighbor of his who had some horses that were good drivers; that Booth remained with him that night, and next morning purchased one of those horses.

In answer to a question, he admitted that he could now recognize the person he treated as the same person he was introduced to—Booth. He had never seen Booth from the time he was introduced to him in Church until that Saturday morning. Herold he had not before seen.

He thought there was something strange about these two persons, from the young man coming down shortly after breakfast and asking for a razor, saying his friend wished to shave himself; and when he was up stairs shortly afterward, he saw that the wounded man had shaved off his moustache. The wounded man, he thought, had a long, heavy beard; whether natural or artificial he did not know. He kept a shawl about his neck, seemingly for the purpose of concealing the lower part of his face. He said he first heard of the murder either on Sunday morning or late on Saturday evening.

He said that Herold—for by that name we spoke of him after the first explanation—asked him the direct road to Dr. Wilmer's, saying he was acquainted with the Doctor. Dr. Mudd described the main traveled road, and was then asked if there was not a nearer way. He replied that there was a road across the swamp, and described it.

Dr. Mudd pointed out to me the track they took, and I went with him a long way into the marsh, and across it on to the hill, where, instead of keeping straight on, they turned square to the left, across a piece of plowed ground, and there all trace of them was lost.

This embraces what Dr. Mudd told me at the several interviews.

Cross-examined by Mr. Ewing.

Dr. Mudd's manner was so very extraordinary, that I scarcely know how to describe it. He did not seem unwilling to answer a direct question; he seemed embarrassed, and at the third interview alarmed, and I found that, unless I asked direct questions, important facts were omitted. I first saw him on Friday, the 21st, and my last interview was on Sunday, I think. We had, perhaps, a dozen interviews in all. It was at the last interview that I told him he seemed to be concealing the facts of the case, which would be considered the strongest evidence of his guilt, and might endanger his safety.

On Sunday Dr. Mudd took us along the road that the two men had taken from his house. They took the direction pointed out by the Doctor until they came to the hill. The marsh there is full of holes and bad places. I thought I discovered, from their tracks, that in going to the right to avoid a bad place they had changed their direction, and got lost.

My impression is that Dr. Mudd said he had first heard of the assassination on the Saturday evening; that somebody had brought the news from Bryantown. The question was asked Dr. Mudd by some person whether any thing had been paid to him for setting the wounded man's leg, and I think he said they had paid him $25.

He said that he had told Dr. George Mudd, I think he said on Sunday, that there had been two suspicious men at his house. The town was full of soldiers and people, coming and going all the time, and the place was in a state of general excitement.

By the JUDGE ADVOCATE.

I understood Dr. Mudd to mean that he recognized the wounded man, while at his house, to be the Booth to whom he had been introduced in November. His expression was that he did not recognize him at first, but, on reflection, he remembered him as the person to whom he had been introduced.

He said that, as he came back in the afternoon, he saw the wounded man going away from the house, hobbling through the mud. Herold had been riding the bay horse, and was going off on it. The roan horse, he supposed, was in the stable. He did not say that he did not see them leave; but from the position he described them as being in, he could not see them the moment after they left the stable.

By MR. EWING.

As near as I can recollect, the words used by Dr. Mudd, in reference to recognizing Booth's photograph, were that he should not have recollected the man from the photograph, and that he did not know him or remember him when he first saw him; but that on reflection he remembered that he was the man who was introduced to him in November last; but he did not say whether this reflection, from which he recognized the wounded man as the one to whom he had been introduced, occurred before or after the man left; but the impression made on my mind was that it was before the man left. He gave as the reason for not remembering him at first that the man was very much worn and debilitated, and that he seemed to make an effort to keep the lower part of his face disguised; but of course the open light of day, the shaving of the face, and the fact that he sometimes slept, gave better opportunities for observation. I do not think he said any thing to indicate that the wounded man at any time entirely threw off his attempt to disguise; but when he came to reflect, he remembered that it was the man to whom he had been introduced; he did not, however, I believe, say that that reflection or memory came to him at any particular moment.

MARY SIMMS (colored.)

For the Prosecution.—May 25.

I know that prisoner yonder, Dr. Samuel Mudd, [pointing to the accused, Samuel A. Mudd.] I was his slave, and lived with him four years; I left him about a month before this Christmas gone. I heard him talk about President Lincoln. He said that he stole in there at night, dressed in woman's clothes; that they lay in watch for him, and if he had come in right they would have killed him. He said nothing about shooting him; he would have killed him, he said, if

he had come in right, but he could not; he was dressed in woman's clothes.

A man named John Surratt and a man named Walter Bowie, visited Dr. Mudd's last summer. Mr. Surratt was a young-looking man, slim made, not very tall, nor very short, and his hair was light. He came very often. Dr. Samuel Mudd and his wife both called him Mr. Surratt; they all called him that. He was there almost every Saturday night to Monday night; and when he would go to Virginia and come back he would stop there. He did not sleep at Dr. Mudd's, but out in the woods. Besides him, there was a Captain White, from Tennessee, they said; a Captain Perry, Lieutenant Perry, Andrew Gwynn, Benjamin Gwynn, and George Gwynn; they all slept in the woods. When they came to the house to eat, Dr. Mudd would put us out to watch if anybody came; and when we told them somebody was coming, they would run to the woods again, and he would make me take the victuals out to them. I would set them down, and stand and watch, and then the rebs would come out and get the victuals. Surratt and Andrew Gwynn were the only two that I saw come out and get them. I have seen Surratt in the house, up stairs and in the parlor, with Dr. Mudd. They never talked much in the presence of the family; they always went off by themselves up stairs.

Some men that were lieutenants and officers, came from Virginia, and brought letters to Dr. Sam Mudd; and he gave them letters and clothes and socks to take back. They were dressed in gray coats, trimmed up with yellow; gray breeches, with yellow stripes down the leg. After Dr. Mudd shot my brother, Elzee Eglent, one of his slaves, he said he should send him to Richmond, to build batteries, I think he said.

Cross-examined by MR. EWING.

It was about four years ago, that Dr. Mudd said that Mr. Lincoln came through, dressed in woman's clothes; he said it at the table. Dr. Mudd never slept in the woods, only the men that used to come there; the bed-clothes were taken out into the woods to them.

I am sure I saw Mr. Surratt there a dozen times last summer. I do not think he slept in the house any time; none of them ever did, but Watt Bowie. The last time I saw Mr. Surratt there, apples and peaches were ripe. I do not know what month it was. He said he was going to Washington then. He took dinner there six or seven times last summer; but when the men from Washington were after them, they got scared, and ate in the woods. Mr. William Mudd, Vincent Mudd, and Albert Mudd saw Mr. Surratt there; they all visited the house while the rebs were about. When Sylvester Mudd and some others came, they would run out of the way. A young man named Albion Brooke saw Mr. Surratt at Dr. Mudd's several times last summer. It was winter when Surratt commenced to come there, and he kept coming, on and off, till summer was out; and after that I did not see him. He used to go to Virginia and come back, and to Washington and back, and every time he would bring the news. Sometimes he would come once a week, and then again he might not come for two weeks.

By Assistant Judge Advocate Bingham.

Albion Brooke was a white man; Dr. Samuel Mudd's wife was his aunt. He sometimes worked out in the field where the colored people were.

ELZEE EGLENT (colored.)

For the Prosecution—May 25.

I know Dr. Samuel Mudd; he was my boss; yonder he is, [pointing to the accused, Samuel A. Mudd.] I was his slave, and lived with him. I left him on the 20th of the August before the last.

Q. Did he say any thing to you before you left him about sending you to Richmond?

A. Yes, sir; he told me the morning he shot me that he had a place in Richmond for me.

Mr. Ewing. I object to that question and the answer.

The Judge Advocate. The object of the question is to show disloyalty.

The Commission overruled the objection.

Witness. He told me he had a place in Richmond for me when I should be able to go away. He did not say what I was to do there. That was the June before the last. He named four more that he said he was going to send to Richmond—Dick and my two brothers, Sylvester and Frank.

I saw men come to Dr. Mudd's, dressed some in black clothes and some in gray; gray jackets, coat-like, and gray breeches. One of them, Andrew Gwynn, I had seen before; the others I did not know. They used to sleep in the woods, about a quarter of a mile off, I reckon, and would come to the house at different times, and go back to the woods. I don't know where they got their victuals, but I have seen victuals going that way often enough; I have seen my sister, Mary Simms, carrying them. That was in the June and July before the last.

Cross-examined by Mr. Ewing.

Nobody but Dr. Mudd and myself were present when he told me he was going to send me to Richmond; he told me so up stairs.

SYLVESTER EGLENT (colored.)

For the Prosecution.—May 25.

I used to live about a quarter of a mile from the house of Dr. Samuel Mudd; I lived with his father.

Q. State whether you heard him say any thing, at any time, about sending men to Richmond; and, if so, what he said, and to whom he was talking.

A. Last August, a twelvemonth ago, I heard him say he was going to send me, Elzee, my brother, Frank, and Dick Gardner, and Lou Gardner to Richmond to build batteries.

Mr. Ewing objected to the question and answer.

The Commission overruled the objection.

Witness. That was the last Friday in the August before last, and I left the next night. Forty head of us went in company.

Cross-examined by Mr. Ewing.

When I heard Dr. Mudd say this he was standing at my old master's front gate, under the oak-tree, where their horses were, talking to Walter Bowie and Jerry Dyer.

MELVINA WASHINGTON (colored.)

For the Prosecution.—May 25.

I used to live with Dr. Samuel Mudd; I was his slave; I see him there, [pointing to the accused, Samuel A. Mudd.] I left him this coming October two years. The last summer I was there I heard him say that President Lincoln would not occupy his seat long. There was a heap of gentlemen in the house at the time, but I do not know who they were. Some had on gray clothes, and some little short jackets, with black buttons, and a little peak on behind. Sometimes they staid in the house, and sometimes slept in the pines not far from Dr. Mudd's spring. Dr. Mudd carried victuals to them sometimes, and once he sent them by Mary Simms. I happened to be at the house one time when they were all sitting down to dinner, and they had two of the boys watching; and when they were told somebody was coming, these men rushed from the table to the side door, and went to the spring.

I heard Dr. Mudd say one day, when he got mad with one of his men, that he would send him to Richmond, but I did not hear him say what he was to do there.

Cross-examined by Mr. Ewing.

Those men that staid in the woods were there for a week or more, and they went away in the night; I do not know where to. I noticed them up at the house seven or eight times during that week, and never saw them there at any other time. I do not know the names of any but Andrew Gwynn. I do not know of any white people that saw these men but Dr. Mudd and his wife, and two colored women, Rachel Spencer and Mary Simms. I did not stay about the house; but when there was company I had to go up on account of the milking, and that was how I happened to see them.

MILO SIMMS (colored.)

For the Prosecution.—May 25.

I was a slave of Dr. Samuel Mudd, and lived with him. There he is, [pointing to the prisoner, Dr. Mudd.] I left his house on the Friday before last Christmas. The last summer I was there, I saw two or three men there, that sometimes staid in the house and sometimes out by the spring, up among the bushes. They had on plaid gray clothes, and one had stripes and brass buttons on. I saw their bed among the bushes; it was fixed under a pine tree; rails were laid at the head and blankets spread out. They got their victuals from Dr. Samuel Mudd's; sometimes he carried them out himself, and sometimes my sister carried them. She would lay them down at the spring, and John Surratt or Billy Simms took them away. I heard John Surratt called by that name in the house; Dr. Samuel Mudd's wife called him so in Dr. Mudd's presence. He was a spare man, slim, pale face, light hair, and no whiskers. When he was in the house, Dr. Mudd told his son and some of the children to stay out of doors and watch, and if anybody was coming to tell him.

Last year, about tobacco-planting time, I heard Ben Gardiner tell Dr. Samuel Mudd, in Beantown, that Abe Lincoln was a God damned old son of a bitch, and ought to have been dead long ago; and Dr. Mudd said that was much of his mind.

Cross-examined by MR. STONE.

I worked in the field, but sometimes was at the house to take the horses from the men who came there. I reckon I am about fourteen years old. I do not know whether I would know Mr. Surratt now; I knew him last summer. He was not shown to me by any one. Dr. Samuel Mudd came out to me and said, "Take Mr. Surratt's horse to the stable and feed him." He staid all night that time. I only saw him there two or three times. Mr. Billy Simms, Mr. Perry, and a man named Charley something, I forget what, came with him. Beantown is about three or four miles from the house; I had been there with Dr. Mudd for some meat when I heard that talk between him and Ben Gardiner. It was not two years ago, it was last summer; there were some more gentlemen present, but I did not know them.

I have never seen Andrew Gwynn with Surratt at Dr. Mudd's house; I have seen them at Dr. Mudd's father's house, with Jerry Dyer and Dr. Blanford. I saw them all there last yea n tobacco-planting time.

RACHEL SPENCER (colored.)

For the Prosecution.—May 25.

I was the slave of Dr. Samuel Mudd. I see him among the prisoners there, [pointing to the accused, Samuel A. Mudd.] I left his house in January last.

I remember some five or six men being there at one time last summer; I think they were dressed in black and blue. Some of them slept in the pines near Dr. Mudd's spring. They got their victuals from his house; Dr. Mudd took them out himself sometimes. The men would come up to the house sometimes, and then I have heard that the boys had to go to the door and watch to see if any body was coming. I only remember the names of Andrew Gwynn and Walter Bowie. There was a young-looking man among them once; I do not know his name; he was not very tall, but slender and fair.

I heard Dr. Mudd tell one of his men that he was going to send him down to Richmond; I don't know what he was to do there.

Cross-examined by MR. STONE.

Those men that were at Dr. Mudd's last summer came all together, staid about a week, and went away together. Their horses were in the stable. I saw them two or three times that week, but I don't remember seeing them before or after. Albion Brooke was there at that time; he used to go with them; they were always together.

WILLIAM MARSHALL (colored.)

For the Prosecution.—May 25.

I was a slave until the year 1863, when I got away from home. I belonged to Mr. Willie Jameston. Of late I have lived near Dr. Samuel Mudd; I see him here now, [pointing to the accused, Dr. Mudd.] I know Benjamin Gardiner, one of his neighbors; he was my wife's master.

Q. State whether you heard any conversation between Benjamin Gardiner and Dr. Samuel A. Mudd about the rebels, and their battle with the Union forces on the Rappahannock.

Mr. EWING objected to the question on the ground heretofore stated by him with reference to similar questions.

The Commission overruled the objection.

A. Yes, sir; I did. On Saturday, soon after the battle at the Rappahannock, I happened to be home. I had every other Saturday. My wife being sick, the Doctor had been to see her, and when he came out Mr. Gardiner met him at the corner of the house, and said to him, "We gave them hell down on the Rappahannock;" and the Doctor said "Yes, we did." Then he said, "Damned if Stonewall ain't the best part of the devil; I don't know what to compare him to."

Q. Who said that he was the best part of the devil.

A. Benjamin Gardiner. The Doctor said Stonewall was quite a smart one. Then Benjamin Gardiner said, "Now he has gone around up in Maryland, and he is going to cross over on the Point of Rocks somewhere"—he did say at that time, but I really forget now, where he was going to cross at the Point of Rocks—"and I would not be the least surprised if very soon from this"—he stated at what time, but I forget at what length of time he said—"he will be down here and take the capital of Washington, and soon have old Lincoln burned up in his house;" and Dr. Mudd said he would not be the least surprised; he made no objection to it.

DANIEL J. THOMAS.

For the Prosecution.—May 18.

I am acquainted with Dr. Mudd. About two months ago, some time in the latter part of March, I had a conversation with Dr. Mudd at John S. Downing's, who lives close by me and about a mile and a quarter from Dr. Mudd's. We were engaged in conversation about the politics of the day. I made a remark to Dr. Mudd that the war would soon be over; that South Carolina was taken, and I thought Richmond would soon be, and that we would soon have peace. He then said that Abraham Lincoln was an abolitionist, and that the whole Cabinet were such; that he thought the South would never be subjugated by abolition doctrine, and he went on to state that the President, Cabinet, and other Union men in the State of Maryland would be killed in six or seven weeks.

Cross-examined by MR. STONE.

Mr. Downing was at home when we had this conversation, though I believe he was out at the time this portion of the conversation took place; he had gone out to the kitchen, or to the wood-pile, or somewhere else. After his return, I asked him if, after having taken the oath of allegiance, he would consider it binding. That was all that occurred after Mr. Downing returned. I did not remain there more than half an hour or three-quarters of an hour; that is the only time I have met Dr. Mudd at Mr. Downing's this year. From Dr. Mudd's conversation he did not seem to be joking, but it is impossible for me to say whether or not he was earnest in what he said. He did not look as if he was angry or speak in malice. I can not judge whether a man is in earnest or not from the language he uses; but I should think a man was in earnest to talk of the President being assassinated.

Q. Did you think at the time that he was in earnest?

A. No, sir. I did not think any such thing would ever come to pass. I thought the President was well guarded, and that it was a want of sense on his part saying so. I laughed to think that the man had no more sense.

When Dr. Mudd first said it, I thought he meant it, but after a day or two I thought he certainly could not have meant it; but after the President was killed, and after hearing that Booth was at his house, I thought he really meant it.

Q. You thought it was a mere joke at the time, from the way he said it?

A. He was laughing at the time, or something like it. I know Dr. Mudd; we went to school together, and when he was a boy he was full of fun and jokes.

I spoke of what Dr. Mudd had said to almost everybody I saw, but everybody laughed at the idea of such a thing. I told Mr. Lemuel Watson, a good Union man, of this conversation before the assassination, and I also wrote to Colonel Holland, Provost Marshal of the Fifth Congressional District of Maryland; but I never received an answer from him. I had written to him several times before, but had never received an answer and I concluded that my letter must have been miscarried. I mailed the letter at Horsehead, and directed it to Ellicott Mills. I mentioned the conversation I had with Dr. Mudd, after the assassination, to my brother, Dr. M. C. Thomas, and Mr. Peter Wood, and to several others in Bryantown, when they were looking for Booth.

I am positive that nothing was said between Dr. Mudd and myself about exempting drafted men, nor had we been speaking of desertions from the rebel army or from the Union army, and that the conversation related is substantially all that occurred.

Two or three weeks after this conversation, but before the assassination, I believe, I mentioned it to Mr. Downing. He said he did not hear it, and he said, " Well, if that be the case, I am glad I was not in there." I thought if he had heard it he would not have said any thing about it. This conversation with Mr. Downing occurred when I met him on the road leading from his house to Horsehead. Mr. Downing said it was only a joke of Dr. Mudd's; that he was always running on his joking ways. When Mr. Downing returned to the room, Dr. Mudd did not say to him that I had been calling the Southern army "our army."

Cross-examined by MR. EWING.

Mr. Downing was out of the room long enough to get some wood, and, to the best of my recollection, he brought in some. We had no further conversation after he came in, only I said, "You are a man who took the oath; do you consider it binding?" He said, "No;" he did not consider it binding; if a man was compelled to take an oath, he did not consider it binding. I told him nobody was going to kill him; it was not compulsory for him to take the oath. He said he thought it was compulsion.

After Mr. Downing came in, Dr. Mudd did not say another word. I just got up and asked Mr. Downing one or two questions; if he had taken the oath, and he said he had taken the oath, but that he was no more loyal than he was before; that he always was a loyal man; that his feeling was for State rights;

but that he did not consider that oath binding upon any person.

Before that I had said to Dr. Mudd that he, having taken the oath, ought not to say such things about the President. He said he did not consider the oath worth a chew of tobacco. It was in consequence of such expressions, and knowing that Mr. Downing had been a justice of the peace, that I wanted to know if he considered the oath binding. I said nothing to Mr. Downing about my being a marshal or deputy marshal, or about my having a commission from General Wallace, or of having received any letters from him.

I told my brother of the conversation I had had with Dr. Mudd at Church or before Church. I told Mr. Watson when he was at my mother's one day. When I mentioned it to him, he laughed heartily; after that I could not help laughing. He said, "Dr. Mudd only did that to scare you. Everybody knows that such a thing is never going to come to pass."

Recalled for the Prosecution.—June 6.

I was at William Watson's door-yard, near Horsehead, on the 1st of June, with John R. Richardson, Benjamin J. Naylor, George Lynch, Lemuel Watson, and William Watson, when James W. Richards, the magistrate, rode up. I did not state to Mr. Richards that I had been asking any of these gentleman for a certificate of the fact that I was the first to give information which led to the arrest of Dr. Samuel Mudd, and that if they would give me a certificate I should be entitled to the reward of $10,000; but what I did say was, that I had been told in Washington, by some of Colonel Baker's men, that I was entitled to so much reward if Dr. Mudd was convicted. But I said that I never expected or looked for a cent, but that I would be very glad to receive the reward if it were so. I knew these fellows said it in a joke, and I told it as a joke. I did not tell Mr. Richards that I had been saying that I was the person who gave the information that led to the arrest of Dr. Mudd. As it had been said that if I had told anybody before the assassination, I would be entitled to a certain part of the reward if Dr. Samuel Mudd was convicted, I inquired of them if they thought I would be entitled to it; but I never did ask them for a certificate of the fact that I had given the information. I told them that I had mentioned it to some persons before and to some since the assassination. I do not myself remember whether it was before or after the assassination.

Q. And you did not ask either of the gentlemen I have named for a certificate of the fact that you were the first person who gave the information which led to Dr. Samuel Mudd's arrest.

A. Never. I just said to them, "You can say I mentioned it before the assassination; you can give me a certificate, and I will have

you summoned to prove it." They said, "No, we did not hear you then." Said I, "Will you give me a piece of paper to show that I mentioned it to you before the assassination?" "No," they said, they did not hear it; because they were afraid I would have them summoned.

Q. What did you ask for a paper for?

A. To certify that I had said such a thing before the arrest of Dr. Mudd.

I certainly did not say to Eli J. Watson, on the 1st of June, before meeting these gentlemen, that I wanted him to certify that I had been the cause of the arrest of Dr. Mudd, or that I had given any information which led to his arrest, and for which I was entitled to $25,000, for I never did give any information which led to the arrest of Dr. Mudd. Dr. Mudd was arrested before I knew it. I never thought of such a thing as being entitled to a reward. I looked upon Colonel Baker's men saying it as a joke at the time. I never looked for or expected such a thing, and more than that, I never would have a reward.

When I was on the stand before, Mr. Stone wanted to know if I had mentioned the conversation with Dr. Mudd to any one before the assassination. When these men told me that I had mentioned this conversation to them before the assassination, I then asked them if they would sign a paper to show the Court that I had mentioned it before. That was my object in asking them to sign, and that is the only paper I asked them to sign.

WILLIAM A. EVANS.

For the Prosecution.—June 5.

About the 1st or 2d of March last—certainly before inauguration day—I saw Dr. Samuel Mudd, with whom I have a slight acquaintance, drive past me as I was driving to the city in the morning. He passed me, I think, about eight miles from the city. He had a fiery horse, and as I wished to take my time, I let him drive past me, but I followed him up to the city, never losing sight of him.

Cross-examined by MR. EWING.

I have seen Dr. Mudd at different times for the last fifteen years, though I never was introduced to him. I have, I think, met Dr. Mudd at different places in the city, and at the National Hotel. Last winter I saw him go into the house of Mrs. Surratt on H Street; I could not say positively where the house is; it may be between Ninth and Tenth Streets, or between Eighth and Ninth Streets; somewhere along there. I asked a policeman, and a lady who was on the sidewalk, whose house it was, and was told it was Mrs. Surratt's. I had seen rebels going in there—Judson Jarboe and others—and I wished to know who lived there. It was a brick house, of perhaps two stories and an attic, and is, I think, between the Patent Office and the President's house, and is on the right-hand side going toward the Capitol.

[The witness, at the request of the counsel, described Mrs. Surratt's house and neighborhood, but did it somewhat indefinitely.]

I was riding down the street, going to see the Rev. J. G. Butler, of the Southern Church, and at the same time call in at the Union Prayer Meeting. There were members of different Churches assembled there, but I could not name any but Ulysses Ward that I saw there. On the same day I saw Mrs. Sophia Pressy and Miss Pumphrey at their houses, and I saw them also at different times during the winter.

I keep a journal of the visits I make, baptisms, deaths, etc., but I did not put Dr. Mudd's name in that, and I could not refer to this journal because it would be impossible for me to get possession of my books now. I was then moderator of the Presbytery of the District of Columbia, and our books are not allowed to be taken out of the churches. The Rev. Henry Highland Garnett, colored, is pastor of that Church now, and the journal of my baptisms, marriages, and deaths is in his possession, but if a hundred such journals were here, they would have no effect in fixing the date when I saw Dr. Mudd go into Mrs. Surratt's house. I visited other families that day, but I can not remember their names now. I am so confused at present that I can not recollect. I have been so confused since the death of President Lincoln that I really at times am bordering on insanity almost. I never got such a shock in my life.

I was in my buggy when I passed Mrs. Surratt's house. Dr. Mudd had on dark-colored clothes, I believe, with some kind of dark-brown overcoat, and a dark slouch hat.

Q. Now state how it is that you are enabled to fix the date from the 1st to the 3d of March as being the day on which you saw Dr. Mudd riding into town.

A. I hold a position in the Post-office Department, and I was making arrangements to come up to the inauguration on the 4th of March; and I was coming up very early on those mornings to do extra work, in order to be present at the inauguration. Dr. Mudd drove on past me. My horse got scared at the time, and was very near throwing me out. I remarked, as he passed by, how rude he was in almost knocking his wheel against my buggy; and I came home and told my wife I was very near being thrown out. I have only one leg, and it is difficult for me to get along. I could not get out of my buggy if the horse ran away.

Q. When did you commence this extra work, so as to be enabled to attend the inauguration?

A. Several days before the inauguration.

Q. Three or four days before?

A. About the latter part of February. I always like to discharge my duty, I have a certain amount of work to do, and I want to do it.

Mr. EWING. We do not want your personal history.

WITNESS. You seem to be so precise, I want to give you every thing connected with it.

Mr. EWING. We are not so precise as to your personal history.

WITNESS. A little of it will not do you any harm.

Mr. EWING. I do not think it will do any good in this case.

WITNESS. We are all free and equal men, and can talk as we please.

Mr. EWING. If the Court wishes this examination continued perpetually, this witness may be indulged in his lucubrations as to his history and answers to every thing except the questions that I propose. I ask the Court to restrain him to enable me to get through the examination.

The PRESIDENT. The witness has been told once that he must reply to the questions.

WITNESS. I have answered every question that he has asked me, to the best of my ability.

The PRESIDENT. We do not want any thing else but answers to the questions.

WITNESS. Very well, I will answer them.

The PRESIDENT. If you do not do as you are directed, we will try ——

WITNESS. And make me do it.

The PRESIDENT. Yes, sir.

WITNESS. Dr. Mudd drove a two-seated carriage; it is what is termed a rockaway.

When I saw Dr. Mudd going into Mrs. Surratt's house, Mr. Judson C. Jarboe was coming out. I saw him shaking hands with a lady at the door as Mudd was going in. I took the lady to be Miss Surratt from her likeness to her mother. Jarboe had murdered one of our citizens, and I wanted to know who lived at the house he was visiting.

I can not say when last I saw Dr. Mudd before the time I have referred to; he passed often on the road during last winter. I think I once saw him coming up with Herold, [pointing to the accused David E. Herold.] It might have been a year ago.

Cross-examined by MR. CLAMPITT.

It might have been about 11 o'clock when I saw Jarboe come out of the house as Mudd was going in.

Q. Did you not say that you were on your way to a prayer meeting at the time?

A. No, sir; I was on my way to see Dr. Butler. I said I was on my way to visit some families, and then in that neighborhood to go to prayer meeting. Being lame, I take pains to arrange my journeys so as not to go over the same ground again.

Cross-examined by MR. AIKEN.

I am a minister now, and have been for fifteen years. I hold a secret commission under the Government to arrest deserters and disloyalists wherever I find them. I am a detective. I wish to discharge my duty toward the Government to the best of my ability, but have never received one cent for any duty of that kind.

[This witness was exceedingly discursive, and his examination was consequently very lengthy. The above narration contains all the material facts testified to.]

JOHN H. WARD.
For the Prosecution.—May 20.

I live in the suburbs of Bryantown, Maryland. On Saturday, the 15th of April, I went to the village as soon as I had finished my dinner, and was there at about 1 o'clock. As soon as I arrived, I observed that the military were in town with Lieutenant Dana, and that there was great excitement among the people as well as the military. I went home, expecting that the soldiers would search the houses. Soon afterward a negro came up and said the President had been assassinated. I immediately left home and went again to the village. There I heard of the assassination. I also heard that the assassin's name was Booth. It was spoken of by everybody at Bryantown; first by the military, and then by the citizens, and it was spread about that Booth was the assassin. I heard this, I suppose, between 1 and 2 o'clock. The village was put under martial law, and many of the people began to be excited about getting home, and made application to the commanding officer to let them go, but he refused to do so. I went home. I think I saw Dr. Samuel Mudd there, but the excitement was so great that I can not say positively that I did.

Cross-examined by MR. EWING.

I could not tell precisely the time I left Bryantown, the second time I went up, but I suppose it was between 2 and 3 o'clock. I did not hear that the President had been assassinated the first time before I left Bryantown; the first intimation I had of it was by the darkey.

"Boose" was the name of the assassin, as spoken by the soldiers who were not familiar with language; they could not say Booth.

By MR. EWING.

Those who spoke audibly, told me that his name was Booth, and those who seemed to have an amalgamation of the languages called it "Boose."

The darkey who told me that the President was assassinated was Charles Bloyce, a brother to the one who has just testified. When he told me that the President had been assassinated, I immediately left home, and went to the village, where I found it a current report. He did not tell me who did it.

My house, I suppose, is four or five miles from Dr. Mudd's. I could not state positively that it was Dr. Mudd I saw; the per-son I supposed was the Doctor I saw about a quarter of 4 o'clock. I am personally acquainted with Dr. Mudd, and have been so for two years and five months.

FRANK BLOYCE (colored.)
For the Prosecution.—May 20.

I live in Charles County, Maryland. about half a mile from Bryantown. I was in Bryantown on Saturday evening after the murder of the President, and saw Dr. Samuel Mudd there between 3 and 4 o'clock. I was in the store buying something when Dr. Mudd came in.

Cross-examined by MR. EWING.

I left Bryantown before night. I do not know what time Dr. Mudd left. Before night the place was guarded, and I heard that the President had been assassinated.

MRS. ELEANOR BLOYCE (colored.)
For the Prosecution.—May 19.

I know the prisoner, Dr. Mudd; he lives about four miles from Bryantown, where I live. I saw him on the 15th of April last, riding into Bryantown late in the afternoon. There was a gentleman with him when he passed. I do not know that they went into town together; they were together until they were out of my sight. It was but a short time until Dr. Mudd returned. When he came back the gentleman was not with him. About eight or ten minutes after I saw him I went into town myself. On arriving there I found the soldiers from Washington, and then I heard of the murder of the President; that he was shot on Friday night at the theater. I did not hear who shot him.

Cross-examined by MR. STONE.

When Dr. Mudd passed the first time, I saw a gentleman with him; when he returned, I did not see the gentleman with him. I was too far from the road to know what kind of looking gentleman he was. I reckon I live about a quarter of a mile from the road. I went to Bryantown in a very short time after he passed my house. I do not think Dr. Mudd staid in Bryantown a quarter of an hour, but I do not know, as I have not any thing to tell by; it was a dark, drizzly, foggy evening, getting late.

I could not tell whether it was an old or young gentleman with the Doctor, he appeared to be riding a bay horse; I think the Doctor was riding a dark-gray horse, but I did not take much notice. They were riding side by side at a tolerable gait, not faster than persons usually ride in the country.

I live on the right of the road that leads up to Dr. Mudd's. There is no road that turns out between my house and Bryantown, and the man that was with Dr. Mudd was obliged to go through Bryantown, or come back the same way as he went. I was not at the door all the time. I happened to be standing at the door when Dr. Mudd passed and the gentleman with him, and when he returned alone.

MRS. BECKY BRISCOE (colored.)

For the Prosecution.—May 19.

I live at Mr. John McPherson's, about a quarter of a mile from Bryantown. I know Dr. Samuel Mudd. On Saturday, the day after the President was murdered, about 3 o'clock, as I was standing in the kitchen-door, I saw the Doctor riding into town with a strange gentleman. The gentleman went toward the bridge, and the doctor kept on to Bryantown, and this gentleman came back again. He kept on down the road to the swamp, when I saw him again. He staid at the swamp till the Doctor came back, in about half an hour, I reckon. The bridge is in sight of the town, about half a mile off. I went to town a very little while after the Doctor came back. I there heard of the murder of the President, but I did not hear until two or three days after that the man who killed him was named Booth.

Cross-examined by MR. STONE.

The swamp is on the other side of the house, just below the barn. Dr. Mudd and this man went along together, and the latter stopped at the bridge and came back again, and went as far as the swamp. I was down in the branch getting willows for Dr. Marshall, but not in the same branch the gentleman was in, but I could see over into that branch. He was sitting there on the horse. I saw him again going up the road with Dr. Samuel Mudd. I think both of them were on bay horses. They passed about 3 o'clock in the afternoon. A boy who was cutting wood at the wood-pile said, "There's a strange man going with Dr. Sam; I don't know who he is."

I started for Bryantown when Dr. Mudd came back. The soldiers were in Bryantown when I got there. I told my mother, who has just testified, that day of having seen this man with Dr. Mudd, and the next day I also told Baker Johnson, Mr. Henry Johnson, and Maria Kirby about it.

MARCUS P. NORTON.

For the Prosecution.—June 3.

By ASSISTANT JUDGE ADVOCATE BURNETT.

I was in in this city, stopping at the National Hotel, from about the 10th of January to the 10th of March last. While there I knew J. Wilkes Booth by sight, having seen him act several times at the theater.

I saw the accused, Samuel A. Mudd, under the following circumstances: A person hastily entered my room, on the morning of the 3d of March, I think. He appeared somewhat excited, made an apology, and said that he had made a mistake; that he wanted to

12

see Mr. Booth. I told him that Booth's room was probably on the floor above, the number I did not know. My room having thus been entered by a person apparently excited, I left my writing and followed the person partly through the hall. As he went down the flight of stairs to the story below, he turned and gave a look at me. It was his hasty apology and hasty departure that made me follow him. On entering the court-room this morning, I pointed out to the Hon. Horatio King the three prisoners I had seen at the National Hotel—Dr. Mudd, Atzerodt, and O'Laughlin. When I pointed them out I did not know their names.

[See testimony of Marcus P. Norton, page 149.]

I recognize the person, Samuel A. Mudd, as the man who entered my room on that occasion. It was either he or a man exactly like him. I am enabled to fix the date when he entered my room, first by the fact of its being immediately before the inauguration, also that it was on the morning of the day on which I was preparing my papers to argue a motion, pending before the Supreme Court, in the case of John Stainthrop and Stephen C. Quinn against Wallis Hollister. I remember the motion was argued on the day the person I speak of entered my room. He had on a black coat. His hat, which he held in his hand, was, I think, a black one, but not a high-crowned hat.

Cross-examined by MR. EWING.

My impression is that it was after I heard the conversation between Booth and Atzerodt that Dr. Mudd entered my room, and I have no doubt it was on the 3d of March. I occupied room No. 77 in the National Hotel at the time. Dr. Mudd was dressed in black; he had on a black coat, no overcoat, I think, and his hat, which he had in his hand, was black; I think it was a hat something like that, [pointing to the black silk hat of the President on the table,] but not so high.

By the COURT.

When Dr. Mudd entered my room he seemed somewhat excited, or perhaps in a hurry rather. He said he had made a mistake in the room, and apologized in that way. The room I then occupied was No. 77. I had perhaps ten days before been removed from room No. 120.

See also the testimony of

DEFENSE OF SAMUEL A. MUDD.

JOHN C. THOMPSON.
For the Defense.—May 26.
By MR. STONE

I reside in Charles County, Maryland. I had a slight acquaintance with a man named Booth; I was introduced to him by Dr. Queen, my father-in-law, about the latter part of October last, or perhaps in November. He was brought to Dr. Queen's house by his son Joseph. None of the family, I believe, had ever seen or heard of him before; I know that I had not. He brought a letter of introduction to Dr. Queen from some one in Montreal, of the name of Martin, I think, who stated that this man Booth wanted to see the county. Booth's object in visiting the county was to purchase lands; he told me so himself, and made various inquiries of me respecting the price of land there, and about the roads in Charles County. I told him that land varied in price from $5 to $50 per acre; poor land being worth only about $5, while land with improvements, or on a river, would be worth $50; but I could not give him much information in regard to these matters, and referred him to Henry Mudd, Dr. Mudd's father, a large land-owner. He also inquired of me if there were any horses for sale in that neighborhood. I told him that I did not know of any, for the Government had been purchasing, and many of the neighbors had been taking their horses to Washington to sell. Booth told me, on the evening of his arrival at Dr. Queen's, that he had made some speculations or was a share-holder in some oil lands in Pennsylvania; and as well as I remember, he told me that he had made a good deal of money out of it, and I did not know but that he came down there for the purpose of investing.

On the next morning, Sunday, I accompanied him and Dr. Queen to Church at Bryantown. I happened to see Dr. Samuel A. Mudd in front of the Church before entering, and spoke to him, and introduced Mr. Booth to him. Mr. Booth staid at Dr. Queen's that night and the next day. About the middle of the December following, if my memory serves me, Mr. Booth came down a second time to Dr. Queen's; he staid one night and left early next morning. I never saw him but on these two occasions, and do not know whither he went when he left Dr. Queen's.

Cross-examined by ASSISTANT JUDGE ADVOCATE BURNETT.

I live about seven or eight miles from Dr. Samuel A. Mudd. I know the Doctor personally, but am not intimately acquainted with him, or with his affairs. I do not know that Dr. Mudd owns lands, or whether he lives upon land that belongs to his father; but I know that his father is an extensive land-holder, and I told Mr. Booth that perhaps he might be able to purchase land from him. I saw the signature of the letter of introduction Booth brought; it was Martin, I believe; the first name I forget. Booth did not buy any lands in that neighborhood, to my knowledge.

DR. WILLIAM T. BOWMAN.
For the Defense.—May 27.
By MR. EWING.

I reside at Bryantown, Charles County, Maryland. Some time in December last I met J. Wilkes Booth at Church, near Bryantown. I was told it was Booth, the tragedian. A few days afterward I saw him again in Bryantown. After speaking to one or two other persons, he asked me if I knew any person who had any land to sell. I told him I had a tract which I should like to dispose of, and took him to the window and pointed out the place to him. I told him the extent and price, etc. He asked me if I had any horses to sell. I told him I had several I would sell. He then said, "I will be down in a couple of weeks and look at your land."

I have heard Dr. Mudd say he would like to sell his land. Last summer, when he could get no hands, he said he would sell. I asked him what he expected to do in case he sold his land; he said he thought of going into business in Benedict, on the Patuxent River; it is in an easterly direction from Bryantown, and is our usual port for Charles County.

Cross-examined by ASSISTANT JUDGE ADVOCATE BINGHAM.

Some four or five days after Booth was there, I saw Dr. Mudd. I told him I thought I should now sell my land. He asked me to whom I expected to sell. I told him there was a man by the name of Booth, who said he was coming down to look at it, when he said, "That fellow promised to buy mine."

By MR. STONE.

The distance from Bryantown to the Patuxent is ten miles. Matthias Point is the nearest crossing on the Potomac from Bryantown, and that is from fifteen to sixteen miles. It is about fifteen miles from Bryantown to Pope's Creek, which is opposite

Matthias Point, on the Potomac, and about three miles and a half from there to Dr. Mudd's. Mr. Henry L. Mudd, the father of Dr. Samuel Mudd, owns a considerable amount of land in that neighborhood.

Cross-examined by ASSISTANT JUDGE ADVOCATE BURNETT.

I live three miles and a half from Dr. Mudd. Dr. Mudd is understood to own the land he lives on, as other people own their land, but I do not know of my own knowledge that it belongs to him.

JEREMIAH DYER.

For the Defense.—May 27.

I have been living in Baltimore for two years; before that I lived from my childhood within half a mile of Dr. Samuel Mudd. I know Sylvester Eglent, who is a servant of Dr. Mudd's father; I also know Frank Eglent, Dick Washington, and Luke Washington. I never heard any conversation in which Dr. Mudd said he would send Sylvester Eglent and his brother Frank Eglent to Richmond. Such a conversation could not have taken place in August, as I left that country on the 1st of August for Baltimore, where I remained until October. I then heard that some thirty or forty of the hands had left, and I went down to hire other hands to secure the crop. I heard, when I got down there, that a man by the name of Turner had started a report that he was going to catch all the negroes in that neighborhood and send them away. I never heard Dr. Mudd say any thing about sending off his hands to Richmond. I never met Dr. Mudd in company with Walter Bowie at his father's house. I know Milo Simms, Melvina Washington, Elzee Eglent, and Mary Simms; they were all, I think, servants of Dr. Mudd's house in 1861.

I know Andrew Gwynn very well. Since 1861 he has been in the rebel army. About he 1st of September, 1861, I was in the neighborhood of Dr. Mudd's house for about a week. We were knocking about in the pines and around there. It was about the time Colonel Dwight's regiment was passing through, and there was a perfect panic in the neighborhood; the report was that everybody was to be arrested. A great many were arrested. Mr. Gwynn and his brother came down in a fright, stating that they had been in the house to arrest them, or had been informed they were on their way there. I also received notice that I was to be arrested. The two Gwynns came down then; I met them there at Dr. Mudd's or my house, I do not know which; the farms are adjoining. For several nights we slept in the pines between his house and mine. That situation was a little inconvenient, and we moved over and lay, I think, one or two nights near his spring. We had some bed-clothing there,

obtained from Dr. Mudd's house and from mine; most of it, I think, from Dr. Mudd's. Our meals were brought us by Dr. Mudd. The Doctor used to bring down a basket containing bread, meat, biscuit, and ham, and the colored girl, Mary Simms, I think, brought a pot of coffee.

There is a large swamp between his house and mine. The first night we were on the other side of the swamp, after that we came within one hundred and fifty or two hundred yards of Mudd's house. The party consisted of Benjamin Gwynn, Andrew Gwynn, and myself. There was at the time a general stampede and panic in the community. A good many left their homes, and went to their friends' houses, or from place to place.

When we were in the pines, I think Mr. Gwynn's horses were left at Dr. Mudd's, and were fed by the boys there; Milo Simms would be likely to attend to them. I remember telling the children to keep a look out, and if any one came to let me know. We were all dressed in citizen's clothes.

Alvin Brook, William Mudd, Vincent Mudd, and Albert Mudd might have come there while we were there, but I do not distinctly remember.

I have known Daniel J. Thomas since he was a boy, and I know his reputation for veracity in that neighborhood is such that very few men there have any confidence in him. His reputation is so bad that I would not believe him under oath.

I have known Dr. Mudd since he was a boy. I have never heard the slightest thing against him. He has always been regarded as a good citizen; he has a good reputation for peace, order, and good citizenship. I have always considered him a kind and humane master. I never knew of any thing to the contrary, except his shooting his servant, which he told me of the same day it happened.

Cross-examined by the JUDGE ADVOCATE.

I have never heard Thomas charged with having sworn falsely. He is a noisy, talkative man, but is unquestionably loyal. I can not say that I have ever heard a man of known loyalty speak of Mr. Thomas as a man they would not believe under oath.

I am not aware that I have been guilty of any disloyalty toward the Government; I certainly never wanted to see two Governments here, and I think I have desired that the Government of the United States might succeed in its endeavors to suppress the rebellion, and I have persuaded young men from going on the other side.

I was a member of a military organization in 1861, the object of which was, I believe, to stand by the State of Maryland in the event of its taking ground against the Government of the United States.

Q. At the time of which you speak, the fall of 1861, was the subject of the Legislature of Maryland passing an ordinance of secession much discussed among you?

A. I do not know; I probably heard the subject spoken of very often, but I do not know that it was discussed to any extent. I may have heard it spoken of in crowds or congregations, but so far as conversing with any particular person on that subject is concerned, I have no knowledge of it.

Q. Did you not suppose that the organization of which you were a member was at that time regarded as disloyal by the Government, and hence feared arrest?

A. I hardly know how to answer that question. That was in the incipiency of the thing, and it was hardly time for men to reflect and give their minds room to see what would be the result of rebellion and civil war; it was in the start, when every thing was wild excitement and enthusiasm; and of course I can hardly answer that question.

I do not know that I particularly rejoiced at the success of the rebels at the first battle of Bull Run. I might have been like a good many others at that time; I suppose my sympathies were with the rebels. When Richmond was taken, my sympathies were on the side of the Government; I wanted to see the war stopped. I believe the United States were pursuing the right course, except in emancipating the slaves; I thought that was wrong.

By MR. EWING.

I have not seen a great deal of Mr. Thomas for the past two or three years; my estimate of his reputation for truth and veracity is based upon my knowledge of that reputation for several years back. I know he has not borne a good reputation for truth and veracity in that neighborhood since he was a boy. I I have heard him spoken of as one who would tattle a great deal, and tell stories, and say a great many things that were not true. The military company of which I have spoken was organized, I think, in 1859, under the authority of Governor Hicks. On the 22d of February, 1860, we were up here in Washington, at the inauguration of the statue.

By the COURT.

Our company broke up immediately on the breaking out of the war, and a great many left and joined the rebel army. I think it was regarded by the Government as a disloyal organization at the breaking out of the war.

Mr. Thomas was, I think, a candidate for a seat in the House of Delegates of Maryland a year or two ago.

By MR. EWING.

I do not think Thomas was nominated; I saw his name in the newspaper, and I saw him at the polls on the day of the election; he was then very confident of his election.

The military organization to which I be-longed was not regarded as a disloyal organization in 1859; we never drilled after the breaking out of the war.

Recalled for the Defense.—May 27.

I know John H. Surratt; I have seen him on his father's place, at Surrattsville. This photograph of him [the one in evidence] is, I think, a good likeness. I have not seen him for a year and a half or two years.

By MR. STONE.

Dr. Mudd does not live on any of the direct roads leading from Washington to the Potomac. A person leaving Washington, intending to strike the Potomac above Pope's Creek or Upper Cedar Point Neck, would go out of his way seven or eight miles to pass Dr. Mudd's. A person starting from here to strike the Potomac at Port Tobacco, would be nearest Dr. Mudd's at Troy, where the main road crosses. That is seven or eight miles from Dr. Mudd's place; so that a person would go out of his way sixteen miles to call at Dr. Mudd's, and by the nearest road it would be ten or twelve miles. Dr. Mudd's house is considerably nearer the Patuxent than the Potomac. All the shipping from his farm is done on the Patuxent. I think Pope's Creek on this side of the Potomac is nearly opposite Matthias Point, in Virginia.

Recalled for the Defense.—May 30.

Cross-examined by ASSISTANT JUDGE ADVOCATE BINGHAM.

In September, 1861, I accompanied Benjamin Gwynn and Andrew Gwynn to Virginia. I think we remained in Richmond four weeks; I was sick there for two weeks. We supposed we were to be arrested, and we went to Richmond to avoid it. We were in the pines at Dr. Mudd's four or five days before we left. I belonged to a cavalry company, but I can not say that it was hostile to the Government and Administration of the United States. I suppose, if Maryland had passed the ordinance of secession, in all probability that company would have been in the rebel army, but I can not say that it was an organization to support Maryland in so doing. I am not aware that I publicly proclaimed myself in favor of the secession of Maryland; I may have done so, but I do not now recollect. I have not been over the lines since the time I have referred to.

I have been at Dr. Mudd's several times during the past two or three years. In going backward and forward from Baltimore, I generally make Dr. Mudd's my head-quarters.

By MR. EWING.

I am brother-in-law to Dr. Mudd. I have two or three sisters in that neighborhood, and I go to see them all. When I returned from Virginia I took the oath of allegiance, and I have never, to my knowledge, violated it.

ALVIN J. BROOK.

For the Defense.—May 27.

By MR. EWING.

I have been living at Calvert College, near Windsor, Maryland, since September last; before that I worked for Dr. Samuel Mudd. I went there in January, 1864. While living at Dr. Mudd's I never saw Captain or Lieutenant Perry, or Captain White, from Tennessee. I know Mr. Benjamin Gwynn and Andrew Gwynn, but I did not see either of them at Dr. Mudd's. I know John H. Surratt; I saw him in Prince George's County last August. While at Dr. Mudd's I never saw nor have I any knowledge of those persons sleeping in the woods at Dr. Mudd's; I never saw any evidence that they did. I was in the stable morning, noon, and night, but I never saw any strange horses there. While living at Dr. Mudd's, I took my meals and slept in the house.

In 1861 I was living at Jerry Dyer's, which is just across the swamp from Dr. Mudd's place. I know of persons sleeping in the woods in 1861, the first year of the war. I know of Jerry Dyer and Benjamin Gwynn dodging about there in the woods. I have not seen Andrew Gwynn since then.

Cross-examined by ASSISTANT JUDGE ADVOCATE BINGHAM.

[Photograph of John H. Surratt exhibited to the witness.]

I know that picture. It is John H. Surratt. I saw him about the middle of August last, about sixteen miles from Dr. Mudd's. No one was at Dr. Mudd's while I was there, but the neighbors round, William A. Mudd, Albert Mudd, and Constantine Mudd. I knew all who came there; there were no strangers. I never saw Booth.

FRANK WASHINGTON (colored.)

For the Defense.—May 27.

By MR. STONE.

I lived the whole of last year at Dr. Samuel Mudd's. I was his plowman; I am working there still. I was there every day, except Sundays and holidays, and I was in the stable night and morning, and at 12 o'clock. I was often at the spring. I took my meals in the kitchen of Dr. Mudd's house.

I know Mr. Andrew Gwynn and Mr. Benjamin Gwynn by sight. It has been four years since I saw Mr. Andrew Gwynn. I never saw any one camped out in the woods at Dr. Mudd's. I never saw any one there called Captain Perry or Lieutenant Perry, or Captain White, and I have never seen any strange horses in the stable. I know Mary Simms.

Q. What do the servants there in the neighborhood think of her character for telling the truth?

A. She was never known to tell the truth.

Q. From her general character among the servants in the neighborhood for telling the truth, would you believe her on oath?

A. No, sir.

Q. How did Dr. Mudd treat his servants?

A. He treated them pretty well.

Q. How did he treat you?

A. He treated me first-rate. I had no fault to find with him.

[Exhibiting a photograph of John H. Surratt.]

I do not know him; I never saw him.

Cross-examined by the JUDGE ADVOCATE.

I have known Mary Simms ever since she was a small girl. Others on the place think of Mary Simms as I do. I was not on the place when Dr. Mudd shot one of his servants. I knew him, but have not seen him since the second year of the war.

[The witness was directed to look at the accused, David E. Herold.]

I never saw him. I do not know any of the prisoners, excepting Dr. Samuel Mudd.

I was home on Saturday, the day the President was killed, when two men called at Dr. Mudd's. I took their horses. I got a glimpse of one of them as he was standing in the door, just as the day was breaking.

Cross-examined by ASSISTANT JUDGE ADVOCATE BURNETT.

Two stray horses came there the day after the assassination; I put them in the stable, and fed them. One was a bay, and the other was a large roan. They came there just about daybreak. At noon the bay was gone, and Dr. Mudd's gray one. I led them out.

Q. Did the little man on the end of the seat there [Herold] ride the bay one, or the Doctor?

A. I do not know; I never saw him on a horse.

Q. You know you took out the bay one and Dr. Mudd's gray?

A. Yes, sir.

I do not know where they went. When I brought out the horses, I went to the field, and did not come back till sundown, and both horses, the bay and the roan, were then gone. Dr. Mudd has only two servants now, myself and Baptist Washington, who is a carpenter.

I get $130 a year wages. I do not know that I shall get any thing for this extra job. No one has promised me any thing for coming here, or said any thing about it. I do not know about any arms being brought to Dr. Mudd's at any time, nor was any thing said that I know about Rachel Spencer burying any arms for Dr. Mudd.

BAPTIST WASHINGTON (colored.)

For the Defense.—May 27.

By MR. STONE.

I worked for Dr. Samuel Mudd last year. I put up a room between his house and the

kitchen. I worked there from either January or February until August, and then came
to Washington, and staid here about a month,
when I went back to Dr. Mudd and staid
there until Christmas. I never heard of
anybody being camped about the spring, or
sleeping in the woods at Dr. Mudd's last
year. I used to be down at the spring pretty
often, but I did not see anybody there. I
do not know Captain Ben. Gwynn or Andrew Gwynn, and I never saw or heard of
Captain White or Captain Perry being at
Dr. Mudd's; nor did I ever know of any
horses belonging to strangers being in the
stable. I did most of my work, sawing-out
and framing, at the stable. I was at the
stable every day while I was at work, excepting Sundays and holidays.

I know Mary Simms, the colored girl, that
lived at Dr. Mudd's. Nobody that knew her
put much confidence in her. Mary Simms
minded the children, and waited on the table
sometimes.

Q. How did Dr. Mudd treat his servants?
A. He always treated his servants very
well, so far as I knew.

Q. How did he treat you?
A. He treated me very well. I was always
very well satisfied with the accommodations
he gave me when I was there.

Cross-examined by ASSISTANT JUDGE ADVOCATE
BINGHAM.

I did not belong to Dr. Mudd, but was hired
out to him. I was the slave of Mrs. Lydia
Dyer, originally of the family of Jerry Dyer.

[Exhibiting to the witness a photograph of John H. Surratt.]

I do not know that man; I never saw him
at Dr. Mudd's that I know.

MRS. MARY JANE SIMMS.

For the Defense.—May 27.

I lived with Dr. Samuel Mudd during the
year 1864, except when I was at my sister's
visiting. I never staid over two or three
weeks at my sisters.

I know Captain Bennett Gwynn and Mr.
Andrew Gwynn. Mr. John H. Surratt I
have seen since. I saw none of those persons at Dr. Mudd's last year; none of them
were in the woods and fed from the house
that I saw or heard of. I visited my sister
last March twelve months, and was at Dr.
Mudd's pretty much all the spring, summer,
and fall.

BENNETT F. GWYNN.

For the Defense.—May 20.

By MR. EWING.

My name is Bennett F. Gwynn. I am
sometimes called Ben. Gwynn. Andrew and
George Gwynn are my brothers. Of Captain
White from Tennessee, Captain Perry, or
Lieutenant Perry, I know nothing. I never
heard of such persons.

About the latter part of August, 1861, I
was with my brother, Andrew J. Gwynn,
Mr. Jerry Dyer, and Alvin Brook, at Dr.
Mudd's place. About that time General
Sickles came over into Maryland, arresting
almost everybody. I was told I was to be
arrested, and I went out of the neighborhood
awhile to avoid it. I went down into Charles
County; staid about among friends there for
a week or so, as almost everybody else was
doing. There was a good deal of running
about that time.

Q. Go on and tell all about it.

Assistant Judge Advocate BINGHAM objected. What occurred in 1861 was not in
issue.

Mr. EWING said that the prosecution had
called four or five witnesses to prove that
several persons, among whom was the witness now on the stand, had been concealed
in the neighborhood of Dr. Mudd's house for
a week, and that their meals were brought
to them by him or his servants, and had
attempted to show that those persons were in
the Confederate service, and that Dr. Mudd
was guilty of treason in assisting them to
secrete themselves, and had stated that that
occurrence took place last year or the year
before. To prove by this witness and others
that no such thing occurred last year or the
year before, might not be regarded as a
complete answer to the allegation, and hence
it was proposed now to show that the transaction referred to took place in 1861, at the
beginning of the war, at a time of general
terror in the community, and that some of
the persons, alleged to have been concealed
there, were not there. To withhold from the
accused the right to prove this would be
denying to him a most legitimate line of
defense.

Assistant Judge Advocate BINGHAM replied,
that the Government had introduced no testimony in regard to any such transaction in
1861; and hence the testimony now proposed to be introduced was irrelevant and
immaterial. If the witness should swear
falsely as to that, it would not be legal
perjury, because it was a matter not in issue. The witness could be inquired of as to
the time when it was stated he had been
there, but not as to what occurred in 1861.

The Commission sustained the objection.

Q. Where did you and the party who were
with you near Dr. Mudd's, sleep?

A. We slept in the pines near the spring.
We had some counterpanes which were furnished by Dr. Mudd, who brought our meals.
We were in the pines four or five days.
While we were there we often went to Dr.
Mudd's house; almost every day, I think.
Our horses, though I do not know positively,
were, I suppose, attended to by Dr. Mudd's
servant. I have not been in Dr. Mudd's
house or near his place since about the 6th
of November, 1861.

Some time from the 5th to the 10th of

November, 1861, I came up to Washington to give myself up, as I was tired of being away from home. When I came here, they said there were no charges filed against me; so I took the oath and went home.

My brother, Andrew Gwynn, has been South, I understand, since August, 1861. He resided some eight or ten miles from my place. He returned once, I understood, last winter, but I did not see him, and did not know it. I have been living in Prince George's County since 1861.

I know John H. Surratt. At the time we were in the pines, he was, I believe, at St. Charles College.

Cross-examined by the JUDGE ADVOCATE.

The parties who were arrested in 1861 were mostly members of volunteer military companies, commissioned by Governor Hicks. I was captain of a cavalry company down there. It was called the Home Guard, and was for the purpose of protection in the neighborhood. There was at that time a great deal of dissatisfaction among the blacks, and those in the neighborhood thought it would be a good plan to organize, and companies were organized all through the counties. I petitioned Governor Hicks, and he gave me a commission.

Q. Was it not understood that these were State organizations, and intended to stand by the State in any disloyal position it might take against the Government?
A. That was my impression of them.
Q. And you were a captain of one of those companies?
A. Yes, sir.
Q. You felt, therefore, that it was likely you would be arrested?
A. I do not know that I did from that. Some of the members of my company were arrested, and I understood there was an order for my arrest, and I left.
Q. You slept there in the pines for the sole purpose of escaping that arrest?
A. Yes, sir. Dr. Mudd knew why we were hiding in the pines, and why he was feeding us there.

By MR. EWING.

The company of which I was captain was organized in Prince George's County, I think, in the winter of 1860. I think we commenced getting it up before the election of Mr. Lincoln. Dr. Mudd was, I think, a member of a company organized in Bryantown, but I do not know it of my own knowledge.

WILLIAM A. MUDD.

For the Defense.—May 30.

By MR. EWING.

I live about a mile and a quarter or a mile and a half from Dr. Samuel Mudd. I never saw any person by the name of Cap-

tain White, or a Captain or Lieutenant Perry, about Dr. Mudd's premises. I did not see Mr. Andrew Gwynn about his premises last year; I have not seen him since he left for the South. I never saw any person staying out in the woods, at Dr. Samuel Mudd's, any time last year. I remember seeing Mr. Bennett Gwynn on his horse, talking with the Doctor. I understood Mr. Gwynn had been scouting. That was in the fall of the first year of the war.

CHARLES BLOYCE (colored.)

For the Defense.—June 3.

By MR. EWING.

I know the prisoner, Dr. Samuel A. Mudd; I was about his house Saturday nights, and some parts of Saturday and Sunday, all last year, except from the 10th of April to the 20th of May, when I went out to haul seine. I commenced going to Dr. Mudd's on the 12th day after Christmas, the same day that Julia Ann Bloyce, my wife, went, and was there every Saturday night and all day Sunday, except when I went to Church. I did not see Ben. or Andrew Gwynn at Dr. Mudd's when the war commenced, about four years ago; I saw them passing along by Mr. Dyer's. I neither saw nor heard any thing of Watt Bowie, John H. Surratt, Captain White of Tennessee, Captain Perry, Lieutenant Perry, or Booth at Dr. Mudd's while I was there; and I do not know of any rebel officers or soldiers being there. I never saw anybody at his house dressed in any kind of uniform.

The colored folks there always laughed at Mary Simms; they said she told such lies they could not believe her. They said the same of Milo Simms. I thought he was a liar, for he used to tell me lies sometimes. I call Dr. Samuel Mudd a first-rate man to his servants; I never saw him whip any of them, nor heard of his whipping them. They did pretty much as they pleased, as far as I saw. I never heard a word of his sending or threatening to send any of his servants to Richmond.

Cross-examined by ASSISTANT JUDGE ADVOCATE BINGHAM.

Q. Did you ever hear any thing about his shooting any of his servants?
A. I did hear that.
Q. Do you think that is first-rate business?
A. I do not know about that.

IMPEACHMENT OF DAN'L J. THOMAS.

JOHN H. DOWNING.

For the Defense.—May 29.

By MR. EWING.

I live near Mount Pleasant, in Charles County, Md. I am very well acquainted with the accused, Samuel A. Mudd, and also with Daniel J. Thomas, both of whom were raised right by me.

Some time this spring, between the 1st and the 15th of March, I think, Daniel Thomas was at my house, and while there Dr. Mudd came in, and staid about half an hour. Dr. Mudd did not, in conversation at that time, say that Abraham Lincoln was an abolitionist, and that the whole Cabinet were such, or that he thought the South would never be subjugated under abolition doctrines, or that the President, and all the Cabinet, and every Union man in the State of Maryland would be killed in six or seven weeks. No such words were spoken in the house to my knowledge, and I staid there all the time. After I had been sitting there half an hour, I got up and walked to the piazza, and Dr. Mudd followed me immediately, and told me his business; that he had come to collect a little doctor's bill, and then went directly home.

Dr. Mudd and Thomas could have had no conversation at that time but what I heard; I was close to them, Thomas sitting between me and Dr. Mudd, and if they had whispered I should have heard it. The President's name was not mentioned during Dr. Mudd's stay, and I do not recollect that Thomas mentioned it while he was at my house, and he had been there two or three hours before Dr. Mudd came, and remained fully an hour after he left. Nor was any reference made to any member of the Cabinet, nor to killing anybody; I am sure I should have remembered it if a word of the kind had been mentioned. Daniel Thomas and I meet each other very frequently, but I never heard him mention a word of the kind to me any time, neither before the assassination nor since.

I do not recollect Dr. Mudd's saying to me on that occasion that he did not consider the oath of allegiance worth a chew of tobacco; to my knowledge nothing of the kind was said. I can not recollect all the conversation; but they commenced talking about detectives, and Daniel Thomas told Dr. Mudd that he was appointed detective, and spoke of several others—Jerry Mudd, Dr. George Mudd, Joe Padgett, I think, and perhaps one of the Hawkinses, who were also detectives; but he said he would never catch anybody; that he would go to their houses because it was his duty, but he would never catch anybody; that he was not bound to catch them.

Cross-examined by ASSISTANT JUDGE ADVOCATE BINGHAM.

Dr. Mudd and Thomas were talking all that half hour; their talk was pretty much about detectives; that is all I recollect of it. I believe it took Thomas pretty much a whole half hour to say that he was a detective, and did not catch anybody; he was telling a whole parcel of foolish things. I had no conversation, none at all; Dr. Mudd and Thomas only were talking. I believe Dr.

Mudd compared Thomas to a jack, because he said he was appointed a Deputy Provost Marshal under Colonel Miller; and said, "I think, Daniel, I am much better educated than you are, and I do not think I am capable of filling that office myself, and I do not think you are." I was irritated when he called Thomas a jack, as it was in my house; I then got up, and Dr. Mudd followed me to the door; he was not half a second behind me. If Mudd called Thomas an abolitionist as well as a jack, I did not hear it. When Mudd called Thomas a jack, he might have been mad at the idea of his being a Deputy Provost Marshal.

By MR. EWING.

It was cold weather at the time, and we sat close by the fire, Thomas between me and Mudd, and I heard every word of the conversation that took place.

DR. JOHN C. THOMAS.
For the Defense.—May 26.

By MR. STONE.

I reside in Woodville, Prince George's County, Md., and have been a practicing physician for nineteen years. I am a brother of Daniel Thomas, who has testified here.

On the Sunday morning after Dr. Mudd's arrest, my brother came to Woodville Church; and as he was just from Bryantown the day before, we asked him the news. He was full of news of the arrest of Dr. Mudd, and the boot having been found with him, etc., and then during the conversation he spoke of what Dr. Mudd had told him a few weeks before, in relation to the assassination of the President. Mr. Sullivan Wood and several other gentlemen were present. He had never mentioned the subject to me before that time, and I am certain that in that same conversation he spoke of Booth's boot being found in Dr. Mudd's house.

I have attended my brother professionally in some serious attacks. About six years ago he had a very serious paralytic attack—partial paralysis of the face and part of the body. He labored under considerable nervous depression for some time before he recovered. He was mentally affected from it. His mind was not exactly right for a long time, and I am under the impression that it is not now at all times; and on these occasions he is credulous and very talkative. He is very apt to tell every thing he hears, and believe every thing he hears. I do not pretend to say that he would tell things that he did not hear, or make up things; but he is very talkative.

His reason may be somewhat affected, and his memory also, when these attacks come on. He has fainting spells, and is confined to his bed; but when he is up, and in the enjoyment of good health, he seems to be rational. These attacks come on at no particular time. When they do come on, he labors under great nervous depression, and has to be stimulated materially sometimes. He has not had an attack now for some time; his health has been better.

Cross-examined by ASSISTANT JUDGE ADVOCATE BINGHAM.

It was on the Sunday after the soldiers were at Bryantown that my brother told me that Dr. Mudd had said that Lincoln, and the whole Cabinet, and all the Union men of Maryland would be killed in a few weeks; that was the first I heard any thing about it.

By the COURT.

My brother seemed to be as rational on that Sunday as I ever saw him; he was not at all excited, and I think he was quite capable of telling the truth on that day. I had no doubt in my mind at that time that Dr. Mudd had said this, though I thought he might probably have said it in joke. At first I thought my brother was jesting, and told him that if it was not true he should not say so, and he said it was certainly true; that Dr. Mudd had made the statement in Bryantown; and I supposed it was so. I do not suppose my brother would swear to any thing that was not true.

JAMES W. RICHARDS.

For the Defense.—June 6.

I live near Horsehead, Prince George's County, Md. On the 1st of June last I met Daniel J. Thomas, in company with John R. Richardson, Benjamin J. Naylor, George Lynch, Lemuel Watson, and William Watson, at the door-yard of Mr. William Watson, near Horsehead. Mr. Thomas said that he had asked Mr. William Watson and Mr. Benjamin J. Naylor for a certificate, stating that he was entitled to the reward, or a portion of the reward, that was offered for the arrest of Booth and his accomplices; and he thought, if he could get a certificate from them to that effect, he would be entitled to a portion of the reward in the event of Dr. Mudd's being convicted, as he (Mudd) was considered one of Booth's accomplices. The reward, Mr. Thomas said, was $10,000; he stated that the certificate was to certify that he informed them concerning Dr. Mudd's arrest. I do not think he wanted a certificate stating that he was the cause of Dr. Mudd's being arrested. He said, if Dr. Mudd was convicted, he was entitled to a portion of the reward.

I have known Daniel J. Thomas for the past five years; his reputation in the community for veracity is very bad. In any thing in which he had a prejudice, or where any money was at stake, I would not believe him under oath.

Cross-examined by ASSISTANT JUDGE ADVOCATE BINGHAM.

When I rode up, Mr. Lemuel Watson remarked to me, "You are a justice of the peace; I am glad you have come; I want you to try a case here. Daniel says he is entitled to so much reward, and I want you to say what you think of it." I do not remember what reply I made to this. Mr. Thomas stated that he had applied to Mr. Watson and Mr. Naylor for a certificate to the effect that he had informed them concerning Dr. Mudd's arrest, and that, if he could get such a certificate, he would be entitled to a portion of the reward. We told him that we thought he was entitled to $20,000, by way of a joke. Both William Watson and myself told him this. I remarked to him that I did not think $10,000 was enough, and I thought he would better take $20,000. Thomas said he would not want me to swear to a lie for him to get $10,000. I understood Thomas pretended to Mr. William Watson that he had told him of the arrest of Dr. Mudd.

By MR. EWING.

I have always been a loyal man, and a hearty supporter of the measures of the Government for the suppression of the rebellion; I voted for Lincoln and Johnson.

In 1861 I met Mr. Thomas on my way from teaching school. He said that he was going to join the Southern army, and that he intended to come back, when Beauregard would cross, and hang a man by the name of Thomas B. Smith. Thomas was not a loyal man at the beginning of the war.

[Mr. EWING offered the following in evidence:]

[OFFICIAL.]

WAR DEPARTMENT,
Washington, April 20, 1865.

One Hundred Thousand Dollars Reward.

The murderer of our late beloved President, Abraham Lincoln, is still at large. Fifty thousand dollars reward will be paid by this department for his apprehension, in addition to any rewards offered by municipal authorities or state executives. Twenty-five thousand dollars reward will be paid for the apprehension of G. A. Atzerodt, sometimes called "Port Tobacco," one of Booth's accomplices. Twenty-five thousand dollars reward will be paid for the apprehension of David E. Herold, another of Booth's accomplices. Liberal rewards will be paid for any information that shall conduce to the arrest of either of the above-named criminals or their accomplices. All persons harboring or screening the said persons, or either of them, or aiding or assisting their concealment or escape, will be treated as accomplices in the murder of the President and the attempted assassination of the Secretary of State, and shall be subject to trial before a military commission, and the punishment of death. Let the stain of innocent blood be removed from the land by the arrest and punishment of the murderers.

All good citizens are exhorted to aid public justice on this occasion. Every man should consider his own conscience charged with this solemn duty, and rest neither night nor day until it be accomplished.

EDWIN M. STANTON,
Secretary of War.

WILLIAM J. WATSON.

For the Defense.—June 9.

By MR. EWING.

I live in the Eighth Election District, Prince George's County, Maryland. I am acquainted, though not intimately, with Daniel J. Thomas. I was in my door yard, near Horsehead, on the 1st of June, with John R. Richardson, Benjamin Naylor, George Lynch, Lemuel Watson, and Daniel J. Thomas. On that occasion, Daniel J. Thomas said, if my memory serves me right, that if Dr. Mudd was convicted upon his testimony, he would then have given conclusive evidence that he gave information that led to the detection of the conspirators.

He said he thought his portion of the reward ought to be $10,000, and he asked me if I would not, as the best loyal man in Prince George's County, give him a certificate of how much I thought he ought to be entitled to.

Cross-examined by ASSISTANT JUDGE ADVOCATE BINGHAM.

I told him I did not think he was entitled to any portion of the reward, and would give him no certificate. I then appealed to his conscience in the most powerful manner I could, and asked him if he believed he was entitled to the reward? I did this three times, but he waived the question every time by saying that Daniel Hawkins said he was entitled to it. He did not say that Daniel Hawkins had told him, but that he had told somebody else so. Thomas then asked Mr. Benjamin J. Naylor, I think, if he did not mention to him and to Arthur D. Gibson, before the killing of the President, the language that Dr. Mudd had used to him. Mr. Naylor said that he had never done it before or after.

When I was appealing to his conscience in regard to the matter, Mr. James Richards, a magistrate in the neighborhood, rode up, and my brother, Joseph L. Watson, or Lemuel Watson as he is called, appealed to him, saying, "There is a contest going on here between Billy and Daniel; you are a magistrate, and I want you to decide it between them." Mr. Richards said, "Lem, let us say that he is entitled to $20,000 of the reward." Mr. Thomas then said, "No, sir, I would not have either of you gentlemen swear falsely, though by your doing so it would give me $20,000." That is what I understood him to say.

By MR. EWING.

Mr. Richards did not offer to take a false oath. He was joking; I am confident of that. Mr. Richards is a true Union man.

By ASSISTANT JUDGE ADVOCATE BINGHAM.

Q. Do you not consider that Daniel J. Thomas is entitled to belief on his oath?
A. I have no reasons bearing on my mind to offer to the Court why I would not; therefore, I must say, I would.
Q. Would you believe him on his oath?
A. I would.
Q. He has as good a reputation for truth as most of his neighbors down there?
A. I should not think he had as good a reputation for truth as most of the neighbors.

Mr. EWING objected to this course of examination as improper. It was not legitimate cross-examination. The witness had been subpoenaed by the Government, and, at the consent of the Judge Advocate, was called by the accused as to a single point, with the understanding that he should be treated as a witness for the accused only to that one point.

The JUDGE ADVOCATE (while not yielding the point that the line of examination pursued was improper) stated that he would agree now to take this witness as one for the prosecution; and the witness was accordingly examined for the prosecution in rebuttal.

By ASSISTANT JUDGE ADVOCATE BINGHAM.

I was not much acquainted with Daniel J. Thomas till 1863. He lives in Charles County, and I in Prince George's. I do not know what kind of a reputation he bore in Charles County, but in my neighborhood they spoke evil of him. They say he tells a good many lies, but I think people tell him as many lies as he tells them. Though some speak well of him, people generally say that his reputation for truthfulness is bad.
Q. I ask you your opinion, whether you consider, from all you hear of his reputation there, that his character for truth is such that he is entitled to be believed on oath?
A. I believe that he is; because if I was to come here and say he was not qualified, I should have to say that half the men around there are not qualified.

By MR. EWING.

Q. Are you able to say that you know what Mr. Thomas's general reputation is, in the community in which he lives, for truth?
A. I think I have stated that it is not good for truth in speaking; but I think he lies more in self-praise, to make the people think a great deal of him, than in any other way. I have never heard of Mr. Thomas telling a lie that would make a difference between man

and man. I have known of no quarrels to be kicked up in my neighborhood about any thing Mr. Thomas has told from one man to another.

Q. Do you know whether Mr. Thomas was a loyal man in the beginning of the war?

A. I do not know. He was represented not, to me; but I suppose if he had been, his feelings would have been coerced by the people by whom he was surrounded.

Q. Do you know who he supported at the last election for President?

A. I do not know; but he electioneered for George B. McClellan.

JOHN C. HOLLAND.

For the Defense.—June 8.

By Mr. Ewing.

I hold the position of Provost Marshal of the draft for the Fifth Congressional District of Maryland. I know Daniel J. Thomas from the fact that he was a drafted man, and I examined him at Benedict, Charles County. I never received a letter from him in which the name of Dr. Mudd was mentioned; nor any letter stating that the President, or any member of his Cabinet, or any Union man in the State of Maryland would be killed. I received a letter from him dated February 9, 1865, but it contained no reference whatever, direct or indirect, to this subject, nor to Dr. Samuel A. Mudd. Mr. Thomas, I believe, was commissioned as an independent detective; that is, commissioned specially by me to arrest drafted men that did not report and deserters, receiving as compensation the reward allowed by law. He was not under pay from the Government. Such commissions were given to any one who applied.

Cross-examined by ASSISTANT JUDGE ADVOCATE BURNETT.

The letter contained a reference to Dr. George Mudd, with whom I am acquainted, but none whatever to Dr. Samuel Mudd; I am not acquainted with him.

RICHARD EDWARD SKINNER (colored.)

For the Defense.—June 27.

I live in Charles County, Md. I am the servant of Mrs. Thomas, the mother of Daniel J. Thomas, whom I have known for thirty years. I know what is thought of him in the community for telling the truth, and he does n't bear a good reputation among gentlemen. I have always been living with him, and I have heard gentlemen say they would not believe him under oath. I do not like to say that I would not believe him when he was under oath.

Mr. Daniel J. Thomas was not a loyal man on the breaking out of the war; since then he has sometimes been loyal, and then again he has not been so; just changeable like.

Cross-examined by the JUDGE ADVOCATE.

I never heard gentlemen speak of Mr. Thomas testifying in a court of justice, and I do not mean to say that Mr. Thomas, when he is on his oath in court, is not to be believed.

JOHN L. TURNER.

For the Defense.—June 9.

By Mr. Ewing.

I live in the lower part Prince George's County, near Magruder's Ferry, on the Patuxent River, six or seven miles from Dr. Mudd's. I have a slight acquaintance with Daniel J. Thomas. He is not regarded as a truthful man by any means in that neighborhood. From his general reputation, I could not believe him under oath, where he was much interested.

Mr. Thomas has been loyal part of the time since the war commenced, but I can not say that he has been so all the time. He has been loyal for the last year or two, but I do not know how he stood at the beginning of the war.

Dr. George D. Mudd has been considered a loyal man throughout the whole war. I have always been a loyal man and a supporter of the Government. I voted for George B. McClellan for President, because I considered him as good a loyal man and as good a Union man as Mr. Lincoln; and as he said that if he were elected the war would only last a few months, I voted for him on that ground.

I know Dr. Sam Mudd. I have known him since he was a boy. His reputation for peace, order, and good citizenship has been very good. I have always considered him a good, peaceable, and quiet citizen, as much so as any man we have among us. I never knew him do any thing in aid of the rebellion.

POLK DEAKINS.

For the Defense.—June 9.

By Mr. Ewing.

I live near Gallant Green, Charles County, Md. I have been acquainted with Daniel J. Thomas ever since I can remember. His reputation in the community for truth-telling is very bad; and if he had any inducement to speak other than the truth, I would not believe him under oath.

In 1861, Mr. Thomas said he was going over into Virginia, and he tried to persuade me to go, but I did not.

JEREMIAH T. MUDD.

Recalled for the Defense.—May 27.

By Mr. Ewing.

I am acquainted with Daniel J. Thomas, and know his reputation in the neighborhood in which he lives; for truth and veracity it is bad; and I do not think I could believe him under oath.

Cross-examined by ASSISTANT JUDGE ADVOCATE BINGHAM.

I base my opinion, as to his general reputation, on my knowledge of him, and on his reputation in the neighborhood. He is known to go riding about the country, telling things that are marvelous and miraculous. I may safely say I have heard as many as ten or a dozen persons speak of his bad reputation for truth and veracity. Among others, I have heard Dr. George Mudd and Mr. Gardiner. I have never heard any one say that Thomas had ever sworn falsely in any court.

By MR. STONE.

Thomas represents himself as a detective, acting under the orders of Colonel Holland; whether such is the fact I do not know.

LEMUEL L. ORME.

For the Defense.—June 6.

By MR. EWING.

I am acquainted with Daniel J. Thomas; I knew him first when he was not more than thirteen or fourteen years of age. He is looked upon in the community in which he lives as a man that hardly ever tells the truth; his reputation for veracity is very bad. I never heard him tell any thing of any length, without betraying himself in a story before he got through; and I have scarcely heard of a man in the neighborhood that would believe any thing he might tell. If he had the least prejudice against a person, I could not believe him under oath.

Cross-examined by ASSISTANT JUDGE ADVOCATE BINGHAM.

If he had a prejudice, and was under oath, I should hardly believe him any how.

By the JUDGE ADVOCATE.

To the best of my knowledge and belief, I have been loyal to the Government during this rebellion. I have never done any thing to oppose the efforts of the Government in suppressing the rebellion; I have always wished that the Union might be sustained, and that the Government might not be broken up, and have always so expressed myself. I had no idea of the South ever forcing the North to go to them; and so far as the Union is concerned, I always expected that, if maintained, it would be by the North.

By MR. EWING.

If words testify any thing, Mr. Thomas has not been a loyal man since the beginning of the war. In the fall of 1861, for a distance of two miles, he talked to me, and advised me to go South with him. He may have changed his sentiments since, but during the first twelve or eighteen months of the war, he was looked upon as a great friend of the South; helping as far as his ability went. He was not looked upon as able to help anybody, but his conversations were all that way.

JOHN H. BADEN.

For the Defense.—June 8.

By MR. EWING.

I live in Anacostia District, Prince George's County, Md. I know the reputation Daniel J. Thomas bears for truth and veracity; he is accounted a very untruthful man; I believe few place any confidence in what he says. From the knowledge I have of his reputation for veracity I would not believe him under oath.

Cross-examined by the JUDGE ADVOCATE.

I have never heard him charged with swearing falsely. I have heard him tell a great deal that was not true, but I never heard him swear to it.

Q. From your knowledge of human character, do you not think there are many men who talk idly and extravagantly, and sometimes untruthfully, who would nevertheless, when under the obligations of an oath, speak the truth?

A. I do not know, sir. I do not place any confidence myself in what I hear him say. I have nothing against Mr. Thomas; I have known him a good while, but I do not put any confidence in what I hear him say.

Q. That is not an answer to my question. Do I understand you to hold that a man who will sometimes speak untruthfully, will necessarily swear to an untruth in a court of justice? Is that your judgment of human character and conduct?

A. Not all.

ELI J. WATSON.

For the Defense.—June 8.

By MR. EWING.

I reside in the Eighth Election District, Prince George's County, Md. I have known Daniel J. Thomas ever since he was a boy. I know his reputation for truth and veracity in the neighborhood in which he lives, and it is very bad. From that general reputation, and my knowledge of his character, I would not believe him under oath.

I saw Mr. Thomas on my farm on the 1st of June; he said he had been a witness against Dr. Mudd, and that Joshua S. Naylor had sworn to put down his oath; he also said that if his oath was sustained, he expected a portion of the reward that the Government was to give for Booth.

Q. And that Joshua S. Naylor had sworn to put down his oath; what do you understand by that?

Assistant Judge Advocate BINGHAM objected to the question, and it was waived.

JOSHUA S. NAYLOR.

For the Defense.—May 30.

By MR. EWING.

I reside in the Eighth Election District, Prince George's County, Md. I have known Daniel J. Thomas since he was a boy. His general reputation for truth and veracity in that neighborhood is bad, and such that I would not believe him under oath. His reputation is that he never tells the truth if a lie will answer his purpose better; and, though it is hard to say it of any man, I could not believe him under oath.

Cross-examined by the JUDGE ADVOCATE.

I can not say that he is reputed to be a loyal and an honest man in his neighborhood. As to his loyalty, he is sometimes one thing and sometimes another, just as the prospects of the different parties seem to be going. During the latter part of the rebellion, he has pretended to be a warm supporter of the Government, and he may have been sincere; but, from what others have told me, he said to them he was not during the early part of the rebellion.

I never heard him speak under oath, and can not say that I have ever heard him charged with swearing falsely.

By MR. EWING.

I have been a supporter of the Government and the Administration of the United States at all times and under all circumstances. Dr. George Mudd I have heard spoken of as a good Union man, and a supporter of the Government in the war against the rebellion

JOHN WATERS.

For the Defense.—May 9.

By MR. EWING.

I live in Charles County, Maryland. I have been loyal to the Union, and a supporter of the Government in the prosecution of the war.

I have known Daniel J. Thomas from a boy. His reputation for truth and veracity has not been very good; I think the people generally regard him as not very truthful.

I am acquainted with the prisoner, Dr. Samuel Mudd; his reputation in the community, as a citizen, has been very good. Before the arrest of Dr. Mudd, I think I saw Mr. Thomas with a hand-bill in his hand, offering a reward for the arrest of the assassins or their accomplices. That, I believe, was on the Tuesday after the assassination of the President.

DANIEL W. HAWKINS.

For the Defense.—June 9.

By MR. EWING.

I am by profession a lawyer. I live about four miles and a half from Bryantown, in Charles County. I have known Mr. Daniel J. Thomas from ten to fifteen years. His general reputation in the community for truth and veracity is not very good. If I were a juror or a judge, I should think it very unsafe to convict on his evidence. I should have very serious doubts about his oath.

I am very well acquainted with Dr. George Mudd; and I can say that I do not know a more loyal man than he in the State of Maryland. My attitude toward the Government during the war has been strictly loyal; and I have been a supporter of the Government in its war measures from the commencement of the rebellion.

JOSEPH WATERS.

For the Defense.—May 9.

By MR. EWING.

I live at Gallant Green, Charles County, Maryland. I have known Daniel J. Thomas from childhood. His general reputation in the community for truth and veracity is very bad; and from my knowledge of his reputation I do not think I could believe him under oath.

I have known Dr. Mudd from childhood. His reputation as a citizen has been very good, as far as I know. I have never known any thing against him. I have not been in any way engaged in aiding the rebellion, but have been a loyal man throughout the war.

FRANK WARD.

For the Defense.—May 9.

By MR. EWING.

I live at Horsehead, Prince George's County, Maryland. I have known Daniel J. Thomas ever since he was a boy. His reputation for veracity in the community is pretty bad. I can not say that Mr. Thomas has been a loyal man throughout the war. He is first one thing and then another; sometimes Union and sometimes disloyal.

Cross-examined by ASSISTANT JUDGE ADVOCATE BINGHAM.

I voted for McClellan. I do not recollect whether I voted for Harris for Congress or not; I certainly did not rejoice at the success of the rebels at the first battle of Bull Run.

By ASSISTANT JUDGE ADVOCATE BURNETT.

I have heard many persons speak in reference to the reputation of Mr. Thomas, but I can not recollect exactly what they said. I live about five miles from Mr. Thomas.

By Mr. Ewing.

My knowledge of his reputation was obtained before this trial commenced.

IN WASHINGTON, December 23, 1864.

Jeremiah T. Mudd.

For the Defense.—May 26.

By Mr. Ewing.

I reside in Charles County, Maryland, about a mile and a half from Dr. Samuel A. Mudd. Dr. Mudd and myself went to Washington together on the morning of the 23d of December last. I recollect the date distinctly, because we got home on the 24th, Christmas eve. It was a little in the night when we arrived in Washington; we put up our horses near the Navy Yard, and went to the Pennsylvania House, registering our names for lodgings. We went to a restaurant on the avenue, now Dubant's, I think, for supper, and staid there possibly an hour. We then went to Brown's Hotel, and afterward to the National Hotel, and there was a tremendous crowd there, and we got separated. I met a friend at the National, conversed with him a short time, then went down the avenue and visited some clothing stores, and returned to the Pennsylvania House. Dr. Mudd came in there shortly after me, and we went to bed. There was no one with him when I first saw him, as he came through the folding doors to the room where I was; but there may have been some few persons in the adjoining room from which he came.

The next morning I went with Dr. Mudd to purchase a cooking stove, and then we separated, he to make some little purchases for himself, and I to buy some clothing, etc.; but we saw each other repeatedly, every ten or fifteen minutes, till about 1 o'clock. Then we went together down to the Navy Yard for our horses, and left the city about 3 o'clock.

Q. Do you know who took the articles which he bought down to his home?

Assistant Judge Advocate Bingham. I object to any inquiry about the articles he bought, or who took them. It is of no consequence.

Mr. Ewing. May it please the Court, it is of a very great deal of consequence. The prosecution has attempted to prove by one witness a meeting between Booth and Dr. Mudd, and an introduction of Booth to Surratt by Dr. Mudd, here in Washington. We expect to be able to show to the Court conclusively, that if there was any such meeting, it must have been at this visit to the city of Dr. Mudd about which we are now inquiring.

In that view, it is of great consequence to the accused to be able to show that he came here on business unconnected with Booth, for the purpose of rebutting the presumption or inference unfavorable to him which might be drawn from the fact of his having met Booth here. That alleged meeting with Booth has been put in evidence as part of the *res gestæ* of the conspiracy; on any other ground, it would have been irrelevant and inadmissible. We have a right to show that Dr. Mudd came to the city that time for other purposes; we have a right to show the acts that he did, in order to establish that his visit was a legitimate business visit to Washington. Therefore it is that we ask who took the things down; and we expect to show that he arranged, before starting from home, to have the things which he was coming here to purchase hauled down, and that therefore he came here on legitimate business.

Assistant Judge Advocate Bingham. If the gentleman had shown that this man was with Booth on that day, I could see something in his argument; but as it is, it does not amount to any thing.

Mr. Ewing. But I assure you we expect to follow this up by testimony which will conclusively establish that he could not have been with Booth upon any other day between that day and the assassination of the President.

Assistant Judge Advocate Bingham. They undertake to prove by this witness that he could not have been with Booth then; this five-minute operation is introduced for that purpose, as I understand. But now, in order to make out something, for some purpose I can not comprehend, they propose to prove that this man bought crockery or something that day in town, and got somebody to haul it home. That has nothing in the world to do with this case. The amount of it all is, that we have introduced testimony here to prove this man's association with Booth in Washington, in another month, at the National Hotel. If they can disprove that, well and good; but it does not tend to disprove it, and does not tend to throw any light on the subject, to show that, in December, (another time altogether than that stated by our witness for the meeting of Booth and Mudd, which the Court will remember was about the middle of January,) Mudd bought certain things, and hired somebody to take them home. All that has nothing to do with the case.

The Commission overruled the objection.

Witness. I took a portion of them myself. The stove was to have been taken down by Mr. Lucas, who had come to the market to sell a load of poultry, and was then in market with his wagon. His taking the stove depended upon his selling his poultry; it was a dull market, and Dr. Mudd and I went three times to see if he had sold out, so that he could take it.

I have known Dr. Mudd from early youth. His general character for peace, order, and good citizenship in the neighborhood in which he resides is exemplary; he has always been amiable and estimable, a good neighbor, honest and correct. I never in all my life heard any thing to the contrary. I think him humane and kind to his servants; I have lived very close to him all my life; he is so regarded universally, I believe. He did not work them hard either; at least they did not do a great deal of work.

I remember Booth being in that county; I saw him at Church at Bryantown in the latter part of November or early in December last. I noticed a stranger there, and inquired who he was, and was told that his name was Booth, a great tragedian. From the description of him, and from his photograph, I am satisfied it was the same man. I only know what I heard others say about his business there—the common talk.

Q. What was the common talk?

Assistant Judge Advocate BINGHAM. The witness need not state what the common talk was. It is not competent evidence to undertake to prove common talk about a party not on trial here.

Mr. EWING. May it please the Court, I know it is the object of the Government to give the accused here liberal opportunities of presenting their defense. I am sure the Judge Advocate does not intend, by drawing the reins of the rules of evidence tight, to shut out testimony which might fairly go to relieve the accused of the accusations made against them. I think it is better, not only for them, but for the Government, whose majesty has been violated, and whose law you are about to enforce, that there should be liberality in allowing these parties to present whatever defense they have to offer. We wish to show that Booth was in that county ostensibly, according to the common understanding of the neighborhood, for the purpose of selecting and investing in lands. We introduce this as explanatory of his meeting with Dr. Mudd, whose family, as we expect to show, were large land-holders, and anxious to dispose of their lands, and I trust to the liberality of the Court to allow us to prove it.

The JUDGE ADVOCATE. I wish certainly the utmost liberality in the introduction of the testimony of the defense here, and I hope the Court will maintain it. If I at any time fall short myself of maintaining that spirit, I trust the Court will do it. I think, however, in this case there is no principle of evidence that will admit the mere talk of a neighborhood. Any fact which any witness knows, tending to show for what purpose Booth was there, no matter what that fact may be, is admissible; but a mere idle rumor, of which you can not take hold, on which you can not cross-question, in regard to which you can not speak, it seems to me, on no principle by which the ascertainment of truth is sought, can be received. I wish to state most distinctly to the Court that I desire the utmost latitude of inquiry indulged in, and that every thing shall be introduced which tends in any manner to illustrate the defense which is made for these prisoners. I wish no technical objection, and shall never make one, and, if made, I trust it will never be sustained by this Court.

The Commission sustained the objection.

Cross-examined by the JUDGE ADVOCATE.

I really do not know Dr. Mudd's reputation for loyalty to the Government of the United States during this war. I have myself heard him say that he did not desire to see two Governments here. I have never known of any disloyal act of his, and never heard of any. I never, that I am aware of, heard any disloyal sentiments expressed by him. I have heard him express sentiments opposed to the policy of the Administration. I do not know that he has been open and undisguised in his opposition to the endeavors of the Government to suppress the rebellion. For the past two or three years our people have had no disposition to talk about the rebellion or the war. For a long time I would seldom talk about it with any one; and would not send to the post-office for my papers perhaps for a week, and then would not read them—just look over them on Sunday. I never heard Dr. Mudd say that the State of Maryland had been false to her duty in not going with other States in the rebellion against the Government; and I never saw Confederate soldiers at his house. I did hear of his shooting one of his servants, and do not doubt that it was true. I heard it was only a flesh wound. I do not know that the boy is lame still; I do not think I have seen him since.

By MR. EWING.

I heard that the servant who was shot was obstreperous; that he had been ordered to do something which he refused to do, and started to go away; that the Doctor had his shot-gun with him, and he thought he would shoot him to frighten him, and make him stop and come back. The Doctor told me so himself. I believe he shot the boy somewhere in the leg.

I have heard Dr. Mudd make use of expressions in opposition to the policy of the Administration, but only in reference to the emancipation policy. He was a large slave-owner—and his father—too, and I suppose did not want to lose his property; this I suppose to be the cause of his uncompromising opposition to the emancipation policy of the Government. I never in my life heard a violent expression from him; it is not in his character; nor did he ever indulge in violent denunciations of the Government.

Recalled for the Defense.—May 27.

By MR. EWING.

I have seen the handwriting of Dr. Samuel A. Mudd frequently, and am acquainted with it.

[Exhibiting to the witness the register of the Pennsylvania House, heretofore produced.]

I recognize his handwriting on the page open before me; it is dated Friday, December 23, 1864. The book is the Pennsylvania House register, with which I am very familiar, having repeatedly registered my name in it for years past. We went into the hotel together, and I registered my name two names above his. I do not know at what hotel Dr. Mudd was in the habit of stopping when he went to Washington. He had some relatives there, and I frequently heard of his staying the night with them. I never was in Washington with him before.

J. H. MONTGOMERY.

For the Defense.—May 29.

By MR. EWING.

I am acquainted with the prisoner, Dr. Samuel A. Mudd. On the 22d of last December, I think, the Thursday morning before Christmas, he asked me if I could bring a stove from Washington for him. I told him that Lucas, who hucksters for me and drives my wagon, could bring it down. Lucas went up on Wednesday, and was to come down on Thursday, but he did not come till Friday, and returned the same day.

FRANCIS LUCAS.

For the Defense.—May 26.

By MR. STONE.

I am a huckster, and live about two miles from Bryantown, Maryland. On Christmas eve last, Dr. Mudd came to me in market and asked me to take a stove down for him; I promised to do so, if I could. He came to me two or three times to tell me not to forget it; and I finally told him it was out of my power to take it.

Cross-examined by ASSISTANT JUDGE ADVOCATE BINGHAM.

I suppose it was about 9 or 10 o'clock on Christmas eve that he came to ask me to haul the stove.

SAMUEL McALLISTER.

For the Defense.—May 26.

By MR. STONE.

I have been a clerk at the Pennsylvania House in this city since the 2d of December last.

[Submitting to the witness an hotel register.]

That is the register of the Pennsylvania House. I have examined it very carefully, and the name of Dr. Samuel A. Mudd does not appear on it for the month of January: I have never, to my knowledge, seen the accused, Samuel A. Mudd, before. He may have stopped at the house and I not know him, but his name would certainly be on the register; for no one is allowed to stop one night without registering his name. Persons often come in to take a meal, and pay when they go out, and do not register their names. I find the name "Samuel A. Mudd" entered under date of December 23, 1864, and also "J. T. Mudd;" they both occupied the same room.

Cross-examined by ASSISTANT JUDGE ADVOCATE BINGHAM.

I do not know who slept with Atzerodt at the Pennsylvania House on the night of the President's assassination; I was in bed that night. The next morning I saw the name of "Samuel Thomas" entered on the book; further than that I do not know. It was the rule of the house that the porter was never to allow a person to go to bed without registering his name; and I have never known the rule to be violated. The register does not show how long Dr. Mudd remained at the house in December; the cash-book would show that.

[By request of Mr. EWING, the witness retired to examine the register of the Pennsylvania House for the name of Dr. Mudd after December 23d.]

I have examined the register from the last entry of Dr. Mudd's name on the 23d of December, 1864, up to this month, May, and his name does not appear at all.

JULIA ANN BLOYCE (colored.)

For the Defense.—May 20

By MR. EWING.

I went to live at Dr. Sam Mudd's on the day they call Twelfth Day after the Christmas before last, and left two days before this last Christmas. I used to cook, and wash, and iron, clean up the house, and sometimes wait on the table. I never saw Andrew Gwynn, nor any Confederate officers or soldiers about Dr. Mudd's house, and never saw a man called Surratt there, nor heard the name mentioned.

[A photograph of John H. Surratt exhibited to the witness.]

I have never seen that man at Dr. Mudd's. I have seen Ben. Gwynn, but I did not see him at Dr. Mudd's last year. I did not hear his name nor Andrew Gwynn's mentioned. Dr. Mudd was very kind to us all. I lived with him a year, and he treated me very kindly; never gave me a cross word, nor any of the rest that I know of. I did not hear of his whipping Mary Simms; he never struck her nor any of the others a lick, through the whole year. I believe she left because Mrs. Mudd told her not to go out walking one Sunday evening; but she would, and the next morning Mrs. Mudd gave her about three licks with a little switch, but the switch was small, and I do n't believe the licks could have hurt her. The general opinion of Mary Simms among the colored people is, that she is not a very great truth-teller. I know she is not, because she told lies on me. The colored folks think the same of Milo Simms as of Mary; if he got angry with you, he would tell a lie on you to get satisfaction.

I never heard Dr. Mudd say any thing against the Government or Mr. Lincoln.

On the day I left, two days before Christmas, Dr. Mudd went away early in the morning, and his wife told me he was gone to Washington to get a cooking stove. Since I left Dr. Mudd's, I have been living in Bryantown with Mr. Ward.

MUDD'S WHEREABOUTS, MARCH 1-5.

FANNIE MUDD.

For the Defense.—June 5.

By MR. EWING.

Dr. Samuel A. Mudd, the accused, is my brother. I know of my brother's whereabouts from the 1st to the 4th of March last. On the 1st of March my sister was taken sick, and on the morning of the 2d my father sent to her room early to know how she felt. She sent him word that she felt very badly, and was afraid she had the small-pox. My father immediately dressed, and went for my brother, and he came there with my father and took breakfast with us. On the 3d, my brother came in between 11 and 12 to see my sister, and took dinner with us. As he had not his medical case with him, having come in from the barn, where he had been stripping tobacco, he went home for it, and came back with the medicine for my sister. On the 4th he came to dinner again, and on the 5th, Sunday, he was at my father's in the evening, in company with Dr. Blanford, my brother-in-law.

I did not see my brother on the 1st of March, but I am pretty sure he was at home. I am confident my brother was not absent from home at any time between the 1st and 5th of March. We live very near, about half a mile distant, and we go backward and forward sometimes twice a day.

I was in the habit of visiting my brother's house very frequently last summer, and the summer previous. I never saw or heard of John H. Surratt being there. I heard of Booth being there once, probably in November; but I did not see him. Since this trial commenced, I have heard that he was there twice.

I knew of three gentlemen, Mr. Jerry Dyer, Andrew Gwynn, and Bennett Gwynn, sleeping in the pines near my brother's house, in 1861; I do not think they secreted themselves except during the night. Mr. Andrew Gwynn was an intimate friend of ours, very fond of music, and he spent two evenings with us at my father's. He left that year, and I have not seen him since, nor have I heard of his being at my brother's. I never heard of a Captain Perry, or Lieutenant Perry, or of any Confederate soldiers being about my brother's house. My father's house is about thirty or thirty-two miles from Washington.

Cross-examined by ASSISTANT JUDGE ADVOCATE BINGHAM.

I think I heard of Booth being at my brother's in the early part of last November. I do not know personally that my brother was at home on the 1st of March; I did not see him at all on that day. I do not know the officer who enrolled the names of those in our neighborhood subject to the draft, nor did I say any thing at all to the enrolling officers as they passed by, or were at my father's house.

By MR. EWING.

I know that it was the 1st of March that my sister was taken sick, because it was Ash Wednesday, and it is customary with Catholics to go to church that day, if possible, to prepare for the penitential season of Lent, and we were Catholics, and were particularly anxious to go to church. My sister attempted to rise that morning, but was not able; and a second time attempted, but was obliged to remain at home.

I did not meet Booth when he was at Bryantown, but I saw him in church; he sat in Dr. Queen's pew, with his family.

MRS. EMILY MUDD.

For the Defense.—June 5.

By MR. EWING.

I live at the house of Mr. Henry L. Mudd, the father of the prisoner, Samuel A. Mudd. On Thursday, the 2d of March, Dr. Samuel Mudd was summoned very early in the morning to see his sister, who was sick, and again on the next day, the 3d. He came over about 12 o'clock that day and dined with us, and finding his sister much worse, he came over again in the evening and brought her some medicine. He was there again on Saturday to see her, and took dinner again; and I think he was there on Saturday afternoon. I am positive of the dates from the fact that the 1st of March, when the prisoner's sister was sick, was Ash Wednesday, and she could not go to church. I am sure that Dr. Samuel Mudd was not from home at any time between the 1st and the 5th of March; he was attending his sick sister, and was not absent from home at all.

I know Andrew Gwynn, but have not seen him since the fall of 1860. He was in the habit of visiting the house of Dr. Mudd's father before that, but has not, to my knowl-

13

edge, been there, or at the house of Dr. Samuel A. Mudd, since 1861. I never knew John H. Surratt, or Lieutenant Perry, or Captain Perry, and never heard of their being at the house of Samuel A. Mudd; nor have I ever known or heard of parties of Confederate officers or soldiers being about Dr. Samuel Mudd's house, and I have been in the habit of going to his house very frequently since 1861. I saw Dr. Mudd on his way home from Bryantown on the Saturday afternoon after the assassination of the President; no one was with him.

Cross-examined by ASSISTANT JUDGE ADVOCATE BINGHAM.

I saw him going by the road by his house toward Bryantown, I expect, between 1 and 2 o'clock; perhaps a little earlier; and I saw him coming back perhaps about 4; but I am not positive as to the time. On the 2d of March, he came to his father's very early, before breakfast; I do not know what time he left; I was sick and did not see him any more; on Friday I did not see him until noon, at dinner. I did not see him at all on Wednesday, the 1st of March, and do not know of myself whether he was abroad or at home on that day, nor do I know whether he was at home or abroad after he left his sister early in the morning of the 2d, until the next day at noon.

BETTY WASHINGTON (colored.)
Recalled for the Defense.—June 5

By MR. EWING.

I went to live at Dr. Samuel A. Mudd's house the week after Christmas, and was there in March last; I know that on the 1st of March, Ash Wednesday, Dr. Mudd was down at the tobacco bed, getting it ready to sow; he was there until about dinner time, and he and Mr. Blanford came in to dinner together. He was out all that afternoon, but was at home at night. I saw him the next morning, Thursday, at breakfast time, and we cut brush all that day, and he was there working with us all day; he laid the brush off for us to dig up. On Friday, he was stripping tobacco in the barn. I saw him on Friday morning, but not at noon; he went from the barn over to his father's to dinner, and came back after we had been to supper.

I saw him on Saturday at breakfast, and after dinner he went to the post-office at Beantown, and came back at night. On Sunday he went to church, and came home Sunday night.

The tobacco bed that he was fixing on the 1st of March is down close to Mr. Sylvester Mudd's. I was working on the bed with him.

I never heard of John H. Surratt while I lived at Dr. Mudd's. If I had heard talk of his name, I should know it. I know Mary Simms who used to live at Dr. Mudd's; all the colored folks about tnere gave her a bad name as a story-teller. Dr. Mudd treated me very well; I have no fault to find with him.

Cross-examined by ASSISTANT JUDGE ADVOCATE BINGHAM.

Dr. Mudd took breakfast at home on Thursday, and he was there all day when we were cutting brush; he was on one side of the path, and we were on the other. I know he was at home to breakfast, dinner, and supper on Thursday.

By MR. EWING.

Q. Are you certain that Dr. Mudd took breakfast at his house on the day after Ash Wednesday?

Assistant Judge Advocate BINGHAM objected to the question as not proper re-examination. The cross-examination had been confined to matters brought out on the examination in chief, and therefore this kind of re-examination was not proper.

Mr. EWING desired to put the question in order to explain a seeming contradiction, and have the matter fully understood.

The Commission sustained the objection.

FRANK WASHINGTON (colored.)
Recalled for the Defense.—June 5.

It is a little better than twelve months since I went to live at Dr. Mudd's house. I was there last March, and I know that on the 1st, which was Ash Wednesday, he was out working with me on the tobacco bed from morning until night; the next day he was about the tobacco bed in the morning and afternoon. On Friday he went to the bed again, but it commenced raining. He then went to the barn to strip tobacco, and he staid in the barn until 12 o'clock, when he went to his father's. On Saturday it rained pretty hard, and he kept the house all day until pretty late in the evening, when he rode up to the post-office at Beantown. On Sunday he went to church.

On Ash Wednesday night, and every other night, Dr. Mudd was at home; Dr. Mudd was also at home Tuesday, the last day of February, and I saw him on Sunday night, the 5th; he was at home.

Cross-examined by ASSISTANT JUDGE ADVOCATE BINGHAM.

I always got up before Dr. Mudd, and I saw him go out of the house early on Thursday morning; I was working with him all that day. He ate his breakfast before I had mine, and he ate his dinner and supper at home.

JOHN F. DAVIS.
For the Defense.—June 5.

By MR. EWING.

I live in Prince George's County, Md., about a mile from the line of Charles County. I know that Dr. Samuel Mudd was at home on the 3d of March, for I went down to see him, and carried him half a dozen small perch. I saw him at his house, within five miles of Bryantown, at about 10 o'clock on Friday morning, the 3d day of March.

THOMAS DAVIS.
Recalled for the Defense.—June 5.
By MR. EWING.

Since the 9th of January I have been living at Dr. Samuel Mudd's. I recollect that he was at home on the 1st of March, because I was sick, and he came into my room to see me. He told me he could not give me any meat on that day because it was Ash Wednesday, the beginning of Lent. He came up to see me twice on that day, in the forenoon and afternoon, and on the 2d of March he came to see me twice, morning and evening. On the 3d I saw him three times, and on the 4th and 5th he came to see me as usual, in the forenoon and afternoon of each day.

Cross-examined by ASSISTANT JUDGE ADVOCATE BINGHAM.

I was sick and confined to my bed at Dr. Mudd's only once last winter; I was taken sick on the 22d of February, and remained sick and confined to the house until about the 15th of March; this is the same sickness that I swore to before the Court a week ago.

By MR. EWING.

Dr. Mudd was up to see me every day during the whole of that time, and generally twice a day. Dr. Mudd did not own a two-horse buggy or rockaway while I lived there; he had no buggy at all.

By ASSISTANT JUDGE ADVOCATE BINGHAM.

He had his father's carriage once on the 17th of April. I do not know what he had while I was sick; I was not out to see.

By MR. EWING.

His father's carriage is a two-horse one. It is a close carriage; not a very heavy one. There is one seat inside, and one outside for the driver; I think it has a window in each side, and opens at the side with a door.

By ASSISTANT JUDGE ADVOCATE BINGHAM.

It has curtains. I said it was a rockaway, but I spoke of it first as a "carriage;" I never heard it called a rockaway.

HENRY L. MUDD, JR.
For the Defense.—June 6.
By MR. EWING.

Of the whereabouts of my brother, Samuel A. Mudd, from the 1st to the 5th of March, I can state that on the 1st of March I did not see him, though he certainly was at home.

On the 2d of March he was at my father's house before breakfast, having come to see my sister, who was sick. I saw him again that day at 4 o'clock. On the 3d of March he was sent for about 10 o'clock, and the boy found him in the barn stripping tobacco. He came about half-past 11 o'clock, remained to dinner, and left about 2 o'clock; I am very positive of this. In the afternoon of the same day he came again, and brought some medicine. I saw him again that evening when I went over to his house to fetch some medicine. On the 4th of March he was again at my father's house to see my sister. On the 5th of March I saw him at church, and he dined at our house. The distance from my father's house to the Navy Yard bridge at Washington is from twenty-seven to thirty miles.

My brother has not owned a carriage of any description since I have known him. My father does not own any buggy; he owns a large two-horse, close carriage, holding four persons inside, two on the driver's seat, and a large seat behind. It is as large as any of the city hacks, and very heavy.

Cross-examined by ASSISTANT JUDGE ADVOCATE BINGHAM.

I distinctly remember my brother being at my father's house on the 3d of March. I was at the barn stripping tobacco, and when I came to my dinner my brother came in immediately afterward, and he asked for some water to wash his hands; I noticed they were covered with the gum of tobacco. My sister was taken sick on the 1st of March, Ash Wednesday; I remember I went to church on that day.

DR. J. H. BLANFORD.
For the Defense.—June 6.
By MR. EWING.

I saw Dr. Mudd at his house on the 1st of March, and I saw him at church on the 5th. Dr. Mudd's father does not own a buggy or rockaway. His carriage is a large, close family carriage; four seats inside and two outside.

MISS MARY MUDD.
For the Defense.—June 9.
By MR. EWING.

On Ash Wednesday, the 1st of March, I was making preparations to go to church, when I was taken very sick. The sickness passed off, and I grew better; but on the 2d of March my father sent for Dr. Samuel Mudd, my brother, and brought him over. My father found him in bed. He remained with us till 7 o'clock, and then returned to his own house.

On Friday morning, the 3d of March, there was an eruption on my face, and my mother, who was much frightened, sent a small colored boy over for my brother, who sent back word that he would be there to dinner. He came between 11 and 12 o'clock and dined with us. Having come from the barn where he was stripping tobacco all day, he brought no medicine. I remember he came directly into my room and washed the tobacco gum off his hands. He left at 2 o'clock, and returned at 4, bringing with him some medicine. On the same day my brother Henry, late in the evening, went over and returned with more medicine. On the 4th, Saturday, my brother came to see me, and dined with us. On the 5th, Sunday, he was at our house in the evening. On Monday, the 6th, he came to see me again; also on Tuesday, the 7th, and on Wednesday I was able to leave my room and did not need his attention any more.

During this time, on one of the days, a negro woman on the place was taken very sick of typhoid pneumonia. My brother saw her every day until the 23d of March. That day I remember very well, because we had a tornado, and his barn was blown down. After that, during the whole of the month, I saw him every two or three days, or heard of him.

I have been in the habit of seeing my brother every day or so, because my mother's health is delicate, and he comes in frequently to see her.

I know of my brother going to Washington on the 23d of March, in company with Lewellyn Gardiner. I remember his being at a party at Mr. George Henry Gardiner's in January, but I do not remember the date. His wife and Mrs. Simms, who boards in the family, were also there. They remained until daybreak. A short time after that, he came with my brother Henry to Giesboro to buy some horses. Those are the only occasions I know of his being away from home between the 23d of December and the 23d of March, and I never heard of his being absent on any other occasion.

My brother never owned a buggy or carriage. My brother has for the past year worn a drab slouch hat. I have never seen him wear a black hat for a year.

I know Andrew Gwynn. I understand he has been in the Confederate service since 1861. I never knew or heard of any Confederate officers, or soldiers, or citizen Confederates, stopping at my brother's house.

I saw Booth in Dr. Queen's pew at church last fall or winter. It was the visit when he purchased the horse of Mr. Gardiner. I do not know of Booth having been at my brother's at that visit. I only heard of it; I did not hear of his staying there over night. I never heard of a second visit until since this trial commenced. Mr. Gardiner does not live more than half a mile, I think, from my brother's. Bryantown is on the road between Dr. Queen's and Mr. Gardiner's. My brother's house is also on that road.

My brother first went to St. John's College in 1849, and he was there in 1850. In 1851 he went to Georgetown College. He was not at home in the months of October, November, and December of 1850, or January, 1851. He never spent any holiday at home except the summer vacation.

IN WASHINGTON, March 23, 1865.

Thomas L. Gardiner.
Recalled for the Defense.—May 29.

By Mr. Ewing.

On the 23d of March last, Dr. Samuel A. Mudd (the accused) and myself came to Washington together. We left home about 8 or 9 o'clock in the morning, and came up to attend the sale of Government condemned horses, which we were told would take place on Friday; but when we got to Mr. Martin's, we heard that the day of sale had been changed to Tuesday, and we were disappointed in attending it.

Dr. Mudd said he wanted to go over in town; so we left our horses at Mr. Martin's, where we had dined, walked across the bridge and up to the Navy Yard gate; then we took a street-car and came up on the avenue. We went to Mr. Young's carriage factory, where Dr. Mudd looked at some wagons, and then around to one or two livery-stables, where Dr. Mudd looked at some second-hand wagons. From there we went round on the island to Mr. Alexander Clark's. Not finding him at home, we went down to his store, staid there with him till dark, and he closed his store, when we returned to his house, and took tea with him. After tea, Mr. Clark, Dr. Mudd, and myself went to Dr. Allen's, remained two or three hours, then returned to Mr. Clark's, and staid all night—Dr. Mudd and myself sleeping together. After breakfast next morning, we accompanied Mr. Clark to his store, and then went to the Capitol and looked at some of the paintings. After this, we took a street-car, returned to Mr. Martin's and ordered our dinner, after which we got our horses and returned home. We were not separated at all during the whole time; we were not out of one another's sight, I am confident, from the time we left Mr. Martin's till we returned. We saw nothing of Booth while there, nor did we go to the National Hotel.

I recollect the contest in our Congressional district, in which Calvert and Harris were the rival candidates. Mr. Harris was running as a peace candidate; I do not know that he was termed a secessionist. Calvert, I understood was the unconditional Union candidate. I can not say whom Dr. Mudd supported at that election. I did not see his ticket, but from a conversation I had with him, I supposed he would support Mr. Calvert. I understood him to say that he thought it would be better to elect Mr. Calvert.

Cross-examined by ASSISTANT JUDGE ADVOCATE BINGHAM.

I understood that Calvert was publicly reputed to be a stronger Union man than Harris.

By ASSISTANT JUDGE ADVOCATE BURNETT.

I do not know that there were three candidates in the field; that Colonel John C. Holland was the unconditional Union candidate in that district, and the others both peace candidates. I know that Colonel Holland was a candidate when Harris was elected the last time.

DR. CHARLES ALLEN.

For the Defense.—June 6.

By MR. EWING.

I am acquainted with the prisoner, Samuel A. Mudd. The last time I saw him was at my office in this city, on the evening of the 23d of March last. He came there in company with Mr. H. A. Clark and Mr. Gardiner; the latter gentleman I had never seen before. I was introduced to him on that evening; I do not know his first name. I understood that he lived in the same section of the country that Dr. Mudd lived in. They came in about 8 o'clock, and remained till between 12 and 1 o'clock at night. There were several other gentlemen in my office, to whom Mr. Clark introduced Dr. Mudd and Mr. Gardiner. I can fix the date of that visit from the fact that a tornado had swept over the city that day, unroofing one or two houses, and killing a negro man; and this was spoken of by us in the evening; by reference to the newspapers I find that it was the 23d. I had seen Dr. Mudd once before, in the early part of 1864, when Mr. Clark first introduced him to me. Those are the only two occasions on which I have seen him.

HENRY A. CLARK.

For the Defense.—June 6.

By MR. EWING.

In the latter part of last March, Dr. Mudd (the accused) and Mr. Gardiner, a neighbor of his, came to my store in this city, between 6 and 7 o'clock in the evening, and went home with me, and took tea at my house. After tea we went around to Dr. Allen's office, and spent the evening there, in company with a number of other gentlemen. Mr. Emerson and Mr. Veighmyer were there. Mr. Gardiner and Dr. Morgan were there for a few minutes, and I think Ethan Allen, but am not positive; and perhaps Mr. Bowman of the Bank of Washington; there were perhaps ten or a dozen. We remained till between 12 and 1 o'clock, playing cards. Dr.

Mudd and Mr. Gardiner went to my house with me; I gave them a bed-room, and they remained together in my house, and went away together the next morning. I have not seen Dr. Mudd on any other occasion this year until yesterday.

I do not know either J. Wilkes Booth, John H. Surratt, or Mr. Weichman. No one bearing either of those names was in company with Dr. Mudd, Mr. Gardiner, and myself at Dr. Allen's, at my house, or any where else. Dr. Mudd was not out of my sight that night from the time he came into the store until he went into his room to bed. There were no strangers about my house in the morning, and there was no one in company with Dr. Mudd and Mr. Gardiner when they left. They came to my house on the day on which a severe storm had occurred, by which a negro boy was killed. I fix the time of their visit by this, for we were talking about it at Dr. Allen's.

Cross-examined by ASSISTANT JUDGE ADVOCATE BINGHAM.

I knew all who were at Dr. Allen's on that evening, but I can not recall them. I spend the evening there often, and am pretty much acquainted with the gentlemen that visit there, but I can not state positively the names of the ten or a dozen that were there that evening

---

AT GIESBORO ON APRIL 11.

HENRY L. MUDD, JR.

For the Defense.—May 29.

By MR. EWING.

I live about three miles from Bryantown, and about three-fourths of a mile from my brother, Samuel A. Mudd; I have lived there all my life. On the 10th of last April, I think it was, my brother, Samuel A. Mudd, and myself left home together and went to Blanford's, ten miles from Washington. We staid there all night, and the next morning Dr. Blanford, Dr. Mudd, and myself went to Giesboro to buy condemned Government horses. Dr. Blanford left us about half-past 10 o'clock, and went to Washington. We remained till about 1 o'clock, and finding no horses that suited us, I proposed to Dr. Mudd to go down to Mr. Martin's, near the bridge, and get some dinner, which we did. Dr. Blanford came in just as we had dined, and we all three returned home. Dr. Mudd and myself were not separated five minutes during that visit. We did not cross the Eastern Branch, or come into Washington or the Navy Yard, nor did I see any thing of John Wilkes Booth during that visit. I know of but two other visits to Washington made by my brother, Samuel A. Mudd, during last winter and spring; the first on the 23d or 24th of

December, in company with Jerry Mudd, and the second visit with Thomas L. Gardiner, about the 23d of March. With the exception of those visits to Washington, and when he went to Giesboro with me, my brother has been at home, and I saw him nearly every day, at least four times a week, at home and at church. A part of last year I was at college; I came home about the 29th of June

I do not know of any Confederate soldiers or other persons having been about my brother's house since my return from college, nor did I ever see or hear of John H. Surratt being there. My father is a large land-owner in the county, and the farm which my brother, the prisoner, holds is between four and five hundred acres.

Cross-examined by ASSISTANT JUDGE ADVOCATE BURNETT.

My father gave that farm to my brother. He has no deed for it, but he can get one any time he wants it. I suppose he is a tenant of my father's.

By MR. EWING.

I always understood that my father set apart that farm for my brother; it is known as my brother's farm, and goes by that name. I know also that six years ago my father bought the land on which Mr. John F. Hardy now lives for my brother, Dr. Samuel Mudd. The house was burned down, and a small one built, which did not suit my brother, and he sold the farm to Mr. Hardy, making the agreement, and selling and receiving the proceeds, although my father held the title.

Recalled for the Defense.—May 31.

By MR. EWING.

I did not say in my previous examination that my brother was a tenant, if that means that he pays rent. I keep my father's accounts, and I know very well that my brother has never paid the first cent of rent for the farm since he has been on it, nor any of the produce of the farm; it was treated as my brother's farm in every respect.

ROBERT F. MARTIN.

For the Defense.—May 29.

By MR. EWING.

I am acquainted with the prisoner, Dr. Samuel A. Mudd, with his brother, Henry L. Mudd, and Dr. Blanford. Dr. Mudd was at my house, on the 23d of March last, with Mr. Lewellyn Gardiner; they took dinner, and left their horses, then went over the river, returned next day to dinner, and got their horses. He was at my house again in April, in company with his brother, Henry Mudd. They had their horse put away, and took dinner.

Dr. Blanford joined them, perhaps between

3 and 4 o'clock, I am not positive, and they all three left together. They said they were going to Giesboro Point to buy horses. I have no means of fixing the date of this visit except from my book, which is at home; but I think it was the 4th of April. Neither Dr. Mudd nor Dr. Blanford was there, to my knowledge, between that time and the assassination of the President.

Cross-examined by ASSISTANT JUDGE ADVOCATE BINGHAM.

I did not register Dr. Mudd's name at all; but a man by the name of Stewart was there that day, and his name was registered; so that the book will show the date.

Recalled for the Defense.—May 30.

By MR. EWING.

Since I was upon the stand yesterday I have referred to my register, and find that it was Jerry Mudd that was at my house on the 4th of April. It must have been on the 11th of April that Dr. Samuel Mudd, his brother Henry, and Dr. Blanford were there; I know it from the fact that, when they had been gone about half an hour, Joshua S. Naylor and Lemuel Orme (whose names are registered on that day) drove up and asked if there was anybody up from Charles County, and I told them that Dr. Mudd and his brother had just left.

I saw Dr. Mudd and Jerry Mudd in market in Washington on the 24th of December last. Dr. Mudd helped me to sell some turkeys; it was a dull market, and he said he thought he could do better than I was doing; so he stood at the stand while I went round the market, but when I came back I do not think he had sold one. He was at my stand twice that day. He inquired of Lucas if he could carry a stove down for him, and Lucas's reply was that, if he sold his poultry, he would; if not, he would have to take it over to me; but he did not sell his poultry, and the stove was not moved that day.

Dr. Mudd was at my house on the 23d of March; his name was registered on that day. He and Mr. Gardiner came together before dinner. They left their horses there, and took them away the next day after dinner. I do not know where they went; I only know they went across the river.

MR. EWING. I now propose to ask the witness, what statement was made by the accused to him, as to the purpose of his visit. Inasmuch as the visit has to be explained, I think, under the rules of evidence, that statement is clearly admissible. There are plenty of authorities for it.

Assistant Judge Advocate BINGHAM. I undertake to say that there is not any authority in the world for it, because that is not in issue.

MR. EWING. It is in issue whether he met Booth in January.

Assistant Judge Advocate BINGHAM. Not

in March. This is in relation to a visit of the 23d of March.

Mr. EWING. It is in issue whether Dr. Mudd met Booth in Washington. We are not confined as to any particular day when the meeting may have occurred. We want to show that he could not have met Booth from the 23d of December down to the time of the assassination of the President; and, in order to show that, we prove his presence at home during all that period, except the visit to Giesboro, and the one night he went to the party; and we follow it by proof as to what the visits were for, and as to what he did, who was with him, and where he went. Now, as a part of the proof, to show the purpose of the visits to Washington, his declarations as to the purpose of the visit made at the time of making the visit are admissible, under the rules of evidence. I will read to the Court an authority on that subject, from 2 Russell on Crimes, p. 750: "Generally speaking, declarations accompanying acts are admissible in evidence as showing the nature, character, and objects of such acts. Thus, where a person enters into land in order to take advantage of a forfeiture to foreclose a mortgage, to defeat a disseizin, or the like, or changes his actual residence, or is upon a journey, or leaves his home, or returns thither, ... his declarations made at the time of the transaction, and expressive of its character, motive, or object, are regarded as verbal acts, indicating a present purpose and intention, and are therefore admitted in proof like any other material acts." The authority is exactly in point. The fact of the journey is legitimately given in evidence by us; and so the object of the journey is legitimate; and, in connection with the object of the journey, his declarations as to its purpose are admissible.

Assistant Judge Advocate BINGHAM. The great trouble is that the gentleman does not read enough. I would yield the point if he could show in the book from which he has read, or in any other book, an authority saying that proof of the kind now offered was admissible, when the point to which it related was not in issue. The rule on the subject is, that if the prosecution prove the declarations and acts of the accused, he may prove all that he said on those occasions, as part of the res gestæ; but there is no such thing in the text he read, or in any other, as that a man may prove what he said at another time and place not involved in the issue, and about which there has been no proof offered by the prosecution. The gentleman says he wants to prove what the prisoner said, as to the object of this journey, in order to show that he was not coming to see Booth. I suppose, if on the 23d of March, he said he was not hunting Booth, and they prove that, and if, when he got back home he said he did not see Booth,

and they prove that, it would be proof of that fact. What authority is there for saying that that can be done? There is no book in the world that says so. The text read by the gentleman does not mean any such thing. If the gentleman can show me a text which says that a defendant may prove an act that has not been put in issue by the accusation, about which no proof has been offered by the prosecution, and prove all he said on that occasion, I shall yield. The same book from which the gentleman read lays down the law, that the party shall not introduce his own declarations on his own motion. The text is, page 750: "Hearsay evidence of a fact is not admissible;" and it goes on to say, "there are, however, certain instances, which it will be the object of this section to point out, where hearsay evidence is admissible." But when? "When hearsay is introduced, not as a medium of proof in order to establish a distinct fact, but as being in itself a part of the transaction in question."

Now, is this transaction in question? How is the fact whether Dr. Mudd came to Washington on the 23d of March or not in question? Is it so on the charge and specification? Not at all. Is it so by any proof offered by the prosecution? Not at all. Our proof is, that in January he was here, and had an interview with Booth, and he is not to disprove that by his mere declarations; and this testimony is offered for no other purpose whatever. It is not to explain any transaction, because there is no transaction calling for explanation. The fact that he came here on the 23d of March is not in evidence against him—it is not a matter of accusation against him—it is not in question; and therefore I say the declarations of that date proposed to be offered in evidence are his declarations, offered in evidence on his own motion, for no purpose except to disprove the testimony offered against him by the prosecution; that he had an interview with Booth in January; and there is no text of any law-book any where that says he can make evidence in that way by his own declarations.

The Commission sustained the objection.

WITNESS. My hotel is about one hundred yards from the Navy Yard bridge, Eastern Branch bridge, and persons going from Bryantown to Washington pass by it. I have a post-office there. I have not seen Dr. Mudd at my house, on his way to or from Washington, since the 24th of December, except on those two occasions. I do not recollect his stopping there on December 24th, but I saw him in market. I attend market pretty regularly, and am not at home much. I suppose I would recollect if he had stopped there at any other time; I can not say positively whether I have heard of his being there, or not. I kept no record of persons coming to my house until the 20th of February.

DR. J. H. BLANFORD.

For the Defense.—May 29.

By MR. EWING.

I live about twelve miles from this city, in Prince George's County, Maryland.

On the 11th of April last, I accompanied Dr. Samuel A. Mudd and his brother, Henry L. Mudd, to Giesboro, to attend a Government sale of horses. We arrived there some time before the hour of sale, and I remained with Dr. Mudd till after 12 o'clock, examining horses. They were very inferior, and Dr. Mudd did not purchase any. Having business in Washington, I left Dr. Mudd about half-past 12; arranging to meet him at 3 o'clock, at Mr. Martin's, near the bridge. I was with Dr. Mudd all the time till half-past 12. I went to Washington, and got back to Mr. Martin's about half-past 2, and found Dr. Mudd there, waiting for me. In about fifteen minutes, probably, we started toward home, and rode together to the road leading to my house, when I went home, and he continued his journey.

His brother was with him when I left him at Giesboro, and was with him at Mr. Martin's when I returned. Mr. Martin's place is on the other side of the Eastern Branch, right in the forks of the road leading to Giesboro and the stage road leading down through the counties, and is not more than fifty or one hundred yards from the bridge. It is a mile and a half, or probably two miles, from the National Hotel, Washington.

During the last eighteen months, I have several times heard Dr. Mudd speak, in general terms, of being dissatisfied with his place, and that he would sell if an advantageous offer were made to him; but I have no knowledge of his making a direct offer to sell his farm.

MUDD'S ABSENCE FROM HOME.

THOMAS DAVIS.

For the Defense.—May 29.

By MR. STONE.

I have lived at Dr. Samuel Mudd's since the 9th of January last, working on his farm. I have been on the plantation all the time, with the exception of one night some time in January. Dr. Mudd has been absent from home only three nights during that time; one night at a party at George Henry Gardiner's, and the other times in Washington. It was on the 26th of January that he went to Mr. Gardiner's; his family accompanied him, and they returned a little after sunrise. The next time he was from home was on the 23d of March, when he went to Washington with Mr. Lewellyn Gardiner to buy some horses. They came back on the

24th. I remember the date because the barn was blown down while he was away, and the 25th was a holiday.

I do not know John H. Surratt, nor John Wilkes Booth; I never heard their names mentioned, nor the name of David E. Herold.

[A likeness of John Wilkes Booth was shown to the witness.]

I never saw that man at Dr. Mudd's while I was living there. I was ill for more than three weeks while I was there, and Dr. Mudd attended me. I took my meals up stairs then, but when I was well I took them with the family, except when late on account of feeding the horses, or doing other things; then I took them by myself. I saw Dr. Mudd every day during all the while I lived there, except the times I have mentioned, when he was absent.

I was at home on Saturday, the 15th of April, and saw two horses there, and heard that two men were there; but I did not see them; I was working in the field. The men left, as near as I can say, between 3 and 4 o'clock in the afternoon. I was there also on the following Friday, at work on the farm. Some soldiers came to the house on that day, and wanted to see Dr. Mudd. He was at his father's, and I went for him. I told him some soldiers were at the house and they wanted to see him, and he came along with me directly. He said nothing to me then about a boot, nor I to him. He came with me as far as the barn, and I went into the field, and he and Mr. Hardy went on toward the house. I never heard Dr. Mudd express any disloyal sentiments.

By MR. EWING.

I did not take breakfast with the family on the day after the President's assassination; I was attending to the horses, and was not ready when the horn was blown; nor did I take dinner with them that day. All I knew about the two men having been there, was that one of them had a broken leg, and one had been to meals, and the other had not.

Cross-examined by ASSISTANT JUDGE ADVOCATE BINGHAM.

That was what I understood about them; I did not see the men. When I came back to the house, about 4 o'clock, the horses were gone, and as I did not hear of the men being there after that, I supposed they were gone.

I saw Dr. Mudd and his wife start to go to Mr. George Henry Gardiner's on the night of the party; they walked in that direction. Mr. Gardiner lives about three-fourths of a mile from Dr. Mudd's.

By MR. EWING.

[Exhibiting to the witness a photograph of John H. Surratt.]

I never saw that man at Dr. Mudd's; I saw him at his own home about five years ago. I have not seen him since the 9th of January, when I went to live at Dr. Mudd's.

BETTY WASHINGTON (colored.)

For the Defense.—May 27.

By MR. STONE.

I went to live at Dr. Samuel Mudd's, as near as I can tell, on the Monday after Christmas, and have been living there ever since. I was a slave before the emancipation in Maryland, and belonged to Mrs. Adelaide Middleton. I have not been away from Dr. Mudd's house a single night since I went to live there. Dr. Mudd has not been away from home at night but three times that I can recollect, but I can not say in what month.

The first time, he and his wife went to a party at Mr. George Henry Gardiner's; they went about sundown, and came back late at night; I do not know what time. The next time was when he went to Giesboro with his brother, Mr. Henry Mudd, to buy some horses. He started in the morning, and came back, I think, next day. I can not think what month it was, but it was since the last Christmas. The last time he went to Washington, he started in the morning, and came back the next day at night. I did not see any one leave the house with him, but I heard that Mr. Gardiner went to Washington with him. I do not know who came back with him. I think it was in the latter part of the month that he went there. He was away, in all, two whole nights and a part of a night.

I did not see the two men that were at Dr. Mudd's lately—Booth and Herold; I saw one of them, the small one. I was standing at the kitchen window, and just saw a glimpse of him going in the direction of the swamp. I did not see any one with him. In three or four minutes after this Dr. Mudd came to the door, and asked if they had gone for the woman to clean up the house. Mrs. Mudd had started off a little girl for a woman to come and clean, as the gentlemen had gone.

I never saw the small man before, and I did not see the large man at all.

[A card photograph of J. Wilkes Booth was shown to the witness.]

If ever I saw that man at Dr. Mudd's, I do not recollect; I never saw anybody like that picture that I can recollect.

Cross-examined by ASSISTANT JUDGE ADVOCATE BINGHAM.

. I do not know where Giesboro is. All that I know about Dr. Mudd's going there is, that he told me he went there, and so did his wife. Mr. Henry Mudd, his brother, was there to go with him, and they started together to buy horses; but he missed the day, and could not buy any.

I think there was a week, or two weeks,

between the time when he went to Giesboro and the next time when he was away all night; but I can not come at it exactly.

AT BRYANTOWN, APRIL 15, 16.

GEORGE BOOZ (colored.)

For the Defense.—May 27.

I live with Mr. Henry L. Mudd. I am attending to his lower place, next to Bryantown, above the road, about half a mile from Mr. John McPherson's.

On Easter Saturday, the 15th of April, I saw Dr. Mudd at my house. I also saw him on the road coming up from toward Bryantown and going toward home. The main road from Bryantown, up to the swamps, goes right through my place. You can go from Bryantown to Dr. Mudd's either by continuing along the main road, or through the plantation path. As Dr. Mudd came from Bryantown he passed through my place by the by-road. I did not see any person with him, either walking or riding. I had been in the swamp looking for my hogs. I had been below, and had crossed the main road, and met Dr. Mudd coming up from Bryantown; I spoke to him. That was between 3 and 4 o'clock in the afternoon. I did not see any one, or pass any one on either road. I did not see any person on horseback standing in the swamp, nor any person at all. If anybody had been standing in the road, I think I should have seen him, as I passed from the big swamp across the main road up to my house, and as I came up to the hill. I also passed near the little swamp, and could have seen if any one had been there.

Dr. Mudd was riding at his usual pace. He very frequently, in going to or coming from Bryantown, would pass through our place, and I would see him. Dr. Mudd, on this occasion, on the Saturday, stopped and spoke a few words, and asked me where I had been, and then kept on.

Cross-examined by ASSISTANT JUDGE ADVOCATE BINGHAM.

When we met, Dr. Mudd was going toward his home. He did not ask me if I had seen anybody, nor did he say any thing about Bryantown. He was riding a bay filly; it was his own horse; I know it well. As I was not looking out for anybody, a person might dismount and I not notice him. Some of the bushes there are as tall as a man's head, or taller.

Recalled for the Defense.—June 7.

I met Dr. Mudd on the by-road leading through our farm on the day after the assassination. I crossed the road just opposite my house, and about three hundred yards from the big elm on the side farthest from Bryantown. Where I crossed the road, I reckon I can see a quarter of a mile in each direction; that is, from and toward Bryantown—a plain, full view. There was no horseman on the road that I saw. If there had been any one going along the road with Dr. Mudd, and he kept on the main road, away from Bryantown, when Dr. Mudd turned up through this by-road, I think I should have seen him; there was nothing to prevent it.

If anybody had been traveling with Dr. Mudd, and kept on the main road when Dr. Mudd turned in at the gate, he would have been pretty nearly at or near the point where and when I crossed the main road, and had he been there I must have seen him.

Susan Stewart.
For the Defense.—June 3.

I live at Mr. John Morris's, about a mile from Bryantown, and not more than a quarter of a mile from George Booz's. I live on the little cut-off road, leading through the farm.

I saw Dr. Samuel Mudd, the prisoner, on Easter Saturday, about 3 or 4 o'clock. He was about fifty yards from the road, inside of the place at which I live. When I saw him, he was just at the corner of the barn, going up toward Mr. Morris's house, riding very slowly by himself. I saw no one with him. It was cloudy and misty, and I think raining a little. Standing at my door, from which I saw Dr. Mudd, I can see a quarter of a mile or more of the main road. I can see from the swamp clear up to the tree called big elm. I did not see Dr. Mudd when he came out of the main road. I did not take particular notice of the main road, but I could have seen very easily if there had been anybody on the main road.

I saw George Booz meet Dr. Mudd that day after he had passed our house.

By Assistant Judge Advocate Bingham.

Dr. Mudd, when I first saw him, was opposite the barn, which is not more than fifty yards from the main road. He was coming up toward our house, but I can not say whether he was coming from the direction of Bryantown or not.

Primus Johnson (colored.)
For the Defense.—June 3.

I saw Dr. Samuel Mudd coming from Bryantown by Mr. Booz's on the Saturday after the President was killed, about 3 o'clock, or a little after. I also saw him when he was going to Bryantown; he was riding by himself. There was a man followed Master Samuel, going toward Bryantown, and this man came back by himself, and he came back before Dr. Samuel Mudd, I reckon, about half an hour. Mr. Booz's is about two miles from Bryantown, and is on the road between Dr. Mudd's and Bryantown.

Leonard S. Roby.
For the Defense.—June 3.

I was in Bryantown on the Saturday after the assassination of the President, about 3 o'clock in the afternoon, and I staid there until night. Before getting to Bryantown, I met a gentleman on the road, who told me of the assassination, but he professed not to believe it. When I got near Bryantown, I found soldiers stationed two or three hundred yards from the village. I made inquiries of them, and learned that such was the fact, and that somebody that belonged to the theater was the assassin; but, though I conversed with several, none of them could give me his name. I was not in Bean's store that day.

I also asked several persons, citizens as well as soldiers, and it was not till a few minutes before I left in the evening that I received the information as to who was the assassin, from Dr. George Mudd.

I know Daniel J. Thomas, and the reputation he bears for truth and veracity in the neighborhood in which he lives. It is such that I would not believe him under oath.

Cross-examined by Assistant Judge Advocate Burnett.

I have known Mr. Thomas from boyhood. My attitude toward the Government during this rebellion has, I believe, been that of a loyal citizen. I have given no assistance or counsel to the enemy in any way, shape, or manner. There are some acts of the Administration I may have spoken of not so pleasantly, but nothing more; but I do not think I have said any thing against the Government in its efforts to put down the rebellion.

I know the man Boyle who murdered Captain Watkins, but I never harbored him at my house. I have only seen him once or twice. He came to my house the morning after our general election, with some ten or a dozen or fifteen. I live not far from the road, and many call after the election. After the general election, on their route homeward, a party called, and Boyle was among them. I did not know him at that time. They staid but a short time. When I heard his name, I had a reason not to want him there, and I was not so particular in my treatment toward those with him, and they left after an hour or two, and I have not seen him since.

By Mr. Ewing.

In what I said of Daniel J. Thomas, I referred to his reputation before the war as well as since. It appears to me he is a kind of man who will imagine things, and then bring himself to believe they are facts, and, believing them, then assert and stand to them to the last that they are facts, and swear to them.

Dr. Joseph Blanford.

For the Defense. — June 3.

By Mr. Ewing.

I am acquainted with the routes from Washington through Surrattsville to Bryantown, and through Surrattsville to Port Tobacco and Pope's Creek. I have traveled these routes several times; I am also familiar with the road from Dr. Mudd's to Bryantown.

[A roughly-drawn map of the locality was offered in evidence, from which it appeared, by the explanation of the witness, that that portion of the road between the elmtree and the swamp, nearly half a mile in length, is visible from the houses of Booz and Murray, and the whole of the road that branches off from the main road, and running by Murray and Booz's houses, is entirely visible from those houses.]

By Assistant Judge Advocate Bingham.

Two weeks ago I made special inspection of these roads, to ascertain what portion of the roads was visible from the houses occupied by Booz and Murray.

I know where the colored people named Bloyce live. The cluster of trees round the houses would obstruct the view of this road, I think. I do not think a person could see any distance from these houses.

By Mr. Ewing.

From the bridge, as indicated on the map, to Bryantown, is not more than a quarter of a mile, and you can look down the road right into the main street of the town. A person coming from the bridge to Dr. Mudd's house would have to pass along the main road by the big elm, or else by the cut-off by John Murray's house.

E. D. R. Bean.

For the Defense. — June 3.

I am a merchant at Bryantown. On the day following the assassination, I believe it was, Dr. Samuel Mudd bought some goods at my store. I sold him some calicoes; this is the only thing that I particularly remember. When I first heard that day that the President was assassinated, I asked by whom, and my impression is that they said it was by Boyle, the man who is said to have killed Captain Watkins, and who had the reputation in that neighborhood of being a desperado.

I can not state positively whether I heard that day that it was Booth or not. Soldiers were in and out of the store that day, and the assassination was the topic of general discussion.

Q. Did you have a conversation with the prisoner, Samuel A. Mudd, that day, as to the assassination of the President?

A. The day I sold him the calico I had some conversation with him, and that circumstance leads me to think it was the day I heard of the assassination.

Q. What was the conversation?

A. I remarked to him that there was very bad news. "Yes," said he, "I am sorry to hear it."

Assistant Judge Advocate Bingham objected to the witness stating the conversation between him and Dr. Mudd; but, inasmuch as the witness had already partly answered the question, he would allow the answer to stand as far as it had gone.

By Mr. Ewing.

Q. What else did Dr. Mudd say in regard to the assassination of the President?

Assistant Judge Advocate Bingham objected to the question, and the Commission sustained the objection.

Q. It was from the conversation you had with Dr. Mudd in regard to the assassination of the President that you are enabled to fix that as the day when he made the purchase of calico?

A. That led me to believe it was the day, because I remember his remarks.

The distance from the Eastern Branch bridge to Surrattsville is about ten miles; from Surrattsville to Bryantown is sixteen miles; from Bryantown to Port Tobacco it is thirteen miles and a half.

Cross-examined by Assistant Judge Advocate Bingham.

I can not state positively when I first heard that it was Booth who had assassinated the President. I also heard that he had been traced within three miles and a half of Bryantown, but I can not say when I first heard it; I certainly did not hear it on Saturday. I think it was Dr. George Mudd that told me on Saturday night that Booth was the murderer.

John Acton.

For the Defense. — June 5.

By Mr. Ewing.

I live about three miles from Bryantown, and about a mile and a quarter from Dr. Samuel Mudd's, on the road from his house to Bryantown. On the day after the President was killed, I saw Dr. Mudd riding toward Bryantown on a gray horse. He was alone when I first saw him, but there was a man overtaking him. In about three-quarters of an hour I saw the man come back. I was about fifty yards from the road when I saw the man returning; and I was there for an hour, more or less, afterward, but did not see Dr. Mudd return toward his house. I could not help seeing him if he had passed along the road.

Cross-examined by Assistant Judge Advocate Bingham.

When I first saw Dr. Mudd and the man, they were a little way apart, and the next thing I saw the man get up to him. I heard no conversation between them. I did not know the man, nor did I notice him much; I noticed the horse more; he rode a bay horse. I can not swear that that man [pointing to the accused, David E. Herold] is the one; he looks more like him than any of the other prisoners, but I can not say that he is the man. It was about 3 or 4 o'clock in the afternoon that I saw him come back alone, on the same road that he had gone down on, not more than an hour before, at most, on the road leading to Dr. Mudd's house. I did not see Dr. Mudd any more that evening.

MASON L. McPHERSON.

For the Defense.—June 5.

By MR. EWING.

I live within three-fourths of a mile of Bryantown. About 2 o'clock on the day after the assassination of the President I went to Bryantown, and was there till 7 or 8 o'clock in the evening. I did not hear any one say that afternoon who had assassinated the President. I heard that Boyle had murdered the Secretary of State—John Boyle, the guerrilla, that had passed through there several times, and had killed Captain Watkins. I made inquiries of some of the soldiers, but they could not tell me who had killed the President. I asked right smart of people, citizens as well as soldiers, but they did not know. I was in Bean's store a short time, and heard the talk there, but nobody mentioned the name of the assassin. There were a good many people in town that day. On Sunday I heard who the supposed murderer was.

On Monday morning, between 8 and 9 o'clock, I guess, I saw Lieutenant Dana in the hotel at Bryantown, in conversation with Dr. George Mudd. They were sitting off to themselves.

I am very well acquainted with Dr. George Mudd's reputation in the community as a Union man. He is as good a Union man as any in the United States.

From general report, I know the reputation of Daniel J. Thomas. His reputation for truth and veracity in the community where he lives is not very good.

Cross-examined by ASSISTANT JUDGE ADVOCATE BINGHAM.

I am confident that it was on Monday morning that Lieutenant Dana had this talk with Dr. George Mudd.

JOHN McPHERSON.

For the Defense.—June 5.

By MR. EWING

I was at Bryantown on Saturday, the day after the assassination of the President, from 2 o'clock till about 6, and heard the talk about the assassination. It was the general topic; but I did not hear who was the assassin. I do not recollect that I made any inquiries about it. On Monday morning I first heard that it was Booth.

I saw Lieutenant Dana at the hotel in Bryantown, on Monday morning, about 8 o'clock, in conversation with Dr. George Mudd. There were some three or four persons in the room. Dr. George Mudd's reputation as a Union man is as good as any man's.

The reputation of Daniel J. Thomas for truth and veracity, in the neighborhood in which he lives, is very bad. I know that people generally think that he is not a truth-telling man.

I am acquainted with the prisoner, Dr. Samuel A. Mudd, and with his general character, as a man of peace, order, and good citizenship. He is considered a very good man, peaceable, and a good citizen.

Cross-examined by the JUDGE ADVOCATE.

I do not recollect whether or not I have ever heard Daniel Thomas charged with having sworn falsely in any case; I have heard him spoken of as rather a bad man, and not apt to speak the truth.

Q. Do I understand you to say, under the oath you have taken, and with the knowledge which you have of Mr. Thomas, and of his life and character, that you would not believe him when speaking under oath before a court?

A. I can not say.

By MR. EWING.

I do not think I have ever heard of Thomas being a witness before this trial.

PETER TROTTER.

For the Defense.—June 5.

By MR. EWING.

I am a blacksmith, and live in Bryantown. I was there on Saturday, the day after the President was killed. I heard the subject of his murder talked of a good deal. There were a good many soldiers there, some twenty-four or twenty-five; they were around my shop the whole afternoon. I inquired of some soldiers if they knew who killed the President, and they said they did not know. They mentioned Boyle as the one that had assassinated the Secretary.

I am acquainted with Daniel J. Thomas; have known him for eight years. His reputation for veracity in the community where he lives is not very good. From my knowledge of his reputation I would believe him under oath in some cases; in others I would not. It would depend upon what it was about. I do not think I would believe him on his oath, and very few in our community would.

Cross-examined by the JUDGE ADVOCATE.

Latterly I have been loyal to the Government, and desired that it should succeed in putting down the rebellion. At first I may have thought a good deal of the rebels, but not for the last eighteen months.

Mr. Thomas is very unpopular in that neighborhood; I never heard him speak much about his loyalty, in any shape or form; I have seen him both ways. Often, when we would hear at Bryantown of some great feat that was done, he would sometimes think one way and sometimes another. I never heard him speak in favor of the rebellion, and never, at any time, have I known him to be at all unfriendly to the Government, or have any sympathy with the rebellion.

Before the last eighteen months, I thought a good deal, but never did any thing unfriendly to the Government; I never spoke much about my feelings. I do not know that I should have thought better of Mr. Thomas if he had been of my way of thinking. I have never taken the oath of allegiance. About three weeks ago I went to take it, but the Captain had no blanks.

I never engaged in blockade-running, and never crossed the military lines without a permit. If Mr. Thomas was under oath in a court of justice, I would believe him if I knew he was speaking the truth. If he was speaking against the rebels, and I had to rely upon him, I do not know that I could bring myself to believe him.

By the COURT.

I am a Scotchman, a British subject, and have never been naturalized. I have used the rights of a citizen, and have voted. The first vote I gave was for Buchanan; afterward I did not vote except for local officers of the county. I have not voted for three years. I do not know why I did not vote on the adoption of the new constitution of Maryland.

By MR. EWING.

Mr. Thomas's reputation for veracity was just the same before the war as now. In the early part of the war he had not the reputation of being a loyal man; I am sure he was not. I came to this country twelve years ago; am thirty-four years of age.

JOHN I. LANGLEY.

For the Defense.—June 5.

By MR. EWING.

I was at Bryantown two or three times on Saturday, the 15th of April; it was sundown when I last left. I heard that the President was assassinated, but did not hear who assassinated him. I did not hear that till Monday morning. There were not many citizens or many soldiers in the town, nor was there much talk about the assassination. Some of the citizens coming in heard that soldiers were there, and that martial law was to be proclaimed, and returned to their homes. I first heard of the assassination from the soldiers. I asked them who had killed the President, and they said they did not know. I did not hear of any one, supposed to be the assassin, being tracked to near Bryantown.

Cross-examined by ASSISTANT JUDGE ADVOCATE BINGHAM.

I heard that the soldiers were in pursuit of the President's assassin.

MARCELLUS GARDINER.

For the Defense.—May 30.

By MR. EWING.

I have heard Dr. Samuel Mudd, on several occasions during the past two years, state that he wanted to sell out.

I was at Reves's Church in our neighborhood on Easter Sunday, the 16th of April, following the murder of the President. The assassination was known and generally talked of; but it is my impression that the name of the assassin was not known. I saw Dr. Samuel Mudd there at church.

Q. State whether you heard Dr. Mudd say any thing as to how he regarded the act of assassination.

Assistant Judge Advocate BINGHAM. I object to introducing Dr. Mudd's declarations.

Mr. EWING. I have brought that before the Court again for the purpose of doing what I failed to do yesterday, calling the attention of the Court specially to the character of the declarations that I expect to prove.

Assistant Judge Advocate BURNETT. It is the rule of military courts, when the counsel states what he expects to prove by a witness, that the witness should withdraw, so that he may not be instructed by the remarks.

[The witness retired from the stand and the court-room.]

Mr. EWING. I expect to prove that Dr. Mudd spoke of the assassination as an atrocious and revolting crime, and a terrible calamity to the country; and that he spoke of it generally among his neighbors at the church in that way. I again call the attention of the Court to the principle upon which I claim that it is applicable; and that is, that Dr. Mudd is charged with concealment of the fact of those men having been there—a concealment extending through Sunday—and that his declarations, showing his feeling with reference to the crime during the time that they allege him to have been acting as accessory to it, are admissible.

The Commission sustained the objection of the Judge Advocate.

DR. GEORGE D. MUDD.

For the Defense.—May 29.

By MR. EWING.

I am a practitioner of medicine in the village of Bryantown, Charles County, Md. Dr. Samuel A. Mudd was a student of medicine under me for many years. His father and my father were first-cousins. I know his reputation in that neighborhood for peace, order, and good citizenship, and I know of none whose reputation is better. As a master, I have always considered him a humane man to his servants, as well as to others. He always, to my knowledge, clothed and fed his servants well, and treated them kindly, as far as I know.

I was at Bryantown the Saturday, the 15th, when the news of the assassination of the President reached there, and remained there all the evening. Lieutenant Dana, on whom I called for information, told me that the party who had attempted the assassination of Secretary Seward was named Boyle, and claimed him to be the same party who assassinated Captain Watkins of Anne Arundel County, and that the party who assassinated the President was supposed to be a man by the name of Booth, but that he thought he had not yet got out of Washington. Boyle, who was known in our region of country, and had been there three or four weeks before, was a noted desperado and guerrilla.

I was at church on Sunday, the 16th; it was then known that the President had been assassinated, but no one, to my knowledge, supposed that Booth had crossed the river; this at least was my impression; I did not make much inquiry relative to it. I saw Dr. Samuel Mudd at church. On returning home he overtook me, and I rode with him as far as his house.

Q. State whether he said any thing to you about any persons having been at his house?

The JUDGE ADVOCATE. You need not answer that question. The Government has not introduced the declarations of the prisoner, Dr. Mudd, at that time.

Mr. EWING. I propose to offer that statement for the purpose of showing that Dr. George Mudd, a resident of Bryantown, and who I will prove is a man of unquestionable loyalty, was informed by the prisoner at the bar that there were two suspicious persons at his house on Saturday morning; he told him of the circumstances of their coming there; expressed to him a desire that he should inform the military authorities, if he thought it advisable, of the fact of their having been there; stated to him that he wished him to take it direct to the military authorities, and not tell it at large about the streets, lest the parties or their friends might assassinate him for the disclosure.

I can imagine no declaration of a prisoner more clearly admissible than this. It accompanies, or is connected with, acts which they have shown of the preceding day, and of subsequent days; it is a part of the very gist of the acts and omissions by which he is sought to be implicated here, and to refuse to allow him to show that he informed the Government, through one of its most loyal friends, of the presence of these men in his house, and his suspicions in regard to them, would be to strip him of a complete and admissible defense. On the subject of such actions—for this statement was an act—I read an authority from Russell on Crimes, vol. 2, p. 750: "When hearsay is introduced, not as a medium of proof, in order to establish a distinct fact, but as being in itself a part of the transaction in question, it is then admissible; for to exclude it might be to exclude the only evidence of which the nature of the case is capable. Thus, in Lord George Gordon's case, on a prosecution for high treason, it was held that the cry of the mob might be received in evidence as part of the transaction. (21 How. St. Tr. 535) And, generally speaking, declarations accompanying acts are admissible in evidence as showing the nature, character, and objects of such acts. Thus, when a person enters into land in order to take advantage of a forfeiture, to foreclose a mortgage, to defeat a disseizin, or the like, or changes his actual residence, or is upon a journey, or leaves his home, or returns thither, or remains abroad, or secretes himself, or, in fine, does any other act material to be understood, his declarations made at the time of the transaction, and expressive of its character, motive, or object, are regarded as verbal acts indicating a present purpose and intention, and are therefore admitted in proof, like any other material facts. They are part of the *res gestæ.*"

In a note to this section, the learned American editor of the work, Judge Sharswood, gives the following, among other decisions, in this country: "*Thus, the declarations of the prisoner may be admitted to account for his silence when that silence would operate against him. The United States v. Craig, 4 Wash. C. C. Rep. 729.*" That is just the case here. "*Whenever the conduct of a person at a given time becomes the subject of inquiry, his expressions, as constituting a part of his conduct and indicating his intention, can not be rejected as irrelevant, but are admissible as part of the res gestæ. Tenney v. Evans, 14 New Hamp. 353.*"

It is to explain his silence up to the time of his making the communication to Dr. George Mudd, and to rebut the evidence of detective Lloyd as to his concealment, on the Tuesday following, of the fact that these two men had ever been at his house, that I propose to introduce that statement in evidence. This statement was made before he could have known that any suspicions were directed against him. It was an act done during the time of that silence and alleged concealment, by reason of which they seek to implicate him as an accessory before and after the fact in the assassination. That conversation with Dr. George Mudd accounts for the silence; that conversation broke the silence. If the fact of his having been silent is to be urged against him, may not the fact that he broke the silence, and communicated all the facts to the military authorities, be introduced in his behalf? I hope the Judge Advocate and the Court will mark the fact that we do not introduce this for the purpose of showing that what Dr. Mudd then said was true. We do not introduce it for the purpose of explaining any thing as to the presence of these men in the house, or the acts they did there; we introduce it simply to show that he communicated, as well as he could, to the military authorities the fact of their presence, and at the same time gave the explanation of his caution then and his silence before. No authority could be more direct upon this point than the authority in *United States* v. *Craig*, 4 Washington Circuit Court Reports, which is briefly stated in the note to Russell, which I before read: "Thus, the declarations of a prisoner may be admitted to account for his silence, where that silence would operate against him."

The JUDGE ADVOCATE. If the Court please, the principle here is almost too well settled to be the subject of discussion. While it is competent for the Government to give in evidence declarations of a prisoner on trial, his confessions, it is not competent for him to do so; that is perfectly clear. But when these confessions are introduced, he has a right to insist that the whole of them shall be given. Now, we have offered no declarations in evidence which were made by the prisoner at the bar on Sunday, the day spoken of by the witness. The ground, then, on which it is sought to introduce them is, that they are part of the *res gestæ*. The *res gestæ* at that moment had been completed. The *res gestæ* in which he was involved, and which is the subject of arraignment on the part of the Government, had closed the day before. That consisted in his having received and entertained these men, and sent them on their way rejoicing, having fed them, having set the leg of the one whose leg was broken, having comforted and strengthened and encouraged them, as far as his hospitality and professional skill could do, to proceed on their journey. That is the *res gestæ*, the transaction on which the Government arraigns him, and that was complete at 4 o'clock on Saturday evening. Now, on a subsequent day, on Sunday, after carefully reviewing his own conduct, he proposes to introduce a line of declaration on his part, nearly twenty-four hours afterward, by which he seeks to relieve himself of the imputation which the law attaches to his previous conduct, which has been the subject of the testimony before this Court. I say it is not competent for him to do so; it is not competent for him to declare the motives by which his previous action was governed, because we have no means of reaching those motives; we have introduced no testimony in regard to them, and we have no means of doing so. The great principle which says that a criminal shall not manufacture testimony for his own exculpation, intervenes and forbids that this Court shall hear that testimony. Any act of the prisoner he may introduce, because in regard to that we ourselves can introduce testimony, but declarations which may have been framed upon careful review of his own conduct, solely for the purpose of his vindication against the accusation which he must have seen would arise from that conduct, can not be heard upon any principle of testimony whatever.

Mr. EWING. The Judge Advocate says that the transaction was wholly closed. Not so. The charge here is a charge of concealment, among others, and the concealment, as they have sought to prove it, was a concealment not only of their presence while they were in the house, but a concealment, extending until Tuesday or Friday, of the fact of their having been there. Two of the witnesses for the prosecution who went there on Tuesday—two out of the four—said, upon their examination in chief, that Dr. Mudd denied that two men had been at his house. That was part of the testimony for the prosecution. It was not irrelevant testimony; it was legitimately applicable to this charge of concealment, which is made in broad and general terms, and which applies as well to his concealing them while they were there as to his concealing their course after they left, and the fact that they had been there. In support of that charge of concealment, as I said before, they have introduced testimony that he denied on Tuesday that they had been there, and now they propose to exclude us from proving that he informed the Government on Sunday that they had been there. It would be most unjust to exclude it, and contrary to the authorities which I have cited, one of which is explicitly and clearly in point.

The JUDGE ADVOCATE. If the gentleman will frame his question so as to bring out simply the conduct of the party in the act he did, I shall not object; but I must object to his declarations.

Mr. EWING. The question has been asked. I can not prove how he informed the Government without proving the words he used. If the witness were the Judge Advocate General, I could not prove that Dr. Mudd had informed him of their presence there without proving what he said to him.

Assistant Judge Advocate BURNETT. The question could certainly be asked, "Did Dr. Samuel A. Mudd direct you to go to the authorities, and inform them that these parties had been there?"

Mr. EWING. I claim more than that; I claim the whole statement.

The Commission sustained the objection of the Judge Advocate.

By MR. EWING.

Q. State whether you communicated to the military authorities in Bryantown the fact of any suspicious persons having been at the house of Dr. Samuel A. Mudd on Saturday.

A. I did to Lieutenant Dana, who was the principal in command of the military there at that time.

Q. When did you communicate it to him?

A. I think it was on Monday morning.

Q. What statement did you make to him?

A. I stated to him that Dr. Samuel A. Mudd had informed me that two suspicious parties came to his house a little before daybreak on Saturday morning; and that one of them had, as he said, a broken leg, which Dr. Samuel Mudd bandaged; that they were laboring under some degree of excitement—more so, he thought, than should arise from a broken leg; that these parties stated that they came from Bryantown, and were inquiring the way to the Rev. Dr. Wilmer's; that while there one of them called for a razor and shaved himself, thereby altering his appearance; that he improvised a crutch or crutches for the broken-legged man, and that they went in the direction of Parson Wilmer's.

I also told the officer that Dr. Samuel Mudd went from his house with the younger of the two men to try and procure a carriage to take them away from his house; that he went down the road toward Bryantown and failed to get one, and that they left his house on horseback. I told him that one bone of the man's leg was broken, said by him to have been by a fall from his horse. All this information I received from Dr. Samuel A. Mudd.

When I was leaving Dr. Samuel Mudd, I told him I would mention the matter to the military authorities at Bryantown, to see what could be made of it. He told me he would be glad if I would; but that, if I could make the arrangements, he would much prefer that he be sent for, and that he would give every information in his power relative to it; that, if it became a matter of publicity, he feared for his life, on account of guerrillas that might be infesting the neighborhood.

Q. By whose authority did you make the communication to him?

A. The mentioning of that matter to me, or any other matter bearing on an assassination, particularly such an assassination as the country and the world now mourn, was my warrant and authority from him, or anybody else who knew me.

Q. Did you make any other communica-

tion to any other military authorities of the facts stated to you by Dr. Samuel A. Mudd?

A. Yes, sir. After that, I was sent for to my house, I think, on Tuesday afternoon. There were four detectives, who asked me to go up in a room with them. They these questioned me very particularly relative to this affair. I stated to them what I have already stated here; and upon my inability to answer all their questions, they ordered their carriage and asked me to direct them the way to Dr. Samuel Mudd's house. I accordingly went with them to Dr. Samuel Mudd's house. Dr. Samuel Mudd was not in the house. I was outside of the door, and saw him coming, and told him, as he entered the house, that the detectives had come there for the purpose of ascertaining the particulars relative to that matter which he had spoken to me about, and that I had made the statement to the military authorities which he had made to me on Sunday, and that they were up there for the purpose of making special inquiry in reference to it. I had already stated to the detectives that I felt confident the Doctor would state the matter just as I had stated it to them, and would not and did not stay in there during their examination.

Q. Can you name the officers that went with you?

A. Lieutenant Lovett, John Lloyd, Gavacan, an Irishman, and Williams was the fourth.

After their conversation with Dr. Samuel Mudd, I think just before they got into their conveyance, they asked me if I could direct them the way to Parson Wilmer's. It was then nearly night. I told them I certainly would, and turning to Dr. Samuel Mudd, who was standing outside the door, I asked him what was the best road to Parson Wilmer's, which he told me, and also stated that there was a bad bridge on that way, which I remember very well.

Before we got to the main road leading to Bryantown, these officers concluded, in consequence, it seems, of my stating to them that it was very little out of the way, to go back by Bryantown to Parson Wilmer's—to go that way, being a much better road, as I thought. Nothing, to my knowledge, was said by either of those officers about Dr. Samuel Mudd having denied that the two men had been at his house.

Q. Did you have any conversation with Dr. Samuel Mudd at the church, or hear his conversation, as to what he knew of the assassination?

A. No, sir; I heard—

Assistant Judge Advocate BINGHAM. You need not state any thing you heard him say there.

Mr. EWING. I think it admissible, as explanatory of the conduct of the accused during the very time of the occurrence of the offenses charged—because, as I said before, one of the offenses charged is concealment, which relates beyond that Sunday—as showing his frame of mind, his information, his conduct.

Assistant Judge Advocate BINGHAM. If the Court please, that is not the point here. Supposing the declaration to be that he did not know any thing about them; the gentleman claims here to prove, on his own motion, the declarations of Dr. Mudd on Sunday at Church. If we had introduced any declarations of Dr. Mudd at that time and place, I admit the well-known rule of law is that whatever he' said, and all that he said at that time, is admissible on his motion; what we did not give, he would have a right to give; but I deny that there is any authority for introducing testimony of this sort as to his declarations at that time about this transaction. That is the question now. The gentleman read a while ago from a text that everybody is familiar with, which has relation to the declarations of third persons not parties to the record. There is not one single line in that text which he read which sustains any position he assumes here in regard to this matter. I desire to read the rule that does apply in regard to the prisoner on trial and his declarations—Wharton's American Criminal Law, vol. 1., p. 358, sec. 699: "Declarations made by a prisoner in his own favor, unless part of the *res gestæ*, are not admissible for the defense. Thus, on an indictment for larceny, the defendant can not give in evidence his declarations, at the time of the arrest, of his claims of ownership in the property taken; and on an indictment against a prisoner for having in his possession coining tools, with intent to use them, he can not give in evidence his declaration to an artificer, at the time he employed him to make such instruments, as to the purpose for which he wished them made. One indicted for murder can not give in evidence his own conversations had after going half a mile from the place of murder; and so, too, when a prisoner, in conversation with a witness, admitted the existence of a particular fact, which tended strongly to establish his guilt, but coupled it with an explanation which, if true, would exculpate him, it was held that the accused could not show that he had made the same statement and explanation to others."

So it goes on all the way through. That is the law in regard to the matter. The man's declarations at the time he committed that murder, being a part of the transaction, were admissible; but after he had gone half a mile they were inadmissible. Here is a party charged with harboring, concealing, and comforting a man, knowing him to be the murderer of the President of the United States. What he said in connection with the fact of his harboring and concealing him at the time to these parties, he has a right to prove, because we have brought out that evidence ourselves. If he said any thing

in addition to what we have proved, he has a right to bring it out. Everybody knows that. But we have introduced no evidence whatever of what he said on Sunday at church. If we had introduced any evidence of that sort, I admit that, on the principles I have before stated, the accused would have a right to give in evidence all that he said at that time and place; but we have not offered any such evidence. If he is allowed to introduce his declarations on Sunday in regard to that transaction, and all that he said then—because the question implies that the witness is to tell all he did say—then he is to be allowed to introduce every declaration he may have .made from that Sunday to this day, to everybody, and at every place; and, as I have before stated to the Court, on that subject, the law has hedged itself about so that criminals shall not make evidence, at their pleasure, in their own behalf, and adduce it in court to exculpate themselves from crime. If there were such a rule as that, there would be an end to the administration of justice, provided the courts should give credence to such testimony.

Mr. EWING. I wish to call the attention of the Court specially to the fact that the declaration as to which I am now inquiring was made during the time of the alleged commission of the offense of concealment. The offense of concealment, as charged, and as attempted to be sustained by the proof on the part of the Government, was a concealment after the fact of the persons having been there, and of the route which they took; in other words, a concealment after their departure as well as during their stay. According to the theory of the prosecution, he was committing that offense during all the time, from Saturday till the following Tuesday; and I say his declarations at the time of the alleged commission of the offense are admissible. The declaration now inquired about was on Sunday, showing his knowledge and frame of mind with reference to the assassination, and therefore I think it admissible. I assure the Court that I do not wish to take up its time by pressing upon it irrelevant or inadmissible testimony; and if I seem pertinacious, it is only because I think we have a right to show what is here offered. I ask the decision of the Court on the objection.

The Commission sustained the objection of the Judge Advocate.

WITNESS. I am acquainted with Daniel J. Thomas. His reputation for veracity has been bad ever since I have known him, and I have known him since he was a boy. From my knowledge of his character for veracity, I would not, if he had a motive to misstate facts, believe him under oath. I consider him an insane man.

I have seen him manifest a sufficiently abnormal condition of mind as would confer in

14

the courts irresponsibility for a criminal act. He is not always so insane as this, however. There seem to have been exacerbations and remissions in his manifestations of insanity. Sometimes I have met him when he was not in a more disordered condition of mind than would indicate eccentricity.

By the COURT.

Q. What is the form of insanity under which Mr. Thomas labors?

A. There is no specific form that I know of, except at times a peculiar excitement and inability to appreciate matters and things as other people do. It is not *dementia*; it is not a monomania; it is not what is called aberration of mind. There are certain forms of insanity which exacerbate and remit, and are known by no specific name as any particular form of insanity.

Q. Do you think the form of insanity under which he is laboring would lead him to imagine that he heard a conversation, for instance, that he never did hear?

A. I have seen him in a mood of mind when I would not doubt but that he would be so insane.

Q. Would he fancy that he heard something said that was not said?

A. Yes, sir; I have known him to labor under the most decided delusions and hallucinations.

Q. Have you known him to narrate things which might have occurred, and which he might have heard, that to your knowledge were purely imaginary, and that he never did hear?

A. Yes, sir, oftentimes.

Q. How long have you entertained the opinion that Mr. Thomas was not of sound mind?

A. I went to a family school in our neighborhood with Mr. Thomas when he was a small boy. I was his senior, perhaps, four or five years. There was something very eccentric and amusing about him at that time, different from other boys, and he was a source of amusement in the way of eccentricity to his schoolmates. Seven or eight years ago, or perhaps longer than that, his insane condition of mind seemed to manifest itself in the estimation of almost everybody in our neighborhood. The common expression was that Dan Thomas was crazy. I have entertained that opinion for seven or eight years, and expressed it over and over again before the war. I have not known of his being objected to as a witness before a court of justice, on the ground that he was not of sound mind, and I have known him to testify under oath on one occasion.

With respect to the reputation of Samuel Mudd for loyalty, from my association with him, I have to consider him as sympathizing with the South. I never knew, however, of any disloyal or treasonable act of his, nor did I ever know of his harboring rebels or per-

sons who were in sympathy with the South. I have generally considered him as very temperate in his discussions and expressions relative to the war. He has contended for the right or legality of secession, but has generally spoken temperately, never using abusive or opprobrious epithets toward the heads of the Government. In saying that he was very temperate in this regard, I must add, if I may be allowed, that he was very much more so than many of the citizens of benighted Charles County, in Southern Maryland.

Q. Were there not certain local military organizations in that neighborhood in the early part of the war? What was their object?

A. There was an organization at Port Tobacco, the object of which, I think, was treasonable. I think it probable, but I am not satisfied of that; that was my impression at the time, though it was said it was for the purpose of quelling insurrections, etc., in the neighborhood. It may have been so. I have regarded Dr. Samuel Mudd, for several months prior to the fall of Richmond and the surrender of the rebel army of Lee, as taking a very handsome prospective view of the downfall of the rebellion. I remember administering an oath to him last year, and was forcibly impressed with the respect and reverence with which he took the oath, making a decided contrast from many others to whom I administered the oath on that occasion; and, so far as I know, he has abided the provisions of that oath.

By MR. EWING.

I administered the oath to Dr. Samuel Mudd, if I remember rightly, when the sense of the people was taken relative to the calling of a convention to frame a new constitution for the State of Maryland, in June or July of last year—I do not remember—or it may have been earlier. I was improvised by two of the judges as the chief judge of the election that day, in the absence of the judge. I think I administered the oath to some two hundred that day. From and after that time, if not before, he has spoken of the downfall of the rebellion as being assured.

Recalled for the Defense.—June 9.

The JUDGE ADVOCATE. This witness is recalled by the defense to prove what was rejected the other day by the Court on objection—the declarations made by the prisoner, Dr. Mudd, on Sunday at church, in regard to the two suspicious men having been at his house. Although I think that the admission of such statement to be irregular, yet wishing that the Court shall have the benefit of every thing which can possibly aid it in arriving at a correct conclusion, I am willing that the statements of the prisoner, made the day after these men had left his house, shall be heard, and taken for what they are worth.

WITNESS. I had very little conversation with Dr. Mudd at church. He remarked that he regarded the assassination of the President, to use his own expression, as a most damnable act. He overtook me on the road after church, and stated to me that two suspicious persons had been at his house; that they came there on Saturday morning a little while before daybreak; that one of them had a broken leg, or a broken bone in the leg, which he bandaged; that they got while there something to eat; that they seemed laboring under some degree, or probably quite a degree, of excitement—more excitement than probably should necessarily result from the injury received; that they said they came from Bryantown, and were inquiring the way to Parson Wilmer's; that while there one of them called for a razor, and shaved himself; I do not remember whether he said shaved his whiskers or moustache, but altered somewhat, or probably materially altered, his features; he did not say which it was that had shaved himself; that he himself, in company with the younger one, or the smaller one of the two, went down the road toward Bryantown, in search of a vehicle to take them away from his house; that he arranged or had fixed for them a crutch or crutches (I do not remember which) for the broken-legged man; and that they went away from his house, on horseback, in the direction of Parson Wilmer's. I do not think he stated what time they went.

When I was about leaving him, he turning into his house, I told him that I would state it to the military authorities, and see if any thing could be made of it. He told me that he would be glad if I would, or that he particularly wished me to do it; but he would much prefer if I could make the arrangement for him to be sent for, and he would give every information in his power relative to the matter; that, if suspicions were warrantable, he feared for his life on account of guerrillas that were, or might be, in the neighborhood.

This was about half-past 11 o'clock in the forenoon, and when I parted with him, I was within fifty yards of his house.

As I left Dr. Samuel Mudd, I went toward Bryantown. I dined at his father's house that day, and on my way toward Bryantown I stopped to see a patient, and it was nightfall before I got to the village of Bryantown. What Dr. Samuel Mudd had told me I communicated to the military authorities at Bryantown next morning.

BENJAMIN GARDINER.

For the Defense.—June 5.

By MR. EWING.

I saw Dr. Samuel Mudd at church on the Sunday after the assassination. I saw him in conversation with his neighbors before the service commenced, which usually begins about 10 o'clock.

Q. Will you state whether or not Dr. Samuel Mudd there mentioned any thing about two suspicious persons having been at his house on Saturday morning?

Assistant Judge Advocate BINGHAM. I object to Dr. Mudd giving his declarations, what he said on Sunday morning at church.

Mr. EWING. It is like the evidence of his informing Dr. George Mudd of the presence of those suspicious persons at his house, which the Court refused to allow to be given in evidence; and which, for the reasons that I then very fully stated, I then thought, and still think, a most important item of testimony, and one most clearly admissible.

Assistant Judge Advocate BINGHAM. I have heretofore stated to the Court the ground of the objection. It is this: that it is the declaration of the prisoner himself, at a time and place about which the prosecution has given no evidence at all; to-wit, his declarations on Sunday at church.

Mr. EWING. But it is during the alleged commission of the crime of concealment, and it is evidence of his having broken that silence, for which they propose to convict him of complicity in the crime.

Assistant Judge Advocate BINGHAM. There is no allegation of time in the charge or specification that is important. The matter of time becomes important by the evidence, and the evidence of the prosecution has not gone to any thing he said or did on Sunday.

Mr. EWING. But the evidence of the prosecution has gone, with one witness, to the fact of his having, as late as Tuesday, concealed the fact of the presence of two suspicious persons at his house.

Assistant Judge Advocate BINGHAM. The evidence has gone to Tuesday as to what he said.

Assistant Judge Advocate BURNETT. As to his misstating the facts—

Mr. EWING. As to his concealing the fact and denying it.

Assistant Judge Advocate BINGHAM. As to what he said; and all he said on Tuesday at that time and place of course is admissible; but that is not Sunday.

The Commission sustained the objection.

Recalled for the Defense.—June 9.

The JUDGE ADVOCATE. This witness is here to prove the declarations made at church by the prisoner, Dr. Mudd, on the Sunday after the assassination. The statement is allowed for the reason stated with respect to the testimony of the previous witness.

By MR. EWING.

I had heard on Saturday evening of the assassination, but it was in such a way that I did not believe it. As I got to church on Sunday morning, I saw the people collected together in the church-yard talking in apparently earnest conversation. It turned out to be about the assassination of the President. As I advanced toward the church, I happened to go where Dr. Samuel Mudd was. I walked up to where he was, and spoke to him, and he spoke to me. I asked him if it was a fact that the President had been assassinated. He then turned around to me from the crowd and said, "Yes, such seems to be the fact;" and he added, "Sir, we ought to immediately raise a home guard, and to hunt up all suspicious persons passing through our section of country and arrest them, and deliver them up to the proper authorities; for there were two suspicious persons at my house yesterday morning" I paid no particular attention to what he said about suspicious persons, because since the war commenced we have always had in our neighborhood deserted soldiers constantly, and detectives and soldiers of the United States, and we could hardly tell who they were.

'Whether Dr. Mudd said any thing further about the assassination or not, I can not tell. Everybody was talking about it until church commenced, and I can not tell whether he said any thing more, or if what I heard was said by others.

DANIEL E. MONROE.

For the Defense.—June 10.

On Sunday, the 16th of April, I heard at Bryantown, from Mr. William Henry Moore, that the man who had assassinated the President was Edwin Booth. Mr. Moore had come from Bryantown that morning. It was about 10 o'clock in the morning that I heard this. Mr. Philip A. Lasser and Mr. Warren were present when Mr. Moore told me. I think he said he heard it from the soldiers. It was some time afterward that I heard the assassins had been traced near Bryantown.

I know Daniel J. Thomas by reputation. The neighbors generally think he is very untruthful. This is not the opinion of one party, but of the community generally. From that reputation I could not believe him under oath.

I approved of the efforts of the Federal Government in its suppression of the rebellion under the Constitution as it formerly stood. I did not approve of the manner in which slavery was abolished. In the last Presidential election I used my influence in favor of Lincoln and Johnson.

JOHN F. DAVIS.

Recalled for the Defense.—June 6.

I was at Dr. Samuel Mudd's house on the Tuesday following the assassination of the President. I went into the field and informed him that Lieutenant Lovett and a party of soldiers were at his house, and had come to see him. When I came up to the house I met Dr. George Mudd. Dr. Samuel Mudd met Dr. George Mudd just at the end of his kitchen.

Q. State what Dr. George Mudd told Dr. Samuel Mudd.

Assistant Judge Advocate BINGHAM. I object to the question.

Mr. EWING. May it please the Court, one of those four officers who testified, contradicting the others, it is true, stated that Dr. Samuel Mudd, on that visit, denied that there had been any persons at his house on Saturday morning. We have proved, in a roundabout sort of a way, owing to the objections that were made, (but still it is proved,) that Dr. Samuel Mudd informed Dr. George Mudd, on Sunday, that there were two suspicious persons at his house on Saturday morning, and requested him to communicate the fact to the military authorities, and have him sent for, if necessary, to give further information on the subject. One, or perhaps more, of those persons who went with Lieutenant Lovett spoke of the fact of Dr. George Mudd having a short conversation with Dr. Samuel Mudd outside the door, before Dr. Samuel Mudd saw the officer and the detectives. I wish to prove by this witness that Dr. George Mudd's whole conversation with Dr. Samuel Mudd was, that, in pursuance of the information which Dr. Samuel Mudd had given him on Sunday, and of his request, he had communicated the facts that Dr. Samuel Mudd stated to him to this officer and the detectives, and that they had come for the purpose of questioning him upon the subject. The purpose of this evidence is twofold: first, to show that Dr. Samuel Mudd knew that these parties had been acquainted by Dr. George Mudd with the circumstance of those two suspicious persons having been at Dr. Samuel Mudd's house on Saturday morning, for the purpose of showing that he could not, after that, as a rational man, have gone into the room and denied that there were two persons in his house on Saturday morning; second, to show that the conversation was not one that was in any manner objectionable, but, on the contrary, in strict pursuance of the request of Dr. Samuel Mudd, and that that was all there was of it. It is true, it is a conversation of Dr. George Mudd with the accused. I do not wish to prove any thing the accused said; I wish to prove merely what Dr. George Mudd stated to him, to show the information he had as to the purpose of this visit, and as to the knowledge of the visitors with reference to those persons, before he entered the room to have his conversation with them.

Assistant Judge Advocate BINGHAM. The witness is asked to state what a third person told the prisoner at the bar, and that I object to as utterly incompetent.

The Commission sustained the objection.

WITNESS. Dr. Samuel Mudd did not betray the least unwillingness to go to the house to see the officer, or manifest any alarm.

JOHN F. HARDY.
For the Defense.—May 29.
By MR. EWING.

I live in Charles County, about two miles and a half from Bryantown. I was with Dr. Samuel Mudd on Friday, a week after the assassination of the President; we dined together at his father's. While there a messenger came for Dr. Samuel Mudd to go to his house. I went with him, and met there Lieutenant Lovett in Dr. Mudd's yard. Dr. Mudd introduced Lieutenant Lovett to me. When we got into the house, Dr. Mudd told the Lieutenant that there was a boot there, and asked him if he wanted it. Lieutenant Lovett said he did. No inquiry had been addressed to him about the boot, or any thing said in my hearing about it before that. Dr. Mudd's wife said that she had found the boot under the bed, in dusting up the room a day or two after the men left.

By ASSISTANT JUDGE ADVOCATE BURNETT.

There was no word said about searching the house before Dr. Mudd spoke of the boot. When we got to the house, I counted twenty-eight horses belonging to the soldiers. I do not know what had occurred in the house before we got there. I think it was Mr. Davis who sent for Dr. Mudd while at his father's.

By MR. EWING.

Dr. Mudd himself gave the boot to the officer. I do not think Dr. Mudd had any conversation with anybody before the fact of the boot being there was mentioned to the officer.

JANE HEROLD
Recalled for the Defense.—June 9.
By MR. EWING.

I live on Eighth Street, east, in this city, not a hundred yards from the Navy Yard gate, and about a quarter of a mile from the Navy Yard bridge. I have lived there eighteen years. It is not on the direct route from the city to the bridge, but it is on one that is very much used. I am not acquainted with the prisoner, Dr. Samuel A. Mudd; I never heard him spoken of in our house, nor by my brother.

MRS. MARY E. NELSON.
For the Defense.—June 9.
By MR. EWING.

David E. Herold, one of the accused, is my brother. I never heard him speak of Dr. Samuel A. Mudd, and never heard the name mentioned in the family until his arrest.

REV. CHARLES H. STONESTREET.
Recalled for the Defense.—June 10.
By MR. EWING.

In the year 1850, I was the President of Frederick College, in Frederick City, Maryland, and the accused, Samuel A. Mudd, was a pupil there. I have recently seen the book, kept by myself, in which his name is entered. At the close of 1850, in December, I think, I was transferred to Georgetown College, and I am under the impression that he was there when I left.

At Frederick College we had one principal vacation, commencing in July and continuing during August; other vacations were only for a few days, during which those pupils that resided at a distance of a hundred miles or so from College did not go home.

Cross-examined by ASSISTANT JUDGE ADVOCATE BINGHAM.

There were no holidays in the fall, and only a few days recess at Christmas. I can not say certainly that Dr. Mudd was there in December. It was the rule not to go away during the temporary vacation, and pupils could not go without the authority of the President.

L. A. GOBRIGHT.
For the Defense.—June 10.
By MR. EWING.

I am telegraphic correspondent of the Associated Press. I was at Ford's Theater on the night of the 14th of April, after the assassination of the President, and heard some persons say positively that it was J. Wilkes Booth who was the assassin, while others said they knew J. Wilkes Booth, and that the man who jumped upon the stage and made his exit differed somewhat in appearance from Booth. So far as I could ascertain, there did not seem to be any certainty at that time, and I was not thoroughly satisfied in my own mind that night as to who was the assassin.

Cross-examined by ASSISTANT JUDGE ADVOCATE BINGHAM.

I was not perfectly satisfied that night that it was J. Wilkes Booth who had killed the President. It was telegraphed over the country that he was the assassin, but not by me; I could tell by whom, if necessary. After I saw the official bulletin the next morning, I came to the conclusion that J. Wilkes Booth was the man.

JAMES JUDSON JARBOE.
For the Defense.—June 7.

I live in Prince George's County. I am usually called Judson Jarboe. I and my brother, William Jarboe, are the only adults of that name in Prince George's County. I do not know and never saw Dr. Samuel Mudd before his arrest. I saw Mrs. Surratt some time in April, since her arrest; I had not seen her before that for two or three years. I have never been at her house on H Street, nor have I ever met her daughter at any house in Washington.

I have known Mr. Evans for several years; he used to live in my neighborhood, and attend a Methodist Church there; I used to see him passing. I have not seen him for a year or two, certainly, till two or three weeks before my arrest. I was standing at the corner of Ninth and G Streets, when Mr. Evans passed by me, walking. I had not seen him before, I think, for a year or two.

Cross-examined by ASSISTANT JUDGE ADVOCATE BINGHAM.

I know John H. Surratt, but have not met him very often. I met him on Seventh Street, in this city, I believe, some time in March last. It was at the restaurant nearly opposite Odd Fellows Hall. There were several gentlemen with Surratt. I just spoke to him, passed the time of day, and passed on. I do not know the persons who were with him. I do not know John Wilkes Booth. I have seen David E. Herold; I recognize him among the prisoners. He was not with Surratt when I saw him at the restaurant. I have not, to my knowledge, met Surratt since. Before that I passed Surratt on the road some time last fall; he was riding alone.

I was arrested on the 15th of April. I do not know that I have been charged with any disloyal conduct down in Maryland, nor do I know for what I was arrested. On the night I was arrested, I was asked some questions by Major Wooster, at Fort Baker, I think. He asked me about a man by the name of Boyle, and if I had not harbored him. I told him I had not. Boyle, he said, was charged with assassination and horse-stealing. I think he said Boyle had killed a Captain Watkins.

I knew Boyle when he was a boy, but I have not seen him for four years. I know he was not harbored on my premises.

Q. How have you stood yourself in relation to this rebellion since it broke out?

A. I do not exactly understand you.

Q. Have you made any declarations against the Government of your country since this rebellion broke out?

A. No, sir.

Q. Have you joined in any glorification down in Prince George's County, Maryland, over rebel victories?

A. No, sir.

Q. Have you wished for the success of the rebellion?

A. O, no, sir; I could not expect that.

Q. Did you want it, whether you expected it or not? Did you want this rebellion—this Southern Confederacy, if you please—to triumph?

Mr. EWING. I will state to the witness that he has the privilege of declining to answer. I do not care about interfering further than that. What I called him to, was one single question of fact.

Assistant Judge Advocate BINGHAM. I have already stated to the witness that if he thinks his answer to any question will criminate him, he can say so, and decline to answer.

The JUDGE ADVOCATE. I do not think a mere wish is such criminality as should be protected from exposure.

Mr. EWING. I think this a species of inquisition, which counsel ought not to indulge in.

The JUDGE ADVOCATE. Loyalty is a question of feeling and conviction, as well as action.

Assistant Judge Advocate BINGHAM. If the witness thinks it will criminate him to make a full and complete answer, he can say so. If he does not think it will criminate him, he must answer the question.

WITNESS. I hardly know what would criminate me here.

Q. I should like to know whether it is your opinion that the Southern Confederation was criminal or not?

A. I do not know much about it.

Q. Have you not expressed yourself that it was all right?

A. What was all right?

Q. The Southern Confederacy and the rebellion?

A. I do not think that I did.

Q. Did you not think that?

A. I think a good many things.

Q. State whether you made an assault upon a man at the election about four years ago, and what you did to him.

A. Are you going to try me for that?

Q. No; but I ask you the question?

A. I have been tried for that same offense twice.

Q. State whether you made an attack, about four years ago, at the time of the election, on a Union man down there, and killed him.

A. There was a pretty smart attack made upon me.

Q. What became of the man?

A. It would be very hard for me to tell now.

Q. Was he killed or not at the time?

A. I understood that he was.

Q. Do you not know who did it?

A. No, I do not know exactly who did it.

Q. Do you know whether you had a hand in killing him?

A. I do not know. I have answered all the questions so often that—

Q. You can answer that question or let it alone. If you say you can not answer it without criminating yourself, you need not.

A. I have answered that several times.

Q. You have not answered me yet.

A. I have answered these questions before other courts; I have been asked these questions over and over.

Q. Did you kill him, or did somebody else kill him?

A. I can not tell you whether some one else did it.

Q. Did you have a hand in it?

No answer.

Q. Where was it that this man was killed?

A. I understood that he was killed at the election.

Q. Do you not know the man was killed? Were you not there?

No answer.

Q. What was the man's name that was killed?

No answer.

Assistant Judge Advocate BINGHAM. I shall not insist on an answer. If you do not wish to answer, you need not answer. It is your privilege to decline or do so.

By Mr. EWING.

Q. Have you any statement you wish to make in regard to the difficulty about which the Judge Advocate has been questioning you? If you have any thing to say to the Court, say it.

A. Well, I do not know. If the Judge wants to know all the particulars about it—

Assistant Judge Advocate BINGHAM. I do not insist on knowing any more. You have declined to answer, as is your right.

WITNESS. I have answered these questions before, and have been tried for that thing by our courts.

Mr. EWING. What was the result?

Assistant Judge Advocate BINGHAM. You need not state.

WITNESS. I was acquitted.

Assistant Judge Advocate BINGHAM. I object to all that.

Mr. EWING. You have been going into the question whether he was tried or not, and I ask him the question in what court he was tried.

Assistant Judge Advocate BINGHAM. The gentleman has made an issue with me. I deny his assertion.

Mr. EWING. The witness can state in what court he was tried.

Assistant Judge Advocate BINGHAM. He can not state where. I did not ask him in what court he was tried. He chose not to answer my questions, and that was all.

Mr. EWING. If the Court please, I think the character of the cross-examination of this witness has been most extraordinary, catching the witness, badgering him with questions, and snapping him up when he started to answer, and undertaking to present to the Court the impression from his answers that he was a felon, and then not allowing the witness to state that he was tried for the offense alleged against him, in a high court of the country, and was acquitted. That is not fair. And, more than that, the gentleman is certainly wrong. He drew out of the witness, on cross-examination, the fact that he was tried. Now, I want to know where he was tried. I want to know whether there was a solemn inquiry into it; and whether he was tried in a high court.

Assistant Judge Advocate BINGHAM. Whether I badgered the witness or the witness badgered me and justice both, is a question that will appear by the record. The point I make is, that I never asked this witness a question whether he was tried.

Mr. EWING. You drew it out.

Assistant Judge Advocate BINGHAM. I did not draw it out of him. What I tried to draw out of him was legitimate; but as the gentleman chooses to arraign me here—

Mr. EWING. I take that back.

Assistant Judge Advocate BINGHAM. I am glad of it. Holding myself as the humblest man here, I beg leave to say, in vindication of my conduct, that there is not a law book on evidence fit to be brought into a court of justice, which does not say that I had the right to ask him whether he had been guilty of murder; and I am not going to let this witness go away from this court with the impression that I have invaded any right of his. I had a right to ask him whether he was guilty of murder, and he had a right, as I told him, to refuse to answer it if he saw fit. Now, what I say to the Court is, that he never answered my questions.

Mr. EWING. You did not ask him whether he was guilty of murder.

Assistant Judge Advocate BINGHAM. I asked him whether he killed a man, and whether he had any thing to do with it.

Mr. EWING. That is not necessarily murder.

Assistant Judge Advocate BINGHAM. If I may ask whether he was guilty of murder, I may ask him whether he killed a man.

Mr. EWING. You did not ask him whether he had committed murder.

Assistant Judge Advocate BINGHAM. The greater includes the less.

Mr. EWING. But you asked the less.

Assistant Judge Advocate BINGHAM. What I say is that the law authorized me to ask squarely whether he was guilty of murder, and he is not to go out of court with the impression that I have invaded any rights of his. I never asked him about any trials. He did not answer my questions. He had a right not to answer them, but I never asked him about trials at all. He never stated whether he had killed the man; he did not even state whether he had a hand in killing the man, and ne would not tell me whether the man was killed at all or not. Now, in that stage of the case, upon that record, the gentleman proposes to prove by parol evidence what appears on record. The man has not admitted yet that anybody was killed; and if nobody was killed, how could he be tried? Then, in the next place, if he was tried, how are you going to prove it by parol? We have not the benefit of any testimony on the subject. The truth is, I do the witness the justice to say that he has not answered my question at all. He has not stated that the man was killed; he has stated that he understood he was killed. He would not state that he himself had a hand in it, and he would not state that he knows the man's name. That is the way it stands, and I object to any thing further about it.

Mr. EWING. He has stated that he was tried, and I now ask him in what court?

Assistant Judge Advocate BINGHAM. I did not ask him if he was tried.

Mr. EWING. He stated that he was tried, and now I ask simply, in what court? I do not ask the result of the investigation.

Assistant Judge Advocate BINGHAM. If there was nobody killed, there was nobody hurt, I reckon.

Q. In what court were you tried?
A. In Prince George's County Court.
Q. Were you, during last spring, winter, or fall, in any house on H Street, in the city of Washington?
A. I do not recollect. I do not think I was in any house on H Street, though.
Q. Have you any acquaintances living on H Street?
A. No, sir, none at all, that I know of.
Q. Have you any acquaintances living on H Street, between Sixth and Seventh?
A. I do not think I have.
Q. Do you know in what part of the city Mrs. Surratt lives?
A. I do not. I never saw her house in my life. I do not know any thing about Mrs. Surratt's residence.

By ASSISTANT JUDGE ADVOCATE BINGHAM.

Q. You say you were tried in a court. What were you tried for?
No answer.
Q. Do you know what you were tried for?
A. I suppose I was tried for what you stated awhile ago.
Assistant Judge Advocate BINGHAM. No, sir; I did not state it at all.
WITNESS. You said I killed a man.
Assistant Judge Advocate BINGHAM. No, I did not.
WITNESS. You asked me if I did not.
Assistant Judge Advocate BINGHAM. I asked you if you did, and you did not answer the question. Now I ask you for what you were tried?
A. I was tried in that case.

Q. What were you tried for? Were you tried for murder?
A. Well, if I understand the case aright, I do not think—
Q. Were you charged in that case with the murder of a Union man?
A. I do not know whether he was a Union man or not.
Q. Was he called a Union man?
A. That I do not know.
Q. But you were tried for murder?
No answer.
Q. In what county?
A. Prince George's.
Q. When?
A. I do not recollect exactly when it was.
Q. Since this rebellion broke out?
A. Yes, I think it was somewhere about the first of the war.

HENRY BURDEN.
For the Defense.—June 8.

By MR. DOSTER.

I know Marcus P. Norton, who testified here to-day. His general reputation for veracity in Troy, New York, is very bad, and I would not believe him under oath.

Cross-examined by the JUDGE ADVOCATE.

I live in Troy, and hold some valuable patents for the manufacture of horseshoes, etc. I have had legal controversies about these patents, and Mr. Norton was engaged as counsel by one of the parties opposed to me in those suits. I have not formed my opinion of him from his conduct in conducting those suits; I did not know him prior to his engaging in those controversies. When I say that Mr. Norton is not to be believed under oath, I think I am expressing what the people of Troy generally think. I derived my knowledge of his character from testimony taken to impeach him in a case tried in Troy.

By ASSISTANT JUDGE ADVOCATE BINGHAM.

A large array of witnesses were called, most of whom I knew, to impeach Mr. Norton. I did not hear the witnesses testify, but I have seen them.

By MR. DOSTER.

It is the general opinion of the people of Troy that Mr. Norton is not to be believed.

D. W. MIDDLETON.
For the Defense.—June 6.

I am clerk of the Supreme Court of the United States. Mr. Marcus P. Norton argued a motion in the Supreme Court in the case of *Willis Hamiston* v. *John Stainthrop, et al*, on the 3d of March, 1864.

[The entry from the court records was read by the witness.]

JUDGE A. B. OLIN.

For the Defense.—June 9.

By MR. DOSTER.

I resided in the city of Troy, New York, about twenty years prior to my coming to this city, two years ago. I knew Marcus P. Norton, a lawyer of that city. Judging by what people say of him in respect to his character for veracity, I should say his reputation was bad, and where his interests, or passions, or prejudices were enlisted, I would not rely upon his testimony under oath.

Cross-examined by the JUDGE ADVOCATE.

The opinion I express has been formed from the speech of those who have been brought into contact with him; generally persons against whom he has been employed as counsel or attorney, or parties litigating in patent suits that he had been connected with.

Q. State whether you have knowledge of the fact that that particular class of suits, probably more than others, excites bitter personal animosity?

A. All the knowledge I have of them mostly arises since the commencement of my duties here as a judge of this District. I had uniformly refused to take employment in that kind of cases, though I had opportunity to do so, and I had very little knowledge of those controversies, except incidentally, until I came here, where appeals are frequently brought from the Commissioner of Patents to the court of which I am a member, and I have seen enough of them to know that they are about as bitter as any controversies in law that I have any knowledge of.

Q. Are not the parties and counsel in these cases extremely censorious in the tone of conversation about each other?

A. I have seen instances of that kind. I know Mr. Burden, of Troy, very well. Mr. Marcus P. Norton has been employed as counsel in opposition to him in patent cases. Mr. Burden is a very wealthy man. He has had several very warmly contested suits. One of them is known all over the country—the suit in reference to the spike machine, his invention for making hook-headed spikes. His controversy with Corning & Co. has been pending now before Chancellor Walworth for ten or twelve years, taking testimony in reference to the damages that he sustained. I believe he has not got through with it. He has had several other very warmly contested suits of the same kind.

Q. Would not the conversation of a man of his fortune and influence, and that of his friends, continued through a series of years, under the influence of excited legal controversies in which this witness was involved against him, afford to your mind some explanation of the reputation which you say exists?

Mr. DOSTER. I object to that question.

The JUDGE ADVOCATE. I wish to get at the grounds of the witness's opinion, and I think this is a legitimate mode of reaching it.

Mr. DOSTER. Judge Olin can scarcely be brought here as an expert as to the character of the testimony of Mr. Burden. It is not material to the issue what Mr. Burden said.

The JUDGE ADVOCATE. It is not an impeachment of Mr. Burden; it is an explanation.

Mr. DOSTER. It is evidently brought here to contradict and invalidate the testimony of Mr. Burden. There can be no other object.

The JUDGE ADVOCATE. I can not take the opinion of Judge Olin without the privilege of looking at the foundation for that opinion, and the question is directed but to that object.

The Commission overruled the objection.

WITNESS. Yes, undoubtedly it would. Mr. Burden is a man of wealth, high social position, and many friends, and he usually speaks his mind freely.

Mr. Norton's reputation, I believe, was very questionable before he had any controversy or connection with Mr. Burden. Mr. Norton is not considered one of the leading lawyers of Troy, and is not classed among lawyers of any considerable attainments, as far as I know. He is, I understand, an ingenious and excellent mechanic, and is probably very efficient in cases of the description in which he is usually employed.

Mr. EWING, by the consent of the Judge Advocate, presented the following agreement entered into between him and the Judge Advocate:

"It is admitted by the prosecution that John F. Watson, John R. Richardson, and Thomas B. Smith, loyal citizens, will testify that they are acquainted with the reputation of Daniel J. Thomas where he lives, and that it is bad; and that, from their knowledge of it, they would not believe him on oath. And, further, that John R. Richardson above named will testify that Daniel J. Thomas (the witness for the prosecution) made the statement on the 1st of June (the National Fast Day,) as sworn to by William J. Watson before the Court this day. And the prosecution agree that this statement be put upon record, and received and weighed by the Court as though said witnesses had actually so testified before it."

TESTIMONY IN REBUTTAL

JOHN F. HARDY.
For the Prosecution.—June 8.

I live about two and a half or three miles from Dr. Mudd, the prisoner at the bar. On Saturday evening, the day after the assassination, just before sundown, I saw Dr. Mudd within a few hundred yards of my house. He said that there was terrible news; that the President and Mr. Seward and his son had been assassinated the evening before. Something was said in that connection about Boyle (the man who is said to have killed Captain Watkins) assassinating Mr. Seward. I remember that Booth's name was mentioned in the same connection, and I asked him if it was the man who had been down there, and was represented as Booth. His reply was that he did not know whether it was that man or some of his brothers; he understood that he had some brothers. That ended the conversation, except that he said it was one of the most terrible calamities that could have befallen the country at this time.

Q. Did you say that it was understood or said that Booth was the assassin of the President?

A. There was some such remark as that made, but I do not exactly remember the remark.

He said nothing to me in that conversation about two strangers having called at his house, and remaining there all day.

When I asked if it was Booth that had been down there, I referred to the stranger that I had seen at church some time before last Christmas, perhaps in November, whose name I was told was Booth. I saw him outside the church; I do not know whether he went into church. I saw him at the same place some time afterward, and asked if it was the same man, and the answer was "Yes." I do not remember whether Dr. Mudd was there on either occasion.

Cross-examined by MR. EWING.

I do not think I asked Dr. Mudd what was the news; he told me there was bad news in the country. He said that he had been to Bryantown and got the news there. I had not heard a word of it before. Dr. Mudd seemed to be in earnest when he spoke of this being a terrible calamity, and I do honestly think he felt the sorrow he expressed. The conversation took place about two hundred yards from my door, and my house is two and a half miles walking distance, or three miles horseback, from Dr. Mudd's. Dr. Mudd came to see me about some rail lumber, about which I had spoken to him some time early in the winter; they were some chestnut-trees, which Dr. Mudd had ordered me to fell and cut up into rails for him.

I can not recall the dates on which I saw Booth in the county. I do not remember any dates at all. I think the two visits were about a month apart, perhaps a little more or less, and the first visit I think must have been some time in November. It strikes me that Booth's visits were before Christmas. I saw him twice on his second visit; on Sunday at church, and on Monday evening I met him riding by himself on the road leading straight to Horsehead.

When Dr. Mudd mentioned the news he had got at Bryantown, he seemed to be somewhat excited, but not more so than the people of the county generally when they first heard it. When I first heard it, I could hardly believe it. I could hardly express my feelings when I heard it; I felt very singular. He seemed to feel sincerely sorry. I do not think he staid ten minutes.

From the position in which we were, I could not notice whether any one rode with him along the main road; there was a bunch of pines on an elevated spot, just above where we were standing, from which the road goes, and then makes a turn, so that I could not see. I heard of no one being with him.

I know where Esquire George Gardiner lives very well; he is the gentleman that is said to have sold a horse to Booth. It is the nearer road from Bryantown to Esquire Gardiner's to go by Dr. Mudd's house, which is a little off the main road, than to go by the main road.

By ASSISTANT JUDGE ADVOCATE BINGHAM.

Dr. Mudd did not tell me how or from whom he had obtained the information that the President had been assassinated the evening before; he simply said he had heard it at Bryantown.

FRANCIS R. FARRELL.
For the Prosecution.—June 8.

I live near Bryantown, and am very well acquainted with Dr. Samuel A. Mudd. He came to my house on Easter Saturday evening last, the day following the assassination of the President, as near as I can judge, between 4 and 5 o'clock. My house is about midway between Dr. Mudd's and Bryantown; he came from the road leading to Bryantown, and turned into the road that leads to my house. I do not know whether he was coming from Bryantown, and did not learn it from his conversation.

Q. While he was at your house, was the assassination of the President a subject of conversation between him and yourself?

A. Yes, sir, he told it there.

Mr. EWING. I object.

The JUDGE ADVOCATE. The gentleman objects to our giving the statements of Dr. Mudd in evidence, I suppose.

Mr. EWING. I object to it on the ground that it is not rebutting evidence.

The JUDGE ADVOCATE. I could offer it on another and distinct ground; that it is, so far as we understand it, a confession on the part of the prisoner—which is at all times competent evidence—and that it has come to our knowledge since the commencement of this trial, and since the close of our testimony on this point. On that ground alone, I think the Court, in the exercise of a sound discretion, would allow it to be introduced; but I think also it is strictly rebutting testimony offered for the defense.

Mr. EWING. I will state to the Court that, if this testimony is admitted, it will be indispensable to the rights of the accused to have one or more witnesses from that neighborhood who have not already been subpenaed.

The Commission overruled the objection.

WITNESS. Mr. Hardy and myself were in the house when Dr. Mudd came there, and Mr. Hardy went out and had some talk with the Doctor; I do not know what. Directly after he went out, he called out to me that the President was assassinated, and also Seward and his son, I think. Then I called out to where Dr. Mudd and Mr. Hardy were, and asked if it was so; I understood the Doctor to say it was.

I asked the question who assassinated the President, and the Doctor replied and said, "A man by the name of Booth." Mr. Hardy then asked him if it was the Booth that was down there last fall. The Doctor said that he did not know whether it was or not; that there were three or four men of the name of Booth, and he did not know whether it was that one or not; he said that if it was that one, he knew him. That was all he said about it, excepting that he said he was very sorry that this thing had occurred—very sorry.

He did not give any particulars of the assassination, and made no allusion to two men having been at his house that morning and during the day. I do n't think he staid over fifteen minutes. I can not say which way he turned when he got on to the main road after he left; neither did I see from which way he came when he turned into the lane leading to my house.

Cross-examined by MR. EWING.

It was Mr. John F. Hardy that was in my house when Dr. Mudd came. Dr. Mudd said that he thought at this time that the killing of the President was the worst thing

that could have happened. That was the only reason he gave why he was sorry, according to my recollection. He said it would make it a great deal worse for the country; I am not certain, but I think he said it would be a great deal worse than while the war was going on. From his appearance, I think he was entirely in earnest in expressing his sorrow for the crime.

I do not know whether any one was with Dr. Mudd on the main road; I can not see any part of it from my house, but there was no one with him in the road leading down to my house, after he left the main road.

Dr. Mudd came to see Mr. Hardy about getting some rail timber, so he said; but he did not get any; Mr. Hardy had let Mr. Sylvester Mudd have the timber. I can not be sure about the time when Dr. Mudd came there; it was cloudy and I could not see the sun; it might have been as late as 5 o'clock; it seemed a short time after he left till it was dark, not more than a couple of hours, any how.

JACOB SHAVOR.

For the Prosecution.—June 12.

Since the summer of 1858, I have known Marcus P. Norton quite intimately. We have both lived in Troy. He has been employed by the firm of Charles Eddy & Co., of which I am a member, for six years, as patent lawyer. He has had, and is still getting, practice in Troy. I know that his reputation, as a man of integrity and truth, is good there; and from my knowledge of his reputation, his conduct, and character, I would fully believe him under oath. In the early part of 1863, an attempt was made to impeach Mr. Norton's credibility as a witness, but it was unsuccessful, and it was so regarded by the public and by myself.

Cross-examined by MR. DOSTER.

Mr. Norton's reputation for veracity among the business men of Troy generally is good. I do know that an unsuccessful attempt to impeach him was made; but I do not know that eighty men in Troy swore that he could not be believed; others in Troy know that, as you yourself know.

We employed Mr. Norton in the Stanley case, and in a number of others; we have more or less every year. In an individual case of my own, I employed another lawyer, and Mr. Norton was a witness. It was an important case, and it was in this case that an attempt was made to impeach Mr. Norton's testimony.

Q. And if this man's testimony had been successfully impeached, you would have lost the case, would you not?

Assistant Judge Advocate BINGHAM objected to the question, and it was waived.

WILLIS HAMISTON.

For the Prosecution.—June 12.

I reside in Troy, and have known Marcus
P. Norton for nine or ten years, intimately
for six. His reputation for truth and integrity, as far as my knowledge extends, is good,
and I would believe him under oath or not.
He was engaged in two patent cases for me,
and is extensively employed in patent cases
in the United States Courts.

Cross-examined by MR. DOSTER.

Mr. Norton is not employed as a witness
in my individual case; he is my lawyer.
There is considerable money involved in it.

HON. HORATIO KING.

For the Prosecution.—June 12.

I reside in Washington City, and have
been an Assistant Postmaster-General and
Postmaster-General. While living here, I
have made the acquaintance of Marcus P.
Norton, of Troy; I have known him quite
intimately for eight or ten years. Before I
left the Department I saw him very frequently, once or twice a year, perhaps oftener; but since I left the department I have
had business with him, and have seen him
oftener, and known more of him, than before. I have always regarded him as scrupulously honest and correct. So far as his
business with me is concerned, I never dealt
with a more truthful man, or one more particular to keep his engagements; and from
my knowledge of him and his character, I
would most unhesitatingly and fully believe
him under oath.

Cross-examined by MR. DOSTER.

I have never lived in Troy, and do not
know Mr. Norton's reputation there. I know
nothing of his reputation for veracity except
as I came in contact with him. My
business with him was in reference to patent
post-rating and canceling stamps. I know
nothing of him beyond that here, but I knew
him quite intimately. I never heard any
one here speak otherwise than favorably of
him. I never heard that his character for
veracity was impeached until the present
time.

By the JUDGE ADVOCATE.

I saw Mr. Norton frequently in March
last; I used to meet him nearly every day
while he was here last winter.

Q. State whether or not, in any of those
conversations, he mentioned to you the singular manner in which some person had
called at his room, asking for Booth.

Mr. DOSTER. I object to that question,
because it is not material to the point in
issue. Besides, it has not been brought out
on the cross-examination.

The JUDGE ADVOCATE. It is entirely competent for me to corroborate the statement
which Mr. Norton made before the assassination of the President, and before there
had arisen any possible motive for the fabrication of this testimony, to show that that
statement was substantially the same, as far
as it went, as that which he has now made
before the Court in regard to the call the
prisoner, Mudd, made at his room, asking
for Booth. I think it is competent to sustain him, assisted as he has been by testimony for the defense.

The Commission overruled the objection.

WITNESS. I recollect perfectly that he
mentioned at the time that some person had
come into the room very abruptly, so much
so as to alarm his sister-in-law, who was in
an adjoining room; I do not remember for
whom he said the person inquired. I think
he told me this some time in March, but I
can not state positively, nor can I state precisely when this entrance was made.

By MR. DOSTER.

Mr. Norton did not, that I remember, mention his having overheard a conversation
between Booth and Atzerodt while he was
there; he first alluded to it in a letter he
wrote to me on the 15th of May.

By ASSISTANT JUDGE ADVOCATE BURNETT.

Q. [Submitting to the witness a letter.] Is
that the letter to which you refer?

A. It is. It was received by me, I presume, on the 17th of May. It bears my indorsement. The letter is dated Troy, New
York, May 15, 1865, addressed to me, and
signed "Marcus P. Norton."

Mr. DOSTER. I object to the reading of
the letter.

Assistant Judge Advocate BURNETT. [To
the witness.] Read the passage of it which
relates to the matter of which you are now
speaking.

WITNESS. It is: "I believe Johnson was
poisoned on the evening of March 3d, or the
morning of March 4th, last. I know of
some things which took place at the National Hotel last winter, between Booth and
strangers to me, which, since the death of
our good President, have thrown me into
alarm and suspicion, and about which I will
talk with you when I see you."

I think that is the first intimation I had
of it; I do not remember Mr. Norton's mentioning that conversation to me before. I
met him nearly every day last winter.

By MR. EWING.

Mr. Norton was here at the inauguration;
I procured tickets for him and his friends
to go into the Capitol, and my impression
is that he did not leave the city until several days afterward. I know that I saw him
after the inauguration, because he spoke of

feeling grateful to me for having procured the tickets for him. I should say it was about the time of the inauguration, though I have no means of fixing the date, that Mr. Norton mentioned to me the fact of a person entering his room. It was the abrupt manner of the person that excited his suspicions, and it alarmed his sister very much. I think he said she was unwilling to remain in the room alone after that.

I do not remember his stating the time, but I think the circumstance occurred just about at the time he told me, because I was in free intercourse with him nearly every day while he was here. I do not remember that he gave me any description of the man, or that he mentioned his inquiring after anybody; I know he told me that he followed the man. He expected the man to go up stairs, but instead of that he went down stairs, and he followed him; he did not say how far, whether down to the office or not. I do not remember whether Mr. Norton spoke of having any conversation with the man, but my impression is that he said the man made some excuse for his abrupt entrance.

WILLIAM WHEELER.

For the Prosecution.—June 9.

By the JUDGE ADVOCATE.

I have known Marcus P. Norton intimately for twelve or fifteen years; I knew him first at school in Vermont, and subsequently at Troy, New York. From my long personal acquaintance with him, I am enabled to state

that his reputation as a man of truth and integrity is good, and from this knowledge of his character I would have no hesitation in believing him under oath.

Cross-examined by MR. DOSTER.

I know by rumor only of one or two cases of attempted impeachment of Mr. Norton, but they were failures. Mr. Norton has a large business at Troy, and is employed by first-class houses.

SILAS H. HODGES.

For the Prosecution.—June 9.

I reside in Washington, and hold the appointment of examiner-in-chief in the Patent Office. I resided for twenty years at Rutland, Vt. I have known Marcus P. Norton for at least eleven years. Some years ago Mr. Norton moved to Troy, and I do not know how he stands there so well as I do at Rutland. Until within the last two or three years I never heard any thing against his reputation, and what I have heard has grown out of litigations in which he has been engaged. Outside of these litigations, I never heard his veracity questioned.

Cross-examined by MR. DOSTER.

I do not know that I can recall any incidents in which I have heard any person speak of Mr. Marcus Norton as a man distinguished for veracity. It is about five years since I left Rutland, and I have known him personally ever since.

TESTIMONY CONCERNING MICHAEL O'LAUGHLIN.

WILLIAM WALLACE.

For the Prosecution.—May 9.

On the 17th of April, I arrested the prisoner, O'Laughlin, at the house of a family named Bailey, on High Street, Baltimore. This was not his boarding-house. I asked him why he was there instead of at his boarding-house; he said that when he arrived in town on Saturday he was told that the officers had been looking for him, and that he went away to a friend of his on Saturday and Sunday night. When he was arrested, he seemed to understand what it was for, and did not ask any questions about it.

Cross-examined by MR. COX.

Q. Did the brother-in-law of the prisoner send for you or go for you to arrest him?

Assistant Judge Advocate BINGHAM objected to the question. The brother-in-law is not the prisoner. The proposition is to show a declaration of the prisoner on his own motion, and at another time and place; it is the declaration of a third person, and I object.

Mr. COX. The object is to show that the prisoner voluntary surrendered himself by sending for the officer. The evidence offered on the part of the prosecution was designed to show that O'Laughlin was avoiding the arrest. In cross-examination, I desire to show that the arrest was made at the instance of the brother-in-law; and I propose to follow that hereafter, by proof that the prisoner himself sent his brother-in-law to communicate his whereabouts to the officer. I think that is legitimate on cross-examination.

Assistant Judge Advocate BINGHAM. It is not cross-examination; it is new matter altogether. We have not offered any evidence of what the prisoner said to his brother-in-law; this witness's testimony was as to what the prisoner said to him.

Mr. COX. It is not the declaration of a fact that I offer, but of an act done by the brother-in-law, on which the officer acted.

The Commission overruled the objection.

WITNESS. I am well acquainted with Mr. Maulsby. He was recommended to me on Sunday evening as a good Union man, one in whom I could put implicit confidence. He knew I was looking for O'Laughlin. I told him I wished him to assist me in getting him. He said he would do all he could to assist me. On Monday morning he came and told me that, if I would go with him, he thought he could find O'Laughlin, and I went with him to the house where we found him.

O'Laughlin, I think, said that when he got to his brother-in-law's house, on Saturday afternoon, he heard that the detectives had been there. He said he knew nothing of the assassination whatever, and could account for his whereabouts during all the time of his stay in Washington by the parties who were with him.

MARSHAL JAMES L. McPHAIL.

For the Prosecution.—May 22.

Michael O'Laughlin, the prisoner, came into our lines about the time of the battles of Antietam and South Mountain. He came in at Martinsburg, I think, about September, 1863. He stated to me that he had taken the oath of allegiance at Martinsburg. I found in the records of my office, this morning, the oath of allegiance of one Michael O'Laughlin, dated Baltimore, June 16, 1863, and signed Michael O'Laughlin, and is, I believe, in the handwriting of the prisoner. I have seen a great deal of his handwriting within the last two or three weeks, and have no doubt the signature is his.

When O'Laughlin was first brought to my office, he stated that he had not reported; he afterward sent for me to correct that error, and to say that he had reported at Martinsburg when he came into our lines, and had there taken the oath of allegiance.

By the COURT.

I only know of O'Laughlin being in the rebel service from his own declarations. Mr. O'Laughlin's family have resided in Baltimore as long as I can remember. I have known them, I suppose, for thirty years.

MRS. MARY VAN TINE.

For the Prosecution.—May 15.

I reside at No. 420 D Street, in this city, and keep rooms to rent. I see two gentlemen here [pointing to the accused, Michael O'Laughlin and Samuel Arnold] who had rooms at my house. I am not positive, but I think it was on the 10th of February last they came. John Wilkes Booth came very often to see the prisoners, O'Laughlin and Arnold, but did not, as a general thing, remain very long. I was told by Arnold, when I inquired, that the gentleman's name was John Wilkes Booth. Sometimes Booth would call when they were out; sometimes he called two or three times before they returned. He generally appeared very anxious for their return. Sometimes, when he found them out, he requested, that if they returned before he called again, that they would come to the stable. Or he sometimes left a note, going into their room to write it. Booth, who frequently came in a carriage, would sometimes inquire for one, sometimes the other, but I think he more frequently inquired for O'Laughlin. The only arms I ever saw in their rooms was a pistol; this I saw only once.

[Photograph of Booth exhibited to the witness.]

I recognize that as a likeness of Booth, but I should not call it a good one. I think him a better looking man than this is. The last time Booth played here, about the 18th or 20th of March last, when he played *Pescara*, I expressed a desire to see him, and Mr. O'Laughlin gave me complimentary tickets.

A man used sometimes to call to see them, and I think he passed one night with them, by his leaving the room very early one morning. I never heard his name. He was not what you would call a gentleman in appearance, but a very respectable-looking mechanic. His skin was hardened like that of a man who had been exposed to the weather, and he had sandy whiskers. I do not see him among the prisoners.

Arnold and O'Laughlin said they were in the oil business, but they did not say that they were connected with Booth in it. Letters occasionally came for them, but not a great many. The letters were sometimes addressed to one, sometimes to the other. Arnold and O'Laughlin left my house, I think, on the Monday following the Saturday on which Booth played at the theater; about the 20th of March.

Cross-examined by MR. COX.

I think these gentlemen had been at my house two or three weeks when they said they were in the oil business. When they left, I understood they were going to Pennsylvania. Nothing was said by them at any time about having abandoned the oil business. They did not stay a great deal in their room, and they were sometimes out all night. I can not say whether Mr. Booth's visits were more frequent during February or March. He was a constant visitor. I never heard any of their conversations.

BILLY WILLIAMS (colored.)

For the Prosecution.—May 15.

I know the prisoner, Mr. O'Laughlin, and I know Mr. Arnold by sight.

In March last I was going by Barnum's Hotel, when Mr. J. Wilkes Booth, the actor, came down the steps and asked me if I would take two letters for him. He told me there was one for O'Laughlin, and the other he said I was to take to the number that was on it. He did not tell me who it was for. There was a colored fellow with me, and I asked him to look at it and see what it was, as I could not read writing. He told me one was for Mr. O'Laughlin, and the other was for Arnold. I took one to Mr. O'Laughlin at the Baltimore Theater, and one I carried to Mr. Arnold. As I was in a hurry, I gave it to a lady who was at the door, and she said she would send it up to him. I saw O'Laughlin at the theater, and gave him his letter there. I said, "Mr. O'Laughlin, here is a letter Mr. Booth gave to me," and I handed it to him.

Mr. Cox. I must object to the whole of this evidence of the delivery of this note to O'Laughlin, and I desire, if the objection is sustained, that it be struck out of the record.

The JUDGE ADVOCATE. If the Court please, it is simply going to establish the intimacy of these men, their close personal relations with each other, as evidenced by their correspondence; and I think, in that point of view, it is clearly competent. We have presented them as visiting each other constantly. Now we are following them to Baltimore, and showing them as corresponding with each other constantly. Both facts go to establish an intimacy which is in accordance with the theory of the prosecution, which is, that they are co-conspirators. We do not offer the contents of the letter; simply the fact of their corresponding with each other.

Mr. Cox. I object to any evidence of the acts of Booth himself. The act of sending a note to an individual, no matter what may be the contents of that note, would be no evidence against that individual, unless the contents were accepted and acted upon by him. The mere fact of intimacy alone is an innocent fact on the part of the accused, and therefore is not evidence, I think, of a conspiracy. I therefore object to it, in the first place, as an act of Booth to which the defendant is not a party at all. He could not help receiving a letter from Booth. The act of receiving a letter was an entirely innocent one. I object, furthermore, that even if it tends to show intimacy, it does not tend to prove the guilt of the party of the charge now made against him.

The Court overruled the objection.

Cross-examined by MR. COX.

I think it was in March that I took the letters, because I heard Tom Johnson say it was March. I never took much notice of the months. It might have been the middle of March or toward the end. Mr. O'Laughlin's letter I took round to the Holliday Street Theater; it was in the afternoon, and I found him in the dress-circle. I know Mr. O'Laughlin right smart.

Cross-examined by MR. EWING.

When Mr. Booth gave me the letters, he said that one was to go up to Fayette Street, above Hart, and I asked a lady at the door, and she read the direction to me. I asked Mr. Booth how his mother was, and he said very well; and he said he was going away to New York at half-past 3 o'clock.

JOHN HAPMAN.

For the Prosecution.—May 18.

[Submitting to the witness a telegraphic dispatch.]

I have seen that dispatch before. It reads:

WASHINGTON, March 13, 1864.

To M. O'Laughlin, Esq., No. 57 North Exeter Street, Baltimore, Md.

Don't fear to neglect your business. You had better come at once.

[Signed] J. BOOTH.

[The original of the foregoing dispatch was offered in evidence.]

This dispatch was sent by telegraph from this city to O'Laughlin, March 13, 1865. We used the old printed forms of the year before, which accounts for the date being 1864. I knew J. Wilkes Booth, and saw him write that message.

Cross-examined by MR. COX.

Q. Can you say whether this is a question or a command, "Don't you fear to neglect your business?"

Assistant Judge Advocate BINGHAM objected to the question. The writing must be its own interpreter.

The Commission sustained the objection.

EDWARD C. STEWART.

For the Prosecution.—May 18.

I am a telegraph operator at the Metropolitan Hotel in this city.

[A telegraphic dispatch was handed to the witness.]

I sent this dispatch myself over the wires to Baltimore; it is:

WASHINGTON, March 27, 1864.

To M. O'Laughlin, Esq., 57 North Exeter Street, Baltimore, Md.

Get word to Sam. Come on, with or without him, Wednesday morning. We sell that day sure. Don't fail.

J. WILKES BOOTH.

[The dispatch was offered in evidence.]

I did not know the man who gave it to me; he wrote it and asked me to send it. I think I should know him if I were to see his photograph.

[The photograph of Booth shown to the witness.]

That is the gentleman who sent it. The true date of the telegram is March 27, 1865, not 1864.

Cross-examined by MR. COX.

This paper does not show that the dispatch was sent last March, it is dated 1864, but that was because we used last year's blanks. I remember sending this very message this year; it was given to me by the gentleman whose photograph has been shown to me.

By the COURT.

I have been an operator at the Metropolitan Hotel about ten months. I was not there in March, 1864.

SAMUEL STREETT.

For the Prosecution.—May 15.

I have known the prisoner, Michael O'-Laughlin, from his youth. About the 1st of April last, I saw him in this city, conversing with John Wilkes Booth. They were conferring together in a confidential manner on the stoop of a house, on the right-hand side of the avenue going toward the Treasury Department; I do not know what house it was. There were three of them in company; Booth appeared to be the speaker of the party, and the third person was an attentive listener. I addressed O'Laughlin first, having known him more familiarly than I did Booth. O'Laughlin called me to one side, and told me that Booth was busily engaged with his friend, or was talking privately. They were conversing in a low tone. The third party, as near as I remember, had curly hair; he had on a slouch hat, and seemed to be in a stooping position, as though talking to Booth in a low tone, or attentively listening to Booth's conversation. [Looking at the prisoners.] I can not swear that the man is here.

Cross-examined by MR. COX.

The house at which I saw Booth and O'Laughlin conversing was, I believe, on the avenue between Ninth and Eleventh Streets; I am not certain about the date, but I think it was nigh on to April. When O'Laughlin made the remark that Booth was engaged with his friend, it is likely that I asked O'Laughlin to propose to Mr. Booth to take a drink, and O'Laughlin's remark, that Booth was engaged with a friend, might have been in reply to my invitation.

BERNARD T. EARLY.

For the Prosecution.—May 15.

I am acquainted with the prisoner, O'-Laughlin, and slightly with Mr. Arnold. I came down to this city from Baltimore on the Thursday before the assassination—the night of the illumination—with Mr. O'Laughlin;

there were four of us in company. Mr. Arnold was not, to my knowledge, on the cars. When we arrived in this city, O'Laughlin asked me to walk with him as far as the National Hotel. He did not take a room there. I do not know that he made inquiries for Booth at the desk, nor did I see him associating with Booth. We stopped that night at the Metropolitan Hotel. On Friday I was with O'Laughlin the greater part of the day. When we got up, we went down and took breakfast at Welch's (Welcker's) on the avenue. After that, all four of us came up the avenue in company. When passing the National Hotel, about 9 o'clock, I think, I stopped to go back to the water-closet. When I came out, Mr. Henderson, one of the company, was sitting down. As I was going out, he called me back, and told me to wait for O'Laughlin, who was gone up stairs to see Booth. We waited, I judge, about three-quarters of an hour, but as he did not come down, we went out without him. In about an hour after that, when we were at a restaurant on the avenue, between Third and Four-and-a-half Streets, O'Laughlin came in. O'Laughlin, Henderson, and myself had supper at Welch's, and the last time I saw O'Laughlin that night was at a restaurant, going out with Mr. Fuller. It was pretty late, but whether it was before or after the assassination I can not say. O'Laughlin had been there for supper. We had been drinking considerably. The name of the present proprietor of the restaurant, I believe, is Lichau. I think, though I would not be certain, that O'Laughlin remained there until after the assassination. However, I distinctly remember seeing him go out in company with Mr. Fuller. Mr. Fuller used to be employed by O'Laughlin's brother in this city.

O'Laughlin returned to Baltimore with me next day, Saturday, by the 3 or half-past 3 o'clock afternoon train. After we arrived in Baltimore, on going down to his house, we met his brother-in-law on the way. He told Mr. O'Laughlin that there had been parties there that morning looking for him. O'Laughlin went into the house, and asked me if I would remain there for awhile; after that he invited me to come in. I went in, and sat in the parlor, while he went up stairs to see his mother; he remained a few minutes, and then came down and said he was not going to stay home that night. I can not say that he appeared to manifest any excitement, except when he heard that there were parties after him because of his known intimacy with Booth, having been acquainted with him, and in the habit of going with him, and from being supposed to be connected with him in the oil business.

Cross-examined by MR. COX.

I came down to Washington with Mr. Henderson, who is, I believe, a Lieutenant in the United States navy, Edward Murphy, O'Laughlin, and myself. I was invited down by Mr. Henderson. He came to the store after me that afternoon, and asked me to come down, with the intention of having a good time, and to see the illumination. I heard Mr. Murphy say that he invited them. Mr. O'Laughlin came to the store with Mr. Henderson, and Henderson invited me to go along with them. We slept at the Metropolitan Hotel on Thursday night. Henderson, Smith, and myself slept together in a three-bedded room, and O'Laughlin, whose name came last as we signed our names, had a room to himself. It was on the same floor as that on which we slept, and the second or third door from our room. It was about 2 o'clock on Friday morning when we went to bed. In the morning I rapped at O'Laughlin's door; I peeped in at the keyhole, and saw that he was in the room and asleep, and I woke him up.

I do not know for what purpose O'Laughlin called to see Booth. After waiting, I suppose, three-quarters of an hour at the National Hotel, during which time we had some cards written by a card-writer, we sent up some cards to Mr. Booth's room for O'Laughlin, that he might take it as a hint, and come down, for we were tired of waiting. The cards were returned with the message that there was nobody in the room. We left the cards with the clerk at the desk. O'Laughlin took a stroll round the city with us, and then four of us had dinner at Welch's; I do not know the hour; it was between 12 and 2. After dinner we took another stroll. Whether O'Laughlin was with me or not I can not say. We had been drinking pretty freely, all of us. Between 4 and 5 O'Laughlin went with me to a friend's house to pay a visit to a lady. I was not well acquainted with the streets, and I asked him to go with me to find the place. The lady invited us to dinner. She took our hats, and we had to stay. We had a second dinner there, and left, I suppose, about 6 o'clock. We returned together to the Lichau House, and were found there by Murphy and Henderson. We staid there until about 7 or 8, and then went to Welch's and had supper. We were there when the procession of the Navy Yard men passed up the avenue. That was perhaps between 8 and 9 o'clock. After that I went back to the Lichau House, and sat there until I went to bed. O'Laughlin was there the best part of the evening. I was there when I heard of the assassination. It was, I believe, about 10 o'clock when I saw O'Laughlin go out with Mr. Fuller, but I could not say whether I saw him there when the news came or not. Mr. Henderson was in the barroom, I believe, but Mr. Murphy had left us on the avenue previous to that.

When we came down on Thursday, it was our intention to go back on Friday; at least I understood so. I guess it was the liquor we had aboard that kept us. We did start to return by the 11 o'clock Saturday morning train. We went as far as the depot, and Mr. Henderson got the tickets. O'Laughlin wanted to go, and I said to Mr. Henderson, "If you press Mike, he will stay until the afternoon." So we all concluded to stay until the next train, at 3 o'clock in the afternoon.

Q. During this visit did you see any thing in Mr. O'Laughlin that betrayed a knowledge of any thing desperate which was to take place?

Assistant Judge Advocate BINGHAM objecting to the question, it was varied as follows:

Q. During this visit, state what his conduct was.

A. His conduct was the same as I usually saw him—jovial and jolly as any of the rest of the crowd.

Q. In good spirits?

A. Yes, sir; he was particularly so coming down in the cars with us that Thursday evening.

Q. No nervousness?

A. No, sir.

When O'Laughlin got to Baltimore and went to his house, he went up stairs, I suppose, to see his mother. On returning he said he would not stay at home that night. The remark he made was, that he would not like to be arrested in the house; that it would be the death of his mother. I told O'Laughlin that I thought it best for him to stay at home until the parties who were looking for him came again; but he said no, it would be the death of his mother if he was taken in the house.

Re-examined by the JUDGE ADVOCATE.

We, all four of us, returned to the Metropolitan Hotel between 1 and 2 o'clock, I suppose, when we went to bed; that is, on Friday morning. After having supper on the Thursday evening, we went to see the illumination, and walked a considerable distance up the avenue. After returning, we went, at the invitation of Mr. Henderson, to the Canterbury Music Hall. O'Laughlin was not separated from us during that night.

JAMES B. HENDERSON.

For the Prosecution.—May 15.

I am acquainted with the prisoner, Mr. O'Laughlin. I saw him in this city on Thursday and Friday, the 13th and 14th of April. I do not know whether he visited J. Wilkes Booth on either of those days, but he told me on Friday that he was to see him that morning.

Cross-examined by MR. COX.

He only told me he was to see Booth, but did not say what for. I can not tell exactly whether he said he had an engagement.

DAVID STANTON.

For the Prosecution.—May 16.

I have seen that man with the black moustache before, [pointing to the accused, Michael O'Laughlin.] I saw him on the 13th of April, the night before the assassination, at the house of the Secretary of War. I saw him pass in the door, and take a position on one side of the hall. I asked him what his business was, and he asked me where the Secretary was, and I told him he was standing on the steps. He said nothing further, but remained there some minutes, until finally I requested him to go out. He followed me out as far as the gate on the left-hand side of the house, and that was the last I saw of him. He did not ask for any one else besides the Secretary, nor did he explain why he was there. At first I supposed he was intoxicated, but I found out, after having some conversation with him, that he was not.

General Grant was in the parlor. He and the Secretary were being serenaded. O'Laughlin could see General Grant from his position. He did not inquire for any one but the Secretary, and after I pointed him out he did not go to him, and did not tell me what his business was. I did not see him go away from the house; there was such a crowd there. That was, I presume, about half-past 10 o'clock.

Cross-examined by MR. COX.

That was the first time I ever saw this man, and I did not see him again until I saw him on the Monitor as a prisoner, on the day on which Booth's body was taken away from the vessel. I can not be sure as to the exact time when I first saw the man; the fireworks commenced at about 9 o'clock, and lasted about an hour and a half, and it was after they were over. He was dressed in a suit of black; dress-coat, vest and pants, and his hat, which was a black slouch hat, I think, he had in his hand. The hall was very well lit up; the parlor, where General Grant was sitting, was also lit up, and I was directly in front of him when I addressed him.

He was inside of the door, about ten feet, standing next to the library door. He was about five feet four inches in hight. When I saw him on the Monitor he stood up, but I had an indistinct view of him there, as it was dark. I thought the man was intoxicated, from the way he came into the house. I inquired, before I went to him, of different members of the family, if they knew him. Finding they did not know him, I addressed him, and requested him to go out, which he did, going after me. There were a good many people about. The Secretary of War and Major Knox were on the door-steps, and this man had got behind them. He had, I think, the same moustache and beard that he has now; I see no change, with the exception of that caused by the want of shaving.

MAJOR KILBURN KNOX.

For the Prosecution—May 16.

I was at the house of the Secretary of War, in this city, on the evening of the 13th of April last, and saw there a man whom I recognize among the prisoners. There he is, [pointing to the accused, Michael O'Laughlin.] I left the War Department at 10 o'clock, after the illumination there was over, and walked up to the Secretary's house. There was a band playing at the house, and on the steps were General Grant, Mrs. Grant, the Secretary, General Barnes and his wife, Mr. Knapp and his wife, Miss Lucy Stanton, and two or three small children. I was standing on the upper steps, talking to Mrs. Grant and the General. Some fireworks were being set off in the square opposite, and I stepped down a little to allow the children to see them. I got down on the step, I think, next to the last one, leaning against the railing, and this man [O'Laughlin] came up to me, after I had been there ten minutes probably, and said, "Is Stanton in?" Said I, "I suppose you mean the Secretary?" He said, "Yes." I think he made the remark, "I am a lawyer in town; I know him very well." I was under the impression he was under the influence of liquor. I told him I did not think he could see him then, and he walked to the other side of the steps, and stood there probably five minutes. I still staid there, I suppose, for about five minutes, and he walked over to me and said, "Is Mr. Stanton in?" and then said, "Excuse me, I thought you were the officer on duty here." Said I, "There is no officer on duty here." He then walked on to the other side of the steps, and walked inside of the hall, the alcove, and stood on the inside step. I saw him standing there, and I walked over to Mr. David Stanton and said, "Do you know that man?" He said he did not. I said to him, "He says he knows the Secretary very well, but he is under the influence of liquor, and you had better bring him out." Mr. David Stanton walked up to him, talked to him a few moments, and then took him down the steps. He went off, and I did not notice him again. He did not say any thing about General Grant. By that time, I think, the General had gone into the parlor.

I think the Secretary stood on the steps outside, and this man stood behind the Secretary, and from where he stood he could see into the parlor. On the left-hand side of the hall, going in, is the library; on the other side is the parlor door. He stood on the side next to the library, and in that position he could have looked into the parlor, and seen who was in there, through the door

The whole house was lighted up, and I feel pretty certain that the prisoner, O'Laughlin, is the man I saw.

Cross-examined by MR. COX.

I do not recollect whether it was moonlight or dark that evening. There was a great crowd round the Secretary's house, and close up to the steps. I did not notice the man until he walked up on the steps and spoke to me, and after he went out again I saw him no more. I did not go inside the hall while he was there. Secretary Stanton was on the left-hand side of the steps, talking to Mrs. Grant, and the man went up on the right-hand side past them, and went in and took a place on the left-hand side. He had on a black slouch hat, a black frock-coat, and black pants; as to his vest I can not say. That was while the fireworks were going on. I had never seen the man before. I have seen him once since in this prison; I came here a week ago last Sunday for the purpose of identifying him.

MR. JOHN C. HATTER.

For the Prosecution.—May 16.

I recognize that man, sitting back there, [pointing to the prisoner, O'Laughlin.] He is the man I saw at Secretary Stanton's house at about 9 o'clock, or after, on the night of the illumination, the 13th of April. I was standing on the steps looking at the illumination, and this man [O'Laughlin] approached me, and asked me if General Grant was in. I told him he was. He said he wished to see him. Said I, "This is no occasion for you to see him. If you wish to see him, step out on the pavement, or on the stone where the carriage stops, and you can see him." That was all that occurred between us. He did not attempt to go into the house. When he spoke to me, he left the steps and walked away toward the tree-box, talking as he went, but I did not understand what he was saying. He seemed to reflect over something, and came back; then he walked off, and I did not see him any more. The house was illuminated, and it was pretty light outside, too.

Cross-examined by MR. COX.

I am a sergeant in the Adjutant-General's service, at the War Department, on duty at the Secretary's room. To my knowledge I had never seen the man before that evening. The next time I saw him was last Sunday week, in prison, in this building. I came down here with Major Eckert and Major Knox. I did not know what I was coming for; but when I was inside the room, and looking round, I saw that man, and I thought to myself, "I see the object of my coming down."

The first time I saw him it was very light, and he had on a dark suit of clothes, with a heavy moustache, black, and an imperial, and the way I took so much notice of him was, while I was speaking to him he was standing a little lower down, and I was looking right in his face.

He wore a dark slouch hat, a little low, and dark dress-coat and dark pantaloons. I should judge him to be about five feet four or five inches. There was a crowd about the house, come to serenade the Secretary; four or five bands were there. The Secretary was in the parlor with General Grant; they had not come out then; there was nobody on the steps but me. Both doors were open, the front door and another door like the front entry, and the gas was fully lit all around.

MARCUS P. NORTON.

For the Prosecution.—June 3.

From about the 10th of January until about the 10th of March, I was stopping at the National Hotel in this city. I knew J. Wilkes Booth, having seen him several times at the theater. I saw the prisoners, George A. Atzerodt and Michael O'Laughlin, at the National Hotel prior to the inauguration of President Lincoln, in company with Booth. I saw Atzerodt twice, and O'Laughlin four or five times, I believe, in conversation with him.

Cross-examined by MR. COX.

When I saw O'Laughlin talking with Booth at the National Hotel, he was in the presence of other people, and in the hall, but there was no one else in company with them. I heard no portion of the conversation. It was during the two months I was there, but I can not fix the precise date.

See also testimony of
Marcus P. Norton.................. page 177
Eaton G. Horner.................. " 284

DEFENSE OF MICHAEL O'LAUGHLIN.

BERNARD J. EARLY.

Recalled for the Defense.—May 25.

By MR. COX.

We left Baltimore on Thursday, the 13th of April, by the half-past 3 o'clock train, and arrived here about half-past 5. After leaving the cars, we went along the avenue to a restaurant kept by Lichau, I think it is called Rullman's Hotel. We remained there but a short time. Mr. Henderson went into the barber's shop to get shaved; while he was in there, Mr. O'Laughlin asked me to walk down as far as the National Hotel with him. I did so; when there, he walked up to the desk and inquired for some person, and told me to wait; he would detain me only a few minutes. I told him that I did not like to wait; that I did not want to miss the rest of the party. He said he would not detain me more than ten or fifteen minutes, and left me standing in the front door. He then went in, and returned again in from three to five minutes. Henderson had not got through with his shaving by the time we got back. We all four then walked up the avenue, I guess as far as Eleventh Street; then returned, and went into Welch's dining-saloon for supper. This saloon is over Wall & Stevens'. We left there about half-past 7, and returned to Rullman's Hotel, and proceeded from there down as far as the corner of Third Street, where O'Laughlin and Murphy left Henderson and me, saying they were going around to see Mr. Hoffman, who was sick, and who lived on B Street. They returned in ten or fifteen minutes with Mr. Daniel Loughran. All five of us then started up the avenue to see the illumination. About Seventh Street, one of the party complained of having sore feet, and said he would not go any further. Seeing a notice of the Canterbury Music Hall performances, we all went there, and got in about at the end of the first piece. It was then getting on for 9 o'clock. We remained there till 10 o'clock, when we proceeded to the Metropolitan Hotel, and from there down to Lichau's or Rullman's Hotel, reaching there about half-past 10. O'Laughlin was with us all the time. We remained at the hotel about an hour, I suppose. As we were there on the steps, Mr. Grillet passed by with a lady, and spoke to Mr. O'Laughlin. We left there with Mr. Giles, one of the men of the house, and went down as far as Second Street. I believe Mr. O'Laughlin is acquainted with the saloons on the corner of B Street and Second. There was a dance or some thing going on there. He took the lead over there and we

followed him. One of the party bought tickets to go back into the ball. We did not stay there more than about an hour; we got tired of the affair and came out. We then went up the avenue, stopped at several places, and went into the Metropolitan Hotel, between 1 and 2 o'clock. We went out again for about five minutes, and returned at about the hour of 2, when we went up stairs to bed. Mr. O'Laughlin was with us all that night.

I do not know where Mr. Stanton's residence is; but I know the situation of the Treasury Building.

Q. Mr. Stanton's house is six squares north of that, and one square east; I ask you if it is possible that Mr. O'Laughlin could have been at Mr. Stanton's at 9 o'clock, or at any time between that and 11 o'clock.

Assistant Judge Advocate BINGHAM objected to the question, and it was waived.

WITNESS. On Friday night, O'Laughlin was in Rullman's Hotel from about supper time until he went out with Mr. Fuller. We had supper at Welch's at about 8 o'clock, and I suppose we staid there from about three-quarters of an hour to an hour. From Welch's we went to Rullman's. Whether Mr. O'Laughlin went out with Mr. Fuller before or after the assassination I can not say, but I distinctly remember his going out with him.

Mr. O'Laughlin had on a dahlia coat—something of a frock—a double-breasted vest, and pantaloons of the same material—a Scotch plaid, purple and green. I made these things for him.

Cross-examined by ASSISTANT JUDGE ADVOCATE BINGHAM.

On Friday evening, about 10 o'clock, I suppose, we were all under the influence of liquor. We might have drank as many as ten times; it was mostly ale, though, that Mr. O'Laughlin and myself drank. I hardly ever saw him drink liquor. I was not separated from O'Laughlin until he went out from Rullman's Hotel. That was about 10 o'clock, or a little after. I next saw him again on Saturday morning. Rullman's Hotel is between Third and Four-and-a-half Streets.

By MR. COX.

I have very seldom, if ever, seen O'Laughlin drink whisky. I have never seen him intoxicated but twice. I have known him slightly for about four years, and intimately for the last ten months.

EDWARD MURPHY.
For the Defense.—May 25.

By M. Cox.

I reside in Baltimore. On the 13th of April last, in company with James B. Henderson, who proposed the trip, Michael O'Laughlin, and Barney Early, I came to Washington. We arrived here about 5 in the afternoon. From the depot we went to Rullman's, had a drink or two, and started for the Metropolitan. We went to several places; took supper at Welch's, somewhere about 8 o'clock. We were there about half an hour, and then came down to Rullman's again. There we met, I think, John Loughran, and took a walk up the street to see the illumination of the Treasury, and stopped on the corner of Ninth Street and the avenue. After standing debating there some time, we went to the Canterbury Music Hall, staid there some time, walked down to the Metropolitan Hotel, and then came back to Rullman's. It was about a quarter to 10 when we got into Rullman's. O'Laughlin was with us all the time. Then we went up to Platz's and back again. That brought us to about half-past 11 or 12. We then started down to Riddle's, on the corner of B and Second Street, where we staid until half-past 12 or 1; from there we went to Dubant's, on the corner of Sixth and the avenue, where we took a hack, and went to the corner of Tenth and the avenue. There is an all-night house there, and we went in and got some refreshments. I suppose it was about half-past 1 when we were there. It was about 2 o'clock when we got to the Metropolitan and registered our names. Before going to bed, we went across the street to Gilson's and got a drink. It made it about half-past 2 when we got to bed. Michael O'Laughlin was with us all the time from leaving the cars until we all went to bed, except that when we first came down, while Henderson was being shaved. O'Laughlin and Early left us for about five minutes and went as far as the National Hotel. They were back before Henderson was shaved; were not gone more than five or six minutes.

I think I know where the house of Mr. Stanton, the Secretary of War, is, and O'Laughlin was no nearer to it that night than the corner of Ninth and the avenue.

I was with him all day Friday and up to 8 o'clock that night, when I went to the Metropolitan Hotel, and did not see him again until Saturday morning. On Saturday I was with him from 9 o'clock in the morning till we went to the depot to go to Baltimore. I did not know of the assassination till 9 o'clock Saturday morning. I never saw O'Laughlin in better spirits in my life than he was during this trip. When we started from Baltimore, it was our intention to go up on Friday afternoon, but we staid in Washington at the solicitation of Mr. Henderson, who wanted to see a lady friend of his that night, and the whole party staid on that account. I remember Mr. Grillet joined us on the steps of the Rullman Hotel on Thursday night.

Recalled for the Defense.—May 25.

By MR. Cox.

I saw O'Laughlin in Baltimore on the Sunday after the assassination, and he told me that the officers were in search of him, and that he was going to surrender himself on the Monday following.

JAMES B. HENDERSON.

Recalled for the Defense.—June 12.

By MR. Cox.

I am an Ensign in the United States Navy. I have been acquainted with the prisoner, Michael O'Laughlin, for about six years. I proposed to him that we should come to Washington on Thursday, the 13th of April, and we left Baltimore at 3:30 on that afternoon, arriving in this city between 5 and 6, I judge. On our arrival, we came up the avenue, and stopped at the Lichau House, or Rullman's Hotel. I went into the barber's shop adjoining to get shaved, and O'Laughlin went up the street in the mean time, but he returned before I had finished shaving, and, with the exception of that, he was not out of my company the whole evening until bedtime. I went up the avenue to look at the illumination. We did not go up as far as Ninth Street. We stopped at the corner of Seventh, and then went back to the Canterbury Music Hall. We reached there about 9 o'clock; after staying there perhaps three-quarters of an hour, we returned to Rullman's Hotel. We got there between 10 and 11, and staid about half an hour there. I retired for the night, at the Metropolitan Hotel, at between 1 and 2 o'clock in the morning.

The avenue was very much crowded. It was almost impossible for a person to get along, and we did not go further west than a little beyond Seventh Street, on Thursday evening; O'Laughlin was not any where in the neighborhood of Franklin Square—Mr. Stanton's; he was with me all the time, except when I was being shaved. I do not know certainly whether he slept at the Metropolitan that night; I saw him in his room, and was there the next morning when they called him. On the Friday afternoon he left me in company with Mr. Early, I think, but I met him again in the evening at Rullman's Hotel. He was there with me until 10 o'clock I should think, and then he went out with a man named Fuller. He was there when the news of the President's assassination came. Our party had arranged to return to Baltimore on Friday morning, but I proposed to them to stay until Friday evening.

Cross-examined by the JUDGE ADVOCATE.

I do not know the name of the street on which Mr. Stanton resides, but I have been shown the house. It was impossible for O'Laughlin to have been there on the evening of Thursday, the 13th of April, for I was with him the whole evening. There was a good deal of free drinking that night by our party, and it was continued until a late hour. It would be impossible for me to say how many drinks we had; I should think not more than ten. They were mostly taken at hotels and restaurants on the avenue. One of the party was drunk—Mr. Early—but the others were sober enough, I think, to be conscious of each other's movements, or presence, or absence.

O'Laughlin left me but for a short time on our arrival in Washington, while I got shaved, and told me he had been to see Booth. That was between 5 and 6 o'clock. I knew of his going to see Booth the next morning at the National Hotel, and I went there to call for him, but found he had left. On going back to Rullman's, I found he was there, and he said he had been to the National Hotel, but Booth was out. I do not know of any other attempt on his part to see Booth, nor do I know his object in seeking that interview.

By MR. COX.

O'Laughlin did not say any thing to me about Booth owing him money, and that he wanted to get some from him. He only told me that he had been to see him; he did not say whether he had seen him or not; and on Friday he said that 'e had been to see him, and he was not at nome.

By the JUDGE ADVOCATE.

I had no particular reason for not returning to Baltimore on Friday; I wanted to stay a little while myself, and asked the others to stay. O'Laughlin himself had not spoken of staying over. It was on the Wednesday that we arranged to come to Washington on the Thursday; I proposed that we should all come down on that day. I do not remember that O'Laughlin made any suggestions about it; I think I asked him to come down. I had been on terms of intimate association with him for only about a week previous to that.

DANIEL LOUGHRAN.

For the Defense.—May 25.

By MR. COX.

I reside in this city. I have known the accused, Michael O'Laughlin, for eighteen or twenty months. On Thursday evening, the 13th of April, at about a quarter past 7, I saw him in front of Rullman's Hotel, on Pennsylvania Avenue, in company with Lieutenant Henderson, Edward Murphy, and Bernard Early. I did not join them then; I went

home to supper. O'Laughlin and Murphy came to my boarding-house, and we met Henderson and Early in front of Adams' Express Office, on Pennsylvania Avenue; that was about 8 o'clock. After we joined them, we went into Platz's Restaurant, and from there to Rullman's Hotel. From Rullman's we went up to the corner of Pennsylvania Avenue and Ninth; it was about 9 o'clock then, for I looked at my watch. We then went into the Canterbury, staid there until 10 or perhaps half-past; from there we went to the Metropolitan Hotel, and then to Rullman's, reaching there probably at half-past 10; perhaps a little earlier or later. Michael O'Laughlin was with me from the time we joined Henderson and Early until we went down to Rullman's Hotel.

I do not know where Mr. Stanton's house is, but I know where Franklin Square is, and I know that O'Laughlin could not have been up there during that time. Mr. Grillet joined us at Rullman's at about half-past 10, and I was with them until after 12 o'clock. O'Laughlin was there all that time.

I saw them the next evening, I judge, between 7 and 8, at Rullman's Hotel; I was there until perhaps half-past 9. I do not know that they went to Welcker's; I heard them speaking about going to supper, but where they went I do not know, nor do I know whether O'Laughlin went to supper. I did not miss him from the time I went there until about half-past 9, when I went home, and saw him no more that night. O'Laughlin wore a plaid vest and pants; the pants he wears now look like the ones. I think he had on a black slouch hat.

By the COURT.

We occupied different seats at the Canterbury play-house; two of us sat on one seat, and the other two sat right behind. I saw them there all the time, and we all left together.

By MR. COX.

O'Laughlin seemed very lively. The remark was made that they had come down from Baltimore to see the illumination and have a good time. I do not think he was intoxicated on Thursday evening; he was lively and merry, but I can not say he was tight or drunk.

GEORGE GRILLET.

For the Defense.—May 25.

By MR. COX.

I reside in Washington, and am solicitor for the New York Cracker Bakery, 96 Louisiana Avenue. I have known the accused, Michael O'Laughlin, one or two years. I saw him on the steps of Rullman's Hotel, between 10 and half-past 10, on the night of Thursday, the 13th of April, and he bowed to me. Lieutenant Henderson and Edward Murphy were with him, and Henry Purdy, the superintendent of the house, was on the porch, I believe. After I had escorted home the lady that was with me, I returned to the house and joined the party, and did not leave them until between 12 and 1 o'clock. I saw O'Laughlin the next morning, and then not until 8 o'clock at night; I staid with them until between 11 and 12. I was at the Lichau House or Rullman's Hotel when I heard the news of the President's assassination. O'Laughlin was there at the time. I did not notice how he behaved when he heard of the assassination. He left shortly after the news came that the President was killed; he and a man named Fuller left together. On that evening I know he had on a Scotch plaid vest and pants; I can not swear positively to the coat, but he had a habit of wearing a sack-coat.

HENRY E. PURDY.

For the Defense.—May 25.

By Mr. Cox.

I am superintendent of Rullman's Hotel in this city. I saw the accused, Michael O'Laughlin, at about half-past 10 on the night of Thursday, the 13th of April, with George Grillet, Loughran, Murphy, and Early; I do not know where they came from. I was principally in the kitchen and the dining-room, and walking around; in the bar only occasionally. Whenever I was in the bar they were there, until a few minutes after 12 o'clock, when I closed up, and they went out at the side door. I am confident that O'Laughlin was with them when they came there at about half-past 10; I have known him about three months. I saw them again on Friday at the same place.

I was standing in front of the door when I heard of the assassination, and I went in and told them what I had just heard from a cavalry sergeant; that the President had been assassinated, and that Booth was the one who had done it. They were all standing together drinking. O'Laughlin was right at the end of the bar, and he was the one I first spoke to when I went in.

When I went in he seemed surprised, and said he had been in Booth's company very often, and people might think he had something to do with it. I do not remember when he individually left that night, but it was after 12 when the whole party was gone. He has staid at my house when he has come down to the city.

By the Court.

Sometimes he would come down pretty often in a week, and sometimes I would not see him for two weeks. On the Thursday night he had dark clothes on; he generally wore dark clothes. I did not take particular notice of his dress, and can not say whether it was the same as that he now wears.

JOHN H. FULLER.

For the Defense.—May 25

By Mr. Cox.

I am engaged in business in this city. I have known the accused, Michael O'Laughlin, for twelve or fourteen years. On Friday, the 14th of April, I saw him at Rullman's on the avenue between 7 and 8 o'clock, and again between 10 and 11. He and I were both there when the news of the President's assassination was brought in, and we left there together to go to the Franklin House, where I was stopping. He staid all night with me, and got up about 8 o'clock next morning, and went with me to New Jersey Avenue, and then to the Lichau House, and there I parted with him; he joining his other friends there. When he heard of the President's assassination, he did not show any fright, nor did he say any thing about Booth; he said he was sorry for it; that it was an awful thing.

Cross-examined by ASSISTANT JUDGE ADVOCATE BINGHAM.

O'Laughlin was stopping at another hotel, but I invited him to go with me that night; he used to go down there with me at times to stay. I do not know where he stopped on Thursday night.

By Mr. Cox.

He used to reside in Washington; his brother was in business here.

JOHN R. GILES.

For the Defense.—June 3.

By Mr. Cox.

I am bar-tender at No. 456 Pennsylvania Avenue, late Rullman's Hotel. I have known the accused, Michael O'Laughlin, personally, about four months. He was at our place on the evening of Thursday, the 13th of April, with Barney Early, Murphy, Lieutenant Henderson, Purdy, and several others. He was there early in the evening, and again about 10 o'clock, and staid till after 11. I joined them when they went out, and was with them until 1 o'clock. They were there again on Friday evening, nearly all the evening. The news of the assassination came in, I think, between half-past 9 and 10; and O'Laughlin was there at that time. He afterward went out with Mr. Fuller. The Lichau House is on Louisiana Avenue, between Four-and-a-half and Sixth Streets, and the Canterbury Music Hall is next door.

Cross-examined by ASSISTANT JUDGE ADVOCATE BINGHAM.

It might have been after 10 o'clock that the news of the President's assassination was brought in—I can not say exactly.

O'Laughlin was at our house on Friday evening from 7 or 8 o'clock till 11. He was out on the pavement, and in and out drinking, but was not away from the house.

P. H. MAULSBY.

For the Defense.—May 26.

By Mr. Cox.

I am a clerk with Eaton Bros. & Co., of Baltimore, and am brother-in-law to the accused, Michael O'Laughlin. O'Laughlin, I believe, came from the South to Baltimore in August, 1862. He came home somewhat sick. He then went with his brother, who was in the produce and feed business, and remained with him until the fall of 1863. His brother then sold the business, but Michael O'Laughlin remained here and received orders, which his brother supplied from Baltimore. O'Laughlin was here off and on from that period up to the 14th of March.

I knew J. Wilkes Booth intimately. Mrs. Booth owns the property in which the O'Laughlin family resides, and Mrs. Booth lived opposite for four years. The boys, Michael and William, were schoolmates of J. Wilkes Booth. To my knowledge, their intimacy has continued for twelve years.

After leaving Washington, the home of Michael O'Laughlin was with me, at 57 North Exeter Street. From the 18th of March to the 13th of April he was with me, and from the 30th of March to the 12th of April, I can speak positively as to his being with me at Baltimore. I know he was at home on the 7th of March, and remained at home some days. I know of his being sent to Washington by his brother on the 13th of March, and on the 14th his brother telegraphed him here respecting a car-load of hay.

[A telegraphic dispatch relating to the hay was read and put in evidence.]

He returned to Baltimore on the following Saturday, and from that time he remained at home till he came to Washington on the 13th of April. In February, I could not state positively as to his being at home. He was at home on the 7th and on the 14th, and my impression is that he was then home for a couple of weeks.

Q. At what time did he arrive at home after the assassination?

A. He came up on Saturday evening; I saw him about 7 o'clock.

Q. Had the officers been to the house then in search of him?

A. They had.

Q. Did you inform him of that?

A. I did.

Q. Then what took place?

A. He told me that—

Assistant Judge Advocate BINGHAM objected to the accused giving his own declarations in evidence, for the reason that he had stated yesterday, in regard to a similar question, in which he had been sustained by the Court, that if such a rule as that were adopted and acted upon by courts, all that a guilty man would have to do, after he had committed a great crime, would be to pour his statements into the ears of all honest people that he met up to the time of his arrest, and then prove those statements on his trial. The law says that he shall not do any such thing, and I object to it on that account.

Mr. Cox stated that he desired to prove by this witness, that the prisoner, Michael O'Laughlin, was informed that the officers had been in pursuit of him; that he informed the witness that he had an engagement on Saturday night, but would communicate with him the next day; that on Monday he did send for him to come to him, and authorized him to procure an officer, and put himself in his custody, declaring all the time his entire innocence of any complicity with this affair.

The JUDGE ADVOCATE said the witness should be instructed that he is not to give the declarations of the prisoner, but simply his acts, in evidence.

Q. You say you informed him on Saturday afternoon that the officers had been in search of him?

A. I did.

Q. Did he protest his innocence?

Assistant Judge Advocate BINGHAM objected to the question. There was no authority in the world for such a question as that; it was a burlesque upon judicial proceedings.

Mr. Cox insisted on the question. If a party flees and avoids arrest, it would certainly be receivable for the prosecution; but if he candidly comes forward and says, "I am not guilty, and I offer myself for investigation and trial," it should equally be receivable for the defense.

The JUDGE ADVOCATE stated that that was not the rule of law. The Government could give the declarations of the accused in evidence, but it did not follow from that that the prisoner could.

Mr. Cox replied that where it was a part of his conduct, he could. He could not prove his innocence by declaring himself so, but where it was a part of his conduct it was receivable upon the question of how far he was conscious of guilt.

The Commission sustained the objection.

WITNESS. On Monday morning Michael O'Laughlin authorized me to procure an officer, and voluntarily surrendered himself.

I have known O'Laughlin for about twelve years.

Q. State his disposition and character; whether he is violent and bad-hearted, or, on the contrary, amiable, mild-tempered, etc.

A. As a boy, he was always a very timid boy. From my observation of twelve years,

I believe him to be the last one who would have any thing—

Assistant Judge Advocate BURNETT. What you believe is not evidence.

Mr. COX. I meant to ask the witness whether, from his knowledge of the accused, he believes him capable of being engaged in any thing of this sort.

Assistant Judge Advocate BINGHAM. I object to his swearing to conclusions. He can state the general character of the accused, but he can not swear to conclusions. This is a matter exclusively for the Court.

WITNESS. I was merely about to speak of his capability, judging from my observation of his disposition.

Assistant Judge Advocate BINGHAM. You can state his disposition.

Q. State what his disposition is as to amiability, peacefulness, etc.

A. I have always regarded him as an amiable boy.

Q. Was he violent on political questions?

A. I never recollect having seen him in a passion in my life. On political questions he has never been violent. I have never heard him express any opinion, except in a very moderate way, on the issues of the times.

Q. There has been some testimony by Mr. Wallace about his arrest of the accused. I would like you to state the facts in regard to that alleged arrest, and what Mr. Wallace had to do with it. In the first place, I will inquire whether Michael had authorized you to go for an officer?

Assistant Judge Advocate BINGHAM. That I object to.

Mr. COX. Then I will ask the witness whether he went for an officer, and whom he procured.

A. The facts in the case are simply these: When I met Michael I suggested to him—

Assistant Judge Advocate BINGHAM. You need not state any thing that you said to Michael.

Q. State what you did after leaving him on Monday morning.

A. On Monday morning he sent for me and said—

Assistant Judge Advocate BINGHAM. You need not state what he said.

Q. What did you do in consequence of what he said to you?

Assistant Judge Advocate BINGHAM objected. The question assumes that the accused told the witness something, and the witness was asked to swear that, in consequence of what the accused told him, he did something else. The counsel had no right to assume any thing here as proof that was not proof; and more especially had he no right to assume as proved what was incapable of being proved—the declarations of his client.

Mr. Cox replied that the whole object of the inquiry was to ascertain, for the satisfac-

tion of the Court, whether the accused, with that consciousness of innocence which would govern a man who was innocent, did really act in accordance with that consciousness, by voluntarily submitting himself to the officers of justice, professing his willingness to submit to an investigation. If the flight, which the prosecution have attempted to prove, was evidence of guilt, certainly it was competent for the defendant to meet that evidence by proof, on the contrary, that there was no flight, no evasion, but a voluntary submission to the officers of the law, with a view of having the merits of the case fairly tried.

The JUDGE ADVOCATE said that the witness might be asked if he did it himself, or if he did it by the prisoner's authority.

Q. State whether you surrendered the accused into the custody of an officer by the authority of the accused himself.

A. I did, sir, most certainly.

On Saturday evening, at 7 o'clock, I met Mr. O'Laughlin and Mr. Early together, just as they returned from Washington. On Sunday morning Mr. Wallace and other officers came to our house in search of O'Laughlin. I believe officers had been there on Saturday, though I had not seen them. On Monday I was sent for by Michael. I went for a hack, and called for Mr. Wallace, who was not then aware of O'Laughlin's whereabouts. I went into the house, Mr. Wallace remaining in the hack, and Michael came out, and I introduced him to Mr. Wallace and Mr. James S. Allison. There was nothing, I believe, said from that time till we reached the Marshal's office.

Q. I ask you to state, further, whether he offered to inform you where he could be found that night, if wanted.

Assistant Judge Advocate BINGHAM objected to the question, and the Commission sustained the objection.

Q. Did you know Booth intimately?

A. Yes, sir.

Q. State whether he was a man of pleasing address.

Assistant Judge Advocate BINGHAM. I object to all that.

Mr. COX. What I desire to show to the Court, and what all the counsel desire, is to have some evidence as to the character of this man, John Wilkes Booth. There is nothing in the case yet to reflect any light at all on that question. If any of these accused should be found guilty of association with him in this serious crime, Booth's influence upon them, whatever it may have been, would not affect the question of their innocence, but it is a consideration, which goes in mitigation of their guilt, that Booth was a man who naturally acquired a great ascendency over young men with whom he associated, and could warp them from the right by means of his control over them. My desire is to introduce some evidence on that subject, and it is the desire of all the counsel for the defense. The question which I propound to the witness is a preliminary question, designed to introduce that subject.

The JUDGE ADVOCATE. It does not mitigate the assassination at all, that it was per-formed by a man of fascinating address and pleasing manners.

Mr. COX. No, but it mitigates the act of the other parties that they were acting under his influence.

The JUDGE ADVOCATE. Not at all.

The Commission sustained the objection.

TESTIMONY CONCERNING SAMUEL ARNOLD.

EATON G. HORNER.

For the Prosecution.—May 18.

On the morning of the 17th of April, Mr. Voltaire Randall and myself arrested the prisoner, Samuel Arnold, at Fortress Monroe. We took him in the back room of the store, where he slept. We there searched his person and his carpet-bag, in which we found a pistol, something like a Colt's. He said he had left another pistol and a knife at his father's, at Hookstown.

Cross-examined by MR. EWING.

Arnold made a statement verbally to us at Fortress Monroe. Before we left Baltimore, a letter was given to us by his father to give him when we should arrest him. We handed him the letter, and he read it. I inquired of him if he was going to do as they asked him to do, and he said that he was. He then gave us a statement and the names of certain men connected with a plan for the abduction of Abraham Lincoln.

Mr. STONE. I object to the declarations of one of the accused against others of the accused, made perhaps to throw the responsibility off his own shoulders on that of the others.

Mr. EWING. The confession of one of the accused in a conspiracy or alleged conspiracy, after the conspiracy has been either executed or abandoned, is not admissible—that is, will not be considered by the Court in weighing the question of the guilt or innocence of those who are associated with him in the charge; but that is a rule of law which should not be so applied as to cut off one of the accused from giving in evidence any statement which he made, accompanying such an incident as his confession of the possession of arms.

MR. STONE. I take it, that is not the rule which governs courts-martial, as it certainly does not govern any other courts in the consideration of evidence. Whatever is not competent evidence is not allowed to go to a jury at all; it is excluded from their consideration entirely; and I take it for granted that this Court, having to determine both the law (under the guidance and advice of the learned Judge Advocate) and the facts of the case, will discard entirely from the record all evidence which is clearly inadmissible, and which ought not to be weighed adversely to a prisoner, because it is impossible for any man, in the nature of things, to discard from his consideration and prevent his judgment from being biased by evidence which is once submitted to him, and which may be in its nature adverse to the prisoner, although it may be incompetent and illegal evidence.

Mr. EWING. The Judge Advocate, in the charges and by the evidence, has sought to associate him with the conspiracy, and one of the links of the association is the arms there. Therefore it seemed to me that any statement he made at that time and place, with reference to his connection with the conspiracy, is legitimate. If the Court will allow me, I will read a short paragraph from Roscoe's Criminal Evidence, page 53:

"Where a confession by one prisoner is given in evidence which implicates the other prisoners by name, a doubt arises as to the propriety of suffering those names to be mentioned to the jury. On one circuit the practice has been to omit their names, (*Fletcher's Case,* 4 C. & P. 250,) but it has been ruled by Littledale, J., in several cases, that the names must be given. Where it was objected, on behalf of a prisoner whose name was thus introduced, that the witness ought to be directed to omit his name, and merely say another person, Littledale, J., said, 'The witness must mention the name. He is to tell us what the prisoner said, and if he left out the name he would not do so. He did not say another person, and the witness must give us the conversation just as it occurred; but I shall tell the jury that it is not evidence against the other prisoner.' (*Hearne's Case,* 4 C & P. 215; *Clewe's Case, Id.* 255.)"

That paragraph evidently contemplates only confessions introduced by the prosecution; but if the course of the examination has been such as to make it the right of a prisoner to introduce a confession or statement, made at a particular moment, on his own behalf, he has just as much right to introduce the confession, even though there be others associated with him in the charge, as the prosecution would have, if it saw fit to do so.

The President, after consultation with the members of the Commission, announced that the objection was overruled.

The question was repeated to the witness.

WITNESS. About three weeks previous to Arnold's going to Fortress Monroe, he said he was at a meeting held at the Lichau House, on Pennsylvania Avenue, between Sixth and Four-and-a-half Streets. J. Wilkes Booth, Michael O'Laughlin, George A. Atzerodt, John H. Surratt, and a man with the *alias* of Moseby, and another, a small man, whose name I could not recollect, were there. I asked him if he ever corresponded with Booth. At first he denied, but on my mentioning the letter that had been found in Booth's trunk, mailed at Huntstown, he admitted that he wrote that letter. In the same conversation he told me about the pistol and knife at his father's farm. We imprisoned him till evening, when we brought him to Baltimore.

Cross-examined by MR. EWING.

In that conversation, Arnold said that Booth had letters of introduction to Dr. Mudd and Dr. Queen, but he said he did not know from whom Booth got the letters. On arriving in Baltimore, we took Arnold to Marshal McPhail's office. At the meeting at which Arnold and others were present an angry discussion took place. Booth, he said, got angry at something he said. Arnold said that if the thing was not done that week that he was there, he would withdraw. Booth got angry at this, and said that he ought to be shot for expressing himself in that way, or he had said enough for Booth to shoot him, or words to that effect, when Arnold said that two could play at that game. Arnold said that he withdrew at that time, and on the 1st of April occupied a position at Fortress Monroe with Mr. W. Wharton.

He did not state, or I do not remember, the precise date of the meeting, and I do not know whether he said he had seen Booth since or not.

Q. But he stated that he had nothing more to do with the conspiracy?

Assistant Judge Advocate BINGHAM objected to the question.

WITNESS. Arnold said that he would withdraw, or would have no connection with the business, if it was not done that week, on which Booth said something to the effect that he would be justified in shooting him for expressing himself in that way. I do not remember that he said after that that he would withdraw. He said that after that he did have nothing more to do with the conspiracy, but accepted a position under Mr. Wharton. He said the purpose of the parties in this conspiracy, up to the time he withdrew, was to abduct or kidnap the President, and take him South, for the purpose of making this Government have

an exchange of prisoners, or something like that. I asked him what he was to do in it, what his part was; I think he said he was to catch the President when he was thrown out of the box at the theater.

On my asking Arnold where he got the arms, he said that Booth furnished the arms for all the men. Arnold said he asked Booth what he should do with the arms; Booth told him to take them and do any thing with them; sell them if he chose. There was a knife and a pistol at his father's, and a pistol he brought with him to Fortress Monroe to sell; that is the one we got in his carpet-bag.

By MR. COX.

From what Arnold said, I do not think that the meeting to which he referred was the first meeting. He said that at that meeting there were some new men that he had not seen before. He said that after discussing the scheme, he came to the conclusion that it was impracticable; that was the word he used. I understood him that he individually abandoned the scheme at that time, but I did not understand that the scheme was abandoned by the party, but that he considered that plan or mode of kidnapping the President as impracticable, and wished to withdraw from having any thing further to do with it. This meeting, I understood Arnold to say, was a week or two, it might have been two or three weeks, before he went to Fortress Monroe. There was no rope found in Arnold's sack.

VOLTAIRE RANDALL.

For the Prosecution.—May 25.

I know the prisoner, Samuel Arnold. When we arrested him, I examined his carpet-sack, and found in it some letters, papers, clothing, a revolver, and some car tridges.

[Submitting to the witness a revolver.]

This is the same revolver; the number is 164,557. I made a memorandum of it at the time, and this is the same. It was loaded then and is now. It is a Colt's navy pistol.

[The pistol was offered in evidence.]

Cross-examined by MR. EWING.

I arrested Arnold at the storehouse of John W. Wharton, near Fortress Monroe. I believe the place is called Old Point; it was not in the fort.

LIEUTENANT WILLIAM H. TERRY

For the Prosecution.—May 18.

I am attached to Colonel Ingraham's office in this city. On the night after the assassination, Mr. William Eaton, who has testified in this case, and who took charge of the trunk of J. Wilkes Booth, placed in my hands the papers found among Booth's effects.

[A letter was handed the witness.]

That is one of the papers, and it was in that envelope. Colonel Taylor marked the envelope "Important," and signed his initials to it.

[The letter was read as follows:]

HOOKSTOWN, BALTO. CO., } March 27, 1865. }

DEAR JOHN: Was business so important that you could not remain in Balto. till I saw you? I came in as soon as I could, but found you had gone to W——n. I called also to see Mike, but learned from his mother he had gone out with you, and had not returned. I concluded, therefore, he had gone with you. How inconsiderate you have been! When I left you, you stated we would not meet in a month or so. Therefore, I made application for employment, an answer to which I shall receive during the week. I told my parents I had ceased with you. Can I, then, under existing circumstances, come as you request? You know full well that the G——t suspicions something is going on there; therefore, the undertaking is becoming more complicated. Why not, for the present, desist, for various reasons, which, if you look into, you can readily see, without my making any mention thereof. You, nor any one, can censure me for my present course. You have been its cause, for how can I now come after telling them I had left you? Suspicion rests upon me now from my whole family, and, even parties in the county. I will be compelled to leave home any how, and how soon I care not. None, no not one, were more in favor of the enterprise than myself, and to-day would be there, had you not done as you have—by this I mean, manner of proceeding. I am, as you well know, in need. I am, you may say, in rags, whereas to-day I ought to be well clothed. I do not feel right stalking about with means, and more from appearances a beggar. I feel my dependence; but even all this would and was forgotten, for I was one with you. Time more propitious will arrive yet. Do not act rashly or in haste. I would prefer your first query, "go and see how it will be taken at R——d, and ere long I shall be better prepared to again be with you. I dislike writing; would sooner verbally make known my views; yet your non-writing causes me thus to proceed.

Do not in anger peruse this. Weigh all I have said, and, as a rational man and a *friend*, you can not censure or upbraid my conduct. I sincerely trust this, nor aught else that shall or may occur, will ever be an obstacle to obliterate our former friendship and attachment. Write me to Balto., as I expect to be in about Wednesday or Thursday, or, if you can possibly come on, I will Tuesday meet you in Balto., at B——. Ever I subscribe myself,

Your friend, SAM.

[The letter was put in evidence.]

WILLIAM McPHAIL.

For the Prosecution.—May 18.

I am acquainted with the handwriting of Samuel Arnold.

[Exhibiting to the witness the letter signed "Sam."]

That has somewhat the appearance of his handwriting, though I think it is rather heavier in some parts of it. I should say it was his handwriting.

Cross-examined by MR. EWING.

I became acquainted with his handwriting from having a confession of his placed in my hands. It was a paper purporting to state all he knew in regard to this affair. It was written in the back room of Marshal James McPhail's office, No. 4 Fayette Street, Baltimore. The paper was handed by me to the Marshal, and I was informed that the officers delivered it to the Secretary of War

GEORGE R. MAGEE.

For the Prosecution.—May 25.

By the JUDGE ADVOCATE.

Q. State to the Court whether you know the prisoner at the bar, Samuel Arnold.
A. I do.
Q. State to the Court whether or not he has been in the military service of the rebels.
Mr. EWING. I object to that question. Arnold is here on trial for having been engaged in a conspiracy to do certain things, and it is not competent for the Government to show (if such be the fact) that before he entered into the conspiracy he was in the military service of the Confederate States. He is not on trial for that. He is on trial for offenses defined clearly in the charge and specification, and it seems to me it is not competent to aggravate the offense of which he is charged, and of which they seek to prove him guilty, by proving that he has been unfaithful to the Government in other respects and at other times, and it can be introduced for no other purpose than that of aggravating his alleged offenses in connection with this conspiracy. That course of testimony would be, in effect, to allow the prosecution to initiate testimony as to the previous character of the accused; and that is a right that is reserved to the accused, and is never allowed to the prosecution. It would do more than that: it would allow them to do what the accused is not allowed on his own behalf on the point of character—that is, to show acts wholly unconnected with the crimes with which he is charged, from which his previous character may be inferred.

The JUDGE ADVOCATE. I think the testimony in this case has proved, what I believe history sufficiently attests, how kindred to each other are the crimes of treason against a nation and the assassination of its chief magistrate. I think of those crimes the one seems to be, if not the necessary consequence, certainly a logical sequence from the other. The murder of the President of the United States, as alleged and shown, was pre-eminently a political assassination. Disloyalty to the Government was its sole inspiration. When, therefore, we shall show, on the part of the accused, acts of intense disloyalty, bearing arms in the field against that Government, we show with him the presence of an *animus* toward the Government which relieves this accusation of much, if not all, of its improbability. And this course of proof is constantly resorted to in criminal courts. I do not regard it as in the slightest degree a departure from the usages of the profession in the administration of public justice. The purpose is to show that the prisoner, in his mind and course of life, was prepared for the commission of this crime; that the tendencies of his life, as evidenced by open and overt acts, lead and point to this crime, if not as a necessary, certainly as a most probable result, and it is with that view, and that only, that the testimony is offered.

Mr. EWING. Can the learned Judge Advocate produce authority to sustain his position?

Assistant Judge Advocate BINGHAM. There is abundance of authority to sustain the position. In Roscoe there is express authority. The book is not here now, but as the gentleman calls for authority, I will state now, and pledge myself to bring the book into the court-room, that Roscoe's Criminal Evidence, about page 85 or 89, contains the express text in the body of it, that when the intent with which a thing is done is in issue, other acts of the prisoner not in issue, to prove that intent, may be given in evidence, and that is exactly the point that is made here by the Judge Advocate General. It is not the point contemplated by the counsel, and, putting it on the ground on which he puts it, nobody contends for it. It is alleged in this charge and specification that this party engaged in this conspiracy to murder the President of the United States, to murder the Secretary of State, to murder the Vice-President, and to murder Lieutenant-General Grant, the commander of the armies in the field under the direction of the President, with intent to aid the rebellion against the United States. The intent is put in issue here by the charge and specification against all these prisoners, and the attempt now made is to establish that intent by proving what? By proving that this man himself was part of the rebellion; that he was in it. I undertake to say that there is no authority which is fit to be read in a court of justice any where that can be brought against it.

I may remark, in this connection, that the general rules of evidence which obtain in the courts of the common law, are always recognized by the military courts. The

ground on which it is put—I state the authority in words—is that on a criminal trial, where the intent is in issue, other acts of the prisoner not in issue may be proved against him by the prosecution, in order to show that intent. The cases are very numerous.

Mr. EWING. Just refer to the allegation.

Assistant Judge Advocate BINGHAM. The gentleman asks me to refer to the allegation. I will. The charge is, "Maliciously, unlawfully, and traitorously, and in aid of the existing armed rebellion against the United States of America, on or before the 6th day of March, A. D. 1865, combining, confederating, and conspiring together," with the persons named in the charge, "and others unknown, to kill and murder, within the Military Department of Washington, and within the fortified and intrenched lines thereof, Abraham Lincoln," etc. Combining, confederating, and conferring together "in aid of the existing armed rebellion against the United States of America," is the allegation; that is the intent.

Mr. EWING. It is an allegation of fact, and not of intent.

Assistant Judge Advocate BINGHAM. I understand the gentleman, but I assert that the words there used, "in aid of the existing armed rebellion against the United States of America," are words of intent; the formality of an indictment is simply departed from. If the charge had followed the common-law form, it would have read, "With intent to aid the existing armed rebellion against the United States, the parties did then and there agree, combine, and confederate together, to kill and murder the President of the United States." These words are not the express terms used, but they are by necessary implication implied; it is nothing but an allegation of intent, and never was any thing else. It is no part of the body of the charge beyond the allegation of intent.

Then comes the specification in regard to the prisoner, Arnold. The first clause of the specification is that the various persons here on trial, "and others unknown, citizens of the United States aforesaid, and who were then engaged in armed rebellion against the United States of America, within the limits thereof, did, in aid of said armed rebellion, on or before the 6th day of March, A. D. 1865, and on divers other days and times between that day and the 15th day of April, A. D. 1865, combine, confederate, and conspire together, at Washington City, within the Military Department of Washington, and within the intrenched fortifications and military lines of the said United States, there being, unlawfully, maliciously, and traitorously to kill and murder Abraham Lincoln," etc., . . . "and, by the means aforesaid, to aid and comfort the insurgents engaged in armed rebellion against the said United States as aforesaid." Is not that the same as saying, "designing and intending thereby to aid and comfort the insurgents engaged in armed rebellion against the United States?" There is the specification, and I should like to know how an intent could be laid any more strongly than that, or more formally than that. It is an allegation of intent, and I say the question stands on authority.

Mr. EWING. If the Court will allow me, I will refer to an authority enunciating the great principle which I claim:

"Evidence will not be admitted on the part of the prosecution to show the bad character of the accused, unless he has called witnesses in support of his character, and even then the prosecution can not examine as to particular act." (Benét on Military Law and Courts-martial, p. 287.)

That is the general principle of law, which is, doubtless, familiar to the Court; but the learned gentleman seeks to take this case out of the general principle, upon the argument that it is alleged in the charge that the crimes for which the accused is being tried, were done with the intent of aiding the rebellion. Now, if, by the practice of military courts, the allegation that these crimes were committed with intent to aid the rebellion, were a necessary allegation, the Court should reject the testimony now offered on the ground of irrelevancy. The acts charged are acts of conspiracy to murder the President, the heads of Government, and the leader of the armies of the United States during the existence of the rebellion; and proof of these acts would be conclusive as to the intent to aid the rebellion; and that evidence of intent would not be in the least aided by proof of service in the Confederate army prior to and unconnected with the acts of conspiracy.

But the allegation of intent here is an *unnecessary* allegation. The crimes charged are the crimes of murder and attempted assassination, and it is unnecessary to go further, and allege that they were done with the intent to aid the rebellion.

If, to support this unnecessary allegation as to intent, the Court should admit evidence which would be inadmissible in the civil courts in a trial on an indictment for the crimes here charged, it would, I think, violate the law of evidence, because the prosecution has seen fit to disregard the rules of pleading. The law of evidence is—and it applies to cases of conspiracy as to all other criminal cases—that the prosecution can show no criminal acts, not part of the *res gestæ* of the offenses charged, unless the offenses charged consist of acts which are not in themselves obviously unlawful, and from the commission of which, therefore, the evil intent can not be presumed—such as uttering forged instruments, or counterfeit money, or receiving stolen goods.

Before any jury, or almost any body of men, proof that a person charged with one crime, and on trial, had before that committed some other crime, would prejudice his cause materially; and it is to avoid that result that this wholesome rule of law has been established.

That the assassination of the President grew out of the spirit of the rebellion, and was one of its monstrous developments, is most true; but the prisoners who are here on trial, are to be tried on evidence admissible under the rules of law, and the accused was not called upon to show here whether or not, a year or eighteen months before this alleged conspiracy was begun, he committed the crime of having taken up arms against his Government. He is not on trial for that, and I think it is unjust to prejudice his case by hearing and recording evidence of it, if such evidence can, in fact, be produced.

I refer the Court, in further support of my objection, to Wharton's Criminal Law, vol. I, p. 297, and Roscoe's Criminal Evidence, p. 76.

Assistant Judge Advocate BINGHAM. I have no desire to delay the Court; but I am very anxious to make good what I said, and to vindicate the proposition of the Judge Advocate General. My proposition was, that when the intent with which a thing was done is put in issue, other acts of the prisoner not in issue on the trial, of the same character, may be given in evidence to prove that intent. Now I propose to read from the book which the gentleman himself has read; but he did not read quite far enough:

"Knowledge and intent, when material, must be shown by the prosecution." (Wharton's American Criminal Law, p. 309, sec. 631.)

It becomes material here, because it is alleged as to the conspirators that they conspired with the intent to aid this rebellion, both in the charge and in the specification; not that they murdered with that intent, but conspired to murder with that intent, to aid the rebellion. The language of this author (Wharton) is, "Knowledge and intent, when material, must be shown by the prosecution. It is impossible, it is true, in most cases, to make them out by direct evidence, unless they have been confessed, but may be gathered from the conduct of the party as shown in proof; and when the tendency of his actions is direct and manifest, he must always be presumed to have designed the result when he acted."

As to guilty knowledge, on the same page of the book, the author says:

"The law in this respect seems to be, that evidence of other acts, or conduct of a similar character, even although involving substantive crimes, is admissible to prove guilty knowledge," even although it shows other crimes not involved before the Court. On the very next page the same author says:

"The same evidence is generally admissible to prove intent as to show guilty knowledge."

That is to say, other acts, although involving substantive crime, may be admitted. On the point the gentleman made, the writer concludes on that question by saying, "That if the crime itself is committed, the intent is necessarily presumed by the law." To be sure it is. But there are two allegations here. One is a conspiracy—

Mr. EWING. To murder the President.

Assistant Judge Advocate BINGHAM. A conspiracy, with intent to aid the rebellion, to murder the President; and then there is the murdering of the President in aid of the rebellion, in pursuance of the conspiracy. Now, we are trying to prove the intent with which they entered into this conspiracy, and executed it. This book, in answer to that suggestion of the gentleman, says:

"A defendant's conduct during the *res gestæ*, as his manner at the time of passing the note, or his having passed by several names, is also admissible for the same purpose; but the intent, the guilty knowledge, must be brought directly home to the defendant; but in no case can evidence tending to show it be admitted, until the *corpus delicti* is first clearly shown." What then? Then it may be.

Mr. EWING. That is the *res gestæ*.

Assistant Judge Advocate BINGHAM. No, as to the intent. What becomes of the objection now? The body of the crime has been proved according to the practice of the common law, as a general thing, and the only exception that I know of, of any note, is the exception made at common law in cases of conspiracy, which the gentleman will remember is written in the text of Starkie. Then what next? In order to prove the intent, you may have other acts of the prisoner, although they involve substantive crime; and the same text and section of Wharton goes on to say:

"On the charge of sending a threatening letter, prior and subsequent letters from the person to the party threatening may be given in evidence, as explanatory of the meaning and intent of the particular letter upon which the indictment is framed." What do you say to that?

Mr. EWING. I say it does not apply at all.

Assistant Judge Advocate BINGHAM. I say it does apply; that sending prior and subsequent letters is a distinctive crime, for which he might also be indicted, and entering into this is a distinctive crime, for which the party may be also arraigned; but when he entered it, he entered into it to aid it, did he not?

Mr. EWING. He did not enter into that to assassinate the President.

Assistant Judge Advocate BINGHAM. Yes, he entered into it to assassinate the President; and everybody else that entered into the rebellion, entered it to assassinate everybody that represented this Government, that either followed the standard in the field, or represented its standard in the councils. That is exactly why it is german.

The Commission overruled the objection.

WITNESS.—I can not state positively of my own knowledge that the accused, Samuel Arnold, has been in the military service of the rebellion. I have seen him in Richmond with the rebel uniform on; whether it was the uniform of a private soldier or an officer, I can not remember. This was in the year 1862.

Cross-examined by MR. EWING.

I would not say positively that it was not in 1861 I saw him. I know he had been ill, but I can not state the year positively. I saw him several times; it was since the rebellion.

JAMES L. McPHAIL.

Recalled for the Prosecution.—May 18.

[Exhibiting the "Sam" letter to the witness.]

I think that letter is in the handwriting of Samuel Arnold; the direction, "J. Wilkes Booth," I should also think is his. I am acquainted with the handwriting of the prisoner, from having received a letter of his from his father, dated the 12th of April, from Fortress Monroe, the writing of which looks similar to that of this letter signed "Sam."

LITTLETON P. D. NEWMAN.

For the Prosecution.—May 18.

I know the accused, Samuel Arnold. On the 9th, 10th, or 12th of September, Mr. Arnold had been helping us to thrash wheat at a neighbor's, and during that time there was a letter brought to him. In that letter there was either a twenty or a fifty-dollar note; I am not positive which. He read the letter, and remarked that he was flush of money, or something to that effect. After having read the letter, he handed it to me, and I read some half a dozen lines, possibly—not more. I did not understand it; it was very ambiguous in its language; and I handed it back to him, and asked him what it meant. He remarked that something big would take place one of these days, or be seen in the paper, or something to that effect. That was about all that occurred.

I do not remember that I saw the signature to the letter; if I did, I do not remember what it was.

The JUDGE ADVOCATE here announced that the testimony on the part of the Government had closed.

See testimony of

DEFENSE OF SAMUEL ARNOLD.

WILLIAM S. ARNOLD.

For the Defense.—May 31.

By Mr. Ewing.

I am brother to the prisoner, Samuel Arnold, and reside at Hookstown, Baltimore County, Md. From the 21st of March up to Saturday, the 25th, my brother was with me in the country, at Hookstown.

We went into Baltimore on Saturday evening, the 25th, and returned to the country again on Sunday, the 26th. We came again into town either on Tuesday or Wednesday. I went to the country again, and came in on Friday night. He went out with me on the 1st of April, and in the afternoon he went to Fortress Monroe.

As I was coming into Baltimore on the 21st, I saw him in the coach going to Hookstown. From the 21st to the 25th, I saw him every day, and he slept with me every night. We arrived in Baltimore on the 25th, between 5 and 6 o'clock. I saw my brother at supper at my father's, and when I went to bed, between 9 and 10 o'clock, he was in bed. When we got up the next morning, I went down to the Government bakery, left him at home, told him I would be back in about half an hour, and we would go out in the country together. When I came back he was home, and between 9 and 10 o'clock that morning we started for the country. He staid there until the 28th or 29th, and I saw him every day and every night. It was on either a Tuesday or a Wednesday that he left, about 8 o'clock. I saw him next on Friday, when I came in from the country to my father's; my brother was there to supper. He was at home at my father's on that night. I did not sleep with him; my brother did; and I slept in the same room. The next day, Saturday, I took him out in the country. We started about 8 o'clock, and came in between 12 and 1 at noon. In the afternoon, between 3 and 4, he left for Fortress Monroe. That was on the 1st of April. I am certain about these dates. Hookstown is about six miles from Baltimore.

Cross-examined by ASSISTANT JUDGE ADVOCATE BURNETT.

I can fix the date of the 21st as being the day on which I saw my brother in the coach going to Hookstown, as I was going to Baltimore, because on that day Mr. Buffington, of the Three-mile House, had a sale of farming utensils, and Mr. Ditch had a sale the day before, at which I bought *some things,* and entered them in my book.

I do not know where my brother was between supper and bedtime on the next Saturday; I went out and left him at home, and he was in bed when I came back. On the following day he went back to Hookstown, and returned to Baltimore on the Tuesday or Wednesday. He gave those arms to me on the 1st of April, when he went to Fortress Monroe. He had had them out in the country from the day he went there, the 21st. The pistol was loaded when it was given to me.

[The pistol found in Arnold's bag at Fortress Monroe shown to the witness.]

That is not the pistol my brother gave to me; he gave me the pistol and knife by themselves. They were not in the valise. I did not give them to anybody, but I remember my father coming to the desk where they were placed, getting them, and taking them to Baltimore. It was a large-sized pistol, something like the one just shown me.

By Mr. Ewing.

On the 20th of March, I saw my brother shoot off two rounds out of the pistol, at the chickens; then he went into the house and reloaded it. I was at the door, and did not see him reload it.

FRANK ARNOLD.

For the Defense.—May 31.

By Mr. Ewing.

The accused, Samuel Arnold, is my brother. I generally reside at my father's in Baltimore. I saw my brother on the 30th and 31st of March last; Thursday and Friday. On the Friday morning I gave him a letter, which came for him from Mr. Wharton, in reference to his application for a situation, telling him to come down, and he went down on Saturday afternoon, the 1st of April, on the Norfolk boat, at about half-past 4. Captain Moffatt of the Eighth Maryland took a state-room with him.

By ASSISTANT JUDGE ADVOCATE BINGHAM.

My brother had made application for employment to Mr. Wharton, but I do not know the date.

JACOB SMITH.

For the Defense.—May 31

By Mr. Ewing.

I live in Hookstown, Baltimore County, Md.; about half a mile from the residence of William S. Arnold, brother of the prisoner, Samuel Arnold. Our farms join. From the 20th to the 22d of March last, up to near the

30th, as near as I can get at it, I saw the prisoner, Samuel Arnold, nearly every day; sometimes three or four times a day.

Cross-examined by ASSISTANT JUDGE ADVOCATE BURNETT.

I can not be sure whether it was the 20th or 22d that I saw him. I do not think it was the 23d or 19th. I have no particular reason for fixing the date; only an indistinct recollection of it. It is just about the same with the 30th; I kept no note of it.

By MR. EWING.

I was over at his brother's place several times during that period. I used to go there for marketing stuff to take to the city; and I used to go right in the field and get it. It was only on those occasions that I saw him on his brother's place, and coming over.

CHARLES B. HALL.

For the Defense.—June 2.

By MR. EWING.

For the past two months I have been at Fortress Monroe, as clerk to Mr. Wharton, a sutler there. His store is outside of the fortification, at what is called "Old Point." I got acquainted with the prisoner, Samuel Arnold, at Mr. Wharton's store. He came there the latter part of March, or 1st of April. He was employed by Mr. Wharton to assist him in book-keeping. I think he staid there two weeks and one day. I saw him every day, but not all the time.

I was engaged in another place part of the time. Mr. Wharton has the contract for Fortress Monroe. I was engaged there from about 7 o'clock until 2. I had business then at the lower store; and at about 5 o'clock I would return.

I can not say positively, but I think it was about the 1st of March that he made the application in writing for employment. I only know of one letter from him, the one I answered, telling him to come, and he came in about a week. Major Stevens, a Government officer, has Arnold's letter. Arnold staid at the lower store and slept at Mr. Wharton's. I saw him every night.

Cross-examined by ASSISTANT JUDGE ADVOCATE BINGHAM.

I was not at all acquainted with him before he came there. He opened the correspondence himself, as far as I know, in March last.

GEORGE CRAIG.

For the Defense.—May 31.

By MR. EWING.

I have lived at Old Point during the past two months, and have been employed as salesman in Mr. Wharton's store. I have

seen the prisoner, Samuel Arnold, there; he was a clerk—chief-clerk, I believe—in the same establishment. He came there on a Sunday morning, some time in the latter part of March or the 1st of April, and remained there about two weeks, up to the time of his arrest. I saw him every day during that time.

MINNIE POLE.

For the Defense.—June 7.

I reside in Baltimore. I am acquainted with the prisoner, Samuel Arnold. I saw him in that city on the 20th, 27th and 28th of April. On the 20th, I saw him in an omnibus, going to Hookstown; and on the 28th, I saw him at our house on his way to Baltimore. I have not seen him since, until now.

EATON G. HORNER.

For the Defense.—June 6.

By MR. EWING.

The facts stated to me by the accused, Samuel Arnold, to which I have testified, were communicated to me by Arnold at Fortress Monroe. He did not speak of any thing that occurred on the boat. The confession of Samuel Arnold, referred to by William McPhail, was written in Marshal McPhail's office.

JOHN W. WHARTON.

For the Defense.—June 7.

By MR. EWING.

I live in the city of Baltimore; my place of business is at Fortress Monroe, outside.

The prisoner, Samuel Arnold, was in my employ from the 2d of April to the 17th, when he was arrested. He was employed by the week as a clerk. I was absent about three days during that time, but I have reason to believe he was there all the time, or I should have been told of his absence. He was employed by me in consequence of a letter received by me from his father; also one from himself.

Q. In that letter did he make any reference to the business in which he had theretofore been engaged?

Assistant Judge Advocate BINGHAM replied, that if the letter were here, it would be utterly inadmissible in regard to any thing contained in it about his former pursuits or whereabouts, and doings of any sort, for the simple reason that a party could not, either in writing or orally, make evidence at his pleasure, to bar the doors of justice against the power of the Government, which he is charged to have offended. Heretofore, testimony had been admitted as to the contents of the letter, so far as to show that Arnold had applied to the witness for employment. That had been admitted, because

16

it seemed perhaps to be fair to the accused without doing injustice to the Government. He had the benefit of that application, but the proposition now made was entirely inadmissible.

Mr. EWING stated that it had been proved that the letter in question was taken from the store of the witness by Major Smith, an officer of the United States, at the time of Arnold's arrest; the Judge Advocate had been requested some days since to produce the letter, and he had been unable to find it; so that if the letter itself would be admissible in evidence, it was now competent to prove its contents by parol. It was a declaration by the prisoner, Arnold, at the time of his application to the witness, as to his having abandoned the business in which he had formerly been engaged. Under the latitude of examination which had been indulged in on the part of the prosecution, this proof might fairly be admitted.

The JUDGE ADVOCATE. We have established that intimacy clearly in their association in Washington. We are simply following them to Baltimore, and showing that there they were in correspondence with each other. It is a fact of the same order, and although it may not have the same force with the other fact, its tendency certainly is in the same direction. We do not offer the contents of the letter; we offer the fact of their correspondence with each other.

The Court sustained the objection.

Each of the counsel for the accused here announced, on behalf of his client, that the defense was closed.

Tuesday, May 16, 1865.

DISCUSSION ON THE DAILY READING OF THE RECORD.

The PRESIDENT. One of the members of the Court has moved that the reading of the record be dispensed with, inasmuch as the counsel on the part of the prisoners are furnished with an official copy of the record, and have an opportunity of examining it during the intervals between the meetings of the Court, and can object to any thing that is incorrect, when they come into Court, if they find any inaccuracies.

Colonel TOMPKINS. Besides, it is very accurately published in the morning papers.

Mr. EWING. If the Court will allow me, I will state that the reporters are not able to furnish us immediately with an official copy of the record; it is always behindhand a day or so; but inasmuch as the record is published quite accurately in the Intelligencer, from the notes of the reporters, if the Court will allow us the privilege at any time, even though it be not the day after the examination of a witness, in case we discover an error, to ask that the witness be recalled, it would be satisfactory, so far as I am concerned. If this arrangement is made, it will be necessary for the Judge Advocate to detain witnesses for, say, two days after their examination, so that we may have time to read the testimony as published in the paper, or as furnished us by the reporters. We have not yet been furnished with the last of yesterday's proceedings, nor has that portion been published in the paper.

The PRESIDENT. I should think a detention of one day would be ample.

Mr. EWING. If the witnesses who were examined yesterday were detained until after the Court meets to-morrow, I think that would be sufficient. The evidence of the last witnesses examined yesterday will probably be published in the Intelligencer to-morrow.

The PRESIDENT. Has the Judge Advocate any objection to that arrangement?

The JUDGE ADVOCATE. I do not wish to embarrass the Court, certainly, by any suggestions of mine. I am as anxious for the dispatch of business as anybody can be; but if this precedent is now established, it will be, I think, not only the first one which has been set in the military service, but the first in the civil service. I never, in my whole life, have been in connection with any court, the proceedings of which were not read over in the hearing of the court itself, before they were declared by the court to be accurate and complete. Although I have as much confidence in the accuracy of our reporters as anybody can have, I think it would be a dangerous example to set, and I would rather see it in any case that has arisen in the military service of the country than in this, where there are so many lives at stake, and where it is so vastly important, not only that there should be strict accuracy, but that the country should feel assured that it is so, and that all the precautions necessary to secure that result, have been resorted to. If it shall be known hereafter, in connection with this trial, that the Court departed from the usages of the service, and did not even have its own record read over, but trusted simply to the reporters for accuracy, it might go very far to shake the confidence of the country in the accuracy of these reports, and would certainly leave an opening for criticism.

General FOSTER. I think the reading should be proceeded with every morning for the purpose of correction, if any correction should be necessary.

The PRESIDENT. I am very much inclined, after hearing the opinion of the Judge Advocate General, to change my first impression on the subject, and I will vote against the proposition, though I thought favorably of it at first.

The motion was then withdrawn, and the record was read and approved.

Thursday, June 8, 1865.

Mr. AIKEN proposed to offer in evidence a telegraphic dispatch from Montreal, Canada, containing an affidavit of John McCullough, made before the Vice-Consul of the United States in Montreal, for the purpose of contradicting a statement made by Louis J. Weichmann, a witness for the prosecution, that he had seen McCullough at Booth's room in the National Hotel on the 2d day of April last.

Assistant Judge Advocate BINGHAM objected to the introduction of the paper. It was a wholly immaterial question whether McCullough ever met Weichmann or not.

Mr. AIKEN claimed that it was competent to disprove any statement made by Weichmann which was not true. Mr. Weichmann had sworn to certain statements which were contradicted in this sworn affidavit of Mr. McCullough. If he was mistaken in such small matters, might he not also be mistaken in the greater matter of the guilt or innocence of some of the accused.

Assistant Judge Advocate BINGHAM replied that this was an illegal mode of attacking a witness. If, on cross-examination, a witness is asked an immaterial question, his answer concludes the party asking the question.

The JUDGE ADVOCATE proposed to read to the Court an authority on this point, as it was raised so often, and might be again; and he wished the authority borne in mind, namely:

"*Irrelevant* questions will not be allowed to be put to a witness on cross-examination, although they relate to facts opened by the other party, but not proved in evidence. Nor can a witness be cross-examined as to any facts which, if admitted, would be collateral and wholly irrelevant to the matters in issue, for the purpose of contradicting him by other evidence, and in this manner to discredit his testimony. And if the witness answers such an irrelevant question before it is disallowed or withdrawn, evidence can not afterward be admitted to contradict his testimony on the collateral matter." (Benét, p. 307.)

Assistant Judge Advocate BINGHAM stated that the same position was sustained by Roscoe's Criminal Evidence, p. 87, from which he read the following extract:

"*Evidence to contradict the opponent witness.*—This may always be given or put in relevant to the issue. But if any opponent's witness be asked questions on cross-examination which are not relevant to the issue—which, as we shall hereafter see, may be done, (p. 146)—the answer must be taken, and he can not be contradicted by other evidence. *Spenceley* v. *DeWillott*, 7 East. 108; *R.* v. *Yewin*, 2 Camp., 638, where a witness was asked whether he had not been charged with robbing the prisoner, his master, which he denied, and Lawrence, J., refused to allow him to be contradicted on this point." (Roscoe's Criminal Evidence, p. 87.)

The Court sustained the objection.

June 8, 1865.

Mr. EWING offered in evidence, on the part of the defense, a copy of General Orders No. 26, War Department, Adjutant-General's Office, Washington, February 2, 1863, as follows:

WAR DEPARTMENT,
ADJUTANT-GENERAL'S OFFICE,
Washington, February 2, 1863.

General Orders No. 26.

The district of country north of the Potomac River, from Piscataway Creek to Annapolis Junction and the mouth of the Monocacy, and south by Goose Creek and Bull Run Mountain to the mouth of the Occoquan, will constitute the Department of Washington, and troops in that department will constitute the Twenty-second Army Corps, to be commanded by Major-General Heintzelman.

By order of the Secretary of War.
L. THOMAS,
Adjutant-General.

Mr. EWING, with the consent of the Judge Advocate, offered as evidence of the same validity, as if the same fact were testified to by Mr. John McCullough, the actor, on the stand, the following telegraphic dispatch:

MONTREAL, June 2, 1865.

To John T. Ford, National Hotel:

I left Washington on Monday evening, March 26th, and have not been there since. You can have my testimony before American Consul here, if requisite.
JOHN McCULLOUGH.

The JUDGE ADVOCATE offered in evidence, for the prosecution, the proclamation of the President of the United States, for the information and government of the army and all concerned, dated September 25, 1862, with accompanying certificate of the Secretary of War, dated May 30, 1865.

[See Appendix, page 673.]

The JUDGE ADVOCATE also offered in evidence, for the prosecution, General Orders No. 100, Adjutant-General's Office, Washington, April 24, 1863, containing "Instructions for the government of the armies of the United States in the field," prepared by Francis Leiber, LL.D., and revised by a Board of Officers, of which Major-General E. A. Hitchcock was president.

[See Appendix, page 410.]

June 12, 1865.

Assistant Judge Advocate BINGHAM offered in evidence certified copies of the journals of the joint sessions of the Senate and the House of Representatives on the 2d Wednesday of February, 1861, and the 2d Wednesday of February, 1865 (certified to be correct copies by the Clerk of the House of Representatives, under the seal of that House,) showing that Abraham Lincoln and Hannibal Hamlin were elected President and Vice-President of the United States, for the term of four years, commencing on the 4th day of March, 1861, and that Abraham Lincoln and Andrew Johnson were elected President and Vice-President of the United States, for the term of four years, commencing on the 4th day of March, 1865.

[Votes for President and Vice-President of the United States for the constitutional term, commencing on the 4th day of March, 1861.

Number of States	33
Number of Electoral Votes	303
Abraham Lincoln, for President	180
John C. Breckinridge, for President	72
John Bell, of Tennessee, for President	39
Stephen A. Douglas, for President	12
Hannibal Hamlin, for Vice-President	180
Joseph Lane, for Vice-President	72
Edward Everett, for Vice-President	39
Herschel V. Johnson, for Vice-President	12

Votes for President and Vice-President of the United States for the constitutional term, commencing on the 4th day of March, 1865.

Number of States (Kansas, West Virginia, and Nevada being added since 1861)	36
Number of Electoral Votes (Virginia, North Carolina, South Carolina, Georgia, Tennessee, Louisiana, Mississippi, Alabama, Arkansas, Florida, and Texas not voting)	233
Abraham Lincoln, for President	212
George B. McClellan, for President	21
Andrew Johnson, for Vice President	212
George H. Pendleton, for Vice-President	21

Certified to as being a correct extract from the Journal of the Senate of the United States of 13th February, 1861, and 8th February, 1865, respectively.

(Signed,) JOHN W. FORNEY.]

BRIGADIER-GENERAL E. D. TOWNSEND.

Recalled for the Prosecution.

Q. Do you know the fact that Abraham Lincoln acted as President of the United States from and after the 4th of March, 1861, until the 15th of April, 1865, when he died?

A. Yes, sir; I had frequent official intercourse with him as President of the United States during that time.

Q. Do you know the fact that Hannibal Hamlin acted as Vice-President during the four years preceding the 4th day of March, 1865?

A. Yes, sir.

Q. And that afterward Andrew Johnson acted as Vice-President until the death of Abraham Lincoln, on the 15th of April, 1865?

A. Yes, sir.

Assistant Judge Advocate BINGHAM offered in evidence a certified copy, under the seal of the Department of State, of the oath of office of Andrew Johnson, as President of the United States, before the Chief-Justice, on the 15th day of April, 1865.

Also a duly certified copy of the resolution of the Senate, dated March 5, 1861, consenting to the appointment, and advising the same, of William H. Seward as Secretary of State of the United States; and, also, a duly certified copy of the commission of William H. Seward as Secretary of State of the United States, dated March 5, 1861, signed by Abraham Lincoln, President of the United States, and attested by J. S. Black, Secretary of State, under the seal of the United States.

June 14, 1865.

Mr. EWING. On behalf of Mr. Stone and myself, who are jointly counsel for Dr. Samuel A. Mudd, and who separately represent other of the defendants, I ask leave to say to the Court, that the arguments in defense of those of the prisoners we represent, can not be made in such manner as to give efficient aid to the Court in its investigation of the questions arising under the charge and specification preferred, unless the said charge and specification are relieved of ambiguity by an opening statement from the Judge Advocate, indicating the offense or offenses, for the commission of which he may claim those of the accused whom we represent should severally be convicted, and the laws creating such offense or offenses, and prescribing the penalties thereof. In support of this suggestion we submit the following reasons:

I There is but one charge, *in form*, against the accused; but, *in fact*, there seem to be four charges, each alleging the commission of a separate and distinct offense, as follows:

1. Maliciously, unlawfully, and in aid of the existing armed rebellion against the United States of America, combining, confederating, and conspiring to kill and murder, within the military department of Washington, and within the defenses of the city, Abraham Lincoln, late, and at the time of conspiring, President of the United States, and Commander-in-chief of the army and navy thereof; Andrew Johnson, then Vice-President of the United States; William H. Seward, Secretary of State; and Ulysses S. Grant, Lieutenant-General of the army, etc.

2. In pursuance of said malicious, unlawful, and traitorous conspiracy, maliciously, unlawfully, and traitorously murdering the said Abraham Lincoln, President, etc.

3. Maliciously, unlawfully, and traitor-

ously assaulting, with intent to kill and murder, the said William H. Seward, Secretary of State, etc.

4. Lying in wait with intent maliciously, unlawfully, and traitorously to kill and murder the said Andrew Johnson, then Vice-President of the United States, and Ulysses S. Grant, Lieutenant-General, etc.

The offenses enumerated, as aforesaid, in the said charge, are separate and distinct, and we, therefore, ask that the Judge Advocate should state, in regard to those of the accused whom we represent, of which of said offenses, under the evidence, he claims they should each be convicted.

II. We further respectfully say we are not advised of the law creating and defining certain of said offenses, as the same are laid in the said charge, and therefore ask that the Judge Advocate specify the law creating said offenses, or the code or system of laws in which the same may be found, that we may be able to present the case of such of the accused as we represent, in a manner conducive to the ends of justice, and therefore more satisfactory to the Court.

The crime of murder—assault with intent to kill and murder, conspiracy to murder, and conspiracy in aid of the rebellion—are well understood and accurately defined by the common or statute law, and for the commission of those crimes just and appropriate penalties have been prescribed; but no laws known to us define the crime of "traitorously" murdering, or of "traitorously" assaulting with intent to kill and murder, or of lying in wait "traitorously" to kill and murder. If the last-named offenses, designated and described in the charge, are created crimes by some code of laws unknown to us, and penalties are prescribed for their commission by such code, it is respectfully submitted that to advise us of what that code is, before we are called upon to present our arguments, could certainly not defeat, and might materially promote the ends of justice.

III. We further respectfully state, that the Constitution of the United States provides that in all criminal prosecutions the accused shall be entitled to be informed of the nature and cause of the accusations against them. That several of the offenses charged are, if they are crimes defined by the Constitution or the laws, offenses in the trial of which rules of evidence are applicable, different in important respects from the general rules of criminal evidence. And the accused have the right now (as they have had the right at all prior stages of this trial) to know for which of the offenses each is severally held, so that counsel and the Court may know what part of the evidence presented against all is applicable to the cases of the accused severally. And that the constitutional guaranty above referred to, in our judgment, entitles the accused to such designation of the specific charges on which it

may be claimed each should be convicted, as well as to an indication of the code of laws by which the last three of the offenses as charged are defined, and their punishments provided.

The Judge Advocate. If the Court please, when I recall the character of the pleadings in this case, the complete distinctness of the charge and of the specification, I confess myself somewhat surprised at the appeal which is now made to the Government on behalf of the counsel for the prisoners. Certainly, if I were to go over the ground again, either orally or by writing, I could not make known to the counsel with more certainty, or with more appropriateness or terseness of language, than has been already employed in these pleadings, the precise offenses with which the prisoners are charged, on which they have been arraigned, in reference to which the entire range of inquiry has been directed, and upon which the judgment of this Court is finally asked.

The general allegation is a conspiracy; and certainly the gentleman would not ask me to expound to him the law of conspiracy, nor to bring from the library here the books which treat upon it. As a professional gentleman of eminence, he is entirely familiar with the range of the authorities on that general subject.

The pleadings proceed, after averring this conspiracy, (in which it is alleged all these prisoners participated,) to set forth clearly and specifically the part which it is believed and alleged each one of them took in the execution of that conspiracy.

The investigation here has carefully followed the line of allegation. We have sought, in every instance, to show, as far as the testimony would enable the Government to do, that these parties, in the execution of the conspiracy, performed precisely the acts which it was charged they had performed.

Now, it can not be possible, in view of these allegations, and in view of the proofs which have been sifted again and again, in the presence of the gentleman and those associated with him, that he can have any doubt, or can feel any embarrassment as to the precise measure and manner of criminality which is charged upon these parties, and upon which the judgment of this Court is invoked. They are all alleged to have participated in the general conspiracy, and in the execution of that conspiracy, so far as the assassination of the President is concerned; and then the particular parts which each one performed therein afterward, either in execution or in the attempt to execute, are set forth. It is for the Court to determine how far the proof sustains these allegations; but it can not be that the gentleman is left with any doubt to embarrass him as to the precise ground on which the judgment of this Court is asked in reference to each of these parties.

Then, as to the law applicable to this case: that is a matter of which the counsel are expected to take notice. We have no special statute to which we can point him. We have the great principles of jurisprudence, which regulate this trial, with which he is familiar, with which all men belonging to his profession are expected and held to be familiar. I do not suppose we shall introduce a solitary authority which will in any manner surprise the gentleman, or with which he is not already perfectly conversant. If I had any such, I should certainly gladly produce it for his inspection and consideration in advance. But I decline making a formal opening on the part of the Government. It is not necessary. It is not in accordance with the practice of military courts, and in this case I have not felt that I was at all required to depart from the usage on that subject. This investigation has been conducted in the frankest and most open manner, and the gentleman is just as familiar as the Judge Advocates, who represent the Government, are with all the facts of this case, on which these parties are sought to be charged. As to the legal inferences which result from those facts, he must be expected also to be advised.

Mr. EWING. I see no answer in the statement of the learned Judge Advocate to the request that I have made. I understand from the Judge Advocate that the only crime charged against these parties is conspiracy. Am I right?

The JUDGE ADVOCATE. A conspiracy, as alleged, to murder the President of the United States, and the members of the Government mentioned, and the execution of that conspiracy as far as it went, and the attempt to execute it as far as alleged.

Mr. EWING. But I ask what crimes are charged? I should like to have them enumerated.

The JUDGE ADVOCATE. I confess that my knowledge of language does not afford me any more distinct designations than those which I have employed in these pleadings.

General KAUTZ. It seems to me this application should have been made when the charge and specification were first read.

Assistant Judge Advocate BURNETT. If the pleadings were not sufficiently distinct, that was the time when a request should have been made to correct them.

Mr. EWING. The application is certainly pertinent now, and it would, of course, have been pertinent at the beginning. I did not see the charge and specification until after my clients had pleaded; nor did I get a seat in the court-room until evidence was being introduced. I have devoted a great deal of time to the study of this charge and specification, and the statement which I have presented is presented in entire good faith, for the purpose of learning whether my clients ——— charged with, and being tried for, four

distinct crimes—to-wit: conspiracy, murder, assault and battery with intent to kill, and lying in wait—or whether they are charged simply with one crime—conspiracy. And after the same deliberate consideration of the charge and specification, I am utterly unable to know in what code or system of laws the crimes of "traitorously murdering," "traitorously lying in wait," "traitorously assaulting with intent to kill," are defined and their punishments provided. I should like an answer to the question, how many distinct crimes are the accused charged with, and what are those crimes? I can not tell, from the charge and specification with certainty.

Assistant Judge Advocate BINGHAM. I understood you to say there were four.

Mr. EWING. It seems to me so, but I should like to know whether I am right in that.

The JUDGE ADVOCATE. I stated, in the brief remarks I submitted, that I regarded them all as charged with conspiring to assassinate the President of the United States, and the various members of the Government named in the pleadings; and they are further charged with having executed that conspiracy, so far as the assassination of the President was concerned, and the attempt to assassinate the Secretary of State, and to have attempted its execution, so far as concerns the lying in wait and other matters, which are distinctly set forth as indicating the individual action of each of these conspirators in connection with the general programme of crime as charged, all being in pursuance of the conspiracy, all alleged to be in aid of the rebellion, and therefore properly charged as "traitorously" done, as well as feloniously done.

Assistant Judge Advocate BINGHAM. I have no hesitation, if the Judge Advocate General will excuse me in making this remark to Mr. Ewing, not at all under the belief that by it I shall do any thing more than to suggest to him what he already knows, that the act of any one of the parties to a conspiracy in its execution, is the act of every party to that conspiracy; and therefore the charge and specification that the President was murdered in pursuance of it by the hand of Booth, is a direct and unequivocal charge that he was murdered by every one of the parties to this conspiracy, naming the defendants by name. We rely for the support of that part of this case upon the general and accepted rules of the common law, as declared in our own courts, as well as in other courts where the common law obtains.

Mr. EWING. I understand that law of conspiracy perfectly well, but I want to renew again my inquiry, whether these persons are charged with the crime of conspiracy alone, and that these acts of murdering, assaulting, and lying in wait, were merely acts done in execution of that conspiracy— .

Assistant Judge Advocate BINGHAM. And not crimes?

Mr. EWING. Or whether they are charged with four distinct crimes in this one charge?

Assistant Judge Advocate BINGHAM. I answer the gentleman again, that where parties are indicted for a conspiracy, and the execution thereof, it is but one crime at the common law, and that, upon all authority, as many overt acts in the execution of that conspiracy as they are guilty of, may be laid in the same count; and I rest it upon the authority of Hale, and Foster, and Hawkins.

Mr. EWING. It is, then, I understand, one crime with which they are charged.

Assistant Judge Advocate BINGHAM. One crime all round, with various parts performed.

Mr. EWING. The crime of conspiracy.

Assistant Judge Advocate BINGHAM. It is the crime of murder as well. It is not simply conspiring, but executing the conspiracy treasonably and in aid of the rebellion.

Mr. EWING. I should like an answer to my question, if it is to be given: How many distinct crimes are my clients charged with and being tried for? I can not tell.

Assistant Judge Advocate BINGHAM. We have told you, it is all one transaction.

The JUDGE ADVOCATE. It may be my misfortune, but I think it is not my fault, if the gentleman has not already the answer which he seeks. I can not give him a better one.

Mr. EWING. Inasmuch as I get no answer intelligible to me in response to that question, a question of the utmost gravity, a question deeply affecting the lives and liberties of those whom I represent, I now respectfully ask an answer to the other branch of the inquiry: By what code or system of laws is the crime of "traitorously" murdering, or "traitorously" assaulting with intent to kill, or "traitorously" lying in wait, defined?

The JUDGE ADVOCATE. I think the common law of war will reach that case. This is a crime which has been committed in the midst of a great civil war, in the capital of the country, in the camp of the Commander-in-chief of our armies, and if the common law of war can not be enforced against criminals of that character, then I think such a code is in vain in the world.

Mr. EWING. Do you base it, then, only on the law of nations?

The JUDGE ADVOCATE. The common law of war.

Mr. EWING. Is that all the answer to the question?

The JUDGE ADVOCATE. It is the one which I regard as perfectly appropriate to give.

Mr. EWING. I am as much in the dark now as to that as I was in reference to the other inquiry.

General WALLACE. I understand Mr. Ewing to make an application that the Court shall direct the Judge Advocate or his assistants to open the case, responding to the questions which he has propounded.

Mr. EWING. That is my application.

The Commission overruled the application.

[Omitted from page 126.]

HENRY HAWKINS (colored.)

For the Defense.—June 13.

By MR. AIKEN.

I have lived at Surrattsville about eleven years. I was formerly a slave of Mrs. Surratt. She always treated me kindly, and she was very good to all her servants. I remember the Government horses breaking away from Giesboro, and that seven of them came to Mrs. Surratt's stable; they were there for a fortnight or more, and then the Government sent for them. I do not know that Mrs. Surratt had a receipt for them, but I know that she bought hay and grain to feed them with.

I have never heard Mrs. Surratt talk in favor of the South; never heard any expressions, loyal or disloyal, from her while I was there. She has often fed Union soldiers that passed her house, and always gave them the best she had; and I do not think she took any pay for it; she took none that I know of. I do not know much about Mrs. Surratt's eyesight being bad, but I heard she could not see some time back, and that she had to wear specs.

Court-Room, Washington, D. C.,
June 29, 1865, 10 o'clock A. M.

The Commission met, with closed doors, pursuant to adjournment.

All the members present; also the Judge Advocate and the Assistant Judge Advocates.

The Commission then proceeded to deliberate upon the evidence adduced in the case of each of the accused.

Pending the deliberation, at 6 o'clock P. M., the Commission adjourned to meet again, with closed doors, on Friday, June 30, at 10 o'clock, A. M.

Court-Room, Washington, D. C.,
June 30, 1865, 10 o'clock A. M.

The Commission met, with closed doors, pursuant to adjournment.

All the members present; also the Judge Advocate and the Assistant Judge Advocates.

The Commission then proceeded to deliberate upon the evidence adduced in the case of each of the accused.

DAVID E. HEROLD.

After mature consideration of the evidence adduced in the case of the accused, DAVID E. HEROLD, the Commission find the said accused—

Of the Specification.....................Guilty.

Except "combining, confederating and cospiring with Edward Spangler;" as to which part thereof..........................Not Guilty.

Of the Charge. ....Guilty.

Except the words of the charge, "combining, confederating, and conspiring with Edward Spangler;" as to which part of the charge, Not Guilty.

And the Commission do, therefore, sentence him, the said David E. Herold, to be hanged by the neck until he be dead, at such time and place as the President of the United States shall direct; two-thirds of the Commission concurring therein.

George A. Atzerodt.

After mature consideration of the evidence adduced in the case of the accused George A. Atzerodt, the Commission find the said accused—

Of the Specification.....................Guilty.

Except "combining, confederating, and conspiring with Edward Spangler;" of this Not Guilty.

Of the Charge...........................Guilty.

Except "combining, confederating, and conspiring with Edward Spangler;" of this Not Guilty.

And the Commission do, therefore, sentence him, the said George A. Atzerodt, to be hanged by the neck until he be dead, at such time and place as the President of the United States shall direct; two-thirds of the Commission concurring therein.

Lewis Payne.

After mature consideration of the evidence adduced in the case of the accused, Lewis Payne, the Commission find the said accused—

Of the Specification.....................Guilty.

Except "combining, confederating, and conspiring with Edward Spangler;" of this Not Guilty.

Of the Charge...........................Guilty.

Except "combining, confederating, and conspiring with Edward Spangler;" of this Not Guilty.

And the Commission do, therefore, sentence him, the said Lewis Payne, to be hanged by the neck until he be dead, at such time and place as the President of the United States shall direct; two-thirds of the Commission concurring therein.

Mrs. Mary E. Surratt.

After mature consideration of the evidence adduced in the case of the accused, Mary E. Surratt, the Commission find the said accused—

Of the Specification.....................Guilty.

Except as to "receiving, sustaining, harboring, and concealing Samuel Arnold and Michael

O'Laughlin," and except as to "combining, confederating, and conspiring with Edward Spangler;" of this.....................Not Guilty.

Of the Charge..........................Guilty.

Except as to "combining, confederating, and conspiring with Edward Spangler;" of this Not Guilty.

And the Commission do, therefore, sentence her, the said Mary E. Surratt, to be hanged by the neck until she be dead, at such time and place as the President of the United States shall direct; two-thirds of the members of the Commission concurring therein.

Michael O'Laughlin.

After mature consideration of the evidence adduced in the case of the accused, Michael O'Laughlin, the Commission find the said accused—

Of the Specification.....................Guilty.

Except the words thereof, "And in the further prosecution of the conspiracy aforesaid, and of its murderous and treasonable purposes aforesaid, on the nights of the 13th and 14th of April, 1865, at Washington City, and within the military department and military lines aforesaid, the said Michael O'Laughlin did there and then lie in wait for Ulysses S. Grant, then Lieutenant-General and Commander of the armies of the United States, with intent then and there to kill and murder the said Ulysses S. Grant;" of said words Not Guilty; and except "combining, confederating, and conspiring with Edward Spangler;" of this.....................Not Guilty.

Of the Charge...........................Guilty.

Except "combining, confederating, and conspiring with Edward Spangler;" of this Not Guilty.

The Commission do, therefore, sentence the said Michael O'Laughlin to be imprisoned at hard labor for life, at such place as the President shall direct.

Edward Spangler.

After mature consideration of the evidence adduced in the case of the accused, Edward Spangler, the Commission find the said accused—

Of the Specification..............Not Guilty.

Except as to the words, "the said Edward Spangler, on said 14th day of April, A. D. 1865, at about the same hour of that day, as aforesaid, within said military department and the military lines aforesaid, did aid and abet him (meaning John Wilkes Booth) in making his escape after the said Abraham Lincoln had been murdered in manner aforesaid;" and of these words..............Guilty.

Of the Charge.....................Not Guilty.

But of having feloniously and traitorously aided and abetted John Wilkes Booth in making his escape after having killed and murdered Abraham Lincoln, President of the United States, he, the said Edward Spangler, at the time of aiding and abetting as aforesaid, well knowing that the said Abraham Lincoln, President as aforesaid, had been murdered by the said John Wilkes Booth, as aforesaid...........................GUILTY.

The Commission do, therefore, sentence the said Edward Spangler to be imprisoned at hard labor for six years, at such place as the President shall direct.

SAMUEL ARNOLD.

After mature consideration of the evidence adduced in the case of the accused, SAMUEL ARNOLD, the Commission find the said accused—

Of the Specification...................GUILTY.

Except "combining, confederating, and conspiring with Edward Spangler;" of this Not GUILTY.

Of the Charge...........................GUILTY.

Except "combining, confederating, and conspiring with Edward Spangler;" of this Not GUILTY.

The Commission do, therefore, sentence the said Samuel Arnold to imprisonment at hard labor for life, at such place as the President shall direct.

SAMUEL A. MUDD.

After mature consideration of the evidence adduced in the case of the accused, SAMUEL A. MUDD, the Commission find the said accused—

Of the Specification...................GUILTY.

Except "combining, confederating, and conspiring with Edward Spangler," of this Not GUILTY; and excepting "receiving, entertaining, and harboring and concealing said Lewis Payne, John H. Surratt, Michael O'Laughlin, George A. Atzerodt, Mary E. Surratt, and Samuel Arnold;" of this..........Not GUILTY.

Of the Charge...........................GUILTY.

Except "combining, confederating and conspiring with Edward Spangler," of this Not GUILTY.

The Commission do, therefore, sentence the said Samuel A. Mudd to be imprisoned at hard labor for life, at such place as the President shall direct.

WAR DEPARTMENT, ADJUTANT-GENERAL'S OFFICE, WASHINGTON, July 5, 1865.

To Major-General W. S. Hancock, United States Volunteers, commanding the Middle Military Division, Washington, D. C.:

WHEREAS, By the Military Commission appointed in paragraph 4, Special Orders No. 211, dated War Department, Adjutant-General's Office, Washington, May 6, 1865, and of which Major-General David Hunter, United States Volunteers, was President, the follow-

ing persons were tried, and, after mature consideration of evidence adduced in their cases, were found and sentenced as hereinafter stated, as follows.

[Here follow the findings and sentences in the case of David E. Herold, George A. Atzerodt, Lewis Payne, and Mary E. Surratt.]

And whereas, the President of the United States has approved the foregoing sentences, in the following order, to wit:

EXECUTIVE MANSION, July 5, 1865.

The foregoing sentences in the cases of David E. Herold, G. A. Atzerodt, Lewis Payne, and Mary E. Surratt, are hereby approved; and it is ordered, that the sentences in the cases of David E. Herold, G. A. Atzerodt, Lewis Payne, and Mary E. Surratt, be carried into execution by the proper military authority, under the direction of the Secretary of War, on the 7th day of July, 1865, between the hours of 10 o'clock, A. M., and 2 o'clock, P. M., of that day.

(Signed)   ANDREW JOHNSON,
President.

Therefore, you are hereby commanded to cause the foregoing sentences in the cases of David E. Herold, G. A. Atzerodt, Lewis Payne, and Mary E. Surratt, to be duly executed, in accordance with the President's order.

By command of the President of the United States.

E. D. TOWNSEND,
Assistant Adjutant-General.

PRESIDENT'S APPROVAL OF THE FINDINGS AND SENTENCES.

EXECUTIVE MANSION, July 5, 1865.

The foregoing sentences in the cases of David E. Herold, G. A. Atzerodt, Lewis Payne, Michael O'Laughlin, Edward Spangler, Samuel Arnold, Mary E. Surratt, and Samuel A. Mudd, are hereby approved, and it is ordered that the sentences of said David E. Herold, G. A. Atzerodt, Lewis Payne, and Mary E. Surratt be carried into execution by the proper military authority, under the direction of the Secretary of War, on the 7th day of July, 1865, between the hours of 10 o'clock, A. M., and 2 o'clock, P. M., of that day. It was further ordered, that the prisoners, Samuel Arnold, Samuel A. Mudd, Edward Spangler, and Michael O'Laughlin be confined at hard labor in the Penitentiary at Albany, New York, during the period designated in their respective sentences.

ANDREW JOHNSON,
President.

EXECUTIVE MANSION, July 15, 1865.

The executive order, dated July 5, 1865, approving the sentences in the cases of Samuel Arnold, Samuel A. Mudd, Edward Spangler, and Michael O'Laughlin is hereby modified, so as to direct that the said Arnold,

Mudd, Spangler, and O'Laughlin, be confined at hard labor in the military prison at Dry Tortugas, Florida, during the period designated in their respective sentences.

The Adjutant-General of the army is di-rected to issue orders for the said prisoners to be transported to the Dry Tortugas, and to be confined there accordingly.

ANDREW JOHNSON,
President.

APPLICATION FOR WRIT OF HABEAS CORPUS IN BEHALF OF MARY E. SURRATT.

WASHINGTON, D. C., July 7, 1865.

To the Hon. Andrew Wylie, one of the Justices of the Supreme Court of the District of Columbia:

The petition of Mary E. Surratt, by her counsel, F. A. Aiken and John W. Clampitt, most respectfully represents unto your Honor, that on or about the 17th day of April, A. D. 1865, your petitioner was arrested by the military authorities of the United States, under the charge of complicity with the murder of Abraham Lincoln, late President of the United States, and has ever since that time been and is now confined on said charge, under and by virtue of the said military power of the United States, and is in the special custody of Major-General W. S. Hancock, commanding Middle Military Division; that since her said arrest your petitioner has been tried, against her solemn protest, by a Military Commission, unlawfully and without warrant, convened by the Secretary of War, as will appear from paragraph 9, Special Orders, No. 211, dated War Department, Adjutant-General's Office, Washington, May the 6th, 1865, and by said Commission, notwithstanding her formal plea to the jurisdiction of the said Commission, is now unlawfully and unjustifiably detained in custody and sentenced to be hanged on to-morrow, July 7th, 1865, between the hours of 10 A. M. and 2 P. M.; your petitioner shows unto your Honor that at the time of the commission of the said offense she was a private citizen of the United States, and in no manner connected with the military authority of the same, and that said offense was committed within the District of Columbia, said District being at the time within the lines of the armies of the United States, and not enemy's territory, or under the control of a military commander for the trial of civil causes. But, on the contrary, your petitioner alleges that the said crime was an offense simply against the peace of the United States, properly and solely cognizable under the Constitution and laws of the United States, by the Criminal Court of this District, and which said court was and is now open for the trial of such crimes and offenses. Wherefore, inasmuch as the said crime was only an offense against the peace of the United States, and not an act of war; inasmuch as your petitioner was a private citizen of the same, and not subject to military jurisdiction, or in any wise amenable to military law; inasmuch as said District was the peaceful territory of the United States, and that all crimes committed within such territory are, under the Constitution and laws of the United States, to be tried only before its criminal tribunals, with the right of public trial by jury; inasmuch as said Com-mission was a Military Commission, organized and governed by the laws of military court-martial, and unlawfully convened without warrant or authority, and when she had not the right of public trial by jury as guaranteed to her by the Constitution and laws of the United States, that, therefore, her detention and sentence are so without warrant against positive law and unjustifiable: wherefore she prays your Honor to grant unto her the United States' most gracious writ of *habeas corpus,* commanding the said Major-General W. S. Hancock to produce before your Honor the body of your said petitioner, with the cause and day of her said detention, to abide, etc., and she will ever pray.

MARY E. SURRATT.

By FREDERICK A. AIKEN, JOHN W. CLAMPITT.

INDORSED.—Let the writ issue as prayed, returnable before the Criminal Court of the District of Columbia, now sitting, at the hour of 10 o'clock A. M., this 7th day of July, 1865. ANDREW WYLIE,
A Justice of the Supreme Court of the District of Columbia.
JULY 7th, 1865.

At half-past 11 o'clock on the morning of the 7th of July, Major-General Hancock, accompanied by Attorney-General Speed, appeared before Judge Wylie in obedience to the writ, and made the following return:

HEAD-QUARTERS MIDDLE MILITARY DIVISION,
WASHINGTON, D. C., July 7, 1865.

To Hon. Andrew Wylie, Justice of the Supreme Court of the District of Columbia:

I hereby acknowledge the service of the writ hereto attached and return the same, and respectfully say that the body of Mary E. Surratt is in my possession, under and by virtue of an order of Andrew Johnson, President of the United States and Commander-in-chief of the Army and Navy, for the purposes in said order expressed, a copy of which is hereto attached and made part of this return; and that I do not produce said body by reason of the order of the President of the United States, indorsed upon said writ, to which reference is hereby respectfully made, dated July 7th, 1865. W. S. HANCOCK,
Maj.-Gen. U. S. Vols., Commanding Middle Div.

THE PRESIDENT'S INDORSEMENT.

EXECUTIVE OFFICE, July 7, 1865, 10 A. M.

To Major-General W. S. Hancock, Commander, etc.:

I, Andrew Johnson, President of the United States, do hereby declare that the writ of *habeas corpus* has been heretofore suspended in such cases as this, and I do hereby especially suspend this writ, and direct that you proceed to execute the order heretofore given upon the judgment of the Military Commission, and you will give this order in return to the writ.

ANDREW JOHNSON, *President.*

The Court ruled that it yielded to the suspension of the writ of *habeas corpus* by the President of the United States.

The sentences were duly carried into execution.

ARGUMENT

ON THE

JURISDICTION OF THE MILITARY COMMISSION,

BY

REVERDY JOHNSON,

Of Counsel for Mrs. Surratt.

Mr. President and Gentlemen of the Commission:

Has the Commission jurisdiction of the cases before it, is the question which I propose to discuss. That question, in all courts, civil, criminal, and military, must be considered and answered affirmatively before judgment can be pronounced. And it must be answered correctly, or the judgment pronounced is void. Ever an interesting and vital inquiry, it is of engrossing interest and of awful importance when error may lead to the unauthorized taking of human life. In such a case, the court called upon to render, and the officer who is to approve its judgment and have it executed, have a concern peculiar to themselves. As to each, a responsibility is involved which however conscientiously and firmly met, is calculated and cannot fail to awaken great solicitude and induce the most mature consideration. The nature of the duty is such that even honest error affords no impunity. The legal personal consequences, even in a case of honest, mistaken judgment, can not be avoided. That this is no exaggeration, the Commission will, I think, be satisfied before I shall have concluded. I refer to it now, and shall again, with no view to shake your firmness. Such an attempt would be alike discourteous and unprofitable. Every member comprising the Commission will, I am sure, meet all the responsibility that belongs to it as becomes gentlemen and soldiers. I therefore repeat that my sole object in adverting to it is to obtain a well considered and matured judgment. So far the question of jurisdiction has not been discussed. The pleas which specially present it, as soon as filed, were overruled. But that will not, because properly it should not, prevent your considering it with the deliberation that its grave nature demands. And it is for you to decide it, and at this time for you alone. The commission you are acting under of itself does not and could not decide it. If unauthorized it is a mere nullity—the usurpation of a power not vested in the Executive, and conferring no authority whatever upon you. To hold otherwise would be to make the Executive the exclusive and conclusive judge of its own powers, and that would be to make that department omnipotent. The powers of the President under the Constitution are great, and amply sufficient to give all needed efficiency to the office. The convention that formed the Constitution, and the people who adopted it, considered these powers sufficient, and granted no others. In the minds of both (and subsequent history has served to strengthen the impression) danger to liberty was no more to be dreaded from the Executive than from any other department of the Government. So far, therefore, from meaning to extend his powers beyond what was deemed necessary to the wholesome operation of the Government, they were studious to place them beyond the reach of abuse. With this view, before entering "on the execution of his office," the President is required to take an oath "faithfully" to discharge its duties, and to the best of his "ability preserve, protect, and defend the Constitution of the United States." He is also liable to "be removed from office on impeachment for and conviction of treason, bribery, or other high crimes and misdemeanors." If he violates the Constitution; if he fails to preserve it; and, above all, if he usurps powers not granted, he is false to his official oath, and liable to be indicted and convicted, and to be impeached. For such an offense his removal from office is the necessary consequence. In such a contingency, "he shall be removed" is the command of the Constitution. What stronger evidence could there be that his powers, all of them, in peace and in war, are only such as the Constitution confers? But if this was not evident from the instrument itself, the character of the men who composed the Convention, and the spirit of the American people at that period, would prove it. Hatred of a monarchy, made the more intense by the conduct of the monarch from whose government they had recently separated, and a deep-seated love of constitutional liberty, made the more keen and active by the sacrifices which had illustrated their revolutionary career, constituted them a people who could never be induced to delegate any executive authority not so carefully restricted and guarded as to render its abuse or usurpation almost impossible. If these observations are well founded—and I suppose they will not be denied—it follows that an executive act beyond executive authority can furnish no defense against the legal consequences of what is done under it. I have said that the question of jurisdiction is ever open. It may be raised by counsel at any stage of the trial, and if it is not, the Court not only may, but is bound to notice it. Unless jurisdiction then exists, the authority to try does not exist, and whatever is done is "*coram non judice*," and utterly void. This doctrine is as applicable to military as to other courts.

O'Brien tells us that the question may be raised by demurrer if the facts charged do not constitute an offense, or if they do not an offense cognizable by a military court, or that it may be raised by a special plea, or under the general one of not guilty. *O'Brien*, 248.

DeHart says: The court "is the judge of its own competency at any stage of its proceedings, and is bound to notice questions of jurisdiction whenever raised." *DeHart III.*

The question then being always open, and its proper decision essential to the validity of its judgment, the Commission must decide before pronouncing such judgment whether it has jurisdiction over these parties and the crimes imputed to them. That a tribunal like this has no jurisdiction over other than military offenses, is believed to be self-evident. That offenses defined and punished by the civil law, and whose trial is provided for by the same law, are not the subjects of military jurisdiction, is of course true. A military, as contradistinguished from a civil offense, must therefore be made to appear, and when it is, it must also appear that the military law provides for its trial and punishment by a military tribunal. If that law does not furnish a mode of trial, or affix a punishment, the case is unprovided for, and, as far as the military power is concerned, is to go unpunished. But as either the civil, common, or statute law embraces every species of offense that the United States, or the States have deemed it necessary to punish, in all such cases the civil courts are clothed with every necessary jurisdiction. In a military court, if the charge does not state a "crime provided for generally or specifically by any of the articles of war," the prisoner must be discharged. *O'Brien*, p. 285. Nor is it sufficient that the charge is of a crime known to the military law. The offender, when he commits it, must be subject to such law, or he is not subject to military jurisdiction. The general law has "supreme and undisputed jurisdiction over all. The military law puts forth no such pretensions; it aims solely to enforce on the *soldier* the additional duties he has assumed. It constitutes tribunals for the trial of breaches of *military duty only*." *O'Brien*, 26, 27. "The one code (the civil) embraces all citizens, whether soldiers or not; the other (the military) has no jurisdiction ever any citizen as such." *Ibid.*

The provisions of the Constitution clearly maintain the same doctrine. The Executive has no authority "to declare war, to raise and support armies, to provide and maintain a navy," or to make "rules for the government and regulation" of either force. These powers are exclusively in Congress. An army can not be raised or have law for its government and regulation except as Congress shall provide. This power of Congress to govern and regulate the army and navy, was granted by the convention without objection. In England, the King, as the generalissimo of the whole kingdom, has this sole power, though Parliament has frequently interposed and regulated for itself. But with us, it was thought safest to give the entire power to Congress, "since otherwise summary and severe punishments might be inflicted at the mere will of the Executive." 8 *Story's Com.*, *sect.* 1192. No member of the Convention, or any commentator on the Constitution since, has intimated that even this Congressional power could be applied to citizens not belonging to the army or navy. In respect, too, to the latter class, the power was conferred exclusively on Congress to prevent that class being made the object of abuse by the Executive—to guard them especially from "summary and severe punishments" inflicted by mere Executive will. The existence of such a power being vital to discipline, it was necessary to provide for it. But no member suggested that it should be or could be made to apply to citizens not in the military service, or be given to any other department, in whole or in part, than Congress. Citizens not belonging to the army or navy were not made liable to military law, or under any circumstances to be deprived of any of the guaranties of personal liberty provided by the Constitution. Independent of the consideration that the very nature of the Government is inconsistent with such a pretension, the power is conferred upon Congress in terms that exclude all who do not belong to "the land and naval forces." It is a rule of interpretation coeval with its existence, that the Government, in no department of it, possesses powers not granted by express delegation or necessarily to be implied from those that are granted. This would be the rule incident to the very nature of the Constitution, but to place it beyond doubt, and to make it an imperative rule, the 10th amendment declares that "the powers not delegated to the United States by the Constitution, nor prohibited by it to the States, are reserved to the States respectively, or to the people." The power given to Congress, "is to make rules for the government and regulation of the land and naval forces." No artifice of ingenuity can make these words include those who do not belong to the army and navy; and they are therefore to be construed to exclude all others, as if negative words to that effect had been added. And this is not only the obvious meaning of the terms, considered by themselves, but is demonstrable from other provisions of the Constitution. So jealous were our ancestors of ungranted power, and so vigilant to protect the citizen against it, that they were unwilling to leave him to the safeguards which a proper construction of the Constitution, as originally adopted, furnished. In this they resolved that nothing should be left in doubt. They determined, therefore, not only to guard him against executive and judicial, but against Congressional abuse. With that view, they adopted the fifth constitutional amendment, which declares that "no person shall be held to answer for a capital or otherwise infamous crime, unless on a presentment or indictment of a grand jury, EXCEPT in *cases arising in the land or naval forces, or in the militia when in active service in time of war or public danger.*" This exception is designed to leave in force, not to enlarge the power vested in Congress by the original Constitution, "to make rules for the government and regulation of the land and naval forces." "The land or naval forces" are the terms used in both, have the same meaning, and until lately, have been supposed by every commentator and judge, to exclude from military jurisdiction offenses committed by citizens not belonging to such forces. Kent, in a note to his 1 Coms., p. 341, states, and with accuracy, that "military and naval crimes, and offenses committed while the party is attached to and under the immediate authority of the army and navy of the United States and in actual service, are not cognizable under the common law jurisdiction of the civil courts of the United States." According to this great authority every other class of persons and every other species of offense, are within the jurisdiction of the civil courts, and entitled to the protection of the proceeding by presentment or indictment, and a public trial in such a court. If the constitutional amendment has not that effect, if it does not secure that protection to all who do not belong to the army or navy, then the provisions in the sixth amendment are equally inoperative. They, "in all criminal prosecutions," give the accused a right to a speedy and public trial; a right to be informed of the nature and cause of the accusation, to be confronted with the witnesses against him, to compulsory process for his witnesses, and the assistance of counsel. The exception in the 5th amendment of cases arising in the land or naval forces applies by necessary implication, at least in part, to this. To construe this as not containing the exception would defeat the purpose of the exception; for the provisions of the 6th amendment, unless they are subject to the exceptions of the 5th, would be inconsistent with the 5th. The 6th is therefore to be construed as if it in words contained the exception. It is submitted that this is evident. The consequence is, that if the exception can be made to include those who, in the language of Kent, are not, when the offense was committed, "attached to and under the immediate authority of the army or navy, and in actual service," the securities designed for other citizens by the 6th article are wholly nugatory. If a military commission, created by the mere authority of the President, can deprive a citizen of the benefit of the guaranties secured by the 5th amendment, it can deprive him of those secured by the 6th. It may deny him the right to a "speedy and public trial," information "of the nature and cause of the accusation," of the right "to be confronted with the witnesses against him," of compulsory process for his witnesses," and of "the assistance of counsel for his defense." That this can be done no one has as yet maintained; no opinion, however latitudinarian, of executive power, of the effect of public necessity, in war or in peace, to enlarge its sphere, and authorize a disregard of its limitations; no one, however convinced he may be of the policy of protecting accusing witnesses from a public examination, under the idea that their testimony can not otherwise be obtained, and

that crime may consequently go unpunished, has to this time been found to go to that extent. Certainly, no writer has ever maintained such a doctrine. Argument to refute it, is unnecessary. It refutes itself. For, if sound, the 6th amendment, which our fathers thought so vital to individual liberty when assailed by governmental prosecution, is but a dead letter, totally inefficient for its purpose whenever the Government shall deem it proper to try a citizen by a military commission. Against such a doctrine the very instincts of freemen revolt. It has no foundation but in the principle of unrestrained, tyrannic power, and passive obedience. If it be well founded, then are we indeed a nation of slaves, and not of freemen. If the Executive can legally decide whether a citizen is to enjoy the guaranties of liberty afforded by the Constitution, what are we but slaves? If the President, or any of his subordinates, upon any pretence whatever, can deprive a citizen of such guaranties, liberty with us, however loved, is not enjoyed. But the Constitution is not so fatally defective. It is subject to no such reproach. In war and in peace, it is equally potential for the promotion of the general welfare, and as involved in and necessary to such welfare, for the protection of the individual citizen. Certainly, until this rebellion, this has been the proud and cherished conviction of the country. And it is to this conviction and the assurance that it could never be shaken that our past prosperity is to be referred. God forbid that mere power, dependent for its exercise on Executive will (a condition destructive of political happiness), shall ever be substituted in its place. Should that unfortunately ever occur, unless it was soon corrected by the authority of the people, the objects of our Revolutionary struggle, the sacrifices of our ancestors, and the design of the Constitution will all have been in vain.

I proceed now to examine with somewhat of particularity the grounds on which I am informed your jurisdiction is maintained.

1st. That it is an incident of the war power.

I. That power, whatever be its extent, is exclusively in Congress. War can only be declared by that body. With its origin the President has no concern whatever. Armies, when necessary, can only be raised by the same body. Not a soldier, without its authority, can be brought into service by the Executive. He is as impotent to that end as a private citizen. And armies, too, when raised by Congressional authority, can only be governed and regulated by "rules" prescribed by the same authority. The Executive possesses no power over the soldier except such as Congress may, by legislation, confer upon him. If, then, it was true that the creation of a military commission like the present is incidental to the war power, it must be authorized by the department to which that power belongs, and not by the Executive, to whom no portion of it belongs. And if it be said to be involved in the power "to make rules for the government and regulation of the land and naval forces," the result is the same. It must be done by Congress, to whom that power also exclusively belongs, and not by the Executive. Has Congress, then, under either power, authorised such a commission as this to try such cases as these? It is confidently asserted that it has not. If it has, let the statute be produced. It is certainly not done by that of the 10th of April, 1806, "establishing articles for the government of the armies of the United States." No military courts are there mentioned or provided for but courts-martial and courts of inquiry. And their mode of appointment and organization, and of proceeding, and the authority vested in them are also prescribed. Military commissions are not only not authorized, but are not even alluded to. And, consequently, the parties, whoever these may be, who, under that act, can be tried by courts-martial or courts of inquiry, are not made subject to trial by a military commission. Nor is such a tribunal mentioned in any prior statute, or in any subsequent one, until these of the 17th of July, 1862, and of the 3d of March, 1863. In the 5th section of the first, the records of "military commissions are to be returned for revision to the Judge Advocate General," whose appointment it also provides for. But how such commissions are to be constituted, what powers they are to have, how their proceedings are to be conducted, or what cases and parties they are to try, is not provided for. In the 38th section of the second, they are mentioned as competent to try persons "lurking or acting as spies." The same absence in the particulars stated in respect to the first is true of this. And as regards this act of 1863, this reflection forcibly presents itself. If military commissions can be created, and from their very nature possess jurisdiction to try all alleged military offenses (the ground on which your jurisdiction, it is said, in part rests), why was it necessary to give them the power, by express words, to try persons "lurking or acting as spies?" The military character of such an offense could not have been doubted. What reason, then, can be suggested for conferring the power by express language than that without it it would not be possessed? Before these statutes a commission, called a military commission, had been issued by the Executive to Messrs. Davis, Holt and Campbell, to examine into certain military claims against the Western Department, and Congress, by its resolution of the 11th of March, 1862 (No. 18), provided for the payment of its awards. Against a commission of that character no objection can be made. It is but ancillary to the auditing of demands upon the Government, and in no way interferes with any constitutional right of the citizen. But until this rebellion a military commission like the present, organized in a loyal State or Territory where the courts are open and their proceedings unobstructed, clothed with the jurisdiction attempted to be conferred upon you—a jurisdiction involving not only the liberty, but the lives of the parties on trial—it is confidently stated, is not to be found sanctioned, or the most remotely recognized,

or even alluded to, by any writer on military law in England or the United States, or in any legislation of either country. It has its origin in the rebellion, and like the dangerous heresy of secession, out of which that sprung, nothing is more certain in my opinion than that, however pure the motives of its origin, it will be considered, as it is, an almost equally dangerous heresy to constitutional liberty, and the rebellion ended, perish with the other, then and forever. But to proceed; such commissions were authorized by Lieutenant-General Scott in his Mexican campaign. When he obtained possession of the City of Mexico, he, on the 17th of September, 1847, re-published, with additions, his order of the 19th of February preceding, declaring martial law. By this order, he authorized the trial of certain offenses by military commissions, regulated their proceedings, and limited the punishments they might inflict. From their jurisdiction, however, he excepts cases "clearly cognizable by court-martial," and in words limits the cases to be tried to such as are (I quote) "not provided for in the act of Congress establishing rules and articles for the government of the armies of the United States," of the 10th of April, 1806. The second clause of the order mentions, among other offenses to be so tried, "assassination, murder, poisoning;" and in the fourth (correctly, as I submit, with all respect for a contrary opinion), he states that "the rules and articles of war" do not provide for the punishment of any one of the designated offenses, "even when committed by individuals of the army upon the persons or property of other individuals of the same, except in the very restricted case in the 9th of the articles." The authority, too, for even this restricted commission—Scott—not more eminent as soldier than civilian—placed entirely upon the ground that the named offenses, if committed in a foreign country by American troops, could not be punished under any law of the United States then in force. "The Constitution of the United States and the rules and articles of war," he said, and said correctly, provided no court for their trial or punishment, "no matter by whom, or on whom" committed. *Scott's Autobiography*, 392.

And he further tells us that even this order, so limited and so called for by the greatest public necessity, when handed to the then Secretary of War (Mr. Marcy) "for his approval," "a startle at the title (martial law order) was the only comment he then, or ever, made on the subject," and that it was "soon silently returned as too explosive for safe handling." "A little later (he adds), the Attorney-General (Mr. Cushing) called and asked for a copy, and the law officer of the Government, whose business it is to speak on all such matters, was stricken with *legal dumbness*," *Ib.* How much more startled and more paralyzed would these great men have been had they been consulted on such a commission as this!—a commission, not to sit in another country, and to try offenses not provided for by any law of the United States, civil or military, but in their own country, and in a part of it where there are laws providing for their trial and punishment, and civil courts clothed with ample powers for both, and in the daily and undisturbed exercise of their jurisdiction; and where, if there should be an attempt at disturbance by a force which they had not the power to control, they could invoke (and it would be his duty to afford it) the President to use the military power at his command, and which everybody knows to be ample for the purpose.

If it be suggested that the civil courts and juries for this District could not safely be relied upon for the trial of these cases, because either of incompetency, disloyalty or corruption, it would be an unjust reflection upon the judges, upon the people, upon the Marshal, an appointee of the President, by whom the juries are summoned, and upon our civil institutions themselves—upon the very institutions on whose integrity and intelligence the safety of our property, liberty and lives, our ancestors thought, could not only be safely rested, but would be safe nowhere else. If it be suggested that a secret trial, in whole or in part, as the Executive might deem expedient, could not be had before any other than a military tribunal, the answer is that the Constitution, "in all criminal prosecutions," gives the accused "the right" to a "public trial." So abhorrent were private trials to our ancestors, so fatal did they deem them to individual security, that they were thus denounced, and, as they no doubt thought, so guarded against as in all future time to be impossible. If it be suggested that witnesses may be unwilling to testify, the answer is that they may be compelled to appear and made to testify.

But the suggestion, upon another ground, is equally without force. It rests on the idea that the guilty only are ever brought to trial —that the only object of the Constitution and laws in this regard is to afford the means to establish alleged guilt; that accusation, however made, is to be esteemed *prima facie* evidence of guilt, and that the Executive should be armed, without other restriction than his own discretion, with all the appliances deemed by him necessary to make the presumption from such evidence conclusive. Never was there a more dangerous theory. The peril to the citizen from a prosecution so conducted, as illustrated in all history, is so great that the very elementary principles of constitutional liberty, the spirit and letter of the Constitution itself repudiate it.

II. Innocent parties, sometimes by private malice, sometimes for a mere partisan purpose, sometimes from a supposed public policy, have been made the subjects of criminal accusation. History is full of such instances. How are such parties to be protected if a public trial, at the option of the Executive, can be denied them, and a secret one, in whole, or in part, substituted? If the names of the witnesses, and their evidence, are not published, what obstacle does it not interpose to establish their innocence? The character of

the witnesses against them may be all important to that end. Kept in prison, with no means of consulting the outer world, how can they make the necessary inquiries? How can those who may know the witnesses be able to communicate with them on the subject? A trial so conducted, though it may not, as, no doubt, is the case in the present instance, be intended to procure the punishment of any but the guilty, it is obvious, subjects the innocent to great danger. It partakes more of the character of the Inquisition, which the enlightened civilization of the age has driven almost wholly out of existence, than of a tribunal suited to a free people. In the palmiest days of that tribunal, kings, as well as people, stood abashed in its presence, and dreaded its power. The accused was never informed of the names of his accusers; heresy, suspected, was ample ground for arrest; accomplices and criminals were received as witnesses, and the whole trial was secret, and conducted in a chamber almost as silent as the grave. It was long since denounced by the civilised world, not because it might not at times punish the heretic (then, in violation of all rightful human power, deemed a criminal), but because it was as likely to punish the innocent as the guilty. A public trial, therefore, by which the names of witnesses and the testimony are given, even in monarchical and despotic Governments, is now esteemed amply adequate to the punishment of guilt, and essential to the protection of innocence. Can it be that this is not true of us? Can it be that a secret trial, wholly or partially, if the Executive so decides, is all that an American citizen is entitled to? Such a doctrine, if maintained by an English monarch, would shake his government to its very center, and, if persevered in, would lose him his crown. It will be no answer to these observations to say that this particular trial has been only in part a secret one, and that secrecy will never be resorted to, except for purposes of justice. The reply is, that the principle itself is inconsistent with American liberty, as recognised and secured by constitutional guaranties. It supposes that, whether these guaranties are to be enjoyed in the particular case, and to what extent, is dependent on Executive will. The Constitution, in this regard, is designed to secure them in spite of such will. Its patriotic authors intended to place the citizen, in this particular, wholly beyond the power, not only of the Executive, but of every department of the Government. They deemed the right to a public trial vital to the security of the citizen, and especially and absolutely necessary to his protection against Executive power. A public trial of all criminal prosecutions they, therefore, secured by general and unqualified terms. What would these great men have said, had they been asked so to qualify the terms as to warrant its refusal, under any circumstances, and make it dependent upon Executive discretion? The member who made the inquiry would have been deemed by them a traitor to liberty, or insane. What would they have said if told that, with a such qualification, the Executive would be able legally to impose it as incidental to Executive power? If not received with derision, it would have been indignantly rejected as an imputation upon those who, at any time thereafter, should legally fill the office.

III. Let me present the question in another view. If such a Commission as this, for the trial of cases like the present, can be legally constituted, can it be done by mere Executive authority?

1. You are a Court, and, if legally existing, endowed with momentous power, the highest known to man, that of passing upon the liberty or life of the citizen. By the express words of the Constitution an army can only be raised, and governed and regulated, by laws passed by Congress. In the exercise of the power to rule and govern it, the act before referred to, of the 10th of April, 1806, establishing the articles of war, was passed. That act provides only for courts-martial and courts of inquiry, and designates the cases to be tried before each, and the laws that are to govern the trial. Military commissions are not mentioned, and, of course, the act contains no provision for their government. Now, it is submitted, as perfectly clear, that the creation of a court, whether civil or military, is an exclusive legislative function, belonging to the department upon which the legislative power is conferred. The jurisdiction of such a court, and the laws and regulations to guide and govern it, is also exclusively legislative. What cases are to be tried by it, how the judges are to be selected, and how qualified, what are to be the rules of evidence, and what punishments are to be inflicted, all solely belong to the same department. The very element of constitutional liberty, recognized by all modern writers on government as essential to its security, and carefully incorporated into our Constitution, is a separation of the legislative, judicial, and executive powers. That this separation is made in our Constitution, no one will deny. Article 1st declares that "All legislative powers herein granted shall be vested in a Congress." Article 2d vests "the Executive power" in a President, and Article 3d, "the judicial power" in certain designated courts, and in courts to be thereafter constituted by Congress. There could not be a more careful segregation of the three powers. If, then, courts, their laws, modes of proceeding, and judgments, belong to legislation (and this, I suppose, will not be questioned), in the absence of legislation in regard to this Court, and its jurisdiction to try the present cases, it has for that purpose no legal existence or authority. The Executive, whose functions are altogether executive, can not confer it. The offenses to be tried by it, the laws to govern its proceedings, the punishment it may award, can not, for the same reason, be prescribed by the Executive. These, as well as the mere constitution of the Court, all exclusively belong to Congress. If it be contended that the Executive has the powers in question, because by implication they are involved in the war power,

or in the President's constitutional function as commander-in-chief of the army, then this consequence would follow, that they would not be subject to Congressional control, as that department has no more right to interfere with the constitutional power of the Executive than that power has a right to interfere with that of Congress. If, by implication, the powers in question belong to the Executive, he may not only constitute and regulate military commissions, and prescribe the laws for their government, but all legislation upon the subject by Congress would be usurpation. That the proposition leads to this result would seem to be clear, and, if it does, that result itself is so inconsistent with all previous legislation, and all executive practice, and so repugnant to every principle of constitutional liberty, that it demonstrates its utter unsoundness. Under the power given to Congress, "to make rules for the government and regulation of the land" forces, they have, from time to time, up to and including the act of the 10th of April, 1806, and since, enacted such rules as they deemed to be necessary, as well in war as in peace, and their authority to do so has never been denied. This power, too, to govern and regulate, from its very nature, is exclusive. Whatever is not done under it, is to be considered as purposely omitted. The words used in the delegation of the power, "govern and regulate," necessarily embrace the entire subject, and exclude all like authority in others. The end of such a power can not be attained, except through uniformity of government and regulation, and this is not to be attained if the power is in two hands. To be effective, therefore, it must be in one, and the Constitution gives it to one—to Congress—in express terms, and nowhere intimates a purpose to bestow it, or any portion of it, upon any other department. In the absence, then, of all mention of military commissions in the Constitution, and in the presence of the sole authority it confers on Congress, by rules of its own enacting, to govern and regulate the army, and, in the absence of all mention of such commissions in the act of the 10th of April, 1806, and of a single word in that act, or in any other, how can the power be considered as in the President? Further, upon what ground, other than those I have examined, can his authority be placed?

I. Is it that the constitutional guaranties referred to are designed only for a state of peace? There is not a syllable in the instrument that justifies, even plausibly, such a qualification. They are secured by the most general and comprehensive terms, wholly inconsistent with any restriction. They are, also, not only not confined to a condition of peace, but are more peculiarly necessary to the security of personal liberty in war than in peace. All history tells us that war, at times, maddens the people, frensies government, and makes both regardless of constitutional limitations of power. Individual safety, at such periods, is more in peril than at any other. Constitutional limitations and guaranties are, then, also absolutely necessary to the protection of the Government itself. The maxim, "*salus populi suprema est lex*," is but fit for a tyrant's use. Under its pretense the grossest wrongs have been committed, the most awful crimes perpetrated, and every principle of freedom violated, until, at last, worn down by suffering, the people, in very despair, have acquiesced in a resulting despotism. The safety which liberty needs, and without which it sickens and dies, is that which law, and not mere unlicensed human will, affords. The Aristotelian maxim, "*Salus publica supremas est lex*"—"Let the public weal be under the protection of the law"—is the true and only safe maxim. Nature, without law, would be chaos; government, without law, anarchy or despotism. Against both these last, in war and in peace, the Constitution happily protects us.

II. If the power in question is claimed under the authority supposed to be given the President in certain cases to suspend the writ of habeas corpus and to declare martial law, the claim is equally, if not more evidently, untenable.

1. Because the first of these powers, if given to the President at all, is given " when, in cases of rebellion or invasion," he deems the public safety requires it. I think he has this power, but there are great and patriotic names who think otherwise. But if he has it, or if it be in Congress alone, it is entirely untrue that its exercise works any other result than the suspension of the writ—the temporary suspension of the right of having the cause of arrest passed upon at once by the civil judges. It in no way impairs or suspemds the other rights secured to the accused. In what court he is to be tried, how he is to be tried, what evidence is to be admitted, and what judgment pronounced are all to be what the Constitution secures, and the laws provide in similar cases, when there is no suspension of the writ. The purpose of the writ is merely, without delay, to ascertain the legality of the arrest. If adjudged legal, the party is detained; if illegal, discharged. But in either contingency, when he is called to answer any criminal accusation, and he is a civilian, and not subject to the articles of war constitutionally enacted by Congress, it must be done by presentment or indictment, and his trial be had in a civil court, having, by State or Congressional legislation, jurisdiction over the crime and under laws governing the tribunal and defining the punishment. The very fact, too, that express power is given in a certain condition of things to suspend the writ referred to, and that no power is given to suspend or deny any of the other securities for personal liberty provided by the Constitution, is conclusive to show that all of the latter were designed to be in force " in cases of rebellion or invasion," as well as in a state of perfect peace and safety.

III. I have already referred to the act of 1806 establishing the articles of war, and said what must be admitted, that it provides for no military court like this. But for argument's sake, let it be conceded that it does. And I then maintain, with becoming confidence and due respect for a different opinion, that it does not embrace the crimes charged against these parties or the parties themselves.

First. The charge is a traitorous conspiracy to take the lives of the designated persons "in aid of the existing armed rebellion." Second. That in the execution of the conspiracy, the actual murder of the late President, and the attempted murder of the Secretary of State, occurred. Throughout the charge and its specification, the conspiracy and its attempted execution are alleged to have been *traitorous*. The accusation, therefore, is not one merely of murder, but of murder designed and in part accomplished, with *traitorous* purpose. If the charge is true, and the intent (which is made a substantial part of it) be also true, then the crime is treason, and not simple murder. Treason against the United States, as defined by the Constitution, can "consist only in levying war against them, or in adhering to their enemies, giving them aid and comfort." *III Art.* This definition not only tells us what treason is, but tells us that no other crime than the defined one shall be considered the offense. And the same section provides that "no person shall be convicted of treason, except on the testimony of two witnesses to the same overt act, or on confession in open court," and gives to Congress the power to declare what its punishment shall be. The offense in the general is the same in England. In that country, at no period since its freedom became settled, has any other treason been recognized. During the pendency of this rebellion (never before), it has been alleged that there exists with us the offense of military treason, punishable by the laws of war. It is so stated in the instructions of General Halleck to the then commanding officer in Tennessee, of the 5th of March, 1863. *Lawrence's Wheaton, Suppt. p.* 41. But Halleck confines it to acts committed against the army of a belligerent, when occupying the territory of the enemy. And he says what is certainly true, if such an offense can be committed, that it "is broadly distinguished from the treason defined in the constitutional and statutory laws, and made punishable by the civil courts." But the term *military treason* is not to be found in any English work or military order, or, before this rebellion, in any American authority.

It has evidently been adopted during the rebellion as a doctrine of military law on the authority of continental writers in governments less free than those of England and the United States, and in which, because they are less free, treason is made to consist of certain specific acts, and no others. But if Halleck is right, and all our prior practice, and that of England, from whom we derive ours, is to be abandoned, the cases before you are not cases of "military treason," as he defines it. When the offense here alleged is stated to have occurred in this District, the United States were not and did not claim to be in its occupation as a belligerent, nor was it pretended that the people of this District were, in a belligerent sense, enemies. On the contrary, they were citizens entitled to every right of citizenship. Nor were the parties on trial enemies. They were either citizens of the District, or of Maryland,

17

and under the protection of the Constitution. The offense charged, then, being treason, it is treason as known to the Constitution and laws, and can only be tried and punished as they provide. To consider these parties belligerents, and their alleged offense military treason, is not only unwarranted by the authority of Halleck, but is in direct conflict with the Constitution and laws which the President and all of us are bound to support and defend. The offense, then, being treason, as known to the Constitution, its trial by a military court is clearly illegal. And this for obvious reasons. Under the Constitution no conviction of such an offense can be had, "unless on the testimony of two witnesses to the same overt act, or on confession in open court." And under the laws the parties are entitled to have "a copy of the indictment and a list of the jury and witnesses, with the names and places of abode of both, at least three entire days before the trial." They also have the right to challenge peremptorily thirty-five of the jury, and to challenge for cause without limitation. And finally, unless the indictment shall be found by a grand jury within three years next after the treason done or committed, they shall not be prosecuted, tried or punished. *Act 30th April,* 1790, 1 *stat. at large,* 118, 119. Upon what possible ground, therefore, can this Commission possess the jurisdiction claimed for it? It is not alleged that it is subject to the provisions stated, and in its very nature it is impossible that it should be. The very safeguards designed by the Constitution, if it has such jurisdiction, are wholly unavailing. Trial by jury in all cases, our English ancestors deemed (as Story correctly tells us), "the great bulwark of their civil and political liberties, and watched with an unceasing jealousy and solicitude." It constituted one of the fundamental articles of Magna Charta—"*Nullus liber homo capiatur nec imprisonetur aut exulet, aut aliquo modo, destruatur,* etc.; *nisi per legae judicium parium suorum, vel per legem terrea.*" This great right the American colonists brought with them as their birth-right and inheritance. It landed with them at Jamestown and on the rock of Plymouth, and was equally prized by Cavalier and Puritan; and ever since, to the breaking out of the rebellion, has been enjoyed and esteemed the protection and proud privilege of their posterity. At times, during the rebellion, it has been disregarded and denied. The momentous nature of the crisis, brought about by that stupendous crime, involving, as it did, the very life of the nation, has caused the people to tolerate such disregard and denial. But the crisis, thank God, has passed. The authority of the Government throughout our territorial limits is reinstated so firmly that reflecting men, here and elsewhere, are convinced that the danger has passed never to return. The result proves that the principles on which the Government rests have imparted to it a vitality that will cause it to endure for all time, in spite of foreign invasion or domestic insurrection; and one of those principles—the choicest one—is the right in cases of "criminal prosecutions to a speedy and public trial by an impartial jury," and in cases of treason

to the additional securities before adverted to. The great purpose of Magna Charta and the Constitution was (to quote Story again) "to guard against a spirit of oppression and tyranny on the part of rulers, and against a spirit of violence and vindictiveness on the part of the people." The appeal for safety can, under such circumstances, scarcely be made by innocence in any other manner than by the severe control of courts of justice, and by the firm and impartial verdict of a jury sworn to do right, and guided solely by legal evidence and a sense of duty. In such a course there is a double security against the *prejudices of judges, who may partake of the wishes and opinions of the Government,* and against the passions of the multitude, who may demand their victim with a clamorous precipitancy." And Mr. Justice Blackstone, with the same deep sense of its value, meets the prediction of a foreign writer. "that because Rome, Sparta, and Carthage have lost their liberties, those of England in time must perish," by reminding him, "that Rome, Sparta, and Carthage, at the time when their liberties were lost, were *strangers to the trial by jury.*" 3 *Bla.,* 379. That a right so valued, and esteemed by our fathers to be so necessary to civil liberty, so important to the very existence of a free government, was designed by them to be made to depend for its enjoyment upon the war power, or upon any power intrusted to any department of our Government, is a reflection on their intelligence and patriotism.

IV. But to proceed: The articles of war, if they provided for the punishment of the crimes on trial, and authorized such a court as this, do not include such parties as are now on trial. And, until the rebellion, I am not aware that a different construction was ever intimated. It is the exclusive fruit of the rebellion.

The title of the act is, "An act for establishing rules and articles for the government of the *armies of the United States.*"

The first section states "the following shall be the rules and articles by which the *armies of the United States shall be governed,*" and every other section, except the 56th and 57th, are, in words, confined to persons belonging to the army in some capacity or other. I understand it to be held by some, that because such words are not used in the two sections referred to, it was the design of Congress to include persons who do not belong to the army. In my judgment, this is a wholly untenable construction; but if it was a correct one, it would not justify the use sought to be made of it in this instance. It would not bring these parties for their alleged crime before a military court known to the act; certainly not before a military commission—a court unknown to the act. The offense charged is a traitorous conspiracy, and murder committed in pursuance of it. Neither offense, conspiracy or murder, if indeed two are charged, is embraced by either the 56th or 57th articles of the statute. The 56th prohibits the relieving "the enemy with money, victuals or ammunition, or knowingly harboring and protecting him." Sophistry itself can not bring the offenses in question, under this article. The 57th prohibits only the "holding correspondence with, or giving intelligence to the enemy, either directly or indirectly." It is equally clear that the offenses in question are not within this provision. But, in fact, the two articles relied upon admit of no such construction as is understood to be claimed. This is thought to be obvious, not only from the general character of the act, and of all the other articles it contains, but because the one immediately preceding, like all those preceding and succeeding it, other than the 56th and 57th, includes only persons belonging to the "armies of the United States." Its language is, "whosoever *belonging to the armies of the United States,* employed in foreign parts," shall do the act prohibited, shall suffer the prescribed punishment. Now, it is a familiar rule of interpretation, perfectly well settled, in such a case, that unless there be something in the following sections that clearly shows a purpose to make them more comprehensive than their immediate predecessor, they are to be construed as subject to the same limitation. So far from there being in this instance, any evidence of a different purpose, the declared object of the statute, as evidenced by its title, its first section, and its general contents, are all inconsistent with any other construction. And when to this it is considered that the power exercised by Congress in passing the statute was merely the constitutional one to make rules for the government and regulation of the *army,* it is doing great injustice to that department to suppose that in exercising it they designed to legislate for any other class. The words, therefore, in the 55th article, "belonging to the armies of the United States," qualifying the immediate preceding word, "whosoever," are applicable to the 56th and 57th, and equally qualify the same word "whosoever" also used in each of them. And, finally, upon this point I am supported by the authority of Lieutenant-General Scott. The Commission have seen from my previous reference to his autobiography that he placed his right to issue his martial law order, establishing, among other things, military commissions to try certain offenses in a foreign country, upon the ground that otherwise they would go unpunished, and his army become demoralized. One of these offenses was murder committed or attempted, and for such an offense he tells us that the articles of war provided no court for their trial and punishment, "no matter by whom or on whom committed." And this opinion is repeated in the 4th clause of his order, as true of all the designated offenses, "except in the very restricted case in the 9th of the article."

V. There are other views which I submit to the serious attention of the Commission.

I. The mode of proceeding in a court like this, and which has been pursued by the prosecution, with your approval, because deemed legal by both, is so inconsistent with the proceedings of civil courts, as regulated for ages by established law, that the fact, I think, demonstrates that persons not belonging to the army can not be subjected to such a jurisdiction. 1. The character of the pleadings. The offense charged is a conspiracy with persons not within the reach of the Court, and some of them in a foreign country, to commit the alleged crime. To give you jurisdiction, the design of the accused and their co-conspirators is averred to have been to aid the rebellion, and to accomplish that end not only by the murder of the President and Lieutenant-General Grant, but of the Vice-President and Secretary of State. It is further averred that the President being murdered, the Vice-President becoming thereby President, and as such, Commander-in-Chief, the purpose was to murder him; and as, in the contingency of the death of both, it would be the duty of the Secretary of State to cause an election to be held for President and Vice-President, he was to be murdered in order to prevent a "lawful election" of these officers; and that by all these means, "aid and comfort" were to be given "the insurgents engaged in armed rebellion against the United States," and "the subversion and overthrow of the Constitution and laws of the United States" thereby effected. That such pleading as this would not be tolerated in a civil court, I suppose every lawyer will concede. It is argumentative, and even in that character unsound. The continuance of our Government does not depend on the lives of any or of all of its public servants. As fact, or law, therefore, the pleading is fatally defective. The Government has an inherent power to preserve itself, which no conspiracy to murder, or murder, can in the slightest degree impair. And the result which we have just witnessed proves this, and shows the folly of the madman and fiend by whose hands our late lamented President fell. He, doubtless, thought that he had done a deed that would subvert the "Constitution and laws." We know that it has not had even a tendency to that result. Not a power of the Government was suspended; all progressed as before the dire catastrophe. A cherished and almost idolized citizen was snatched from us by the assassin's arm, but there was no halt in the march of the Government. That continued in all its majesty wholly unimpeded. The only effect was to place the nation in tears, and drape it in mourning, and to awake the sympathy, and excite the indignation of the world.

II. But this mode of pleading renders, it would seem, inapplicable, the rules of evidence known to the civil courts. It justifies, in the opinion of the Judge Advocate and the Court (or what has been done would not have been done), a latitude that no civil court would allow, as in the judgment of such a court the accused, however innocent, could not be supposed able to meet it. Proof has been received, not only of distinct offenses from those charged, but of such offenses committed by others than the parties on trial. Even in regard to the party himself, other offenses alleged to have been previously committed by him can not be proved. At one time a different practice prevailed in England, and does now, it is believed, in some of the Continental governments. But since the days of Lord Holt (a name venerated by lawyers and all admirers of enlightened jurisprudence), it has not prevailed in England. In the case of Harrison, tried before that judge for murder, the counsel for the Government offered a witness to prove some felonious design of the prisoner three years before. Holt indignantly exclaimed, "Hold! hold! what are you doing now? How can he defend himself from charges of which he has no notice? And how many issues are to be raised to perplex me and the jury? Away! away! that ought not to be—that is nothing to the matter." 12 *State Trials*, 833–874. I refer to this case, not to assail what has been done in these cases contrary to this rule, because I am bound to infer that before such a commission as this the rule has no legal force. If, in a civil court, then, these parties would be entitled to the benefit of this rule, one never departed from in such courts, they would not have had proved against them crimes alleged to have been committed by others, and having no necessary or legal connection with those charged. With the same view, and not denying the right of the Commission in the particular case I am about to refer to, but to show that the Constitution could not have designed to subject citizens to the practice, I cite the same judge to prove that in a civil court those parties could not have been legally fettered during their trial. In the case of *Cranbum*, accused as implicated in the "assassination plot," on trial before the same judge, Holt put an end to what Lord Campbell terms "the revolting practice of trying prisoners in fetters." Hearing the clanking of chains, though no complaint was made to him, he said, "I should like to know why the prisoner is brought in ironed." "Let them be instantly knocked off. When prisoners are tried they should stand at their ease." 13 *State Trials*, 221, 2d Campbell, *Lives Chief Justices*, 140. Finally, I deny the jurisdiction of the Commission, not only because neither Constitution or laws justify, but, on the contrary, repudiate it, but on the ground that all the experience of the past is against it. Jefferson, ardent in the prosecution of Burr, and solicitous for his conviction, from a firm belief of his guilt, never suggested that he should be tried before any other than a civil court. And in that trial, so ably presided over by Marshall, the prisoner was allowed to "stand at his ease;" was granted every constitutional privilege, and no evidence was permitted to be given against him but such as a civil court recognizes; and in that case, as in this, the overthrow of the Government was the alleged purpose, and yet it was not intimated in any quarter that he could be tried by a military tribunal. In England, too, the doctrine on which this prosecution is placed is unknown. Attempts were made to assassinate George the Third and the present Queen, and Mr. Percival, then Prime Minister, was assassinated as he entered the House of Commons. In the first two instances, the design was to murder the commander-in-chief of England's army and

navy, in whom, too, the whole war power of the Government was also vested; in the last, a secretary, clothed with powers as great, at least, as those that belong to our Secretary of State; and yet, in each, the parties accused were tried before a civil court, no one suggesting any other. And during the period of the French Revolution, when its principles, if principles they can be termed, were being inculcated in England to an extent that alarmed the Government, and caused it to exert every power it was thought to possess to frustrate their effect, when the writ of *habeas corpus* was suspended, and arrests and prosecutions resorted to almost without limit, no one suggested a trial, except in the civil courts. And yet the apprehension of the Government was, that the object of the alleged conspirators was to subvert its authority, bring about its overthrow, and subject the kingdom to the horrors of the French Revolution, then shocking the nations of the world. Hardy, Horne Tooke, and others, were tried by civil courts, and their names are remembered for the principles of freedom that were made triumphant mainly through the efforts of "that great genius," in the words of a modern English statesman (Earl Russell), "whose sword and buckler protected justice and freedom during the disastrous period;" having "the tongue of Cicero and the soul of Hampden, an invincible orator and an undaunted patriot." *Erskine*.

As it was, these trials were conducted in so relentless a spirit, and, as it was thought, with such disregard of the rights of the subject, that the administration of the day were not able to withstand the torrent of the people's indignation. What would have been their fate, individually as well as politically, if the cases had been tried before a military commission, and life taken? Can it be that in this particular an American citizen is not entitled to all the rights that belong to a British subject? Can it be that with us Executive power at times casts into the shade and renders all other power subordinate? An American statesman, with a world-wide reputation, long since gave answer to these inquiries. In a debate in the Senate of the United States, in which he assailed what he deemed an unwarranted assumption of Executive power, he said, "the first object of a free people is the preservation of their liberties, and liberty is only to be maintained by constitutional restraints and just divisions of political power." "It does not trust the amiable weaknesses of human nature, and, therefore, will not permit power to overstep its prescribed limits, though benevolence, good intent, and patriotic intent come along with it." And he added, "Mr. President, the contest for ages has been to rescue liberty from the grasp of Executive power." "In the long list of the champions of human freedom there is not one name dimmed by the reproach of advocating the extension of Executive authority." Thoughts so eloquently expressed appeal with subduing power to every patriotic heart, and demonstrate that Webster, if here, would be heard raising his mighty voice against the jurisdiction of this Commission—a jurisdiction placed upon Executive authority alone. But it has been urged that martial law warrants such a commission, and that such law prevails here. The doctrine is believed to be alike indefensible and dangerous. It is not, however, necessary to inquire whether martial law, if it did prevail, would maintain your jurisdiction, as it does not prevail. It has never been declared by any *competent* authority, and the civil courts we know are in the full and undisturbed exercise of all their functions. We learn, and the fact is doubtless true, that one of the parties, the very chief of the alleged conspiracy, has been indicted, and is about to be tried before one of those courts. If he, the alleged head and front of the conspiracy, is to be and can be so tried, upon what ground of right, of fairness, or of policy can the parties who are charged to have been his mere instruments be deprived of the same mode of trial? It may be said that in acting under this commission you are but conforming to an order of the President, which you are bound to obey. Let me examine this for a moment. If that order merely authorizes you to investigate the cases and report the facts to him and not to pronounce a judgment, and is to that extent legal, then it is because the President has the power himself, without such a proceeding, to punish the crime, and has only invoked your assistance to enable him to do it the more justly. Can this be so? Can it be that the life of a citizen, however humble, be he soldier or not, depends in any case on the mere will of the President? And yet it does, if the doctrine be sound. What more dangerous one can be imagined? Crime is defined by law, and is to be tried and punished under the law. What is murder, treason, or conspiracy, and what is admissible evidence to prove either, are all legal questions, and many of them, at times, difficult of correct solution. What the facts are may also present difficult inquiries. To pass upon the first, the Constitution provides courts consisting of judges selected for legal knowledge, and made independent of Executive power. Military judges are not so selected, and so far from being independent, are absolutely dependent on such power. To pass upon the latter, it provides juries as being not likely to "partake of the wishes and opinions of the Government." But if your function is only to act as aids to the President, to enable him to exercise his function of punishment, and as he is under no obligation by any law to call for such aid, he may punish upon his own unassisted judgment, and without even the form of a trial. In conclusion, then, gentlemen, I submit that your responsibility, whatever that be, for error, in a proceeding like this, can find no protection in Presidential authority. Whatever it be, it grows out of the laws, and may, through the laws, be enforced. I suggested in the outset of these remarks that that responsibility in one contingency may be momentous. I recur to it again, disclaiming, as I did at first, the wish or hope that it would cause you to be wanting in a single particular of what you may believe to be your duty, but

to obtain your best and most matured judgment. The wish and hope disclaimed would be alike idle and discourteous; and I trust the Commission will do me the justice to believe that I am incapable of falling into either fault.

Responsibility to personal danger can never alarm soldiers who have faced, and will ever be willing in their country's defense to face, death on the battle-field. But there is a responsibility that every gentleman, be he soldier or citizen, will constantly hold before him, and make him ponder—responsibility to the Constitution and laws of his country and an intelligent public opinion—and prevent his doing anything knowingly that can justly subject him to the censure of either. I have said that your responsibility is great. If the commission under which you act is void and confers no authority, whatever you may do may involve the most serious personal liability. Cases have occurred that prove this. It is sufficient to refer to one. Joseph Wall, at the time the offense charged against him was committed, was Governor and commander of the garrison of Goree, a dependency of England, in Africa. The indictment was for the murder of Benjamin Armstrong, and the trial was had in January, 1802, before a special court, consisting of Sir Archibald McDonald, Chief Baron of the Exchequer; Lawrence, of the King's Bench, and Rocke, of the Common Pleas. The prosecution was conducted by Law, then Attorney General, afterward Lord Ellenborough. The crime was committed in 1782, and under a military order of the accused, and the sentence of a regimental court-martial. The defense relied upon was, that at the time the garrison was in a state of mutiny, and that the deceased took a prominent part in it; that, because of the mutiny, the order for the court-martial was made, and that the punishment which was inflicted and said to have caused the death, was under its sentence. The offense was purely a military one, and belonged to the jurisdiction of a military court, if the facts relied upon by the accused were true, and its judgment constituted a valid defense. The court, however, charged the jury, that if they found that there was no mutiny to justify such a court-martial or its sentence, they were void, and furnished no defense whatever. The jury so finding, found the accused guilty, and he was soon after executed. 28 *St. Tr.*, 51, 178. The application of the principle of this case to the question I have considered is obvious. In that instance want of jurisdiction in the court-martial was held to be fatal to its judgment as a defense for the death that ensued under it. In this, if the Commission has no jurisdiction, its judgment for the same reason will be of no avail, either to Judges, Secretary of War, or President, if either shall be called to a responsibility for what may be done under it. Again, upon the point of jurisdiction, I beg leave to add that the opinion I have endeavored to maintain is believed to be the almost unanimous opinion of the profession, and certainly is of every judge or court who has expressed any.

In Maryland, where such commissions have

been and are held, the Judge of the Criminal Court of Baltimore recently made it a matter of special charge to the grand jury. Judge Bond told them: "It has come to my knowledge that here, where the United States Court, presided over by Chief Justice Chase, has always been unimpeded, and where the Marshal of the United States, appointed by the President, selects the jurors, irresponsible and unlawful military commissions attempt to exercise criminal jurisdiction over citizens of this State, not in the military or naval service of the United States, nor in the militia, who are charged with offenses either not known to the law, or with crimes for which the mode of trial and punishment are provided by statute in the courts of the land. That it is not done by the paramount authority of the United States, your attention is directed to article 5, of the Constitution of the United States, which says: 'No person shall be held to answer for a capital or otherwise infameus crime, unless on a presentment or indictment of a grand jury, except in cases arising in the land or naval forces, or in the militia when in actual service in time of war or public danger.'" *Such persons exercising such unlawful jurisdiction are liable to indictment by you, as well as responsible in civil actions to the parties.* In New York, Judge Peckham, of the Supreme Court of that State, and speaking for the whole bench, charged the grand jury as follows:

"The Constitution of the United States, Article 5, of the amendments, declares that 'no person shall be held to answer for a capital or otherwise infamous crime, unless on presentment or indictment of a grand jury, except in cases arising in the land or naval forces, or in the militia, when in actual service in time of war or public danger.'

"Article 6 declares that, 'in all criminal prosecutions, the accused shall enjoy the right to a speedy and public trial.'

"Article 3, section 2, declares that 'the trial of all crimes, except in cases of impeachment, shall be by jury,' etc.

"These provisions were made for occasions of great excitement, no matter from what cause, when passion, rather than reason, might prevail.

"In ordinary times, there would be no occasion for such guards, as there would be no disposition to depart from the usual and established modes of trial.

"A great crime has lately been committed that has shocked the civilized world. Every right-minded man desires the punishment of the criminals, but he desires that punishment to be administered according to law, and through the judicial tribunals of the country. No star-chamber court, no secret inquisition, in this nineteenth century, can ever be made acceptable to the American mind.

"If none but the guilty could be accused, then no trial could be necessary—execution should follow accusation.

"It is almost as necessary that the public should have undoubted faith in the purity of criminal justice, as it is that justice in fact be administered with integrity.

"Grave doubts, to say the least, exist in the minds of intelligent men as to the constitutional right of the recent military commissions at Washington to sit in judgment upon the persons now on trial for their lives before that tribunal. Thoughtful men feel aggrieved that such a commission should be established in this free country, when the war is over, and when the common-law courts are open and accessible to administer justice, according to law, without fear or favor.

"What remedy exists? None whatever, except through the power of public sentiment.

"As citizens of this free country, having an interest in its prosperity and good name, we may, as I desire to do, in all courtesy and kindness, and with all proper respect, express our disapprobation of this course in our rulers in Washington.

"The unanimity with which the leading press of our land has condemned this mode of trial, ought to be gratifying to every patriot.

"Every citizen is interested in the preservation, in their purity, of the institutions of his country; and you, gentlemen, may make such presentment on this subject, if any, as your judgment may dictate."

The reputation of both of these judges is well and favorably known, and their authority is entitled to the greatest deference.

Even in France, during the consulship of Napoleon, the institution of a military commission for the trial of the Prince Duc d'Enhien, for alleged conspiracy against his life, was, to the irreparable injury of his reputation, ordered by Napoleon. The trial was had, and the Prince was at once convicted and executed. It brought upon Napoleon the condemnation of the world, and is one of the blackest spots in his character. The case of the Duke, says the eminent historian of the Consulate and the Empire, furnished Napoleon "a happy opportunity of saving his glory from a stain," which he lost, and adds, with philosophic truth, that it was "a deplorable consequence of *violating the ordinary forms of justice,*" and further adds, "to defend social order by conforming *to the strict rules and forms of justice,* without allowing any feeling of revenge to operate, is the great lesson to be drawn from these tragical events." *Thier's History, etc.,* 4 vol., 818, 822.

Upon the whole, then, I think I shall not be considered obtrusive if I again invoke the Court to weigh well all that I have thought it my duty to urge upon them. I feel the duty to be upon me as a citizen sworn to do what I can to preserve the Constitution, and the principles on which it reposes. As counsel of one of the parties, I should esteem myself dishonored if I attempted to rescue my client from a proper trial for the offense charged against her, by denying the jurisdiction of the Commission, upon grounds that I did not conscientiously believe to be sound. And, in what I have done, I have not more had in view the defense of Mrs. Surratt, than of the Constitution and the laws. In my view, in this respect, her cause is the cause of every citizen. And let it not be supposed that I am seeking to secure impunity to any one who may have been guilty of the horrid crimes of the night of the 14th of April. Over these the civil courts of this District have ample jurisdiction, and will faithfully exercise it if the cases are remitted to them, and guilt is legally established, and will surely award the punishment known to the laws. God forbid that such crimes should go unpunished! In the black catalogue of offenses, these will forever be esteemed the darkest and deepest ever committed by sinning man. And, in common with the civilized world, do I wish that every legal punishment may be legally inflicted upon all who participated in them.

A word more, gentlemen, and, thanking you for your kind attention, I shall have done. As you have discovered, I have not remarked on the evidence in the case of Mrs. Surratt, nor is it my purpose; but it is proper that I refer to her case, in particular, for a single moment. That a woman, well educated, and, as far as we can judge from all her past life, as we have it in evidence, a devout Christian, ever kind, affectionate and charitable, with no motive disclosed to us that could have caused a total change in her very nature, could have participated in the crimes in question it is almost impossible to believe. Such a belief can only be forced upon a reasonable, unsuspecting, unprejudiced mind, by direct and uncontradicted evidence, coming from pure and perfectly unsuspected sources. Have we these? Is the evidence uncontradicted? Are the two witnesses, Weichmann and Lloyd, pure and unsuspected? Of the particulars of their evidence I say nothing. They will be brought before you by my associates. But this conclusion in regard to these witnesses must be, in the minds of the Court, and is certainly strongly impressed upon my own, that, if the facts which they themselves state as to their connection and intimacy with Booth and Payne are true, their knowledge of the purpose to commit the crimes, and their participation in them, is much more satisfactorily established than the alleged knowledge and participation of Mrs. Surratt. As far, gentlemen, as I am concerned, her case is now in your hands.   REVERDY JOHNSON.

JUNE 16, 1865.

As associate counsel for Mrs. Mary E. Surratt, we concur in the above.

FREDERICK A. AIKEN,
JOHN W. CLAMPITT

ARGUMENT

ON THE PLEA TO THE

JURISDICTION OF THE MILITARY COMMISSION,

BY

THOMAS EWING, Jr.

JUNE 23, 1865.

May it please the Court : The first great question—a question that meets us at the threshold—is, do you, gentlemen, constitute a court, and have you jurisdiction, as a court, of the persons accused, and the crimes with which they are charged? If you have such jurisdiction, it must have been conferred by the Constitution, or some law consistent with it, and carrying out its provisions.

1. The 5th article of the Constitution declares:

"That the judicial power of the United States shall be vested in one Supreme Court, and in such *inferior courts* as Congress may, from time to time, ordain and establish;" and that "the judges of both Supreme and *inferior courts* shall hold their offices during good behavior."

Under *this* provision of the Constitution, none but courts ordained or established by Congress can exercise judicial power, and those courts must be composed of judges who hold their offices during good behavior. They must be independent judges, free from the influence of Executive power. Congress has not "ordained and established" you a court, or authorized you to call these parties before you and sit upon their trial, and you are not " *judges* " who hold your offices during good behavior. You are, therefore, no court under the Constitution, and have no jurisdiction in these cases, unless you obtain it from some other source, which overrules this constitutional provision.

The President can not confer judicial power upon you, for he has it not. The *executive*, not the *judicial*, power of the United States is vested in him. His mandate, no matter to what man or body of men addressed, to try, and, if convicted, to sentence to death a citizen, not of the naval or military forces of the United States, carries with it no authority which could be pleaded in justification of the sentence. It were no better than the simple mandate to take A B, C D, E F, and G. H, and put them to death.

2. The President, under the 5th *amendment* to the Constitution, may constitute courts pursuant to the Articles of War, but he can not give them jurisdiction over citizens. This article provides that "no person shall be held to answer for a capital or otherwise infamous crime, unless on a presentment or indictment of a grand jury, *except in cases arising in the land or naval forces, or in the militia when in actual service in time of war or public danger.*"

The presentment and indictment of a grand jury is a thing unknown and inconsistent with your commission. You have nothing of the kind. Neither you nor the law officers who control your proceedings seem to have thought of any such thing. These defendants did not and do not belong to the " *land or naval forces*" of the United States—nor were they " *militia, in time of war or public danger, in actual service.*" The Constitution, therefore, in the article above cited, expressly says: *You shall not hold them to answer* to any of the capital and infamous crimes with which they are charged.

Is not a single, direct, constitutional prohibition, forbidding you to take jurisdiction in these cases, sufficient? If it be not, read the provision of the 3d section of the 3d article. It is as follows:

"The trial of all crimes, except in cases of impeachment, shall be *by jury.*"

But lest this should not be enough, in their anxious care to provide against the abuses from which England had recently escaped, and which were still fresh in the memories of men—as the Star Chamber, the High Commission Courts, and their attendant enormities—the framers of the Constitution further provided, in the 6th amendment, that—

"In all criminal prosecutions the accused shall enjoy the right to a speedy and public trial *by an impartial jury* of the State and district wherein the crime shall have been committed."

Now, whence, and what, is the authority which overrules these distinct constitutional prohibitions, and empowers you to hold these citizens to answer, *despite the mandates* of the Constitution forbidding you?

Congress has not attempted to grant you the power; Congress could not grant it. A law to that effect, against the constitutional prohibition, would be merely void. Congress has authorized the suspension of the writ of *habeas corpus*, as the Constitution permits (Art. 1, Sec. 9); but the Constitution does not thereby permit the military to try, nor has Congress attempted to deliver over to the military for *trial, judgment, and execution, American citizens*, not in the land or naval forces or in the militia in actual service, *when accused of crime.* Congress and the President, the law-making power, were incompetent to this, and have not attempted it. Whence, then, comes the dispensation with the constitutional prohibition? Where and whence is the affirmative grant of jurisdiction under which you propose to try, and, if convicted, pass sentence upon these men, citizens of the United States—not soldiers, not militia-men—but citizens, engaged in the ordinary avocations of life? I am not permitted to know. *Congress* has not in any form attempted to violate or impair the Constitution. They have suspended the writ of *habeas corpus;* this goes to imprisonment—not trial, conviction, or punishment. This is the extreme limit to which the law-making power is permitted to go, and it is only in cases of strong necessity that this is permitted. Congress has repealed so much of the 102d section of the act of September 24, 1789, as required that in all capital cases twelve petit jurors should be summoned from the county in which the offense was committed (par. 221, sec. 102, repealed July 16, 1862, page 1164, sec. 22), but has preserved all other legal provisions made in aid of the Constitution to protect citizens from the oppression of unregulated and unrestrained Executive power. The accused shall be tried upon an indictment or presentment of a grand jury. If two or more crimes of a like nature be charged, they must be set forth *in separate counts.* (Act of February 26, 1853, sec. 117.) You may not compel an accused to answer to a loose story or accusation of *several crimes in one count.* If the crime charged be treason, which this paper approaches more nearly than anything else, the accused shall have a copy of the indictment, and a list of the jury, and of all the witnesses to be produced on the trial for proving the said indictment (mentioning the names and places of abode of such witnesses and jurors), delivered unto him at least three entire days before he shall be tried for the same; and in other capital offenses, shall have such copy of indictment and list of the jury two entire days, at least, before the trial. (Act of April 30, 1790, sec. 24, p. 221.)

Against this array of constitutional and legal prohibition and regulation, I know of nothing that can be adduced, except, perhaps, an Executive order authorizing, by direct mandate or implication, the thing to be done which the Constitution forbids you to do. If you be proceeding in obedience to such Executive mandate, and if that give jurisdiction, still you proceed in a form and manner which the Constitution and law expressly forbid. If my clients be charged with treason or murder (and I conjecture they are charged with murder, at least), they must be proved to have been *present, aiding in or actually committing the overt act, or alleged murder.* For either of these the punishment on conviction is death. The Judge Advocate has been unable, in the cases of Arnold and Mudd, to present any evidence *remotely approaching* that prescribed by the Constitution and the laws as the condition of conviction; and yet I am led to infer that he will claim a conviction of one or both of them on the proof presented. What is the profession, on this and on the other side of the Atlantic, to think of such administration of criminal jurisprudence?—for this, the first of our State trials, will be read with avidity everywhere. I ask the officers of the Government to think of this carefully *now,* lest two or three years hence they may not like to hear it named.

But we may mistake the whole case as it presents itself to the mind of the Judge Advocate. We are here as counsel for the accused, but are not allowed to know explicitly with what crime, *defined by law,* any one of them is charged, or what we are here to defend. No crime known to the law is legally charged in the paper which is here substituted for an indictment. In this paper three distinct crimes are strongly hinted at in a single charge, to each of which different rules of law and evidence are applicable, and different penalties are attached; and I had wished to know, so that I might shape the defense of my clients accordingly, for *which* alleged or intimated crime any one, or each, or all of them, are to be tried. The information has been denied us. The Judge Advocate puts these parties on trial, and refuses (in the most courteous terms) to advise their counsel on what law or authority he rests his claim to jurisdiction; of what crime he intends to convict each or any of the defendants; in what laws the crimes are defined and their punishments prescribed; or on what proof, out of the wild jungle of testimony, he intends to rest his claim to convictions.

But it has been said, and will perhaps be said again, in support of this jurisdiction, that the necessities of war justify it—and *"silent leges inter arma."* So said the Roman orator when Rome had become a military despotism, and ceased forever to have liberty, and when she retained law only as the gift or by the permission of the ruling despot. "*The law is silent amid arms.*" Yes, it is so in a conquered country, when the victorious general chooses to put the law to silence; for he is an autocrat, and may, if he chooses, be a despot. But how extravagant is the pretense that a bold, and spirited, and patriotic people, because they rise in their majesty and send forth conquering armies to rescue the republic, thereby forfeit all constitutional and legal protection of life, liberty, and property!

Cases have often arisen, in which robber bands, whose vocation is piracy on the high seas, or promiscuous robbery and murder on land—*hostes humani generis*—may be lawfully put to the sword without quarter, in battle, or hung on the yard-arm, or otherwise put to death, when captured, according to the necessities of the case, without trial or other conviction, except the knowledge of the commanding general that they were taken *flagrante bello,* and that they are pirates or land robbers. A military court may be called, but it is *advisory* merely; the *general* acts, condemns, and executes. But the *Constitution* of the United States has nothing to do with this. It does not protect pirates or marauders who are enemies of the human race; or spies, or even ene-mies taken in battle. It protects, not bellig-erent enemies, but only citizens and those persons not citizens who, in civil life, seek and claim its protection, or aliens who are en-gaged in its military or other service. The power of the commanding general over these classes is restrained only by the *usages* of war among civilized nations. But these defend-ants are not charged as spies or pirates, or armed and organized marauders, or enemies captured in war, or persons in the land or na-val service of the United States. They belong to none of these classes, over whom military discretion or martial law extends, unless they extend over and embrace *all* the people of the United States.

But if the jurisdiction in this case exist, whether by law or by the power of arms, I re-gret that a Military Commission should be charged with the trial of these causes. The crimes are, as far as hinted at and written about in the charge and specifications, all cognizable in our civil courts. Those courts are open, un-obstructed, without a single impediment to the full and perfect administration of justice—ready and prompt, as they always are, to per-form the high duties which the well-known principles of law under the Constitution de-volve on them. What good reason can be given in a case like this, to a people jealous of their rights, for a resort here and now to military trials and military executions? We are at the advent of a new, and I trust a suc-cessful, Administration. A taint such as this—namely, the needless violation of the constitutional rights of the citizen—ought not to be permitted to attach to and infect it. The jurisdiction of this Commission has to be sought *dehors* the Constitution, and against its express prohibition. It is, therefore, at least of doubtful validity. If that jurisdic-tion do not exist; if the doubt be resolved against it by our judicial tribunals, when the law shall again speak, the form of trial by this unauthorized Commission can not be pleaded in justification of the seizure of prop-erty or the arrest of person, much less the in-fliction of the death penalty. In that event, however fully the recorded evidence may sus-tain your findings, however moderate may seem your sentences, however favorable to the accused your rulings on the evidence, your sentence will be held *in law* no better than the rulings of Judge Lynch's courts in the ad-ministration of lynch law. When the party now in power falls—as in the vicissitudes of things it must one day fall, and all the sooner for a reckless use of its present power—so it will be viewed by that party which succeeds it. This is to be expected, and, indeed, hoped; but if, unfortunately, this proceeding be then accepted and recorded as a precedent, we may have fastened on us a military despotism. If we concede that the exercise of jurisdiction claimed is *now* necessary, and for the best pos-sible object, before we consent that it stand as a precedent in our jurisprudence, we should recall to mind the statesmanlike and almost prophetic remarks of Julius Cæsar, in the Ro-

man Senate, on the trial of Lentulus and his accomplices in Catiline's conspiracy: "*Abuses often grow from precedents good in principle; but when the power falls into hands of men less en-lightened or less honest, a just and reasonable pre-cedent receives an application contrary to justice and reason.*" It is to be remembered that crim-inal trials involving capital punishment were not then within the competency of the Roman Senate; and neither the Consul nor the Sen-ate, nor both of them, had the right to con-demn a Roman citizen without the concurrence of the people.[*]

If you believe you possess the power of life and death over the citizens of the United States in States where the regular tribunals can be safely appealed to, still, for the sake of our common country and its cherished institu-tions, do not press that power too far. Our ju-dicial tribunals, at some future day, I have no doubt, will be again in the full exercise of their constituted powers, and may think, as a large proportion of the legal profession think now, that your jurisdiction in these cases is an unwarranted assumption; and they may treat the judgment which you pronounce, and the sentence you cause to be executed, as your own unauthorized acts.

This assumption of jurisdiction, or this use of a legitimate jurisdiction, not created by law, and not known to the law or to legal men, has not for its sanction even the plea of *necessity*. It may be *convenient*. Conviction may be easier and more certain in this Military Commission than in our constitutional courts. Inexperi-enced as most of you are in judicial investi-gations, you can admit evidence which the courts would reject, and reject what they would admit, and you may convict and sentence on evidence which those courts would hold to be wholly insufficient. Means, too, may be re-sorted to by detectives, acting under promise or hope of reward, and operating on the fears or the cupidity of witnesses, to obtain and in-troduce evidence, which can not be detected and exposed in this military trial, but could be readily in the free, but guarded, course of investigation before our regular judicial tribu-nals. The Judge Advocate, with whom chiefly rests the fate of these citizens, is learned in the law, but from his position he can not be an impartial judge, unless he be more than man. He is the PROSECUTOR, in the most extended sense of the word. As in duty bound, before this Court was called, he received the reports of detectives, pre-examined the witnesses, pre-pared and officially signed the charges, and as principal counsel for the Government, con-trolled on the trial the presentation, admis-sion and rejection of evidence. In our courts of law, a lawyer who has heard his client's story, if transferred from the bar to the bench, may not sit in the trial of the cause, lest the ermine be sullied through the partiality of counsel. This is no mere theoretical objec-tion—for the union of prosecutor and judge works practical injustice to the accused. The

---

[*] Cicero, who was Consul, Cato, Silanus, and others of their associates in the Senate, were afterward tried for the murder of the conspirators, convicted, and banished.

Judge Advocate controls the admission and rejection of evidence—knows what will aid and what will injure the case of the prosecution, and inclines favorably to the one, and unfavorably to the other. The defense is met with a bias of feeling and opinion on the part of the judge who controls the proceedings of the Court, and on whom, in great measure, the fate of the accused depends, which morals and law alike reject. Let it not be supposed I censure or reflect on any one, for I do not. The wrong suffered by the parties accused has its root in the vice of this system of trial, which I have endeavored to expose.

Because our Chief, so venerated and beloved (and no one venerated and loved him more than I), has fallen by the hand of a ruthless assassin, it ought not to follow that the Constitution and law should be violated in punishing men suspected of having compassed his death, or that men not *legally* found guilty should be sacrificed in vengeance as victims generally because of the crime.

There may be a lurking feeling among men which tends to this harshness of retribution, regardless of the innocence of those on whom vengeance may fall. Tending to this feeling, exciting or ministering to it, was the two days' testimony which, without other apparent point or purpose, detailed the horrors of the Libby Prison; and the evidence that, in 1861, one of my clients took part in the rebellion; and the further testimony (which we showed was utterly fabulous) that another of my clients, in 1863 or 1864, entertained rebel officers and soldiers, and corresponded with rebels in Richmond. As if to say: "What matters it how we try, or whether we legally try at all, provided we convict and execute men who have been associated with, or in sympathy with, monsters such as those?" Homer makes Achilles immolate, at the funeral pyre of Patroclus, twelve Trojan captives, simply because they *were* Trojans, and because Patroclus had fallen by a Trojan hand. If that principle of judicial action be adopted here, it were surely not too much to sacrifice to the *manes* of one so beloved and honored as our late Chief Magistrate a little lot of rebel sympathizers, because, like the assassin, some of them, at some time, participated in the rebellion, or gave aid and comfort to rebels. If this course of reasoning do not develop the object of that strange testimony, I know not how to read it. Indeed, a position taken by the learned Assistant Judge Advocate, in discussing my objection to the part of that evidence which relates to my clients, goes to this—and even beyond it—namely, that participation in the rebellion was participation in the assassination, and that the rebellion itself formed part of the conspiracy for which these men are on trial here.

ARGUMENT

IN

DEFENSE OF DAVID E. HEROLD.

BY

FREDERICK STONE, ESQ.

May it please the Court:

At the earnest request of the widowed mother and estimable sisters of the accused, I have consented to act as his counsel in the case now before the Court.

It is a source of some embarrassment to the counsel for the accused that the Judge Advocate General has seen fit not to open this case with a brief statement of the law upon which this prosecution is founded. It would have been a great, and, as he thinks, proper assistance to the accused and his counsel to have known with more accuracy than is set out in the charge, the special offense for which he is arraigned. In the absence of such opening statement, the accused can only discuss the law on which he supposes the Judge Advocate to rely.

While the counsel for the accused does not, and can not, concede the question of jurisdiction, it is not proposed by him to discuss the question of the jurisdiction of this Court over the accused in this case, except so far as may be necessary incidentally in discussing the effect of General Order No. 141. The question of the general jurisdiction he will leave in abler hands.

But, supposing this Court should be entirely satisfied that they have jurisdiction, another, and, as the counsel for the accused thinks, a more important question arises; and that question is: What is the law governing the several offenses with which the accused stands charged, and what is the law prescribing the punishment thereof? I shall first consider what is the law governing the case as to the crime and the punishment, upon the hypothesis that martial law generally was in force in the District of Columbia on the 14th of April, 1865, and still so continues in force; and I shall, in the second place, consider whether martial law did, in fact, exist within the District of Columbia on the 14th of April, and does now exist, and to what extent.

In time of peace, the civil law is administered by civil tribunals, whose mode of procedure and jurisdiction are clearly defined; in time of war, justice is administered in the enemy's country, occupied by the belligerent, and also in that part of the belligerent's own country which is under martial law, by military commissions, according to a system of jurisprudence sometimes called the common law of war. In this changed condition of things, the military commission supersedes the civil tribunal, and the common law of war supersedes the civil law; but the rules of the common law of war are as clearly defined as are those of the civil law, and the jurisdiction of the military commission is as accurately defined as the jurisdiction of the civil tribunal. The common law of war determines the manner in which a military commission, charged with its administration, shall be organized, the mode in which proceedings before it shall be conducted, the rules by which it shall determine questions of evidence arising in the course of the trial, and the penalty to which it shall subject the accused upon conviction.

By this law a military commission must be organised in the manner in which courts-martial are organized, and its proceedings must conform to the manner of proceedings before courts-martial, and be conducted according to the rules prescribing the mode and manner of conducting proceedings before these tribunals.

By the same common law of war, the jurisdiction of a military commission as to persons and offenses is also limited and defined. A military commission possesses no power to try a person in the army or navy of the United States for any offense provided for in the articles of war. It has no jurisdiction in the case of a soldier charged with disobedience of orders, desertion, etc. Offenses of this nature, and committed by persons subject to military law, are expressly cognizable before the military courts created by that law, and known as courts-martial. If, in time of peace, a soldier commit an offense against the civil law not provided for in the articles of war, he is surrendered up to the civil jurisdiction to be tried; and if he commit such an offense in time of war in a district subject to martial law, he will be tried by military commission, which, in such district, supersedes the civil courts in the administration of justice. It is, therefore, apparent that everything in the organization of the military commission, or in the manner of conducting proceedings before it, from the filing of the charges and specifications, down to the final decision of the court, and its jurisdiction as to persons, is not entirely within the discretion of the Commander-in-Chief or of the commission itself, but is subject to the established rules and principles of the common law of war, which calls it into existence, to administer justice according to those rules and principles.

What are these rules and principles? They are clearly indicated in article 6 of General Order No. 100 (already in evidence in this case), which is as follows:

"All civil and penal law shall continue to take its usual course in the enemy's places and territories under martial law, unless interrupted or stopped by order of the occupying military power; but all functions of the hostile government—legislative, executive or administrative—whether of a general, provincial or local character, cease under martial law, or continue only with the sanction, or, if deemed necessary, the participation, of the occupier or invader."

This order proves that, in the enemy's country, under martial law, the civil and penal law shall remain as the rule of conduct and law of the people, unless interrupted by express command. In the absence of any command interrupting the operation of the civil and penal law, what is the law over that portion of the enemy's territory to which this order refers? Martial law certainly prevails, because the territory referred to is described as territory under martial law. The civil and penal law of the country also prevails, because the order expressly declares that it shall continue. It is apparent, therefore, that two systems of jurisprudence prevail at the same time on the same territory; one, the system which martial law establishes, and known as the system of the common law of war, and the other, the system in force over the territory at the time of its conquest. But the latter system, although prevailing, can not be enforced, except by the conqueror, for the article further provides that all the "functions of the hostile government, legislative, executive or administrative, whether of a general, provincial or local character, cease under martial law, or continue only with the sanction, or if deemed necessary, the participation, of the occupier or invader."

Judicial power is one of the functions of government, and is specifically designated in the order by the word "administrative." All the functions of the government, including the administrative functions, must cease under martial law; but still, by the terms of the order, the civil and penal law shall continue and take its course, and be administered. By whom? By what tribunals? The civil courts can no longer exercise functions of their administering the law, and military courts administer, not civil and penal law, but military law and the common law of war. Article 18 of the order referred to says:

"Military jurisdiction is of two kinds: first, that which is conferred and defined by statute; second, that which is derived from the common law of war."

How, then, can a military jurisdiction administer civil and penal law? There is but one solution to the difficulty, and it is in the application of the principle lying at the foundation of the common law of war, and determining the system of jurisprudence known by that name, and it is this: That where, by virtue of the existence of martial law, the common law of war is required to be administered, the civil and penal law of the territory subject to martial law becomes part of that common law of war, and, as such, is to be administered by military tribunals, under military modes of procedure, with the same effect in securing the rights of litigants and the punishment of crimes as if administered by civil tribunals, according to the modes provided and adopted in the civil courts.

I do not mean to contend that the code of the common law of war is exclusively made up of the civil and penal law of the country which has become subject to martial law, but that the civil and penal law becomes a part of the common law of war in all cases to which it is applicable. Under martial law many acts become crimes which are innoxious and innocent in time of peace and under the civil code, and which are not, therefore, provided against in the civil and penal law.

In regard to the trial of persons arraigned for any of this class of crimes, the Commission must conform in its action, as nearly as may be, to the authenticated precedents of the common law of war, and administer justice with sound discretion; but in regard to the trial of persons arraigned for offenses created and recognized by the civil and penal law, the Commission must administer, as part of the common law of war, the civil and penal law as it is written. The civil and penal law becomes part of the common law of war by the fact of the inauguration of martial law.

It is true the operation of this principle may be interrupted by order of the occupying military power, in the exercise of an authority derived from, and limited by, the military necessity; but the right to interrupt the operation of the principle by special order, shows that the principle continues in force until the interrupting order is promulgated. It may, however, be contended that a special order in such case is not necessary according to the laws of war, and would not be required except for the mandate of section 6, above quoted from. If this is true, then the principle for which I have contended should be stated with a qualification, and the civil and penal law of the country subject to martial law becomes a part of the common law of war, except as to such parts thereof as military necessity requires should be suspended. Section 8 of General Order No. 100 provides as follows:

"Martial law in a hostile country consists in the suspension, by the occupying military authority, of the civil and criminal law, and of the domestic administration and government of the occupied place or territory, and the substitution of military rule and force for the same, as well as in the dictation of general laws, as far as military necessity *requires* this suspension or dictation."

According, then, to this section of the order, the civil and penal law is suspended only as far as military necessity requires a suspension.

The rule, therefore, is that the civil and penal law shall continue in force, and the exception is as to such parts thereof as military necessity may require to be suspended. This necessity, as is well understood, is not a condition in which the suspension of the civil and penal law would be more convenient to the occupying military power, or would simply gratify the caprice of the commander, but a condition in which such suspension is imperatively demanded to meet the exigencies of war, and absolutely required to conduct that war successfully. Military necessity is thus defined by section 14 of General Order No. 100:

"Military necessity, as understood by modern civilized nations, consists in the necessity of those measures which are *indispensable* for securing the ends of the war, and which are lawful according to the modern law and usages of war."

That portion of the civil and penal law suspended in the enemy's country subject to martial law, on the ground of military necessity, must, therefore, be such portions of said law as it is indispensable to suspend for securing the ends of the war, and which it is also lawful to suspend according to the modern law and usages of war.

Sections 3 and 6, above quoted, of General Order No. 100, by their terms, refer only to the "enemy's country," but they indicate the effect of martial law upon the system of jurisprudence to be administered wherever martial law prevails. That effect will be greater or less in modifying or suspending the civil and penal laws of the various territories that may be subject to martial law, according to the measure of the necessity existing in each.

Section 5 of General Order No. 100 provides as follows:

"Martial law should be less stringent in places and countries fully occupied and fairly conquered. Much greater severity may be exercised in places or regions where active hostilities exist, or are expected, and must be prepared for. Its most complete sway is allowed even in the commander's own country, when face to face with the enemy, because of the absolute necessities of the case, and of the paramount duty to defend the country against invasion."

It is apparent, therefore, that the effect of martial law in modifying and changing the civil and penal code, or the civil administration of the district or territory in which it prevails, depends upon the military necessity growing out of the condition of things existing in such territory or district. And if in any portion of the conquered and occupied territory of the enemy the civil and penal law is allowed to continue, certainly in such portions of the commander's own country as may be declared subject to martial law, the civil and penal law should not be interrupted, unless some extraordinary and overwhelming necessity arises to justify it.

I will not enter into the inquiry suggested by section 5, quoted above, as to whether or not martial law can prevail in the commander's own country in any case other than that referred to in the article, to-wit: when face to face with the enemy, and to which condition this article would seem to limit the rightful exercise of that law. But conceding that it may prevail within the commander's country, where hostile armies are not arrayed against each other on its soil, and war is not in actual progress, what, under such circumstances, is its effect in interrupting or suspending the civil and penal law? I concede, for the purpose of this argument, that it establishes the common law of war as suspending the civil and penal law, that it substitutes a military tribunal for civil courts, and the summary process of military arrests for the ordinary mode and form of civil arrests; but, when the military court is convened and organized, what law is it required to administer? The answer is obvious: it is to administer the common law of war. What part of the civil and penal law has been excluded from that common law of war and suspended under the force of a necessity making such suspension indispensable for securing the ends of the war?

This Commission is sitting not only in the commander's own country, but in the capital of that country. Before it met, the last hostile gun of the war had been fired, a thousand miles away. During its session 200,000 veterans have returned from the field, and passed in review in sight of the windows of this court-room, their faces homeward turned, their swords sheathed, their work accomplished. No enemy now remains in arms against the Government of the country; but the war is over, and peace restored. Again, I ask, what military necessity renders a suspension of the civil and penal law of the United States, in the capital of the United States indispensable for securing the ends of war?

The second inquiry which I propose to make before this Commission, is, whether martial law did exist on the 14th of April, 1865, in the city of Washington, and if so, to what extent, and whether it does now exist? The only evidence before the Commission of the existence of martial law in the city of Washington, on the 14th of April last, is the proclamation of the President of the United States, issued in September, 1862. That proclamation is in these words:

"That during the existing insurrection, and as a necessary measure for suppressing the same, all rebels and insurgents, their aiders and abettors, within the United States, and all persons discouraging volunteer enlistments, resisting militia drafts, or guilty of any disloyal practice, affording aid and comfort to rebels against the authority of the United States, shall be subject to martial law, and liable to trial and punishment by courts-martial or military commission."

It appears clearly, from General Order No. 100, that martial law is not, if I may use such an expression, an unbending code; that it can be made, in the discretion of the commander, more or less stringent, as the exigencies of the case may require. It also is apparent, from the same General Order, that martial law in the commander's own country, must exist by virtue of some proclamation or announcement. To what extent, then, does it appear that martial law was declared by the proclamation of the President of September, 1862, and which is sometimes designated as General Order No. 141? The President of the United States, if he had the right to issue the proclamation at all. had the right to limit its duration and the persons to whom it should apply. In the exercise of this constitutional right, the President did both; he limited the time of existence of martial law, as well as the persons to whom it is applied. By the terms of that order declaring martial law, the existence of that martial law is made to depend entirely on the existence of the rebellion. It required no order to annul or revoke it; it carried, if I may use such an expression, its own death-warrant upon its face. "During the existing insurrection, and as a necessary measure for its suppression," persons guilty of affording aid and comfort to the rebels are liable to be tried by courts-martial or military commission. Had the President of the United States intended that the crime of aiding the insurgents by giving to them aid and comfort, which occurred during the rebellion, should be punished after the rebellion had ceased, apt words were at hand so to express the order; but the order is not so expressed; both the crime and the punishment are made to depend upon the existence of the rebellion. That order, too, only touches a particular class of crimes. It does not touch the crime of murder, of an assault with intent to kill, of aiding or abetting in a murder, or aiding or abetting the escape of a murderer from justice, or of a conspiracy to murder. The same facts make the crime, and the same punishment follows conviction, and the same mode of punishment exists after the issue of that order as did before.

Loyal civil courts in the city of Washington have been constantly, since the issue of that proclamation, in session, with full and ample power and authority to try the crimes of murder, of conspiracy to murder, of assault with intent to kill and murder, and of aiding and abetting in the escape of a murderer. The jurisdiction of the civil courts over all such crimes last above enumerated has been left untouched and undisturbed by that order. There has been no hour since the issue of that proclamation that the Supreme Court of the District of Columbia has not had full and ample powers to try every crime enumerated in the charge in this case. Upon the suppression of the rebellion, that proclamation expired, and became from that and continues to this hour a dead letter upon the statute book, and that martial law which it inaugurated can never again exist in the capital of the country until the Commander-in-Chief, in the exercise of his constitutional powers, shall again declare it.

But supposing the proclamation to be still in force, supposing it to be as valid this day as it was on the day it was issued, still the fact remains that it only applies to one single class of persons and to one single crime, and that crime is aiding and abetting the rebellion. And if this Commission should conclude that

General Order No. 141 is still in force, and that they derive their power and authority to hear and determine these cases by virtue of that general order, still the fact remains that they have only the power under that order to try the naked crime of aiding and abetting the rebellion.

The charge in this case consists of several distinct and separate offenses embodied in one charge. The parties accused are charged with a conspiracy in aid of the rebellion, with murder, with assault with intent to kill, and with lying in wait. It is extremely doubtful from the language of the charge and the specification, under which of the following crimes the accused, Herold, is arraigned and now on his trial, viz.:

I. Whether he is on trial for the crime of conspiracy to overthrow the Government of the United States, as punishable by the act of the Congress of the United States, as passed the 31st of July, 1861; or,

II. Whether he is on his trial for giving aid. and comfort to the existing rebellion, as punishable by the act of Congress passed the 17th of July, 1862; or,

III. Whether he is on trial for aiding and abetting the murder of Abraham Lincoln, President of the United States.

His counsel well understands the legal definition of the three crimes above mentioned, but does not understand that either to the common law or to the law of war is known any one offense comprised of the three crimes mentioned in this charge. He knows of no one crime of a conspiracy to murder and an actual murder, all in aid of the rebellion, distinct and separate from the well-known and defined crimes of murder, of conspiracy in aid of the rebellion, or of giving aid and comfort to the rebellion as defined by the acts of Congress. It is extremely doubtful, from the language of this charge, whether the murder of the President of the United States is not referred to as the mere means by which the conspirators gave aid and comfort to the rebellion—whether it was not merely the overt act by which the crime of aiding the rebellion was completed.

If the crime of aiding and abetting the rebellion, as laid in the charge and specification, is only laid as the inducement to the crime of murder, then the crime as laid in the charge and specification does not come within the terms of the proclamation of September, 1862. It is the actual crime, and not the motives which induced it, that confers the jurisdiction. In the first general specification of the charge we find the following words used: "And by the means aforesaid" (referring to the murder of the President, Vice-President, the Secretary of State, and the Lieutenant-General), "to aid and comfort the insurgents in armed rebellion against the United States as aforesaid, and thereby to aid in the subversion and overthrow of the Constitution and laws of the United States." In that sentence the murder of the President of the United States and the rest of the crimes aforesaid are merely spoken of as the means, and not as the end.

The ambiguity in the charge and the first general specification is not relieved by the special specification against the accused, Herold. The special specification against him uses these terms:

"And in further prosecution of the said unlawful, murderous and traitorous conspiracy, and in pursuance thereof, and with the intent aforesaid," etc.

The special specification then goes on to charge Herold with two matters: first, with aiding and abetting in the murder of the President of the United States; and second, with aiding and abetting Booth in his escape from justice after the murder.

The language of the charge and of the general specification, as well as of the special specification, leaving it doubtful whether the accused is charged with all three or any one, it is necessary for his counsel to present his defenses to all three of the crimes mentioned in the charge and specification.

First, as to the crime of conspiracy. What evidence is there of the accused, Herold, having conspired to murder the President, or to aid the rebellion and overthrow the Constitution and laws of the United States? The evidence upon that point consists of but very few facts.

The first that it is necessary to notice is the testimony of Weichmann, who says that he saw Herold once at Mrs. Surratt's house since he went there to board, which was in November, 1864. It is hardly possible that this Commission will take a single visit of a young man to a house, where there were both young men and young ladies, as evidence of complicity in a conspiracy of so grave and heinous a character, especially as the same witness deposes that Herold was a previous acquaintance of the Surratts, as he had seen him before they moved to town, down in the country, at a serenade there some eighteen months before.

The same witness (Weichmann) also deposes that once in the winter of 1865, he, Holahan, Atzerodt, and this boy Herold went to the theater to see Booth play; that, on leaving the theater and going down the street, he (the witness, Weichmann) and Holahan going in advance, they found that they had outwalked the other three of the party; that the witness (Weichmann) returned, and found Booth, Atzerodt, and Herold in a restaurant, and, to use his expression, "in close conversation near a stove," and upon his going in they invited him to take a drink. If the fact of two persons going to a theater to see a popular play, and leaving that theater with the addition of a third, and stopping at a restaurant and taking a drink, or standing all three as (in the witness' opinion) in confidential conversation, is an evidence of conspiracy, probably half of the population of Washington city during the winter could be convicted on the same testimony.

The only other testimony is that of John M. Lloyd, who deposes that John Surratt and Atzerodt, some weeks before the assassination, passed his house, and that on their return Herold was with them, Herold being in a buggy alone; that they stopped at his house and took drinks; that John Surratt took him (Lloyd) out by himself, apart from Herold, and out of Herold's sight and hearing, and handed him (Lloyd) two carbines. There is no evidence whatever in Lloyd's testimony that Herold had the most remote knowledge that Surratt had given Lloyd the carbines.

There is one other point which was given in evidence by the Government, and that is the testimony of the witness Taltavull, the restaurant keeper, who deposes that one night, either Friday, the night of the assassination, or Thursday, the night before it, Herold came into his restaurant and asked if Booth had been there.

Fifty people could probably be convicted if facts like these were sufficient to convict; but they do not give, either separately or collectively, the slightest evidence that this boy Herold ever conspired with Booth and others in aid of the rebellion, and for the overthrow of the Government of the United States. They show nothing that might not have occurred to any one, perfectly consistent with the most perfect innocence. The term "confidential communication" is the witness' (Weichmann's) own construction. He meant only to say that the three were talking together—that after leaving the theater, where they had been, the three stopped and went into a restaurant, and that he found them there talking together near a stove. So much for the conspiracy.

In the special specification there are two things charged. The first is the murder of the President of the United States; the second, aiding and abetting Booth in his escape from justice after the murder. An accessory after the fact is thus defined: "An accessory after the fact is one who, when knowing a felony to have been committed by another, receives, relieves, comforts or assists the felon." There is no reasonable doubt, from the evidence in this case, that the accused, Herold, was guilty of aiding and abetting Booth in his escape from justice. It is not the object of the counsel for the accused either to misrepresent the law (which would be useless in the presence of the able and learned Judge Advocates who are conducting this case on the part of the Government), or to attempt to misrepresent the facts that have been disclosed in the evidence, which would be equally useless before this Court. Of the fact that this boy, Herold, was an aider and abettor in the escape of Booth, there is no rational or reasonable doubt. He was clearly guilty of that crime, and must abide by its consequences. But the accused, by his counsel, altogether denies that he was guilty of the murder of Abraham Lincoln, President of the United States, or that he aided and abetted in the murder of Abraham Lincoln, President of the United States, as set forth in the specification and the charge.

Herold is charged in the charge with the murder of the President. It is shown, as clearly as the sun shines, that he did not do the murder with his own hands, that he did not strike the mortal blow; and the only question that can arise under the charge and specification, and the evidence, in this cause, is whether he was such an aider and abettor as would make him equally guilty with the party who did strike the blow; and in order to arrive at a satisfactory conclusion whether he did so aid and abet in the murder of the President of the United States, it is necessary to examine what will constitute an aider and abettor.

An aider and abettor, termed in the law a principal in the second degree, is thus defined: "Principals in the second degree are those who are present aiding and abetting at the commission of the fact. To constitute principals in the second degree there must be, in the first place, a participation in the act committed, and, in the second place, presence, either actual or constructive, at the time of its commission." *Wharton's American Criminal Law, 4th edition,* ? 116.

What is that "actual or constructive" presence is thus explained in the same book, ? 124: "It is not necessary that the party should be actually present, an ear or eye-witness of the transaction. He is, in construction of law, present aiding and abetting if, with the intention of giving assistance, he be near enough to afford it should the occasion arise."

Now, did the accused, in the language of the law, participate in the act? Did he strike the illustrious victim the fatal blow? Did he point or hold the weapon? Did he open the door of that accursed box? Did he bar that outer door? Did he clear the passage of the theater? Did he stop or attempt to stop pursuit? Was he even in the theater at the time the fatal deed was done? To all these questions the evidence answers, distinctly and emphatically, no.

As to the second branch of the definition of a principal in the second degree, was he constructively present? He was not actually present, as we have seen above. Was he, then, constructively present? That is to say, in the language last quoted from Wharton, was he, "with the intention of giving assistance," "near enough to afford it, should the occasion arise?" What says the evidence on this point? John Fletcher, the only witness who mentions Herold at all on the 14th of April, 1865, says that he saw Herold at twenty-five minutes past ten o'clock that night, riding on horseback, slowly, on Pennsylvania avenue, near Willard's Hotel, coming from the direction of Georgetown; that his horse seemed to be somewhat, though not very, tired, and gave evidences of having been ridden. The main portion of the testimony places the assassination of the President at fifteen minutes after ten o'clock. That the assassination took place in the midst of a crowded theater, there is no controversy or dispute.

Now, what possible assistance could the accused have rendered to a murder committed in Ford's theater about the time that he was riding slowly down the middle of Pennsylvania avenue? No living man saw Herold nearer Ford's theater, on that fatal night, than the witness, Fletcher. Every circumstance attending that dreadful act has been minutely detailed to this Court by witnesses who were present. What possible assistance could the accused, Herold, have rendered to the murderer? The only time that he was seen on that night, and about the

18

time of the murder, he was fully half a mile from the scene of the dreadful tragedy.

In order to convict him of being near enough to give aid, should the occasion arise, the Court must be satisfied of the nature of the aid that he was able to give. What aid could he have possibly given? Was he near enough to hand Booth another pistol in case the first missed fire? Was he near enough to prevent assistance being given to the lamented President in case the first shot did not take effect? Was he in a situation to give the murderer aid in his escape from the theater? As far as this testimony discloses, Herold was entirely unarmed. Can the Court conceive any possible assistance that, under these circumstances, he, on the outside of the theater, in the middle of the principal street of Washington, half a mile from the theater, about the time the murder was committed, could have given Booth in the murder, or even in his escape?

To constitute an aider and abettor, the accused must have been in a situation to render aid. Booth might have supposed him to be in a situation, the accused might have supposed himself even to be in a situation to render aid; but it is not sufficient, unless the Court are satisfied, from the evidence brought before them, that he was actually and positively in a situation where he could have rendered aid in the commission of the act; and, in support of this position, I refer to 9 *Pickering's Reports* p. 496:

"To be present aiding and abetting the commission of a felony, the abettor must be in a situation where he may actually aid the perpetrator. It is not enough that he is at a place appointed, where the perpetrator erroneously supposes he might render aid."

But it may be argued that the accused said to Jett, a witness produced from the State of Virginia, "We are the assassinators of the President." If the Court will examine, they will find that this declaration was qualified one moment after it was made; that, pointing to Booth, the accused said, "Yonder is the assassinator." Herold is on trial for his acts, and not for his words. It is shown conclusively, in this case, that Booth, and not Herold, assassinated the President. If Jett heard accurately the words used by Herold, taken in connection with the facts disclosed to this Court, they only disclosed to Jett the character of the party. Declarations are only a means to arrive at the true character of acts. They must be taken in connection with the facts of every case; and it is clear, from every particle of testimony in this case, that Herold was not the "assassinator" of the President; and even if he used the words as repeated by Jett, the meaning is clear enough; he meant to designate and point out to Jett, the witness, the character of the party that he was with.

But it may be urged that the flight of Herold is evidence of his guilt. It is true that flight, unexplained, is always regarded as evidence of guilt, but not conclusive evidence.

"By the common law, flight was regarded so strong a presumption of guilt, that, in cases of treason and felony, it carried forfeiture of the person's goods, whether he was found guilty or acquitted. These several acts, in all their modifications, are indicative of fear, which, however, may spring from causes very different from that of conscious guilt. Mr. Justice Abbott, on the trial of Donnall for the murder of Mrs. Downing, observed, in his charge to the jury, that a person, however conscious of innocence, might not have the courage to stand a trial, but might, though innocent, think it best to consult his safety by flight." *Wharton*, 4th ed., sec. 714.

But what guilt in this case is the flight of Herold evidence of? He is found with Booth, and his flight in this case is not only evidence, but constitutes the guilt that he has acknowledged; it constitutes the guilt of his aiding in the escape of Booth, but no more. It by no means follows, because he aided Booth to escape, that he aided him to kill the President. It is bad reasoning to conclude that because he was guilty of one crime he was guilty of others.

But it may be asked, why did he leave in the dead hour of the night with a murderer? A slight glance at the relative character of the two men may explain this difficulty. John Wilkes Booth, as appears from all the evidence in this case, was a man of determined and resolute will, of pleasing, fascinating manners, and one who exercised great influence and control over the lower orders of men with whom he was brought in contact. He was a man of means, quite a prominent actor, fine in personal appearance and manners, and an adept in athletic and manly exercises. All the force of his mind, all his means, and his time in the winter of 1865, were devoted to get agents to aid in his desperate enterprise. In his search he met with Herold, then out of employment, and he at once marked him for his own.

Who is Herold, and what does the testimony disclose him to be? A weak, cowardly, foolish, miserable boy. On this point there is no conflict. Dr. McKim, who probably knew him best, and in whose employ he had been, declares that his mind was that of a boy of eleven years of age, although his age actually was about 22—not naturally vicious, but weak, light, trifling, easily persuaded, good tempered, ready to laugh and applaud, and ready to do the bidding of those around him. Such a boy was only wax in the hands of a man like Booth.

But though Booth exercised unlimited control over this miserable boy, body and soul, he found him unfit for deeds of blood and violence; he was cowardly; he was too weak and trifling; but still he could be made useful. He knew some of the roads through Lower Maryland, and Booth persuaded him to act as guide, foot-boy, companion. This accounts for their companionship.

There is one piece of evidence introduced by the Government that should be weighed by the Commission. It is the declaration of Booth, made at the time of his capture: "I declare, before my Maker, that this man is innocent." Booth knew well enough, at the time he made that declaration, that his hours, if not his minutes, were numbered. In natures the most depraved, there seems to be left some spark of a better humanity, and this little remnant of a better nature urged Booth to make that declaration while it was yet time to do so. What did he mean by that declaration? Not that Herold was not guilty of the act of aiding and assisting him (Booth) to escape; but what he did mean, and what he tried to convey, was, that Herold was guiltless of the stain of blood being upon his hands, either as an accessory before the fact to the murder of the President, or as an aider and abettor in that murder, or any other deed of violence. That is what he meant.

I should mention here, what I might more properly, perhaps, have mentioned in another place, that I think it has been made clear from the testimony, that Dr. Merritt, who said Herold was in Canada between the 15th and 20th of February last, was manifestly mistaken. Merritt was positive as to the location of the time, and if he did not see him there during that time, he did not see him at all. He did not profess to have been introduced to him, or to have had conversation with him, nor was he pointed out to him, as Merritt says, by name; but the sum of his testimony is, that between the 15th and 20th of February last, a man was pointed out to him whose name was Harrison, and who, he thinks, was the prisoner Herold. It appears, from the testimony of his little sister, as well as that of Mrs. Jenkins, that Herold was at home on the 15th of February; it appears conclusively, from the testimony of Mrs. Potts, that he was at home, as she paid him some money and took his receipt, on the 18th of February; and it appears equally conclusively from the testimony of Captain Edmonds, an officer in the navy, that he was at home on the 20th of the same month, showing clearly that Herold was not in Canada; that Dr. Merritt was mistaken; it was some other man; more than probable Surratt, who was called very frequently by his middle name of Harrison.

It has been intimated by one of the Assistant Judge Advocates that "where parties are indicted for a conspiracy and the execution thereof, it is but one crime at the common law; and that, upon all authority, as many overt acts in the execution of that conspiracy as they are guilty of may be laid in the same count." To this doctrine the accused can not assent. The crime of conspiracy is thus defined by Mr. Sergeant Talfourd:

"The offense of conspiracy consists, according to all authorities, not in the *accomplishment* of any unlawful or injurious purpose, nor in any one act moving toward that purpose, but in the actual concert and agreement of two or more persons to effect something, which, being so concerted and agreed, the law regards as the object of an indictable conspiracy." *Per Bayley J.*, 2 *Barnewall and Alderson*, 205.

If this decision is correct—and of its correctness I think there can be no doubt—the crime of conspiracy becomes complete upon the concert and agreement. The overt act is not essential to the completion of the crime.

In *Wharton's American Criminal Law*, section 2,385, the law is thus set out:

"It is usual to set out the overt acts, that is to say, those acts which may have been done by any one or more of the conspirators in pursuance of the conspiracy, and in order to effect the common purpose of it; but this is not requisite, if the indictment charge what is in itself an unlawful conspiracy. The offense is complete on the consummation of the conspiracy, and the overt acts, though it is proper to set them forth, may be either regarded as matters of aggravation, or discharged as surplusage."

It seems to me clear from these authorities that the conspiracy to commit a crime, and the actual commission of that crime, are nowhere regarded in the eye of the law as constituting but one offense. They do, in fact, constitute two separate and distinct offenses, and the party may be indicted for them both, or for either of them separately. The prevailing doctrine in this country is, that where the conspiracy is to commit a felony, if the felony is afterward committed, the conspiracy merges in the felony, conspiracy being regarded by all the writers as a misdemeanor merely.

Again, if upon a conspiracy being entered into to commit murder, the murder is afterward actually committed by one of the conspirators, it is not a conclusion of law that the murder is committed also by the other co-conspirators.

Another principle here comes in. To the crime of murder, there may be principals and accessories before and after the fact. A co-conspirator may be an accessory before the fact, but it does not follow, because he is a co-conspirator, that he is an accessory before the fact. What is an accessory before the fact, is thus defined:

"An accessory before the fact, is one who, though absent at the time of the commission of the felony, doth yet procure, counsel, command, or abet another to commit such felony."

Now, where is the evidence that Herold procured, counseled, commanded, or abetted Booth to assassinate the President of the United States?

I beg leave again to refer the Court to the case of the *Commonwealth* vs. *Knapp*, 9 *Pickering's Reports*, 518:

"The fact of the conspiracy being proved against the person is to be weighed as evidence in the case having a tendency to prove that the prisoner aided, but it is not in itself to be taken as a legal presumption of his having aided unless disproved by him. It is a question of evidence for the consideration of the jury."

Should, then, the Court determine that Herold was one of the conspirators, it is not to be taken of itself as any conclusive evidence that he aided or abetted in any manner the murder.

This case is being tried by the rules of evidence as known to the common law and the general principles of that law applicable to criminal cases. I beg leave to call the attention of the Court to one of the most important and most thoroughly established rules of the common law in the investigation of all crimes, and that rule is this: That whenever upon any question there should arise in the minds of the investigating tribunal any reasonable doubt, the accused should have the benefit of that doubt. This rule has met with the unqualified approbation of every judge in England and America whose name adorns the judicial history of either country. While I do not contend that the Court should for a moment examine the record for the purpose of raising capricious doubts, still, whenever the record does present a case of reasonable doubt, I insist that the accused shall have the benefit of that doubt. Apply this principle to the main charge in this case: Can the Court say, from the evidence before them, that, on the night of the 14th of April, 1865, the accused, Herold, was in a situation where he could render aid in the actual murder of the President? Taking into consideration the mode and manner of the execution of that murder, and Herold's position from the time of its commission, it seems to me that it is almost, if not quite, clear that he was not in a situation where he could render such aid. Can the Court say, beyond a reasonable doubt, then, that he was an accessory before the fact? Can they say that Herold did procure, counsel, command, or abet Booth to kill and murder the President of the United States? If so, what word or deed of Herold's can they point to in this record that does amount to procuring, counseling, commanding or abetting? There is clearly none. The feeble aid that he could render to any enterprise was rendered in accompanying and aiding Booth in his flight, and nothing beyond. That of itself is a grave crime, and carries with it its appropriate punishment.

I beg leave to conclude this defense with a quotation from *Benet on Military Law and Courts-martial*:

"Where the punishments for particular offenses are not fixed by law, but left discretionary with the courts, the above mandate of the Constitution must be strictly kept in view, and the benign influence of a mandate from a still higher law ought not to be ignored, that justice should be tempered with mercy."

DAVID E. HAROLD.

ARGUMENT

IN

DEFENSE OF EDWARD SPANGLER,

BY

THOMAS EWING, Jr.

Mr. President and Gentlemen of the Commission:

In presenting to you this morning the case of the accused, Edward Spangler, I shall confine myself to a discussion of the evidence, leaving whatever I may see fit to say on the question of jurisdiction, and on the character of the charges and specifications to the occasion when my argument in the case of Mudd is presented.

Preliminary to a consideration of the specific items of testimony against Edward Spangler, I will briefly refer to and ask consideration of the evidence as to his character, his occupation, his relations to Booth, and Booth's habits of resorting to the theater and fraternizing with its employees.

John T. Ford says, on his cross-examination:

Q. [By Mr. Ewing.] State what were the duties of the accused, Edward Spangler, on the stage.

A. Spangler was employed as a stage hand, frequently misrepresented as the stage carpenter of the theater. He was a laborer to assist in the shoving of scenery into its place, and removing it within the groves, as the necessity of the play required. These were his duties at night, and during the day to assist in doing the rough carpenter work incidental to plays to be produced.

Q. State his relations to Booth, as far as you have known them to be together at all.

A. He seemed to have a great admiration for Booth. I have noticed that, in my business on the stage with the stage manager. Booth was a peculiarly fascinating man, and controlled the lower class of people, such as Spangler belonged to, I suppose, more than ordinary men would—a man who excelled in all manly sports.

And on his second examination, Ford says:

Q. How long have you known the accused, Edward Spangler?

A. Nearly four years, I think.

Q. Was he in your employ through that time?

A. Most of that time.

Q. State what his character is for peace, good nature and kindness.

A. He was always regarded as a very good-natured, kind, willing man. His only fault was occasionally participating in drinking

liquor more than he should have done—disposed to drink at times—not so as to make him vicious, but more to unfit him to work.

Q. Is he a quarrelsome man?

A. I never knew him to be but in one quarrel since he has been in my employ, and that was through drink.

Q. Was he faithful in attending to his duties?

A. Very; a good, efficient drudge; always willing to do anything; I never found him unwilling.

Q. Was he a man that was trusted with the confidence of others?

A. I should think not to any extent. He had no self-respect. He was not one who had many associates. He usually slept in the theater—a man who rarely slept in a bed.

Q. A harmless man?

A. Very harmless—always esteemed so, I think, by all the company around the theater; often the subject of sport and fun; but never, except on one occasion, did I know him to be engaged in a quarrel.

Q. How was he as to politics? Was he a man of intense feeling?

A. I never knew anything of his political sentiments in this city. In Baltimore he was known to be a member of the American Order. I never heard an expression of political sentiment from him.

Gifford says [cross-examination]:

Q. What were his relations with Booth?

A. Nothing that I know of, further than friendly. Everybody about the house was friendly with him.

Q. With Booth?

A. Yes, sir, actors and all; they were all friendly with him. He had such a very winning way that it made every person like him. He was a good-natured and jovial kind of man. The people about the house, as far as I knew, all liked him.

Q. Was he much in the habit of frequenting the theater?

A. Sometimes I have seen him there for a week, and then he would go off, and I would not see him for a couple of weeks. Then he would come again for a week, perhaps, and after that I would not see him for a couple of weeks or ten days, or something of that sort. When the house was open, he had free access all through the house.

276

Q. Day and night?

A. Yes, sir; except when the house was locked up and the watchman was there; he had no access to it then.

Q. Was not Spangler a sort of a drudge for Booth?

A. He appeared so; he used to go down and help him to hitch his horse up, and such things, I am told; I have seen him once or twice hitching the horse up myself.

It is to be remarked here, that a stable a few yards from the back of the theater, and from the doors of the negro women, Mrs. Turner and Mrs. Anderson, was used by Booth for his horses and buggy, from early in January until the assassination, and Burroughs and Spangler, employed at the theater, attended to the drudgery at the stable.

Burroughs ("Peanuts") says [cross-examination]:

Q. Was not Spangler in the habit of bridling, and sadling, and hitching up Booth's horse?

A. When I was not there he used to hitch him up.

Q. Was he not in the habit of holding him, too, when you were not about?

A. Yes, sir; and he used to feed him when I was not about.

While calling the attention of the Court to the evidence as to the relations existing between Spangler and Booth, I desire it also to mark the fact that in the great volume of testimony as to the letters, conversations, meetings, associations, acts done, and things said which have been adduced as evidence in these cases, there is not the slightest indication that Spangler ever met Booth except in and around the theater, that he ever got a note or a message from him, or ever saw or heard of any one of the persons suspected to have been associated with Booth, in either the conspiracy to capture or that to assassinate the President and the heads of the Government.

Now, in the light of the above-recited evidence, I am certain there is nothing shown to have been said or done by anybody prior to the moment of assassination—outside of the testimony of Sergeant Joseph M. Dye and John F. Sleickman—tending at all to show that Spangler had any intimation of Booth's guilty purpose, or was in any way, even innocently, instrumental in effecting it. Let us briefly consider the several items of evidence of acts done and things said prior to the conversation with Booth, narrated by Sleickman, and consultation with him noticed by Sergeant Dye, which have been adduced here as evidences of Spangler's guilt.

1. He repaired Booth's stable, in January, Burroughs says. What of that? He was a rough carpenter, and a drudge at the theater, and the stable was near at hand. The incident is unworthy of further notice or comment.

2. He sold Booth's horse and buggy several days before the assassination, at the horse market or at a livery stable. (Burroughs'.) The same witness says he prepared them for sale, and went with Spangler, and that Gifford sent them to make the sale. And Gifford says he received and J. R. Ford receipted for the money,

and he (G.) paid it over to Booth. This item is at least as good against Gifford and "Peanuts" as against Spangler, and amounts to nothing against either.

3. There was found in Spangler's carpetsack, at his boarding-house, on the 17th of April (the day of his arrest), rope 81 feet long, some letter paper, and a shirt-collar. (Rosch.) The rope was offered in evidence; the letter paper and shirt collar were not. The rope was just like forty or fifty others used about the theater as "border ropes," and to "haul up lumber to the top dressing rooms, because the stairs are so narrow the timber can not be got up that way." (Carland). "The border ropes are seventy to eighty feet long—not less than 80 feet." (Lamb.) "They are of just the same material, texture and size as this." (Carland, Lamb, Raybold.) "We used such ropes as this at the time of the Treasury Guards' ball, to stretch from the lobby to the wings, to hang on it the colors of different nations." (Raybold.) "This rope has evidently been in use." (Carland, Lamb, Raybold). "Sometimes we use them, and a great many of them, and then again we have to take them down, and they lie up there on the scene loft until we need them again." (Raybold). From the evidence, it appears probable Spangler stowed away this rope to use on his frequent fishing excursions as a crab line. Gifford says:

Q. State whether you know anything of the accused, Edward Spangler, being accustomed to crabbing and other fishing during the recesses of his engagement.

A. I never saw him at it; but I have known him to tell me that he went crabbing—that he would go down to the Neck on Saturday night, and stay until Monday morning, and come home on Monday morning. I have never seen him at it myself; but I know that is what he told me, and I have seen others who said the same thing—that they had been crabbing together.

Q. [Exhibiting to the witness the rope]. Will you state whether that rope is such a one as might be used in that sport?

A. They have a line something of this sort, and small lines tied on to it about that distance [three feet], with pieces of meat attached, and as they go along they trail it along. I have seen them at it, although I have never done anything at it myself. They pull up the crabs as they go along, and let the line go down, and dip them up out of the boat.

And John T. Ford says:

Q. State whether or not you know anything of the prisoner, Spangler, having been in the habit of going to Baltimore, and for what, during the spring.

A. I know that he had lived in Baltimore, and buried his wife there some eight or ten months, or probably a year ago, while in my employ, and that he considered Baltimore his home, and usually spent the summer months, during the vacation of the theater, there, chiefly in crabbing and fishing. He was a great fisher and crabber. I know nothing positive of my own knowledge as to that. I only heard that, and we used to plague him about it.

Q. [Exhibiting to witness the coil of rope found in a carpet-sack at the house where Spangler took his meals.] Look at that rope, and see whether or not it might be used for any such purpose, and in what way.

A. I suppose that could be used as a crab line, though it is rather short for that purpose. I have seen some as short used. I have read that the length of this is eighty feet, but I do not know from its appearance.

Q. This is such a rope as you have seen used by amateurs in that sport?

A. Yes, sir; I have seen such ropes. I frequently go fishing in the summer.

While it is unquestionably true that, so far as the evidence goes, Spangler may have got this rope for some purpose other than that suggested, it is also true that there are many other uses for which we can more readily imagine he got it than for the assassination plot. In the devilish scheme of that conspiracy I can imagine no use for a rope eighty feet long. It could not have been provided for lariats, for there was then no grass; nor for halters, for it would make a half score. If, however, it had been provided for any purpose connected with the conspiracy, it would have been kept at the theater, or the stable, and not off at a remote boarding house. It is easier to imagine him frugal enough to provide for his home, in Baltimore, a clothes line or a bed cord, than foolish enough to provide for the assassin's scheme an article so unnecessary as an eighty-foot rope. My only embarrassment in this point of the case arises from a failure to show that he fairly got title to the rope; but in this embarrassment I find consolation in reflecting that I am not called on to show what he meant to do with the shirt collar and the letter paper—which would have been a much more difficult task.

4. Two boxes had always been thrown into one when the President came to the theater on several former occasions during the season. (H. Clay Ford). Except while taking out the partition, Spangler was not in the box as it was being prepared and decorated. (H. Clay Ford). But Burroughs says:

Q. What was he doing?

A. Harry Ford told me to go in with Spangler and take out the partition of the box, as the President and General Grant were coming there. I then went after Spangler.

Q. Do you remember whether, while Spangler was doing that, he said anything in regard to the President?

A. He made remarks and laughed.

Q. What were they?

A. He said, "Damn the President and General Grant."

Q. While damning the President, or after damning him, did he say anything else?

A. I said to him, "What are you damning the man for—a man that has never done any harm to you?" He said he ought to be cursed when he got so many men killed. I stayed there until they took the partition out, and sat down in the box.

Q. Did you observe what else they did in the box?

A. No, sir. Spangler said it would be a nice place to sleep in after the partition was down. That is all I recollect.

Judge Advocate omitted to ask his witness (Jake Ritterspack) as to this conversation, so that it rests on the evidence of "Peanuts" only. I do not think it goes a great way toward establishing Spangler's connection with the conspiracy, or calls for special comment. But I will present a set-off to this exhibition of ill feeling toward the President by Spangler, at being called away from his work on the stage to do an extra job in fixing the box, by his equally strong exhibition of good feeling, when, as the President entered the theater, "he clapped his hands and stamped his feet, and seemed as pleased as anybody to see the President come in." (James.)

5. Burroughs further says, between five and six o'clock Friday evening, Booth came with his horse to the stable and called for Spangler and wanted a halter. That Spangler sent Ritterspack up stairs for one; that Maddox was there with them, and Spangler wanted to take the bridle and saddle off, but Booth would not let him, but that he (Spangler) did afterward take them off. The fact that Booth wanted the saddle and bridle left on, and Spangler wanted to take them off, and did subsequently do it, indicates that Spangler had, up to that time, no intimation of Booth's need of the horse that night.

6. I have no doubt that the actual and the apparent preparations in and about the President's box for the assassination, more than all other circumstances combined, led the Government to arrest Spangler and put him on trial as a conspirator. They were sufficient to direct suspicion against him and to justify his arrest, for in them they appeared to the casual observer the hand of a mechanic in aid of Booth's plan. But the evidence has wholly cleared the defendant of that suspicion. These actual and apparent preparations were:

1. A quarter of an inch hole bored through the door of box 7, which was the closed door when the two boxes, 7 and 8, were thrown into one for the President's party. This hole was bored with a gimlet, and enlarged on the outside with a penknife. (Plant, Ferguson, Olin.) A gimlet was found in Booth's room, after he fled, about the size of the hole, but it was lost or mislaid, and, therefore, could not be fitted to the hole. Booth occupied box 7 one night, about two weeks before the assassination. (Raybold.) "He secured box No. 7 three or four times during the season before the assassination, but I can not say whether he occupied it or not." "Sometimes he would use it and sometimes he would not." "He always engaged that box." (H. Clay Ford.) The fact that Booth apparently brought the gimlet, bored the hole, and carried the gimlet to his room again, leaves this item of testimony not only of no effect against Spangler, but of great significance in his favor. For, if Booth had a confidant and confederate in this rough carpenter, the work would have been done by Spangler, or, at least, with Spangler's tools.

2. The hole in the plastering, two by three

inches, into which the brace rested which fastened the outer door leading from the dress-circle into the little passage from which the doors open into the private boxes. This hole was cut with a penknife, apparently, from the scratches down the wall. (Rathbone.) It was not cut into the brick, but about an inch, or an inch and-a-half, into the plaster. It would take ten or fifteen minutes to do it with a penknife. (Gifford.) That passage was pretty dark, even when the door is opened. (H. Clay Ford.) If done with a knife, even with the door opened, it would make no noise sufficient to attract attention. (Gifford.) This item, like the last, tends in Spangler's favor, and not against him. For a carpenter, with tools at hand, would have made the hole with a chisel, rather than with a penknife. The chips which fell from whittling one side of the gimlet-hole, and the plastering from the hole in the wall, were not on the floor next morning. (Judge Olin.) This indicates that the work was done in advance, or on some one of the occasions when Booth occupied box 7, opposite the door of which the hole in the wall was cut.

3. A penknife was found in the President's box next morning. This was used on Friday afternoon by Harry Ford, in cutting the strings to tie up the flags and the picture of Washington, and was left by him accidentally in the box. (H. Clay Ford.)

4. The screws which fastened the keepers of the locks on the doors of 7 and 8, were so loose that the doors could be easily pushed open, even when locked. (Judge Olin.) The theory of the prosecution was that the screws were drawn by Spangler, in advance, in aid of Booth's plan. Raybold says that several weeks before the assassination, he burst open the door of box 8 to admit Mr. Merrick, and that after that the lock was not repaired and wouldn't fasten the door; but Merrick says it was the door of box 7. This conflict of evidence is of no consequence, however, because O'Bryon, the usher, says:

A. In box 8 the keeper was wrenched off, broken off in some way; I do not know how. I was absent one evening; I was at home sick, and when I came again I found that it was broken off, but the door itself was pretty tight at the top, and I never thought of speaking about it. All I had to do was to close the door, and the door itself would shut tight, and I do not know that I ever said anything about it.

Q. When did you first notice that the keeper of the door of box 8 was broken?

A. On the first occasion that I went into the box afterward; I can not tell when that was.

Q. Was it before the assassination?

A. Oh yes, sir, some time.

Q. About how long before?

A. That I could not say.

Q. Which door was used when the Presidential party was occupying the two boxes?

A. The door of box 8.

Q. How was it generally left after the party entered?

A. Always open.

Q. Do you know whether the door leading into the passage, which separates the two boxes from the wall, had a lock upon it?

A. No, sir, it had no lock.

And Plant, an expert, unconnected with the theater, who, a few days ago, examined the keepers of both boxes, says:

A. I examined the keepers on boxes 7 and 8. To all appearances they had both been forced. The woodwork in box 8 is shivered and splintered by the screws. In box 7 I could pull the screw with my thumb and finger; the tap was gone clear to the point. I could force it back with my thumb. In box 4, which is directly under box 8, the keeper is gone entirely.

Q. State whether or not, according to your professional opinion, the keepers of the locks in boxes 7 and 8 were made loose by an instrument, or by force applied to the outside of the doors?

A. I should judge by force.

Q. Is there any appearance of an instrument having been used to draw the screws in either of those boxes?

A. I could see no such evidence.

5. A square pine stick, about four feet long, and beveled at one end, with which the outer door was braced, was picked up in the box that night. (Jaquette.) Through the beveled end are driven two lath nails, bent at the ends, which Gifford, the carpenter, says might have been put there to hold that end against the door, but which obviously were not put there for any such purpose, as they were wholly unnecessary for that purpose, and were not driven into the door. In the other end are two large nails, which, he says, could have been of no use to hold the butt end in the hole. The stick had evidently been prepared for some other use. It is doubtful whether it was the stick that Booth used, as it was found, not in the passage, but in the box (Jacquette); and Major Rathbone says: "I found the door barred by a heavy piece of plank;" and "My impression was, it was a different piece of wood." Whether this is in fact the bar is of no apparent importance. The members of the Court have observed that the wall forms with the door, when shut, an acute angle, and are doubtless satisfied that a strong stick or piece of plank, anywhere from three to five feet long, would answer well to bar the door. But if this was the bar, it was not prepared by Spangler for the purpose, for he, a carpenter, would not have driven the nails in the butt end.

These three acts of preparation—the boring the hole in the door, the cutting the hole in the plaster, and providing the brace—were acts of mere drudgery, which, if Spangler had been a conspirator, Booth would naturally have called on him to do; and the fact that Booth certainly did one, and probably did the others, and the presumption that Spangler did neither, tend strongly to the conclusion that he was not in the plot when these preparations were made.

Ritterspack, in his last examination, said that just before he and Spangler went home to supper, on the day of the assassination, and about six o'clock in the evening, they were at work together on the stage, and saw a stranger in the dress circle smoking a cigar. He called

Spangler's attention to him, but he said "he had no charge on that side of the theater, and no right to order the man out." That presently the stranger entered one of the lower private boxes opposite the President's box, when Spangler said something, in consequence of which the man left. The Assistant Judge Advocate objected to the witness saying what it was Spangler said to the stranger to make him leave. Doubtless this man was there inspecting the President's box for Booth, and *possibly* cutting the hole in the wall, and bringing in the bar. Had Spangler been in the conspiracy, would Booth have needed the services of this inspector and assistant?

We now come to the consideration of the testimony of Sleickman, referred to above.

Q. Do you know J. Wilkes Booth?

A. Yes, sir.

Q. Did you or not see him on that night, and if so, at what hour and under what circumstances?

A. I saw him about nine o'clock, I guess it was. He came up on a horse and came in a little back door to the theater. Ned Spangler was standing there by one of the wings, and Booth said to him, "Ned, you will help me all you can, won't you?" and Ned said, "Oh, yes."

Q. I understand you to say that as Booth came up to the door with his horse, he said that?

A. When he came in the door after he got off the horse.

Q. How long was that before the President was shot?

A. I should judge it to be about an hour and a-half.

Q. Did you observe the horse afterward, by whom it was held?

A. I did not.

Q. You did not see Booth any more?

A. I just got a glimpse of him as he was going out the first entrance on the right-hand side.

Q. What hour was that when you saw him going out of the first entrance?

A. About half-past ten o'clock, I think. That was after he shot the President.

Q. How close were you to Booth and Spangler when Booth said those words to him on entering the theater, from the door?

A. About as far as I am from you. [A distance of about eight feet.]

Q. How far was Spangler from him?

A. Spangler was standing as close to him as the gentleman next to you is to you. [About three feet.]

Q. He spoke, then, in a loud voice?

A. Yes, sir.

Q. Could he have seen you from where he was standing?

A. Oh, yes.

Now this evidence is flatly contradicted by the evidence of J. L. Debonay, the "responsible utility" man.

In his second examination he says:

Q. Did you see anything of Mr. Sleickman when Booth said he wanted Spangler to hold his horse, and you went over for Spangler?

A. They were both standing at the same

place, very near, close to each other, on the opposite side of the stage.

Q. That is, on the left-hand side of the stage looking to the audience?

A. Yes, sir; and the same side that the President's box was on.

Q. Did Mr. Sleickman go over to the door?

A. I did not see him go over there.

Q. Did you see Spangler go over?

A. Yes, sir; because I went right behind him, pretty close.

Q. Did you see Spangler go out of the door?

A. Yes, sir.

Q. Did you see Booth then come in?

A. I did.

Q. How long was it after Spangler went out before Booth came in?

A. About a minute, or a minute and a-half—not longer than that.

Q. How far were you from the door?

A. I was about half-way between the back door and the green-room—about eighteen or twenty feet, I suppose.

Q. Did you hear any conversation between Spangler and Booth?

A. I did not.

Q. Did you hear anything to indicate that there was conversation going on between them?

A. No, sir.

Q. Did Booth meet Spangler inside of the door?

A. He was standing at the door; he was on the outside. The door was about half open when Spangler went out.

Q. Would you have seen any person who followed Spangler, and went out, too?

A. Yes, sir; I think I should have seen any one.

Q. And you did not see Sleickman?

A. I did not.

Q. When Booth came in, what did he do?

A. He went under the stage to the opposite side, and he went out the side door.

Q. How do you know that he went out of the side door?

A. Because I went under the stage and crossed to the opposite side myself.

Q. Did you go under with Booth?

A. Yes, sir; I went under with him.

It may be suggested that the conversation between Booth and Spangler occurred at some time during the play, *prior* to the time when Booth rode up to the back door and called for Spangler to hold his horse. But, if that be claimed, I assert that the evidence shows conclusively that *Booth came to the door with his horse but once that night during the play.* And in support of that assertion I here refer the Court to each item of evidence (except that of Sleickman and Debonay, the conflicting witnesses), as to Booth entering the theater by the back door during the performance.

1. John Miles, colored, whose place was in the flies, from which he could see out of the window down into the alley by the door, says:

Q. Did you see J. Wilkes Booth there?

A. I saw him when he came there.

Q. What hour did he come? Tell us all you saw.

A. He came there, I think, between nine and

ten o'clock, and he brought a horse from the stable and came to the back door and called "Ned Spangler" three times out of the theater. Ned Spangler went across the stage to him. After that I did not see what became of Booth, and never noticed him any more until I heard the pistol go off.

Cross-examined by Mr. EWING:

Q. Was the play going on when Booth rode up and called for Spangler?

A. They had just closed a scene, and were getting ready to take off that scene at the time he called for Spangler. Spangler was at the second groove then, and pushed a scene across. Booth called him three times.

Q. Where were you then?

A. Up on the flies, about three and one-half stories from the stage.

Q. Do you know who held the horse?

A. John Peanuts held him; he was lying on a bench, holding the horse, when I noticed him. I was at the window pretty nearly all the time from the time Booth brought the horse until he went away. Every time I looked out the window, John Peanuts was lying on the bench holding the horse. I did not see any one else hold him.

2. Joseph Burroughs ("Peanuts") says:

Q. Did you see him on the afternoon of the 14th of April?

A. I saw him when he brought his horse to the stable, between five and six o'clock.

Q. Did you see him again at a later hour that evening?

A. I saw him on the stage that night.

Q. Did you or not see him when he came with his horse, between nine and ten o'clock that night?

A. No, sir; I did not see him when he came up the alley with his horse.

Q. Did you see the horse at the door?

A. I saw him when Spangler called me out there to hold the horse.

Q. Did you see Booth when he came there with his horse?

A. No, sir; I did not see him.

Q. Did you hear him call for Ned Spangler?

A. No, sir; I heard Debonay calling Ned, that Booth wanted him.

3. Mary Ann Turner (colored) says:

Q. Did you know John Wilkes Booth?

A. I knew him when I saw him.

Q. Will you state what you saw of him on the afternoon of the 14th of April last?

A. That afternoon I saw him, I think, to the best of my recollection, between three and four o'clock, standing in the back door of Ford's Theater, with a lady by his side; I did not take any particular notice of him at that time, but I turned from the door, and I saw no more of him until, to the best of my recollection, between seven and eight, or near about eight, o'clock that night, when he brought a horse up to the back door, and opened the door, and called for a man by the name of "Ned" three times, to the best of my recollection, not more than three times; this "Ned" came to him, and I heard him say to "Ned," in a low voice, "Tell Maddox to come here." I then saw Maddox come; he (Booth) said something in a

very low voice to this Maddox, and I saw Maddox reach out his hand and take the horse; but where "Ned" went I can not tell; this Booth went on into the theater.

Cross-examined by Mr. EWING:

Q. How far is your house from the back door of the theater?

A. My front door fronts to the back of the theater; it comes out into the open alley, which leads up to the door; there is another house between mine and the theater; the two houses are adjoining, and my house stands as far from the door of the theater as from here to the post. [About twenty-two feet.] I think it would allow that space for the two houses.

4. Mary Jane Anderson.

Q. Does your house adjoin that of Mrs. Turner, who has just testified?

A. Yes, sir; my house and her's are adjoining. He came up to the theater door, this gentleman did, with the horse by the bridle. He pushed the door open, and said something in a low tone, and then in a loud voice he called "Ned," four times. There was a colored man up at the window, and he said: "Mr. Ned, Mr. Booth calls you." That is the way I came to know it was Mr. Booth. It was dark, and I could not see his face. When Mr. Ned came, Booth said to him, in a low tone, "Tell Maddox to come here." Then Mr. Ned went back, and Maddox came out.

Q. How long was it from the time that Booth rode up there until the people said he had shot the President?

A. I suppose it was about an hour—not quite an hour—from the time he came up there to the time they said the President was shot. I think it was almost an hour, but I do not think it was quite an hour.

These six witnesses (including Sleickman and Debonay) are all who have testified to Booth's coming to, or entering, the back door of the theater that night. Every one of them, except Sleickman and Burroughs, refers to his calling loudly several times for Spangler. Burroughs, who was too remote from the door to hear Booth calling for Spangler, fixes it as being the same time, by saying that he heard Debonay repeat Booth's call for Spangler; and Sleickman says it was when Booth came up with his horse to the back door that he saw him and heard him talk to Spangler. If Booth had previously, during the play, come up the alley to the back door with his horse, Mrs. Turner, Mrs. Anderson and John Miles, from their positions adjacent to and overlooking that part of the paved alley, would certainly have seen or heard, and noticed him or the horse; and if Booth had entered the theater previously during the play, and stopped by the scenes to talk to Spangler, surely some one else, on that small, thronged stage, would have seen or heard him. It would have been, of itself, a trifling incident; but on the day following the assassination, when it was established that Booth was the murderer, I venture to say there was not a man or woman in the city of Washington, who ever saw Booth, who did not recall when and where he or she saw the assassin last. And, therefore, I feel safe in asserting that, had he rode up to the back door and gone into the theater at any other time that night than the one time fixed by the concurrent testimony of so many witnesses, we would have learned it in this investigation; for every step the villain took about the theater that night is recounted in the evidence before us.

If, then, he was there but once, what credence can be given to Sleickman's evidence as to Booth's statement to Spangler and the reply? I claim that the evidence overthrows it. If the issue as to it were to be settled by a consideration only of Sleickman's evidence with the flatly contradictory evidence of Debonay, I might reasonably claim an even balance of testimony, as the two witnesses were apparently equally credible. But Debonay's evidence is consistent with, and supported by, the other evidence of the case, and Sleickman's is not. For, if Sleickman's statement be true, some other man, not disclosed by the proof, must have held Booth's horse while this colloquy was going on in the theater. Mrs. Turner, in her confused statement, says, in substance, that after Booth came up, Spangler first held the horse a few minutes, and from that time it was held by the same man who held him at the time of the assassination, to-wit, Burroughs, whom she mistook for Maddox, one of the witnesses for the prosecution. She testifies the horse was held all the time, and if any one else had held him, surely he would not have escaped the vigilant and incessant search of the Government.

But grant Booth did say to Spangler, "Ned, you will help me all you can, won't you?" and Ned replied, "Oh, yes," all said in a loud tone, and in sight and hearing of Sleickman. If there were preceding incidents in proof showing Spangler's knowledge of Booth's guilty purpose, this alleged colloquy might be regarded as a link in a chain of evidence against him. But of itself, unaccompanied with the slightest evidence or ground of presumption of Spangler's previous knowledge of Booth's purpose, and followed (as we will see in this discussion of the evidence), by not the slightest act, or arrangement, or apparent intent of co-operation in the crime, or the escape, it should, I think, be treated by the Court (if it be thought to have occurred), as on Spangler's part nothing but the unwitting response of a drudge to a remark of one he looked up to as a superior, whom he was accustomed to serve, and of which he knew not the special intent. Had he known Booth's purpose, and meant to aid his escape, would he not have got a substitute to shove the scenes, and been in the passage, or at the door, ready to help baffle the pursuers? Or would he not, at least, when he heard the pistol fired, have crossed to the passage and opened the door which Withers, and Ritterspack, and Stewart say was shut when Booth reached it? Is it possible he would have stood motionless (as Ritterspack and James say he did), remote from the passage and the door, and thus leave Booth to the hazard of his flight, unaided? Would he, as Debonay says he did, instead of following Booth to see him off, have shoved back the scene behind which he stood,

so as to allow free exit for the crowd who sprang on the stage to follow and catch the assassin, and *himself* run for water for the President? His whole conduct before and after the shot was fired shows that if that remark was in fact made to him by Booth, he was wholly ignorant of its imputed meaning.

I here desire to call attention of the Court to a fact in the evidence which, to my mind, *conclusively* shows that if Booth did in fact say that to Spangler, and get that reply, still Spangler neither knew Booth's criminal purpose nor was a party to its execution. That fact is, that Booth knocked "Peanuts" down as he took the horse from him, and fled. Now, I assert that if the evidence shows that Booth intended for Spangler, or assigned to him any part to perform in the conspiracy, it was to hold his horse in the alley at the back door, *and nothing else whatever.* That Spangler failed to do that, but stuck to his duties on the stage, is evidence drawn from *his* conduct that he was no party willing to aid and abet the crime. That Booth knocked the horse holder down is evidence equally conclusive from *his* conduct that Spangler was not intrusted with the secret of the crime to be committed, nor relied on to knowingly aid and abet it. For he, in all probability, thought it was Spangler, and not "Peanuts," who held his horse. He had left him with Spangler, who did not call "Peanuts" to hold him until Booth had passed under the stage and out the side entrance (Debonay), to return on the stage no more until fleeing from his pursuers. As Booth fled he could not have seen Spangler on the stage; and the night was so dark he did not distinguish "Peanuts" from Spangler, both being of near the same hight and frame. It was so dark that Mrs. Simms and Mrs. Turner both took "Peanuts" for Maddox—a man less like him than Spangler is—though he was but a few yards off, holding the horse an hour. And surely Booth, rushing from the glare of the stage, into the blinding darkness of that night, wild with excitement and passion, would not scrutinize the features of his horse boy. He knocked "Peanuts" over, supposing him to be Spangler, thus showing a fear that Spangler would pursue him, and thus, in the midst of his own crime, giving us convincing evidence of Spangler's innocence.

The other item of evidence tending to show that Spangler knew of Booth's purpose and was consenting, advising, or aiding to accomplish it, is the testimony of Sergeant Jos. M. Dye, which I will now consider. He says he saw a roughly-dressed man standing on the pavement, just outside the door of the theater, from twenty-five or thirty minutes past nine, till ten minutes past ten, by the time of the theater clock. That Booth frequently whispered to this man during that time, and that just as the call was made by Booth's other and unknown companion, at ten minutes past ten, from the clock in the theater hall, Booth whispered to this roughly-dressed man and entered the theater. The roughly-dressed man was not seen to leave by the Sergeant, who himself at that time left and went with a friend to a grocery around the corner, where in fifteen minutes, or less, news came that the President was shot. He could describe no article of the roughly-dressed man's clothing, but a black slouch hat, thought him five feet eight or nine inches high, heavily built, and dressed in worn clothes. He recollects distinctly, and asserts most postively, that this man wore *a heavy black mustache.* He did not recollect the color of his eyes, his hair, or any of his clothes, nor knew whether he wore an overcoat. He says (pointing to Spangler), "If that man had a mustache, it would be just the appearance of the face exactly."

It is fortunate for the accused that this witness states with certainty three circumstances, by means of which the theory that this man was Spangler has been completely overthrown.

1. He says (six times in the course of his evidence) that the man he saw had a mustache, and said also it was black and heavy.

Miles, Sleickman, Burroughs, Maddox and Gifford, witnesses for the prosecution, who all saw Spangler during the play, said he wore no mustache then, and they never saw him wear one. Maddox saw him in his place three or four minutes before the assassination, and *then* he wore none. Buckingham, Withers, and Ferguson, witnesses for prosecution, and Goenther, Harry Ford, and others, for defense, who saw him daily, say they never saw him wearing a mustache. If he had been in front of the theater that night for three-quarters of an hour, wearing a heavy *black* mustache, *red-headed as he is,* no one can doubt that many of the employees and *habitues* of the theater who knew him would have noticed his grotesque disguise, and having their attention drawn to the subject by the daily publication of testimony on this point, would have offered themselves as witnesses against him.

2. Sergeant Dye also says, this man remained on the pavement just at the front entrance of the theater constantly from twenty-five or thirty minutes past nine until ten minutes past ten by the theater clock, including a part of the second act, the whole interval between the second and third acts, and that part of the third act before ten minutes past ten—for he speaks of the "rush" coming down to drink after he had been there some time, and returning some time before he left.

If the man had been Spangler, Buckingham, the door-keeper, who was at the ticket window all the evening, would in all probability have noticed him; or Maddox, who was in front of and in the ticket office during the evening, but neither saw him. During all the interval between the acts, before he held Booth's horse, Burroughs (Peanuts) was in front of the theater, but did not see him. Sleickman was in front ten or fifteen minutes before the close of the second act, and *he* did not see him there; nor did Debonay, who was on the pavement front about five minutes before the assassination.

Gifford, on cross-examination, says:

Q. You were in front of the theater during the performance of the second act?

A. During the performance of the second act

I was in front, I think, to the best of my knowledge.

Q. All the time?

A. No, sir; not all the time. I would walk in, and may be stay five or ten minutes, and then walk out again.

Q. State whether or not you saw the prisoner, Spangler, at any time during that play, in front of the theater.

A. I did not see him in front of the theater.

We have not only this negative evidence of persons who were in front of the theater, or in the passage during the time named by Sergeant Dye, but we have also further negative evidence on the same point in the fact that Spangler is shown, by many witnesses, not to have been missed from his place that night, and that his duties on the stage were such as to require his constant presence at his post, and make an absence of three-quarters of an hour impossible, without marring the play and attracting attention of employees and actors to the fact of his absence. On this point John T. Ford, the proprietor of the theater, says:

Q. State whether or not his duties were such as to require his presence upon the stage during the whole of the play.

A. Strictly so. His absence for a moment might imperil the success of the play, and cause dissatisfaction to the audience. It is very important to the effect of a play that the scenery should be well attended to in all its changes; and he is absolutely important there every moment from the time the curtain rises until it falls. There are intervals, it is true, but he can not judge how long or how brief a scene may be.

Q. What were his duties in the intervals between the scenes?

A. To be prepared for the next change; to be ready at his scene; to remain on the side where the stage carpenter had assigned him as his post of duty. Emergencies often arise during an act that require extra service of a stage hand.

But, though the negative evidence above referred to would, in my opinion, be quite sufficient to relieve Spangler of the suspicion of being the person seen by Sergeant Dye, fortunately an *alibi* is shown conclusively by the concurrent testimony of many witnesses for the prosecution and the defense, which testimony shows, beyond all doubt, that he was not only not in front of the theater in consultation with Booth, but was, throughout the play, until the fatal shot, at his post on the side opposite and most remote from the passage and the door by which the murderer escaped—on that part of the stage where, from his position, he would be least able to aid the villain's flight.

John Miles (colored) says he saw Booth ride up to the back door about three-quarters of an hour before the President was shot, and heard him call Spangler three times: and that he looked down from the "flies," and saw Spangler in his place, shoving a scene across on the second groove. Debonay says:

When Booth rode up he came to the alley door and called for Spangler; he called me first; but whether he came on a horse or not, I do not know. He said to me, "Tell Spangler to come to the door and hold my horse." I did not see a horse, though.

Q. What did you do?

A. I went over to where Mr. Spangler was, on the left hand side, at his post, and called him from his post. Said I, "Mr. Booth wants you to hold his horse." He then went to the door, went outside, and was there about a minute, and Mr. Booth came in. He asked me if he could get across the stage. I told him no, the dairy scene was on; that he would have to go under the stage, and come upon the other side. About the time that he got upon the other side, Spangler called to me, "Tell Peanut John to come here and hold this horse; I have not time; Mr Gifford is out in the front of the theater, and all the responsibility of the scenes lies on me." I went on the other side and called John, and John went there and held the horse, and Spangler came in and returned to his post again.

Q. Did you see Spangler any more that evening?

A. I did, three or four times that evening.

Q. Where?

A. On the stage.

Q. In his proper position?

A. Yes, sir.

Q. At what time during the play?

A. I could not say, for certain, what times. It was between and during the acts.

Q. Did you see him about the time the shot was fired?

A. I saw him about two minutes before that, I think.

Q. Where was he then?

A. He was on the same side I was on—the same side as the President's box.

Maddox says:

Q. Where was Spangler's position on the stage?

A. His position was on the left-hand side of the stage.

Q. The same side that the President's box was on?

A. Yes, sir; he has always been on that side since I have been about the theater.

Q. Did you see Spangler that night?

A. Yes, sir, I did.

Q. State at what times you saw him, and where he was during the performance.

A. I saw him pretty nearly every scene. If he had not been there I should certainly have missed him. I do not recollect of seeing him away from the flats at all. He may have been away, but I can not say.

Q. Where were you at the moment the President was assassinated?

A. I was in the first entrance, left hand.

Q. That is the side the President's box is on?

A. Yes, sir.

Q. Did you see Spangler very shortly before that?

A. Yes, sir, I think I did. I saw him standing at his wing when I crossed the stage with the will, while the second scene of the third act was on.

Q. You saw him in his place, then?

A. Yes, sir.

Q. How long was that before the President was assassinated?

A. I think that was about three or four minutes; it could not have been longer than that before, but I will not say positively.

Ritterspack says:

Q. Where were you standing when you heard the pistol fired?

A. In the center of the stage.

Q. Where was Spangler then?

A. He was at the same place, just about ready to shove off the scenes, and I was standing there and listening to the play.

Q. Which was nearest the door, you or Spangler?

A. I was.

Henry M. James says:

Q. State your position and the position of Edward Spangler, if you know what it was, at that time.

A. I was standing ready to draw off the flat, and Mr. Spangler was standing opposite to me on the stage at the time it happened.

Q. You heard the shot fired?

A. Yes, sir.

Q. From the position you were in, you could not then see the President's box?

A. I could not. There was a flat between me and the President.

Q. From the position Spangler was in, could he see it?

A. No sir.

Q. Could he see the front part of the stage on which Booth jumped?

A. No sir. He was standing behind the scene.

Q. On which side of the center of the stage? On the side toward that on which the President's box was?

A. Mr. Spangler was on the side toward the President's box.

Q. Had you seen him previously during the play?

A. I had often seen him every time there was anything to do there; I did not notice him any other time, only when the scenes had to be changed I saw him there at his post.

On cross-examination, Gifford says:

Q. State at what times during the performance you were on the stage that night?

A. I was on the stage until the curtain went up at each act. When the curtain was down I would go around on to the stage, to see that everything was right, and then go out again.

Q. State at what times during that evening, when you came on the stage between the acts, you saw Mr. Spangler.

A. I could not state the time. I should judge the last time I saw him was at about half-past nine o'clock.

Q. State whether you saw him each time you came on the stage. A. Yes, sir; I saw him each time.

Q. He was your subordinate, I believe?

A. Yes, sir. Thus we have Miles and Debonay, who saw him at his place when Booth called for him; Debonay, who saw him in his proper place three or four times after that, before the assassination, "between and during the scenes;" Maddox, who saw him "pretty nearly every scene;" Ritterspack and James, who saw him "where he ought to be to do the work he had to do, behind the scenes ready to shove his flat, at the moment the shot was fired;" James, who during the play, "had often seen him, every time there was anything to do there;" and Gifford, who was on the stage between each act, and each time saw him subordinate there, once, twenty minutes before the assassination.

If any member of this Court should be called on two months hence to prove his presence here during any hour of this day's session, he could hardly bring as much positive evidence, or more or better negative evidence of the fact, than has been presented here to show that Spangler was on the stage throughout the hour preceding the assassination. Either the positive or the negative evidence on this point taken alone shows beyond a possibility of doubt that it was not Spangler whom Sergeant Dye saw in front of the theater from half-past nine till ten minutes past ten that night.

I do not mean at all to discredit Sergeant Dye's testimony as to seeing a man in front of the theater that night in consultation with Booth, or as to that man resembling Spangler. Greenawalt says a man, who called himself Thomas, came to the Pennsylvania House at two o'clock that night and stayed until morning, who resembled Spangler "somewhat;" but that he had darker hair, cut down half over his ears, was of heavy body, wore a black heavy mustache, and "his beard came front, and was cut down from the mustache up; but it was either that way or whiskers all round. I know he had whiskers in front. "He describes him too, as wearing a black, worn slouch hat, such as Sergeant Dye describes the man in consultation with Booth to have had, being the only article of clothing either Greenawalt or Dye describes. It is highly probable both saw the same man. That Spangler is not the man Greenawalt saw is certain from his description of his person, and also from the fact that Spangler slept in the carpenter shop adjoining the theater that night. (Carland.)

I have thus presented to the Court all the evidence taken before it on both sides, which in any way illustrates the acts done and words spoken up to the moment of the assassination, having any relation to the accused. I will now proceed to discuss the evidence as to his conduct from that moment to his arrest, on the 17th of April.

Colonel Stewart says that he pursued Booth through the passage which passes between the green and dressing rooms and the stage, and got within twenty feet of the back door at the end of the passage, when Booth dashed out, and *the door slammed shut*; that he reached the door next after Booth, and opened it and rushed out; that in the passage he passed several actors and actresses, who were greatly agitated; that instantly after the door slammed shut he saw a man within three feet of the door, who seemed composed, and was turning from the door toward him; "that that man resembled Spangler more than he did any of the other prisoners; Spangler makes the impression of that man's visage as I caught it as I was going along very rapidly."

.Q. And you swear now simply to a mere impression, hardly a fixed opinion, as to his being the person?

A. I do not undertake to swear positively that that person sitting there was the person I saw. I do say that I saw a person there, and I see no person among these prisoners who calls to mind the appearance of that person except the one I have indicated, and that one, I am told, is Mr. Spangler.

Q. I wish to know how strongly you are of opinion, or under the impression, that that was probably the man, or whether you are under that impression?

A. I am decided in my opinion that the person now referred to resembles the person I saw there.

Colonel Stewart further says that he thinks the person had some beard, but not heavy enough to attract marked attention, and was in a position where he *might* have shut the door. But the Court will recollect that the person described was turning in *just the opposite* way from that in which a man's body would naturally be turned by the act of slamming the door.

This testimony is of not much value on this point:

1. Because Captain Stewart does not recognize the prisoner as the man, and because he describes the person he saw as having beard, which the prisoner had not.

2. Because he could not, in the nature of things, recognize the stranger he so hurriedly saw, were he to see him again.

3. Because Ritterspack says he saw Booth open the door and shut it, and that *he* was then the first who opened the door after Booth, and *he left it open*, and that a very large man (Capt. Stewart) followed him. The evidence of Ritterspack, on this point, is strengthened by that of Ferguson and Smith, who testify that Booth ran off the stage before Stewart got on it, and that Stewart turned and looked up at the President's box before pursuing Booth.

4. Because Ritterspack says Spangler was on the other side of the stage, near the center, behind the scenes, when the shot was fired, and did not go to the door. James' testimony strengthens Ritterspack's on this point. Both were in view of Spangler when the shot was fired, and between him and the door, and he could not have gone to it without their seeing him go. Neither saw him move.

2. Ritterspack says when the shot was fired Spangler was standing behind the scene waiting the time to shove in, and he was between him and the door, listening to the play. That he could not tell what had happened, for neither he nor Spangler could see the President's box, nor the front of the stage, where they stood. That some cried "Stop that man!" That after he rushed out and returned, Spangler was standing in the same place, and "looked the same as if he was crying, a kind of scared." He then hit me on the face with the back of his hand, and he said, "Don't say which way he went. " I asked him what he meant by slapping me in the mouth, and he said, "For God' s sake, thus up, and that was the last he said."

Gifford, to whom Ritterspack says he told

this at Carroll Prison, says he only told him he had forgotten to tell something in his first examination, and that he (Gifford) *certainly* would have recollected this had it been told him. Carland, to whom Ritterspack said he told it on the night of the assassination, says he told him that he said to Spangler, *as Booth ran along the passage*, "That's Mr. Booth," and Spangler slapped him and said, "You don't know who it is—it may be Mr. Booth, or it may be some one else." Lamb, to whom, Ritterspack said he told it next day, says he told him substantially the same he told Carland the night before, and says that Ritterspack was grumbling at Spangler for slapping him. All three of these witnesses assert most positively that Ritterspack did not represent Spangler as saying, "Don't say which way he went."

At the time Ritterspack told these gentlemen of the conversation with Spangler, the theater had been taken possession of by the military authorities, and general suspicion directed to the employees, under the belief that Booth had accomplices among them. Each employee was doubtless scanning the reported conduct of his fellows, and especially that of Burroughs and Spangler, Booth's horse holders. Ritterspack's statement was one they would be likely to weigh and recollect. If Carland and Lamb recollect aright what Ritterspack told them, there can be no question but that his statement of the conversation, made on the witness stand, is incorrect. For if the conversation did occur between him and the accused, he would recollect and tell it more exactly that night and next day than he would after undergoing a month's confinement, and alarm, and detective discipline, in Carroll Prison.

The evidence of Dabonay, in his second examination, tends strongly to show that Spangler had shoved his scene back and got on the front of the stage before Ritterspack could have returned and held the reported conversation. He says:

Q. State to the Court again where you were standing when the shot was fired in the theater on the night of the 14th of April.

A. I was standing on the left-hand side, first entrance.

Q. You mean the side the President's box was on?

A. Yes, sir.

Q. How long was it after you saw Mr. Stewart run out after Booth, before you saw the accused, Edward Spangler; and where did you see him, and what did you see him do?

A. The first time I saw him he was moving his scene, I think. They shoved the scene back to give the whole of the stage to the people who came on. I do not know who assisted him.

Q. How long was that after Mr. Stewart had left the stage?

A. I guess it was about a minute and a-half, or two minutes.

Q. Was it long enough for Mr. Stewart to have got out of the back door?

A. *I think he had just about time to get to the back door before they shoved the scenes.*

Q. What did Spangler do then?

A. He came in front on the stage, with the

rest. There was a cry for water, and I started to the green-room, and he started the same way. About half a dozen of us went to get some water to carry it to the private box.

Q. How far did Spangler go after the water? Did he go into the green-room?

A. We all went into the green-room; about half a dozen of us went into the green-room. By that time the stage was full of people. Maddox says he saw Booth just as he left the stage, and that he then "ran on the stage and heard the call for water."

This evidence of Debonay and Maddox, and the statements of Carland and Lamb, and the strong improbability of Spangler's standing, still amid the great commotion, render it nearly certain that Spangler was not in his place behind the scene when Ritterspack returned; and that if anything was said between them, it was as stated by Ritterspack to Carland and Lamb. If that be so, of what significance were Spangler's acts or words? He was not in position to see Booth when he jumped on the stage, and ran off, for the scene was between them. He heard nothing but the shot, followed by the cry, "Stop that man," as the assassin, bending forward, hatless, fled through the bewildered crowd in the narrow passage opposite. How would he know it was Booth instantly, when Booth's name had not then been called (Ritterspack) and when men who knew Booth well, and saw him leap on the stage and face the audience in the glare of the foot-lights, shouting "*Sic Semper Tyrannis!*" before he fled, did not recognize him? (Gobright) And if he did recognize Booth, how could he know what had been done? And what could be more natural or apparently innocent than his telling Ritterspack, who cried, "That's Mr. Booth! "Shut up, you don't know who it is. It may be Mr. Booth and may be some one else!"

But even if Ritterspack's last statement be true (which I think it clearly is not), and Spangler was still standing behind the scene, and said, "Shut up, don't say which way he went!" "For God's sake, shut up," he only knew that Booth had fled, and was being pursued. He had seen nothing, and was stunned by the clamor and excitement. He, probably, did not think that Booth had committed crime, or know what crime had been committed, or how Booth was connected in it. It was a stupid, ineffective exclamation—for Ritterspack was not then pursuing Booth, but dozens of others were.

But whatever view we take of Ritterspack's evidence, Captain Stewart's faint recognition of Spangler as the man he met at the door, falls to the ground, for Withers, who knows Spangler well, and saw Booth open and shut the door, did not see Spangler there, and from Spangler's position when the shot was fired, as sworn to by both Ritterspack and James, who were both between him and the door, and who did not notice him move, it is certain he was not at the door when Stewart ran down the passage.

3. After the assassination, John Miles (colored) came down from the flies, three stories above the stage, and met Spangler and several

others at the back door, "and I asked him who it was that held the horse, and he told me to 'hush, not to say nothing,' and I did not say anything more, though I knew who it was, because I saw the boy (Peanuts) holding the horse. He said 'hush don't say anything to me,' or 'hush don't say anything about it.'"

Mary Jane Anderson (colored) says that a short time after Booth had gone, she went to the door of the theater, where some people were standing, and said to Mr. Spangler, "That gentleman (Booth) called you, and he said 'no he did not— he did not call me,' and I said 'he did call you,' and I kept on saying so. With that he walked down the alley." It was probably not fear of the authorities, but of the infuriated people, which led Spangler to this effort to conceal the fact that Booth called him, and that he took the horse. It is as consistent with the theory of his innocence as of his guilt, and therefore amounts to nothing.

4. Carland says Spangler usually slept in the theater—that on Friday night he slept in the carpenter shop, which is part of the theater building. Lamb says he was in the theater all day Saturday, and saw Spangler there through the day. Carland says Spangler slept in his room Saturday night, adjoining the theater, saying there was talk of burning the theater, and he was "afraid to stay in it alone, as he was a heavy sleeper;" and that he was arrested there that night and discharged Sunday morning. Sunday afternoon he saw him again, near the theater, and went with him visiting some friends; and there, hearing that he was to be arrested again, he (Spangler) went to the Detective Police office, and learned it was not so. During this time he had no money. He was arrested Monday, and up to that time was at his meals, as usual, at a boarding house where he had taken them for five or six months (Boigi, Goenther), and where his carpet-sack remained, with the rope in it. During these three days and nights there is not a word or act of Spangler's shown in evidence which does not indicate a consciousness of innocence.

There are several circumstances and general considerations I will now present to the Court remotely affecting the case of the accused, and with it the question of the probable complicity of any of the men connected with the theater in the horrid crime of the conspiracy.

It will be recollected that Chester, the New York actor, says that in the latter part of December, or early in January, Booth solicited him to engage in a scheme to *capture* the President, and said he proposed to do it at Ford's Theater, which the President frequently visited, and that he wanted *him* to open the back door at a preconcerted signal, "and that it must be some one connected or acquainted with that theater who could take part in it." I offered to show that by the "some one connected or familiar with Ford's Theater," was meant Chester himself, by showing Booth's repeated solicitations to Ford, in January and February, to employ that actor, but the Judge Advocate objected, and the objection was sustained. That inference, however, is clearly deducible from Chester's own statement.

I also proposed to show that from its construction an escape could be more readily made from the private boxes of Ford's Theater, than from those of the other principal theaters here; but the Judge Advocate again objected, and his objection was sustained.

It is fit I should advert to these rulings of the Court, to show it that if Chester's evidence is without explanation, it is so by reason of its own rulings. I do not feel, however, that, as it stands, that evidence is of weight against the accused. It is rather in his favor, for the only thing Chester said Booth wanted him to do is a thing which Spangler could easily have done, without of itself attracting suspicion, and which would have greatly aided Booth's escape, but which Booth did for himself—opening the back door after the shot was fired.

It has been generally thought that Booth could not have accomplished the crime and then escape without one or more accomplices employed about the theater. I feel safe in saying not only that it *does not* appear he *had* one, but also that it *does* appear he did not *need* one.

1. Booth was an actor of some distinction, who had played at Ford's, and had, through professional courtesy, as well as his engaging manners, free access to the theater at all hours and by every entrance, when it was open. He had, therefore, abundant opportunities to make his preparations about the President's box, unobserved and unaided.

2. The leap from the box *needed no rehearsal.* It is one which any man of good strength and action could make with safety. Had it not been—apparently through a providence of God —that the villain's spur caught in the folds of one of our country's battle flags, which adorned the box, he would have made the leap with ease. John T. Ford says:

Q. State to the Court whether, from your knowledge of Booth, the leap from the box upon the stage would be a difficult one.

A. By no means, I think. He excelled in everything of that kind. He had a reputation for being a great gymnast. He introduced, in some Shakesperian plays, some of the most extraordinary and outrageous leaps, deemed so by the critics and condemned by the press at the time.

3. The passage leading to the alley door, by which Booth escaped, was always kept clear of furniture and other obstructions during the play. Hess, Gifford, Maddox, James, Ford and others testify, most emphatically, to that. C. D. Hess, the manager of Grover's Theater, a rival of Ford's, says:

Q. State whether or not it is customary in theaters to keep the passage-way between the scenes and the green-room and the dressing room clear.

A. Yes, sir; that is a point of excellence in a stage carpenter. If he keeps a clean stage and his scenes well put away, the passage as clear as possible, we look upon him as a careful man.

And John T. Ford says:

Q. Then I understand the prisoner, Spangler, would not be charged with the duty of keeping the passage-way in order?

A. That was no duty of his, unless specially assigned to him by the stage carpenter; he was subordinate entirely to the stage carpenter.

Q. Now state whether or not that passage-way is generally obstructed in any way.

A. It should never be obstructed. My positive orders are to keep it always clear and in the best order. It is the passage-way used by all the parties coming from the dressing rooms. Where a play was performed like the *American Cousin*, the ladies were in full dress, and it was absolutely necessary that there should be no obstruction there, in order that the play should be properly performed. Coming from the dressing rooms and the green-room of the theater, every one had to use that passage.

I have no doubt that Booth, knowing the passage would be clear, was confident that, with his bowie-knife drawn, he would meet with no resistance from the unarmed men and women who might flock from the green-room in wonder and amazement at the shot and shouts. If so, he would not have wanted or provided any help, except some one to hold his horse, which "Peanuts" did, and some one to open the door for him and shut it on his pursuers, which nobody did but himself.

4. C. D. Hess, the manager of Grover's Theater, says:

Q. State whether you were in the habit of seeing John Wilkes Booth during the last season before the assassination of the President.

A. Yes, sir, very frequently.

Q. State whether he ever made any inquiry of you in regard to the President's attending your theater.

A. He did make such an inquiry.

Q. When?

A. On the day before the assassination.

Q. State the circumstances under which the inquiry was made.

A. He came into the office some time during the afternoon, I think, of Thursday, interrupted me and the prompter of the theater in reading a manuscript, seated himself in a chair, and entered into conversation on the subject of the illumination. There was to be a general illumination of the city on Thursday night, and he asked me if I intended to illuminate. I told him yes, I would illuminate to a certain extent that night, but that the next night would be my great night of the illumination, that being the celebration of the fall of Sumter. He asked me the question—my impression is, his words were, "Do you intend," or "Are you going to invite the President?" I think my reply was, "Yes, that reminds me I must send that invitation." I had it in my mind for several days to invite the Presidential party down on that night—on the night of the 14th.

Q. Was there anything marked in Booth's manner in making the inquiry of you?

A. It struck me as rather peculiar, his entering in the manner that he did; he must have observed that we were busy, and it was not usual for him to come in and take a seat unless he was invited. He did upon that occasion, and made such a point of it that we were both considerably surprised. He pushed the matter so far that I got up and put the manuscript away and entered into conversation with him.

It is probable from this that Booth would have attempted the assassination of the President in Grover's Theater, had he gone there instead of to Ford's on that fatal night; and it *tends* to show that he had no accomplices at either theater.

I have now presented to the Court every point in the evidence which seems to me may, by any possibility, be relied on as indicating guilty knowledge of or participation by Spangler in the conspiracy, or any of its crimes. From the natural partiality of a counsel to his client, I may not have noticed all that bears against him, or presented it in its true light, but I have earnestly sought, in this discussion, to show all that is of weight for or against him, extenuating nothing. I can see in the evidence no ground for such suspicion as would, in the civil courts, lead a grand jury to present him for trial, and believe that, so far from his guilt being established beyond a reasonable doubt, a review of the evidence will leave, in few candid minds, a reasonable doubt of his innocence.

EDWARD SPANGLER.

By his Counsel.

ARGUMENT

IN DEFENSE OF MRS. MARY E. SURRATT,

BY

FREDERICK A. AIKEN, ESQ.

Of Counsel for Mrs. Surratt.

Mr President and Gentlemen of the Commission:

For the lawyer as well as the soldier, there is an equally pleasant duty—an equally imperative command. That duty is to shelter from injustice and wrong the innocent, to protect the weak from oppression, and to rally at all times and on all occasions, when necessity demands it, to the special defense of those whom nature, custom, or circumstance may have placed in dependence upon our strength, honor and cherishing regard. That command emanates and reaches each class from the same authoritative and omnipotent source. It comes from a Superior, whose right to command none dare question, and none dare to disobey. In this command there is nothing of that *lex talionis* which nearly two thousand years ago nailed to the cross its Divine Author.

"Therefore, all things whatsoever ye would that men should do to you, do ye even so unto them; for this is the law and the prophets."

God has not only given us life, but He has filled the world with everything to make life desirable; and when we sit down to determine the taking away of that which we did not give, and which, when once taken, we can not restore, we consider a subject the most solemn and momentous within the range of human thought and human action.

Profoundly impressed with the innocence of our client, we enter upon this last duty in her case with the heartfelt prayer that her honorable judges may enjoy the satisfaction of not having a single doubt left on their minds in granting her an acquittal, either as to the testimony affecting her, or by the surrounding circumstances of the case.

The first point that naturally arises in the presentation of the defense of our client, is that which concerns the plea that has been made to the jurisdiction of this Commission to try her—a plea which by no means implies any thing against the intelligence, fairness, or integrity of the brilliant and distinguished officers who compose the Court, but which merely touches the question of the *right* of this tribunal, under the authority by which it is convoked. This branch of her case is left to depend upon the argument already submitted by her senior counsel, the *grande decus columenque* of his profession, and which is exhaust-

ive of the subject on which it treats. Therefore, in proceeding to the discussion of the merits of the case against her, the jurisdiction of the Court, for the sake of argument, may be taken as conceded.

But, if it be granted that the jurisdiction is complete, the next preliminary inquiry naturally is as to the principles of evidence by which the great mass of accumulated facts is to be analyzed and weighed in the scales of justice and made to bias the minds of her judges; and it may be here laid down as a *concessum* in the case that we are here in this forum, constrained and concluded by the same process, in this regard, that would bind and control us in any other Court of *civil* origin, having jurisdiction over a crime such as is here charged. For it is asserted in all the books that courts-martial must proceed, so far as the acceptance and the analysis of evidence is concerned, upon precisely those reasonable rules of evidence which time and experience, *ab antico*, surviving many ages of judicial wisdom, have unalterably fixed as unerring guides in the administration of the criminal law. Upon this conceded proposition it is unnecessary to consume time by the multiplication of references. We are content with two brief citations from works of acknowledged authority.

In Greenleaf it is laid down, "that courts-martial are bound, *in general*, to observe the rules of the law of evidence by which the courts of criminal jurisdiction are governed." 8 *Greenleaf, sec.* 467.

This covers all the great *general* principles of evidence, the points of difference being wholly as to minor matters.

And it is also affirmed in Benet, "that it has been laid down as an indisputable principle, that whenever a legislative act erects a new jurisdiction, without prescribing any particular rules of evidence to it, the common law will supply its own rules, from which it will not allow such newly-erected Court to depart. The rules of evidence, then, that obtain in the criminal courts of the country, must be the guides for the courts-martial; the end sought for being the truth, these rules laid down for the attainment of that end, must be intrinsically the same in both cases. These rules constitute the law of evidence, and involve the quality, admissibility, and effect of evidence and its application to the purposes of truth." *Benet, pp.* 226, 227.

Therefore, all the facts that tend against the accused, and all those that make for her, are to be weighed and are to operate upon her conviction or acquittal precisely as they would in a court of law. If they present a case such as would there convict her, she may be found guilty here; and if, on the other hand, the rules of law upon these facts would raise any presumption or create any doubt, or force any conclusions that would acquit her in a court of law, then she must be discharged, upon the same principles, by this Commission. This is a point which, in our judgment, we can not too strongly impress upon the minds of her judges. The extraordinary character of the crime; the assassination that removed from us the President of the United States, makes it most desirable that the findings of this tribunal shall be so well founded in reason as to satisfy and secure public confidence and approval; for many of the most material objects of this prosecution, and some of the most important ends of justice, shall be defeated and frustrated if convictions or acquittals, and more especially the former, shall be adjudged upon grounds that are notoriously insufficient.

Such a course of action would have a tendency to draw sympathy and support to the parties thus adjudged guilty, and would rob the result of this investigation of the wholesome support of professional and public opinion. The jurisdiction of the Commission, for example, is a matter that has already provoked considerable criticism and much warm disapproval; but in the case of persons clearly found to be guilty, the public mind would easily overlook any doubts that might exist as to the regularity of the Court in the just sentence that would overtake acknowledged criminals. Thus, if Booth himself and a party of men clearly proved, by ocular evidence or confession, to have aided him, were here tried and condemned, and, as a consequence, executed, not much stress, we think, would be laid by many upon the irregularity of the mode by which they should reach that just death which all good citizens would affirm to be their deserts. But the case is far different when it affects persons who are only suspected, or against whom the evidence is weak and imperfect; for if citizens may be arraigned and convicted for so grievous an offense as this upon insufficient evidence, every one will feel his own personal safety involved, and the tendency would be to intensify public feeling against the whole process of the trial. It would be felt and argued that they had been condemned upon evidence that would not have convicted them in a civil court, and that they had been deprived, therefore, of the advantages which they would have had for their defense. Reproach and contumely upon the Government would be the natural result, and the first occasion would arise in all our history for such demonstrations as would be sure to follow the condemnation of mere citizens, and particularly of a woman, upon evidence on which an acquittal would fol-

low in a civil court. It is, therefore, not only a matter of the highest concern to the accused themselves as a question of personal and private right, but also of great importance upon considerations of general public utility and policy, that the results of this trial, as affecting each of the accused, among them Mrs. Surratt, shall be rigidly held within the bounds and limitations that would control in the premises, if the parties were on trial in a civil court upon an indictment equivalent to the charges and specifications here. Conceding, as we have said, the jurisdiction for the purposes of this branch of the argument, we hold to the principle first enunciated as the one great, all-important, and controlling rule that is to guide the Commission in the findings they are now about to make. In order to apply this principle to the case of our client, we do not propose to range through the general rules of evidence with a view to seeing how they square with the facts as proven against her. In the examination of the evidence in detail, many of these must from necessity be briefly alluded to; but there is only one of them to which we propose in this place to advert specifically, and that is the principle that may be justly said to lie at the foundation of all the criminal law—a principle so just, that it seems to have sprung from the brain of Wisdom herself, and so undoubted and universal as to stand upon the recognition of all the times and all the mighty intellects through and by which the common law has been built up. We allude, of course, to that principle which declares that "every man is held to be innocent until he shall be proven guilty"—a principle so natural that it has fastened itself upon the common reason of mankind, and been immemorially adopted as a cardinal doctrine in all courts of justice worthy of the name. It is by reason of this great, underlying legal tenet that we are in possession of the rule of law, administered by all of the courts, which, in mere technical expression, may be termed "the presumption of innocence in favor of the accused." And it is from hence that we derive that further application of the general principle, which has also become a rule of law and of universal application wherever the common law is respected (and with which we have more particularly to deal), by which it is affirmed, in common language, that in any prosecution for crime "THE ACCUSED MUST BE ACQUITTED WHERE THERE IS A REASONABLE DOUBT OF HIS GUILT." We hardly think it necessary to adduce authorities for this position before any tribunal. In a civil court we certainly should waive the citations, for the principle as stated would be assumed by any civil judge, and would, indeed, be the starting point for any investigation whatever. Though a maxim so common and conceded, it is fortified by the authority of all the great lights of the law. Before reference, however, is made to them, we wish to impress upon the minds of the Court another and important rule which we shall have occasion to refer to:

"The evidence in support of a conspiracy is generally *circumstantial.*" *Russell on Crimes, vol.* 2, § 698.

In regard to circumstantial evidence, all the best and ablest writers, ancient and modern, agree in treating it as wholly inferior in cogency, force, and effect, to *direct* evidence. And now for the rule which must guide the jury in all cases of reasonable doubt:

"If evidence leave reasonable ground for doubt, the conclusion can not be morally certain, however great may be the preponderance of probability in its favor." *Wills on Circumstantial Evidence. Law Library, vol.* 41.

"The burden of proof in every criminal case is on the Government to prove all the material allegations in the indictment; and if, on the whole evidence, the jury have a reasonable doubt whether the defendant is guilty of the crime charged, they are bound to acquit him. If the evidence leads to a reasonable doubt, that doubt will avail in favor of the prisoner." *1st Greenleaf, sec* 34—*Note.*

Perhaps one of the best and clearest definitions of the meaning of a "reasonable doubt" is found in an opinion given in Dr. Webster's case by the learned and accurate Chief-Justice of Massachusetts. He said:

"The evidence must establish the truth of the fact to a reasonable and moral certainty; a certainty that convinces and directs the understanding, and satisfies the reason and judgment of those who are bound to act conscientiously upon it." *Commonwealth* vs. *Webster,* 5 *Cush.,* 320.

Far back in the early history of English jurisprudence we find that it was considered a most serious abuse of the common law "that justices and their officers, who kill people by false judgment, be not destroyed as other murderers, which King Alfred caused to be done, who caused forty-four justices in one year to be hanged for their false judgment. He hanged Freburne because he judged Harpin to die, whereas the jury were in *doubt* of their verdict; *for in doubtful cases* we ought rather to save than to condemn."

The spirit of the Roman law partook of the same care and caution in the condemnation of those charged with crime. The maxim was:

"*Satius est, impunitum relinqui fecinus nocentis, quam innocentem damnare.*"

That there may be no mistake concerning the fact that this Commission is bound as a jury by these rules, the same as juries in civil courts, we again quote from Benet:

"It is in the province of the Court (Court-martial) to decide all questions on the admissibility of evidence. Whether there is *any* evidence is a question for the Court as judges, but whether the evidence is sufficient is a question for the Court as jury to determine, and this rule applies to the admissibility of every kind of evidence, written as well as oral." *Benet,* pp. 225, 226.

These citations may be indefinitely multiplied, for this principle is as true in the law as any physical fact in the exact sciences. It is not contended, indeed, that *any* degree of doubt is sufficient to acquit, but the doubt must be of a reasonable nature, so as to overset the moral evidence of guilt; a mere *possibility* of innocence will not suffice, for, upon human testimony, no case is free from possible innocence. Even the most direct evidence of crime may possibly be mistaken. But the doubt required by the law must be so consonant with reason as, in analogous circumstances, would affect the action of a reasonable creature concerning his own affairs. We may make the nature of such a doubt clearer to the Court by alluding to a very common rule in the application of the general principle in certain cases, and the rule will readily appeal to the judgment of the Court as a remarkable and singularly beautiful example of the inexorable logic with which the law applies its own unfailing reason.

Thus, in cases of conspiracy, and some others, where many persons are charged with joint crime, and where the evidence against most of them must, of necessity, be circumstantial, the plea of "reasonable doubt" becomes peculiarly valuable to the separate accused, and the mode in which it is held it can best be applied is the test whether the facts as proved, circumstantial, as supposed, can be made to consist just as reasonably with a theory that is essentially different from the theory of guilt.

If, therefore, in the development of the whole facts of a conspiracy, all the particular facts against a particular person can be taken apart and shown to support a reasonable theory that excludes the theory of guilt, it can not be denied that the moral proof of the latter is so shaken as to admit the rule concerning the presumption of innocence. For surely no man should be made to suffer because certain facts are proved against him, which are consistent with guilt, when it can be shown that they are also, and more reasonably, consistent with innocence. And, as touching the conspiracy here charged, we suppose there are hundreds of innocent persons, acquaintances of the actual assassin, against whom, on the social rule of "*noscitur a sociis,*" mercifully set aside in law, many facts might be elicited that would corroborate a suspicion of participation in his crime; but it would be monstrous that they should suffer from that theory when the same facts are rationally explainable on other theories.

The distinguished Assistant Judge Advocate, Mr. Bingham, who has brought to the aid of the prosecution, in this trial, such ready and trenchant astuteness in the law, has laid the following down as an invariable rule, and it will pass into the books as such:

"A party who conspires to do a crime may approach the most upright man in the world, with whom he had been, before the criminality was known to the world, on terms of intimacy, and *whose position in the world was such that he might be on terms of intimacy with reputable gentlemen.* It is the *misfortune* of a man that is approached in that way; *it is not his crime,* and *it is not* COLORABLY *his crime either.*"

This rule of construction, we humbly submit, in connection with the question of doubt, has a direct and most weighty bearing upon the case of our client. Some indication of the mode in which we propose to apply it may be properly stated here. Now, in all the evidence, there is not a shadow of direct and positive proof which connects Mrs. Surratt with a participation in this conspiracy alleged, or with any knowledge of it. Indeed, considering the active part she is charged with taking, and the natural communicativeness of her sex, the case is most singularly and wonderfully barren of even circumstantial facts concerning her. But all there is, is circumstantial. Nothing is proved against her, except some few detached facts and circumstances, lying around the outer circle of the alleged conspiracy, and *by no means* necessarily connected with guilty intent or guilty knowledge.

It becomes our duty to see:
1. What these facts are.
2. The character of the evidence in support of them, and of the witnesses by whom they are said to be proven. And,
3. Whether they are consistent with a reasonable theory by which guilt is excluded.

We assume, of course, as a matter that does not require argument, that she has committed no crime at all, even if these *facts* be proved, unless there is the necessary express or implied criminal *intent*, for guilty knowledge and guilty intent are the constituent elements, the principles of all crime. The *intent* and malice, too, in her case must be *express*, for the facts proved against her, taken in themselves, are entirely 'and perfectly innocent, and are not such as give rise to a necessary *implication* of malice. This will not be denied. Thus, when one commits a violent homicide, the law will *presume* the requisite malice; but when one only delivers a message, which is an innocent act in itself, the guilty knowledge, malice and intent, that are absolutely necessary to make it criminal, must be expressly proven before any criminal consequences can attach to it. And, to quote, "Knowledge and intent, when material, must be shown by the prosecutor." *Wharton's American Criminal Law, sec.* 631. The intent to do a criminal act, as defined by Bouvier, implies and means a pre-conceived purpose and resolve, and determination to commit the crime alleged. To quote again: "But the intent or guilty knowledge must be brought directly home to the defendant." *Wharton's American Criminal Law, sec.* 635. When an act, *in itself indifferent*, becomes criminal, if done with a particular intent, then the intent must be proved and found." 3 *Greenleaf, sec.* 13.

In the light of these principles, let us examine the evidence as it affects Mrs. Surratt.
1. What are the acts she has done? The specification against her, in the general charge, is as follows:
"And in further prosecution of the said conspiracy, Mary E. Surratt did, at Washington city, and within the military department and military lines aforesaid, on or before the 6th day of March, A. D. 1865, and on divers other days and times between that day and the 20th day of April, A. D. 1865, receive, entertain, harbor and conceal, aid and assist the said John Wilkes Booth, David E. Herold, Lewis Payne, John H. Surratt, Michael O'Laughlin, George A. Atzerodt, Samuel Arnold, and their confederates, with knowledge of the murderous and

traitorous conspiracy aforesaid, and with intent to aid, abet and assist them in the execution thereof, and in escaping from justice after the murder of the said Abraham Lincoln, as aforesaid."

The first striking fact proved is her acquaintance with J. Wilkes Booth—that he was an occasional visitor at her house. From the evidence, if it is to be relied on, it distinctly appears that this acquaintance commenced the latter part of last January, in the vicinage of three months only before the assassination of the President, and, with slight interruptions, it was continued down to the day of the assassination of the President. Whether he was first invited to the house and introduced to the family by Weichmann, John H. Surratt, or some other person, the evidence does not disclose. When asked by the Judge Advocate "whom did he call to see," the witness, Weichmann, responded, "He generally called for Mr. Surratt—John H. Surratt—and, in the absence of John H. Surratt, he would call for Mrs. Surratt."

Before calling the attention of the Commission to the next evidence of importance against Mrs. Surratt, we desire to refresh the recollection of the Court as to the time and manner, and by whom, according to the testimony of Lloyd, the carbines were first brought to his (Lloyd's) house.

From the official record the following is taken:
Q. Will you state whether or not, some five or six weeks before the assassination of the President, any, or all of these men, about whom I have inquired, came to your house?
A. They were there.
Q. All three together?
A. Yes; John H. Surratt, Herold and Atzerodt were there together.
Q. What did they bring to your house, and what did they do there?
A. When they drove up there, in the morning, John H. Surratt and Atzerodt came first; they went from my house, and went toward T. B., a post-office kept about five miles below there. They had not been gone more than half an hour when they returned with Herold; then the three were together—Herold, Surratt and Atzerodt.
Q. What did they bring to your house?
A. I saw nothing until they all three came into the bar-room. I noticed one of the buggies—the one I supposed Herold was driving or went down in—standing at the front gate. All three of them, when they came into the bar-room, drank, I think, and then John Surratt called me into the front parlor, and on the sofa were two carbines, with ammunition. I think he told me they were carbines.
Q. Anything beside the carbines and ammunition?
A. There was a rope and also a monkey-wrench.
Q. How long a rope?
A. I can not tell. It was in a coil—a right smart bundle—probably sixteen or twenty feet.
Q. Were those articles left at your house?
A. Yes, sir; Surratt asked me to take care

of them, to conceal the carbines. I told him there was no place there to conceal them, and I did not wish to keep such things in the house.

Q. You say that he asked you to conceal those articles for him?

A. Yes, sir; he asked me to conceal them. I told him there was no place to conceal them. He then carried me into a room that I had never been in, which was just immediately above the store room, as it were in the back building of the house. I had never been in that room previous to that time. He showed me where I could put them, underneath the joists of the house—the joists of the second floor of the main building. This little unfinished room will admit of anything between the joists.

Q. Were they put in that place?

A. They were put in there according to his directions.

Q. Were they concealed in that condition?

A. Yes, sir; I put them in there. I stated to Colonel Wells through mistake, that Surratt put them there; but I put them in there myself. I carried the arms up myself.

Q. How much ammunition was there?

A. One cartridge-box.

Q. For what purpose, and for how long, did he ask you to keep these articles?

A. I am very positive that he said he would call for them in a few days. He said he just wanted them to stay for a few days and he would call for them.

It also appears in evidence against Mrs. Surratt, if the testimony is to be relied on, that on the Tuesday previous to the murder of the President, the 11th of April, she met John M. Lloyd, a witness for the prosecution, at Uniontown, when the following took place:

Question by the Judge Advocate:

Q. Did she say anything to you in regard to those carbines?

A. When she first broached the subject to me, I did not know what she had reference to; then she came out plainer, and I am quite positive she asked me about the "shooting irons." I am quite positive about that, but not altogether positive. I think she named "shooting irons," or something to call my attention to those things, for I had almost forgotten about their being there. I told her that they were hid away far back—that I was afraid the house would be searched, and they were shoved far back. She told me to get them out ready; they would be wanted soon.

Q. Was her question to you first, whether they were still there, or what was it?

A. Really, I can not recollect the first question she put to me. I could not do it to save my life.

On the afternoon of the 14th of April, at about half-past five, Lloyd again met Mrs. Surratt, at Surrattsville, at which time, according to his version, she met him by the wood-pile, near the house, and told him to have those shooting irons ready that night, there would be some parties calling for them, and that she gave him something wrapped in a piece of paper, and asked him to get two bottles of whisky ready also. This message to Mr. Lloyd

is the second item of importance against Mrs. Surratt, and in support of the specification against her. The third and last fact that makes against her in the minds of the Court, is the one narrated by Major H. W. Smith, a witness for the prosecution, who states that while at the house of Mrs. Surratt, on the night of the 17th of April, assisting in making the arrest of its inmates, the prisoner, Payne, came in. He (Smith) stepped to the door of the parlor and said: "Mrs. Surratt, will you step here a minute?" As Mrs. Surratt came forward, he asked her the question, "Do you know this man?" She replied, quoting the witness' language, "Before God, sir, I do not know this man, and I have never seen him." An addition to this is found in the testimony of the same witness, as he was drawn out by the Judge Advocate. The witness repeats the language of Mrs. Surratt, "Before God, I do not know this man, and have never seen him, and did not hire him to dig a gutter for me." The fact of the photographs and card of the State arms of Virginia have ceased to be of the slightest importance, since the explanations given in evidence concerning them, and need not be alluded to. If there is any doubt as to whom they all belonged, reference to the testimony of Misses Surratt and Fitzpatrick will settle it.

These three circumstances constitute the part played by the accused, Mary E. Surratt, in this great conspiracy. They are the acts she has done. They are all that two months of patient and unwearying investigation, and the most thorough search for evidence that was probably ever made, has been able to develop against her. The acquaintance with Booth, the message to Lloyd, the non-recognition of Payne, constitute the sum total of her receiving, entertaining, harboring, and concealing, aiding, and assisting those named as conspirators and their confederates, with knowledge of the murderous and traitorous conspiracy, and with intent to aid, abet, and assist them in the execution thereof, and in escaping from justice. The acts she has done, in and of themselves, are perfectly innocent. Of themselves they constitute no crime. They are what you or I, or any of us might have done. She received and entertained Booth, the assassin, and so did a hundred others. She may have delivered a message to Lloyd—so have a hundred others. She might have said she did not know Payne—and who within the sound of my voice can say that they know him now? They are ordinary and commonplace transactions, such as occur every day and to almost everybody. But as all the case against her must consist in the guilty intent that will be attempted to be connected with these facts, we now propose to show that they are not so clearly proven as to free them from great doubt, and, therefore, we will inquire.

2d. How are these acts proven? *Solely* by the testimony of Louis J. Weichmann and John M. Lloyd. Here let us state that we have no malice toward either of them, but if in the analysis of their evidence we should seem to be severe, it is that error and duplicity may be exposed, and innocence protected.

We may start out with the proposition that a body of men, banded together for the consummation of an unlawful act against the Government, naturally would not disclose their purpose and hold suspicious consultations concerning it in the presence continually of an innocent party. In the light of this fair presumption, let us look at the ACTS OF WEICHMANN, as disclosed by his own testimony. Perhaps the most singular and astonishing fact that is made to appear is his omnipresence and co-action with those declared to be conspirators, and his professed and declared knowledge of all their plans and purposes. His acquaintance with John H. Surratt commenced in the fall of 1859, at St. Charles College, Maryland. In January, 1863, he renewed his acquaintance with him in this city. On the 1st of November, 1864, he took board and lodgings with Mrs. Surratt, at her house, No. 541 H street, in this city. If this testimony be correct, he was introduced to Booth on the 15th day of January, 1865. At this first, very first meeting, he was invited to Booth's room, at the National, where he drank wine and took cigars at Booth's expense. After consultation about something in an outer passage between Booth and the party alleged to be with him by Weichmann, they all came into the room, and for the first time business was proceeded with in his presence. After that he met Booth in Mrs. Surratt's parlor and in his own room, and had conversations with him. As near as Weichmann recollects, about three weeks after his introduction, he met the prisoner, Atzerodt, at Mrs. Surratt's. (How Atzerodt was received at the house will be referred to.) About the time that Booth played Pescara, in the "Apostate," at Ford's theater, Weichmann attended the theater in company with Surratt and Atzerodt. At the theater they were joined by Herold. John T. Holahan, a gentleman not suspected of complicity in the great tragedy, also joined the company at the theater. After the play was over, Surratt, Holahan and himself went as far as the corner of Tenth and E streets, when Surratt, noticing that Atzerodt and Herold were not with them, *sent Weichmann* back for them. He found them in a restaurant near by, in conversation with Booth, by whose invitation Weichmann took a drink. After that the entire party went to Kloman's, on Seventh street, and had some oysters. The party there separated, Surratt, Weichmann and Holahan going home. In the month of March last the prisoner, Payne, according to Weichmann, went to Mrs. Surratt's house and *inquired for* John H. Surratt. "I myself," says Weichmann, "went to open the door, and he inquired for Mr. Surratt. I told him Mr. Surratt was not at home, but I would introduce him to the family, and did introduce him to Mrs. Surratt—under the name of Wood." What more? By Weichmann's request Payne remained in the house all night. He had supper served to him in the privacy of Weichmann's own room. More than that, Weichmann went down into the kitchen and got the supper and carried it up to him himself, and as nearly as he recollects, it was about eight weeks previous to the assassination. Payne remained as Weichmann's guest until the

next morning, when he left in the early train for Baltimore. About three weeks after that Payne called again. Says Weichmann, "I again went to the door, and *I again* ushered him into the parlor;" but says he had forgotten his name, and only recollected that he had given the name of *Wood* on the former visit, when one of the ladies called Payne by that name. He who had served supper to Payne in his own room, and had spent a night with him, could not recollect for three weeks the common name of "Wood," but recollects with such distinctness and particularity scenes and incidents of much greater age, and by which he is jeopardizing the lives of others. Payne remained that time about three days, representing himself to the family as a Baptist preacher; that he had been in prison in Baltimore about a week, and that he had taken the oath of allegiance and was going to become a good loyal citizen. To Mrs. Surratt this seemed eccentric, and she said "he was a great looking Baptist preacher." "They looked upon it as odd, and laughed at it." It seems from Weichmann's testimony that he again shared his room with Payne, and when returning from his office one day, and finding a false mustache on the table in his room, he took it and threw it into his toilet box, and afterward with a box of paints, in his trunk, and the mustache was subsequently found in Weichmann's baggage. When Payne, according to Weichmann's testimony, inquired, "Where is my mustache?" Weichmann said nothing, but "thought it rather queer that a Baptist preacher should wear a mustache." He says he did not want it about his room; "thought no honest person had any reason to wear a false mustache," and as no *"honest person"*(?) should be in possession of it, he locked it up in his *own trunk.* Weichmann professes throughout his testimony the greatest regard and friendship for Mrs. Surratt and her son. Why did he not, on this occasion, and while his suspicions were aroused—if *he* is an honest man, why did he not go to Mrs. Surratt and communicate them at once? She, an innocent and guileless woman, not knowing what was occurring in her own house; he, the friend, coming into possession of important facts, and not making them known to her, the head of the household, but claiming *now*, since this overwhelming misfortune has fallen upon Mrs. Surratt, that, while reposing in the very bosom of the family as a friend and confidant, he was a spy and an informer! and that, we believe, is the best excuse the prosecution is able to make for him. His account and explanation of this mustache would be treated with contemptuous ridicule in a civil court. But this is not all. Concede Weichmann's account of the mustache to be true, and if it was not enough to rouse his suspicions that all was not right, he states that, on the same day, he went to Surratt's room and found Payne seated on the bed with Surratt, playing with bowie-knives, and surrounded with revolvers and spurs. Miss Honora Fitzpatrick testifies that Weichmann was treated by Mrs. Surratt "more like a son than a friend." Poor return for motherly care! Guilty knowledge of and participation in crime or in wild schemes for the capture of the President, would be a good excuse for not making all this known to Mrs. Surratt. In speaking of the spurs and pistols, Weichmann *knew* that there were *just eight spurs*, and two long navy revolvers. Bear in mind, we ask you, gentlemen of the Commission, that there is no evidence before you showing that Mrs. Surratt knew anything about these things. It seems farther on, about the 19th of March, that Weichmann went to the Herndon House with Surratt to engage a room. He says he afterward learned that it was for Payne, from Atzerodt, but contradicts himself in the same breath by stating that he inquired of Atzerodt if he was going to see Payne at the Herndon House. His intimate knowledge of Surratt's movements between Richmond and Washington, fixing the dates of the trips with great exactitude; of Surratt's bringing gold back; of Surratt's leaving on the evening of the 3d of April for Canada, spending his last moments here with Weichmann; of Surratt's telling Weichmann about his interviews with Davis and Benjamin in all this knowledge concerning himself, and associations with those named as conspirators, he is no doubt truthful as far as his statements extend, but when he comes to apply some of this knowledge to others, he at once shakes all faith in his testimony bearing upon the accused.

"Do you remember," the question was asked him, "early in the month of April, of Mrs. Surratt having sent for you and asking you to give Mr. Booth notice that she wished to see him?"

when he delivered the message. One of two things to which he swears in this statement can not be true: 1. That he met John McCullough in Booth's room, for we have McCullough's sworn statement that at that time he was not in the city of Washington, and if, when he delivered the message to Booth, McCullough was in the room, it could not have been on the 2d of April.

"St. Lawrence Hall,
"Montreal, June 3, 1865.

"I am an actor by profession, at present fulfilling an engagement at Mr. Buckland's theater, in this city. I arrived here on the 12th of May. I performed two engagements at Ford's theater, in Washington, during the past winter, the last one closing on Saturday evening, 25th of March. I left Washington on Sunday evening, 26th March, and have not been there since. I have no recollection of meeting any person by the name of Weichmann.

"JOHN McCULLOUGH.

"Sworn to and subscribed before me, at the United States Consulate General's in Montreal, this third day of June, A. D. 1865.

"C. H. POWERS,
"U. S. Vice Consul General."

If he can be so mistaken about those facts, may he not be in regard to the whole transaction? It is also proved by Weichmann that before Mrs. Surratt started for the country, on the 14th of April, Booth called; that he remained three or four minutes, and then Weich-

mann and Mrs. Surratt started for the country.

All this comes out on his first examination in chief. The following is also told in his first cross-examination: Mrs. Surratt keeps a boarding house in this city, and was in the habit of renting her rooms out, and that he was upon very intimate terms with Surratt; that they occupied the same room; that when he and Mrs. Surratt went to Surrattsville on the 14th, she took two packages, one of papers, the contents of the other were not known. That persons have been in the habit of going to Mrs. Surratt's and staying a day or two; that Atzerodt stopped in the house only one night; that the first time Payne came to the house he was dressed genteelly, like a gentleman; that he heard both Mrs. Surratt and her daughter say that they did not care about having Atzerodt brought to the house; and at the conclusion, in swearing as to Mrs. Surratt's character, he said it was exemplary and lady-like in every particular, and apparently, as far as he could judge, she was all the time, from the 1st of November up to the 14th of April, "doing her duties to God and man." It also distinctly appears that Weichmann never had any conversation with Mrs. Surratt touching any conspiracy. One thing is apparent to our minds, and it is forced upon us, as it must be upon every reasonable mind, that in order to have gained all this knowledge Weichmann must have been within the inner circle of the conspiracy. He knows too much for an innocent man, and the conclusion is perfectly irresistible that if Mrs. Surratt had knowledge of what was going on, and had been, with others, a *particeps criminis* in the great conspiracy, she would have certainly done more than she did or has been shown against her, and Weichmann would have known it. How does her non-recognition of Payne, her acquaintance with Booth, and the delivery of the message to Lloyd, compare with the long and startling array of facts proved against Weichmann out of his own mouth? All the facts point strongly to him as a co-conspirator.

Is there a word on record of conversation between Booth and Mrs. Surratt? That they did converse together, we know; but if anything treasonable had passed between them, would not the quick ears of Weichmann have caught it, and would not he have recited it to this Court?

When Weichmann went, on Tuesday, the 11th of April, to get Booth's buggy, he was not asked by Mrs. Surratt to get ten dollars. It was proffered by Booth, according to Weichmann, and he took it. If Mrs. Surratt ever got any money from Booth, she paid it back to him. It is not her character to be in any one's debt.

There was no intimacy with Booth, as Mrs. Surratt has proved, but only common acquaintance, and such as would warrant only occasional calls on Booth's part, and only intimacy would have excused Mrs. Surratt to herself in accepting such a favor, had it been made known to her. Moreover, Miss Surratt has attested to remarks of her brother, which prove that intimacy of Booth with his sister and mother were not desirable to him.

The preceding facts are proven by statements made by Weichmann during his first examination. But, as though the Commission had not sufficiently exposed the character of one of its chief witnesses in the role of grand conspirator, Weichmann is re-called and farther attests to the genuineness of the following telegram:

"NEW YORK, March 23d, 1865.— *To Weichmann, Esq., 541 H street:* Tell John telegraph number and street at once."

[Signed,]   "J. BOOTH."

What additional proof of confidential relations between Weichmann and Booth could the Court desire? If there was a conspiracy planned and maintained among the persons named in the indictment, Weichmann must have had *entire* knowledge of the same, else he had not been admitted to that degree of knowledge to which he testifies; and in such case, and in the alleged case of Mrs. Surratt's complicity, Weichmann *must* have known the same by circumstances strong enough to exclude doubt, and in comparison with which all present facts of accusation would sink into insignificance.

We proceed to the notice and review of the second chief witness of the prosecution against Mrs. Surratt, John M. Lloyd. He testifies to the fact of a meeting with Mrs. Surratt at Uniontown on the 11th of April, 1865, and to a conversation having occurred between Mrs. Surratt and himself, in regard to which he states : "I am *quite positive* she asked me about the 'shooting irons;' I am quite positive about that, but not altogether positive; I *think* she named shooting irons, or something to call my attention to those things, for I had almost forgotten about their being there." Q. "Was her question to you first, whether they were there, or what was it?" A. "Really, I can not recollect the first question she put to me—I could not do it to save my life." The question was asked Lloyd, "During this conversation, was the word carbine mentioned?" He answered, "No." "She finally came out, but can not be determined about it—that she said shooting irons—asked me in relation to them." The question was then asked: "Can you swear, on your oath, that Mrs. Surratt mentioned the words 'shooting irons' to you at all?" A. "I am very positive she did." Q. "Are you *certain ?* " A. "I am very positive that she named shooting irons on both occasions. Not so positive as to the first as I am about the last."

Here comes in the plea of "reasonable doubt." If the witness himself is not absolutely positive as to what occurred, and as to the conversation that took place, how can the jury assume to act upon it as they would upon a matter personally concerning themselves?

On this occasion of Mrs. Surratt's visit to Uniontown, three days before the assassination, where she met Lloyd, and where this conversation occurred between them, at a time when Lloyd was, by presumption, sober and not intoxicated, he declares definitely before the Commission that he is unable to recollect the conversation, nor parts of it, with distinctness. But on the 14th of April, and at a time when, as testified by his sister-in-law, he was more than ordinarily affected by intoxicating drink —and Capt. Gwynn, James Lusby, Knott, bar-

keeper, and others, corroborate the testimony as to his absolute inebriation—he attests that he positively remembers that Mrs. Surratt said to him : "Mr. Lloyd, I want you to have those shooting irons ready." "That persons would' call for them." "That was the language she made use of, and she gave me this other thing to give to whoever called."

In connection with the fact that Lloyd can not swear positively that Mrs. Surratt mentioned "shooting irons" to him at Uniontown, bear in mind the fact that Weichmann sat in the buggy on the same seat with Mrs. Surratt, and he swears he heard nothing about "shooting irons." Would not the quick ears of Weichmann have heard the remark had it been made?

The gentlemen of the Commission will please recollect that these statements were rendered by a man addicted to excessive use of intoxicating liquors; that he was even inordinately drunk at the time referred to; that he had voluntarily complicated himself in the concealment of the arms by J. H. Surratt and his friends; that he was in a state of maudlin terror when arrested, and when forced to confess, that for two days he maintained denial of all knowledge that Booth and Herold had been at his house; and that at last, and in the condition referred to, he was coerced by threats to confess, and in a weak and common effort to exculpate himself by the accusation of another, he proceeded to place blame upon Mrs. Surratt by statements of conversation already cited. Notwithstanding his utter denial of all knowledge of Booth and Herold having called at his house, it afterward appears, by his own testimony, that immediately Herold commanded him (Lloyd) "for God's sake, make haste and get those things," he comprehended *what* "things" were indicated, without definition, and brought forth both carbines and whisky. He testifies that J. H. Surratt had told him, when depositing the weapons in concealment in his house, that they would soon be called for, but did not instruct him, it seems, by whom they would be demanded.

All facts connecting Lloyd with the case, tend to his implication and guilt, and to prove that he adopted the *dernier resort* of guilt—accusation and inculpation of another. In case Lloyd were innocent and Mrs. Surratt the guilty co-adjutrix and messenger of the conspirators, Lloyd would have been able to cite so much more open and significant remarks and acts of Mrs. Surratt that he would not have been obliged to recall, in all perversion and weakness of uncertainty, so common and unmeaning deeds and speech as his testimony includes.

It is upon these considerations that we feel ourselves safe and reasonable in the position that there are facts and circumstances, both external and internal, connected with the testimony of Weichmann and Lloyd, which, if they do not destroy, do certainly greatly shake their credibility, and which, under the rule that will give Mrs. Surratt the benefit of all reasonable doubts, seem to forbid that she should be convicted upon the unsupported evidence of these two witnesses. But even admitting the facts to be proven as above recited, it remains to be seen where is the guilty knowledge of the contemplated assassination; and this brings us to the inquiry whether these facts are not explainable so as to exclude guilt.

From one of the most respected of legal authorities the following is taken: "Whenever, therefore, the evidence leaves it indifferent which of several hypotheses is true, or merely establishes some finite probability in favor of one hypothesis rather than another, such evidence can not amount to proof. The maxim of the law is that it is better that ninety-nine offenders should escape than that one innocent man should be condemned." *Starkie on Evidence.*

The acts of Mrs. Surratt must have been accompanied with a criminal intent in order to make them criminal. If any one supposes that such intent existed, the supposition comes alone from inference. If disloyal acts and constant disloyal practices; if overt and open action against the Government on her part had been shown down to the day of the murder of the President, it would do something toward establishing the inference of criminal intent. On the other hand, just the reverse is shown. The remarks here of the learned and honorable Judge Advocate are peculiarly appropriate to this branch of the discussion, and, with his authority, we waive all others:

"If the Court please, I will make a single remark. I think the testimony in this case has proved, what I believe history sufficiently attests, how kindred to each other are the crimes of treason against a nation and the assassination of its Chief Magistrate. I think of those crimes, the one seems to be, if not the necessary consequence, certainly a logical sequence from the other. The murder of the President of the United States, as alleged and shown, was pre-eminently a political assassination. Disloyalty to the Government was its sole, its only inspiration. When, therefore, we shall show, on the part of the accused, acts of intense disloyalty, bearing arms in the field against that Government, we show, with him, the presence of an *animus* toward the Government which relieves this accusation of much, if not all, of its improbability. And this course of proof is constantly resorted to in criminal courts. I do not regard it as in the slightest degree a departure from the usages of the profession in the administration of public justice. The purpose is to show that the prisoner, in his mind and course of life, was prepared for the commission of this crime; that the tendencies of his life, as evidenced by open and overt acts, lead and point to this crime, if not as a necessary, certainly as a most probable result, and it is with that view, and that only, that the testimony is offered."

Is there anything in Mrs. Surratt's mind and course of life to show that she was prepared for the commission of this crime? The business transacted by Mrs. Surratt at Surrattsville, on the 14th, clearly discloses her only purpose in making the visit. Calvert's letters, the package of papers relating to the estate, the business with Nothe, would be sufficiently clear to most minds, when added to the fact that the other unknown package had been handed to Mrs. Offutt; that, while at Surrattsville, she made no inquiry for, or allusion to, Mr. Lloyd, and was ready to return to Washington when Lloyd drove up to the house. Does not this open wide the door for the admission of the plea of "reasonable doubt?" Had she really been engaged in assisting in the great crime, which makes an epoch in our country's history, her only object and most anxious wish would have been to see Lloyd. It was no ruse to transact important business there to cover up what the uncharitable would call the real business. Calvert's letter was received by her on the forenoon of the 14th, and long before she saw Booth that day, or even before Booth knew that the President would be at the theater that night, Mrs. Surratt had disclosed her intention to go to Surrattsville, and had she been one moment earlier in her start, she would not have seen Booth at all. All these things furnish powerful presumptions in favor of the theory that, if she delivered the message at all, it was done innocently.

In regard to the non-recognition of Payne, the third fact adduced by the prosecution against Mrs. Surratt, we incline to the opinion that, to all minds not fore-judging the testimony of Miss A. E. Surratt, and various friends and servants of Mrs. Surratt, relative to physical causes, might fully explain and account for such ocular remissness and failure. In times and on occasions of casual meeting at intimate acquaintances on the street, and of common need for domestic uses, the eyesight of Mrs. Surratt had proved treacherous and failing. How much more liable to fail her was her imperfect vision on an occasion of excitement and anxiety, like the night of her arrest and the disturbance of her household by military officers, and when the person with whom she was confronted was transfigured by a disguise which varied from the one in which she had previously met him, with all the wide difference between a Baptist parson and an earth-soiled, uncouthly dressed digger of gutters? Anna E. Surratt, Emma Offutt, Eliza Holahan, Honora Fitzpatrick, Anna Ward, and a servant, attest all to the visual incapacity of Mrs. Surratt, and the annoyance she experienced therefrom, in passing friends without recognition in the daytime, and from inability to sew or read even on a dark day, as well as at night. The priests of her church, and gentlemen who have been friendly and neighborhood acquaintances of Mrs. Surratt for many years, bear witness to her untarnished name and discreet and Christian character, and absence of all imputation of disloyalty, to her character for patriotism. Friends and servants attest to her voluntary and gratuitous beneficence to our soldiers stationed near her; and, "in charges for high treason, it is pertinent to inquire into the humanity of the prisoner toward those representing the Government" is the maxim of the law; and, in addition, we invite your attention to the singular fact that of the two officers who bore testimony in this matter, one asserts that the hall, wherein Payne sat, was illuminated by a full head of gas; the other that the gaslight was purposely dimmed. The uncertainty of this witness, who gave testimony relative to the coat of Payne, may also be recalled to your notice.

Should not this valuable testimony of loyal and moral character shield a woman from ready belief, on the part of judges who judge her worthiness in every way, that within the few, few moments in which Booth detained Mrs. Surratt from her carriage, already waiting, when he approached and entered the house, she became so converted to diabolical evil as to hail with ready assistance his terrible plot, which must have been framed (if it were complete in his intent at that hour, half-past two o'clock), since the hour of eleven that day?

If any part of Lloyd's statements is true, and Mrs. Surratt did verily bear to his or Mrs. Offutt's hands the field-glass, enveloped in paper, by the evidence itself, we may believe she knew not the nature of the contents of the package; and, had she known, what evil could she, or any other, have attached to a commission of so common a nature? No evidence of individual or personal intimacy with Booth has been adduced against Mrs. Surratt; no long and apparently confidential interviews; no indications of a private comprehension mutual between them; only the natural, and not frequent, custom on the part of Booth—as any other associate of her son might and doubtless did do—of inquiring through the mother, whom he would request to see, of the son who, he would learn, was absent from home. No one has been found who could declare any appearance of the nursing or mysteriously discussing of anything like conspiracy within the walls of Mrs. Surratt's house. Even if the son of Mrs. Surratt, from the significancies of associations, is to be classed with the conspirators, if such body existed, it is monstrous to suppose that the son would weave a net of circumstancial evidences around the dwelling of his widowed mother, were he never so reckless and sin-determined; and that they (the mother and the son) joined hands in such dreadful pact, is more monstrous still to be thought.

A mother and son associate in crime! and such a crime as this half of the civilized world never saw matched, in *all* its dreadful bearings! Our judgments can have hardly recovered their unprejudiced poise since the shock of the late horrors, if we can contemplate with credulity such a picture, conjured by the unjust spirits of indiscriminate accusation and revenge. A crime which, in its public magnitude, added to its private misery, would have driven even the Atis-haunted heart of a Medici, a Borgia, or a Madame Bocarme to wild confession before its accomplishment, and daunted even *that* soul, of all the recorded world the most eager for novelty in license, and most unshrinking in sin— the indurated soul of Christina of Sweden; such a crime as profoundest plotters within padded walls would scarcely dare whisper; the words forming the expression of which, spoken aloud in the upper air, would convert all listening boughs to aspens, and all glad sounds of nature to shuddering wails. And *this* made known, even surmised, to a woman! a *mater familias*, the good genius, the "*placens uxor*" of a home where children had gathered all

the influences of purity and the reminiscences of innocence, where RELIGION watched, and the CHURCH was MINISTER and TEACHER.

Who—were circumstantial evidence strong and conclusive, such as only time and the slow weaving fates could elucidate and deny—who will believe, when the mists of uncertainty which cloud the present shall have dissolved, that a woman born and bred in respectability and competence—a Christian mother, and a citizen who never offended the laws of civil propriety; whose unfailing attention to the most sacred duties of life has won for her the name of "a proper Christian matron;" whose heart was ever warmed by charity; whose door unbarred to the poor, and whose Penates had never cause to veil their faces;—who will believe that she could so suddenly and so fully have learned the intricate arts of sin? A daughter of the South, her life associations confirming her natal predilections, her individual preferences inclined, without logic or question, to the Southern people, but with no consciousness nor intent of *disloyalty* to her *Government*, and causing no exclusion from her friendship and active favors of the people of the loyal North, nor repugnance in the distribution among our Union soldiery of all needed comforts within her command, and on all occasions.

A strong but guileless-hearted woman, her maternal solicitude would have been the first denouncer, even abrupt betrayer, of a plotted crime in which one companion of her son could have been implicated, had cognizance of such reached her. Her days would have been agonized and her nights sleepless, till she might have exposed and counteracted that spirit of defiant hate which watched its moment of vantage to wreak an immortal wrong—till she might have sought the intercession and absolution of the Church, her refuge, in behalf of those she loved. The brains, which were bold, and crafty, and couchant enough to dare the world's opprobrium in the conception of a scheme which held as naught the lives of men in highest places, never imparted it to the intelligence, nor sought the aid nor sympathy of any living woman, who had not, like Lady Macbeth, "unsexed herself"—not though she were wise and discreet as Maria Theresa or the Castilian Isabella. *This woman knew it not.* This woman, who, on the morning preceding that blackest day in our country's annals, knelt in the performance of her most sincere and sacred duty at the confessional, and received the mystic rite of the Eucharist, knew it not. Not only would she have rejected it with horror, but such proposition, presented by the guest who had sat at her hearth as the friend and convive of her son, upon whose arm and integrity her widowed womanhood relied for solace and protection, would have roused her maternal wits to some sure cunning which would have contravened the crime and sheltered her son from the evil influences and miserable results of such companionship.

The mothers of Charles the IX and of Nero could harbor, underneath their terrible smiles, schemes for the violent and unshriven deaths, or the moral vitiation and decadence which would painfully and gradually remove lives sprung from *their own*, were they obstacles to their demoniac ambition. But *they* wrought their awful romances of crime in lands where the sun of supreme civilization, through a gorgeous evening of Syberitish luxury, was sinking, with red tents of revolution, into the night of anarchy and national caducity. In our own young nation, strong in its morality, energy, freedom, and simplicity, assassination can never be indigenous. Even among the desperadoes and imported lazzaroni of our largest cities, it is comparatively an infrequent cause of fear.

The daughters of women to whom, in their yet preserved abodes, the noble mothers who adorned the days of our early independence are vividly remembered realities and not haunting shades—the descendants of earnest seekers for liberty, civil and religious, of rare races, grown great in heroic endurance, in purity which comes of trial borne, and in hope born of conscious right, whom the wheels of Fortune sent hither to transmit such virtues—the descendants of *these* have no heart, no ear for the diabolisms born in hot-beds of tyranny and intolerance. No descendant of these, no woman of this temperate land could have seen, much less *joined*, her son, descending the sanguinary and irrepassable paths of treason and murder, to ignominious death, or an expatriated and attainted life, worse than the punishing wheel and bloody pool of the poets' hell.

In our country, where reason and moderation so easily quench the fires of insane hate, and where "*La Vendetta*" is so easily overcome by the sublime grace of forgiveness, no woman could have been found so desperate as to sacrifice all spiritual, temporal, and social good, self, offspring, fame, honor, and all the *desiderata* of life, and time, and immortality, to the commission, or even countenance, of such a deed of horror as we have been compelled to contemplate the two past months.

In a Christian land, where all records and results of the world's intellectual, civil and moral advancement mold the human heart and mind to highest impulses, the theory of old Helvetius is more probable than desirable.

The natures of all born in equal station are not so widely varied as to present extremes of vice and goodness, but by the effects of rarest and severest experience. Beautiful fairies and terrible gnomes do not stand by each infant's cradle, sowing the nascent mind with tenderest graces or vilest errors. The slow attrition of vicious associations and law-defying indulgences, or the sudden impetus of some terribly multiplied and social disaster, must have worn away the susceptibility of conscience and self respect, or dashed the mind from the hight of these down to the deeps of despair and recklessness, before one of *ordinary* life could take counsel with violence and crime. In no such manner was the life of our client marked. It was the parallel of nearly all the competent masses; surrounded by the scenes of her earliest recollections, independent in her condition, she was satisfied with the *mundus* of her daily pursuits,

and the maintenance of her own and children's *status* in society and her church.

Remember *your* wives, mothers, sisters and gentle friends, whose graces, purity and careful affection ornament and cherish and strengthen your lives. Not widely different from *their* natures and spheres have been the nature and sphere of the woman who sits in the prisoner's dock to-day, mourning with the heart of Alcestis her children and her lot; by whose desolated hearthstone a solitary daughter wastes her uncomforted life away in tears and prayers and vigils for the dawn of hope; and this wretchedness and unpitied despair have closed like a shadow around one of earth's common pictures of domestic peace and social comfort, by the one sole cause—suspicion fastened and fed upon the facts of acquaintance and mere fortuitous intercourse with that man in whose name so many miseries gather, the assassinator of the President.

Since the days when Christian tuition first elevated womanhood to her present free, refined and refining position, man's power and honoring regard have been the palladium of her sex. Let no stain of injustice, eager for a sacrifice to revenge, rest upon the reputation of the men of our country and time.

This woman, who, widowed of her natural protectors; who, in helplessness and painful severe imprisonment, in sickness and in grief ineffable, sues for justice and mercy from your hands, may leave a legacy of blessings, sweet as fruition-hastening showers, for those you love and care for, in return for the happiness of fame and home restored, though life be abbreviated and darkened through this world by the miseries of this unmerited and woeful trial. But long and chilling is the shade which just retribution, slow creeping on with its "*pede claudo*," casts around the fate of him whose heart is merciless to his fellows bowed low in misfortune and exigence.

Let all the fair womanhood of our land hail you with a pæon of joy that you have restored to her sex, in all its ranks, the ægis of impregnable legal justice which circumvallates and sanctifies the threshhold of home and the privacy of home life against the rude irruptions of arbitrary and perhaps malice-born suspicion, with its fearful attendants of arrest and incarceration, which in this case have been sufficient to induce sickness of soul and body.

Let not this first State tribunal in our country's history, which involves a woman's name, be blazoned before the world with the harsh tints of intolerance, which permits injustice. But as the benignant heart and kindly judging mind of the world-lamented victim of a crime which wound, in its ramifications of woe, around so many fates, would himself have counseled you, let the heralds of PEACE and CHARITY, with their wool-bound staves, follow the fasces and axes of JUDGMENT and LAW, and without the sacrifice of any innocent Iphigenia, let the ship of State lanch with dignity of unstained sails into the unruffled sea of UNION and PROSPERITY.

MARY E. SURRATT.

By FREDERICK A. AIKEN, of Counsel.
REVERDY JOHNSON,
JOHN W. CLAMPITT, Associate Counsel.

ARGUMENT

IN

DEFENSE OF GEORGE A. ATZERODT.

BY

W. E. DOSTER, ESQ.

May it please the Court:

The prisoner, George A. Atzerodt, is charged with the following specification: "And in further prosecution of said conspiracy, and its traitorous and murderous designs, the said George A. Atzerodt did, on the night of the 14th of April, A. D. 1865, and about the same hour of the night aforesaid, within the military department and military lines aforesaid, lie in wait for Andrew Johnson, then Vice-President of the United States aforesaid, with the intent, unlawfully and maliciously, to kill and murder him, the said Andrew Johnson." In support of this specification the prosecution has submitted the following testimony: The testimony of Weichmann and Miss Surratt, that he was frequently seen in company with Booth at the house of Mrs. Surratt. The testimony of Greenawalt, that Atzerodt had interviews with Booth at the Kimmell House, and that the prisoner once said, the 1st of April, "Greenawalt, I am pretty near broke, though I have friends enough to give me as much money as will keep me all my life. I am going away one of these days, but I will return with as much money as will keep me all my lifetime." The testimony of Marcus P. Norton, that he overheard him in conversation with Booth, in which it was said, about the evening of the 3d of March, that, "If the matter succeeded as well with Johnson as it did with old Buchanan, the party would be terribly sold;" and, also, that "The character of the witnesses would be such that nothing could be proved by them." The testimony of Col. Nevins, that he was asked by the prisoner, between four and five of the afternoon of the 12th of April, at the Kirkwood House, to point out Mr. Johnson while at dinner. The testimony of John Fletcher, that on or about April 3d, the prisoner owned a horse and saddle, which he afterward said was sold in Montgomery county, and which was afterward found near Camp Barry Hospital, on the night of the 14th of April. The testimony of Fletcher, also, that on the evening of the 14th, the prisoner got a dark bay mare at Naylor's (which he had brought there in the morning), rode her away at half-past six, brought her back at eight, returned again at ten, ordered his mare, took a drink; said, "If this thing happens to-night, you will hear of a present;" and of the mare, "She is good on a retreat;" that he then rode to the Kirkwood House, came out again, went

300

along D street, and turned up Tenth street. The testimony of Thomas L. Gardner, that the same dark bay one-eyed horse found near Camp Barry, was sold by his uncle, George Gardner, to Wilkes Booth. Testimony of John L. Toffey, that the same horse was found at twelve and a half A. M., Saturday, the 15th of April, near Camp Barry, about three-quarters of a mile east of the Capitol. The testimony of Washington Briscoe, that on the evening of the 14th, between twelve and half-past twelve, the prisoner got into the cars near the Navy Yard, and asked him three times to let him sleep in the store; that he was refused, and said he was going to the Kimmell House. The testimony of Greenawalt, again, that he came to the Kimmell House at two P. M., and in company with a man by the name of Thomas, and hesitated to register his name, and went away in the morning, about five, without paying his bill. Testimony of Lieutenant Keim, that he slept in the same room with Atzerodt that night at the Kimmell House, and when Keim spoke of the assassination, he said "it was an awful affair," and that on the Sunday before he saw a knife in his possession—"a large bowie-knife in a sheath"—and that Atzerodt remarked, "If one fails, I want the other." Testimony of Wm. Clendenin, that he found a knife similar to the one seen by Keim, in F street, between Eighth and Ninth streets, opposite the Patent Office, at six o'clock of the morning after the assassination. Testimony of Robert Jones and John Lee, that Atzerodt took a room at the Kirkwood House, No. 126, and that in it, on the morning of the 15th, were found a coat containing a loaded pistol and a bowie-knife, and a handkerchief marked with the name of J. Wilkes Booth. Testimony of Provost Marshal McPhail, that Atzerodt confessed he threw his knife away near the Herndon House; that he pawned his pistol at Caldwell's store, at Georgetown, and borrowed ten dollars, and that the coat and arms at the Kirkwood House belonged to Herold. Testimony of Sergeant Gemmill, that he arrested Atzerodt near Germantown, and that he denied having left Washington recently, or having had anything to do with the assassination. Testimony of Hezekiah Metz, that on the Sunday following the assassination Atzerodt said at his house, "If the man had followed Gen. Grant that was to have followed him, he would have been killed." To negative this specification the defense has submitted the following testimony: The testimony of Somerset Leaman, that the prisoner said at the house of Mr. Metz, when asked whether Gen. Grant was killed, "No, I do not suppose he was. If he was killed, he would have been killed probably by a man that got on the same train of cars that he did," and that he never used the language imputed to him by Mr. Metz; that he was confused, but that the daughter of Mr. Metz, to whom he was paying his addresses, was showing him the cold shoulder on that day. The same confirmed by James E. Leaman. The testimony of James Keleher, proprietor of a livery stable, corner of Eighth and E streets, that Atzerodt hired a dark bay mare from his stable at half-past two o'clock on the afternoon of the 14th, wrote his name in a large hand, did not hesitate to put down his name, willingly gave references, told him he lived in Port Tobacco, and was a coachmaker by trade, and gave the names of John Cook and Stanley Higgins as references. Testimony of Samuel Smith, that the bay mare was returned about eleven o'clock on the evening of the 14th, very much in the same condition as when she went out: no foam on her. Samuel McAllister, that the prisoner rode up to the Kimmell House about ten o'clock on the evening of the 14th, and called to the black boy to hold his mare. Samuel McAllister further recognises the knife found opposite the Herndon House, and the new revolver pawned at Caldwell's, as having been in the possession of Atzerodt, but does not recognize the coat found at the Kirkwood House, in Atzerodt's room, nor any of its contents. Provost Marshal McPhail's testimony, to show the coat and arms belonged to Herold. The testimony of Mrs. Naylor, to show that the handkerchief in the pocket of the coat in Atzerodt's room was marked with the name of Herold's sister. The testimony of Hartman Richter, that the prisoner came to his house in Montgomery county, Maryland, made no effort to escape, worked in the garden, and went about among the neighbors. Testimony of Somerset Leaman, that he is of respectable family, and visited the most respectable families in Montgomery county. Of Samuel McAllister, again, that he was generally considered a coward. Of Washington Briscoe, that he was a noted coward. Of Lewis C. Hawkins, that he is a notorious coward. Of Henry Brawner, that he is a well-known coward. Testimony of Governor Farwell, that he came to the President's room, at the Kirkwood, immediately after the assassination; could have seen anybody lying in wait, but saw no one; remained there half an hour, but no one attempted to enter by violence. Testimony of William A. Browning, private secretary to Mr. Johnson, that the Vice-President was in his room from five for the balance of the evening. Testimony of Matthew J. Pope, that Atzerodt was, on the 12th, about noon, at his stable, trying to sell a horse, and remained there until he went off with John Barr. Testimony of John Barr, that he met Atzerodt on that day; knows it was on the 12th, because the same day, by his memorandum, he made two spring blocks. Testimony of Henry Brawner and Lewis C.

Hawkins, to show that, on the 3d of March he was at Port Tobacco. Testimony of Judge Olin and Henry Burden, that they do not believe Marcus P. Norton on oath.

Now, the prisoner submits that the testimony adduced by the prosecution fails utterly to support the specification, but corroborates his own statement in every particular. First, the specification charges him with "lying in wait" for Andrew Johnson, the Vice-President of the United States, "within the military department and military lines aforesaid." The evidence on this point of "lying in wait" is altogether circumstantial. Colonel Nevins says he inquired for President Johnson on the afternoon of the 12th, between four and five. This decrepit gentleman, sixty years of age, acknowledges that he never saw the prisoner after that until the day he gave his testimony, about six weeks afterward, although he saw him but for a minute at the time of the conversation, and describes him as looking exactly as he did then. Now, all the other witnesses say that Atzerodt is much thinner; all of them, even his most intimate friends, have had difficulty in recognizing him, and yet this peremptory old gentleman, with failing eyesight, says he looks just the same, although he saw him but for a moment, and then not again for six weeks. The testimony of this witness, besides the natural anxiety of a Government officer to serve his Government, and of an old one to retrench his waning importance, is incredible on the face of it; but if it were not, it is absolutely contradicted, beyond a doubt, by the witnesses for the defense. Matthew Pope, a livery-stable keeper, near the Navy Yard, says a man came to his stable and tried to sell him a horse on the noon of the same day in April. He can not recognize the prisoner, neither can he give the date, only he knows that he left his umbrella, and that he went off with John Barr, and was there between four and five. John Barr, being called, very well remembers that the person who left his umbrella, and who rode off from Pope's stable, was Atzerodt, who went home with him to supper; and he knows it was the day that he made two spring blocks for Sanderson & Miller, and he sees by reference to his book that it was the 12th of April.

The testimony of Col. Nevins must, therefore, fall to the ground; and while it is conceded that some one out of the multitude at the Kirkwood may have asked the Colonel this common question, it is certain that this man was not Atzerodt, for at the given hour and day he was a mile from the house. The second point brought in support of this specification is the declaration of Marcus P. Norton, a lawyer, from Troy, New York, to the effect that he saw Atzerodt in company with Booth, he thinks, on the evening of the 3d of March, at the National, and heard it said that, "If the matter succeeded as well with Johnson as it did with old Buchanan, the party would be terribly sold;" also the words, "The character of the witnesses would be such that nothing could be proved by them." Now, the prisoner says that this testimony is a deliberate falsehood. To prove that on the 2d and 3d days of March he was not in

Washington, he brought Henry Brawner, proprietor of the Brawner House, at Port Tobacco, who says he knows that about that time he was at home; and Lewis P. Hawkins confirms the declaration. Neither of these two is absolutely certain of the date, for in country towns people can seldom prove their exact whereabouts on a given day three months back. This alone would be sufficient to throw doubt on the statements of Norton. But there is other evidence that he was deliberately making testimony. He says that on the same day he saw Dr. Mudd asking for Booth. Dr. Mudd has shown that on that day he was not at the National Hotel, nor in Washington city. This ingenious fabricator of testimony (in whose mind the bad character of himself as witness seems to dominate, and who, therefore, appears to put his own thoughts into the mouths of others), chose the 3d of March, the day before the inauguration, to give his story the probability which arises from connecting conversation with a given place. He appears, before he wove this fine perjury, to have omitted reading the testimony of Conover, who says the name of Andrew Johnson was not joined in the plot until after the inauguration, and that at that time the name of Mr. Hamlin was on the list; and so he perpetrated an egregious blunder. And he seems to have forgotten how strange it would seem, if, after having heard these things at the very time, eight years ago, when a plot was suspected to poison Mr. Buchanan, he should neither have suspected nor informed of such a plot, nor how curious an instance of memory that he should remember words exactly for three months, and faces, although he is short-sighted, and yet remembers no others. As we might conclude from internal evidence, the man is a notable false witness. It is in evidence that he takes patent cases, and, if he can not win by argument, he takes the witness-box and swears them through. Mr. Henry Burden, an old, wealthy and honorable gentleman, swears he would not believe him under oath, and that his reputation for veracity is very bad. Justice Abraham B. Olin, of the Supreme Court of this District, formerly member of Congress from Troy, swears he has never had any difference with Norton, but his reputation for veracity is sufficiently bad, and he would not believe him under oath. It is true they have brought here three witnesses to bolster up this false character. One never knew him at all at Troy. The other knew him at Troy, but is a client who has the very case pending in which Norton's testimony was attempted to be impeached. It is not likely, then, that he would swear away the character of his own witness. The third, Horatio King, knew him only in business relations at Washington city.

The internal evidence of Norton's testimony, its falsity in the matter of Dr. Mudd, its proven falsity in the time of Atzerodt's visit to the National, and his known reputation as a false witness, leaves no shadow of doubt that his testimony is the offspring of a desire to distinguish himself on the witness-stand, and that Atzerodt never met Booth at the National on the 3d of March, nor had the alleged conversation with

him. The third strong point of the prosecution is, that Atzerodt left room No. 126, at the Kirkwood House, taking the key along, and in his room was found a coat, containing a bowie-knife, a pistol, loaded, and handkerchiefs marked with the name of J. Wilkes Booth, together with notes on the Ontario Bank, in the name of Booth, and memoranda showing they once belonged to Booth. The coat and all its contents were disposed of by the prosecution itself. McPhail swears Atzerodt told him the coat and arms all belonged to Herold. The clerk at the Kirkwood swears somebody called for Atzerodt in the afternoon. It was Herold who visited Atzerodt, and left the coat in his room. One handkerchief is marked with the name of Mary E. Naylor, the sister of Herold. Another is marked "H," the initial of Herold. But why did Atzerodt suffer this coat and arms to be in his room? Because he was in a plot to capture the President. In so far he was the colleague of Herold and Booth. No farther. Because, for this purpose, to capture the President, and to be used in defense, he carried the knife and pistol which McAllister used to keep for him—the same knife he threw away and the same pistol he pawned—and, therefore, he suffered Herold to leave his armor for the same reason he carried his own. But why did Atzerodt go away with the key and never come back? Because he did not want to be arrested. Because he was not guilty of aiding in the assassination of Mr. Lincoln. Because he was in the plot so far as to capture the President, and when he was ordered to kill the Vice-President and refused, he was unable to resolve either to inform the authorities, for fear of Booth, or to do the deed for fear of being hung; and so he just abandoned the room as he abandoned everything else connected with the conspiracy. Had he been able to resolve to carry out his allotted duty, he would naturally have taken the coat of Herold and put it on, and used the arms. Had he been able to resolve to fly at once, he would have removed all traces of his participation. One reason of leaving without paying was because it appears he had no money, and the reason for leaving the coat was because it did not belong to him, and he had no reason to conceal what could not implicate him. But the main reason, we must admit, was that he was between two fires, which brought out his native irresolution, and so he cut the Gordian knot by running away. We shall see that he left the Kimmell House, without paying his bill, the next morning. It was for the same reason—he had no money until after he had pawned his pistol at Georgetown.

The fourth point of the prosecution is that Atzerodt lodged in the same house with the Vice-President, and the relative situation of the rooms was favorable to assassination. Probably five hundred people roomed at the Kirkwood the same night, and had rooms which enabled the owners to command the room occupied by the Vice-President. The Vice-President's room is the first on the right-hand side, after reaching the landing of the second floor. It is a room which nobody can help passing, either going down or coming up. It is impossible to get a room lower than that in the house. That Atzerodt, therefore, might, in passing, have entered it, is saying that everybody in the house might have done the same. But this room, No. 126, is about as remote from Mr. Johnson's as possible. It is in a different wing, and removed by many perplexing turns and four flights of stairs. It is very evident, at a moment's inspection, that any one desirous of lying in wait for the Vice-President could not well have missed his purpose farther, and that with that intent he would have sought, at least, a room on the same floor. But the actual fact is better than suppositions. Mr. Browning tells us that the Vice-President was in his room from five in the evening to ten at night, and that there were, therefore, six hours in which the deed could have been done. In all that time we have no evidence that Atzerodt was at the Kirkwood House, except the statement of Fletcher, the hostler at Naylor's stables, who says he followed Atzerodt, and saw him dismount at the Kirkwood, stay five minutes, and come out again. What was he doing there? He was taking a drink at the bar. It is impossible to show this. The barkeeper does not remember the faces of all who take a drink. If he was lying in wait, why did it take him but five minutes? But if he tried to kill Mr. Johnson, if he tried to get into his room, why is it not shown in evidence? If he was in any way prevented from getting into his room, why was it not shown in evidence? Governor Farwell, who went first to the Vice-President's room after the assassination, saw no one lying in wait; he was not told by the President there had been anybody lying in wait; the lock had not been tampered with; no attempt whatever was made; the Vice-President was in his room six hours, but at the very time when the President was shot he was left undisturbed, even by a knock, in his room. And why? Because Atzerodt refused to go and kill him. Because Atzerodt, during the evening, kept up appearances, but backed out. Because the instrument which was to have assassinated the Vice-President was either too conscientious or afraid to do it. During the whole half hour following no one attempted to kill him, no one was seen lying in wait. Why? Because there had been and there was no one lying in wait. He who was to do it was somewhere else, getting drunk. A fifth point alleged in corroboration of his guilt is, that, on his arrest by Sergeant Gemmill, he gave a false name, denied having left Washington recently, and said he had nothing to do with the assassination. In the last statement he but told the truth. Assassination and murder were things for which he was not by nature intended, and he had nothing to do with it. As for giving a false name, it appears the Sergeant understood his name to be Atwood, and had been ordered to arrest Atwood, and finally says he did not really understand the name, it was in German. Certainly he might say he had not left Washington recently. He knew that he had been in a plot to capture the President, and he knew that he had been a colleague of the President's murderer in another scheme, and, of course, he was afraid to confess his part then and there. Any presumption of guilt that might arise from these circumstances is negatived by Richter, his cousin, at whose house he was staying. He tells us that he worked in the garden; saw the neighbors; made no attempt to escape, nor was he in an unusual frame of mind. He was, doubtless, in that frame of mind when one, who had been on the verge of being dragged into murder for gold, had fled from the temptation and been saved— a happy and a tranquil mood. Finally, that he stated to Metz, "Gen. Grant would have been killed, if the man had followed that was to have followed him," is denied by the two brothers, Leaman, who state he said: "That Grant, if he was killed, must have been killed by somebody that got into the same car"—an innocent and most truthful proposition; and any remarks he made at that time about his "Having more trouble than he would ever get rid of," even supposing the words had not reference to the love matters which immediately preceded it, are by no means so much a sign of guilt as the honest expression of fear, lest one who has been a colleague in a lesser crime may get into difficulty about a greater, of which he was innocent.

The sixth point is, that Atzerodt said to Fletcher, on the evening of the 14th, after 10: "If this thing happens to-night you will hear of a present;" and also in reference to the mare: "She is good on a retreat;" and that the Sunday before he said to Lieut. Keim, at the Kimmell House, after finding his knife: "If one fails, I shall want the other." On the first occasion both parties had been drinking, and Fletcher says he thought Atzerodt half drunk, while the other remark was made after each party had taken three cocktails. So that, even if we credit the drunken memories of the witnesses, we can not do more than ascribe it to pot valor, pointing to the possible desperate melee of an attempt to capture.

All the evidence to prove that the prisoner was lying in wait to assassinate Mr. Johnson may be summed up thus: On the same evening that the President was assassinated he had a room at the same hotel as the Vice-President, in which were found arms and the name of the President's murderer. He was before seen with the murderer, and used expressions indicating expectation of gold and the use of his arms, and afterward he fled the city, and said he had trouble on his mind. These circumstances are nothing by themselves. Any friend of Booth's might have carried arms, stayed at the Kirkwood, had Booth's coat in his room, said he expected to be rich, and afterward said he had troubles. These things might have naturally happened to John Ford, the manager of the theater; to Junius Brutus Booth; to any other friend of Booth's, innocent of the plot as the babe unborn. These circumstances are only important if it is proved that the person who is involved in them either tried to murder Mr. Johnson or was prevented. That proven, the arms are the tools of murder, the coat the coat of an accomplice, the talk of gold an expression of intention, the talk of trouble a confession of guilt. But if it is not shown that an attempt was made to murder, or that it was impossible to attempt murder; and if, on the contrary, it is shown that there was every opportunity for murder, and nothing in the world to prevent it, then these circumstances lose all their force, and we are bound to believe that where there was every opportunity and no attempt, there was no intention and no lying in wait.

Adopting the theory that Atzerodt intended to murder, and lying in wait to murder, we are met at every step with denials. Thus, if he was lying in wait, why did he not stay at the Kirkwood House during the evening? Why did nobody see him lie in wait? Why did he come out of the Kirkwood at about ten minutes after ten without having tried to attack the Vice-President? Why did he not enter the room? Why, at 10:20, was he drinking at the Kimmell House? Why, in short, was he riding about town instead of waiting outside the Vice-President's room? There is only one theory that will make everything agree: Atzerodt backed out. He would have liked the money for capturing, but he did not like to be hung for murder. He never heard of murder before that evening at eight, or he would long before have hid himself. When he did hear it he had firmness enough to object. Coward conscience came to his rescue. But Booth threatened to kill, and he knew well enough he was the man to close the mouth of any one who troubled him. So he went off, driven like a poor frail being between irresolution and fear; took drinks, feigned to be doing his part, talked valiantly while the rum was in his throat, promised gloriously, galloped around fiercely, looked daggers, and when the hour struck did nothing and ran away. This, gentlemen, is the history in a small compass—*venit, videt, fugit.* He tried to become a hero, but he was only a coachmaker.

Look at the face of this impossible Brutus, and see whether you can see therein that he is—

" For dignity composed and high exploits."

Why, gentlemen, this hero, who, under the influence of cocktail courage, would capture Presidents and change the destinies of empires, is the same fleet-footed Quaker, famous in Port Tobacco for jumping out of windows in bar-room fights; an excellent leader—of a panic, this son of arms who buries his knife in a gutter and revolves his revolvers into a greenback. Well might it have been said to Booth:

" O, Cassius, you are yoked to a lamb
That carries anger as the flint bears fire;
Who much enforced shows a hasty spark,
And straight is cold again."

He has the courage of vanity and of folly. As long as he could be seen on intimate terms with Booth about hotels, it did his soul good to be so great a confederate; and as long as he could see a bold stroke by which he might suddenly change the coachmaker into a prince, he was, doubtless, brave. But when he heard of murder, conceived to himself his going into the Vice-President's room and stabbing him to the

heart, the pigeon-liver asserted itself, the prince was gone, and the habits of the tavern-brawler re-appeared. Nor was he a natural boaster. He was simply the Curius of the conspiracy, who could neither keep his own secrets nor those of others; who was big with the portentous future, although he knew not what it was; who exchanged his wrath for a sudden prudence; and so as he imitated his prototype, "*Repente glorians maria montesque policeri cœpit,*" so he afterward imitated him by pointing out Booth, and informing, under the promise of mercy, upon his fellows. There is, then, no evidence whatever that he was "lying in wait to kill Mr. Johnson, with the intent, unlawfully and maliciously, to kill and murder him." There is only one other clause of the specification that deserves notice—the allegation that the lying in wait was "about the same hour of the night," viz.: Ten o'clock and fifteen minutes, on the evening of the 14th of April. Let us see, again, where the prisoner was at this time, 10:15. Fletcher says he came to Naylor's stable at ten. He then asked him whether he would have a drink. Fletcher said yes. They went down to Thirteen-and-a-half and E street, to the Union Hotel, and took a drink apiece; went back to the stable, and had some conversation about the mare. Meanwhile the boy had got the wrong horse, and had to go back and get the mare. Then they had some conversation about Herold. Then he rode down E, past Thirteen-and-a-half street, and finally came to the Kirkwood House. Fletcher says that he rode so slowly that he kept up with him. Now, believing what is improbable, that Fletcher did keep up with a man on horseback for three squares (for from Naylor's to the corner of Thirteen-and-a-half and E streets is one square, and to Twelfth and E two squares, and to Twelfth and Pennsylvania avenue three squares), we are further obliged to believe that, in fifteen minutes, Atzerodt ordered a horse, walked two squares, waited for two drinks, paid for them, held two conversations, mounted, dismounted, had a horse changed, and, afterward, rode three squares so slowly that a hostler could follow him. It is not possible. At 10:15 Atzerodt was either not yet at the Kirkwood House, or else Mr. Fletcher made a mistake in his time. His course after this was as follows : Fletcher says he rode up D in the direction of Tenth; yet at this very time, about ten, McAllister says he came with his mare to the Kimmell House, "rode up to the door, and called the black boy out to hold his horse." Now, the Kimmell is on C street, near Four-and-a-half, and, of course, when he rode down D he went to the Kimmell.

Thus we now know what he was doing at the time Payne was at Mr. Seward's, and at the time Booth shot the President. He was riding round from bar-room to bar-room; and it is very plain he was now in liquor. He was half tight when Fletcher saw him, and yet took another drink with him. He went to the Kirkwood and took another drink; he went to the Kimmell and took another. Certainly, of getting drunk, of riding from tavern to tavern, of guzzling like a Falstaff, of having an inextinguishable thirst—of this he is guilty; but of lying in wait for the President at 10:15, we are paying him an undeserved compliment.

There is, therefore, no part of the specification proven, but the immediate contrary. During the whole of that evening, as far as the evidence throws any light on his conduct, instead of lying in wait near the Vice-President to murder him, he was standing over the different bars, from the Union House to the Kimmell, with the intent then and there, unlawfully and maliciously, to make Atzerodt drunk. Thus much of the specification.

There is one suggestion I will answer before I leave the specification. Why, if he was so cowardly, so halting, so irresolute a character, did Booth employ him? Booth employed him for an emergency which he was perfectly competent to meet. In the plot of the capture, the part assigned to the prisoner was to furnish the boat to carry the party over the Potomac. For this his experience in a seaport town fitted him. This required no resolution and no courage. For participation in the President's assassination he could never have been intended. Booth, as these men all agree, as his own conduct shows, was ambitious to carry off the glory of this thing. Payne says Booth remarked, he "wanted no botching with the President and Gen. Grant." As for the rest, therefore, of the Cabinet, he probably had no concern; he was far more interested in his own part than in others. When he, therefore, told Atzerodt to take charge of the Vice-President, he must have known that the prisoner had not the courage, and therefore did not care particularly whether he accomplished it or not, only so he himself could attain the desired immortal infamy. He wanted Atzerodt as the *Charon*, the ferryman of the capture, and, *after the failure*, reserved him for greater things, *the duties of Orcus*, which he was incompetent to perform.

The charge is divisible into two separate and distinct allegations. First, "For maliciously, unlawfully, traitorously and in aid of the armed rebellion against the United States, combining, confederating and conspiring with Booth, Surratt, Davis, etc., to kill and murder Abraham Lincoln, General Grant, Andrew Johnson and William H. Seward, on or before the 6th day of March."

The substance of this allegation is, that as early as the 6th of March there was a project on foot to kill the President and the heads of State; and, to involve the prisoner, it must be shown that as early as March 6th he was advised of and agreed to it. Now, what evidence is there that there was a conspiracy to kill the President as early as March the 6th? Chester, the actor, says he knew of a plot to capture in the latter end of February. Weichmann, the chief witness for the prosecution, states that as late as the middle of March—about the 16th or 18th, he thinks—about three weeks before the assassination, John Surratt, Booth, Atzerodt and Payne, took a ride into the country, armed, and returned. What does this show, but that two weeks after the 6th of March it was the intention of Booth to capture the President at the Soldiers' Home, and abduct him? Before

and during the early part of March, Atzerodt was at Brawner's Hotel, at Port Tobacco, and could have known nothing of it, even had the plot existed. As late as the 18th of March, as was shown in the cases of O'Laughlin and Arnold, there was a project to capture, from which they backed out. As late as the 18th of March Booth admits the sale of horses, the detection of parties, and fixes the time of the abandonment of the scheme. Payne said he never knew of any plot to assassinate until the evening of the 14th, at eight o'clock, at a meeting held at the Herndon House, while Atzerodt confirms it in all his confession, that the evening of the 14th day of April was the first time he ever heard of a plot to kill the heads of State. The only evidence against this is the testimony of Norton, who declares that on the 3d of March, Booth and Atzerodt spoke as follows: "If the matter succeeded as well with Johnson as it did with old Buchanan, the party would be terribly sold;" from which it might be inferred that on that date assassination was broached to Atzerodt. Fortunately we know that this Norton is an egregious falsifier, as it was shown that neither Atzerodt nor Dr. Mudd was in Washington that day, and he himself is proved not worthy of being believed on oath.

The prisoner, therefore, can not be found guilty of the first member of the charge.

The second member of the charge is, in substance, as follows: "For, on the 14th of April, A. D. 1865, with John Wilkes Booth and John Surratt, maliciously, unlawfully and traitorously assaulting, *with intent to kill and murder*, William H. Seward, *and lying in wait to kill and murder* Vice-President Johnson and Gen. Grant."

This charges Atzerodt with being an accomplice of Payne in the assault on Mr. Seward, and an accomplice of whoever was lying in wait for Gen. Grant and Vice-President Johnson. Now, it was proved beyond a shadow of doubt, under the specification, that Atzerodt himself was not lying in wait for President Johnson, nor was anybody else shown to be lying in wait for him. Atzerodt is, therefore, neither principal nor accessory to the lying in wait for Vice-President Johnson. But was he not an accomplice or accessory to Payne's assault of Mr. Seward, or to Booth's killing of the President? If so, he must have been accessory either before the fact or after the fact. An accessory before the fact is "one who, being at the time of the crime committed, doth yet procure, counsel or command another to commit a crime." Now, was Atzerodt the one who procured, counseled or commanded either Booth or Payne? Certainly not. The position Atzerodt held was one of subordinate; he was the procured, the counseled, the commanded, as far as we can judge of the different characters, as far as we know that Booth was the ringleader; as far as we know that in all the dealings Atzerodt was the slave, and Payne and Booth the masters.

Was Atzerodt, then, accessory after the fact? There is greater plausibility of this, but no evidence. "An accessory after the fact may be where a person, knowing a felony to have been committed, receives, relieves, comforts or assists the felon." Did Atzerodt in any way help

Booth or Payne after the felony was committed? No; he never saw either of them after the meeting at eight o'clock until he met Payne on the monitor. Instead of assisting them, he kept getting drunk; instead of helping them across the river, the sergeant says only two passed the bridge, viz.: Booth and Herold; instead of showing by his horse he had assisted, his horse came back just in the same condition as it went away, and that at eleven o'clock; instead of comforting or relieving them across the river, he went to Washington Briscoe, and finally to bed at the Kimmell House, instead of receiving; he first told McPhail and Wells Booth had gone in the direction of Bryantown, and confessed the whole affair, and had them all arrested. The assistance he has rendered the assault and murder is such neither of the principals has any occasion for gratitude; and, therefore, he can not be found guilty of being an accessory after the fact, neither helping Booth nor Payne. But the prosecution have laid great stress on a big bay horse, with large feet, and blind in one eye.

They show that such a horse was found saddled (near Camp Barry), and without a rider, at twelve o'clock on the night of the assassination. They show that this horse was brought to Naylor's stable by Atzerodt and another man on the 3d of April, to be sold and kept there until the 12th of April; that on the 14th, Atzerodt came to the stable again and said he had sold the horse in Montgomery county; that Fletcher, the hostler, swears the horse, saddle and bridle Atzerodt said he sold, are the same found near Camp Barry. Well, what, if this testimony be true, is the conclusion? One conclusion is, that Atzerodt told a lie; for how, if he sold this horse in Montgomery county on the 12th, comes he to Camp Barry on the 14th? Well, let us concede that Atzerodt lied. We are not trying him for his veracity. He is not bound to tell every hostler how he disposes of his horses. But the second conclusion the prosecution draws is, that Payne rode this horse, and that Atzerodt *furnished* him the horse. Let us examine what ground there is for the conclusion. According to Fletcher, the horse when brought to Naylor's in April did not belong to Atzerodt. He belonged to the gentleman with him, who "left him in Atzerodt's care to sell." He was, therefore, factor of the gentleman in the horse business, and took the horse away on the 12th. The negro who saw the horse Payne rode, says he was a "big bay, very stout." But was this horse not belonging to some one else? Was the horse found at Camp Barry ever ridden by Payne? The truth of the whole matter is this: The horse brought to Naylor's was bought by Booth of Mr. Gardiner, living in Prince George's county, in the latter part of last November, according to the evidence of Thomas Gardiner. On April 3d, Atzerodt went to Naylor's with Booth, and was ordered to sell him there. The saddle and all belonged to Booth. It was the same big bay which Atzerodt, on the 12th, tried to sell to Matthew Pope, at the Navy Yard, for Booth. On the 12th, Atzerodt, not succeeding in selling him, returned him to Booth, and that is the last connection that Atzerodt ever had

with the horse. He tried to sell, and could not, and so gave him back to Booth. Here ends the brokerage and the responsibility of Atzerodt. Whether Booth ever gave this horse to Payne, and where he kept him until that evening, are questions that Payne alone can answer. It is probable that this horse was kept for two days in the stable in the rear of Ford's, and on that night given to Payne. But there is no evidence that Atzerodt gave Payne a horse over which he had ceased to have control, and which belonged to Booth. On the contrary, it is shown that Atzerodt was never seen in company with that horse after the 12th, and never claimed to be the owner. Any inference of complicity, therefore, drawn from this horse is turning horse-brokerage into murder. The prisoner, then, being neither guilty as accessory before nor after the fact, neither counseling nor aiding Payne and Booth before, nor assisting and receiving Payne and Booth after the fact, can not be found guilty of any branch of the charge.

What is, then, the plain, unvarnished truth of Atzerodt's part in this conspiracy? I will briefly relate it. During the latter part of February, John Surratt and Booth wanted a man who understood boating, and could both get a boat and ferry a party over the Potomac on a capture. Surratt knew Atzerodt, and under the influence of great promises of a fortune, the prisoner consented to furnish the boat, and do the ferrying over. The plot was attempted the 18th of March, and failed. Booth, however, kept his subordinates uninformed of his plans, except it was understood that the President was to be captured. Meanwhile, everybody was waiting for Booth. On the 18th of March Atzerodt went to the Kimmell House. On the 1st of April he talked of future wealth. On the 6th he spoke to Lieut. Keim, over their liquor, of "using one, if the other failed." On the 12th he stayed at the Kirkwood, and tried to sell the bay horse at Pope's. On the 14th Booth unfolded his plans at the Herndon House, and Atzerodt refused. From the Herndon House he went to Oyster Bay and took drinks till ten. At ten he took a drink with Fletcher at the Union; at ten minutes after ten he took a drink at the Kirkwood; at twenty minutes after ten he took a drink at the Kimmell House, and rode about the city. At eleven he returned his horse; at twelve he was at the Navy Yard; at two he went to bed. Next morning at five he got up and went to Georgetown, pawned his pistol, and went to Mr. Metz'. On the 16th (Sunday) he took dinner at Metz'. On Sunday evening he went to Hartman Richter's. On the 19th he was arrested. Thus ends this history, which, under a greater hand, might have become a tragedy, but with the prisoner has turned into a farce.

Before I close, it is my duty to submit some reflections as to the nature of the crime and the nature of the penalty, in case you should find him guilty, which I hold can not be done under the evidence. This man is principal in an attempt to abduct the President of the United States. He has assaulted no one; he has sheltered no one that did assault. He has killed no one, nor has he sheltered any one that did kill. You can, therefore, only find him guilty of a crime for which he is not on trial. If it be argued, that although the prisoner ran away, he intended to kill Mr. Johnson, the answer is, intention can only be inferred from acts. "It is a universal rule that a man shall be taken to intend that which he does." *Hale, P. C.*, 229. And the converse of this is true, that a man shall not be taken to intend what he does not do. *Exteriora acta indicunt animis secreta.* 8 Cb., 146. And, therefore, as we know he ran away we are bound to infer that he had no intention of murder. If it be argued that, although neither guilty as accessory in felony nor principal in treason, he is yet guilty of the conspiring, which is the essence of the offense, the answer is, the conspiracy in which he was engaged is not the conspiracy for which he is on trial; and that as soon as he knew of the latter he hastened to dissolve all connection with the conspirators.

As for the punishment, supposing he could be found guilty of either the charge or the specification, the offense, in either case would only be technical, and have damaged no one; and even supposing he were proven guilty of the charge and specification, he has already turned states-evidence to the Provost Marshal, and therefore his punishment would fall under the practice usual in the courts of justice, that one who confesses has an equitable right to the leniency of the court. His case, however, rests on no such slender ground. Instead of conspiring to kill, he refused to kill; and instead of lying in wait to murder, he intoxicated himself at the appointed hour, and next morning ran away. He is guilty solely of what he confesses—of conspiring to abduct the President—and of that can be found guilty only under a new indictment.

I claim, therefore, at your hands an unqualified acquittal. That he did wrong in conspiring to capture, is admitted. That he should be punished for it whenever tried for it, is also admitted. But that he is innocent of both charge and specification, as now laid, is so transparent, that his acquittal will, I trust, be urged by the Judge Advocate as a matter of form, if it were not also a matter of justice.

STATEMENT BY GEORGE A. ATZERODT,

Read by his counsel, W. E. Doster, Esq.

The prisoner, Atzerodt, submits the following statement to the Court:

I am one of a party who agreed to capture the President of the United States, but I am not one of a party to kill the President of the United States, or any member of the Cabinet, or General Grant, or Vice-President Johnson. The first plot to capture failed; the second—to kill—I broke away from the moment I heard of it.

This is the way it came about: On the even-

ing of the 14th of April I met Booth and Payne at the Herndon House, in this city, at eight o'clock. He (Booth) said he himself should murder Mr. Lincoln and General Grant, Payne should take Mr. Seward, and I should take Mr. Johnson. I told him I would not do it; that I had gone into the thing to capture, but I was not going to kill. He told me I was a fool; that I would be hung any how, and that it was death for every man that backed out; and so we parted. I wandered about the streets until about two o'clock in the morning, and then went to the Kimmell House, and from there pawned my pistol at Georgetown, and went to my cousin's house, in Montgomery county, where I was arrested the 19th following. After I was arrested, I told Provost Marshal Wells and Provost Marshal McPhail the whole story; also told it to Capt. Monroe, and Col. Wells told me if I pointed out the way Booth had gone I would be reprieved, and so I told him I thought he had gone down Charles county in order to cross the Potomac. The arms which were found in my room at the Kirkwood House, and a black coat, do not belong to me; neither were they left to be used by me. On the afternoon of the 14th of April, Herold called to see me and left the coat there. It is his coat, and all in it belongs to him, as you can see by the handkerchiefs, marked with his initial, and with the name of his sister, Mrs. Naylor. Now I will state how I passed the whole of the evening of the 14th of April. In the afternoon, at about two o'clock, I went to Keleher's stable, on Eighth street, near D, and hired a dark bay mare and rode into the country for pleasure, and on my return put her up at Naylor's stable. The dark bay horse which I had kept at Naylor's before, on about the 3d of April, belonged to Booth; also the saddle and bridle. I do not know what became of him. At about six in the evening, I went to Naylor's again and took out the mare, rode out for an hour, and returned her to Naylor's. It was then nearly eight, and I told him to keep the mare ready at ten o'clock, in order to return her to the man I hired her from. From there I went to the Herndon House. Booth sent a messenger to the "Oyster Bay," and I went. Booth wanted me to murder Mr. Johnson. I refused. I then went to the "Oyster Bay," on the Avenue, above Twelfth street, and whiled away the time until nearly ten. At ten I got the mare, and having taken a drink with the hostler, galloped about town, and went to the Kimmell House. From there I rode down to the depot, and returned my horse, riding up Pennsylvania Avenue to Keleher's. From Keleher's, I went down to the Navy Yard to get a room with Wash. Briscoe. He had none, and by the time I got back to the Kimmell House it was nearly two. The man Thomas was a stranger I met on the street. Next morning, as stated, I went to my cousin Richter's, in Montgomery county.   GEORGE A. ATZERODT.

ARGUMENT

IN

DEFENSE OF LEWIS PAYNE,

BY

W. E. DOSTER, ESQ.

May it please the Court:

I. There are three things in the case of the prisoner, Payne, which are admitted beyond cavil or dispute:

1. That he is the person who attempted to take the life of the Secretary of State.

2. That he is not within the medical definition of insanity.

3. That he believed what he did was right and justifiable.

The question of his identity and the question of his sanity are, therefore, settled, and among the things of the past. The sole question that remains is, how far shall his convictions serve to mitigate his punishment? I use the word punishment deliberately, and with the consciousness that in so doing I admit that if he is a responsible being he ought to be punished. And I say it, because I can not allow my duties as counsel to interfere with my convictions as a man so far as to make me blind to the worth of the life of a distinguished citizen, and the awful consequences of an attempt to take it away. If, indeed, such an attempt be allowed to go without rebuke, then it seems to me the office is but a perilous exposure to violence; then the highest compensation for public services is the distinction which follows assassination, and then our public servants are but pitiable and defenseless offerings to sedition. And surely, if any public servant deserved to be excepted from that fate, it was he, the illustrious and sagacious statesman, who, during a long life of arduous services, has steadfastly checked all manner of factious and public discontent; who, in the darkest days of discord, has prophesied the triumph of concord, and who at all times has been more ready to apply antidotes than the knife to the nation's wounds. How far, then, shall the conviction of the prisoner that he was doing right go in extenuation of his offense? That we may accurately, and as fully as the occasion demands, understand the convictions of the prisoner, I invite your attention to a sketch of his life, the customs under which he was reared, and the education which he received. Lewis Thornton Powell is the son of the Rev. Geo. C. Powell, a Baptist minister, at present supposed to live at Live Oak Station, on the railroad between Jacksonville and Tallahassee, in the State of Florida, and was born in Alabama in the year 1845. Besides himself, his father had six daughters

and two sons. He lived for some time in Worth and Stewart counties, Georgia, and in 1859 moved to Florida. At the breaking out of the war, but four years ago, the prisoner was a lad of sixteen, engaged in superintending his father's plantation and a number of slaves. We may safely presume that, occupied in the innocent pursuits of country life, he daily heard the precepts of the Gospel from his father; that, in the society of his sisters, the hardy life of a planter was softened by the charms of a refined and religious circle, and that, in the natural course of events, he would be to-day, as he was then, a farmer and an honest man. But, in 1861, war broke out—war, the scourge and pestilence of the race. The signal, which spread like a fire, was not long in reaching Live Oak Station. His two brothers enlisted, and Lewis, though but sixteen, enlisted in Capt. Stuart's company, in the Second Florida Infantry, commanded by Col. Ward, and was ordered to Richmond.

Let us pause a moment in this narrative, and consider what, in the eyes of this Florida boy, was the meaning of war, and what the thoughts that drove him from a pleasant home to the field of arms. At another time I might picture to you the scene, but too familiar, of his taking leave; a mother, like the mothers of Northern boys, shedding tears, less bitter, because she was dedicating a son to her country; sisters, whose sorrow, like the sorrow of the sisters of Northern boys, was alleviated with pride that they had a brother in the field; the father's blessing; the knapsack filled with tributes of affection, to be fondled by distant bivouac fires, and the heavy sigh, drowned in the rolling of the drum. But this is not a stage for effect. We know this was mistaken pride and sorrow in a mistaken cause, though the object of them was a son and brother, and we must not consider them, though the boy was but sixteen when he launched on the terrible sea of civil war.

In the State of Florida were two separate races—one white and the other black—of which the one was slave to the other, and Lewis belonged to the race which was master. It was a custom of this State for masters to whip their slaves, sell them, kill them, and receive the constant homage which the oppressed offer to the powerful. It was the custom of this State to whip and burn men who preached against the custom. It was the custom to defend this institution in meeting-houses, at political gatherings, in family prayers. It was the custom to hunt fugitives with bloodhounds—even those who tried to help them to freedom.

In this custom the prisoner was bred; education made it a second nature; politicians had taught him to find it in the Constitution, preachers had taught him to find it in the Bible, the laws taught him to regard it as property, habit had made it a very part of his being. In the eyes of the lad, the war meant to abolish this custom and upheave society from its foundations. His inheritance was to be dissipated, his vassals equals, his laws invaded, his religion confounded, his politics a heresy, his habits criminal. Hereafter, to strike a slave was to be an assault, to sell one felony, to kill one murder. For this, then, the lad was going to fight—*the defense of a social system.* That was the reason. It was a traditional political precept of the State in which the prisoner lived, that the State, like its elder sisters, had reserved the right of divorcing itself at pleasure from the Union, and that great as the duty of a citizen might be to the Union, his first duty was to Florida. Schoolmasters taught that the relative rights of State and Nation had been left unsettled; politicians taught that the local power was greater than the central, and in support of it men were sent to Washington. The war, in the eyes of the boy, meant to reverse this, to subordinate the State to the Nation, the Governor to the President, Tallahassee to Washington City. And, therefore, he was going to fight; *to defend State rights.* That was the second reason.

It was a deep-seated conviction of the people in this State that their blood and breeding were better than the blood and breeding of Northerners; that they had more courage, more military prowess, and were by nature superiors. This conviction the war threatened to overthrow, this boast the war was to vindicate, this superiority was, by the war, intended to be proved. And this was the third reason he was going to fight—*to show that he was a better man than Northerners.*

There was a frantic delusion among these people that Northern men were usurping the Government, were coveting their plantations, were longing to pillage their houses, ravage their fields, and reduce them to subjection. The war was to defend mother, sister, home, soil, and honor, and beat back an insolent invader. This was the fourth reason—*to repel invasion.* These were, in the mind of this lad, the *incentives* to war. Let us not pass unnoticed how he was schooled in the *instincts* and *morals* of war. Under the code of slavery we know that the murder of a companion with a bowie-knife or in a duel was an index of spirit; the torture of negroes evidence of a commanding nature; concubinage with negroes a delicate compliment to wives; spending wealth earned by other men in luxuriance, chivalric; gambling the sweet reprieve for confinement to plantations. Instead of morals was sprung up a code of honor—perhaps a false, but surely an exacting and imperious code, that kept bowie-knives in the belt and pistols in the pocket, and had no hesitation in using them when slavery was assailed, and a code that remembered friends and never forgave enemies. These, then, were the morals and instincts of the lad—it is right to kill negroes, right to kill abolitionists; it is only wrong to break promises, to forget a friend, or forgive an enemy; and to do right is to be ready with bowie-knife and pistol.

Now let me ask whether in the wide world there is another school in which the prisoner could so well have been trained for assassination as in this slave aristocracy? The stealthiest Indian that ever shot from ambush was not so well instructed in the social use of his knife; the deadliest Gheber that ever strangled his victim had not the animosity which comes from power in danger of losing its slaves, nor the cheap regard for human life which comes from trading in and killing slaves. All the horrible accomplishments of assassination, which Machiavel says are three—"fierceness of nature, resolute undertakings, and having had one's hands formerly in blood," are his by religion, by politics, by law, by education, and by custom. And who is responsible for this training of the lad? Standing, as we do to-day, at the end of a four years, war, having just heard again recited tales of prisoners starved, cities infected, cities burned, prisons undermined—things that seem unparalleled in the barbarity of all ages—and all by men who, four years ago, sat side by side with us, and seemed no different, we now know, what we never dreamt of, that this is the spirit of slavery, stripped of its disguise. In rebellion we now recognize the master never taught to obey; in arson of cities we see again the fagot and the stake; in Libby and Andersonville we see again the slave-pen; in captures the bloodhound and the lash; in assassination the social bowie-knife and pistol; and in this prisoner *the legitimate moral offspring of slavery, State rights, chivalry, and delusion.*

But who is to blame that he, with five millions more, was so instructed, so demoralized, so educated to crime? Is it his father and mother? They found their precepts in the Bible; they gave their son but the customs they had themselves inherited. Is it the society of Florida? It was a society that ruled this country until within four years, and occupied the seats of Government. Is it the laws of Florida? They were but rescripts of the Constitution. Is it the Constitution? That is but the creation of our forefathers. Who, then, is responsible that slavery was allowed to train assassins? I answer, it is we; we, the American people; we who have cherished slavery, have compromised with it, have for a hundred years extended it, have pandered to it, and have at last, thanks be to God, destroyed it. Let us, then, not shrink from our responsibility. If there be any Southerner here who has sought to foster slavery, he is in part father of the assassin in this boy. If there be any Northerner here who has been content to live with slavery, he is also in part father of the assassin in this boy. If there be any American that has been content to be a citizen of a slaveholding republic, he is part father of the assassin in this boy. Nay, all of us—such as he is we have made him—the murderous, ferocious, and vindictive child of by-gone American Constitution and laws. And what is to be the fate of our offspring? Let us see. That it is criminal, let us reform it; that it is deluded, let us instruct it. But let us not destroy it, for therein we punish others for our own crimes. Let the great American people rather speak thus: "For twenty years we have sent you to a wicked school, though we knew not the wickedness thereof, until our own child rebelled against us. Now we have torn down the school-house and driven out the master. Hereafter you shall be taught in a better school, and we will not destroy you, because you learnt but as instructed."

II. But there is another school before him—the school of war. At Richmond his regiment joined the army of Gen. Lee, and was joined to A. P. Hill's corps; with it he shared the fate of the rebel army, passed through the Peninsular campaign, the battles of Chancellorsville and Antietam. Here he heard that his two brothers were killed at Murfreesboro. Finally, on the 3d of July, 1863, in the charge upon the Federal center, at Gettysburg, he was wounded, taken prisoner, and detailed as a nurse in Pennsylvania College Hospital.

Let us pause again to consider the effect of two years' campaigning as a private in the army of Gen. Lee upon the moral nature of the accused. He was one of that army who made trinkets and cups out of the bones of Union soldiers—an army where it was customary to starve prisoners by lingering agonies, which supplied its wants by plundering the dead, which slew men after surrender, that was commanded by officers who had violated their sacred oaths to the United States, and who taught their subordinates that such violation was justifiable; an army who were taught by Jackson that God was the champion of their cause; an army that held the enemy in quest of "booty and beauty;" an army which believed no means that helped the cause of Southern independence unjustifiable, but glorious; an army who for two years explained victory by the righteousness of the cause—finally, an army that held the person and Cabinet of the President in holy execration. Surely he could not pass through these two terrible years without being in his moral nature the same as the army of which he formed a part. He is now eighteen, and the last two years have formed his character. He also abhors the President of the Yankees; he also believes that victory comes because God is just; he also believes that nothing is bad so the South be free; he also regards a Federal as a ravisher and robber; he also prays with Jackson to God for the victory. He further believes in Heaven and General Lee; dresses himself in the clothes of Union dead; stands guard over starving prisoners; also has his cup carved out of some Federal skull. Besides, he has learned the ordinary soldier's lessons, to taste blood and like it; to brave death and care nothing for life; to hope for letters and get none; to hope for the end of the war and see none; to find in victory no more than the beginning of another march; to look for promotion and get none; to pass from death and danger to idleness and corruption; to ask for furloughs and get none, and finally, to despair, and hope for death to end his sufferings. The slave-driver has now become a butcher; the slaveholder a pillager; he who found divine authority to support slavery in sermons now finds it in action; he who was led by fanatical politicians is now led by fanatical generals; and he who had once only the instincts, has now the practice and habit of shedding Northern blood. These two years of carnage and suffering, from sixteen to eighteen, when the character is mobile and pliable, and which he would have naturally spent at college among poets and mythologies and tutors, are spent on picket, with fierce veterans, in drunken quarrels, with cards, with oaths, in delirious charges, amid shot and shell, amid moaning wounded and stinking dead, until, at eighteen, he has the experience of a Cambronne, the ferocity of an Attilla, and the cruelty of a Tartar. This, gentlemen, is the horrible demoralization of civil war. It makes loyalty a farce, justifies perjury, dignifies murder, instills ferocity, scorns religion and enjoins assassination as a duty. And whose fault is it that he was so demoralized, and so educated in public vices, instead of public virtues, on the field of war? Let us be just, and not shrink from the inquiry. Was it our forefathers who sowed the seed of discord in the charter of Union? If so, then let their memories pay the penalty; but spare the fruit which has involuntarily ripened in the heart of this boy. Was it the Southern leaders? Then let them pay the penalty; but spare their ignorant and misguided tool. Was it Generals Lee and Jackson and Hill, who were his immediate models and tutors in crime? Then punish them; but spare their pupil. Was it, perhaps, fanatical malcontents among Northern men who first lighted the torch of war? Then extirpate them from the land; but spare the boy whose passions caught fire, and burnt until they consumed him. Rest, then, the responsibility of this war with whom it will—with the living or dead, with the vicissitudes of things or in the invisible plans of God—it is not with this plastic boy, who came into the world in the year of the annexation of Texas, has lived but four administrations, and is younger than the last compromise with slavery. *He is the moral product of the war*, and belongs to them who first began it.

Now, I hear it said, true, the boy has been a rebel soldier, and we can forgive him; but we can not forgive assassins. Let us, for a moment, compare a rebel soldier with the prisoner, and see wherein they differ. The best rebel soldiers are native Southerners. So is he. The best rebel soldiers have for four years longed to capture Washington, and put its Government to the sword. So has he. The best rebel soldiers have fought on their own hook, after the fashion of the provincials during the Revolution, finding their own knives, their own horses, their own pistols. So has he. The best rebel soldiers have fired at Mr. Lincoln and Mr. Seward, have approached the city by stealth from Baltimore, and aimed to destroy the Government by a sudden blow. So has he. The best rebel soldiers have picked off high officers of the Government—Kearney, Stevens, Baker, Wadsworth, Lyon, Sedgwick. So has he.

What, then, has he done that every rebel soldier has not tried to do? Only this: he has ventured more; he has shown a higher courage, a bitterer hate, and a more ready sacrifice; he has aimed at the head of a department, instead of the head of a corps; he has struck at the head of a nation, instead of at its limbs; he has struck in the day of his humiliation, when nothing was to be accomplished but revenge, and when he believed he was killing an oppressor. As Arnold Vinkelried was braver than all the combined legions of Switzerland, when he

"Felt as though himself were he
On whose sole arm hung victory;"

as Leonidas, who threw himself in the gap of Thermopylæ, was braver than all the Grecian hosts; as Mucius Seaevola was the bravest of the Roman youth when he approached Porsena with intent to assassinate, and said: "*Hostis hostem occidere volui; nec ad mortem minus animi est, quam fuit ad cædem. Et facere et pati fortia, Romanum est;*" so was this youth braver than all the rebel hosts when he came to offer up his life by killing the chief of the enemy.

As Harmedius and Aristogeton were more careless of their lives than the rest of the Athenian youth when they killed Hippias and Hipparchus, as Brutus said on the market place: "As I slew my best lover for the good of Rome, I have the same dagger for myself when it shall please my country to need my death;" so was this boy more ready to offer up his life for what he believed to be the good of his country. And as Gerard was the bitterest Catholic of the Netherlands when he slew the Prince of Orange; Ravaillac the bitterest enemy of the Protestants when he slew Henry IV.; as Jacques Clement was the bitterest Catholic when he killed Henry III; as Orsini was the most bitter Italian when he tried to kill Louis Napoleon, so this boy, remembering his two slaughtered brothers, was the bitterest Southerner of all that defied the Government.

Courage, then, martyrdom, inextinguishable hate for oppression, are his sins. Now, if courage be a crime, then have you and I, and all of us, who have braved death, been criminals? Then are the emblems of valor, which a grateful country has placed upon your shoulders and breasts, but marks of crime. Is readiness to be sacrificed for the common good a crime? Then are the millions of heroic youths, who have left the plow and girded on the sword for four years, but criminals; then is our banner but the flag of crime; then are our battlefields but loathsome scenes of general fratricidal murder. Is, then, undying hatred for what is believed to be oppression a crime? Then was our Revolution but successful crime. Then were the struggles of Tyrol, of Hungary, of Venice, of Greece, but unsuccessful crimes. Then was Byron a traitor to Greece, Garibaldi a traitor to Austria, Kossuth a traitor to Austria, Hofer a traitor to Austria, and Washington a traitor to England. Mark, throughout the history of the world, there is no lesson taught in clearer language than that the noblest deed of men is to free the world of oppressors.

But I hear a student of history reply: True; but they must have been oppressors. Granted; but who is to be the judge? There can be no one but the assassin himself. It is he, and he only, who takes the risk of becoming a deliverer, or a foul and parricidal murderer. Let us, then, see what these people were, against whom he aimed his blow and what they appeared to him. In truth, if you seek for characters in history, you will find none further removed from the oppressors than our late President and the Secretary of State. The one was the great emancipator, the deliverer of a race from bondage, the great *salvator*, the deliverer of a nation from civil war. The other was the great pacificator, the savior from foreign war, the uniter of factions, the constant prophet and messenger of good will and peace. This is how they seemed to us; but such were they not in the eyes of this boy, or of five millions of his fellow-countrymen. To them, the one appeared a usurper of power, a violator of laws, a cruel jester, an invader, a destroyer of life, liberty and property; the other a cunning time-server, an adviser in oppression, and a slippery advocate of an irrepressible conflict. These Southern men had long borne power, and, in their obscurity, felt the envy for greatness which once cried:

"Ye gods! It doth amaze us,
A man of such a feeble temper should
So get the start of the majestic world
And bear the palm alone."
    *   *   *
"Why man, he doth bestride the narrow world
Like a colossus, and we petty men
Walk under his huge legs, and peep about
To find ourselves dishonorable graves."

This was his idea of Mr. Lincoln and Mr. Seward. This was what he heard in Florida, among the village politicians. This was what he read in the Richmond papers, in the orders of the generals, in the gossip of the camp-fire, in the letters that he got from home. Every farmer by whose well he filled his canteen told him that; every Southern lass that waved her handkerchief toward him repeated it; his mother in mourning told it; every prisoner returned from Northern prisons told it; every wayside cripple but confirmed it. Lincoln, the oppressor, was in the air, it was in the echo of the drum, it was in the whizzing of the shell, it came on every breeze that floated from the North. Wonderful was his error; strange, indeed, is it that charity and liberty should be thus misconstrued. Let us, then, remember that if he was wrong he erred on the side of courage, on the side of self-sacrifice, and on the side of hatred to what he believed to be oppression; that he differs from the Southern army simply because he surpassed it in courage; that he differed from a patriot and a martyr, simply because he was mistaken in his duty.

If, then, you praise men because they kill such as they believe oppressors, you must praise him; if you praise men who are ready to die for their country, you will praise him; and if you applaud those who show any courage superior to the rest of mankind you will applaud him.

III. But there is a third school before him. From Gettysburg he was sent to West Building

Hospital, Pratt street, Baltimore, and remained until October, 1863, when, seeing no hope of an exchange, he deserted for his regiment, and, walking through Winchester, met a regiment of cavalry at Fauquier. Not being able to get through our lines, he was joined to this arm of the service, and remained in that service until January 1, 1865. On that day, as we see by the narrative of Mrs. Grant, he saved the lives of two Union soldiers. About the same time he, like many of the Southern soldiers, began to despair of the Confederacy, came to Alexandria, sold his horse, gave his name as Payne, took the oath of allegiance as a refugee from Fauquier, went to Baltimore, took a room at the house of Mrs. Branson, the lady he had met at Gettysburg, and resolved to wait for the return of peace. Now, let us see what he learned in the third school.

The rebel cavalry of Northern Virginia, as we now know, was considered, in the Southern army, the *elite* of their horsemen. Dismounted cavalrymen of the army of the Potomac were sent to Northern Virginia, re-mounted and then returned to their commands. In the spirit of war, however, they differed materially from the rest of the Southern forces. First, they came intimately in contact with the people of Loudon and Fauquier, who had suffered most from the war, and whose hatred of Northern troops was more bitter, so that they fought rather from personal hate, and in individual contests, than from political sentiments, and in battle. Accordingly, whatever edge of acrimony was wanting in the temper of Powell he gained at the houses of ruined slaveholders in Leesburg, Aldie, Middleburg, and Upperville. It was also the custom of those soldiers, and esteemed honorable from their stand-point, to capture quartermasters and paymasters, lie in wait for bearers of dispatches and important generals, and to make sudden attacks and hurried retreats. Accordingly, if he wanted a certain feline intrepidity in planning and escaping—a capacity to approach by stealth, execute with rapidity, and hurry off before his victims had recovered from their consternation—we may well believe that he learned it in this third school. And who is responsible for the third school? His Colonel? Then let him be punished. His Captain? He is now at liberty. General Lee? Then let him abide the consequences. Jefferson Davis, who commissioned them? Then let the blow fall on him. This boy comes here with no marvellous spirit of fury, that we should wonder and say, where has he learnt all this? Where among men are savages formed like this? He comes here fresh from Northern Virginia, with all its sorrow and all its bitterness. On the tablets of his memory are written curses of many a ruined master; in his ears are ringing the cries of women and children, and the moans of dying men. Before his eyes are visions of burning barns, ravaged fields, a people prostrate, humble, starving, homeless—a land once beautiful, now a barren waste, peopled by famine, disease, and ruin—and these have brought him here to seek a quick revenge. We know that we have done these things righteously, with malice to-

ward none, for the salvation of the State and for liberty. But the wail of woe and lamentation is not the less piercing; the thirst for a dire, bitter and consuming revenge, is not the less keen. As the woes of Normandy brought Charlotte Corday to the chamber of Murat, as the humiliations of France brought Louvel to the side of the Duke de Berri, as the ravages in Thuringia brought Stapps to Napoleon at Schonbronn, so is the prisoner at the bar the messenger of Virginia's sorrow and bitterness to the chamber of the Secretary of State. And how are we to meet those woes and bitterness and their deluded messenger? In anger? That were only to confess that we were wrong in inflicting them. No; rather let us say, "What we have done was more in love than in hate. Let us forget the past. For your sorrows there is sympathy—for your bitterness there is charity. From henceforward let there be peace, and let the great sacrifice which we have paid you make us forever even."

IV. But there is a fourth school before him—the school of necessity.

Arrived at Baltimore and having taken up his residence with Mrs. Branson, he looked around for something to do. He had no trade or profession. The period in which he would have learned one was spent in the army; and we know how abhorrent it was to men of the South to engage in manual labor; and as his hands attest, he has never engaged in any. Accordingly, in perplexity about his future—for the little money he got for his horse was fast going—he whiled away the time in reading medical books and brooding in his chamber. While in this condition, unable to get home, unable to see how he was to live at Baltimore, the fracas occurred by which he was arrested, brought before the Provost Marshal, and ordered north of Philadelphia.

Picture to yourself the condition of this unfortunate victim of Southern fanaticism, suddenly again cast into the street and exiled from Baltimore, a stranger, sundered from his only friends, in a strange land. He thinks of his own home in far-off Florida, but between him and it are a thousand miles and a rebel army on whose rolls he is a deserter. He thinks of rejoining that army, but between him and it is a Union army. He thinks of the unknown North into which he is banished, but his fingers refuse the spade; he thinks of a profession, but the very dream of one is now a mockery; he thinks of going where no one knows him, but he fears that after all the curse of secession will follow him; he thinks of eluding the authorities and staying at Baltimore, but then he is afraid of compromising his friends, and leaves them. Everywhere the sky is dark. Among Northern men he is persecuted, for he is a rebel; among Southern men at Baltimore he is despised, for he is a recreant Southerner; among Southern men at home he is a by-word, for he is a deserter. The earth seems to reject him, and God and man to be against him.

Now, if there be any man in this Court who has ever wandered, penniless, houseless, friendless, in that worst of solitudes, the streets of a strange city, with hunger at his stomach, and a great sense of wrong at his heart, in rags, and these very rags betraying him as a thing to be despised and spurned; afraid of meeting at every corner the peering eyes of a Government detective; too proud to beg, and, when hunger overcame pride, rejected with a frown, that man will understand how the prisoner felt in the beginning of March, 1865. If there be any man who has ever been hunted down by misery in his youth, and before much sorrow had made the burden easy, until he wondered why he was born, and hid his face in his hands, praying to God to end his pain forever, he also can understand how, in the fulness of suffering, he has been brother to the accused.

Well, indeed, had it been for him if some angel of mercy had on that day, as he wandered a hungry specter through the streets of Baltimore, with flashing eyes and disordered hair, stretched forth her hand and said: "Here is bread; take, eat, and live." A loaf of bread might have saved him; a single word of kindness might have saved him; the gracious lick of a friendly dog might have saved the glow of a once generous heart from going out forever. We have all, my friends, had these turning points in our lives, and we all reckon back to a time when we stood in the midst of gloom, and suddenly it was glorious day, for we found a plank and reached the shore. His Creator, in His inscrutable wisdom, thought it good there should be no ray of light, no beckoning hand, no hope for the prisoner. Perhaps it had been better if he had dragged himself to the pier and ended his career in suicide. It was ordered that his very weakness should make him the prey of a human devil. We can already foresee the consequences. He is desperate, anxious for death, only he is a soldier, and he will not die ingloriously, after having faced death an hundred times. He is pursued by the Government in which he had confided, and for which he had deserted his own; pursued, tracked, followed like an outlaw among mankind. He will show that Northern Government that he is not a dog, and that Southern Government that he is not a traitor; and give him but a chance, and he will, with one stroke, pay off the scores he owes the abolitionists, restore himself in the eyes of his comrades in arms, and throw himself into the arms of a pitiful eternity.

And who is to blame that he was urged to desperation and consequent revenge? I answer, this civil war. The civil war took him from the magnolias and orange groves of Florida, and left him a waif upon the pavements of a Northern city. The civil war took the independent farmer from his fields, and left him a beggar among strangers. The civil war took him from honest pursuits and professions, and left him to make his living without any other accomplishments than dexterity in murder. The civil war forbade him a home among Northern men, after it had taken him away from his home in the South. The civil war made him an outcast and a fugitive on the face of the earth; took the bread out of his mouth, and gave him the alternative of dying obscurely by his own hand, or notoriously by the death of a public officer.

V. The education of our farmer's boy is now complete. He has been in four schools. Slavery has taught him to wink at murder, the Southern army has taught him to practice and justify murder, cavalry warfare has taught him to love murder, necessity has taught him resolution to commit murder. He needs no further education; his four terms are complete, and he graduates an assassin! And of this college we, the re-united people of the United States, have been the stern tutors, guides and professors. It needs now only that some one should employ him.

I need not pursue this dolorous history further. You know the rest. If you did not know it, you could infer it from what has gone before. That he should meet Booth at Barnum's Hotel, enter into his plans eagerly, and execute them willingly, are matters of course. That he should care nothing for money, but only for revenge; that he should hate the Lincoln Government like a slaveholder; that he should enter the house of a cabinet officer like a guerrilla; that he should try to murder, and justify his murder like a Southern soldier; that he should then give himself up willingly, as one who exchanges the penalties of assassination for suicide; that he should sit here like a statue, and smile as one who fears no earthly terrors, and should tell the doctors, calmly and stoically, that he only did what he thought was right—all these things are as certain to follow as use, education and employment necessity.

Now, in considering the condition of Powell at this crisis, I do not ask you to believe he was insane. That is a declaration of mental disease of which I am no judge. I only ask you to believe that he was human—a human being in the last stage of desperation, and obeying self-preservation, nature's first law. It is acknowledged by all that the possession of reason only makes man responsible for crime. Now, there are two ways in which reason is vanquished. One is when the passions make war against reason and drive her from her throne, which is called insanity. Another is when the necessities of the body overcome the suggestions of the mind, a state in which the reason is a helpless captive. And if you find that while his reason was so in captivity, he surrendered to temptation, I am sure you will set it to the credit, not of reason, but of the body, whose wants were imperious while there was yet no reason in it, in childhood, and which will again exist without reason after death.

At the beginning of the war, Powell, one night, secured a pass and went to the theater at Richmond. It was the first play that Powell ever saw, and he was spellbound with that magical influence wielded by the stage over such, to whom its tinsel is yet reality. But he was chiefly attracted by the voice and manner of one of the actors. He was a young man of about twenty-five, with large, lustrous eyes, a graceful form, features classical and regular as a statue, and a rich voice that lingered in the ears of those who heard him. Although only a private soldier, Powell considered himself the equal of any man, and after the play was over sought and gained an introduction to the actor.

Never were two natures thrown together so different, yet so well calculated, the one to rule, the other to be ruled. The soldier was tall, awkward, rough, frank, generous and illiterate. The actor was of delicate mold, polished, graceful, subtle, with a brilliant fancy, and an abundant stock of reading. Each was what the other was not, and each found in the other an admirer of the other's qualities. The actor was pleased to have a follower so powerful in his muscles, and Powell was irresistibly drawn to follow a man so wondrously fascinating and intellectual. They saw enough of one another to form a close intimacy, and confirm the control of the actor over Powell, and parted, not to meet for nearly four years.

In the twilight of that memorable day in March, which I have described, Powell was dragging himself slowly along the street past Barnum's Hotel—a poor creature overcome by destiny. Suddenly a familiar voice hailed him. Looking up the steps, he saw the face of the Richmond actor. The actor on his side expressed astonishment to find Powell in such a plight—for the light in the eyes of a desperate man needs no translation—and in that distant city. Powell answered him in few words: "Booth, I want bread—I am starving." In ordinary circumstances, I do not doubt but Booth would have said, come in and eat; but just now he was filled with a mighty scheme, for he had just been to Canada, and was lying in wait for agents. So he did not give him to eat; he did not tell him to go and die, but he seized with eagerness upon this poor man's hunger to wind about him his accursed toils, saying, "I will give you as much money as you want, but first you must swear to stick by me. It is in the oil business.' An empty stomach is not captious of oaths, and Powell then swore that fatal oath, binding his soul as firmly to Booth as Faust to Mephistopheles, and went in and feasted. Next morning Booth gave him money enough to buy a change of clothing and keep him for a week. Powell now became anxious to know what plan it was that was to make him rich, but Booth answered evasively that it was in the oil business. He knew well enough that he had to do with a desperate man, but he knew, also, that any proposition of a guilty character might as yet be rejected. He must get full control of this desperate tool, and instil into his nature all the subtle monomania of his own. Accordingly he proceeded to secure every thought and emotion of Powell. With a master pencil he painted before the eyes of this boy the injuries of the South and the guilt of her oppressors. He reminded him of devastated homes, negroes freed, women ravished, the graves of his brothers on a thousand hillsides. He reminded him that he was a traitor to the Southern cause, and that it was necessary he should regain the favor of his country. He pointed out to him his desperate condition—a fugitive from his friends, and an exile among strangers. He touched him upon his pride, and showed him how he was born a gentleman, and ought to live as a gentleman. He touched upon his helplessness, and showed him that there was no hope for him, in peace or war, in heaven or earth, except by rendering a great service to the South. He touched upon his melancholy, and said if he must die, he should offer up his life in a manner that would bequeath his name as a blessing to posterity. Powell now awoke from the depth of despair to the highest pinnacle of agonized excitement. It was as if he had been breathing that subtle Eastern poison, wherein the victim sees swimming before his eyes a vision of more than celestial felicity, but far off and unattainable. What wonder he swam in dreams of delicious pain! Instead of that former melancholy, he felt an eager desire to live. Instead of that long torpor, he felt all the old wounds bleeding again, and burned to avenge the South. Instead of laboring like a negro, he saw a vague vision of rolling in boundless wealth. Instead of being cursed by his kinsmen, he was fired with zeal to be cherished as one of her chief martyrs. Instead of being the toy of fortune, he dreamed of being her conqueror. But yet he saw no avenue to all this, and, spell-bound as he was, turned to his tormentor, who held him as firmly as ever Genii did their fabled imps, for the explanation, for the means and quick road to happiness. Booth saw his victim was ready, and hastened to impart his mysterious plans. The first plan was to go to Washington, take a ride with confederates, on horseback, to the Soldiers' Home, capture the President, and deliver him to the Rebel authorities. This failed. The second plan was to kill the heads of the State—a plan first broached to Payne on the evening of the 14th of April, at eight o'clock.

Booth, on the evening of the 14th, at eight o'clock, told him the hour had struck; placed in his hands the knife, the revolver, and the bogus package of medicine; told him to do his duty, and gave him a horse, with directions to meet beyond the Anacosta bridge; and he went and did the deed. I have asked why he did it. His only answer is: "Because I believed it my duty."

VI. Now, let us not be deceived by the special name of assassination, and confound it with the conscientious killing of what is believed to be an oppressor. When we read of assassination we involuntarily bring to mind examples of men hired by statesmen to make away with princes. There is the Italian perfumer, Rogeri, of Catherine de Medici; there is Orloff, of Catherine, and Alexander, of Russia; we think of the tools used by Tiberius, by Richard III, Philip the II, by Mary of Scotland, by Louis XI, and our minds are filled with associations with State murders accomplished by tigers in human shape killing for gold.

But there is another type of assassination and of so-called assassins. That comes to pass when a fanatic, religious or political, deems it his duty to offer up his life in exchange for the life he believes to be a public enemy. This is the Sand of Kotzebue, the Corday of Murat, the Count Ankerstroem of Gustavus III, the Brutus of Cæsar, the Gerard of Orange, the Ravaillac of Henry IV—men who may ally themselves with others, but who receive their orders immediately, as they believe, from God himself.

The first order kills for money, it is hired by princes, it would for money kill its employers, it uses concealment, it is ashamed, it strikes in masks and dominoes, and when caught gives way to despair. Not so the second order. It glories in its deed, it goes joyfully to its own death, it has commandments from Heaven, it stabs without changing its dress, it makes no effort to escape, it gladly delivers itself up; on trial it is composed as on the eve of triumph, it justifies its crime, it makes no defense, and longs for death, saying, in the words of Corday, "To-morrow I hope to meet Brutus and the other patriots in Elysium."

It needs no argument to show to which class the prisoner belongs. He did, indeed, consort with others, but he lent his ear only, as one would say:

"What is that you would impart to me ?
If it be aught toward the general good
Set honor in one eye and death in the other,
And I will look on both indifferently ;
For, let the gods so speed me, as I love
The name of honor more than I fear death."

You have not shown that any gold has soiled his motive. You have shown that he gained from others plans, made with them agreements of time and place; but the motive, the spirit, the self-sacrifice, the courage, the justification, the longing for death is all his own. He alone says he thought it was his duty.

I say he is the fanatic, and not the hired tool; the soldier who derived his orders from conscience, and who, in the applause of that tribunal, smiles at all earthly trials. How else do you explain his bearing? He smiles at all that you can do against him. To him the clanking of these chains is the sweet music of his triumph. The efforts of the prosecution and its bitter witnesses to convict him are but the confirmation of his glory. The power and majesty of the Government brought upon his head seem but clear and pleasant praises of his deed. He lives in that land of imagination where it seems to him legions of the souls of Southern soldiers wait to crown him as their chief commander. He sits here like a conqueror; for four weeks he has held his head erect when all others have quailed; he meets the stare of curiosity as a king might face his subjects; he keeps his state even in his cell, and the very keepers, in admiration, acknowledge him their master. Now, I know I dare not call him mad—the doctors have forbidden it. I might say that if ever man fell within that definition of Chief-Justice Shaw of insanity, "A very common instance is where a person fully believes the act he is doing is done by the immediate command of God, and he acts under the delusive but sincere belief that what he is doing is by command of a superior power, which supersedes all human laws and the laws of nature," this is the man. But the doctors have said he is not insane, and though he fills the legal definition he does not fill the medical, and, therefore, I can not hope that you will hold him insane.

But I appeal from medical definitions and from legal definitions to your good sense, and I ask you to explain for me the riddle of this man's conduct in any other way than that he is a political fanatic; a monomaniac on the subject of his duty—call him sane or insane—yet one who is responsible only to that God from whom he derives his commandments. Before another tribunal, where all his previous life might be inquired into, and where time would be given for all this mystery to be unraveled, I do not hesitate to say I could convince the judges beyond a doubt that he is no more responsible for what he has done to the laws of the United States than a Chinaman whom custom and religion give the right to strangle his daughters. You have not the time, and I must end the inquiry. But as you are sworn to try this man on your consciences, so I charge you to give him the benefit of his.

Gentlemen, when I look at the prisoner, and see (as it has been my duty for four weeks to see) the calm composure with which he has gone through the horrors of this trial; the cheerful and firm fortitude with which he has listened to the evidence against him, and with which he has endured the gaze of the public, as well as the ignominy of fetters; the frank and honest way in which he speaks of his crime, as a thing revolting in itself, but due to a cause which he thinks holy; and, more than all, the settled conviction, which robs the trial of all terrors, that he has but obeyed the voice of custom, education, and conscience; and the calm serenity with which he regards all pains that men can inflict upon him as contemptible, and part of his duty to endure, I can not help being proud—though blood is on his hands—that such fortitude, unparalleled in history, is the growth of American soil; and I can not help wishing that throughout all the coming vicissitudes of life, in all perplexities and doubts, on all occasions of right and wrong, in all misconstructions and trials, I may have so cheering, so brave, so earnest a conviction that I have done my duty.

And what is this duty? What is this doing right? Ask the Indian, as he returns to his wigwam, laden with the dripping scalps of the dispossessors of his soil, why he has done it, and he will answer you, with a flourish of his tomahawk and his face turned toward Heaven, that he is doing right—the Great Spirit has commanded it. Ask the Hindoo, as he disembowels some English officer by the Ganges, and riots in his blood, the reason of his crime, and he will tell you it is his duty, he is doing right—the Brahmins have decreed it. Consult the records of Vendee, and see why Charette and Gastou murdered the Republican soldiery in ambuscades and thickets, and you will find they entered, at the bar of the Parisian Court, the plea that they were doing right; it was their duty. Now go through the devastated South; speak with a few of the five millions, and ask them why they have thirsted for and taken Northern blood in secret places, murdered stragglers, waylaid orderlies, and killed by stealth, and they will answer you, pointing to the charred remains of some ancestral home and some neighboring hill dotted with graves: Because it was our duty; because we felt bound in conscience to do it.

Let us not undervalue the force of conscience. It is man's sole director, his highest judge, his last resort. Without it he is but an erring wanderer, tossed by every wind of passion, interest, and caprice. With it, his course is as certain and regular as the stars. In labor it cheers him; in pleasure it restrains him; to all manner of good it prompts him; from all manner of evil it defends him. In peace it teaches him to labor; in war to fight; for religion it tells him to fear God; for his country it says, protect and defend it; for himself it says, thy country, thy home, thy friends first, and thyself last. It is this spark of heavenly fire which has supported martyrs at the stake; which has sustained good men on the scaffold; which brought liberty and preserved it in this land for you and me and all of us. Let us, then, respect it, even when it speaks in a voice which we can not understand. Let us honor it as the same voice which directs us, even when it directs others to a grievous fault. We are but men. The same God who created us all, may reconcile all that, and find in our difference but ignorance on the one side and ignorance on the other. And if we dare to judge the dictates of conscience, do we not arrogate to ourselves the prerogatives of the Sovereign Lawgiver of the Universe, who gave the rule, "Judge not, that ye be not judged?" Therefore, considering that we have the limit set, and that we can not go beyond without becoming in turn transgressors, let us leave that cause with Him who measures the conduct of men by no standard of success, but by obedience to the invariable dictates of conscience. For us it is enough that we are weak judges of weak men. If we were beasts, unconscious of the sacred limits of right and wrong, we might excuse him; if we were Gods and superior to destiny, we might destroy him; but as we are men who know our duties, but also our weakness, often seek good but do evil, therefore let us do the work of man to man—punish and reform him.

VII. Gentlemen, I have done with narrative and reflections. We now know that this Florida boy is not a fiend, but an object rather of compassion. We now know that slavery made him immoral, that war made him a murderer, and that necessity, revenge, and delusion made him an assassin. We now know that in all regards he is like us, only, that he was taught to believe right what we were taught to believe wrong; and that if we had been taught in his school, we would be like him, and if he had been taught in ours, he would be like us. We know that, from his point of view, he justifies the murder of our Secretary of State; we know that, from our standpoint, we would gladly have seen, for four years, the death of the rebel Secretary of State. We know that we were on the side of the Government, because we were born North; we know that he was against it, because he was born South; and that had we been born South we would have been in his place, and had he been born North he would be in ours. We know, also, that all the enemy desired the death of the President, and that he surpassed them only in courage; and that if we forgive them who killed our brothers, we must, in consistency, forgive him who tried to kill Mr. Seward, because he thought

Mr. Seward guilty of murdering his brothers.

We know, further, that this man desires to die, in order to gain the full crown of martyrdom; and that, therefore, if we gratify him, he will triumph over us; but if we spare him, we will triumph over him. We know, also, that the public can gain nothing by his death from the example; for if he die as he lived, there will be more anxious to emulate his bravery, as Adam Luc, a deputy from Ments, who, on the death of Corday, fired with admiration, wrote to the tribunal requesting to die like Charlotte Corday, while the multitude exclaimed: "She is greater than Brutus." But if he is suffered to live, he will receive the worst punishment—obscurity—and the public will have nothing to admire. We also know, and we can not consider it too much, that he has killed no man, and that if he be put to death we shall have the anomaly of the victim surviving the murderer; and that, under the laws, this man can be punished only for assault and battery with intent to kill, and, therefore, imprisoned. We know, also, that we are at the end of a civil war, a time when it is desirable there should be no farther mention or remembrance of fraternal strife. If we put this man to death, he will live forever in the hearts of his comrades, and his memory will forever keep our brethren from us. If, moreover, we put him to death, we will show that war is still in our hearts, and that we are only content to live with them because we have subdued them.

Finally, we know that if we let him live and teach him better, we show the whole world that this war was carried on to undeceive a deluded people and to maintain the supremacy of the laws, so that, now that the laws are supreme, we may begin with reform; but if we put him to death we show only that we are vindictive, and use our victory only to gratify our anger. Let him, then, live. His youth asks it, fraternity asks it, the laws ask it, our own sins ask it, the public good demands it. Because you and I taught him the code of assassination in slavery; because you and I brought about a civil war, which practiced him in assassination and made him justify it; because you and I spurned him from us when he sought refuge with us, and bade him destroy himself, ignobly, by his own hand, or grandly, by assassination; because, in short, you and I have made this boy what he is, therefore, lest we who are really ourselves guilty of this attempt at murder, should perpetrate a real murder, let him live, if not for his sake, for our own. Take from the refugee his desperation, and you have the cavalryman; take from the cavalryman his hate, and you have the soldier of Hill; take from the soldier his martial habits, and you have the slave-holder; take from the slaveholder his slavery, and you have again the pure and simple child, who, four years ago, went singing in innocence over the land.

Before I close, one word from myself. I have heretofore spoken of the prisoner as his counsel; I may also speak of him in my character as a man; and I can testify that in the four weeks' acquaintance I have had, hearing him converse with freedom and explain all his secret thoughts, in spite of the odious crime with which he is charged, I have formed an estimate of him little short of admiration, for his honesty of purpose, freedom from deception and malice, and courageous resolution to abide by the principles to which he was reared. I find in him none of that obstinacy which perseveres in crime because it is committed, and hopes to secure admiration in a feigned consistency. Neither is there about him a false desire of notoriety, nor a cowardly effort to screen himself from punishment; only one prominent anxiety—that is, lest people should think him a hired assassin, or a brute; an aversion to being made a public spectacle of, and a desire to be tried at the hands of his fellow-citizens.

Altogether, I think we may safely apply to him, without spurious sympath' or exaggeration, the words which were sa d of Brutus—

> "This was the noblest Roman of them all
> All the conspirators, save only he,
> Did that they did in envy of great Cæsar;
> He only, in a general honest thought,
> And common good to all, made one of them.
> His life was gentle, and the elements
> So mixed in him, that nature might stand up
> And say to all the world, "This was a man!"

I commit him, then, without hesitation, to your charge. You have fought on the same fields, and as you have never been wanting in mercy to the defeated, so I know you will not be wanting in mercy to him. You have all commanded private soldiers, and as you could estimate the enthusiasm of your own men, so you will know how to estimate the enthusiasm of those who fought against you. The lives of all of you have shown that you were guided in all perplexities by the stern and infallible dictates of conscience and duty, and I know that you will understand and weigh in your judgment of the prisoner, dictates and duties so kindred to your own.   LEWIS PAYNE.

ARGUMENT

ON THE

LAW AND EVIDENCE IN THE CASE OF DR. SAM'L A. MUDD,

BY

THOMAS EWING, Jr.

May it please the Court: If it be determined to take jurisdiction here, it then becomes a question vitally important to some of these parties—a question of life and death—whether you will punish only offenses created and declared by *law*, or whether you will make and declare the past acts of the accused to be crimes, which acts the law never heretofore declared criminal: attach to them the penalty of death, or such penalty as may seem meet to you; adapt the evidence to the crime and the crime to the evidence, and thus convict and punish. This, I greatly fear may be the purpose, especially since the Judge Advocate said, in reply to my inquiries, that he would expect to convict "*under the common law of war.*" This is a term unknown to our language—a *quiddity*—wholly undefined and incapable of definition. It is, in short, just what the Judge Advocate chooses to make of it. It may create a fictitious crime, and attach to it arbitrary and extreme punishment, and who shall gainsay it? The *laws* of war—namely, our *Articles* of War—and the habitual practice and mode of proceeding under them, are familiar to us all; but I know nothing, and never heard or read of a common law of war, as a code or system under which military courts or commissions in this country can take and exercise jurisdiction not given them by express legal enactment or constitutional grant. But I still hope the *law* is to govern, and if it do, I feel that my clients are still safe.

I will now proceed to show you, that on the part of one of my clients—Dr. Mudd—no crime known to the law, and for which it is pretended to prosecute, can possibly have been committed. Though not distinctly informed as to the offense for which the Judge Advocate claims conviction, I am safe in saying, that the testimony does not point to treason, and if he is being tried for treason, the proceedings for that crime are widely departed from. The prosecution *appears* to have been instituted and conducted under the proclamation of the Secretary of War, of April 20, 1865. This makes it a crime, punishable with death, to harbor or screen Booth, Atzerodt, or Herold, or to aid or assist them to escape. It makes it a crime to do a *particular act*, and punishes that crime with death. I suppose we must take this *proclamation as law.* Perhaps it is part of what the Judge Advocate means when he speaks of the "common law of war." If this be so, my

clients are still safe, if we be allowed to construe it *as laws are construed by courts of justice.* But I will show, first, that Dr. Mudd is not, and can n t possibly be, guilty of any offense known to the law.

1. Not f treason. The overt act attempted to be alleged is the murder of the President. The proof is conclusive, that at the time the tragedy was enacted Dr. Mudd was at his residence in the country, thirty miles from the place of the crime. Those who committed it are shown to have acted for *themselves*, not as the instruments of Dr. Mudd. He, therefore, can not be charged, according to law and upon the evidence, with the commission of this overt act. Th re are not two witnesses to prove that he did commit it, but abundant evidence to show negatively that he did not.

Chief Justice Marshall, in delivering an opinion of the Court in Burr's case, says: "Those only who perform a part, and who are leagued in the conspiracy, are declared to be traitors. To complete the definition both circumstances must concur. They must "*perform a part*" which will furnish the *overt act*, and they must be *leagued* with the conspiracy." 4 Cr., 474.

Now, as to Dr. Mudd, there is no particle of evidence tending to show that he was ever leagued with traitors in their treason; that he had ever, by himself, or by adhering to, and in connection with, others, levied war against the United States. It is contended that he joined in compassing the death of the President ("*the King's death*"). *Foster*, p. 149, speaking of the treason of compassing the king's death, says: "From what has been said it followeth, that in every indictment for this species of treason, and indeed for levying war and adhering to the king's enemies, an *overt act must be alleged and proved.*" 4 Cr., 490.

The only *overt act* laid in these charges against Mudd is the act of assassination, at which it is claimed he was constructively present and participating. His presence, and participation, or procurement, must be *proved* by *two witnesses*, if the charge be treason; and such presence, participation, or procurement, be the *overt act.*

Chief Justice Marshall, in Burr's case (*Dall.,* 500), says: "Collateral points, say the books, may be proved according to the course of the common law; but is this a collateral point? Is the fact without which the accused does not participate in the guilt of the assemblage, if they were guilty (or in any way in the guilty act of others), a collateral point? This cannot be. The presence of the party, when presence is necessary, being part of the overt act, must be positively proved by two witnesses. No presumptive evidence, no facts from which presence may be conjectured or inferred, will satisfy the Constitution and the law. If procurement take the place of presence, and become part of the overt act, then no presumptive evidence, no facts from which the procurement may be conjectured or inferred, can satisfy the Constitution and the law. The mind is not to be led to the conclusion that the individual was present by a train of conjectures or inferences, or of reasoning. *The fact itself must be proved by two witnesses,* and must have been committed within the district."

2. Not of murder. For the law is clear, that, in cases of treason, presence at the commission of the overt act is governed by the same principle as constructive presence in *ordinary felonies,* and has no other latitude, greater or less, except that in proof of treason *two* witnesses are necessary to the overt act, and one only in murder and other felonies. "A person is not constructively present at an overt act of treason, unless he be aiding and abetting at the fact, or ready to do so, if necessary." 4 *Cr.*, 492. Persons not sufficiently near to give assistance are not principals. And although an act be committed in pursuance of a previous concerted plan, those who are not present, or so near as to be able to afford aid and assistance, at the time when the offense is committed, are not principals, but accessories before the fact. *Wharton Am. Crim. Law,* 112 to 127.

It is, therefore, perfectly clear, upon the law as enacted by the Legislature and expounded by jurists, that Dr. Mudd is not guilty of participating in the murder of the President; that he was not actually or constructively present when the horrid deed was done, either as a traitor, chargeable with it as an overt act, or a conspirator, connected as a principal felon therewith.

3. The only other crimes defined by law for the alleged commission, of which the Judge Advocate may, by possibility, claim the conviction of the accused, are: 1st. The crime of *treasonable conspiracy,* which is defined by the law of 21st July, 1861, and made punishable by fine not exceeding $6,000, and imprisonment not exceeding six years. 2d. The crime of being an *accessory before, or after the fact* to the crimes of murder, and of assault with intent to kill. That the accused is not guilty of either of these crimes, will be clearly shown in the discussion of the evidence which follows.

4. Admitting the Secretary's proclamation to be law, it, of course, either supersedes or defines the unknown something or nothing which the Judge Advocate calls "the common law of war." If so, it is a definite, existing thing, and I can defend my clients against it; and it is easy to show that Dr. Mudd is not guilty of violating that proclamation. He did not, *after the date of the proclamation,* see either of the parties named therein—dress the wound of Booth or point out the way to Herold—and the proclamation relates to *future* acts, not to *past.*

5. But of the *common law of war,* as distinct from the usages of Military Courts, in carrying out and executing the Articles of War, I know nothing, and on examining the books, I find nothing. All that is written down in books of law or authority I am, or ought to be, prepared to meet; but it were idle and vain to search for and combat a mere phantom of the imagination, without form and void.

I now pass to a consideration of the evidence, which I think will fully satisfy the Court that Dr. Mudd is not guilty of treasonable conspiracy, or of being an accomplice, before or after the fact in the felonies committed.

The accused has been a practising physician, residing five miles north of Bryantown, in Charles county, Maryland, on a farm of about five hundred acres, given to him by his father. His house is between twenty-seven and thirty miles from Washington, and four or five miles east of the road from Washington to Bryantown. It is shown by Dr. George Mudd, John L. Turner, John Waters, Joseph Waters, Thomas Davis, John McPherson, Lewellyn Gardiner, and other gentlemen of unimpeached and unquestionable loyalty, who are in full sympathy with the Government, that he is a man of most exemplary character—peaceable, kind, upright, and obedient to the laws. His family being slaveholders, he did not like the anti-slavery measures of the Government, but was always respectful and temperate in discussing them, freely took the oath of allegiance prescribed for voters (Dr. George Mudd), supported an Union candidate against Harris, the secession candidate, for Congress (T. L. Gardiner), and for more than a year past regarded the rebellion a failure. (Dr. George Mudd.) He was never known or reported to have done an act or said a word in aid of the rebellion, or in countenance or support of the enemies of the Government.

An effort was made, over all objections and in violation, I respectfully submit, of the plainest rules of evidence, to blacken his character as a citizen, by showing that he was wont, after the war broke out, to threaten his slaves to send them to Richmond "to build batteries." But it will be seen hereafter, that all that part of the testimony of the same witnesses, which related to the presence of Surratt and of rebel officers at the house of the accused, was utterly false. And Dyer, in presence of whom Eglent says the threat was made to him, swears he was not in the country then, and no such threat was ever made in his presence. The other colored servants of the accused, Charles and Julia Bloyce, and Betty and Frank Washington, say they never heard of such threats having been made; and J. T. Mudd and Dr. George Mudd, and his colored servants Charles and Julia Bloyce, and Betty and Frank Washington, describe him as being remarkably easy, unexacting and kind to all about him—slaves and freemen.

From this brief reference to the evidence of the character of the accused, I pass to a consideration of the testimony adduced to prove his connection with the conspiracy.

And, first, as to his *acquaintance with Booth*. J. C. Thompson says, that early in November last Booth went to the house of witness' father-in-law, Dr. William Queen, four or five miles south of Bryantown, and eight or ten from Dr. Mudd's, and presented a letter of introduction from a Mr. Martin, of Montreal, who said he wanted to see the county. It does not appear who Martin was. Booth said his business was to invest in land and to buy horses. He went with Dr. Queen's family to a church next day, in the neighborhood of Bryantown, and was there *casually* introduced, before service, by Thompson, to the accused. After service Booth returned to Queen's house, and stayed until the next morning, when he left. While at Queen's, he made inquiries of Thompson as to horses for sale, the price of lands, their qualities, the roads to Washington, and to the landings on the Potomac; and Thompson told him that the father of Dr. Samuel Mudd was a large landholder, and might sell part of his land. On Monday morning, after leaving Dr. Queen's, Booth came by the house of the accused, who went with him to the house of George Gardiner, to look at some horses for sale. The accused lives about one-quarter of a mile from Gardiner's (Mary Mudd, Thomas L. Gardiner), and on the most direct road to that place from Dr. Queen's, through Bryantown. (Mary Mudd, Hardy.) There Booth bought the one-eyed saddle-horse which he kept here, and which Payne rode after the attempted assassination of Mr. Seward. Mudd manifested no interest in the purchase, but after it was made Booth directed the horse to be sent to Montgomery's Hotel, in Bryantown, and Booth and the accused rode off together in the direction of the house of the accused, which was also the direction of Bryantown. Witness took the horse to Bryantown next morning, and delivered him in person to Booth there. Witness says the horse was bought on *Monday*; but he thinks in the latter part of November; though he says he is "one of the worst hands in the world to keep dates."

Thompson further says, that after Booth's first introduction and visit to Dr. Queen's, "he came there again, and stayed all night, and left very early next morning. I think it was about the middle of December following his first visit there."

There is nothing whatever to show that Mudd saw Booth on this *second* visit, or at any other time, in the country, prior to the assassination; but a great deal of evidence that he never was at Mudd's house, or in his immediate neighborhood, prior to the assassination, except once, and on his first visit. I will refer to the several items of testimony on this point.

1st. Thomas L. Gardiner says he was back and forth at Mudd's house, sometimes every day, and always two or three times a week, and never heard of Booth being there, or in the neighborhood, after the purchase of the horse and before the assassination.

2d. Mary Mudd says she saw Booth one Sunday in November at church, in Dr. Queen's pew, and with his family, and that she heard of his being at the house of her brother, the accused, on that visit, but did not hear that he stayed all night; and that on the same visit he bought the horse of Gardiner. She lives at her father's, on the farm adjoining that of accused, and was at his house two or three times a week, and saw him nearly every day on his visits to his mother, who was an invalid, and whose attending physician he was; and never saw or heard of Booth, except on that one occasion, before the assassination.

3d. Fanny Mudd, sister of the accused, living with her father, testifies to the same effect.

4th. Charles Bloyce was at the house of the accused Saturday and Sunday of each week of last year until Christmas Eve (except six weeks in April and May), and never saw or heard of Booth's being there.

5th. Betty Washington (colored) lived there from Monday after Christmas until now, and never saw or heard of Booth there before the assassination.

6th. Thomas Davis lived there from 9th of January last. Same as above.

Nor is there any evidence whatever of Booth's having *stayed all night* with the accused on the visit when the horse was bought of Gardiner, or at any other time, except that of Col. Wells, who says, that after Mudd's arrest, "he said, in answer to another question, that he met Booth sometime in November. I think he said he was introduced by Mr. Thompson, a son-in-law of Dr. Queen, to Booth. I think he said the introduction took place at the chapel or church on Sunday morning; that, after the introduction had passed between them, Thompson said, Booth wants to buy farming lands; and they had some little conversation on the subject of lands, and then Booth asked the question, whether there were any desirable horses that could be bought in that neighborhood cheaply; that he mentioned the name of a neighbor of his who had some horses that were good travelers; *and that he remained with him that night, I think, and the next morning purchased one of those horses*." Now, it will be recollected that Thompson says Booth stayed at Dr. Queen's on that visit Saturday night and Sunday night, and Thomas L. Gardiner says the horse was bought *Monday morning*. So that, if Col. Wells is correct in recollecting what Mudd said, then Thompson must be wrong. It is more probable that Thompson is right, as to Booth's having spent Sunday night at Queen's. Thompson's testimony is strengthened, too, by that of Mary Mudd, Fanny Mudd, and Charles Bloyce, who would, in all probability, have heard the fact of Booth spending Sunday night at the house of the accused, had he done so; but they did not hear it.

It is here to be observed, that though the accused was not permitted to show, by Booth's declarations *here*, that he was contemplating and negotiating purchases of lands in Charles county, yet evidence was admitted as to his declarations made *there* to that effect. Dr. Bowman, of Bryantown, says that Booth negotiated with him, on one of these visits, for the purchase of his horses, and also talked of buying horses. And a few days after witness had negotiated with Booth for the sale of his farm, he met Dr. Mudd, and spoke of the negotiation with Booth, and Mudd said, "*Why that fellow promised to buy my land.*" It is also shown by Dr. Blanford, Dr. Bowman, M. P. Gardiner, and Dyer, that Mudd, for a year past, wanted to sell his land, and quit farming.

This, then, is all that is shown of any meeting between Mudd and Booth in that country before the assassination—a casual introduction at church on Sunday in November—Booth going next morning to Mudd's, talking of buying his farm, and riding with him a quarter of a mile to a neighbor's to buy a horse, and their going off together toward Mudd's and Bryantown, where the horse was delivered to Booth next morning.

We will now turn to consider the evidence as to the accused's acquaintance with *John H. Surratt.* If he knew Surratt at all, the fact is not shown by, nor inferable from, the evidence. Miss Surratt was educated at Bryantown, before the war, and her family lived at Surrattsville, and kept the hotel there (which is on the road from Dr. Mudd's house to Washington), until they removed, in October last, to a house on H street, in this city, where they have since resided. (Miss Surratt, Holahan, Weichmann). Dr. Mudd *probably* had met Surratt at the hotel at Surrattsville, or, before the war, at Bryantown, while his sister was at school; but it is not shown by credible testimony that he knew him at all. Let us examine the evidence on this point.

1st. *Mary Simms,* formerly Dr. Mudd's slave, says that a man whom Dr. and Mrs. Mudd called *Surratt* was at Mudd's house from almost every Saturday night until Monday night through the latter part of the *winter*, and through the spring and summer of *last year* until apples and peaches were ripe, when she saw him no more; and that on the last of November she left Dr. Mudd's house. That he *never slept in the house,* but took dinner there six or seven times. That *Andrew Gwynn, Bennett Gwynn,* Capt. Perry, Lieut. Perry, and Capt. White, of Tennessee, slept with Surratt in the pines near the spring, on bed-clothes furnished from Dr. Mudd's house, and that they were supplied by witness and by Dr. Mudd with victuals from the house. That William Mudd, a neighbor, and Rachel Spencer, and Albin Brooke, members of Mudd's household, used to see Surratt there then. She says that the lieutenants and officers had epaulettes on their shoulders, gray breeches with yellow stripes, coat of same color and trimming. Their horses were kept in Dr. Mudd's stable, by Milo Simms.

2d. *Milo Simms,* brother of Mary, fourteen years old, formerly slave of Dr. Mudd, left there Friday before last Christmas. Saw *two or three men* there *last summer,* who slept at the

spring near Dr. Mudd's house. Bedding taken from the house; meals carried by *Mary Simms,* generally, though they sometimes ate in the house, and they all slept at the spring, except one called John Surratt, who slept once in the house. Don't say how long they stayed. It was in "planting tobacco time." He attended their horses in Dr. Mudd's stable.

3d. Rachel Spencer, slave of Dr. Mudd and cook at his house, left him early in January, 1865; saw five or six men around Dr. Mudd's house *last summer;* slept in the pines near the house, and were furnished with meals from it. Were dressed in black and blue. *Were there only a week, and never saw them there before or since.* She heard no names of the men except *Andrew Gwynn* and *Watt Bowie.* That *Albin Brooke* lived at Dr. Mudd's then, and was with these men occasionally.

4th. Elzee Eglen, formerly Dr. Mudd's slave, left him 20th August, 1863; saw a party sleeping in the pines, by the spring, near the house, *summer before last.* Knew *Andrew Gwynn,* and he was one of them; did not recollect any other names. *Mary Simms* carried them meals, and *Milo Simms* attended the horses in Dr. Mudd's stable. Some wore gray clothes with brass buttons, but without other marks—some black clothes. Did not say how many there were, nor how long they stayed.

5th. Melvina Washington, formerly Dr. Mudd's slave, left him October, 1863; saw party sleeping in the pines near the house *summer before last;* victuals furnished from the house. Party stayed there *about a week,* and then left. Some were dressed in gray, and some in short jackets with little peaks behind, with black buttons. She saw them seven or eight times during one week, and then they all left, and *she never saw any of them at* any other time *except during that week.* That *Andrew Gwynn's* name was the only one she heard; that *Mary Simms* used to tell her, when the men were there, the names of others, but she had forgotten them.

That these five witnesses all refer to the same party of men and the same year is certain, from the fact that Elzee Eglen says that Mary Simms carried the party he describes as being there in the summer of 1863, their victuals, and that Milo Simms kept their horses in the stable, and Melvina Washington says Mary Simms used to tell her the names of the party which she describes as being there in 1863; and also from the fact that all of them, except Milo Simms, named *Andrew Gwynn* as being one of the party. I will not waste the time of the Court in pointing out to it in detail the discrepancies in their evidence apparent from the foregoing synopsis of their testimony; and therefore, only calling its attention to the fact that all of these witnesses were living with Dr. Mudd during and after the year 1861 (Dyer), down to the several dates given above, when they respectively left, I will proceed to show from the evidence *what* and *when* the occurrences really were about which they have testified.

1st. Ben. Gwynn (named by Mary Simms as one of the party) says:

Q. Will you state whether during last summer, in company with Captain White, from Tennessee, Captain Perry, Lieut. Perry, Andrew Gwynn, and George Gwynn, or either of them, you were about Dr. Samuel A. Mudd's house for several days? A. I was not. I do not know any of the parties named, and I never heard of them, except Andrew Gwynn and George Gwynn.

Q. Were you with your brothers, Andrew Gwynn and George Gwynn, about Dr. Mudd's house last year? A. No, sir. I have not been in Dr. Mudd's house since about the first of November, 1861. I have not been on his place, or nearer his place than church, since about the 6th of November, 1861.

Q. Where did you and the party who were with you near Dr. Mudd's sleep? A. We slept in the pines near the spring.

Q. How long were you there? A. Four or five days. I left my neighborhood, and went down there and stayed around in the neighborhood—part of the time at his place, and part of the time elsewhere. He fed us there—gave us something to eat, and had some bed-clothing brought out of the house. That was all.

He further said, that the party was composed of his brother, Andrew Gwynn, and Jerry Dyer, who, on the breaking out of the war, were, like all the people of that section, panic-stricken, and apprehending arrest; that he came up to Washington on the 10th of November, gave himself up, found there were no charges against him, took the oath, and went back home. That John H. Surratt, when this party were there, was at college, and witness never saw him in Charles county then or since. That his brother, *Andrew Gwynn*, went South in the fall of 1861, and was never, to his knowledge, back in that county but once since, and that was last winter sometime. He corrected his statement as to *when* the party were there, and fixed it in August, 1861.

2d. Jerry Dyer, brother-in-law of the accused, testifies to the same as Ben. Gwynn. Says he and the two Gwynns were members of companies organized by authority of Governor Hicks for home protection in 1860; were present on parade in Washington at the inauguration of a statue, on the 22d of February, 1860. When the war broke out the companies were disbanded; many of the members going South, and many of those who remained in Charles county scattering about from rumors of arrests; that there was a general panic in the county then, and almost everybody was leaving home and "dodging about;" that while he and the two Gwynns slept in the pines these three or four days, Mary Simms carried them victuals from the house, and Milo Simms attended to the horses in Mudd's stables; that they were dressed in citizens' clothing; that Andrew Gwynn went South in the fall of 1861; witness never heard of his being back since; that Surratt was not there then, nor, so far as he knows, since.

3d. William Mudd, a near neighbor of the accused, named by Mary Simms as having seen the party she describes, says he saw Benjamin Gwynn there in 1861, but saw none of the others, then or since.

4th. Albin Brooke, referred to by Mary Simms and Rachel Spencer as having seen the party they describe (and by Mary Simms as having seen Surratt especially), says he knows Surratt, having met him in another county once, and knew Benjamin Gwynn and Andrew Gwynn, but that he never saw Surratt with any of the men named by Mary Simms at Dr. Mudd's, nor heard of his having ever been there; never heard of Andrew Gwynn being back from Virginia since 1861. That he lived at Dr. Mudd's from the 1st of January to between the 1st and the 15th of September of last year, and was at the stable morning, noon, and night, each day, and was about the spring daily; while there, never saw any strangers' horses in the stable, nor any signs about the spring of persons sleeping there; but that, while living near Dr. Mudd's, in the summer of 1861, he knew of Ben. and Andrew Gwynn and Dyer sleeping in the pines there.

5th. Mrs. Mary Jane Simms boarded, or was a guest, at Dr. Mudd's all last year, except through March; knew Andrew, Ben. and George Gwynn, and George Surratt. Never saw or heard of any of them there, nor of any of them sleeping in the pines.

6th. Frank Washington (colored) lived at Dr. Mudd's all last year; knew Andrew Gwynn by sight; never saw or heard of him or Surratt (of whom a photograph was shown him), or of any of the men named by Mary Simms, being there, or of any men being there in uniform; at the stable three times daily, and often at the spring; and saw no strange horses in the stable; saw no signs of men sleeping about the spring.

7th. Baptist Washington, carpenter, at work there putting up kitchen, etc., from February till Christmas last year, except the month of August; same as above, except as to knowledge of Andrew Gwynn. (Photograph of Surratt shown him.)

8th. Charles Boyce (colored), at Dr. Mudd's through every Saturday and Sunday all last year, except from 10th April to 20th May; same as Frank Washington, except as to knowing Andrew Gwynn.

9th. Julia Ann Bloyce (colored cook), there from early in July to 23d December, 1864; same, substantially, as Frank Washington; knew Ben. and Andrew Gwynn. (Photograph of Surratt shown witness.)

10th. Emily Mudd and Fanny Mudd live on adjoining farm to Dr. Mudd, at his father's; at his house almost daily for years; knew of the party in the pines in 1861, composed of Dyer and the two Gwynns; knew Andrew Gwynn well; never heard of his being back from Virginia since 1861, nor of Surratt ever being at Dr. Mudd's, nor of any of the others named by Mary Simms, except the Gwynns, in 1861.

11th. Henry L. Mudd, jr., brother of the accused, living at his father's; same as above as to Surratt.

None of the five witnesses, whose testimony has been shown false in all essential parts by the evidence of the twelve witnesses for defense, referred to above said that Surratt was one of the party sleeping in the pines, except Mary and Milo Simms. These two witnesses are shown to have established reputations as liars, by the evidence of Charles Bloyce, Julia Ann Bloyce, and Frank, Baptist and Betty Washington. So all that testimony for the prosecution, of the "intelligent contrabands," who darkened the counsels of the court in this case, is cleared away. The only part of it at all admissible under the rules of evidence, or entitled to the consideration of the Court, was that showing Surratt was intimate with Mudd, and often at his house last year and year before; and that, like nearly all the rest of their testimony, has been conclusively shown to be false.

Another witness, who testifies to implicate Mudd as an associate of Surratt, is William A. Evans, who said he saw Mudd some time last winter enter a house on H street, just as Judson Jarboe, of Prince George's county, was going out of it; and that Jarboe was then shaking hands with a young lady, whom witness took to be a daughter of Mrs. Surratt, from her striking likeness to her mother, he having known or seen all the family; and that he stopped a policeman on the street, and asked whose house it was, and he said, "Mrs. Surratt's;" and that he drove up to the pavement, and asked also a lady who lived near by and she said the same. He said this house was between Eighth and Ninth, or Ninth and Tenth—he was not perfectly certain as to the streets, but *was certain* it was between the Patent Office and the President's. Through an hour's cross-examination, he fought by equivocation, or pleading defect of memory, against fixing any circumstance by which I could learn, directly or indirectly, the day or the month when it occurred, and, finally, he could only say it was "sometime last winter." Although his attention had been so strongly attracted to the house, he first said it was on one side of the street and then on the other; and could not tell whether it had any porch or any portico, nor describe its color, nor whether it had a yard in front, nor whether it was near the center of the square, nor describe a single house on either side of the same square. He said he knew Dr. Samuel Mudd, having met him first at Bryantown church, in *December*, 1850.

Every material thing he did say, which was susceptible of being shown false, has been so shown.

1st. Mrs. Surratt's house is not between the Patent Office and the President's, but next the corner of Sixth. (Weichmann, Holahan, Miss Surratt.)

2d. Miss Surratt, an only daughter, says she never saw or heard of Samuel Mudd being at her mother's house, nor heard his name mentioned in the family, and never met Judson Jarboe there or elsewhere before the assassination.

3d. Miss Fitzpatrick, who boarded at Mrs. Surratt's from the 6th of October last to the assassination, and Holahan, who was there from the first week of February last, never saw either Mudd or Jarboe there, or heard of either being there, or the name of either mentioned in the family.

4th. Weichmann who boarded there through last winter, never heard of Mudd being at the house.

5th. Judson Jarboe says he never was at Mrs. Surratt's house, or met Dr. Mudd or Miss Surratt in Washington before the assassination.

6th. Mary Mudd says Samuel Mudd was at Frederick College, at Fredericktown, Maryland, in December, 1850, and was not at home during the collegiate year, beginning in September of that year; and Rev. Dr. Stonestreet, who was president of that college until December of that year, testifies the accused was then entered as a student there, and could not by the rules of the college have gone home.

This witness, Evans, boasted often to the Court that he was a minister of the Gospel, and reluctantly admitted, on cross-examination, that he was also one of the secret police. In his reckless zeal as a detective, he forgot the ninth commandment, and bore false witness against his neighbor. It is to be hoped his testimony that he is a minister of the Gospel is as false as his material evidence. I feel bound in candor to admit, however, that his conduct on the stand gave an air of plausibility to *one* of his material statements—that for a month past he has "been on the verge of insanity."

I have now presented and considered all the testimony going to show that Mudd ever met Surratt at all, and all that he ever met Booth, before the assassination, and after the first visit Booth made to Charles county—except the testimony of Weichmann, which I will now consider.

That witness says that about the middle of January last, he and Surratt were walking down Seventh street one night, and passed Booth and Mudd walking up the street, and just after they had passed, Mudd called, "Surratt, Surratt." Surratt turned and recognised Mudd as an old acquaintance, and introduced Mudd to witness, and then Mudd introduced Booth to witness and Surratt. That soon after the introduction, Booth invited them all to his room at the National Hotel, where wine and cigars were ordered. That Dr. Mudd, after the wines and cigars came, called Booth into the passage, and they stayed there five to eight minutes, and then both came and called Surratt out, and all three stayed there about as long as Mudd and Surratt had stayed, both interviews together making about ten to twenty minutes. On returning to the room, Dr. Mudd seated himself by witness, and apologised for their private conversation, saying, "that Booth and he had some private business — that Booth wished to purchase his farm." And that, subsequently, Booth also apologised to him, giving the same reason for the private conversation. Booth at one time took out the back of an envelope, and made marks on it with a pencil. "I should not consider it writing, but more in the direction of roads or lines." The three were at the time seated round a center table in the middle of the room. "The room was very large—half the size of this court room." He was standing, when this was done, within eight feet of them, and Booth was talking in a low tone, and Surratt and Mudd looking on the paper, but witness heard no word of the conversation. About twenty minutes after the second return from the passage, and after a good deal of general conversation, they all walked round to the Pennsylvania House, where the accused sat with witness on a lounge, and talked about the war, "expressed the opinion that the war would soon be over, and talked like a Union man." Soon after getting there, Booth bid the accused good night, and after Booth left, witness and Surratt followed, at about half-past ten o'clock.

It will be observed that the only men spoken of by this witness as having seen the accused on this occasion are, Booth, who is dead, and Surratt, who is a fugitive from the country. So there is no one who can be called to confirm or confute his statements, as to the fact of these men being together, or as to the character of the interview. But there was *one fact* about which he said he could not be mistaken, and by means of which his evidence against Mudd is utterly overthrown. That is, he alleges the meeting was about the middle of January, and fixes the time with certainty by three distinct circumstances:

1st. He made a visit to Baltimore about the middle of January, and near the date of this meeting.

2d. He had, *before the meeting*, got a letter, which he received on the 16th *of January.*

3d. It was after the Congressional holidays, and Congress had resumed its session. He recollects this fact of itself, and is confirmed in his recollection by the fact that Booth's room was one a member of Congress had occupied before the holidays, and which was given Booth, as he learned, until the member, who had been delayed beyond the time of the reassembling of Congress, should return. Booth told him this.

In refutation of this evidence, we have proved, beyond all controversy, that Dr. Mudd was not in Washington *from the 23d of December to the 23d of March.*

On the 23d of December he came to Washington with J. T. Mudd, who says they left their horses at the Navy Yard, and went into the city at dark, on the street cars, and registered at the Pennsylvania House. They then went out and got supper at a restaurant, and then went to the Metropolitan Hotel and stayed there together a quarter of an hour, and then to the National, where witness met a friend, and became separated in the crowd from the accused. Witness strolled out and went back to the Pennsylvania House, to which accused returned in a few minutes after he got there. He saw and heard no one with the accused, though there *might* have been persons with him in the front part of the room (which was separated from where witness sat by open folding doors), without witness seeing them. Witness and accused then went to bed; were together all next day; were about the market together, and at the

store making purchases; were not at the National Hotel, and left the city about one o'clock in the afternoon of the 24th, and returned home together. Witness never saw Booth, except on his visit to Bryantown in November. We have shown by the evidence of Lucas, Montgomery, Julia Bloyce and Jerry Mudd, that accused came here on that visit on a sufficient and legitimate business errand—to purchase a cooking stove and other articles, which he bought here then.

On the 23d of March, Lewellyn Gardiner said accused again came to Washington with him to attend a sale of condemned horses, but that the sale did not occur at that time. They got to Washington at four or five P. M., left their horses at Martin's, beyond the Navy Yard, and went about looking at some wagons for sale, and went then to the Island to the house of Henry Clark, where they took tea. They spent the evening at Dr. Allen's playing whist; slept together that night at Clark's, and after breakfast next morning went through the Capitol, looking at the paintings in the Rotunda, and returned to Martin's at dinner, and after dinner left and returned home. Accused was not separated from or out of sight of witness five minutes during the whole visit, and did not go to any of the hotels or to the post-office, or see or inquire for Booth. Dr. Allen, Clark, Martin, Thomas Davis, Mary Mudd, Henry Mudd and Betty Washington confirm witness as to the objects or incidents of the visit.

On the 11th of April, three days before the assassination, while Booth, as appears by the hotel register, was at the National in this city, accused came to Giesboro to attend the sale of Government horses, which he and Lewellyn Gardiner had come on the 23d of March to attend. Though in sight of Washington, he did not come into the city, but took dinner at Martin's, and after dinner left and returned home. On this visit he stayed all night at Blanford's, twelve miles from the city, coming up, but not returning. (Lewellyn Gardiner, Henry L. Mudd, Dr. Blanford, Martin, Davis, Betty Washington, Mary Mudd.)

On the 26th of January, he went with his wife to the house of his neighbor, George H. Gardiner, to a party, and stayed till daylight. (Betty Washington, Thomas Davis, Mary Mudd.) Except for one night on the occasion of each of those four visits—two to Washington, one to Giesboro, and one to Gardiner's—accused was not absent from home a night from the 23d of December until his arrest. (Betty Washington, Thomas Davis, Henry L. Mudd, Mary Mudd, Frank Washington.)

After the evidence for the defense above referred to had been introduced, refuting and completely overwhelming Weichmann's testimony and all inferences as to Dr. Mudd's complicity with Booth, which might be drawn from it, a new accuser was introduced against him on the same point, in the person of *Marcus P. Norton*, who said that at half-past 10 o'clock on the morning of the 3d of March, as he was preparing his papers to go to the Supreme Court to argue a motion in a patent case there pending, (which motion the record of the Court shows he *did* argue on that day), a stranger abruptly entered his room and as abruptly retired, saying he was looking for Mr. Booth's room; and though witness never saw Dr. Mudd before or since, until the day of his testifying, he says that stranger is the prisoner at the bar. He could not tell any article of the stranger's clothing except a black hat. *Wm. A. Evans*, a part of whose evidence we have hereinbefore considered, comes to the support of Norton by saying that early on the morning of either the 1st, or 2d, or 3d of March (witness is certain it was one of those three days), Dr. Mudd passed witness on the road from Bryantown to Washington, a few miles from the city, driving a two-horse rockaway, and there was a man in with him, but whether a black or a white man witness could not recollect. Fortunately for the accused, the 1st day of March was Ash Wednesday—the first day of Lent—a religious holiday of note and observance in the community of Catholics among whom he lived. Fortunately for him, too, his sister Mary was taken ill on that day, and required his medical attendance (at her father's house, on the farm adjoining his own, thirty miles from Washington) each day, from the 2d to the 7th of March, inclusive. By the aid of these two circumstances we have been able to show, by Thomas Davis, that accused was at home at work on the 28th of February—the day before Ash Wednesday; by Dr. Blanford, Frank Washington and Betty Washington, that he was there at work at home on the 1st of March; by Mary, Fanny, Emily and Henry L. Mudd, Betty and Frank Washington and Thomas Davis, that he was there on the 2d, 3d, 4th and 5th of March, at various hours of each day. At or within two hours of the time when Norton says he saw the accused enter the room at the National (half past 10 A. M., 3d of March), Mary, Emily, Fanny and Henry L. Mudd, Frank and Betty Washington, Thomas and John Davis, all testify most emphatically to having seen him at his house, on his farm, or at his father's house adjacent to his own—six hours' ride from Washington! We have shown, too, by Mary Mudd, that the accused has always worn a lead-colored hat whenever she has seen him this year, and that she has seen him almost daily; and by Henry Mudd, Dr. Blanford and Mary Mudd, that neither he nor his father owns a rockaway. Now, Norton either saw the accused enter his room on the morning of the 3d of March, or not at all, for his evidence, clinched as to the date by the record of the Supreme Court, excludes the supposition that he *could* have been mistaken *as to the day*. Nor can these eight witnesses for the defense be mistaken as to the day, for the incidents by which they recollect Mudd's presence at home, fix the time in their memories exactly. With all this evidence before the Court, it can not hesitate to hold the *alibi* established beyond all cavil.

The only other item of evidence as to anything done or said by Dr. Mudd, or by anybody, before the assassination, tending in the least to show him implicated in the conspiracy, is the evidence of *Daniel J. Thomas*, who says that several weeks before the assassination he met Mudd

at the house of his neighbor, Downing, and there, in the course of conversation, Mudd said (laughingly) that "Lincoln and his whole Cabinet, and every Union man in the State of Maryland, would be killed within six weeks." Witness said he wrote to Col. John C. Holland, provost marshal of that district, at Ellicott's Mills, before the assassination, advising him of Mudd's statement. But Col. Holland says he got a letter from witness about that time, and there was not a word of the statement in it, nor a reference to the accused, nor to any statement by anybody about killing anybody. Thomas says he told his brother, Dr. Thomas, of the declaration before the President was killed, but his brother says emphatically he did not tell him until after Mudd's arrest—the boot found at Mudd's house having been named in the same conversation. Thomas says he told Mr. Downing about it before the assassination, but Downing says emphatically he did not tell him a word about it *at any time*. Downing also says that he himself was present every moment of the time Mudd and Thomas were together at his house, and heard every word said by either of them, and Mudd did not make that statement, nor refer to the President, or the Cabinet, or the Union men of Maryland, at all, nor say a word about anybody being killed. He says, however, Mudd, when Thomas was bragging and lying about being a provost marshal, did tell him, "he was a jack," which insult was doubtless an incentive to the invention of the calumny. But it was not the *only* incentive. Thomas knew that if that lie could be palmed off on the Judge Advocate and the Court for truth, it might lead to Mudd's arrest and conviction as one of the conspirators. He had, on Tuesday, before Mudd's arrest, and before this lie was coined and circulated, been posting handbills, containing the order of the War Department offering liberal rewards for any information leading to the arrest of Booth's accomplices, and he then doubtless conceived the idea of at once getting reward in money from the Government for his information, and revenge on Mudd for his insult in Downing's house.

That he gave that evidence corruptly is shown by Wm. Watson, John R. Richardson and Benjamin Naylor, who say that Thomas, after testifying against Mudd, went to see them, and said that "*if Dr. Mudd was convicted upon his testimony, he would then have given conclusive evidence that he gave the information that led to the detection of the conspirator!*" "*He then asked Mr. Benjamin J. Naylor if he did not mention to him and Gibbons, before the killing of the President, the language that Dr. Mudd had used. Mr. Naylor said that he had never done it before or after!*" "*He said his portion of the reward ought to be $10,000—and asked me (Watson) if I would not, as the best loyal man in Prince George's county, give him a certificate of how much he ought to be entitled to.*" The testimony of Richards, and of Eli J. Watson, coupled with Thomas' testimony in denial of these statements, fill the record of infamy of this false witness.

To accumulate evidence that Thomas' statement is utterly unreliable, the defense brought over twenty of his neighbors, who testified that he could not be believed on oath—among whom were Naylor, Roby, Richards, Orme, Joseph Waters, John Waters, J. F. Watson, Eli Watson, Smith, Baden, Dickens, Hawkins, Monroe and others, of undisputed loyalty, nearly all of whom had known him from boyhood. His brother, Dr. Thomas, testifies that he is at times deranged; and Dr. George Mudd says that he is mentally and morally insane. And, although Thomas' evidence was the most important in the case against Dr. Mudd, the Judge Advocate has not seriously attempted to sustain him—has not tried to show that he ever told or hinted at this story to anybody before the assassination—and has not asked one of the scores of witnesses for the prosecution in attendance from Thomas' neighborhood a question as to his reputation for veracity—except Wm. Watson, who said it was decidedly bad. A feeble attempt was made to sustain him, by endeavoring to show that he was a zealous supporter of the Administration, and that, *therefore*, the general voice of his community was against him. But we showed that he was a rebel at the beginning of the war, and an opponent of the Administration at the last election—and then the Judge Advocate dropped him!

This is all the evidence of every act or word done or said by any body, prior to the assassination, tending in the remotest degree to connect Mudd with the conspiracy. It consists, in large part, of the testimony of the five negroes, as to the Confederate officers frequenting Mudd's house last year and the year before—two of them, Milo and Mary Simms, as to Surratt's visiting his house last year—of Evans, as to Mudd's going to Surratt's house last winter—of Evans and Norton, as to Mudd's being here on the 3d of March—of Weichmann, as to the interview between Mudd, Booth and Surratt, about the middle of January, and of Thomas, as to Mudd's prediction of the assassination in March. I venture to say that rarely in the annals of criminal trials has the life of an accused been assailed by such an array of false testimony as is exhibited in the evidence of these nine witnesses—and rarely has it been the good fortune of an innocent man, arraigned and on trial for his life, to so confute and overwhelm his accusers. I feel it would be a waste of time, and an imputation on the intelligence of the Court to delay it with fuller discussion of the evidence of these witnesses, and feel sure it will cast their testimony from its deliberations, or recollect it only to reflect how foully and mistakenly the accused has been assailed.

Having now discussed all the evidence adduced that calls for discussion, or may by possibility be relied on as showing Mudd's acquaintance with Booth, or connection with the conspiracy, and having, I think, shown that there is no reliable evidence that he ever met Booth before the assassination but once on Sunday, and once the day following, in November last, I will proceed to a consideration of the testimony relied on to show that he knowingly aided the escape of the assassin.

First. Why did Booth go to Dr. Mudd's and stop there from daybreak till near sundown on his flight? I answer, because he had a broken leg, and needed a physician to set it. And as to the *length* of the stay, the wonder is he was able to ride off on horseback with his broken and swollen limb at all—not that he took ten hours' rest. The Court will observe from the map in evidence, that Booth, taking Surrattsville in his route to Pope's creek, opposite Matthias Point, where he crossed the Potomac (Capt. Doherty), traveled at least eight or ten miles out of his way to go, after leaving Surrattsville, by Dr. Mudd's. (See Dyer's testimony.) Would he have gone that far out of his route to the Potomac crossing if he had not broken his leg? Or was it part of his plan to break it? Obviously, he could not in advance have planned to escape by crossing the *Patuxent*, nor to evade his pursuers by lying concealed in Charles county, within six hours' ride of Washington. He must, as a sane man, have contemplated and planned escape across the Potomac into Virginia, and thence South or abroad; and it could never have been part either of the plan of abduction, or of that of assassination, to go the circuitous route to a crossing of the Potomac by Bryantown or Dr. Mudd's. So that the fact of Booth going to the house of the accused and stopping to get his leg set and to rest, does not necessarily lead to any conclusion unfavorable to the accused.

Booth got there, with Herold, about daybreak (Frank Washington). He usually wore a mustache (see photograph), but he then wore heavy whiskers, and had his face muffled in a shawl, so as to disguise him. The disguise was kept up all day. (Col. Wells.) He was taken to a lounge in the hall, and then to a front room up stairs. where the broken bone was set, where a fee of $25 was paid for the service, and where, it is probable, he slept most of the day. They represented that the leg had been broken by a fall of the horse; that they had come from Bryantown, and were going to Parson Wilmer's. After breakfast accused went to his field to work. Herold, whom Mudd had never met (Colonel Wells), came down to breakfast and dinner with the family, and after dinner he and Mudd went off together to the house of Mudd's father to get a family carriage to take the wounded man to the house of Parson Wilmer, five miles off, at Piney Chapel. (Lovett Wells.) Now, can any man suppose for a moment that Mudd, at this time, had the slightest suspicion or intimation of the awful tragedy of the night before? Could he, knowing or suspecting the crime or the criminal, have thus recklessly given himself up to arrest and trial, by publicly aiding the escape of the assassin? Could he have been ready to expose his old father to suspicion by thus borrowing his carriage, which would have been noticed by every man, woman and child on the road, to carry off the assassin? Impossible! I need nothing more of the Court than its consideration of this fact, to clear the accused of all suspicion of having, up to that time, known or suspected that a crime had been committed by the crippled stranger, whom he was thus openly and kindly seeking to aid.

But the carriage could not be got, and Mudd and Herold rode off toward Bryantown to get one there. Col. Wells thinks the accused told him that Herold turned back when getting one and a-half miles from the elder Mudd's house, saying he could take his friend off on horseback.

Betty Briscoe and Eleanor Bloyce, however, say they saw a man riding toward Bryantown with the accused, who turned back at the bridge at the edge of the town.

Mudd made some purchases of calico and other articles, and heard of the assassination. (Bean.) It was not generally known then among the citizens who was the assassin. (Bean, Roby, Trotter, B. W. Gardiner, M. L. McPherson, John McPherson.) In fact it was not generally known with certainty at the theater, or in Washington, Friday night, whether Booth was the murderer. (Gobright.) In Bryantown it was commonly understood that Boyle, a noted desperado of that region, who assassinated Capt. Watkins last fall, was one of the assassins. (M. L. McPherson, Bean, Trotter, Roby.) It was not known that the murderer had been tracked into that neighborhood. (Bean, Dr. Geo. Mudd.) Lieutenant Dana told Dr. Geo. Mudd, Saturday afternoon, that Boyle assassinated Mr. Seward, and Booth the President, but that he thought Booth had not then got out of Washington. Even next day (Sunday) it was reported there that it was *Edwin Booth* who killed the President.

The accused left Bryantown about four o'clock to return home. *Betty Briscoe* says the same man who had turned back at the bridge stopped in the edge of a branch, which the road crosses a couple of hundred yards from the bridge, until Mudd returned from the town, and then they rode off together across the branch, "up the road." But *Booz* says he saw Mudd a couple of hundred yards beyond that crossing leisurely going through the farm *Booz* lives on, by a near-cut which he usually traveled, *alone;* and that he would himself have probably noticed the man at the crossing, which was in full view of where he was, had he been waiting there; and would have *certainly* noticed him had he been with Mudd traveling the main road, when Mudd turned into the cut-off through the farm—but he saw no one but the accused. *Susan Stewart* also saw Mudd in the by-road returning home alone, and did not see any man going the main road, which was in full view. I call the attention of the Court to the plat by which the branch and these roads are shown, and to the fact that there is no road turning off from the main road between Booz's place and Bryantown, except the side road by Booz's house. If further refutation of the testimony of Betty Briscoe on this point be required, it is found in the evidence of *Primus Johnson*, who saw Herold pass the elder Mudd's in the main road, going toward the house of the accused, and some time after that, himself caught a horse in the pasture, and rode toward Bryantown, and met and passed Dr. Mudd coming leisurely from Bryantown, *alone, at Booz's farm;* and that from the time he saw Herold until he met and passed Mudd was full an hour and a-half. And in the evidence of *John Acton*, who was on the roadside, three miles from Bryantown, when Herold passed, at between three and four o'clock, and who remained there an hour, and Dr. Mudd did not go by in that time. Acton also says, that, between the time Herold and Mudd went

toward Bryantown and the time Herold returned alone, was but three-quarters of an hour. From the fact that Herold could not have ridden to the bridge and back in that time (six miles), it seems highly probable that he did not go to the bridge, but turned back about where Colonel Wells thinks Mudd said he did. But however that may be is not important, as it is certain from the evidence of these four witnesses that Herold did not wait at the branch for Mudd's return from Bryantown.

As Mudd rode home, he turned out of his way to see his neighbor, *Hardy* (who lives half-way between the house of the accused and Bryantown), about some rail-timber he had engaged there. The house is not in view of the road, a clump of pines intervening. He told Hardy and Farrell of the news. Hardy says:

"He said to me that *there was terrible news now*, that the President and Mr. Seward and his son had been assassinated the evening before. Something was said in that connection about Boyle (the man who is said to have killed Captain Watkins) assassinating Mr. Seward. I remember that Booth's name was mentioned in the same connection, and I asked him if Booth was the man who had been down there. His reply was that he did not know whether it was that man or one of his brothers; he understood that he had some brothers. That ended the conversation, except that *he said it was one of the most terrible calamities that could have befallen the country at this time.*

"Q. Did you say that it was understood or said that Booth was the assassin of the President? A. There was some such remark made, but I do not exactly remember the remark."

They both say he seemed heartily sorry for the calamity, and that he said he had just come from Bryantown, and heard the news there. Hardy says he stayed there only about ten minutes, and left just about sundown. Farrell corroborates Hardy as to the conversation, except that he reports nothing as to Boyle's name being mentioned; but he says the conversation was going on when he joined Hardy and Mudd. He says the house is less than a quarter of a mile off the road, and that accused stayed there about fifteen minutes.

Now, I ask the Court, what is there up to this point to indicate that Mudd knew or had any suspicion that the broken-legged man was implicated in the crime? If there is anything in proof showing that fact, I fail to find it. True, he had met Booth twice in November— five months before. Had seen him that dark, cloudy morning, at day-break, faint with fatigue and suffering, muffled in his shawl and disguised in a heavy beard; had ministered to him in the dim light of a candle, whose rays struggled with the dull beams of the opening day; had seen him, perhaps, sleeping in the darkened chamber, his mustache then shaved off, his beard still on, his effort at concealment still maintained. (Wells.) And here let me remind the Court, that there is nothing in the evidence showing that Booth *spoke a word*, but where either of the men are referred to as saying anything, "the smaller man" was the spokesman. Let it be remembered, too, that Booth was an actor, accustomed by years of professional practice to disguise his person, his features, and his tones, so that if Mudd had been an intimate associate, instead of a mere casual acquaintance, it would have been easy for Booth to maintain a disguise even when subjected to close scrutiny under circumstances favorable to recognition. If the Court will also consider with what delicacy a physician and a gentleman would naturally refrain from an obtrusive scrutiny of a patient coming to his house under the circumstances, they will appreciate how easy it was for Booth to avoid recognition, and how probable that Mudd had no suspicion who his patient was. Had he recognized Booth before he went to Bryantown, and heard there that name connected with the "terrible calamity," would he have jogged quietly home, stopping to chat with Booz, to look after his rail-timber, to talk of the names of the assassins with his neighbors? Unless the Court start out with the hypothesis of guilt, and substitute unsupported suspicion for proof—which I respect them too highly to fear for a moment they will do—they can not charge him with a recognition of Booth before he returned home from Bryantown.

Hardy says it was about sundown when Mudd left; Farrell says about 5 o'clock. He had two miles to ride home. It must have been sundown when he got home, and the men had just gone. Betty Washington says that three or four minutes after Herold (the last of the two) disappeared toward the swamp, Mudd came through the hall to the kitchen, and was then first seen by her after his return from Bryantown. The other servants had not come from the field when the men started, and we are, therefore, left to that one witness to show that the statement of Simon Gavacan, one of the detectives, who says "*he thinks*" Mudd said he went with them part of the way, is incorrect. It is inconsistent, too, with Mudd's statement to Col. Wells on the subject, which is as follows: "The Doctor said that as he came back to the house he saw the person, that he afterward supposed to be Herold, passing to the left of the house, and toward the barn or the stable; that he did not see the other person at all after he left him at the house, which was about 1 o'clock, I think." This statement, and that of Betty Washington, last above quoted, coincide with, and strengthen each other.

It is true, Dr. Mudd did say to all, who asked him, that he had shown Herold the way to Parson Wilmer's by the short route, but this was in the morning, soon after the parties reached the house, and before the idea of the carriage appears to have been suggested. This is shown by the statement of Col. Wells, who says that the accused, *in the same conversation in which he said that Booth and Herold had just gone from the house as he came up*, told him that " Herold, the younger of them, asked him the direct route to Piney Chapel, Dr. Wilmer's, saying that he was acquainted with Dr. Wilmer." He described the main traveled road, which leads to the right of his house, and was then asked if there was not

a shorter or nearer road. He said, " Yes; there is a road across the swamp that is about a mile nearer, I think;" he said it was five miles from his house to Piney Chapel by the direct road, and four miles by the marsh, and undertook to give him (as he said) a description by which they could go by the nearer route. He said that the directions were these: "They were to pass down by his barn, inclining to the left, and then pass straight forward in a new direction across the marsh, and that, on passing across the marsh, they would come to a hill; keeping over the hill, they would come in sight of the roof of a barn, and, letting down one or two fences, they would reach the direct road."

The accused meant, of course, that this inquiry and explanation occurred before his return to the house from Bryantown, and so Col. Wells understood him, for he so in effect says. The statement of the accused to Dr. George Mudd, the next day after Booth left, is to the same effect. He said: "That these parties stated that they came from Bryantown, and were inquiring the way to the Rev. Dr. Wilmer's," thus putting their inquiry for the route to Parson Wilmer's in direct connection with their early explanation as to whence they came.

I have no doubt that Gavacan, the detective, recollects an *inference* which he, and, perhaps, also his associate detective, Williams, drew from Dr. Mudd saying that he had shown Herold the route to Parson Wilmer's; that he showed it as Booth and Herold were leaving. But the inferences of detectives, under the strong stimulus of prospective rewards, are inferences generally of guilt; and that these gentlemen were not free from the weaknesses of their profession, and that they grossly misrepresented Dr. Mudd in other important statements, will presently be shown to the satisfaction of the Court.

Now, if Mudd did not know, when he talked with Hardy about the assassination, and spoke of Booth in connection with it, that the assassin was at his house—as I think the evidence shows he did not—then when did he first suspect it? Col. Wells says his *inference* was, from something the accused said, that he suspected the crippled man to be Booth before he left the premises. The evidence not only shows that when Mudd returned Booth had gone out of sight, but it also shows what fact it was that, added to the undue excitement of the strangers, and to the fact that the crippled man shaved off his moustache, thoroughly aroused his suspicion. It was the fact that *his wife said to him, after they left, that, as the crippled man came down to go, his false whiskers became detached from his face.* (Lieut. Lovett.) *When* she told him this, and what he said or proposed to do, *was not shown* by the prosecution, and, by the rules of evidence, *could not be* by the defense. But that was a fact which could not probably have been communicated to Mudd by his wife until Booth had gone.

In the evidence adduced as to Mudd's subsequent conduct and statements, I need only call the attention of the Court to two points, for in it there is nothing else against him: 1st. He did not tell, on *Tuesday*, that the boot was there, far down in the leg of which was found, by the officers, "J. Wilkes," written in pale ink. I answer, the boot was not found by his wife until several days after the assassin left, and was then found in sweeping under the bed. (Hardy.) We have every reason to suppose it was not found until after Tuesday, for the accused, on Friday, before a question was asked, or a word communicated to him, *told of the boot himself, and had it produced,* and said, in presence of his wife, it was found by her after the officers were there before. (Hardy.)

2d. Of the three detectives who went to the house of accused Tuesday, *Williams* says: Accused denied throughout that two men had been there; yet he says, on cross-examination, that accused, in the same conversation, pointed out the route the men had taken toward Wilmer's. *Gavacan* said he at first denied two men had passed there, and then admitted it. Lloyd says he denied it from beginning to end, on Tuesday. But *Lieut. Lovett,* who went with and in command of these detectives, speaking of this interview on Tuesday, says: "*We first asked whether there had been any strangers at his house, and he said there were.*" The three detectives are manifestly mistaken; either from infirmity of memory, or from some less pardonable cause, they have failed to recollect and truthfully render what Dr. Mudd did say on that subject.

The commentators upon the law of evidence give a caution which it may be well for the Court to observe. They admonish us how easy it is for a corrupt witness to falsify a conversation of a person accused, and as the accused can not be heard, how difficult, if not impossible, contradiction is. How easy for an honest witness to misunderstand, or in repeating what was said, to substitute his own language or inference for the language which was really used, and thus change its whole meaning and import. In no case can the caution be more pertinent than in this. The very phrensy of madness ruled the hour. Reason was swallowed up in patriotic passion, and a feverish and intense excitement prevailed most unfavorable to a calm, correct hearing and faithful repetition of what was said, especially by the suspected. Again, and again, and again the accused was catechised by detectives, each of whom was vieing with the other as to which should make the most important discoveries, and each making the examination with a preconceived opinion of guilt, and with an eager desire, if not determination, to find in what might be said the proofs of guilt. Again, the witnesses against the accused have testified under the strong stimulus of a promised reward for information leading to arrest and followed by convictions. (See order of Secretary of War.) At any time and in any community, an advertisement of rewards to informers would be likely to be responded to—at a time, and on an occasion like this, it would be a miracle if it failed of effect. In view of these considerations, the Court can not be too vigilant in its scrutiny of the evidence of these detectives, or too circumspect in adjusting the influence to be given to it.

No more effective refutation of this statement, that Mudd denied on Tuesday that two strangers had been at his house, can be given than to ask how came Lieut. Lovett and the detectives at Dr. Mudd's? They did not scent out the track for themselves. They were at Bryantown on Saturday, and were at fault, and had they been let alone, would probably have remained at fault, and not have gone to Dr. Mudd's. By whom and when was the information given which brought them there? The next morning after the startling news of the assassination reached him, the accused went to Dr. George Mudd, a man of spotless integrity and veracity, and of loyalty unswerving through all the perilous and distressing scenes of the border war, and fully informed him of all that had occurred—the arrival of the two strangers, the time and circumstances under which they came, what he had done for them, the suspicions he entertained, when they departed, and what route they had taken; and requested him, on his behalf and in his name, to communicate this information to the military authorities on his return that day to Bryantown. Dr. George Mudd *did* make the communication as requested, on Monday morning, to Lieut. Dana, and further informed him of Dr. Samuel Mudd's desire to be sent for any further information which it might be in his power to give. In consequence of this, *and of this alone,* Lieut. Lovett and the detectives did, on *Tuesday,* go to the house of the accused, accompanied by Dr. George Mudd, who prefaced his introduction by informing the accused that, in accordance with his request, he had brought Lieut. Lovett and the detectives to confer with him in reference to the strangers who had been at his house Saturday. Of these facts there is no doubt or dispute. They stand too prominently upon the record to be ignored or evaded. But for this information the detectives would not have been at the house of the accused at all. They came at his request, and when they came it is absurd and idle to say that he denied, almost in the presence of Dr. George Mudd, who had been his messenger and was then in the house, that the two strangers had been there. On the contrary, the evidence shows he imparted all he knew, and pointed out the route which the strangers took when they left—but which Lieut. Lovett and the detectives did not at once pursue, because they chose to consider his statement uncandid, and intended to put them upon a false scent. Indeed, so accurate was the description given by the accused to Lieut. Lovett, Tuesday, of the persons who had been at his house, that *the lieutenant says he was satisfied, from Mudd's description, they were Booth and Herold.*

It was in great part by reason of Dr. Mudd's having delayed from Saturday night until Sunday noon to send to the authorities at Bryantown information as to the suspected persons who had been at his house, that he was arrested and charged as a conspirator; and yet I assert this record shows *he* moved more promptly in communicating his information than they did in acting on it. His message was communicated to Lieut. Dana Monday morning. *Tuesday*, Lieut. Lovett and the detectives came, and that officer got such information from Dr. Mudd as convinced him the suspected persons were Booth and Herold, and yet it was not until Col. Wells came, on *Saturday*, that an energetic effort was made to find the route of the assassin. On that day, Dr. Mudd himself went with that officer, and followed the tracks on the route indicated beyond the marsh into a piece of plowed ground, where the tracks were lost. But Col. Wells had got the general direction, and it was in consequence of the information sent by the accused to the authorities the day after Booth left his house, that he was tracked to the Potomac.

But the evidence does not show that Dr. Mudd delayed at all in communicating his information, for it does not show *when* his wife told him of the false whisker of the crippled man. But, admit she told him on Saturday evening, as soon as the men left. It was four miles to Bryantown, and his wife may have feared to be left alone that night. Boyle, who haunted that neighborhood, was understood by Dr. Mudd to have been one of the assassins (Hardy), and may not his or his wife's fears of the vengeance of that desperado have prevented him *communicating his suspicions direct and in person* to the officer at Bryantown? He told Dr. George Mudd next day, when asking him to go to the authorities with the information, to caution them not to let it be publicly known that *he* had volunteered the statement, lest he might be assassinated in revenge for having done it.

Having thus presented and discussed somewhat in detail the testimony in this case, I now ask the indulgence of the Court while I briefly review some of its leading features.

Booth and Mudd met first in November last at church, near Bryantown, casually, and but for a few minutes. Their conversation was in presence of many others, including men of unquestioned loyalty. Next morning, Booth left Dr. Queen's, rode by Mudd's, talked of buying his farm, got him to show him over to Gardiner's, a quarter of a mile off, where he bought a horse, Mudd manifesting no interest in the purchase. They rode away together toward Mudd's house, and toward Bryantown, where Gardiner found Booth next morning at the village hotel. Booth was again at Dr. Queen's in the middle of December. But the evidence shows that he did not go into Mudd's neighborhood, or seek or see him. So far as we dare speak from the evidence—and we should dare speak from nothing else—that is all the intercourse between Mudd and Booth in that neighborhood before the assassination.

What was there in that to attract attention or excite remark toward Mudd more than to Dr. Queen or Mr. Gardiner, or any other gentleman in Charles county, to whom Booth had been introduced, and with whom he had conversed? All that is shown to have passed between them was perfectly natural and harmless, and nothing is to be presumed which was

not shown. True, they *might* have talked of and plotted assassination; but *did* they? Is there, in the intercourse which had thus far occurred, any incident from which such a deduction could be drawn, or which would justify a suspicion that any such thing was thought of or hinted at? Nor did they ever meet again *anywhere* before the assassination, unless the testimony of Weichmann is to be accepted as true, which, upon this point, at least, is quite unworthy of credence. He swears to having met Dr. Mudd and Booth, in the city of Washington, about the middle of January—certainly after the holidays. But it is in proof by many witnesses, who can not be mistaken, have not been impeached, and who unquestionably stated the truth, that Dr. Mudd was from home but one night from the 23d of December to the 23d of March, and that night at a party in his own neighborhood. If this be so, and there is no reason to doubt it, then Weichmann's statement can not be true. The mildest thing that can be said of him, as of Norton, is, that he was mistaken in the man. That which was attempted to be shown by this contradicted witness (Weichmann) was, that Dr. Mudd and Booth, who were almost strangers to each other, met Surratt, to whom Booth was unknown, at the National Hotel, and within half an hour after the meeting, plotted the assassination of the President, his Cabinet, the Vice-President, and General Grant—all this in Washington, and in the presence of a man whom one of the supposed conspirators knew to be an employee of the War Department, and had reason to believe was a Government detective! It is monstrous to believe any such thing occurred. It outrages all that we have learned of the philosophy of human nature, all that we know of the motives and principles of human actions. And yet, if Mudd was not then and there inducted into the plot, he never was. He never saw Booth again until after the assassination, and never saw any of the other conspirators at all. Twice, then, and twice only—unless the Court shall accept the testimony of Weichmann against the clear proofs of an *alibi*, and then only three times—he and Booth had met. None of these meetings occurred later than the 15th of January. They are shown to have been *accidental* and *brief*. The parties had but little conversation, and portions of that little have been repeated to the Court. So far as it has been disclosed, it was as innocent as the prattle of children, and not a word was breathed that can be tortured into criminality—not a word or an act that betokens malign purposes. Against how many scores of loyal persons, even in this community, may stronger evidence be adduced than against Mudd, if the mere fact of meeting and conversing with Booth is to be accepted as evidence of guilt? Booth was a guest at the National Hotel—intelligent, agreeable, of attractive manner, with no known blemish on his character as a man or a citizen. He had the *entree* of the drawing-rooms, and mingled freely with the throngs that assembled there. His society, so far from being shunned, was courted; and the fairest ladies of the land, the daughters of distinguished statesmen and patriots deemed it no disparagement to them to accept his escort and attentions. It is not extravagant to say, that hundreds of true, Union-loving, loyal people in this and in other cities, were on terms of cordial and intimate association with him. And why should they not have been? He was under no suspicion. They did not shun him. Why should Mudd? And why shall what was innocent in them be held as proof of guilt in him? Let it be remembered, in this connection, that Dr. Mudd's house was searched and his papers seized; that Surratt's house was seized and searched; that all the effects of Booth, Atzerodt, Arnold, Herold, Spangler, and Mrs. Surratt, that could be found, were seized and examined; and among them all not a letter, a note, a memorandum, not the scrape of a pen by any person or in any form, has been found implicating Dr. Mudd. Let it further be remembered, that all these persons have been subjected to repeated examinations, under appalling circumstances, by various officials of the Government, eager to catch the faintest intimation of Mudd's complicity, and that not one of them has mentioned or hinted at his name. Let it also be remembered, that anonymous letters have been picked up in railroad cars, found in pigeon-holes at hotels, rescued from the waves, and that the continent has been traversed and the ocean vexed in search of proofs of the conspiracy, its instigators, leaders, and abettors, and that in all this written and oral testimony there is not a word making the remotest allusion to Dr. Mudd. The probabilities are as a thousand to one that he never knew, or heard, or imagined, of a purpose, much less plotted in a conspiracy, either to capture or to assassinate the President. There is not only a failure to show his connection affirmatively, but, if the rules of law be reversed, and guilt be presumed until innocence be shown, then, I say, he has carried his proofs in negation of complicity to a point as near demonstration as it is possible for circumstantial evidence to reach. I once more concede, that (if the Court accept Weichmann's statement) it is *possible* he may have talked treason and plotted assassination with Booth and Surratt, but it is indefinitely removed from the probable; and neither liberty nor life is to be forfeited upon either probabilities or possibilities. I can not bring myself to fear that this Commission will sanction what, in my judgment, would be so shocking and indefensible a conclusion.

If he and Booth had, at the alleged meeting in January, confederated for the perpetration of one of the most stupendous and startling crimes in the annals of human depravity, who can doubt that frequent meetings and consultations would thereafter have occurred, and that they would have increased in frequency as the time for the consummation of the atrocious plot approached? Yet, though within six hours' ride of each other, they had no meetings, no consultations, no intercourse, no communication, no concert, but were in total ignorance of each other's movements and purposes. Mudd was here the 23d of March, but he was not here for the purpose of seeing Booth, nor did he see him. He made no inquiry for him; did not call at his hotel; saw none of his associates; did not speak of him; did not, so far as appears, even think of him. On the 11th of April, only three days before the frightful tragedy was enacted, Mudd was at Giesboro, in sight of Washington. Booth was then at the National Hotel; and if Mudd was leagued with him, that was the time of all others, from the conception to the consummation of the deed, when he would have seen and conferred with him. If Mudd was a conspirator, he knew of Booth's presence here then; yet he did not come to the city—did not inquire for Booth, see him, hold communication with him, learn whether he was in Washington or Boston, Nassau or London. Three days only before the frightful tragedy—three days before the world was astounded by its enactment! Imagine, if you can—if he was a conspirator—what a tumult of thought and emotion must have agitated him then—what doubts and misgivings—what faltering and rallying of resolution—what invocations to "stop up the access and passage to remorse"—and then ask your own hearts and judgments if it is natural, or possible, that, at such a moment and under such circumstances, he could quietly have transacted the business that brought him to Geisboro, then turn his back upon Washington, indifferent to the failure or success of the events with which his own life, the happiness of his family, and all that was dear to him on earth, were bound up? If a conspirator, he knew what had been, and what was to be, done. He knew that the hour for the bloody business was at hand, and that everything depended upon the secrecy and success of its execution. Yet he was indifferent. He sought no interview with his supposed confederates—gave them no counsel or assistance—took no precautions for security—gave no signs of agitation or concern—but, in sight of the place and the agents selected for the enactment of the horrible deeds, turned his back upon them all, with an indifference that bordered upon idiocy, quietly trafficked at Geisboro, and returned to the seclusion of his family and farm. You know, gentlemen, that this is impossible. You know that it could not have happened without outraging every law of human nature and human action. You know that at such an hour his soul would have been shaken with the maddest storm and tempest of passion, and that no mere business affair on earth could have seduced his thoughts for a moment from the savage slaughter he had in hand. It would have engrossed all his thoughts, and shaped all his actions. No one can, in the strong light of the evidence, believe he *was* a conspirator.

I then confidently conclude that Dr. Mudd can not be convicted as a principal in the felony. He did not participate in its commission, and was more than thirty miles distant from the scene when it was committed. He can not be convicted as an accessory before the fact, for the evidence fails to show that he had any knowledge or suspicion of an intention to commit it. If, then, he is to be held responsible at all, it is an accessory after the fact. Does the evidence implicate him in that character? What is an accessory after the fact?

An accessory after the fact is when a person, knowing a felony to have been committed, receives, relieves, comforts, or assists him whom he knows to be the felon. He must know that the felon is guilty to make him an accessory. 1 *Chitt. Crim. Law*, 264.

Any assistance given to him to hinder *his being apprehended*, tried, or punished, is sufficient to convict the offender—as lending him a horse to escape his pursuers; but the assistance or support must be given in order to favor an illegal escape. 1 *Chitt. Crim. Law*, 265. If a man receives, harbors, or otherwise assists to elude justice, *one whom he knows to be guilty of felony*, he becomes thereby an accessory after the fact in the felony. 1 *Bishop's Crim. Law*, 487. Obviously, a man to be an accessory after the fact *must be aware of the guilt of his principal;* and, therefore, one can not become an accessory by helping to escape a prisoner convicted of felony, *unless he has notice of the conviction, or at least of the felony committed.* 1 *Bishop's Crim. Law*, 488. The charge against an accessory consists of two parts: First, of the felonious situation of th principal : and, secondly, of the guilty knowledge and conduct of the accessory. It will thus be seen that *knowledge of the crime committed, and of the guilt of the principal who is aided,* and aid and assistance *after acquiring that knowledge,* are all necessary to charge one as accessory after the fact.

Now let us apply the facts to the law, and see whether Dr. Mudd falls within the rule. On the morning after the assassination, about daybreak, Booth arrived at his house. He did not find the doctor on watch for him, as a guilty accomplice, expecting his arrival, would have been, but he and all his household were in profound sleep. Booth came with a broken leg, and his companion, Herold, reported that it had happened by the fall of his horse, and that they had come from Bryantown, and were going to Parson Wilmer's. The doctor rose from his bed, assisted Booth into the house, laid him upon a sofa, took him up stairs to a bed, set the fractured bone, sent him a razor to shave himself, permitted him to remain there to sleep and rest, and had a pair of rude crutches improvised for his use. For all this he received the ordinary compensation for services rendered to strangers. He then went to his field to work. After dinner, while the day was still dark, and Booth still resting disguised in his chamber, Mudd left the house with Herold. Even though he had known of the assassination, and that his patient was the

assassin, none of these acts of assistance would have made him an accessory after the fact. "*If a person supply a felon with food, or other necessaries for his sustenance, or professionally attend him sick or wounded, though he know him to be a felon, these acts will not be sufficient to make a party an accessory after the fact.*" *Wharton's American Criminal Law*, p. 73. But he did not know, and had no reason to suspect, that his patient was a fugitive murderer. The most zealous advocate would not venture to assert that the evidence warrants such conclusion; much less will it be assumed by one acting under the solemn responsibilities of judge. Down, then, to the time Mudd left home with Herold, after dinner, the evidence affords no pretext for asserting he was an accessory after the fact.

But if he was not then an accessory, he never was. It is shown that Herold turned back on the way to Bryantown, and when Mudd returned, he and Booth had gone. And the evidence does not show that he suspected them of having been guilty of any wrong, until his wife told him, after they had gone, that the whiskers of the crippled man fell off as he came down stairs to go. True, Booth was guilty, and Mudd had shown his companion the route to Wilmer's; which was the only thing done by Mudd, from first to last, that could have implicated him, *even had he from the first known the crime and the criminal.* But when he did that, he did not know either; for he did not know the crime until he went to Bryantown, nor have even the least suspicion of the criminal, until after Booth had gone. I have read you the law—the *scienter* must be shown. Things not appearing and not existing stand before the law in the same category; and the guilty knowledge not appearing in evidence, in the eye of the law it does not exist. In this case it is not only not shown, but is negatived by the evidence. The conclusion most unfavorable to Mudd which the evidence can possibly justify is, that, having had his suspicions thoroughly aroused Saturday night, he delayed until Sunday noon to communicate them to the authorities. "*If A knows B hath committed a felony, but doth not discover it, this doth not make A an accessory after the fact.*" 1st *Hale's Pleas of the Crown*, 618. "*Merely suffering a felon to escape will not charge the party so doing—such amounting to a mere omission.*" *Whar. Am. Crim. Law*, 73.

Can, then, Dr. Mudd be convicted as a conspirator, or an accessory before or after the fact, in the assassination? If this tribunal is to be governed in its findings by the just and time-honored rules of law, he can not; if by some edict higher than constitutions and laws, I know not what to anticipate or how to defend him. With confidence in the integrity of purpose of the Court and its legal advisers, I now leave the case to them.   SAM'L. A. MUDD.

ARGUMENT

IN

DEFENSE OF MICHAEL O'LAUGHLIN AND SAM'L ARNOLD,

BY

WALTER S. COX, ESQ.

Mr. President and Gentlemen of the Commission:

I have appeared before you as the sole counsel of the prisoner, Michael O'Laughlin, and, in part, represent the accused, Samuel Arnold. I now rise to their defense, deeply impressed with the gravity of their situation, and the importance of the duty it imposes.

For myself, I would say, that, born and nurtured under the ægis of the Federal Government, and schooled from childhood in that all-embracing patriotism which knows no section nor party when the interests or glory of my country is in question, I have been second to none, in attachment to the Federal Union, and in hostility to the rebellion which menaced its existence. I need hardly add, that no one could have more deplored and execrated the odious crime wrought upon the Chief Magistrate of the nation at a moment when the rewards of peace and sectional reconciliation were about to crown his arduous and patriotic labors. Nor was I willing to connect my humble name with this defense until I felt assured that the accused, for whom my service was first invited, was merely the victim of compromising appearances, but was wholly innocent of the great offense. And now that I have heard the evidence produced to you, I am strong in the conviction that, even if it appear that these *two* accused were ever beguiled, for a moment, to listen to the suggestions of this restless schemer, Booth, yet there is no blood on their hands, and they are wholly guiltless of all previous knowledge of, or participation in, that "arch deed of malice" which plunged the nation into mourning. I feel, therefore, that I stand here, not as the defender of assassins, but to rescue the innocent from the opprobrium of this great crime and a death of infamy.

I can not forbear the remark that, upon this trial, both the accused and their counsel have labored under disadvantages not incident to the civil courts, and unusual even in military trials. In both the civil courts and courts-martial the accused receives not only a copy of the charge, or indictment, in time to prepare his defense, but also a list of the witnesses with whom he is to be confronted. And, in the civil courts, it is usual for the prosecutor to state in advance the general nature of the case he expects to establish, and the general scope of the evidence he expects to adduce. By this the accused is enabled not only to apply intelligently the test of cross-examination, but also to know and show how much credit is due to the witnesses who accuse him. In this case the accused were aroused from their slumbers on the night before their arraignment, and, for the first time, presented with a copy of the charge. For the most part, they were unable to procure counsel until the trial had commenced; and, when counsel were admitted, they came to the discharge of their duties in utter ignorance of the whole case which they were to combat, except as they could gather it from the general language of the charge, as well as, for the most part, wholly unacquainted with the prisoners and their antecedents; and the consequence is, that the earlier witnesses for the Government were allowed to depart with little or no cross-examination, which, subsequent events show, was of vital importance to elicit the truth, and reduce their vagueness of statement to more of accuracy. And, I may add, that important parts of this testimony have consisted of the always suspicious statements of informers and accomplices, brought from remote places, whose antecedents and characters it is impossible for the prisoners to trace.

I am constrained, further, to notice the manner in which the trial has been conducted, and which, I think, can hardly have a parallel. The accused were arraigned upon a single charge. It described one offense of some kind, but, however specific in form, it seems to have been intended, like a purser's shirt, to fit every conceivable form of crime which the wickedness of man can devise. The crime is laid at Washington; yet we have wandered far away, like mariners who have lost their compass and can not see the polar star. We have been carried to the purlieus of Toronto and Montreal, and have skirted the borders of New York and Vermont, touching at Ogdensburg and St. Albans; have passed down the St. Lawrence, and out to sea; inspected our ocean shipping; have visited the fever hospitals of the British islands; have returned to the prison-pen of Andersonville; have seen the camp at Belle Isle and the historical Libby, and penetrated the secret councils of Richmond; have passed thence to the hospitals of the West, and ascended the

888

Mississippi, and, at length, terminated this eccentric career in the *woods* of New York Under
a charge against these prisoners of conspiring
to kill the President, and others, in Washington, Jefferson Davis and his associates have
been tried, and, in the judgment of many, convicted of starving, poisoning, arson, and other
crimes too numerous to mention.

I have apprehended that the counsel for the
accused would appear in a false position, from
their apparent acquiescence in this wide range
of inquiry, and, therefore, feel it due to myself, at least, to explain. I, for my part, have
felt no interest whatever in resisting the exposure of the misdeeds of the rebel authorities
and agents. My only concern has been to show
that my clients had nothing to do with the conspiracy set forth in this charge. To the best
of my ability, I have scrutinised and sifted
the evidence of that conspiracy, so far as necessary to their defense. With regard to other
matters, foreign to this issue, I have to say, in
the first place, the charge was artfully framed,
with a view to admit them in evidence. It imputes that the accused conspired, with Jefferson
Davis and others, to kill and murder the President, etc., *with intent to aid and comfort the insurgents, etc., and thereby aid in the subversion and
overthrow of the Constitution and laws of the
United States.* And, on the principle that other
acts, constituting distinct offenses, were sometimes admitted as proof of intent, these subjects, foreign to the main issue, have been put
in evidence. Although this seems to me a total
misapplication of the rule of practice, yet, the
Court having settled the principle in favor of
the prosecution in the early part of the trial,
it became useless to object to each separate
item coming within it afterward. It would
have been to tilt with windmills, for by no
possible ingenuity can these foreign matters be
used to the prejudice of the accused. I have
supposed that the only object of introducing
them was to bring to the public, in the shape
of sworn testimony, information of the practices of the rebel leaders, to which, however irregular the proceeding, I had no objection to
interpose. I can not, for a moment, suppose
that the object was to inflame prejudice against
the accused, because of their supposed remote
connection with the authors of all these evils,
and, for want of higher victims, to make them
the scapegoats for all the atrocities imputed to
the rebellion; to immolate them, to hush the
clamors of the public for a victim, or to ap-
pease the Nemesis that has recorded the secrets
of the Southern prison-houses, or the deadly
deeds wrought through fire and pestilence; for
such a proceeding would disgrace this Government in the eyes of all Christendom, as much
as assassination would disgrace the spurious
Government which has just vanished into thin
air.

To come to the issue before this Commission:
I had intended to confine myself to a simple
review of the evidence; but the anomalous
character of the charge, the uncertainty in
which we are left with reference to the positions to be taken by the Government, and the
general course of the investigation pursued,
admonish me that I should present some legal
considerations, at least, of a general character.
This Commission sits by authority of the order
of the President, offered in evidence, of September 24, 1862, which declared martial law
against all rebels and insurgents, their aiders
and abettors, and all guilty of any disloyal practice, affording aid and comfort to rebels against
the authority of the United States. The question of jurisdiction having been discussed at
length already, I shall not enter upon the question whether this Court has jurisdiction to try
the accused upon this charge, but, assuming
that for argument's sake, I shall endeavor to
ascertain the grounds and limits of that jurisdiction, and the mode in which it is to be exercised; and, with this view, shall first submit
some general reflections upon the character of
the offenses set forth in the charge and specification, as they are known to, and punishable
by, the civil law of the land, and then endeavor
to ascertain how far this Commission, in dealing with them, is to be guided and restrained
by that law.

Below the grade of treason, crimes are
ranged under two general heads, viz.: *felonies*
and misdemeanors. The class of felonies embraces the more heinous offenses, such as murder, arson, robbery, rape, etc.; and the idea
of felony is generally associated with that of
capital punishment, though, in point of fact,
they are not inseparably connected. The class
of misdemeanors embraces the offenses of lower
degrees, such as perjury, battery, libels, public
nuisances, and *conspiracies,* and, in short, all
crimes less than felonies. See 1 *Russell on
Crimes, pp.* 44, 45.

A *conspiracy,* then, belongs to the lower grade
of crime, and this whatever may be its object,
whether to commit a felony or a misdemeanor.
See 2 *Bishop on Criminal Law, sec.* 202.

A word as to the rationale of this rule. The
criminal law takes no notice of a mere mental
intent, unaccompanied by an act. It would be
equally impossible for human wisdom to scrutinize the operations of the mind with that
accuracy essential to justice, and to adapt a
scale of punishments to offenses which have
no visible proportions, no tangible effects.
Besides which the law makes a charitable allowance for that repentance and change of purpose which may intervene at any stage between
the first conception and the consummation of
crime. Between the intent and the consummation lies the wide region of *attempts* from the
first feeble preparation or movement, to the
striking of the deadly blow. A *conspiracy* is
scarcely more than an intent, at least in its
earliest stage. It is but the intent of several,
mutually communicated, perhaps with mutual
excitement, and encouragement, and consultation, and the chances of its falling short of an
overt attempt are multiplied just in proportion to
the number of wills between which concert is
necessary to successful action. If it can be
properly said to advance beyond a mere intent,
it is in the nature of an *attempt,* but it is so
manifestly inchoate and elementary, leaving
so wide a scope for the working of that lingering good which may prompt to change of pur-

pose, that the law wisely places it in the lower grade of offenses. "All indictable *attempts* (says *Bishop, vol.* 1, *sec.* 628), whether to commit felony or misdemeanor, are *misdemeanors.*" As the idea of capital punishment is ordinarily associated with that of felony, though the more appropriate idea is that of forfeiture of property, so with misdemeanor is associated the punishment of fine and imprisonment only. Says *Bishop, vol.* 1, *sec.* 626: "The ordinary and appropriate *common law* punishment *for misdemeanor* is fine and imprisonment, or either of them, at the discretion of the Court. It is inflicted in all cases in which the law has not provided some other specific penalty."

So much for the case of a conspiracy to commit a felony. How is it with a conspiracy to commit treason?

In looking at this charge and specification, one may doubt whether the terms "in aid of the said rebellion" are predicated of the conspiring, confederating, and combining, or of the acts charged to have been done in pursuance of said conspiracy and combination, etc. Inasmuch as giving aid and comfort to the enemies of the United States is one form of treason, it may be supposed that a mere unexecuted conspiracy may amount to giving aid and comfort to the enemies of the Government, and thereby become treason, and it may be supposed that to show such a conspiracy alone would be to make out a substantive case of treason, and that a party might be convicted thereof under this charge, although the evidence might show him to be not guilty of the crimes actually perpetrated in pursuance of the alleged conspiracy. Let us inquire, then, what is the law of treason.

The murder of the President of the United States, considered in itself, is no more, in the eye of the law, than the murder of any other citizen. Whether, however, that murder, perpetrated for the very object of overthrowing the Government or aiding its enemies, is treason, is a different question. I do not require to discuss that question. I pause, however, to remark that the term *"enemies,"* in this part of the Constitution, has been understood and adjudged to mean *public* and not *domestic* enemies. And Congress have legislated in exact accordance with this view; for in the act to suppress insurrection, to punish treason and rebellion, etc., of July 17, 1862, they provide, in the first section, that any one who shall commit the crime of treason, and shall be adjudged guilty thereof, shall suffer death; and in the second section, that any one convicted of giving aid and comfort to the existing rebellion, shall be punished by fine or imprisonment, or both. But whether murder, committed with the intent charged, is treason, either in the sense of levying war or of giving aid and comfort to the enemies of the United States, is immaterial to my present purpose. All that I need to maintain is, that a mere *conspiracy* to do this is *not* treason.

The Constitution, in art. 8, sec. 8, declares that treason against the United States shall consist only in levying war against them, or in adhering to their enemies, giving them aid and

comfort, and no person shall be convicted of treason unless on the testimony of two witnesses to the *same overt act*, or on confession in open court. To constitute treason, therefore, there must be an *overt act*. In the case of Bollman and Swartout, 4 *Cr., S. C. R.*, 75, in which these parties were charged with levying war against the United States in combination with Aaron Burr, the Supreme Court said, "To constitute that specific crime for which the prisoners now before the Court have been committed, war must be actually levied against the United States. However flagitious may be the crime of *conspiring* to subvert by force the Government of our country, such conspiracy *is not treason*. To conspire to levy war, and actually to levy war, are distinct offenses. The first must be brought into open action by the assemblage of men for a purpose treasonable in itself, or the fact of levying war can not have been committed." Again, "in the case now before the Court, a design to overturn the Government of the United States in New Orleans by force would have been, unquestionably, a design which, if carried into execution, would have been treason, and the assemblage of a body of men for the purpose of carrying it into execution would amount to levying war against the United States; *but no conspiracy for this object, no enlisting of men to effect it, would be an actual levying of war.*" In conformity with the principles now laid down, have been the decisions heretofore made by the judges of the United States. Judge Chase, in the case of Fries, stated the opinion of the Court to be, "that if a body of people *conspire and meditate an insurrection to resist or oppose the execution of any statute of the United States by force, they are only guilty of a high misdemeanor;* but if they proceed to carry such intention into execution by force, they are guilty of the treason of levying war," etc. So much for that species of treason which consists of *levying war*. The same rule prevails as to the other form, viz.: adhering to the enemy, and giving them aid and comfort. In the case of the *United States* vs. *Pryor*, 3 *Washington Circuit Court Reports*, p. 234, in which the accused was charged with adhering to the enemy, and giving them aid and comfort, by purchasing provisions for them, Judge Washington said: "That the prisoner went from the British seventy-four to the shore with an intention to procure provisions for the enemy, is incontestably proved, and, indeed, is not denied by his counsel. If this constituted the crime of treason, the motives which induced him to attempt the commission of it, and by which there are the strongest reasons to believe he was most sincerely actuated, would certainly palliate the enormity of it. But the law does not constitute such an act treason, even although these motives had not existed; and although *intentions and feelings as guilty as ever stained the character of the most atrocious traitor* were proved against the prisoner, can it be seriously urged that if a man, *contemplating an adherence to the enemy, by supplying them with provisions, should walk toward the market-house to purchase, or into his own fields to slaughter, whatever he might find there, but should, in fact, do neither the one nor the other of the intended acts, he has committed an overt act of adhering to the enemy? Certainly not. All rests in intention merely,* which our law of treason, in no instance, *professes to punish.*"

Thus we find it adjudged by the highest authorities, that under our Constitution, mere intention, or preparation, or conspiracy, to levy war or adhere to and aid and comfort the enemies of the Government, does not constitute treason, but *misdemeanor* only, and Congress seem clearly to recognize this view in their legislation, for by the act entitled "An act to define and punish certain conspiracies," approved July 21st, 1861, they enact "that if two or more persons, within any State or Territory of the United States, shall conspire together to overthrow, or to put down, or to destroy by force, the Government of the United States, or to levy war against the United States, or to oppose by force the authority of the United States," etc., "each several person so offending shall be guilty of a high crime, and upon conviction thereof, in any District or Circuit Court of the United States having jurisdiction thereof, shall be punished by a fine not less than $500, and not more than $5,000; or by imprisonment with or without hard labor, as the court shall determine, for a period not less than six months, nor greater than six years, or by both fine and imprisonment."

In other words, the offense is declared to be a high misdemeanor, and has annexed to it, by this law, the punishment appropriate to that degree of crime.

It results, then, that a mere conspiracy to commit either treason or felony, in this country, is a mere misdemeanor. Of course, these remarks apply only to unexecuted conspiracies. If the conspiracy to commit treason or felony be executed by the actual commission of the intended crime, it is held that the *misdemeanor is merged in the higher crime.* And the law is conceded to be, that if parties join and *continue* in a conspiracy, and different parts are assigned to the different members, and are executed, wholly or partially, each is responsible for everything done in pursuance of the common design.

But if, after a conspiracy is organized, but unexecuted, any party involved therein should withdraw and abandon it, and refuse to have any further connection with it, he is not responsible for any act done by the others in prosecution of the objects of the conspiracy afterward.

A conspirator may be said to be a compound of a principal and an accessory before the fact. Conspirators mutually incite, encourage, advise and instruct each other to the commission of a crime, and are thus accessories before the fact, and at the same time each expects to act as principal in some way or other.

In the case of a principal, so long as an act rests in bare intention, it is not punishable. So, if a man start out to commit a crime, as in the case put by Judge Washington in the case of the *United States* vs. *Pryor,* before cited, of a man going to market to purchase provisons, or going to his field to slaughter cattle for the enemy, but doing neither in fact.

And in the case of an accessory before the fact—that is, one who counsels, persuades or commands the commission of a crime—it is laid down in *Wharton's American Criminal Law,* citing 1 *Hale,* 618, that "the procurement (by an accessory) must *continue* till the consummation of the offense, for if *the procurer of a felony repent,* and before the felony is committed actually countermand his order, and the principal, notwithstanding, commit the felony, the original contriver will not be an accessory." The conspirator, then, who withdraws from a conspiracy before the same is executed, is in the position of a principal who has repented before acting, and of a procurer who has incited or ordered a crime, and withdrawn his order before it was acted upon. And his case is evidently still stronger where he was not the *principal conspirator,* who has incited and procured others, but was only one of the *subordinates,* himself incited and procured by others, and where, after yielding for the time to their influence, he withdraws from and resists their solicitations. The responsibility of such a person for the results of the conspiracy, had he remained in it, would have been less, morally, than that of the principal, and by his withdrawal is so much the more easily got rid of.

Another proposition to be borne in mind is, that if parties conspire for one object, however criminal, and some of them commit a crime different from that contemplated by the original conspiracy, the others are not involved in their guilt. The proposition is too evident for argument. An illustration of it is found in 1 *Bishop on Criminal Law,* section 265. He says: "Obviously, if two or more persons are lawfully together, and one of them commits a crime without the concurrence of the others, the rest are not thereby involved in guilt. So, if they are unlawfully together, or if several persons are in the actual perpetration, by a concurrent understanding, of some crime, and one of them, of his sole volition, not in pursuance of the main purpose, does another thing criminal, but in no way connected with this, *he only* is liable. Thus, if numbers are together, poaching, and join in an attack on the game-keeper and leave him senseless, then if one of them returns and steals the game-keeper's money, this one only can be convicted of the robbery."

So, in the analogous case of an accessory, it is said (1 *Hale,* 617), "If the accessory order or advise one crime, and the principal intentionally commit another, as, for instance, *to burn a house,* and instead of that he commit *a larceny,* or to commit a crime against A, and instead of that he commit the same crime against B, the accessory will not be liable."

These are the general principles which I desired to premise in reference to the general nature of crimes, and which might be applicable, more or less to this case.

I need scarcely add, that a material variance between the charge and the proof, as where one crime is charged and another proved, is fatal to the prosecution, and entitles the accused to an acquittal. Thus, if a burglary be alleged to have been committed in the house of J. Y., and it turned out in evidence to be the dwelling-house of J. S., the defendant must be acquitted for the variance. (*Archbold,* 95.)

So, in indictment for larceny of the goods of H, when they were proved to be the goods of H and E, the variance was admitted to be fatal. (*Commonwealth* vs. *Trimmer*, 1 *Mass. Rep.*, 476.)

So, a conspiracy against A is not sustained by proof of conspiracy against B or against the public generally. (See *Wharton*.) So, if a person be indicted for one species of killing, as by poisoning, he can not be convicted by evidence of a species of death entirely different, as by shooting, starving or strangling. (1 *Russell on Crimes*, 557.)

Still less can a conviction be had by proof of an offense which is entirely different in character.

While upon an indictment for a murder a man may be convicted of manslaughter, the essential crime being the homicide, it is very plain that he could not be convicted of an assault, false imprisonment or abduction; and upon a charge of conspiracy to murder, he could not be convicted of conspiracy to imprison or to abduct.

The same rule prevails in courts-martial. De Hart says (p. 364): "It is a distinction which runs through the whole criminal law, that it is enough to prove so much of the indictment as shows that the defendant has committed a *substantive crime therein specified;* but the offense, however, of which he is convicted must *be of the same class* with that with which he is charged." The general principles of the common law on this subject are adopted in the military code.

Let us next consider how far tribunals sitting by virtue of martial law can depart from the established law of the land in its distinctions between crimes and in its scale of punishments.

Military law, says De Hart (p. 17), is a rule for the government of military persons only; but *martial law* is understood to be that state of things when, from the force of circumstances, the military law is indiscriminately applied to all persons whatsoever. And Greenleaf says (vol. 3, p. 469, etc.): "It [martial law] extends also to a great variety of cases not relating to the discipline of the army, such as plots against the sovereign, intelligence to the enemy, and the like. It is founded *on paramount necessity,* and is proclaimed by a military chief, and when it is imposed upon a city or other territorial district, all their inhabitants and all their actions are brought within the sweep of its dominion." Almost everything in the shape of authority on the subject of martial law relates to that law as exercised in a foreign and hostile country. Even in that case it has certain limitations.

General Halleck, in his work on international law and the laws of war, in treating of the effects of military occupation, says (chap. 32, sec. 6):

"Although the laws and jurisdiction of the conquering State do not extend over such foreign territory, yet the laws of war confer upon it ample power to govern such territory, and to punish all offenses and crimes therein, by whomsoever committed. The trial and punishment of the guilty parties may be left to the ordinary courts and authorities of the country, or they may be referred to special tribunals organized for that purpose by the Government of military occupation, etc. It must be remembered that the authority of such tribunals has its source not in the laws of the conquering, nor in those of the conquered State, but, like any other powers of the Government of military occupation, in the laws of war; and *in all cases not provided for by the laws actually in force in the conquered territory,* such tribunals must be governed and guided by the principles of universal public jurisprudence." This plainly implies that where the cases are provided for by the local law, that should guide in the administration of criminal justice.

Professor Lieber, in his *Instructions for the Government of the Armies of the United States in the Field,* adopted by the War Department, says:

"Martial law in a hostile country *consists in the suspension by the occupying military authority of the criminal and civil law* and of the domestic administration and government *in the occupied place or territory,* and in the *substitution of military rule and force for the same,* as well as in the dictation of general laws, *as far as military necessity requires this suspension, substitution, or dictation."*

And Benet, p. 14, thus lays down the rule: "Martial law, then, is that military rule and authority which exists in time of war in relation to persons and things *under and within the scope of active military operations in carrying on the war, and which extinguishes or suspends civil rights and the remedies founded on them, for the time being, so far as it may appear to be necessary in order to the full accomplishment of the purpose of the war, the party who exercises it being liable in an action for any abuse of the authority thus conferred.* It is the application of military government—the government of force—to persons and property within the scope of it, according to the laws and usages of war, to the exclusion of the municipal Government in all respects *where the latter would impair the efficiency of military law or military action."*

The exercise of martial law is capable of being abused. It must, therefore, have some limits. It has no code but one single, vital, fundamental principle, which is alike its justification and its limit; and that is, necessity—not state nor political necessity, but *military* necessity. It is the same principle announced by Sir Boyle Roche, a member of the Irish Parliament and a breeder of Irish bulls, who, in the debate on the suspension of the *habeas corpus* act, said "he was in favor of surrendering a part of the Constitution, and even the whole of it if necessary, in order to save the remainder." As this alone justifies the suspension of the civil law of the land at all, so that suspension can not be legitimately carried further than is necessary to the efficiency of *military action* or *military law—i. e.,* of the law governing the military force.

If this is true of a military occupation of an enemy's country, how infinitely more binding in the case of martial law prevailing at home! When an enemy's country is conquered, all political powers therein cease, and a suspension of judicial functions also generally results.

22

There must be offenses unprovided for in such a state of things which can only be taken cognizance of by military courts established in virtue of the martial law, which is established and proclaimed by the very presence of a hostile army. Of course, revolts, insurrections, and plots against the conquering power would be wholly unprovided for in the laws of the conquered State, and must be necessarily dealt with by martial law. But all this is different when martial law exists at home. Treason, conspiracy, murder, in short, every crime, is already provided for by the civil law. When the law martial undertakes to deal with such offenses, it finds them already accurately defined in the written or common law of the land, and the appropriate punishment affixed by the same. It may find, and it certainly does find in the present case, legal courts duly constituted and in unobstructed operation. It invades the domain of the latter, wrests from them their jurisdiction, and seeks to deal with crimes which, I may say, it does not understand, for which it has no definitions, no graduated scale of penalties.

Clearly, nothing can justify this but the most urgent military necessity, and the requirements of *active military operations must be the measure of that departure from the civil law,* which would be legitimate and which could not be taken notice of subsequently, by that law, as an abuse.

In a beleaguered city, under martial law, one who is detected in signaling the enemy, or doing any thing to cripple the defenders, secretly or openly, may be shot down without trial, or dealt with by a military commission in the most summary way. But no one would maintain that such a commission could place a petty larceny, by a civilian, on the same footing as murder, and visit it with the death penalty. It would be a criminal abuse of power, simply because wholly unnecessary to the efficiency of military operations. And even acts of military hostility, committed during a period of invasion and siege, could not, after the enemy is repulsed, the siege raised, the danger passed, be punished by summary execution without trial.

The argument on this head may be summed up thus: The law of the land defines certain crimes. It establishes a distinction and gradation among them, and visits them with appropriate punishments. It also establishes the mode in which the accused shall be tried, and certain guarantees of fairness and justice. These distinctions between crimes and punishments and these guarantees are the right alike of the innocent and guilty, the injured public and the accused. If it be absolutely necessary to the repulse of a foreign or the reduction of a domestic enemy, by the military power of the country, persons within the scope of its operations may be both tried and punished in a manner different from the course of the civil law. But without such necessity they can not be so tried. And if the situation require such *trial,* still, *without such necessity,* the military authority *can not ignore but must adhere to, observe, and be guided by the civil law, in its distinctions between*

crimes, and in its measure of punishment. To disregard it without overruling military necessity, is unnecessarily to infringe public and private rights, and this is military oppression, which Professor Lieber says is not martial law, but is the abuse of the power that law confers.

Granting, then, for the sake of argument, that at the time of the President's assassination, when the rebellion was not yet subdued, when it was possible for its flickering and expiring hopes to be revived by this startling event, when the mysterious plot seemed to be aimed directly at the power of the Government to effect the purpose of the war, to suppress the rebellion and perpetuate its own existence, it was necessary to employ the machinery of martial law to pursue and bring to justice the perpetrators of the murder, and on account of difficulties, supposed or real, in the trial of the accused in a civil court, to subject them to a *trial* by a military commission, still the question recurs, how is this commission to deal with the accused? Now that "grim-visaged war hath smoothed his wrinkled front," that "bruised arms are hung up for monuments," that the only military *action* in progress consists in the disbanding and dispersion of the national forces, that even the rancors of civil strife are yielding to an universal aspiration for peace and fraternal union, can any man, on his conscience, say, that any *military exigency* requires this Commission to ignore the law of the land in regard to crimes and punishments, to condemn and punish, as treason, that which is not treason by the Constitution; to confound felonies with treason on the one side, or misdemeanors, on the other; to try for one offense and convict of another; to inflict punishments disproportionate to the crime, in view of the proportion between them established by the common law and universal understanding? Most clearly not. It will not do to assume that martial law, once conceded to be in force, has no limit. It is begging the whole question to assume that to concede the necessity of martial law is to concede the necessity of all its rigors and harsh contrasts with the civil law. In the able argument of Judge-Advocate Burnett on the plea of jurisdiction, on the trial of the Chicago conspirators, he says:

"Martial law can never be restricted by any defined lines, because it is the law of necessity, the law of self-defense, of self-preservation; it is a law to meet the *exigencies and necessities of great, unexpected emergencies in time of war;* and whatever law or rule of action becomes necessary to meet these emergencies is martial law."

He also cites Professor Greenleaf, who, in speaking of the difference between martial and military law, says:

"The tribunals of *both* are alike bound by the *common law of the land in regard to the rules of evidence, as well as to other rules of law, so far as they are applicable to the manner of proceeding;*" and adds: "As, for illustration, martial law, as now being administered, is, giving these prisoners a fair, impartial hearing, according to the strict rules of the civil law, in all questions of evidence, argument, etc.; it gives them the benefit of counsel, of processes to compel the attendance of witnesses; it allows them a clear and public trial, in open day, before their peers, and before just and honorable men. But under other circumstances and greater emergencies, it might have demanded that they be shot down in the streets, and without trial and without hearing, as in case they had gone forward in this conspiracy, attacked our camps, undertaken to release our prisoners, and burn the city."

Now, on what ground can martial law admit a trial at all? On what ground can its courts be bound to observe the common law rule of evidence and proceeding? On no other but this: That, by the law of the land, this is one of the rights of the accused of which he can not be deprived, unless there be a military necessity for it. But what reason is there applicable to form, which does not apply, with ten-fold force, to matters of substance? If the accused is entitled to be tried according to the forms of the common law, as far as applicable, how much more is he entitled to be judged and punished according to that law, where no departure from it, in that respect, is required by any military emergency.

But the Government officers seem to have tasked their ingenuity to invent a new species of crime—traitorous murder, traitorous conspiracy—murder which is something more than murder, yet something less than treason; a hybrid between them, partaking of both. On the same principle, stealing a percussion cap, with intent to use it against the Government, would be traitorous larceny, instead of petty larceny. And when we inquire by what code it is to be judged and punished, we are referred to the *common law of war.*

The common law of war! What a convenient instrument for trampling upon every constitutional guarantee, every sacred right of the citizen! There is no invention too monstrous, no punishment too cruel, to find authority and sanction in such a common law. Is it possible that American citizens can be judged and punished by an unwritten code, that has no definitions, no books, no judges or lawyers; which, if it has any existence, like the laws of the Roman Emperor, is hung up too high to be read?

I deny that the common law of war has anything to do with treason, or anything traitorous, *as such.* Treason, in any shape, is an offense against the civil government. The acts constituting the offense are dealt with by martial law, not as treason, but only as they interfere with military rule and operations. Such offenses as those charged are unknown to any common law of war. In short, the only common law of war, which can be admitted in this country against civilians, is the common law of the land, so far modified, only, as the military emergency of the hour requires.

I conclude, then, that, supposing this Commission to have lawful jurisdiction over the persons of the accused, for the purpose of trying them upon this charge, still the Commission are bound, in ascertaining the nature of the offense made out by the evidence, if any be proven, and in affixing a punishment to it, to follow and be guided by the law of the land, as administered in the civil courts.

The application of these general principles I shall reserve until I shall have discussed the evidence.

The evidence offers a very wide field to one inclined to collate, weigh, and comment on it, in detail, but I shall notice only so much as seems material to my case.

First, then, what are some of the facts in relation to the alleged conspiracy? The assassination of the President and other heads of Government, may have been discussed in the South, as a measure of ultimate resort, to retrieve the fortunes of the Confederacy, when at their lowest ebb; the rebel agents in Canada may have individually signified their approval of the measure, in the abstract, long since; but I undertake to maintain, upon the evidence, that there never was any final determination on the part of any person or persons, with whom any of these accused can possibly be connected, actually to attempt the life of the President, or other functionary, until a few days—about one week—before the murder; that no conspiracy for that object, such as is charged against the accused, was formed, or, at least, had any active existence, at any time during the month of March, as imputed in the charge and specification; and that if any conspiracy had ever been organized, for such object, at an earlier period, it did not contemplate the event, otherwise than contingently, and upon a contingency which never arrived until the period I have named, and was, meanwhile, completely in suspense and abeyance.

The specification imputes that the accused were incited and encouraged to the murder by Davis, Thompson, Clay, and others, and this is of the very essence of the charge.

The theory of the prosecution is, that Booth, who is acknowledged to have been the head, and front, and soul of the conspiracy, if there was one, was only the hireling tool of these rebel emissaries. I think he was probably something more, but it will not vary the result. I think he was probably actuated not only by the sordid hope of reward, but by a misguided, perverted ambition. Of moderate talents, but considerable ambition, of strong will and passions, and high nervous organization, accustomed to play parts, and those of a tragic character, he had contracted perverted and artificial views of life and duty, and aspired to be the Brutus, in real life, that he had been or seen on the boards. He well knew, however, that the act he contemplated would be execrated all the world over, except, *possibly,* among those whom he intended to serve. Therefore, whether pecuniary reward or false glory was his object, he could hope for neither until he was secure of their approbation. Whatever his principle of action, he was wholly without motive for so desperate an undertaking until he had, or supposed he had, the approval of the rebel authorities. When does the evidence tend to show that this was given? On this subject three principal witnesses have testified for the Government. None of them carry farther back than January last, the date when even an individual approval of the scheme of assassination was expressed by any of the rebel agents in Canada. The first witness, Richard Montgomery, represents Jacob Thompson as saying, in the summer of 1864, that he had his agents throughout the Northern States, and could, at any time, have President Lincoln, or any of his advisers, put out of the way. But it was only in the middle of January last that Thompson informed him that a distinct proposition for the President's assassination had been made to him, and that he was in favor of it, but was determined to defer his answer until he had consulted his Government at Richmond, and he was then only waiting their approval. Although the witness was in constant intercourse with those men in Canada, going back and forth, until shortly before his testimony was given, he was not able to state when these rebel agents considered themselves authorized to act in this matter. But in a conversation with Tucker, a few days after the assassination, the latter said, "it was too bad that the boys had not been allowed to act when they wanted to," which would indicate that the approval waited for from Richmond was not received in time for earlier action, and this the witness distinctly states to be his impression. He inferred from Tucker's remark that the approval had been received, and that the attempt had been delayed for its arrival.

In all this, Montgomery agrees exactly with Conover. The latter states that Thompson spoke to him in February on the subject of the removal of the President and others from office, by killing them, and offered him the chance of immortalizing himself and saving the country by embarking in the enterprise; that these conversations were repeated all through the month of February, and in that month he stated he was awaiting dispatches from Richmond. The witness inquired if he thought the plan would receive the approbation of the Government at Richmond, and Thompson replied that he thought it would, but he would know in a few days. The witness knew nothing of the arrival of such dispatches, until about the 6th or 7th of April, when Surratt arrived in Canada with dispatches from Mr. Benjamin and Mr. Davis. The witness was present in Thompson's room, with Surratt, when Thompson laid his hand upon the papers, brought by the latter from Richmond, and said, "This makes the thing all right,' referring, as the witness says, to the assent of the Richmond authorities, that is, to the assassination project. On cross-examination the witness says distinctly that he understood this to be the first official approval they had received from Richmond of the plan to assassinate the President, and he knew of no other.

And this evidence, as far as it fixes the date of Surratt's arrival in Canada, and its probable object, is corroborated by Weichmann, who has testified that Surratt arrived in Washington, from Richmond, on the 3d of April, with money in his pocket, and professing to have seen Benjamin and Davis, and to have been assured by them that Richmond would not be evacuated, and that he left, on the same evening, for Montreal, where he would probably arrive on the 5th or 6th.

There is an apparent discrepancy between the testimony of Dr. Merritt and that of Conover, which I here proceed to notice.

He represents that he was present at a meeting of a number of the rebel emissaries, in Montreal, in the middle of February last, at which George N. Sanders, after discussing the projected assassination, read a letter which he said he had received from "the President of our Confederacy," meaning Jefferson Davis, expressing approbation of whatever measures they might take to accomplish the object. Conover, on the other hand, had had conversations with Thompson all through the month of February, and no dispatches had then arrived of the purport stated by Merritt. But that Merritt is wholly mistaken, and his testimony wholly unreliable, in this particular, is clear, from several considerations:

First. The witness did not read the letter, nor does he pretend to repeat its language, nor can he distinguish very clearly between the language of the letter and that of Sanders himself. He says, at first: "Which letter justified him (Sanders) in making any arrangements that he could to accomplish the object." This was the witness' construction of the letter, not its terms. When asked for its language he could not give a word of it, but said it was in substance, "That if the people in Canada and the Southerners in the States were willing to submit to be governed by such a tyrant as Lincoln, he did not wish to recognize them as friends or associates, or something like that." This was the whole of the witness' unprompted account of the substance of the letter. He is asked, however, the leading question, "And you say that in that letter he expressed his approbation of whatever measures they might take to accomplish this object?" To this he answers, "Yes." But he had said nothing of the sort. He had merely said that the letter justified such measures. Still later he says: "When he (Sanders) read the letter he spoke of Mr. Seward, and I inferred that that was partially the language of the letter; I think it was, that if those parties, the President, Vice-President and Cabinet, or Mr. Seward, could be disposed of, it would satisfy the people of the North that they (the Southerners) had friends in the North, and that a peace could be obtained on better terms than it could otherwise be obtained," etc. It will be found that, in the course of his testimony, he gives three different versions of the substance of the letter. He does not pretend to say the assassination was mentioned, in terms, in the letter, and he is evidently unable to distinguish clearly between the language of Sanders and that of Davis, and, on the whole, we are left in complete uncertainty whether we have the conclusions of the witness or those of Jefferson Davis.

But, secondly, it is perfectly certain that Jefferson Davis never would have written such a letter as this is described to be, to George N. Sanders. It is apparent, from the whole testimony, that Jacob Thompson and Clement C.

Clay were the principal emissaries of the rebel Government in Canada. They represented themselves to Montgomery to be invested with full powers to do anything they might deem expedient for the benefit of their cause. Thompson seemed to have had the principal financial agency, though Clay is also said to have had the funds used in the frontier raids. Thompson certainly was the controlling authority in regard to the assassination; the proposition was made to *him*, *he* consulted his Government and expected their approval. No others than these professed to have any authority or control over the frontier operations; and Sanders evidently acted a subordinate part and had the entire confidence of no one, Clay describing him as a very *good man to do their dirty work*, but not *one to whom everything could be safely communicated*. It was, therefore, of all things, one of the most unlikely, that a dispatch, so important as the one described by the witness, would be addressed by Davis to Sanders.

Thirdly. It was equally unlikely that Thompson and Clay would not even be privy to the fact, but would be actually excluded from the confidence of Davis and Sanders. And yet, if the witness is correct, this is the case. For when he is called on to repeat the names of those present at the meeting at which Sanders read his confidential missive, he names ten persons, but omits both Thompson and Clay. In proof that this omission was intentional and not accidental, it is to be noted, that the witness afterward spoke to Clay in Toronto about the letter Sanders had read in Montreal, and states, as a noteworthy fact, that Clay seemed to understand the nature and character of the letter, which remark would never have occurred to the witness, had Clay been present and heard the letter read, and handled and perused it himself when it was passed round at the meeting, as he says it was.

But finally, on this head, the testimony of this witness, as to the subsequent proceedings of the rebel agents, clearly corroborates Conover. It is clear, that no steps were taken on the strength of this letter of Davis, in pursuance of the object supposed to be sanctioned by it, for nearly two months afterward. But the witness Merritt states, that he was in Toronto, on the 5th and 6th of April; that on the 6th, he met Harper and several other rebels, and Harper told him they were going to the States, and were going to kick up the damnedest row that had ever been heard of yet, and afterward said, that if he [the witness] did not hear of the death of Old Abe, of the Vice-President, and of General Dix in less than ten days, he might put him [Harper] down as a damned fool. He afterward ascertained that Harper had in fact left on the 8th of April for the States.

Now, it will be remembered that, according to Weichmann, Surratt passed through Washington on the 3d of April for Canada, where he probably arrived on the 5th, and that, on the 6th or 7th, according to Conover, Jacob Thompson spoke of the dispatches carried by him as conveying the needful authority. This fact could easily be communicated, by telegraph,

to the rebels in Toronto, and there is a perfect correspondence between their declarations and actions, on the 6th of April and after, and Conover's story, that the sanction of the Richmond authorities to the assassination scheme was communicated, for the first time, in the dispatches carried by Surratt to Canada, about the 5th of April. Thus, in the end, there is seen to be a substantial accord between all the three witnesses, on the important question, when the formal sanction of the Richmond authorities was received in Canada, and when, consequently, for the first time, they were in a condition to give their formal and official approval to the proposed assassination.

By whom the proposition was originally made to Thompson is involved in profound mystery, or, at most, is left to conjecture. If it came from Booth, both his conduct and that of the rebel band in Canada show that it was a mere offer, unaccepted, unacted upon, and that its acceptance, and the granting the authority it invited, was an open question, from the month of December to the 5th of April. Booth was reported to have been in Canada in the fall, and as late as December last, but since that time none of the testimony shows any immediate intercourse between him and the rebel emissaries there. And although Harper, Caldwell, and Randall, and Ford are mentioned by Merritt, as parties whom he understood to be implicated in the plot, we hear of no stir or activity among them until the 6th of April. It seems, therefore, very clear, upon this testimony, that this date was the earliest period at which any positive design was formed for the assassination.

The testimony of Mrs. Mary Hudspeth may seem to conflict with this theory, and, therefore, requires some examination. That she is sincere in her statements, I have no reason to doubt; but that she is mistaken seems to me very probable. In the month of November last, she saw two strangers, whom she had never met before, and has never met since, in a street car in New York city, one of them disguised by false whiskers. Some six months afterward, she is shown a photograph taken of Booth, without disguise, and undertakes to recognize it as that of one of the persons in question. This is one improbability in her story. Again, she represents that they had an earnest conversation, one stating that he would leave for Washington on the second day after, and the other being very angry that it had not fallen to him to go to Washington; and all this in a car which she represents as crowded—a second improbability, if the conversation was serious. Next, these important letters are dropped carelessly on the floor and left there. The conduct of these men would seem to justify the judgment Gen. Dix was half inclined to pronounce on the transaction, viz.: that it was a hoax got up for the *Sunday Mercury*; particularly, when we consider that, though one of the letters looks in terms to immediate action, yet nothing followed having the remotest reference to the subject matter, for five months afterward.

But let us compare dates. Mrs. Hudspeth says the circumstance she relates occurred on the day when General Butler left New York. Major Eckert says the order to leave New York was sent to General Butler on the 11th of November; that he applied for permission to remain until the next Monday, which was the 14th. The inference would be that General Butler left on the 14th, and that Mrs. Hudspeth's adventure occurred on that day, and, as one of the parties she speaks of was to leave for Washington on the second day after, Wednesday, the 16th, would be the day fixed for his departure. But a little uncertainty is thrown upon this by the dispatch of General Dix, of the 17th, to C. A. Dana, Esq., in which he says: "The party who dropped the letter was heard to say he would start for Washington on Friday night." This would be the 18th. If, then, Mrs. Hudspeth is correct in saying that one of the parties said he would leave for Washington the day after to-morrow, and so reported to General Dix, and he properly understood her, it must have been on Wednesday, the 16th, that the meeting in the car occurred, and either her recollection is at fault, as to date, or General Butler left on the 16th instead of the 14th. At all events, we are safe in fixing either the 14th or 16th as the date of the occurrence; no evidence points to any other date. Now, if we turn to the testimony of Mr. Bunker, clerk of the National Hotel, we will find that Booth arrived in Washington and registered at that hotel on the 14th of November, and left again on the 16th.

If he arrived here on the 14th, he could not possibly have been riding in a street car in New York, at an hour when the brokers' offices were open, to one of which Mrs. Hudspeth was then going with some gold, and the fact is also inconsistent with the declaration made by the party at the time, that he was to leave for Washington two days after; and again, if Booth started from Washington on the 16th, as the National Hotel book shows he did, it was equally impossible for him to have had the pleasure of Mrs. Hudspeth's company, in the street cars of New York, on the same day in business hours; for even Sir Boyle Roche declared that nothing could be in two places at the same time, except a bird. I conclude, therefore, that this was a case of mistaken identity, like others which have been developed in the course of this trial—that Mrs. Hudspeth is wholly mistaken in identifying Booth as the person encountered by her in the car; and if this be so, then her evidence does not point to anybody now under accusation, and is wholly immaterial; and if it further be judged probable, as it seems to me to be, that the occurrence testified to was designed merely to mystify the public, its value as evidence in this case, of course, falls below zero.

But if the letter found by Mrs. Hudspeth had a serious character, and the individual who dropped it was really Booth, what then? It says, among other things, "The English gentleman, Harcourt, must not act hastily—remember, he has ten days." Again, "Do anything but fail, and meet us at the appointed place *within the fortnight.*" Whatever the plot darkly alluded to, its *complete consummation*

within ten days or a fortnight is clearly contemplated. Now, this is no such conspiracy as the present charge is intended to embrace; for the evidence for the Government shows that the rebel authorities, at a much later period, had not incited and encouraged or even approved formally any plot of assassination, but instead, that the proposition had been made *to them* and was only held under advisement. No such plot had been sanctioned by them in November, and it is such a plot only that this charge deals with. If there really was any such plot as the letter hints at, it evidently failed and was abandoned, for it was to be consummated within ten days. Nothing was done in furtherance of the design, and in December we find Booth, according to Cleary's information to Montgomery, *again in Canada.*

Again, it does not appear from the evidence, as far as I remember, that as early as November, Booth was even acquainted or had any intercourse with Payne, Atzerodt, Herold or Surratt, who are evidently considered by the Government his principal accomplices in the crime which is the subject of this charge. On the contrary, it is shown, as to Surratt, by the Government witness, Weichmann, that Booth was only introduced to him on the 15th of January last. If, therefore, the letter found by Mrs. Hudspeth tends to show any conspiracy existing as far back as November, looking to the murder of the President, it must have been a conspiracy wholly different from that with which these accused are charged—one which wholly failed or was abandoned *immediately;* and, therefore this evidence is not inconsistent with the theory I have announced, that there was no active, living, breathing conspiracy in February or March, or until April, and no determination by any one, connected with any conspiracy, to assail the life of the President or of other heads of Government. This, then, I take to be incontrovertibly established by the evidence on the part of the Government.

But in the interval between the proposition said to have been made in or before January, 1865, to the rebel agents in Canada, to assassinate the President and others, and the formal sanction to the scheme in April, what was brewing?

It is evident that in this interval Booth was revolving and maturing another project, of an entirely different character; one which, as between two hostile nations, was perfectly legitimate, and involved no breach of the law of nations, and one which the Confederate authorities had as much right to attempt as they had to do anything within the scope of belligerent rights, and one to which the special sanction of the Richmond authorities was wholly unnecessary. That was the *capture of the President, and, perhaps, others, and their abduction to Richmond, with a view of forcing an exchange of prisoners.* The scheme, though not innocent, might almost be called harmless, from its perfect absurdity and impracticability. But Booth had become possessed with the idea, and was a monomaniac on the subject. He would admit no difficulties, and, like a madman, sought to dragoon his friends into the scheme with threats of ruin and even death. Al this is proved by the testimony of the Government witness, by Booth's declarations, made in the prosecution of his design, in the very act of enlisting adherents for his project, or rather, I should say, of *conscripting* them, for cajolery was less a means and instrument, than threats, of effecting his object.

Samuel Knapp Chester testifies that about the 24th or 25th of November, Booth took a walk with him in New York, and told him he had a big speculation on hand, and some time after repeated the statement; that still later Booth wrote to him from Washington that he was speculating in farms in Lower Maryland, in which he was sure to coin money, saying that the witness must join him; that late in *December or early in January*, he walked with the witness in an unfrequented portion of Fourth street, in New York, and there disclosed the nature of the great speculation he was engaged in; that it was a large conspiracy to *capture* the heads of the Government, including the President, and to take them to Richmond. He assigned to Chester the part which he wished him to perform, threatened to implicate him in it anyhow, and that if he attempted to betray the plot he would be hunted down through life. Subsequently, in January, Booth wrote several times to Chester, and remitted money to him, urging him to come to Washington. Still later, he saw Chester in New York in February, and repeated his solicitations, and spoke of his efforts to engage one John Matthews in the enterprise, saying that he would not have cared if he had sacrificed him, in consequence of his refusal to join him, as he was a coward, and not fit to live—all which indicates the insane state of Booth's mind on this subject. Subsequently, the witness states, Booth told him he had given up the particular project of capturing the President and heads of Government, and *that it had fallen through in consequence of some of the parties backing out. Still later, he informed him that in consequence of this, he was selling off the horses he had bought for the purpose.* When was this project given up? The witness thought he was so informed in February, but we shall see that he was mistaken in the month, both by the date of the sale of the horses and the date when some of the parties backed out. Who were the parties that backed out? Booth did not give their names, but this omission is supplied by the statement of Arnold, made after his arrest, which was elicited from the Government witness, Eaton G. Horner. From this it appears, that on the 1st of April, Arnold went to Fortress Monroe to accept a situation. Some time before that—the witness can not remember whether it was a week or two or three weeks—he attended a meeting in Washington, in reference to the projected capture of the President, in order to take him South, and thereby compel the Government to make an exchange of prisoners. Arnold declared that he would withdraw from the scheme unless it was effected that week, whereupon Booth threatened to shoot him. Arnold considered the scheme impracticable, and did withdraw, and had nothing more to do with it, and Booth told him to sell the arms that had been furnished him, or do what he chose with

them. It has been proved, by Mrs. Van Tyne, that Arnold gave up his room at her house about the 18th of March, and by other witnesses, as we shall hereafter see, more at large, that he left Washington finally on or before the 20th of March. So that, according to his confession, he was the party, or one of the parties, who backed out from this insane scheme of capture, and it must have fallen through and been abandoned somewhere about the middle of March. This is corroborated by other evidence. Weichmann shows that on a certain day, which at first he could not fix with certainty, vacillating between the 18th and 25th, but which he finally fixed to be the 16th, Booth, Payne and John Surratt came into Mrs. Surratt's in a state of great anger and excitement, and Surratt exclaimed, "My prospects are gone, my hopes are blighted; I want something to do. Can you get me a clerkship?" Booth and Payne manifested similar excitement, and all three went off together. On Surratt's return he informed the witness that Payne had gone to Baltimore and Booth to New York. By the hotel register it appears that Booth did leave on the 21st. All this demonstrates that at this time some mysterious scheme of theirs had failed. The sale of the horses is another circumstance. Surratt had told Weichmann that he had two horses, which he kept at Howard's stable, which Booth afterward told him were his. From the testimony of Brooke Stabler, who kept Howard's stable, it appears that on the 29th of March, Booth paid the livery of these horses for the month, and that Atzerodt, who had been allowed before the use of the horses, took them away on the 31st, and shortly after brought them back, at different times, separately, for sale. This, then, was about the period when Booth must have informed Chester he was selling off his horses, and the backing out of parties to the abduction scheme, and its consequent falling through and abandonment must have been shortly before, and about the middle of March. We shall see hereafter that Booth still clung to this project all through the month of March, and made one or two spasmodic efforts to rally his forces, but without success. The abandonment and failure were complete about the middle of that month. On the 1st of April, Booth went to New York and was there a week, evidently having then finally abandoned the scheme of capture. According to Conover, this scheme of capture had been talked of in Canada in the month of February. It is probable, however, that it was deemed too impracticable to attract much attention. In fact, its failure might easily have been predicted. It was only necessary for the parties concerned to assemble and arrange to put it in motion, for the whole thing to fall to pieces, and this was exactly the result of the first general meeting of the conspirators. But Booth adhered to it with the infatuation of a half insane man, which both his original conception of and his mode of prosecuting this scheme, prove to have been.

But suddenly the scenes are all shifted, and the curtain rises upon a new drama, a bloody tragedy. On the 3d of April, during Booth's absence, John H. Surratt arrives in Washing ton with these ominous dispatches from Richmond, freighted with doom to the unconscious victim of all these contrivances, and with ruin and infamy to all the authors of his fate. Booth was then in New York. Bunker shows that he left the National on the 1st, and Chester saw him in New York on the 7th. Surratt started for Montreal, and probably saw Booth on the way, or else he received news from Canada after Surratt's arrival there; for he came to Washington on the 8th, and the hellish plot of murder must have been concocted, and all its details arranged by him, between that time and the moment of its execution. In its execution, not a single trace is seen of any of the Canadian rebels, nor is there the slightest ground furnished by the evidence, for believing that more than three or four persons, besides Booth himself, were immediately concerned in the commission of the crime.

Now, what part had Arnold or O'Laughlin in the final tragedy? As to Arnold, the matter seems too plain for doubt or argument. Mrs. Van Tyne shows that he gave up his room at her house about the 18th or 20th of March. His brother, William S. Arnold, met him on the way to his house, in Hookstown, on the 21st, where he remained till Saturday, the 25th. On the afternoon of that day, he went to Baltimore with the same brother, supped with him, and slept in the same room with him, and returned with him to the country on the following morning. He there remained until Tuesday or Wednesday, the 28th or 29th, when he returned to Baltimore, and on the way stopped at the house of another witness, Miss Minnie Pole. On the 30th and 31st, Thursday and Friday nights, he was at his father's house, and his brother, Frank, slept with him, William also sleeping in the room, on Friday night. On Saturday morning he went to the country with his brother, returned in the middle of the day, and on the same afternoon went to Fortress Monroe. He had previously made application, by letter, for a situation there. The testimony of his brother, as to his stay in the country, is confirmed by that of Jacob Smith, a neighbor. Then it appears from the testimony of Mr. Wharton, who employed him as clerk, and of Charles B. Hall, a fellow-clerk, that he was constantly in the store at Fortress Monroe, in daily attendance, and faithfully discharging his duty, from the time of his arrival, the 2d of April, to the 17th, the date of his arrest. It was, therefore, physically impossible for him to participate in the murder or assaults in Washington. Nor is there the slightest evidence, or even pretense, that he had any part to perform, in the execution of the deadly plot, at *Fortress Monroe*, or was otherwise engaged there, than in the peaceful duties of his clerkship.

The case of O'Laughlin is equally free from doubt. The specific charge against him is, that, in pursuance of the general design of the conspiracy, he did, on the nights of the 13th and 14th of April, lie in wait for General Grant, with intent *then and there* to murder him; and the whole evidence on the subject shows a mistake of identity that would be ridiculous but for the serious consequences it involves to the accused. On the evening of the 13th, a large crowd assembled in front of Secretary Stanton's, in compliment to him and General Grant. About half-past ten o'clock, and while the crowd were still there, according to Mr. David Stanton and Major Knox, a stranger inquired of the latter where the Secretary was, and afterward lounged into the hall and peered into the parlor, and, on being questioned by Mr. David Stanton, repeated his inquiry, and being told that the Secretary was on the steps, and being requested to leave, quietly walked out. Neither of these witnesses has any recollection that General Grant was inquired for at all. Why the Government, with this information, did not charge the lying in wait to have been for Secretary Stanton, is a matter of astonishment. The whole evidence applicable to General Grant is that of Mr. Stanton's messenger, John G. Hatter, who simply relates that about nine o'clock, or a little after, a man approached him, on the step, and inquired for Grant, and, on being told that he could not see him, walked off. This was, probably, some half-intoxicated and, perhaps, half-demented stranger, who was actuated by the same curiosity that brought a large part of the crowd assembled there on that occasion, and, but for the tragedy of the next night, the circumstance would never have been thought of again. But when the President was shot, Mr. Seward was assaulted, and the Vice-President apparently waylaid, it naturally occurred to every one that the members of the Cabinet had, probably, all been exposed to the common danger, and the affair of the mysterious stranger's visit was recalled, and when Booth was discovered to be the assassin of the President, and his associates were arrested, these witnesses went to examine them with a natural suspicion of finding among them a would-be assassin of Secretary Stanton or General Grant. Mr. David Stanton recognized O'Laughlin as the man on the monitor, although he says he had a very indistinct view of him, because it was so dark. Major Knox and Hatter visited him in prison, and both under the same conviction that the person seen at Mr. Stanton's must have had something to do with the conspiracy, undertook to identify the accused as the man. Two of these witnesses describe his coat as a black dress coat, and one as a frock; all say he had black pants. None of them had ever seen the individual before.

This is only one of several instances of mistaken identity exhibited in the trial. Dr. Merritt located Herold in Canada, where he never was in his life, from the 15th to the 20th of February, when he was clearly proved to have been here on both those days, collecting rent, and signing his own name to the receipts. The same thing occurred in regard to Dr. Mudd, whom Evans swears to having seen in Washington on the 1st, 2d or 3d of March, whereas, he is proved to have been many miles distant on each of those days.

But this whole story about the lying in wait for General Grant is blown to the wind by the testimony of the defense. Let us trace the accused by the light of this testimony. In the first place, he was invited, with two others, Murphy and Early, by Ensign Henderson, to come to Washington, on Thursday, the 13th of April, the occasion of the general illumination. This is sworn to by all three of these parties. They arrived in Washington between five and six o'clock, and first stopped at Rullman's Hotel. While one of the company stopped to be shaved, the accused went with Early to the National Hotel, and there inquired for some person, and, perhaps, went in search of him, but returned to the door in from three to five minutes. This is proven by Early. The accused stated to Henderson afterward that he had been to see Booth, but not whether he had seen him; and there is no proof that he had, but the contrary is sufficiently shown by the short time spent in the hotel. The accused and Early then returned to Rullman's before Henderson had finished shaving, and there rejoined him and Murphy. This is sworn to by all three—Murphy, Early and Henderson—and Murphy says that Early and the accused were not gone more than five or six minutes. They then lounged up Pennsylvania avenue, and went into Welcher's saloon. These details are given by both Early and Murphy, and though Henderson is more general, he confirms them, as to the accused having been in company, all the time, with these parties. Leaving Welcher's about eight o'clock, they returned to Rullman's, and were shortly after joined by Daniel Loughran, who is now added as a fourth witness. The whole party of five then strolled up Pennsylvania avenue to look at the illumination. They all agree as to having passed Seventh street. Those not residing here, and not familiar with the streets, speak only of going a little beyond Seventh, but Loughran, who resides here, fixes the end of the walk at Ninth street, and all agree that they did not go beyond it. They then turned back. Henderson, Early and Loughran all fix the hour of this movement to be nine o'clock, about. Loughran looked at his watch, because he wished to go as far as the Treasury, and some of the party remarked that it was too late. They then went to the Canterbury Music Hall, and remained about an hour or three-quarters, which brought them to about ten o'clock. All four swear that O'Laughlin went there with them, and remained with them, and returned with them to Rullman's, after stopping at the Metropolitan, about ten o'clock—a little sooner or later. There they remained from half an hour to an hour. At half-past ten, Grillet passed with a lady, and shortly after eleven o'clock returned, found them in the same place, and joined them. He, Early, Murphy and Loughran mention the circumstance, and this brings a fifth witness on the stage. In addition to these, Purdy, the manager, and Giles, the bar-tender of Rullman's Hotel, both swear that he was at the hotel, one fixing the hour at about ten, and the other at about half-past ten, and remained with the other parties until after eleven. Here, then, are seven witnesses, of whom four swear they were in company with the accused at the hour fixed by Hatter of his waylaying General Grant at Mr. Stanton's, and all the evening af-

terward, and that they were not for a moment nearer to Mr. Stanton's than a point which must be a full mile distant, and their testimony is added to by three other witnesses, making seven, who locate the accused still farther off from the scene of his supposed murderous designs, between the hours of ten and eleven o'clock, when the other Government witnesses profess to have seen him. Six of the party were with the accused until between twelve and one o'clock that night, and the casual accessions to the company having left, the accused, Henderson, Murphy and Early, according to their concurrent testimony, retired, at the Metropolitan Hotel, toward two o'clock in the morning. On Friday morning the accused was roused by Early and Henderson. The same party of four breakfasted at Welcher's, and strolled on the avenue to the National Hotel, and entered there about nine o'clock. There the accused went up stairs in search of Booth, and, as he did not return for some time, a half or three-quarters of an hour, the party left, thinking he might have gone to Rullman's. Not finding him there, they returned to the National, and sent up their cards to Booth's room, but no one was there. The cards being left at the office, they returned to Rullman's, where they were joined by the accused in about an hour. This would be in the neighborhood of eleven o'clock, and the accused then stated to Henderson that he had not found Booth, that he was out. All the rest of the morning the accused was in company with all three of his friends, and, in the afternoon, he only parted with the others, to go with Early, between four and five o'clock, to visit a lady. Early speaks fully of this, and Henderson says he was with the accused all day, except a part of the afternoon, when he went off with Early. Early and the accused paid the visit, and returned about six o'clock, and rejoined the others at the hotel (Rullman's). So Early states, and Henderson confirms it, and Murphy states that he was with them until eight o'clock, when they went to supper, and he parted with them until next day. Meanwhile, Early, Henderson and the accused went to Welcher's to supper, and returned to Rullman's, where they remained until after the news of the President's assassination. Early does not remember how late this was, and does not remember the hour of O'Laughlin's leaving there with Fuller; but Grillet, Purdy, Henderson, Fuller and Giles all swear that O'Laughlin was at Rullman's, in their company, when the news of the President's assassination reached there. It was communicated to O'Laughlin and the others by Purdy, who had heard it at the door. Shortly after O'Laughlin left Rullman's, in company with Fuller, who had been in his brother's employ, and, on his invitation, he spent the night with him. Early on Saturday morning the accused joined the same party, and was with them until their departure for Baltimore, in the afternoon train, as testified by Early and Murphy.

Now, to return to Thursday evening. One Government witness fixed nine, and the other two, half-past ten o'clock, as the hour at which the accused was seen lurking about Mr. Stanton's. As to the first hour, we have four, and as to the second hour, the same, with three others, making seven respectable witnesses, of different pursuits, casually meeting, and in no wise implicated or interested themselves; two of them called by the Government, and so accredited as worthy of belief, and one of these an officer in the United States navy, and all of them wholly unimpeached, all intimately acquainted with the accused, who establish an *alibi* beyond the possibility of question. It is physically impossible that they can be mistaken; they can not be disbelieved without imputing deliberate perjury to them all. It is morally impossible that they can be perjured. On the other hand, nothing is further from impossible, nothing is easier, than for all the Government witnesses to have been mistaken. A minute's view at night, of a stranger, whom they had never beheld before, furnished them all the knowledge upon the strength of which, weeks after, they assumed to identify him in the obscurity of an iron-clad, and the shades of a dungeon. It were folly to dwell longer on the comparison between the two kinds of evidence. But look for a moment at the gross improbability of the story. It is evident that the different parts of this plot were to be executed simultaneously—it was essential to success. It is also evident that Friday night was the first time fixed for its execution. Nothing tends to show any earlier attempt, made or contemplated. On Friday night the murder occurred; on the same night Mr. Seward was assaulted; on Friday afternoon Booth called to see the Vice-President, evidently not to assassinate him then, but to learn of his whereabouts; and if any such part as the assassination of Gen. Grant was assigned to O'Laughlin, Friday night was the time assigned for its execution. It is evident that if he had made the attempt on Thursday, successfully or not, it would have thwarted the whole scheme, for it would have put every one else on his guard. And the prosecution felt the stress of this consideration, for they have added Friday, the 14th, in the specification, because this was absolutely necessary in order to connect the accused with the actual execution of the conspiracy, although they had not a scintilla of proof to justify it. The story becomes still more improbable when we are required to believe that this small and feeble man ventured, single-handed, into a brilliantly lit house to assault Mr. Stanton or General Grant, or both, where he could hardly fail to be seized, with a crowd at the front to intercept his retreat, and wholly ignorant of the exit by the rear. It may be said that he was then simply reconnoitering for a more favorable opportunity. But the charge is, that he lay in wait on that night with intent, *then and there* to kill and murder General Grant; and if that is disproved, the whole is disproved, for it has not been even attempted to show waylaying on Friday night, the 14th of April. For this reason it is almost battling wind-mills to attempt to controvert that part of the charge relating to Friday night. There is nothing to answer or refute. It is sufficient, however, to refer to the evidence already analysed, which shows that from six o'clock until after the assassination, the accused was quietly engaged with the companions before named, remote from the scenes of blood and danger, until after the whole tragedy was over. General Grant, meanwhile, was far away, although he had been expected and announced to appear at Ford's theater on Friday night, and the change of purpose was probably only known to the conspirators by his actual absence. The accused was not at the theater, nor at Secretary Seward's, nor at the Kirkwood, nor anywhere else where it can be conceived that any part of the massacre was to be performed. No conceivable part in the enterprise can be assigned to him. Indeed, it is evident that he designed, as the others did, to return to Baltimore on Friday morning, and was only detained by the persuasions of Henderson. Did his conduct indicate any complicity in, or knowledge of, the impending crime? Was he silent, or excited, or nervous, betraying the fatal truth in his cups, bursting with the big and fatal secret which could not be contained? On the contrary, he is represented as in the finest spirits, cheerful, composed, and light-hearted, mingling in the merry revel with his boon companions, evidently all unconscious of the impending evil.

But he went to see Booth on two occasions—Thursday afternoon and Friday morning. It does not appear that he saw him on either; the contrary is rather shown. But suppose he had seen him. The afternoon and the morning visit were both before Booth even knew that the President was to be at Ford's theater on Friday night, for it appears that he only received the information at the theater at noon on that day. Before that hour, O'Laughlin had rejoined his companions, and was not out of the company of some of them the whole day afterward. Now, after Booth learned of the President's arrangements for the evening, and laid his plans for the murder, if the accused had any connection with him whatever in this scheme, why did not Booth go after him, seek him out, and assign him his part? Either he did not know of his presence here, or he did not regard him as an accomplice.

But could the accused really desire better proof of his innocence than the fact of his visit to Booth affords? Can anybody conceive that with the knowledge of the intended murders, still more, expecting to participate in them, he would have gone openly, in a public hotel, to visit the intended leader in the crime, in company with several persons, one of them an officer in the navy, on the very day of the intended attempt? Could such infatuation be imputed to any man in his senses? Would not a guilty man, or one with guilty knowledge only, have sought a covert interview, well knowing that suspicion would attach to every one seen in intercourse with Booth about the time of his crime, and that the sleuth-hounds of justice would soon be upon his trail?

And when he received the news of the assassination, what was his conduct? Did he betray guilt by agitation, and excitement and flight? Nothing of the sort. He was naturally startled, and the thought naturally occurred, that as he had been intimate with Booth, and had only that morning gone openly to call on him, he might be suspected. But still he betrayed none of the terrors of guilt. He went quietly to sleep at the house or lodgings of a friend. The party had no particular lodgings, and seem all to have scattered that night. O'Laughlin stayed with Fuller. He joined his friends the next morning, and they went quietly home together. On reaching home he was informed that the officers of justice were in search of him. His suspicion, expressed in Washington, was realized, and he found himself involved in trouble. No man—the most innocent—could avoid emotion in some degree, under such circumstances. But his demeanor was wholly irreconcilable with guilt. He absented himself from home that night for a reason that was creditable to him, vis.: that his arrest there might be the death of his mother; and no one can believe that a youth governed by these filial sentiments could be so steeped in depravity as to have had any share in the conception or execution of the diabolical crime of Booth. The officers were at his lodgings in search of him on Saturday and on Sunday. On Sunday he informed Murphy of the fact, and stated that he meant to surrender himself on Monday, and on that day he did so, through his brother-in-law, Mr. Maulsby. Throughout, his declarations were that he was innocent of any connection with the crime, and could account for every moment of his time spent in Washington; and that he has done.

It is, therefore, apparent that neither Arnold nor O'Laughlin had anything to do with the execution of the alleged conspiracy, and that they even *could* not have had any knowledge of the intended murders.

Furthermore, it appears that for nearly a month before the assassination they had no personal intercourse with Booth. Arnold was in Baltimore and the neighborhood from the 21st to the 31st of March, and from that time at Fortress Monroe. He was not in Washington at all. And though his letter, offered in evidence, would seem to show that Booth had been to see him at his home, it also shows that no interview was had, nor is any correspondence shown, except the letter in question. This letter evidently shows a rupture of former relations with Booth. "When I left you, you stated we would *not meet in a month or so.*" "I told my parents *I had ceased with you. Can I, then, under existing circumstances, come as you request?*" Such are the terms of the letter. And, in effect, we know that he did not come as requested, but, on the contrary, accepted a situation, and went to Fortress Monroe on the 1st of April, and this was the last even of his correspondence with Booth, and this completed and sealed the rupture. As to O'Laughlin, no intercourse of any sort is shown with Booth after the 18th of March. On that day he went home, according to Mr. Maulsby, and remained there with him ever since. Mr. Bunker, who speaks of O'Laughlin's frequent visits to Booth, admits that he did

not recollect his coming during the last few days of Booth's stay. Those last few days were the week before the assassination. The previous week Booth was in New York, and could not have been seen here by the accused. Bunker's testimony is so vague as to dates, that it can not be weighed for a moment against the positive testimony of Mr. Maulsby. The same may be said of Streett, who thinks he remembers seeing the accused in conversation with Booth in the streets, well on to the 1st of April, which might have been before his departure on the 18th of March. It is true that Booth telegraphed to him on the 27th to come to Washington on the 29th, but it does not appear that he ever received the telegram, and it is certain he did not respond to or comply with its request. Some time in March it also appears that a letter was sent from Booth to O'Laughlin, but whether in the beginning or end, or what were its contents, is a matter of perfect uncertainty, as it is, also, whether he ever noticed it. On O'Laughlin's own part, no single act of intercourse is shown, between March 18th and April 18th, when he came to Washington, evidently in the most complete and happy ignorance of the mischief that was brewing.

If, then, Arnold and O'Laughlin ever were connected with Booth in a conspiracy for any object, before the middle of March, it is clear that, about that time, they wholly withdrew from and abandoned it, while it was wholly unexecuted, if not merely in embryo. And this being the case, according to the principles heretofore laid down, they were not parties, in *law* or in *fact*, to any act subsequently done.

But let us see what evidence there is to connect them with any conspiracy.

First, as to O'Laughlin. I maintain that there is no competent legal evidence to show him implicated in any conspiracy whatever. Throw out of the case the confession of Arnold, and any statements made by him casually to third persons—which, I shall show, are not evidence against O'Laughlin—what remains? No one can pretend that there is any direct evidence. If any, it is circumstantial. A conspiracy may be proved by circumstances, but by what kind of circumstances? *Russell on Crimes,* 2 vol., p. 698, says:

"The evidence in support of an indictment for a conspiracy is generally circumstantial; and it is not necessary to prove any direct concert, or even any meeting of the conspirators, as the actual fact of conspiracy may be collected from the collateral circumstances of the case." "If, therefore, two persons *pursue, by their own acts, the same objects, often by the same means, one performing one part of the act, and the other another part of the same act,* so as to complete it, with a view to the attainment of the object they were pursuing, *the jury are at liberty to draw the conclusion that they had been engaged in a conspiracy to effect that object.* In a case where a husband and wife and their servants were indicted for a conspiracy to ruin the trade of the prosecutor, who was the king's card-maker, the evidence against them was that they had, at several times, given money to the prosecutor's apprentices to put grease into the paste, which had spoiled the cards; but there was no account given that ever more than one at a time was present, though *it was proved that they had all given money in their turns;* it was objected that this could not be conspiracy, on the ground that several persons might do the same thing without having any previous communication with each other. But it was ruled that the defendants being all of a family, and concerned in the making of cards, it (*i. e.* these acts done in pursuance of a common object) would be evidence of a conspiracy." Now, it is evident in this case, that the mere fact of belonging to this family, and even being concerned in the same trade, would not have begun to be evidence to implicate any one. It was the *doing of acts in pursuance of the common end,* which was the circumstantial proof admitted, aided by showing a common motive.

Now, in the case under trial, what single act or declaration of O'Laughlin can be shown looking to any common end or object between him and Booth? Is his personal intimacy adduced? But not only had that no necessary connection with any criminal design, but it is proved that it could not have originated in anything of the sort. They were opposite neighbors in Baltimore, had been schoolmates in boyhood, in the same neighborhood, and between themselves and their families an uninterrupted intimacy had subsisted for many years. If intimacy were any evidence of complicity with Booth, it would hardly be possible to assign any limits to the scope of this conspiracy. His profession, no less than his personal qualities, necessarily made him many acquaintances. Others were more intimate with him than the accused—McCulloch, Wentworth, and others, shared his room at the National Hotel. Yet they seem to have attracted no suspicion.

Can the circumstance of O'Laughlin's presence in Washington and his occupying a room at Mrs. Van Tyne's be relied on? It has been shown that he formerly resided in Washington, was in the employment of his brother, then in business here, and that he has constantly had to visit Washington since, to make collections, solicit orders, and deliver merchandise, and that on the very day of his last visit, a month before the assassination, he came down for his brother, upon business, about which he was telegraphed the next day. In this state of affairs, nothing was more natural than that he should occupy a room with a fellow-townsman, Arnold; but that that had no reference to anything in which Booth or Arnold was concerned, an examination of dates will show. Mrs. Van Tyne does not profess to know anything of the relations between Arnold and O'Laughlin, nor could she know which of them was actually present in her lodgings at any particular time. But she fixes the beginning of this occupancy on the 10th of February. Now, Mr. Maulsby shows that O'Laughlin was at home on the 14th of February, and remained there two weeks—that is, to the end of the month. So that, as far as appears, he was in Washington but four days during the whole month of February; and, by looking at Bunker's testimony, it will be

seen that Booth was absent from Washington at that time. Indeed, he was absent for twelve days before the room was taken at Mrs. Van Tyne's, and so continued, if I understand Bunker's evidence aright, for twelve days afterward. The book shows that he left on the 28th of January, and arrived again on the 22d of February, though there is some confusion on this point. It can hardly be understood, then, how his occupancy of this room could have any reference to schemes Booth was prosecuting here. It certainly had no necessary connection with them, and can not be called as an act done in furtherance of them, without much more proof. Where O'Laughlin was in the beginning of March, is not very clear, but it is certain that he was at home on the 7th, and so continued until the 13th, when he spent five days in Washington. Now, this is everything in the case, in the shape of acts or declarations of O'Laughlin. No man can deny that his intimacy with Booth, and his stay in Washington, were perfectly consistent with utter ignorance of anything illicit in progress, and are fully accounted for on other grounds. He might, for aught that appears, have been guilelessly keeping up a social intimacy with the friends of his boyhood, and Booth may not have whispered his designs to him, as he did not to others equally or more intimate with him. This intimacy, therefore, can not be called an act done in pursuance of the conspiracy, and tending to prove it against O'Laughlin. Consider, moreover, what else has not been proved against him. While the prosecution have sought to show, and will doubtless maintain, that Mrs. Surratt's house was the headquarters of the alleged conspiracy, that John Surratt, Payne, Atzerodt, and perhaps Spangler and Herold, were the principal accomplices of Booth, they have not shown that O'Laughlin was ever at that house, or was ever known to any of those parties. When arrested, no arms were found on him, nor anything indicating any deadly or illegal purpose, of any kind.

Now, if I am right in my position that no act or word of O'Laughlin himself has been shown, nor any independent fact, connecting him with any conspiracy, then it is very plain that no act or declaration of any third person is competent evidence against him. The rule of law, under this head, is too plain to be misunderstood.

The *fact of conspiracy* between A and B can never be proved against A by the mere declarations of B; but if it once be proved by the declarations or acts of A himself, then B's declarations, accompanying some act done in furtherance of the common design, would be evidence, but they would not be evidence if made casually, or after the conspiracy is either executed or abandoned.

Thus, Professor Greenleaf says (vol. I, § III): "The same principles apply to the acts and declarations of one of a company of conspirators, *in regard to the common design,* as affecting his fellows. Here a foundation must first be laid by proof sufficient, in the opinion of the judge, to establish, *prima facie, the fact of conspiracy* between the parties, or proper to be laid before the jury, as tending to establish that fact. *The connection of the individual in the unlawful enterprise being thus shown,* every act and declaration of each member of the confederacy, *in pursuance of the original concerted plan,* is, in contemplation of law, the act and declaration of them all," etc. "Sometimes, for the sake of convenience, the acts and declarations of one are admitted in evidence, before sufficient proof is given of the conspiracy, the prosecutor undertaking to furnish such proof of conspiracy in a subsequent stage of the cause. But this rests in the discretion of the judge, and is not permitted, except under peculiar and urgent circumstances, *lest the jury should be misled to infer the fact itself, of the conspiracy, from the declarations of strangers.* And here, also, care must be taken that the acts and declarations thus admitted be those only which were made and done during the pendency of the criminal enterprise, and *in furtherance of its object.*"

If they took place at a subsequent period, and are, therefore, merely narrative of past occurrences, they are, as we have just seen, to be refused.

And, as Russell says [v. 2, p. 697]: "But what one of the party may have been heard to say at some other time, as to the share which some of the others had in the execution of the common design, or as to the object of the conspiracy, can not, it is conceived, be admitted as evidence to affect them, on their trial for the same offense."

It is clear, then, that Arnold's oral confession is not admissible against O'Laughlin, for two reasons, viz.: first, because no conspiracy between them had first been proved by other evidence; and next, because it was not made in furtherance or prosecution of any conspiracy, but as to a past transaction. It is pure hearsay, inadmissible because of the double chance of mistakes—mistake in the witness as to the third person's declarations, and mistake of the third person himself. The same is to be said of casual remarks made by him to third persons, as to the nature of his or their business, not made in the prosecution and furtherance of that business.

On the same principle, neither could any act or declaration of Booth be evidence against him. We have nothing of this sort but the sending of a letter, the contents of which are entirely unknown, and the sending of the telegrams of March 13 and March 27, asking him to come to Washington. But without proof of conspiracy, from another source, this would be inadmissible against O'Laughlin. Otherwise, it would be in the power of any man to ruin an enemy, by writing to him or telegraphing to him in terms which assumed the existence of some guilty plot between them; and these acts are consistent with the theory of a mere attempt to persuade him into a conspiracy, which he would not yield to. If, then, these acts of Booth, and declarations of Arnold be rejected as evidence, the case is utterly bare of proof against O'Laughlin of any conspiracy whatever.

But suppose all these acts and declarations admitted, let us see what they prove; and in considering them, I treat the cases of Arnold and O'Laughlin together.

If I have been correct in my analysis of the proof, I have shown, that no active design against the life of the President was on foot, between January and the early part of April; and I have further shown, from the evidence of the Government, that during that interval, Booth was contriving an entirely different project—the capture of the President and others. It has further appeared that that project was abandoned, and the date of its abandonment is fixed about, by facts referred to by Booth, to-wit: the defection of some of the parties, the sale of horses, etc., and that date is ascertained to have been about the middle of March.

Now, it is clear, that if any connection is shown between Booth on one hand, and O'Laughlin and Arnold on the other, it existed only during the period when this absurd project of capture was agitated, and terminated with that. Their fitful stay in Washington was only between February 10th and March 18th. By Arnold's confession, it would appear that he, and if he is not mistaken, O'Laughlin, attended one meeting about the middle of March, to consider the plan of capture; but so immature was the plan, and so slight his connection with it, that he did not even know the names of the others at the meeting—two in number—besides Booth, Surratt and Atzerodt. At that meeting, as might have been expected, the difficulties of the scheme became apparent, and a rupture ensued between him and Booth; the whole scheme fell through, and he and O'Laughlin, immediately after, left for Baltimore. Booth told him he might sell the arms he had given him; and, in fact, it is proved that he gave part of them away, shortly after, to his brother. As to O'Laughlin, this confession proves nothing but his presence at this single meeting. This was the beginning and the end of their connection with Booth in any scheme whatever of a political character; and, in this, it is evident that he was the arch-contriver, and they the dupes. And when they had once escaped his influence, although he still evidently clung to his design, and telegraphed and wrote, and called to see them, it is evident that they refused to heed the voice of the charmer, charm he never so wisely. From O'Laughlin he received no response at all; from Arnold, only the letter offered in evidence. There are expressions in the letter which look to a contingent renewal of their relations in the future; but they were employed to parry his importunities for the present. Certainly, *all connection ceased from that time.*

If, therefore, any conspiracy at all be proved, by the utmost latitude of evidence, against these two accused, it was a mere unacted, stillscheme, scarce conceived before abandoned, of a nature wholly different from the offense described in this charge, the proof of which does not sustain this charge, and of which the accused could not be convicted upon this trial; for this Court, as we have seen, is bound by the rules of evidence which prevail in others, and one of the most important is, that the proof must correspond with the charge or indictment, and show the same offense, or the accused is entitled to acquittal.

And there is no evidence which connects these two accused with that dreadful conspiracy which forms the subject of this charge. There is nothing to show that during their brief intercourse with Booth, in Washington, that nefarious design was agitated at all, certainly none that it was even disclosed to *them;* and if such conspiracy had any existence, it was in a state of slumber and suspense, awaiting that sanction without which it had no motive, nor end, nor aim, nor life.

I state, then, the following conclusions as established, viz.:

1. That the accused, Samuel Arnold and Michael O'Laughlin, had no part whatever in the execution of the conspiracy set forth in this charge and its specification.

2. That if they were implicated in such conspiracy, they withdrew from it and abandoned it while yet wholly unexecuted, and resting merely in intention, and are not responsible for any of the acts subsequently done in pursuance of it.

3. That there is no legal and complete evidence implicating O'Laughlin in any conspiracy whatever, and none implicating either O'Laughlin or Arnold in the conspiracy charged.

4. That if there is evidence against them of any conspiracy, it is of one wholly different from that set forth in the charge and specification, and upon these they must be wholly acquitted.

I, therefore, claim for them an absolute and unqualified acquittal. That the accused were wrong in ever joining the rebellion against their Government, no one will deny; that they were wrong in ever listening for a moment, if they ever did, to any proposition from that wicked schemer, Booth, inimical to their Government, no one will deny. But it would be to insult the intelligence of this Court to waste time in showing that this Court are not sitting in judgment on all the errors in the lives of these accused, but to decide the single question whether they are guilty of conspiracy to kill and murder the President, Vice-President, Secretary of State, and General in command of the armies of the United States, and of the acts charged against them severally in pursuance of said conspiracy.

And now, Mr. President and gentlemen, with all the sense of responsibility the occasion is fitted to inspire, I commit to you the lives, liberties, and good names of my clients, to be dealt with by you according to the law and evidence, without partiality, favor, or affection.

       MICHAEL O'LAUGHLIN,
       SAMUEL ARNOLD.

ARGUMENT

IN REPLY TO THE SEVERAL

ARGUMENTS IN DEFENSE OF MARY E. SURRATT

AND OTHERS, CHARGED WITH CONSPIRACY AND THE MURDER OF ABRAHAM LINCOLN, LATE PRESIDENT OF THE UNITED STATES, ETC.

BY THE

HON. JOHN A. BINGHAM,

Special Judge Advocate.

May it please the Court:

The conspiracy here charged and specified, and the acts alleged to have been committed in pursuance thereof, and with the intent laid, constitute a crime the atrocity of which has sent a shudder through the civilized world. All that was agreed upon and attempted by the alleged inciters and instigators of this crime constitutes a combination of atrocities with scarcely a parallel in the annals of the human race. Whether the prisoners at your bar are guilty of the conspiracy and the acts alleged to have been done in pursuance thereof, as set forth in the charge and specification, is a question the determination of which rests solely with this honorable Court, and in passing upon which this Court are the sole judges of the law and the fact.

In presenting my views upon the questions of law raised by the several counsel for the defense, and also on the testimony adduced for and against the accused, I desire to be just to them, just to you, just to my country, and just to my own convictions. The issue joined involves the highest interests of the accused, and, in my judgment, the highest interests of the whole people of the United States.

It is a matter of great moment to all the people of this country that the prisoners at your bar be lawfully tried and lawfully convicted or acquitted. A wrongful and illegal conviction or a wrongful and illegal acquittal upon this dread issue would impair somewhat the security of every man's life, and shake the stability of the republic.

The crime charged and specified upon your record is not simply the crime of murdering a human being, but it is the crime of killing and murdering, on the 14th day of April, A. D. 1865, within the military department of Washington and the intrenched lines thereof, Abraham Lincoln, then President of the United States, and commander-in-Chief of the army and navy thereof; and then and there assaulting, with intent to kill and murder, William H. Seward, then Secretary of State of the United States; and then and there lying in wait to kill and murder Andrew Johnson, then Vice-President of the United States, and Ulysses S. Grant, then Lieutenant-General and in command of the armies of the United States, in pursuance of a treasonable conspiracy entered into by the accused with one John Wilkes Booth, and John H. Surratt, upon the instigation of Jefferson Davis, Jacob Thompson, and George N. Sanders, and others, with intent thereby to aid the existing rebellion and subvert the Constitution and laws of the United States.

The rebellion, in aid of which this conspiracy was formed and this great public crime committed, was prosecuted for the vindication of no right, for the redress of no wrong, but was itself simply a criminal conspiracy and gigantic assassination. In resisting and crushing this rebellion the American people take no step backward, and cast no reproach upon their past history. That people now, as ever, proclaim the self-evident truth that whenever government becomes subversive of the ends of its creation, it is the right and duty of the people to alter or abolish it; but during these four years of conflict they have as clearly proclaimed, as was their right and duty, both by law and by arms, that the Government of their own choice, humanely and wisely administered, oppressive of none and just to all, shall not be overthrown by privy conspiracy or armed rebellion.

What wrong had this Government or any of its duly constituted agents done to any of the guilty actors in this atrocious rebellion? They themselves being witnesses, the Government which they assailed had done no act, and attempted no act, injurious to them, or in any sense violative of their rights as citizens and men; and yet for four years, without cause of complaint or colorable excuse, the inciters and instigators of the conspiracy charged upon your record have, by armed rebellion, resisted the lawful authority of the Government, and attempted by force of arms to blot the Republic from the map of nations. Now that their battalions of treason are broken and flying before the victorious legions of the Republic, the chief traitors in this great crime against your Government, secretly conspire with their hired confederates to achieve by assassination, if possible, what they have in vain attempted by wager of battle, the overthrow of the Government of the United States and the subversion of its Constitution and laws. It is for this secret conspiracy in the interest of the rebellion, formed at the instigation of the chiefs in that rebellion, and in pursuance of which the acts charged and specified are alleged to have been done, and with the intent laid, that the accused are upon trial.

The Government, in preferring this charge, does not indict the whole people of any State or section, but only the alleged parties to this unnatural and atrocious conspiracy and crime. The President of the United States, in the discharge of his duty as Commander-in-Chief of the army, and by virtue of the power vested in him by the Constitution and laws of the United States, has constituted you a military court, to hear and determine the issue joined against the accused, and has constituted you a court for no other purpose whatever. To this charge and specification the defendants have pleaded, first, that this court has no jurisdiction in the premises; and, second, not guilty. As the Court has already overruled the plea to the jurisdiction, it would be passed over in silence by me but for the fact, that a grave and elaborate argument has been made by counsel for the accused, not only to show the want of jurisdiction, but to arraign the President of the United States before the country and the world as a usurper of power over the lives and the liberties of the prisoners. Denying the authority of the President to constitute this Commission is an averment that this tribunal is not a court of justice, has no legal existence, and therefore no power to hear and determine the issue joined. The learned counsel for the accused, when they make this averment by way of argument, owe it to themselves and to their country to show how the President could otherwise lawfully and efficiently discharge the duty enjoined upon him by his oath to protect, preserve, and defend the Constitution of the United States, and to take care that the laws be faithfully executed.

An existing rebellion is alleged and not denied. It is charged that in aid of this existing rebellion a conspiracy was entered into by the accused, incited and instigated thereto by the chiefs of this rebellion, to kill and murder the executive officers of the Government, and the commander of the armies of the United States, and that this conspiracy was partly executed by the murder of Abraham Lincoln, and by a murderous assault upon the Secretary of State; and counsel reply, by elaborate argument, that although the facts be as charged, though the conspirators be numerous and at large, able and eager to complete the horrid work of assassination already begun within your military encampment, yet the successor of your murdered President is a usurper if he attempts by *military force* and martial law, as Commander-in-Chief, to prevent the consummation of this traitorous conspiracy in aid of this treasonable rebellion. The civil courts, say the counsel, are open in the District. I answer, they are closed throughout half the Republic, and were only open in this District on the day of this confederation and conspiracy, on the day of the traitorous assassination of your President, and are only open at this hour by force of the bayonet. Does any man suppose that if the military forces which garrison the intrenchments of your capital, fifty thousand strong, were all withdrawn, the rebel bands who this day infest the mountain passes in your vicinity would allow this Court, or any court, to remain open in this District for the trial of these their confederates, or would permit your executive officers to discharge the trust committed to them, for twenty-four hours?

At the time this conspiracy was entered into, and when this Court was convened and entered upon this trial, the country was in a state of civil war. An army of insurrectionists have, since this trial began, shed the blood of Union soldiers in battle. The conspirator, by whose hand his co-conspirators, whether present or absent, jointly murdered the President on the 14th of last April, could not be and was not arrested upon civil process, but was pursued by the military power of the Government, captured and slain. Was this an act of usurpation?—a violation of the right guaranteed to that fleeing assassin by the very Constitution against which and for the subversion of which he had conspired and murdered the President? Who in all this land is bold enough or base enough to assert it?

I would be glad to know by what law the President, by a military force, acting only upon his military orders, is justified in pursuing, arresting, and killing one of these conspirators, and is condemned for arresting in like manner and by his order subjecting to trial, according to the laws of war, any or all of the other parties to this same damnable conspiracy and crime, by a military tribunal of justice—a tribunal I may be pardoned for saying, whose integrity and impartiality are above suspicion, and pass unchallenged even by the accused themselves.

The argument against the jurisdiction of this Court rests upon the assumption that, even in time of insurrection and civil war, no crimes are cognizable and punishable by military commission or court-martial, save crimes committed in the military or naval service of the United States, or in the militia of the several States when called into the actual service of the United States. But that is not all the argument; it affirms that, under this plea to the jurisdiction, the accused have the right to demand that this Court shall decide that it is not a judicial tribunal, and has no legal existence.

This is a most extraordinary proposition, that the President, under the Constitution and laws of the United States, was not only not authorized, but absolutely forbidden to constitute this Court, for the trial of the accused, and, therefore, the act of the President is void, and the gentlemen who compose the tribunal, without judicial authority or power, and are not, in fact or in law, a court.

That I do not misstate what is claimed and attempted to be established on behalf of the accused, I ask the attention of the Court to the following as the gentleman s (Mr. Johnson's) propositions:

That Congress has not authorized, and, under the Constitution, can not authorize the appointment of this Commission.

That this Commission has, "as a court, no legal existence or authority," because the President, who alone appointed the Commission, has no such power.

That his act "is a mere nullity, the usurpation of a power not vested in the Executive, and conferring no authority upon you."

We have had no common exhibition of law-learning in this defense, prepared by a Senator of the United States; but, with all his experience, and all his learning and acknowledged ability, he has failed, utterly failed, to show how a tribunal, constituted and sworn, as this has been, to duly try and determine the charge and specification against the accused, and, by its commission, not authorized to hear or determine any other issues whatever, can rightfully entertain, or can, by any possibility, pass upon the proposition presented by this argument of the gentleman for its consideration.

The members of this Court are officers in the army of the United States, and, by order of the President, as Commander-in-Chief, are required to discharge this duty, and are authorized, in this capacity, to discharge no other duty, to exercise no other judicial power. Of course, if the commission of the President constitutes this a court for the trial of this case only, as such court it is competent to decide all questions of law and fact arising in the trial of the case. But this Court has no power, as a Court, to declare the authority by which it was constituted null and void, and the act of the President a mere nullity, a usurpation. Has it been shown by the learned gentleman, who demands that this Court shall so decide, that officers of the army may lawfully and constitutionally question, in this manner, the orders of their Commander-in-Chief, disobey, set them aside, and declare them a nullity and a usurpation? Even if it be conceded that the officers, thus detailed by order of the Commander-in-Chief, may question and utterly disregard his order, and set aside his authority, is it possible, in the nature of things, that any body of men, constituted and qualified as a tribunal of justice, can sit in judgment upon the proposition that they are not a court for any purpose, and finally decide judicially, as a court, that the Government which appointed them was without authority? Why not crown the absurdity of this proposition by asking the several members of this Court to determine that they are not men—living, intelligent, responsible men! This would be no more irrational than the question upon which they are asked to pass. How can any sensible man entertain it! Before he begins to reason upon the proposition he must take for granted, and, therefore, decide in advance, the very question in dispute, to-wit, his actual existence.

So with the question presented in this remarkable argument for the defense; before this Court can enter upon the inquiry of the want of authority in the President to constitute them a court, they must take for granted and decide the very point in issue, that the President had the authority, and that they are in law and in fact a judicial tribunal; and, having assumed this, they are gravely asked, as such judicial tribunal, to finally and solemnly decide and declare that they are not in fact or in law a judicial tribunal, but a mere nullity and nonentity. A most lame and impotent conclusion!

As the learned counsel seems to have great reverence for judicial authority, and requires precedent for every opinion, I may be pardoned for saying that the objection which I urge against the possibility of any judicial tribunal, after being officially qualified as such, entertaining, much less judicially deciding, the proposition that it has no legal existence as a court, and that the appointment was a usurpation, and without authority of law, has been solemnly ruled by the Supreme Court of the United States.

That Court say: "The acceptance of the judicial office is a recognition of the *authority* from which it is derived. If a court should enter upon the inquiry (whether the *authority* of the Government which established it existed), and should come to the conclusion that the Government under which it acted had been put aside, it would cease to be a court, and be *incapable* of pronouncing a judicial decision upon the question it undertook to try. If it decides at all, as a court, it necessarily affirms the existence and *authority* of the Government under which it is exercising judicial power." *Luther vs. Borden*, 7 *Howard*, 40.

That is the very question raised by the learned gentleman in his argument, that there was no *authority* in the President, by whose act alone this tribunal was constituted, to vest it with judicial power to try this issue; and, by the order upon your record, as has already been shown, if you have no power to try this issue, for want of authority in the Commander-in-Chief to constitute you a court, you are no court, and have no power to try any issue, because his order limits you to this issue, and this alone.

It requires no very profound legal attainments to apply the ruling of the highest judicial tribunal of this country, just cited, to the point raised, not by the pleadings, but by the argument. This Court exists as a judicial tribunal by authority only of the President of the United States; the acceptance of the office is an acknowledgement of the validity of the authority conferring it, and, if the President had no authority to order, direct and constitute this Court to try the accused, and, as is claimed, did, in so constituting it, perform an unconstitutional and illegal act, it necessarily results that the order of the President is void and of no effect; that the order did not, and could not, constitute this a tribunal of justice,

23

and, therefore, its members are incapable of pronouncing a judicial decision upon the question presented.

There is a marked distinction between the question here presented, and that raised by a plea to the jurisdiction of a tribunal whose existence, as a court, is neither questioned nor denied. Here, it is argued, through many pages, by a learned Senator, and a distinguished lawyer, that the order of the President, by whose authority alone this Court is constituted a tribunal of military justice, is unlawful; if unlawful it is void and of no effect, and has created no court; therefore, this body, not being a court, can have no more power as a court, to decide any question whatever, than have its individual members power to decide that they, as men, do not in fact exist.

It is a maxim of the common law—the perfection of human reason—that what is impossible the law requires of no man.

How can it be possible that a judicial tribunal can decide the question that it does not exist, any more than that a rational man can decide that he does not exist?

The absurdity of the proposition, so elaborately urged upon the consideration of this Court, can not be saved from the ridicule and contempt of sensible men by the pretense that the Court is not asked judicially to decide that it is not a court, but only that it has no jurisdiction; for it is a fact not to be denied that the whole argument for the defense, on this point, is, that the President had not the lawful authority to issue the order by which alone this Court is constituted, and that the order for its creation is null and void.

Gentlemen might as well ask the Supreme Court of the United States, upon a plea to the jurisdiction, to decide, as a court, that the President had no lawful authority to nominate the judges thereof severally to the Senate, and that the Senate had no lawful authority to advise and consent to their appointment, as to ask this Court to decide, as a court, that the order of the President of the United States constituting it a tribunal for the sole purpose of this trial was not only without authority of law, but against and in violation of law. If this Court is not a lawful tribunal, it has no existence, and can no more speak as a court than the dead, much less pronounce the judgment required at its hands, that it is not a court, and that the President of the United States, in constituting it such to try the question upon the charge and specification preferred, has transcended his authority, and violated his oath of office.

Before passing from the consideration of the proposition of the learned Senator, that this is not a Court, it is fit that I should notice that another of the counsel for the accused (Mr. Ewing) has also advanced the same opinion, certainly with more directness and candor, and without any qualification. His statement is, "You," gentlemen, "are no court under the Constitution." This remark of the gentleman can not fail to excite surprise, when it is remembered that the gentleman, not many months

since, was a general in the service of the country, and as such in his department in the West proclaimed and enforced martial law by the constitution of military tribunals for the trial of citizens not in the land or naval forces, but who were guilty of military offenses, for which he deemed them justly punishable before military courts, and accordingly he punished them. Is the gentleman quite sure, when that account comes to be rendered for these alleged unconstitutional assumptions of power, that he will not have to answer for more of these alleged violations of the rights of citizens by illegal arrests, convictions, and executions, than any of the members of this Court? In support of his opinion that this is no court, the gentleman cites the 3d article of the Constitution, which provides. "that the judicial power of the United States shall be vested in one Supreme Court, and such inferior courts as Congress may establish," the judges whereof "shall hold their offices during good behavior."

It is a sufficient answer to say to the gentleman, that the power of this Government to try and punish military offenses by military tribunals is no part of the "judicial power of the United States," under the 3d article of the Constitution, but a power conferred by the 8th section of the 1st article, and so it has been ruled by the Supreme Court in *Dynes* vs. *Hoover*, 20 *Howard*, 78. If this power is so conferred by the 8th section, a military court authorized by Congress, and constituted as this has been, to try all persons for military crimes in time of war, though not exercising "the judicial power" provided for in the 3d article, is nevertheless a court as constitutional as the Supreme Court itself. The gentleman admits this to the extent of the trial by courts-martial of persons in the military or naval service, and by admitting it he gives up the point. There is no *express* grant for any such tribunal, and the power to establish such a court, therefore, is *implied* from the provisions of the 8th section, 1st article, that "Congress shall have power to provide and maintain a navy," and also "to make rules for the government of the land and naval forces." From these grants the Supreme Court infer the power to establish courts-martial, and from the grants in the same 8th section, as I shall notice hereafter, that " Congress shall have power to declare war," and "to pass all laws necessary and proper to carry this and all other powers into effect," it is necessarily implied that in time of war Congress may authorize military commissions, to try all crimes committed in aid of the public enemy, as such tribunals are *necessary* to give effect to the power to make war and suppress insurrection.

Inasmuch as the gentleman (Gen. Ewing) for whom, personally, I have a high regard as the military commander of a western department, made a liberal exercise, under the order of the Commander-in-Chief of the army, of this power to arrest and try military offenders not in the land or naval forces of the United States, and inflicted upon them, as I am informed, the extreme penalty of the law, by virtue of his military jurisdiction, I wish to know whether he proposes, by his proclamation of the personal responsibility awaiting all such usurpations of judicial authority, that he himself shall be subjected to the same stern judgment which he invokes against others—that, in short, he shall be drawn and quartered for inflicting the extreme penalties of the law upon citizens of the United States in violation of the Constitution and laws of his country? I trust that his error of judgment in pronouncing this military jurisdiction a usurpation and violation of the Constitution may not rise up in judgment to condemn him, and that he may never be subjected to pains and penalties for having done his duty heretofore in exercising this rightful authority, and in bringing to judgment those who conspired against the lives and liberties of the people.

Here I might leave this question, committing it to the charitable speeches of men, but for the fact that the learned counsel has been more careful in his extraordinary argument to denounce the President as a usurper than to show how the Court could possibly decide that it has no judicial existence, and yet that it has judicial existence.

A representative of the people and of the rights of the people before this Court, by the appointment of the President, and which appointment was neither sought by me or desired, I can not allow all that has here been said by way of denunciation of the murdered President and his successor to pass unnoticed. This has been made the occasion by the learned counsel, Mr. Johnson, to volunteer, not to defend the accused, Mary E. Surratt, not to make a judicial argument in her behalf, but to make a political harangue, a partisan speech against his Government and country, and thereby swell the cry of the armed legions of sedition and rebellion that but yesterday shook the heavens with their infernal enginery of treason and filled the habitations of the people with death. As the law forbids a Senator of the United States to receive compensation, or fee, for defending, in cases before civil or military commissions, the gentleman volunteers to make a speech before this Court, in which he denounces the action of the Executive Department in proclaiming and executing martial law against rebels in arms, their aiders and abettors, as a usurpation and a tyranny. I deem it my duty to reply to this denunciation, not for the purpose of presenting thereby any question for the decision of this Court, for I have shown that the argument of the gentleman presents no question for its decision as a Court, but to repel, as far as I may be able, the unjust aspersion attempted to be cast upon the memory of our dead President, and upon the official conduct of his successor.

I propose now to answer fully all that the gentleman (Mr. Johnson) has said of the want of jurisdiction in this Court, and of the alleged usurpation and tyranny of the Executive, that the enlightened public opinion to which he appeals may decide whether all this denunciation is just—whether indeed conspiring against the whole people, and confederation and agreement in aid of insurrection to murder all the executive officers of the government, can not be checked

or arrested by the Executive power. Let the people decide this question; and in doing so, let them pass upon the action of the Senator as well as upon the action of those whom he so arrogantly arraigns. His plea in behalf of an expiring and shattered rebellion is a fit subject for public consideration and for public condemnation.

Let that people also note, that while the learned gentleman (Mr. Johnson), as a volunteer, without pay, thus condemns as a usurpation the means employed so effectually to suppress this gigantic insurrection, the New York *News*, whose proprietor, Benjamin Wood, is shown by the testimony upon your record to have received from the agents of the rebellion twenty-five thousand dollars, rushes into the lists to champion the cause of the rebellion, its aiders and abettors, by following to the letter his colleague (Mr. Johnson), and with greater plainness of speech, and a fervor intensified, doubtless, by the twenty-five thousand dollars received, and the hope of more, denounces the Court as a usurpation and threatens the members with the consequences!

The argument of the gentleman, to which the Court has listened so patiently and so long, is but an attempt to show that it is unconstitutional for the Government of the United States to arrest upon military order and try before military tribunals and punish upon conviction, in accordance with the laws of war and the usages of nations, all criminal offenders acting in aid of the existing rebellion. It does seem to me that the speech in its tone and temper is the same as that which the country has heard for the last four years uttered by the armed rebels themselves and by their apologists, averring that it was unconstitutional for the Government of the United States to defend by arms its own rightful authority and the supremacy of its laws.

It is as clearly the right of the republic to live and to defend its life until it forfeits that right by crime, as it is the right of the individual to live so long as God gives him life, unless he forfeits that right by crime. I make no argument to support this proposition. Who is there here or elsewhere to cast the reproach upon my country that for her crimes she must die? Youngest born of the nations! is she not immortal by all the dread memories of the past—by that sublime and voluntary sacrifice of the present, in which the bravest and noblest of her sons have laid down their lives that she might live, giving their serene brows to the dust of the grave, and lifting their hands for the last time amidst the consuming fires of battle! I assume, for the purposes of this argument, that self-defense is as clearly the right of nations as it is the acknowledged right of men, and that the American people may do in the defense and maintenance of their own rightful authority against organized armed rebels, their aiders and abettors, whatever free and independent nations anywhere upon this globe, in time of war, may of right do.

All this is substantially denied by the gentleman in the remarkable argument which he has here made. There is nothing further from my purpose than to do injustice to the learned gentleman or to his elaborate and ingenious argument. To justify what I have already said, I may be permitted here to remind the Court that nothing is said by the counsel touching the conduct of the accused, Mary E. Surratt, as shown by the testimony; that he makes confession at the end of his arraignment of the Government and country, that he has not made such argument, and that he leaves it to be made by her other counsel. He does take care, however, to arraign the country and the Government for conducting a trial with closed doors and before a secret tribunal, and compares the proceedings of this Court to the Spanish Inquisition, using the strongest words at his command to intensify the horror which he supposes his announcement will excite throughout the civilized world.

Was this dealing fairly by this Government? Was there anything in the conduct of the proceedings here that justified any such remark? Has this been a secret trial? Has it not been conducted in open day, in the presence of the accused, and in the presence of seven gentlemen learned in the law, who appeared from day to day as their counsel? Were they not informed of the accusation against them? Were they deprived of the right of challenge? Was it not secured to them by law, and were they not asked to exercise it? Has any part of the evidence been suppressed? Have not all the proceedings been published to the world? What, then, was done, or intended to be done, by the Government, which justifies this clamor about a Spanish Inquisition?

That a people assailed by organized treason over an extent of territory half as large as the continent of Europe, and assailed in their very capital by secret assassins banded together and hired to do the work of murder by the instigation of these conspirators, may not be permitted to make inquiry, even with closed doors, touching the nature and extent of the organization, ought not to be asserted by any gentleman who makes the least pretensions to any knowledge of the law, either common, civil or military. Who does not know that at the common law all inquisition touching crimes and misdemeanors, preparatory to indictment by the grand inquest of the State, is made with closed doors?

In this trial, no parties accused, nor their counsel, nor the reporters of this Court, were at any time excluded from its deliberations when any testimony was being taken; nor has there been any testimony taken in the case with closed doors, save that of a few witnesses who testified, not in regard to the accused or either of them, but in respect to the traitors and conspirators not on trial, who were alleged to have incited this crime. Who is there to say that the American people, in time of armed rebellion and civil war, have not the right to make such an examination as secretly as they may deem necessary, either in a military or civil court?

I have said this, not by way of apology for anything the Government has done or attempted to do in the progress of this trial, but to expose the animus of the argument, and to repel the accusation against my country sent out to the world by the counsel. From anything that he has said, I have yet to learn that the American people have not the right to make their inquiries secretly, touching a general conspiracy in aid of an existing rebellion, which involves their nationality and the peace and security of all.

The gentleman then enters into a learned argument for the purpose of showing that, by the Constitution, the people of the United States can not, in war or in peace, subject any person to trial before a military tribunal, whatever may be his crime or offense, unless such person be in the military or naval service of the United States. The conduct of this argument is as remarkable as its assaults upon the Government are unwarranted, and its insinuations about the revival of the inquisition and secret trials are inexcusable. The Court will notice that the argument, from the beginning almost to its conclusion, insists that no person is liable to be tried by military or martial law before a military tribunal, save those in the land and naval service of the United States. I repeat, the conduct of this argument of the gentleman is remarkable. As an instance, I ask the attention, not only of this Court, but of that public whom he has ventured to address in this tone and temper, to the authority of the distinguished Chancellor Kent, whose great name the counsel has endeavored to press into his service in support of his general proposition, that no person save those in the military or naval service of the United States is liable to be tried for any crime whatever, either in peace or in war, before a military tribunal.

The language of the gentleman, after citing the provision of the Constitution, "that no person shall be held to answer for a capital or otherwise infamous crime unless on a presentment or indictment of a grand jury, except in cases arising in the land or naval forces, or in the militia, when in actual service in time of war or public danger," is, "that this exception is designed to leave in force, not to enlarge, the power vested in Congress by the original Constitution to make rules for the government and regulation of the land and naval forces; that the land or naval forces are the terms used in both, have the same meaning, and until lately have been supposed by every commentator and judge to exclude from military jurisdiction offenses committed by citizens not belonging to such forces." The learned gentleman then adds: "Kent, in a note to his 1st Commentaries, 341, states, and with accuracy, that 'military and naval crimes and offenses, committed while the party is attached to and under the immediate authority of the army and navy of the United States, and in actual service, are not cognizable under the common-law jurisdiction of the courts of the United States.'" I ask this Court to bear in mind that this is the only passage which he quotes from this note of Kent in his argument, and that no man possessed of common sense, however destitute he may be of the exact and varied learning in the law to which the gentleman may rightfully lay claim, can for a moment entertain the opinion that the distinguished chancellor of New York, in the passage just cited, intimates any such thing as the counsel asserts, that the Constitution excludes from military jurisdiction offenses committed by citizens not belonging to the land or naval forces.

Who can fail to see that Chancellor Kent, by the passage cited, only decides that military and naval crimes and offenses committed by a party attached to and under the immediate authority of the army and navy of the United States, and in actual service, are not cognisable under the common-law jurisdiction of the courts of the United States? He only says they are not cognisable under its common-law jurisdiction; but by that he does not say or intimate, what is attempted to be said by the counsel for him, that "all crimes committed by citizens are by the Constitution excluded from military jurisdiction," and that the perpetrators of them can under no circumstances be tried before military tribunals. Yet the counsel ventures to proceed, starting upon this passage quoted from Kent, to say that, "according to *this* great authority, every other class of persons and every other species of offenses are within the jurisdiction of the civil courts, and entitled to the protection of the proceeding by presentment or indictment and the public trial in such a court."

Whatever that great authority may have said elsewhere, it is very doubtful whether any candid man in America will be able to come to the very learned and astute conclusion that Chancellor Kent has so stated in the note or any part of the note which the gentleman has just cited. If he has said it elsewhere, it is for the gentleman, if he relies upon Kent for authority, to produce the passage. But was it fair treatment of this "great authority"—was it not taking an unwarrantable privilege with the distinguished chancellor and his great work, the enduring monument of his learning and genius, to so mutilate the note referred to, as might leave the gentleman at liberty to make his deductions and assertions under cover of the great name of the New York chancellor, to suit the emergency of his case, by omitting the following passage, which occurs in the same note, and absolutely excludes the conclusion so defiantly put forth by the counsel to support his argument? In that note Chancellor Kent says:

"*Military* law is a system of regulations for the government of the armies in the service of the United States, authorized by the act of Congress of April 10, 1806, known as the Articles of War, and *naval* law is a similar system for the government of the navy, under the act of Congress of April 23, 1800. But *martial* law is quite a distinct thing, and is founded upon paramount necessity, and proclaimed by a *military chief*."

However unsuccessful, after this exposure, the gentleman appears in maintaining his monstrous proposition, that the American people are by their own Constitution forbidden to try the aiders and abettors of armed traitors and rebellion before military tribunals, and subject them, according to the laws of war and the usages of nations, to just punishment for their great crimes, it has been made clear from what I have already stated, that he has been eminently successful in mutilating this beautiful production of that great mind; which act of mutilation, every one knows, is violative alike of the laws of peace and war. Even in war the divine creations of art and the immortal productions of genius and learning are spared.

In the same spirit, and it seems to me with the same unfairness as that just noted, the learned gentleman has very adroitly pressed into his service, by an extract from the autobiography of the war-worn veteran and hero, General Scott, the names of the late Secretary of War, Mr. Marcy, and the learned ex-Attorney-General, Mr. Cushing. This adroit performance is achieved in this way: after stating the fact that General Scott in Mexico proclaimed martial law for the trial and punishment by military tribunals of persons guilty of "assassination, murder and poisoning," the gentleman proceeds to quote from the Autobiography, "that this order, when handed to the then Secretary of War (Mr. Marcy) for his approval, 'a startle at the title (martial law order) was the only comment he then or ever made on the subject,' and that it was 'soon silently returned as too explosive for safe handling.' 'A little later (he adds) the Attorney-General (Mr. Cushing) called and asked for a copy, and the law officer of the government, whose business it is to speak on all such matters, was stricken with *legal dumbness*.'" Thereupon the learned gentleman proceeds to say: "How much more startled and more paralyzed would these great men have been had they been consulted on such a commission as this! A commission, not to sit in another country, and to try offenses not provided for in any law of the United States, civil or military, then in force, but in their own country, and in a part of it where there are laws providing for their trial and punishment, and civil courts clothed with ample powers for both, and in the daily and undisturbed exercise of their jurisdiction."

I think I may safely say, without stopping to make any special references, that the official career of the late Secretary of War (Mr. Marcy) gave no indication that he ever doubted or denied the constitutional power of the American people, acting through their duly constituted agents, to do any act justified by the laws of war, for the suppression of a rebellion or to repel invasion. Certainly there is nothing in this extract from the Autobiography which justifies any such conclusion. He was startled, we are told. It may have been as much the admiration he had for the boldness and wisdom of the conqueror of Mexico as any abhorrence he had for the trial and punishment of "assassins, poisoners and murderers," according to the laws and usages of war.

But the official utterances of the ex-Attorney-General, Cushing, with which the gentleman doubtless was familiar when he prepared this argument, by no means justify the attempt here made to quote him as authority against the proclamation and enforcement of martial law in time of rebellion and civil war. That distinguished man, not second in legal attainments to any who have held that position, has left an official opinion of record touching this subject. Referring to what is said by Sir Mathew Hale, in his History of the Common Law, concerning martial law, wherein he limits it, as the gentleman has seemed by the whole drift of his argument desirous of doing, and says that it is "not in truth and in reality law, but something indulged rather than allowed as a law—the necessity of government, order and discipline in an army," Mr. Cushing makes this just criticism: "This proposition is a mere composite blunder, a total misapprehension of the matter. It confounds *martial law* and *law military*; it ascribes to the former the uses of the latter; it erroneously assumes that the government of a body of troops is a necessity more than of a body of civilians or citizens. It confounds and confuses all the relations of the subject, and is an apt illustration of the incompleteness of the notions of the common-law jurists of England in regard to matters not comprehended in that limited branch of legal science. * * * Military law, it is now perfectly understood in England, is a branch of the law of the land, applicable only to certain acts of a particular class of persons, and administered by special tribunals; but neither in that nor in any other respect essentially differing as to foundation in constitutional reason from admiralty, ecclesiastical or indeed chancery and common law. * * It is the system of rules for the government of the army and navy established by successive acts of Parliament. * * * * * Martial law, as exercised in any country by the commander of a foreign army, is an element of the *jus belli*.

"It is incidental to the state of solemn war, and appertains to the law of nations. * * Thus, while the armies of the United States occupied different provinces of the Mexican republic, the respective commanders were not limited in authority by any local law. They allowed, or rather required, the magistrates of the country, municipal or judicial, to continue to administer the laws of the country among their countrymen; but in subjection, always, to the military power, which acted summarily and according to discretion, when the belligerent interests of the conqueror required it, and which exercised jurisdiction, either summarily or by means of military commissions for the protection or the punishment of citizens of the United States in Mexico. *Opinions of Attorneys-General*, vol. viii, 866–869.

Mr. Cushing says, "That, it would seem, was one of the forms of martial law;" but he adds, that such an example of martial law administered by a foreign army in the enemy's country "does not enlighten us in regard to the question of martial law in one's own country, and as administered by its military commanders. That is a case which the law of nations does not reach. Its regulation is of the domestic resort of the organic laws of the country itself, and regarding which, as it hap-

pens, there is no definite or explicit legislation in the United States, as there is none in England.

"Accordingly, in England, as we have seen, Earl Grey assumes that when martial law exists it has no legal origin, but is a mere fact of necessity, to be legalized afterward by a bill of indemnity, if there be occasion. I am not prepared to say that, under existing laws, such may not also be the case in the United States." *Ibid.*, 870.

After such a statement, wherein ex-Attorney-General Cushing very clearly recognizes the right of this Government, as also of England, to employ martial law as a means of defense in a time of war, whether domestic or foreign, he will be as much surprised when he reads the argument of the learned gentleman wherein he is described as being struck with *legal dumbness* at the mere mention of proclaiming martial law, and its enforcement by the commander of our army in Mexico, as the late Secretary of War was startled with even the mention of its title.

Even some of the reasons given, and certainly the power exercised by the veteran hero himself, would seem to be in direct conflict with the propositions of the learned gentleman.

The Lieutenant-General says, he "excludes from his order cases already cognizable by court-martial, and limits it to cases not provided for in the act of Congress establishing rules and articles for the government of the armies of the United States." Has not the gentleman who attempts to press General Scott into his service argued and insisted upon it, that the commander of the army can not subject the soldiers under his command to any control or punishment whatever, save that which is provided for in the articles?

It will not do, in order to sustain the gentleman's hypothesis, to say that these provisions of the Constitution, by which he attempts to fetter the power of the people to punish such offenses in time of war within the territory of the United States, may be disregarded by an officer of the United States in command of its armies, in the trial and punishment of its soldiers in a foreign war. The law of the United States for the government of its own armies follows the flag upon every sea and in every land.

The truth is, that the right of the people to proclaim and execute martial law is a necessary incident of war, and this was the right exercised, and rightfully exercised, by Lieutenant-General Scott in Mexico. It was what Earl Grey has justly said was a "fact of necessity," and I may add, an act as clearly authorized as was the act of fighting the enemy when they appeared before him.

In making this exception, the Lieutenant-General followed the rule recognized by the American authorities on military law, in which it is declared that "many crimes committed even by military officers, enlisted men, or camp retainers, can not be tried under the rules and articles of war. Military Commissions must be resorted to for such cases, and these commissions should be ordered by the same authority, be constituted in a similar manner, and their proceedings be conducted according to the same general rules as general courts-martial." *Benet*, 15.

There remain for me to notice, at present, two other points in this extraordinary speech: first, that martial law does not warrant a military commission for the trial of military offenses—that is, offenses committed in time of war in the interests of the public enemy, and by concert and agreement with the enemy; and second, that martial law does not prevail in the United States, and has never been declared by any competent authority.

It is not necessary, as the gentleman himself has declined to argue the first point—whether martial law authorizes the organization of military commissions by order of the Commander-in-Chief to try such offenses, that I should say more than that the authority just cited by me shows that such commissions are authorized under martial law, and are created by the commander for the trial of all such offenses, when their punishment by court-martial is not provided for by the express statute law of the country.

The second point—that martial law has not been declared by any competent authority, is an arraignment of the late murdered President of the United States for his proclamation of September 24, 1862, declaring martial law throughout the United States; and of which, in Lawrence's edition of *Wheaton on International Law*, p. 522, it is said: "Whatever may be the inference to be deduced, either from Constitutional or International Law, or from the usages of European governments, as to the legitimate depository of the power of suspending the writ of *habeas corpus*, the virtual abrogation of the judiciary in cases affecting individual liberty, and the establishment as *matter of fact* in the United States, by the Executive alone, of martial law, not merely in the insurrectionary districts, or in cases of military occupancy, but throughout the entire Union, and not temporarily, but as an institution as permanent as the insurrection on which it professes to be based, and capable on the same principle of being revived in all cases of foreign as well as civil war, are placed beyond question by the President's proclamation of September 24, 1862." That proclamation is as follows:

"BY THE PRESIDENT OF THE UNITED STATES OF AMERICA—A PROCLAMATION.

"Whereas, it has become necessary to call into service not only volunteers, but also portions of the militia of the States, by a draft, in order to suppress the insurrection existing in the United States, and disloyal persons are not adequately restrained by the ordinary processes of law from hindering this measure, and from giving aid and comfort in various ways to the insurrection: Now, therefore, be it ordered, that during the existing insurrection, and as a necessary means for suppressing the same, all rebels and insurgents, their aiders and abettors, within the United States, and all persons discouraging volunteer enlistments, 'resisting militia drafts, or guilty of any disloyal practice, affording aid and comfort to rebels, against the authority of the United States, shall be subject to martial law, and liable to trial and punishment by courts-martial or military commission.

"Second. That the writ of *habeas corpus* is suspended in respect to all persons arrested, or who are now, or hereafter during the rebellion shall be, imprisoned in any fort, camp, arsenal, military prison, or other place of confinement, by any military authority, or by the sentence of any court-martial or military commission.

"In witness whereof, I have hereunto set my hand, and caused the seal of the United States to be affixed.

"Done at the city of Washington, this 24th day of September, A. D. 1862, and of the independence of the United States the eighty-seventh.   "ABRAHAM LINCOLN

"By the President:

"WILLIAM H. SEWARD, Secretary of State."

This proclamation is duly certified from the War Department to be in full force and not revoked, and is evidence of record in this case; and but a few days since a proclamation of the President, of which this Court will take notice, declares that the same remains in full force.

It has been said by another of the counsel for the accused (Mr. Stone) in his argument, that admitting its validity, the proclamation ceases to have effect with the insurrection, and is terminated by it. It is true the proclamation of martial law only continues during the insurrection; but inasmuch as the question of the existence of an insurrection is a political question, the decision of which belongs exclusively to the political department of the Government, that department alone can declare its existence, and that department alone can declare its termination, and by the action of the political department of the Government every judicial tribunal in the land is concluded and bound. That question has been settled for fifty years in this country by the Supreme Court of the United States: First, in the case of Brown *vs.* the United States, 8 *Cranch;* also in the prize cases, 2 *Black*, 641. Nothing more, therefore, need be said upon this question of an *existing* insurrection than this: The political department of the Government has heretofore proclaimed an insurrection; that department has not yet declared the insurrection ended, and the event on the 14th of April, which robbed the people of their chosen Executive, and clothed this land in mourning, bore sad but overwhelming witness to the fact that the rebellion is not ended. The fact of the insurrection is not an open question to be tried or settled by parol, either in a military tribunal or in a civil court.

The declaration of the learned gentleman who opened the defense (Mr. Johnson), that martial law has never been declared by any competent authority, as I have already said, arraigns Mr. Lincoln for a usurpation of power. Does the gentleman mean to say that, until Congress authorizes it, the President can not proclaim and enforce martial law in the suppression of armed and organized rebellion? Or does he only affirm that this act of the late President is a usurpation?

The proclamation of martial law in 1862 a usurpation! though it armed the people in that dark hour of trial with the means of defense against traitorous and secret enemies in every State and district of the country; though by its use some of the guilty were brought to swift and just judgment, and others deterred from crime or driven to flight; though by this means the innocent and defenseless were protected; though by this means the city of the gentleman's residence was saved from the violence and pillage of the mob and the torch of the incendiary. But, says the gentleman, it was a usurpation, forbidden by the laws of the land!

The same was said of the proclamations of blockade, issued April 19 and 27, 1861, which declared a blockade of the ports of the insurgent States, and that all vessels violating the same were subjects of capture, and, together with the cargo, to be condemned as prize. Inasmuch as Congress had not then recognized the fact of civil war, these proclamations were denounced as void. The Supreme Court decided otherwise, and affirmed the power of the Executive thus to subject property on the seas to seizure and condemnation. I read from that decision:

"The Constitution confers upon the President the whole executive power; he is bound to take care that the laws be faithfully executed; he is Commander-in-Chief of the army and navy of the United States, and of the militia of the several States when called into the actual service of the United States. * * Whether the President, in fulfilling his duties as Commander-in-Chief in suppressing an insurrection, has met with such armed hostile resistance, and a civil war of such alarming proportions as will compel him to accord to them the character of belligerents, is a question to be decided *by him*, and this Court must be governed by the decisions and acts of the political department of the Government to which this power was intrusted. He must determine what degree of force the crisis demands.

"The proclamation of blockade is itself official and conclusive evidence to the Court that a state of war existed which demanded and authorized a recourse to such a measure under the circumstances peculiar to the case." 2 *Black*, 670.

It has been solemnly ruled by the same tribunal, in an earlier case, "that the power is confided to the Executive of the Union to determine when it is necessary to call out the militia of the States to repel invasion," as follows: "That he is necessarily constituted the judge of the existence of the exigency in the first instance, and is bound to act according to his belief of the facts. If he does so act, and decides to call forth the militia, his orders for this purpose are in strict conformity with the provisions of the law; and it would seem to follow as a necessary consequence, that

every act done by a subordinate officer, in obedience to such orders, is equally justifiable. The law contemplates that, under such circumstances, orders shall be given to carry the power into effect; and it can not, therefore, be a correct inference that any other person has a just right to disobey them. The law does not provide for any appeal from the judgment of the President, or for any right in subordinate officers to review his decision, and in effect defeat it. Whenever a statute gives a discretionary power to any person, to be exercised by him upon his own opinion of certain facts, it is a sound rule of construction, that the statute constitutes him the sole and exclusive judge of the existence of those facts." 12 *Wheaton*, 31.

In the light of these decisions, it must be clear to every mind that the question of the existence of an insurrection, and the necessity of calling into requisition for its suppression both the militia of the States, and the army and navy of the United States, and of proclaiming martial law, which is an essential condition of war, whether foreign or domestic, must rest with the officer of the Government who is charged by the express terms of the Constitution with the performance of this great duty for the common defense and the execution of the laws of the Union.

But it is further insisted by the gentleman in this argument, that Congress has not authorized the establishment of military commissions, which are essential to the judicial administration of martial law, and the punishment of crimes committed during the existence of a civil war, and especially, that such commissions are not so authorized to try persons other than those in the military or naval service of the United States, or in the militia of the several States, when in the actual service of the United States. The gentleman's argument assuredly destroys itself, for he insists that the Congress, as the legislative department of the government, can pass no law which, either in peace or war, can constitutionally subject any citizen in the land or naval forces, to trial for crime before a military tribunal, or otherwise than by a jury in the civil courts.

Why does the learned gentleman now tell us that Congress has not authorized this to be done, after declaring just as stoutly that by the fifth and sixth amendments to the Constitution no such military tribunals can be established for the trial of any person not in the military or naval service of the United States, or in the militia, when in actual service, for the commission of any crime whatever in time of war or insurrection? It ought to have occurred to the gentleman when commenting upon the exception in the fifth article of the Constitution, that there was a reason for it very different from that which he saw fit to assign, and that reason, manifestly upon the face of the Constitution itself, was, that by the eighth section of the first article, it is expressly provided that Congress shall have power to make rules for the government of the land and naval forces, and to provide for organizing, arming and disciplining the militia, and for *governing* such part of them as may be employed in the service of the United States, and that, inasmuch as military discipline and order are as essential in an army in time of peace as in time of war, if the Constitution would leave this power to Congress in peace, it must make the exception, so that rules and regulations for the government of the army and navy should be operative in time of peace as well as in time of war; because the provisions of the Constitution give the right of trial by jury IN TIME OF PEACE, in all criminal prosecutions by indictment, in terms embracing every human being that may be held to answer for crime in the United States: and therefore, if the eighth section of the first article was to remain in full force IN TIME OF PEACE, the exception must be made; and accordingly, the exception was made. But by the argument we have listened to, this Court is told, and the country is told, that IN TIME OF WAR—a war which involves in its dread issue the lives and interests of us all—the guarantees of the Constitution are in full force for the benefit of those who conspire with the enemy, creep into your camps, murder in cold blood, in the interests of the invader or insurgent, the Commander-in-Chief of your army, and secure to him the slow and weak provisions of the civil law, while the soldier, who may, when overcome by the demands of exhausted nature, which can not be resisted, have slept at his post, is subject to be tried upon the spot by a military tribunal and shot. The argument amounts to this: that as military courts and military trials of civilians in time of war are a usurpation and tyranny, and as soldiers are liable to such arrests and trial, Sergeant Corbett, who shot Booth, should be tried and executed by sentence of a military court; while Booth's co-conspirators and aiders should be saved from any such indignity as a military trial! I confess that I am too dull to comprehend the logic, the reason, or the sense of such a conclusion! If there is any one entitled to this privilege of a civil trial, at a remote period, and by a jury of the District, IN TIME OF CIVIL WAR, when the foundations of the Republic are rocking beneath the earthquake tread of armed rebellion, that man is the defender of the republic. It will never do to say, as has been said in this argument, that the soldier is not liable to be tried in time of war by a military tribunal for any other offense than those prescribed in the rules and articles of war. To my mind, nothing can be clearer than that citizen and soldier alike, in time of civil or foreign war, after a proclamation of martial law, are triable by military tribunals for all offenses of which they may be guilty, in the interests of, or in concert with, the enemy.

These provisions, therefore, of your Constitution for indictment and trial by jury in civil courts of all crimes are, as I shall hereafter show, silent and inoperative in time of war when the public safety requires it.

The argument to which I have thus been replying, as the Court will not fail to perceive, nor that public to which the argument is addressed, is a labored attempt to establish the proposition, that, by the Constitution of the United States, the American people can not, even in a civil war the greatest the world has ever seen, employ martial law and military tribunals as a means of successfully asserting their authority, preserving their nationality, and securing protection to the lives and property of all, and especially to the persons of those to whom they have committed, officially, the great trust of maintaining the national authority. The gentleman says, with an air of perfect confidence, that he denies the jurisdiction of military tribunals for the trial of civilians in time of war, because neither the Constitution nor laws justify, but on the contrary repudiate them, and that all the experience of the past is against it. I might content myself with saying that the practice of all nations is against the gentleman's conclusion. The struggle for our national independence was aided and prosecuted by military tribunals and martial law, as well as by arms. The contest for American nationality began with the establishment, very soon after the firing of the first gun at Lexington, on the 19th day of April, 1775, of military tribunals and martial law. On the 30th of June, 1775, the Continental Congress provided that "whosoever, *belonging to the continental army,* shall be convicted of holding correspondence with, or giving intelligence to the enemy, either indirectly or directly, shall suffer such punishment as by a court-martial shall be ordered." This was found not sufficient, inasmuch as it did not reach those *civilians* who, like certain civilians of our day, claim the protection of the civil law in time of war against military arrests and military trials for military crimes. Therefore, the same Congress, on the 7th of November, 1775, amended this provision by striking out the words "belonging to the continental army," and adopting the article as follows:

"*All persons* convicted of holding a treacherous correspondence with, or giving intelligence to the enemy, shall suffer death, or such other punishment as a general court-martial shall think proper."

And on the 17th of June, 1776, the Congress added an additional rule:

"That all persons, not members of, nor owing allegiance to, any of the United States of America, who should be found lurking as spies in or about the fortifications or encampments of the armies of the United States, or any of them, shall suffer death, according to the law and usage of nations, by the sentence of a court-martial, or such other punishment as a court-martial shall direct."

Comprehensive as was this legislation, embracing, as it did, soldiers, citizens and aliens, subjecting all alike to trial for their military crimes by the military tribunals of justice, according to the law and the usage of nations, it was found to be insufficient to meet that most dangerous of all crimes, committed in the interests of the enemy, by citizens, in time of war, the crime of conspiring together to assassinate, or seize and carry away, the soldiers and citizens who were loyal to the cause of the country. Therefore, on the 27th of February, 1778, the Congress adopted the following resolution:

"*Resolved,* That whatever inhabitants of these States shall kill, or seize, or take, any loyal citizen or citizens thereof, and convey him, her, or them, to any place within the power of the enemy, or shall ENTER INTO ANY COMBINATION for such purpose, or attempt to carry the same into execution, or hath assisted or shall assist therein; or shall, by giving intelligence, acting as a guide, or, in any manner whatever, aid the enemy in the perpetration thereof, he shall suffer death, by the judgment of a court-martial, as a traitor, assassin, or spy, if the offense be committed within seventy miles of the headquarters of the grand or other armies of these States, where a general officer commands." *Journals of Congress*, vol. II, pp. 459, 460.

So stood the law until the adoption of the Constitution of the United States. Every well-informed man knows that, at the time of the passage of these acts, the courts of justice, having cognizance of all crimes against persons, were open, in many of the States, and that, by their several constitutions and charters, which were then the supreme law for the punishment of crimes committed within their respective territorial limits, no man was liable to conviction but by the verdict of a jury. Take, for example, the provisions of the Constitution of North Carolina, adopted on the 10th of November, 1776, and in full force at the time of the passage of the last resolution by Congress above cited, which provisions are as follows:

"That no freeman shall be put to answer any criminal charge but by indictment, presentment or impeachment."

"That no freeman shall be convicted of any crime but by the unanimous verdict of a jury of good and lawful men, in open court, as heretofore used."

This was the law in 1778 in all the States, and the provision for a trial by jury, every one knows, meant a jury of twelve men, impanneled and qualified to try the issue in a civil court. The conclusion is not to be avoided that these enactments of the Congress, under the confederation, set aside the trial by jury within the several States, and expressly provided for the trial, by court-martial, of "any of the inhabitants" who, during the revolution, might, contrary to the provisions of said law, and in aid of the public enemy, give them intelligence, or kill any loyal citizens of the United States, or enter into any combination to kill or carry them away. How comes it, if the argument of the counsel be true, that this enactment was passed by the Congress of 1778, when the constitutions of the several States, at that day, as fully guaranteed trial by jury to every person held to answer for a crime, as does the Constitution of the United States at this hour? Notwithstanding this fact, I have yet to learn that any loyal man ever challenged, during all the period of our conflict for independence and nationality, the validity of that law for the trial, for military offenses, by military tribunals, of all offenders, as the law, not of peace, but of war, and absolutely essential to the prosecution of war. I may be pardoned for saying that it is the accepted common law of nations that martial law is, at all times, and everywhere, essential to the successful prosecution of war, whether it be a civil or a foreign war. The validity of these acts of the Continental and Con-

federate Congress I know was challenged, but only by men charged with the guilt of their country's blood.

Washington, the peerless, the stainless, and the just, with whom God walked through the night of that great trial, enforced this just and wise enactment upon all occasions On the 30th of September, 1780, Joshua H. Smith, by the order of General Washington, was put upon his trial before a court-martial, convened in the State of New York, on the charge of there aiding and assisting Benedict Arnold, in a combination with the enemy, to *take, kill* and *seize* such loyal citizens or soldiers of the United States as were in garrison at West Point. Smith objected to the jurisdiction, averring that he was a private citizen, not in the military or naval service, and, therefore, was only amenable to the civil authority of the State, whose constitution had guaranteed the right of trial by jury to all persons held to answer for crime. *Chandler's Criminal Trials*, vol. II, p. 187. The Constitution of New York, then in force, had so provided; but, notwithstanding that, the Court overruled the plea, held him to answer, and tried him. I repeat that, when Smith was thus tried by court-martial, the Constitution of New York as fully guaranteed trial by jury in the civil courts, to all civilians charged and held to answer for crimes within the limits of that State, as does the Constitution of the United States guarantee such trial within the limits of the District of Columbia. By the second of the Articles of Confederation each State retained "its sovereignty," and every power, jurisdiction and right not *expressly* delegated to the United States in Congress assembled. By those Articles there was no express delegation of judicial power; therefore, the States retained it fully.

If the military courts, constituted by the commander of the army of the United States under the Confederation, who was appointed only by a resolution of the Congress, without any *express* grant of power to authorize it—his office not being created by the act of the people in their fundamental law—had jurisdiction in every State to try and put to death "any inhabitant" thereof who should *kill* any loyal citizen, or enter into "any combination" for any such purpose therein in time of war, notwithstanding the provisions of the Constitution and laws of such States, how can any man conceive that, under the Constitution of the United States, which is the Supreme law over every State, anything in the Constitution and laws of such State to the contrary notwithstanding, and the supreme law over every Territory of the Republic as well, the Commander-in-Chief of the army of the United States, who is made such by the Constitution, and, by its supreme authority, clothed with the power and charged with the duty of directing and controlling the whole military power of the United States, in time of rebellion or invasion, has not that authority?

I need not remind the Court that one of the marked differences between the Articles of Confederation and the Constitution of the United States was, that, under the Confederation, the Congress was the sole depository of all federal power. The Congress of the Confederation, said Madison, held "the command of the army." *Fed.*, *No.* 38. Has the Constitution, which was ordained by the people the better "to insure domestic tranquillity and to provide for the common defense," so fettered the great power of self-defense against armed insurrection or invasion that martial law, so essential in war, is forbidden by that great instrument? I will yield to no man in' reverence for or obedience to the Constitution of my country, esteeming it, as I do, a new evangel to the nations, embodying the democracy of the New Testament, the absolute equality of all men before the law, in respect of those rights of human nature which are the gift of God, and, therefore, as universal as the material structure of man. Can it be that this Constitution of ours, so divine in its spirit of justice, so beneficent in its results, so full of wisdom, and goodness, and truth, under which we became one people, a great and powerful nationality, has, in terms or by implication, denied to this people the power to crush armed rebellion by war, and to arrest and punish, during the existence of such rebellion, according to the laws of war and the usages of nations, secret conspirators who aid and abet the public enemy?

Here is a conspiracy, organized and prosecuted by armed traitors and hired assassins, receiving the moral support of thousands in every State and district, who pronounced the war for the Union a failure, and your now murdered but immortal Commander-in-Chief a tyrant; the object of which conspiracy, as the testimony shows, was to aid the tottering rebellion which struck at the nation's life. It is in evidence that Davis, Thompson, and others, chiefs in this rebellion, in aid of the same, agreed and conspired with others to poison the fountains of water which supply your commercial metropolis, and thereby murder its inhabitants; to secretly deposit in the habitations of the people and in the ships in your harbors inflammable materials, and thereby destroy them by fire; to murder by the slow and consuming torture of famine your soldiers, captives in their hands; to import pestilence in infected clothes to be distributed in your capital and camps, and thereby murder the surviving heroes and defenders of the republic, who, standing by the holy graves of your unreturning brave, proudly and defiantly challenge to honorable combat and open battle all public enemies, that their country may live; and, finally, to crown this horrid catalogue of crime, this sum of all human atrocities, conspired, as charged upon your record, with the accused and John Wilkes Booth and John H. Surratt, to kill and murder in your capital the executive officers of your Government and the commander of your armies. When this conspiracy, entered into by these traitors, is revealed by its attempted execution, and the foul and brutal murder of your President in the capital, you are told that it is unconstitutional, in order to arrest the further execution of the conspiracy, to interpose the military power of this government for the arrest, without civil process, of any of the parties thereto, and for their trial by a military tribunal of justice. If any such rule had obtained during our struggle for independence, we never would have been a nation. If any such rule had been adopted and acted upon now, during the fierce struggle of the past four years, no man can say that our nationality would have thus long survived.

The whole people of the United States, by their Constitution, have created the office of President of the United States and Commander-in-Chief of the army and navy, and have vested, by the terms of that Constitution, in the person of the President and Commander-in-Chief, the power to enforce the execution of the laws, and preserve, protect, and defend the Constitution.

The question may well be asked: If, as Commander-in-Chief, the President may not, in time of insurrection or war, proclaim and execute martial law, according to the usages of nations, how he can successfully perform the duties of his office—execute the laws, preserve the Constitution, suppress insurrection, and repel invasion?

Martial law and military tribunals are as essential to the successful prosecution of war as are men, and arms, and munitions. The Constitution of the United States has vested the power to declare war and raise armies and navies exclusively in the Congress, and the power to prosecute the war and command the army and navy exclusively in the President of the United States. As, under the Confederation, the commander of the army, appointed only by the Congress, was by the resolution of that Congress empowered to act as he might think proper for the good and welfare of the service, subject only to such restraints or orders as the Congress might give; so, under the Constitution, the President is, by the people who ordained that Constitution and declared him Commander-in-Chief of the army and navy, vested with full power to direct and control the army and navy of the United States, and employ all the forces necessary to preserve, protect, and defend the Constitution and execute the laws, as enjoined by his oath and the very letter of the Constitution, subject to no restriction or direction save such as Congress may from time to time prescribe.

That these powers for the common defense, intrusted by the Constitution exclusively to the Congress and the President, are, in time of civil war or foreign invasion, to be exercised without limitation or restraint, to the extent of the public necessity, and without any intervention of the Federal judiciary or of State constitutions or State laws, are facts in our history not open to question.

The position is not to be answered by saying you make the American Congress thereby omnipotent, and clothe the American Executive with the asserted attribute of hereditary monarchy—the king can do no wrong. Let the position be fairly stated—that the Congress and President, in war as in peace, are but the agents of the whole people, and that this unlimited power for the common defense against armed rebellion or foreign invasion is but the power of the people intrusted exclusively to the legislative and executive departments as their agents, for any and every abuse of which these agents are directly responsible to the people—and the demagogue cry of an omnipotent Congress, and an executive invested with royal prerogatives, vanishes like the baseless fabric of a vision. If the Congress corruptly, or oppressively, or wantonly abuse this great trust, the people, by the irresistible power of the ballot, hurl them from place. If the President so abuse the trust, the people by their Congress withhold supplies, or by impeachment transfer the trust to better hands, strip him of the franchises of citizenship and of office, and declare him forever disqualified to hold any position of honor, trust, or power under the government of his country.

I can understand very well why men should tremble at the exercise of this great power by a monarch whose person, by the Constitution of his realm, is inviolable, but I can not conceive how an American citizen, who has faith in the capacity of the whole people to govern themselves, should give himself any concern on the subject. Mr. Hallam, the distinguished author of the *Constitutional History of England*, has said:

"Kings love to display the divinity with which their flatterers invest them, in nothing so much as in the instantaneous execution of their will, and to stand revealed, as it were, in the storm and thunderbolt when their power breaks through the operation of secondary causes and awes a prostrate nation without the intervention of law."

How just are such words when applied to an irresponsible monarch! How absurd, when applied to a whole people, acting through their duly appointed agents, whose will, thus declared, is the supreme law, to awe into submission and peace and obedience, not a prostrate nation, but a prostrate rebellion! The same great author utters the fact which all history attests, when he says:

"It has been usual for all governments during actual rebellion, to proclaim martial law for the suspension of civil jurisdiction; and this anomaly, I must admit," he adds, "is very far from being less indispensable at such unhappy seasons where the ordinary mode of trial is by jury, than where the right of decision resides in the court." *Const. Hist.*, vol. I, ch. 5, p. 826.

That the power to proclaim martial law and fully or partially suspend the civil jurisdiction, Federal and State, in time of rebellion or civil war, and punish by military tribunals all offenses committed in aid of the public enemy, is conferred upon Congress and the Executive, necessarily results from the unlimited grants of power for the common defense to which I have already briefly referred. I may be pardoned for saying that this position is not assumed by me for the purposes of this occasion, but that early in the first year of this great struggle for our national life I proclaimed it as a representative of the people, under the obligation of my oath, and, as I then believed, and still believe, upon the authority of the

great men who formed and fashioned the wise and majestic fabric of American government.

Some of the citations which I deemed it my duty at that time to make, and some of which I now re-produce, have, I am pleased to say, found a wider circulation in books that have since been published by others.

When the Constitution was on trial for its deliverance before the people of the several States, its ratification was opposed on the ground that it conferred upon Congress and the Executive unlimited power for the common defense. To all such objectors—and they were numerous in every State—that great man, Alexander Hamilton, whose words will live as long as our language lives, speaking to the listening people of all the States, and urging them not to reject that matchless instrument which bore the name of Washington, said:

"The authorities essential to the care of the common defense are these: To raise armies; to build and equip fleets; to prescribe rules for the government of both; to direct their operations; to provide for their support. These powers ought to exist WITHOUT LIMITATION; because it is impossible to foresee or define the extent and variety of national exigencies, and the correspondent extent and variety of the means which may be necessary to satisfy them.

"The circumstances that endanger the safety of nations are infinite; and for this reason no constitutional shackles can wisely be imposed on the power to which the care of it is committed. ✱ ✱ ✱ This power ought to be under the direction of the same councils which are appointed to preside over the common defense. ✱ ✱ ✱ It must be admitted, as a necessary consequence, that there can be no limitation of that authority which is to provide for the defense and protection of the community, in any manner essential to its efficacy; that is, any matter essential to the formation, direction or support of the national forces."

He adds the further remark:

"This is one of those truths which, to a correct and unprejudiced mind, carries its own evidence along with it; and may be obscured, but can not be made plainer by argument or reasoning. It rests upon axioms as simple as they are universal—the *means* ought to be proportioned to the *end*; the persons from whose agency the attainment of any *end* is expected, ought to possess the means by which it is to be attained." *Federalist*, No. 23.

In the same great contest for the adoption of the Constitution, Madison, sometimes called the Father of the Constitution, said:

"Is the power of declaring war necessary? No man will answer this question in the negative. ✱ ✱ ✱ Is the power of raising armies and equipping fleets necessary? ✱ ✱ ✱ It is involved in the power of self-defense. ✱ ✱ ✱ With what color of propriety could the force necessary for defense be limited by those who can not limit the force of offense? ✱ ✱ ✱ The means of security can only be regulated by the means and the danger of attack. ✱ ✱ ✱ It is in vain to oppose constitutional barriers to the impulse of self-preservation. It is worse than in vain, because it plants in the Constitution itself necessary usurpations of power." *Federalist*, No. 41.

With this construction, proclaimed both by the advocates and opponents of its ratification, the Constitution of the United States was accepted and adopted, and that construction has been followed and acted upon, by every department of the Government to this day.

It was as well understood then in theory as it has since been illustrated in practice, that the judicial power, both Federal and State, had no voice and could exercise no authority in the conduct and prosecution of a war, except in subordination to the political department of the Government. The Constitution contains the significant provision, "The privilege of the writ of *habeas corpus* shall not be suspended, unless when in cases of rebellion or invasion the public safety may require it."

What was this but a declaration, that in time of rebellion, or invasion, the public safety is the highest law?—that so far as necessary the civil courts (of which the Commander-in-Chief, under the direction of Congress) must be silent, and the rights of each citizen, as secured in time of peace, must yield to the wants, interests and necessities of the nation? Yet we have been gravely told by the gentleman, in his argument, that the maxim, *salus populi suprema est lex*, is but fit for a tyrant's use. Those grand men, whom God taught to build the fabric of empire, thought otherwise, when they put that maxim into the Constitution of their country. It is very clear that the Constitution recognizes the great principle which underlies the structure of society and of all civil government; that no man lives for himself alone, but each for all; that if need be some must die, that the State may live, because at best the individual is but for to-day, while the commonwealth is for all time. I agree with the gentleman in the maxim which he borrows from Aristotle, "Let the public weal be under the protection of the law;" but I claim that in war, as in peace, by the very terms of the Constitution of the country, the public safety is under the protection of the law; that the Constitution itself has provided for the declaration of war for the common defense, to suppress rebellion, to repel invasion, and by express terms, has declared that whatever is necessary to make the prosecution of the war successful, may be done, and ought to be done, and is therefore constitutionally lawful.

Who will dare to say that in time of civil war "no person shall be deprived of life liberty and property, without due process of law?" This is a provision of your Constitution, than which there is none more just or sacred in it; it is, however, only the law of peace, not of war. In peace, that wise provision of the Constitution must be, and is, enforced by the civil courts; in war, it must be, and is, to a great extent, inoperative and disregarded. The thousands slain by your armies in battle were deprived of life "without due process of law." All spies arrested, convicted and executed by your military tribunals in time of war are de-

prived of liberty and life "without due process of law;" all enemies captured and held as prisoners of war are deprived of liberty "without due process of law;" all owners whose property is forcibly seized and appropriated in war are deprived of their property "without due process of law." The Constitution recognizes the principle of common law, that every man's house is his castle; that his home, the shelter of his wife and children, is his most sacred possession; and has therefore specially provided, "that no soldier shall *in time of peace* be quartered in any house, without the consent of its owner, nor in time of war, but in a manner to be prescribed by law [III Amend.]; thereby declaring that, in time of war, Congress may by law authorize, as it has done, that without the consent and against the consent of the owner, the soldier may be quartered in any man's house, and upon any man's hearth. What I have said illustrates the proposition, that in time of war the civil tribunals of justice are wholly or partially silent, as the public safety may require; that the limitations and provisions of the Constitution in favor of life, liberty and property are therefore wholly or partially suspended. In this I am sustained by an authority second to none with intelligent American citizens. Mr. John Quincy Adams, than whom a purer man or a wiser statesman never ascended the chair of the Chief Magistracy in America, said in his place in the House of Representatives, in 1836, that:

"In the authority given to Congress by the Constitution of the United States to declare war, all the powers incident to war are by necessary implication conferred upon the Government of the United States. Now the powers incident to war are derived, not from their internal, municipal source, but from the laws and usages of nations. There are, then, in the authority of Congress and of the Executive, two classes of powers altogether different in their nature, and often incompatible with each other, the war power and the peace power. The peace power is limited by regulations and restricted by provisions prescribed within the Constitution itself. The war power is limited only by the laws and usage of nations. This power is tremendous; it is strictly constitutional, but it breaks down every barrier so anxiously erected for the protection of liberty, of property, and of life."

If this be so, how can there be trial by jury for military offenses in time of civil war? If you can not, and do not, try the armed enemy before you shoot him, or the captured enemy before you imprison him, why should you be held to open the civil courts and try the spy, the conspirator and the assassin, in the secret service of the public enemy, by jury, before you convict and punish him? Why not clamor against holding imprisoned the captured armed rebels, deprived of their liberty without due process of law? Are they not citizens? Why not clamor against slaying, for their crime of treason, which is cognisable in the civil courts, by your rifled ordnance and the leaden hail of your musketry in battle, these public enemies, without trial by jury? Are they not citizens?

Why is the clamor confined exclusively to the trial by military tribunals of justice of traitorous spies, traitorous conspirators, and assassins hired to do secretly what the armed rebel attempts to do openly—murder your nationality by assassinating its defenders and its executive officers? Nothing can be clearer than that the rebel captured prisoner, being a citizen of the republic, is as much entitled to trial by jury before he is committed to prison, as the spy, or the aider and abettor of the treason by conspiracy and assassination, being a citizen, is entitled to such trial by jury, before he is subjected to the just punishment of the law for his great crime. I think that in time of war the remark of Montesquieu, touching the civil judiciary, is true: that "it is next to nothing." Hamilton well said, "The Executive holds the sword of the community; the judiciary has no direction of the strength of society; it has neither force nor will; it has judgment alone, and is dependent for the execution of that upon the arm of the Executive." The people of these States so understood the Constitution, and adopted it, and intended thereby, without limitation or restraint, to empower their Congress and Executive to authorize by law, and execute by force, whatever the public safety might require, to suppress rebellion or repel invasion.

Notwitstanding all that has been said by the counsel for the accused to the contrary, the Constitution has received this construction from the day of its adoption to this hour. The Supreme Court of the United States has solemnly decided that the Constitution has conferred upon the Government authority to employ all the means necessary to the faithful execution of all the powers which that Constitution enjoins upon the Government of the United States, and upon every department and every officer thereof. Speaking of that provision of the Constitution which provides that "Congress shall have power to make all laws that may be necessary and proper to carry into effect all powers granted to the Government of the United States, or to any department or officer thereof," Chief Justice Marshall, in his great decision in the case of McCulloch *vs.* State of Maryland, says:

"The powers given to the Government imply the ordinary means of execution, and the Government, in all sound reason and fair interpretation, must have the choice of the means which it deems the most convenient and appropriate to the execution of the power. • • • The powers of the Government were given for the welfare of the nation; they were intended to endure for ages to come, and to be adapted to the various crises in human affairs. To prescribe the specific means by which Government should, in all future time, execute its power, and to confine the choice of means to such narrow limits as should not leave it in the power of Congress to adopt any which might be appropriate and conducive to the end, would be most unwise and pernicious." 4 *Wheaton,* 420. Words fitly spoken! which illustrated at the time of their utterance the wisdom of the Constitution in providing this general grant

of power to meet every possible exigency which the fortunes of war might cast upon the country, and the wisdom of which words, in turn, has been illustrated to-day by the gigantic and triumphant struggle of the people during the last four years for the supremacy of the Constitution, and in exact accordance with its provisions. In the light of these wonderful events, the words of Pinckney, uttered when the illustrious Chief Justice had concluded his opinion, "The Constitution of my country is immortal!" seem to have become words of prophesy. Has not this great tribunal, through the chief of all its judges, by this luminous and profound reasoning, declared that the Government may by law authorize the Executive to employ, in the prosecution of war, the ordinary means, and all the means necessary and adapted to the end? And in the other decision, before referred to, in the 8th of Cranch, arising during the late war with Great Britain, Mr. Justice Story said:

"When the legislative authority, to whom the right to declare war is confided, has declared war in its most unlimited manner, the executive authority, to whom the execution of the war is confided, is bound to carry it into effect. He has a discretion vested in him as to the manner and extent, but he can not lawfully transcend the rules of warfare established among civilized nations. He can not lawfully exercise powers or authorize proceedings which the civilized world repudiates and disclaims. The sovereignty, as to declaring war and limiting its effects, rests with the Legislature. The sovereignty, as to its execution, rests with the President." *Brown vs. United States,* 8 *Cranch,* 153.

Has the Congress, to whom is committed the sovereignty of the whole people to declare war, by legislation restricted the President, or attempted to restrict him, in the prosecution of this war for the Union, from exercising all the "powers" and adopting all the "proceedings" usually approved and employed by the civilized world? He would, in my judgment, be a bold man who asserted that Congress has so legislated; and the Congress which should by law fetter the executive arm when raised for the common defense, would, in my opinion, be false to their oath. That Congress may prescribe rules for the government of the army and navy, and the militia when in actual service, by articles of war, is an express grant of power in the Constitution, which Congress has rightfully exercised, and which the Executive must and does obey. That Congress may aid the Executive by legislation in the prosecution of a war, civil or foreign, is admitted. That Congress may restrain the Executive, and arraign, try, and condemn him for wantonly abusing the great trust, is expressly declared in the Constitution. That Congress shall pass all laws *necessary* to enable the Executive to execute the laws of the Union, suppress insurrection, and repel invasion, is one of the express requirements of the Constitution, for the performance of which the Congress is bound by an oath.

What was the legislation of Congress when

treason fired its first gun on Sumter? By the act of 1795 it is provided that whenever the laws of the United States shall be opposed, or the execution thereof obstructed, in any State, by combinations too powerful to be suppressed by the ordinary course of judicial proceeding, or by the powers vested in the marshals, it shall be lawful by this act for the President to call forth the militia of such State, or of any other State or States, as may be necessary to suppress such combinations and to cause the laws to be executed. 1st *Statutes at Large*, 424. By the act of 1807 it is provided that in case of insurrection or obstruction to the laws, either of the United States or of any individual State or Territory, where it is lawful for the President of the United States to call forth the militia for the purpose of suppressing such insurrection or of causing the laws to be duly executed, it shall be lawful for him to employ for such purpose such part of the land or naval forces of the United States as shall be judged necessary. 2d *Statutes at Large*, 443.

Can any one doubt that, by these acts, the President is clothed with full power to determine whether armed insurrection exists in any State or Territory of the Union, and, if so, to make war upon it with all the force he may deem necessary or be able to command? By the simple exercise of this great power it necessarily results that he may, in the prosecution of the war for the suppression of such insurrection, suspend, as far as may be necessary, the civil administration of justice by substituting in its stead martial law, which is simply the common law of war. If, in such a moment, the President may make no arrests without civil warrant, and may inflict no violence or penalties on persons (as is claimed here for the accused), without first obtaining the verdict of juries and the judgment of civil courts, then is this legislation a mockery, and the Constitution, which not only authorized but enjoined its enactment, but a glittering generality and a splendid bauble. Happily the Supreme Court has settled all controversy on this question. In speaking of the Rhode Island insurrection the Court say:

"The Constitution of the United States, as far as it has provided for an emergency of this kind, and authorized the general Government to interfere in the domestic concerns of a State, has treated the subject as political in its nature, and placed the power in the hands of that department." * * * * "By the act of 1795 the power of deciding whether the exigency has arisen upon which the Government of the United States is bound to interfere is given to the President."

The Court add:

"When the President has acted, and called out the militia, is a Circuit Court of the United States authorized to inquire whether his decision was right? If it could, then it would become the duty of the Court, provided it came to the conclusion that the President had decided incorrectly, to discharge those who were arrested or detained by the troops in the service of the United States." * * * * "If the judicial power extends so far, the guaran-

tee contained in the Constitution of the United States is a guarantee of anarchy and not of order." * * * "Yet, if this right does not reside in the courts when the conflict is raging, if the judicial power is, at that time, bound to follow the decision of the political, it must be equally bound when the contest is over. It can not, when peace is restored, punish, as offenses and crimes, the acts which it before recognized and was bound to recognize as lawful." *Luther vs. Borden*, 7 *Howard*, 42, 43.

If this be law, what becomes of the volunteer advice of the volunteer counsel, by him given without money and without price, to this Court, of their responsibility—their *personal* responsibility—for obeying the orders of the President of the United States, in trying persons accused of the murder of the Chief Magistrate and Commander-in-Chief of the army and navy of the United States in time of rebellion, and in pursuance of a conspiracy entered into with the public enemy? I may be pardoned for asking the attention of the Court to a further citation from this important decision, in which the Court say the employment of military power, to put down an armed insurrection, "is essential to the existence of every Government, and is as necessary to the States of this Union as to any other Government; and if the Government of the State deem the armed opposition so formidable as to require the use of military force and the declaration of MARTIAL LAW, we see no ground upon which this Court can question its authority." *Ibid.* This decision, in terms, declared that, under the act of 1795, the President had power to decide, and did decide, the question so as to exclude further inquiry whether the State Government, which thus employed force and proclaimed martial law, was the Government of the State, and, therefore, was permitted to act. If a State may do this, to put down armed insurrection, may not the Federal Government as well? The reason of the man who doubts it may justly be questioned. I but quote the language of that tribunal, in another case before cited, when I say the Constitution confers upon the President the whole executive power.

We have seen that the proclamation of blockade, made by the President, was affirmed by the Supreme Court as a lawful and valid act, although its direct effect was to dispose of the property of whoever violated it, whether citizen or stranger. It is difficult to perceive what course of reasoning can be adopted, in the light of that decision, which will justify any man in saying that the President had not the like power to proclaim martial law in time of insurrection against the United States, and to establish, according to the customs of war among civilized nations, military tribunals of justice for its enforcement, and for the punishment of all crimes committed in the interests of the public enemy.

These acts of the President have, however, all been legalized by the subsequent legislation of Congress, although the Supreme Court decided, in relation to the proclamation of blockade, that no such legislation was necessary.

By the act of August 6, 1861, ch. 63, sec. 3, it is enacted that:

"All the acts, proclamations and orders of the President of the United States, after the 4th of March, 1861, respecting the army and navy of the United States, and calling out, or relating to, the militia or volunteers from the States, are hereby approved in all respects, legalized and made valid to the same extent, and with the same effect, as if they had been issued and done under the previous express authority and direction of the Congress of the United States." 12 *Stat. at Large*, 326.

This act legalized, if any such legalization was necessary, all that the President had done from the day of his inauguration to that hour, in the prosecution of the war for the Union. He had suspended the privilege of the writ of *habeas corpus*, and resisted its execution when issued by the Chief Justice of the United States; he had called out and accepted the services of a large body of volunteers for a period not previously authorized by law; he had declared a blockade of the Southern ports; he had declared the Southern States in insurrection; he had ordered the armies to invade them and suppress it; thus exercising, in accordance with the laws of war, power over the life, the liberty and the property of the citizens. Congress ratified it, and affirmed it.

In like manner, and by subsequent legislation, did the Congress ratify and affirm the proclamation of martial law of September 25, 1862. That proclamation, as the Court will have observed, declares that, during the existing insurrection, all rebels and insurgents, their aiders and abettors within the United States, and all persons guilty of any disloyal practice affording aid and comfort to the rebels against the authority of the United States, shall be subject to martial law, and liable to trial and punishment by courts-martial or *military commission;* and, second, that the writ of *habeas corpus* is suspended in respect to all persons arrested, or who are now, or hereafter during the rebellion shall be, imprisoned in any fort, etc., by any military authority, or by the sentence of any court-martial or *military commission.*

One would suppose that it needed no argument to satisfy an intelligent and patriotic citizen of the United States that, by the ruling of the Supreme Court cited, so much of this proclamation as declares that all rebels and insurgents, their aiders and abettors, shall be subject to martial law, and be liable to trial and punishment by court-martial or military commission, needed no ratification by Congress. Every step that the President took against the rebels and insurgents was taken in pursuance of the rules of war, and was an exercise of martial law. Who says that he should not deprive them, by the authority of this law, of life and liberty? Are the aiders and abettors of these insurgents entitled to any higher consideration than the armed insurgents themselves? It is against these that the President proclaimed martial law, and against all others who were guilty of any disloyal practice affording aid and comfort to rebels against the authority of

the United States. Against these he suspended the privilege of the writ of *habeas corpus;* and these, and only such as these, were, by that proclamation, subjected to trial and punishment by court-martial or military commission.

That the proclamation covers the offense charged here, no man will, or dare, for a moment deny. Was it not a disloyal practice? Was it not aiding and abetting the insurgents and rebels to enter into a conspiracy with them to kill and murder, within your Capital and your intrenched camp, the Commander-in-Chief of our army, your Lieutenant-General, and the Vice-President and the Secretary of State, with intent thereby to aid the rebellion, and subvert the Constitution and laws of the United States? But it is said that the President could not establish a court for their trial, and, therefore, Congress must ratify and affirm this proclamation. I have said before that such an argument comes with ill grace from the lips of him who declared, as solemnly, that neither by the Congress nor by the President could either the rebel himself or his aider or abettor be lawfully and constitutionally subjected to trial by any military tribunal, whether court-martial or military commission. But the Congress did ratify, in the exercise of the power vested in them, every part of this proclamation. I have said, upon the authority of the fathers of the Constitution, and of its judicial interpreters, that Congress has power, by legislation, to aid the Executive in the suppression of rebellion, in executing the laws of the Union when resisted by armed insurrection and in repelling invasion.

By the act of March 3, 1863, the Congress of the United States, by the first section thereof, declared that during the present rebellion the President of the United States, whenever in his judgment the public safety may require it, is authorized to suspend the writ of *habeas corpus* in any case throughout the United States or any part thereof. By the fourth section of the same act, it is declared that any order of the President, or under his authority, made at any time during the existence of the present rebellion, shall be a defense in all courts to any action or prosecution, civil or criminal, pending or to be commenced, for any search, seizure, arrest, or imprisonment, made, done, or committed, or acts omitted to be done, under and by virtue of such order. By the fifth section it is provided, that, if any suit or prosecution, civil or criminal, has been or shall be commenced in any State court against any officer, civil or military, or against any other person, for any arrest or imprisonment made, or others trespasses or wrongs done or committed, or any act omitted to be done at any time during the present rebellion, by virtue of or under color of any authority derived from or exercised by or under the President of the United States, if the defendant shall, upon appearance in such court, file a petition stating the facts upon affidavit, etc., as aforesaid, for the removal of the cause for trial to the Circuit Court of the United States, it shall be the duty of the State court, upon his giving security, to proceed no further in the cause or prosecution.

Thus declaring that all orders of the President, made at any time during the existence of the present rebellion, and all acts done in pursuance thereof, shall be held valid in the courts of justice. Without further inquiry, these provisions of this statute embrace Order 141, which is the proclamation of martial law, and necessarily legalize every act done under it, either before the passage of the act of 1863 or since. Inasmuch as that proclamation ordered that all rebels, insurgents, their aiders and abettors, and persons guilty of any disloyal practice affording aid and comfort to rebels against the authority of the United States, at any time during the existing insurrection, should be subject to martial law, and liable to trial and punishment by *military commission*, the sections of the law just cited declaring lawful all acts done in pursuance of such order, including, of course, the trial and punishment by military commission of all such offenders, as directly legalized this order as it is possible for Congress to legalize or authorize any executive act whatever. 12 *Stat. at Large*, 755-6.

But after assuming and declaring with great earnestness in his argument that no person could be tried and convicted for such crimes, by any military tribunal, whether a court-martial or a military commission, save those in the land or naval service in time of war, the gentleman makes the extraordinary statement that the creation of a military commission must be authorized by the legislative department, and demands, if there be any such legislation, "let the statute be produced." The statute has been produced. The power so to try, says the gentleman, must be authorized by Congress, when the demand is made for such authority. Does not the gentleman thereby give up his argument, and admit, that if the Congress has so authorized the trial of all aiders and abettors of rebels or insurgents for whatever they do in aid of such rebels and insurgents during the insurrection, the statute and proceedings under it are lawful and valid? I have already shown that the Congress have so legislated by expressly legalizing Order No. 141, which directed the trial of all rebels, their aiders and abettors, by military commission. Did not Congress expressly legalize this order by declaring that the order shall be a defense in all courts to any action or prosecution, civil or criminal, for acts done in pursuance of it? No amount of argument could make this point clearer than the language of the statute itself. But, says the gentleman, if there be a statute authorizing trials by military commission, "Let it be produced."

By the act of March 3, 1863, it is provided in section thirty that in time of war, insurrection, or rebellion, murder and assault with intent to kill, etc., when committed by persons in the military service, shall be punishable by the sentence of a court-martial or *military commission*, and the punishment of such offenses shall never be less than those inflicted by the laws of the State or District in which they may have been committed. By the 38th section of the same act, it is provided that all

persons who, in time of war or rebellion against the United States, shall be found lurking or acting as spies in or about the camps, etc., of the United States, or elsewhere, shall be triable by a *military commission*, and shall, upon conviction, suffer death. Here is a statute which expressly declares that all persons, whether citizens or strangers, who in time of rebellion shall be found acting as spies, shall suffer death upon conviction by a military commission. Why did not the gentleman give us some argument upon this law? We have seen that it was the existing law of the United States under the Confederation. Then, and since, men not in the land or naval forces of the United States have suffered death for 'this offense upon conviction by courts-martial. If it was competent for Congress to authorize their trial by courts-martial, it was equally competent for Congress to authorize their trial by military commission, and accordingly they have done so. By the same authority the Congress may extend the jurisdiction of military commissions over all military offenses or crimes committed in time of rebellion or war in aid of the public enemy; and it certainly stands with right reason, that if it were just to subject to death, by the sentence of a military commission, all persons who should be guilty merely of lurking as spies in the interests of the public enemy in time of rebellion, though they obtained no information, though they inflicted no personal injury, but were simply overtaken and detected in the endeavor to obtain intelligence for the enemy, those who enter into conspiracy with the enemy, not only to lurk as spies in your camp, but to lurk there as murderers and assassins, and who, in pursuance of that conspiracy, commit assassination and murder upon the Commander-in-Chief of your army within your camp and in aid of rebellion, should be subject in like manner to trial by military commission. *Stat. at Large* 12, 786-'7, *ch.* 8.

Accordingly, the President having so declared, the Congress, as we have stated, have affirmed that his order was valid, and that all persons acting by authority, and consequently as a court pronouncing such sentence upon the offender as the usage of war requires, are justified by the law of the land. With all respect, permit me to say that the learned gentleman has manifested more acumen and ability in his elaborate argument by what he has omitted to say than by anything which he has said. By the act of July 2, 1864, cap. 215, it is provided that the commanding general in the field, or the commander of the department, as the case may be, shall have power to carry into execution all sentences against guerrilla marauders for robbery, arson, burglary, etc., and from violation of the laws and customs of war, as well as sentences against spies, mutineers, deserters, and murderers.

From the legislation I have cited, it is apparent that military commissions are expressly recognized by the law-making power; that they are authorized to try capital offenses against citizens not in the service of the United States, and to pronounce the sentence of death upon them; and that the commander of a department,

24

or the commanding general in the field, may carry such sentence into execution. But, says the gentleman, grant all this to be so; Congress has not declared in what manner the court shall be constituted. The answer to that objection has already been anticipated in the citation from Benet, wherein it appeared to be the rule of the law martial that in the punishment of all military offenses not provided for by the written law of the land, military commissions are constituted for that purpose by the authority of the commanding officer or the Commander-in-Chief, as the case may be, who selects the officers of a court-martial; that they are similarly constituted, and their proceedings conducted according to the same general rules. That is a part of the very law martial which the President proclaimed, and which the Congress has legalized. The Proclamation has declared that all such offenders shall be tried by military commissions. The Congress has legalised the same by the act which I have cited; and by every intendment it must be taken that, as martial law is by the Proclamation declared to be the rule by which they shall be tried, the Congress, in affirming the act of the President, simply declared that they should be tried according to the customs of martial law; that the commission should be constituted by the Commander-in-Chief according to the rule of procedure known as martial law; and that the penalties inflicted should be in accordance with the laws of war and the usages of nations. Legislation no more definite than this has been upon your statute-book since the beginning of the century, and has been held by the Supreme Court of the United States valid for the punishment of offenders.

By the 32d article of the act of 23d April, 1800, it is provided that "all crimes committed by persons belonging to the navy which are not specified in the foregoing articles shall be punished according to the laws and customs in such cases at sea." Of this article the Supreme Court of the United States say, that when offenses and crimes are not given in terms or by definition, the want of it may be supplied by a comprehensive enactment such as the 32d article of the rules for the government of the navy; which means that courts-martial have jurisdiction of such crimes as are not specified, but which have been recognized to be crimes and offenses by the usages in the navies of all nations, and that they shall be punished according to the laws and customs of the sea. *Dynes vs. Hoover*, 20 *Howard*, 82.

But it is a fact that must not be omitted in the reply which I make to the gentleman's argument, that an effort was made by himself and others in the Senate of the United States, on the 3d of March last, to condemn the arrests, imprisonments, etc., made by order of the President of the United States in pursuance of his proclamation, and to reverse, by the judgment of that body, the law which had been before passed affirming his action, which effort most signally failed.

Thus we see that the body which by the Constitution, if the President had been guilty of the misdemeanors alleged against him in this argument of the gentleman, would, upon presentation of such charge in legal form against the President, constitute the high court of impeachment for his trial and condemnation, has decided the question in advance, and declared upon the occasion referred to, as they had before decided by solemn enactment, that this order of the President declaring martial law and the punishment of all rebels and insurgents, their aiders and abettors, by military commission, should be enforced during the insurrection, as the law of the land, and that the offenders should be tried, as directed, by military commission. It may be said that this subsequent legislation of Congress, ratifying and affirming what had been done by the President, can have no validity. Of course it can not if neither the Congress nor the Executive can authorize the proclamation and enforcement of martial law, in the suppression of rebellion, for the punishment of all persons committing military offenses in aid of that rebellion. Assuming, however, as the gentleman seemed to assume, by asking for the legislation of Congress, that there is such power in Congress, the Supreme Court of the United States has solemnly affirmed that such ratification is valid. 2 *Black*, 671.

The gentleman's argument is full of citations of English precedent. There is a late English precedent bearing upon this point—the power of the legislature, by subsequent enactment, to legalize executive orders, arrests, and imprisonment of citizens—that I beg leave to commend to his consideration. I refer to the statute of 11 and 12 Victoria, ch. 35, entitled "An act to empower the lord lieutenant or other chief governor or governors of Ireland, to apprehend and detain until the first day of March, 1849, such persons as he or they shall *suspect* of conspiring against her Majesty's person and government," passed July 25, 1848, which statute in terms declares that all and every person and persons who is, are, or shall be, within that period, within that part of the United Kingdom of England and Ireland called Ireland, at or on the day the act shall receive her Majesty's royal assent, or after, by warrant for high treason or treasonable practices, or *suspicion* of high treason or treasonable practices, signed by the lord lieutenant, or other chief governor or governors of Ireland for the time being, or his or their chief secretary, for such causes as aforesaid, may be detained in safe custody, without bail or main prize, until the first day of March, 1849; and that no judge or justice shall bail or try any such person or persons so committed, without order from her Majesty's privy counsel, until the said first day of March, 1849, any law or statute to the contrary notwithstanding. The 2d section of this act provides that, in cases where any persons have been, *before* the passing of the act, arrested, committed, or detained for such cause by warrant or warrants signed by the officers aforesaid, or either of them, it may be lawful for the person or persons to whom such warrants have been or shall be directed, to detain such person or persons in his or their custody in any place whatever in Ireland; and that such person or persons to whom such warrants have been or shall be directed shall, be deemed and taken, to all intents and purposes, lawfully authorized to take into safe custody and be the lawful jailors and keepers of such persons so arrested, committed, or detained.

Here the power of arrest is given by the act of Parliament to the governor or his secretary; the process of the civil courts was wholly suspended; bail was denied and the parties imprisoned, and this not by process of the courts, but by warrant of the chief governor or his secretary; not for crimes charged to have been committed, but for being *suspected* of treasonable practices. Magna charta it seems opposes no restraint, notwithstanding the parade that is made about it in this argument, upon the power of the Parliament of England to legalize arrests and imprisonments made before the passage of the act upon an executive order, and without colorable authority of statute law, and to authorize like arrests and imprisonments of so many of six million of people as such executive officers might *suspect* of treasonable practices.

But, says the gentleman, whatever may be the precedents, English or American; whatever may be the provisions of the Constitution; whatever may be the legislation of Congress; whatever may be the proclamations and orders of the President as Commander-in-Chief, it is a usurpation and a tyranny in time of rebellion and civil war, to subject any citizen to trial for any crime before military tribunals, save such citizens as are in the land or naval forces, and against this usurpation, which he asks this Court to rebuke by solemn decision, he appeals to public opinion. I trust that I set as high value upon enlightened public opinion as any man. I recognize it as the reserved power of the people which creates and dissolves armies, which creates and dissolves legislative assemblies, which enacts and repeals fundamental laws, the better to provide for personal security by the due administration of justice. To that public opinion upon this very question of the usurpation of authority, of unlawful arrests, and unlawful imprisonments, and unlawful trials, condemnations, and executions by the late President of the United States, an appeal has already been taken. On this very issue the President was tried before the tribunal of the people, that great nation of freemen who cover this continent, looking out upon Europe from their eastern and upon Asia from their western homes. That people came to the consideration of this issue, not unmindful of the fact that the first struggle for the establishment of our nationality could not have been, and was not, successfully prosecuted without the proclamation and enforcement of martial law, declaring, as we have seen, that any inhabitant who, during that war, should kill any loyal citizen, or enter into any combination for that purpose, should, upon trial and conviction before a military tribunal, be sentenced as an assassin, traitor, or spy, and should suffer death, and that in this last struggle for the maintenance of American nationality, the President but followed the example of the illustrious Father of his Country. Upon that issue the people passed judgment on the 8th day of last November, and

declared that the charge of usurpation was false. From this decision of the people there lies no appeal on this earth. Who can rightfully challenge the authority of the American people to decide such questions for themselves? The voice of the people, thus solemnly proclaimed, by the omnipotence of the ballot, in favor of the righteous order of their murdered President, issued by him for the common defense, for the preservation of the Constitution, and for the enforcement of the laws of the Union, ought to be accepted, and will be accepted, I trust, by all just men, as the voice of God.

May it please the Court: I have said thus much touching the right of the people, under their Constitution, in time of civil war and rebellion, to proclaim through their Executive, with the sanction and approval of their Congress, martial law, and enforce the same according to the usage of nations.

I submit that it has been shown that, by the letter and spirit of the Constitution, as well as by its contemporaneous construction, followed and approved by every department of the Government, this right is in the people; that it is inseparable from the condition of war, whether civil or foreign, and absolutely essential to its vigorous and successful prosecution; that according to the highest authority upon Constitutional law, the proclamation and enforcement of martial law are "usual under all Governments in time of rebellion;" that our own highest judicial tribunal has declared this, and solemnly ruled that the question of the necessity for its exercise rests exclusively with Congress and the President; and that the decision of the political departments of the Government, that there is an armed rebellion and a necessity for the employment of military force and martial law in its suppression, concludes the judiciary.

In submitting what I have said in support of the jurisdiction of this honorable Court, and of its Constitutional power to hear and determine this issue, I have uttered my own convictions; and for their utterance in defense of my country, and its right to employ all the means necessary for the common defense against armed rebellion and secret treasonable conspiracy in aid of such rebellion, I shall neither ask pardon nor offer apology. I find no words with which more fitly to conclude all I have to say upon the question of the jurisdiction and Constitutional authority of this Court, than those employed by the illustrious Lord Brougham to the House of Peers in support of the bill before referred to, which empowered the Lord Lieutenant of Ireland, and his deputies, to apprehend and detain, for the period of seven months or more, all such persons within that island as they should *suspect* of conspiracy against Her Majesty's person and Government. Said that illustrious man: "A friend of liberty I have lived, and such will I die; nor care I how soon the latter event may happen, if I can not be a friend of liberty without being a friend of traitors at the same time—a protector of criminals of the deepest dye—an accomplice of foul rebellion and of its concomitant, civil war, with all its atrocities and all its fearful consequences." *Hansard's Debates,* 3d series, vol. 100, p. 635.

May it please the Court: It only remains for me to sum up the evidence, and present my views of the law arising upon the facts in the case on trial. The questions of fact involved in the issue are:

First, did the accused, or any two of them, confederate and conspire together, as charged? and,

Second, did the accused, or any of them, in pursuance of such conspiracy, and with the intent alleged, commit either or all of the several acts specified?

If the conspiracy be established, as laid, it results that whatever was said or done by either of the parties thereto, in the furtherance or execution of the common design, is the declaration or act of all the other parties to the conspiracy; and this, whether the other parties, at the time such words were uttered or such acts done by their confederates, were present or absent—here, within the intrenched lines of your capital, or crouching behind the intrenched lines of Richmond, or awaiting the results of their murderous plot against their country, its Constitution and laws, across the border, under the shelter of the British flag.

The declared and accepted rule of law in cases of conspiracy is that—

"In prosecutions for conspiracy it is an established rule that where several persons are proved to have combined together for the same illegal purpose, any act done by one of the party, in pursuance of the original concerted plan, and in reference to the common object, is, in the contemplation of law as well as in sound reason, the act of the whole party; and, therefore, the proof of the act will be evidence against any of the others, who were engaged in the same general conspiracy, without regard to the question whether the prisoner is proved to have been concerned in the particular transaction." *Phillips on Evidence,* p. 210.

The same rule obtains in cases of treason: "If several persons agree to levy war, some in one place and some in another, and one party do actually appear in arms, this is a levying of war by all, as well those who were not in arms as those who were, if it were done in pursuance of the original concert, for those who made the attempt were emboldened by the confidence inspired by the general concert, and therefore these particular acts are in justice imputable to all the rest." 1 *East., Pleas of the Crown,* p. 97; *Roscoe,* 84.

In *Ex parte Bollman and Swartwout,* 4 *Cranch,* 126, Marshall, Chief Justice, rules: "If war be actually levied—that is, if a body of men be actually assembled, for the purpose of effecting, by force, a treasonable purpose, all those who perform any part, *however minute, or however remote from the scene of action,* and who are actually leagued in the general conspiracy, are to be considered as traitors."

In *United States* vs. *Cole et al.,* 5 *McLean,* 601, Mr. Justice McLean says: "A conspiracy is rarely, if ever, proved by positive testimony. When a crime of high magnitude is about to be perpetrated by a combination of individuals, they do not act openly, but covertly and se-

cretly. The purpose formed is known only to those who enter into it. Unless one of the original conspirators betray his companions and give evidence against them, their guilt can be proved only by circumstantial evidence. *
* It is said by some writers on evidence that such circumstances are stronger than positive proof. A witness swearing positively, it is said, may misapprehend the facts or swear falsely, but that circumstances can not lie.

"The common design is the essence of the charge; and this may be made to appear when the defendants steadily pursue the same object, whether acting separately or together, by common or different means, all leading to the same unlawful result. And where *prima facie* evidence has been given of a combination, the acts or confessions of one are evidence against all. * * * It is reasonable that where a body of men assume the attribute of individuality, whether for commercial business or for the commission of a crime, that the association should be bound by the acts of one of its members, in carrying out the design."

It is a rule of the law, not to be overlooked in this connexion, that the conspiracy or agreement of the parties, or some of them, to act in concert to accomplish the unlawful act charged, may be established either by direct evidence of a meeting or consultation for the illegal purpose charged, or more usually, from the very nature of the case, by circumstantial evidence. 2 *Starkie,* 232.

Lord Mansfield ruled that it was not necessary to prove the actual fact of a conspiracy, but that it might be collected from collateral circumstances. *Parson's Case,* 1 *W. Blackstone,* 392.

"If," says a great authority on the law of evidence, "on a charge of conspiracy, it appear that two persons by their acts are pursuing the same object, and often by the same means, or one performing part of the act, and the other completing it, for the attainment of the same object, the jury may draw the conclusion there is a conspiracy. If a conspiracy be formed, and a person join in it afterward, he is equally guilty with the original conspirators." *Roscoe,* 415.

"The rule of the admissibility of the acts and declarations of any one of the conspirators, said or done in furtherance of the common design, applies in cases as well where only part of the conspirators are indicted, or upon trial, as where all are indicted and upon trial. Thus, upon an indictment for murder, if it appear that others, together with the prisoner, conspired to commit the crime, the act of one, done in pursuance of that intention, will be evidence against the rest." 2d *Starkie,* 237.

They are all alike guilty as principals. *Commonwealth* vs. *Knapp,* 9 *Pickering,* 496; 10 *Pickering,* 477; 6 *Term Reports,* 528; 11 *East.,* 584.

What is the evidence, direct and circumstantial, that the accused, or either of them, together with John H. Surratt, John Wilkes Booth, Jefferson Davis, George N. Sanders, Beverley Tucker, Jacob Thompson, William C. Cleary, Clement C. Clay, George Harper and George Young, did combine, confederate, and conspire, in aid of the existing rebellion, as charged, to kill and murder, within the military department of Washington, and within the fortified and intrenched lines thereof, Abraham Lincoln, late, and, at the time of the said combining, confederating and conspiring, President of the United States of America, and Commander-in-Chief of the army and navy thereof; Andrew Johnson, Vice-President of the United States; William H. Seward, Secretary of State of the United States; and Ulysses S. Grant, Lieutenant-General of the armies thereof, and then in command, under the direction of the President?

The time, as laid in the charge and specification, when this conspiracy was entered into, is immaterial, so that it appear by the evidence that the criminal combination and agreement were formed before the commission of the acts alleged. That Jefferson Davis, one of the conspirators named, was the acknowledged chief and leader of the existing rebellion against the Government of the United States, and that Jacob Thompson, George N. Sanders, Clement C. Clay, Beverley Tucker, and others named in the specification, were his duly accredited and authorized agents, to act in the interests of said rebellion, are facts established by the testimony in this case beyond all question. That Davis, as the leader of said rebellion, gave to those agents, then in Canada, commissions in blank, bearing the official signature of his war minister, James A. Seddon, to be by them filled up and delivered to such agents as they might employ to act in the interests of the rebellion within the United States, and intended to be a cover and protection for any crimes they might therein commit in the service of the rebellion, is also a fact established here, and which no man can gainsay. Who doubts that Kennedy, whose confession, made in view of immediate death, as proved here, was commissioned by those accredited agents of Davis to burn the city of New York? That he was to have attempted it on the night of the Presidential election, and that he did, in combination with his confederates, set fire to four hotels in the city of New York on the night of the 25th of November last? Who doubts that, in like manner, in the interests of the rebellion, and by the authority of Davis, these, his agents, also commissioned Bennett H. Young to commit arson, robbery and the murder of unarmed citizens in St. Albans, Vermont? Who doubts, upon the testimony shown, that Davis, by his agents, deliberately adopted the system of starvation for the murder of our captive soldiers in his hands, or that, as shown by the testimony, he sanctioned the burning of hospitals and steamboats, the property of private persons, and paid therefor, from his stolen treasure, the sum of thirty-five thousand dollars in gold? By the evidence of Godfrey Joseph Hyams it is proved that Thompson—the agent of Jefferson Davis—paid him money for the service he rendered in the infamous and fiendish project of importing pestilence into our camps and cities, to destroy the lives of citizens and soldiers alike, and into the house of the Presi-

dent for the purpose of destroying his life. It may be said, and doubtless will be said, by the pensioned advocates of this rebellion, that Hyams, being infamous, is not to be believed. It is admitted that he is infamous, as it must be conceded that any man is infamous who either participates in such a crime or attempts in anywise to extenuate it. But it will be observed that Hyams is supported by the testimony of Mr. Sanford Conover, who heard Blackburn and the other rebel agents in Canada speak of this infernal project, and by the testimony of Mr. Wall, the well-known auctioneer of this city, whose character is unquestioned, that he received this importation of pestilence (of course without any knowledge of the purpose), and that Hyams consigned the goods to him in the name of J. W. Harris, a fact in itself an acknowledgment of guilt; and that he received, afterward, a letter from Harris, dated Toronto, Canada West, December 1, 1864, wherein Harris stated that he had not been able to come to the States since his return to Canada, and asked for an account of the sale. He identifies the Godfrey Joseph Hyams, who testified in court as the J. W. Harris who imported the pestilence. The very transaction shows that Hyams' statement is truthful. He gives the names of the parties connected with this infamy (Clement C. Clay, Dr. Blackburn, Rev. Dr. Stuart Robinson, J. C. Holcombe, all refugees from the Confederacy in Canada), and states that he gave Thompson a receipt for the fifty dollars paid to him, and that he was by occupation a shoemaker; in none of which facts is there an attempt to discredit him. It is not probable that a man in his position in life would be able to buy five trunks of clothing, ship them all the way from Halifax to Washington, and then order them to be sold at auction, without regard to price, solely upon his own account. It is a matter of notoriety that a part of his statement is verified by the results at Newbern, North Carolina, to which point, he says, a portion of the infected goods were shipped, through a sutler, the result of which was that nearly two thousand citizens and soldiers died there, about that time, with the yellow fever.

That the rebel chief, Jefferson Davis, sanctioned these crimes, committed and attempted through the instrumentality of his accredited agents in Canada—Thompson, Clay, Tucker, Sanders, Cleary, etc.—upon the persons and property of the people of the North, there is positive proof on your record. The letter brought from Richmond, and taken from the archives of his late pretended Government there, dated February 11, 1865, and addressed to him by a late rebel Senator from Texas, W. S. Oldham, contains the following significant words: "When Senator Johnson, of Missouri, and myself waited on you, a few days since, in relation to the project of annoying and harrassing the enemy, by means of burning their shipping, towns, etc., there were several remarks made by you upon the subject, which I was not fully prepared to answer, but which, upon subsequent conference with parties proposing the enterprise, I find can not apply

as objections to the scheme. First, the 'combustible materials' consist of several preparations, and not one alone, and can be used without exposing the party using them to the least danger of detection whatever.   *   *
* Second, there is no necessity for sending persons in the military service into the enemy's country, but the work may be done by agents.
*   *   * I have seen enough of the effects that can be produced to satisfy me that in most cases, without any danger to the parties engaged, and, in others, but very slight, we can, first, burn every vessel that leaves a foreign port for the United States; second, we can burn every transport that leaves the harbor of New York, or other Northern port, with supplies for the armies of the enemy in the South; third, burn every transport and gunboat on the Mississippi river, as well as devastate the country of the enemy, and fill his people with terror and consternation.
*   *   * For the purpose of satisfying your mind upon the subject, I respectfully, but earnestly, request that you will give an interview with General Harris, formerly a member of Congress from Missouri, who, I think, is able, from conclusive proofs, to convince you that what I have suggested is perfectly feasible and practicable."
. No one can doubt, from the tenor of this letter, that the rebel Davis only wanted to be satisfied that this system of arson and murder could be carried on by his agents in the North successfully and without detection. With him it was not a crime to do these acts, but only a crime to be detected in them. But Davis, by his indorsement on this letter, dated the 20th of February, 1865, bears witness to his own complicity and his own infamy in this proposed work of destruction and crime for the future, as well as to his complicity in what had before been attempted without complete success. Kennedy, with his confederates, had failed to burn the city of New York. "The combustibles" which Kennedy had employed were, it seems, defective. This was "a difficulty to be overcome." Neither had he been able to consummate the dreadful work without subjecting himself *to detection.* This was another "*difficulty* to be overcome." Davis, on the 20th of February, 1865, indorsed upon this letter these words: "Secretary of State, at his convenience, see General Harris, and learn what plan he has for *overcoming the difficulties heretofore experienced. J. D.*"
This indorsement is unquestionably proved to be the handwriting of Jefferson Davis, and it bears witness on its face that the monstrous proposition met his approval, and that he desired his rebel Secretary of State, Benjamin, to see General Harris and learn how to overcome *the difficulty heretofore experienced,* to wit: the inefficiency of "the combustible materials' that had been employed, and the liability of its agents to detection. After this, who will doubt that he had endeavored, by the hand of incendiaries, to destroy by fire the property and lives of the people of the North, and thereby "fill them with terror and consternation;" that he knew his agents had been unsuccess-

ful; that he knew his agents had been detected in their villainy and punished for their crime; that he desired, through a more perfect "chemical preparation," by the science and skill of Professor McCulloch, to accomplish successfully what had before been unsuccessfully attempted?
The intercepted letter of his agent, Clement C. Clay, dated St. Catharine's, Canada West. November 1, 1864, is an acknowledgment and confession of what they had attempted, and a suggestion made through J. P. Benjamin, rebel Secretary of State, of what remained to be done, in order to make the "chemical preparations" efficient. Speaking of this Bennett H. Young, he says; "You have doubtless learned through the press of the United States, of the raid on St. Alban's by about twenty-five Confederate soldiers, led by Lieutenant Bennett H. Young; of their attempt and failure to burn the town; of their robbery of three banks there of the aggregate amount of about two hundred thousand dollars; of their arrest in Canada, by United States forces; of their commitment and the pending preliminary trial." He makes application, in aid of Young and his associates, for additional documents, showing that they acted upon the authority of the Confederate States Government, taking care to say, however, that he held such authority at the time, but that it ought to be more explicit, so far as regards the particular acts complained of. He states that he met Young at Halifax in May, 1864, who developed his plans for retaliation on the enemy; that he, Clay, recommended him to the rebel Secretary of war; that after this, "Young was sent back by the Secretary of War with a commission as Second Lieutenant to execute his plans and purposes, but to report to Hon. —— and myself." Young afterward "proposed passing through New England, burning some towns and robbing them of whatever he could convert to the use of the Confederate Government. This I approved as justifiable retaliation. He attempted to burn the town of St. Alban's, Vermont, and would have succeeded but for the failure of the *chemical preparation* with which he was armed. He then robbed the banks of funds amounting to over two hundred thousand dollars. That he was not prompted by selfish or mercenary motives, I am as well satisfied as I am that he is an honest man. He assured me before going that his effort would be to destroy towns and farm-houses, but not to plunder or rob; but he said if, after firing a town, he saw he could take *funds* from a bank, or any house, and thereby might inflict injury upon the enemy and benefit his own Government, he would do so. He added most emphatically, that *whatever* he took should be turned over to the Government or *its representatives in foreign lands.* My instructions to him were, to destroy whatever was valuable; not to stop to rob, but if, after firing a town, he could seize and carry off money or treasury or bank notes, he might do so upon condition that they were delivered to the proper authorities of the Confederate States"—that is, to Clay himself.
When he wrote this letter, it seems that this accredited agent of Jefferson Davis was as strongly impressed with the *usurpation and de-*

potism of Mr. Lincoln's administration as some of *the advocates* of his aiders and abettors seem to be at this day; and he indulges in the following statement: "All that a large portion of the Northern people, especially in the Northwest, want to resist the *oppressions* of the *despotism* at Washington, is a *leader*. They are ripe for resistance, *and it may come soon after the Presidential election*. At all events, it must come, if our armies are not overcome, or destroyed, or dispersed. No people of the Anglo-Saxon blood can long endure *the usurpations and tyrannies of Lincoln*." Clay does not sign the dispatch, but indorses the bearer of it as a person who can identify him and give his name. The bearer of that letter was the witness, Richard Montgomery, who saw Clay write a portion of the letter, and received it from his hands, and subsequently delivered it to the Assistant Secretary of War of the United States, Mr. Dana That the letter is in Clay's handwriting, is clearly proved by those familiar with it. Mr. Montgomery testifies that he was instructed by Clay to deliver this letter to Benjamin, the Rebel Secretary of State, if he could get through to Richmond, and to tell him what names to put in the blanks.

This letter leaves no doubt, if any before existed in the mind of any one who had read the letter of Oldham, and Davis' indorsement thereon, that "the chemical preparations" and "combustible materials" had been tried and had failed, and it had become a matter of great moment and concern that they should be so prepared as, in the words of Davis, "to overcome the difficulties heretofore experienced;" that is to say, complete the work of destruction, and secure the perpetrators against personal injury or detection in the performance of it.

It only remains to be seen whether Davis, the procurer of arson and of the indiscriminate murder of the innocent and unoffending, necessarily resultant therefrom, was capable also of endeavoring to procure, and in fact did procure, the murder, by direct assassination, of the President of the United States and others charged with the duty of maintaining the Government of the United States, and of suppressing the rebellion in which this arch-traitor and conspirator was engaged.

The official papers of Davis, captured under the guns of our victorious army in his rebel capital, identified beyond question or shadow of doubt, and placed upon your record, together with the declarations and acts of his co-conspirators and agents, proclaim to all the world that he was capable of attempting to accomplish his treasonable procuration of the murder of the late President, and other chief officers of the United States, by the hands of hired assassins.

In the fall of 1864, Lieutenant W. Alston addresses to "His Excellency" a letter, now before the Court, which contains the following words:

"I now offer you my services, and if you will favor me *in my designs*, I will proceed, as soon as my health will permit, to rid *my* country of some of her deadliest enemies, by strik-ing at the very *hearts' blood* of those who seek to enchain her in slavery. I consider nothing *dishonorable* having such a tendency. All I ask of you is, to favor me by granting me the necessary papers, etc., to travel on. * * * *I am perfectly familiar with the North*, and feel confident that I can *execute* anything I undertake. I was in the raid last June in Kentucky, under General John H. Morgan; * * * was taken prisoner; * * * escaped from them by dressing myself in the garb of a citizen. * * * I went through to the Canadas, from whence, by the assistance of *Colonel J. P. Holcomb*, I succeeded in working my way around and through the blockade. * * * I should like to have a *personal* interview with you in order to perfect the arrangements before starting."

Is there any room to doubt that this was a proposition to *assassinate*, by the hand of this man and his associates, such persons in the North as he deemed the "deadliest enemies" of the rebellion? The weakness of the man who for a moment can doubt that such was the proposition of the writer of this letter, is certainly an object of commiseration. What had Jefferson Davis to say to this proposed assassination of the "deadliest enemies" in the North of his great treason? Did the atrocious suggestion kindle in him indignation against the villain who offered, with his own hand, to strike the blow? Not at all. On the contrary, he ordered his private secretary, on the 29th of November, 1864, to indorse upon the letter these words: "Lieutenant W. Alston; accompanied raid into Kentucky, and was captured, but escaped into *Canada*, from whence he found his way back. Now offers his services to rid the country of some of its *deadliest enemies*; asks for papers, etc. Respectfully referred, by direction of the President, to the honorable Secretary of War." It is also indorsed for attention, "By order. (Signed) J. A. Campbell, Assistant Secretary of War."

Note the fact in this connection, that Jefferson Davis himself, as well as his subordinates, had, before the date of this indorsement, concluded that Abraham Lincoln was "the deadliest enemy" of the rebellion. You hear it in the rebel camp in Virginia in 1863, declared by Booth, then and there present, and assented to by rebel officers, that "Abraham Lincoln must be killed." You hear it in that slaughter-pen in Georgia, Andersonville, proclaimed among rebel officers, who, by the slow torture of starvation, inflicted cruel and untimely death on ten thousand of your defenders, captives in their hands—whispering, like demons, their horrid purpose, "Abraham Lincoln must be killed." And in Canada, the accredited agents of Jefferson Davis, as early as October, 1864, and afterward, declared that "Abraham Lincoln must be killed" if his re-election could not be prevented. These agents in Canada, on the 13th of October, 1864, delivered, in cipher, to be transmitted to Richmond by Richard Montgomery, the witness, whose reputation is unchallenged, the following communication:

"OCTOBER 13, 1864.

"We again urge the immense necessity of our gaining immediate advantages. Strain every nerve for victory. We now look upon the re-election of *Lincoln* in November as almost certain, and we need to whip his hirelings to prevent it. Besides, with *Lincoln* re-elected, and his armies victorious, we need not hope even for recognition, much less the help mentioned in our last. Holcomb will explain this. Those figures of the Yankee armies are correct to a unit. *Our friends shall be immediately set to work as you direct.*"

To which an official reply, in cipher, was delivered to Montgomery by an agent of the state department in Richmond, dated October 19, 1864, as follows :

"Your letter of the 13th instant is at hand. There is yet time enough to colonize many *voters* before November. A blow will shortly be stricken here. It is not quite time. General Longstreet is to attack Sheridan without delay, and then move north as far as practicable toward unprotected points. This will be made instead of movement before mentioned. He will endeavor to assist the *Republicans* in collecting their ballots. Be watchful and assist him."

On the very day of the date of this Richmond dispatch Sheridan was attacked, with what success history will declare. The Court will not fail to notice that the *re-election of Mr. Lincoln* is to be prevented if possible, by any and every means. Nor will they fail to notice that *Holcomb* is to "explain this "—the same person who, in Canada, was the friend and advisor of *Alston*, who proposed to Davis the assassination of the "deadliest enemies" of the rebellion.

In the dispatch of the 18th of October, which was borne by Montgomery, and transmitted to Richmond in October last, you will find these words : "Our friends shall be immediately set to work as you direct." Mr. Lincoln is the subject of that dispatch. Davis is therein notified that his agents in Canada look upon the re-election of Mr. Lincoln in November as almost certain. In this connection he is assured by those agents, that the *friends* of their cause are to be set to work as Davis *had directed.* The conversations, which are proved by witnesses whose character stands unimpeached, disclose what "work" the "friends" were to do under *the direction of* Davis himself. Who were those "friends," and what was "the work" which his agents, Thompson, Clay, Tucker and Sanders had been directed to set them at? Let Thompson answer for himself. In a conversation with Richard Montgomery in the summer of 1864, Thompson said that he *had his friends*, confederates, all over the Northern States, who were ready and willing to go any lengths for the good of the cause of the South, and he could at any time have the *tyrant Lincoln*, or *any other of his advisers* that he chose, *put out of his way;* that they would not consider it a *crime* when done for the cause of the Confederacy." This conversation was repeated by the witness in the summer of 1864 to Clement C. Clay, who immediately stated: "That is so; we are all devoted to our cause and ready to go any length—to do anything under the sun."

At and about the time that these declarations of Clay and Thompson were made, *Alston*, who made the proposition, as we have seen, to Davis,

to be furnished with papers *to go North* and rid the Confederacy of some of its "deadliest enemies," was in Canada. He was doubtless one of the "friends" referred to. As appears by the testimony of Montgomery, Payne, the prisoner at your bar, was about that time in Canada, and was seen standing by Thompson's door, engaged in a conversation with Clay, between whom and the witness some words were interchanged, when Clay stated he (Payne) was one of *their friends*—" we trust him." It is proved beyond a shadow of doubt that in October last John Wilkes Booth, the assassin of the President, was also in Canada, and upon intimate terms with Thompson, Clay, Sanders, and other rebel agents. Who can doubt, in the light of the events which have transpired, that he was one of the "friends" to be "set to work," as Davis had already directed—not, perhaps, as yet to assassinate the President, but to do that other work which is suggested in the letter of Oldham, indorsed by Davis in his own hand, and spread upon your record—the work of the secret incendiary, which was to "fill the people of the North with terror and consternation." The other "work" spoken of by Thompson—putting the *tyrant Lincoln* and *any of his advisers out of the way*, was work doubtless to be commenced only after the re-election of Mr. Lincoln, which they had already declared in their dispatch to their employer, Davis, was with them a foregone conclusion. At all events, it was not until after the Presidential election in November that Alston proposed to Davis to go North on the work of assassination ; nor was it until after that election that Booth was found in possession of the letter which is in evidence, and which discloses the purpose to assassinate the President. Being assured, however, when Booth was with them in Canada, as they had already declared in their dispatch, that the re-election of Mr. Lincoln was certain, in which event there would be no hope for the Confederacy, they doubtless entered into the arrangement with Booth as one of their "friends," that as soon as that fact was determined he should go "to work," and as soon as might be "rid the Confederacy of the tyrant Lincoln and of his advisers."

That these persons named upon your record, Thompson, Sanders, Clay, Cleary and Tucker, were the agents of Jefferson Davis, is another fact established in this case beyond a doubt. They made affidavit of it themselves, of record here, upon the examination of their "friends," charged with the raid upon St. Albans, before Judge Smith, in Canada. It is in evidence, also, by the letter of Clay, before referred to.

The testimony, to which I have thus briefly referred, shows, by the letter of his agents, of the 13th of October, that Davis had before directed those agents to set his *friends to work.* By the letter of Clay it seems that his direction had been obeyed, and his friends had been set to work, in the burning and robbery and murder at St. Albans, in the attempt to burn the city of New York, and in the attempt to introduce pestilence into this capital and into the house of the President. It having appeared, by the letter of Alston, and the indorsement thereon, that Davis had in November entertained the proposition of sending agents, that is to say, "friends," to the North, to not only "spread terror and consternation among the people" by means of his "chemical preparations," but also, in the words of that letter, "to strike," by the hands of assassins, "at the heart's blood" of the deadliest enemies in the North to the confederacy of traitors; it has also appeared by the testimony of many respectable witnesses, among others the attorneys who represented the people of the United States and the State of Vermont, in the preliminary trial of the raiders in Canada, that Clay, Thompson, Tucker, Sanders and Cleary declared themselves the agents of the Confederacy. It also clearly appears by the correspondence referred to, and the letter of Clay, that they were holding, and at any time able to command, blank commissions from Jefferson Davis to authorize *their friends* to do whatever work they appointed them to do, in the interests of the rebellion, by the destruction of life and property in the North.

If a *prima facie* case justifies, as we have seen by the law of evidence it does, the introduction of all declarations and acts of any of the parties to a conspiracy, uttered or done in the prosecution of the common design, as evidence against all the rest, it results, that whatever was said or done in furtherance of the common design, after this month of October, 1864, by either of these agents in Canada, is evidence not only against themselves, but against Davis as well, of his complicity with them in the conspiracy.

Mr. Montgomery testifies that he met Jacob Thompson in January, at Montreal, when he said that "a proposition had been made to him to rid the world of the tyrant Lincoln, Stanton, Grant, and some others; that he knew the men who had made the proposition were bold, daring men, able to execute what they undertook; that he himself was in favor of the proposition, but had determined to defer his answer until he had consulted his government at Richmond; that he was then only awaiting their approval." This was about the middle of January, and consequently more than a month after Alston had made his proposition direct to Davis, in writing, to go North and rid their Confederacy of some of its "deadliest enemies." It was at the time of this conversation that Payne, the prisoner, was seen by the witness standing at Thompson's door in conversation with Clay. This witness also shows the intimacy between Thompson, Clay, Cleary, Tucker, and Sanders.

A few days after the assassination of the President, Beverley Tucker said to this witness "that President Lincoln deserved his death long ago; that it was a pity he didn't have it long ago, and it was too bad that the boys had not been allowed to act when they wanted to." This remark undoubtedly had reference to the propositions made in the fall to Thompson, and also to Davis, to rid the South of its deadliest enemies by their assassination. Cleary, who was accredited by Thompson as his confidential agent, also stated to this witness that Booth was one of the party to whom Thompson had referred in the conversation in January, in which he said he knew the men who were ready to rid the world of the tyrant Lincoln, and of Stanton and Grant. Cleary also said, speaking of the assassination, "that it was a pity that the whole work had not been done," and added, "they had better look out—we are not done yet;" manifestly referring to the statement made by his employer, Thompson, before in the summer, that not only the tyrant Lincoln, but Stanton and Grant, and others of his advisers, should be put out of the way. Cleary also stated to this witness that Booth had visited Thompson twice in the winter, the last time in December, and had also been there in the summer.

Sanford Conover testified that he had been for some time a clerk in the war department at Richmond; that in Canada he knew Thompson, Sanders, Cleary, Tucker, Clay, and other rebel agents; that he knew John H. Surratt and John Wilkes Booth: that he saw Booth there upon one occasion, and John H. Surratt upon several successive days; that he saw Surratt (whom he describes) in April last, in Thompson's room, and also in company with Sanders; that about the 6th or 7th of April Surratt delivered to Jacob Thompson a dispatch brought by him from Benjamin, at Richmond, enclosing one in cipher from Davis. Thompson had before this proposed to Conover to engage in a plot to assassinate President Lincoln and his cabinet, and on this occasion he laid his hand upon these despatches and said, "This makes the thing all right," referring to the assent of the rebel authorities, and stated that the rebel authorities had consented to the plot to assassinate Lincoln, Johnson, the Secretary of War, Secretary of State, Judge Chase, and General Grant. Thompson remarked further that the assassination of these parties would leave the Government of the United States entirely without a head; that there was no provision in the Constitution of the United States by which they could elect another President, if these men were put out of the way.

In speaking of this assassination of the President and others, Thompson said that it was only removing them from office, that the killing of a tyrant was no murder. It seems that he had learned precisely the same lesson that Alston had learned in November, when he communicated with Davis, and said, speaking of the President's assassination, "he did not think anything dishonorable that would serve their cause." Thompson stated at the same time that he had conferred a commission on Booth, and that everybody engaged in the enterprise would be commissioned, and if it succeeded, or failed, and they escaped into Canada, they could not be reclaimed under the extradition treaty. The fact that Thompson and other rebel agents held blank commissions, as I have said, has been proved, and a copy of one of them is of record here.

This witness also testifies to a conversation with William C. Cleary, shortly after the surrender of Lee's army, and on the day before the President's assassination, at the St. Lawrence Hotel, Montreal, when, speaking of the rejoicing in the States over the capture of Richmond,

Cleary said, "they would put the laugh on the other side of their mouth *in a day or two*." These parties knew that Conover was in the secret of the assassination, and talked with him about it as freely as they would speak of the weather. Before the assassination he had a conversation, also, with Sanders, who asked him if he knew Booth well, and expressed some apprehension that Booth would "make a failure of it; that he was desperate and reckless, and he was afraid the whole thing would prove a failure."

Dr. James B. Merritt testifies that George Young, one of the parties named in the record, declared in his presence, in Canada, last fall, that Lincoln should never be inaugurated; that they had friends in Washington, who, I suppose, were some of the same friends referred to in the dispatch of October 13, and whom Davis had directed them "to set to work." George N. Sanders also said to him "that Lincoln would keep himself mighty close if he did serve another term;" while Steele and other confederates declared that the tyrant never should serve another term. He heard the assassination discussed at a meeting of these rebel agents in Montreal in February last. "Sanders said they had *plenty of money* to accomplish the assassination, and named over a number of persons who were ready and willing to engage in undertaking to remove the President, Vice-President, the Cabinet, and some of the leading generals. At this meeting he read a letter, which he had received from Davis, which justified him in making any arrangements that he could to accomplish the object." This letter the witness heard read, and it, in substance, declared that if the people in Canada, and the Southerners in the States, were willing to submit to be governed by such a tyrant as Lincoln, he didn't wish to recognize them as friends. The letter was read openly; it was also handed to Colonel Steele, George Young, Hill and Scott to be read. This was about the middle of February last. At this meeting Sanders named over the persons who were willing to accomplish the assassination, and among the persons thus named was Booth, whom the witness had seen in Canada in October; also, George Harper, one of the conspirators named on the record, Caldwell, Randall, Harrison and Surratt.

The witness understood, from the reading of the letter, that if the President, Vice-President and Cabinet could be disposed of, it would satisfy the people of the North that the Southerners had *friends* in the North; that a peace could be obtained on better terms; that the rebels had endeavored to bring about a war between the United States and England, and that Mr. Seward, through his energy and sagacity, had thwarted all their efforts; that was given as a reason for removing him. On the 5th or 6th of last April this witness met George Harper, Caldwell, Randall, and others, who are spoken of in this meeting, at Montreal, as engaged to assassinate the President and Cabinet, when Harper said they were going to the States to make a row, such as had never been heard of, and added, that "if I (the witness) did not

hear of the death of Old Abe, of the Vice-President and of General Dix in less than ten days, I might put him down as a fool. That was on the 6th of April. He mentioned that Booth was in Washington at that time. He said they had plenty of friends in Washington, and that some fifteen or twenty were going."

This witness ascertained, on the 8th of April, that Harper and others had left for the States. The proof is, that these parties could come through to Washington, from Montreal or Toronto, in thirty-six hours. They did come, and within the ten days named by Harper, the President was murdered! Some attempts have been made to discredit this witness (Dr. Merritt), not by the examination of witnesses in court, not by any apparent want of truth in the testimony, but by the *ex parte* statements of these rebel agents in Canada, and their hired advocates in the United States. There is a statement upon the record, verified by an official communication from the War Department, which shows the truthfulness of this witness, and that is, that, before the assassination, learning that Harper and his associates had started for the States, informed, as he was, of their purpose to assassinate the President, Cabinet and leading generals, Merritt deemed it his duty to call, and did call, on the 10th of April, upon a Justice of the Peace, in Canada, named Davidson, and gave him the information, that he might take steps to stop these proceedings. The correspondence on this subject with Davidson has been brought into Court. Dr. Merritt testifies, further, that after this meeting in Montreal he had a conversation with Clement C. Clay, in Toronto, about the letter from Jefferson Davis, which Sanders had exhibited, in which conversation Clay gave the witness to understand that he knew the nature of the letter perfectly, and remarked that he thought "the end would justify the means." The witness also testifies to the presence of Booth with Sanders in Montreal, last fall, and of Surratt in Toronto in February last.

The Court must be satisfied, by the manner of this and other witnesses to the transactions in Canada, as well as by the fact that they are wholly uncontradicted in any material matter that they state, that they speak the truth, and that the several parties named on your record (Davis, Thompson, Cleary, Tucker, Clay, Young, Harper, Booth and John H. Surratt), did combine and conspire together, in Canada, to kill and murder Abraham Lincoln, Andrew Johnson, William H. Seward and Ulysses S. Grant. That this agreement was substantially entered into by Booth and the agents of Davis in Canada as early as October there can not be any doubt. The language of Thompson at that time, and before, was that he was in favor of the assassination. His further language was, that he knew the men who were ready to do it; and Booth, it is shown, was there at that time, and, as Thompson's secretary says, was one of the men referred to by Thompson.

The fact that others, beside the parties named on the record, were, by the terms of the conspiracy, to be assassinated, in nowise affects the case now on trial. If it is true that these parties did conspire to murder other parties, as well as those named upon the record, the substance of the charge is proved.

It is also true that, if, in pursuance of that conspiracy, Booth confederated with Surratt and the accused, killed and murdered Abraham Lincoln, the charge and specification is proved literally, as stated on your record, although their conspiracy embraced other persons. In law the case stands, though it may appear that the conspiracy was to kill and murder the parties named in the record and others not named in the record. If the proof is that the accused, with Booth, Surratt, Davis, etc., conspired to kill and murder one or more of the persons named the charge of conspiracy is proved.

The declaration of Sanders, as proved, that there was plenty of money to carry out this assassination, is very strongly corroborated by the testimony of Mr. Campbell, cashier of the Ontario Bank, who states that Thompson, during the current year preceding the assassination, had upon deposit, in the Montreal Branch of the Ontario Bank, six hundred and forty nine thousand dollars, beside large sums to his credit in other banks in the province.

There is a further corroboration of the testimony of Conover as to the meeting of Thompson and Surratt in Montreal, and the delivery of the dispatches from Richmond, on the 6th or 7th of April, first, in the fact, which is shown by the testimony of Chester, that in the winter, or spring, Booth said he himself, or some other party, must go to Richmond; and, second, by the letter of Arnold, dated 27th of March last, that he preferred Booth's first query, that he would first go to Richmond and see how they would take it, manifestly alluding to the proposed assassination of the President. It does not follow, because Davis had written a letter in February, which, in substance, approved the general object, that the parties were fully satisfied with it; because it is clear there was to be some arrangement made about the funds; and it is also clear that Davis had not before as distinctly approved and sanctioned this act as his agents, either in Canada or here, desired. Booth said to Chester, "We must have money; there is money in this business, and, if you will enter into it, I will place three thousand dollars at the disposal of your family; but I have no money myself, and must go to Richmond," or one of the parties must go, "to get money to carry out the enterprise." This was one of the arrangements that was to be "made right in Canada." The funds at Thompson's disposal, as the banker testifies, were exclusively raised by drafts of the Secretary of the Treasury of the Confederate States upon London, deposited in their bank to the credit of Thompson.

Accordingly, about the 27th of March, Surratt did go to Richmond. On the 3d of April he returned to Washington, and the same day left for Canada. Before leaving, he stated to Weichmann that when in Richmond he had had a conversation with Davis and with Benjamin. The fact in this connection is not to be overlooked, that on or about the day Surratt arrived in Montreal, April 6th, Jacob Thompson, as the cashier of the Ontario Bank states, drew of these Confederate funds the sum of one hundred and eighty thousand dollars in the form of certificates, which, as the bank officer testifies, "might be used anywhere."

What more is wanting? Surely no word further need be spoken to show that John Wilkes Booth was in this conspiracy; that John H. Surratt was in this conspiracy; and that Jefferson Davis and his several agents named, in Canada, were in this conspiracy. If any additional evidence is wanting to show the complicity of Davis in it, let the paper found in the possession of his hired assassin, Booth, come to bear witness against him. That paper contained the secret cipher which Davis used in his State Department at Richmond, which he employed in communicating with his agents in Canada, and which they employed in the letter of October 13th, notifying him that "their friends would be set to work *as he had directed.*" The letter in cipher found in Booth's possession, is translated here by the use of the cipher machine now in Court, which, as the testimony of Mr. Dana shows, he brought from the rooms of Davis' State Department in Richmond. Who gave Booth this secret cipher? Of what use was it to him if he was not in confederation with Davis?

But there is one other item of testimony that ought, among honest and intelligent people at all conversant with this evidence, to end all further inquiry as to whether Jefferson Davis was one of the parties, with Booth, as charged upon this record, in the conspiracy to assassinate the President and others. That is, that on the fifth day after the assassination, in the city of Charlotte, North Carolina, a telegraphic dispatch was received by him, at the house of Mr. Bates, from John C. Breckinridge, his rebel Secretary of War, which dispatch is produced here, identified by the telegraph agent, and placed upon your record in the words following:

"GREENSBORO', April 19, 1865.

"*His Excellency, President Davis:*

"President Lincoln was assassinated in the theater in Washington on the night of the 14th inst. Seward's house was entered on the same night and he was repeatedly stabbed, and is probably mortally wounded.

"JOHN C. BRECKINRIDGE."

At the time this dispatch was handed to him, Davis was addressing a meeting from the steps of Mr. Bates' house, and after reading the dispatch to the people, he said: "If it were to be done, it were *better* it were well done." Shortly afterward, in the house of the witness, in the same city, Breckinridge, having come to see Davis, stated his regret that the occurrence had happened, because he deemed it unfortunate for the people of the South at that time. Davis replied, referring to the assassination, "Well, General, I don't know; if it were to be done at all, it were *better* that it were well done; and if the same had been done to Andy Johnson, the beast, and to Secretary Stanton, the job would then be *complete.*"

Accomplished as this man was in all the arts of a conspirator, he was not equal to the task—as happily, in the good providence of God, no mortal man is—of concealing, by any form of words, any great crime which he may have meditated or perpetrated either against his Government or his fellow-men. It was doubtless furthest from Jefferson Davis' purpose to make confession. His guilt demanded utterance; that demand he could not resist; therefore his words proclaimed his guilt, in spite of his purpose to conceal it. He said, "If it were to be done, it were *better* it were *well done*." Would any man, ignorant of the conspiracy, be able to devise and fashion such a form of speech as that? Had not the President been murdered? Had he not reason to believe that the Secretary of State had been mortally wounded? Yet he was not satisfied, but was compelled to say, "it were *better* it were *well done*"—that is to say, all that had been agreed to be done had not been done. Two days afterward, in his conversation with Breckinridge, he not only repeats the same form of expression—"if it were to be done it were *better* it were *well done*"—but adds these words: "And if the same had been done to Andy Johnson, the beast, and to Secretary Stanton, the *job* would *then be complete*." He would accept the assassination of the President, the Vice-President, of the Secretary of State, and the Secretary of War, as a complete execution of the "job" which he had given out upon contract, and which he had "made all right," so far as the pay was concerned, by the dispatches he had sent to Thompson by Surratt, one of his hired assassins. Whatever may be the conviction of others, my own conviction is that Jefferson Davis is as clearly proven guilty of this conspiracy as is John Wilkes Booth, by whose hand Jefferson Davis inflicted the mortal wound upon Abraham Lincoln. His words of intense hate, and rage, and disappointment, are not to be overlooked—that the assassins had not done their work *well;* that they had not succeeded in robbing the people altogether of their Constitutional Executive and his advisers; and hence he exclaims, "If they had killed Andy Johnson, the beast!" Neither can he conceal his chagrin and disappointment that the War Minister of the Republic, whose energy, incorruptible integrity, sleepless vigilance, and executive ability had organized day by day, month by month, and year by year, victory for our arms, had escaped the knife of the hired assassins. The job, says this procurer of assassination, was not well done; it had been *better* if it had been well done! Because Abraham Lincoln had been clear in his great office, and had saved the nation's life by enforcing the nation's laws, this traitor declares he must be murdered; because Mr. Seward, as the foreign Secretary of the country, had thwarted the purposes of treason to plunge his country into a war with England, he must be murdered; because, upon the murder of Mr. Lincoln, Andrew Johnson would succeed to the Presidency, and because he had been true to the Constitution and Government, faithful found among the faithless of his own State, clinging to the falling pillars of the Republic

when others had fled, he must be murdered; and because the Secretary of War had taken care by the faithful discharge of his duties, that the Republic should live and not die, he must be murdered. Inasmuch as these two faithful officers were not also assassinated, assuming that the Secretary of State was mortally wounded, Davis could not conceal his disappointment and chagrin that the work was not "well done," that the "job was not complete!"

Thus it appears by the testimony that the proposition made to Davis was to kill and murder the deadliest enemies of the Confederacy—not to kidnap them, as is now pretended here; that by the declaration of Sanders, Tucker, Thompson, Clay, Cleary, Harper, and Young, the conspirators in Canada, the agreement and combination among them was to kill and murder Abraham Lincoln, William H. Seward, Andrew Johnson, Ulysses S. Grant, Edwin M. Stanton, and others of his advisors, and not to kidnap them; it appears from every utterance of John Wilkes Booth, as well as from the Charles Selby letter, of which mention will presently be made, that, as early as November, the proposition with him was to kill and murder—not to kidnap.

Since the first examination of Conover, who testified, as the Court will remember, to many important facts against these conspirators and agents of Davis in Canada, among others, the terrible and fiendish plot, disclosed by Thompson, Pallen, and others, that they had ascertained the volume of water in the reservoir supplying New York city, estimated the quantity of poison required to render it deadly, and intended thus to poison a whole city, Conover returned to Canada, by direction of this Court, for the purpose of obtaining certain documentary evidence. There, about the 9th of June, he met Beverley Tucker, Sanders, and other conspirators, and conversed with them. Tucker declared that Secretary Stanton, whom he denounced as "a scoundrel," and Judge Holt, whom he called "a bloodthirsty villain," could protect themselves, as long as they remained in office, by a guard, but that would not always be the case, and, by the Eternal! he had a large account to settle with them." After this, the evidence of Conover here having been published, these parties called upon him, and asked him whether he had been to Washington and had testified before this Court. Conover denied it; they insisted, and took him to a room, where, with drawn pistols, they compelled him to consent to make an affidavit that he had been falsely personated here by another, and that he would make that affidavit before a Mr. Kerr, who would witness it. They then called in Mr. Kerr to certify to the public that Conover had made such a denial. They also compelled this witness to furnish, for publication, an advertisement, offering a reward of five hundred dollars for the arrest of the "infamous and perjured scoundrel" who had recently personated James W. Wallace under the name of Sanford Conover, and testified to a tissue of falsehoods before the Military Commission at Washington, which advertisement was published in the papers.

To these facts Mr. Conover now testifies, and also discloses the fact that these same men published, in the report of the proceedings before Judge Smith, an affidavit purporting to be his, but which he never made. The affidavit which he in fact made, and which was published in a newspaper at that time, produced here, is set out substantially upon your record, and agrees with the testimony upon the same point given by him in this Court.

To suppose that Conover ever made such an affidavit, voluntarily, as the one wrung from him as stated, is impossible. Would he advertise for his own arrest, and charge himself with falsely personating himself? But the fact can not evade observation, that, when these guilty conspirators saw Conover's testimony before this Court in the public prints, revealing to the world the atrocious plots of these felon conspirators, conscious of the truthfulness of his statements, they cast about at once for some defense before the public, and devised the foolish and stupid invention of compelling him to make an affidavit that he was not Sanford Conover, was not in this Court, never gave this testimony, but was a practicing lawyer in Montreal! This infamous proceeding, coupled with the evidence before detailed, stamps these ruffian plotters with the guilt of this conspiracy.

John Wilkes Booth having entered into this conspiracy in Canada, as has been shown, as early as October, he is next found in the city of New York, on the 11th day, as I claim, of November, in disguise, in conversation with another, the conversation disclosing to the witness, Mrs. Hudspeth, that they had some matter of personal interest between them; that upon one of them the lot had fallen to go to Washington; upon the other to go to Newbern. This witness, upon being shown the photograph of Booth, swears "that the face is the same" as that of one of those men, who, she says, was a young man of education and culture, as appeared by his conversation, and who had a scar, like a bite, near the jaw-bone. It is a fact, proved here by the Surgeon-General, that Booth had such a scar on the side of his neck. Mrs. Hudspeth heard him say he would leave for Washington the day after to-morrow. His companion appeared angry because it had not fallen on him to go to Washington. This took place after the Presidential election in November. She can not fix the precise date, but says she was told that General Butler left New York on that day. The testimony discloses that General Butler's army was, on the 11th of November, leaving New York. The register of the National Hotel shows that Booth left Washington on the early morning train, November 11, and that he returned to this city on the 14th. Chester testifies positively to Booth's presence in New York early in November. This testimony shows most conclusively that Booth was in New York on the 11th of November. The early morning train on which he left Washington would reach New York early in the afternoon of that day. Chester saw him there early in November, and Mrs. Hudspeth not only identifies his picture, but describes his person. The scar upon his neck, near his

jaw, was peculiar, and is well described by the witness as like a bite. On that day Booth had a letter in his possession which he accidentally dropped in the street car in the presence of Mrs. Hudspeth, the witness, who delivered it to Major-General Dix the same day, and by whom, as his letter on file before this Court shows, the same was transmitted to the War Department, November 17, 1864. That letter contains these words:

"DEAR LOUIS: The time has at last come that we have all so wished for, and upon you every thing depends. As it was decided, before you left, we were to cast lots; we accordingly did so, and you are to be the Charlotte Corday of the 19th century. When you remember the fearful, solemn vow that was taken by us, you will feel there is no drawback. *Abe* must *die*, and *now*. You can choose your weapons—*the cup, the knife, the bullet.* The cup failed us once, and might again. Johnson, who will give *this,* has been like an enraged demon since the meeting, because it has not fallen upon him to rid the world of the monster. * * * You know where *to find your friends.* Your *disguises* are so perfect and complete, that, without *one* knew your *face,* no police telegraphic dispatch would catch you. The English gentleman, *Harcourt,* must not act hastily. Remember he has ten days. *Strike for your home, strike for your country; bide your time, but strike sure.* Get introduced; congratulate him; listen to his stories (not many more will the brute tell to earthly friends); do anything but fail, and meet us at the appointed place within the fortnight. You will probably hear from me in Washington. Sanders is doing us no good in Canada.

"CHAS. SELBY."

The learned gentleman (Mr. Cox), in his very able and carefully considered argument in defense of O'Laughlin and Arnold, attached importance to this letter, and, doubtless, very clearly saw its bearing upon the case, and, therefore, undertook to show that the witness, Mrs. Hudspeth, must be mistaken as to the person of Booth. The gentleman assumes that the letter of General Dix, of the 17th of November last, transmitting this letter to the War Department, reads that the party who dropped the letter was heard to say that he would start to Washington on Friday night next, although the word "next" is not in the letter; neither is it in the quotation which the gentleman makes, for he quotes it fairly; yet he concludes that this would be the 18th of November.

Now, the fact is, the 11th of November last was Friday, and the register of the National Hotel bears witness that Mrs. Hudspeth is not mistaken; because her language is, that Booth said he would leave for Washington day after to-morrow, which would be Sunday, the 13th, and if in the evening, would bring him to Washington on Monday, the 14th of November, the day on which, the register shows, he did return to the National Hotel. As to the improbability which the gentleman raises, on the conversation happening in a street car, crowded with people, there was nothing that transpired, although the conversation was earnest, which enabled the witness, or could have enabled any one, in the absence of this letter, or of the subsequent conduct of Booth, to form the least idea of the subject-matter of their conversation. The gentleman does not deal altogether fairly in his remarks touching the letter of General Dix; because, upon a careful examination of the letter, it will be found that he did not form any such judgment as that it was a hoax for the *Sunday Mercury*, but he took care to forward it to the Department, and asked attention to it; when, as appears by the testimony of the Assistant Secretary of War, Mr. Dana, the letter was delivered to Mr. Lincoln, who considered it important enough to indorse it with the word "Assassination," and file it in his office, where it was found after the commission of this crime, and brought into this Court to bear witness against his assassins.

Although this letter would imply that the assassination spoken of was to take place speedily, yet the party was *to bide his time*. Though he had entered into the preliminary arrangements in Canada; although conspirators had doubtless agreed to co-operate with him in the commission of the crime, and lots had been cast for the chief part in the bloody drama, yet it remained for him, as the leader and principal of the hired assassins, by whose hand their employers were to strike the murderous blow, to collect about him and bring to Washington such persons as would be willing to lend themselves for a price to the horrid crime, and likely to give the necessary aid and support in its consummation. The letter declares that Abraham Lincoln must die, and *now*, meaning as soon as the agents can be employed, and the work done. To that end you will bide *your time*. But says the gentleman, it could not have been the same conspiracy charged here to which this letter refers. Why not? It is charged here that Booth with the accused and others conspired to kill and murder Abraham Lincoln—that is precisely the conspiracy disclosed in the letter. Granted that the parties on trial had not then entered into the combination; if they at any time afterward entered into it they became parties to it, and the conspiracy was still the same. But, says the gentleman, the words of the letter imply that the conspiracy was to be executed within the fortnight. Booth is directed, by the name of Louis, to meet the writer within the fortnight. It by no means follows that he was to strike within the fortnight, because he was to meet his co-conspirator within that time, and any such conclusion is excluded by the words, "Bide your time." Even if the conspiracy was to be executed within the fortnight, and was not so executed, and the same party, Booth, afterward by concert and agreement with the accused and others, did execute it by "striking sure" and killing the President, that act, whenever done, would be but the execution of the same conspiracy. The letter is conclusive evidence of so much of this conspiracy as relates to the murder of President Lincoln. As Booth was to do anything but fail, he immediately thereafter sought out the agents to enable him to strike sure, and execute all that he had agreed with Davis and his co-confederates in Canada to do —to murder the President, the Secretary of State, the Vice-President, General Grant, and Secretary Stanton.

Even Booth's co-conspirator, Payne, now on his trial, by his defense admits all this, and says Booth had just been to Canada, "was filled with a mighty scheme, and was lying in wait for agents." Booth asked the co-operation of the prisoner, Payne, and said: "I will give you as much money as you want; but first you must swear to stick by me. It is in the oil business." This, you are told by the accused, was early in March last. Thus guilt bears witness against itself.

We find Booth in New York in November, December and January, urging Chester to enter into this combination, assuring him that there was *money* in it; that they had "friends on the other side;" that if he would only participate in it he would never want for money while he lived, and all that was asked of him was to stand at and open *the back door of Ford's theater*. Booth, in his interviews with Chester, confesses that *he is without money himself*, and allows Chester to reimburse him the $50 which he (Booth) had transmitted to him in a letter for the purpose of paying his expenses to Washington as one of the parties to this conspiracy. Booth told him, although he himself was penniless, "*there is money in this*—we have friends on the other side;" and if you will but engage, I will have three thousand dollars deposited at once for the use of your family.

Failing to secure the services of Chester, because his soul recoiled with abhorrence from the foul work of assassination and murder, he found more willing instruments in others whom he gathered about him. Men to commit the assassinations, horses to secure speedy and certain escape, were to be provided, and to this end Booth, with an energy worthy of a better cause, applies himself. For this latter purpose he told Chester he had already expended $5,000. In the latter part of November, 1864, he visits Charles county, Maryland, and is in company with one of the prisoners, Dr. Samuel A. Mudd, with whom he lodged over night, and through whom he procures of Gardner one of the several horses which were at his disposal, and used by him and his co-conspirators in Washington on the night of the assassination.

Some time in January last, it is in testimony, that the prisoner, Mudd, introduced Booth to John H. Surratt and the witness, Weichmann; that Booth invited them to the National Hotel; that when there, in the room to which Booth took them, Mudd went out into the passage, called Booth out and had a private conversation with him, leaving the witness and Surratt in the room. Upon their return to the room, Booth went out with Surratt, and upon their coming in, all three, Booth, Surratt, and Samuel A. Mudd, went out together and had a conversation in the passage, leaving the witness alone. Up to the time of this interview, it seems that neither the witness nor Surratt had any knowledge of Booth, as they were then introduced to him by Dr. Mudd. Whether Surratt had in fact previously known Booth, it is not important to inquire. Mudd deemed it necessary, perhaps a wise precaution, to introduce Surratt to Booth; he also deemed it necessary to have a private conversation with Booth shortly afterward, and directly upon that to have a conversation together with Booth and Surratt alone. Had this conversation, no part of which was heard by the witness, been perfectly innocent, it is not to be presumed that Dr. Mudd, who was an entire stranger to Weichmann, would have deemed it necessary to hold the conversation secretly, nor to have volunteered to tell the witness, or rather pretend to tell him, what the conversation was; yet he did say to the witness, upon their return to the room, by way of apology, I suppose, for the privacy of the conversation, that Booth had some private business with him and wished to purchase his farm. This silly device, as is often the case in attempts at deception, failed in the execution; for it remains to be shown how the fact that Mudd had private business with Booth, and that Booth wished to purchase his farm, made it at all necessary or even proper that they should both volunteer to call out Surratt, who up to that moment was a stranger to Booth. What had Surratt to do with Booth's purchase of Mudd's farm? And if it was necessary to withdraw and talk by themselves secretly about the sale of the farm, why should they disclose the fact to the very man from whom they had concealed it?

Upon the return of these three parties to the room, they seated themselves at a table, and upon the back of an envelope Booth traced lines with a pencil, indicating, as the witness states, the direction of roads. Why was this done? As Booth had been previously in that section of country, as the prisoner in his defense has taken great pains to show, it was certainly not necessary to anything connected with the purchase of Mudd's farm that at that time he should be indicating the direction of roads to or from it; nor is it made to appear, by anything in this testimony, how it comes that Surratt, as the witness testifies, seemed to be as much interested in the marking out of these roads as Mudd or Booth. It does not appear that Surratt was in anywise connected with or interested in the sale of Mudd's farm. From all that has transpired at this meeting at the hotel, it would seem that this plotting the roads was intended, not so much to show the road to Mudd's farm, as to point out the shortest and safest route for flight from the capital, by the houses of all the parties to this conspiracy, to their "friends on the other side."

But, says the learned gentleman (Mr. Ewing), in his very able argument in defense of this prisoner, why should Booth determine that his flight should be through Charles county? The answer must be obvious, upon a moment's reflection, to every man, and could not possibly have escaped the notice of the counsel himself, but for the reason that his zeal for his client constrained him to overlook it. It was absolutely essential that this murderer should have his co-conspirators at convenient points along his route, and it does not appear in evidence that by the route to his friends, who had then fled from Richmond, which the gentleman (Mr. Ewing) indicates as the more direct, but of which there is not the slightest evidence whatever, Booth had co-conspirators at an equal distance from Washington. The testimony discloses, further, that on the route selected by him for his flight there is a large population that would be most likely to favor and aid him in the execution of his wicked purpose, and in making his escape. But it is a sufficient answer to the gentleman's question, that Booth's co-conspirator Mudd lived in Charles county.

To return to the meeting at the hotel. In the light of other facts in this case, it must become clear to the Court that this secret meeting between Booth, Surratt, and Mudd was a conference looking to the execution of this conspiracy. It so impressed the prisoner—it so impressed his counsel, that they deemed it necessary and absolutely essential to their defense to attempt to destroy the credibility of the witness Weichmann.

I may say here, in passing, that they have not attempted to impeach his general reputation for truth by the testimony of a single witness, nor have they impeached his testimony by calling a single witness to discredit one material fact to which he has testified in this issue. Failing to find a breath of suspicion against Weichmann's character, or to contradict a single fact to which he testified, the accused had to fly to the last resort, an *alibi*, and very earnestly did the learned counsel devote himself to the task.

It is not material whether this meeting in the hotel took place on the 23d of December or in January. But, says the counsel, it was after the commencement or close of the Congressional holiday. That is not material; but the concurrent resolution of Congress shows that the holiday commenced on the 22d December, the day before the accused spent the evening in Washington. The witness is not certain about the date of this meeting. The material fact is, did this meeting take place—either on the 23d of December or in January last? Were the private interviews there held, and was the apology made, as detailed, by Mudd and Booth, after the secret conference, to the witness? That the meeting did take place, and that Mudd did explain that these secret interviews, with Booth first, and with Booth and Surratt directly afterward, had relation to the sale of his farm, is confessedly admitted by the endeavor of the prisoner, through his counsel, to show that negotiations had been going on between Booth and Mudd for the sale of Mudd's farm. If no such meeting was held, if no such explanation was made by Mudd to Weichmann, can any man for a moment believe that a witness would have been called here to give any testimony about Booth having negotiated for Mudd's farm? What conceivable connection has it with this case, except to show that Mudd's explanation to Weichmann for his extraordinary conduct was in exact accordance with the fact? Or was this testimony about the negotiations for Mudd's farm intended to show so close an intimacy and intercourse with Booth that Mudd could not fail to recognize him when he came flying for aid to his house from the work of assassination? It would be injustice to the able counsel to suppose that.

I have said that it was wholly immaterial whether this conversation took place on the 23d of December or in January; it is in evidence that in both those months Booth was at the National Hotel; that he occupied a room there; that he arrived there on the 22d and was there on the 23d of December last, and also on the 12th day of January. The testimony of the witness is, that Booth said he had just come in. Suppose this conversation took place in December, on the evening of the 23d, the time when it is proved by J. T. Mudd, the witness for the accused, that he, in company with Samuel A. Mudd, spent the night in Washington city. Is there anything in the testimony of that or any other witness to show that the accused did not have and could not have had an interview with Booth on that evening? J. T. Mudd testifies that he separated from the prisoner, Samuel A. Mudd, at the National Hotel early in the evening of that day, and did not meet him again until the accused came in for the night at the Pennsylvania House, where he stopped. Where was Dr. Samuel A. Mudd during this interval? What does his witness know about him during that time? How can he say that Dr. Mudd did not go up on Seventh street in company with Booth, then at the National; that he did not on Seventh street meet Surratt and Weichmann; that he did not return to the National Hotel; that he did not have this interview, and afterward meet him, the witness, as he testifies, at the Pennsylvania House? Who knows that the Congressional holiday had not in fact commenced on that day? What witness has been called to prove that Booth did not on either of those occasions occupy the room that had formerly been occupied by a member of Congress, who had temporarily vacated it, leaving his books there? Weichmann, I repeat, is not positive as to the date, he is only positive as to the fact; and he disclosed voluntarily, to this Court, that the date could probably be fixed by a reference to the register of the Pennsylvania House; that register can not, of course, be conclusive of whether Mudd was there in January or not, for the very good reason that the proprietor admits that he did not know Samuel A. Mudd, therefore Mudd might have registered by any other name. Weichmann does not pretend to know that Mudd had registered at all. If Mudd was here in January, as a party to this conspiracy, it is not at all unlikely that, if he did register at that time in the presence of a man to whom he was wholly unknown, his kinsman not then being with him, he would register by a false name. But if the interview took place in December, the testimony of Weichmann bears as strongly against the accused as if it had happened in January. Weichmann says he does not know what time was occupied in this interview at the National Hotel; that it probably lasted twenty minutes; that, after the private interviews between Mudd and Surratt and Booth, which were not of very long duration, had terminated, the parties went to the Pennsylvania House, where Dr. Mudd had

rooms, and after sitting together in the common sitting-room of the hotel, they left Dr. Mudd there about 10 o'clock, P. M., who remained during the night. Weichmann's testimony leaves no doubt that this meeting on Seventh street and interview at the National took place after dark, and terminated before 10 o'clock, P. M. His own witness, J. T. Mudd, after stating that he separated from the accused at the National Hotel, says after he had got through a conversation with a gentleman of his acquaintance, he walked down the Avenue, went to several clothing stores, and "after a while" walked round to the Pennsylvania House, and "very soon after" he got there Dr. Mudd came in, and they went to bed shortly afterward. What time he spent in his "walk alone" on the Avenue, looking at clothing; what period he embraces in the terms "after a while," when he returned to the Pennsylvania House, and "soon after" which Dr. Mudd got there, the witness does not disclose. Neither does he intimate, much less testify, that he saw Dr. Mudd when he first entered the Pennsylvania House on that night after their separation. How does he know that Booth and Surratt and Weichmann did not accompany Samuel A. Mudd to that house that evening? How does he know that the prisoner and those persons did not converse together some time in the sitting-room of the Pennsylvania Hotel? Jeremiah Mudd has not testified that he met Doctor Mudd in that room, or that he was in it himself. He has, however, sworn to the fact, which is disproved by no one, that the prisoner was separated from him long enough that evening to have had the meeting with Booth, Surratt, and Weichmann, and the interviews in the National Hotel, and at the Pennsylvania House, to which Weichmann has testified? Who is there to disprove it? Of what importance is it whether it was on the 23d day of December or in January? How does that affect the credibility of Weichmann? He is a man, as I have before said, against whose reputation for truth and good conduct they have not been able to bring one witness. If this meeting did by possibility take place that night, is there anything to render it improbable that Booth, and Mudd, and Surratt did have the conversation at the National Hotel to which Weichmann testifies? Of what avail, therefore, is the attempt to prove that Mudd was not here during January, if it was clear that he was here on the 23d of December, 1864, and had this conversation with Booth? That this attempt to prove an *alibi* during January has failed, is quite as clear as is the proof of the fact that the prisoner was here on the evening of the 23d of December, and present in the National Hotel, where Booth stopped. The fact that the prisoner, Samuel A. Mudd, went with J. T. Mudd on that evening to the National Hotel, and there separated from him, is proved by his own witness, J. T. Mudd; and that he did not rejoin him until they had retired to bed in the Pennsylvania House is proved by the same witness, and contradicted by nobody. Does any one suppose there would have been such assiduous care to prove that the prisoner was with his kinsman all the time on the 23d of December in Washington, if they had not known that Booth was then at the National Hotel, and that a meeting of the prisoner with Booth, Surratt, and Weichmann on that day would corroborate Weichmann's testimony in every material statement he made concerning that meeting?

The accused having signally failed to account for his absence after he separated from his witness, J. T. Mudd, early in the evening of the 23d of December, at the National Hotel, until they had again met at the Pennsylvania House, when they retired to rest, he now attempts to prove an *alibi* as to the month of January. In this he has failed, as he failed in the attempt to show that he could not have met Booth, Surratt and Weichmann on the 23d of December.

For this purpose the accused calls Betty Washington. She had been at Mudd's house every night since the Monday after Christmas last, except when here at court, and says that the prisoner, Mudd, has only been away from home three nights during that time. This witness forgets that Mudd has not been at home any night or day since this Court assembled. Neither does she account for the three nights in which she swears to his absence from home. First, she says he went to Gardner's party; second, he went to Giesboro, then to Washington. She does not know in what month he was away, the second time, all night. She only knows where he went, from what he and his wife said, which is not evidence; but she does testify that when he left home and was absent over night, the second time, it was about two or three weeks after she came to his house, which would, if it were three weeks, make it just about the 15th of January, 1865; because she swears she came to his house on the first Monday after Christmas last, which was the 26th day of December; so that the 15th of January would be three weeks, less one day, from that time; and it might have been a week earlier according to her testimony, as, also, it might have been a week earlier, or more, by Weichmann's testimony, for he is not positive as to the time. What I have said of the register of the Pennsylvania House, the headquarters of Mudd and Atzerodt, I need not here repeat. That record proves nothing, save that Dr. Mudd was there on the 23d of December, which, as we have seen, is a fact, along with others, to show that the meeting at the National then took place. I have also called the attention of the Court to the fact that if Mudd was at that house again in January, and did not register his name, that fact proves nothing; or, if he did, the register only proves that he registered falsely; either of which facts might have happened without the knowledge of the witness called by the accused from that house, who does not know Samuel A. Mudd personally.

The testimony of Henry L. Mudd, his brother, in support of this *alibi*, is, that the prisoner was in Washington on the 23d of March, and on the 10th of April, four days before the murder! But he does not account for the absent night in January, about which Betty Washing-

ton testifies. Thomas Davis was called for the same purpose, but stated that he was himself absent one night in January, after the 9th of that month, and he could not say whether Mudd was there on that night or not. He does testify to Mudd's absence over night three times, and fixes one occasion on the night of the 20th of January. In consequence of his own absence one night in January, this witness can not account for the absence of Mudd on the night referred to by Betty Washington.

This matter is entitled to no further attention. It can satisfy no one, and the burden of proof is upon the prisoner to prove that he was not in Washington in January last. How can such testimony convince any rational man that Mudd was not here in January, against the evidence of an unimpeached witness, who swears that Samuel A. Mudd was in Washington in the month of January? Who that has been examined here as a witness knows that he was not?

The Rev. Mr. Evans swears that he saw him in Washington last winter, and that at the same time he saw Jarboe, the one coming out of, and the other going into, a house on H street, which he was informed on inquiry, was the house of Mrs. Surratt. Jarboe is the only witness called to contradict Mr. Evans, and he leaves it in extreme doubt whether he does not corroborate him, as he swears that he was here himself last winter or fall, but can not state exactly the time. Jarboe's silence on questions touching his own credibility leaves no room for any one to say that his testimony could impeach Mr. Evans, whatever he might swear.

Miss Anna H. Surratt is also called for the purpose of impeaching Mr. Evans. It is sufficient to say of her testimony on that point that she swears negatively only—that she did not see either of the persons named at her mother's house. This testimony neither disproves, nor does it even tend to disprove, the fact put in issue by Mr. Evans. No one will pretend, whatever the form of her expression in giving her testimony, that she could say more than that she did not know the fact, as it was impossible that she could know who was, or who was not, at her mother's house, casually, at a period so remote. It is not my purpose, neither is it needful here, to question in any way the integrity of this young woman.

It is further in testimony that Samuel A. Mudd was here on the 3d day of March last, the day preceding the inauguration, when Booth was to strike the traitorous blow, and it was, doubtless, only by the interposition of that God who stands within the shadow and keeps watch above his own, that the victim of this conspiracy was spared that day from the assassin's hand that he might complete his work and see the salvation of his country in the fall of Richmond and the surrender of its great army. Dr. Mudd was here on that day (the 3d of March) to abet, to encourage, to nerve his co-conspirator for the commission of this great crime. He was carried away by the awful purpose which possessed him, and rushed into the room of Mr. Norton at the National Hotel in search of Booth, exclaiming excitedly:

every nerve for victory. We now look upon the re-election of *Lincoln* in November as almost certain, and we need to whip his hirelings to prevent it. Besides, with *Lincoln* re-elected, and his armies victorious, we need not hope even for recognition, much less the help mentioned in our last. Holcomb will explain this. Those figures of the Yankee armies are correct to a unit. *Our friends shall be immediately set to work as you direct.*"

To which an official reply, in cipher, was delivered to Montgomery by an agent of the state department in Richmond, dated October 19, 1864, as follows :

" Your letter of the 18th instant is at hand. There is yet time enough to colonize many *voters* before November. A blow will shortly be stricken here. It is not quite time. General Longstreet is to attack Sheridan without delay, and then move north as far as practicable toward unprotected points. This will be made instead of movement before mentioned. He will endeavor to assist the *Republicans* in *collecting their ballots.* Be watchful and assist him."

On the very day of the date of this Richmond dispatch Sheridan was attacked, with what success history will declare. The Court will not fail to notice that the *re-election of Mr. Lincoln* is to be prevented if possible, by any and every means. Nor will they fail to notice that *Holcomb* is to "explain this "—the same person who, in Canada, was the friend and advisor of *Alston,* who proposed to Davis the assassination of the "deadliest enemies" of the rebellion.

In the dispatch of the 18th of October, which was borne by Montgomery, and transmitted to Richmond in October last, you will find these words: "Our friends shall be immediately set to work as you direct." Mr. Lincoln is the subject of that dispatch. Davis is therein notified that his agents in Canada look upon the re-election of Mr. Lincoln in November as almost certain. In this connection he is assured by those agents, that the *friends* of their cause are to be set to work as Davis *had directed.* The conversations, which are proved by witnesses whose character stands unimpeached. disclose what "work" the "friends" were to do under *the direction* of Davis himself. Who were these "friends," and what was "the work " which his agents, Thompson, Clay, Tucker and Sanders had been directed to set them at ? Let Thompson answer for himself. In a conversation with Richard Montgomery in the summer of 1864, Thompson said that he *had his friends,* confederates, all over the Northern States, who were ready and willing to go any lengths for the good of the cause of the South, and he could at any time have the *tyrant Lincoln,* or *any other of his advisers* that he chose, *put out of his way;* that they would not consider it a *crime* when done for the cause of the Confederacy." This conversation was repeated by the witness in the summer of 1864 to Clement C. Clay, who immediately stated: "That is so ; we are all devoted to our cause and ready to go any length—to do anything under the sun."

At and about the time that these declarations of Clay and Thompson were made, *Alston,* who made the proposition, as we have seen, to Davis,

to be furnished with papers *to go North* and rid the Confederacy of some of its "deadliest enemies," was in Canada. He was doubtless one of the "friends" referred to. As appears by the testimony of Montgomery, Payne, the prisoner at your bar, was about that time in Canada, and was seen standing by Thompson's door, engaged in a conversation with Clay, between whom and the witness some words were interchanged, when Clay stated he (Payne) was one of *their friends*—"we trust him." It is proved beyond a shadow of doubt that in October last John Wilkes Booth, the assassin of the President, was also in Canada, and upon intimate terms with Thompson, Clay, Sanders, and other rebel agents. Who can doubt, in the light of the events which have transpired, that he was one of the "friends" to be "set to work," as Davis had already directed—not, perhaps, as yet to assassinate the President, but to do that other work which is suggested in the letter of Oldham, indorsed by Davis in his own hand, and spread upon your record—the work of the secret incendiary, which was to " fill the people of the North with terror and consternation." The other "work" spoken of by Thompson—putting the *tyrant Lincoln* and *any of his advisers out of the way,* was work doubtless to be commenced only after the re-election of Mr. Lincoln, which they had already declared in their dispatch to their employer, Davis, was with them a foregone conclusion. At all events, it was not until after the Presidential election in November that Alston proposed to Davis to go North on the work of assassination ; nor was it until after that election that Booth was found in possession of the letter which is in evidence, and which discloses the purpose to assassinate the President. Being assured, however, when Booth was with them in Canada, as they had already declared in their dispatch, that the re-election of Mr. Lincoln was certain, in which event there would be no hope for the Confederacy, they doubtless entered into the arrangement with Booth as one of their " friends," that as soon as that fact was determined he should go "to work," and as soon as might be " rid the Confederacy of the tyrant Lincoln and of his advisers."

That these persons named upon your record, Thompson, Sanders, Clay, Cleary and Tucker, were the agents of Jefferson Davis, is another fact established in this case beyond a doubt. They made affidavit of it themselves, of record here, upon the examination of their "friends," charged with the raid upon St. Albans, before Judge Smith, in Canada. It is in evidence, also, by the letter of Clay, before referred to.

The testimony, to which I have thus briefly referred, shows, by the letter of his agents, of the 13th of October, that Davis had before directed those agents to set his *friends to work.* By the letter of Clay it seems that his direction had been obeyed, and his friends had been set to work, in the burning and robbery and murder at St. Albans, in the attempt to burn the city of New York, and in the attempt to introduce pestilence into this capital and into the house of the President. It having appeared, by the letter of Alston, and the indorsement thereon, that Davis had in November entertained the proposition of sending agents, that is to say, "friends," to the North, to not only "spread terror and consternation among the people" by means of his "chemical preparations," but also, in the words of that letter, " to strike," by the hands of assassins, "at the heart's blood" of the deadliest enemies in the North to the confederacy of traitors; it has also appeared by the testimony of many respectable witnesses, among others the attorneys who represented the people of the United States and the State of Vermont, in the preliminary trial of the raiders in Canada, that Clay, Thompson, Tucker, Sanders and Cleary declared themselves the agents of the Confederacy. It also clearly appears by the correspondence referred to, and the letter of Clay, that they were holding, and at any time able to command, blank commissions from Jefferson Davis to authorize *their friends* to do whatever work they appointed them to do, in the interests of the rebellion, by the destruction of life and property in the North.

If a *prima facie* case justifies, as we have seen by the law of evidence it does, the introduction of all declarations and acts of any of the parties to a conspiracy, uttered or done in the prosecution of the common design, as evidence against all the rest, it results, that whatever was said or done in furtherance of the common design, after this month of October, 1864, by either of these agents in Canada, is evidence not only against themselves, but against Davis as well, of his complicity with them in the conspiracy.

Mr. Montgomery testifies that he met Jacob Thompson in January, at Montreal, when he said that "a proposition had been made to him to rid the world of the tyrant Lincoln, Stanton, Grant, and some others; that he knew the men who had made the proposition were bold, daring men, able to execute what they undertook; that he himself was in favor of the proposition, but had determined to defer his answer until he had consulted his government at Richmond; that he was then only awaiting their approval." This was about the middle of January, and consequently more than a month after Alston had made his proposition direct to Davis, in writing, to go North and rid their Confederacy of some of its "deadliest enemies." It was at the time of this conversation that Payne, the prisoner, was seen by the witness standing at Thompson's door in conversation with Clay. This witness also shows the intimacy between Thompson, Clay, Cleary, Tucker, and Sanders.

A few days after the assassination of the President, Beverley Tucker said to this witness "that President Lincoln deserved his death long ago; that it was a pity he didn't have it long ago, and it was too bad that the boys had not been allowed to act when they wanted to."

This remark undoubtedly had reference to the propositions made in the fall to Thompson, and also to Davis, to rid the South of its deadliest enemies by their assassination. Cleary, who was accredited by Thompson as his confidential agent, also stated to this witness that Booth was one of the party to whom Thompson had referred in the conversation in January, in which he said he knew the men who were ready to rid the world of the tyrant Lincoln, and of Stanton and Grant. Cleary also said, speaking of the assassination, "that it was a pity that the whole work had not been done," and added, "they had better look out—we are not done yet;" manifestly referring to the statement made by his employer, Thompson, before in the summer, that not only the tyrant Lincoln, but Stanton and Grant, and others of his advisers, should be put out of the way. Cleary also stated to this witness that Booth had visited Thompson twice in the winter, the last time in December, and had also been there in the summer.

Sanford Conover testified that he had been for some time a clerk in the war department at Richmond; that in Canada he knew Thompson, Sanders, Cleary, Tucker, Clay, and other rebel agents; that he knew John H. Surratt and John Wilkes Booth: that he saw Booth there upon one occasion, and John H. Surratt upon several successive days; that he saw Surratt (whom he describes) in April last, in Thompson's room, and also in company with Sanders; that about the 6th or 7th of April Surratt delivered to Jacob Thompson a dispatch brought by him from Benjamin, at Richmond, enclosing one in cipher from Davis. Thompson had before this proposed to Conover to engage in a plot to assassinate President Lincoln and his cabinet, and on this occasion he laid his hand upon these despatches and said, "This makes the thing all right," referring to the assent of the rebel authorities, and stated that the rebel authorities had consented to the plot to assassinate Lincoln, Johnson, the Secretary of War, Secretary of State, Judge Chase, and General Grant. Thompson remarked further that the assassination of these parties would leave the Government of the United States entirely without a head; that there was no provision in the Constitution of the United States by which they could elect another President, if these men were put out of the way.

In speaking of this assassination of the President and others, Thompson said that it was only removing them from office, that the killing of a tyrant was no murder. It seems that he had learned precisely the same lesson that Alston had learned in November, when he communicated with Davis, and said, speaking of the President's assassination, "he did not think anything dishonorable that would serve their cause." Thompson stated at the same time that he had conferred a commission on Booth, and that everybody engaged in the enterprise would be commissioned, and if it succeeded, or failed, and they escaped into Canada, they could not be reclaimed under the extradition treaty. The fact that Thompson and other rebel agents held blank commissions, as I have said, has been proved, and a copy of one of them is of record here.

This witness also testifies to a conversation with William C. Cleary, shortly after the surrender of Lee's army, and on the day before the President's assassination, at the St. Lawrence Hotel, Montreal, when, speaking of the rejoicing in the States over the capture of Richmond,

Cleary said, "they would put the laugh on the other side of their mouth *in a day or two*." These parties knew that Conover was in the secret of the assassination, and talked with him about it as freely as they would speak of the weather. Before the assassination he had a conversation, also, with Sanders, who asked him if he knew Booth well, and expressed some apprehension that Booth would "make a failure of it; that he was desperate and reckless, and he was afraid the whole thing would prove a failure."

Dr. James B. Merritt testifies that George Young, one of the parties named in the record, declared in his presence, in Canada, last fall, that Lincoln should never be inaugurated; that they had friends in Washington, who, I suppose, were some of the same friends referred to in the dispatch of October 13, and whom Davis had directed them "to set to work." George N. Sanders also said to him "that Lincoln would keep himself mighty close if he did serve another term;" while Steele and other confederates declared that the tyrant never should serve another term. He heard the assassination discussed at a meeting of these rebel agents in Montreal in February last. "Sanders said they had *plenty of money* to accomplish the assassination, and named over a number of persons who were ready and willing to engage in undertaking to remove the President, Vice-President, the Cabinet, and some of the leading generals. At this meeting he read a letter, which he had received from Davis, which justified him in making any arrangements that he could to accomplish the object." This letter the witness heard read, and it, in substance, declared that if the people in Canada, and the Southerners in the States, were willing to submit to be governed by such a tyrant as Lincoln, he didn't wish to recognize them as friends. The letter was read openly; it was also handed to Colonel Steele, George Young, Hill and Scott to be read. This was about the middle of February last. At this meeting Sanders named over the persons who were willing to accomplish the assassination, and among the persons thus named was Booth, whom the witness had seen in Canada in October; also, George Harper, one of the conspirators named on the record, Caldwell, Randall, Harrison and Surratt.

The witness understood, from the reading of the letter, that if the President, Vice-President and Cabinet could be disposed of, it would satisfy the people of the North that the Southerners had *friends* in the North; that a peace could be obtained on better terms; that the rebels had endeavored to bring about a war between the United States and England, and that Mr. Seward, through his energy and sagacity, had thwarted all their efforts; that was given as a reason for removing him. On the 5th or 6th of last April this witness met George Harper, Caldwell, Randall, and others, who are spoken of in this meeting, at Montreal, as engaged to assassinate the President and Cabinet, when Harper said they were going to the States to make a row, such as had never been heard of, and added, that "if I (the witness) did not

hear of the death of Old Abe, of the Vice-President and of General Dix in less than ten days, I might put him down as a fool. That was on the 6th of April. He mentioned that Booth was in Washington at that time. He said they had plenty of friends in Washington, and that some fifteen or twenty were going."

This witness ascertained, on the 8th of April, that Harper and others had left for the States. The proof is, that these parties could come through to Washington, from Montreal or Toronto, in thirty-six hours. They did come, and within the ten days named by Harper, the President was murdered! Some attempts have been made to discredit this witness (Dr. Merritt), not by the examination of witnesses in court, not by any apparent want of truth in the testimony, but by the *ex parte* statements of these rebel agents in Canada, and their hired advocates in the United States. There is a statement upon the record, verified by an official communication from the War Department, which shows the truthfulness of this witness, and that is, that, before the assassination, learning that Harper and his associates had started for the States, informed, as he was, of their purpose to assassinate the President, Cabinet and leading generals, Merritt deemed it his duty to call, and did call, on the 10th of April, upon a Justice of the Peace, in Canada, named Davidson, and gave him the information, that he might take steps to stop these proceedings. The correspondence on this subject with Davidson has been brought into Court. Dr. Merritt testifies, further, that after this meeting in Montreal he had a conversation with Clement C. Clay, in Toronto, about the letter from Jefferson Davis, which Sanders had exhibited, in which conversation Clay gave the witness to understand that he knew the nature of the letter perfectly, and remarked that he thought "the end would justify the means." The witness also testifies to the presence of Booth with Sanders in Montreal, last fall, and of Surratt in Toronto in February last.

The Court must be satisfied, by the manner of this and other witnesses to the transactions in Canada, as well as by the fact that they are wholly uncontradicted in any material matter that they state, that they speak the truth, and that the several parties named on your record (Davis, Thompson, Cleary, Tucker, Clay, Young, Harper, Booth and John H. Surratt), did combine and conspire together, in Canada, to kill and murder Abraham Lincoln, Andrew Johnson, William H. Seward and Ulysses S. Grant. That this agreement was substantially entered into by Booth and the agents of Davis in Canada as early as October there can not be any doubt. The language of Thompson at that time, and before, was that he was in favor of the assassination. His further language was, that he knew the men who were ready to do it; and Booth, it is shown, was there at that time, and, as Thompson's secretary says, was one of the men referred to by Thompson.

The fact that others, beside the parties named on the record, were, by the terms of the conspiracy, to be assassinated, in nowise affects the case now on trial. If it is true that these parties did conspire to murder other parties, as well as those named upon the record, the substance of the charge is proved.

It is also true that, if, in pursuance of that conspiracy, Booth confederated with Surratt and the accused, killed and murdered Abraham Lincoln, the charge and specification is proved literally, as stated on your record, although their conspiracy embraced other persons. In law the case stands, though it may appear that the conspiracy was to kill and murder the parties named in the record and others not named in the record. If the proof is that the accused, with Booth, Surratt, Davis, etc., conspired to kill and murder one or more of the persons named the charge of conspiracy is proved.

The declaration of Sanders, as proved, that there was plenty of money to carry out this assassination, is very strongly corroborated by the testimony of Mr. Campbell, cashier of the Ontario Bank, who states that Thompson, during the current year preceding the assassination, had upon deposit, in the Montreal Branch of the Ontario Bank, six hundred and forty nine thousand dollars, beside large sums to his credit in other banks in the province.

There is a further corroboration of the testimony of Conover as to the meeting of Thompson and Surratt in Montreal, and the delivery of the dispatches from Richmond, on the 6th or 7th of April, first, in the fact, which is shown by the testimony of Chester, that in the winter, or spring, Booth said he himself, or some other party, must go to Richmond; and, second, by the letter of Arnold, dated 27th of March last, that he preferred Booth's first query, that he would first go to Richmond and see how they would take it, manifestly alluding to the proposed assassination of the President. It does not follow, because Davis had written a letter in February, which, in substance, approved the general object, that the parties were fully satisfied with it; because it is clear there was to be some arrangement made about the funds; and it is also clear that Davis had not before as distinctly approved and sanctioned this act as his agents, either in Canada or here, desired. Booth said to Chester, "We must have money; there is money in this business, and, if you will enter into it, I will place three thousand dollars at the disposal of your family; but I have no money myself, and must go to Richmond," or one of the parties must go, "to get money to carry out the enterprise." This was one of the arrangements that was to be "made right in Canada." The funds at Thompson's disposal, as the banker testifies, were exclusively raised by drafts of the Secretary of the Treasury of the Confederate States upon London, deposited in their bank to the credit of Thompson.

Accordingly, about the 27th of March, Surratt did go to Richmond. On the 3d of April he returned to Washington, and the same day left for Canada. Before leaving, he stated to Weichmann that when in Richmond he had had a conversation with Davis and with Benjamin. The fact in this connection is not to be overlooked, that on or about the day Surratt

arrived in Montreal, April 6th, Jacob Thompson, as the cashier of the Ontario Bank states, drew of these Confederate funds the sum of one hundred and eighty thousand dollars in the form of certificates, which, as the bank officer testifies, "might be used anywhere."

What more is wanting? Surely no word further need be spoken to show that John Wilkes Booth was in this conspiracy; that John H. Surratt was in this conspiracy; and that Jefferson Davis and his several agents named, in Canada, were in this conspiracy. If any additional evidence is wanting to show the complicity of Davis in it, let the paper found in the possession of his hired assassin, Booth, come to bear witness against him. That paper contained the secret cipher which Davis used in his State Department at Richmond, which he employed in communicating with his agents in Canada, and which they employed in the letter of October 13th, notifying him that "their friends would be set to work *as he had directed*." The letter in cipher found in Booth's possession, is translated here by the use of the cipher machine now in Court, which, as the testimony of Mr. Dana shows, he brought from the rooms of Davis' State Department in Richmond. Who gave Booth this secret cipher? Of what use was it to him if he was not in confederation with Davis?

But there is one other item of testimony that ought, among honest and intelligent people at all conversant with this evidence, to end all further inquiry as to whether Jefferson Davis was one of the parties, with Booth, as charged upon this record, in the conspiracy to assassinate the President and others. That is, that on the fifth day after the assassination, in the city of Charlotte, North Carolina, a telegraphic dispatch was received by him, at the house of Mr. Bates, from John C. Breckinridge, his rebel Secretary of War, which dispatch is produced here, identified by the telegraph agent, and placed upon your record in the words following:

"GREENSBORO', April 19, 1865.
"His Excellency, President Davis:

"President Lincoln was assassinated in the theater in Washington on the night of the 14th inst. Seward's house was entered on the same night and he was repeatedly stabbed, and is probably mortally wounded.

"JOHN C. BRECKINRIDGE."

At the time this dispatch was handed to him, Davis was addressing a meeting from the steps of Mr. Bates' house, and after reading the dispatch to the people, he said: "If it were to be done, it were *better* it were well done." Shortly afterward, in the house of the witness, in the same city, Breckinridge, having come to see Davis, stated his regret that the occurrence had happened, because he deemed it unfortunate for the people of the South at that time. Davis replied, referring to the assassination, "Well, General, I don't know; if it were to be done at all, it were *better* that it were well done; and if the same had been done to Andy Johnson, the beast, and to Secretary Stanton, the job would then be *complete.*"

street, but that he did not go to 9th street.
The other witnesses swear he went to 9th
street. He swears he went to Canterbury
about nine o'clock, after going back from 7th
street to Rullman's. Loughran swears that
O'Laughlin was with him at the corner of the
Avenue and 9th street at nine o'clock, and
went from there to Canterbury, while Early
swears that O'Laughlin went up as far as 11th
street, and returned with him and took supper
at Welcker's, about eight o'clock. If these
witnesses prove an *alibi*, it is really against
each other. It is folly to pretend that they
prove facts which make it impossible that
O'Laughlin could have been at the house of
Secretary Stanton, as three witnesses swear
he was, on the evening of the 18th of April,
looking for General Grant.

Has it not, by the testimony thus reviewed,
been established *prima facie* that in the months
of February, March and April, O'Laughlin
had combined, confederated, and agreed with
John Wilkes Booth and Samuel Arnold to
kill and murder Abraham Lincoln, William
H. Seward, Andrew Johnson, and Ulysses S.
Grant? Is it not established, beyond a shadow
of doubt, that Booth had so conspired
with the rebel agents in Canada as early as
October last: that he was in search of agents
to do the work *on pay*, in the interests of the
rebellion, and that in this speculation Arnold
and O'Laughlin had joined as early as February;
that then, and after, with Booth and
Surratt, they were in the "oil business," which
was the business of assassination by contract
as a speculation? If this conspiracy on the
part of O'Laughlin with Arnold is established,
even *prima facie*, the declarations and acts of
Arnold and Booth, the other conspirators, in
furtherance of the common design, is evidence
against O'Laughlin as well as against Arnold
himself, or the other parties. The rule of law
is, that the act or declaration of one conspirator,
done in pursuance or furtherance of the
common design, is the act or declaration of
all the conspirators. 1 *Wharton*, 706.

The letter, therefore, of his co-conspirator,
Arnold, is evidence against O'Laughlin because
it is an act in the prosecution of the common
conspiracy, suggesting what should be done in
order to make it effective, and which suggestion,
as has been stated, was followed out.
The defense has attempted to avoid the force
of this letter by reciting the statement of
Arnold, made to Horner at the time he was
arrested, in which he declared, among other
things, that the purpose was to abduct President
Lincoln and take him South; that it was
to be done at the theater by throwing the
President out of the box upon the floor of the
stage, when the accused was to catch him.
The very announcement of this testimony excited
derision that such a tragedy meant only
to take the President and carry him gently
away! This pigmy to catch the giant as the
assassins hurled him to the floor from an elevation
of twelve feet! The Court has viewed
the theater, and must be satisfied that Booth,
in leaping from the President's box, broke his
limb. The Court can not fail to conclude that

this statement of Arnold was but another silly
device, like that of "the oil business," which,
for the time being, he employed to hide from
the knowledge of his captor the fact that the
purpose was to murder the President. No
man can, for a moment, believe that any one
of these conspirators hoped or desired, by such
a proceeding as that stated by the prisoner, to
take the President alive in the presence of
thousands assembled in the theater after he had
been thus thrown upon the floor of the stage,
much less to carry him through the city, through
the lines of your army, and deliver him into
the hands of the rebels. No such purpose was
expressed or hinted by the conspirators in Canada,
who commissioned Booth to let these assassinations
on contract. I shall waste not a
moment more in combatting such an absurdity.

Arnold does confess that he was a conspirator
with Booth in this proposed murder: that
Booth had a letter of introduction to Dr. Mudd;
that Booth, O'Laughlin, Atzerodt, Surratt, a
man with an alias, "Mosby," and another
whom he does not know, and himself, were
parties to this conspiracy, and that Booth had
furnished them all with arms. He concludes
this remarkable statement to Horner with the
declaration that at that time, to wit, the first
week of March, or four weeks before he went
to Fortress Monroe, he left the conspiracy, and
that Booth told him to sell his arms if he chose.
This is sufficiently answered by the fact that,
four weeks *afterward*, he wrote his letter to
Booth, which was found in Booth's possession
after the assassination, suggesting to him what
to do in order to make the conspiracy a success,
and by the further fact that at the very
moment he uttered these declarations, part of
his arms were found upon his person, and the
rest not disposed of, but at his father's house.

A party to a treasonable and murderous
conspiracy against the government of his country
can not be held to have abandoned it because
he makes such a declaration as this, when
he is in the hands of the officer of the law, arrested
for his crime, and especially when his
declaration is in conflict with and expressly
contradicted by his written acts, and unsupported
by any conduct of his which becomes a citizen
and a man.

If he abandoned the conspiracy, why did he
not make known the fact to Abraham Lincoln
and his constitutional advisers that these men,
armed with the weapons of assassination, were
daily lying in wait for their lives? To pretend
that a man who thus conducts himself for
weeks after the pretended abandonment, volunteering
advice for the successful prosecution
of the conspiracy, the evidence of which is in
writing, and about which there can be no mistake,
has, in fact, abandoned it, is to insult the
common understanding of men. O'Laughlin
having conspired with Arnold to do this murder,
is, therefore, as much concluded by the
letter of Arnold of the 27th of March as is Arnold
himself. The further testimony touching
O'Laughlin, that of Streett, establishes the fact
that about the 1st of April he saw him in confidential
conversation with J. Wilkes Booth, in
this city, on the Avenue. Another man, whom

the witness does not know, was in conversation. O'Laughlin called Streett to one side, and told him Booth was busily engaged with his friend—was *talking privately* to his friend. This remark of O'Laughlin is attempted to be accounted for, but the attempt failed; his counsel taking the pains to ask what induced O'Laughlin to make the remark, received the fit reply: "I did not see the interior of Mr. O'Laughlin's mind; I can not tell." It is the province of this Court to infer why that remark was made, and what it signified.

That John H. Surratt, George A. Atzerodt, Mary E. Surratt, David E. Herold, and Louis Payne, entered into this conspiracy with Booth, is so very clear upon the testimony, that little time need be occupied in bringing again before the Court the evidence which establishes it. By the testimony of Weichmann we find Atzerodt in February at the house of the prisoner, Mrs. Surratt. He inquired for her or for John when he came and remained over night. After this and before the assassination he visited there frequently, and at that house bore the name of " Port Tobacco," the name by which he was known in Canada among the conspirators there. The same witness testifies that he met him on the street, when he said he was going to visit Payne at the Herndon House, and also accompanied him, along with Herold and John H. Surratt, to the theater, in March, to hear Booth play in "The Apostate." At the Pennsylvania House, one or two weeks previous to the assassination, Atzerodt made the statement to Lieutenant Keim, when asking for his knife which he had left in his room, a knife corresponding in size with the one exhibited in Court, " I want that; if one fails I want the other," wearing at the same time his revolver at his belt. He also stated to Greenawalt, of the Pennsylvania House, in March, that he was nearly broke, but had friends enough to give him as much money as *would see him through*, adding, " I am going away some of these days, but will return with as much gold as will keep me all my lifetime." Mr. Greenawalt also says that Booth had frequent interviews with Atzerodt, sometimes in the room, and at other times Booth would walk in and immediately go out, Atzerodt following.

John M. Lloyd testifies that some six weeks before the assassination, Herold, Atzerodt, and John H. Surratt came to his house at Surrattsville, bringing with them two Spencer carbines with ammunition, also a rope and wrench. Surratt asked the witness to take care of them and to conceal the carbines. Surratt took him into a room in the house, it being his mother's house, and showed the witness where to put the carbines, between the joists on the second floor. The carbines were put there according to his directions, and concealed. Marcus P. Norton saw Atzerodt in conversation with Booth at the National Hotel about the 2d or 3d of March; the conversation was confidential, and the witness accidentally heard them talking in regard to President Johnson, and say that " the class of witnesses would be of that character that there could be little proven by them." This conversation may throw some light on the

fact that Atzerodt was found in possession of Booth's bank book !

Colonel Nevins testifies that on the 12th of April last he saw Atzerodt at the Kirkwood House; that Atzerodt there asked him, a stranger, if he knew where Vice-President Johnson was, and where Mr. Johnson's *room was*. Colonel Nevins showed him where the room of the Vice-President was, and told him that the Vice-President was then at dinner. Atzerodt then looked into the dining-room, where Vice-President Johnson was dining alone. Robert R. Jones, the clerk at the Kirkwood House, states that on the 14th, the day of the murder, two days after this, Atzerodt registered his name at the hotel, G. A. Atzerodt, and took No. 126, retaining the room that day, and carrying away the key. In this room, after the assassination, were found the knife and revolver with which he intended to murder the Vice-President.

The testimony of all these witnesses leaves no doubt that the prisoner, George A. Atzerodt, entered into this conspiracy with Booth; that he expected to receive a large compensation for the service that he would render in its execution; that he had undertaken the assassination of the Vice-President for a price; that he, with Surratt and Herold, rendered the important service of depositing the arms and ammunition to be used by Booth and his confederates as a protection in their flight after the conspiracy had been executed; and that he was careful to have his intended victim pointed out to him, and the room he occupied in the hotel, so that when he came to perform his horrid work he would know precisely where to go and whom to strike.

I take no further notice now of the preparation which this prisoner made for the successful execution of this part of the traitorous and murderous design. The question is, did he enter into this conspiracy? His language, overheard by Mr. Norton, excludes every other conclusion. Vice-President Johnson's name was mentioned in that secret conversation with Booth, and the very suggestive expression was made between them that " little could be proved by the witnesses." His confession in his defense is conclusive of his guilt.

That Payne was in this conspiracy is confessed in the defense made by his counsel, and is also evident from the facts proved, that when the conspiracy was being organized in Canada by Thompson, Sanders, Tucker, Cleary, and Clay, this man Payne stood at the door of Thompson; was recommended and indorsed by Clay with the words, " We trust him; " that after coming hither he first reported himself at the house of Mrs. Mary E. Surratt, inquired for her and for John H. Surratt; remained there for four days, having conversation with both of them; having provided himself with means of disguise, was also supplied with pistols and a knife, such as he afterward used, and spurs, preparatory to his flight; was seen with John H. Surratt, practicing with knives such as those employed in this deed of assassination, and now before the Court; was afterward provided with lodging at the Herndon House at the instance of Surratt; was visited there by Atzerodt, and attended Booth and Surratt to Ford's theater, occupying with those parties the box, as I believe and which we may readily infer, in which the President was afterward murdered.

If further testimony be wanting that he had entered into the conspiracy, it may be found in the fact sworn to by Weichmann, whose testimony no candid man will discredit, that about the 20th of March, Mrs. Surratt, in great excitement, and weeping, said that her son John had gone away not to return, when about three hours subsequently, in the afternoon of the same day, John H. Surratt re-appeared, came rushing in a state of frenzy into the room, in his mother's house, armed, declaring he would shoot whoever came into the room, and proclaiming that his prospects were blasted and his hopes gone; that soon Payne came into the same room, also armed and under great excitement, and was immediately followed by Booth, with his riding-whip in his hand, who walked rapidly across the floor from side to side, so much excited that for some time he did not notice the presence of the witness. Observing Weichmann, the parties then withdrew, upon a suggestion from Booth, to an upper room, and there had a private interview. From all that transpired on that occasion, it is apparent that when these parties left the house that day, it was with the full purpose of completing some act essential to the final execution of the work of assassination, in conformity with their previous confederation and agreement. They returned foiled—from what cause is unknown—dejected, angry, and covered with confusion.

It is almost imposing upon the patience of the Court to consume time in demonstrating the fact, which none conversant with the testimony of this case can for a moment doubt, that John H. Surratt and Mary E. Surratt were as surely in the conspiracy to murder the President as was John Wilkes Booth himself. You have the frequent interviews between John H. Surratt and Booth, his intimate relations with Payne, his visits from Atzerodt and Herold, his deposit of the arms to cover their flight after the conspiracy should have been executed; his own declared visit to Richmond to do what Booth himself said to Chester must be done, to-wit, that he or some of the party must go to Richmond in order to get funds to carry out the conspiracy; that he brought back with him gold, the price of blood, confessing himself that he was there; that he immediately went to Canada, delivered dispatches in cipher to Jacob Thompson from Jefferson Davis, which were interpreted and read by Thompson in the presence of the witness Conover, in which the conspiracy was approved, and, in the language of Thompson, the proposed assassination was "made all right."

One other fact, if any other fact be needed, and I have done with the evidence which proves that John H. Surratt entered into this combination; that is, that it appears by the testimony of the witness, the cashier of the Ontario, Bank, Montreal, that Jacob Thompson, about the day that these dispatches were delivered, and while Surratt was then present in Canada, drew from that bank of the rebel funds there on deposit the sum of one hundred and eighty thousand dollars. This being done, Surratt finding it safer, doubtless, to go to Canada for the great bulk of funds which were to be distributed among these hired assassins than to attempt to carry it through our lines direct from Richmond, immediately returned to Washington, and was present in this city, as is proven by the testimony of Mr. Reid, *on the afternoon of the 14th of April,* the day of the assassination, booted and spurred, ready for flight whenever the fatal blow should have been struck. If he was not a conspirator and a party to this great crime, how comes it that from that hour to this no man has seen him in the capital, nor has he been reported anywhere outside of Canada, having arrived in Montreal, as the testimony shows, on the 18th of April, four days after the murder? Nothing but his conscious coward guilt could possibly induce him to absent himself from his mother, as he does, upon her trial. Being one of these conspirators, as charged, every act of his in the prosecution of this crime is evidence against the other parties to the conspiracy.

That Mary E. Surratt is as guilty as her son of having thus conspired, combined and confederated to do this murder, in aid of this rebellion, is clear. First, her house was the headquarters of Booth, John H. Surratt, Atzerodt, Payne and Herold. She is inquired for by Atzerodt; she is inquired for by Payne, and she is visited by Booth, and holds private conversations with him. His picture, together with that of the chief conspirator, Jefferson Davis, is found in her house. She sends to Booth for a carriage to take her, on the 11th of April, to Surrattsville, for the purpose of perfecting the arrangement deemed necessary to the successful execution of the conspiracy, and especially to facilitate and protect the conspirators in their escape from justice. On that occasion Booth, having disposed of his carriage, gives to the agent she employed ten dollars, with which to hire a conveyance for that purpose. And yet the pretence is made that Mrs. Surratt went on the 11th to Surrattsville exclusively upon her own private and lawful business. Can any one tell, if that be so, how it comes that she should apply to *Booth* for a conveyance, and how it comes that he, of his own accord, having no conveyance to furnish her, should send her ten dollars with which to procure it? There is not the slightest indication that Booth was under any obligation to her, or that she had any claim upon him, either for a conveyance or for the means with which to procure one, except that he was bound to contribute, being the agent of the conspirators in Canada and Richmond, whatever money might be necessary to the consummation of this infernal plot. On that day, the 11th of April, John H. Surratt had not returned from Canada with the funds furnished by Thompson!

Upon that journey of the 11th, the accused, Mary E. Surratt, met the witness, John M. Lloyd, at Uniontown. She called him; he got out of his carriage and came to her, and she whispered to him in so low a tone that her attendant could not hear her words, though Lloyd, to whom they were spoken, did distinctly hear them, and testifies that she told him he should have those "shooting-irons" ready, meaning the carbines which her son and Herold and Atzerodt had deposited with him, and added the reason, "for they would soon be called for." On the day of the assassination she again sent for Booth, had an interview with him in her own house, and immediately went again to Surrattsville, and then, at about six o'clock in the afternoon, she delivered to Lloyd a field-glass and told him "to have two bottles of whisky and the carbines ready, as they would be called for that night." Having thus perfected the arrangement, she returned to Washington to her own house, at about half-past eight o'clock in the evening, to await the final result. How could this woman anticipate, on Friday afternoon, at six o'clock, that these arms would be called for and would be needed that night, unless she was in the conspiracy and knew the blow was to be struck, and the flight of the assassins attempted by that route? Was not the private conversation which Booth held with her in her parlor on the afternoon of the 14th of April, just before she left on this business, in relation to the orders she should give to have the arms ready?

An endeavor is made to impeach Lloyd. But the Court will observe that no witness has been called who contradicts Lloyd's statement in any material matter; neither has his general character for truth been assailed. How, then, is he impeached? Is it claimed that his testimony shows that he was a party to the conspiracy? Then it is conceded by those who set up any such pretence that there was a conspiracy. A conspiracy between whom? There can be no conspiracy without the co-operation or agreement of two or more persons. Who were the other parties to it? Was it Mary E. Surratt? Was it John H. Surratt, George A. Atzerodt, David E. Herold? Those are the only persons, so far as his own testimony or the testimony of any other witness discloses, with whom he had any communication whatever on any subject immediately or remotely touching this conspiracy before the assassination. His receipt and concealment of the arms are unexplained evidence that he was in the conspiracy.

The explanation is that he was dependent upon Mary E. Surratt; was her tenant; and his declaration, given in evidence by the accused herself, is that "she had ruined him, and brought this trouble upon him." But because he was weak enough, or wicked enough, to become the guilty depositary of these arms, and to deliver them on the order of Mary E. Surratt to the assassins, it does not follow that he is not to be believed on oath. It is said that he concealed the facts that the arms had been left and called for. He so testifies himself, but he gives the reason that he did it only from apprehension of danger to his life. If he were in the conspiracy, his general credit being unchallenged, his testimony being uncontradicted in any material matter, he is to be believed, and can not be disbelieved if his testimony is substantially corroborated by other reliable witnesses. Is he

not corroborated touching the deposit of arms by the fact that the arms are produced in court, one of which was found upon the person of Booth at the time he was overtaken and slain, and which is identified as the same which had been left with Lloyd by Herold, Surratt and Atzerodt? Is he not corroborated in the fact of the first interview with Mrs. Surratt by the joint testimony of Mrs. Offut and Louis J. Weichmann, each of whom testified (and they are contradicted by no one), that on Tuesday, the 11th day of April, at Uniontown, Mrs. Surratt called Mr. Lloyd to come to her, which he did, and she held a *secret* conversation with him? Is he not corroborated as to the last conversation on the 14th of April by the testimony of Mrs. Offut, who swears that upon the 14th of April she saw the prisoner, Mary E. Surratt, at Lloyd's house, approach and hold conversation with him? Is he not corroborated in the fact, to which he swears, that Mrs. Surratt delivered to him at that time the field-glass wrapped in paper, by the sworn statement of Weichmann, that Mrs. Surratt took with her on that occasion two packages, both of which were wrapped in paper, and one of which he describes as a small package about six inches in diameter? The attempt was made by calling Mrs. Offut to prove that no such package was delivered, but it failed; she merely states that Mrs. Surratt delivered a package wrapped in paper to her after her arrival there, and before Lloyd came in, which was laid down in the room. But whether it was *the* package about which Lloyd testifies, or the other package of the *two* about which Weichmann testifies, as having been carried there that day by Mrs. Surratt, does not appear. Neither does this witness pretend to say that Mrs. Surratt, after she had delivered it to her, and the witness had laid it down in the room, did not again take it up, if it were the same, and put it in the hands of Lloyd. She only knows that she did not see that done; but she did see Lloyd with a package like the one she received in the room before Mrs. Surratt left. How it came into his possession she is not able to state; nor what the package was that Mrs. Surratt first handed her; nor which of the packages it was she afterward saw in the hands of Lloyd.

But there is one other fact in this case that puts forever at rest the question of the guilty participation of the prisoner, Mrs. Surratt, in this conspiracy and murder; and that is, that Payne, who had lodged four days in her house, who, during all that time, had sat at her table, and who had often conversed with her, when the guilt of his great crime was upon him, and he knew not where else he could so safely go to find a co-conspirator, and he could trust none that was not, like himself, guilty, with even the knowledge of his presence, under cover of darkness, after wandering for three days and nights, skulking before the pursuing officers of justice, at the hour of midnight, found his way to the door of Mrs. Surratt, rang the bell, was admitted, and upon being asked, "Whom do you want to see?" replied, "Mrs. Surratt." He was then asked by the officer, Morgan, what he came at that time of night for, to which he re-

plied, "to dig a gutter in the morning; Mrs. Surratt had sent for him." Afterward he said "Mrs. Surratt knew he was a poor man and came to him." Being asked where he last worked, he replied, "sometimes on 'I' street," and where he boarded, he replied, "he had no boarding-house, and was a poor man who got his living with the pick" which he bore upon his shoulder, having stolen it from the intrenchments of the Capital. Upon being pressed again why he came there at that time of night to go to work, he answered that he simply called to see what time he should go to work in the morning. Upon being told by the officer, who, fortunately, had preceded him to this house, that he would have to go to the Provost Marshal's office, he moved and did not answer, whereupon Mrs. Surratt was asked to step into the hall and state whether she knew this man. Raising her right hand, she exclaimed, "Before God, sir, I have not seen that man before; I have not hired him; I do not know anything about him." The hall was brilliantly lighted.

If not one word had been said, the mere act of Payne, in flying to her house for shelter, would have borne witness against her strong as proofs from Holy Writ. But when she denies, after hearing his declarations that she had sent for him, or that she had gone to him and hired him, and calls her God to witness that she had never seen him, and knew nothing of him, when in point of fact, she had seen him for four successive days in her own house, in the same clothing which he then wore, who can resist for a moment the conclusion that these parties were alike guilty?

The testimony of Spangler's complicity is conclusive and brief. It was impossible to hope for escape after assassinating the President, and such others as might attend him in Ford's theater, without arrangements being first made to aid the flight of the assassin, and, to some extent, prevent immediate pursuit.

A stable was to be provided close to Ford's theater, in which the horses could be concealed, and kept ready for the assassin's use whenever the murderous blow was struck. Accordingly, Booth secretly, through Maddox, hired a stable in the rear of the theater, and connecting with it by an alley, as early as the 1st of January last, showing that at that time he had concluded, notwithstanding all that has been said to the contrary, to murder the President in Ford's theater, and provide the means for immediate and successful flight. Conscious of his guilt, he paid the rent for this stable through Maddox, month by month, giving him the money. He employed Spangler, doubtless for the reason that he could trust him with the secret, as a carpenter to fit up this shed, so that it would furnish room for two horses, and provided the door with lock and key. Spangler did this work for him. Then it was necessary that a carpenter, having access to the theater, should be employed by the assassin to provide a bar for the outer door of the passage leading to the President's box, so that when he entered upon his work of assassination he would be secure from interruption from the rear. By the evidence it is shown that Spangler was in the box

in which the President was murdered on the afternoon of the 14th of April, and when there damned the President and General Grant, and said the President ought to be cursed, he had got so many good men killed, showing not only his hostility to the President, but the cause of it, that he had been faithful to his oath, and had resisted that great rebellion, in the interest of which his life was about to be sacrificed by this man and his co-conspirators. In performing the work, which had doubtless been intrusted to him by Booth, a mortise was cut in the wall. A wooden bar was prepared, one end of which could be readily inserted in the mortise and the other pressed against the edge of the door, on the inside, so as to prevent its being opened. Spangler had the skill and the opportunity to do that work and all the additional work which was done.

It is in evidence that the screws in "the keepers" to the locks on each of the inner doors of the box occupied by the President were drawn. The attempt has been made, on behalf of the prisoner, to show that this was done some time before, accidentally, and with no bad design, and had not been repaired by reason of inadvertence; but that attempt has utterly failed, because the testimony adduced for that purpose relates exclusively to but one of the two inner doors, while the fact is that the screws were drawn in both, and the additional precaution taken to cut a small hole through one of these doors, through which the party approaching, and while in the private passage would be enabled to look into the box and examine the exact posture of the President before entering. It was also deemed essential, in the execution of this plot, that some one should watch at the outer door, in the rear of the theater, by which alone the assassin could hope for escape. It was for this work Booth sought to employ Chester in January, offering $3,000 down of the money of his employers, and the assurance that he should never want. What Chester refused to do, Spangler undertook and promised to do. When Booth brought his horse to the rear door of the theater, on the evening of the murder, he called for Spangler, who went to him, when Booth was heard to say to him, "Ned, you'll help me all you can, won't you?" To which Spangler replied, "Oh, yes."

When Booth made his escape, it is testified by Colonel Stewart, who pursued him across the stage and out through the same door, that, as he approached it, some one slammed it shut. Ritterspaugh, who was standing behind the scenes when Booth fired the pistol and fled, saw Booth run down the passage toward the back door, and pursued him; but Booth drew his knife upon him and passed out, slamming the door after him. Ritterspaugh opened it and went through, leaving it open behind him, leaving Spangler inside, and in a position from which he readily could have reached the door. Ritterspaugh also states that very quickly after he had passed through this door he was followed by a large man, the first who followed him, and who was, doubtless, Colonel Stewart. Stewart is very positive that he saw this door slammed; that he himself was constrained to open it, and

in opening it. He also testi-
...ached the door a man stood
...e thrown it to with his
...e witness believes, was
...itterspaugh has sworn
...hind him when he
first followed by
Who slammed
It was not
Booth, for
...ounting
...s that
out.
or
...rred
...e very
, upon the
...e. The door
...gh being asked
...d answered. Rit-
. I came back on the
...eft Edward Spangler; he
...ace with his hand, and said,
...ich way he went.' I asked him
...eant by slapping me in the mouth.
..., 'For God's sake, shut up.'"

...he testimony of Withers is adroitly handled,
...o throw doubt upon these facts. It can not
avail, for Withers says he was knocked in the
scene by Booth, and when he "come to" he got
a side view of him. A man knocked down
and senseless, on "coming to" might mistake
anybody, by a side view, for Booth.

An attempt has been made by the defense to
discredit this testimony of Ritterspaugh, by
showing his contradictory statements to Gifford,
Carlan and Lamb, neither of whom do, in fact,
contradict him, but substantially sustain him.
None but a guilty man would have met the witness with a blow for stating which way the assassin had gone. A like confession of guilt
was made by Spangler when the witness Miles,
the same evening, and directly after the assassination, came to the back door, where Spangler was standing, with others, and asked Spangler who it was that held the horse, to which
Spangler replied: "Hush; don't say anything
about it." He confessed his guilt again when
he denied to Mary Anderson the fact, proved
here beyond all question, that Booth had called
him when he came to that door with his horse,
using the emphatic words, "No; he did not; he
did not call me." The rope comes to bear witness against him, as did the rope which Atzerodt, and Herold, and John H. Surratt, all
carried to Surrattsville, and deposited there
with the carbines.

It is only surprising that the ingenious counsel did not attempt to explain the deposit of the
rope at Surrattsville by the same method that
he adopted in explanation of the deposit of
this rope, some sixty feet long, found in the
carpet-sack of Spangler, unaccounted for, save
by some evidence which tends to show that he
may have carried it away from the theater.

It is not needful to take time in the recapitulation of the evidence, which shows conclusively that David E. Herold was one of these
conspirators. His continued association with
Booth, with Atzerodt, his visits to Mrs. Sur-

ratt's, his attendance at the theater with Payne,
Surratt and Atzerodt, his connexion with Atzerodt on the evening of the murder, riding with
him on the street in the direction of, and near
to, the theater at the hour appointed for the
work of assassination, and his final flight and
arrest, show that he, in common with all the
other parties on trial, and all the parties named
upon your record not upon trial, had combined
and confederated to kill and murder in the interests of the rebellion, as charged and specified
against them.

That this conspiracy was entered into by all
these parties, both present and absent, is thus
proved by the acts, meetings, declarations and
correspondence of all the parties, beyond any
doubt whatever. True, it is circumstantial evidence, but the Court will remember the rule
before recited, that circumstances can not lie;
that they are held sufficient in every court
where justice is judicially administered to establish the fact of a conspiracy. I shall take
no further notice of the remark made by the
learned counsel who opened for the defense,
and which has been followed by several of his
associates, that, under the Constitution, it requires two witnesses to prove the overt act of
high treason, than to say, this is not a charge
of high treason, but of a treasonable conspiracy, in aid of a rebellion, with intent to kill
and murder the Executive officer of the United
States, and commander of its armies, and of
the murder of the President, in pursuance of
that conspiracy, and with the intent laid, etc.
Neither by the Constitution, nor by the rules of
the common law, is any fact connected with
this allegation required to be established by
the testimony of more than one witness. I
might say, however, that every substantive
averment against each of the parties named
upon this record has been established by the
testimony of more than one witness.

That the several accused did enter into this
conspiracy with John Wilkes Booth and John
H. Surratt, to murder the officers of this Government named upon the record, in pursuance
of the wishes of their employers and instigators in Richmond and Canada, and with intent
thereby to aid the existing rebellion and subvert the Constitution and laws of the United
States, as alleged, is no longer an open question.

The intent as laid was expressly declared
by Sanders in the meeting of the conspirators
at Montreal in February last, by Booth in Virginia and New York, and by Thompson to Conover and Montgomery; but if there were no
testimony directly upon this point, the law
would presume the intent, for the reason that
such was the natural and necessary tendency
and manifest design of the act itself.

The learned gentleman (Mr. Johnson) says
the Government has survived the assassination
of the President, and thereby would have you
infer that this conspiracy was not entered into
and attempted to be executed with the intent
laid. With as much show of reason, it might
be said that because the Government of the
United States has survived this unmatched
rebellion, it therefore results that the rebel con-

had some difficulty in opening it. He also testifies that as he approached the door a man stood near enough to have thrown it to with his hand, and this man, the witness believes, was the prisoner Spangler. Ritterspaugh has sworn that he left the door open behind him when he went out, and that he was first followed by the large man, Colonel Stewart. Who slammed that door behind Ritterspaugh? It was not Ritterspaugh; it could not have been Booth, for Ritterspaugh swears that Booth was mounting his horse at the time; and Stewart swears that Booth was upon his horse when he came out. That it was Spangler who slammed the door after Ritterspaugh may not only be inferred from Stewart's testimony, but it is made very clear by his own conduct afterward, upon the return of Ritterspaugh to the stage. The door being then open, and Ritterspaugh being asked which way Booth went, had answered. Ritterspaugh says: "Then I came back on the stage, where I had left Edward Spangler; he hit me on the face with his hand, and said, 'Don't say which way he went.' I asked him what he meant by slapping me in the mouth. He said, 'For God's sake, shut up.'"

The testimony of Withers is adroitly handled, to throw doubt upon these facts. It can not avail, for Withers says he was knocked in the scene by Booth, and when he "come to" he got a side view of him. A man knocked down and senseless, on "coming to" might mistake anybody, by a side view, for Booth.

An attempt has been made by the defense to discredit this testimony of Ritterspaugh, by showing his contradictory statements to Gifford, Carlan and Lamb, neither of whom do, in fact, contradict him, but substantially sustain him. None but a guilty man would have met the witness with a blow for stating which way the assassin had gone. A like confession of guilt was made by Spangler when the witness Miles, the same evening, and directly after the assassination, came to the back door, where Spangler was standing, with others, and asked Spangler who it was that held the horse, to which Spangler replied: "Hush; don't say anything about it." He confessed his guilt again when he denied to Mary Anderson the fact, proved here beyond all question, that Booth had called him when he came to that door with his horse, using the emphatic words, "No; he did not; he did not call me." The rope comes to bear witness against him, as did the rope which Atzerodt, and Herold, and John H. Surratt, had carried to Surrattsville, and deposited there with the carbines.

It is only surprising that the ingenious counsel did not attempt to explain the deposit of the rope at Surrattsville by the same method that he adopted in explanation of the deposit of this rope, some sixty feet long, found in the carpet-sack of Spangler, unaccounted for, save by some evidence which tends to show that he may have carried it away from the theater.

It is not needful to take time in the recapitulation of the evidence, which shows conclusively that David E. Herold was one of these conspirators. His continued association with Booth, with Atzerodt, his visits to Mrs. Surratt's, his attendance at the theater with Payne, Surratt and Atzerodt, his connexion with Atzerodt on the evening of the murder, riding with him on the street in the direction of, and near to, the theater at the hour appointed for the work of assassination, and his final flight and arrest, show that he, in common with all the other parties on trial, and all the parties named upon your record not upon trial, had combined and confederated to kill and murder in the interests of the rebellion, as charged and specified against them.

That this conspiracy was entered into by all these parties, both present and absent, is thus proved by the acts, meetings, declarations and correspondence of all the parties, beyond any doubt whatever. True, it is circumstantial evidence, but the Court will remember the rule before recited, that circumstances can not lie; that they are held sufficient in every court where justice is judicially administered to establish the fact of a conspiracy. I shall take no further notice of the remark made by the learned counsel who opened for the defense, and which has been followed by several of his associates, that, under the Constitution, it requires two witnesses to prove the overt act of high treason, than to say, this is not a charge of high treason, but of a treasonable conspiracy, in aid of a rebellion, with intent to kill and murder the Executive officer of the United States, and commander of its armies, and of the murder of the President, in pursuance of that conspiracy, and with the intent laid, etc. Neither by the Constitution, nor by the rules of the common law, is any fact connected with this allegation required to be established by the testimony of more than one witness. I might say, however, that every substantive averment against each of the parties named upon this record has been established by the testimony of more than one witness.

That the several accused did enter into this conspiracy with John Wilkes Booth and John H. Surratt, to murder the officers of this Government named upon the record, in pursuance of the wishes of their employers and instigators in Richmond and Canada, and with intent thereby to aid the existing rebellion and subvert the Constitution and laws of the United States, as alleged, is no longer an open question.

The intent as laid was expressly declared by Sanders in the meeting of the conspirators at Montreal in February last, by Booth in Virginia and New York, and by Thompson to Conover and Montgomery; but if there were no testimony directly upon this point, the law would presume the intent, for the reason that such was the natural and necessary tendency and manifest design of the act itself.

The learned gentleman (Mr. Johnson) says the Government has survived the assassination of the President, and thereby would have you infer that this conspiracy was not entered into and attempted to be executed with the intent laid. With as much show of reason, it might be said that because the Government of the United States has survived this unmatched rebellion, it therefore results that the rebel conspirators waged war upon the Government with no purpose or intent thereby to subvert it. By the law, we have seen that without any direct evidence of previous combination and agreement between these parties, the conspiracy might be established by evidence of the acts of the prisoners, or of any others with whom they co-operated, concurring in the execution of the common design. *Roscoe*, 416.

Was there co-operation between the several accused in the execution of this conspiracy? That there was, is as clearly established by the testimony as is the fact that Abraham Lincoln was killed and murdered by John Wilkes Booth. The evidence shows that all of the accused, save Mudd and Arnold, were in Washington on the 14th of April, the day of the assassination, together with John Wilkes Booth and John H. Surratt; that on that day Booth had a secret interview with the prisoner, Mary E. Surratt; that immediately thereafter she went to Surrattsville to perform her part of the preparation necessary to the successful execution of the conspiracy, and did make that preparation; that John H. Surratt had arrived here from Canada, notifying the parties that the price to be paid for this great crime had been provided for, at least in part, by the deposit receipts of April 6th for $180,000, procured by Thompson, of the Ontario Bank, Montreal, Canada; that he was also prepared to keep watch, or strike a blow, and ready for the contemplated flight; that Atzerodt, on the afternoon of that day, was seeking to obtain a horse, the better to secure his own safety by flight, after he should have performed the task which he had voluntarily undertaken by contract in the conspiracy—the murder of Andrew Johnson, then Vice-President of the United States; that he did procure a horse for that purpose at Naylor's and was seen about nine o'clock in the evening to ride to the Kirkwood House, where the Vice-President then was, dismount, and enter. At a previous hour Booth was in the Kirkwood House, and left his card, now in evidence, doubtless intended to be sent to the room of the Vice-President, and which was in these words: "Don't wish to disturb you. Are you at home? J. Wilkes Booth." Atzerodt, when he made application at Brooks' in the afternoon for the horse, said to Weichmann, who was there, he was going to ride in the country, and that "he was going to get a horse and send for Payne." He did get a horse for Payne, as well as for himself; for it is proven that on the 12th he was seen in Washington, riding the horse which had been procured by Booth, in company with Mudd, last November, from Gardner. A similar horse was tied before the door of Mr. Seward on the night of the murder, was captured after the flight of Payne, who was seen to ride away, and which horse is now identified as the Gardner horse. Booth also procured a horse on the same day, took it to his stable in the rear of the theater, where he had an interview with Spangler, and where he concealed it. Herold, too, obtained a horse in the afternoon, and was seen between nine and ten o'clock riding with *Atzerodt* down the Avenue from the Treasury,

then up Fourteenth and down F street, passing close by Ford's theater.

O'Laughlin had come to Washington the day before, had sought out his victim, General Grant, at the house of the Secretary of War, that he might be able with certainty to identify him, and at the very hour when these preparations were going on, was lying in wait at Rullman's, on the Avenue, keeping watch, and declaring, as he did, at about ten o'clock P. M., when told that the fatal blow had been struck by Booth, "I don't believe Booth did it." During the day, and the night before, he had been visiting Booth, and doubtless encouraging him, and at that very hour was in position, at a convenient distance, to aid and protect him in his flight, as well as to execute his own part of the conspiracy by inflicting death upon General Grant, who happily was not at the theater nor in the city, having left the city that day. Who doubts that, Booth having ascertained in the course of the day, that General Grant would not be present at the theater, O'Laughlin, who was to murder General Grant, instead of entering the box with Booth, was detailed to lie in wait, and watch and support him.

His declarations of his reasons for changing his lodgings here and in Baltimore, after the murder, so ably and so ingeniously presented in the argument of his learned counsel (Mr. Cox), avail nothing before the blasting fact that he did change his lodgings, and declared "he knew nothing of the affair whatever." O'Laughlin, who lurked here, conspiring daily with Booth and Arnold for six weeks to do this murder, declares "he knew nothing of the affair." O'Laughlin, who said he was "in the oil business," which Booth and Surratt, and Payne and Arnold, have all declared meant this conspiracy, says he "knew nothing of the affair." O'Laughlin, to whom Booth sent the dispatches of the 13th and 27th of March— O'Laughlin, who is named in Arnold's letter as one of the conspirators, and who searched for General Grant on Thursday night, laid in wait for him on Friday, was defeated by that Providence "which shapes our ends," and laid in wait to aid Booth and Payne, declares "he knows nothing of the matter." Such a denial is as false and inexcusable as Peter's denial of our Lord.

Mrs. Surratt had arrived at home, from the completion of her part of the plot, about half-past eight o'clock in the evening. A few moments afterward she was called to the parlor, and there had a private interview with some one unseen, but whose retreating footsteps were heard by the witness Weichmann. This was doubtless the secret and last visit of John H. Surratt to his mother, who had instigated and encouraged him to strike this traitorous and murderous blow against his country.

While all these preparations were going on, Mudd was awaiting the execution of the plot, ready to faithfully perform his part in securing the safe escape of the murderers. Arnold was at his post at Fortress Monroe, awaiting the meeting referred to in his letter of March 27th, wherein he says they were not "to meet for a month or so," which month had more than expired on the day of the murder, for his letter and the testimony disclose that this month of suspension began to run from about the first week in March. He stood ready with the arms which Booth had furnished him to aid the escape of the murderers by *that route*, and secure their communication with their employers. He had given the assurance in that letter to Booth, that although the Government "suspicioned them," and the undertaking was "becoming complicated," yet "a time more propitious would arrive" for the consummation of this conspiracy in which he "was one" with Booth, and when he would "be better prepared to again be with him."

Such were the preparations. The horses were in readiness for the flight; the ropes were procured, doubtless, for the purpose of tying the horses at whatever point they might be constrained to delay, and to secure their boats to their moorings in making their way across the Potomac. The five murderous camp knives, the two carbines, the eight revolvers, the Derringer, in Court and identified, all were ready for the work of death. The part that each had played has already been in part stated in this argument, and needs no repetition.

Booth proceeded to the theater about nine o'clock in the evening, at the same time that Atzerodt, Payne and Herold were riding the streets, while Surratt, having parted with his mother at the brief interview in her parlor, from which his retreating steps were heard, was walking the avenue, booted and spurred, and doubtless consulting with O'Laughlin. When Booth reached the rear of the theater, he called Spangler to him (whose denial of that fact, when charged with it, as proven by three witnesses, is very significant), and received from Spangler his pledge to help him all he could, when with Booth he entered the theater by the stage door, doubtless to see that the way was clear from the box to the rear door of the theater, and look upon their victim, whose exact position they could study from the stage. After this view, Booth passes to the street, in front of the theater, where, on the pavement with other conspirators yet unknown, among them one described as a low-browed villain, he awaits the appointed moment. Booth himself, impatient, enters the vestibule of the theater from the front, and asks the time. He is referred to the clock, and returns. Presently, as the hour of ten approached, one of his guilty associates called the time; they wait; again, as the moments elapsed, this conspirator upon watch called the time; again, as the appointed hour draws nigh, he calls the time; and finally, when the fatal moment arrives, he repeats in a louder tone, "Ten minutes past ten o'clock." Ten minutes past ten o'clock! The hour has come when the red right hand of these murderous conspirators should strike, and the dreadful deed of assassination be done.

Booth, at the appointed moment, entered the theater, ascended to the dress-circle, passed to the right, paused a moment, looking down, doubtless to see if Spangler was at his post, and approached the outer door of the close passage leading to the box occupied by the President, pressed it open, passed in, and closed the passage door behind him. Spangler's bar was in its place, and was readily adjusted by Booth in the mortise, and pressed against the inner side of the door, so that he was secure from interruption from without. He passes on to the next door, immediately behind the President, and there stopping, looks through the aperture in the door into the President's box, and deliberately observes the precise position of his victim, seated in the chair which had been prepared by the conspirators as the altar for the sacrifice, looking calmly and quietly down upon the glad and grateful people whom by his fidelity he had saved from the peril which had threatened the destruction of their government, and all they held dear this side of the grave, and whom he had come upon invitation to greet with his presence, with the words still lingering upon his lips which he had uttered with uncovered head and uplifted hand before God and his country, when on the 4th of last March he took again the oath to preserve, protect and defend the Constitution, declaring that he entered upon the duties of his great office "with malice toward none—with charity for all." In a moment more, strengthened by the knowledge that his co-conspirators were all at their posts, seven at least of them present in the city, two of them, Mudd and Arnold, at their appointed places, watching for his coming, this hired assassin moves stealthily through the door, the fastenings of which had been removed to facilitate his entrance, fires upon his victim, and the martyr spirit of Abraham Lincoln ascends to God.

"Treason has done his worst; nor steel nor poison,
Malice domestic, foreign levy, nothing
Can touch him further."

At the same hour, when these accused and their co-conspirators in Richmond and Canada, by the hand of John Wilkes Booth, inflicted this mortal wound which deprived the republic of its defender, and filled this land from ocean to ocean with a strange, great sorrow, Payne, a very demon in human form, with the words, of falsehood upon his lips, that he was the bearer of a message from the physician of the venerable Secretary of State, sweeps by his servant, encounters his son, who protests that the assassin shall not disturb his father, prostrate on a bed of sickness, and receives for answer the assassin's blow from the revolver in his hand, repeated again and again, rushes into the room, is encountered by Major Seward, inflicts wound after wound upon him with his murderous knife, is encountered by Hansell and Robinson, each of whom he also wounds, springs upon the defenseless and feeble Secretary of State, stabs first on one side of his throat, then on the other, again in the face, and is only prevented from literally hacking out his life by the persistence and courage of the attendant Robinson. He turns to flee, and, his giant arm and murderous hand for a moment paralyzed by the consciousness of guilt, he drops his weapons of death, one in the house, the other at the door, where they were taken up, and are here now to bear witness against him. He attempts escape on the horse which Booth and Mudd had procured of Gardner—with what success has already been stated.

Atzerodt, near midnight, returns to the stable of Naylor the horse which he had procured for this work of murder, having been interrupted in the execution of the part assigned him at the Kirkwood House, by the timely coming of citizens to the defense of the Vice-President, and creeps into the Pennsylvania House at two o'clock in the morning with another of the conspirators, yet unknown. There he remained until about five o'clock, when he left, found his way to Georgetown, pawned one of his revolvers, now in court, and fled northward into Maryland.

He is traced to Montgomery county, to the house of Mr. Metz, on the Sunday succeeding the murder, where, as is proved by the testimony of three witnesses, he said that if the man that was to follow Gen. Grant had followed him, it was likely that Grant was shot. To one of these witnesses (Mr. Leaman) he said he did not think Grant had been killed; or if he had been killed, he was killed by a man who got on the cars at the same time that Grant did; thus disclosing most clearly that one of his co-conspirators was assigned the task of killing and murdering Gen. Grant, and that Atzerodt knew that Gen. Grant had left the city of Washington, a fact which is not disputed, on the Friday evening of the murder, by the evening train. Thus this intended victim of the conspiracy escaped, for that night, the knives and revolvers of Atzerodt, and O'Laughlin, and Payne, and Herold, and Booth, and John H. Surratt, and, perchance, Harper and Caldwell, and twenty others, who were then here lying in wait for his life.

In the meantime Booth and Herold, taking the route before agreed upon, make directly after the assassination, for the Anacostia bridge. Booth crosses first, gives his name, passes the guard, and is speedily followed by Herold. They make their way directly to Surrattsville, where Herold calls to Lloyd, "Bring out those things," showing that there had been communication between them and Mrs. Surratt after her return. Both the carbines being in readiness, according to Mary E. Surratt's directions, both were brought out. They took but one. Booth declined to carry the other, saying that his limb was broken. They then declared that they had murdered the President and the Secretary of State. They then make their way directly to the house of the prisoner Mudd, assured of safety and security. They arrived early in the morning before day, and no man knows at what hour they left. Herold rode toward Bryantown with Mudd about three o'clock that afternoon, in the vicinity of which place he parted with him, remaining in the swamp, and was afterward seen returning the same afternoon in the direction of Mudd's house; about which time, a little before sundown, Mudd returned from Bryantown toward his home. This village, at the time Mudd was in it, was thronged with soldiers in pursuit of the murderers of the President, and although great care has been taken by the defense to deny that any one said in the presence of Dr. Mudd, either there or elsewhere on

that day, who had committed this crime, yet it is in evidence by two witnesses, whose truthfulness no man questions, that upon Mudd's return to his own house, that afternoon, he stated that Booth was the murderer of the President, and Boyle the murderer of Secretary Seward, but took care to make the further remark that Booth had brothers, and he did not know which of them had done the act. When did Dr. Mudd learn that Booth had brothers? And what is still more pertinent to this inquiry, from whom did he learn that either John Wilkes Booth or any of his brothers had murdered the President? It is clear that Booth remained in his house until some time in the afternoon of Saturday; that Herold left the house alone, as one of the witnesses states, being seen to pass the window; that he alone of those two assassins was in the company of Dr. Mudd on his way to Bryantown. It does not appear when Herold returned to Mudd's house. It is a confession of Dr. Mudd himself, proven by one of the witnesses, that Booth left his house on crutches, and went in the direction of the swamp. How long he remained there, and what became of the horses which Booth and Herold rode to his house, and which were put into his stable, are facts nowhere disclosed by the evidence. The owners testify that they have never seen the horses since. The accused give no explanation of the matter, and when Herold and Booth were captured they had not these horses in their possession. How comes it that, on Mudd's return from Bryantown, on the evening of Saturday, in his conversation with Mr. Hardy and Mr. Farrell, the witnesses referred to, he gave the name of Booth as the murderer of the President and that of Boyle as the murderer of Secretary Seward and his son, and carefully avoided intimating to either that Booth had come to his house early that day, and had remained there until the afternoon; that he left him in his house and had furnished him a razor with which Booth attempted to disguise himself by shaving off his mustache? How comes it, also, that, upon being asked by those two witnesses whether the Booth who killed the President was the one who had been there last fall, he answered that he did not know whether it was that man or one of his brothers, but he understood he had some brothers, and added, that if it was the Booth who was there last fall, *he knew that one*, but concealed the fact that this man had been at his house on that day, and was then at his house, and had attempted, in his presence, to disguise his person? He was sorry, very sorry, that the thing had occurred, but not so sorry as to be willing to give any evidence to these two neighbors, who were manifestly honest and upright men, that the murderer had been harbored in his house all day, and was probably at that moment, as his own subsequent confession shows, lying concealed in his house or near by, subject to his call. This is the man who undertakes to show by his own declaration, offered in evidence against my protest, of what he said afterward, on Sunday afternoon, the 16th, to his kinsman, Dr. George D. Mudd, to whom he then stated that the assassination of the President was a most damnable act—a conclusion in which most men will agree with him, and to establish which his testimony was not needed. But it is to be remarked that this accused did not intimate that the man whom he knew the evening before was the murderer had found refuge in his house, had disguised his person, and sought concealment in the swamp upon the crutches which he had provided for him. Why did he conceal this fact from his kinsman? After the church services were over, however, in another conversation on their way home, he did tell Dr. George Mudd that two suspicious persons had been at his house, who had come there a little before daybreak on Saturday morning; that one of them had a broken leg, which he bandaged; that they got something to eat at his house; that they seemed to be laboring under more excitement than probably would result from the injury; that they said they came from Bryantown, and inquired the way to Parson Wilmer's; that while at his house one of them called for a razor and shaved himself. The witness says, "I do not remember whether he said that this party shaved off his whiskers or his mustache, but he altered somewhat, or probably materially, his features." Finally, the prisoner, Dr. Mudd, told this witness that he, in company with the younger of the two men, went down the road toward Bryantown in search of a vehicle to take the wounded man away from his house. How comes it that he concealed in this conversation the fact proved, that he went with Herold toward Bryantown and left Herold outside of the town? How comes it that in this second conversation, on Sunday, insisted upon here with such pertinacity as evidence for the defense, but which had never been called for by the prosecution, he concealed from his kinsman the fact which he had disclosed the day before to Hardy and Farrell, that it was Booth who assassinated the President, and the fact which is now disclosed by his other confessions given in evidence for the prosecution, that it was Booth whom he had sheltered, concealed in his house, and aided to his hiding place in the swamps? He volunteers as evidence his further statement, however, to this witness, that on Sunday evening he requested the witness to state to the military authorities that two suspicious persons had been at his house, and see if anything could be made of it. He did not tell the witness what became of Herold, and where he parted with him on the way to Bryantown. How comes it that when he was at Bryantown on the Saturday evening before, when he knew that Booth was then at his house, and that Booth was the murderer of the President, he did not himself state it to the military authorities then in that village, as he well knew? It is difficult to see what kindled his suspicions on Sunday, if none were in his mind on Saturday, when he was in possession of the fact that Booth had murdered the President, and was then secreting and disguising himself in the prisoner's own house.

His conversation with Gardner on the same Sunday at the church is also introduced here to relieve him from the overwhelming evidences of his guilt. He communicates nothing to Gardner of the fact that Booth had been in his house; nothing of the fact that he knew the day before that Booth had murdered the President; nothing of the fact that Booth had disguised or attempted to disguise himself; nothing of the fact that he had gone with Booth's associate, Herold, in search of a vehicle, the more speedily to expedite their flight; nothing of the fact that Booth had found concealment in the woods and swamp near his house, upon the crutches which he had furnished him. He contents himself with merely stating "that we ought to raise immediately a home guard, to hunt up all suspicious persons passing through our section of country and arrest them, for there were two suspicious persons at my house yesterday morning."

It would have looked more like aiding justice and arresting felons if he had put in execution his project of a home guard on Saturday, and made it effective by the arrest of the man then in his house who had lodged with him last fall, with whom he had gone to purchase one of the very horses employed in his flight after the assassination, whom he visited last winter in Washington, and to whom he had pointed out the very route by which he had escaped by way of his house, whom he had again visited on the 3d of last March, preparatory to the commission of this great crime, and who he knew, when he sheltered and concealed him in the woods on Saturday, was not merely a suspicious person, but was, in fact, the murderer and assassin of Abraham Lincoln. While I deem it my duty to say here, as I said before, when these declarations, uttered by the accused on Sunday, the 16th, to Gardner and George D. Mudd, were attempted to be offered on the part of the accused, that they are in no sense evidence, and by the law were wholly inadmissible, yet I state it as my conviction that, being upon the record upon motion of the accused himself, so far as these declarations to Gardner and George D. Mudd go, they are additional indications of the guilt of the accused, in this, that they are manifestly suppressions of the truth and suggestions of falsehood and deception; they are but the utterances and confessions of guilt.

To Lieutenant Lovett, Joshua Lloyd, and Simon Gavacan, who, in pursuit of the murderer, visited his house on the 18th of April, the Tuesday after the murder, he denied positively, upon inquiry, that two men had passed his house, or had come to his house on the morning after the assassination. Two of these witnesses swear positively to his having made the denial, and the other says he hesitated to answer the question he put to him; all of them agree that he afterward admitted that two men had been there, one of whom had a broken limb, which he had set; and when asked by this witness who that man was, he said he did not know—that the man was a stranger to him, and that the two had been there but a short time. Lloyd asked him if he had ever seen any of the parties, Booth, Herold and Surratt, and he said he had never seen them; while it is positively proved that he was acquainted with John H. Surratt, who had been in his house; that he knew Booth and had introduced Booth to Surratt last winter. Afterward, on Friday, the 21st, he admitted to Lloyd that he had been introduced to Booth last fall, and that this man, who came to his house on Saturday, the 15th, remained there from about four o'clock in the morning until about four in the afternoon; that one of them left his house on horseback, and the other walking. In the first conversation he denied ever having seen these men.

Colonel Wells also testifies that, in his conversation with Dr. Mudd on Friday, the 21st, the prisoner said that he had gone to Bryantown, or near Bryantown, to see some friends on Saturday, and that as he came back to his own house he saw the person he afterward supposed to be Herold passing to the left of his house toward the barn, but that he did not see the other person at all after he left him in his own house, about one o'clock. If this statement be true, how did Dr. Mudd see the same person leave his house on crutches? He further stated to this witness that he returned to his own house about four o'clock in the afternoon; that he did not know this wounded man; said he could not recognize him from the photograph which is of record here, but admitted that he had met Booth some time in November, when he had some conversation with him *about lands* and horses; that Booth had remained with him that night in November, and on the next day had purchased a horse. He said he had not again seen Booth from the time of the introduction in November up to his arrival at his house on the Saturday morning after the assassination. Is not this a confession that he did see John Wilkes Booth on that morning at his house, and knew it was Booth? If he did not know him, how came he to make this statement to the witness: that "he had not seen Booth *after* November *prior* to his arrival there on the Saturday morning?"

He had said before to the same witness, he did not know the wounded man. He said further to Colonel Wells, that when he went up stairs after their arrival, he noticed that the person he *supposed* to be Booth had shaved off his mustache. Is it not inferable from this declaration that he *then* supposed him to be Booth? Yet he declared the same afternoon, and while Booth was in his own house, that Booth was the murderer of the President. One of the most remarkable statements made to this witness by the prisoner was that he heard for the first time on Sunday morning, or late in the evening of Saturday, that the President had been murdered! From whom did he hear it? The witness (Colonel Wells) volunteers his "impression" that Dr. Mudd had said he heard it after the persons had left his house. If the "impression" of the witness thus volunteered is to be taken as evidence—and the counsel for the accused, judging from their manner, seem to think it ought to be—let this question be answered: how could Dr. Mudd have made that impression upon anybody truthfully, when it is proved by Farrell and Hardy that on his return from Bryantown, on Saturday afternoon, he not only stated that the President. Mr. Seward and his son had been assassinated, but that Boyle had assassinated Mr. Seward, and Booth had

assassinated the President? Add to this the fact that he said to this witness that he left his own house at one o'clock, and when he returned the men were gone, yet it is in evidence, by his own declarations, that Booth left his house at four o'clock on crutches, and he must have been there to have seen it, or he could not have known the fact.

Mr. Williams testifies that he was at Mudd's house on Tuesday, the 18th of April, when he said that strangers had *not* been that way, and also declared that he heard, *for the first time*, of the assassination of the President on Sunday morning, at church. Afterward, on Friday, the 21st, Mr. Williams asked him concerning the men who had been at his house, one of whom had a broken limb, and he confessed they had been there. Upon being asked if they were Booth and Herold, he said they were not—*that he knew Booth*. I think it is fair to conclude that he did know Booth, when we consider the testimony of Weichmann, of Norton, of Evans, and all the testimony just referred to, wherein he declares, himself, that he not only knew him, but that he had lodged with him, and that he had himself gone with him when he purchased his horse from Gardner last fall, for the very purpose of aiding the flight of himself, or some of his confederates.

All these circumstances taken together, which, as we have seen upon high authority, are stronger as evidences of guilt than even direct testimony, leave no further room for argument, and no rational doubt that Dr. Samuel A. Mudd was as certainly in this conspiracy as were Booth and Herold, whom he sheltered and entertained; receiving them under cover of darkness on the morning after the assassination, concealing them throughout that day from the hand of offended justice, and aiding them, by every endeavor, to pursue their way successfully to their co-conspirator. Arnold, at Fortress Monroe, and in which direction they fled until overtaken and Booth was slain.

We next find Herold and his confederate Booth, after their departure from the house of Mudd, across the Potomac, in the neighborhood of Port Conway, on Monday, the 24th of April, conveyed in a wagon. There Herold, in order to obtain the aid of Captain Jett, Ruggles and Bainbridge, of the Confederate army, said to Jett, "We are the assassinators of the President;" that this was his brother with him, who, with himself, belonged to A. P. Hill's corps; that his brother had been wounded at Petersburg; that their names were Boyd. He requested Jett and his rebel companions to take them out of the lines. After this, Booth joined these parties, was placed on Ruggles' horse, and crossed the Rappahannock river. They then proceeded to the house of Garrett, in the neighborhood of Port Royal, and nearly midway between Washington city and Fortress Monroe. where they were to have joined Arnold. Before these rebel guides and guards parted with them, Herold confessed that they were traveling under assumed names—that his own name was Herold, and that the name of the wounded man was John Wilkes Booth, "who had killed the President." The rebels left Booth at Garrett's, where Herold re-visited him from time to time, until they were captured. At two o'clock on Wednesday morning, the 26th, a party of United States officers and soldiers surrounded Garrett's barn, where Booth and Herold lay concealed, and demanded their surrender. Booth cursed Herold, calling him a coward, and bade him go, when Herold came out and surrendered himself, was taken into custody, and is now brought into Court. The barn was then set on fire, when Booth sprang to his feet, amid the flames that were kindling about him, carbine in hand, and approached the door, seeking, by the flashing light of the fire, to find some new victim for his murderous hand, when he was shot, as he deserved to be, by Sergeant Corbett, in order to save his comrades from wounds or death by the hands of this desperate assassin. Upon his person was found the following bill of exchange:

"No. 1492. The Ontario Bank, Montreal Branch. Exchange for £61 12s. 10d. Montreal, 27th October, 1864. Sixty days after sight of this first of exchange, second and third of the same tenor and date, pay to the order of J. Wilkes Booth £61 12s. 10d. sterling, value received, and charge to the account of this office. H. Stanus, manager. To Messrs. Glynn, Mills & Co., London."

Thus fell, by the hands of one of the defenders of the republic, this hired assassin, who, for a price, murdered Abraham Lincoln, bearing upon his person, as this bill of exchange testifies, additional evidence of the fact that he had undertaken, in aid of the rebellion, this work of assassination by the hands of himself and his confederates, for such sum as the accredited agents of Jefferson Davis might pay him or them, out of the funds of the Confederacy, which, as is in evidence, they had in "any amount" in Canada for the purpose of rewarding conspirators, spies, poisoners and assassins, who might take service under their false commissions, and to do the work of the incendiary and the murderer upon the lawful representatives of the American people, to whom had been intrusted the care of the republic, the maintenance of the Constitution, and the execution of the laws.

The Court will remember that it is in the testimony of Merritt, and Montgomery, and Conover, that Thompson, and Sanders, and Clay, and Cleary, made their boasts that they had money in Canada for this very purpose. Nor is it to be overlooked or forgotten that the officers of the Ontario Bank, at Montreal, testify that during the current year of this conspiracy and assassination, Jacob Thompson had on deposit in that bank the sum of six hundred and forty-nine thousand dollars, and that these deposits to the credit of Jacob Thompson accrued from the negotiation of bills of exchange drawn by the Secretary of the Treasury of the so-called Confederate States on Frazier, Trenholm & Co., of Liverpool, who were known to be the financial agents of the Confederate States. With an undrawn deposit in this bank of four hundred and fifty-five dollars, which has remained to his credit since October last, and with an unpaid bill of exchange drawn by

the same bank upon London, in his possession, and found upon his person, Booth ends his guilty career in this work of conspiracy and blood in April, 1865, as he began it in October, 1864, in combination with Jefferson Davis, Jacob Thompson, George N. Sanders, Clement C. Clay, William C. Cleary, Beverley Tucker, and other co-conspirators, making use of the money of the rebel confederation to aid in the execution and in the flight, bearing, at the moment of his death, upon his person, their money, part of the price which they paid for his great crime, to aid him in its consummation, and secure him afterward from arrest, and the just penalty which, by the law of God and the law of man, is denounced against treasonable conspiracy and murder.

By all the testimony in the case, it is, in my judgment, made as clear as any transaction can be shown by human testimony, that John Wilkes Booth and John H. Surratt, and the several accused, David E. Herold, George A. Atzerodt, Lewis Payne, Michael O'Laughlin, Edward Spangler, Samuel Arnold, Mary E. Surratt and Samuel A. Mudd, did, with intent to aid the existing rebellion, and to subvert the Constitution and laws of the United States, in the month of October last, and thereafter, combine, confederate and conspire with Jefferson Davis, George N. Sanders, Beverley Tucker, Jacob Thompson, William C. Cleary, Clement C. Clay, George Harper, George Young, and others unknown, to kill and murder, within the military department of Washington, and within the intrenched fortifications and military lines thereof, Abraham Lincoln, then President of the United States, and Commander-in-Chief of the army and navy thereof; Andrew Johnson, Vice-President of the United States; William H. Seward, Secretary of State, and Ulysses S. Grant, Lieutenant-General, in command of the armies of the United States; and that Jefferson Davis, the chief of this rebellion, was the instigator and procurer, through his accredited agents in Canada, of this treasonable conspiracy.

It is also submitted to the Court, that it is clearly established by the testimony that John Wilkes Booth, in pursuance of this conspiracy, so entered into by him and the accused, did, on the night of the 14th of April, 1865, within the military department of Washington, and the intrenched fortifications and military lines thereof, and with the intent laid, inflict a mortal wound upon Abraham Lincoln, then President and Commander-in-chief of the army and navy of the United States, whereof he died; that, in pursuance of the same conspiracy, and within the said department and intrenched lines, Lewis Payne assaulted, with intent to kill and murder, William H. Seward, then Secretary of State of the United States; that George A. Atzerodt, in pursuance of the same conspiracy, and within the said department, laid in wait, with intent to kill and murder Andrew Johnson, then Vice-President of the United States; that Michael O'Laughlin, within said department, and in pursuance of said conspiracy, laid in wait to kill and murder Ulysses S. Grant, then in command of the armies of the United States; and that Mary E. Surratt.

26

David E. Herold, Samuel Arnold, Samuel A. Mudd and Edward Spangler did encourage, aid and abet the commission of said several acts in the prosecution of said conspiracy.

If this treasonable conspiracy has not been wholly executed; if the several executive officers of the United States and the commander of its armies, to kill and murder whom the said several accused thus confederated and conspired, have not each and all fallen by the hands of these conspirators, thereby leaving the people of the United States without a President or Vice-President, without a Secretary of State, who alone is clothed with authority by the law to call an election to fill the vacancy, should any arise, in the offices of President and Vice-President; and, without a lawful commander of the armies of the republic, it is only because the conspirators were deterred by the vigilance and fidelity of the executive officers, whose lives were mercifully protected, on that night of murder, by the care of the Infinite Being, who has, thus far, saved the Republic, and crowned its arms with victory.

If this conspiracy was thus entered into by the accused; if John Wilkes Booth did kill and murder Abraham Lincoln in pursuance thereof; if Lewis Payne did, in pursuance of said conspiracy, assault, with intent to kill and murder, William H. Seward, as stated, and if the several parties accused did commit the several acts alleged against them, in the prosecution of said conspiracy, then it is the law that all the parties to that conspiracy, whether present at the time of its execution or not, whether on trial before this Court or not, are alike guilty of the several acts done by each in the execution of the common design. What these conspirators did in the execution of this conspiracy by the hand of one of their co-conspirators they did themselves; his act, done in the prosecution of the common design, was the act of all the parties to the treasonable combination, because done in execution and furtherance of their guilty and treasonable agreement.

As we have seen this is the rule, whether all the conspirators are indicted or not; whether they are all on trial or not. "It is not material what the nature of the indictment is, provided the offense involve a conspiracy. Upon indictment for murder, for instance, if it appear that others, together with the prisoner, conspired to perpetrate the crime, the act of one, done in pursuance of that intention, would be evidence against the rest." 1 *Whar.*, 706. To the same effect are the words of Chief Justice Marshall, before cited, that whoever leagued in a general conspiracy, performed any part, however MINUTE, or however REMOTE, from the scene of *action*, are guilty as principals. In this treasonable conspiracy, to aid the existing armed rebellion, by murdering the executive officers of the United States and the commander of its armies, all the parties to it must be held as principals, and the act of one, in the prosecution of the common design, the act of all.

I leave the decision of this dread issue with the Court, to which alone it belongs. It is for you to say, upon your oaths, whether the accused are guilty.

I am not conscious that in this argument I have made any erroneous statement of the evidence, or drawn any erroneous conclusions; yet I pray the Court, out of tender regard and jealous care for the rights of the accused, to see that no error of mine, if any there be, shall work them harm. The past services of the members of this honorable Court give assurance that, without fear, favor or affection, they will discharge with fidelity the duty enjoined upon them by their oaths. Whatever else may befall, I trust in God that in this, as in every other American court, the rights of the whole people will be respected, and that the Republic in this, its supreme hour of trial, will be true to itself and just to all, ready to protect the rights of the humblest, to redress every wrong, to avenge every crime, to vindicate the majesty of law, and to maintain inviolate the Constitution, whether assailed secretly or openly, by hosts armed with gold, or armed with steel.

APPENDIX.

OPINION

ON THE

CONSTITUTIONAL POWER OF THE MILITARY

TO TRY AND EXECUTE THE

ASSASSINS OF THE PRESIDENT.

BY ATTORNEY GENERAL JAMES SPEED.

ATTORNEY GENERAL'S OFFICE,
Washington, July —, 1865.

SIR: You ask me whether the persons charged with the offense of having assassinated the President can be tried before a military tribunal, or must they be tried before a civil court.

The President was assassinated at a theater in the city of Washington. At the time of the assassination a civil war was flagrant, the city of Washington was defended by fortifications regularly and constantly manned, the principal police of the city was by Federal soldiers, the public offices and property in the city were all guarded by soldiers, and the President's House and person were, or should have been, under the guard of soldiers. Martial law had been declared in the District of Columbia, but the civil courts were open and held their regular sessions, and transacted business as in times of peace.

Such being the facts, the question is one of great importance—important, because it involves the constitutional guarantees thrown about the rights of the citizen, and because the security of the army and the government in time of war is involved; important, as it involves a seeming conflict between the laws of peace and of war.

Having given the question propounded the patient and earnest consideration its magnitude and importance require, I will proceed to give the reasons why I am of the opinion that the conspirators not only may but ought to be tried by a military tribunal.

A civil court of the United States is created by a law of congress, under and according to the Constitution. To the Constitution and the law we must look to ascertain how the court is constituted, the limits of its jurisdiction, and what its mode of procedure.

A military tribunal exists under and according to the Constitution in time of war. Congress may prescribe how all such tribunals are to be constituted, what shall be their jurisdiction and mode of procedure. Should Congress fail to create such tribunals, then, under the Constitution, they must be constituted according to the laws and usages of civilized warfare. They may take cognizance of such offenses as the laws of war permit; they must proceed according to the customary usages of such tribunals in time of war, and inflict such punishments as are sanctioned by the practice of civilized nations in time of war. In time of peace, neither Congress nor the military can create any military tribunals, except such as are made in pursuance of that clause of the Constitution which gives to Congress the power "to make rules for the government of the land and naval forces." I do not think that Congress can, in time of war or peace, under this clause of the Constitution, create military tribunals for the adjudication of offenses committed by persons not engaged in, or belonging to, such forces. This is a proposition too plain for argument. But it does not follow that because such military tribunals can not be created by Congress under this clause, that they can not be created at all. Is there no other power conferred by the Constitution upon Congress or the military, under which such tribunals may be created in time of war?

That the law of nations constitutes a part of the laws of the land, must be admitted. The laws of nations are expressly made laws of the land by the Constitution, when it says that "Congress shall have power to define and punish piracies and felonies committed on the high seas and offenses against the laws of nations." To *define* is to give the limits or precise meaning of a word or thing in being; to make, is to call into being. Congress has power to *define*, not to make, the laws of nations; but Congress has the power to make rules for the government of the army and navy. From the very face of the Constitution, then, it is evident that the laws of nations do constitute a part of the laws of the land. But very soon after the organization of the Federal Government, Mr. Randolph, then Attorney General, said: "The law of nations, although not specifically adopted by the Constitution, is essentially a part of the law of the land. Its obligation commences and runs with the existence of a nation, subject to modification on some points of indifference." (See opinion Attorney General, vol. 1, page 27.) The framers of the Constitution knew that a nation could not maintain an honorable place among the nations of the world that does not regard the great and essential principles of the law of nations as a part of the law of the land. Hence Congress may define those laws, but can not abrogate them, or as Mr. Randolph says, may "modify on some points of indifference."

That the laws of nations constitute a part of the laws of the land is established from the face of the Constitution, upon principle and by authority.

But the laws of war constitute much the greater part of the law of nations. Like the other laws of nations, they exist and are of binding force upon the departments and citizens of the Government, though not defined by any law of Congress. No one that has ever glanced at the many treatises that have been published in different ages of the world by great, good and learned men, can fail to know that the laws of war constitute a part of the law of nations, and that those laws have been prescribed with tolerable accuracy.

Congress can declare war. When war is declared, it must be, under the Constitution, carried on according to the known laws and usages of war among civilized nations. Under the power to define those laws, Congress can not abrogate them or authorize their infraction. The Constitution does not permit this Government to prosecute a war as an uncivilized and barbarous people.

As war is required by the frame-work of our Government to be prosecuted according to the known usages of war among the civilized nations of the earth, it is important to understand what are the obligations, duties and responsibilities imposed by war upon the military. Congress, not having defined, as under the Constitution it might have done, the laws of war, we must look to the usage of nations to ascertain the powers conferred in war, on whom the exercise of such powers devolve, over whom, and to what extent do those powers reach, and in how far the citizen and the soldier are bound by the legitimate use thereof.

The power conferred by war is, of course, adequate to the end to be accomplished, and not greater than what is necessary to be accomplished. The law of war, like every other code of laws, declares what shall not be done, and does not say what may be done. The legitimate use of the great power of war, or rather the prohibitions upon the use of that power, increase or diminish as the necessity of the case demands. When a city is besieged and hard pressed, the commander may exert an authority over the non-combatants which he may not when no enemy is near.

All wars against a domestic enemy or to repel invasions, are prosecuted to preserve the Government. If the invading force can be overcome by the ordinary civil police of a country, it should be done without bringing upon the country the terrible scourge of war; if a commotion or insurrection can be put down by the ordinary process of law, the military should not be called out. A defensive foreign war is declared and carried on because the civil police is inadequate to repel it; a civil war is waged because the laws can not be peacefully enforced by the ordinary tribunals of the country through civil process and by civil officers. Because of the utter inability to keep the peace and maintain order by the customary officers and agencies in time of peace, armies are organized and put into the field. They are called out and invested with the powers of war to prevent total anarchy and to preserve the Government. Peace is the normal condition of a country, and war abnormal, neither being without law, but each having laws appropriate to the condition of society. The maxim *enter arma silent leges* is never wholly true. The object of war is to bring society out of its abnormal condition; and the laws of war aim to have that done with the least possible injury to persons or property.

Anciently, when two nations were at war, the conqueror had, or asserted, the right to take from his enemy his life, liberty and property: if either was spared, it was as a favor or act of mercy. By the laws of nations, and of war as a part thereof, the conqueror was deprived of this right.

When two governments, foreign to each other, are at war, or when a civil war becomes territorial, all of the people of the respective belligerents become by the law of nations the enemies of each other. As enemies they can not hold intercourse, but neither can kill or injure the other except under a commission from their respective governments. So humanizing have been, and are the laws of war, that it is a high offense against them to kill an enemy without such commission. The laws of war demand that a man shall not take human life except under a license from his government; and under the Constitution of the United States no license can be given by any department of the Government to take human life in war, except according to the law and usages of war. Soldiers regularly in the service have the license of the government to deprive men, the active enemies of their government, of their liberty and lives; their commission so to act is as perfect and legal as that of a judge to adjudicate, but the soldier must act in obedience to the laws of war, as the judge must in obedience to the civil law. A civil judge must try criminals in the mode prescribed in the Constitution and the law; so, soldiers must kill or capture according to the laws of war. Non-combatants are not to be disturbed or interfered with by the armies of either party except in extreme cases. Armies are called out and organized to meet and overcome the active, acting public enemies.

But enemies with which an army has to deal are of two classes:

1. Open, active participants in hostilities, as soldiers who wear the uniform, move under the flag, and hold the appropriate commission from their government. Openly assuming to discharge the duties and meet the responsibilities and dangers of soldiers, they are entitled to all belligerent rights, and should receive all the courtesies due to soldiers. The true soldier is

proud to acknowledge and respect those rights, and ever cheerfully extends those courtesies.

2. Secret, but active participants, as spies, brigands, bushwhackers, jayhawkers, war rebels and assassins. In all wars, and especially in civil wars, such secret, active enemies rise up to annoy and attack an army, and must be met and put down by the army. When lawless wretches become so impudent and powerful as not to be controlled and governed by the ordinary tribunals of a country, armies are called out, and the laws of war invoked. Wars never have been and never can be conducted upon the principle that an army is but a *posse comitatus* of a civil magistrate.

An army, like all other organized bodies, has a right, and it is its first duty, to protect its own existence and the existence of all its parts, by the means and in the mode usual among civilized nations when at war. Then the question arises, do the laws of war authorize a different mode of proceeding, and the use of different means against secret active enemies from those used against open active enemies?

As has been said, the open enemy or soldier in time of war may be met in battle and killed, wounded or taken prisoner, or so placed by the lawful strategy of war as that he is powerless. Unless the law of self-preservation absolutely demands it, the life of a wounded enemy or a prisoner must be spared. Unless pressed thereto by the extremest necessity, the laws of war condemn and punish with great severity harsh or cruel treatment to a wounded enemy or a prisoner.

Certain stipulations and agreements, tacit or express, betwixt the open belligerent parties, are permitted by the laws of war, and are held to be of very high and sacred character. Such is the tacit understanding, or it may be usage, of war, in regard to flags of truce. Flags of truce are resorted to as a means of saving human life, or alleviating human suffering. When not used with perfidy, the laws of war require that they should be respected. The Romans regarded ambassadors betwixt belligerents as persons to be treated with consideration and respect. Plutarch, in his *Life of Cæsar*, tells us that the barbarians in Gaul having sent some ambassadors to Cæsar, he detained them, charging fraudulent practices, and led his army to battle, obtaining a great victory.

When the Senate decreed festivals and sacrifices for the victory, Cato declared it to be his opinion that Cæsar ought to be given into the hands of the barbarians, that so the guilt which this breach of faith might otherwise bring upon the State might be expiated by transferring the curse on him who was the occasion of it.

Under the Constitution and laws of the United States, should a commander be guilty of such a flagrant breach of law as Cato charged upon Cæsar, he would not be delivered to the enemy, but would be punished after a military trial. The many honorable gentlemen who hold commissions in the army of the United States, and have been deputed to conduct war according to the laws of war, would keenly feel it as an insult to their profession of arms for any one to say that they could not or would not punish a fellow-soldier who was guilty of wanton cruelty to a prisoner, or perfidy toward the bearers of a flag of truce.

The laws of war permit capitulations of surrender and paroles. They are agreements betwixt belligerents, and should be scrupulously observed and performed. They are contracts wholly unknown to civil tribunals. Parties to such contracts must answer any breaches thereof to the customary military tribunals in time of war. If an officer of rank, possessing the pride that becomes a soldier and a gentleman, who should capitulate to surrender the forces and property under his command and control, be charged with a fraudulent breach of the terms of surrender, the laws of war do not permit that he should be punished without a trial, or, if innocent, that he shall have no means of wiping out the foul imputation. If a paroled prisoner is charged with a breach of his parole, he may be punished if guilty, but not without a trial. He should be tried by a military tribunal, constituted and proceeding as the laws and usages of war prescribe.

The law and usage of war contemplate that soldiers have a high sense of personal honor. The true soldier is proud to feel and know that his enemy possesses personal honor, and will conform and be obedient to the laws of war. In a spirit of justice, and with a wise appreciation of such feelings, the laws of war protect the character and honor of an open enemy. When by the fortunes of war one open enemy is thrown into the hands and power of another, and is charged with dishonorable conduct and a breach of the laws of war, he must be tried according to the usages of war. Justice and fairness say that an open enemy to whom dishonorable conduct is imputed, has a right to demand a trial. If such a demand can be rightfully made, surely it can not be rightfully refused. It is to be hoped that the military authorities of this country will never refuse such a demand, because there is no act of Congress that authorizes it. In time of war the law and usage of war authorize it, and they are a part of the law of the land.

One belligerent may request the other to punish for breaches of the laws of war, and, regularly, such a request should be made before retaliatory measures are taken. Whether the laws of war have been infringed or not, is of necessity a question to be decided by the laws and usages of war, and is cognizable before a military tribunal. When prisoners of war conspire to escape, or are guilty of a breach of appropriate and necessary rules of prison discipline, they may be punished, but not without trial. The commander who should order every prisoner charged with improper conduct to be shot or hung, would be guilty of a high offense against the laws of war, and should be punished therefor, after a regular military trial. If the culprit should be condemned and executed, the commander would be as free from guilt as if the man had been killed in battle.

It is manifest, from what has been said, that military tribunals exist under and according to the laws and usages of war, in the interest of justice and mercy. They are established to save human life, and to prevent cruelty as far as possible. The commander of an army in time of war has the same power to organize military tribunals and execute their judgments that he has to set his squadrons in the field and fight battles. His authority in each case is from the law and usage of war.

Having seen that there must be military tribunals to decide questions arising in time of war betwixt belligerents who are open and active enemies, let us next see whether the laws of war do not authorize such tribunals to determine the fate of those who are active, but secret, participants in the hostilities.

In Mr. Wheaton's *Elements of International Law*, he says: "The effect of a state of war, lawfully declared to exist, is to place all the subjects of each belligerent power in a state of mutual hostility. The usage of nations has modified this maxim by legalizing such acts of hostility only as are committed by those who are authorized by the express or implied command of the State; such are the regularly commissioned naval and military forces of the nation and all others called out in its defense, or spontaneously defending themselves, in case of necessity, without any express authority for that purpose. Cicero tells us in his offices, that by the Roman feudal law no person could lawfully engage in battle with the public enemy without being regularly enrolled, and taking the military oath. This was a regulation sanctioned both by policy and religion. The horrors of war would indeed be greatly aggravated, if every individual of the belligerent States were allowed to plunder and slay indiscriminately the enemy's subjects, without being in any manner accountable for his conduct. *Hence it is that, in land wars, irregular bands of marauders are liable to be treated as lawless banditti, not entitled to the protection of the mitigated usages of war as practiced by civilized nations.*" (*Wheaton's Elements of International Law*, page 406, 3d edition.)

In speaking upon the subject of banditti, Patrick Henry said, in the Virginia Convention, "The honorable gentleman has given you an elaborate account of what he judges tyrannical legislation, and an *ex post facto* law (in the case of Josiah Phillips); he has misrepresented the facts. That man was not executed by a tyrannical stroke of power; nor was he a Socrates; he was a fugitive murderer and an outlaw; a man who commanded an *infamous banditti*, and *at a time when the war was at the most perilous stage* he committed the most cruel and shocking barbarities; he was an enemy to the human name. Those who declare war against the human race may be struck out of existence as soon as apprehended. He was not executed according to those beautiful legal, ceremonies which are pointed out by the laws in criminal cases. The enormity of his crime did not entitle him to it. I am truly a friend to legal forms and methods, but, sir, the occasion warranted the measure. A pirate, an outlaw, or a common enemy to all mankind, may be put to death at any time. It is justified by the *law of nature and nations.*" (3d volume *Elliott's Debates on Federal Constitution,* page 140.)

No reader, not to say student, of the law of nations, can doubt but that Mr. Wheaton and Mr. Henry have fairly stated the laws of war. Let it be constantly borne in mind that they are talking of the law in a state of war. These banditti that spring up in time of war are respecters of no law, human or divine, of peace or of war, are *hostes humani generis,* and may be hunted down like wolves. Thoroughly desperate and perfectly lawless, no man can be required to peril his life in venturing to take them prisoners—as prisoners, no trust can be reposed in them. But they are occasionally made prisoners. Being prisoners, what is to be done with them? If they are public enemies, assuming and exercising the right to kill, and are not regularly authorized to do so, they must be apprehended and dealt with by the military. No man can doubt the right and duty of the military to make prisoners of them, and being public enemies, it is the duty of the military to punish them for any infraction of the laws of war. But the military can not ascertain whether they are guilty or not without the aid of a military tribunal.

In all wars, and especially in civil wars, secret but active enemies are almost as numerous as open ones. That fact has contributed to make civil wars such scourges to the countries in which they rage. In nearly all foreign wars the contending parties speak different languages and have different habits and manners; but in most civil wars that is not the case; hence there is a security in participating secretly in hostilities that induces many to thus engage. War prosecuted according to the most civilized usage is horrible, but its horrors are greatly aggravated by the immemorial habits of plunder, rape and murder practiced by secret, but active participants. Certain laws and usages have been adopted by the civilized world in wars between nations that are not of kin to one another, for the purpose and to the effect of arresting or softening many of the necessary cruel consequences of war. How strongly bound are we, then, in the midst of a great war, where brother and personal friend are fighting against brother and friend, to adopt and be governed by those laws and usages.

A public enemy must or should be dealt with in all wars by the same laws. The fact that they are public enemies, being the same, they should deal with each other according to those laws of war that are contemplated by the Constitution. Whatever rules have been adopted and practiced by the civilized nations of the world in war, to soften its harshness and severity, should be adopted and practiced by us in this war. That the laws of war authorized commanders to create and establish military commissions, courts or tribunals, for the trial of offenders against the laws of war, whether they be active or secret participants in the hostilities, can not be denied. That the judgments of such tribunals may have been some times harsh, and sometimes even tyrannical, does not prove that they ought not to exist, nor does it prove that they are not constituted in the interest of justice and mercy. Considering the power that the laws of war give over secret participants in hostilities, such as banditti, guerrillas, spies, etc., the position of a commander would be miserable indeed if he could not call to his aid the judgments of such tribunals; he would become a mere butcher of men, without the power to ascertain justice, and there can be no mercy where there is no justice. War in its mildest form is horrible; but take away from the contending armies the ability and right to organize what is now known as a Bureau of Military Justice, they would soon become monster savages, unrestrained by any and all ideas of law and justice. Surely no lover of mankind, no one that respects law and order, no one that has the instinct of justice, or that can be softened by mercy, would, in time of war, take away from the commanders the right to organize military tribunals of justice, and especially such tribunals for the protection of persons charged or suspected with being secret foes and participants in the hostilities. It would be a miracle if the records and history of this war do not show occasional cases in which those tribunals have erred; but they will show many, very many cases in which human life would have been taken but for the interposition and judgments of those tribunals. Every student of the laws of war must acknowledge that such tribunals exert a kindly and benign influence in time of war. Impartial history will record the fact that the Bureau of Military Justice, regularly organized during this war, has saved human life and prevented human suffering. The greatest suffering, patiently endured by soldiers, and the hardest battles gallantly fought during this protracted struggle, are not more creditable to the American character than the establishment of this bureau. This people have such an educated and profound respect for law and justice—such a love of mercy—that they have, in the midst of this greatest of civil wars, systematized and brought into regular order, tribunals that before this war existed under the law of war, but without general rule. To condemn the tribunals that have been established under this bureau, is to condemn and denounce the war itself, or justifying the war, to insist that it shall be prosecuted according to the harshest rules, and without the aid of the laws, usages and customary agencies for mitigating those rules. If such tribunals had not existed before, under the laws and usages of war, the American citizen might as proudly point to their establishment as to our inimitable and inestimable constitutions. It must be constantly borne in mind that such tribunals and such a bureau can not exist except in time of war, and can not then take cognizance of offenders or offenses where the civil courts are open, except offenders and offenses against the laws of war.

But it is insisted by some, and doubtless with honesty, and with a zeal commensurate with their honesty, that such military tribunals can have no constitutional existence. The argument against their constitutionality may be shortly, and I think fairly, stated thus:

Congress alone can establish military or civil judicial tribunals. As Congress has not established military tribunals, except such as have been created under the articles of war, and which articles are made in pursuance of that clause in the Constitution which gives to Congress the power to make rules for the government of the army and navy, any other tribunal is and must be plainly unconstitutional, and all its acts void.

This objection thus stated, or stated in any other way, begs the question. It assumes that Congress alone can establish military judicial tribunals. Is that assumption true?

We have seen that when war comes, the laws and usages of war come also, and that during the war they are a part of the laws of the land. Under the Constitution, Congress may define and punish offenses against those laws, but in default of Congress defining those laws and prescribing a punishment for their infraction, and the mode of proceeding to ascertain whether an offense has been committed, and what punishment is to be inflicted, the army must be governed by the laws and usages of war as understood and practiced by the civilized nations of the world. It has been abundantly shown that these tribunals are constituted by the army in the interest of justice and mercy, and for the purpose and to the effect of mitigating the horrors of war.

But it may be insisted that though the laws of war, being a part of the law of nations, constitute a part of the laws of the land, that those laws must be regarded as modified so far, and whenever they come in direct conflict with plain constitutional provisions. The following clauses of the Constitution are principally relied upon to show the conflict betwixt the laws of war and the Constitution:

"The trial of all crimes, except in cases of impeachment, shall be by the jury; and such trial shall be held in the State where the said crime shall have been committed; but when not committed within any State, the trial shall be at such place or places as the Congress may by law have directed." (*Art. III of the original Constitution, sec. 2.*)

"No person shall be held to answer for a capital or otherwise infamous crime unless on a presentment or indictment of a grand jury, except in cases arising in the land or naval forces, or in the militia when in actual service, in time of war or public danger; nor shall any person be subject for the same offense to be twice put in jeopardy of life or limb, nor shall be compelled, in any criminal case, to be witness against himself, nor be deprived of life, liberty or property, without due process of law; nor shall private property be taken for public use without just compensation." (*Amendments to the Constitution, Art. V.*)

"In all criminal prosecutions, the accused shall enjoy the right of a speedy and public trial by an impartial jury of the State and district wherein the crime shall have been committed, which district shall have been previously ascertained by law, and be informed of the nature and cause of the accusation; to be confronted with the witnesses against him, to have compulsory process for obtaining witnesses in his favor; and to have the assistance of counsel for his defense." (*Art. VI of the amendments to the Constitution.*)

These provisions of the Constitution are intended to fling around the life, liberty and property of a citizen all the guarantees of a jury trial. These constitutional guarantees can not be estimated too highly, or protected too sacredly. The reader of history knows that for many weary ages the people suffered for the want of them; it would not only be stupidity, but madness in us not to preserve them. No man has a deeper conviction of their value, or a more sincere desire to preserve and perpetuate them than I have.

Nevertheless, these exalted and sacred provisions of the Constitution must not be read alone and by themselves, but must be read and taken in connexion with other provisions. The Constitution was framed by great men—men of learning and large experience, and it is a wonderful monument of their wisdom. Well versed in the history of the world, they knew that the nation for which they were forming a government would, unless all history was false, have wars, foreign and domestic. Hence the government framed by them is clothed with the power to make and carry on war. As has been shown, when war comes, the laws of war come with it. Infractions of the laws of nations are not denominated *crimes*, but *offenses*. Hence the expression in the Constitution that "Congress shall have power to define and punish * * *offenses* against the law of nations." Many of the *offenses* against the law of nations for which a man may, by the laws of war, lose his life, his liberty or his property, are not *crimes*. It is an offense against the law of nations to break a lawful blockade, and for which a forfeiture of the property is the penalty, and yet the running a blockade has never been regarded a crime; to hold communication or intercourse with the enemy is a high offense against the laws of war, and for which those laws prescribe punishment, and yet it is not a *crime;* to act as a spy is an offense against the laws of war, and the punishment for which in all ages has been death, and yet it is not a crime; to violate a flag of truce is an offense against the laws of war, and yet not a crime of which a civil court can take cognizance; to unite with banditti, jayhawkers, guerrillas or any other unauthorized marauders is a high offense against the laws of war; the offense is complete when the band is organized or joined. The atrocities committed by such a band do not constitute the offense, but make the reasons, and sufficient reasons they are, why such banditti are denounced by the laws of war. Some of the offenses against the laws of war are crimes, and some not. Because they are crimes they do not cease to be offenses against those laws; nor because they are not crimes or misdemeanors do they fail to be offenses against the laws of war. Murder is a crime, and the murderer, as such, must be proceeded against in the form and manner prescribed in the Constitution; in committing the murder an offense may also have been committed against the laws of war; for that offense he must answer to the laws of war, and the tribunals legalized by that law.

There is, then, an apparent but no real conflict in the constitutional provisions. *Offenses* against the laws of war must be dealt with and punished under the Constitution, as the laws of war, they being part of the law of nations direct; *crimes* must be dealt with and punished as the Constitution, and laws made in pursuance thereof, may direct.

Congress has not undertaken to define the code of war nor to punish offenses against it. In the case of a spy, Congress has undertaken to say who shall be deemed a spy, and how he shall be punished. But every lawyer knows that a spy was a well-known offender under the laws of war, and that under and according to those laws he could have been tried and punished without an act of Congress. This is admitted by the act of Congress, when it says that he shall suffer death "according to the law and usages of war." The act is simply declaratory of the law.

That portion of the Constitution which declares that "no person shall be deprived of his life, liberty or property without due process of law," has such direct reference to, and connection with, trials for *crime* or *criminal* prosecutions, that comment upon it would seem to be unnecessary. Trials for offenses against the laws of war are not embraced or intended to be embraced in those provisions. If this is not so, then every man that kills another in battle is a murderer, for he deprived a "person of life without that due process of law" contemplated by this provision; every man that holds another as a prisoner of war is liable for false imprisonment, as he does so without that due process of law contemplated by this provision; every soldier that marches across a field in battle array is liable to an action of trespass, because he does it without that same due process. The argument that flings around offenders against the laws of war these guarantees of the Constitution would convict all the soldiers of our army of murder; no prisoners could be taken and held; the army could not move. The absurd consequences that would of necessity flow from such an argument show that it can not be the true construction—it can not be what was intended by the framers of the instrument. One of the prime motives for the Union and a Federal Government was to confer the powers of war. If any provisions of the Constitution are so in conflict with the power to carry on war as to destroy and make it valueless, then the instrument, instead of being a great and wise one, is a miserable failure, a *felo de se.*

If a man should sue out his writ of *habeas corpus*, and the return shows that he belonged to the army or navy, and was held to be tried for some offense against the rules and articles of war, the writ should be dismissed, and the party remanded to answer to the charges. So, in time of war, if a man should sue out a writ of *habeas corpus*, and it is made appear that he is in the hands of the military as a prisoner of war, the writ should be dismissed and the prisoner remanded to be disposed of as the laws and usages of war require. If the prisoner be a regular unoffending soldier of the opposing party to the war, he should be treated with all the courtesy and kindness consistent with his safe custody; if he has offended against the laws of war, he should have such trial and be punished as the laws of war require. A spy, though a prisoner of war, may be tried, condemned and executed by a military tribunal without a breach of the Constitution. A bushwhacker, a jayhawker, a bandit, a war rebel, an assassin, being public enemies, may be tried, condemned and executed as offenders against the laws of war. The soldier that would fail to try a spy or bandit after his capture, would be as derelict in duty as if he were to fail to capture; he is as much bound to try and to execute, if guilty, as he is to arrest; the same law that makes it his duty to pursue and kill or capture, makes it his duty to try according to the usages of war. The judge of a civil court is not more strongly bound under the Constitution and the law to try a criminal than is the military to try an offender against the laws of war.

The fact that the civil courts are open does not affect the right of the military tribunal to hold as a prisoner and to try. The civil courts have no more right to prevent the military, in time of war, from trying an offender against the laws of war than they have a right to interfere with and prevent a battle. A battle may be lawfully fought in the very view and presence of a court; so a spy, a bandit or other offender against the law of war, may be tried, and tried lawfully, when and where the civil courts are open and transacting the usual business.

The laws of war authorize human life to be taken without legal process, or that legal process contemplated by those provisions in the Constitution that are relied upon to show that military judicial tribunals are unconstitutional. Wars should be prosecuted justly as well as bravely. One enemy in the power of another, whether he be an open or a secret one, should not be punished or executed without trial. If the question be one concerning the laws of war, he should be tried by those engaged in the war; they and they only are his peers. The military must decide whether he is or not an active participant in the hostilities. If he is an active participant in the hostilities, it is the duty of the military to take him a prisoner without warrant or other judicial process, and dispose of him as the laws of war direct.

It is curious to see one and the same mind justify the killing of thousands in battle because it is done according to the laws of war, and yet condemning that same law when, out of regard for justice and with the hope of saving life, it orders a military trial before the enemy are killed. The love of law, of justice and the wish to save life, of justice and the wish to save life and suffering, should impel all good men in time of war to uphold and sustain the existence and action of such tribunals. The object of such tribunals is obviously intended to save life, and when their jurisdiction is confined to offenses against the laws of war, that is their effect. They prevent indiscriminate slaughter; they prevent men from being punished or killed upon mere suspicion.

The law of nations, which is the result of the experience and wisdom of ages, has decided that jayhawkers, banditti, etc., are offenders against the laws of nature and of war, and as such amenable to the military. Our Constitution has made those laws a part of the law of the land. Obedience to the Constitution and the law, then, requires that the military should do their whole duty; they must not only meet and fight the enemies of the country in open battle, but they must kill or take the secret enemies of the country, and try and execute them according to the laws of war. The civil tribunals of the country can not rightfully interfere with the military in the performance of their high, arduous and perilous, but lawful duties. That Booth and his associates were secret active public enemies, no mind that contemplates the facts can doubt. The exclamation used by him when he escaped from the box on to the stage, after he had fired the fatal shot, *sic semper tyrannis*, and his dying message, "Say to my mother that I died for my country," show that he was not an assassin from private malice, but that he acted as a public foe. Such a deed is expressly laid down by Vattel, in his work on the law of nations, as an offense against the laws of war, and a great crime. "I give, then, the name of assassination to a treacherous murder, whether the perpetrators of the deed be the subjects of the party whom we cause to be assassinated or of our own sovereign, or that it be executed by any other emissary introducing himself as a suppliant, a refugee or a deserter, or, in fine, as a stranger." (*Vattel*, 339.)

Neither the civil nor the military department of the Government should regard itself as wiser and better than the Constitution and the laws that exist under or are made in pursuance thereof. Each department should, in peace and in war, confining itself to its own proper sphere of action, diligently and fearlessly perform its legitimate functions, and in the mode prescribed by the Constitution and the law. Such obedience to and observance of law will maintain peace when it exists, and will soonest relieve the country from the abnormal state of war.

My conclusion, therefore, is, that if the persons who are charged with the assassination of the President committed the deed as public enemies, as I believe they did, and whether they did or not is a question to be decided by the tribunal before which they are tried, they not only can, but ought to be tried before a military tribunal. If the persons charged have offended against the laws of war, it would be as palpably wrong for the military to hand them over to the civil courts, as it would be wrong in a civil court to convict a man of murder who had, in time of war, killed another in battle.

I am, sir, most respectfully, your obedient servant,

JAMES SPEED,
Attorney General.

To the President

INSTRUCTIONS

GOVERNMENT OF ARMIES OF THE UNITED STATES IN THE FIELD.

GENERAL ORDERS, NO. 100.

WAR DEPARTMENT,
ADJUTANT GENERAL'S OFFICE,
Washington, April 24, 1863. }

The following "Instructions for the Government of Armies of the United States in the Field," prepared by Francis Lieber, L. L D., and revised by a Board of Officers, of which Major-General E. A. Hitchcock is President, having been approved by the President of the United States, he commands that they be published for the information of all concerned.

BY ORDER OF THE SECRETARY OF WAR:

E. D. TOWNSEND,
Assistant Adjutant General.

SECTION I.

Martial Law—Military Jurisdiction—Military Necessity—Retaliation.

1. A place, district or country occupied by an enemy, stands, in consequence of the occupation, under the martial law of the invading or occupying army, whether any proclamation declaring martial law, or any public warning to the inhabitants has been issued or not. Martial law is the immediate and direct effect and consequence of occupation or conquest.

The presence of a hostile army proclaims its martial law.

2. Martial law does not cease during the hostile occupation, except by special proclamation, ordered by the Commander-in-Chief, or by special mention in the treaty of peace concluding the war, when the occupation of a place or territory continues beyond the conclusion of peace as one of the conditions of the same.

3. Martial law in a hostile country consists in the suspension, by the occupying military authority, of the criminal and civil law, and of the domestic administration and government in the occupied place or territory, and in the substitution of military rule and force for the same, as well as in the dictation of general laws, as far as military necessity requires this suspension, substitution or dictation.

The commander of the forces may proclaim that the administration of all civil and penal law shall continue, either wholly or in part, as in times of peace, unless otherwise ordered by the military authority.

410

4. Martial law is simply military authority exercised in accordance with the laws and usages of war. Military oppression is not martial law; it is the abuse of the power which that law confers. As martial law is executed by military force, it is incumbent upon those who administer it to be strictly guided by the principles of justice, honor and humanity—virtues adorning a soldier even more than other men, for the very reason that he possesses the power of his arms against the unarmed.

5. Martial law should be less stringent in places and countries fully occupied and fairly conquered. Much greater severity may be exercised in places or regions where actual hostilities exist, or are expected and must be prepared for. Its most complete sway is allowed—even in the commander's own country—when face to face with the enemy, because of the absolute necessities of the case, and of the paramount duty to defend the country against invasion.

To save the country is paramount to all other considerations.

6. All civil and penal law shall continue to take its usual course in the enemy's places and territories under martial law, unless interrupted or stopped by order of the occupying military power; but all the functions of the hostile government—legislative, executive or administrative—whether of a general, provincial or local character, cease under martial law, or continue only with the sanction, or if deemed necessary, the participation of the occupier or invader.

7. Martial law extends to property, and to persons, whether they are subjects of the enemy or aliens to that government.

8. Consuls, among American and European nations, are not diplomatic agents. Nevertheless, their offices and persons will be subjected to martial law in cases of urgent necessity only: their property and business are not exempted. Any delinquency they commit against the established military rule may be punished as in the case of any other inhabitant, and such punishment furnishes no reasonable ground for international complaint.

9. The functions of Ambassadors, Ministers or other diplomatic agents, accredited by neutral powers to the hostile government, cease, so far as regards the displaced government; but the conquering or occupying power usually recognizes them as temporarily accredited to itself.

10. Martial law affects chiefly the police and collection of public revenue and taxes, whether imposed by the expelled government or by the invader, and refers mainly to the support and efficiency of the army, its safety, and the safety of its operations.

11. The law of war does not only disclaim all cruelty and bad faith concerning engagements concluded with the enemy during the war, but also the breaking of stipulations solemnly contracted by the belligerents in time of peace, and avowedly intended to remain in force in case of war between the contracting powers.

It disclaims all extortions and other transactions for individual gain; all acts of private revenge, or connivance at such acts. Offenses to the contrary shall be severely punished, and especially so if committed by officers.

12. Whenever feasible, martial law is carried out in cases of individual offenders by military courts; but sentences of death shall be executed only with the approval of the Chief Executive, provided the urgency of the case does not require a speedier execution, and then only with the approval of the chief commander.

13. Military jurisdiction is of two kinds: first, that which is conferred and defined by statute; second, that which is derived from the common law of war. Military offenses under the statute law must be tried in the manner therein directed; but military offenses which do not come within the statute must be tried and punished under the common law of war. The character of the courts which exercise these jurisdictions depends upon the local laws of each particular country.

In the armies of the United States the first is exercised by courts-martial, while cases which do not come within the "Rules and Articles of War," or the jurisdiction conferred by statute on courts-martial, are tried by military commissions.

14. Military necessity, as understood by modern civilized nations, consists in the necessity of those measures which are indispensable for securing the ends of the war, and which are lawful according to the modern law and usages of war.

15. Military necessity admits of all direct destruction of life or limb of *armed* enemies, and of other persons whose destruction is incidentally *unavoidable* in the armed contests of the war; it allows of the capturing of every armed enemy, and every enemy of importance to the hostile government, or of peculiar danger to the captor; it allows of all destruction of property, and obstruction of the ways and channels of traffic, travel or communication, and of all withholding of sustenance or means of life from the enemy; of the appropriation of whatever an enemy's country affords necessary for the subsistence and safety of the army, and of such deception as does not involve the breaking of good faith either positively pledged, regarding agreements entered into during the war, or supposed by the modern law of war to exist. Men who take up arms against one another in public war, do not cease, on this account, to be moral beings, responsible to one another and to God.

16. Military necessity does not admit of cruelty, that is, the infliction of suffering for the sake of suffering or for revenge, nor of maiming or wounding except in fight, nor of tortures to extort confessions. It does not admit of the use of poison in any way, nor of the wanton devastation of a district. It admits of deception, but disclaims acts of perfidy; and, in general, military necessity does not include any act of hostility which makes the return of peace unnecessarily difficult.

17. War is not carried on by arms alone. It is lawful to starve the hostile belligerent, armed or unarmed, so that it leads to the speedier subjection of the enemy.

18. When the commander of a besieged place expels the non-combatants, in order to lessen the number of those who consume his stock of provisions, it is lawful, though an extreme measure, to drive them back, so as to hasten on the surrender.

19. Commanders, whenever admissible, inform the enemy of their intention to bombard a place, so that the non-combatants, and especially the women and children, may be removed before the bombardment commences. But it is no infraction of the common law of war to omit thus to inform the enemy. Surprise may be a necessity.

20. Public war is a state of armed hostility between sovereign nations or governments. It is a law and requisite of civilised existence that men live in political, continuous societies, forming organized units, called states or nations, whose constituents bear, enjoy and suffer, advance and retrograde together, in peace and in war.

21. The citizen or native of a hostile country is thus an enemy, as one of the constituents of the hostile state or nation, and as such is subjected to the hardships of the war.

22. Nevertheless, as civilization has advanced during the last centuries, so has likewise steadily advanced, especially in war on land, the distinction between the private individual belonging to a hostile country and the hostile country itself, with its men in arms. The principle has been more and more acknowledged that the unarmed citizen is to be spared in person, property and honor as much as the exigencies of war will admit.

23. Private citizens are no longer murdered, enslaved or carried off to distant parts, and the inoffensive individual is as little disturbed in his private relations as the commander of the hostile troops can afford to grant in the overruling demands of a vigorous war.

24. The almost universal rule in remote times was, and continues to be with barbarous armies, that the private individual of the hostile country is destined to suffer every privation of liberty and protection, and every disruption of family ties. Protection was, and still is with uncivilized people, the exception.

25. In modern regular wars of the Europeans, and their descendants in other portions of the globe, protection of the inoffensive citizen of the hostile country is the rule; privation and disturbance of private relations are the exceptions.

26. Commanding generals may cause the

magistrates and civil officers of the hostile country to take the oath of temporary allegiance, or an oath of fidelity to their own victorious government or rulers, and they may expel every one who declines to do so. But whether they do so or not, the people and their civil officers owe strict obedience to them as long as they hold sway over the district or country, at the peril of their lives.

27. The law of war can no more wholly dispense with retaliation than can the law of nations, of which it is a branch. Yet civilized nations acknowledge retaliation as the sternest feature of war. A reckless enemy often leaves to his opponent no other means of securing himself against the repetition of barbarous outrage.

28. Retaliation will, therefore, never be resorted to as a measure of mere revenge, but only as a means of protective retribution, and, moreover, cautiously and unavoidably; that is to say, retaliation shall only be resorted to after careful inquiry into the real occurrence, and the character of the misdeeds that may demand retribution.

Unjust or inconsiderate retaliation removes the belligerents farther and farther from the mitigating rules of a regular war, and by rapid steps leads them nearer to the internecine wars of savages.

29. Modern times are distinguished from earlier ages by the existence, at one and the same time, of many nations and great governments related to one another in close intercourse.

Peace is their normal condition; war is the exception. The ultimate object of all modern war is a renewed state of peace.

The more vigorously wars are pursued, the better it is for humanity. Sharp wars are brief.

30. Ever since the formation and co-existence of modern nations, and ever since wars have become great national wars, war has come to be acknowledged not to be its own end, but the means to obtain great ends of state, or to consist in defense against wrong; and no conventional restriction of the modes adopted to injure the enemy is any longer admitted; but the law of war imposes many limitations and restrictions on principles of justice, faith and honor.

SECTION II.

Public and private property of the enemy—Protection of persons, and especially women; of religion, the arts and sciences—Punishment of crimes against the inhabitants of hostile countries.

31. A victorious army appropriates all public money, seizes all public movable property until further direction by its government, and sequesters for its own benefit or that of its government all the revenues of real property belonging to the hostile government or nation. The title to such real property remains in the abeyance during military occupation, and until the conquest is made complete.

32. A victorious army, by the martial power inherent in the same, may suspend, change, or abolish, as far as the martial power extends, the relations which arise from the service due,

according to the existing laws of the invaded country, from one citizen, subject, or native of the same to another.

The commander of the army must leave it to the ultimate treaty of peace to settle the permanency of this change.

33. It is no longer considered lawful—on the contrary, it is held to be a serious breach of the law of war—to force the subjects of the enemy into the service of the victorious government, except the latter should proclaim, after a fair and complete conquest of the hostile country or district, that it is resolved to keep the country, district, or place permanently as its own, and make it a portion of its own country.

34. As a general rule, the property belonging to churches, to hospitals, or other establishments of an exclusively charitable character, to establishments of education, or foundations for the promotion of knowledge, whether public schools, universities, academies of learning or observatories, museums of the fine arts, or of a scientific character—such property is not to be considered public property in the sense of paragraph 31; but it may be taxed or used when the public service may require it.

35. Classical works of art, libraries, scientific collections, or precious instruments, such as astronomical telescopes, as well as hospitals, must be secured against all avoidable injury, even when they are contained in fortified places while besieged or bombarded.

36. If such works of art, libraries, collections, or instruments belonging to a hostile nation or government, can be removed without injury, the ruler of the conquering state or nation may order them to be seized and removed for the benefit of the said nation. The ultimate ownership is to be settled by the ensuing treaty of peace.

In no case shall they be sold or given away, if captured by the armies of the United States, nor shall they ever be privately appropriated, or wantonly destroyed or injured.

37. The United States acknowledge and protect, in hostile countries occupied by them, religion and morality; strictly private property; the persons of the inhabitants, especially those of women; and the sacredness of domestic relations. Offenses to the contrary shall be rigorously punished.

This rule does not interfere with the right of the victorious invader to tax the people or their property, to levy forced loans, to billet soldiers, or to appropriate property, especially houses, land, boats or ships, and churches, for temporary and military uses.

38. Private property, unless forfeited by crimes or by offenses of the owner, can be seized only by way of military necessity, for the support or other benefit of the army or of the United States.

If the owner has not fled, the commanding officer will cause receipts to be given, which may serve the spoliated owner to obtain indemnity.

39. The salaries of civil officers of the hostile government who remain in the invaded territory, and continue the work of their office, and can continue it according to the circum-

stances arising out of the war—such as judges, administrative or police officers, officers of city or communal governments—are paid from the public revenue of the invaded territory, until the military government has reason wholly or partially to discontinue it. Salaries or incomes connected with purely honorary titles are always stopped.

40. There exists no law or body of authoritative rules of action between hostile armies, except that branch of the law of nature and nations which is called the law and usages of war on land.

41. All municipal law of the ground on which the armies stand, or of the countries to which they belong, is silent and of no effect between armies in the field.

42. Slavery, complicating and confounding the ideas of property (that is of a *thing*), and of personalty (that is of *humanity*), exists according to municipal or local law only. The law of nature and nations has never acknowledged it. The digest of the Roman law enacts the early dictum of the pagan jurist, that " so far as the law of nature is concerned, all men are equal." Fugitives escaping from a country in which they were slaves, villains or serfs, into another country, have, for centuries past, been held free and acknowledged free by judicial decisions of European countries, even though the municipal law of the country in which the slave had taken refuge acknowledged slavery within its own dominions.

43. Therefore, in a war between the United States and a belligerent which admits of slavery, if a person held in bondage by that belligerent be captured by, or come as a fugitive under, the protection of the military forces of the United States, such person is immediately entitled to the rights and privileges of a freeman. To return such person into slavery would amount to enslaving a free person, and neither the United States nor any officer under their authority can enslave any human being. Moreover, a person so made free by the law of war is under the shield of the law of nations, and the former owner or State can have, by the law of post-liminy, no belligerent lien or claim of service.

44. All wanton violence committed against persons in the invaded country, all destruction of property not commanded by the authorized officer, all robbery, all pillage or sacking, even after taking a place by main force, all rape, all wounding, maiming or killing of such inhabitants, are prohibited under the penalty of death, or such other severe punishment as may seem adequate for the gravity of the offense. A soldier, officer or private, in the act of committing such violence, and disobeying a superior ordering him to abstain from it, may be lawfully killed on the spot by such superior.

45. All captures and booty belong, according to the modern law of war, primarily, to the government of the captor. Prize money, whether on sea or land, can now only be claimed under local law.

46. Neither officers nor soldiers are allowed to make use of their position or power in the hostile country for private gain, not even for

commercial transactions otherwise legitimate. Offenses to the contrary committed by commissioned officers will be punished with cashiering, or such other punishment as the nature of the offense may require; if by soldiers, they shall be punished according to the nature of the offense.

47. Crimes punishable by all penal codes, such as arson, murder, maiming, assaults, highway robbery, theft, burglary, fraud, forgery and rape, if committed by an American soldier in a hostile country against its inhabitants, are not only punishable as at home, but in all cases in which death is not inflicted, the severer punishment shall be preferred.

SECTION III.

Deserters—Prisoners of War—Hostages—Booty on the Battle-field.

48. Deserters from the American army, having entered the service of the enemy, suffer death if they fall again into the hands of the United States, whether by capture, or being delivered up to the American army; and if a deserter from the enemy, having taken service in the army of the United States, is captured by the enemy, and punished by them with death or otherwise, it is not a breach against the law and usages of war, requiring redress or retaliation.

49. A prisoner of war is a public enemy armed or attached to the hostile army for active aid, who has fallen into the hands of the captor, either fighting or wounded, on the field or in the hospital, by individual surrender or by capitulation.

All soldiers, of whatever species of arms; all men who belong to the rising en masse of the hostile country; all those who are attached to the army for its efficiency and promote directly the object of the war, except such as are hereinafter provided for; all disabled men or officers on the field or elsewhere, if captured; all enemies who have thrown away their arms and ask for quarter, are prisoners of war, and as such exposed to the inconveniences as well as entitled to the privileges of a prisoner of war.

50. Moreover, citizens who accompany an army for whatever purpose, such as sutlers, editors, or reporters of journals, or contractors, if captured, may be made prisoners of war, and be detained as such.

The monarch and members of the hostile reigning family, male or female, the chief, and chief officers of the hostile government, its diplomatic agents, and all persons who are of particular and singular use and benefit to the hostile army or its government, are, if captured on belligerent ground, and if unprovided with a safe-conduct granted by the captor's government, prisoners of war.

51. If the people of that portion of an invaded country which is not yet occupied by the enemy, or of the whole country, at the approach of a hostile army, rise, under a duly authorized levy, en masse to resist the invader, they are now treated as public enemies, and if captured, are prisoners of war.

52. No belligerent has the right to declare that he will treat every captured man in arms of a levy en masse as a brigand or bandit.

If, however, the people of a country, or any portion of the same, already occupied by an army, rise against it, they are violators of the laws of war, and are not entitled to their protection.

53. The enemy's chaplains, officers of the medical staff, apothecaries, hospital nurses and servants, if they fall into the hands of the American army, are not prisoners of war, unless the commander has reasons to retain them. In this latter case, or if, at their own desire, they are allowed to remain with their captured companions, they are treated as prisoners of war, and may be exchanged if the commander sees fit.

54. A hostage is a person accepted as a pledge for the fulfillment of an agreement concluded between belligerents during the war, or in consequence of a war. Hostages are rare in the present age.

55. If a hostage is accepted, he is treated like a prisoner of war, according to rank and condition, as circumstances may admit.

56. A prisoner of war is subject to no punishment for being a public enemy, nor is any revenge wreaked upon him by the intentional infliction of any suffering, or disgrace, by cruel imprisonment, want of food, by mutilation, death, or any other barbarity.

57. So soon as a man is armed by a sovereign government, and takes the soldier's oath of fidelity, he is a belligerent; his killing, wounding, or other warlike acts, are no individual crimes or offenses. No belligerent has a right to declare that enemies of a certain class, color or condition, when properly organized as soldiers, will not be treated by him as public enemies.

58. The law of nations knows of no distinction of color, and if an enemy of the United States should enslave and sell captured persons of their army, it would be a case for the severest retaliation, if not redressed upon complaint.

The United States can not retaliate by enslavement; therefore, death must be the retaliation for this crime against the law of nations.

59. A prisoner of war remains answerable for his crimes committed against the captor's army or people, committed before he was captured, and for which he has not been punished by his own authorities.

All prisoners of war are liable to the infliction of retaliatory measures.

60. It is against the usage of modern war to resolve, in hatred and revenge, to give no quarter. No body of troops has the right to declare that it will not give, and therefore will not expect, quarter; but a commander is permitted to direct his troops to give no quarter, in great straits, when his own salvation makes it *impossible* to cumber himself with prisoners.

61. Troops that give no quarter have no right to kill enemies already disabled on the ground, or prisoners captured by other troops.

62. All troops of the enemy known or discovered to give no quarter in general, or to any portion of the army, receive none.

63. Troops who fight in the uniform of their enemies, without any plain, striking, and uniform mark of distinction of their own, can expect *no quarter.*

64. If American troops capture a train containing uniforms of the enemy, and the commander considers it advisable to distribute them for use among his men, some striking mark or sign must be adopted to distinguish the American soldier from the enemy.

65. The use of the enemy's national standard, flag, or other emblem of nationality, for the purpose of deceiving the enemy in battle, is an act of perfidy by which they lose all claim to the protection of the laws of war.

66. Quarter having been given to an enemy by American troops, under a misapprehension of his true character, he may, nevertheless, be ordered to suffer death, if, within three days after the battle, it be discovered that he belongs to a corps which gives no quarter.

67. The law of nations allows every sovereign government to make war upon another sovereign state, and, therefore, admits of no rules or laws different from those of regular warfare, regarding the treatment of prisoners of war, although they may belong to the army of a government which the captor may consider as a wanton and unjust assailant.

68. Modern wars are not internecine wars, in which the killing of the enemy is the object. The destruction of the enemy in modern war, and, indeed, modern war itself, are means to obtain that object of the belligerent which lies beyond the war.

Unnecessary or revengeful destruction of life is not lawful.

69. Outposts, sentinels, or pickets are not to be fired upon, except to drive them in, or when a positive order, special or general, has been issued to that effect.

70. The use of poison in any manner, be it to poison wells, or food, or arms, is wholly excluded from modern warfare. He that uses it puts himself out of the pale of the law and usages of war.

71. Whoever intentionally inflicts additional wounds on an enemy already wholly disabled, or kills such an enemy, or who orders or encourages soldiers to do so, shall suffer death, if duly convicted, whether he belongs to the army of the United States, or is an enemy captured after having committed his misdeed.

72. Money and other valuables on the person of a prisoner, such as watches or jewelry, as well as extra clothing, are regarded by the American army as the private property of the prisoner, and the appropriation of such valuables or money is considered dishonorable, and is prohibited.

Nevertheless, if *large* sums are found upon the persons of prisoners, or in their possession, they shall be taken from them, and the surplus, after providing for their own support, appropriated for the use of the army, under the direction of the commander, unless otherwise ordered by the Government. Nor can prisoners claim, as private property, large sums found and captured in their train, although they had been placed in the private luggage of the prisoners.

73. All officers, when captured, must surrender their side-arms to the captor. They may be restored to the prisoner in marked cases, by

the commander, to signalize admiration of his distinguished bravery, or approbation of his humane treatment of prisoners before his capture. The captured officer to whom they may be restored can not wear them during captivity.

74. A prisoner of war, being a public enemy, is a prisoner of the government, and not of the captor. No ransom can be paid by a prisoner of war to his individual captor, or to any officer in command. The government alone releases captives, according to rules prescribed by itself.

75. Prisoners of war are subject to confinement or imprisonment such as may be deemed necessary on account of safety, but they are to be subjected to no other intentional suffering or indignity. The confinement and mode of treating a prisoner may be varied during his captivity, according to the demands of safety.

76. Prisoners of war shall be fed upon plain and wholesome food, whenever practicable, and treated with humanity.

They may be required to work for the benefit of the captor's government, according to their rank and condition.

77. A prisoner of war who escapes may be shot, or otherwise killed in his flight; but neither death nor any other punishment shall be inflicted upon him simply for his attempt to escape, which the law of war does not consider a crime. Stricter means of security shall be used after an unsuccessful attempt at escape.

If, however, a conspiracy is discovered, the purpose of which is a united or general escape, the conspirators may be rigorously punished, even with death; and capital punishment may also be inflicted upon prisoners of war discovered to have plotted rebellion against the authorities of the captors, whether in union with fellow-prisoners or other persons.

78. If prisoners of war, having given no pledge nor made any promise on their honor, forcibly or otherwise escape, and are captured again in battle, after having rejoined their own army, they shall not be punished for their escape, but shall be treated as simple prisoners of war, although they will be subjected to stricter confinement.

79. Every captured wounded enemy shall be medically treated, according to the ability of the medical staff.

80. Honorable men, when captured, will abstain from giving to the enemy information concerning their own army, and the modern law of war permits no longer the use of any violence against prisoners, in order to extort the desired information, or to punish them for having given false information.

SECTION IV.

Partisans—Armed enemies not belonging to the hostile army — Scouts—Armed prowlers— War rebels.

81. Partisans are soldiers armed and wearing the uniform of their army, but belonging to a corps which acts detached from the main body for the purpose of making inroads into the territory occupied by the enemy. If captured, they are entitled to all the privileges of the prisoner of war.

82. Men, or squads of men, who commit hostilities, whether by fighting, or inroads for destruction or plunder, or by raids of any kind, without commission, without being part and portion of the organized hostile army, and without sharing continuously in the war, but who do so with intermitting returns to their homes and avocations, or with the occasional assumption of the semblance of peaceful pursuits, divesting themselves of the character or appearance of soldiers—such men, or squads of men, are not public enemies, and, therefore, if captured, are not entitled to the privileges of prisoners of war, but shall be treated summarily as highway robbers or pirates.

83. Scouts, or single soldiers, if disguised in the dress of the country, or in the uniform of the army hostile to their own, employed in obtaining information, if found within or lurking about the lines of the captor, are treated as spies, and suffer death.

84. Armed prowlers, by whatever names they may be called, or persons of the enemy's territory, who steal within the lines of the hostile army, for the purpose of robbing, killing, or of destroying bridges, roads, or canals, or of robbing or destroying the mail, or of cutting the telegraph wires, are not entitled to the privileges of the prisoner of war.

85. War rebels are persons within an occupied territory who rise in arms against the occupying or conquering army, or against the authorities established by the same. If captured, they may suffer death, whether they rise singly, in small or large bands, and whether called upon to do so by their own, but expelled, government or not. They are not prisoners of war; nor are they, if discovered and secured before their conspiracy has matured to an actual rising, or to armed violence.

SECTION V.

Safe-conduct — Spies — War traitors — Captured messengers—Abuse of the flag of truce.

86. All intercourse between the territories occupied by belligerent armies, whether by traffic, by letter, by travel, or in any other way, ceases. This is the general rule, to be observed without special proclamation.

Exceptions to this rule, whether by safe-conduct, by permission to trade on a small or large scale, or by exchanging mails, or by travel from one territory into the other, can take place only according to agreement approved by the government, or by the highest military authority.

Contraventions of this rule are highly punishable.

87. Ambassadors, and all other diplomatic agents of neutral powers, accredited to the enemy, may receive safe-conducts through the territories occupied by the belligerents, unless there are military reasons to the contrary, and unless they may reach the place of their destination conveniently by another route. It implies no international affront if the safe-

conduct is declined. Such passes are usually given by the supreme authority of the State, and not by subordinate officers.

88. A spy is a person who secretly, in disguise or under false pretense, seeks information with the intention of communicating it to the enemy.

The spy is punishable with death by hanging by the neck, whether or not he succeed in obtaining the information or in conveying it to the enemy.

89. If a citizen of the United States obtains information in a legitimate manner, and betrays it to the enemy, be he a military or civil officer, or a private citizen, he shall suffer death.

90. A traitor under the law of war, or a war-traitor, is a person in a place or district under martial law who, unauthorized by the military commander, gives information of any kind to the enemy, or holds intercourse with him.

91. The war traitor is always severely punished. If his offense consists in betraying to the enemy anything concerning the condition, safety, operations or plans of the troops holding or occupying the place or district, his punishment is death.

92. If the citizen or subject of a country or place invaded or conquered gives information to his own government, from which he is separated by the hostile army, or to the army of his government, he is a war traitor, and death is the penalty of his offense.

93. All armies in the field stand in need of guides, and impress them if they can not obtain them otherwise.

94. No person having been forced by the enemy to serve as a guide, is punishable for having done so.

95. If a citizen of a hostile and invaded district voluntarily serves as a guide to the enemy, or offers to do so, he is deemed a war traitor, and shall suffer death.

96. A citizen serving voluntarily as a guide against his own country commits treason, and will be dealt with according to the law of his country.

97. Guides, when it is clearly proved that they have misled intentionally, may be put to death.

98. All unauthorized or secret communication with the enemy is considered treasonable by the law of war.

Foreign residents in an invaded or occupied territory, or foreign visitors in the same, can claim no immunity from this law. They may communicate with foreign parts, or with the inhabitants of the hostile country, so far as the military authority permits, but no further. Instant expulsion from the occupied territory would be the very least punishment for the infraction of this rule.

99. A messenger carrying written dispatches or verbal messages from one portion of the army, or from a besieged place, to another portion of the same army, or its government, if armed, and in the uniform of his army, and if captured, while doing so, in the territory occupied by the enemy, is treated by the captor as a prisoner of war. If not in uniform, nor a soldier, the circumstances connected with his capture must determine the disposition that shall be made of him.

100. A messenger or agent who attempts to steal through the territory occupied by the enemy, to further in any manner the interests of the enemy, if captured, is not entitled to the privileges of the prisoner of war, and may be dealt with according to the circumstances of the case.

101. While deception in war is admitted as a just and necessary means of hostility, and is consistent with honorable warfare, the common law of war allows even capital punishment for clandestine or treacherous attempts to injure an enemy, because they are so dangerous, and it is so difficult to guard against them.

102. The law of war, like the criminal war regarding other offenses, makes no difference on account of the difference of sexes, concerning the spy, the war traitor, or the war rebel.

103. Spies, war traitors and war rebels are not exchanged according to the common law of war. The exchange of such persons would require a special cartel, authorized by the government, or, at a great distance from it, by the chief commander of the army in the field.

104. A successful spy or war traitor, safely returned to his own army, and afterward captured as an enemy, is not subject to punishment for his acts as a spy or war traitor, but he may be held in closer custody as a person individually dangerous.

SECTION VI.

Exchange of prisoners—Flags of truce—Flags of protection.

105. Exchanges of prisoners take place—number for number—rank for rank—wounded for wounded—with added condition for added condition—such, for instance as not to serve for a certain period.

106. In exchanging prisoners of war, such numbers of persons of inferior rank may be substituted as an equivalent for one of superior rank as may be agreed upon by cartel, which requires the sanction of the government, or of the commander of the army in the field.

107. A prisoner of war is in honor bound truly to state to the captor his rank; and he is not to assume a lower rank than belongs to him, in order to cause a more advantageous exchange; nor a higher rank, for the purpose of obtaining better treatment.

Offenses to the contrary have been justly punished by the commanders of released prisoners, and may be good cause for refusing to release such prisoners.

108. The surplus number of prisoners of war remaining after an exchange has taken place is sometimes released either for the payment of a stipulated sum of money, or, in urgent cases, of provision, clothing, or other necessaries.

Such arrangement, however, requires the sanction of the highest authority.

109. The exchange of prisoners of war is an act of convenience to both belligerents. If no general cartel has been concluded, it can not be demanded by either of them. No belligerent is obliged to exchange prisoners of war.

A cartel is voidable so soon as either party has violated it.

110. No exchange of prisoners shall be made except after complete capture, and after an accurate account of them, and a list of the captured officers has been taken.

111. The bearer of a flag of truce can not insist on being admitted. He must always be admitted with great caution. Unnecessary frequency is carefully to be avoided.

112. If the bearer of a flag of truce offer himself during an engagement, he can be admitted as a very rare exception only. It is no breach of good faith to retain such a flag of truce, if admitted during the engagement. Firing is not required to cease on the appearance of a flag of truce in battle.

113. If the bearer of a flag of truce, presenting himself during an engagement, is killed or wounded, it furnishes no ground of complaint whatever.

114. If it be discovered, and fairly proved, that a flag of truce has been abused for surreptitiously obtaining military knowledge, the bearer of the flag thus abusing his sacred character is deemed a spy.

So sacred is the character of a flag of truce, and so necessary is its sacredness, that while its abuse is an especially heinous offense, great caution is requisite, on the other hand, in convicting the bearer of a flag of truce as a spy.

115. It is customary to designate by certain flags (usually yellow), the hospitals in places which are shelled, so that the besieging enemy may avoid firing on them. The same has been done in battles, when hospitals are situated within the field of the engagement.

116. Honorable belligerents often request that the hospitals within the territory of the enemy may be designated, so that they may be spared. An honorable belligerent allows himself to be guided by flags or signals of protection as much as the contingencies and the necessities of the fight will permit.

117. It is justly considered an act of bad faith, of infamy or fiendishness, to deceive the enemy by flags of protection. Such act of bad faith may be good cause for refusing to respect such flags.

118. The besieging belligerent has sometimes requested the besieged to designate the buildings containing collections of works of art, scientific museums, astronomical observatories or precious libraries, so that their destruction may be avoided as much as possible.

SECTION VII.

The Parole.

119. Prisoners of war may be released from captivity by exchange, and under certain circumstances, also by parole.

120. The term parole designates the pledge of individual good faith and honor to do, or to omit doing, certain acts after he who gives his parole shall have been dismissed, wholly or partially, from the power of the captor.

121. The pledge of the parole is always an individual, but not a private, act.

122. The parole applies chiefly to prisoners of war whom the captor allows to return to their country, or to live in greater freedom within the captor's country or territory, on conditions stated in the parole.

123. Release of prisoners of war by exchange is the general rule; release by parole is the exception.

124. Breaking the parole is punished with death when the person breaking the parole is captured again.

Accurate lists, therefore, of the paroled persons must be kept by the belligerents.

125. When paroles are given and received, there must be an exchange of two written documents, in which the name and rank of the paroled individuals are accurately and truthfully stated.

126. Commissioned officers only are allowed to give their parole, and they can give it only with the permission of their superior, as long as a superior in rank is within reach.

127. No non-commissioned officer or private can give his parole except through an officer. Individual paroles not given through an officer are not only void, but subject the individuals giving them to the punishment of death as deserters. The only admissible exception is where individuals properly separated from their commands, have suffered long confinement without the possibility of being paroled through an officer.

128. No paroling on the battle-field; no paroling of entire bodies of troops after a battle, and no dismissal of large numbers of prisoners, with a general declaration that they are paroled, is permitted or of any value.

129. In capitulations for the surrender of strong places or fortified camps, the commanding officer, in cases of urgent necessity, may agree that the troops under his command shall not fight again during the war, unless exchanged.

130. The usual pledge given in the parole is not to serve during the existing war, unless exchanged.

This pledge refers only to the active service in the field, against the paroling belligerent or his allies actively engaged in the same war. These cases of breaking the parole are patent acts, and can be visited with the punishment of death; but the pledge does not refer to internal service, such as recruiting or drilling the recruits, fortifying places not besieged, quelling civil commotions, fighting against belligerents unconnected with the paroling belligerents, or to civil or diplomatic service for which the paroled officer may be employed.

131. If the Government does not approve of the parole, the paroled officer must return into captivity, and should the enemy refuse to receive him, he is free of his parole.

132. A belligerent government may declare, by a general order, whether it will allow paroling, and on what conditions it will allow it. Such order is communicated to the enemy.

133. No prisoner of war can be forced by the hostile government to parole himself, and no government is obliged to parole prisoners of war, or to parole all captured officers, if it paroles any. As the pledging of the parole is an individual act, so is paroling, on the other hand, an act of choice on the part of the belligerent

27

184. The commander of an occupying army may require of the civil officers of the enemy, and of its citizens, any pledge he may consider necessary for the safety or security of his army, and upon their failure to give it, he may arrest, confine or detain them.

SECTION VIII.

Armistice—Capitulation.

185. An armistice is the cessation of active hostilities for a period agreed upon between belligerents. It must be agreed upon in writing, and duly ratified by the highest authorities of the contending parties.

186. If an armistice be declared, without conditions, it extends no further than to require a total cessation of hostilities, along the front of both belligerents.

If conditions be agreed upon, they should be clearly expressed, and must be rigidly adhered to by both parties. If either party violates any express condition, the armistice may be declared null and void by the other.

187. An armistice may be general, and valid for all points and lines of the belligerents; or special, that is, referring to certain troops or certain localities only.

An armistice may be concluded for a definite time, or for an indefinite time, during which either belligerent may resume hostilities on giving the notice agreed upon to the other.

188. The motives which induce the one or the other belligerent to conclude an armistice, whether it be expected to be preliminary to a treaty of peace, or to prepare during the armistice for a more vigorous prosecution of the war, does in no way affect the character of the armistice itself.

189. An armistice is binding upon the belligerents from the day of the agreed commencement; but the officers of the armies are responsible from the day only when they receive official information of its existence.

140. Commanding officers have the right to conclude armistices binding on the district over which their command extends, but such armistice is subject to the ratification of the superior authority, and ceases so soon as it is made known to the enemy that the armistice is not ratified, even if a certain time for the elapsing between giving notice of cessation and the resumption of hostilities should have been stipulated for.

141. It is incumbent upon the contracting parties of an armistice to stipulate what intercourse of persons or traffic between the inhabitants of the territories occupied by the hostile armies shall be allowed, if any.

If nothing is stipulated, the intercourse remains suspended, as during actual hostilities.

142. An armistice is not a partial or a temporary peace; it is only the suspension of military operations to the extent agreed upon by the parties.

143. When an armistice is concluded between a fortified place and the army besieging it, it is agreed by all the authorities on this subject that the besieger must cease all extension, perfection or advance of his attacking works as much so as from attacks by main force.

But as there is a difference of opinion among martial jurists, whether the besieged have the right to repair breaches or to erect new works of defense within the place during an armistice, this point should be determined by express agreement between the parties.

144. So soon as a capitulation is signed, the capitulator has no right to demolish, destroy or injure the works, arms, stores or ammunition in his possession, during the time which elapses between the signing and the execution of the capitulation, unless otherwise stipulated in the same.

145. When an armistice is clearly broken by one of the parties, the other party is released from all obligation to observe it.

146. Prisoners, taken in the act of breaking an armistice, must be treated as prisoners of war, the officer alone being responsible who gives the order for such a violation of an armistice. The highest authority of the belligerent aggrieved may demand redress for the infraction of an armistice.

147. Belligerents sometimes conclude an armistice while their plenipotentiaries are met to discuss the conditions of a treaty of peace; but plenipotentiaries may meet without a preliminary armistice; in the latter case the war is carried on without any abatement.

SECTION IX.

Assassination.

148. The law of war does not allow proclaiming either an individual belonging to the hostile army, or a citizen, or a subject of the hostile government, an outlaw, who may be slain without trial by any captor, any more than the modern law of peace allows such international outlawry; on the contrary, it abhors such outrage. The sternest retaliation should follow the murder committed in consequence of such proclamation, made by whatever authority. Civilized nations look with horror upon offers of rewards for the assassination of enemies, as relapses into barbarism.

SECTION X.

Insurrection—Civil War—Rebellion.

149. Insurrection is the rising of people in arms against their government, or a portion of it, or against one or more of its laws, or against an officer or officers of the government. It may be confined to mere armed resistance, or it may have greater ends in view.

150. Civil war is war between two or more portions of a country or State, each contending for the mastery of the whole, and each claiming to be the legitimate government. The term is also sometimes applied to war of rebellion, when the rebellious provinces or portions of the State are contiguous to those containing the seat of government.

151. The term rebellion is applied to an insurrection of large extent, and is usually a war

between the legitimate government of a country and portions or provinces of the same who seek to throw off their allegiance to it, and set up a government of their own.

152. When humanity induces the adoption of the rules of regular war toward rebels, whether the adoption is partial or entire, it does in no way whatever imply a partial or complete acknowledgment of their government, if they have set up one, or of them, as an independent or sovereign power. Neutrals have no right to make the adoption of the rules of war by the assailed government toward rebels the ground of their own acknowledgment of the revolted people as an independent power.

153. Treating captured rebels as prisoners of war, exchanging them, concluding of cartels, capitulations or other warlike agreements with them; addressing officers of a rebel army by the rank they may have in the same; accepting flags of truce, or, on the other hand, proclaiming martial law in their territory, or levying war taxes or forced loans, or doing any other act sanctioned or demanded by the law and usages of public war between sovereign belligerents, neither proves nor establishes an acknowledgment of the rebellious people, or of the government which they may have erected, as a public or sovereign power. Nor does the adoption of the rules of war toward rebels imply an engagement with them extending beyond the limits of these rules. It is victory in the field that ends the strife and settles the future relations between the contending parties.

154. Treating, in the field, the rebellious enemy according to the laws and usages of war has never prevented the legitimate government from trying the leaders of the rebellion or chief rebels for high treason, and from treating them accordingly, unless they are included in a general amnesty.

155. All enemies in regular war are divided into two general classes; that is to say, into combatants and non-combatants, or unarmed citizens of the hostile government.

The military commander of the legitimate government, in a war of rebellion, distinguishes between the loyal citizen in the revolted portion of the country and the disloyal citizen. The disloyal citizens may further be classified into those citizens known to sympathize with the rebellion, without positively aiding it, and those who, without taking up arms, give positive aid and comfort to the rebellious enemy, without being bodily forced thereto.

156. Common justice and plain expediency require that the military commander protect the manifestly loyal citizens, in revolted territories, against the hardships of the war as much as the common misfortune of all war admits.

The commander will throw the burden of the war, as much as lies within his power, on the disloyal citizens of the revolted portion or province, subjecting them to a stricter police than the non-combatant enemies have to suffer in regular war; and if he deems it appropriate, or if his government demands of him that every citizen shall, by an oath of allegiance, or by some other manifest act, declare his fidelity to the legitimate government, he may expel, trans-

fer, imprison or fine the revolted citizens who refuse to pledge themselves anew as citizens obedient to the law, and loyal to the government.

Whether it is expedient to do so, and whether reliance can be placed upon such oaths, the commander or his government have the right to decide.

157. Armed or unarmed resistance by citizens of the United States against the lawful movements of their troops is levying war against the United States, and is therefore treason.

———

GENERAL ORDERS, NO. 141.

War Department,
Adjutant General's Office,
Washington, September 25, 1862.

The following Proclamation by the President is published for the information and government of the Army and all concerned:

"BY THE PRESIDENT OF THE UNITED STATES OF AMERICA.

"A PROCLAMATION.

"Whereas, It has become necessary to call into service not only volunteers, but also portions of the militia of the States by draft, in order to suppress the insurrection existing in the United States, and disloyal persons are not adequately restrained by the ordinary processes of law from hindering this measure and from giving aid and comfort in various ways to the insurrection. Now, therefore, be it ordered:

"First. That during the existing insurrection, and as a necessary measure for suppressing the same, all rebels and insurgents, their aiders and abettors, within the United States, and all persons discouraging volunteer enlistments, resisting militia drafts, or guilty of any disloyal practice, affording aid and comfort to rebels against the authority of the United States, shall be subject to martial law, and liable to trial and punishment by courts-martial or military commission.

"Second. That the writ of *habeas corpus* is suspended in respect to all persons arrested, or who are now, or hereafter during the rebellion shall be, imprisoned in any fort, camp, arsenal, military prison or other place of confinement by any military authority, or by the sentence of any court-martial or military commission.

"In witness whereof, I have hereunto set my hand, and caused the seal of the United States to be affixed.

"Done at the city of Washington, this twenty-fourth day of September, in the year of
[L. S.] our Lord one thousand eight hundred and sixty-two, and of the Independence of the United States the eighty-seventh.

"ABRAHAM LINCOLN.

"By the President:

"William H. Seward, Secretary of State.

"By order of the Secretary of War.

"L. THOMAS, Adjutant General.

"Official."

AFFIDAVITS

LOUIS J. WEICHMANN AND CAPT. G. W. DUTTON.

COL. H. L. BURNETT, *Judge Advocate, Cincinnati, Ohio:*

Colonel—I stated before the Commission, at Washington, that I commenced to board with Mrs. Surratt in November, 1864. As a general thing, I remained at home during the evenings, and, consequently, I heard many things which were then intended to blind me, but which now are as clear as daylight. The following facts, which have come to my recollection since the rendition of my testimony, may be of interest:

AFFIDAVIT OF LOUIS J. WEICHMANN.

I once asked Mrs. Surratt what her son John had to do with Dr. Mudd's farm; why he made himself an agent for Booth (she herself had told me that Booth desired to purchase Mudd's farm). Her reply was, that "Dr. Mudd and the people of Charles county had got tired of Booth, and that they had pushed him on John." Before the fourth of March, she was in the habit of remarking that "*something* was going to happen to old Abe which would prevent him from taking his seat; that Gen. Lee was going to execute a movement which would startle the *whole world.*" What that movement was she never said.

A few days after, I asked her why John brought such men as Herold and Atzerodt to the house, and associated with them? "O, John wishes to make use of them for his *dirty work,*" was her reply. On my desiring to know what the dirty work was, she answered that "John wanted them to clean his horses." He had two at that time. And once, when she sent me to Brooks, the stabler, to inquire about her son, she laughed, and remarked that "Brooks considered John Surratt, and Booth, and Herold, and Atzerodt a party of young gamblers and sports, and that she wanted him to think so." Brooks has told me since the trial that such was actually the case, and that at one time he saw John H. Surratt with three one-hundred dollar notes in his possession.

When Richmond fell and Lee's army surrendered, when Washington was illuminated, Mrs. Surratt closed her home and wept. Her house was gloomy and cheerless. To use her own expression, it was "indicative of her feelings."

On Good Friday I drove her into the country, *ignorant* of her purpose and intentions. We *started* at about half-past two o'clock in the afternoon. Before leaving, she had an interview with John Wilkes Booth in the parlor. On the way down she was very lively and cheerful, taking the reins into her own hands several times, and urging on the steed. We halted once, and that was about three miles from Washington, when, observing that there were pickets along the road, she hailed an old farmer, and wanted to know if they would remain there all night. On being told that they were withdrawn at about eight o'clock in the evening, she said she "was glad to know it." On the return, I chanced to make some remark about Booth, stating that he appeared to be without employment, and asking her when he was going to act again. "Booth is done acting," she said, "and is going to New York very soon, never to return." Then turning round, she remarked: "Yes, and Booth is crazy on *one subject,* and I am going to give him a good scolding the next time I see him." What that "one subject" was, Mrs. Surratt never mentioned to me. She was very anxious to be at home at nine o'clock, saying that she had made an engagement with some gentleman who was to meet her at that hour. I asked her if it was Booth. She answered neither yes nor no.

When about a mile from the city, and having from the top of a hill caught a view of Washington swimming in a flood of light, raising her hands, she said, "I am afraid all this rejoicing will be turned into mourning, and all this glory into sadness." I asked her what she meant. She replied that after sunshine there was always a storm, and that the people were too proud and licentious, and that God would punish them.

The gentleman whom she expected at nine o'clock on her return, called. It was, as I afterward ascertained, Booth's last visit to Mrs. Surratt, and the third one on that day. She was alone with him for a few minutes in the parlor. I was in the dining room at the time, and as soon as I had taken tea, I repaired thither. Mrs. Surratt's former cheerfulness had left her. She was now very nervous, agitated and restless. On my asking her what was the matter, she replied that she was very nervous, and did not feel well. Then looking at me, she wanted to know which way the torchlight procession was going that we had seen on the Avenue. I remarked that it was a procession of the arsenal employees, who were going to serenade the President. She said that she would like to know, as she was very much interested in it. Her nervousness finally increased so much that she chased myself and the young ladies who were making a great deal of noise and laughter, to our respective rooms.

When the detectives came, at three o'clock the next morning, I rapped at her door for permission to let them in.

"For God's sake, let them come in! I expected the house to be searched," said she.

When the detectives had gone, and when her daughter, almost frantic, cried out:

"Oh, Ma! just think of that man's (John W. Booth) having been here an hour before the assassination! I am afraid it will bring suspicion upon us."

"Anna, come what will," she replied, "I am resigned. I think that J. Wilkes Booth was only an instrument in the hands of the Almighty to punish this proud and licentious people."

LOUIS J. WEICHMANN.

Sworn and subscribed before me this 11th day of August, 1865.

CHAS. E. PANCOAST,
Alderman.

AFFIDAVIT CONCERNING CERTAIN STATEMENTS MADE BY DR. SAM'L A. MUDD, SINCE HIS TRIAL.

CAMP FRY, WASHINGTON, D. C.,
August 22, 1865.

BRIG.-GEN. JOSEPH HOLT,
Judge Advocate General, U. S. A.:

SIR—I am in receipt of your communication of this date, in which you request information as regards the truthfulness of certain statements and confessions reported to have been made by Dr. Mudd while under my charge, *en route* to the Dry Tortugas.

In reply, I have the honor to state that my duties required me to be constantly with the prisoners, and during a conversation with Dr. Mudd, on the 22d of July, he confessed that he knew Booth when he came to his house with Herold, on the morning after the assassination of the President; that he had known Booth for some time, but was afraid to tell of his having been at his house on the 15th of April, fearing that his own and the lives of his family would be endangered thereby. He also confessed that he was with Booth at the National Hotel on the evening referred to by Weichmann in his testimony; that he came to Washington on that occasion to meet Booth, by appointment, who wished to be introduced to John Surratt; that when he and Booth were going to Mrs. Surratt's house to see John Surratt, they met, on Seventh street, John Surratt, who was introduced to Booth, and they had a conversation of a private nature. I will here add that Dr. Mudd had with him a printed copy of the testimony pertaining to his trial, and I had, upon a number of occasions, referred to the same. I will also state that this confession was voluntary, and made without solicitation, threat or promise, and was made after the destination of the prisoners was communicated to them, which communication affected Dr. Mudd more than the rest; and he frequently exclaimed, "Oh, there is now no no hope for me." "Oh, I can not live in such a place."

Please acknowledge the receipt of this letter.

I am, General, very respectfully,
Your obedient servant,
GEORGE W. DUTTON,
Capt. Co. C, 10th Reg't V. R. C., com'dg Guard.

Sworn and acknowledged at Washington, D. C., this 23d August, 1865, before me.
G. C. THOMAS,
Notary Public.

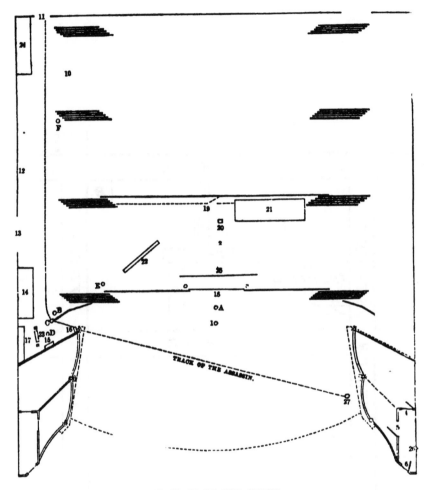

DIAGRAM OF THE STAGE.

The above is a diagram of the stage, with properties, as it stood at the time of the assassination.

The number of persons required upon the stage during the performance is as follows: 19 actors and actresses, 4 scene-shifters, 1 stage carpenter, 1 assistant stage carpenter, 1 property man, 1 gas man, 1 (back) door-keeper, 1 prompter, making a total of 29 persons passing and repassing upon the stage and through the passages and green-room which connects with the stage by the passage through which the assassin passed.

A—"Asa Trenchard," (Mr. Harry Hawk.)
B—Miss Laura Keene.
C—Mr. Ferguson.
D—Gas Man.
E—Stage Manager, (Mr. Wright.)
F—Mr. Wm. Withers, Jr., (Leader of Orchestra.)

1—First scene.
2—Second "
3—Box of President.
4—Door to box.
5— "   "   "
6—Entrance to passage.
7—First entrance to right.
8—Second "   "
9—Third "   "
10—Fourth "   "
11—Back door to alley.

12—Scenery in pile.
13—Door to dressing-rooms.
14—Scenery in pile.
15—Governor to gas-lights.
16—Prompter's desk.
17—Scenery in pile.
18—Center door in scene.
19—Fence, with gate.
20—Martin-house.
21—Set dairy, (12 ft. by 12 ft., 3 feet deep.)
22—Bench.
23—Small table and two chairs.
24—Covered stairway to basement.
25—Set piece, to mask center door.
26—Hole in the wall, to fasten door, (3 ft. 6 in. from corner.)
27—Torn place in carpet, (two feet from lower box.)

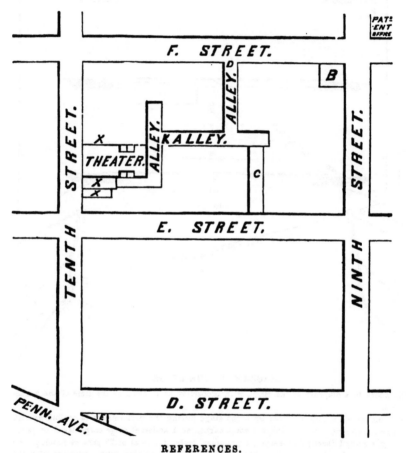

REFERENCES.

B—Herndon House.   C—Vacant lot communicating with the alley of the Theater.   D—Alley communicating with F Street.   K—Alley by which Booth escaped.   X—Restaurants.

Lightning Source UK Ltd.
Milton Keynes UK
UKHW020756081118
331957UK00010B/1145/P